Also by Francine Klagsbrun

Too Young to Die: Youth and Suicide

Voices of Wisdom: Jewish Ideals and Ethics for Everyday Living

Free to Be . . . You and Me (editor)

Married People: Staying Together in the Age of Divorce

*Mixed Feelings: Love, Hate, Rivalry, and Reconciliation
Among Brothers and Sisters*

Jewish Days: A Book of Jewish Life and Culture Around the Year

The Fourth Commandment: Remember the Sabbath Day

LIONESS

LIONESS

*Golda Meir
and the Nation of Israel*

Francine Klagsbrun

Schocken Books, New York

A portion of this book originally appeared in different form in *Hadassah*
magazine (September/October 2017).

Library of Congress Cataloging-in-Publication Data
Name: Klagsbrun, Francine, author.
Title: Lioness : Golda Meir and the nation of Israel / Francine Klagsbrun.
Description: New York : Schocken Books [2017]
Identifiers: LCCN 2017004908 (print). LCCN 2017006101 (ebook).
ISBN 9780805242379 (hardcover). ISBN 9780805243505 (ebook).
Subjects: LCSH: Meir, Golda, 1898–1978. Women prime ministers—
Israel—Biography.
Classification: LCC DS126.6.M42 K53 2017 (print). LCC DS126.6.M42
(ebook). DDC 956.9405/3092 [B]–dc23
LC record available at lccn.loc.gov/2017004908

www.schocken.com

Jacket photograph of Golda Meir by Kahana/Camera Press/Redux
Jacket design by Janet Hansen

Printed in the United States of America
First Edition
2 4 6 8 9 7 5 3 1

What a lioness was your mother
Among the lions!
Crouching among the great beasts,
She reared her cubs.

—Ezekiel 19:2

For Sarah and Eric,
Eliana, Benji, and Ari.
And for Sam.

Contents

Cast of Characters

ABDULLAH BIN HUSSEIN. First king of Jordan, 1946–1951.

YIGAL ALLON. Israeli general during the 1948 Israeli-Arab War; held a variety of ministerial positions during the 1960s and 1970s, including deputy prime minister and minister of education and culture in Golda's government; architect of the Allon Plan for territories captured during the 1967 Six-Day War.

SHULAMIT ALONI. Feminist and civil rights advocate; member of the Knesset and founder of the Ratz Party; held a variety of ministerial positions in the 1990s.

MEIR AMIT. Director of the Mossad, 1963–1968.

YASSER ARAFAT. Chairman of the Palestine Liberation Organization, 1969–2004; leader of the Fatah political party.

ZALMAN ARANNE. Labor leader; minister of education and culture, 1955–1960, 1963–1969; close colleague of Golda's.

MOTTI ASHKENAZI. A captain in the Israel Defense Forces who led a protest movement against Golda's government after the 1973 Yom Kippur War.

HAFEZ AL-ASSAD. President of Syria, 1971–2000.

SHAUL AVIGUR. Commander of Mossad l'Aliyah Bet, which smuggled Jews into mandatory Palestine; a founder and head of Nativ, an underground organization that maintained contact with Soviet Jews.

MENACHEM BEGIN. Leader of the right-wing political parties Herut, Gahal, and Likud; Israel's sixth prime minister, 1977–1983.

DAVID BEN-GURION. Chairman of the executive committee of the Jewish Agency in pre-state Israel; first prime minister of Israel, 1948–1954 and 1955–1963; considered its founding father.

RACHEL YANAIT BEN-ZVI. Zionist leader in pre-state Israel and together with her husband, Yitzhak Ben-Zvi (Israel's second president, 1952–1963), an important early influence on young Golda.

ERNEST BEVIN. British Labour Party leader; foreign secretary during the last days of the British mandate in Palestine.

WILLY BRANDT. Chancellor of West Germany, 1969–1974.

HANNA CHIZICK. Pioneer and agricultural laborer in pre-state Israel; member of the kibbutz Merhavia; wife of Meir Dubinsky.

SIR ALAN CUNNINGHAM. The last British high commissioner in mandatory Palestine, 1945–1948.

MOSHE DAYAN. Charismatic Israeli general; minister of defense in the governments of Levi Eshkol (during the Six-Day War) and Golda Meir (during the Yom Kippur War).

SIMCHA DINITZ. Close aide to Golda; director general of the prime minister's office, 1969–1973; ambassador to the United States, 1973–1979.

MEIR DUBINSKY. Member of the Milwaukee Poalei Zion; ardent early suitor of Golda's.

ABBA EBAN. Diplomat and Israeli spokesman; Israel's first ambassador to the United States and the United Nations; minister of foreign affairs, 1966–1974.

ILYA EHRENBURG. Soviet Jewish journalist.

ADOLF EICHMANN. Nazi war criminal captured by Israel in 1960; executed following trial in 1962.

DAVID "DADO" ELAZAR. Chief of general staff of the Israel Defense Forces during the Yom Kippur War; forced to resign in its aftermath.

ARIE LOVA ELIAV. Secretary-general of Israel's Labor Party; proponent of Palestinian nationalism.

LEVI ESHKOL. Third prime minister of Israel, 1963–1969.

ISRAEL GALILI. Chief of staff in the pre-state Haganah; minister without portfolio in Golda's government and one of her closest advisers.

LEONARD GARMENT. American attorney who served in the Nixon and Ford administrations; liaison between the government and the American Jewish community during the 1970s.

MORDECHAI GAZIT. Director general of the prime minister's office during Golda's premiership.

NAHUM GOLDMANN. President of the World Jewish Congress, 1948–1977.

ELIYAHU GOLOMB. Leading statesman in pre-state Israel; a founder of the Haganah and commander in it.

REGINA HAMBURGER-MEDZINI. Golda's best childhood friend; immigrated to mandatory Palestine with her and maintained lifelong ties.

DAG HAMMARSKJÖLD. United Nations secretary-general, 1953–1961.

ISSER HAREL. Director of Mossad, 1952–1963; replaced by Meir Amit.

HUSSEIN BIN TALAL. King of Jordan, 1953–1999.

VLADIMIR "ZEEV" JABOTINSKY. Right-wing Zionist leader and theoretician; founder of the Revisionist Party in 1925.

LOU KADAR. Golda's assistant, secretary, and confidante for almost thirty years.

BERL KATZNELSON. Visionary and moral authority in pre-state Israel.

HENRY KISSINGER. U.S. national security adviser and secretary of state during the Nixon and Ford administrations.

ABRAHAM ISAAC KOOK. First Ashkenazi chief rabbi of mandatory Palestine and influential religious thinker.

ZVI YEHUDAH KOOK. Son of Abraham Isaac Kook and the spiritual force behind the Gush Emunim settler movement.

YOSSEL KOPILOV. Philosopher-barber, close friend in Golda's youth, immigrated to mandatory Palestine with her and remained a family friend until his death.

SHEYNA MABOVITCH KORNGOLD. Golda's older sister (1889–1972).

BRUNO KREISKY. Chancellor of Austria, 1970–1983.

PINHAS LAVON. Served in several ministerial positions in the 1950s; as minister of defense was accused of running a failed covert operation in Egypt that became known as the Lavon Affair.

BLUMA NAIDITCH MABOVITCH. Golda's mother (1867–1951).

MOSHE YITZHAK MABOVITCH. Golda's father (1864–1944).

ADA MAIMON-FISHMAN. Politician, feminist leader in pre-state Israel; head of Women Workers' Council; director of Girls' Training Farm at Ayanot.

AYA PINKERFELD MEYERSON (MEIR). Menahem's second wife; mother of Amnon, Daniel, and Gideon.

CHANA LUTSKY MEYERSON (MEIR). Menahem's first wife; mother of Meira.

MENAHEM MEYERSON (MEIR). Golda's son (1924–2014).

MORRIS MEYERSON. Golda's husband (1893–1951).

SHIFRA MEYERSON. Morris's mother.

VYACHESLAV MOLOTOV. Minister of foreign affairs in the Soviet Union, 1939–1949; deputy premier, 1942–1957.

GAMAL ABDEL NASSER. President of Egypt, 1956–1970.

SHIMON PERES. Eighth prime minister of Israel, 1984–1986, 1995–1996; ninth president of Israel, 2007–2014; served in several other ministerial positions from the 1970s through the 1990s.

YITZHAK RABIN. Fifth prime minister of Israel, 1974–1977, 1992–1995; chief of general staff of Israel Defense Forces during Six-Day War; ambassador to America, 1968–1973.

SARAH MEYERSON REHABI. Golda's daughter (1926–2010); mother of Naomi and Shaul.

DAVID REMEZ. Minister of transportation, 1948–1950; minister of education, 1950–1951; Golda's mentor and lover.

WILLIAM P. ROGERS. U.S. secretary of state, 1969–1973; formulator of the 1969 Rogers plan for peace between Israel and its Arab neighbors and of the 1970 plan that ended the war of attrition between Egypt and Israel.

ANWAR EL-SADAT. President of Egypt, 1970–1981.

PINHAS SAPIR. Held many ministerial positions from the 1950s through the 1970s, including minister of finance, 1969–1974, and minister of trade and industry, 1970–1972.

ZEEV SHAREF. Secretary of the Israeli government, 1948–1957; held several ministerial positions in the 1960s and 1970s, including minister of housing, 1969–1974; with his wife, Henya, was a close friend of Golda's.

MOSHE SHARETT (SHERTOK). Second prime minister of Israel, 1954–1955; foreign minister, 1948–1956.

RACHEL KATZNELSON SHAZAR. Zionist pioneer; editor of the monthly magazine *Dvar Hapoelet* (The woman worker speaks); wife of Zalman Shazar.

ZALMAN SHAZAR (RUBASHOV). Third president of Israel, 1963–1973; author, poet, and editor in chief of the newspaper *Davar*, 1944–1949; Golda's lover.

JOSEPH SISCO. Assistant U.S. secretary of state, 1969–1976.

CLARA "TZIPKA" MABOVITCH STERN. Golda's younger sister (1902–1981).

MARIE SYRKIN. American journalist, author, and editor of *Jewish Frontier*; Golda's close friend and biographer.

ISADORE TUCHMAN. Milwaukee Zionist activist; a member of the Jewish labor movement Poalei Zion.

MEYER WEISGAL. American Jewish journalist and playwright; president of the Weizmann Institute of Science, 1966–1969, and founding president of the Diaspora Museum; good friend of Golda's.

CHAIM WEIZMANN. First president of Israel, 1949–1952; prominent British chemist; Zionist activist; and president of the Zionist Organization, 1920–1931 and 1935–1946.

ZVI ZAMIR. Director of the Mossad, 1968–1974.

ELI ZEIRA. Director of Amman, Israel's military intelligence, before and during the Yom Kippur War.

YAAKOV ZERUBAVEL. A leader of the Poalei Zion movement in pre-state Israel.

BARUCH ZUCKERMAN. Zionist activist; head of the Poalei Zion Central Committee in New York; friend of Golda and Morris.

"Call Me Golda"

Two wooden figurines stand side by side on my desk. One is of an austere woman, strong-jawed, long-nosed, in a suit with a high-neck blouse and well-below-the-knees skirt, her hair, made of black yarn, pulled back in a bun, her eyes staring straight ahead, her face unsmiling. I don't remember when I acquired it, maybe during the 1980s, on a visit to Israel. The other, larger, cruder, hand carved, and painted, shows a big-busted woman in a long blue dress and yellow apron, her prominent nose and thick dark eyebrows setting off pink lips that are spread across her face in a broad closed-mouth smile. I bought that figure on eBay, where it was advertised as a "Yiddishe Mama."

Both, of course, are of Golda Meir, the fourth prime minister of Israel, and both are true. Single-minded in her dedication to Zionism and Israel, Golda gained a reputation for her toughness, will of steel, and unwavering principles. Whether with a co-worker or the head of a foreign government, she carried herself with the air of someone who knows she is right. An irate stare from her could wither the strongest official and her disapproval send fear through the heart of the most seasoned politician. She was unyielding in defending her nation, a formidable foe to anyone out to harm her people. She was also everyone's loving grandmother, or so she often presented herself. She hovered over her state, as though prepared at the first sign of trouble to gather its inhabitants under her ample apron. Her charm, when turned on, could disarm the most antagonistic adversary; her homey anecdotes and quick wit spread an aura of warm camaraderie. "Your grandson says you are the best gefilte fish maker in Israel," a reporter called out at a news conference. "My grandson . . . I'm afraid he's not very objective about me. I'm not very objective about him either," she shot back. When someone publicly mentioned her chicken soup, thousands requested her recipe, and her office accommodated them all.

That combination of strength tempered by a grandmotherly demeanor and severity leavened by humor helped her gain and hold on to the power she wielded for decades.

The contradictions in the way she presented herself to the world typify many other contradictions about Golda Meir. The ultimate insider—she was the only prime minister to have held the state's two other key posts, labor minister and foreign minister—she was also an outsider: a woman reaching for the highest leadership roles in a male-dominated society, an émigré from the United States in an Eastern European–oriented culture. An opponent of the organized feminist movement, she became a worldwide icon for what women could achieve and a poster figure for feminism itself. A dyed-in-the-wool socialist, she developed tight friendships with some of the wealthiest American Jewish capitalists, and they doted on her. Poorly educated, with a limited Hebrew vocabulary and a prosaic speaking style, she held audiences spellbound with her talks, most of them unwritten. One of the most famous women in the world, winner of numerous awards, she lived unpretentiously in a small house that she shared with her son and his family in a middle-class neighborhood. And a premier who claimed to know nothing of military matters, she made crucial military decisions that helped save her country during two wars.

She began life in the waning days of tsarist Russia, a repressed land pulsing with the first sparks of revolution. Her memories of that land were of pogroms and Cossacks (although she had never directly witnessed either) and, mostly, of a Jewish people hemmed in and held back, too weak to determine its own destiny. Like millions of Eastern European Jews, her parents moved the family to the United States, where they settled in Milwaukee. Her experience there became more than memories. It shaped much of her life's thinking. The American democracy she learned about in school, the socialism she saw enacted in the Milwaukee of her day, the can-do atmosphere of the nearby western frontier, and the exuberant optimism of a still-young country stayed with her long after she left that land behind her.

Brimming with Zionist zeal, she left it for the unfamiliarity of mandatory Palestine. And although she came to the States regularly, sometimes for months at a time, she never again identified as an American. For almost sixty years, she devoted herself to constructing a homeland for the Jewish people, creating, among other things, a progressive system of legislation that helped meld hundreds of thousands of immigrants from a hundred different countries into a single nation. The socialist Labor

Zionist Party she first joined as a young woman in Milwaukee became the predominant force in the land, representing its trade unions, running its medical clinics, and supervising its schools. As Golda rose in the party's hierarchy, she rose also in the nation's leadership, and as her role and reputation in Israel grew, she became known throughout the world: the intrepid leader of the Jewish state who smoked nonstop and didn't hesitate to say what was on her mind, and the delightful old lady who never seemed too tired to meet with one more statesman or appear on one more television show to promote her viewpoint. She was especially adored by American Jews, many of whom knew her as "our Golda," and by Americans in general. To this day, her name elicits comments about her charisma, intelligence, and idealism.

And herein lies perhaps the greatest paradox in Golda Meir's life: outside Israel, she remains a revered figure. American libraries and political centers bear her name, philanthropies give Golda Meir awards, and children's books about her appear regularly. Within Israel, large segments of the population—mainly the intelligentsia—dislike her, and much of the media rarely refers to her favorably.

From the height of popularity, with a rating of almost 90 percent when she took office in 1969 as Israel's prime minister, she was, essentially, forced to resign after the Yom Kippur War in October 1973. The country was taken by surprise in that war, and many blamed Golda Meir and her government for its unpreparedness. Even more, she was and continues to be held responsible for not preventing the war by making peace with Egypt beforehand. With time, Israeli disapproval has spread retroactively to other aspects of her administration and personality. What had once been seen as her fearlessness in standing up to the big powers of her era—the United States and the Soviet Union—came to be viewed as arrogance. What had been regarded as conviction was branded self-righteousness. What had been called firmness became inflexibility. To a great extent, the labels represent a backlash against a woman who exerted enormous power in a society traditionally run by men. But the labels also reflect the enduring pain of the October War. Although in the end Israel won the war, more than twenty-five hundred soldiers lost their lives, and scores of others suffered grievous wounds. In that sense, the maternal Golda, protector of her people, became to her critics the mother who failed to forestall the disaster.

As an American, I grew up with a positive view of Golda Meir. She was part of the landscape of an Israel I loved and visited many times and whose history I came to know well through years of study of Jewish life and Hebrew texts. When I began researching this biography, the attacks against her, particularly vociferous each year on the anniversary of the Yom Kippur War, came as something of a surprise. How could a woman so admired everywhere in the world be so disliked by people in her own country? I sought to answer that question and at the same time to fully understand the abiding trauma caused by a war fought more than forty years ago. Consequently, that war and the period leading up to it became an important part of my study.

But the Yom Kippur War does not define Golda Meir. She lived a long and remarkable life, which was intertwined with every aspect of the building and growth of the State of Israel. Many of the most controversial issues at the core of Israeli existence today had their origins in her day: the quandary of how to handle the territories captured during the Six-Day War of 1967, the establishment of settlements on the West Bank, the Palestinian question, the social and cultural divide separating Israeli Jews whose families emanated from different parts of the globe, the challenge of large-scale terrorism, and more. Yet although her basic story has been told many times, it has not been told in the kind of breadth and detail her complex life deserves.

There have been numbers of biographies in Hebrew and English written about Golda Meir, including her autobiography composed for her by the writer Rinna Samuel. I have read them all and relied on the best of them. But I was after something more in writing this book: a comprehensive narrative based on original Hebrew as well as English sources that would present an in-depth view of this multifaceted woman. Golda did not make it easy to uncover her life or private thinking. She kept no diaries, was a sporadic letter writer—neglecting to answer most letters or simply scribbling notes at the bottom of those received—and revealed little of her inner self in that ghostwritten autobiography. She warned her assistants and bodyguards never to divulge what they knew about her even after her death, when, she predicted, journalists and historians would hound them for information. She wanted her history known only as she chose to tell it.

Nevertheless, this has been a good time to undertake an expansive biography of Golda Meir. A large number of resources, such as the Israel State Archives, Israel Defense Forces Archives, British National Archives, U.S. National Archives, presidential libraries, and others have declassified files that had been top secret for decades. I have studied more than a thousand documents, telephone transcripts, minutes of American, Israeli, British, and Russian government meetings, political party records, magazine and newspaper reports, films, personal papers, oral histories, diaries, cables, and private family letters—some never published anywhere. I have read hundreds of books and articles connected to Israeli life and traveled to and from Israel to interview dozens of people, among them high-ranking American and Israeli government officials, national security chiefs, diplomats, politicians, and others who worked with Golda or knew her well. I spent considerable time with her son, daughter, daughter-in-law, and assistant for almost thirty years, all of whom have since passed away, and met with her grandsons and other relatives, former neighbors, and bodyguards.

This book aims to present a balanced portrait of Golda Meir and to examine her life as it unfolded within the context of her own times. My hope is that her story and the story of the Israel of that era will resonate for current-day readers, providing a deeper understanding of the roots of today's Israel. I hope also that this telling will shine a light on some of the most dramatic and far-reaching moments in that nation's history and illuminate the singular woman and leader so often at the heart of them.

A WORD ABOUT THE USE of her name: Men in public life are almost uniformly referred to by their last names, as in Washington, Lincoln, or Ben-Gurion, whereas women are frequently called by their first names, an informality that tends to diminish the woman's status. But Golda Meir is different. Her first name identified her everywhere; she owned it and promoted it, allowing others to feel they knew her intimately even while she rose in stature and influence. When asked how she wanted to be addressed, she would answer, "Call me Golda." And so the world did. And so she is named throughout this book.

PART ONE

STUBBORN ROOTS

1

The Carpenter's Daughter

The Eighth Constitutional Convention of the American Federation of Labor and Congress of Industrial Organizations (AFL-CIO) in 1969 took place at the Hotel Traymore in Atlantic City, New Jersey. Speakers during the convention week included the former vice president of the United States Hubert Humphrey, the African American civil rights activist Bayard Rustin, and the U.S. secretary of labor, George Shultz. On the morning of the third day of meetings, October 6, Golda Meir, prime minister of the State of Israel, addressed the plenary.

As Mrs. Meir walked slowly to the podium, audience members saw a familiar figure: square set, standing about five feet five inches tall, silver-streaked hair pulled back in a signature bun, thick brows, no makeup, and a protruding nose that was the delight of cartoonists. Golda, as she had come to be known everywhere, was dressed that morning in the same chevron-patterned jacket and skirt, collarless blouse, and large beads in which she had been seen three days earlier when visiting her hometown of Milwaukee. Her no-nonsense laced shoes supported thick legs, one swollen slightly out of proportion to the other. A big black leather handbag hung from her arm.

The more than three thousand delegates and visitors who filled the convention hall represented every major labor union in the United States and a considerable number of foreign ones. Some carried small placards, while others held up large banners, all bearing their union names—Associated Actors and Artistes of America, International Ladies' Garment Workers' Union, Amalgamated Meat Cutters and Butcher Workmen of North America, and many more. The audience waited expectantly while the speaker stood silently at the podium, shielding her eyes with one hand from the glare of television lights and calmly looking around the room, as though searching for someone she knew.

She turned to George Meany, president of the labor federation, who had introduced her. "My dear friend, Mr. Meany," she began, then back to the hall, "my many good friends here on the dais, and friends in the audience: I have been looking around for the Carpenters' sign. That is the one my father belonged to."

The audience rose to its feet as wild cheers erupted. "The applause continued for fifteen minutes," recalled Amos Eiran, a senior diplomat at the Israeli embassy at the time. "It wouldn't have mattered what she said after that. She may have been a head of state, but her father was a union man, and they saw her as one of them."

As she had many times before and would again, Golda Meir invoked her humble origins and strong ties to working people to capture her audience. This was not simple playacting or sheer political manipulation, although the prime minister was well versed in both. Her working-class roots evoked her deepest sense of self; she could identify with her listeners almost as much as they identified with her.

"Don't forget that you are the daughter of a carpenter," her elder sister admonished her whenever she was elected to a new office or received an honor. "Don't forget that we knew hunger." Golda didn't forget. She spoke with pride of her modest beginnings and often credited them with having shaped her life, no matter how far from them life took her.

SHE WAS BORN Golda Mabovitch in Kiev, Russia, on May 3, 1898. Six years before her birth, her father, Moshe Yitzhak Mabovitch, had left Pinsk in the region of Belorussia, where he and his family lived with his wife's parents, to find work in the Ukrainian city of Kiev. After the illness and death of a baby girl, his grieving wife, Bluma, and their young daughter, Sheyna, joined him in the small flat where he had been staying.

For Russia's Jews, Kiev was a city of conflicting messages, drawing them in with one hand and pushing them away with the other. Established in the ninth century amid the hills and ravines along the Dnieper River, it quickly became a major center of commerce between Europe and central Asia. Among the merchants who flocked to it were traders from the small, powerful kingdom of Khazaria. Tradition has it that a century earlier, the ruler of this kingdom, the nobility, and a large proportion of the population had converted to Judaism. Some historians believe that Khazars, including the Jews of that land, might have been among Kiev's first settlers and influenced its growth as a trading post. During the next several centuries, the Jews of Kiev developed a community that boasted at least one Talmudic expert, known as Moses of Kiev.

By the thirteenth century, whatever benefits Kiev's Jews might have derived from their connection to Khazaria were long forgotten. That odd little kingdom had all but disappeared, and as one principality after another won control of the city, a pattern set in that was repeated again and again. A ruler would expel the Jews, as the ruler of Lithuania did in 1495, pressured by Christian merchants, who felt threatened by Jewish competitors. Soon the Jews would be invited back, as they were eight years later, because the city's economy suffered without Jewish businessmen. Kiev's anti-Semitism, like anti-Jewish sentiments throughout Christian Europe, ran full and strong, but the city had additional justifications: its many monasteries and churches and its great Byzantine Cathedral of St. Sophia, inspired by the Hagia Sophia in Constantinople, made it a "holy city" to its Russian Orthodox residents. Jews did not belong there, except for the economic benefits they might generate.

When Catherine the Great of Russia annexed large parts of Poland and Lithuania into the Russian Empire in the late eighteenth century, hundreds of thousands of Jews who lived in those territories came under Russian domination. Catherine confined members of the Jewish population of the expanded empire to the areas they had been in at the time of the annexation—the Pale of Jewish Settlement, it was called—and forbade them by law to settle elsewhere. At first, Kiev, like most of Ukraine, fell inside the Pale, but bending to the complaints of Christian burghers about "the increase of *zhidy*," Catherine's grandson Tsar Nicholas I once again outlawed Jews. Under later tsars, the law was liberalized from time to time to allow various categories of Jewish artisans, merchants, or bankers to settle in Kiev, but the basic decree of exclusion remained in effect.

Yet for all the restrictions, Jews continued to flock to Kiev, seeking to make their homes in this thriving city. Most came to escape the stifling poverty of the villages and *shtetlach*, the small towns, that stretched through the Pale. Merchants attended the huge trade fairs held in Kiev every year and managed, legally or illegally, to remain. Students came to study at the city's schools and stayed beyond graduation. Doctors, lawyers, and other professionals permitted to practice for a while found ways to establish themselves permanently. Aiding the deceptions were constant changes in residency laws that confused even the authorities. And then bribery flourished; the chief of police headed the list of officials who could be paid off to turn a temporary permit into a lasting one.

By 1892, when the carpenter Moshe Mabovitch and his family arrived in Kiev, it had a Jewish community of more than fourteen thousand members—about 11 percent of the city's total population—several synagogues, a Jewish hospital for the poor, Jewish philanthropic organizations, and a Jewish cemetery. Moshe had more legitimate reasons than many to obtain a residency permit. His father, Meir Zelig Mabovitch, had served in the army of Tsar Nicholas I, a badge of honor that gave soldiers' spouses and descendants the right to dwell outside the Pale. Moshe's mother and sister already lived in Kiev because of that privilege. Although Golda was born long after Meir Zelig died, she'd heard enough about him to regard him in adulthood as "one of the personalities that people my childhood." His background is a weave of fact and family lore, its strands impossible to separate.

The family narrative places him among thousands of Jewish boys kidnapped or torn from their parents to serve for twenty-five years in the tsar's army. American Jews often have the mistaken notion that their forebears who fled Russia in the early twentieth century did so to escape just such a fate. In fact, the kidnapping of Jewish children for military service occurred in only one period, from 1827 to 1855, during the reign of Tsar Nicholas I, when Meir Zelig could have lived. The mass exodus of Russian Jews in later years might have stemmed in part from people fleeing military service—which, after Nicholas, extended for six years— but its key cause was the poverty and oppression Jews suffered. Still, the era of the kidnapped children had such a devastating effect that it remained etched into Jewish consciousness as a symbol of tsarist Russia.

Until Nicholas, Jews were not deemed capable or loyal enough for military duty. He changed that, determined to use the army as a means to integrate the Jews in his empire into Russian life and at the same time convert them to the Russian Orthodox faith. To this end, he established quotas for conscripts from individual Jewish communities, forcing community leaders to choose between drafting adult men or young boys to fill their quotas. Because Jewish men of the time tended to marry young and have babies quickly, the leaders preferred to take children rather than uproot fathers from their families. Known as Jewish cantonists, these children would be trained far from home in military cantons, or settlements, along with the children of Russian soldiers, before serving their conscription term.

The Jewish elders shamelessly protected the wealthy and influential in their communities by filling their quotas with children from poor and marginal families. Jewish *khappers*, or snatchers, grabbed boys off the streets or forced their way into homes to abduct children for the draft.

So it was, as the family tells it, that "two men with long beards" nabbed Meir Zelig while he was walking outdoors and pressed him into military service. He was thirteen years old.

The family narrative continues: Meir Zelig resisted every attempt to convert him, even when he was made to kneel on a stone floor for hours. So devout was he that in all his years in the army, he refused to eat any food that was not kosher, limiting himself to bread and uncooked vegetables. Nevertheless, when he finally returned home, a man of twenty-six, he still worried that he might have sinned inadvertently and as atonement slept for years on a bench in an unheated synagogue using a bare stone for a pillow. Eventually, Meir Zelig married and had thirteen children with his wife, Tzippe, only three of whom survived into adulthood, Moshe and two younger daughters.

Golda Meir grew up with few religious sentiments, but she remained impressed with the stories her father told about the unflinching resolve of the pious grandfather she had never met.

Meir Zelig's army service might have been Moshe's ticket out of the Pale; his own skills as a carpenter would be his entrée to permanent residency in Kiev. Jewish artisans like him had the right to establish households in Kiev on condition that they qualified as masters in their field by producing an acceptable piece of work. While Moshe prepared for the master's exam, he, Bluma, and Sheyna lived in grinding poverty and constant fear of the *oblavy*, police hunts that swept through every neighborhood, expelling Jews who did not have proper papers. He finally produced a fine chess table and received his permanent residency permit. With that, he had high hopes of establishing a furniture workshop and changing his fortune.

It would not happen. A quiet man who could be stubborn in his opinions, Moshe was also an inveterate optimist, "an innocent," Golda said, "much given to believing in people," a trait that made him an easy mark for one unscrupulous business partner after another and often left his family destitute.

When Moshe and Bluma set up house in Kiev, most of the city's Jews lived in its poorest neighborhoods, the densely populated districts of Podol and Ploskaia near the port, or Lybed, which stretched from the upper city to the railroad tracks below. Houses in these areas fell victim to frequent fires and flooding, and rented apartments were often nothing more than one room without running water or a dank, airless basement. The Mabovitch family moved from one such hovel to another as Moshe struggled to find work. "Jewish craftsmen," the newspaper *Kievskii Tele-graf* wrote, "poke about anywhere they can, from house to house, just in case someone might have some work, but they find things little better here than where they came from."

Decades later, Sheyna remembered the "cold and hunger" of Kiev, a cold that entered her bones and a hunger that never left her. She remembered the tiny, dark single room that served as the family's bedroom as well as eating room and the chairs she slept on instead of a bed. She also remembered the sounds of her parents shouting at each other in the sorrows of their daily existence. Shrewd, quick-tempered Bluma had little patience for her husband's failures. It didn't help either that his mother, Bubbe Tzippe, came to live with the family from time to time. Golda later described this grandmother as a "tall woman with a tight, withered face." A fanatical housewife, Tzippe cast a critical eye on her daughter-in-law's household management, provoking angry arguments between the women that added to Bluma's bitterness. This was not the life she had imagined when she and Moshe married after a love-at-first-sight romance almost unheard of among their relatives and friends.

Bluma reveled in telling the story of that romance to her daughters, who never tired of hearing it or questioned the veracity of any part of it. As the saga went, for some unknown reason Moshe, who was born in the Ukrainian town of Berdichev, had to report for military service in Pinsk, which might have been an army recruitment center. Bluma, living in Pinsk, saw the tall, good-looking youth and was instantly smitten. A lively, pretty redhead, she was the eldest of the six children—five girls and a boy—of Menachem Naiditch, a Pinsk tavern owner, and his wife, Pesse Feigel, and used to getting her way. (Menachem had two other living children, a girl and a boy, from his first wife, who had died in a household fire.) The parents, however, were less than happy about her choosing a mate, in an era when marriages were arranged through a *shad-chan*, a marriage broker. They hired a *shadchan* anyway, to make inquiries about Bluma's young man, and were pleased to learn that Moshe had studied for a while at a reputable yeshiva in the town of Slonim before apprenticing himself to a carpenter.

Nevertheless, Menachem Naiditch opposed the marriage. "There will be no artisans in our family," he declared, refusing, with the pride of a tavern owner, to have his daughter wed a carpenter who could do no better than work with his hands. He finally agreed to the match after his mother, known in the family as Bubbe Golde, convinced him that the man was a mensch, and, besides, "it's not a tragedy to be a carpenter . . . from a carpenter it's possible to become a merchant." Moshe never did become a merchant; he remained a carpenter all his life.

After the marriage, the couple lived with Bluma's parents in Pinsk, the custom for newlyweds. So many younger sisters and other relatives filled the home that family members sometimes had to sleep three to a bed. They subsisted, as did others in the town, on weekday meals of potatoes and beans, with an occasional meat or fish dish for the Sabbath and holidays. Yet compared with the difficulties of Kiev, those years in Pinsk came to be seen by Bluma as almost luxurious. Sheyna, their first child, was born in 1889, about a year after their marriage, and some three years later they set out on their own for Kiev.

Compounding the hardships they endured in that city were the deaths of a string of babies. In addition to the loss of their daughter Sorele, in the course of their marriage Bluma bore and lost four sons. Two died from unknown causes within weeks of each other, one around the age of two, the other at six months. Another boy might have been accidentally smothered to death after Bluma tried to treat a cold by rubbing oil and turpentine on his body and swaddling him so tightly that the fumes probably caused him to suffocate. A fourth baby, born in Golda's lifetime, seems to have developed an infection after an unsanitary circumcision. Bluma was not alone in these tragedies of childbirth. Unsanitary conditions and lack of a decent sewage system in the overcrowded Jewish areas of Kiev led to widespread epidemics and deaths.

NOT ALL THE JEWS in Kiev shared in the losses or the poverty. At the other extreme of the economic scale, and other parts of town, dwelled Jewish business magnates, some among the wealthiest inhabitants of Kiev. The writer Sholem Aleichem, who lived in Kiev for many years, gave it the fictitious name Yehupetz and referred often in his stories to actual wealthy Jewish families there. One of them, the Brodsky family, known throughout the Russian Empire for its vast sugar-refining enterprises, helped finance the city's most important Jewish institutions. Other Jewish entrepreneurs made their fortunes in the liquor and tobacco industries, in shipping, or in trading on the Kiev stock exchange. Many owned large mansions in the upper city, an area graced by wide boulevards.

Although Moshe and Bluma lived worlds apart from the likes of a Brodsky or the others, their lives crossed those of one well-to-do family in a way that would affect Golda's well-being. Named Yanovsky, the family resided in a large, elegant house surrounded by a flowering garden. With the birth of their eleventh child, a girl named Simka, Mrs. Yanovsky's strength gave out. She sought a wet nurse and found her in Bluma Mabovitch, who had recently lost one of her baby boys and had "enough milk in her breasts to nurse two children." Mrs. Yanovsky interviewed Bluma, liked her, and not only paid her to nurse her baby but also had the family moved to a larger, lighter apartment on a respectable street so that little Simka would be looked after in a healthy and relaxed environment. Taking no chances, Mrs. Yanovsky sent an aide to teach Bluma how to care for an infant.

Simka remained with the Mabovitch family until she was about a year old. Because of the basics of cleanliness and hygiene that Bluma learned during that time, when Golda was born a midwife in a "crisp white gown" attended her, unlike the untrained old grandmother who had helped bring Sheyna into the world nine years earlier. And whereas Sheyna rarely received a full bath before she was a year old, the new baby was bathed two or three times a week. Nor was this child tightly swaddled as the others had been. She could grow freely and develop naturally.

From the start, family mythology surrounded little Goldie, as everyone called her. She bore the name of Bubbe Golde, the great-grandmother long regarded as the family matriarch. It was Bubbe Golde who influenced her son, Menachem Naiditch, to allow his daughter Bluma to marry Moshe the carpenter. It was Bubbe Golde, more than anyone, to whom Bluma turned for comfort when her babies died. It was Bubbe Golde whose counsel relatives and neighbors far and wide sought when they had a troubling problem. It was Bubbe Golde of whom people said, admiringly, she has "a man's mind." In the future, people were to repeat incessantly that Golda Meir was "the only man in the cabinet," supposedly the words of Israel's prime minister David Ben-Gurion. She hated the description. "What does it really mean?" she asked. "That it's better to be a man than a woman, a principle on which I don't agree at all . . . Men always feel so superior!"

In the great-grandmother's day, and long afterward, attributing a "man's mind" to a woman was considered a compliment. This woman had the will of an absolute monarch and the confidence of a trapeze artist. According to family lore, she habitually put salt instead of sugar in her tea so that she would take the taste of the *goless*, the Diaspora, and its salty tears with her into the next world. She lived in this world for many years, leaving it only at the age of ninety (some said ninety-four). Alert to the end, she pronounced the traditional confessional to a rabbi, blessed each family member, arranged for psalms to be read aloud upon her death, shut her eyes, and breathed her last at the close of the Sabbath.

AS GOLDIE MABOVITCH GREW UP, her parents often told her that she looked like the great-grandmother with deep-set eyes whose name she carried. Sheyna went further. "Whoever remembers Bubbe Golda, and knows my sister Golda," she wrote in a memoir, "must believe that personality traits can be passed on from one generation to the next."

Some of those traits showed up early in Goldie's life. From Sheyna's accounts, she was a lively, bright child, curious about her environment and set in her ways. In keeping with Bubbe Golde's legendary stubbornness, a classic family story tells of a power struggle between Golda and her mother when she was about five years old. With no toys in the poverty-stricken home, Golda cherished a little notebook her mother had given her, in which she would try to copy letters from a book. One day, absorbed in her notebook, she failed to respond when her mother called her repeatedly. Irritated, Bluma tore the notebook to shreds. The distraught child cried for days. "Promise to obey me and I will buy you another notebook," Bluma ordered. Golda would neither promise nor ask for a replacement. Finally, Bluma relented and bought her daughter a new notebook. Golda had made no concessions. "There's a *dybbuk* in her," relatives said.

But childhood did not begin with battles. After the many losses Moshe and Bluma had suffered during the years following Sheyna's birth, they took great delight in the pretty, healthy new daughter who broke the chain of death. For a while at least, she experienced the warmth and indulgence of grateful parents. Sheyna never forgot how her mother would comb Golda's long, curly hair dotingly, gathering it into a tuft at the top of her head, "like a little crown," while the small girl stood in front of a mirror admiring herself. Golda's hair would always remain a source of pride and comfort to her. "It was streaked and lined with white," the journalist Ruth Gruber recalled about the adult Golda. "And you know she'd stand in the bathroom and there was a big mirror there and she'd brush and brush it in front of the mirror." David Harman, a family friend who had lived in Golda's house as a student, remembered that when mulling over a problem, she would often wash her hair, sometimes at one or two o'clock in the morning. "Somehow the washing of the hair and the brushing out of the hair, which was very long, was a way for her to think things over," he said. And maybe on some level to evoke those fleeting childhood feelings of basking in her mother's love.

Sheyna was jealous of her new sister, jealous of the hair combing and the kisses her mother lavished on this little girl, whom she called her "golden child." Within a few years, however, Golda would suffer similar feelings when a new baby supplanted her in her parents' affections.

Bubbe Tzippe, dying from typhus, had come to live out her final days with her son's family. Gone now was the resentment Bluma once felt toward her mother-in-law, replaced by a veil of sorrow that spread across the household at the old woman's suffering. Tzippe died a painful death, and on the day of her burial Bluma gave birth to a baby girl, whom she and Moshe named Tzipka, after her. (Both names are diminutives of the biblical Zipporah.) It was January 20, 1902, and Golda was three and a half. Pushed from her throne as youngest child, she soon acquired her own air of sadness and neglect. Her aloneness stirred Sheyna's compassion. With no interest in the new baby, who seemed to cry all the time, she drew close to her little sister, becoming her guardian and mentor and, as Golda would later discover, extending her supervision throughout life as a self-appointed, and often self-righteous, voice of conscience.

During these years, from Golda's birth through Tzipka's, the economic situation at home often skirted on the dire. At times Sheyna, who attended a school she loved, went to classes without eating all day. And Golda would remember her mother cooking porridge on rare occasions as a special treat and her resentment once when her mother made her give up a part of her small portion to baby Tzipka, who had finished her own and was crying for more. Golda was always "a little too cold outside and a little too empty inside," she said of those bleak days.

Moshe entered into a new partnership, which lasted until he discovered that the partner had cheated him out of his share of the income. The family moved again, to Lukianovka, an area on the outskirts of the city, known for its fortresslike prison. Here Moshe managed a building in exchange for a rent-free apartment. Soon another opportunity arose. The government began to expand its educational system and to commission craftsmen to create furniture for new schools and libraries. Moshe submitted an anonymous bid, as required, and received a contract for library tables and benches.

With great optimism—a trait he never seemed to lose—Moshe moved the family to a larger apartment, where the three girls slept in the one bedroom and the parents in the dining room. He opened a workshop, borrowed money to buy supplies, and hired two workers for the project. He delivered the furniture on time, confident of his workmanship, only to have large parts of it rejected. When he returned home that evening, his family saw a broken man. He regarded himself the victim of anti-Semitism once he had revealed his name and the authorities realized he was Jewish.

By 1902, Kiev's anti-Semitism was, in fact, becoming more open, and violent, with rumors of pogroms flying everywhere. Much later, whenever people asked Golda Meir about her early childhood in Kiev, she would tell them, in slightly different versions, about an image of that city that remained in her mind. She remembered her family living on the first floor of a building with a stairway in the entrance that led to a neighbor's home on the second floor. Aside from this neighbor, the building held no other Jewish families. When word of a possible pogrom reached the two families, the fathers prepared to protect their homes however possible. In one of Golda's descriptions, she and the neighbor's daughter, a girl about her age, watched their fathers frantically at work. In another, several children stood by. In one, the fathers boarded the front door to barricade the entrance; in another, they boarded the windows while Cossacks on horseback galloped down the street toward them. Regardless of how the details varied, in the telling the memory of the terror remained the same. "I can hear the sound of that hammer now," she would say, "and I can see the children standing in the streets, wide-eyed and not making a sound, watching the nails being driven in."

The pogrom did not take place. Indeed, Golda would never witness a pogrom. But her childhood fear of pogroms was real, and it reflected a fear always present in Russian Jewish lives, especially in Kiev with its history of expulsions and anti-Jewish activity.

Those fears and his most recent business failures convinced Moshe that life in Kiev had nothing more to offer. Passover in 1902 was a dreary affair, with the family having to rely on the holiday clothing and food Bluma's parents sent from Pinsk. At the next festival, Shavuot, fried fish and dry bread made up the only fare on the holiday table. With his wife and daughters sitting at that table, Moshe announced his decision: he would go to America to work and return with the money he earned, while the rest of the family would stay with the relatives in Pinsk.

In planning his exodus from the land of the tsars, Moshe was joining more than two million Jews streaming out of the Russian Empire at the end of the nineteenth and the beginning of the twentieth centuries toward the promised land of milk and honey far across the seas. "In the early 1900's," Golda would say, "to the Jews America was a kind of bank where you went to pick up the dollars scattered on the sidewalks and came back with your pockets full."

Bluma packed up the family's few belongings and with her three girls, aged fourteen, four and a half, and one year, left Kiev for Pinsk early in 1903. For them, Pinsk was home, where Bluma had grown up and Sheyna lived as a baby. For Moshe, it symbolized defeat. He had left his in-laws' protective nest to strike out on his own and had to return to it a failure, almost penniless. He sold his tools, settled his business dealings in Kiev, and arrived in Pinsk two weeks after his family. With some of the money from his sales, he journeyed to America, arriving in New York on December 2, 1903. The wife and children he left behind would have to manage as well as they could.

Ninety-five years later, on a freezing day in November 1998, the small Jewish community that had emerged in Kiev after the ravages of the Holocaust and Soviet occupation placed a commemorative plaque on a building at 5 Basseyna Street, proclaiming that Golda Meir had lived there. City records list that address for "I. Mabovitch" (probably for Izok, derived from Moshe's middle name) in the years 1901, 1902, and 1903. Situated in the center of the city, considered then as now one of its better neighborhoods, the building might have held the family's last apartment in Kiev, when Moshe still had dreams of success.

Not far from that building and facing it stands a statue of Sholem Aleichem, his hand lifting his hat, as though in greeting. City guides tell tourists that the famous Jewish author is tipping his hat to the famous Jewish prime minister, both warmly embraced among Kiev's noted sons and daughters. It is an irony about a city that Sholem Aleichem left after witnessing a pogrom in 1905, and of which Golda Meir's one lasting memory would be the sound of nails boarding up her home in anticipation of a murderous mob.

PINSK WAS DIFFERENT. This was a Jewish town, a shtetl, where in 1897 more than twenty thousand Jews made up almost three-quarters of the population and by 1914 the number had risen to almost thirty thousand. Jews did not need special permission to live here; located in Belorussia in western Russia, it lay in the heart of the Pale of Jewish Settlement. In this town, during the 1890s, "no one dared start pogroms," a historian of the city wrote. "Jewish self-confidence was high." Ten years earlier, when pogroms plagued much of Russia, Pinskers had banded together for self-defense so that "butchers, coachmen and porters" were able to chase off mobs of peasants from surrounding areas.

Unlike Kiev, which boasted picturesque hills and bluffs and broad boulevards with stately homes in its wealthier areas, Pinsk, with its squat wooden houses and many unpaved streets, had little to commend it physically. It "was not a pleasant town to live in," wrote Chaim Weizmann, later Israel's first president, who came to the city when he was eleven to study at a Russian high school. "Low-lying, malarial, it was . . . mud in the spring and autumn, ice in the winter, dust in the summer." Built along the marshlands of two rivers, the Pripet and the Pina, Pinsk was known for its muddy swamps, the *blotte*, as they were called in Yiddish. Golda would remember those swamps when she became a young pioneer trying to maneuver her way through the unpaved, muddy paths in the kibbutz Merhavia, where she lived. But even those, she said, weren't as treacherous as the *Pinsker blotte* during spring thaws and autumn rains. One day, walking alone in Pinsk as a child, she stepped into a mud hole with one foot. When it got stuck, she tried using the other foot to extricate herself and got doubly stuck. She had to stand in mud up to her knees until a passerby freed her.

Some fifteen Jewish families laid the foundations for the city in 1506, close to the castle of a Polish prince who could offer them protection. It grew slowly until it became part of the Russian Empire in the late eighteenth century. With its increasing numbers, the town spread eastward, turning the nearby community of Karlin into a suburb of Pinsk. Golda had an aunt in Karlin, which became home also to some of the city's more well-heeled Jewish families, like the Weizmanns.

Although plenty of Pinsk Jews, like those throughout the Pale, suffered the relentless poverty of shtetl life and the community had a system of public support for those who needed it, the town boasted a better economy than many other shtetlach. Its waterways provided work for Jews as fishermen, porters, and stevedores in the summertime, and in the winter the frozen rivers could be chopped into massive chunks of ice to be sold to householders for storage in their ice cellars. With the growth of railroads in the region, wealthy Jewish entrepreneurs built factories that employed thousands of Jewish laborers to make matches, candles, soap, and other products that they shipped to all parts of the empire. The city had merchants who traded in timber and salt, and a variety of artisans who labored as carpenters, housepainters, watchmakers, and tailors. This was a town of Jewish workers, and some did well for themselves.

Zeide (Grandfather) Menachem Naiditch owned a tavern, a respected calling, several notches above manual laborer or artisan like his son-in-law Moshe. One of six taverns in town, it was situated near the waterfront alongside two others. All remained almost empty during most of the week but bustled with business on market days—Sunday and Wednesday—when Jews and gentiles from neighboring villages brought their wares to sell in town. Sundays were the best days financially. After attending church, the village farmers, often called *mujiks* ("little men" in Russian), crowded into the taverns to drink vodka and eat rolls and fried fish. By the end of the day, as the drinking outpaced the eating, tavern owners had to calm their customers to prevent violence, which might quickly turn against the local Jewish population. Tall, thin, straight backed, with a thick beard and soothing, reticent manner, Menachem Naiditch seemed suited to that role.

The tavern was part of a large brick building that housed the Naiditch family, far more spacious than any place Golda had lived in. A deep pit belowground held an ice cellar, where ice purchased from the river workers and covered with straw stayed frozen through the summer. The tavern room, on the first floor, had two long tables, shelves along the walls for food storage, and iron beams to hold the liquor casks. A small hallway led to the kitchen, dominated by its big Russian stove, which heated the house while serving a slew of other purposes. In its interior, women baked and cooked the family meals; in an enclosed space beneath it, they fattened geese, which they used on the holidays of Hanukkah and Passover; and on its top they dried fish and kept dishes warm on the Sabbath. On that broad, flat top also, children in the family slept close together for warmth on bitter winter nights. For Golda, that space became a hideout from which to observe family events.

Four small bedrooms branched off the central room, each packed now with Golda's married aunts and their families. So packed, in fact, that Bluma soon rented a room for her and her daughters nearby in the house of a *shochet*, a ritual slaughterer, joining the rest of the family at the Naiditch home on Friday nights and Saturdays to celebrate the Sabbath.

Golda later remembered those Sabbaths with the sentimentality of someone who has moved far from religious observance but still feels affection for many of the traditions. The central room, she said, became a "palace," filled with "Sabbath light." Its long wooden tables, unwashed all week, were scrubbed clean for the large family that would gather around them. Bubbe Pesse Feigel, a "short, fat" woman with a hairnet on her head and soot on her face from standing at the stove all week, a woman who ordinarily barely opened her mouth except to complain about her lot in life, was suddenly transformed into a "Sabbath grandmother" with a spotless face and festive clothes. The burdens of work and worry dropped away for a time, neighbors came by to visit, and the room filled with the sounds of conversation and song. Years later, Golda Meir's home, with its constant streams of guests on Saturday mornings and afternoons, would reflect those childhood days.

One of the taverns next to Menachem Naiditch's belonged to Leibe Shertok, whose son Yaakov became one of the first pioneers to immigrate to Palestine from Pinsk and whose grandson Moshe Shertok (later Sharett) would work closely with Golda Meir through much of their lives. Menachem and Leibe shared a warm and unusual friendship considering their business rivalry and different backgrounds. Shertok was Jewishly educated with a sophisticated sense of humor; Naiditch serious and reserved, and word had it that he could barely read or write.

"There was another Naiditch family in Pinsk that was more famous," Golda recalled. "I don't come from that famous family." Her Naiditch grandfather "was a simple man . . . an honest and good man." People often called him "Menachem Goldes," after his formidable mother, Golde, the powerhouse in the clan. Golda Meir named her son Menahem, for this grandfather, and commented that he, too, was a "Menahem Goldes."

It might have been in keeping with that simple, mostly illiterate grandfather that Golda received no formal education during her Pinsk years, between the ages of five and eight. To be sure, she was a girl, and few Jewish families of that generation regarded education for girls a necessity. Had one of Bluma's baby boys lived past infancy, at the age of four he would certainly have started attending *heder,* the traditional Jewish school. As notorious as many of these schools were for their ill-trained teachers and squalid classrooms, they still managed to implant in their young students a lifelong familiarity with Jewish texts. Had this imaginary little boy been lucky, he might have studied at the modern *heder* that had gained ground under the influence of the Haskalah, the Jewish Enlightenment. In it, teachers taught in Hebrew instead of Yiddish, and courses included secular subjects such as Russian literature, along with religious ones.

Golda had none of those opportunities for study. Nor, as she advanced in years, did she attend a primary school in Pinsk as many young girls did. Her mother "was a good woman," she would say, "but she didn't want me to have any education; she thought that was for men only." She was referring to her high school years, but the words also suited her early ones. Aside from issues of gender, little in Golda's immediate environment encouraged study. When she wanted to copy the letters of the Hebrew alphabet from a book, one of the only books she could find in her grandfather's home was a *siddur,* a prayer book. Yet this was a time in Jewish life when thousands of people in the shtetlach were reading the works of the great Yiddish storytellers Mendele Moykher Sforim, Sholem Aleichem, and I. L. Peretz and when, on a more everyday level, romance novels in Yiddish and Hebrew had become widely popular. Pinsk itself was a vibrant cultural center noted for its rabbis, scholars, and political thinkers. When Jews in small communities pictured a larger world than any they had known, they described it as "even beyond Pinsk."

Sheyna pitied the little sister she saw wandering about with nothing to do except household chores. She had arranged her life differently. In Kiev, she had discovered a progressive school for poor children and had been old enough and strong-willed enough to attend it despite her mother's desire to have her learn a trade. She was able to help Golda learn to read and write in Yiddish and even master some arithmetic, the extent of the girl's schooling until the family moved to America.

Golda Meir would become one of Israel's most effective speakers; she could make an audience cry simply by reading aloud from a phone book, her colleagues said. Yet she never attained the reservoir of Jewish intellectual knowledge that came to the male founders of the state from their earliest days: David Ben-Gurion, who sat on his grandfather's knees to learn new Hebrew words every day; Berl Katznelson, Labor Zionist hero, whose father's library held stacks of Hebrew journals and books for the boy to rummage through; Moshe Shertok, who inherited a love of learning and languages from his tavern-owning grandfather and his father after that. Golda had no such models.

Growing into childhood in Pinsk, little Goldie acquired two nicknames. Sometimes she was called *die alte kup,* the old head or wise one, a reflection of her seriousness and common sense as a child; early photographs of her show an unsmiling, somber girl with eyes gazing steadfastly into the camera. Her other nickname, less flattering, was Golda *der gilgul.* A *gilgul* in Yiddish and Hebrew can mean something that rolls around and around, or, more likely in Golda's case, a soul that has transmigrated into the body of a human, another way of saying that she had an uncontrollable spirit within, a *dybbuk*, that pushed her to strong-headedness.

"My mother . . . didn't know psychology," the adult Golda said. "How could she not understand what she did to me when she called me 'Golda the gilgul'? As a child I was certain, and frightened at the thought, that when I grew up and improved my life, I would still always bear this dreadful nickname, 'Golda the gilgul.'"

Golda had other fears that Bluma exacerbated. Across from the Nai-ditch house, a monastery rose from a hill near the river, and in front of it sat "wild-haired and wild-eyed" cripples, begging for alms and praying aloud with eerie melodies that remained with Golda for decades. The beggars terrified her, as did the monastery, the symbol of an unfamiliar Christian world, and as much as possible she avoided the area. Bluma capitalized on the terror by threatening the child that if she misbehaved, the fearsome beggars would haunt her dreams.

It was the kind of folklorish talk, like the *gilgul* nickname, that generations of Old Country mothers, hardly schooled in modern child-rearing techniques, utilized to keep their children in check. Bluma was far from an ideal mother, but for her, as for most shtetl women, daily existence demanded strength, toughness, and a level of aggressiveness. To support her daughters while her husband was away, earning next to nothing, she assisted her sisters in small shops they opened in town and started her own modest business baking bread and cakes that she sold door-to-door to wealthy householders. At some point, she and the children moved to an apartment in a poor, dirty alleyway close to a local police station. It had one room and a sooty kitchen with a large Russian stove built into the wall. Her life did not lend itself to insights into her daughters' fears and feelings, even had she been so inclined. But the lack led to constant misunderstandings and angry arguments with them.

The conflicts intensified as the world around them became more dangerous. On Easter Sunday, April 19, 1903, the eighth day of Passover, a murderous pogrom erupted in the city of Kishinev that stunned Jews everywhere. Through the lens of post-Holocaust eyes, the number of dead may seem negligible; the violence limited. But in its time, Kishinev served as a turning point in Russian Jewish history, becoming a symbol of Jewish vulnerability and a catalyst for Jewish self-defense.

A few months before the pogrom, a young Christian boy had been found murdered in a village near Kishinev and a young woman died of unknown causes in a Jewish hospital. With those deaths, a fiercely anti-

Semitic newspaper editor, Pavolachi Krushevan, launched a campaign of blaming the Jews with the old canard of "ritual murders" to acquire blood for Passover ceremonies. "Death to the Jews," his headlines screamed, and bands of teenage boys joined by adults took up the slogan, murdering and mutilating the Jews of Kishinev. The attacks were bloody and savage—nails driven through heads, eyes gouged out, women raped and their breasts chopped off. By the time the violence ended, three days after it started, almost fifty people were dead, more than five hundred injured, and thousands of families left homeless. Most contemporaries accused the Russian government of instigating the horrors, and though later historians have shown this not to be the case, national and local forces were both inept and slow to quell the riots.

Russia's Jews responded to news of the pogrom with despair. In the Mabovitch household, as in thousands of others, adult family members undertook an all-day fast in sympathy with the victims. Five-year-old Goldie insisted on joining them. According to her younger sister, Tzipka, drawing on family legend, she announced to her parents, "You fast for the adults, and I will fast for the little children."

When word of the terror spread, it aroused outrage in the Western world. In Paris and London, Jews, joined by gentiles, held massive protest meetings, and in Germany the kaiser conveyed his personal concern to the tsar. In the United States, President Theodore Roosevelt agreed to send a petition to the tsar signed by thirteen thousand Americans (it never reached him). But the most powerful aftermath of the pogrom came in the form of a long poem written by Chaim Nachman Bialik, the greatest Hebrew poet of his time. Called "In the City of Slaughter," it began by describing the obscenities of the Kishinev massacre and went on to depict, with bitter sarcasm, the weakness of the Jews themselves, particularly of the men who watched in terror and did nothing as their wives and daughters were violated.

Bialik's burning accusations fired the souls of Russia's Jewish youth and became a rallying cry for self-defense, a cry also for rebellion against Tsar Nicholas II. Scores of Jews had already been stirred by an antitsarist fever sweeping Russia's liberal circles, and now they identified more ardently than ever with the revolutionary cause. In Pinsk, teenage Sheyna Mabovitch joined the frenzy. Through her experiences, Golda, although too young to understand all the politics, received her first lessons in Jewish activism.

Sheyna joined with other young people to form a study group of ten, with teachers from various political movements. The opportunities to become part of one or another of those movements were almost limitless. In muddy alleyways and twisting roads branching off the "big street" that ran through the town, groups representing every manner of social activity held secret, illegal meetings to study, plot, and sing songs of a new day to come.

There were Jewish revolutionaries who identified more readily with the Russian intelligentsia or the militant Socialist Revolutionary Party than with their Jewish heritage. Like the Russian rebels, they opposed the tsar's autocratic rule and sought to better the lot of peasants and proletariat. For these young people, the pogroms seemed less a Jewish issue than a demonstration of the tsar's failures.

There was the highly influential Bund (General Jewish Workers' Union in Lithuania, Poland, and Russia), a Jewish socialist workers' party for whom the oppressive conditions of Jewish life in Russia cried out for a new Jewish society on that soil. Bundists predicted that when the tsarist government was replaced by a socialist one, anti-Semitism would disappear and Jews would enjoy full rights.

And there was an array of Zionist groups, the Bund's chief political opponents, although much smaller and weaker than the Bund. For Zionists, the only way Jews could combat discrimination was by having a land of their own, which to most meant Eretz Yisrael, the historic Land of Israel. The Bundists accused the more middle-class Zionists of "bourgeois utopianism" that ignored the needs of the struggling Jewish masses in Russia. The Zionists accused the Bundists of blindness in not recognizing that Jews could never lead normal lives outside their own land.

The Zionist idea had taken hold in Pinsk and other parts of the Pale after pogroms swept Russia in 1881 and 1882. One of the earliest Pinsk Zionists, Yaakov Shertok, had joined a tiny group of student dreamers from many parts of the Russian Empire to head toward the Ottoman-controlled Holy Land. They called themselves BILU, from the initials of the biblical phrase "Beit Yaakov lechu venelcha" (House of Jacob, let us go up). Other early pioneers were part of a larger, more organized movement, the Hovevei Zion, or lovers of Zion. Unprepared for the desolation they found and untrained in physical labor, many of the young idealists from both groups fell ill and left, disillusioned. Most of those who remained depended on funds from the wealthy Parisian banker Baron Edmond de Rothschild to sustain their settlements. Yet they did build settlements and are remembered in Zionist history as founders of almost thirty permanent modern Jewish agricultural colonies in Palestine.

When the dark-eyed, black-bearded Viennese journalist Theodor

Herzl appeared on the Jewish scene, filled with rage at Europe's pernicious anti-Jewishness, Zionism took a turn that reshaped the entire movement. Under Herzl's direction, the First Zionist Congress met in Basel, Switzerland, in 1897, the same year the Bund was established. Beyond the building of farms and settlements, the goal now became to establish a political state in Palestine, a national home for the world's Jews. Sparked by Herzl, a new Zionist excitement spread through the towns and cities of Eastern Europe.

But as Sheyna, who took up the Zionist cause, soon discovered, that camp was also split into opposing, often bitter sides. Some groups, known as territorialists, argued that after the Kishinev slaughter times were too pressing to concentrate only on Palestine as a homeland, and while that land remained the ultimate hope, Jewish leaders needed to seek other options for the present. Others passionately insisted that only Palestine could serve as a haven for the Jewish people. Sheyna eventually found her way to the socialist Poalei Zion (Workers of Zion) movement, a synthesis of socialism and Zionism developed by its leader, Ber Borochov, and the influential theoretician Nachman Syrkin, whose daughter was to become one of Golda's closest friends.

These were exciting times for Sheyna. She received her first lessons in revolutionary tactics from Chaya Weizmann Lichtenstein, Chaim Weizmann's sister, at their parents' home. (Chaim was away most of this time, working in Geneva.) It was an unusual home, open to all the competing revolutionary groups. A large tree in the center of its garden provided cover for the activists who gathered beneath it to talk and argue, or quickly switch to singing and dancing when warned of a police raid.

The tradition Pinsk Jews had of defending themselves against pogroms made them especially aggressive after Kishinev. Jewish revolutionaries murdered men they suspected of being "agents provocateurs," government infiltrators into their secret organizations, and assassinated policemen who had killed Jews. Everybody knew that whatever a person's political affiliation, a Jew fleeing the police could find asylum in any Jewish home.

They were dangerous times. As Sheyna and her small circle became more sophisticated in their studies, they left the Weizmann meeting ground and branched out into the various movements they joined. Groups met in synagogues on Friday nights after services and in members' homes when they knew parents would be away. At a meeting Sheyna hosted, her mother returned unexpectedly to find her home filled with young conspirators. "Mother understood very well that this was no time to call me to account," Sheyna said. Instead, Bluma hurried outside and for an hour paced around the house, ready to warn the rebels if she saw any sign of the police.

Not that Bluma approved of Sheyna's activities. From where they lived, near the police station, they could hear the screams of young women and men being brutally beaten, and Bluma feared for her daughter's safety and for the safety of the family. She fought with Sheyna about her activities, and even locked her out one night when the teenager came home particularly late. To no avail. Angry at her mother's incessant harassment, Sheyna moved in with her favorite aunt, Chaya, and quickly returned when that household turned out to be stricter than her own. In the end, she did not budge from her mission, and Bluma reluctantly kept guard when gatherings took place at their home—usually on Saturday mornings—her eyes peeled for the police.

And Golda? How much of the tumult around her could she assimilate? Too young to understand everything, she watched Sheyna and her friends from her hideout on top of the stove and grasped enough to give her, in Sheyna's words, a "whip" with which to threaten her sister during their own quarrels.

"I'll tell everything to Maxim the policeman," she would yell.

"What will you tell him?" Sheyna would ask.

"I'll tell him that you and your comrades shout, 'Down with the tsar and his regime,'" Golda would reply. Explaining what she could, Sheyna would caution that such words could get her exiled to Siberia. Burly Maxim never arrested anyone, but the young people felt certain that he passed on information to higher officials.

Despite her childish threats, Golda adored her older sister. From those early years onward, Sheyna would remain for her "a shining example," her "dearest friend," and "the one person whose praise and approval—when I won them, which was not easy—meant most to me." Even so, as an adult, she had to acknowledge that Sheyna's single-mindedness in pursuing her ends had caused their mother great pain. For now, however, Sheyna's convictions became her own.

These were romantic times for Sheyna. On a visit to her aunt Chaya, she met a neighbor's son, a young revolutionary named Shamai Korngold, and fell head over heels in love. Sheyna knew of Shamai by reputation as a leader of the territorialist Socialist Zionist group. He bore the code name Copernicus and often disguised himself to avoid police capture. Out of disguise, he cut a dashing figure in Sheyna's eyes, dressed in his black Russian peasant shirt and peaked cap, the uniform of young revolutionaries.

The grandson of a noted rabbi in Pinsk, Shamai had been the pride of his family, a talented student especially gifted in mathematics. With the revolutionary currents washing across Russia, he gave up his studies to throw himself into the struggle, giving up also any semblance of his family's strict religious observance. To make that point, he arranged a political meeting in his home on Yom Kippur, the holiest day on the Jewish calendar, when his parents were in synagogue, leaving behind a trail of cigarette smoke (an activity prohibited on that day). His behavior, which shattered his parents, reflected the contempt many young revolutionaries felt toward traditional religious practices. Golda knew Shamai through his frequent visits to the Mabovitch household. Years later, in America, after he and Sheyna married, he would play a unique role in her life.

They were dramatic times. On January 9, 1905, Father Gapon, a St. Petersburg priest, led tens of thousands of workers and their families on a peaceful march to the tsar's Winter Palace with a petition requesting civil liberties for all citizens. The government dispatched soldiers, who shot into the crowd, killing more than a hundred and wounding several hundred more. A stunned population labeled the day "Bloody Sunday" and reacted with fury, staging mass protests and labor strikes, with peasants lashing out against landlords' estates. As the country turned into a cauldron of rage and rebellion, Russian and Jewish revolutionary groups were exhilarated in a newfound sense that their dreams of a better world might soon be realized.

To contain the commotion, in a brutal crackdown, the government called up mounted military troops, despised by the Jews as dreaded Cossacks. In reality, these were not replicas of the bloodthirsty Cossacks of Russia's early days; they were usually groups of peasants who served in the army as cavalrymen and were sent to keep order. But the Jews experienced enough cruelty from them to view them in the same light as the Cossacks of old. Golda remembered playing with friends in a narrow lane on a winter evening when suddenly "a troop of Cossacks galloped through. They didn't even slow down. They just jumped their horses over us . . . we were scared almost to death."

Nevertheless, with their increasing confidence, Jewish leaders in the town insisted on defending their rights. At a meeting with the chief of police on September 22, a Jewish spokesman declared that the only means to restore order is "equality for the Jews." By the next month, that equality seemed close at hand. On October 17, the tsar issued a manifesto promising his people civil liberties and the right to elect a legislature with power to enact and veto laws. Golda's aunt Chaya broke the news to the family, joyfully shouting in Yiddish, "Mir hubin a constituzia" (We have a constitution). Victory parties burst out in Pinsk and around the land.

Exciting times. Dangerous, romantic, dramatic times. And then everything fell apart. "For no group in Russia would the fall from triumph come so suddenly as it did for the Jews," writes the historian Jonathan Frankel.

Within days of the October Manifesto, pogroms descended on Kiev and Kishinev, Odessa, Zhitomer, Minsk, Belostok, and dozens of other cities and towns. Historians estimate that in the last two weeks of October alone, 690 anti-Jewish pogroms erupted. The *pogromshchiki*, who defended the tsar or simply opposed change—peasants, shopkeepers, janitors—blamed the Jews for sparking the revolution. They were joined by hoodlums and gangs out to loot and murder. Although, this time again, the government did not instigate the pogroms, many local officials looked the other way.

The pogroms did not reach Pinsk, but Bluma was now desperate. With unrest everywhere, the authorities were mercilessly seeking out Jewish revolutionaries. She and her girls had to leave Pinsk, not wait for Moshe to return.

"Take us away," she wrote to him. "We can no longer live here."

Moshe had been struggling to send money home from the meager income of three dollars a week he had been earning in New York. By 1905, however, he was living in Milwaukee, Wisconsin, where he had found a job as a carpenter working on the Milwaukee Railroad. He wrote to Bluma that he could now manage to bring the family to America and they should start preparing for the journey.

They left Pinsk in April 1906, immediately after Passover. At the train station, family members gathered for anguished farewells, the grandparents Menachem Naiditch and Pesse Feigel, Aunt Chaya, the many cousins. Everyone promised to write regularly, and Zeide Naiditch pleaded with his grandchildren not to forget their *Yiddishkeit*, their Jewishness, in their distant land. Golda never saw any of them again.

"SO WHAT DID I TAKE with me from there? Fear, hunger and fear," Golda Meir would say, "fear of Cossacks in Pinsk and the dreadful cries from the police station." Always in the recounting, her memories of early childhood in Russia emphasized the troubles, the "poverty, pogroms, and political repression." Such memories suited the broader Zionist goals that dominated her life. But she also carried with her other impressions, less openly expressed, as she left her childhood land: the activism, not only the fears, of the Jews of Pinsk; the revolutionary fervor that had inspired her sister and other young Jews; the *Yiddishkeit*, so important to her grandfather, that had surrounded her every day; the close connections shtetl Jews had with one another. They, too, would have their influence as her life developed.

2

An American Girl

In leaving Russia, Bluma and her girls followed a pattern typical of hundreds of thousands of other émigrés. First to depart were the men in the family, the husbands and fathers, often elder sons, who then worked in America's cities to earn enough money to send for wives, mothers, children, and other relatives. It might take years before these men could pay for their family's passage. In the meantime, many lived as boarders in dismal tenement apartments that held several people to a room, with a single bathroom located in the hallway or outside the building, while back home women like Bluma carried the full burden of supporting themselves and their children. When the men had scraped together the necessary funds, they sent home money or steamship tickets, the cherished *shifskarten* that would enable the family to join them. Now the women left, clutching children and the few bags of belongings they could manage and maneuvering their way through a maze of railroad stations, inspection centers, and cramped steerage departments aboard dilapidated ships.

For Golda and her family, emigration problems began with Moshe's leave-taking three years earlier. To cross the border out of tsarist Russia, the head of a household was required to buy a passport, which also listed all other family members. Having sold his carpenter's tools, Moshe had enough to pay for the passport but not for the ship's passage or other travel expenses. He turned for advice to some of the shady "agents" who, along with legitimate travel agents, had sprouted like weeds all over the empire as emigration swelled. The worst of these people, known by the Yiddish *agenten shvindler*, or swindling agents, were skilled at duping trusting and desperate emigrants. Moshe was lucky. The agents he hired found a woman eager to be reunited with her husband in America who could afford to pay Moshe's way but did not have a passport for her and her three daughters. She and her girls adopted the Mabovitch name on Moshe's passport and traveled with him as his "wife and children."

That, of course, left his legitimate wife and daughters without passports when their turn came to exit Pinsk in the spring of 1906. Through the network of illegal agents, they arranged to assume fake identities of their own and steal across the border from Russia into Galicia, Poland, a common practice among emigrants. The first step took them by train to the town of Grajewo, in the Russian-controlled part of Poland. There they were to take another train for a short trip across the border. The scene as it unfolded became embedded in family history.

It was nighttime, and they were tired and hungry. An old woman who met them at the station led them to a nearby house to await their train. Suddenly, as they ate the meager meal provided, a man burst into the house shouting that the police would have to be bribed because they had heard that some Jews planned to steal across the border. Moreover, he insisted, Bluma and the girls would be safer leaving that evening and traveling through the forest by horse and wagon instead of waiting for the train. Bluma was no fool. She understood immediately that a horse and wagon cost less than a train and the money saved would end up in the agents' pockets. With the kind of strength and shrewdness her daughters would come to admire in her, she announced indignantly that they had been promised train travel, and if that did not happen, they would return to Pinsk, the money they still owed unpaid.

Early the next morning, the family traveled across the border into Galicia by train, as originally promised. For this trip, Bluma took on the identity of a woman of twenty; Sheyna became a twelve-year-old; Golda, five; and Tzipka pretended to be another woman's child. Somewhere in that crossing, Bluma bribed the local police, as required, and somewhere their baggage was lost, or more likely stolen. Bluma would sigh over their missing bags for years.

The family spent the next two days in a large, wooden barrack in Galicia waiting for a train to carry them to Antwerp, Belgium. Moshe had sailed from Liverpool to New York. Bluma and the girls would board a boat in Antwerp for Quebec, Canada, and from there travel by train to Milwaukee. (They might have chosen Quebec because of its less daunting immigrant processing center than New York's Ellis Island.) The barrack was cold and unheated, packed with other refugees, and primitive in its facilities. Dirty mattresses for sleeping lay scattered about the floor, water had to be brought in from the outside, and just one outhouse served everyone.

"Only last night and the night before," Sheyna reflected, "we enjoyed a sense of security; here we felt helpless . . . We tasted the condition of immigrants. What lay ahead for us?"

Far ahead, in Golda's future, were to be encounters with wave after wave of immigrants landing in Israel. Through her own experience, she knew the loneliness and sense of dislocation they felt, and she would be angry when some of them accused her of not understanding their needs.

They finally boarded the train to Antwerp, where two shipping company officials met them and led them to a large immigration center. There, for the first time since leaving Russia, they bathed, ate decent meals, and slept in clean, comfortable beds. Such centers existed in most of Europe's port cities. Shipping companies that had once provided only the barest necessities to poor refugees had learned that it was more profitable for them to treat their wards humanely before they embarked than to have the U.S. government return sick travelers to their countries of origin at the companies' expense.

The family had assumed their own names again, and on the evening of their second day at the center they heard themselves called for their assigned ship, the S.S. *Montreal*. They left the next morning, Wednesday, May 16. The ship's passenger manifest prepared for the U.S. Immigration Services lists among its "Hebrew" passengers "Blume Mabowitz" and "Scheine," "Golde," and "Zipa," daughters, with their approximate years of birth. In a column headed "whether in possession of $50.00, and if less, how much?" the sum of $12.00 appears opposite Bluma's name.

Now they embarked on a sea voyage that mirrored the voyages of myriad immigrants who traveled steerage across the Atlantic at the start of the twentieth century. They were assigned a tiny, airless compartment, deep in the ship's bowels. Their wooden beds, in narrow bunks one above the other, had straw-filled mattresses without sheets. When a bell rang, people stood up in their compartments—steerage had no dining room—holding the cup and plate they had been given, while a crew member doled out food from huge kettles. Most people were too sick from the tossing of the ship and the stench of the cabins to eat the unappetizing food in any event; at one point, Sheyna fainted from hunger and had to be revived by the ship's doctor. Bluma finally managed to scrounge some scraps of potatoes and onions from the kitchen and find a way to prepare a "stew" they could keep down. With it all, Golda remained healthy, able to stay on the deck for hours. She would make that crossing many times in the years ahead, often in inclement weather, with no sign of seasickness. Her constitution proved strong from the start.

Twelve days after leaving Antwerp, the ship docked in Quebec, where the four family members boarded a train out of Canada, toward Moshe and their new life. After changing trains in Chicago, they finally stepped, somewhat bewildered, into the hustle and bustle of Milwaukee's railroad station. All told, from the time they left Russia until they arrived in Milwaukee, they had been traveling for six weeks, from after Passover to the eve of the festival of Shavuot on May 29.

MILWAUKEE. MOSHE HAD NEVER HEARD of the place before leaving Pinsk. "Everybody who was anybody had either gone or was going to New York," wrote Marcus Ravage, a Romanian immigrant. Some also went to Boston, Philadelphia, Chicago, or other large cities. But Milwaukee?

Moshe's move to that city appears to have been arranged by the Industrial Removal Office (IRO), one of a variety of organizations created to cope with the tide of Jewish immigrants pouring into New York. Often working closely with the Hebrew Immigrant Aid Society (HIAS), the IRO had the specific task of steering newcomers away from large East Coast cities to the south and west. Its lofty goal, according to its general manager, was to allow the immigrants to find "their own salvation," a romantic way of describing the organization's calculated efforts to redirect the lives of the new arrivals.

The avalanche of poverty-stricken Russian and Polish Jews that descended on Manhattan's Lower East Side stunned the established New York Jewish community. Proud descendants of parents or grandparents who had come to the United States from central Europe years earlier, most of these "German Jews," as they were called, had ambivalent attitudes toward their co-religionists. They felt it their duty to aid the new immigrants, and they did, admirably, through philanthropic works, educational programs, and social services. But they were also embarrassed by the foreign-looking newcomers whom many considered "ignorant, superstitious . . . quarrelsome, unclean." The establishment Jews worried about the effect the dirt-poor Yiddish-speaking masses might have on their own standing among Christian Americans. And they hoped that by being dispersed, away from the congestion of big-city ghettos to small communities, the new arrivals might become Americanized more quickly.

In the end, those efforts barely paid off. In the twenty-one years of the IRO's existence, it dispersed only about seventy-nine thousand immigrants out of the millions who flocked to America's shores. Once they reached New York, most Jewish immigrants preferred to remain there.

Moshe seems to have been one of the IRO's successes. Among the records the agency kept are boxes of "removal ledgers" listing people sent out of New York. As with similar immigrant records, the handwritten names are frequently misspelled or distorted. One name and age listed on a ledger for September 1904 is "M. Mayowitz, 38." The surrounding entries indicate that this person was married, a carpenter, from Russia, had lived in New York City at 45 East Seventh Street for about nine to twelve months, and was sent to Milwaukee, Wisconsin. It is likely that this is Golda's father, Moshe, who would have been in his late thirties at the time. Having arrived in New York in December 1903 and never earning more than a few dollars a week, he would have been ripe for "removal" to Milwaukee. There, from his job as a carpenter in the workshops of the Milwaukee Railroad, he managed to purchase steamship tickets for the family.

As a result of Moshe's decision—and in some sense courage—to move yet again to another unfamiliar location, Golda Mabovitch would not grow up in the slums and ghettos of New York or other large eastern cities as did the vast majority of immigrant Jewish children from Russia. She would spend those years in a relatively small town in the Midwest, whose population of about 300,000 included only about 9,000 Jews when she arrived, and though her home would be in the Jewish quarter, it would also be in an area of the country surrounded by dairy farms and wide prairies, an area where the pioneer spirit of old still inspired people to push westward, to pursue their dreams in new places. She could not help but be touched by the openness around her.

The tall slender man who met Golda and the others at the train station in Milwaukee looked nothing like the father and husband they remembered. Dressed strangely to their eyes, he had also lost his beard and with it his Jewish appearance. The wife and daughters Moshe greeted at the train station looked nothing like the nostalgic mental images he had of them. They seemed such "greenhorns" with their shawls and long, dark dresses, rumpled and soiled from the many weeks of traveling, and with no personal belongings to speak of. During his three years away from them, he had come to feel himself quite the American. They had Old Country poverty written all over them.

Moshe hired an automobile to take the family to his lodgings, the "first time I saw what I thought was a wagon without a horse," Golda said. She felt overwhelmed by the newness about her—the neat rows of one-story clapboard houses they passed, the sounds of a language she didn't know, the father she scarcely remembered. The friendly landlady at the house where he boarded, a Mrs. Badner, who had arrived from Poland about a year earlier, greeted them warmly and made them as comfortable as possible, although all five would have to sleep in Moshe's tiny, shabby furnished room. He had neglected to find an apartment for them.

Before looking for one even now, Moshe—who had changed his name to Morris outside the family—took them on a shopping expedition to Schuster's department store, part of a chain located in Milwaukee neighborhoods. For him, as for every immigrant, dressing like an American was vital to becoming one. He asked the salesperson for pretty dresses for the little girls, something light and fluffy, and for Bluma a white shirtwaist and dark skirt—the current fashion—along with a simple everyday outfit. For Sheyna he chose a frilly blouse, a shiny dark skirt, and a hat covered with flowers. She was horrified.

Over the past two years, she had worn only long black dresses with long sleeves and high collars, the dress of revolutionaries and the color of mourning. She had been in mourning since the day in 1904 when her aunt came to their apartment in Pinsk to announce that Theodor Herzl had died. She was not alone in that practice. Rachel Yanait, one of the early pioneers in Palestine and later the wife of Israel's second president, Yitzhak Ben-Zvi, wore only one black dress for an entire year, in mourning for Herzl, and other young women demonstrated their Zionist loyalty in similar ways. For Sheyna, shedding her black clothes and donning a frivolous blouse and flowered hat was tantamount to shedding her entire identity.

"This is how we dress in America," Moshe retorted, when she objected to the clothes. He knew of her revolutionary activities in Pinsk and wanted it made clear that she lived in the United States now. To Golda's mind, the hostility that would dominate the relationship between her father and her elder sister during most of their years in the United States began that day, when he insisted she wear American-style clothes.

Unlike Sheyna, Golda loved her new clothes and began to love what she saw around her. The city traffic, the well-dressed people, the five-story department stores—which seemed skyscrapers to her—the penny ice cream cones sold in bakeries, the wooden Indians outside cigar stores, the electric lights, trolleys, soda pop, and other wonders of this new world enthralled her. For the first time in her short life, she felt a sense of freedom, or, more precisely, a lack of fear.

In later years, Golda told and retold of her first Labor Day, in September, a little less than four months after she arrived in Milwaukee. Her father, who had become a proud union member, planned to march with his carpenters' group in the traditional Labor Day Parade and invited his family to watch the festivities. When little Tzipka spotted the mounted police leading the parade, she began to tremble and scream, "It's the Cossacks, the Cossacks are coming!" She became so agitated that she spiked a high fever and had to stay in bed for days. Golda, on the other hand, recognized the deeper significance of the event: "Police on horseback were actually escorting the marchers, instead of dispersing them and trampling them underfoot." The story became emblematic for her of how profoundly she appreciated the ideals of her new country.

Milwaukee served as a fine example of American freedom for a young girl born into the tyranny of Russia. The area, which began as a native American village in the seventeenth century and became a French trading post in the eighteenth, gained its lasting German character in the nineteenth. The bulk of German immigrants thronged the city after the German revolution of 1848 failed to win political reforms from the princes of their various German states. These "forty-eighters," now persecuted in their own country, gave their newfound home a flavor of their own liberalism. As the German community increased, its progressive ideas—along with its huge breweries and noisy beer gardens—came to dominate Milwaukee life.

The early German Jews and especially the later Eastern European immigrants who settled in Milwaukee strengthened the city's traditions of socialism and liberalism. While Golda attended elementary school, Milwaukee elected a socialist mayor and the nation's first socialist congressman—Victor Berger. The socialist reign in Milwaukee stretched through her years there, with Berger returned to Congress four times, and a second socialist mayor, Dan Hoan, holding office for more than twenty years.

Milwaukee's socialism differed from the radical revolutionary rhetoric Golda had heard from her sister in Russia. The emphasis here was on social justice, on reform more than revolution, on gradually building a new society instead of violently overthrowing the old one. The emphasis was on aiding the town's numerous small German American craftsmen, helping its Jewish factory workers, cleaning up the poorest neighborhoods, and fighting the widespread corruption of the Republican and Democratic Parties. With their moderate messages, socialist leaders reached beyond the working classes to businesspeople who would not ordinarily have supported them. They spread their ideas by blanketing the city with bundles of leaflets in several languages, including Yiddish, and publishing a popular daily newspaper, *The Milwaukee Leader*.

Could Golda as a young schoolgirl have understood or even known about the ideas and aims of Milwaukee's socialists? Not likely at first. But she would have been aware of the liberalism so prevalent in the city, aware, for example, of the street corner "soap boxing" that took place on Friday nights and Saturday afternoons, when people of every political stripe gave impromptu speeches to anyone who would listen. In a few years, she would mount a soapbox of her own, and as she became devoted to Socialist Zionism, she and her group would work closely with the city's socialists.

For now, she and her family moved into the Jewish "ghetto" centered on Walnut Street, where most of the Eastern European immigrants lived—the more prosperous German Jews had settled farther east—and everyone spoke Yiddish. "Jews ran small businesses then, groceries, delicatessens," Robert Hess, a Milwaukee lawyer from an immigrant Jewish background, recalled. "Life was hard, complicated, but also simple . . . a guy could take a girl out to a free lunch counter, where for fifty cents you could get a glass of beer and as much as you wanted to eat."

Not far from the Mabovitch dwelling at 615-623 Walnut Street stood six synagogues, a Jewish old-age home, and the city's much-used Settlement House, later renamed the Abraham Lincoln House. German Jews had established "the Settlement" to teach new immigrants the "American way" of doing things, and as much as the Eastern Europeans resented their patrons' condescending airs, they also took advantage of the English classes, cooking lessons, singing groups, and dances held in the house. Housewives all over the city, and far beyond it, swore by Lizzie Black Kander's *Settlement Cookbook*, first published in 1901 with the title *The Way to a Man's Heart*. It is hard to picture the book in Bluma's kitchen, however. She was too set in her ways and too busy running her own little store to pay attention to some German Jewish lady's recipes, let alone seek the way to the heart of a husband who, she quickly discovered, could still barely earn a livelihood, even in America, even in Milwaukee.

The idea for the store came to Bluma when the only apartment she and Moshe could find to rent had two rooms and a tiny kitchen with a long corridor leading to a vacant shop a few doors away. With her usual self-assurance and no experience at all, she plunged headlong into establishing a small business, first a dairy, then a grocery store. Nor did it faze her that she had to compete with more than ninety groceries and delicatessens in the Jewish quarter. With help from neighborhood women, she learned to stock what Milwaukeeans liked, cover fresh produce so it wouldn't spoil, and use a cash register. Moshe regarded the store as women's work and would have nothing to do with it. Sheyna took an even more adamant stand. "Suddenly become a storekeeper?" she declared. "For this I came to America?" She was a revolutionary, after all, a member of the proletariat, not the middle classes.

It fell on Golda to mind the store mornings when Bluma made trips to the wholesale markets to buy fruits and vegetables. Golda hated the job, especially after she began school. Because of it, she would frequently be late to classes or miss a day altogether and feel miserable about that. Always indifferent to her girls' education, Bluma shrugged off her daughter's bitter complaints, shrugged off also the truant officer who showed up to explain that in America children were required to attend school regularly. Her attitude infuriated Golda, who did not want to notice, any more than did the others, that without Bluma's struggling store there would be little to sustain them.

As poor as the family was, however, it never suffered the grinding squalor of the tenements of New York and other large cities. In this midwestern town, peeling frame houses with dark rooms still had open-air porches and a patch of green in the back. Compared with the dwellings Golda remembered in Kiev and Pinsk, the Milwaukee apartment seemed "the height of luxury" even without electricity and an indoor bathroom. She, Sheyna, and Bluma scrubbed the place clean until "light dazzled our eyes and a lightness entered our hearts," Sheyna rhapsodized.

The lightness quickly faded for Sheyna. She had trouble learning English (and spoke it with a thick Yiddish accent all her life), could not make a go of one job after another, and quarreled constantly with her parents. When she finally found work as a seamstress in a small factory in Chicago, Golda would wheedle her father into inviting Sheyna home for a visit. Without that invitation, she knew her sister would never show up. After Sheyna pricked her finger with a sewing needle and it became badly infected, she had to return to Milwaukee for medical care. "When it hurts, they always run home," Bluma greeted her sarcastically. But

Golda happily welcomed Sheyna and for weeks helped her dress and groom herself, thrilled to be able to draw close to her idol. After Sheyna recuperated, she found a job running a sewing machine in a small local shop and moved to a tiny apartment not far from the family.

THROUGH IT ALL, GOLDA EXCELLED as a student. She was enrolled at the Fourth Street School, a handsome three-story Romanesque Revival structure, all brick and limestone, with wide staircases and large double-hung windows that allowed light into the classrooms. It had been built on "Brewers' Hill" some fifteen years earlier to provide the children of both managers and workers in the nearby beer factories an equal education. As the Jewish immigrant community grew and German residents moved to other areas, Jewish children like Golda filled the classrooms, learning the customs of their new land.

During assemblies, students smartly saluted the U.S. flag and recited the Pledge of Allegiance to "one nation indivisible." In an era when Americans expressed little cynicism about patriotism or doubted their country's manifest destiny in the world, the school's civics books, like those throughout the nation, assured young readers that "they will be glad they live in the United States when they know more of its government and the governments of some other countries," and history texts breathlessly described the drama in Philadelphia when "the bell in the high tower above the hall began to ring" and the people cried out, "It is done! They have signed the Declaration of Independence."

In another era, Golda would weep with joy as she signed Israel's independence declaration. "When I studied American history as a schoolgirl," she would say, "and I read about those who signed the Declaration of Independence, I couldn't imagine these were real people doing something real. And there I was sitting down and signing a declaration of independence." Her powerful emotional ties to the United States began with those earliest lessons in citizenship and would remain with her through life, even as they became more complex and more hidden.

She loved school. "She was always first to answer all the questions the teachers asked. She was always the one who knew more than the others," her closest grade school chum, Regina Hamburger (later Medzini), said. The two girls lived on the same street, and they would walk to and from classes together, do their homework together, and often sleep at each other's house. Summers they worked as messenger girls at Gimbels department store for three dollars a week, walking for almost an hour each way to save the five-cent tramway fare. "Every penny we earned we gave to our parents," Regina attested. Golda's family especially needed the money she made. "They were very poor . . . there were times when really the question of food was a problem."

As Regina pictured her in their youth, Golda was "very serious minded." Although she had many friends in school, she didn't play with them after school. She was too busy working in her mother's store and, if she had spare time, reading. More than twice a week, she and Regina borrowed books from the public library—Tolstoy, Dostoyevsky, and other writers "far beyond us," Regina recalled. It's a surprising slice of memory about Golda, whom critics mocked in adult life as someone who rarely read a book of any sort. Occasionally, Golda and Regina might splurge on a silent movie or vaudeville act for a nickel or dime. One spring, when Golda was ten and Regina nine, the girls saw a production of *Uncle Tom's Cabin* at the local Bijou Theater, probably with free tickets from school. The play so affected the impressionable Golda that she jumped out of her seat to shout at the cruel Simon Legree. She enjoyed telling about that incident later; she liked the image it projected of her.

Another school friend, Sara Feder, whose parents ran a delicatessen near the Mabovitch store, remembered gaining "school fame" shortly before graduation, when she and Golda debated other students on the question of who was the better Civil War general, Ulysses S. Grant or Robert E. Lee. They backed Grant and won.

American history, the public library, a classic play, department store work—Golda was slipping easily into American life outside her home.

Inside the scene was different. There, anger and yelling between her parents and sister took over again, this time centered on the arrival of Sheyna's friend Shamai Korngold from Russia. Bluma and Moshe (less vociferously) firmly opposed any romance between the two. True, Bluma had chosen her own spouse without serious parental interference, but that happened in another place and time. It pained her that in America, where Sheyna had a chance to rise above the poverty that had darkened their lives and marry someone with a future, she refused to budge from her past.

Sheyna stood her ground. She rented a room for Shamai in Milwaukee and helped him find work in a cigarette factory. They began studying English at night and attending lectures and meetings together. Then, shocking to both, Sheyna became ill with tuberculosis, the dread "white plague." People called it *di Yiddishe proletarishe krenk*, the disease of the

Jewish working class, for it grew and spread in the unsanitary conditions of factories and workshops where scores of Jews labored.

Sheyna entered the National Jewish Hospital for Consumptives in Denver, Colorado, as a free patient. She left home less than two years after the family had settled in Milwaukee, a frightened young woman of eighteen, with only Golda and Shamai to see her off at the train station. Still furious with her, Bluma and Moshe refused to join them. Long after she and they would reconcile, Sheyna could relive the anguish she felt during her early days in Denver. "If a daughter leaves for a sanatorium without a coin in her pocket," she said, "they could have written first and sent a few dollars as well." They could and should have, but they lacked the ability, or will, to understand the daughter who, in their eyes, had rebelled against them at every turn.

Golda alone kept contact with Sheyna. She corresponded faithfully and secretly, channeling her mail through Regina and another neighbor. With the country experiencing a severe recession in 1907 and 1908, her letters carried depressing news. "I can tell you that Pa does not work yet and in the store is not very busy," she wrote in 1908 and soon again, "Pa isn't working."

But for the most part she tried to lift Sheyna's spirits. When she could, she enclosed stamps so that Sheyna could write to her, and when the puritanical Sheyna worried about where her sister obtained money for those stamps, Golda assured her that she had saved it from her lunch money. In fact, she had "borrowed" the necessary coins from her mother's household till.

HER HAPPIEST LETTER TOLD OF her first "public work," organizing a group of schoolmates to provide textbooks to poor children. Accounts of that episode, like many narratives of Golda's childhood, have an almost mythic cast, often told and repeated. Untold, however, is the background for this narrative, the real issue that prompted Golda's actions and the recognition those actions received.

Although Milwaukee public schools charged no tuition, students were required to pay for their textbooks. Traditionally, they bought second-hand books or received them from older siblings, but in the spring of 1908 the textbook committee of the Milwaukee school board began a review to determine which texts might be outdated and in need of replacement. The very idea of replacement, which meant that children could no longer count on used books in those subjects, set off a firestorm of protest from parents and politicians. For months, newspapers carried editorials and news stories on the topic, sometimes allotting them equal space with pieces about the presidential hopefuls William Howard Taft and William Jennings Bryan.

Despite controversy, on June 3 the full board accepted the committee's recommendations to replace eleven books. With school opening in September, *The Milwaukee Journal* noted that there had been 146 applicants for free books by people who could not afford new ones, 80 of the applicants from the "Russian Jewish section of the Sixth ward," Golda's neighborhood.

To young Golda, the situation called for action. With Regina's help, she rounded up a group of girls and formed a club with the ambitious name American Young Sisters' Society to raise textbook money for the following year. Club members sent out invitations to their entire district announcing a public meeting and somehow managed to finagle a small hall for the event. On the scheduled Saturday evening, with dozens in attendance, Golda "said a speech from my head" explaining the purpose of the group, she wrote to Sheyna. Afterward, she recited two Yiddish poems, "Der Schneider" (The tailor) and "Die zwei Korbones" (The two sacrifices), followed by little sister Tzipka, known now as Clara, who also recited a Yiddish poem. Their parents beamed with pride, while a sympathetic audience contributed generously to the cause.

"We had the greatest success that there ever was in Packen Hall. And the entertainment was Grand," Golda boasted in a letter to Sheyna on August 2, 1909.

A month later, a news story about the group appeared prominently in *The Milwaukee Journal*. It carried the headline "Children Help Poor in School" and the subhead "Little Sisters' Society Is Well Organized." The project "was organized Dec. 5, 1908, at 623 Walnut St.," the paper said, giving Golda's address. "The children are not of rich parentage . . . To every child, perhaps, the 3 cents a week that constitutes the dues, means some little childish wish unfulfilled." With the money collected, the children had bought fifteen books and, after taking applications from parents, distributed them to the neediest. Coincidentally, advertisements surrounding the article offered children's socks on sale for "7 cents" and shoes for "95 cents," reinforcing the value of the children's three-cent-a-week contributions. At the end, the column listed the members and officers of the club, with "Goldie Mabowetz, president," and Clara Mabowetz a member. An accompanying photograph showed thirteen serious-looking young girls and the notation that "President Goldie Mabowetz is in top row, fourth from right."

Here, at age eleven, was the earliest glimmer of Golda Meir's formidable lifelong skills at organizing and fund-raising—and attracting public notice.

In Denver, Sheyna experienced no such triumphs. The only pleasant interlude in her hard life was the arrival of Shamai, who had been struggling in Chicago during these difficult economic times. She lined up a job for him washing dishes in the sanatorium kitchen, which he supplemented with evening work as a presser in a hotel laundry. As her year as a patient ended, Sheyna found work doing odd jobs at the Agnes Memorial Sanatorium, a private hospital for the wealthy.

While shoveling snow one day outside the sanatorium, she began to cough up blood. She would need to be rehospitalized and applied this time to Denver's Jewish Consumptives' Relief Society (JCRS), which accepted the most serious tubercular cases. Charles Friend, secretary of the Milwaukee branch of the Federated Jewish Charities (FJC), sent a letter on April 3, 1909, on her behalf. Although the FJC had been paying for her care, he wrote, "We cannot continue to support this young woman in the future . . . The case of Miss Mabovitz is particularly sad since she has no one to whom she may look for any aid. While she has parents living in Milwaukee, they are unwilling to assist her and they are in financial straits also." Her break with her parents had become part of the public record.

Sheyna, who had taken the name Jennie, was admitted to the JCRS on April 22 and remained there for three months. After her discharge, she and Shamai—he had become "Sam"—married, although her doctors strongly advised against it because of her illness. Their daughter, Judith, was born a year later, in 1910.

Meanwhile, Golda continued her studies at the Fourth Street School and in 1912 graduated valedictorian of her class. At the ceremony, she noticed her father's "moist" eyes as he looked at his middle daughter in her white graduation dress. Her grandfather had barely been literate, and here she was, the first member of their family to graduate from school. But the tender moment passed quickly. She had expected to go on to high school, then study to become a schoolteacher. Bluma had other expectations. Golda could go to a secretarial school, as her friend Regina was planning to do, and learn to type so that she could find an office job. Moreover, Milwaukee did not permit schoolteachers to be married. Did that mean, Bluma harangued her, that Golda wanted to be an old maid?

In later years, Golda would speak warmly of her mother and quote her frequently as a wellspring of maternal wisdom. Colleagues rolled their eyes when they related anecdotes that she told and retold about the older woman. When she was a young girl and the family very poor, one story went, she would refuse to wash the dishes for fear something would break. But once, when her mother was ill, Golda had to do the dishes. "Goldele," her mother said after that, "now you really should be beaten, because if you didn't know how to do it and you didn't, that's one thing; but you did know and you didn't do it. For that, you ought to be hit." The adult Golda admired the lesson behind the story and found it worth repeating often, especially to her staff.

The teenage Golda considered her mother's lessons a burden and the rejection of her school plans intolerable. For her, the prospect of office work was "worse than death." To make matters worse, her father backed her mother, preaching his own lesson in practicality: It doesn't pay to be too clever. Men didn't like smart girls.

Golda persevered, no less driven than her mother or sister to get her own way. Defying her parents, she enrolled in North Division High School on September 3, 1912. Secretly, she planned to join Sheyna in Denver, where she could continue her studies without interference. To earn extra money for the venture, she and Regina started teaching English to new immigrants at ten cents a lesson. From the first, Sheyna urged Golda on in her plans. She loved the thought of having her sister with her and, though she might not admit it, also relished her victory over her parents, knowing that Golda would leave them to join her.

A series of letters from Sheyna to "My dear Goldie," and signed "Jennie," track the sisters' plotting as circumstances evolved in both their lives. Sheyna wrote in English because she knew Golda preferred that, although she still had difficulty with the spelling and language. "I surely thought you would be with us by this time," she wrote in August, before Golda's school began, "but I think you'll have to wait for a while yet, for the longer we are here, the more we get into debts." Sam, who had been out of work, had finally found a night job as a janitor for the telephone company, and she hoped that would soon ease their financial situation. "Did you change your mind yet about coming?" she asked, hoping the answer would be no. And, with big sister concern, "Would you be afraid to go on the train all by yourself?"

Learning that Golda had actually started high school, Sheyna wrote on October 8 how "very happy," although astonished, she was to hear that news. "Tell me the truth," she pushed, "how many times did you shout and how many times were you about to commit suicide untill [*sic*] you won the battle." For her part, she remained estranged from their parents. In thanking Golda for a gift she sent to little Judith, Sheyna wondered how her sister could have paid for it, "for I know that all the money you used to earn Mr. and Mrs. Mabowitz used to take away from you," she said, bitterly referring to her parents by their last name. (Bluma and Moshe would not meet Judith, their first grandchild, until she was about four years old, when they finally made their peace with Sheyna.)

Sometime that year, Bluma had opened a new store on Tenth Street, a delicatessen, where Morris worked as a butcher, and the family lived in the apartment overhead. Sheyna wanted to know how Golda had taken to the move. "Is there anybody sleeping with you upstairs?" she asked, adding, "I know you are afraid to sleep alown [*sic*]," a portent, perhaps, of Golda's habit later in life of phoning friends or assistants in the middle of the night and inviting them to her home to keep her company.

But now a new turn of events sent sparks flying in Milwaukee. Like Mrs. Bennet in *Pride and Prejudice*, whose "business [in] life was to get her daughters married," Bluma, disappointed in her elder daughter's marriage, was making it her business to get *this* one properly married and cared for. She lined up a fairly well-to-do man more than twice Golda's age, a Mr. Goodstein, whom Golda knew slightly from his visits to the store and who agreed to wait a few years for her to grow up. Golda's unhappy news brought an immediate response from Denver, this time from Shamai: "My advice is that you should get ready and come to us."

Yet, unhappy as she felt at home, Golda hesitated. She also followed a practice that throughout her life drove friends and relatives to distraction. Busy with other activities, or simply negligent, she failed to answer letters she received, often waiting to accumulate almost a dozen from one person before responding. A friend later called her not writing "almost a disease" that like other diseases should have a Latin name so that "it might sound more mysterious." Irritated at not hearing from her, Sheyna wrote on November 29, "Don't know what to think of your silence. The matter was so importine [*sic*] and you don't answer." And making it clear that she needed Golda as much as Golda needed to get away, she continued, "Please, have pity on me, don't keep me onknown [*sic*] about your resolution." With still no response, Shamai took over. "Well Goldie," he asked impatiently, "do you ever expect to be heare [*sic*] . . . If you wouldn't then we will have to spend the money for something else."

Within a few weeks, the matter seemed resolved. Whatever her doubts, Golda had made her decision, and Sheyna could write ecstatically on December 13, "You have no idia [*sic*] how happy we all are that you are willing to come." Reversing their earlier roles, she enclosed stamps, because she sensed that Golda had run out of funds, and she promised to send money for a train ticket. "The main thing is that nobody shall ever know about your plans," she warned, adding, "Goldie, see to be brave, don't show with any action or word what you are going to do . . . Get ready little by little."

The conspiracy was coming to fruition; the plans under way. Yet, again, Golda held back. She wanted to flee, but she worried about leaving her parents so abruptly and abandoning their little sister, Clara. Neither she nor Sheyna had been close to Clara, but with Sheyna away and Clara part of Golda's Young Sisters group, she felt some responsibility for the girl, and she wrote to Sheyna about her concerns. Sheyna reassured her: "I knew that Clara will bother you, but I don't see any reason why. It never entered my mind that you should not write home even if you would go away without their knowledge." Their lives, it pleased Sheyna to say, had improved greatly. Shamai had bought a dry-cleaning shop, and they were moving to a nice house on Julian Street in West Denver, with a living room, bedroom, kitchen, and bathroom. "We have a room and bed ready for you," she wrote, and she would send money to a friend to buy Golda's train ticket for her.

All that was left for Golda now was to work out the logistics of her flight, and this she did with Regina. Little by little, as Sheyna had advised, she gathered the clothes she would need into a bundle. On a designated February evening in 1913, she lowered the bundle through her second-story bedroom window to Regina, who was waiting below to carry it to the baggage room in the railway station. Golda prepared a note for her parents to read the next day after her departure, asking their forgiveness, but saying simply, "I am going to live with Sheyna, so that I can study." Before she went to bed, she gently kissed her sleeping little sister goodbye. The next morning, she left for school as usual but headed instead to Union Station to board a train to Denver.

Without having checked the schedule, she had to wait almost all day for the train, terrified that once her parents read her note, they would find her and force her home. Luckily for her, by the time they understood what had happened and rushed to the station, she had left. Reflecting on that day years later, Golda said, "I had done something that deeply wounded my mother and father, but that was truly essential for me."

3

"Dearest Gogo"

Sheyna was there to greet Golda as she stepped off the train at Denver's Union Station. The little sister she had left behind, Sheyna observed, had developed into a pretty, serious-looking girl, with a slim figure, deep-set eyes, and a head of thick chestnut hair. True, her nose was "a little too large," yet it suited her face, and clearly her firm mouth, although not delicate, was where her "obstinacy resided." Would Sheyna be able to influence this blossoming young woman the way she had managed the child of the past?

The sisters boarded the yellow Denver Tramway streetcar out toward the city limits and their stop in West Denver. From there they walked a block or two, lugging Golda's bag of belongings, to Sheyna's house at 1606 Julian Street. It was a humble home, in one half of a duplex (two one-story houses attached by a common wall), for which the Korngolds paid a monthly rent of ten dollars, a modest sum even in those days. If Golda had one of its two main rooms, as Sheyna had promised her, Sheyna, Shamai, and little Judith all slept in the other. A small kitchen and bathroom completed the layout.

The house fronted on an open field in an area so undeveloped that the health department could post a notice for people to "bury your dead chickens and stop throwing them out in the alley." But it also sat at the edge of the Jewish quarter, with its kosher butcher shops, small synagogues, and immigrant Jewish families much like those Golda had known in Milwaukee. In this city, also, upper-crust German Jews lived in the east side of town, rarely mingling with the Russian west siders.

German-speaking Jews had accompanied the first wave of adventurers rushing to Colorado in search of gold in the "Pike's Peak or Bust" mania of the mid-nineteenth century. Instead of prospecting for that precious metal, most of the Jews became merchants and traders who supplied the miners with necessary goods. By the turn of the century, the small German Jewish community in Colorado had become so integrated and assimilated that almost every town and city had a Jewish mayor or councilman.

Soon a different group poured into this state, the "consumptives," tubercular patients who came to "chase the cure" in the high altitude and dry, clean air of the Rocky Mountain region. So many of the ill crowded into Denver that the town's German Jews felt called upon to establish a hospital for them. They opened the National Jewish Hospital for Consumptives in 1899. Although it was nonsectarian, the majority of its patients were Jewish, half of them Russian immigrants like Sheyna. It didn't take long after that for Denver's west side Jews to form their own hospital, the Jewish Consumptives' Relief Society, which opened in 1904. Nor did it take long for competition to develop between the two hospitals, reflecting the antagonisms between German Jews and Eastern Europeans that hovered over all of American Jewish life.

More than enough sick people flocked to town to fill both hospitals, however, and although both urged patients to return home after treatment, a good number of discharged "lungers," like Sheyna, stayed on. When Golda arrived, Denver had a population of 225,000 with about 8,000 Jews, many of them former patients.

Golda enrolled in North High School, some twenty blocks from the Korngold home, getting up early to walk there every day. After classes, she hurried downtown to help Shamai in a small business he had opened, the Wisconsin Cleaning and Pressing Shop, where she pressed clothes and waited on customers, freeing him to leave for his nighttime job as a janitor at Mountain States Telephone and Telegraph Company. Busy as she was, she managed to do well in school, accumulating A's in such subjects as English, Latin, algebra, and ancient history (with a C in mechanical drawing). She also made friends easily among the largely gentile school population. Carl Ginn, a classmate who became a prominent Denver educator, had fond memories of the two of them strolling around nearby Sloan Lake, "a little flirtatiously," he told friends. After she became Israel's prime minister, he dutifully praised her "strong leadership" as a student, but what he actually remembered was that "she had great ankles," visible beneath her long skirts. This, about ankles that became noted later in life for their thick shapelessness. But the Golda of these years looked vastly different from the leader the world would come to know. This was an attractive young woman with a vibrant personality who could have made even less than perfect ankles appear "great" to an admirer.

Her best high school girlfriend, Minnie Willens, belonged, with her, to a minority of Jewish students in the school. Minnie idolized Golda, the more popular and confident of the two. One evening at a gathering, Golda, surrounded as she often was by other young people, did not get a chance to speak to Minnie alone. Hurt and awed by her friend, Minnie penned an emotional letter to her from home. "I respect and love you for your independent spirit," she wrote. "I know Goldie that it is in you to make your life a real success. You are one of those very few who can and will make the world at least a little bit brighter by your presence." She, on the other hand, "did not seem to make friends readily." She trusted only Golda with her innermost thoughts and confidences.

One of those confidences she shared in a later letter concerned a social meeting Minnie had with a non-Jewish boy. Already pragmatic, Golda cautioned that from a romantic viewpoint the relationship had no future. Minnie took her words to heart. He may be "a nice fellow," she wrote, "but as you say, 'men *cannot* be mere friends,'" and following Golda's advice, she had decided to cut off the friendship before it escalated.

Attached as she became to her new friends, Golda kept in contact with her closest pal, Regina. "Reggie," as she signed many of her newsy letters, was attending business school and working for a while at the socialist newspaper *The Milwaukee Leader*. "Say Goldie," she admonished, about six months after her friend's flight to Denver, "why don't you write your mother oftener than you do? . . . You are driving her mad by not writing . . . remember she is your mother."

After striking a blow for independence by secretly leaving home, Golda had no desire to be weighted down by obligations to write to her parents regularly. Bluma, on the other hand, having broken with Sheyna, longed to remain part of Golda's life and might have tried using Regina to achieve that end.

Regina also sent good news about Golda's parents. "You just ought to see the swell house they furnished up," she reported a year into Golda's stay in Denver. "Why your mother lives like a millionaire now." The "swell house" was connected to Bluma's success with her store, now called Miller and Mabowitz Delicatessen. Some months later Regina elaborated: "Clara and your mother and father are all well and living like kings in a nice home with pretty furniture and a grand $375.00 piano. Clara is still as much a baby as when you left . . . But now she is much taken up with the Camp Fire Girls."

Clara had benefited from being the only child at home. More secure financially, and still smarting from their struggles with Sheyna and

Golda, the Mabovitch parents made fewer demands on her, even indulging her with piano lessons—an immigrant Jewish family's quintessential sign of advancement. She, in turn, became something of an all-American girl, with her involvement in the nonsectarian Camp Fire Girls. Clara remained an American all her life, the only family member who did not settle in Israel.

Golda followed the news from home eagerly, but she increasingly felt herself pulled in a different direction, her mind buzzing with new ideas she had begun to hear regularly in her sister's kitchen.

Although Sheyna had settled into a comfortable domestic life caring for her husband and small daughter, she and Shamai still held on to the early socialist and Zionist beliefs they had been drawn to in Russia. The couple had joined the Denver chapter of the Socialist Territorialists, one of several small Zionist groups in the city. They also became active in the Aid Association of the Ex-patients of the JCRS, involved in raising money for TB victims. Through their affiliations, they became friendly with many members of the Jewish community, gradually turning their home into a meeting place for the city's intelligentsia.

Former patients of the major sanatoriums, recovering and not quite recovered patients, children of patients, anarchists, socialists, would-be poets, and dreamers—most of them lonely young Jewish immigrant men, far from family and home—congregated around Sheyna's square oak kitchen table on evenings and weekends. In broken English and fluent Yiddish, they discussed—more often argued about—philosophy and current events, literature and politics. Their gatherings served as a small-town version of New York's Lower East Side cafés, where immigrant voices could be heard late into the night shouting at each other about every conceivable subject. At Sheyna's, Golda heard for the first time about such philosophers as Hegel and Schopenhauer, about anarchism and Emma Goldman, about the literary merits of Sholem Aleichem and Mendele Moykher Sforim.

She watched and listened as the young people downed cup after cup of tea with lemon while their talk roamed from one topic to another: the woman's suffrage movement was gaining momentum. A month after Golda's arrival in Denver and on the day before Woodrow Wilson's inauguration as president, thousands of suffragists marched on Washington to protest his lack of support for their cause. Should women be given the vote? What about other rights? In Europe, political tensions were mounting among the big powers, Russia, France, Germany, England.

How would their differences affect the Jews? In America, in the city of Atlanta, a young Jewish pencil factory superintendent named Leo Frank was being accused of murdering a Christian employee, Mary Phagan. Would the accusation trigger a wave of anti-Semitism in this country? Everyone had an opinion on every subject.

Most intriguing to fifteen-year-old Golda were the discussions about Zionism and socialism. The majority of American Jews had little interest in Zionism, except, perhaps, to put a few coins in the blue-and-white tin Jewish National Fund *pushke* that some kept beside their other charity boxes. Most were too preoccupied with building the American dream for their families to devote themselves to building a new home for the Jewish people in a faraway land. But many of the young people meeting in the Korngold home had carried their ideologies and passions with them from the Old Country. Their debates about Zionism, Socialist Zionism, and territorialism were the same they'd had in Pinsk or Minsk or the many other places they had left in the Pale of Eastern Europe. For them, the issues remained as real as ever.

Golda was especially moved by the news drifting back from Palestine about the first kibbutzim, the collective agricultural settlements of Degania and Kinneret that had been established near the Sea of Galilee. The people there were living the socialist ideals of sharing and equality that the people around her merely talked about. And these pioneers had come to that desolate land to work the soil with their own hands, not very different from the American pioneers who conquered the West. The reports she heard had an air of romance that excited her imagination and helped shape her vision of a future she wanted for herself.

Her status at the gathering started to change. At first, she had just listened to the words swirling around her, awed by these "older" people in their twenties. With time and growing confidence, she dove into the discussions, even disagreed on matters. She made friends in the group and joined them at a dizzying round of lectures, concerts, and picnics while keeping up her schoolwork and after-school chores. But as she became socially freer, Sheyna began to pull tighter to hold her in place. Golda needed to get to bed earlier, spend more time on her homework, watch out for her reputation, with so many men in the group. If Sheyna felt jealous of her sister's mounting popularity, she covered those feelings with concerned nagging about the girl's welfare. Golda placated her by taking on the task of disinfecting teacups after the visitors left at the end of an evening.

Regina once said that out of five men who met Golda, "four fell in love with her." One of the men whose attention she caught during these heady Denver days was Yossel Kopilov, ten years her senior, who had come to Denver from Chicago, where he worked as a barber. He did menial work, he often said, to keep his mind free for thinking, and he took great pride in the philosophical essays he occasionally published in Yiddish magazines. A short man, with a limp that had resulted from a childhood accident, he had been an ardent Zionist in his native Russia and might have been in Denver for a Zionist convention when he and Golda met. They struck up an instant and intense friendship that would last their lifetimes. Although platonic on Golda's side, she probably sensed an undercurrent of romantic longing on Yossel's, or as she advised Minnie, "men cannot be mere friends."

After he left Denver, Yossel wrote to her frequently, long, high-flown letters, some in English, others in Yiddish. "By what fate, by what 'will of the wisp,' were we brought to Denver, met, befriended and write now letters?" he asked shortly after he returned to Chicago, explaining that "the more frequent we think of this coincidence . . . the stronger must be the ties of our friendship." He signed, "Your best friend Yossel." In a later letter, he mentioned a new essay subject he was "flirting" with and wrote, "Dear Golda, you know my flirtation is not empty-hearted, not of a frivolous character." Some of his letters took the tone of an older brother, offering Golda sympathetic advice. "You are my sister in moods, a sister in grief and sorrow," he wrote when she expressed some unhappiness in her life. And he spoke of his own sadness at seeing a woman he once loved, Ida, marry another man. For her part, Golda felt free to write at some length about the true love of her life, who was also Yossel's good friend.

His name was Morris Meyerson, and he seemed a most unlikely choice for the vivacious, outgoing Golda. Quiet and soft-spoken, he had little to say in the political shouting matches that went on in Sheyna's house. His heart belonged to the arts—music, poetry, literature, drama. Hardly glamorous, he was short and balding, with round spectacles and a self-effacing manner. But Golda admired him enormously "for his gentleness, his intelligence," and "his soul." He seemed so much older than she, so much more mature, although he had barely passed twenty, and he led her into a world of culture she'd never experienced before. "From him," she was to say, "I learned all the beautiful things."

Morris had moved to Denver to be with his half sister Sarah, who suffered for years from tuberculosis. His mother, Shifra, from Vitebsk in Belorussia, had a sad history. She had married twice, both times to men who died young. She'd had two children, Sarah and Bertha, with her first husband—whose family name was Gluzumitsky—and two more, Morris and his older sister, Rae, with her second husband, Moshe. That man's last name in Russia is unknown, but he and the rest of the family took the name Meyerson when they arrived in America around 1904—a year after Moshe Mabovitch—and settled in West Philadelphia. About eleven or twelve when his father died, Morris went to work early to help support his mother and sisters. When Golda met him, and for some time afterward, he worked sporadically as a sign painter.

Morris found his way to Sheyna's square table through Sarah's friendship with Sheyna; most likely the two women met at the National Jewish Hospital for Consumptives. Unlike Sheyna, Sarah struggled continually with her illness, feeling at times so weak that "it was an exertion to dress or comb," she wrote to her half sister, Rae. When Morris and his mother moved to Denver to be near Sarah, Rae remained in Philadelphia with her husband, Louis Broudo, but the women kept up a lively correspondence.

As elder sisters, Sarah and Rae might have influenced Morris in his cultural interests. Certainly they shared those interests, at times somewhat pretentiously. Sick as she often felt, Sarah, with her husband, Salomon Leon Skoss, joined a literary circle, and she passed along to Rae her strong opinions about everything she read. When Rae wrote that she liked the plays of George Bernard Shaw, Sarah responded, "I confess I have not much regard for him. He appears to me to be a bigoted, audacious parvenu." On the subject of "women's fight for emancipation," Sarah recommended the writings of Charlotte Perkins Gilman. And for Skoss's college graduation, she told Rae, she planned to surprise him with the complete works of the Russian writer Dmitri Pisareff, while Morris bought him an "excellent set" of "Taine's English Literature" (a reference to Hippolyte Taine's *History of English Literature*). It's unlikely that Golda had heard of any of these works.

Morris also seemed to share some family personality traits the sisters discussed. Rae blamed herself for not being able to express her thoughts well in public. Sarah admitted to the same failing but pointed out that "our family, beginning with mother, suffer even more than others with self-analysis and self-condemnation." In a similar vein of "self-condemnation," Morris would later ask Golda, "Have you ever stopped to think whether your Morris has the one attribute without which all other refinements are worthless, namely, 'the indomitable will'?" Sarah herself, she complained to Rae, had inherited a "cursed coldness and reserve" from their mother, which prevented her from showing the "tenderness" she truly felt inside.

But if Sarah disliked those qualities in herself, Golda found them endearing in Morris. His reserve, his self-doubts, and his reluctance to draw attention to himself set him apart from other young men she knew. "He was one of the purest spirits I have ever met," a Zionist leader later said of him. "He was always searching his soul; he was full of doubt of its existence." Golda's admiration would shore up Morris's confidence. His "pure spirit" would calm her restlessness and bring a quiet softness into her often frenetic days.

They began to spend as much time together as they could, attending free band concerts in City Park, taking long, contemplative walks, and sharing intimacies about themselves. In the evenings, they appeared at lectures on philosophy and history. He compiled lists of books for her to read and explained the subtleties of musical compositions. She was entranced by his mind, his erudition; he by her energy and vitality. "Ours was a great love," she said years later, long after the last embers of that love had turned to ash.

She wrote to Regina about Morris's "beautiful soul," which compensated for his plain looks. Regina wondered whether she planned to return to Milwaukee to pursue her teacher training course. Or, maybe "the matrimonial course appeals to you better with the man you love. I do not blame you."

Actually, Golda did not yet have matrimony on her mind, but she was about to give up her high school course of study, and not because of Morris. Sheyna was now making their life together impossible. Tiny and delicate-featured, Sheyna made up in assertiveness for what she lacked in physical stature. "She was a hard person," Regina said. "A real hard, tight pest," another close family friend, Nomi Zuckerman, labeled her. "She thought she knew everything." As Golda began to test her wings, Sheyna cracked down forcefully. She scolded if Golda stayed out too late, ordered her about, and watched her every step "like a hawk," Golda complained. Of course, Golda herself was also "a little domineering," Sheyna's daughter, Judith, recalled about that period. But Sheyna's unconditional belief in her own convictions—the inflexibility she'd shown as a rebellious teenager—prevented her from understanding this teenager's willfulness.

Issues came to a head after an all-out quarrel one evening. "Very well, I'll leave," Golda announced, and headed out the door. To both sisters' surprise, Sheyna did nothing to stop her. "Stubbornness," Sheyna later said, was "embedded in both our natures since childhood," but "most stubborn" was Golda. Whether true, after that evening's blowout, the stubborn girl would crawl out from under her stubborn sister's domination and take her first serious steps toward self-sufficiency.

"Now Goldie," Sheyna wrote to her a few years later, remembering the break, "no matter what happened between us, as much as I can see, the old love is preserved. I hope so, anyway." In any event, she went on, "there was a good deal of wrong and guilt on both sides."

The sisters' love eventually did get preserved, although differently than it had been. For the present, neither made a move to undo what had happened. Golda found herself with no clothes, except for the black skirt and white blouse she had been wearing, no home, and no means of support. She gratefully accepted an offer from two of Sheyna's friends, both in advanced stages of TB, to move into their one-room apartment for as long as she wished. She slept in a tiny niche and spent most of her nights in the bathroom, where she could keep the light on as she tried to work her way through the pile of books Morris had recommended.

From Regina, June 18, 1914: "Dearest Goldie, I have your letter of June 14th, which caused me much worry. What has happened? Don't you stay with Jennie any more? . . . Why did you write such a sad lonly [sic] letter? I supposed something of grave importance must have happened because I know my proud Goldie would not write me thus otherwise."

Proud Goldie had dropped out of school on June 5, before the semester ended, and gone to work at a laundry that specialized in washing lace curtains. She soon found a better job in a department store, taking measurements for custom-made skirt linings. With the little money she made, she rented a tiny room of her own. Loosed from Sheyna's watchful eye, she could spend as much time as she liked with Morris and her other friends. By August, she sounded happier in her letters to Regina, who wrote how glad she was that Goldie was now free to do as she pleased.

As free as she might have been, Golda felt "as lonely as I was independent," cut off as she had become from her entire family. When she received a letter from her father urging her to return home, she jumped at the opportunity. Emphasizing her mother's need for her, Moshe broke the angry silence he had maintained throughout her stay in Denver. Golda regretted having to leave Morris, who had to remain in Denver to support his mother and sister, but the young lovers promised to write regularly until they could be reunited.

"Well! The cat came back," Regina wrote to Morris on December 26, 1914. Golda had returned to Milwaukee a short time earlier, and all she could talk about was "in Denver we did this and in Denver we did that," with no interest at all in "Beerwaukee." With tongue in cheek Regina asked, "Mr. Myerson, do you know a party by the name of Morris? . . . I sure wish that I could see him personally because the way he was portrayed to me he is not human but superhuman and I think that his wings must be sprouting."

Smitten with Morris, and even more so at a distance, Golda plied Regina with details of his many virtues. At home, she grew furious when she discovered that her mother had Clara steam open some of his letters and translate them into Yiddish for her. She decided to have Morris send future missives to Regina's address. Other than Bluma's intrusion on her privacy, she found her home life transformed. More comfortable financially than they had been, and more attuned now to American ways, the Mabovitch parents took for granted that Golda would return to school and continue her studies as she planned. She reentered North Division High School (which, strangely, has no record of her leaving) and within a short time was voted vice president of the junior class.

But the household had changed also in other fundamental ways. Feeling more magnanimous with their greater economic security, Bluma and Moshe opened their apartment to an assortment of visitors. Some came from Palestine, *shlichim*, or emissaries, sent primarily to raise money for the struggling Yishuv, the Jewish settlement there. With no money for hotels, these men (and an occasional woman) slept in people's homes as they traveled from state to state and town to town to deliver their message. The Mabovitch living room couch became a favorite resting place in Milwaukee, and Bluma's cooking an added bonus. Additional guests included Yiddish writers on lecture tours and members of Jewish fraternal organizations overseas. Closer to home, the Mabovitch apartment became a hangout for Golda's friends. "Her parents would give a whole crowd of us supper. I don't know how they managed," recalled Sadie Ottenstein, who lived on Ninth Street, across an alley from Golda. "Whatever happened, the family always seemed to have wine."

Most satisfying to Golda, she developed a new bond with her father. The outbreak of World War I in 1914 brought miseries to the Jews of Palestine, which was under Turkish rule. And in Europe, both German and Russian armies persecuted and slaughtered Jews in their paths as they battled each other. Reports of massacres and deportations throughout Eastern Europe horrified American Jews, so many of whom had family in the war areas. They responded to the crisis by creating relief organizations, which later became part of the Joint Distribution Committee (JDC). Golda and her father threw themselves into working for the People's Relief Committee formed in Milwaukee by an assortment of labor groups. They went house to house knocking on doors to plead for donations and helped organize balls and bazaars to raise money. Their work together gave Golda a chance to spend time alone with her quiet, introverted father. It gave him a chance to accept his daughter as a competent young woman moving into a world of her own.

Isadore Tuchman, a businessman and Zionist activist, ascribed Golda's entry into that world to a chance meeting he had with her in 1915. He saw her chairing a meeting of a Zionist literary society she had joined. "The hall was fairly full," he recalled, "when I noticed this striking girl on the platform surrounded by old women . . . I thought what on earth is this young girl doing with these old women! She doesn't belong at all! So I got in touch with her and asked if she'd join our movement."

The movement was Poalei Zion (Workers of Zion), the worldwide Labor Zionist (also called Socialist Zionist) organization whose roots went back to Russia and to which Sheyna and Shamai had been close. Influenced by them and fresh from Denver and its accounts of pioneer settlements, Golda might well have found her way to the movement's Milwaukee branch without Tuchman's urging. But she always credited him with having inspired and guided her. When he died in October 1974, shortly after Golda resigned as prime minister, she sent a telegram to his widow: "Just learned about passing away my beloved and admired Chaver Tuchman. I learned much from him." Like other members of the movement, he remained a lifelong *chaver*, a comrade and friend.

As a Zionist organization, Poalei Zion aimed to help build up the Land of Israel. As a socialist labor group, it stood for social justice and support of the working classes. Yet it was more than the sum of its parts. Although always significantly smaller than the General Zionist organization in the United States or such women's groups as Hadassah, it established a meaningful place in the social and cultural lives of Eastern European Jewish immigrants. The Milwaukee branch of Poalei Zion, founded in 1906, sponsored literary lectures like the one Golda chaired, campaigned hard for socialist candidates during local elections, developed educational programs, arranged public debates with opponents, and organized fund-raising balls and picnics. In its early days, it tried to introduce Hebrew and Yiddish courses into the public schools but failed because of opposition from German Jews, who complained that "it is audacious on the part of a group of greenhorns to demand this." It did get the public library to include books in those languages on its shelves.

For Golda and other young people, the town's Poalei Zion became a home away from home, the center of their social activities. "Lincoln Park was our hangout," recalled Sadie Ottenstein. "The girls would pack lunches, and we'd form a large circle so the fellows could buy them." Every cent raised went to the Labor Zionist cause. It didn't take long for Golda to become totally caught up in the group's activities. An article in the Milwaukee Yiddish newspaper, *Milwauker Wochenblat*, of September 24, 1915, lists her along with other committee members helping to organize the Poalei Zion tenth annual fund-raising ball. Another, later, has her on the "arrangements committee" planning the movement's regional conference. She regularly attended the group's meetings and lectures, sometimes, a friend remembered, as "the only girl there." Urged by Isadore Tuchman, she became a teacher in the movement's local *folkschule* (folk school), a secular, Yiddish-speaking school where children learned about Jewish culture and nationalism. It was the only formal teaching she would ever do.

The folk schools were the pride of the national Labor Zionist movement. The first one opened in New York in 1910 with the formidable title of Yidishe Nazional Radikale Shuln, Jewish National Radical Schools, and proved so popular that branches around the country established similar institutions, calling them simply folk schools. When Golda began teaching in 1915, the Milwaukee school had 120 students. A year later it had 150, and she had acquired the title of school secretary. Classes met on Saturday afternoons, Sunday mornings, and one additional afternoon a week at the Abraham Lincoln House, the Jewish Settlement headquarters on Ninth and Vine Streets. Golda taught courses in Yiddish reading and literature and some Jewish history. Her childhood school friend Sara Feder ran the singing and music programs.

A photograph of the *folkschule* staff in 1916 shows Golda standing at one end of a line of male teachers and Sara at the other. Next to Golda is a markedly short, slight man named Meir Dubinsky, and therein lies another "men *cannot* be mere friends" tale of Golda's youth.

A few years older than Golda, Dubinsky worked as a presser for the clothing firm of David Adler & Son and devoted most of his free time to Poalei Zion activities. Working alongside Golda in the *folkschule* for two years, he fell helplessly in love with her. She might have enjoyed his devotion and affection for a while, and possibly had a romance with him, but in the end she relegated him to the role of friend and brother, much as she had Yossel Kopilov. Dubinsky (Golda never called him by his first name) agreed to accept that role, but in a series of letters he wrote to her, from the time they taught together until he left Milwaukee for Palestine, and even after she had married, he recounted his love and sadness at not having won her. He wrote in Yiddish, the favored language of the Poalei Zion group.

Looking back to their years at the school, Dubinsky invoked hazy images of moments together, like vanishing shadows of the past. In one letter, addressed to "Darling Golda," he recalled seeing Golda crying while sitting under a tree with Sheyna and his own reluctance to tell her how he felt in front of her sister. "My heart is deflated; it has been torn into little pieces," he wrote. Another time, while reading a book, he remembered that she had once recommended that book to him. It was a "lovely summer night," and she was sitting on the steps of her father's house. "There I was standing and looking at you, and I was happy when sometimes you threw me a glance. I was then overcome by emotion and seized by a powerful longing. After such a look from you, and even more, when there was no look—Oh! How I suffered and suffer even now." Some letters refer to Golda by the code name Buzie, an allusion to a Sholem Aleichem story she would have known. With the biblical title "Song of Songs," the story tells of a young man's forbidden love for his beautiful niece, nicknamed Buzie, with whom he had been raised as brother and sister. Dubinsky remembered Golda saying, "I'll remain your sister until the end," and like the lover in the story he realized that he could never act on his true feelings. Instead, he would have to regard himself as her brother.

"After a short stroll, we agreed to remain friends forever," he wrote in a reminiscence. Golda had her way again. She had deflected his romantic love and established a friendship that was later to prove vital for her and Morris.

MORRIS WAS NEVER FAR FROM Golda's thoughts even as she immersed herself in her newfound friends and activities. They began exchanging letters as soon as she arrived in Milwaukee; he is the only correspondent of that period whose letters do not begin by chastising her for not having written. They wrote in English and addressed each other lovingly, he frequently using the nickname Gogele or Gogo for her. (The name probably came from Sheyna's daughter, Judith, who as a baby called Golda "Goga.") Golda's letters brim with news about her life; his often reflect on what she has told him while claiming that he has nothing much to write himself. When she wrote that she had become a "sister" to some of the men she met, he remarked approvingly that "other people seem to discern your real worth, your sisterly goodness." When she described the meetings in which she participated, he teased her, writing, "Getting up to ask questions at a socialist meeting—the nerve of a girl!" When she called her appearance in a photograph of herself with a group of their friends "awful," he chided her, "You know well that I, like any lover, am bound to differ with you. To me it is very beautiful and I just can't lift my eyes from it." And with a touch of pique, he added, "And ask Yossel whether he placed his hand on your shoulder purposely to show me how well he is taking the part of your protector." He wanted it clear to his friend Yossel that she was *his* girl.

The tenor of the letters through much of 1915 reflects the tenor of the relationship the two had in Denver. Morris is the protector, the mentor; Golda, seemingly insecure, seeks his approval. In February, about two months after she left Denver, she received a letter from Shamai, scolding her for having abandoned him and Sheyna while there. She wrote to Morris in distress. Shamai's opinion mattered to her. Later in life, Sheyna and Shamai's son, Yona, depicted his aunt and his father as "very close, very open with each other about what they thought." At this juncture, she felt hurt and humiliated by Shamai's attacks. Morris reassured her: "Don't mind, Goldie, what Korngold or anybody else will say about you . . . Radical as he would have people believe he is, he couldn't digest the idea of a modern, sensible girl striking for her independence."

She was his "little girl," he told her, and she need rely on no one but him. He was "head over heels" in love, longing to "fondle" and "kiss" her "beautiful head," sending his kisses "sailing through the ethereal blue," declaring after they had been months apart that he will "dwell in the bughouse forever" if he doesn't see her soon. Girlishly, she worried that he might find her "uninteresting" and "unattractive" or doubt the "sincerity of her love," concerned if he seemed moody or downhearted. "Goldie is worrying her head off on account of the letters you send her," Regina wrote to Morris. "You have no idea how much she loves you."

Stubborn, headstrong Golda was all tenderness and vulnerability when it came to Morris.

But her life was changing and so was she. As she plunged more deeply into the Labor Zionist cause, it took over her days and nights. "You better not be telling me anymore of such stuff as staying up until three and the like," Morris wrote to her in mock disapproval, after she described working for a Poalei Zion event. She also became ever more fascinated by the emissaries from Palestine who stayed at her parents' home or whose lectures she attended. One of the men who impressed her most during that year away from Morris was Yitzhak Ben-Zvi, who had arrived in the United States with his friend David Ben-Gurion. They came to promote a program called Hechalutz (the Pioneer) aimed at recruiting Americans to immigrate to the Land of Israel and join the collectives there. Both members of the Palestine Poalei Zion Party, they had been arrested and banished from Palestine by its Turkish rulers, who had turned violently against Zionism and other nationalist movements after the world war broke out.

The "two Bens," as they were called, made an odd-looking pair, Ben-Gurion short and stocky with unruly hair, Ben-Zvi a tall, lanky, bookish fellow with a mustache and small beard, both sporting their Turkish fez hats. For their mission, they divided up the United States, each traveling to different locales. When Ben-Gurion fell ill with diphtheria and had to drop out for a while, Ben-Zvi continued, and on August 5, 1915, he spoke in Milwaukee.

Golda would likely have been in the audience that Thursday evening. Zionism, he tried to convey to his listeners, did not mean simply helping the suffering Jews of Russia, Palestine, or other countries with money and aid. It meant creating a new future for Jews in a land of their own. And Labor Zionism called for Jews to build that land themselves, with their own labor, for only by living and working in the land would they secure their rights to it. After his talk, an audience member asked whether there would be enough room in Palestine for the thousands of pioneers Ben-Zvi might inspire to move there. His answer came in a dry notation in his diary: "At the end of the evening, five people registered for the program."

American Jews were not rushing to sign up to be pioneers. After all the travels and lectures the two Bens made, they recruited only about a hundred volunteers between them. But for Golda, Ben-Zvi's words and those of other emissaries—she would meet Ben-Gurion later—struck a receptive chord. In Denver, she had heard accounts of the agricultural settlements being built. Now pioneers who had seen those settlements or actually worked in them made the theoretical ideas and stories come alive with possibility.

Warm, likable Ben-Zvi visited the Mabovitch home several times. He sang Hebrew and Yiddish songs with the family and spoke to them about the Yishuv and the people in it. Among the figures he described, Rachel Yanait—who was to become his wife in a few years—most fired Golda's imagination. Rachel, born Golda Lishanski in Ukraine, had immigrated to Palestine in 1908 after hearing within herself a clarion call to "get up and go to Eretz Israel!" There she Hebraized her name and, poverty stricken, settled in Jerusalem, where she became devoted to its Poalei Zion group. Along with Ben-Zvi and Ben-Gurion, she helped found Hashomer, the Yishuv's Jewish self-defense organization, and served actively in it. Golda would later work as an equal with Rachel, but she would always look up to her as a symbol of the courage and ingenuity of Israel's early pioneer women.

What Golda learned she excitedly transmitted to Morris. By the summer of 1915, she had begun to write glowingly of the idealists who gave up their material comforts to live and labor in the Land of Israel. She described Palestine as the only solution to the sufferings of Jews around the world. She hinted broadly about the prospect of living there herself—themselves. Morris responded at first casually, far removed from the issues that so ignited her.

"I do not know whether to say that I am glad or sorry that . . . you seem to be so enthusiastic a nationalist," he wrote in August. "I am altogether passive in the matter, though I give you full credit for your activity . . . The idea of Palestine or any other territory for the Jews is, to me, ridiculous. Racial persecution does not exist because some nations have no territories but because nations exist at all." In short, "I do not care particularly as to whether the Jews are going to suffer in Russia or the Holy Land." Years later, their son, Menahem, would say of Morris, "In principle and by temperament he was an internationalist, a pacifist, and an anarchist." For him, the perfect world was one in which religions and states ceased to exist.

Despite Morris's strong words, Golda persisted in her enthusiasm. He responded to her Zionist fervor with amusement, missing the emotional granite at its base. "Yes, Gogele, I shall even consider a trip to Palestine (or the North Pole for that matter) with you," he wrote. "But why we need go there now I don't know. We shall roll there, cost prepaid, after we have died of some Latin disease and been buried under four ft. of sod." More soberly, almost defensively, he added, "As to that group of 'idealists'—why you need not envy them . . . After they have eaten their bread in the sweat of their brows, perhaps Nature won't seem the 'kindest mother still.' They shall feel her cruelty, her ugliness . . . and begin to see that to a great extent there is far more poetry in artificial city life than in 'Back to Nature.'"

Golda, of course, had not been admiring a Thoreau-like "back to nature" movement. Her "idealists" might at times have exaggerated the rewards of agricultural work, but they suffered the "cruelty" of nature for a specific purpose, to fashion a nation. Not yet ready to acknowledge Golda's commitment to Zionist ideology, Morris chose to ignore it. He did add, as an afterthought, "But of course I shall be tickled to go with you any time you say the word," not anticipating that her "word" would mean permanent settlement in Palestine.

In the meantime, the more pressing issue the lovers faced was how and when to be reunited. As early as January 1915, Golda wrote to Yossel in Chicago to ask impatiently when he thought Morris might come to Milwaukee. Yossel understood "the soul of one who is in love," but he knew that Morris faced many obstacles. By summertime, Morris was lamenting that the time was still "so very far off" when he would be able to leave his mother to be with Golda. "I would not for a moment have her imagine that her only son is going to desert her in her old age," he wrote on October 5. A week later he offered an alternative plan: Goldie could come to Denver after she graduated from high school in February. If she could not find a school to attend there for the teacher training program she planned, she could at least stay with him and his family for a few months. He would provide "all the necessary expenses."

She replied immediately. She would not accept his money, nor would she come to Denver and "be a burden to his family." Behind the refusal lay her unspoken resolution: she would not compromise the independence she had fought so hard to achieve, first from her parents and then from Sheyna, by living with Morris's family. Hurt by her response, he didn't mince words: "Such an attitude as yours will constantly be building frigid barriers between our love; it was the very reason for your estrangement from your sister; the sooner you modify it the less danger of our love sharing a similar fate." He had fully supported her flight from her sister at the time but was distressed now to have that streak of iron independence directed at him. This was no longer the "little girl" he had mentored in Denver.

In November, Morris surprised Golda by deciding to leave his mother in Denver after all and go to Milwaukee to be with her. Ever mindful of his "duty," he gave his mother a sum of cash before he left and arranged to send money to her on a regular basis from the work he did. It was a triumph for Golda. Thrilled with the turn of events, she rushed the good news off to Regina, who had moved to Chicago that summer with her family. "I'm the luckiest person on earth," she wrote. Regina replied by return mail, "Oh Goldie, I am so glad, so glad. How I wish I were there to seal your happiness with a few kisses."

GOLDIE HAD ANOTHER CAUSE for happiness. A few months earlier, she had been accepted as a full-fledged member of Poalei Zion, although she had not yet turned eighteen, the age required for membership. The Milwaukee chapter's leaders admired her for the hard work she did for them, administering the *folkschule*, arranging social events, and raising money. By nature and commitment, she was to remain a member of this party for her entire life. Over the years, it would split and unify, have various political incarnations, and assume different names—Ahdut Ha'avoda, Mapai, Labor—but at its core it would retain the essence of the Poalei Zion, the Labor Zionist organization she joined at the age of seventeen.

With Golda ensconced in the movement, Morris had little choice but to put aside his antinationalist stance and become involved also if he wanted to see her at all. In his memoir of Milwaukee's Poalei Zion, Louis Perchonok mentioned Morris ("Goldie's intended husband") along with Golda, Meir Dubinsky, Sara Feder, and others as one of the young people who infused new energy into the organization in the midst of the war. Morris also taught at the *folkschule* for a time and joined its picnics and outings, but he stayed in the background. "He never talked," one of the group's members said. "He just went where Goldie went."

Golda graduated from North Division High School on February 4, 1916. In the earnest language of high school publications, her yearbook, *The Tattler*, said of her, "Those about her/From her shall read the perfect ways of honor." Shortly before the graduation, a small item appeared in the *Milwauker Wochenblat* noting that "Goldie Mabovitz, one of the more active young ladies in the Jewish Settlement, is graduating from North Side High School this week." It then simply listed "the other Jewish graduates."

4

The Path to Palestine

Goldie Mabovitch's ambition to become a teacher lasted barely a year after high school. She entered the Wisconsin State Normal School in October 1916 to prepare for the career she had always planned and left after two semesters. Too much outside the walls of academia beckoned her; too much within the Labor Zionist firmament tugged at her soul.

For one thing, Zionism received a newfound respectability in America after the outbreak of the Great War, as contemporaries called World War I, with membership numbers everywhere jumping. The largest Zionist group, the Zionist Organization of America, which had only 12,000 members in 1914, would leap to 120,000 by 1918. The International Poalei Zion, although always small and on the margins, would more than double its size in those four years, from an enrollment of 2,000 in 1914 to more than 5,000 members at the end of the war. Certainly, these figures represented only a minuscule proportion of the almost three million Jews in America at the time, but even many of those who did not officially join the Zionist movement sympathized as they never had before with the idea of a national home for their people. The anti-Jewish brutalities in Eastern Europe evoked profound pain throughout the community.

At the same time, the American Poalei Zion itself grew in prestige. When party leaders from Palestine and Eastern Europe escaped to American shores from the devastations overseas, they catapulted the American branch to the center of the worldwide organization, giving it new authority. Even David Ben-Gurion, a Yishuv leader in Palestine, had to receive his tour schedule and payment arrangement from the group's New York office whenever he came to the States. He also had to subject himself—unhappily—to the decisions of local chapter heads, including some who refused to invite him because they found his flat, cerebral lecture style uninspiring to their members. On the other hand, the very presence of the two Bens and other exiled leaders heightened the prominence of the American Poalei Zion group.

As the group's star rose, so did Golda's, and now a new enterprise brought added stature to both: the creation of the American Jewish Congress, a democratically elected assembly to represent all American Jews. From the start of the war, a number of Jewish leaders began planning such a congress to speak for the Jewish community at an eventual peace conference afterward. The idea was that American Jews would vote for delegates to the congress and that body would make the case for Jewish rights in all parts of the world. For Zionists, that also meant the right to a homeland in Palestine.

Like so much else in American Jewish life, getting the project off the ground pitted the established German Jewish leadership against the Eastern European immigrant population. The conflict, wrote the memoirist Perchonok, "personified the struggle of the folk masses against the rule of the wealthy individual." Traditionally, the American Jewish Committee (AJC), run by patrician German Jewish leaders—Jacob Schiff, Felix Adler, and other powerful men—had represented the Jewish community in America. They could not imagine a popularly elected body sharing their guardianship. Moreover, the committee had always taken an anti-Zionist stand, viewing Zionism as a form of separatism that exposed Jews to accusations of dual loyalty, allegiance to another country aside from America. A Jewish congress that included Zionists "promised dangerous results for the entire race," Schiff declared.

As the battle lines shaped up, Bundists and other anti-Zionist socialists sided in opposing the congress with the wealthy capitalists of the AJC, ordinarily their natural enemies, while the Poalei Zion and various labor groups joined with mainstream Zionist organizations in favor of it. Golda became part of an "army" of Poalei Zion members who devoted their waking hours to whipping up excitement for the congress in the Jewish immigrant community. At the same time, Ben-Gurion, Ben-Zvi, and other Yishuv leaders who had come to America talked it up at rallies around the country. Pressured from all sides, the American Jewish Committee and its allies finally agreed in the spring of 1917 to participate in the proposed congress. The "masses" had won: every "Jew and Jewess 21 years of age and over" received the right to vote for delegates to the congress.

In Milwaukee, the spotlight turned on teenage Golda Mabovitch.

A consortium of organizations invited her to serve on the city's executive board that oversaw elections to the congress, the youngest member there. Milwaukee was entitled to nominate four candidates, of whom two would be chosen as the congress delegates. When voters elected two Zionists and two non-Zionist candidates, Golda campaigned tirelessly to have the Zionist nominees selected as final delegates. She gave speeches everywhere, at meeting halls and school auditoriums, movie theaters and street corners. A favorite family anecdote has it that when word reached her father that she was going to "make a spectacle of herself" by speaking at a street corner gathering, he threatened to pull her off her soapbox by her hair. She defied him, but after he heard her, he returned home awestruck and said to his wife, "I don't know where she gets it from."

She could transfix listeners. "She would move people to tears and herself as well," a party member recalled. "We used to stand off-stage with huge man's-sized handkerchiefs" for her to use. As Perchonok described her, she was "free of stage fright, courageous, and possessing a vast reservoir of energy." She never wrote a speech ahead of time; she seemed to know instinctively how to tug on the collective heartstrings of an audience with simple, straightforward language, a mixture of plain talk and passion that served her all her life.

Her most memorable performance occurred in late May, during the festival of Shavuot. She and members of her group had campaigned at various synagogues, but one large congregation, Beth Israel, denied them permission to speak and invited instead a Reform rabbi and non-Zionist to preach about the holiday. Golda acted quickly. She stood on a bench outside the synagogue, and as congregants left the service, she called out, "My dear fellow Jews, we are very sorry that we are detaining you at the exit of a sacred place. But it is not our fault. It is the fault of your leaders—the presidents and the trustees, who closed the door to our people." Some of the congregants objected to the intrusion, but Zionist sympathizers outnumbered them. Golda and her *chaverim* delivered their message and "left the place in triumph."

Elections for the congress were held on June 10, 1917, in polling stations set up in synagogues, schools, camps, and Jewish centers all over America. More than 300,000 people, a cross section of American Jews, voted, about 4,000 of them in Milwaukee. The Milwaukee voters chose as their delegates the Hebrew poet and Zionist Ephraim Lisitzky and the non-Zionist Charles Friend, president of the Hebrew Relief Association (who, eight years earlier, had written on behalf of Sheyna's application to the Jewish Consumptives' Relief Society in Denver). In the end, the congress was postponed until December 1918, after the war. By then, Lisitzky had moved away, and Nathan Sand, a Poalei Zion stalwart, took his place.

Almost every account of Golda's life, including her own, erroneously portrays her as a delegate to that historic congress, whereas every list of delegates indicates that she did not hold that position, nor was she nominated for it. She did serve as a Milwaukee delegate to the Poalei Zion convention that met in Philadelphia a week after the congress. She attended sessions at both conventions and might have confused the two in her mind later, leading to the widespread misconception. But the congress was important for Golda in other ways. Through her relentless work on its behalf, her presence on the executive board, and her fiery speeches, Golda made her name known to Socialist Zionist leaders far beyond Milwaukee. "It was the beginning of her becoming famous," Isadore Tuchman said.

A PERSON WHO TOOK CREDIT for helping to spread that fame was another Yishuv leader come to America to escape the Turks, Yaakov Zerubavel. Born in Ukraine, Zerubavel had been a key figure in the Poalei Zion movement in that country before going to Palestine. Like Ben-Gurion and Ben-Zvi, he traveled from city to city in the United States, speaking on behalf of Poalei Zion. In Palestine, he flaunted a thick black square-cut beard, which he replaced with a bushy mustache when he fled. With his lively Yiddish and warm manner, he became a popular speaker on the Jewish immigrant lecture circuit.

"In Milwaukee," he wrote in a memoir, "I met a young *chavera* who worked as a teacher—Golda came to my attention at members' meetings, because of her modest and pleasant bearing. In my conversations with her, I noted her inner spiritual strength, the hidden power within her, her honesty, and her alert thinking." Impressed, Zerubavel tried to persuade Golda to devote her full time to organizational activities, but, he wrote admiringly, she preferred to "remain in the shadows" and not call attention to herself.

It would seem an odd description of the Golda who spoke out self-confidently to promote her party's positions and later emerged as one of the world's best-known figures. But at each step of her career, Golda disavowed even a whiff of ambition, always portraying herself as unworthy of the role being offered her, always accepting it only as a duty. In part that stance was a conceit of the times and of her Labor Zionist milieu. One didn't stoop to seeking recognition; it was thrust upon you, and you accepted it self-deprecatingly. In part her attitude stemmed from Golda herself, picking her way as a woman through untrodden trails. She belonged to an age in which women tended to mask their aspirations with diffidence and an air of dependency while pursuing their underlying goals with resolute determination. That pattern, a combination of ambition coated with a veneer of modesty, was beginning to emerge in these early career years. Zerubavel saw only the modesty and gallantly sought to encourage the ability he spotted beneath the self-effacing exterior.

He told Ben Shapiro, founder of Chicago's Poalei Zion, to "save" Golda from the "country," the boondocks of Milwaukee, where she was "wasting" her abilities. In New York, he demanded that Baruch Zuckerman, head of the organization's central committee, turn his attention to the matter of "Golda from Milwaukee" and involve her in national activities. Golda already knew Shapiro from her many visits to Chicago. She also knew Zuckerman, who had run the People's Relief program around the country and stayed with her parents when he came to Milwaukee. But a recommendation from the influential Zerubavel heightened their interest in Golda and helped her make the leap from the local to the national platform.

Throughout 1917, Zerubavel kept up a correspondence in Yiddish with her as he traveled around the country. "My dear devoted *chavera* and friend," he would open his letters, reporting on his activities. "I strongly wish that you should continue in your work," he limned from St. Louis. "In you I see a good, interesting person. And while you are a woman, this makes it even more important, for personal as well as societal reasons." In one letter, he referred to her as his "colleague" and in another to how good it made him feel "to talk things over" with her. He made her feel his equal—she, a novice in a provincial town, and he, a central party chief in Europe and America.

After the Russian Revolution exploded in February 1917, the Poalei Zion in Russia summoned its old leaders from the various countries where they lived. Zerubavel decided to return "on behalf of our work there," he wrote to Golda. With the tsarist regime crushed, the world's Jews were sure their long persecuted brothers and sisters in Russia would finally be free to live full lives as Jews and Russians. Along with the Poalei Zion theorist Ber Borochov—who had fled Russia for America after the failed revolution of 1905—Zerubavel and others hurried back to rebuild the Socialist Zionist movement that had originated there and through it create a homeland in Palestine.

At a farewell party for Zerubavel in Milwaukee, Golda begged him "with a sad and serious face" not to take lightly the dangers of the sea. And before he and Borochov departed from New York, she sent him a long telegram pleading with the seas to be quiet and calm until the men reached their destination. It was a novel and dramatic gesture, bound to catch its recipient's attention. Zerubavel had treated her as an equal, and now she showed him that she accepted that equality, presenting herself—in an image she would cultivate over the years—as a motherly, concerned friend and not only a party comrade.

He wrote from New York to thank her warmly and hope that they would meet again "in the flesh, wherever." He wrote to her from Russia, in December, after the Bolsheviks had overthrown the Kerensky government that replaced the tsarist regime. "Russia," he said, "is now a bloodied, tragic place," and he mentioned the sudden death of Borochov, who had succumbed to pneumonia shortly after they arrived. Zerubavel soon moved to Poland, where he became an important party leader, and didn't return to live in Palestine until the 1930s. By then, he had moved far into the extreme left wing of the Labor Zionist Party and was never again accepted by Ben-Gurion—or Golda.

BY THE TIME ZERUBAVEL LEFT for Russia, Golda had come to a life decision. She would not be a "parlor Zionist," one of those people who talked about Zionism while living out their lives in the comforts of America. She would leave that land and settle in Palestine, a pioneer, like Zerubavel or Rachel Yanait or the two Bens. But then there was Morris.

"What if he hadn't gone with you to Palestine?" she was asked later.

"I would have gone alone, but heart-broken," came the answer.

Morris no longer doubted that the idea of living in Palestine that Golda had floated by him in their exchange of letters had taken firm hold. He understood perfectly that she had made up her mind and would not change it; he had to make up his own about how badly he wanted to be with her. Adding to his burden was Golda's nonstop immersion in the work and the party. After giving up the normal school, she took a part-time job as a library assistant at twenty cents an hour, leaving her free to pack her days, and most of her nights, with Poalei Zion meetings, lectures, and fund-raising. Aware of her schedule, her friend Yossel wondered in a letter whether she wasn't "spreading yourself too thin."

To please Golda, Morris also devoted more time to party activities. He "excelled as an active worker," Perchonok said, and even took on the job of secretary of the Milwaukee branch. Still, there was no keeping up with Golda. It didn't help that Morris's mother, Shifra, came to Milwaukee for a visit during the summer of 1917. She had become embittered over the years with her poverty and her dependence on her children for financial support. She had never adjusted to Morris's moving away and leaving her in Denver, nor was she happy with his "amorous adventures," for which she placed "all the blame . . . on Goldie's shoulders," in the words of her daughter Sarah.

On August 17, Sarah wrote a long letter to her sister Rae reporting on their mother's visit. She had heard from "Mrs. Korengold"—Sheyna— that it was not going well. Shifra was "very much displeased with Milwaukee as a whole." With no friends there and Morris working during the day and going out in the evening, she felt "miserable." Moreover, "she hates the Mabovitzes because she considers them so much below herself . . . She also dislikes the mother because she thinks that a Mabovitz no matter how good is unworthy of her Morris." A devoted mother's prophetic response, as it were, to all those in the future who would wonder why the formidable Golda chose the mild, unassuming Morris.

In a revealing description of the two lovers, Sarah continued, "Goldie is pretty, young and attractive and has loads of admirers, both male and female. She is being complimented on all sides and naturally getting somewhat spoiled. Nevertheless she thinks the world of Morris and loves him dearly. But she is a very ardent Poaleinist and puts her ideal above her personal life and hence there is some friction between her and Morris." As for Morris, she went on, he was not much of an "ist" of any kind. As an "educated and well developed fellow," he could see the "narrowness of all the movements," and therefore could not adjust to them. What he would like would be "to get married, have his Goldie near him and together enjoy good music, lectures," and "have a circle of more or less refined friends" with whom he could have serious discussions.

"The friction" between Morris and Golda, Sarah concluded, was "nothing but youths' or lovers' troubles." As they grew older, they would find that "all of married life if not all of life in general is nothing but a series of compromises." What Sarah didn't know was that Golda would not easily make compromises, then or ever. Instead, she dealt with the "friction" Sarah spoke of by leaving Morris and moving to Chicago.

She lived with the Shapiros, Raizel and Ben, and their two young daughters in a four-room apartment at 1306 South Lawndale Avenue, close to the hub of Jewish life on Chicago's Twelfth Street. Regina had moved to Chicago about a year earlier, as did Sheyna and her family, and Yossel lived and worked in the suburb of Evanston. Based on her library experience in Milwaukee, Golda found part-time work at a branch of the Chicago Public Library. But her life centered on Poalei Zion head-quarters at 3322 Douglas Boulevard, bordered by the sprawling Douglas Park. Chicago had a much larger and more influential chapter of the party than Milwaukee. At times, Golda would be at meetings until 4:00 in the morning. "Then she would take medication before going to sleep, because she was afraid she would wake up with a migraine headache," the Shapiros' daughter Judy recalled. Raizel would have to "noodge" her to get her up in the morning.

With it all, her mind was on Morris. On the eve of the Jewish New Year, September 16, 1917, Meir Dubinsky, still longing for her, sent a letter from Milwaukee. She had written to him from Chicago that she was still "searching" and had not yet "found herself." He saw in "every word, every line" of that letter "the old despair, the old sorrow." Yet he had come to a crushing conclusion: "It is evident that you don't want to tear yourself away from him"—Morris. "I choke myself with quiet tears: she is returning to be married," he wrote.

Dubinsky was right. Intoxicated as she was with Poalei Zion, Golda still wanted Morris. Nor could he bring himself to give her up. "The boy is head over heels in love, and spends all his time and energy on it," Sarah wrote to Rae. To keep Golda, Morris had made the momentous decision to go to Palestine with her. They would be married as soon as possible.

Before that marriage took place, a near-miraculous event happened in the Jewish world. On November 2, 1917, the British government issued the Balfour Declaration, announcing that it views "with favour the establishment in Palestine of a national home for the Jewish people." The announcement took the form of a letter from the British foreign secretary, Arthur Balfour, to the Zionist financier Lionel Walter Roth-schild. More ambiguously, it also indicated that "nothing shall be done which may prejudice the civil and religious rights of existing non-Jewish communities in Palestine," promises to Jews and Arabs that would cause difficulties later.

For the present, Arabs railed against the declaration, and Zionists hailed it as a glorious coup. Much of the credit for it belonged to Chaim Weizmann, the world Zionist leader and Russian-born British scientist (whose sister Chaya had taught revolutionary tactics to Sheyna and her comrades). Weizmann had devised a formula for manufacturing synthetic acetone, a key ingredient in producing the smokeless powder, cordite, crucial for the ammunition England desperately needed in the war. As a result, he had developed close relationships with Balfour and other government officials, and they respected him and his Zionist positions. They seemed to believe also—with an exaggerated view of Jewish influence—that by backing the Zionist cause, they could win the support of Jews in the United States and with it greater support from the American government for a major British presence in the Holy Land after the war.

Elated Jews in the United States, Canada, Britain, and other European countries held parades and exuberant demonstrations of gratitude in front of British and American consulates. Golda joined in the festivities, but with a touch of skepticism. Not long after the declaration was issued, Baruch Zuckerman and Nachman Syrkin visited Milwaukee, where Syrkin lectured about it to a wildly enthusiastic audience. The next morning, Golda, back in Milwaukee, took Zuckerman aside and asked, "Can we be sure the British will not deceive us, if it is beneficial for them?" Zuckerman was "shocked" at this question nobody else he knew had raised. In light of the problems the Jews were to face under the British mandate, he would regard Golda's question as an indication even in her youth of her "sharp sense of politics and diplomacy." More likely it presaged her lifelong suspicion of government powers outside her own land and her refusal to trust the fate of the Jewish people to any of them.

The Balfour Declaration opened the way for another Zionist achievement. After complicated negotiations earlier in the war, the British government had agreed to the creation of a Jewish legion, a fighting force of Jewish volunteers to help the British oust the Ottoman Turks from Palestine. With the U.S. entry into the conflict in April 1917 and then the Balfour Declaration, the U.S. government allowed American Jews—those not eligible for the regular draft—to volunteer for the legion and form Jewish battalions within the framework of the British army. Golda wanted to volunteer and was disappointed that women were not accepted.

Some two thousand Jews from many groups and all parts of the United States and Canada joined the Jewish Legion, making up the Thirty-Ninth Battalion of the Royal Fusiliers. In Chicago, Ben Shapiro left Raizel to become part of the legion, and in Milwaukee, Golda's mother had gifts for each young legionnaire as he departed for service: a hand-embroidered bag to hold his prayer shawl and phylacteries, and another bag filled with her homemade cookies.

Meir Dubinsky, Golda's rejected lover, was among the volunteers. "I must join the fight," he wrote to her as he prepared to leave Milwaukee. And as Private Dubinsky in Plymouth, England, he couldn't resist a final flourish: "But if it is my fate to fall somewhere on a hill of my land, felled by an enemy bullet and with blood flowing, I will recall your name." Then he sent regards to Morris. He was not felled by an enemy bullet, and continued to write to Golda, always yearning for her answers, which were always slow in coming.

The American battalion saw action only once, on September 22, 1918, a month before the war ended, when it helped the British drive the Turks out of northern Palestine. Its existence, however, had symbolic meaning. For the first time in almost two thousand years, a Jewish combat unit went into battle in uniform and under its own flag to fight for the goals of its people.

AT THE END OF THE whirlwind of changes that made up the year 1917, Golda and Morris were married. Their marriage certificate lists them as Morris Myerson and Golda Mabowehz, ages twenty-four and nineteen. His occupation is "sign painter"; the space for hers is blank. Golda had planned on having a strictly civil ceremony, as befit her socialist identity. Her mother wouldn't hear of it, and after much arguing and yelling, the older woman prevailed. On December 24, the couple had a traditional Jewish ceremony under a chuppa (wedding canopy), conducted by Rabbi Solomon Isaac Scheinfeld, an Orthodox rabbi and preeminent scholar in the Milwaukee Jewish immigrant community. Scheinfeld was also a dedicated Zionist and had worked with Golda on the executive board planning the American Jewish Congress. He spoke warmly about her and delighted Bluma by having some of her homemade cake, a great honor coming from someone who rigorously observed Jewish dietary laws and ordinarily would not eat anything outside his own home.

Golda donned the "plainest of plain" dresses, of a light gray crepe de chine, reported Sadie Ottenstein—"we didn't know from chiffon then." Some years earlier, she had reprimanded Sadie for using face powder; it was not fitting for a serious Labor Zionist to wear makeup. "But I did powder my nose again, Goldie or no Goldie," Sadie said. Golda never did powder hers or wear makeup, not even at her wedding. Only a few guests attended the modest affair—Yossel, Meir Dubinsky (alas!) and his elder brother Joseph, Sadie and her husband, Regina, and some family members. As single men, Yossel and Morris had pooled their resources to buy an eleventh-edition *Encyclopaedia Britannica* with the understanding that whoever married first would keep it. It now became the property of Golda and Morris, later passed on to their children.

Writing to Golda two weeks after the marriage, Raizel reflected, "I was sure that on your wedding day all your doubts would end and a new life would unfold for you, a life of satisfaction and happiness."

If Golda had doubts about the marriage, she barely had time to notice. Within a month or two, she began traveling for the national Poalei Zion, giving speeches, raising money, and organizing chapters. Her father was outraged. "Who leaves a new husband and goes on the road?" he shouted at her. But as she took off on her travels and left Morris alone for weeks at a time, Golda rationalized that he understood that she "couldn't say no to the movement." Maybe he did. Or maybe he understood that she didn't want to say no, for to her the exhausting movement work was also exhilarating. It had become her life.

She worked for a salary of fifteen dollars a week plus expenses. Like other party emissaries, she never stayed in hotels, always sleeping at the homes of *chaverim*. She and Morris had rented a small apartment at 534 Ninth Street, to which she sent a steady stream of postcards and letters, in English or Yiddish. While she was away, he decorated the rooms with cutout pictures from magazines, and when she returned, he always had flowers on the table. He worked when he could, taught at the *folkschule*, and in his free time listened to music or went to the library, and, according to friends, took care of all the household needs, including buying Golda's clothes.

"Dearest," she addressed him in her English notes or, in the Yiddish ones, "My dear Meir'ke," the diminutive of "Meir," his Yiddish name. Even the fact that she wrote to him in Yiddish had party connotations. The two had always spoken and corresponded in English, but an emphasis on Yiddish had gained momentum in the movement, urged on by Chaim Zhitlowsky, a dynamic Russian-born Yiddishist who had settled in America. The Yiddish focus resulted from an ongoing debate within the Zionist community about whether Yiddish or Hebrew should be the national language of the Jewish people. In Palestine, the Yishuv had chosen Hebrew. The American Poalei Zion Party had not taken an official position, but its leaders, almost all from Eastern Europe, wanted "to ensure the equal rights of Yiddish" in the Diaspora and Palestine. Yiddish was the tongue of the Jewish masses, its proponents argued, the folk language Jews had spoken among themselves in country after country.

Golda fully accepted the party's Yiddish ideology and had begun making an effort to use it instead of English in her correspondence. It *was* an effort because, although she spoke the language fluently, she had never been formally schooled in it as she had been in English, and writing was more difficult than speaking. In that effort, she reversed the Americanization pattern typical of most immigrant Jewish children, who consciously chose to move away from the "old" language of their parents to their newer American one.

Fluent in all aspects of Yiddish, Yossel had encouraged Golda from the start to use it in her letters to him. Regina, who, under Golda's influence, had joined Chicago's Poalei Zion chapter, struggled to conform to the Yiddish trend but had to admit, in a Yiddish postscript to an English letter she sent to Golda, that she "wrote much faster and better in English." Still, she closed with her Yiddish name, "Rivka."

Later Golda would discover that she had made the wrong decision, moved in the wrong direction. Hebrew was the language of the new country she was going to, and Hebrew was the language she should have put greater energies into learning. Yiddish would not stand her in good stead.

At the time, however, she wrote to Morris from Pittsburgh and Johnstown, Cleveland, and other cities, sometimes in English, often in Yiddish. From Chicago, she told him she was going to run a "basket picnic" with the *chaverim* and from Buffalo that she was waiting for *chaverim* to take her to Niagara Falls, a small break in the day's work. For the most part, the letters and cards said little, just urged him to take care of himself, sent "lots of kisses," and promised that "I will soon be with you" as she moved on to the next town. After a while, she began to sell shares in a daily Yiddish newspaper the party planned to publish. Although it already published a monthly paper, *Der Yiddisher Kaempfer*, which had financial problems, party leaders hoped that the new paper, *Die Zeit*, would promote the party's ideology on a daily basis. They were mistaken; once published, the paper lasted less than two years. But as it was being launched, Golda became so wrapped up in the work that even the patient Morris complained, and she felt called upon to apologize.

"My dear, you are right, I only write to you about shares. In my next letter, tomorrow, I'll write to you about myself," she said. Lest she sound too contrite, she added, "But you also don't write anything about yourself." It was not a promising exchange for a young marriage.

In the spring of 1918, less than a year after their wedding, Golda became pregnant and had an abortion. Not yet twenty, forging ahead in her party, and planning to move to Palestine, she would not allow herself to have a child at this point. Whatever Morris might have felt about the matter, the two enlisted the aid of his sister Sarah, who accompanied Golda to Chicago for the procedure.

Abortions were illegal in Illinois, and obtaining one could be dangerous. Chicago newspapers told of thousands of deaths resulting from "criminal abortions" and of doctors and midwives arrested because of them. Nevertheless, a woman seeking an abortion would be able to find a practitioner easily enough through ads that promised success in treating "women's problems" and drugstores that pointed women to "private hospitals" in the city. Having made up her mind, Golda was willing to take the risk.

Afterward, Sarah's husband, Leon Skoss, "rushed off" a check for fifty dollars to the couple, because Sarah indicated how badly they needed the money. In a Yiddish letter to "Beloved Meir and Golda," Skoss wanted to know with "no beating around the bush" how Golda felt. "I would like to say something about the subject of birth control," he wrote, "but since you didn't ask my advice, I don't find it necessary to offer it. All I hope is that everything went smoothly."

Golda had given little thought to how difficult the experience must have been for Sarah and Skoss. Sarah had passionately wished for a child but had been forbidden by her doctors to become pregnant because of her persistent tuberculosis. Sadly, two years after Golda's abortion, Sarah disobeyed medical advice and died in childbirth delivering a healthy baby girl.

The abortion behind her, Golda informed Sheyna about it. The reaction was swift and vehement. "I was thunderstruck," Sheyna wrote. "I was hurt and angered to the utmost depths to learn that you people did it." The hurt and anger, probably exacerbated by the fact that Golda had not consulted her first, turned into a fierce tongue-lashing: "And taking all your 'considerations' into consideration I still cannot see any good, strong reason for it. You are not sick, you have no difficulties. Your poverty I think is also a matter of mismanagement when you both work. I don't see how you should be so much in debt and your social activities remind me of the society ladies, they too cannot bear children, for it will take time away from their activities."

Sheyna knew how to twist the knife. She had to know that comparing Golda, the resolute socialist, to a society lady would cut deeply. And she had more cutting things to say: "Don't you know that your activities in comparison to Motherhood is [sic] not worthwhile to speak about? What do you do with your activities? You teach the masses, and do you know anything to teach them? ... The woman that bears children and tries her best to bring them up properly does more towards humanity than you with your activities."

Sheyna the revolutionary had become Sheyna the earth mother. The radical sister who had been Golda's first model for activism and rebellion sounded as conventional as their own mother. Toward the end of her letter, Sheyna scolded Golda about the couple's plans to give up their apartment and move in with the Mabovitch parents. "You never liked her ways," she wrote about their mother, "and I'm sure she doesn't like yours." Again, Golda followed her own wishes. From late in that year and through the next, she mailed her letters to Morris from the road to 1311 Chestnut Street, her parents' most recent address.

She sent her most enthusiastic letters from Philadelphia and the American Jewish Congress, held from December 15 to December 18 in 1918. More than a year and a half had passed since American Jews chose delegates to the congress, and six weeks had gone by since Germany's surrender and the armistice on November 11 ending World War I. Newspapers that week were filled with stories about the deposed German kaiser, who attempted suicide, and the global flu epidemic that had taken more lives throughout the world than had the entire war. Golda had been ill with the flu earlier, in October. Raizel had been sick for several weeks with the "fashionable illness," as she called it, and Dubinsky had to be hospitalized for some time. At the height of the epidemic, group meetings in Milwaukee and other cities were prohibited, theaters and halls shut, and children kept home from school, but the congress took place as scheduled.

Five thousand people attended the opening session, held in Philadelphia's opera house, with another ten thousand milling about outside. Colonel Harry Cutler of the American Jewish Committee called the session to order at 2:30 p.m., and the philanthropist Nathan Straus introduced it, demanding the human rights of Jews everywhere.

For the Zionists present, the highlight came two days later, when a resolution on Palestine was read out loud. Calling for a national home for the Jewish people under the trusteeship of Great Britain, the resolution was adopted with thunderous acclamation. Delegates rose from their seats and sang "Hatikvah," while Nathan Straus shouted joyously from the platform, "The Jewish People Lives!" Afterward, everyone sang "The Star-Spangled Banner" and waved Jewish and American flags.

"I tell you," Golda wrote to Morris, "that some moments reached such heights that after them one could have died happy. You should have been in the Hall when the resolution for Palestine was adopted. There were only two votes against it—German Jews." Then, with special pride, "The Poalei Zion played a tremendous part in the Congress. Everybody says they set the tone."

During other sessions Golda attended, the congress chose ten men to represent Jewish interests at the Paris Peace Conference convening the following month, among them Nachman Syrkin, one of Poalei Zion's own. In all, the American Jewish Congress of 1918 marked a unique moment in Jewish history, the only time the American Jewish community voted democratically for delegates to a major convention. Golda would credit that event as the beginning of her political life.

The excitement didn't end with the close of the congress. Less than a week later, Golda took part in the Poalei Zion conference in the same city, from December 24 through December 29. According to Isadore Tuchman, the two served as delegates to this convention, and "when she appeared among delegates . . . everybody seen [sic] that she was more than the average girl." When Golda speaks, "her mouth is gold," he would say.

As she finished attending all her meetings, Golda managed a postcard to Regina. "This is the life," she exclaimed, and the congress "the most wonderful thing that could be imagined." From Evanston, Yossel wrote that he looked forward to a long talk with her about it, "like a religious Greek who awaits the Oracle at Delphi."

She would have little time to satisfy Yossel's interests. With the convention behind her, she quickly resumed her travels. Then, back in Milwaukee, she took on a new project: organizing a massive protest against anti-Jewish pogroms in Poland.

At the congress, Louis Marshall, president of the American Jewish Committee, spoke from the podium of daily reports that he and other Jewish leaders received about murders, rapes, and other atrocities against Jews going on in the new state of Poland, formed after the war, and other areas of Eastern Europe. Jews throughout America began mobilizing to show their solidarity with Polish and Russian co-religionists. In Milwaukee, a conference held by representatives of more than fifty Jewish organizations elected Golda secretary of a protest committee, the Milwaukee branch of the National Committee for the Defense of Jews in Eastern Europe.

At 3:00 p.m. on Wednesday, May 28, 1919, a parade of several thousand men, women, and children marched through Milwaukee to the music of a band followed by an honor guard carrying "the Stars and Stripes and the Zionist colors, sky blue and white," *The Milwaukee Sentinel* reported. So many people participated that it took "more than an hour for the marchers to pass a given point," and when the parade moved to a protest meeting at the North Side Auditorium, every seat was taken, every inch of standing room filled, and a "great crowd outside" tried in vain to gain admission. Golda's protest committee's planning had paid off. The violence in Poland lasted through 1920, when the new Polish state became more stable and the pogroms eased up.

Marching in the protest parade on that May afternoon, Golda decided the time had come to move to Palestine. In some ways, it was an odd moment for that decision. The very fact of the march and the massive protests around the country attested to the growing strength and influence of American Jews. But for Golda the march also pointed up the limitations of life in America. Protesting wasn't enough. She needed to act directly in helping to shape the Jewish future, and she could do that only by working in Palestine to build a homeland.

What did Golda know about the land to which she was about to commit her life? For the most part, her image of Palestine reflected the ideals of the pioneers she knew—Ben-Zvi, Zerubavel, and Ben-Gurion—and others such as Rachel Yanait whom she had heard about. In memory, looking back, she would say that she had been drawn to the philosophy of Aaron David Gordon, who left white-collar work in Russia when he was close to fifty to till the soil in Palestine. He lived and wrote in the small workers' village of Ein Ganim near the agricultural colony of Petach Tikvah and later in the kibbutz Degania, preaching the "religion of labor" and the redemptive power of returning to the land. With his long white beard and spartan lifestyle, he became a symbol of the pioneer movement, spiritual leader for a generation of seekers.

Undoubtedly, also, Golda had read two popular Yiddish books about Palestine that had reached best-seller status in Zionist circles. The first, *Yizkor*, edited by Ben-Gurion and A. Hashin in 1916, commemorated the watchmen who had been killed protecting Jewish settlements. In romantic and elegiac terms, it applied the traditional language of the Yizkor memorial service to the fallen heroes of the Yishuv. The second book, *Eretz Israel*, by Ben-Gurion and Ben-Zvi, was a thick, handsome volume filled with information about the Land of Israel, which Morris liked enough to send as a gift to his sister and brother-in-law.

Occasionally, Golda received letters from Poalei Zion comrades in Palestine that described the situation there, most notably from her friend Dubinsky, who had stayed on after the Jewish Legion ended. In his most recent letters, he had stopped complaining about his unrequited love for Golda and begun mentioning a woman named Hanna. She was Hanna Chizick, from a family known in the Yishuv for its courage and devotion to the Zionist cause. He would marry Hanna before Golda moved to Palestine and from time to time report on events there.

Golda did not expect to find an idyllic land flowing with milk and honey. She expected to work hard and live up to the pioneer ideals she so admired. But she lacked knowledge of the harsh realities beyond the ideals. She knew little about the daily life of the majority of Yishuv Jews, of workers in the towns, and particularly women, who struggled to earn a living and often went hungry because they could not find employment. And although she knew the land was not empty and there had been several clashes with the Arabs living there, she believed, as most Zionists did, that the Arabs would come to accept the Jews once they understood the benefits Jewish immigration would bring. Like the others, she looked ahead optimistically to a Palestine freed with the war's end from Turkey and placed under British control.

Once Golda resolved to make the move to Palestine, Regina and Yossel jumped on board. A few months earlier, Regina had written, "Hurry up Goldie and get ready to go, I am ready at any time." Her family opposed the move, and when the departure became imminent, an aunt yelled at her, "Are you crazy? All Jews live in America, so you have to go to that wilderness?" But she had firmly decided, she told her friend. Yossel wrote to Golda and Morris sweetly, "My deepest wish is to be there with you. Joy is at the threshold." His older brother, Beryl, had given him funds to buy a one-way ticket to Palestine, admonishing, "We don't have the money for you to come back." As for Morris, he continued to so absorb himself in party activities that his sister complained of a lack of intimacy in his letters. What satisfaction did he derive from being "body and soul" in the movement? she wondered.

They were all saving money for the great adventure. Aside from her regular job at a chemical company, Regina worked in a shoe store on Saturdays, sending Golda "bargains" such as a pair of "pink slippers with blue birds on them." Golda supplemented her income with odd jobs, one of them at the Gridley Dairy Company. Fifty years later, in a letter to the chief executive officer of Borden Milk meant to encourage that company's business with Israel, she mentioned that she shared a personal tie with him, having worked for Borden at Gridley's in Milwaukee. It was the kind of detail Golda enjoyed pulling out of her past when useful.

Regina had once told Golda that Yossel seemed so lonely at times she wished "there were another Goldie in this world for him to marry." Now, while preparing for Palestine, Regina and Yossel married—as close as he could come, perhaps, to "another Goldie." In the fall of 1920, the four friends moved to New York to earn higher wages and complete their travel arrangements, sharing a rented apartment on Riverside Drive, not far from Columbia University. Golda found a job as a librarian and Regina as a secretary at *The Menorah Journal*, a Jewish literary magazine. With New York the nerve center of Poalei Zion in America, Golda spent every free moment she could at party headquarters on the Lower East Side. Morris painted signs when he could find work and spent his free time walking the city streets, happy to be surrounded by bookstores, museums, theaters, culture. The most important thing he planned to take to his new home was his phonograph and records.

By early spring of 1921, the travelers had amassed enough money to buy tickets on the S.S. *Pocahontas*, scheduled to depart on May 22. They gave up their apartment and set out to say their good-byes to family and friends. Before going to Milwaukee, Golda stopped off in Chicago to see Sheyna and Shamai. What happened there took her by surprise. The older sister who appeared to have embraced convention-ality announced suddenly that she, too, would go to Palestine, taking along her ten-year-old daughter, Judith, and three-year-old son, Chaim. Shamai, who worked for a Yiddish newspaper, would have to stay behind to support them with his earnings until he could join them. He agreed to the arrangement—they seem to have spoken of such a possibility before—but he pleaded with Sheyna to wait until the situation in Pal-estine calmed down. A year earlier, an Arab uprising in Jerusalem had killed a number of Jews and injured many others. On May 1 of this year, more serious violence erupted, starting in the northern settlements and spreading through the country.

Sheyna would hear nothing of delay; she had made her decision. It was a decision motivated by a mixture of things. Jealousy, probably, of the younger sister who had far surpassed her and was leaving now to live out the Zionist dreams that she, Sheyna, had instilled in her years earlier. A perception, also, that if she didn't grab this moment, if she didn't go with her sister to that distant land, she never would. That and the old stubbornness she and Golda shared.

Golda went on to Milwaukee, where she took an emotional leave of her parents, Moshe, unable to hold back tears, and Bluma, looking "small and withdrawn," and of her younger sister, Clara. A student at the University of Wisconsin, Clara would be the only one of the three sisters who attended college. Golda and Morris met up again with Regina and Yossel in New York for the last few days before departure and were joined there by a disparate group of people making the journey also. They numbered twenty-two in all, including several women, like Sheyna, traveling alone with children.

The excitement mounted. Baruch Zuckerman and his wife, Nina, who had become Golda's close friends, put the group up in their Bronx apartment, where everyone slept on the floor in whatever space could be found. A few days before their departure, the Poalei Zion *chaverim*—the comrades Golda had worked with these last several years—threw a farewell party for all of them, with speeches and toasts to their future. About a month earlier, in April, the *Jewish Daily Press* noted that "Milwaukeeans who have received passports to go to Eretz Yisroel are Mr. and Mrs. Goldie Meyerson." The appellation fit the couple. Golda had been the force that led her marriage to this point and the force that led her friends to uproot themselves, leave their families and the comforts of America behind them, disregard the dangers ahead, and venture into a new life.

MANY YEARS LATER ALBERTA SZALITA, a prominent psychiatrist researching the subject of leadership, interviewed Golda Meir, then Israel's prime minister. "How would you explain your rise to leadership?" Dr. Szalita asked.

"I don't know anything about leadership," Golda replied, typically eschewing theoretical talk. "I can only tell you that I was going to the theater one evening and got on an elevator. Nobody in the elevator bothered to move. So I pressed the button. That's all I can say about leadership."

Golda had pressed the button for her group and herself, and they were on the move.

PART TWO

ASCENT

5

"New Jews"

At midnight on July 7, 1921, James J. Prendergast of Dorchester, Massachusetts, received a terrifying phone call. His son, James Daniel Prendergast, an engineer aboard the U.S. mail steamer *Pocahontas*, had apparently thrown himself overboard as the ship neared Naples, Italy. Shocked, James senior appealed to his congressman, James A. Gallivan, for an investigation, arguing that the boy "was too good a Catholic" to take his own life. Gallivan sent the Prendergast letter and a newspaper report of the incident to the State Department and about two weeks later received word that young Mr. Prendergast had suffered from "nervous prostration and mental depression" and had jumped overboard.

Goldie Meyerson and her little group aboard the S.S. *Pocahontas* had heard rumors about the death of the engineer Prendergast, but by the time it occurred, so many disasters had beset their steamship that they took this one in stride. The saga of the *Pocahontas* began when Golda and her party arrived at the steamer on their scheduled departure date and had to return to shore and the friends who had bade them farewell because of a strike by the crew. The next day, May 23, 1921, with the strike supposedly settled, they embarked on their journey, headed first to Naples. What they didn't know, and never would learn, was that a nationwide maritime strike had begun a few weeks earlier, on May 1, and was still in progress. The International Seamen's Union (ISU) had called the strike in response to shipowners' plans to lower seamen's wages now that World War I had ended. Most of the *Pocahontas* crew does not appear to have belonged to the ISU, but key troublemakers among them might have been members of other unions sympathetic to the strike.

And trouble they made. Barely out of the harbor, the ship started to list, its engine and boilers damaged. At the same time, the passengers, many of them vacationers on their way to Italy, found their food inedible and their drinking water mixed with seawater. It took an unheard-of full week for the steamer to reach Boston from New York and another nine days there for the captain to have the ship repaired. Meanwhile, three members of Golda's group, a young bride and an elderly couple, decided to go back; they'd had enough excitement. Golda prevailed on the others not to give up, arguing that if they returned home now and settled into their old lives, "I don't know whether we will ever decide again to go."

With the boat mended, the group left Boston Harbor in high spirits, only to find the trip now worse than before. The mutineers flooded the engine room, opened the portholes so that water ruined most of the supplies on board, disabled the rudder, and set mysterious fires. When the ship limped into the next port, Ponta Delgada in the Azores, the first assistant, G. W. Hinckley, ringleader of the conspirators, started smashing windows and shouting, "God damn you, if we can't sink you we'll break you up." For their treachery, the captain arrested Hinckley and two of his men, holing them up on board in irons until the voyage ended.

Unaware of the labor battles, Golda and her entourage knew only that the voyage had become a nightmare. They found some relief during the weeklong stopover for repairs at Ponta Delgada, where they met the small Jewish community on the island. But back on board, they had to cope with new traumas. The ship's electric icebox was destroyed so that meat and other perishables had to be thrown overboard and everyone subsist on rice and salty tea. One of the passengers died, another broke her leg, and the captain's brother went mad and had to be locked in his cabin. And the poor engineer Prendergast was found at the bottom of the sea with both hands tied and a large pipe between them so that he couldn't swim, his death nevertheless ruled a suicide—rather than the homicide it probably was—by a State Department eager to be done with the whole sorry business of the S.S. *Pocahontas*.

The ship finally reached Naples on Monday, July 4, some six weeks after it left New York on what should have been a two-week voyage. Forty years later, in July 1961, Golda Meir, then Israel's foreign minister, held a reunion of the group that had made the voyage with her, inviting also their families. Only a handful showed up; others had died, were too infirm, or had returned permanently to the United States. Those who came spent a nostalgic evening with Golda, reminiscing and singing their hearts out with the pioneer songs of their youth. About a decade after that, Mrs. Meir, now prime minister and celebrating her fiftieth anniversary in the Land of Israel, again invited *Pocahontas* participants and their families to commemorate their journey. This time, the guests included Elisha Kally, son of her old friend Yossel Kopilov. With him were his wife and his son Yossi, named for his grandfather, who had died years earlier.

In the summer of 1921, Yossel, Regina, Golda, Morris, and the rest of their companions disembarked from the cursed *Pocahontas* in Naples, eager to make their way to Palestine. It would remain a difficult passage. With the unrest in that land, they could not go directly to Jaffa, as they had planned. Ordinarily, because Jaffa did not yet have a harbor, passengers would disembark at sea and Arab boatmen would load them and their baggage into boats and row them ashore. Now the Arabs refused to carry Jews. Accordingly, after five days in Naples the group traveled by train to the port city of Brindisi. There they would board a ship to Alexandria, Egypt, take a train again to El Qantara, and then another train to Tel Aviv.

In Brindisi, they met a group of young Lithuanian Jews, also on their way to Palestine. The minute Golda spotted these young people, she spoke admiringly of them as "real" *halutzim*, authentic pioneers. They had trained in Zionist youth camps in Europe, spoke Hebrew fluently, and were well versed in agricultural skills. Equally impressed, Yossel described these people in a letter to Shamai as "new Jews . . . Real Hercules who are ready to build a land on just foundations with their backs." Compared with them, he felt "small and unworthy."

In earlier years, in the United States, Jacob Schiff and the other elite German Jewish philanthropists had hoped to make "new Jews" out of the masses of Eastern European immigrants by helping them to assimilate into Christian America. The "new Jew" in Zionist imagination was a more impressive breed of person, a strong, proud Spartan who had left home and parents behind, "negating the Diaspora," in contemporary parlance, by discarding all traces of the beaten-down ghetto Jew. He—the term was most often applied to men—was brave and altruistic, engaged in agriculture instead of intellectual life or traditional Jewish trades. Posters of the period and later depicted such men and their female counterparts as tanned, muscular, smiling pioneers carrying hoes or bushels of wheat as they tamed the wilderness and made the deserts of Palestine bloom. They were ideal images that the complexities of reality would diminish, but they were the ideals that drew waves of newcomers to the Land of Israel.

The "real Hercules," as Yossel called the Lithuanians, fit the image of new Jews and the kind of *halutzim* Golda longed to emulate. She tried to strike up an acquaintance with them aboard the ship to Alexandria, only to be rebuffed. The austere Lithuanians looked down on her and her little band, regarding them as soft, bourgeois Americans, incapable of holding up under the rigors of life in Palestine. With no money for the third-class cabins that Golda's group enjoyed, these hardy souls slept on the ship's deck, and Golda quickly decided that she and her comrades needed to show solidarity by doing the same. The others very reluctantly went along with her—"none dared oppose her," in Sheyna's words— even though giving up their cabins also meant giving up hot meals in the dining room. Sheyna and Regina secretly bribed the dining room supervisor to sneak the children in for meals after hours.

In the course of the three-day journey, the standoffish Lithuanians gradually thawed. They exchanged life stories with the Americans and joined them in singing Yiddish and Hebrew pioneer songs and dancing the hora on deck. Golda was in her glory; for the first time, she felt part of the inner circle of pioneers, an accomplishment that she, at least, regarded as worth the discomforts she had caused her friends.

The discomforts worsened during the last leg of the journey. Alexandria, where Golda's group left the ship, teemed with flies and beggars in filthy rags pulling at them for alms, and the train rides to El Qantara and then Tel Aviv were ordeals of unbearable heat and thirst, of the sting of windswept sand in their eyes and the grit of it in their mouths, of hard, dirty benches and crying children and more beggars, of the sight through unwashed windows of mile after mile of the arid deserts of the Sinai Peninsula so different from the green plains of Wisconsin. Their first encounter with the Middle East dismayed them, and the situation got no better when they finally alighted from the train in Tel Aviv, on Thursday, July 14, 1921, at the height of a severe heat wave.

The small shack of a train station appeared to have been built in the middle of a blazing no-man's-land. Friends they had expected to meet them at the station had not shown up. (It would later emerge that these friends were in Jerusalem arranging their return passage to Chicago; life here had proved too difficult.) "Well, Golda, you wanted to come to Eretz Yisrael. Here we are. Now we can all go back," Yossel said, with some attempt at humor. Nobody laughed. The romantic Tel Aviv of their dreams, the "Hill of Spring," as its name meant, looked as far as their eyes could see like a desolate flatland of sand surrounded by more sand in the shape of dunes.

While they were wondering what to do next, a tall, lanky man named

Barash approached them to say in Yiddish that he owned a hotel on nearby Lilienblum Street. They gratefully agreed to follow him there. Spirits rose when everyone had a chance to eat, bathe, and settle into the hotel's large, light rooms, but plummeted again after Golda and some others discovered the blood of bedbugs in their beds. Nor did it help to have dinner the next evening with their Chicago friends—who had completed their plans to return to the States—and find that a chunk of soap had accidentally been mixed into the hamburgers served, making them repulsive.

Within a few days, Golda and the others set out to find a place to live and a means of earning a living. The Tel Aviv they saw as they wended their way through its streets held out more promise than the stark desert of their first impression. This was a city on the go, growing so quickly that everywhere workers were leveling sand, paving sidewalks, and constructing new buildings. Its rapid growth had made apartments so difficult to find and rents so high that tents and huts had been set up on the seashore and other areas for struggling new arrivals.

It had begun modestly as a garden suburb of the overcrowded ancient Arab port of Jaffa, where many Jews worked as merchants and artisans, professionals or business owners. Sixty Jewish families had bought several acres of dunes north of Jaffa, mostly with money borrowed from the Jewish National Fund, the Zionists' major land development organization. On April 11, 1909, they drew lots to divide up the land. From the start, they aspired to imbue their new quarter with a European flavor along the lines of a Parisian suburb. By 1910, several large streets had been laid out and given the names of notable Jews, such as Herzl, Ahad Ha'am, and the broad, tree-lined Rothschild Boulevard. A water tower had been installed, providing homes with running water, and houses had begun to emerge from the sand in a jumble of eclectic styles. The burgeoning neighborhood suffered a severe setback during World War I, when the Turks expelled all its Jews. But the area itself remained intact, and when the British gained control of Palestine at the end of the war, former Tel Aviv residents hurried back.

On May 10, 1921, two months before Golda and her group showed up, Tel Aviv and its surrounding neighborhoods were incorporated as an independent municipality, in charge of many of its own taxes and administrative activities. It "has become the first Hebrew city in the world," Morris wrote proudly to his family. "It is a city in which everyone is Jewish, with self-government, a Hebrew police force and schools." And its

Jewish mayor, Meir Dizengoff, rode about regally on a white horse. "It is going to be a modern and beautiful town," Morris concluded his letter.

As Morris, Golda, and their friends searched for lodgings, they might have noticed, side by side with people in everyday work clothes, women in fashionable European-style garments and prosperous-looking men having their shoes shined in the street. Had they the time, they might have gone swimming in one of the popular beach areas being developed along the sea, attended a lecture offered at the imposing Herzliya Gymnasium, a Hebrew high school at the end of Herzl Street, or enjoyed a concert in the Shulamit music school. But they would have been conscious, also, of the open-air markets in nearby Jaffa, where Tel Aviv residents nonchalantly shopped, oblivious to the swarms of flies coating often rotting, unwrapped foods. They would have seen piles of garbage littering even some of the best streets—although strict laws forbade that—and discovered that the city's sole letter carrier often didn't bother to deliver the mail.

Their new home, they would have found, was an amalgam of a rough-and-tumble frontier town, budding cultural mecca, and developing urban community. Much of Golda's future life was to take place here as she and it grew and changed.

Golda and Morris, Regina and Yossel, and Sheyna and her children managed to rent a two-room apartment together in an old section, Neve Zedek (Oasis of Justice), the first Jewish neighborhood established next to Jaffa even before Tel Aviv came into being. With its narrow alleys, low stucco houses, and winding, mostly unpaved streets, it had the air of a European shtetl more than a modern quarter, yet the newness of the city projected itself even there. Their flat was behind the Eden cinema, the only movie house in town, but also the most important culture center in the country. The week they arrived in Tel Aviv, Ibsen's *Nora* was being performed in Hebrew, prominently advertised in the local newspapers.

The group had to pay three months' rent in advance for their apartment, and for that they received, aside from their two small rooms, a tiny kitchen, a closed veranda that served as a dining space, and a toilet in the outside yard, shared with about forty other people. With no electricity, they used a kerosene lamp for light, and they cooked on a Primus stove, also fueled by kerosene. Despite the inconveniences, they were luckier than the many new immigrants scrounging for places to live.

They were lucky also in finding work. Unemployment was rife, "with crowds of Jewish workers coming every week from Europe," Morris wrote in his letter home. Golda rejected an offer to teach English at the Herzliya high school, not wanting to tie herself to a steady job. Instead, she gave private English lessons, for which, Morris indicated, "there was a high demand." Morris got a job with a British commercial company in Lydda, a small town about a half hour's bus ride from Tel Aviv. The pay was low—thirteen dollars a week—but reasonable, within the Tel Aviv economy, he wrote. Regina lined up a high-paying position as a stenographer, and Yossel eventually found work in a barbershop. Sheyna kept house for them all.

And for this group, as for everyone in Tel Aviv, the recent Arab riots formed a backdrop of fear along with a determination to keep the British on their side. "True, one feels the English government quite heavily in the country but this does not frighten me," Golda wrote to Shamai on August 24, in a letter urging him to come to Palestine soon. "England will not choose the Arabs instead of us to colonize the land." The note of defiance in her letter reflected some actual waffling on Britain's part.

After the war, Jews had reason for optimism in regard to the British. At the San Remo conference in April 1920, the victorious Allies awarded England a mandate over Palestine, incorporating in their edict the words of the Balfour Declaration. With that, Zionists felt they had the approval of both Britain and the international community for encouraging Jewish immigration and continuing to purchase land. When the aristocratic English Jew and Zionist Herbert Samuel became high commissioner of Palestine, the picture seemed rosier than ever.

The Arabs saw a much darker image. Although many had benefited from Jewish agricultural skills and the need for extra labor, a number of fellaheen, or small farmers, had been displaced by Arab landlords' sale of land to the Jews. But land was not the key issue in the view of the historian Walter Laqueur; only a small percentage of the land the Jews bought came from the fellaheen. The Arabs objected to the increasing Jewish presence "because they anticipated that the Jews intended one day to become masters of the country and that as a result they would be reduced to the status of a minority." So when the Zionists spoke of finding ways for the two groups to work together for the benefit of all, the Arabs insisted that the Jews had no right to the country in the first place, and therefore they could see no reason to seek compromises.

Twice during 1920, while Golda was still in America making final plans for her move to Palestine, Arab rioters attacked Jews. The Jewish folk hero Joseph Trumpeldor died in one of those attacks, in the northern settlement of Tel Hai. The most lethal Arab uprising burst out in May 1921, in the heart of Jaffa, leaving forty-seven Jews and forty-eight Arabs dead and several hundred people wounded. Among those killed was the well-known Jewish writer Yosef Chaim Brenner.

Stunned by the violence, the British began reassessing their commitment to the Balfour Declaration. The high commissioner, Herbert Samuel, whose appointment had so delighted Palestinian Jews, infuriated them by placing a temporary ban on all Jewish immigration to Palestine. In the Arab community, on the other hand, even people who did not condone the attacks on Jews lauded their benefits. As one Arab executive noted, no longer did the British use the word "Palestine" only in connection with Zionism. They had also begun to "feel the existence of the Palestinian people."

It was when news of these riots reached America that Shamai had pleaded in vain with Golda and Sheyna not to make their journey. Now, a month after landing in Tel Aviv, Golda and her group still sensed the tense aftereffects of the riots. Refugees from Jaffa continued to come to Tel Aviv, and Hebrew newspapers still emphasized the need to help them; committees had been formed to assist the wounded with shoes and clothing and to find employment for some who did not yet have the ability to work hard. When Golda wrote to Shamai that August, she recognized the strengthened Arab position and understood the vacillating English one. Nevertheless, she believed, as she said, that the British would choose the Jews over the Arabs. That would happen, she told Shamai, "if we will not go away" but hold steadfast in their commitment. And although economic conditions had become more difficult, "if one wants one's own land, and if one wants it with one's whole heart, one must be ready for this." Her message: "I cannot leave, and you must come."

For Golda, not leaving meant only one thing—working the land on a collective settlement. The place she set her sights on was Merhavia in the northern Valley of Jezreel, an area known in Hebrew simply as Ha'Emek, the Valley. Merhavia—God's Open Spaces—was technically a *kvutza*, a forerunner of the kibbutz and smaller in size, but the terms became interchangeable with time and Merhavia was frequently referred to as a kibbutz. Golda chose Merhavia because Dubinsky, whose love she had spurned but whose friendship she still valued, had settled there and invited her and Morris to join him.

Dubinsky had helped form the collective in the summer of 1920 together with some of his American comrades from the Jewish Legion and a few pioneers from Russia and Poland. Before that, it had been a failed cooperative farm whose members abandoned the area after tormented years of suffering with mosquito-infested swamps, widespread malaria, and constant attacks from Arab snipers in nearby villages. The Zionist movement, which had purchased the land in 1910, sent pioneers to the area to try to make a go of it after that failure, but groups of settlers came and went until Dubinsky and his group took up the challenge.

Twice, this new, struggling community rejected the Meyersons' application for membership. Having applied after arriving in Tel Aviv in July, they were told to wait until after the Jewish New Year in the fall, when the *kvutza* would have a better idea of how many new people it could take. When they applied a second time, only two members voted to admit them, one, their friend Dubinsky.

Ironically, the mostly American-born members held Golda's American roots against her. Too "spoiled," they pronounced her, too "soft" to withstand the tough physical labor required. Like the Lithuanians in Brindisi, they themselves had become "new Jews," who had shed their American bourgeois values. A second strike against Golda and Morris was their marriage. Most of the men, still bachelors, preferred to admit unmarried women. Moreover, the socialist kibbutz world viewed marriage as an outmoded institution and a married couple as unbalancing the larger group intimacy. "There was a need . . . to hide the family unit," a kibbutz veteran recalled. The kibbutz community mattered more than any individual in it.

Golda fought on all fronts, reapplying, arguing her case, and appearing at the kibbutz to be "looked over" by the group. With their third application, she and Morris were accepted for a trial period. Bent on proving her mettle, she worked a threshing machine for the first time in her life, picked almonds in a grove until her hands turned yellow, and dug deep holes in the rocky ground to plant saplings near the entrance gate, barely able to move her fingers afterward. She never let on how exhausted she felt as she joined the others in the dining room to eat the tasteless "chick-pea mush." After about a month's trial, she and Morris became permanent members.

In December, Morris wrote a long, detailed letter to his mother describing their surroundings. To reassure her, he put the best face he could on the small, struggling *kvutza*, exaggerating the good points and omitting most negatives. Merhavia's grounds, he wrote, occupied thirty-five hundred *dunams* of land (about nine hundred acres) beneath stately mountains. The actual farm where members lived and worked was built around a square yard about an acre long, surrounded by a thick protective fence. It had four stone buildings for inhabitants, left over from the first cooperative settlers, a communal shower, small bakery, kitchen and dining room, and a granary, barn, stable, chicken coop, and garage. (Golda would later label all those buildings little more than "shacks.") He proudly mentioned that the shower "even had warm water" and the kitchen running water but skipped the fact that the kitchen lacked basic utensils, the toilets were outside and some distance away, and everyone had been warned not to wear white when going out at night, to avoid Arab snipers. The farm had forty cows, fifteen horses, and some chickens and ducks, and the group was planning to acquire twenty-five beehives to produce honey. Many kinds of trees had been planted around the buildings, he wrote, and there were fig and olive groves. He neglected to mention that it would be years before the new plantings grew into actual trees that could provide shade over the sunbaked earth. No mention either of the mud the settlers had to slog through all winter (reminding Golda of the mud holes in Pinsk), the malaria-infested marshes they still had to drain, or the gnats and flies, known as *barhash*, that tormented them in the summer, forcing them to smear Vaseline on the exposed parts of their bodies and cover themselves with clothes from head to toe despite the grueling sun, and even then they were bitten sick. Morris noted that the kibbutz had thirty-two members at the time, twenty men and twelve women, among them three married couples. The couples had larger rooms than the single people, "very beautiful, with white-washed walls and stone floors," he said, as though describing a rustic hotel. (Golda would speak of the sparse room that Morris decorated with flowers, the only thing that made it look "nicer.") And he praised the kibbutz system of sharing work so that each member had a turn at doing everything, from washing laundry to plowing the fields. "You should have seen your Morris," he ended, "driving two mules that are hitched to a carriage loaded with manure or walking behind them plowing . . . really as an experienced farmer from birth."

Despite his exaggerations, Morris's enthusiasm in those early kibbutz days was real. He enjoyed "spiritual satisfaction" in the hard labor that left his body "feeling warm and his blood rushing with a surge of life," he wrote. He had a sense also that the "frantic and troubled" lives he and Golda had led until then might calm down in the quiet peace of farm living. He should have anticipated, but didn't, that Golda would become as immersed in kibbutz operations as she had been in organizational activities back in Milwaukee. He should have anticipated that, given her nature, her promise to "no longer be constantly on the move" once they reached Palestine could never be fulfilled. The sadness of Morris's life was that when it came to Golda, he always set himself up for disappointment.

But at the beginning in Merhavia, he seemed optimistic. He must have been especially pleased that the gramophone and classical record collection he had brought with them from America became the hit of the kibbutz. The record player, a "modern" machine without the large exterior horn typical of earlier models, was the first of its type on the collective and a phenomenon to all who saw it.

Sarah Lishanski, older sister of Rachel Yanait Ben-Zvi and, like her, an admired and dedicated pioneer, wrote to Rachel about her unforgettable experience at Merhavia because of the Meyersons. The couple—"who had arrived a while ago from America"—invited her to their room along with a group of Americans and others on the kibbutz. They had brought with them "some kind of instrument called a victorula" (Victrola, the trade name of the phonograph), made up of "a small box with a motor inside that plays in an amazing and beautiful way." She heard many types of music, she wrote, but the pieces that left the greatest impression were the "Hebrew melodies of Heifetz, the well-known musician, and the opera Tosca." She had returned to her room at one in the morning and could not fall asleep because of her excitement.

Golda had seen the excitement the gramophone caused among their neighbors when she lived in Tel Aviv. On leaving, she had given it to Sheyna but soon demanded it back. Sheyna complied resentfully. Alone with her children in their flat, she found comfort in the music and the neighbors' visits to hear it. "How could one have the heart to take our single musical instrument away from us?" she wrote in her memoirs. Golda's answer at the time was that the kibbutz needed the record player more than Sheyna did. That might have been, but Golda also needed the kind of attention it fetched her. Years later, she wrote facetiously that she sometimes wondered whether the kibbutz members might have been happy to "accept the dowry without the bride," the phonograph without its owner, so popular had it been.

Along with the gramophone, Golda had another ticket into the kibbutz community. During the first, hardest weeks, she was taken under the wing of Hanna Chizick, Dubinsky's wife. Hanna had immigrated to Palestine from Ukraine as a teenager in 1906, part of a family of twelve children, who with their parents all settled in the land. When Golda met her, she already had a reputation as a dedicated pioneer who did hard agricultural labor in various villages. About a year earlier, she had been overcome by the death of her younger sister Sarah during the Arab attacks at Tel Hai. Despairing and ill, she had gone to Vienna to recover, then back to Palestine and her companion Dubinsky at Merhavia. They married shortly afterward.

If Hanna knew of Dubinsky's earlier passion for Golda, she didn't say so. Golda always credited her with smoothing the way in Merhavia. "It was not easy then for a young American girl, unaccustomed to physical work and without knowledge of Hebrew, to become adjusted and acclimatized," she said. "As a latecomer who had little knowledge of the spadework done by the earlier arrivals, I may have been troubled by a feeling of inferiority. Hanna made me feel that I, too, could learn some branch of agriculture."

Hanna left Merhavia in early 1923 to join a women workers' farm in the cooperative settlement of Nahalat Yehuda, not far from Tel Aviv, and Dubinsky followed her there. By then, any "inferiority" Golda might have felt had long since disappeared. She had reverted to her Milwaukee self, organizing, controlling, demanding, and flourishing despite illnesses, disagreements with her comrades, and the daily struggle for subsistence.

She threw herself into everything. She did the physical labor required of her, took her turn in the kitchen, learned to bake bread, and became an expert in the poultry yard, putting aside her fear of chickens and other animals. She participated in weekly meetings of the entire *kvutza*, when every aspect of the collective was discussed, sat up late into the night around the long wooden dining hall table talking with the others, and sang and danced with verve at kibbutz parties.

She also didn't hesitate to change what she decided needed changing. If the comrades had greasy hands—which they wiped on their clothes—after peeling the herring they ate daily, she made sure the herring was peeled in the kitchen before they received it; if they had been eating cold preserved foods for breakfast, she began cooking hot oatmeal instead; if they drank their tea from chipped, rusted enamel cups, she bought more sanitary drinking glasses (not realizing how quickly they would break). She wore the same kind of work dress as the other women, a slab of rough woven fabric tied around her waist, but she insisted on ironing it every evening so that it looked fresh in the morning. And she introduced the custom of spreading a white sheet over the dining table on Friday evenings for the Sabbath meal, placing a few wildflowers in the center. A hopelessly middle-class American? The "witch," as some of her angrier comrades labeled her? Certainly she loved the socialist values of kibbutz life in which everybody shared everything, but she was never one to elevate theory over practicality. Usually she got her way.

What neither she nor any of the others were able to do, however, was transform the tiny, strapped *kvutza* into the successful kibbutz it would become later. The small budget the collective received from the Jewish National Fund and the modest income it generated from producing milk and other farm products barely sustained it. The handwritten minutes of the weekly meetings reflect the persistent pressures members felt. The tractor required gasoline, reported Chaver Mandelblatt at a spring meeting in 1922, but "there is only a little bit of money left," and it is needed to "keep the *kvutza* going until the end of the summer." On the other hand, without the tractor, the fields could not be plowed and readied for planting the next year's crops. What to do? Or how to handle the constant turnover in membership? People left Merhavia all the time because of its harsh living conditions and a restlessness that drove the young pioneers from one place to another. As a result, the *kvutza* often found itself shorthanded. Should the total number of members be increased to compensate for these departures? as Chaver Kremer suggested. Should standards be lowered for accepting new applicants? Every question required a committee to investigate and reach a compromise that would keep the group vital a little longer, and a little longer still.

Golda's American background contributed to the collective's economic welfare on at least one occasion, when she gave English lessons to the daughter of a grocer named Blumenfield in the neighboring *moshav* (workers' cooperative village). Instead of paying her, he set up a monthly credit in his store for the *kvutza*, which the comrades used to buy such luxuries as potatoes, salt, and Quaker Oats, known as "Kwoker."

Her larger contribution came by way of chickens and eggs. Chaver Friedman had complained that it was "impossible" for him both to tend the garden with the vegetables it grew and to handle the chicken coop, which required much time and effort. Moreover—another kibbutz conundrum—the coop "was in a state of terrible disrepair," but there was also a need to have someone learn the techniques of poultry breeding to increase the farm's production. The *kvutza* voted to postpone repair of the chicken house and first have somebody study poultry. The task fell to Golda. She spent a few weeks at the agricultural preparatory farm of Ben Shemen, east of Tel Aviv, and on her return took over the poultry yard. Under her supervision, a new five-hundred-egg incubator yielded more chicks than the kibbutz had ever bred. She became so caught up in raising poultry that at one point, ill with a high fever and unable to water the ducks, she hallucinated about seeing a room filled "with dead ducks." But she took pleasure in her expertise and the recognition it gave her.

Less than a year after the Meyersons arrived at Merhavia, the *kvutza* elected Golda to its three-person central steering committee. She was in good company. The committee head, David Yizraeli, had been a devoted member of the Poalei Zion in America and so influential in the *kvutza* that he had his own glass for tea tucked away in the communal cupboard, one of the few privileged with such private property. With that position and a newfound participation in conferences outside the collective, Golda took the first steps on her political career ladder in the Land of Israel.

THE NAMES OF THE VENERABLE women at a woman's conference she attended in Haifa in September 1922 would slip away from collective Jewish memory for decades, to be reclaimed by Jewish feminists only in the late twentieth and early twenty-first centuries: Manya Shochat, Ada Maimon-Fishman, Rachel Yanait Ben-Zvi, Hanna Chizick, and others formed the core of activist women who devoted themselves to improving the conditions of working women in the farms and towns of Palestine. Golda attended the conference with Hanna Chizick and by then had probably met Rachel, whom she had long admired from afar. Manya Shochat and Ada Maimon were newer acquaintances. Shochat, a radical labor leader and feminist, was a founder of the country's first independent agricultural collective, the small settlement of Sejera in the Galilee. As one of the few female members of the elite Hashomer (Watchman) association that protected the settlements, she could be seen riding her horse from place to place, garbed in the flowing headpiece and robes of a Bedouin man. Maimon was less colorful but equally ardent in her commitment to women's rights. She had worked as an agricultural laborer, founded a girls' agricultural school, and was the prime mover behind the Haifa conference.

These women and other attendees had been among the group of

male and female immigrants that became known as the Second Aliyah workers. (*Aliyah*, Hebrew for "ascent," is the word used for immigration to Palestine and later Israel.) The First Aliyah generally refers to the Hovevei Zion, the lovers of Zion, and other early settlers who began arriving during the 1880s and establishing *moshavot*, agricultural villages built around privately owned farms. Some of these people were motivated by religious ideals, some by a desire to till the soil in the ancient Land of Israel (although many would use Arab laborers for the actual work). Members of the Second Aliyah started entering Palestine around 1904, during a period of pogroms in Eastern Europe, and continued for the next decade, until 1914 and the beginning of World War I. Of perhaps thirty-five thousand Jews who came at that time, only about five thousand were dedicated young *halutzim*, the Zionist workers committed to reclaiming the land with their own physical labor. Small as their numbers were, however, their creativity and drive shaped the nature of the country for decades, and their role became almost mythical in the history of Zionism. Pioneers like Golda, who immigrated after the war into the early 1920s, were part of the Third Aliyah. Golda would later say that the Second Aliyah workers originated the basic institutions and programs that would form the foundations of the Jewish state—Jewish labor, collective living, an emphasis on Hebrew—and "bequeathed" this "torah" (teaching) to the Third Aliyah members, who "accepted it with a full heart and with joy."

Golda idolized the movers and shakers of the Second Aliyah group, men like Ben-Gurion, Ben-Zvi, and Zerubavel. Now she was getting to know their female counterparts, women concerned with the plight of other women workers in the hard-knocks world of the Yishuv.

For women it *was* an especially hard world. Many who came as pioneers, hoping to plow the land, dig the ditches, build the roads—to be "new Jews" alongside the men—often found themselves ridiculed and pushed instead into the traditional female roles of cooking, cleaning, and child care. And as hard as they labored even at these jobs, their work always remained lower in status than the "productive" men's work.

By 1914, numbers of these women pioneers and other female workers had united to form a budding women's movement to address women's employment problems and other areas of inequality in the Yishuv. Although interrupted by the war, the movement coalesced afterward, with Ada Maimon one of its most influential leaders. In the winter of 1921, the women's movement formed its operating arm, the Women

Workers' Council, Moetzet Hapoalot in Hebrew. Elected secretary-general, Maimon suggested that only a limited number of women be invited to the council's next conference, in Haifa, so that it could be a serious working meeting. From what she had heard, Golda Meyerson was the kind of woman who should be included. She was young, politically smart, and willing to work hard.

Thirty-two delegates and eight members of the executive committee gathered for the Haifa conference. Through most of it, Golda simply listened and said nothing. Her turn to present came in the sixth session, devoted to the role of mothers in educating and caring for children in communal settlements.

"What happens when a woman has children, but she also has an opportunity to participate in community work?" she asked in her brief talk. It was an issue that would haunt her for years. If a woman feels "she is stealing time from her children" by working, should she give up the work? In some of the newer *kvutzot*, children lived and studied in children's houses, cared for by women assigned that responsibility, leaving both parents free to work. Could that child-care arrangement be applied to city life? The answers were not forthcoming.

Toward the close of the conference, Golda was elected to the secretariat—part of the executive body—along with Ada Maimon, Hanna Chizick, Elisheva Kaplan (who would become the wife of Levi Eshkol, Israel's third prime minister), and others, a mix of new members with older, established ones. She was also placed on a committee with Manya Shochat and Ada Maimon to represent the council in areas involving public works. She told the assembly modestly how very "happy" she was "to have had the privilege of being at this conference."

Ada Maimon seemed delighted to have Golda in the fold and began writing to her soon afterward to encourage her to assume additional responsibilities. In October, she asked permission from Merhavia for Golda to leave to attend another meeting. In December, she reported to her friend Hayuta Bussel that at a recent executive committee meeting Golda Meyerson, "as an American girl," had "complete confidence" that the council would be able to raise money for its women's farms from Americans. Golda's suggestion had led to serious fund-raising discussions in the council. Ada appreciated Golda's vitality and practical approach to problems, and Golda appreciated Ada's experience and interest in her. That interest increased as the second convention of the Histadrut, the general federation of labor, approached.

Established in 1920, the Histadrut had been designed—to a great extent by Ben-Gurion—to unify all aspects of labor in the Yishuv. Eventually, it would be the most powerful institution in pre-state Israel and afterward, in charge of schools and hospitals, of producing food and building highways. Now, in its early years, it focused on the well-being of Jewish laborers and particularly on work and housing for new immigrants. It was dominated by two political parties: Ahdut Ha'avoda (Unity of Labor) and Hapoel Hatzair (The Young Worker). Ahdut Ha'avoda, now Golda's party, had been created when the Palestine branch of her beloved Poalei Zion merged with some smaller groups of labor parties. Hapoel Hatzair, an early workers' party, refused to join that union and remained independent. Although separate, the two parties worked together to establish the Histadrut and then competed for influence over it.

Because the women workers' movement did not have a party of its own, it had no official representation at the Histadrut's founding convention or on the organization's central council. Ada Maimon won that representation for the women by publicly threatening that if they did not receive it, they would create a separate women's party, drawing women away from the established parties. To prevent such a split, the Histadrut agreed to reserve two places on its council for the women's group.

The second general convention of the Histadrut would take place in Tel Aviv in February 1923, and Maimon set about arranging for as many members of the women's council as possible to attend. She manipulated to have Golda represent the Haifa area, which included the Jezreel Valley, where Merhavia lay, and then campaigned hard to win votes for her. Elected, Golda looked forward with excitement to the convention.

Back home in Merhavia, Morris had become increasingly disenchanted with kibbutz life. The enthusiasm of his first letters to his family in America metamorphosed into bitterness in the later ones. "Ah, Palestine, Palestine, you beggarly little land, what will become of you?" he wrote. "How ironic sound the fine words at Poalei Zion meetings about a free workers' Palestine." Whatever idealism he might have felt when he began his adventure with Golda was gone now, stifled by a daily routine he had come to despise. He couldn't stand kibbutz life, Golda later told the journalist Oriana Fallaci: "He couldn't stand eating at the communal table . . . He couldn't stand the hard work. He couldn't stand the climate and the feeling of being part of a community. He was too individualistic, too introverted, too delicate." He wanted privacy. He wanted to be able to have a glass of tea alone without having to traipse to the dining hall to get it. He wanted to wear his own clothes instead of having to take every garment from the communal laundry. He wanted to read, enjoy music, discuss art instead of listening to the *chaverim* endlessly dissect kibbutz ideology.

He wanted his Goldie. His dreams of a new beginning had dissipated, like the early morning dew on the soil he barely had energy left to till. When she was home, in the *kvutza*, she often spent her evenings conversing or singing with the others or having midnight snacks with the watchmen after their guard duty. And these days, she was away at conferences and meetings much of the time, leaving Morris alone and lonely.

THE HISTADRUT CONVENTION she left him to attend in February had prestige written all over it. Golda was one of 120 delegates to it chosen by the six thousand members of the Histadrut. The convention opened in a festive atmosphere on the evening of Wednesday, February 7, at the Eden cinema in Tel Aviv, near where Golda and Morris had lived. Hundreds of people crammed into the theater, and throngs of others outside strained to get a glimpse of the proceedings. The stage held only a table covered with a green cloth for speakers to use. Pictures of Theodor Herzl and Karl Marx hung side by side, with photographs above them of Ber Borochov and Aaron David Gordon, philosophers of the Labor Zionist movement.

The renowned American Reform rabbi Judah L. Magnes, who would become chancellor of Hebrew University, greeted the assembly and spoke of this group's connection with Jewish workers in America. If the Palestinian Jews wished to develop close ties to the Americans, he advised, they needed "to regard them not only as a source of money, but also as their brothers and sons of Israel." His words resonated with Golda, who would refer to them a little later.

Early Friday morning, as Ben-Gurion began his report on various Histadrut departments, loud applause suddenly interrupted him. Albert Einstein had entered the auditorium. Having completed a six-month trip to Asia, Einstein was spending twelve days in Palestine before returning to his native Germany, the only visit he would ever make there or, later, to Israel. "The future of this land and the future of our entire race are in your hands," he told his listeners, thrilling them with pride.

After Einstein left and the excitement died down, Ben-Gurion resumed his report, which continued through the day. When he reached the subject of the Women Workers' Council, he noted that even within the labor movement, which fully subscribed to the equality of men and women, working women had not achieved their rightful place. "The very existence and the need for the existence of a special institution to protect the interests of women workers do not add to our honor," he said, but such an institution had to exist because of continuing discrimination against working women.

While Ben-Gurion's words conveyed great sympathy for the problems of female workers in the villages and towns, they also hinted at a struggle to come. How independent should the Women Workers' Council be? Were his words actually a guarded warning, as feminists of a later generation would argue, against turning the council into a power center for women within the Histadrut?

One of seventy delegates chosen to speak, Golda presented her talk on Sunday morning during the convention's fifth session. Speaking in Yiddish (her Hebrew far too weak), she began by praising the achievements of the Histadrut leaders, all of them part of the Second Aliyah. "For us, the newcomers, it is hard even to comprehend the depth of the great work done and to give it its proper due," she said. She went on to establish her own credentials. "Dr. Magnes was right," she said, with the authority of a former American, "workers in America should not be seen as only a financial resource." They should also be regarded as a "living body" that can carry the Zionist idea forward, and therefore the Histadrut needed to strengthen its connection with them. Then, as she had at the Haifa conference two months earlier, she raised the question most on her mind, about working mothers and the care and education of their children, which she saw as "one of the most important tasks of the Histadrut."

Not until the end of her talk did she turn to the subject of the Women Workers' Council: "It is a sad and shameful fact that we are forced to create a special organization to deal with the woman worker's issues . . . The conference should create the right conditions for the woman worker so that we will no longer need that special institution."

Yehuda Sharett, a musician and younger brother of Moshe Sharett—one of the party's key players—described Golda's appearance in a letter to his brother, who was in London. "She was filled with grace," he wrote, "a treasure" for Ahdut Ha'avoda. Unlike Hayuta Bussel or Rachel Yanait or the other women in the council, with their "long, shapeless" dresses, she wore simple, pretty clothes, decorated with "embroidery around the neck." And she spoke in a clear voice, "looking straight ahead," with such feeling that the entire hall "grew silent." A humor magazine published the next day called Golda a "singer," in the sense of being a performer. Indeed, her "performance" had smitten Yehuda and some of the more senior party members such as Yitzhak Tabenkin, a leader of the kibbutz movement, who seemed to so enjoy listening to her that Yehuda told him, jokingly, "It's too late, she's married."

Undoubtedly, Ada Maimon had a much different reaction to Golda Meyerson's talk. She and the other women rightly might have expected Golda to present herself as a delegate of the council, which had worked hard to get her elected to the convention. Instead, in her maiden appearance before the most important institution in the Labor Zionist movement, she spoke about other things and kept her ideas about the representation of working women until last, almost as an afterthought. Even then, she echoed Ben-Gurion's wishes that the working women's issues become resolved within the Histadrut and not by a separate institution—one that Maimon and the others considered crucial to furthering women's rights. Golda Meyerson had signaled her independence from the women's group.

As the convention days passed, Ada Maimon could not help but notice Golda's natural sociability and easy mingling among the delegates. She could not help but recognize that this young woman, who had caught her party leaders' attention, had her eyes set on broader horizons outside the Women Workers' Council. In elections to the Histadrut council at the convention's end, Golda was chosen along with Ada to fill the two seats allocated to the women workers' movement. Ada represented Hapoel Hatzair and Golda Ahdut Ha'avoda, her selection bypassing such senior and better-known party members as Rachel Yanait Ben-Zvi and Hanna Chizick. She had made her mark.

Within two months of returning to Morris and Merhavia, Golda left again. Party leaders, impressed with what they had seen of her, asked her to guide a visiting English dignitary around her area of the country. Ethel Snowden, a prominent socialist and politician, was also the wife of the influential British Labour Party leader Philip Snowden. Moshe Sharett found her "conceited," he wrote to Berl Katznelson from London, but he recognized that she could be important to them. Golda had no problem with her. They conversed freely in English (a relief for Golda, struggling with her Hebrew), and the tour gave her a chance to explore many parts of her region.

Snowden had written a book on feminism and was an active suffragist

in England, a subject they might have discussed. Golda had paid scant
attention to the woman's suffrage movement in the United States. Pioneers like Rachel Yanait, she held, did more "to further the cause of our
sex than even the most militant of suffragists in the United States or
England." Rachel herself "never had a special interest in suffragism," she
told an interviewer, nor did large numbers of the female workers in the
Yishuv. Their pioneer work in Palestine filled their lives and saturated
their emotions, leaving little room for other causes.

With the success of the tour, Golda became the party's first choice to
escort other visiting English-speaking VIPs.

In May, another conference beckoned, this one a gathering during the
festival of Shavuot of delegates from all the kibbutzim in the country.
It took place at Degania, the mother *kvutza*, the first to be established.
Golda had the high honor of being chosen by her kibbutz to represent it,
yet at this conference she both publicly embarrassed herself and infuriated a cadre of women.

The embarrassment came when she stood up to speak in Yiddish as
she had at the Histadrut convention. Joseph Beltz, one of the early pioneers, broke into her first words. "It's enough that you speak Yiddish in
Tel Aviv," he shouted, "in Degania—no!" Hebrew was the language of
the Jewish people in their land, the language of books and newspapers, of
schoolchildren and politicians. But Golda had a difficult time learning it
and, in fact, would never become as proficient in it as she was in English
and Yiddish. Despite Beltz's admonition, she delivered her brief talk in
Yiddish. What she said riled the women present.

She had taken it on herself to defend women doing kitchen work in the
kibbutzim. The comrades needed to "change attitudes and strengthen
people's recognition that the kitchen is the branch of work upon which
the entire life of the *kvutza* depends," she argued. Her words reflected
what she often said to the women at Merhavia when they griped about
their kitchen duties: "Why is it so much better to work in the barn and
feed the cows rather than in the kitchen and feed your comrades?" In
reality, Golda knew exactly why women in the *kvutzot* preferred the barn
to the kitchen and why it was hard to elevate the status of kitchen work.
She knew of how these pioneer women and others before them had been
relegated to the kitchen when they wanted to till the fields and drain
the marshes. She knew, as a member of the Women Workers' Council,
of the women's efforts to gain the equality the Zionist revolution had
promised them but failed to deliver.

She knew all that, but to her pragmatic mind there was nothing demeaning about kitchen work; it simply called for feeding *kvutza* members in as efficient a manner as possible. In taking that position, she was aligning herself again with the broader group, the Histadrut, the party, this time the *kvutza*, and not with the specific goals of women. She was distancing herself, once more, from women's unique issues, as she had at the Histadrut convention.

Ada Maimon had made a similar statement about kitchen work. "Preparing food and caring for a family—whether one's own or the larger family of working comrades—were no less important jobs than feeding cows," she wrote in a brief history of women workers, but she added something Golda did not: "But it must always be remembered that domestic tasks were not the exclusive responsibility of women." Indeed, at the Degania conference Yitzhak Tabenkin voiced the same thought. To free women from feeling they have sole responsibility for the kitchen, he said, "men should also be assigned to this work." Golda would certainly have agreed with him and Ada, yet she had neglected to make that point herself.

She did make a concession on the subject of women and the kitchen, forty years after the Degania convention. Speaking in 1960 to a gathering of Third Aliyah veterans, Golda recounted her two "sins" at the Degania convention of 1923, speaking Yiddish and defending kitchen work for women on the kibbutzim. It had taken a long time for her comrades to forgive her for the last sin, she confessed, yet at the time she believed she was just conveying simple "common sense."

This time she was willing to concede that "if, God forbid, the women pioneers of the Second Aliyah and the Third had acted only on the basis of common sense," they would not have left behind the great legacy they had, in all branches of work and all aspects of building the land.

There had been rumors for some time that the Meyersons were leaving their *kvutza* at Merhavia. There would also be rumors, never confirmed, that the couple left Merhavia because Golda had a love affair there with an older man who would later become a physician in Tel Aviv. The one verifiable fact was that by the time Golda returned from Degania in May 1923, it had become inevitable that her stay in Merhavia would end soon. Miserable with his life in the kibbutz, Morris had also become physically ill. He suffered from recurrent bouts of malaria and developed a rupture that would require surgery. Added to that, he had received a barrage of letters from his mother and sister, urging him to return to the States and even offering to pay his way. Complicating matters further, Golda very much wanted to have a baby, but Morris refused to do so unless they left the kibbutz. Longing for privacy himself, he would rear a child only in the privacy of his own home and not within a collective where the community made all decisions.

Given little choice, Golda agreed to leave Merhavia. The couple packed their few belongings and moved to Tel Aviv in September 1923. Looking back years later, she would refer to the "tragedy" of having had to give up the pioneer life she had so loved for Morris. She never spoke of the ever deteriorating economic situation that would ultimately lead to the *kvutza*'s disintegration. She never mentioned the despair of the steering committee at the failure of others in the kibbutz to assume decision-making responsibilities. The harsh reality was that had Golda stayed on at Merhavia, she would have had to leave anyway in a few years, when the enterprise collapsed for lack of money and leadership.

She left the kibbutz in tears with the hope that when Morris regained his health, they would return permanently. That plan didn't work out, and the next few years would become the darkest of her young life. When she reflected on her time at Merhavia, and especially through the lens of the grim years that followed, it seemed a golden age of promise and idealism, its severe shortcomings brushed aside.

6

The Dark Years

Tel Aviv had changed in the two years since Golda left it. Its population had jumped to close to seventeen thousand and within a year would more than double. The frenetic construction she had witnessed when she first set foot in the town had continued at a faster pace than ever. New houses and small shops crowded one another on narrow streets, and cafés—some nothing more than a tiny room with chairs on the sidewalk—dotted the main avenues. The pride of the town now was the Casino, a flamboyant coffeehouse at the end of Allenby Street, built on stilts dug into the sand below. Everybody who was anybody came to dance to the music of its band and listen to the sounds of the breaking waves in the background. Among its regulars, the great Zionist essayist and philosopher Ahad Ha'am could be seen ordering his favorite ice cream.

Two years earlier, about the time Golda and her group reached Palestine, Pinhas Rutenberg, an engineer and one of the prime builders of the Yishuv, received a concession from the British mandatory government to build an electric power station in Tel Aviv, the first in the country, lighting up the city and adding to its self-conscious modernity.

For Golda, the electricity, the hubbub of construction, and the gaiety of the Casino and other coffeehouses held little joy. After the open spaces of Merhavia, Tel Aviv seemed "unbearably small, noisy and crowded." Least bearable was her sense of defeat as she and Morris took up residence with Sheyna and her family. Golda, who had led Sheyna to Palestine, been the commanding presence in her little group of Americans, and gained the notice of some of the most prominent leaders in the Yishuv labor movement, had to swallow her pride and depend once again on her sister. Meanwhile, after volunteering at Hadassah Hospital, Sheyna had received a paying job there as supervisor of its kitchen. "I found great satisfaction in my work," she wrote.

Shamai arrived from America in 1922 and joined his family in an apartment Sheyna had rented, with the luxury of a private bathroom, and there the Meyersons joined them. For a while, Shamai earned a decent living as a part-time bookkeeper at a construction site, after which he became involved in a cooperative shoe factory that would eventually fail.

Golda and Morris were barely on speaking terms, each secretly blaming the other for their circumstance. Much later, Marie Syrkin, Golda's close friend and first biographer, speculated on why the strong-willed Golda did not have the strength to end the marriage then. She concluded that torn with guilt at having persuaded Morris to come to Palestine, Golda "was bound by his bondage," his emotional dependency on her. She might also have been bound by a fear of striking out completely on her own in a place she still did not know well. Added to that, ending marriage in divorce was not quite acceptable, even in the Roaring Twenties and even among young socialists who often referred to their mates as "life partners" instead of the bourgeois "husband" and "wife." A divorce still raised eyebrows; a divorcée was still someone to be pitied or looked down upon.

For the time being, the situation was helped by the man who would later become Golda's lover, some might say the true love of her life, David Remez. She had impressed him along with other Yishuv leaders at the Histadrut convention and met him again one day in Tel Aviv. After learning that she had left the kibbutz, he offered her a job in the Public Works Office, which he headed.

The Public Works, part of the Histadrut, oversaw the country's expanding road and construction projects. In earlier years, the British had supplied the funds for building roads, largely to provide employment for the immigrants streaming into the country. When the Histadrut took over that function, it aimed to develop the country and at the same time give workers a share in the economy, in true socialist fashion. Remez seemed well suited to the position of director. Born in Russia, he had studied law in Constantinople, where he met Ben-Gurion and Ben-Zvi, and come to Palestine in 1913 as part of the Second Aliyah. In his commitment to Labor Zionist ideals, he put aside his books and went to work as a laborer in the country's orange groves and vineyards, afterward moving to Tel Aviv with his wife, Luba. Highly intellectual, he was also a poet and linguist who coined Hebrew names for some of the country's rapidly sprouting industries: "Zim" for the biggest commercial navigation company in the land; "Mashbir," the largest supplier of food and machinery for the Histadrut; "El Al," the national airline; and other, everyday words, for launching a ship, for a bulldozer, a road sign, and dozens more.

Shabtai Teveth, Ben-Gurion's biographer, describes Remez as "intelligent, clever, and possessed of a wonderful sense of humor; the sparkle in his eye and his charm endeared him to all who knew him." In the gossipy world of the Yishuv, he was known as something of a ladies' man, and word had it that one of the people to whom he had especially "endeared" himself was a young secretary in the Jerusalem branch of the Public Works bureau, Gusta Strumpf. Born in Germany, Strumpf rented a room in the Remez apartment after she came to Palestine. She left to work on a kibbutz, became ill, went to Europe to recover, and upon her return to Palestine joined the Public Works Office. With her knowledge of German and familiarity with Western ways, Strumpf became important to the Histadrut leaders in dealing with bank managers and heads of various financial institutions, many of whom came from Germanic backgrounds. In some ways, Golda's life after Merhavia would follow the contours of Strumpf's. Her fluency in English and understanding of America led her to a similar role as a contact with Western officials, mostly British and American. She would work in the Public Works Office and other Histadrut projects, sometimes alongside Gusta, and she, too, would form an attachment to David Remez.

All that was in the future, however. For the present, Remez offered her a low-level job as a cashier in the Tel Aviv branch of the bureau. With unemployment rampant and Morris still recovering from his illnesses, she jumped at the opportunity. Yitzhak Rabin's mother, Rosa Cohen, held the more elevated position of bookkeeper in the same branch. Later Golda would reflect on "whether a person has as deep and lasting a memory of an easy period in life as of a hard, trying one." Certainly, the months she spent with the Public Works department in Tel Aviv, in a cramped room in a nondescript building, were hard and trying. The organization stretched out in all directions, expanding its building projects but assuming increasing debt to finance them, providing work for the unemployed by hiring untrained laborers and managers—they didn't even know how to build a second story on a building, Golda would say— and constantly running out of money to pay anybody.

As the cashier, Golda had to face the workers arriving for their paychecks at the week's end. The Tel Aviv branch manager, Shraga Gorochovsky, would write her a coded note. If the "tail" of his signature pointed up, it meant she could pay the workers; down signified no pay-roll. Without money for their salaries, Golda would become the target of the workers' wrath. "If somebody would ask me what I did" at that job, Golda remembered, "I would say that what stands out most is that I cried. I cried when I had to pay and didn't have with what to pay." She cried frequently, a trait that would stay with her: the tough woman not afraid to show emotion or to use it to get her way.

One day, a group of workers burst into Gorochovsky's office shouting and threatening him. "Why didn't you say something?" Golda asked him afterward. "They were pushing and shoving you, and you're not to blame." Gorochovsky's answer would become part of her repertoire, a testimony to the idealism of that early period. "Golda," he replied. "I receive ten and a half lires a month. Every morning I drink coffee and eat bread . . . I'm not sure that those workers and their children even have breakfast. If I were sure, I would have chased them out of the office."

On another occasion, the company received promissory notes to finance a teachers' academy it was constructing, but the bank refused to exchange the notes for cash. So Golda found a different way of obtaining money—on the black market, from "a Jew on the corner of Lilienblum Street." Unfortunately, the man took 20 or 25 percent off the top, leaving little for the building company.

Then, gradually, almost imperceptibly at first, things began to improve. Among the immigrants to Palestine, a wave of newcomers arrived from Poland, most of them settling in Tel Aviv. The period became known later as the Fourth Aliyah, or, more specifically to the Polish Jews, the Grabski aliyah. Władisław Grabski, Poland's prime minister, had imposed heavy taxes and other harsh economic measures that particularly affected Polish Jews, inciting them to flee by the thousands. With the U.S. doors shut to mass immigration, the Polish refugees headed toward Palestine, bringing with them new capital and entrepreneurial skills. In Tel Aviv and other towns, they built houses, set up shops as shoemakers and tailors, opened small factories, and sold soft drinks on the streets. They were not the storied pioneers of the Second or Third Aliyah, whose souls were bound up in the soil. But these urbanized Polish immigrants helped usher in a period of prosperity and optimism that touched the entire country.

David Remez took advantage of the changing circumstances to reorganize the almost bankrupt Public Works Office under a new name, Solel Boneh (Paving and Building), and devise large-scale construction projects, such as a bridge over the Yarkon River, a commercial building in Haifa, and, most impressive, the Hebrew University in Jerusalem. (The building firm felt special pride when the university officially opened in April 1925 with Lord Balfour, architect of the Balfour Declaration, as its guest of honor.) Remez offered work in the Jerusalem office to both Golda and Morris, who had recovered from his illnesses, and in the summer of 1924 they moved to a poor Jerusalem quarter on the fringes of an ultra-Orthodox neighborhood. With a kitchen on the outside in a tin shack and no gas or electricity, their tiny two-room apartment made for a grim home, dependent on an oil stove for heat and a kerosene lamp for light. When Morris used some of the first money he made to buy a "beautiful lampshade with goat's fur inside it," a neighbor related, Golda "almost put the thing around his neck." But she was pregnant, and their spirits lifted with expectation. She continued to work for some months, and on November 23, 1924, they celebrated the birth of a son. They named him Menahem, after her mother's father.

When Menahem was about six months old, Golda left Morris in Jerusalem and with the baby returned to Merhavia. Was she testing the waters for a more permanent separation from her husband? Was she so driven to return to kibbutz life or so sad away from it that she made the move, although she knew Morris would never agree to join her? Her motives are unclear, but if she expected to recapture the exuberance of her earlier years in the kibbutz, she would be greatly disappointed. Merhavia was disintegrating, and with its lack of funds and disorganized leadership it showed little joy in receiving a single mother and her child. Golda was assigned to caring for four or five kibbutz babies, including Menahem. The children slept in one room and she in a smaller one next door, alert to their crying or wakefulness at night, feeding and bathing them during the day. She liked to tell later of putting alcohol in the tin bathtub after each bath to disinfect the water—there was only one tub for all—and being laughed at by her comrades, as she had been earlier for her "American" ways.

But the camaraderie of earlier times did not materialize, nor did her intense engagement in communal operations, although she struggled to maintain contact with labor leaders. She had turned down the opportunity to represent them at an international workers' conference in Amsterdam in the spring of 1924, probably because of her pregnancy. She did manage to be included in several Histadrut activities the following year, each useful to her in a different way. In the winter of 1925, even before she went to Merhavia, she began serving on a committee investigating the sensitive issue of Yishuv defense. Sensitive, because it involved the old, prestigious Hashomer, the Watchman's league that had protected lives and property in the early settlements, and a more recent secret defense organization, the Haganah, placed under the aegis of the Histadrut. Officially, the Hashomer had been incorporated into the Haganah, but it continued to operate independently. Determined to have absolute unity under Histadrut control, Ben-Gurion convened a committee, which included Golda, to examine the situation. After several meetings, the committee concluded that Hashomer and its allies must stop their activities and turn their weapons over to the Haganah, handing Ben-Gurion an important victory. For Golda, the meetings also meant getting acquainted with a committee member, Shneur Zalman Rubashov, known as Shazar, who was to become the third president of Israel. The two would become "extremely close friends," in her words, a guarded reference to another romance in her life.

The second political act took place on May 14, 1925, probably shortly after Golda arrived in Merhavia. She represented the Women Workers' Council at a Tel Aviv conference of the Histadrut secretariat. She listened while Ben-Gurion, Ben-Zvi, Remez, and the other powerful male executives argued about loans the Solel Boneh had taken out. When the discussion turned to a campaign to raise money from American Jewish labor groups, Golda spoke up to reassure the assembly that Americans could generally be counted on for funds. An American who promised thirty thousand dollars may not pay that entire sum, she held, but there was "no reason to believe he would pay only ten thousand dollars." She suggested that all money raised in this campaign go to Solel Boneh, even if it was solicited for other purposes. "American comrades will understand us," she assured them. "We have only to explain to them." Her contribution to the debate was minor, her position very junior, but her words helped reinforce the image Golda had begun to establish for herself as an authority on all things American.

Her American "expertise" might also have been the reason she received an invitation to attend another Histadrut executive meeting in Tel Aviv a few months later. Abraham Cahan, editor of the New York *Forverts* (*Forward*), the largest-circulating Yiddish newspaper in the world, was visiting Palestine from America for the first time. A long-standing Bundist, Cahan had taken a strong anti-Zionist stand, and the Histadrut leadership hoped to change his mind. Yitzhak Eilam, who later worked closely with Golda in the Histadrut, met her for the first time at that meeting. "Her Hebrew was weak" was his first impression. Afterward, he and Golda visited her friend Hanna Chizick at the women workers' farm she directed in northern Tel Aviv. To get there, they had to travel by horse and carriage for several hours on unpaved roads, the carriage unexpectedly driven by Hanna's husband and Golda's admirer from youth, Meir Dubinsky. The meeting, the trip, and the pleasant visit with her friends brought home to her how limited her life had become.

In a letter to David Remez on August 9, 1925, Ruth HaCohen, an influential Solel Boneh bookkeeper, informed him that "Golda is here in Jerusalem, permanently, it seems." Unsatisfied by the kibbutz interlude and unfulfilled by her few political forays, Golda had decided to return to Morris and devote herself to attempting to save her marriage by becoming a full-time wife and mother. By trying very hard, she reasoned, "I would succeed."

For a few months, Golda and Morris alternated times in the Solel Boneh office, one working while the other stayed home with the baby. They also rented out one of their two rooms for a little extra income. Both arrangements ended when their daughter, Sarah, was born on May 17, 1926. The next year and a half became one of the lowest points of Golda's entire life. With Morris's single income, the couple could barely make ends meet, and often didn't. Her days became cycles of unpaid bills and pleas with the grocer for bread on credit and with the butcher for a small piece of chicken for the children's soup. In their dismal, unheated flat, Menahem and Sarah constantly suffered from sore throats and runny noses, and Golda ran around trying to get medicines she couldn't afford to buy. Occasionally, Shamai came to Jerusalem with some fruit or cheese Sheyna sent for the family, but when the treat ended, the hunger returned. Golda had moved to Palestine to become a new Jew, cultivating the land with her toil, and had reverted instead to the worst of her mother, the shtetl Jew endeavoring simply to subsist. In Palestine, "we lived in more poverty than even back in Pinsk," she recalled.

Behind many of her economic woes was the fast-approaching collapse of Solel Boneh. The bubble of prosperity that had accompanied the Fourth Aliyah burst quickly. Too many immigrants bore down on the country at once, too few jobs existed to go around, and too little capital had been generated to sustain the vast building projects that had been the Histadrut's most important undertaking. As an economic depression set in, Jewish immigration to Palestine dropped precipitously and emigration rose. The crisis reached a peak in 1927, when twenty-seven hundred Jewish immigrants entered the country and seven thousand left it.

Within the Solel Boneh "family," as the staff saw itself, an air of desperation had already begun to spread in 1926. The company had expanded with a whirlwind of building ventures during the boom days, borrowing huge sums, which it expected to repay through new contracts. When those dried up, it was left with a burden of debts and little recourse for reducing them. "The reason we could fulfill our contracts in Jerusalem," the branch manager Nahum Lifshits admitted at a meeting in August, "is that since Passover [in April] we have not paid out one penny of our obligations in cash." Contractors received payment in promissory notes, workers in credit slips.

In years to come, Golda would praise the ideals of the Solel Boneh of those days. It functioned not only as a construction company, she would say, but also as a "pioneer" in its own right, laboring to build the country, absorb its immigrants, and provide a decent living for Jewish workers without concern for profit. Struggling in real time, however, was another matter. When Menahem reached nursery school age, "he no longer wanted to eat at home. It appears the food we had wasn't very good." So Golda arranged to do laundry for a nursery school in exchange for the tuition. She laundered at night while her children slept, heating pails of water in which she scrubbed towels, bibs, and diapers on her metal washboard. For a while, she taught English at Miss Kallen's, a progressive school where the Jewish elite sent their children. She was miserable.

And isolated. Theoretical issues she had raised in the past became personal. How can a woman participate in public life when she has young children to care for? she had asked at the women workers' convention. The kibbutz provided an answer with its communal child care, she had pointed out, but city women had no such support. Now here she was, a woman who had dreamed of living on a kibbutz and found herself trapped in the city scrubbing diapers and arguing with shopkeepers.

With great effort, she struggled to stay in touch with Histadrut leaders beyond the few meetings she attended. She wrote to Berl Katznelson, the most eminent of them all, the ideologist behind her labor party, and apparently conveyed her unhappiness, because he, in turn, wrote to a mutual friend, Lily Zadek: "I received a letter from Golda. Her situation is bad, and she's lonely. Perhaps you will write to her? You understand, don't give her the feeling that I told you this." The historian Anita Shapira, Berl's biographer, cites this letter, among other things, as an indication of the special affection he had for Golda from the earliest days. To Yehudit Simhonit, who was to become a member of Israel's First Knesset, Golda once confided that it took a long time for Katznelson's wife to be convinced that there had been no romance between her and him. There is no evidence of any. He appreciated her, as did the other members of the Histadrut's inner circle, even when she no longer held a place at the center of the action.

Occasionally, she poured out her unhappiness to her friend Regina, who lived in Jerusalem and worked as a secretary for the Zionist organization. Regina had suffered troubles of her own. Shortly after she and Golda arrived in Palestine, she divorced Yossel Kopilov, whom she had married before they left America. Both of them remarried shortly after their breakup, and they seem to have remained friends. Yossel met his future wife, Dina Kaplan, who had come alone from Russia, while visiting Golda and Morris at Merhavia. Regina married Moshe Medzini, the Jerusalem bureau chief of the Hebrew newspaper *Haaretz*, which had moved its headquarters to Tel Aviv. Medzini and Golda would have strong political differences, but they managed to get along, and Golda's friendship with Regina lasted her lifetime. It felt natural to her during her lonely Jerusalem days to turn to Regina for solace.

In the midst of her gloom and the dreadful economic conditions of 1926, her parents sold their store in America and immigrated to Palestine. They longed to be with their two elder daughters, and they expected their youngest, Clara, to join them after finishing her studies at the University of Wisconsin. With the little money they had, they bought ten *dunams* (a little over two acres) of land in Herzliya, an agricultural village a few miles north of Tel Aviv. It was an unusual move: few parents, especially from America, followed their children to the Land of Israel. For the most part, young people who came alone as *halutzim* left their parents and the old ways behind them as they carved out new lives. Moshe and Bluma chose to start over themselves; as a result, Golda's and Sheyna's children had the experience, denied many others in the pre-state period, of growing up with grandparents nearby. They would carry warm memories well into their older ages of the entire family spending Passover and other festivals at their grandparents' home in Herzliya, of melodies they sang together, and of sleeping on the floor, the only available space, with all their cousins around them.

In an unexpected reversal of roles, Golda and Sheyna, the rebel daughters, lived working-class lives in the city while their parents became the real pioneers, staking out their home on the dangerous frontier. Herzliya, which was to grow into a bustling city close to Tel Aviv, appeared to be nothing but sand and open skies at the time, vulnerable to attack from Arab villages around it. Moshe regularly took his turn standing guard, along with younger members of the community. The move to Palestine energized him. He built his house largely with his own hands, planted an orange grove, and raised chickens in his yard. He had a beautiful singing voice, and when he discovered that the local synagogue lacked a cantor, he volunteered for that assignment. He also became head of his district's administrative committee.

People who knew Moshe in those years portrayed him as sitting silently at settlers' meetings, "listening intently to the discussions and only occasionally asking permission to speak." When he did speak, it was "like someone cutting through rock," slowly, with simple words in Yiddish mixed with Russian and English. If he had a communal request to make of the village's larger governing council, he would get directly to the point and hurry out afterward "with a warm handshake."

Moshe was a simple, "good-hearted man . . . who liked others as they liked him," Golda would say lovingly. Her feelings toward her mother remained mixed, as they had been in her youth. Bluma could carp and criticize, never attempting to hide any displeasure she felt toward her daughter. Yet for all Moshe's appealing goodness, Bluma, as usual, brought in much-needed income by cooking and serving hot lunches to neighborhood workmen, including Arabs. She spoke to them, as she did to everyone, in Yiddish.

Visiting her parents in Herzliya when she could get away, Golda sometimes stopped off in Tel Aviv to see friends and catch up with Histadrut news. Curiously, she seems to have had little contact with the Women Workers' Council, which, beginning in 1926, went through a series of crises. At their root lay the pervasive question that had surfaced when Golda first joined the organization: How independent should—and could—the women's council be within the Histadrut? The complex disagreements and open squabbles surrounding that question became so twisted and entwined that even members could not pick apart the political differences from the ideological ones.

Many of the quarrels revolved around Ada Maimon, the main force behind the Women Workers' Council and a fierce feminist and defender of independence for the women's group. Although Maimon's single-minded devotion to the problems of women workers was sincerely felt, her struggle to expand the women's authority in the Histadrut was also "not free of party influence," writes the Israeli scholar Bat-Sheva Margalit Stern, an expert on that period. As a member of Hapoel Hatzair, she reflected her party's rivalry with the larger Ahdut Ha'avoda Party and its desire to limit that party's dominance in the labor federation. The women who opposed Maimon in the various skirmishes all belonged to Ahdut Ha'avoda. These women also cared greatly about women workers' matters, but their loyalties lay primarily with their party and the broader issues of the Histadrut.

One of the major battle arenas, which would eventually affect Golda, concerned the means of raising money abroad for women workers in Palestine. Maimon had made connections with WIZO, the Women's International Zionist Organization, a General Zionist group, not driven by any particular political party. Rachel Yanait, always prominent in Ahdut Ha'avoda, had close ties to the Pioneer Women's Organization of America, later called Pioneer Women. It had been founded by women from Poalei Zion, Golda's former party in America and the forerunner of Ahdut Ha'avoda. Ada resented Rachel's establishing links for the women's council with a politically oriented group; Rachel ignored Ada's objections and went about organizing the American women and gathering funds. The infighting became so intense that by the end of 1925 the entire leadership of the Women Workers' Council resigned and the Histadrut executive committee had to appoint interim heads to keep the group going. About half a year later, in April 1926, the third convention of the women workers' movement organized a new executive body for the Women Workers' Council. Known as the "active secretariat," it had two members at its head, one from each party. Still, the quarrels continued, well into 1927.

Enter Golda Meyerson. In her account, she met David Remez in Tel Aviv one rainy day as she stood outside the Histadrut building talking to an acquaintance. To her surprise and delight, he asked her if she would like to return to work and invited her to become secretary of the Women Workers' Council, representing Ahdut Ha'avoda. The scholar Bat-Sheva Margalit Stern labels that invitation "swooping from above." Golda had been plucked for the position from among the far more experienced women in her party, such as Rachel Yanait and Hanna Chizick. She attracted the male Histadrut establishment because unlike Ada Maimon, who was a "nuisance" to them with her outspoken demands, Golda "was an obedient, loyal candidate . . . and a person who did not stand out for any prominent feminist tendencies." True enough. With an eye on the future, Golda had no desire to defy party leaders.

Yet the story is more complex than that. In fact, Chizick, Yanait, and other Ahdut Ha'avoda women showed as much loyalty to the party as did Golda; Maimon often accused them of destroying the Women Workers' Council with their political tendencies. Golda, however, offered something else: she had youth and vitality; she knew English fluently and understood Americans, much needed for fund-raising; and she could captivate audiences when she spoke, as demonstrated by the Histadrut convention. From the viewpoint of the party executives, Golda could invigorate the women's council while also strengthening the party's position in it.

Ada, who had resigned several times as secretary of the council representing Hapoel Hatzair, seemed prepared to return but with Golda's appointment would not. Instead, Elisheva Kaplan joined Golda as the council heads from the two parties.

Golda's decision to accept the position offered symbolized also her decision to live apart from Morris. "Golda should never have married," Regina said, "because she wasn't someone who could stay at home and be a wife." She had thought having children would bring her and Morris closer, but it didn't. In early 1928, she moved to Tel Aviv with the children, while Morris remained in Jerusalem. The final separation was to come ten years later, but Golda had acknowledged to herself that "the marriage was a failure."

7

A Star Is Born

It happened quickly. From the sense of marking time but standing still, Golda found every moment of her time packed with motion. From the loneliness of being on the outside looking in, she moved to the center of activity. From the helplessness of a poverty-stricken housewife, she became a world traveler heralded for her strength and good sense. When she left Jerusalem, she left behind a kind of domestic life she would never again experience and entered a public life that, as she later told a journalist, "put me on the path which led me to sitting in the Prime Minister's office . . . talking to you."

Within the next few years, she would write of the guilt she suffered being the type of woman "who cannot remain at home." In an essay in *The Plough Woman*, a collection of memoirs by women pioneers, she put into words the dilemmas of working mothers like her for generations to come. Her piece, "Borrowed Mothers," speaks of the "inner struggles and the despairs of the mother who goes to work" as being "without parallel in human experience." It laments that the "clever things the child says reach the mother at second hand," because a "borrowed" mother substitutes for her. And it describes the "superhuman effort of the will" it takes for a mother to withstand the "look of reproach" from her child as she leaves to go off to work.

She meant everything she wrote. Yet she also recognized that her "nature and being" demanded "something more" than children and family and that she, like many women who chose to work outside their homes, could not "let her children narrow down her horizons" or "divorce herself from the larger social life." She had raised these issues back at the women workers' conference in 1922. She now gave in to the fact that much as she wanted children, she also had to have that larger life.

She rented a two-room apartment for her and the children in a shabby, peeling building with a small balcony overlooking the sea. Even though it stood on an unpaved street, with sand up to its doorstep, and even without gas and electricity and with a couch serving as Golda's bed while the children shared the bedroom, the new apartment far exceeded the old one in Jerusalem. With Morris's salary and her own steady, if modest, one from the Histadrut, Golda no longer had to scrounge for basic necessities. In keeping with the socialist ideals of the labor movement, Histadrut salaries followed a "family wage" system in which a worker's salary accorded to need: a janitor with five children might earn considerably more than a top Histadrut executive with no children. But Golda's wages were a little different. In addition to her base pay, she received a two-and-a-half-lire supplement under the category of medical assistance for her children. Sarah was a sickly child, and the extra money helped defray medical expenses. It also helped pay for a nanny, not the kind of benefit openly broadcast in a socialist society, but a testament to how strongly the Histadrut leaders wanted Golda at work.

The move to Tel Aviv had the added advantage of bringing Golda and the children closer to Sheyna in the city and Golda's parents in Herzliya. Much of the time, Sheyna, rather than hired help, became the "borrowed" mother who cared for Golda's children along with her own, while Golda absorbed herself in her work.

She left early every morning to work in a low red building with a few small rooms, where everybody used first names and dressed informally, women in casual skirts and blouses, men in khaki pants and open-collared shirts with short sleeves. At thirty, she was an attractive woman, but with no makeup and her hair severely parted in the center and off her face, she was beginning to take on the set features of the later, iconic Golda Meir. The recreational smoking she had begun years earlier quickly turned into chain-smoking; she rarely let a moment pass without a cigarette—usually an unfiltered Chesterfield—in her hand. ("Don't have the cigarette dangling from your mouth," she once advised a woman portraying her in a play. Golda didn't dangle it. She held it between her first two fingers, puffed it to the end, snuffed it out, and took another.)

Her tasks as secretary of the Women Workers' Council included helping to raise money for agricultural training farms where young immigrant women could learn the necessary skills for working the land. With her often expressed concern about urban women workers, she also took a special interest in nursery and kindergarten programs for the children of city working mothers. In 1928, she reported to a labor movement convention about a model day-care center in Tel Aviv that cared for some thirty-five children from seven in the morning until five in the evening. Their mothers, she wrote, could feel secure at work, knowing their children were in good hands.

Golda's children felt secure at home, and when their mother joined them after work, they found her loving and attentive. At the end of her workday, she cooked, cleaned, mended clothes, took them to their doctors' appointments, and did the other motherly chores expected of her. The problem was that many of her workdays had no end, and most often she was not with the children, tied up several evenings a week with meetings that could extend until one or two in the morning. The children rejoiced when she had to stay home for a day because of one of the throbbing migraines that plagued her all her life, a misery she shared with her mother and Sheyna.

The worst times for the children came when Golda began traveling out of the country to attend conventions or raise money. Worse still, her travels coincided with Sarah's deteriorating health caused by a misdiagnosed kidney disease. At one point, Sarah became so ill that Golda did not work for six weeks, caring for her. Sarah could recall having blood drawn from her veins and being conscious of a frightened Golda standing nearby weeping softly. She also remembered feeling lonely and abandoned when Golda considered her well enough to leave and go abroad. "She would travel and leave behind a very sick child for long months. It didn't bother her to go away. Today I don't understand how she did this. I would not leave my children that way."

Sarah's negative comment is one of the few criticisms about their mother she and her brother, Menahem, ever made in public. They conceded that as children they had "resented it very much" when Golda left them for long periods, but as adults they defended and protected her. To Golda's confessions of remorse over what her grown children "really have in their hearts" because of her "neglect" of them in earlier years, their dutiful answers always emphasized their pride in her and their gratitude for the enriched lives she gave them. (This in contrast to the activist Manya Shochat's daughter, who, at age seventy, wrote in an Israeli newspaper that she never forgave her mother and father, Israel Shochat, for putting the concept of "homeland" ahead of a home for their children.) Morris's presence in the children's lives during their early years helped greatly. Although he lived in Jerusalem, he spent weekends with the family in Tel Aviv, sharing the traditional Friday evening Sabbath dinner with them and preparing breakfast on Saturday mornings. Later, when he moved in with them for some years, he devoted himself fully to the children. "Meyerson was more of a father to them than she was a mother," a former babysitter sniffed disapprovingly.

Golda's mother and sister spouted the severest criticisms. "She is a public person, not a homebody. Should we rejoice in this?" Sheyna wrote with sarcasm to her husband, Shamai, who had temporarily returned to the United States to earn the family income. The attacks stung, but for all the guilt they might have engendered, Golda knew she was exactly where she wanted to be, doing—at least for the time being—exactly what she wanted to do.

In a letter penned during one of her trips out of the country, she tried to explain herself: "I ask only one thing, that I be understood and believed. My social activities are not an accidental thing; they are an absolute necessity for me . . . Do I have to justify myself?" Yet, she went on, "you can understand how hard it is for me to leave. But in our present situation I could not refuse to do what was asked of me."

That she "could not refuse" became Golda's standard explanation for projects that she would not have wanted to refuse. She assured Sheyna that if she had been convinced that cutting off her outside connections, as she once did, "at Morris' insistence," would be better for the children, she would not hesitate to do so. But "I am doubtful," she said. It had not worked then, and she had no reason to believe it could ever work.

And so, in spite of family censure and her declared misgivings, Golda Meyerson undertook a string of missions outside the Land of Israel.

The first voyage, to Berlin during the summer of 1928, began with a tug-of-war between Golda and Ada Maimon. As a result of Maimon's strong links to WIZO, she had been invited to attend its annual international convention in Berlin on July 5 and 6. Golda and other women in the Women Workers' Council objected to WIZO's attempt to bypass their organization by inviting Ada on its own in that way. When the council members demanded that two women attend, one from each political party—Ahdut Ha'avoda and Hapoel Hatzair—Ada interpreted their demands as a lack of confidence in her. The internal fighting became such that, unable to resolve the matter, the women's group brought it before the male Histadrut's executive committee in the middle of June.

Golda opened the discussion by informing the committee of Ada's announcement that she would not attend the convention if two women were sent. Irritated with Ada, Ben-Gurion wanted to know "how it happened that in only one institution of the Histadrut," meaning the women's council, "others," like WIZO, "decided who the delegates should be." Ada objected immediately: "I have fought against that and I have advised WIZO that they must not turn directly to me, but to the Women Workers' Council." As if Ada had not spoken, Golda repeated the idea that WIZO must be made to understand that it needed to work with the institution and not with individuals. And she drove home the point again that "Ada said she saw no need for another person to go with her to watch over her," placing the onus for the dispute on Ada. This was not the Golda who had once spoken sweetly and shyly at the women council's convention. Here was a hard-hitting politician in the making, maneuvering to win her battle and unconcerned about where the chips might fall.

She did win. The committee decided that two people should attend the WIZO convention and that Ada needed to be one of them. Golda would be the second.

The convention did not begin well for her. The WIZO women objected to her presence as a representative of the Women Workers' Council. They had invited Maimon as an individual to report on farm areas for training women workers, which they might finance, and they had little other interest in the women's council. "It was very good that Golda attended the convention, for a number of reasons, but she didn't get much pleasure from being there," Zalman Shazar, in Berlin with the Histadrut executive, wrote to his wife, Rachel. "She had some unpleasant hours." The WIZO women ended their coldness toward Golda only after several days.

Shazar wrote to his wife regularly on this trip, as on others, lively, gossipy letters, filled with the latest labor movement activities abroad. He omitted mentioning one thing, however: his growing intimacy with their mutual friend Golda Meyerson.

Golda had first noticed Shazar in 1924 at a May Day rally, shortly after she and Morris left Merhavia. A short, slender man (he would become heavier over the years) with magnetic dark eyes, he had captured her attention in his high-collared Russian embroidered shirt—the *rubashka*—and sash, the popular revolutionary style of dress adopted by Jewish workers in Palestine. The dramatic and passionate speech he gave, complete with gesticulations, held her in thrall. By the time they served together on the investigative defense committee in 1925, she knew enough about him to be dazzled by his intellect and erudition. Russian born, nine years older than she, he had been reared in a Hasidic environment, studied Talmud and Jewish history in Russia, and later received degrees in history and philosophy from German universities. He made his first journey to Palestine in 1911 and worked on the settlement at Merhavia that preceded Golda's kibbutz there. In that year, he met and fell in love with the beautiful Rachel Bluwstein, who became known simply as Rachel, one of the country's most beloved poets. A year after settling permanently in Palestine, he joined the editorial staff of *Davar*, a newly created daily Hebrew newspaper that would be the voice of Labor Zionism for decades.

Shazar's affair with Rachel the poet had ended by the time Golda met him. The Rachel he married—Rachel Katznelson—had plain features and a keen mind that matched his in many respects. They had one child, Rhoda, born with Down syndrome. The difficulties of rearing her drained them physically and psychologically, particularly Rachel, who had "no rest day or night," she would say. In spite of her sorrow and exhaustion, she founded and edited *Dvar Hapoelet*, the key publication of the women workers' movement. She also edited *The Plough Woman*, the anthology in which Golda's essay on motherhood appeared. Rachel and Golda worked together closely on the Women Workers' Council and got along well. When Golda was away, as she would be in Berlin, Rachel filled in for her.

Golda was not Shazar's only romantic interest. Nevertheless, he and Rachel had a warm and supportive relationship. "Rachele," he addressed her affectionately in his letters; "Zalmanke," she called him. When, in one of her letters, Rachel voiced some suspicion about his fidelity, Zalman responded reassuringly. "Give me your hand from afar," he wrote. "Kiss me and be with me as I am with you." Rachel appears to have accepted his assurances, maybe because she believed him or maybe because in the revolutionary, antibourgeois atmosphere of pre-state Israel extramarital affairs were not uncommon. Almost all the Yishuv leaders—from Ben-Gurion to Berl to Moshe Sharett—had intimate ties outside their marital bonds, and almost everyone knew about them. But the marriages usually lasted.

Shazar opened the door for Golda into a world of intellectual excitement, comparable to what Morris had once done for her on a lesser scale. With Shazar, the cultural vitality was accompanied by traits Morris lacked—the enthusiasm of a Zionist activist and the energy of a restless mind. Given the coldness between Golda and Morris now, Shazar's warmth and exuberance filled the emotional emptiness in her life. Their friendship would remain intact over the years, even when each had other romances. Almost a quarter of a century later, in 1945, at a time when Golda was sick, Shazar wrote from Paris to "Goldenu, dearest of my dears," to say how much he missed her. "I never knew if you really knew my feelings," he wrote, "so how do I know now?" Afterward, during her years as labor minister, when they traveled about Israel together, they always "held hands in the backseat of her car," her driver noticed. "It was very sweet." Their affection lasted through their lives.

Now in Berlin, which Shazar knew well, the two found time to be alone with each other. They also attended many meetings together. After the snubs she had initially received at the WIZO convention, Golda could feel good about being included among the Histadrut elite who were attending conferences in Europe at the time. Aside from Ben-Gurion, Ben-Zvi, and Shazar, other big-name Labor Zionists included Abraham Hartzfeld, Shlomo Kaplansky, Israel Marminski (later Marom), and Joseph Sprinzak. Ada Maimon, also present, might have felt less than happy about Golda's inclusion and what it signified—her easy acceptance by the highest-ranking Histadrut leaders so rapidly after her years away from extended public activity.

From Berlin, Golda went to Brussels, where she spoke briefly at a socialist women's convention. But the main attraction for her and the other Histadrut leaders, who joined her there, was the opening of the Socialist International convention on August 5, 1928. Ben-Gurion commented in his diary that "the small nations had spaces reserved for them at the front of the hall," but no room had been left for the Palestinian Jewish delegates, and in the afternoon's parade of socialist youths with their "sea of banners" from all parts of the world "the flag of the Jewish people was missing." One day, he and the others fantasized, there would be such a flag; meanwhile, the Labor Zionists had to make themselves known to the world's socialists, their main purpose for attending the convention.

Golda reveled in the event. On her first journey outside Palestine, and after settling there only seven years earlier, she participated in a major socialist convention, listening to speeches by the likes of Arthur Henderson, the British Labour Party politician and soon to be Nobel Peace Prize winner, and Léon Blum, who would become the first Jewish premier of France. At the end, the convention chose her to serve on a committee dealing with women's issues. On her way back to Palestine, she stopped off in Paris, her stay in that city another first, and left for home on August 15, arriving, as she always would after traveling, with small gifts for the children—and plans to go abroad again.

FROM RACHEL KATZNELSON SHAZAR IN Tel Aviv to her husband, Zalman, in Berlin, concerning their daughter, Rhoda, September 6, 1928:

"Rhodela was sick for two weeks. Now it has passed . . . Two days and two nights she ran a high fever . . . The illness began with a small wound on her leg that I didn't care for properly and it became infected . . . Golda showed great compassion. She came here the first time, filled with stories to tell me from her trip, at the very moment when I didn't know what to do, and she ran with me to the Kupat Holim [the Histadrut-owned medical clinic] and every necessary place."

Notwithstanding Golda's liaison with Shazar or the suspicions Rachel might have had about it, the two women remained friends. Having worked together at the Women Workers' Council, the two also shared an understanding of the party conflicts in that organization. Less politically driven than Golda, Rachel was even more distressed than she by the constant fighting among the women. "Sometimes I feel a need not only to leave the organization but also to proclaim out loud" about the women's "disgraceful" behavior, she wrote to Shazar. "There are no worse relationships than the relationship among women in organizations," she, a woman long devoted to women's causes, continued despondently. "I have the desire after one of these 'pleasant' meetings to go some place else where I will not have to deal with this anymore."

In the women's attempts to run their organization independently of the men who dominated the Histadrut, but less experienced than the men in the power plays that often accompany organizational life, the women had become increasingly enmeshed in ideological and personal disputes. Ironically, that gave the men even more control over the women's organization. Now, with Golda and Ada back from Europe, the women's differences were about to burst into an open explosion that neither Rachel nor any of the others could smother.

The immediate issue centered on a planned fund-raising trip for Golda to the United States, scheduled for late September 1928. Ben-Gurion had noted the need to send someone to that country for six months to work with the Pioneer Women's organization there, emphasizing that "Golda should . . . be involved." At the Women Workers' Council, Ada objected that not one but two women should go to America, just as two had gone to the Berlin WIZO convention, one from each political party. "Golda adamantly opposed this idea," Rachel wrote to Shazar. "Now there is a stalemate." Unable to agree among themselves, the women turned, as usual, to the male Histadrut executive committee, and as might be expected, Golda emerged victorious.

"I do not understand why this activity had to cause so much commotion," Yosef Aharonowitz rebuked Maimon at the executive meeting of

September 20 after she presented her position. David Remez, consistently Golda's supporter, went further. "From Ada's words, I can judge the atmosphere in the Women Workers' Council," he said. "I do not want to carry this hostile spirit to an organization in America." Therefore only one emissary should be sent to the United States and that person should be "Golda Meyerson."

After much further debate, in which Golda craftily said almost nothing, a vote of 5 to 3 supported sending her, and only her, on the mission.

Move ahead two months. Although Golda should have been in America by October 11, to attend a Pioneer Women's conference, for a variety of reasons she has not yet left. At a Histadrut executive meeting on November 5, Maimon turns in anger to Ben-Gurion. "I am asking Ben-Gurion why he agreed to send two women to Berlin, when it was not necessary, but here, when every additional comrade would be useful," he regards one alone as sufficient. The reason, she contends, is that the decision to send only one person was purely political, demonstrated by the selection of Golda Meyerson, a member of Ahdut Ha'avoda, the Histadrut's majority party. Her argument finally leads to a new decision: two women will go to America, one of them Golda Meyerson and the second, from the Hapoel Hatzair Party, to be chosen at the next meeting.

With that, Maimon surprises everyone by refusing now to accept the addition of a second woman, even one from her own party. She asks that the minutes reflect her feelings, namely, that the way the question was handled, the selection of Golda Meyerson, and the later decision to add a second comrade demonstrate that the executive committee arrived at its decision not based on what is useful and good but, she repeats, "only and completely from a political standpoint."

Maimon might have been hurt that she wasn't named immediately as the second person to go to the United States; she was probably also genuinely irritated by the role politics had played in the entire process. Either way, she was enraged at Golda, who, with the backing of the executive committee, had a few months earlier pushed herself into the Berlin WIZO convention and was now holding center stage in the American drama. Ada would not go to America, she declared, nor would anyone from her party. "In my opinion, a person who has any self respect would not accept this mission from the executive committee," she said, and in a direct slap at Golda, added, "And in the future I will regard any mission by Golda as strictly partisan."

If Maimon wanted to be seen as choosing the high moral road, rising above politics, and concerned only for the Women Workers' Council, she might have achieved her goals among her own party members. From a practical standpoint, however, she hurt herself and her party. Golda could happily go off alone to the familiar terrain of the United States, free to pursue her fund-raising and political agendas without having to account to Ada or her party.

But the victory had its drawbacks. She would have to leave her children for at least six months, the longest separation from them she had yet experienced. She probably could have taken them with her, but then child-care concerns would have limited her ambitions. "Always," she wrote in her *Plough Woman* essay, a mother who works outside her home "has the feeling that her work is not as productive as that of a man, or even of an unmarried woman." Ada Maimon, unmarried, without children, could devote all her time and energy to her work. Zalman Shazar, with a wife at home to care for his disabled child, had been in Europe since July and would not return home until he finished his Histadrut activities there in February or March. In going on this voyage without the children, Golda could accomplish as much as any man or unmarried woman. Even so, she would have to pay a price. The working mother suffered from a "double pull," an "alternating feeling of unfulfilled duty—today toward her family, the next day toward her work." For Golda, distance from her family lightened this "burden" in many ways but made it harder to bear in others.

Instead of including the children on her trip, she arranged for Morris to be transferred from Jerusalem to Tel Aviv, where he could care for them. Ben-Gurion's diary records on October 8 that Golda should have been in America by now, "but she cannot depart until Meyerson is settled in his work." In parentheses, it adds that "he is a bookkeeper and can correspond in English, but does not know how to use a typewriter," a pathetic summary of his standing among Yishuv leaders. He received part-time work as an English translator for the Histadrut executive committee.

GOLDA FINALLY SET OUT ON her journey in mid-November. She arrived aboard the S.S. *Aquitania* on December 1, 1928, in a city and country at the height of prosperity, ecstatic about the ever-rising stock market. In less than a year, that giddiness would come crashing down, transformed into America's most devastating depression. At the time, no one predicted the fall, and even in faraway Palestine the socialist labor movement leaders hoped to tap into the riches of the New World. They looked for funding to an American federation of Jewish trade unions organized as the United Hebrew Trades, or Geverkshaften in Yiddish. Since the early 1920s, the Histadrut had been raising funds from the Geverkshaften, through campaigns headed by emissaries from Palestine. As part of her job in America, Golda joined the current emissaries, Chaim Arlosoroff, David Bloch, and Israel Marminski.

Less than a month after she arrived in the States, she appeared with them at a convention in New York, marking the fifth anniversary of the Geverkshaften campaign. On her first trip back to the land of her youth, she spoke before an audience of more than five hundred, larger than any she'd had before. Her knees shook with nervousness, but her voice remained steady as she delivered her Yiddish "greetings from a *chavera*"—an appealing young woman engaging a sea of mostly male, mostly seasoned organization men. Instead of a formal speech, she created a "fable" about Jews who emigrated from Russia. The majority settled in America, and only a small number went to Palestine, she related. No one believed these two groups could unite, but then the Palestinian Jewish workers began digging a tunnel to reach their "American brothers," and the Americans heard the sound of their axes. The wall separating the two groups began to tumble, and a union of the workers of both countries emerged. The audience loved the story with its stirring message of oneness in the labor movement. Golda "brought the convention to its highest pitch of enthusiasm," a Yiddish American newspaper reported.

She would continue to devote time to the Histadrut fund-raising campaign, but on this trip she would direct her greatest efforts toward the Pioneer Women. In the distant future, after she became Golda Meir, Israel's national leader, she was to say, dismissively, that Pioneer Women and the Women Workers' Council "were the first and last women's organizations for which I ever worked." Yet in the arc of her life, Pioneer Women, with which she would work intermittently for the next several years, served as more than just a "first and last." Her activities with this organization formed the fulcrum of who she was at the time and who she became later. Although she had left America behind her, it was there, in that country, among these women and because of them that her star began to shine most brightly.

The Pioneer Women's group prided itself on being different from other Zionist women's organizations in the United States. Its members, mostly immigrant women, spoke Yiddish and identified with the working classes, in contrast to the middle- and upper-class English-speaking women of Hadassah, the largest American Zionist organization. Its purpose was to raise money for the Women Workers' Council in Palestine and in the process to absorb the pioneer culture and ideals of that group. Rachel Yanait had been the inspiration for the Pioneer Women when she wrote to an American friend, Sophie Udan, in 1924, seeking funds to dig a well to water a tree nursery in Jerusalem where young female pioneers might plant saplings. Udan and six other New York women raised the money and began to form themselves into a Labor Zionist organization. The "well story" became their founding narrative.

The women in the new group had been part of the Socialist Zionist Poalei Zion Party, Golda's party when she lived in the United States. Men dominated that party and opposed the idea of a separate women's organization, but the women insisted, pointing out that the men outnumbered and overshadowed them, confining them mostly to childcare activities. A year after forming their group, they sought approval at a Poalei Zion convention for the creation of an autonomous women's organization, and in 1926 they held their first convention, electing Leah Biskin their national secretary. Nevertheless, they kept a close affiliation with the larger Poalei Zion movement.

Golda promoted that affiliation. When Rachel Yanait, who was in the States as the Histadrut liaison early in 1928, seemed to support a move to separate completely from Poalei Zion, Golda answered her firmly. "I do not believe that an independent women's organization in America will be able to exist," she wrote in Yiddish. "No matter, I do not think that at the present time we should have one." She suggested that Yanait "rethink the matter" and "make it clear" to the members. Golda's position in this debate paralleled the one she had taken earlier in regard to keeping the Women Workers' Council part of the Histadrut, positions that did not endear her to women who sought greater independence for their groups. Her response fit into a pattern that was to thread itself through her career. Unity in the movement, the party, the community, the larger whole, would invariably take precedence over individuals or special interests, including women's interests. Years later, in 1949, with Pioneer Women at a peak of membership, Golda, still pursuing wholeness, insisted at the organization's convention in Philadelphia that it combine with a now weakened Poalei Zion to form one large Socialist Zionist movement. The women indignantly turned her down.

When Golda came to work with the Pioneer Women at the end of 1928, the organization had grown from its seven-woman beginnings to three thousand members and several dozen clubs around the country. (Hadassah had thirty-seven thousand members and 285 chapters.) The members knew of her; in her American years, she had crisscrossed the country selling shares in the Labor Zionist newspaper *Die Zeit* and organizing Poalei Zion events. She stood out from other emissaries the Histadrut sent to raise money, men and women with thick European accents and an air of contempt for capitalist, "soft" Americans. "The entire movement here is worthless," Manya Shochat had complained back in 1921 about the American branch of Poalei Zion. Golda understood American Jews. She spoke their language, straightforward and to the point, in Milwaukee-accented English and Russian-tinged Yiddish. She radiated American confidence and optimism, and audiences responded to her with warm enthusiasm. As her popularity grew, the process of mythologizing her in America began.

Dvorah Rothbard, later president of the Pioneer Women, remembered a cold, blustery day in Buffalo in 1929, when Golda came to speak and visited a Labor Zionist *folkschule* where Rothbard's husband taught. The news spread "like a flash" that "our own Golda from Milwaukee, who made aliyah in 1921," had arrived as an emissary from the Histadrut. When Golda took over the class, "she won the hearts of the young ones and the admiration of the teachers." The Detroit member Fannie Goren was so thrilled when Golda kissed her that "she didn't wash her face for a week."

Golda traveled around the United States and Canada, through New England and the Midwest, spending long hours on buses and trains, going from one Pioneer Women's club to another, sleeping at the homes of members, sometimes sharing the bed of a *chavera*, if there was no other room. Wherever she went, she taught the women the latest songs of the *halutzot*, brought them anecdotes and gossip from the Yishuv, and pushed them hard to meet the quotas needed to raise money for the women workers' farms in Palestine. If they didn't have the necessary funds, she sternly advised them to "do housework for one another or make lokshen [noodles] and sell it."

After seven hardworking months in the States, she went to Zurich, Switzerland, to attend the Sixteenth Zionist Congress—her first worldwide Zionist Congress—and also participate in a WIZO conference there. Her American stay had been a resounding hit. David Bloch, who toured with her for the Geverkshaften campaign, informed the Histadrut leaders that Golda "greatly succeeded," not only because of her "personal abilities, but also due to her Americanness." The Pioneer Women collected $36,500 in their campaign, topping the previous year, in large part, they said, because of Golda Meyerson.

While Golda was away, Morris resigned from his half-time position with the Histadrut executive committee. His departure reflects the sadness of his life. He was leaving, he informed the finance committee head, Shlomo Kaplansky, on March 20, 1929, largely because the work demanded more hours of him than he could give; in a separate letter, he also let it be known that he had not been paid for the full amount of time he worked. In an internal memo, with copies to Golda and others, nobody on the finance committee seemed to remember exactly what salary had been promised Morris. They did remember that Golda had requested he be given the job, because she did not want him to receive a salary without actually working.

Golda had been separated from her children for almost nine months, about a quarter of three-year-old Sarah's lifetime. She had moved to a larger apartment before she left, with an extra room that she rented to a woman who would also look after the children. Even with that help, the main responsibility for the children fell on Morris and Sheyna, who made no effort to hide her disfavor with a litany of complaints: "She neglects herself and us." "Her first duty is to the family," and so on. Her disapproval of Golda, however, did not prevent her from leaving her two oldest children in Palestine while she went with her youngest to Battle Creek, Michigan, to train as a dietitian. Shamai, who was working in America again, encouraged her to join him, and when Golda suggested, "Perhaps you understand me now," Sheyna responded that *her* husband "understands and helps me because he is all my life." She would not give her sister the slightest break.

The Land of Israel to which Golda returned in the late summer of 1929 had been shaken by a new outburst of Arab violence. Word of Arab disturbances had reached her and the other delegates in Zurich even before the Zionist Congress dispersed. There had been great excitement during the congress earlier when the delegates united to form the Jewish Agency, a body that would represent world Jewry—Zionists and non-Zionists—in working with the British to establish a Jewish national home in Palestine. With much fanfare and celebration Chaim Weizmann was elected the agency's first president. Then news of the riots arrived, smothering hopes and forcing world Jewish attention onto the Arab-Jewish conflict. "If there was ever an event in the annals of the Yishuv which can be called 'traumatic,'" writes the historian Anita Shapira, "it was the 1929 riots."

Eight years had passed since the violence of 1921, a quiet period in which the Jews had become fairly complacent about Arab acceptance of their presence in the land. There had been skirmishes and tensions around the Western Wall in Jerusalem, an area sacred to Jews as the last remnant of the Second Temple and to Arabs as bordering on the al-Aqsa Mosque, Islam's third-holiest site, but these clashes had been brief. Suddenly, in the early morning of Friday, August 23, a quarrel over worship at the wall turned into bloody attacks by thousands of Arabs, spreading from Jerusalem to Hebron to Safed and other areas across the country.

The Arab throngs attacked with stones, sticks, firearms, and particularly knives, which they could conceal easily. A surgeon at Hadassah Hospital reported that the first group of victims he treated "suffered mostly dagger wounds." And in Hebron, where Jews had lived alongside Muslims for hundreds of years, wild mobs stormed through town, massacring people with knives and hatchets, chopping off heads and hands. As they moved from house to house, they also raped and pillaged and set fire to buildings with people in them. Among their victims were religious yeshiva students from the United States, who had no chance of defending themselves.

Underlying the atrocities lay Arab fears of being displaced and hatred of the "foreigners" settling the land, the same attitudes that had sparked the 1921 riots. In the years since then, although the Yishuv had not reached its expectations—a mass immigration of Jews from around the world never materialized—it did expand in many areas. By the late 1920s, the Arabs could see that the Zionists had gained strength and were striking permanent roots in the country. The violence lasted about a week, with neither the Haganah nor the British police handling it effectively. When it ended, 133 Jews and 116 Arabs had been killed, and 339 Jews and 232 Arabs injured.

Golda returned to Tel Aviv from Zurich toward the last days of the riots. Like other Yishuv leaders who had been away, she headed almost immediately to Haganah headquarters. She also had a personal connection with some of its units. In Herzliya, the frontier town where her parents lived, Haganah members had used the Mabovitch home to secretly store their weapons. In a trick of fate, Golda, the activist, was safely in Europe during the worst of the riots, while her parents, who had come to Palestine to be with her and Sheyna, faced real danger from the Arab villages surrounding their neighborhood. When the Haganah evacuated most of the people in their area, Golda's father insisted on remaining and standing guard at night, and her mother on staying home with him, a demonstration of courage Golda would refer to as a model for herself.

ON HER RETURN, GOLDA PICKED up her duties in the Women Workers' Council. Some two months later, she and Ada Maimon began to lock horns again in a series of explosive meetings. The topic once more: the ties between the Women Workers' Council and WIZO.

The matter of the Women Workers' Council had come up at the WIZO conference in Zurich, but WIZO was left hanging as to the exact nature of its financial arrangement with the council. Golda opposed any WIZO involvement. She made her position clear at a meeting of the Histadrut executive committee on October 11 and would not budge from it subsequently. WIZO, she argued, was part of the General Zionist movement; the Histadrut represented Labor Zionism. Allowing WIZO to support women's training farms was tantamount to the Histadrut's ceding control of those farms to that group. Moreover, the Pioneer Women, who also raised money for the farms, would disapprove.

While the men on the executive committee searched for a compromise—after all, WIZO money was not to be rejected lightly—Golda rammed her position through the Women Workers' Council. Furious, Maimon and her followers in Hapoel Hatzair complained to Ben-Gurion. In a jab at Golda, he demanded that the executive committee be shown the minutes of the women's last meeting, which she had dominated. Golda Meyerson, it was turning out, was not quite as malleable as he and the other executives might have expected when they first invited her to head the council.

Something else was also afoot. Ben-Gurion, Berl Katznelson, and others had been working intensely to effect a merger between the two opposing labor parties in the Histadrut, Ahdut Ha'avoda and Hapoel Hatzair, and a continuation of the battle between Golda and Ada could destroy the process. Nevertheless, the battle went on . . . and on.

At a Histadrut executive committee meeting in November, Golda asserted in a tone of finality that "as a formal matter, the issue is over. The women's council decided not to enter into an agreement with WIZO." Then, unaware, she slipped from the third person to the first. "Because I think it is unnecessary and hurtful to the Pioneer Women." Incensed, Maimon and her supporters resigned from the Women Workers' Council, threatening to start a competing women's organization. Ben-Gurion became livid at the threat. Golda continued to hold her ground. And the strains among the three moved close to a breaking point in December.

First came a bitter exchange between Ben-Gurion and Maimon, in which he labeled her group's threat a "criminal act in the Histadrut." She snapped back that "no one can think me less a Histadrut person than you, and I will do it if the executive committee does not come to a decision."

Next a convoluted debate raged about how to rearrange and reelect the women's council secretariat in such a way that the Hapoel Hatzair group that had resigned could be readmitted. Golda maintained that changes could not be made at this point. "There are some things that cannot be undone," she pronounced. Ben-Gurion, seeking to pacify Ada after the previous outburst, turned on Golda, stating sharply that "for the sake of peace many things can be undone." Remez, quick to defend Golda, commented that "in addition to peace, there is also justice and principles," to which Ben-Gurion shot back, "You can compromise on many things . . . for the sake of the institution's work," implying that Golda's obstinacy interfered with the women council's work.

Finally, Golda and Ben-Gurion faced off. Irritated with her high-handedness, he asked, seemingly in all innocence, what the women's council had actually accomplished, particularly for city women. He knew, as did the others, that the council had done little to help city women, in spite of Golda's interest in them; most of its activities had been on behalf of women's agricultural farms. Unfazed, as though unaware of the provocation behind Ben-Gurion's dart, Golda admitted that not enough had been done for city women, but she listed one by one the council's various other accomplishments and its plans for the future. Nobody listening doubted that this woman had complete charge of the situation, and of the Women Workers' Council.

Two weeks later, she offered to give up that charge. A new reality had set in and begun to change the face of the Histadrut. On January 6, 1930, the long-awaited merger between Ahdut Ha'avoda and Hapoel Hatzair took place at a convention that ended the next day in a joyous procession of delegates and leaders singing and dancing in the streets. The new, united party, called Mapai (Mifleget Poalei Eretz Israel), the Land of Israel Workers' Party, would be the largest party in the Yishuv, control the Histadrut, and eventually dominate the entire Zionist movement. In that context, it seemed pointless to Golda to continue heading the women's council, with its turmoil and tensions.

She had been a delegate at the founding Mapai convention and then elected to its central board, one of fifteen people given that authority, including Berl Katznelson and David Remez. She was one of only two women on the board—the other, Ada Maimon, always her rival, yet always participating alongside her in labor movement projects. "I have had the feeling for some time already that I am not succeeding, and I am not confident that I am doing what is necessary," she said at a meeting of the Women Workers' Council on January 9, three days after the Mapai convention. "Therefore, I do not see any possibility of continuing my participation in the work of the secretariat." It was not an official resignation, but by late March, Ben-Gurion would write in his diary that Golda had informed him that she was busy with her children and could not work for the secretariat full-time, nor was she proficient enough in Hebrew. These seem strange excuses for someone who left her children for months while she traveled and who had been speaking Hebrew—albeit a weak Hebrew—at meetings. But Golda wanted out. Heading the women's council had not been a happy, or successful, experience for her.

She left her position as secretary of the Women Workers' Council in April 1930, although she kept her affiliation with the group. A year later, the Women Workers' Council signed the financial agreement with WIZO she had so vehemently opposed.

GOLDA'S RESIGNATION from the secretariat did not prevent her from receiving a prestigious new assignment: to represent Mapai at the Conference of Socialist Women in London. "Golda is conducting a highly successful campaign among the women workers of England," Ben-Gurion wrote to his wife, Paula, on June 23. "Her talk . . . created a great impression." The talk lasted only five minutes, but it so impressed the more than one thousand delegates attending the conference that she was bombarded with invitations to speak at branches throughout Britain. Essentially, she reported to a Mapai meeting later, the socialist women "knew nothing about Eretz Israel. They have heard only that the Jews are chasing out Arabs and socialists need to oppose that." She suggested to her colleagues that they invite some of the women to Palestine, particularly those living in cooperatives. Showing them the Yishuv's achievements would go a long way toward gaining their support; "one visit to Israel is worth a hundred speeches," she was to say.

She had planned to return home after the women's conference, but pleased with her success there, Ben-Gurion prevailed on her to remain in London and attend the Imperial Labour Conference, an international gathering of socialist delegates. It was an important gathering for the Jewish leaders at this moment. After the Arab uprising the previous spring, the British government, under the Labour leader Ramsay MacDonald, had appointed a commission headed by Sir Walter Shaw to investigate the cause and effects of the disturbances. The commission results, published in March 1930, blamed the Arabs for the violence but presented Jewish immigration and land sales as threats to them and recommended restricting immigration quotas. Shocked and angered, the Zionist community viewed the report as a blatant retreat from the Balfour Declaration's promise of a Jewish homeland in Palestine. It came as a particularly bitter pill for the Labor Zionists, emanating as it did from the British Labour government.

If Golda had expected Ben-Gurion to address the report in his speech at the Imperial Labour Conference, she was disappointed. He spoke for forty-five minutes in broad, general terms, "without particular sharpness toward the government," she reported. She, on the other hand, gave a blistering fifteen-minute talk in which she portrayed the painful condition of the Jewish community after the Arab attacks and lashed out at the British proposal to curtail Jewish immigration. "I do not trust the socialism of someone who convinces himself that socialism can exist . . . even though an entire nation does not have its own land," she told the many socialist leaders present.

After she spoke, the Austrian socialist Friedrich Adler mumbled that he felt he had been personally attacked. A British Labour representative accused her of being too "tragic," exaggerating the impact of the riots and the response of the British government. But Ben-Gurion was swept away. "I trembled at her daring words," he wrote. "Her speech shook the conference. She spoke with pride, assertiveness, bitterness, pain, and good sense. Although I had heard of her success at the women's conference and other gatherings . . . her speech was an enormous surprise for me."

Gone were their differences from the Women Workers' Council. Gone too, Golda's shame about an incident of long ago. When she still lived in America, David Ben-Gurion had come to Milwaukee to speak and was scheduled to have lunch the next day at the Mabovitch home. Golda had gone to a concert with Morris instead of attending his lecture, and as a result the lunch had been canceled. Someone who did not bother to hear Ben-Gurion speak should not have the privilege of having lunch with him, she was told. It broke her heart then that she had missed the opportunity to meet him. Now she had won what she had longed for since that day and would continue to seek for much of her life: his approval.

8

Pioneer Woman

Ben-Gurion and the other Histadrut decision makers would have liked Golda to go back to America immediately after she returned from London in the summer of 1930; she was the country's best emissary to American women. She resisted. For one thing, she didn't want to leave the children again. For another, this seems to have been when Sheyna was in the States studying nutrition, and Golda would have felt a need to keep an eye on her sister's children in Palestine as her sister had cared for hers. Then there was the matter of Zalman Shazar, with whom she had developed a deep bond in the past few years. He had been slated to go to the States for a fund-raising campaign, but a question had arisen about whether he could leave his newspaper position at *Davar*. She seemed hesitant to depart while he remained in Palestine.

Golda's affair with Zalman Shazar was not unknown to the people closest to her, most notably David Remez. Shazar and Remez were good friends. Remez and Golda had a tight relationship, although it might not have become romantic yet. A few months earlier, Remez had written her an angry letter about her attachment to Shazar. He was jealous. Or bitter, because, romantic or not, theirs had been a warm, intimate tie.

The letter used code names for people, a practice the two would continue. "Gershon" referred to Morris; "Chaya" was Golda. "We always avoid talking about serious things," he wrote early in the letter. "I don't know why, but first there was no opportunity and then I don't want to cause a scene, and Zalman had the same feeling." Then he went on to talk about serious things: "Golda, the trouble with you is you were raised on praises. No question you are successful. I don't question you in your social earnestness. You are not a *mensch*. For you, there is no individual. It's only the masses . . . Particularly the way you act to your friends is unforgivable."

His words echoed thoughts her friend Yossel had expressed long ago in Milwaukee. "I don't believe Golda misses anybody," he had written to Morris. "She addresses herself to all of humanity. To miss somebody means speaking to only one person at a single moment." Golda valued causes above friendships, both men contended, and her friends felt slighted. Actually, the current scene seemed a replay of Golda's youthful experience—men fascinated by her, competing for her attention, and irritated at not fully receiving it while she turned from one to another. Then it was Yossel and Dubinsky, now Remez and Shazar. Morris always inhabited the middle: the man she loved at that time; the man she treated badly at this time. Remez's letter reveals just how badly she treated Morris and how far their marriage had deteriorated.

"You're impressed by Zalman. I dare say Zalman has a wife that loves him . . . Gershon has a wife that ignores him . . . True, Gershon is a very difficult person, but you made him what he is today . . . Before you were famous, it wasn't any better . . . You are ready so you say to give your entire life to Gershon for the sake of the children. Why do you make yourself ridiculous, Chaya . . . What kind of atmosphere can there be in the home when . . . the father comes home and she rests on one sofa and he on the other?" About Morris, he continued, "Don't forget in the nice words Gershon said to you, there's more love and devotion than in the beautiful phrases your friends give you."

Remez's solicitousness toward Morris appears strange, if not hypocritical, considering his own marriage and long-standing affair with Gusta Strumpf, who gave birth to a son generally known to be his. And while supposedly defending Morris, he also dwelled martyr-like on his personal feelings: "I'll suffer. I'm used to suffering . . . you ran away with him."

Golda's response, if any, remains unknown. Despite the reprimands from Remez, in the fall of 1931 she finally agreed to leave her family again and go to the States for another fund-raising campaign. Shazar journeyed there shortly afterward on the same mission. Aside from working for the campaign, he would attend Columbia University in New York for additional advanced study.

Golda arrived in New York aboard the S.S. *Europa* on October 13, traveling, as she had earlier, on her "Government of Palestine" passport. She couldn't have chosen a worse time. The Great Depression that struck the city and the country shortly after she left two years earlier had changed the face of America. More than thirteen million people had lost their jobs, and more than ten thousand banks failed. In New York City, where soup kitchen lines snaked around street corners, almost two million people received some form of public welfare. The Jewish community everywhere was hit hard, with thousands of new requests for help pouring into charities at the very moment that hospitals, nursing homes, orphanages, and other services had to close for lack of funds. As jobs became scarce, anti-Semitism, always brewing beneath the surface, became blatant. JEWS NEED NOT APPLY signs appeared on storefronts and accompanied want ads. Businesses and law firms shut their doors so firmly against Jews that men in well-tailored suits and ties could be seen shuffling on breadlines. They don't accept Jews into colleges, Golda reported home, and even when they do, what kind of work will Jewish graduates find?

Membership in Zionist institutions plummeted. The Zionist Organization of America, which had topped 100,000 members after the Balfour Declaration in 1917, dropped to little more than 8,000 by the 1930s, and Hadassah would reach a low of 23,349 members. Beset by economic miseries, American Jews did not have money to spend on membership dues or their minds set on Zionist fantasies.

In this environment, Golda plunged into her fund-raising tasks for the Geverkshaften and other Labor campaigns, and especially for the Pioneer Women, trying to wear blinders to the economic realities around her. She based herself in the small cluttered Pioneer Women's office at 1133 Broadway in Manhattan's garment district but spent the next months traveling.

A sample from her 1932 tour schedule in the Pioneer Women's files tells the story:

> KANSAS CITY—Tuesday, Wed. Thurs. Fri—19–22 January; TULSA, OKLA.—Sunday, Mon.—24–25 January; DALLAS, TEX.—Wed. Thurs.—27–28 January; SAN ANTONIO, TEX.—Fri. Sat. Sun.—29–31 January; LOS ANGELES SAN FRANCISO PETALUMA—Wed. till Sunday—3–14 February; SEATTLE, WASH.—16–17 February; COLGARY—Friday—19 February; EDMONTON—Sat. Sun. Mon.—20–22 February; SASKATOON—Wed. 24 February.

The tour continues with the same packed days to Winnipeg, St. Paul, Minneapolis, Sioux City, Omaha, Iowa City, Cleveland, Columbus, Detroit, Toronto, and Hamilton, ending in Pittsburgh on April 3. Not really ending, because on April 14, the women's organization held a reception for her at the Hotel Pennsylvania in Manhattan, another occasion for her to speak and for them to raise money. And a few weeks later, donning her hat as a representative of the Histadrut, she appeared in Philadelphia before a conference of the International Ladies' Garment Workers' Union (ILGWU) attended by 150 delegates and almost three thousand visitors. Reporting on the event, *Davar* noted with pride that May 3 was a "big day at the conference," because Norman Thomas, leader of the American Socialist Party, addressed the gathering and so did the Histadrut's own Golda Meyerson. The convention responded enthusiastically to Golda, who spoke in Yiddish and English, the newspaper related, and afterward the delegates voted unanimously to actively support the work of the Histadrut.

It was an extraordinary commitment by the union to Labor Zionism, and a tribute to Golda, given the strains of the Depression—membership in the ILGWU had fallen from 120,000 in 1928 to 33,000 in 1932. For Golda, it marked the beginning of a lifetime lovefest with American labor unions. Regardless of that success, the grueling pace of travels continued in May, this time to the East Coast. From Boston, she appeared at the nearby cities of Dorchester, Roxbury, and Chelsea, where she spoke in the name of the Histadrut. In New Haven, in addition to appearing at the Pioneer Women's club, she met with Hadassah women, to familiarize them with her group's work. In Baltimore, she added a Zionist youth group to her other meetings and attended a banquet in her honor. Cleveland, Detroit, Toronto, and Buffalo appeared on her schedule for the remainder of the month.

"You undoubtedly already know the lot of an emissary," she wrote to her comrades in the Women Workers' Council back home. "Three or four meetings in the course of a day, talks until the early morning hours, day after day and week after week." She didn't know whether she had aged since her last visit to America, she wrote sardonically—she was only thirty-four—or whether the work had actually become harder, but the past months had depleted her strength. She hesitated to commit herself to a longer stay, although the Pioneer Women very much wanted her to continue.

By June, she no longer had a choice. An ominous telegram arrived from Morris: "Sarah ill. Suggest you return." The mysterious kidney disease had progressed to the point that the child could no longer eat, and her face had swollen out of shape.

Family lore has it that Golda hurried home frantically, and in the course of some weeks she and Morris made the agonizing decision for her to take Sarah to America for medical treatment, although the pediatrician warned that the little girl was too sick to travel and might die on the way. In this memory, Golda then requested that she be sent as an emissary to the Pioneer Women in America so that she might carry out her plans for her daughter. In reality, Golda seems to have decided quickly that she would go home to get her children and return to the States with both of them so that Sarah could receive expert care and she could continue the work she had begun with the American women. "The knowledge that she will remain with us gave great pleasure to all the *haverot* and the entire movement," the Pioneer Women wrote to the Women Workers' Council, before Golda even left the States.

She arrived in Tel Aviv in early July. Though worried about her daughter, she quickly got back into the whirl of Yishuv activity after feeling out of the mainstream in America, attending executive meetings of the Histadrut and Women Workers' Council. She reported to the council, with satisfaction, that the Pioneer Women had formed thirteen new youth clubs and grown its membership and, even in the "hard situation" in the States, had matched the sum raised the previous year. She also notified the women that the Pioneer Women had prevailed on her to become national secretary of the organization. Golda needed the salaried position of secretary (comparable to executive director) to help support her and the children in America. As a Histadrut emissary, she had received only minimal pay, covering basic expenses.

Morris would remain behind. He had been living again in Jerusalem, where he ran a bookstore on Jaffa Road with money raised by Sheyna's husband, Shamai. The children, who lived with him during Golda's most recent American stay, loved to visit the store and receive gifts of new books from their father. Eventually, it would fail, as did most of his enterprises, this time due to theft by a dishonest clerk and—more likely—Morris's lack of business acumen. Some months after Golda and the children left, he moved into the home of Baruch Zuckerman, head of Poalei Zion in America, with whom Golda had worked closely. The Zuckermans immigrated to Jerusalem in the fall of 1932, but Zuckerman still spent most of his time on party activities outside the country. "Everyone thought Morris Meyerson was our father, because our father was never home," recalled Nomi Zuckerman, the younger of his two daughters. To her, Morris would always be "a kind, gentle human being, who knew everything in the world . . . a tragic, lonely figure."

THE TWO-WEEK VOYAGE TO THE United States gave Golda her first extended uninterrupted time with the children in years. Following the route she had taken previously, they boarded their ship, the S.S. *Bremen*, at Cherbourg, France. In their small, tourist-class cabin, she slept on a deck chair while the children used the bunks. During the day, she played shuffleboard with Menahem or read and sang to both children. Sarah might have been too ill to fully appreciate the precious hours with her mother, unhindered by meetings or speeches, but for eight-year-old Menahem the journey stood out as an idyllic moment in time that would rarely be duplicated.

They disembarked in New York on August 27, 1932, and headed directly to the spacious Brooklyn apartment of Fanny and Jacob Goodman, where they were to live for the next year. Jacob Goodman had run a restaurant that became a hangout for writers and musicians during Golda's earlier American years. He and Fanny were part of her close circle of Poalei Zion *chaverim*, comrades who became extended family to her and her children. Golda arranged to have Sarah enter Beth Israel Hospital on the Lower East Side of Manhattan, and within six weeks the child who had been close to death was "miraculously" cured. Although she had kidney problems, the nature of her illness had been misdiagnosed, and with proper food and treatment she left the hospital "in perfect health," Golda wrote to Morris.

But the children's ordeal was just beginning. They spoke little English, lived in unfamiliar surroundings with a family they barely knew, and saw their mother disappear, sometimes all day and far into the night when she attended meetings, at times for weeks or even months when she traveled the country raising money.

"It was not a good time," Sarah said with rueful understatement. During their first week of school—she and Menahem both entered the first grade in the local public school—Golda helped the children by sitting in class with them, translating the teacher's words into Hebrew. In Tel Aviv, she and Morris had spoken English to each other and Yiddish to the children so that they would know that language along with the Hebrew they would pick up automatically. When their English improved in America, she spoke to them only in Hebrew to ensure that they did not forget that language.

Once Golda launched into her frenetic work schedule, the children "went wild." Menahem, especially, vented his rage at his mother by quarreling constantly with her, at one point furiously piling up all the furniture against the door to his room, locking himself in and her out. After almost a year at the Goodmans', the family moved to Hamilton Street in Manhattan to stay with Malka Sheinkman, a divorcée, and her son. Menahem remembered attending P.S. 192 with his sister and feeling that, abandoned as they were by their mother, he had to be the "big brother" to Sarah. That didn't stop him, however, from being jealous of Sarah, who endeared herself to others, and tormenting her because of his rage at Golda.

They did have some good experiences in the States. When she could, Golda took them to movies and museums or to visit relatives. Her younger sister, Clara, lived in Bridgeport, Connecticut, a fairly short train ride from New York. She had married a man she met at the University of Wisconsin, Fred Stern, and had a young son, Daniel David. Sharp and caustic, Fred was a Communist, vehemently opposed to all forms of nationalism. He informed Golda on their first meeting, two years earlier, that he considered Zionism a reactionary movement. Clara, as feisty and opinionated as her two older sisters, had announced that she would not join the family in Eretz Yisrael. As it happened, she did not even visit that land until 1950, when she would see her ill mother for the first time in twenty-five years. By then, her life had been overwhelmed with pain. Her son died at the age of eighteen, and her husband, always bitter, suffered a severe illness that caused him to lose a leg and remain bedridden for years.

But in 1932, when Menahem and Sarah visited their aunt Tzipka—the family still used her Yiddish name—the sorrows lay in the future, and Clara and Fred welcomed them cordially. Morris's family in Philadelphia also greeted them with affection. They met their grandmother Morris's mother, Shifra, for the first time. In earlier days, she had disliked the Mabovitch family and Golda, but she had adjusted to the marriage and her son's move to Palestine. Most likely she and the other family members knew nothing about the difficulties between Morris and Golda. The children also met Morris's sister Rae and her husband, Lou Broudo. They had reared Marcella, the daughter of Rae's deceased sister Sarah, for six years, until her father, Leon Skoss, remarried and could care for her. It comforted the children to have relatives they could visit. Yet their abiding memory of those years in America was of loneliness. "We were always lonesome for mother because we saw very little of her," Sarah said.

Golda's lasting memory was of "the smell of railway stations and the sound of my own voice." The steady stream of long-distance railway travel did not begin immediately, however. For much of the first year, she worked primarily out of the Pioneer Women's office, which had moved a few blocks to 1225 Broadway, taking trips out of town to give lectures, attend meetings, or organize the perennial bazaars, raffles, and dances that supplied the bread and butter of money raising. On a trip to Toronto at the end of October, she was officially elected to her position as national secretary at the Pioneer Women's fourth biennial convention. During those autumn months, one of the most beautiful seasons in New York, she also found time to be with Shazar, who was still studying at Columbia, but by Thanksgiving he had returned to Tel Aviv while his wife, Rachel, came to join Golda as an emissary in America.

Good, kind, trusting Rachel wrote glowingly to her husband about Golda a month after her arrival: "It may be redundant to tell you what a powerful impression Golda's work has made on me now that I see it up close. I went with her to several meetings in which she participated, and I simply do not remember when I've received such an impression of a public leader." Then, with sympathy, "In general, she has many difficulties in her life, and that is crystal clear." Was she referring to Golda's difficulties with her husband, her unhappy children, or the totality of her private life compared with her public one? She assumed Shazar would know. In the same letter, she alluded to Golda's continued lack of confidence in her Hebrew-speaking abilities. Rachel accepted an invitation to speak at a forthcoming celebration of the working woman in the Land of Israel to be held by an American cultural organization that promoted Hebrew. Golda refused, because she still did not feel competent in the language.

Golda and Rachel divided the work for the Pioneer Women between them. For the time being, Golda would concentrate on New York and surrounding regions, and Rachel would travel to the more distant places. In a return letter, Shazar advised Rachel to "stay only in hotels," even though she didn't like hotels, because "they are less wearying than being a guest in the homes of the *chaverot.*"

In fact, emissaries like Rachel and Golda, who had not reached Shazar's level of eminence, had little say in the matter of their lodging. Money was scarce, and the Pioneer Women members insisted on playing hosts. Golda almost always stayed in members' homes on short or long trips. When she didn't, the *chaverot* noticed and commented. Norma Salz was a young girl when Golda visited the Pioneer Women's group in Buffalo, New York, on May 12, 1931. "Golda slept in my bed that night," Salz recalled, remembering the excitement of the event. "So many women across the country can say the same thing." But the following year, when Golda came to Buffalo again, she stayed at a hotel. "What a grumbling went on because of this. 'How could she spend the money? How will we get her from the hotel?'" Decades later, in 1975, Salz traveled to Israel on the same plane as Golda. Receiving permission to speak to the then-retired prime minister, she told Golda about the "scandal" that had erupted when she stayed at the Hotel Lafayette in Buffalo in 1932. The bill had come to seven dollars. "The women accused you of squandering the funds," she said, and they both laughed.

It was an insignificant sum in 1975, but for American women prying out nickels and dimes for the cause in the depressed 1930s, $7.00 spent on a hotel meant that much less toward reaching the quota they had set for themselves, a sum always difficult to meet. (The Newark, New Jersey, chapter planned to raise $165.00 between October 1933 and July 1934. It collected $17.40.) Under the circumstances, few of the women could appreciate the toll travel extracted from their emissaries and how wearying it was for them to be houseguests, expected to talk until all hours with hosts who could never get enough of them.

Meanwhile, Golda's expenses came under scrutiny from a different quarter. Beba Idelson, the current secretary of the Women Workers' Council in Palestine, complained in a letter that Golda had charged too much of her work expenses to the council instead of to the Pioneer Women. When Golda objected indignantly in her response that she felt her integrity was being questioned, Beba replied in a similar vein. "It's too bad that you understood my letter to mean something other than what was intended," she wrote, regretting also that Golda took the matter so "personally." The issue was that Golda had gone to the States to work for the Pioneer Women but, instead of confining her activities to that organization, had involved herself in the Women Workers' Council and many other labor areas and billed accordingly. "Is it forbidden to say that our expenses are too high?" an irritated Beba wrote.

As usual, Golda had viewed the women's organizations through the prism of the larger Labor Zionist movement and took it upon herself to strengthen that movement as a whole in America. She continued to raise money for the Geverkshaften campaign. She worked with youth groups, speaking at Poalei Zion conventions for young people and at chapters of Avukah, a student Zionist organization. She involved herself in the League for Labor Israel, a newfound advocacy group for Labor Zionism, and she attempted to invigorate the American Poalei Zion Party, which had declined over the years. For her many activities, she charged more of her expenses to the Women Workers' Council than its members deemed fair, irking them also by how much she undertook outside the women's spheres.

Her main work, however, was still in those spheres. After Rachel left for Palestine, Golda embarked again on her Pioneer Women tours. She traveled for five months to the West Coast and Canada, beginning after the festival of Sukkot in the fall of 1933, returned to New York for a month to celebrate Passover with the children, then took off again to cities on the East Coast. She gave dozens of talks, organized hundreds of programs, met with thousands of women, danced untold numbers of horas.

To attract new, younger members, she pressed to have the organization move away from using Yiddish as its sole language and reach out to English-speaking girls and women. Many of the older members regarded speaking Yiddish a matter of principle, a way of identifying with Jewish tradition. Golda and her friends had once also tried to speak Yiddish on principle before immigrating to Palestine, only to discover that the accepted language of the Yishuv was Hebrew. To these women, she argued that an organization based on Yiddish in an English-speaking land would soon disappear. She won her argument. With the blessings of the national board, she helped establish English-speaking clubs everywhere she went. Some clubs called themselves "Young Pioneer Girls"; many others became known as "Golda Meyerson clubs."

As much as she could, she capitalized on her knowledge of America and Americans. When the Pioneer Women received an invitation from some of the most conservative gentile women's groups—Daughters of the American Revolution, Colonial Dames, and the like—to participate in a women's fair at the New York Armory, she jumped at the opportunity. Coming across the name "Pioneer Women" in the phone book, those women had assumed the group boasted early American pioneer ancestry. Golda grasped the mistake but persuaded her skeptical board to accept the invitation and pay the required fee for a booth. To the amazement of the sponsors, the booth displayed handicrafts from the Jews in Palestine, and Golda, at her most charming, told them about her life in the Midwest and about the new frontier she and others were forging in their ancient homeland. The booth became one of the most popular attractions at the fair, giving the aristocratic Christian women their first exposure to Zionism.

With each of Golda's accomplishments, her myth grew. To be sure, members knew she could be demanding, an "aggressive, impatient woman" who might "hit the ceiling" if they disappointed her or didn't follow her directions. She could also be humorlessly puritanical. Many remembered her refusal to permit them to play cards in order to raise money. At one meeting in a private home in Chicago, the "husbands closeted themselves in a room to play cards," while the women gathered in another to await Golda's arrival. There was "a quick hiding of the cards and the money from the card table as the bell rang and it was announced that she was coming up the stairs." Nobody dared get caught by a disapproving Golda.

Just the same, as one woman rationalized, "We were her family, and she was ours, and one has the right to demand the maximum of family." Golda made them feel as though they *were* family, speaking to them intimately, directly, with no airs, "from her heart straight to ours," another said. With her fervor and unadorned speech and with the example of her life, she gave them a sense of purpose, a feeling of living in a special time and sharing in a great social experiment.

To these women, Golda symbolized the pioneer par excellence, as she had to the gentile ladies at the fair. She was the Jewish *halutza* and the American frontier woman wrapped in one. Both had left the comforts of home to follow a dream and cultivate an untamed land. Some members of the Pioneer Women would join Golda in that land at a later time. Most would remain in America, supporting the cause, raising money, and adulating the woman who had the courage to do what they did not. From those years in the 1930s through all the years of her life, the Pioneer Women claimed her as "our Golda."

MARIE SYRKIN WOULD SAY that she, like others, came under Golda's "spell." The two women met sometime in 1932 and quickly became fast friends. The intellectual Syrkin, a poet and journalist, was drawn to the activist Golda. "She's everything I'm not," she later told an interviewer. "I really admired this kind of person—though I'm much cleverer than she is—but she had virtues that seemed to me so impressive." Among those virtues was Golda's "impassioned and persuasive" speech making. "All that subsequently became the trite rhetoric of Zionist oratory—

making the desert bloom, renewing an oppressed people in a just, cooperative society—was both challenge and revelation when she spoke," Syrkin would recall. She had heard about Golda's oratory abilities long before the two met. Her father, Nachman Syrkin, had been one of Golda's Zionist heroes and mentors. When Marie was barely twenty, he told her about a young woman in the movement, about a year older than she, "who is a remarkable speaker." He then said to Marie, "I thought you would be like that." His words always made her feel guilty, as though she had somehow failed the father she adored.

By any standards, Marie Syrkin was no failure. She spoke five languages, wrote witty poetry, contributed articles to intellectual Jewish publications, and, following her first trip to Palestine in 1933, helped launch the influential Labor Zionist journal *Jewish Frontier*. At the time she and Golda met, she was wed to her third husband, the celebrated poet Charles Reznikoff, had a son by a former marriage, and had tragically lost another son, at age two, to illness. Having recently suffered the anxiety of Sarah's kidney ailment, Golda could relate to Marie's sorrow over her lost child. Beyond that, she saw in Marie a kindred spirit, bright, lively, openly committed to Labor Zionism, and forthright in her opinions. "I always come away from conversations with Marie refreshed," she told her son.

Marie became Golda's closest female friend, one of the few people to whom she trusted her most intimate secrets. Marie kept those secrets out of the biography she wrote of Golda in 1955 (later updating and expanding it) but pointed out when sending Golda the manuscript of the work that it suffered "from the fact that so little personal detail . . . can be given," elaborating on that detail in parentheses as "the kind of thing that gives human interest—what was the hero's love life, etc." Obviously, she wrote, omitting that kind of detail was "unavoidable at this stage and for this biographer." When, more than thirty years later, long after Golda's death, a different biography revealed—and exaggerated—such details, Syrkin suggested in a letter to Golda's children that they find a way to "privately influence the big Jewish agencies not to sponsor it in any way."

Not long after the two women met, Golda turned to Marie for help in writing articles and speeches. Writing had never been Golda's forte. She still so rarely even answered letters that Rachel Katznelson Shazar had felt it necessary to urge Beba Idelson to continue sending news of the Women Workers' Council to Golda even if she received no reply. Marie might have composed some of the editorials and articles that appeared over Golda's name as editor of the *Pioneer Women's Journal* and later prepared many of her written essays. In speech making, Golda was at her best when she spoke simply and clearly in her own words without a written text, but when she needed a text for more formal talks, Marie often also provided that. Syrkin never publicly took or received credit for her ghostwriting.

Golda enjoyed other friendships during her stint in America, although none on the level of Marie Syrkin. She renewed her ties to Sara Feder, one of her early school chums from Milwaukee who had become a Pioneer Women leader. When Golda worked in the Midwest, Sara could see that she felt "harassed and tired from the difficult pioneering task," and she and her husband provided her with some "respite" in their Chicago home. Leah Biskin, the first secretary of Pioneer Women and daughter of a well-known Detroit Zionist family, invited Golda and the children to visit with the family during the weeklong Passover holiday in 1933. She so admired Golda that she returned to Palestine with her at the end of Golda's American assignment. Never married, she lived with the family at various times for years, helping to care for the children, who came to regard her as "practically like an aunt." Then there were countless Pioneer Women leaders and members with whom Golda stayed in touch through her life—not confidantes, but comrades she enjoyed catching up with when she had a chance.

At the height of her travels for the Pioneer Women, Golda wrote an article in Yiddish reflecting on her journeys and the women she had worked with as she went from town to town. It was an odd, disjointed piece, hopping from subject to subject. Still it received a good amount of attention, appearing prominently in the Socialist Zionist newspaper *Der Yiddisher Kaempfer* and reprinted in Hebrew in *Davar*, the Yishuv's Labor Zionist newspaper.

What stands out most in the article is Golda's description of "feminists." There were feminists who didn't want to join the Pioneer Women because they considered themselves already liberated, she wrote. For such women, "independence grows in proportion to their war against the species 'man.'" Instead of taking part in an organization that worked with men, they preferred to segregate themselves completely by "not allowing men to participate in their discussions and always standing guard against this 'enemy.'" There were other "avowed feminists" who did join but wanted to "shrink" the group's programs by avoiding strong connections to the party or the Histadrut and concentrating on women's issues. Golda, having learned from experience, she noted sarcastically, that "the more extreme the feminism," the less faith it had in "women's intellectual and practical abilities," was not surprised by the feminists' claims that the fuller programs were "too much" for the women or would "frighten" them.

In contrast to these "feminists," the article discusses how other women who joined the organization gained from being in it. There were women from Russia whose "god was the Russian Revolution and the concept of world freedom." They had never thought about Jewish freedom, but when they entered the Pioneer Women, the spark that had been within them "burst into flame." Other women "knew nothing and felt nothing outside their own four walls: their husband, their children. Accidentally, they joined the movement, which gave them a new soul and new spirit."

For these women and others, the group served as a learning environment, teaching them to "rely on their own judgments . . . and to believe in their own strengths." And with their newfound confidence, the women developed closer ties to the Histadrut. They were able to accept advice from men in that organization without fear that "they will dominate us." At the same time, many of the male comrades who had looked down on women as being "less intelligent and capable than men," and therefore needing guidance, learned to work with the women as equals. Can anyone then deny, Golda asked, "that the emancipation of the woman in the end also emancipates the man"?

Taken as a whole, the article reveals as much about Golda as it does about the women she worked with during these pivotal American years. It tells readers that under her direction the organization played a critical role in "emancipating" its members by giving them the self-respect they needed to work as equals with men. It also picks up on one of Golda's favorite themes—that no matter how self-reliant the women became, they did not allow anyone to "shrink" the group's programs to women's interests only, but remained devoted to the larger labor movement.

The piece makes it apparent that with her unquestioning self-confidence Golda is separating herself from the mainstream members she led, women who needed an organization to help them find their voices. Even more obviously, she sets herself apart from the "feminists," whom she portrayed as radicals, viewing men as their "enemy."

That image of feminists is the most puzzling part of the article. Judging by her own life, Golda might appear to be the consummate feminist.

From the illegal abortion she had early in her marriage, to her independence from her husband both financially and emotionally, to her willingness to leave her children for months at a time in pursuit of her work, Golda broke the traditional mold for women. In fact, a few years earlier, she had participated with other women in a rally at the Kupat Holim, the national medical clinic, to create a committee to deal with abortion needs and rights, a daring and "very very feminist matter" at that time, recalled Yehudit Simhonit. Moreover, Golda complained often about the lack of sufficient activity among women workers. At one Women Workers' Council meeting, she reported with disapproval that for a recent Histadrut mission to the Diaspora, "not a single *chavera* agreed to go." She, on the other hand, almost always agreed to go, rarely allowing anything to stand in the way of her determination and loyalty to her missions.

Why then define herself in opposition to feminists? The answer lies in Golda's personal goals. The women's organizations—the Women Workers' Council and the Pioneer Women—had served as her entrée into the political life of the Yishuv, the only avenues available to a woman taking her first large steps toward leadership. Rejecting feminism by ridiculing its extremes, as she did, was Golda's way of securing the next steps as she prepared to advance in the male-dominated world of Labor politics. In this world, feminism carried little weight; even concentrating primarily on women's concerns could be a barrier to moving ahead. Ada Maimon, dedicated to her women's agricultural farm in Ayanot; Hanna Chizick, heading hers in Tel Aviv; Rachel Yanait Ben-Zvi, helping to found the Pioneer Women; Rachel Katznelson Shazar, editing a prestigious women's newspaper; Beba Idelson, serving as secretary of the Women Workers' Council for forty years—each devoted herself to improving the lot of women in pre-state Palestine and later. Another generation of women would venerate these early feminists, but in their own era they would remain on the sidelines, respected by male leaders but relegated to their chosen areas. Golda had different objectives for her future. She aimed to be at the center of her country's life and not in its margins, at the heart of Labor Zionism and not on the periphery. From her perspective, she could achieve her goals by sharply differentiating herself from other strong women while taking on the wider interests of the party and the movement.

Her article leaves behind some troubling questions, however. Might she have attained the same goals without the exaggerated depictions of "feminists"? Was it necessary to attack the whole, as she did, or could she have acknowledged moderate feminists, who were not very different from her? Did her attacks help her career or simply alienate her from feminists over the decades? The questions hang in the air.

As her mission drew to a close, Golda became restless and eager to return to the Land of Israel. "I'm still doing this crazy work of mine," she wrote to Berl Katznelson in January. "I no longer have the energy or patience for this kind of work." She longed "to soar to the Land at least for one good discussion" with her comrades in the Histadrut. She was to continue with her "crazy" work until the end of the summer. Then, despite pleas to stay on, she packed up the children and departed, first having made all the arrangements for a forthcoming Pioneer Women convention.

The Mapai leader Joseph Sprinzak described the Pioneer Women as the "liveliest and best-organized" group in the Labor Zionist constellation, due to Golda Meyerson. But after she left the United States in early August 1934, Golda never again headed a women's organization.

9

Black Clouds Rising

Golda was still in America on June 16, 1933, when Chaim Arlosoroff was murdered. Young, brilliant Arlosoroff headed the Jewish
Agency's political department and was seen as destined for greatness in
the Labor Zionist hierarchy. Two men shot him in cold blood as he and
his wife, Sima, strolled along Tel Aviv's beachfront. His death, several
hours after the shooting, sent shock waves through the world Jewish
community.

Golda knew Arlosoroff through his work in the party and from his
activities as a Histadrut emissary in America when she was there in 1928.
Like almost all members of the Histadrut, she had no doubt that his
assailants came from the Revisionist Party, bitter opponents of the Labor
Zionists. Indeed, Sima later testified that she recognized one of the Revisionists, Abraham Stavsky.

The Labor Zionists had many reasons to suspect the Revisionists,
not least of them their distrust of Vladimir Jabotinsky, who founded
the movement in 1925. Gifted and charismatic, Jabotinsky had been the
spirit behind the Jewish Legion that fought the Turks under the command of the British army during World War I. His stance toward the
British changed when he perceived them as pulling away from the Balfour Declaration after the Arab riots of the 1920s. Viewing himself as
falling in a direct line with Theodor Herzl, he demanded that Britain
fully implement the declaration and establish a Jewish national home in
Palestine on all the land promised, including the territory of Transjordan
(later Jordan), which the British had created in 1921. He spoke openly
of forming a self-governing Jewish state in Palestine with a permanent
Jewish majority, a goal the Zionist leaders held as well but camouflaged,
leaving it unarticulated.

As for those Zionist leaders, Jabotinsky called for a "revision" of their
policy of building up the land, "dunam by dunam . . . farmstead by farmstead," in favor of a global approach of encouraging mass immigration

and settling the entire area. He especially opposed the Labor Zionist dedication to socialism and the working classes—the ideals Golda
most valued. Zionism and nationhood, he held, had to take precedence
over everything, including class struggles and social concerns. With his
approval, Revisionists broke up labor union strikes in the Yishuv, arguing
that they diverted attention from the more important national needs.

Jabotinsky's emphasis on nationalism frightened and repelled the
other Zionist groups. All over Europe, nationalism was on the march,
with dire consequences for democratic governments. Adolf Hitler had
manipulated his way to power in Germany in 1933 with his National
Socialist Party and rapidly set in motion his first anti-Jewish policies.
In Italy, Benito Mussolini and his fascists had controlled the government since 1922. In Spain, internal political wrangles would lead in a
few years to civil war and the dictatorship of Francisco Franco. To be
sure, Jabotinsky did not align himself with dictatorships, but numbers
of his followers took on the trappings of fascism, particularly within the
Revisionist youth movement Betar. Members of the movement's most
aggressive and violent faction, led by the radical Abba Ahimeir, stomped
through the streets in brown-shirted uniforms, complete with breeches,
boots, and belts. Influenced by them, the party newspaper, *Hazit Ha'am*
(The people's front), spouted praise for Hitler, except—it allowed—for
his anti-Semitism.

Behind the ideological clashes between the Labor Zionists and the
Revisionists lay another, deeper conflict: a struggle for control over
Zionism as a whole. Incited by British actions, an all-out war for that
control began shaping up during the summer of 1931 at the Seventeenth
Zionist Congress in Basel, Switzerland. The Shaw Commission report
had criticized both the Jews and the Arabs in regard to the 1929 riots.
Following up on that report, the British colonial secretary, Lord Passfield, issued a White Paper in October 1931 severely restricting Jewish
immigration and land purchases. Zionists of every stripe reacted with
dismay and fury. In protest, Chaim Weizmann, the force behind the Balfour Declaration, resigned as president of the Zionist Organization, his
position as a close ally of the British much weakened by the White Paper.

At the Basel congress, Jabotinsky had relentlessly attacked Weizmann
and the General Zionists he led for having cooperated too fully with
the British. It became obvious to the Labor Zionists that the Revisionist leader was positioning himself and his faction to become the major
force within Zionism. To combat that, during the next two years, Ben-

Gurion and the others launched an intensive campaign among Zionists throughout the world to win votes for Mapai. By the Eighteenth Zionist Congress, held in Prague in 1933, Labor had amassed 44 percent of the votes and emerged as the dominant party in the Zionist movement. It would hold that position for more than forty years, through all stages of Golda's political career.

In spite of Labor's political victory, its battle with the Revisionists continued. Golda, in the States, threw herself into that battle as best she could. She blasted Jabotinsky in writing as a "general" hungry for recognition and power and his followers for using Mussolini-like tactics, attacks that landed her on the Revisionist hate list. At a Histadrut fundraiser in New York, members of the group loudly disrupted a speech she gave and, after continuing their heckling during a talk by the guest speaker, Norman Thomas, were forced from the auditorium one by one.

Arlosoroff's murder pained Golda deeply and the more so when the British arrested the Revisionists Abraham Stavsky, Zvi Rosenblatt, and Abba Ahimeir for their part in the crime. "We had the suspicion from the first moment," she wrote in a letter to the Women Workers' Council. "Even so, news of the arrests makes life impossible." The idea that a Jew would kill another Jew within the Yishuv as a result of political extremism pushed her to despair, she said. "How much more are we going to experience in our lifetimes?"

More than seventy thousand people marched in procession at Arlosoroff's funeral. Although Stavsky and Rosenblatt were found guilty at their trial, and Stavsky condemned to death, both were later acquitted for insufficient evidence. Revisionist leaders consistently denied any connection to the murder and accused the Labor Zionists of mounting a blood libel against them. Almost fifty years later, in 1982, Menachem Begin, then Israel's prime minister and once a Betar leader, appointed a state commission to reexamine the case. It was never solved.

The turmoil and tension in the wake of Arlosoroff's slaying tore at the soul of the Yishuv. Even before the murder, Mapai members had begun reacting to Revisionist strikebreaking with violence of their own. At a Revisionist gathering in Tel Aviv on Passover in 1933, thousands of Histadrut workers descended on young Betar members who paraded in the streets wearing their brown uniforms and injured some of the youngest ones. The next day's Labor newspaper *Davar* blared, "Tel Aviv Insists: 'Remove Hitler's Vile Uniforms from Our Midst.'" After Arlosoroff's death, the atmosphere of hate and hysteria intensified to the point that an explosive civil war between Labor on the left and the Revisionists on the right seemed but a match stroke away.

Fearful for the future, some of the Mapai leaders Golda most admired—Berl Katznelson, David Remez, and others—called on party members to stop their violence before the situation got completely out of hand. Younger party chiefs, particularly kibbutz and labor union heads, fiercely opposed these established leaders, comparing the current predicament to the events that had recently swept Germany. Had the German Social Democrats fought the Nazis, these activists argued, Hitler's seizure of the government might have been stopped in its tracks. By the same token, unless Mapai struck back, the Revisionists would gain the upper hand.

Golda followed the debates closely from America. Despite her opposition to the Revisionists, from the start she supported the Mapai moderates who opposed using force. Before she had a chance to express her opinion within Mapai circles, another eruption shook the Yishuv. After Stavsky's acquittal on July 20, 1934, word reached Mapai that he was to be honored in Tel Aviv's Great Synagogue on the following Saturday by being called to the Torah. As he rose for his honor, party workers planted in the congregation hurled stones, prayer books, and broken benches at him. The police had to be called to quell the rioting, which spread into the streets.

When Golda arrived in Palestine in early August, she learned that the Revisionists had put out peace feelers to Mapai and her comrades were deliberating an answer. Nevertheless, in October, fifteen hundred Mapai workers in Haifa burst into a closed meeting of eighty to a hundred Revisionists, shouting and throwing stones. This time Golda could respond, and she did, strongly condemning the violence. "There are times when I am ashamed to be in a movement like this," she railed at a Mapai central committee meeting, "to organize 1,500 people in order to chase 80 Revisionists away from a closed meeting, this is false heroism." She wanted to know, she said, "How were our people able to sing that night in Haifa? The young men who took part in this event should at least have felt ashamed." Always conscious of Diaspora reactions, she added, "When I was away from Eretz Yisrael, I could say many times with a clear conscience that we are a large community and there are certainly in our midst youths who get out of control . . . but I did not believe that we could organize such things. Now I know that what I said was a lie and I will never say that again."

Ben-Gurion's attitude was less transparent. He had passionately denounced Jabotinsky—once even labeling him "Vladimir Hitler"—and he never condemned violence the way Golda did. He insisted, rather, that its use be regulated by party leaders and not left to the whim of workers. Given his ambivalence, he took those leaders by surprise when he sent word from London in October that he and Jabotinsky had been meeting and had agreed on several areas of peace between the movements. Even Berl Katznelson, who supported such a peace, objected to Ben-Gurion's acting on his own in that way at a time when the party was so split in its attitude to the Revisionists. Telegrams for and against the pact with Jabotinsky flooded Ben-Gurion's office. Among them was one from the Histadrut executive committee signed by David Remez, Golda Meyerson, and other key people. After taking stock of the situation, the signers signaled their support for Ben-Gurion and indicated that opinions within the party were settling down and would be sorted out in the next few days.

In fact, nothing was settled. Ben-Gurion's "October surprise" led to months of heated debates in the Labor community. In the end, he agreed to a referendum on his pact with Jabotinsky to be held among all Histadrut members. Golda campaigned hard, along with Berl and others, to win backing for Ben-Gurion. But in March 1935, nearly 60 percent voted against the London agreements—"most unfortunately," Golda was to say decades later. After that, no other meeting of minds occurred between the two groups. The violence tapered off for a while, only to resurface in a different and bloodier form within a few years.

TEL AVIV, THAT CHAMELEONIC CITY, had reinvented itself again in the two years of Golda's absence. The hum of human activity and the rhythm of new construction permeated the air as Jews from Germany and Austria flocked to the land in the wake of the Nazi expansion in those countries. Hitler had not yet devised his "Final Solution," and Germany strove only to rid itself of its Jews. In 1933, thirty-five thousand new immigrants entered Palestine, and in 1935 sixty-nine thousand arrived, the largest number that had ever come in a single year. They would become known as the Fifth Aliyah. Many of the first arrivals from Germany and Austria had been members of Zionist youth groups and now joined collective settlements or established their own farms. But the bulk of new immigrants settled in Tel Aviv. Almost overnight, it seemed, the small urban center blossomed into a sophisticated metropolis with a population of eighty-six thousand, a third of the entire Jewish population in the land.

Along with their sorrows, the newcomers brought their energy and skills and the customs they had lived with. In 1934, the twenty-fifth anniversary of the city's founding, it boasted three daily newspapers, ninety-four hotels, more than fifteen hundred factories, and 178 cafés and coffee shops, most with the flavor (and whipped cream) of Vienna or the atmosphere of Berlin. Houses designed in the German Bauhaus, or International Style, appeared everywhere. Built of white or tan concrete, with low, clean geometric lines set off by curving balconies, the new structures turned Tel Aviv into the most avant-garde of cities. The "all Hebrew" town that Morris had once proudly described to his family came to be known as the White City, a symbol of hope to be dressed "in a gown of concrete and cement," the poet Nathan Alterman wrote.

Perhaps it was the contradiction between the ominous events in Germany that Golda followed with mounting anxiety and the newly booming Tel Aviv economy, so different from the depressed American one she had just left. Or maybe it was simply being home after her great success in the States, having to face Morris and the problems of her domestic life again. But even caught up as she was in the Revisionist maelstrom, Golda seemed at first at loose ends. At a Mapai central committee meeting, Ben-Gurion suggested that she work closely with him on the Mapai executive board. David Remez, who had become secretary-general of the Histadrut, wanted her for Histadrut work. Pulled from both sides, without a clear direction in either, Golda announced that she would enter the kibbutz Ein Harod the following week, for "personal reasons." She had never given up the fantasy—a "hidden yearning," her daughter called it—of returning to kibbutz life. But it *was* only fantasy, never to be realized.

She settled instead in Tel Aviv, which was to remain her base for the rest of her life, joining a cooperative workers' building project in the northern part of the city. Called Me'onot Ovdim (Workers' Dwellings), its apartments became home to many prominent Histadrut leaders and working people. There were six buildings in a complex, each one standing on stilts, with a cafeteria and "culture room" on its ground floor, and between buildings large gardens provided gathering places for residents after work. Golda and the children moved in to a three-room apartment facing the sea on the third floor of 254 Hayarkon Street, nicer than any home they'd ever had. Sarah and Menahem shared one room, another was rented out, and Golda slept on a pullout bed in the "living room," as she had in previous apartments.

Her longtime friend Yossel Kopilov occupied an apartment near hers, with his second wife, Adena, and sons Elisha and Uzzi. Both Golda and Morris had kept strong ties to Yossel over the years; it was she, Elisha said, who persuaded his parents to move in to the workers' complex. Yossel had dwelled in Tel Aviv since his arrival in 1921, and there he opened a barbershop, the occupation he had cultivated in the States that gave him time to read and occasionally write.

For Golda and the children, Yossel seemed a godsend. Every Saturday morning, he arrived at their home at eleven o'clock for a cup of tea, played chamber music records, and read aloud to Menahem and Sarah. In memory, they could hear him fifty years later reciting from James Joyce's *Ulysses*, passages they didn't understand but loved because they loved Yossel. Morris, who worked in Haifa during the early 1930s, would join the family for the weekend, arriving on Friday evenings and sharing Yossel's Saturday visits.

The workers' homes where Golda and Yossel lived made up just one part of the Histadrut's broad-based community, the workers' socialist "paradise" it was steadily expanding. Menahem and Sarah attended Beit Hinuch, a Histadrut-affiliated school for workers' children, eating lunch there every day with food produced by Histadrut-run companies. Golda and Morris deposited their money in the Histadrut's Bank Hapoalim, the workers' bank, and held medical insurance through the Histadrut's Sick Fund. And Solel Boneh, where Morris worked sporadically, was the Histadrut's construction and contracting company. Here, within the Histadrut's encircling arms, Golda came as close as she ever would to replicating the cooperative life of a kibbutz, where all members' needs were handled communally. As it was with kibbutz life, those who didn't belong to the Histadrut were left out, to fend for themselves.

Very much part of the Histadrut, Golda became a member of the Va'ad Hapoel, its executive committee, and within a year was appointed to the organization's secretariat, its innermost circle. Urged by Ben-Gurion, the executive committee of Mapai also added her to its roster. With those positions, she had a place among the Yishuv's most influential leaders and policy makers. But as she settled in, her start-up job didn't reflect her growing power and prestige. At her suggestion and Remez's insistence, she organized a tourist bureau to handle visiting dignitaries—particularly from Britain and the United States—whom she might win over to the

Zionist cause, and others, such as labor union chiefs, who could be a source of future funding. True to form, however, she quickly branched out to myriad activities, her finger in every proverbial Yishuv pie.

Kupat Holim, the workers' sick fund, provided clinics and medical services to Histadrut members; Golda was on its board of supervisors and in 1937 became board chairman. The Mutual Aid department coordinated social services and unemployment benefits for working people; Golda eventually served as its director. The Women Workers' Council created the broad, new Organization for Working Mothers; Golda was elected one of its heads. In fact, she remained involved in all the council's projects, even though she no longer chaired its executive committee: she represented the group at International Women's Day events that celebrated women workers, often along with her old rival Ada Maimon; she helped found a company, Haboneh, that managed the council's property; and she worked on the editorial board of *Dvar Hapoelet*, the women workers' newspaper that Rachel Shazar edited. Golda, Rachel wrote to Shazar, was one of her "good" editors; Beba Idelson made her "blood boil."

Somehow, Golda even managed to leave her mark on one of the most exciting cultural happenings of the day, concerts by the Palestine Symphony Orchestra. During a trip to America, she took the first plane ride of her life, between Los Angeles and San Francisco ("I was excited and a little nervous," she told her children), and on the plane met the violinist Bronislaw Huberman. He spoke of starting a symphony orchestra in Palestine, where the many Jewish musicians forced out of Germany could play. Golda promised to help him in any way she could. On December 26, 1936, the Palestine Symphony Orchestra, with its guest conductor Arturo Toscanini, gave its inaugural concert at a gala in Tel Aviv. Keeping her promise, Golda influenced the Histadrut to sponsor a series of concerts for workers that over the years became a hallmark of the orchestra.

With it all, she attended meetings, as she always had, seemingly endlessly, day and night. One night, while conducting a vote on some current issue, through the haze of a smoke-filled room, she saw Menahem and Sarah sitting on a bench in the back, their hands raised to be counted among the "all in favor" votes. She had left them at home without a babysitter, promising that she would be back early. After hours of waiting for her return and trying to amuse themselves, they simply got dressed and slipped off to the meeting.

Dozens of Histadrut executive meetings record the presence of Golda

Meyerson. Relatively few of those minutes record Mrs. Meyerson's participation at any length in discussions and debates. When she speaks, it is usually to report on one of her travel missions or to state an opinion briefly. It might have been expected that someone as strong-minded as Golda, and so adept at public speaking, would have had more to say at these meetings. But Golda was developing a pattern that was to mark her behavior and leadership style through all the public offices she held. She listened. Through meeting after meeting and discussion upon discussion, she often just sat and listened. She listened to every argument and every side of every argument. Finally, when she heard everything she felt she needed to hear on a subject, she would make up her mind about what she believed and how she wanted to act. And once that mind was made up, almost nothing could change it. Even admirers often cited her refusal, or inability, to change after coming to a decision as a sign of her "inflexibility." Even critics saw it as a basis for her power.

Here is Amos Manor, head during the 1950s and early 1960s of the Shin Bet, Israel's internal secret service, who worked closely with Golda for many years: "Everybody knew that once Golda said something, even if she was wrong, you almost could not change her attitude. But that very trait gave her great credibility. People felt that she believed in what she said and that she spoke with the authority of that belief, even if she turned out to be mistaken. This was her strength."

Attending executive meetings during the 1930s, Golda had not yet acquired the wide credibility or authority that would give her that strength later. She was still learning, developing her listening skills, and speaking her mind infrequently, still on her way.

Alongside Golda at many meetings sat David Remez. The two had adjoining rooms in the Histadrut executive committee building at 115 Allenby Street, close to Yossel's barbershop. From time to time, Golda might have stopped in to chat with Yossel or share a cup of tea with him, but increasingly her emotional world centered on Remez. He was, she would later say, "one of the very few" of her comrades with whom she discussed "personal, nonpolitical matters." His son, Aharon, who became aware of the couple's long-lasting affair, added that "she saw in him a man who understood her, from the public and the personal side." Remez knew of—and resented—her romance with Shazar, but whatever the nature of their relationship earlier, as they worked closely together, it turned amorous.

In her late thirties, Golda came across as "very attractive," in the opinion of a colleague, Eliyahu Sacharov, who had an office next to hers. He worked for the Haganah, which had made its headquarters in the Histadrut executive building. Although "her nose was prominent, it didn't dominate her face as it did in later years," he said. "She always dressed nicely and in good taste," he observed, "but she didn't try to hide her femininity." Not that she exploited her womanliness, he hastened to add, but "the fact that she was a woman contributed to her centrality in the male world in which she worked." Some of her female colleagues were less generous about the way she handled her womanliness. In the gossip mill of Yishuv society, her romances with Remez and Shazar—and whispers of several others—made for steady grist, and as she advanced professionally, rumors circulated that she was "easy to get" and sleeping her way to the top.

Without a doubt, Remez helped her as she climbed up the political hierarchy. A dozen years her senior, as secretary-general he had become one of the most powerful men in the Histadrut, second only to Ben-Gurion. He guided Golda and had the authority to promote her, as he did "rapidly . . . from one position to another," her co-worker Yitzhak Eilam noted. But nobody could honestly question her qualifications for those positions or her ability to execute them, and certainly not her capacity for hard work. "She devoted herself without end to her work," Sacharov said. "The light burned in her office until all hours of the night." From her first days in the land, and before becoming romantically linked with her, Remez viewed Golda as an "important force," with "great potential," impressed by her "confidence, her great performance," his son said.

Golda admired Remez's intellect and knowledge, as she did Shazar's. Always, she felt herself drawn to such creative and brainy men. They helped fill the intellectual gap in her background, broadening her identity and strengthening her sense of self. And she found them exciting to be with, especially men like Shazar and Remez who belonged to the Second Aliyah, that pioneer period she had revered since girlhood. She never spoke openly about her romantic ties, except, perhaps, to Marie Syrkin. "Look," her friend Regina told an interviewer in regard to Remez, "I knew about it, but we never discussed it. She was also very friendly with Shazar. Very." But, she said, "she was reticent about such things." Reticent enough that she cautioned her drivers and secretaries never to reveal anything they knew, not even after her death.

Sitting together at one meeting after another, she and Remez passed notes to each other, like schoolkids scribbling behind a teacher's back.

Some of their missives were in Yiddish, most in Hebrew, with several misspellings on Golda's part. On small scraps of paper, the two teased each other and flirted. "After I left the executive committee, I waited until your conference ended *only* because I wanted to see you," Golda wrote, "and you didn't even wait a minute for me. But that's all right." Or, "I have to leave in an hour: I'm telling you this so you won't be suspicious of me," she scrawled. They laughed together at some of their long-winded comrades. "This is Mariminsra's straight line between two points," she wrote sarcastically in one note, with a drawing of curvy lines circling back and forth between two black dots. In another, "I'm afraid I'll get home for Sarahle's eighteenth birthday," although her daughter Sarah had not even reached twelve. Sometimes she touched on profoundly personal matters between them. "You said precious and amazing things to me yesterday," she wrote, contrite and blaming herself for a misunderstanding between them. "But you also said something else— that in a very difficult time for you . . . my friendship did not stand the test. It doesn't matter that I can prove to you that you're not right. It's enough that you think that way. That thought and feeling wipe out my right to the precious words you said to me." Sometimes she kibitzed. "There was a song in the IWW [Industrial Workers of the World] against the rich and their promises to the workers," she dashed off in Hebrew, giving the song's words in English, "You'll have pie in the sky when you die."

Remez kept all the notes together with his state and personal papers. Taken as a whole, they show two youthful, vibrant people, deeply committed to their work and each other. If Remez was the mentor and Golda the student in a number of areas, they functioned as equals in others, sharing private ideas, hurts, and laughter. They enjoyed being the ultimate insiders in the dominant Labor Zionist world, and they enjoyed feeling a little outside it, above their comrades as they secretly jotted their thoughts and opinions to each other. For Golda, this relationship afforded deep satisfaction, especially in contrast to her stagnant marriage. For Remez, although married to a woman he professed to love, "the warm, personal bonds" that developed between him and Golda, his son said, "lasted all the days of his life."

ALONG WITH EVERYTHING ELSE, Golda traveled incessantly in these days, to attend conferences, give speeches, and—the perennial—raise money for the Histadrut. Back and forth she went, zigzagging between her home in Palestine and distant lands, sometimes remaining away for many months. Despite her brutal schedule, Ben-Gurion pressured her to take on more. "If only Golda could have headed this project," he would write in his diary, convinced that whatever she did would turn out well.

In September 1935, she attended the Nineteenth Zionist Congress in Lucerne, Switzerland; on November 27, she arrived in New York; in May 1936, she flew to Canada; by July 23 of that year, she met with Ben-Gurion in Paris; in August, she was back in Palestine, reporting to the Histadrut executive committee. She took off again for London in mid-February 1937, on to America in March, went to the Twentieth Zionist Congress in Zurich from the third to the twenty-first of August, returned home at the end of that month, and left for the States once more in mid-October, arriving in New York on November 5 on an Italian liner, the *Roma*, and remaining through the spring. On July 16, 1938, she appeared at an international conference in Évian, France, and reported on it in Tel Aviv on July 21; from the end of November of that year until the middle of February 1939, she traveled with Remez to London, Warsaw, and Paris; and in August 1939, she took part in the Twenty-First Zionist Congress in Geneva, the last congress before the outbreak of World War II.

All told, from the time she returned to Palestine from the States in August 1934 until the end of August 1939, the months and weeks she spent away from her home and family added up to a full two of those five years. Menahem, approaching his teens, painted a picture of his mother packing as she readied herself for yet another trip. Its thick, heavy brush-strokes and dark, somber colors "reflected my mood," he remembered, seventy years later.

Aside from Sheyna, her usual standby, and Morris at home as often as possible, Golda almost always had a woman living with the family and caring for the children when she left the country or steeped herself in meetings. Some of the time it was Leah Biskin, former secretary of the Pioneer Women, who settled in Palestine after she followed Golda there in 1934. After Golda's autobiography appeared in 1975, she received a letter from Aliza London, a mutual friend, reprimanding her for not mentioning Leah in the book. "You told me that Leahke was like a sister to you," London wrote. "And truly, like a sister, she helped care for your children when you were busy at meetings until late in the night, and in the morning she made sure that you rested while she awakened the children and sent them off to school. She also cared for the children when you traveled on missions outside the Land. And more and more and more." Golda included little in her book about friends, other than those in her political world.

Another live-in friend, also not mentioned, was Nomi Zuckerman, who moved in with the family in 1937 while attending a teachers' seminary in Tel Aviv. "When Golda was home," Nomi said, "she always baked a cake for Shabbat. It made her feel like a mother." She "could be very, very crisp with people," Nomi also said, but with the children "she was never cold . . . no matter how busy she was. If she needed to be left alone to work, she said so, and they more or less understood." Still, they "missed her, they loved her, they wanted her around like other mothers."

According to Nomi, Golda found it very hard to leave the children, "always worrying about what was happening with them." Yet she did leave on her continual voyages, passionate in her commitment to her work. Later she spoke about that passion to an interviewer. She was in western Canada, laboring very hard "at meetings, morning, noon, and night." A good friend who lived in the area suggested they have breakfast at Golda's hotel and relax, without talking about Eretz Israel for a change. Golda happily agreed. They met and drank tea—and stared silently at each other. Golda finally said, "What do you want to talk about if not Eretz Israel? There is nothing else to talk about." The men Golda loved, the friends she made, the conversations she held, all had close ties to her work, and more than ever her work equaled her life.

She was away from the Land of Israel when the Arab revolt began in 1936. Seven quiet years had gone by since the last uprising in 1929. For the Jews, it had been a period of growth and optimism. After their despair at the Passfield White Paper of 1930 restricting Jewish immigration, they hailed an "interpretation" of the White Paper issued on February 13, 1931, in the form of a letter from the British prime minister, Ramsay MacDonald, to Chaim Weizmann. A tribute to Weizmann's charm, influence, and powers of persuasion among the British, the letter essentially repealed the limitations of the White Paper and reaffirmed the promises of the Balfour Declaration. Weizmann, who had resigned as president of the Zionist Organization in protest against the White Paper, was reelected at the Nineteenth Zionist Congress in 1935.

But what the Jews celebrated, the Arabs despised. They especially resented the numbers of Jewish immigrants flowing into the country as the situation in Germany worsened. They could see the growth year after year. In 1931, about 175,000 Jews lived in the land, and they made

up only about 17 percent of the entire population. By 1935, their numbers had soared to almost 400,000, and they constituted about 33 percent of the population. And the figures kept accelerating: a full quarter
of the newcomers had arrived between 1934 and 1935 alone. Always
fearful of the Jews becoming a majority in the land, Arab leaders saw in
the escalating numbers a red flag and a call to arms.

Looking around at the world situation, the Arabs found sufficient reason to push against the British at this time. Again and again, Britain had
responded to acts of aggression with little more than weak verbal protests. It did nothing to stop Mussolini and his Italian fascists from invading Ethiopia. Nor did it or any democratic country prevent Japan from
invading China in the early 1930s or Germany from entering the Rhine-
land in 1936. In the Middle East, England gave Iraq its independence in
1932 and signed a treaty with Egypt leading toward independence after
rioting and strikes there. From the Arab perspective, the prospect of
ending British support for Zionist goals seemed promising.

The "disturbances," as the British called them, began with attacks
against individual Jews. The first came on April 15, 1936, when two
Arabs shot and killed a Jewish poultry merchant. Four days later—on
"bloody Sunday"—nine Jews were murdered in Jaffa and others injured.
As the terror escalated, it involved Arab swords and rifles, land mines
and bombs. Under cover of night, armed bands set fires to granaries and
fields that laborers had cultivated for years and chopped down thousands
of trees painstakingly planted. In the cities—Tel Aviv, Jerusalem, and
others—Arabs ambushed buses, hurled grenades at cars, blew up marketplaces, and indiscriminately shot at passersby. "I kissed the children
good-bye in the morning knowing that I might well never come home
again," Golda recalled.

But this uprising also took a different tack from others before it. Along
with the violence, Arab leaders, headed by the grand mufti, Haj Amin
al-Husseini, called for a general strike of all Arab workers. Under the
supervision—and watchful eye—of the mufti and the multiparty Arab
Higher Committee, which he led, Arab workers stayed away from their
jobs at farms and citrus groves, paralyzed the port at Jaffa, refused to
man buses and trucks, and absented themselves from other daily labor,
losing their livelihoods in the process. It was the first such unified action
by the Arabs against the Jews. No longer the random violence of earlier
riots, it came closer to an organized national movement—their Revolt,
the Arabs called it.

The Jewish community suffered from the strike, but it also gained strength. Jews replaced striking Arab laborers, giving new immigrants much-needed work; they produced the foods Arab farmers had supplied; and they built a port of their own in Tel Aviv, a simple offshore jetty that would grow to become the first Jewish port in two thousand years. The Haganah, which had been weak and ineffectual during the riots of 1929, took an active role in defending the settlements and, as a special police force, worked closely with the British in controlling the violence. In performing that work, they received arms from the British and training that would be invaluable to them in the future.

To prevent the British from blaming the Jews equally with the Arabs for the fighting, Ben-Gurion instituted a policy of restraint, *havlagah*, in Hebrew. It meant defending themselves but not initiating attacks or retaliating against Arab aggression. The Revisionists, who equated such restraint with weakness, did hit hard on several occasions and seek revenge, but they remained in the minority.

The strike petered out after six months without achieving Arab goals and under pressure from the heads of neighboring Arab states, who had been promised a new British investigation into the situation. And so, once again, His Majesty's government dispatched a royal commission to probe the dispute between Jews and Arabs in Palestine. Headed by Lord William Robert Peel, the six commission members arrived in Jerusalem on November 11, 1936. After checking in to the elegant King David Hotel, they drove to the British War Cemetery on Mount Scopus, all of them dressed in top hats and tails.

Five days later, commission members began holding hearings at Jerusalem's Palace Hotel, interviewing mandate officials and leaders on both sides of the conflict. Although Golda was interviewed, the topic assigned her—Arab and Jewish women—was peripheral to the main issues under discussion. The commission members, all men, seemed to assume that male leaders could address substantive Yishuv matters; a woman should be questioned on women's subjects. More significant were the commission's tours and extensive hearings that continued until mid-January 1937. It published its much-anticipated conclusions in July, in a report that ran to 404 pages.

For the first time, the mandate government acknowledged that the Jews and Arabs could not live together peacefully on the same piece of land. Neither could either group get all it wanted. Palestine would have to be divided, "partitioned" into two independent states, one Jewish, one

Arab. "Half a loaf is better than no bread," the report inanely quoted an English proverb. The proposal gave the Jews a tiny space, less than a quarter of western Palestine. It included most of the Galilee, the Jezreel Valley, and the central coastal plain as far south as the town of Ashdod. The Arabs were to receive almost all the remainder of the land, more than 70 percent, including the mountain areas, the Negev, and the Gaza Strip, with the expectation that they would join with Transjordan in the east to form a single, large Arab state. Britain was assigned Jerusalem, Bethlehem, and surrounding areas, with a corridor to the Jaffa port, and responsibility for holy places in the region.

To implement the recommendations, the report suggested that an "exchange of population" accompany the transfer of land, so that most Arabs leave the areas under Jewish control and the Jews abandon Arab lands. As an example of how that might work smoothly, it cited population exchanges between Greece and Turkey in the aftermath of World War I. Presented so benignly here, the concept of population transfer would become one of the most incendiary issues between Arabs and Jews over the years.

Almost simultaneously with the Peel report, the government published a White Paper endorsing the commission's recommendations. The two documents triggered an uproar within the Zionist camp, causing deep chasms and searing conflicts. Everybody knew that the minuscule state proposed fell far short of Zionist goals. The question to be decided was whether it made sense to accept that state "here and now" or to continue along the path followed until that time, counting on immigration and settlement to create a Jewish majority in the land. Chaim Weizmann and Ben-Gurion avidly supported partition. "A Jewish State, the idea of independence in Palestine," Weizmann told a colleague, "is such a lofty thing that it ought to be treated like the Ineffable Name, which is never pronounced in vain." Ben-Gurion envisioned a state that, no longer subject to British limitations, could accept millions of new immigrants. Besides, as he wrote to his son, Amos, such a partial Jewish state "is not the end, but the beginning," that with time could grow "either by mutual agreement with our Arab neighbors or *by some other means*," including force if absolutely necessary.

Golda opposed the Peel proposal with every fiber of her being. She spoke of that opposition at a council meeting of the Labor World Alliance, or Ihud, an umbrella organization of Mapai and its counterparts, the Poalei Zion groups around the world. Meeting in Zurich between

July 9 and August 7, 1937, the council aimed to hammer out a Labor Zionist position on partition. Golda spoke in Yiddish, the language the delegates shared, her words rooted in pragmatic considerations. Yes, she could agree with Ben-Gurion that in the course of the next fifteen years two million Jews might come to the new state. But what will happen later, when the boundaries allotted the Jewish state have not changed? "I want a Jewish state," she said, "but I do not want to reach a time when I or my son after me will be forced to tell Jews knocking at the gates of this state that there is no place left for them." While Ben-Gurion welcomed the thought of admitting many more immigrants in the present, Golda looked optimistically to a future when the small territory assigned the Jews would no longer have the capacity to absorb new people.

She could not know then that the "knocking at the gates" would come not in fifteen years but within a year or two as darkness descended over Europe, or that the prospect of saving thousands of Jews in the present would have been more than enough reason to leap at partition.

Taking up the Peel recommendations about transfer, Golda said, "I am ready to accept that the Arabs will leave Eretz Israel, and my conscience will be absolutely clear. But is such a thing possible?" And if they remained, "that would not mark the end of the Arab problem but the beginning. Would we create a constitutional law against them? No! We would have to promise all of them full citizenship rights without any racial differences." She was never blind to the Arab presence in the land or the need to treat the Arabs equally in a Jewish state. But she also never wavered in her belief that by right the land the pioneers had reclaimed belonged to the Jewish people. The Arabs had vast territories in the region, she was to argue time and again. Eretz Israel was the Jewish homeland.

She ended as she began, with the meagerness of the space. "Only wars change borders," she said, picking up on Ben-Gurion's thoughts. "Maybe there will be a war in the near future, but how do we know that in such a war, the borders will change in our favor?"

In taking her stand, Golda clashed not only with Ben-Gurion but also with her lover David Remez and her colleague Moshe Sharett. But she aligned herself with Berl Katznelson, Yitzhak Tabenkin (leader of most Mapai kibbutz groups), and many others in the labor movement. She also found allies in an odd consortium of right- and left-wing factions opposed to partition. Religious Zionists refused to surrender Jewish authority over Jerusalem, and the more extreme Right, led by the Revisionists, forbade relinquishing any part of the historic Land of

Israel. On the left, supporters of a binational state, where Jews and Arabs might live together harmoniously, would not hear of formal division. And in America, mainstream Zionist organizations regarded the Peel plan with its minute Jewish state unreasonable. "I don't like it," wrote Henrietta Szold, president of Hadassah, and many American Zionists agreed with her.

Golda spoke again at the Twentieth Zionist Congress on August 9, a short talk in Yiddish that picked up most of her earlier themes. "We knew that many Arabs live in Eretz Israel," she explained, "and still we always said that all Jews who are compelled or wish to come, have a right to, as long as we do not impinge on the rights of the Arabs who live here." Now, she went on, she was astounded at the number of loyal Zionists who speak of "our great good fortune" at being given a Jewish state with all the trappings of sovereignty. "The truth of the matter is," she said with even more bitterness than she had shown before, "they are giving us nothing; they are only robbing us of our land."

The congress closed, after a week of debates, with a resolution for the Zionist Executive to open negotiations with the British government for a better partition plan. In the end, that resolution along with all the angst and arguing amounted to nothing. A Pan-Arab congress categorically rejected the Peel recommendations. After a subsequent failed commission, the issue fell off the British agenda.

Later, after the devastation of the Holocaust, Golda would apologize for having opposed partition in 1937. "Ben-Gurion, in his greater wisdom . . . was right," she would write. "Had the partition scheme been shelved because of us . . . I would not have been able to sleep nights on account of the responsibility for what happened in Europe." She felt a need to apologize, and she acted correctly in doing so. Yet, in reality, the issue did not hinge simply on who had been right and who wrong. Both camps, those for and those against partition, sought the best way to achieve Zionist goals in circumstances that offered no clear-cut solutions. Only after the fact did the wisdom of accepting even a tiny state shine through. The tragedy of the Peel Commission comes from the reality that at the time nothing the Jews could have done would have made a difference. The Arabs rejected the partition scheme, and the British abandoned it.

THE ARABS TURNED TO violence again, fiercer and bloodier than before. This time, in reaction to the Peel report, it was aimed at the British as well as the Jews. The renewed fighting began on September 26, 1937, when Arab gunmen assassinated Lewis Andrews, the popular British acting district commissioner of the Galilee, and escalated from there. Arab guerrillas derailed trains, sabotaged roads, bombed trucks, and murdered Jews and British alike. "One must not allow oneself to be terrorized by the gangs of bandits," Golda wrote to the American Labor Zionist leader Isaac Hamlin. The Americans had collected funds to replace a kibbutz truck blown up by the Arabs. "I attended the funeral, where I witnessed three *chaverim* murdered and bloody. I shall never forget this image."

Even so, Golda embarked on an ambitious project for the Histadrut, raising money for a new maritime venture. The reawakened Arab rebellion reinforced the conviction of Zionist leaders that the Yishuv needed to become as self-sufficient as possible. What better path toward self-sufficiency than through the sea? With the constantly expanding Tel Aviv port, the Yishuv developed "a sea psychology," Golda would say, stirring up visions of Hebrew ships coming and going, many carrying immigrants to their new homeland.

David Remez set out to transform those visions into actuality with a broad shipping enterprise called Nachshon. "Berl Katznelson created the name 'Nachshon,'" he wrote to Golda. "To know its meaning, look in the Aggadah book, volume 1, page 13." The Aggadah, the book of legends, compiled by the poet Chaim Nachman Bialik, tells of how the biblical Nachshon ben Aminadav stepped into the Red Sea before anyone as the Israelites escaped from Egypt. Golda had already publicized a small Jewish shipping line, the "SS Tel-Aviv," when she headed the country's tourist bureau. Nachshon would be a much greater undertaking. In Remez's lofty vision, it would have a fleet of twenty-five vessels that included fishing boats, freighters for trading with foreign countries, and passenger ships. Eventually, the project was to lead to fisheries and canning industries and the employment of "tens of thousands of Jews."

Golda so bought into the fantasies that for a time she "ate, drank, slept and talked shipping and fishing." In reality, the enterprise would turn into much hard work and frustration. Its story comes through in an assortment of correspondence and reports. Herein a few snippets.

A letter from London in March 1937 finds Golda writing to Remez before leaving for the States on her first Nachshon fund-raising foray. She seems uncharacteristically ill prepared, requesting a map and "material and information" to use in her presentations and asking that the "formal" papers she requires about establishing the association be prepared for her.

The "Memorandum and Articles of Association of Nakhshon Limited" in April spells out the company's goals and share offering, making Golda's work official.

The Wisconsin Jewish Chronicle of December 10 carries a long article on "Mrs. Goldie Myerson, a former Milwaukeean," with a photograph, detailing the Nachshon enterprise and her goal of raising $550,000 from American Jews through the sale of stock. With her glowing descriptions of how "the sea opens to us a new country . . . a territory where we don't have to fight for every inch," she sells about fifteen thousand shares at $5 each.

A letter to Golda in May 1938 from Gusta Strumpf, Remez's former mistress, now manager of Nachshon. The women are trying to procure ships, and Gusta fears that Remez is being taken in by the "bluff" of a crook who wants to be a partner. Remez "trusts everyone," she confides to Golda. If the women feel competitive, it doesn't show—at least in writing.

A series of letters from the New York lawyer Maurice Boukstein advising Golda "to be as cautious as possible" in considering the purchase of two ships, "Prince David" and "Prince Henry," from the Canadian government. "Million dollar deals, and this appears to be a million dollar proposition, are not done in haste," he writes. After much tangling, the deal fell through, to Golda's great disappointment.

Golda's report to the Nachshon administration in August 1938 about her second trip to America, when she sold another thirty thousand shares. She complains that nobody had prepared her for a meeting with a Jew named Zimori, an executive in the giant United Fruit Company. At the last minute, she'd had to change her plans and stay in New York an extra week in order to see him several times. But after a flurry of excitement, nothing came of that contact either.

A letter from Gusta to Remez on December 13, 1939. "I very much want to give up my work in Nachshon," it informs him.

The high hopes of a majestic navy had not been realized. Nachshon never came into being. But it did lay the basis for Israel's future maritime industry. For Golda, it provided important experience in meeting high-powered American businessmen. "The rich Jews are very strange," she told her Histadrut comrades. If someone comes to them for business, "it has to be one hundred percent about business." But if you interest such a person in a specific project, "it is possible to excite him about that sub-ject." She would perfect her technique of engaging rich Jews in the years ahead, providing the groundwork for her unique contribution to creat-ing the Jewish state. And although she moved away from the maritime enterprise, she remained knowledgeable about many aspects of it. Berl Katznelson dubbed her "Capitain" for her role in attempting to purchase two beautiful ships and launch a fleet to conquer the seas.

Had it worked out, Nachshon might have helped carry Jews fleeing Nazi brutality to the Land of Israel, but no matter how many ships it might have purchased, it could not have saved the vast numbers of those desperate refugees; the British restricted their entry to Palestine, and almost no other countries would have them. That truth became evident in the summer of 1938 at a posh French resort town, Évian-les-Bains, on the shores of Lake Geneva. There, at the behest of the U.S. president, Franklin Delano Roosevelt, delegates of thirty-two of the world's nations assembled at the Hôtel Royal to discuss the refugee problem in Europe.

Roosevelt had announced plans for his International Conference on Refugees on March 22, eleven days after Germany occupied Austria and began almost immediately to persecute its 200,000 Jews. Germany itself had already passed more than a hundred laws against the Jews, depriv-ing them of their citizenship, their livelihood, and any form of normal life. In convoking the conference, Roosevelt was responding to pressure from the press and the public, particularly the Jewish community. Yet instead of a high-ranking diplomat to head the American delegation, he chose a friend and former chief executive of U.S. Steel, Myron C. Taylor, about whom the most Golda could say was that he seemed "a man of good intentions." The president also indicated in his invitation to the nations that none "would be expected or asked to receive a greater number of emigrants than is permitted by its existing legislation," deflat-ing Jewish hopes for an increase in worldwide immigration quotas. Still, expectations for the conference ran high.

Golda attended as an observer for the Histadrut along with several Zionist officials. Shazar came as a reporter for *Davar*. Without a state of their own to represent, the Jews could not receive official invitations. Golda reported to the Histadrut executive afterward that the conference, which began on July 6, had been poorly prepared, with "no order to the day and no program." Lack of organization soon gave way to much greater disappointment as nation after nation explained why it could not offer shelter to the refugees.

Lord Winterton, head of the British delegation, described his country's "overseas territories," without mentioning Palestine, lest he kindle Arab rage. Some of those territories were "already overcrowded," he said, "while in others again local political conditions" hinder immigration. Only after Palestine had been named by others as the most reasonable land of refuge did he mention it directly and then only to assert that "Palestine is not a large country," and while Britain did not plan to discontinue Jewish immigration there altogether, it needed to "subject it to certain restrictions." He did hold out the possibility of settling some refugees in Kenya and other East African territories instead.

Australia announced, "As we have no real racial problem, we are not desirous of importing one." Switzerland railed against the stream of Austrian refugees flowing its way, declaring that it "has as little use for these Jews as has Germany." Canada said it might accept certain classes of agricultural workers. France and Argentina spoke of their pride in having saved lives and could do no more. Peru had a ban on admitting doctors, lawyers, and other intellectuals, and various Central American states declared that they could not accept "traders" either. The United States indicated that for the first time it would accept its full quota of 27,370 refugees a year from Germany and Austria combined, but no more. Only one country, the Dominican Republic, offered to take a large number of refugees—100,000—and give them an agricultural area to cultivate. It was unclear whether the area could really be developed.

After the meetings ended, Golda appeared at a press conference in the hotel's lavish private dining room. She spoke emotionally, her words heavy with sorrow and rage. "Everybody expresses sympathy for us, but the situation is still tragic," she said. "Even if there truly is a desire at this conference to solve the Jewish problem, it stems from a feeling of 'cast them away from before my eyes,'" an allusion to Pharaoh's words to Moses in the Hebrew Bible. "They want to push the Jews into a distant corner," she continued, "so that they won't be an obstacle and won't need to be spoken about any longer. But we in Eretz Israel are creating not a corner for hiding but a homeland."

Alone before a barrage of reporters, seeming to personify the Jewish people alone on the world stage, she spoke of the Zionist dream and so stirred her listeners that afterward they crowded around her with questions about Palestine and Zionism. At some point, she uttered words that have been quoted often: "There is only one thing I hope to see before I die, and that is that my people should not need expressions of sympathy anymore."

She recalled those words much later, after she retired as prime minister. Looking back, she spoke of the Évian conference as a turning point in her life. "I realized then," she told a young journalist, "that a world which is not necessarily anti-Semitic—because Hitler was denounced at the conference and there was considerable pro-Jewish sentiment— could stand by and see others who were weaker victimized . . . We can't depend on any others."

One group at the conference would have cynically agreed with her. Uninvited, they had come from Nazi Germany as observers. When they returned to Berlin, they informed Hitler that he could do whatever he wished with the Jews. No nation would stop him.

10

"And the Heart Breaking"

For some weeks, while Golda was in America on her Nachshon mission, Morris harbored dreams of a full rapprochement between them, a miraculous renewal of the conjugal bonds that long ago had frayed close to the breaking point. His hopes stemmed from an agreement they seemed to have reached after one of her travels. They would "bury the hatchet of past grievances" and try again to live together harmoniously. Morris knew it would be different this time from their early marital years. He spelled out their new relationship in a florid poem qua prayer he wrote to her heralding "this day of days when two souls sprang into refreshed life and out of their dead ashes." Theirs would be "a great adventure," an "edifice dedicated to Eternal Friendship." Now, as he wrote in a follow-up letter, "the days of silence, reserve and aloofness are over and past." Now they were "paving the way for a warm open-hearted comradeship." He would correspond with her regularly, and she could answer him as though she were "dropping in for half an hour's chat with a good old friend." And when she completed her work abroad, she could return home "as the fourth pal of a happy family."

Pals. Old friends. A family unit. That is the relationship they appear to have decided on, a companionable one centered on the children. It was an arrangement that worked well for Golda. With Morris living at home keeping the children's lives running smoothly, he could also keep her informed of their growth and activities. "What will you send your daughter for her birthday?" he asked in one of his letters. (Golda, away, consistently missed the children's birthdays.) He suggested "a very fine edition of 'Les Miserables,' abridged for children, with beautiful illustrations." In another letter, he described the children's busy day, attending school and still managing to practice their musical instruments before supper—Sarah the violin and Menahem the cello. "Lovely, wonderfully lovely children, is all I can say," he wrote, allowing her to feel part of the family and proud of it.

Morris fully accepted the arrangement they had worked out. "Let's lose our egos for the welfare of these children born of our former love," he wrote to her, "and a newer, more enduring love may be the gain." He believed in what he said and planned to abide by it. Yet he couldn't. He could not rein in that "former love" he still felt for Golda despite all that had been between them. For weeks, throughout April 1937, along with family stories, he poured out his heart in letters that brimmed with adulation and longing, unabashed sentimentality, and a large dose of self-pity. He wrote in English, the language they spoke to each other. "My dear Goldele," he began some letters. Or "Goldele mine," or "Goldele dearest," or "Goldele my beloved."

In a long letter penned on April 1, during the Passover festival, he plied her with questions about people she'd seen and work she had done. She probably wouldn't answer "such trivialities," he acknowledged, yet "I do want to know everything about you—from the kind of dress you wore on a certain occasion to the triumphs and obstacles met with in your work, and to the more subtle moods of your inner . . . emotional self." For, he assured her, "everything that is connected with your dear self is of vital interest to me."

He continued his letter the next day, "the last day of Pesach," beginning with a homey description of everyone sleeping late on the holiday, including "Leake" (Leah Biskin, who lived with them then). They planned to have dinner at the home of Golda's longtime friend from Chicago Raizel (who remarried a Hebrew scholar after her husband, Ben Shapiro, died) and the next day at Sheyna's. They themselves had few visitors. "The attraction of the house being gone why should anyone want to come?" he asked. "I do not seem to matter to anyone in the whole wide world. Do I mind? Hardly. I am already inured to loneliness . . . With you my life is full and needs no one else; without you, all is emptiness and nothing can matter."

He ended plaintively: "Do you ever think of me these days, Goldele, and how, and in what light?" He signed, "Forever yours, Goldele of my heart, with treasure hoards of love."

The letters grew more heated and needy as the days progressed. "The whole complex of my being is as ever continuously athrill under the sway and charm of your glorious femininity, that has been holding me captive for near a quarter of a century," he wrote on April 4, while apologizing for having skipped a day of communicating with her. His teeth were aching; he had a burning pain in his right lung and a nagging cough. "Add to that an emotional state that nearly amounts to a good old-fashioned nervous break-down, and you'll have a flashlight portrait of your poor, old, bald-headed Morris, in his forty-fourth year—a lump of nerves smarting from the arrow-stings of past afflictions, and with nothing but brooding fear, doubt, and uncertainty for the future." The cure for all that ailed him, however, was simple. "O Goldie, my own, how I need your bodily presence in these moments of dejection! . . . [A] look of yours could still the thumping heart; the music of your voice would calm the feverish brain."

On April 5, he was looking forward to the next day's mail and a letter from Golda, from whom he had not yet heard. In the meantime, he wanted her to "be happy in the knowledge that I love you with a love unending." By April 7, he still had no word from her, but he knew the "cherished letter" would come soon. He signed off as "your passionately lovelorn Morris."

Two weeks later, the long-anticipated letter from America arrived. In it, Golda informed Morris coolly and briefly that she could not in any way reciprocate the feelings he had expressed. Pretending even to approach the level of intimacy he desired would be "untruthful" for her. That was not what she had in mind when they agreed to attempt a new beginning. Morris was shattered. "I no longer know what I am to you," he wrote to her on April 15. "That is, I do know, that I mean as little to you as heretofore—except, that you are prepared not to scowl at me so . . . And I've fed my soul with sweet delusions, not reckoning the impregnable wall that I was up against. It seems that it will not be my lot ever to break that wall." Even so, he looked for some crack in the barrier she had set up. "Shall I still express a hope for better moments, or is all futility and frustration?" he asked, pathetically, willing to accept the slightest crumb of affection Golda might toss his way. With little expectation, however, he ended, "And shall I without any words of endearment sign, as you do, just—your Morris?"

Golda's coldness and Morris's gloom would seem to have signaled the end of their tortured marriage. Surprisingly, it did not. Rumor had it that at one point Morris had left for good, but the children were so distressed that Golda had to ask him back. That may be why when she returned briefly to Tel Aviv in the summer of 1938, after the Évian conference, their relationship again improved. In the fall, she was writing to him from London with open despair about the world situation. She had gone to England with Remez on Nachshon business and planned to continue on to Warsaw and Paris. Having received nothing but a brief telegram from Morris and the children since arriving in London, she was "very worried" about all of them. True, she said, she had written only once from England herself, but her time had been taken up with constant meetings "and the heart breaking with all that is happening" in the countries of Europe. Among the most heartbreaking happenings at the moment was the horrendous treatment of Jews in Germany. "When one hears the stories from Germany from people who have just come from there," she told Morris, "one feels he has no right to live at all."

Many of the stories she would have heard now concerned Kristallnacht, the Night of Broken Glass, on November 9 and 10, 1938, when Nazi mobs throughout Germany and Austria smashed the windows of thousands of Jewish shops and homes, murdered almost a hundred Jews, and set fire to some two hundred synagogues. At the same time, thousands of Jewish men were arrested and sent to concentration camps, where many were beaten and tortured before being forced to buy their way out and leave the country. Some historians view the attacks as a direct consequence of the failure of the Évian conference. Joseph Burg, then a young member of the National Religious Party, in Berlin at the time, later noted in his autobiography that Remez and Golda happened to be there that night, on their way from a Zionist Executive meeting in London. No evidence other than Burg's report places Golda at the Kristallnacht scene, but Remez was there (and because of him Burg might have assumed Golda's presence). In a letter to his wife, Remez described the Berlin rampage as the first pogrom he had ever seen, too painful to write about. "Tens of Hitler youth chased after one Jew, who kept running and falling," and this while crowds of people looked on.

What he portrayed to his wife, he also conveyed to Golda, who found the actions he and others described almost "impossible to imagine." They lived in a "barbarous world," she wrote to Morris. "As one walks in the street all you see are newspaper posters about Jews in Germany," with each story worse than the one before. "I want to be with you and the children now," she wrote, the misery around her making her long for the security of home and family. She signed her letter, "Love—your Goldie."

A few days later, having finally heard from Morris, she replied with an affectionate, newsy letter. She expressed sympathy for his various physical ailments, writing—without a hint of irony, considering her own packed schedule—that he was "run down" and "will have to take a vacation and have a good rest." She was "so happy" also to receive a letter from the children. "Morris dear," she wrote, sounding like any concerned wife and mother, "please see that Menachem's [sic] teeth are taken care of, also see about his Hebrew lessons. We must help him get thru this year. It will be terrible for him if he doesn't make it." Never as good a student as his sister, Menahem had been struggling with his Hebrew studies. Golda had even asked Yossel's son Elisha to help him with his schoolwork.

Through much of the letter, Golda's thoughts dwelled on the pressing problems of the Jews and England's steady retreat from the Balfour Declaration. The children "don't know how happy they should be that they are still young and do not fully grasp how miserable and cruel this world is," she wrote. She had attended a session of Parliament on November 24 and "could not control my tears when I heard the cynical talk of our 'friend' MacDonald"—Malcolm MacDonald, the British colonial secretary. "What is going to become of us?" she went on. "The press here, too, is against us. There is no doubt that it is all inspired by the Government. They are ready to sell us out as they have the Chechs [sic]," an allusion to Prime Minister Neville Chamberlain's appeasement of Hitler in the Munich Agreement, forcing Czechoslovakia to cede its industrially rich Sudetenland to Germany.

Then a stunning question: "What do you think about our taking a German child? Reports we get here from there are enough to drive one mad." After Kristallnacht, the Jewish Agency had asked the British government to allow ten thousand German and Austrian Jewish children to enter Palestine. Although the British had not yet agreed to the request, as she told the children in a separate letter, she wanted to pursue the idea. "I would like you to consult with Father about our taking one of these children," she wrote to them. "I think we have an obligation to do that. Decide if you want a boy or girl and of what age. It seems to me that it would have to be someone in your age group." It was a bewildering thought coming as it did from a woman who rarely spent time at home with her own children and whose marriage was an on-again, off-again matter.

Yet the very fact that Golda would think about taking in a child suggested that in spite of every setback she still regarded the marriage as intact. Decisive in so many areas, she had been incapable of making a clean break with Morris. She might have felt guilty about his life in Palestine, as Marie Syrkin observed years earlier. Or, for all her attachments to other men, she might have had a residue of feeling for the first man she had loved. (She would keep his love letters all her life, and his photograph the only one near her bed.) On the most fundamental level, Morris's presence had made possible the life she led, with its long absences from home.

The marriage was to last just a short while longer. The plan to house a German Jewish child never materialized: the British turned down the request to allow a contingent of German Jewish children into Palestine. In August 1939, when Golda traveled to Geneva, Morris went to America for several months, his first trip back since leaving the States. "Picture my reunion with Grandmother, after eighteen years," he wrote to the children. "She had given up hope of ever seeing her only son again." Eighty years old and almost totally blind, she was to have a cataract operation (a complicated procedure at the time), one of his reasons for returning. Described by a family member as "hunched over, brooding," Morris spent most of his time in Philadelphia with his sister Rae and her husband, Lou Broudo. In his letters, he asked the children to keep him informed about Golda. Contacts between the two had become limited.

When the final break came, probably in 1940, with Golda aged forty-two and Morris forty-seven, he moved out of the family's apartment into a rented one-room flat, where the children visited him regularly. The separation made sense now for Golda. Living at home, not traveling during the war years, and with the children in their teens, she had less need for Morris to maintain their family life. For his part, Morris might have decided at last that he could not break through the "impregnable wall" that was Golda and he wanted out. Still, they were never divorced, remaining permanently separated. According to some observers, Morris refused to give Golda a divorce, out of "spite." Golda, on the other hand, always insisted that she had no interest in a divorce or remarriage. The "idea never entered my head," she told a journalist. However honest that statement, she might have found that being "Mrs. Meyerson," or "Mrs. Meir," served as a protective coat of armor, freeing her from the stigma of divorce while allowing her to live as she wished without having to relinquish her independence.

The children were distraught when told of the separation. Sarah withdrew into herself, but Menahem reacted with rage, blaming Golda for the failure of the marriage. He pulled away from friends, did poorly in school, and then dropped out altogether, also quitting the Labor Zionist youth group to which he belonged, a special punishment for his mother. He spent many hours practicing his cello, drawing close to his father, the music lover. Eventually, he would become a professional cellist. Sarah also left her studies after a few years, before completing high school, and together with her Labor Zionist youth group prepared to enter a kibbutz.

Some time after the split, Morris was sent by the Solel Boneh to work on construction projects in Iran and other Middle Eastern sites. From Abadan, he wrote in Hebrew to Menahem of his "troubled existence" and of a "life utterly unhinged and frustrated," which had been his "lot now for oh so many ages." From Bahrain, he complained of the winter's icy winds that "become unbearable" especially in the small huts where he and other workers lived. Unhappy as he was, he managed to compile a detailed list of classical records by Beethoven, Chopin, Mozart, and others that he bought at a fraction of the price they would have cost at home, proud of Menahem's musical career and firmly connected to it. He continued to take great pride and interest in both his children, and once back in Tel Aviv he never again left the Land of Israel, not wanting to be far from them.

When Golda wrote to Morris from London that the children were too young to grasp the world's cruelties, she might have intended to say little in her letters to them about the situation of the Jews in Europe. But anguished over reports constantly flowing out of Germany and other lands, she could think of almost nothing else. "One can go crazy" with the news, she wrote to them shortly after Kristallnacht. "They have taken everything from the Jews," leaving them with nothing, no means of subsistence. She'd heard that Chaim Weizmann was running around the offices of the British government, "from one minister to the next, pleading with them to do something, with no success. Each one says that it is truly terrible, but he can do nothing." And at this very moment, she lamented, the British government wanted to further reduce Jewish immigration to Palestine. At a recent meeting of the Histadrut executive, she and the others concluded that "the whole world has abandoned us, and we can rely only on ourselves." She had felt that way after the Évian conference, and in the months and years ahead she was to repeat those words often—"we can rely only on ourselves"—until they became almost like a mantra, her response to one crisis after another.

Every day the forces of darkness gained ground. While Hitler tightened the noose around the necks of German and Austrian Jews, he also forcibly had Jews in Germany who were Polish nationals deported to Poland, no matter how many years they had lived in Germany. The Polish government, no friend of the Jews, refused to accept these people, and for months they lived in makeshift shelters in the no-man's-land of a German-Polish border town called Zbąszyń, penniless, hungry and freezing, ignored by the government, and helped only by Poland's Jewish community. "I was in London then," Prime Minister Golda Meir was to tell a reunion of Israelis from Pinsk, her childhood home, more than thirty years later. "I decided in my heart that I would not return home without seeing these Jews." She went with Remez from London to Poland and witnessed the condition of the refugees. "That night," she would tell the Pinsk gathering, "I determined that no matter what, I would do everything to make sure Jews would never again have to live under foreign powers and suffer."

Golda and Remez also went to Warsaw, where they met with members of Hechalutz, a Zionist training camp. Golda wanted very much to visit Pinsk, but she fell ill and had to spend two weeks in Lodz recuperating, after which her Polish visa expired and the Polish government would not renew it. She little suspected that she had lost her last opportunity to see Pinsk or her relatives there again. Only one distant family member, a grandson of her grandmother's sister, would survive the Shoah.

When she returned to Palestine in February 1939, the second, more intense phase of the Arab rebellion was winding down. After the Arabs attacked the British along with the Jews in late 1937, the British began using the full power of His Majesty's military to subdue the attackers, ruthlessly, when deemed necessary. Among other things, British forces destroyed rebel homes, bombed entire villages, and executed terrorists. They also worked closely with Jewish defense units, including the special Jewish Settlement Police force (*Notrim* in Hebrew), which patrolled the roads and protected settlements. Although the British knew that many of the Jewish forces belonged to the Haganah, the Yishuv's underground army, they preferred to ignore that fact because they needed the help.

Soon after the second round of Arab terror began, the British outlawed the Arab Higher Committee and deported five of its members. The sixth, the mufti, Haj Amin al-Husseini, who had instigated much of the rioting, escaped to Lebanon (disguised as a Bedouin or, some said, a woman), where he continued to consolidate his power. Meanwhile, vicious infighting among key Arab families and political parties caused havoc among the Palestinian Arabs, further aiding the British in suppressing the revolt.

There was a paradox in the British behavior. Militarily their soldiers crushed the Arab rebels with a powerful show of force, while politically the government leaned ever closer toward the Arabs and away from the Jews. The contradiction was not accidental. The British wanted to operate from a position of strength even when appeasing the Arabs, with an eye toward maintaining their authority in Palestine and the colonies. They also wanted to end the revolt quickly so that they could then placate the Arabs with political concessions that might prevent future uprisings.

Toward the Jews, British leaders held ambivalent views. After the appearance of the Peel report, while Golda and the others debated the pros and cons of partition, the government had its own internal disagreements. The Foreign Office, always partial to the Arabs, opposed the concept of a Jewish state, even truncated as it would be under the Peel plan. The Colonial Office, especially when Sir William Ormsby-Gore headed it, showed more sympathy for Zionist goals and the idea of an independent state. Bitter fighting between the two departments left the Zionists confused about their standing and future government policies. Confusion turned to discouragement when Malcolm MacDonald replaced Ormsby-Gore as colonial secretary in May 1938. MacDonald, who had previously seemed devoted to the promises of the Balfour Declaration—and whose father, Ramsay MacDonald, had been a Zionist supporter—adopted many of the pro-Arab views of the Foreign Office. When the British government sent another commission—the Woodhead Commission—to reexamine the Peel recommendations, the Zionist leaders rightly sensed that their plans to negotiate with the British about partition would disappear along with any government thoughts about dividing the land between Arabs and Jews.

"If we must offend one side," Prime Minister Chamberlain said in April 1939, "let us offend the Jews rather than the Arabs." Ben-Gurion fathomed his reasoning. As he wrote to his wife, Paula, "Even if Britain makes trouble for us in Palestine, it is inconceivable that the Jews will be on Hitler's side. Not so the Arabs. They have to be bought off." The British hoped to buy them off with the White Paper on Palestine they issued on May 17, a document the Jews in the Yishuv and elsewhere regarded as one of the blackest in modern history. It limited Jewish immigrants to just seventy-five thousand over the next five years, after which the Arabs would have to give their permission for any further immigration. It forbade Jews to buy any Arab lands in some areas and severely restricted them in others, and it proposed that an independent Palestinian state come into being within ten years. The Jews would be a minority in that state.

Even though Golda and other Zionist leaders had been aware beforehand of the direction the White Paper would take, the document in its entirety dropped like a bombshell on them. The British appeared to have rewarded the Arabs for their violence after all. Moreover, they had broken faith with the Balfour Declaration with its promise of a Jewish national home in Palestine, violating the mandate they had received from the League of Nations. All this at a time when Jews were desperately trying to flee the expanding Nazi brutality in Europe.

Golda had written to Morris months earlier of her worry that the British government would sell out the Jews in Palestine to the Arabs, as it had sold out Czechoslovakia to the Germans. She was to use that analogy many times in the future as Israel confronted one large power after another. She was not alone in making the comparison now; many Jews expressed the same sense of betrayal. In Great Britain itself, Winston Churchill, a dissident in his own Conservative Party, railed at his party's prime minister, Neville Chamberlain, "What will our potential enemies think?" He answered himself, "This is another Munich."

About two weeks before the White Paper was published, Golda stayed up almost all night to write a long article for *Dvar Hapoelet*, the periodical of the Women Workers' Council. Her feelings in turmoil with the dreadful news pouring in daily from Europe, she wrote with passion of "Jewish children scattered everywhere in the world" and "Jewish mothers in many countries . . . asking for one thing only: take our children away, take them to any place you wish, only save them from this hell!" But she also wrote of the one place she believed where, no matter what, children could be safe. If "we rescue them from the hell of the Diaspora and bring them here, to this country—even today, with the situation in the country what it is, with the shooting and explosion and all the political difficulties. Here our children will be safe. Here they'll be safe for their mothers and here they'll be safe for the Jewish people."

During these years, while curbing immigration into Palestine, the British had organized a unique rescue operation that carried youngsters by trains and boats from Germany, Austria, Czechoslovakia, and Poland to foster homes in England. About ten thousand children were saved through these *Kindertransports*, as they were called—the same number the British had refused to allow into Palestine earlier under a special program. Grateful as she might have been for the humanitarian British action, Golda did not regard it as a real solution. "Children who are crossing today or crossed a year ago from Germany to Austria and from Austria to Czechoslovakia and from Czechoslovakia to England—who can be sure and who can assure . . . mothers that by getting their children out of one hell they have not got them into another," she wrote prophetically.

The only hope for Europe's Jews lay in Palestine, with the workers of the Yishuv, Golda emphasized, and therefore they had to fight a war, their own type of war, against British restrictions: "Only one thing is absolutely certain . . . our war in this country, our Zionist war, must be different from the war of every other nation. Any other nation entering a war doesn't dream and can't imagine that in the war period itself it will have to build, to construct, to develop. We cannot afford to wage war without constructing . . . Indeed the whole meaning of our war is construction, carrying on, extending, expanding."

And with that effort, they would win, she assured readers. "It is inconceivable that we shall not succeed in our work here, in our defense of every single settlement, even the smallest, if we have before us the image of thousands of Jews in the various concentration camps in the various countries. Therein lies our strength."

When Golda composed those words, Hitler's "Final Solution" was almost two years away. But if no one could yet conceive of the depths of what the Nazis had in store for the Jews, Golda and the other Zionist leaders knew enough about persecutions and concentration camps and savageries against the Jewish people to resist the British White Paper as forcefully as they could, short of using actual force. They held strikes, signed petitions, drew up manifestos, and marched in protest, Golda often leading the way, her face grim and determined. In one mass demonstration in Jerusalem, the police tried to intervene, and in the ensuing melee dozens of demonstrators were injured and a British officer lay dead. Still, the protests continued. New settlements sprang up under cover of darkness, with the hastily erected "stockades and watchtowers" (a fence on the outside and a guard tower within) that became symbols of their rapid growth. "We will build and go on building!" Golda promised in her *Dvar Hapoelet* article. For the Zionists, new settlements served as the ammunition for their war.

Clandestine immigration was its hallmark. The Zionists called it Aliyah Bet, Immigration B, a "parallel" form of admitting refugees to Palestine to evade immigration quotas. The British called it illegal immigration. Either way, Golda was in the thick of it.

On the dark, moonless night of August 15 to 16, 1939, Shaul Avigur and a co-worker slipped into Golda's apartment on Hayarkon Street.

The rugged, taciturn Avigur, already known for his courage, headed the Mossad l'Aliyah Bet, the organization that ran the immigrant operation. Involved in every detail of the work, he had decided on this night to monitor the landing of the illegal ship *Dora* from the shortwave radio center in the Meyerson apartment. The *Dora*, previously a cattle boat, had picked up three hundred immigrants in Amsterdam and crammed in almost two hundred more in Antwerp, the only refugee ship to make its way to Palestine from Holland and Belgium before World War II. It had been a rough two-week journey for the rickety boat and its passengers. They hit a fierce storm as they reached the Bay of Biscay but managed to push on through the Strait of Gibraltar, turn east, and pull in at the coast of the kibbutz Shefayim, north of Tel Aviv.

When the vessel reached its destination, the commander on the ground, David Nameri, signaled its arrival. The signals were relayed to the wireless in the Meyerson apartment, where Avigur could receive and send coded messages to the boat. In one heart-stopping moment for everyone in the flat, a British police boat with searchlights ablaze almost spotted the immigrant ship as it neared the coast, but the ship stayed hidden in the blackness of the night. When all seemed safe, it dropped off its passengers, who silently made their way on foot to Kfar Shmaryahu, a nearby agricultural village. The captain lifted anchor and sailed westward into the dark, to begin another mission. "In the early morning hours," Avigur reported years later, "we said good night to our hosts, Golda Meir and Leah Biskin, and went about our business."

Golda was glad to be part of the operation and not simply on the sidelines receiving reports. Some years later, at the end of the war, when the immigration battle had accelerated, the British broke the code used in communications to and from the illegal ships. The switch to a new code was quickly made and word of the change sent to the central transmitting station in Tel Aviv. "Within an hour," wrote Ehud Avriel, a major figure in the Aliyah Bet operation, "radio-operators of our far-flung network, from Stockholm to New York, from the high seas to the Tel Aviv flat of Golda Meir, all switched over to the new code." She had remained engaged in smuggling refugees into Palestine throughout the war years and beyond them.

The Mossad l'Aliyah Bet, an arm of the Haganah, began its secret refugee operation in the spring of 1939. (Later the organization evolved into the Mossad, Israel's intelligence agency.) Even before that, illegal ships were making their hazardous way to Palestine's shores, a few sponsored by private entrepreneurs, who often took advantage of the predicament of the refugees, more launched by Jabotinsky's Revisionists. And therein lies some background.

After the talks between Ben-Gurion and Jabotinsky failed, the divide between the Labor Zionists and the Revisionists became unbridgeable. In September 1935, at a worldwide convention in Vienna, the Revisionists formed the New Zionist Organization. From then on, they regarded themselves as freed from the authority of mainstream Zionist groups or the policies of the Jewish Agency and its chairman, Ben-Gurion. Eventually, a right-wing breakaway unit from the Haganah called the Irgun Z'vai Leumi (National Military Organization) developed into the Revisionists' defense organization. During the Arab revolt, that group, known in English as the Irgun or IZL and in Hebrew as Etzel, refused to abide by the policy of restraint, *havlagah*, that Zionist leaders had adopted. Fighting Arab terror with terror of their own, Irgun members detonated bombs in crowded Arab bus stations and marketplaces and randomly killed Arab men, women, and children in retaliation for Arab murders of Jews. With the renewal of the Arab rebellion, the Haganah fought more aggressively than it had before, but it never resorted to the extremism of the Irgun.

Golda despised that extremism. "The notion of attacking Arabs indiscriminately, regardless of whether or not they were the particular perpetrators of an outrage, was morally abhorrent to me," she was to say. In 1939, she signed a declaration against terror issued by leading voices in the Yishuv. "Do Not Murder," its headline announced. Addressed "to the Yishuv and to the Youth," it acknowledged the pain the recently issued White Paper had caused but urged—as Golda had urged in her article—that the Jews focus their energies on building the land. "Do not murder—this commandment from the infancy of an ancient people . . . still applies today," the declaration stated. It called for unity of the Yishuv in defending the national home from "terror within as from its enemies without." Henrietta Szold signed the declaration, as did Berl Katznelson and the writer S. Y. Agnon. Golda's name appears beneath theirs, along with many others, including the philosopher Martin Buber and the scholar Gershom Scholem.

But if the Revisionist terror aroused Jewish disgust, the Revisionist role in the illegal immigration saga became a model for others. It was the Revisionists who organized some of the earliest clandestine boatloads of immigrants to Palestine. At first, Ben-Gurion and other Zionist leaders opposed the smuggling operations. During the many months of British deliberations about dividing Palestine into Jewish and Arab states, the Zionist leaders wanted to avoid clashes with the mandatory government. If there were to be a Jewish state, they needed to cooperate with Great Britain. The Revisionists, who adamantly refused to give any part of the land to the Arabs, had no such compunctions. The Zionist leaders' reservations fell by the wayside when the White Paper effectively ended the hope for a Jewish state and slammed shut the gates of Palestine.

The Haganah now undertook the course the Revisionists had set of smuggling in as many refugees as it could. The operations for both groups involved grave dangers, cunning intrigue, and the participation of people the British would not suspect of being involved—like Golda Meyerson, the Histadrut executive who spoke fluent English and often met with them on Yishuv matters. Each voyage called for raising money to procure ships—and even then most were dilapidated and barely seaworthy—gathering passengers from different lands and locations to designated embarkation points, and sneaking through the waters out of sight and range of British patrols. When the British captured a ship, they sometimes forced it to turn back; more often during these prewar years, they allowed the refugees to stay in Palestine but deducted their numbers from the quota of legal immigrant certificates issued.

Regardless of risks, the odysseys continued. Some tens of thousands of *maapilim*, another term for the unauthorized immigrants, made it to Palestine between 1937 and 1939, arriving on either Haganah or Revisionist ships.

THE TWENTY-FIRST ZIONIST CONGRESS that met in Geneva, Switzerland, on August 16–25, 1939, had an air of grim determination. To the Zionist delegates who gathered for plenary sessions at the city's imposing Opera House, the future appeared bleak as the shadow of war closed in on them. Some dubbed the popular Café Lyric, where they met for coffee and conversation, "Café Panic." On a picture postcard showing the League of Nations, Golda wrote to Sarah that the Swiss people "are so very quiet. They don't have the worries we do. If only the League of Nations were a living body, our situation would also be much better."

Early in the conference, Nahum Goldmann, a world Zionist leader with whom Golda would later have many dealings, summed up the dire condition of Europe's Jews, which the League of Nations had done little to alleviate: "Thousands of Jews are wandering about like hunted animals to the no-man's-lands between borders . . . Hundreds of thousands of Jews are sentenced to jail, tortured and murdered in concentration camps, subject to illnesses and unimaginable pressures and troubles . . . for no wrongdoing other than their one and only crime—the crime of belonging to the most ancient roots of human civilization."

In keeping with that reality, much of the convention discussions centered on the British White Paper of May 17. "A Rabbi from America spoke yesterday against 'illegal' immigration," Golda wrote to the children, "and Berl Katznelson replied in a wonderful and great speech."

The "Rabbi from America" was Abba Hillel Silver, a Reform rabbi from Cleveland, Ohio, who was fast becoming one of the most important leaders of American Zionism. Golda would clash with him at a later time but also come to respect him. Tall, aristocratic in demeanor, confident of his position, and powerful in his oratory, Silver warned that the Yishuv was not strong enough to confront the mandatory government with illegal acts. Earlier Ben-Gurion had declared that Jews "must conduct ourselves as though we were the state in Palestine, and we must carry this through in order that we become the state in Palestine," a declaration to which Golda thoroughly subscribed. Silver responded that in their current situation, without a state, Jews would do best to cooperate with Britain and have faith that the White Paper would prove only temporary. Katznelson, short and stocky, lacking Silver's presence or rhetorical skills and gulping water throughout his hour-long presentation, nonetheless electrified the audience. He portrayed the refugees as standing at the forefront of the Zionist fight and prodding the conscience of the world. Why was it legitimate for governments to violate their promises, he asked angrily, while the lifesaving immigration of Jews is considered "illegal"? He received a standing ovation.

"The entire Congress felt that, at this terrible hour, it is good that there is someone who can present our case so well," Golda wrote to the children.

In quieter moments, Golda went about her routine Labor Zionist activities, meeting especially with delegates from European youth organizations. In a separate session that lasted into the early morning hours, she and the other Palestinian labor delegates met with Histadrut emissaries working in Poland, Galicia, Germany, Austria, Czechoslovakia, and other European countries. They had to decide whether the emissaries should go back to those countries in these dangerous times or return home to Palestine. The emissaries themselves insisted that they must continue their assignments in spite of dangers, and after the congress they went back to their posts. Three months later, most would leave those posts and return to Palestine.

When the discussion turned to America, Golda urged the labor leaders to "prepare both for the possibility of war and the possibility of peace," but either way they needed to continue the Geverkshaften campaign to raise money in America for the Yishuv. She suggested that with good planning they could get many young American volunteers to come to Palestine for Aliyah Bet and other activities. Moreover, "it is necessary to find an American comrade who will go on a mission to Germany," she said. The suggestions were naive and unrealistic, based in part on America's neutrality at this point in Europe's conflict but also on the desperate need for help in the immigration struggle as one country after another fell into Nazi hands. No other country but the United States could be counted on to supply manpower, Remez added.

Given a choice by Remez of whether to go to the States again as an emissary, Golda chose to return home. She was to remain in Palestine for the next six years, her longest stay there throughout her life without traveling abroad. She had been scheduled to fly back by plane with four other Histadrut leaders, including Remez and Katznelson, but as war fever mounted and the situation became chaotic, she and the others left by ship from Marseilles.

A few days earlier, on August 23, while the congress was still in session, it received news of the nonaggression pact the Soviet Union and Germany had signed. The alliance between these two powerful countries made war almost palpable, with Eastern Europe more vulnerable than ever and France, Great Britain, and other central and western countries in immediate danger. Golda said good-bye to her European colleagues not knowing whether she would see any of them again yet planning with them to maintain contact. In an emotional farewell, Chaim Weizmann could only pray that they would "all meet again alive" to continue their work, he said, and "who knows, perhaps from out of the darkness a new light will shine on us." When he ended his talk with the words "Au revoir in peace," the hall erupted in sustained applause. He embraced Ben-Gurion and other colleagues before walking slowly from the platform, while people wept and hundreds of hands reached out to him.

Golda was not yet home when Germany invaded Poland on September 1, 1939, unleashing the bloodiest conflict in history, World War II.

11

Life and Death

By the time Golda reached home, England and France had declared war on Germany. In mandatory Palestine, people were starving. With borders closed because of the war, few imports or exports could enter or leave the country, and with British restrictions on immigration the stream of money and people to create work dried up. Unemployment soared, reaching as many as fifty thousand in the Jewish community—out of a population of a little more than half a million—and people with jobs lived in constant fear of losing them. In meeting after agonizing meeting, the Histadrut executive committee thrashed about for solutions to the emergency.

Golda argued for a dream she'd held for decades: a commune-like arrangement for city families comparable to that in the kibbutzim. Histadrut members (which included the majority of working people), she suggested, "should give up having kitchens in their own homes," and instead adults should share common kitchens while the children would "all eat at school, and whoever couldn't pay for it wouldn't have to pay, and whoever could only pay less than the full price would pay less." With this scheme, "we should all be equal as regards the food we eat."

This was Golda's persistent—and hopelessly utopian—vision of how a socialist society should be conducted. It fit well with her long-standing attachment to the family wage system, in which no matter what type of work Histadrut members did, they were paid according to their needs and the numbers of dependents in their families. On that one, she went to battle with the nurses in the Kupat Holim, the Histadrut hospital, and lost. They insisted on being paid as professionals based on their training and experience, not on a family scale, and the Histadrut finally gave in to them. Golda disapproved (turning many nurses into enemies) and stubbornly clung to her belief in the family wage long after it had proved unworkable. Likewise, she pressed hard for the communal kitchen, which her colleagues rejected as impractical.

More realistically, while Golda was away, the Histadrut had instituted an emergency tax, called a *mifdeh*, or redemption payment, that required every employed worker to donate one day's pay a month to an unemployment fund in addition to their dues and other payments. The first time the *mifdeh* was levied, the workers contributed to it willingly; some even helped to collect it. A second *mifdeh* also worked fairly smoothly, but as unemployment rose and people with jobs struggled to feed their families in the depressed economy, many bridled at paying a third emergency tax. Golda understood that she would have to involve herself personally in this collection and impose still another, a fourth taxation, on an even larger scale.

They were a hard sell, these last two taxes. To make their case, the Histadrut executives met with an influential group of workers' representatives. Angry complaints reverberated from one end of the room to the next. It was unfair to burden working people any further, participants argued. If the situation were reversed, would the others take on the same degree of responsibility? Pushed too hard, everyone predicted, workers might simply leave the Histadrut altogether. Unfazed, Golda lit back with—what was fast becoming—her trademark blend of idealism, emotion, and not a little guilt provocation.

"Generally, I'm not a coward," she said, "but when I meet an unemployed worker and hear his complaints and accusations . . . I have nothing to say to him . . . I have a right to work, I have a right to my salary, I also have my own troubles. But an unemployed person has the same rights as I . . . He has been in the land as many years; he has the same children and the same privilege. For some reason Fate has decreed that I should have food while he shouldn't." Fate had also allowed her listeners to keep their jobs while their comrades had not, her words implied. As for the person who might threaten to abandon the Histadrut because of these taxes, she had only disdain. "What will he gain by leaving the Histadrut? Do you think the Histadrut is not strong enough to evict someone who is able to think in such terms?" she warned.

At other meetings, she squelched any thoughts of a bailout from American Jews. "We shall not go to the Jews of the Diaspora to seek relief," she declared. "Our topic of discussion with them cannot be the matter of unemployment, the matter of hunger." Instead, "we must be able to proclaim the nature of their special mission: to aid in the building of the country rather than in sending doles to the poor."

The rhetoric was fine, but it didn't feed the hungry, and the Histadrut leaders soon came under attack from other quarters. A group of professional union chiefs in Tel Aviv, all members of the Mapai Party, escalated criticisms they had been making for some years of the Tel Aviv branch of their party and of the local Histadrut-run labor council. (With Mapai the dominant party in the Histadrut, party members headed most of the Histadrut's various institutions.) Known as Faction B, these union leaders might have remained just a rebellious minority in Mapai had they not received support from a prestigious movement in the party that represented most of the kibbutzim in the country. It was called Hakibbutz Hameuhad, the United Kibbutz.

Headed by Yitzhak Tabenkin, Hakibbutz Hameuhad gained much of its power from its authenticity. Here were the pioneers, the *halutzim*, who had come to Palestine to transform the land and had remained on the soil, living communal lives in kibbutzim that others like Ben-Gurion, Berl Katznelson, and Golda herself had given up as they immersed themselves in politics and public works. When Hakibbutz Hameuhad, then, allied itself with the Tel Aviv trade unionists—the whole now called Faction B—in attacking Mapai and the Histadrut, the leaders of those organizations had to take serious notice.

The criticism: The Histadrut and Mapai Party chiefs had strayed far from the socialist roots of the country. They lived in towns, they worked as professional politicians, and they had lost touch with ordinary people's struggles. Worse, in this time of severe crisis they had failed to allay the misery of the unemployed. Faction B called for more militant action, strikes, and, if necessary, violence against employers and the wealthy. Although it offered few practical programs, it won over many young people in its noisy opposition to established leaders.

"Fifty or sixty men came to the executive committee . . . and demanded to see the secretary [Remez]," Golda Meyerson reported at a party meeting about an incident at the Histadrut in late September 1939. When they were told they would have to wait for half an hour, "they burst" into Remez's office with demands. These men, led by the discontented union leaders of Tel Aviv, insisted that food be distributed immediately to the starving workers and their families and shelter provided for those who could not pay their rent. A short time later, the union leaders sent a letter to the Histadrut executive committee with an ultimatum: they would resign from their positions—leaving behind chaos from the angry unemployed—if they did not receive a positive response within a week.

Golda was enraged. "Do we have one party or several parties?" she barked at them. The Tel Aviv rebels, Mapai members themselves, had attacked the Histadrut and Mapai as though they had no stake in either institution. And did they really think, as their actions implied, that the Histadrut leaders didn't care about the unemployment crisis or could solve the problem if they truly wanted to? To add to her ire, when the Mapai central committee discussed the union leaders' conduct at their meeting, several members present did not wholeheartedly condemn it. The men should not have invaded Remez's office, they conceded, but—a significant "but"—they had good reasons to lash out at the party and the Histadrut. Nothing said at the meeting cast the slightest blame on Golda; her name did not even come up. Nevertheless, with her hand in every major social service institution in the Histadrut, she chose to interpret the lukewarm condemnation of the union chiefs as reflecting a lack of confidence in her.

So she quit. On November 1, she announced her resignation as a representative of the Mapai central committee to the Histadrut executive, declaring that she had concluded after the last meeting of the central committee that she "could not continue." It was a brilliant maneuver. In that one act, she shifted the conversation from conflicts in the party to Golda Meyerson and the party's need for her. To be sure, resigning in protest was not a unique practice. As the historian Tuvia Friling put it, "Ben-Gurion resigned 140 times; 139 of those resignations were rejected," and only one, the final one, accepted. Golda would also resign many times as a ploy to get her way, but this resignation, one of her earliest, pushed her front and center in the dispute and the party.

For the next three weeks, the agendas of party meetings list "the resignation of comrade Golda Meyerson" as a principal item for discussion. Most of the discussions came in the form of requests for Golda to change her mind and her responses about why she could not. To perform her work effectively, she avowed, she needed to know that she had the full support of her colleagues. "There may be people who can work in the absence of such feeling," she explained, coating her steely determination with self-effacement, another trademark technique, "but . . . I don't have that kind of self-confidence." The determination won, as it always would. On December 6, the central committee resolved unanimously "to request that Golda Meyerson take back her resignation." She "reluctantly" agreed to do so.

She had forced the issue and gained the backing she wanted. Now she plunged into the fourth *mifdeh* campaign, more secure and confident of her pivotal position in the party. She needed all the confidence she could muster for that struggle with antagonistic workers who felt they'd been taxed more than they could bear. At a meeting of the Histadrut executive in mid-December, Golda proposed that the fourth *mifdeh* raise 100,000 Palestinian pounds, using most of the money to create jobs for the unemployed and a small proportion for "direct aid," to feed hungry children. She also proposed linking the new tax to a basic "single tax" that included dues and sick fund and pension fund payments required for membership. With that linkage, "not a single member will be relieved of his share of the burden unless he's prepared to leave the Histadrut," she declared.

To promote the new tax, Golda stumped from factory to factory to the point of exhaustion, pressuring, cajoling, pleading, shouting, bullying, demanding in every way possible that the levy be paid. When people argued that the Histadrut would lose members because of her taxes, she snapped that if she had to choose between an unemployed member leaving out of despair and a bank employee quitting because of too many taxes, she was willing to let the bank employee go. When some accused her of having a "sadistic streak" and being "against the workers," she tightened her lips, adjusted her face into a cold mask of indifference, and pounded home her message. Unemployment caused a "blot on the community and chiefly on the labor federation," and they, the workers, must "wipe out this shame."

She put herself on the line throughout what she termed "the loathed *mifdeh* drives" and in the end succeeded mightily. She raised the necessary funds, and the Histadrut remained intact. The campaign proved, in her words, "that this labor federation had the will and power to decide on something and carry it out."

And the same could be said of Golda Meyerson.

BUT FACTION B DID NOT let up in its opposition. Just when the unemployment emergency began to taper off, a new party crisis developed. To fill its wartime needs, England began constructing military bases, roads, airfields, and other necessary facilities. This seemed an excellent opportunity for Jewish workers to find employment. Word quickly spread, however, that people seeking jobs needed *protectia*, pull, with the powers that be in the Histadrut. Moreover, when Solel Boneh, the Histadrut's construction company, received a contract from the British army for a major project, rumor had it that the company hired many more Arab workers than Jewish ones because it could pay the Arabs lower wages. In the bitter atmosphere that prevailed, nobody took note of the fact that the British had made hiring Arab workers a condition for giving Solel Boneh the contract, part of Britain's attempt to keep the Arabs on its side in its fight against Germany.

Angry Tel Aviv union leaders distributed a pamphlet decrying the unfair treatment of Jewish laborers, egging on the unemployed. On the morning of June 13, 1940, a mass of men, including several union leaders, barged into the Histadrut office of Berl Repetur, who handled job distributions, and announced that they would not permit him to leave until he agreed to change hiring policies. The incident ended in a standoff, but furious at the union chiefs who had incited it, all of them Mapai members, a party council held an internal trial for the five main instigators. Golda gave a detailed testimony before the party judges describing how she arrived for work at nine that Sunday morning and saw that a mob had invaded Repetur's office. She was especially irritated that not one person found a way "to speak, to listen, to discuss," instead of stubbornly holding Repetur in his office. "What have we come to?" she cried out in disgust.

During the trial, the union leaders, speaking in the name of the destitute workers, denounced the Histadrut and the party as bureaucracies whose heads had become professional politicians—party hacks—selling out earlier idealism. That "holier than thou" attitude galled Golda, who retorted, again, as if personally attacked. You are no less professional politicians than I, she challenged them. Your children are not starving. You are not dividing your last crusts of bread with the destitute. What gives you the right to attack me in this way? Given Golda's impeccable socialist credentials and reputation for hard work and plain living, the opposition had trouble refuting her. The Mapai court found the union leaders guilty and evicted them from the party and the Histadrut.

In the next months, as Britain expanded its war activities and needed more laborers, the economic situation began to improve. Mapai infighting quieted down for a while, but the cracks in party unity remained, and not far from the surface anger continued to boil.

GREAT BRITAIN AT WAR POSED a cruel dilemma for Golda and her colleagues. The White Paper had been issued only four months earlier, and despite war pressures the British determined to carry it out to the letter. In fact, the war had made limitations on Jewish immigration and land purchase more urgent in British eyes. One after another the Arab nations began lining up behind Germany: Iraq would rebel against England and form a pro-Nazi government, Egypt flirted shamelessly with the Axis powers (Germany, Japan, and Italy), and the mufti, who had fled Jerusalem, collaborated enthusiastically with Hitler, urging the Muslim world to support the führer. Under these circumstances, the British sought to fend off a rebellion by Palestinian Arabs by adhering closely to the White Paper.

How were the Jews in Palestine to respond to such severity on the part of the British, the very people who were also bravely fighting the Jews' worst enemy in Europe? Ben-Gurion came up with a proper slogan, arguably the most famous of his pronouncements: "We must assist the English in their war as if there were no White Paper, and resist the White Paper as if there were no war." For all the fame surrounding the manifesto, Golda was to say later that the only reason she and others "didn't laugh" at it was that it came from Ben-Gurion. On an emotional level, how were people to split their feelings in order to oppose England at the same time that they supported it? More practically, the Yishuv did not have the physical resources or ability to fight against the British, and their ability to fight for them depended on Britain itself.

But they could demonstrate their anger. On February 27, 1940, new British land regulations gave the Jews so few areas in which to acquire land—about 5 percent of western Palestine—that Ben-Gurion described the space as "a small Pale of Settlement similar to that which existed in tsarist Russia." Golda marched at protests, dressed in the standard white shirt and dark skirt she wore to work, walking briskly toward the front, with thousands behind. At any sign of violence, the police cracked down with force, injuring some demonstrators and arresting others. After the arrests of several demonstrators, Golda, Remez, and Meir Grabovsky, a Histadrut leader, met in Jerusalem with the chief secretary of Palestine.

Golda began by describing the many achievements the Jews had made in Palestine. The secretary noted that the British Empire's protection had made those accomplishments possible. A placard in the demonstrations that really angered him, he said, read, "Hitler is beating us in front and England is stabbing us in the back." They did not want to speak of England and Hitler in one breath, they countered, but how could they not react strongly to the unfair British laws?

"He was a young, very alert man, who gave the impression of being an intelligent person, not without feelings," Golda related to the Histadrut executive committee. "But he truly believed that England was justified in its actions."

"I said to him: 'Let us grant that you feel justified,'" she continued. "'But if we don't accept that, a third party will have to decide.'"

"His answer to that: 'The sides are the Arabs and you, the Empire makes the decisions.'"

So much for being a small people challenging a large colonial power. Such encounters, time and again, convinced Golda and the other leaders that the relationship the Yishuv had with the mandate government in the 1920s and 1930s had ended. True, as the secretary said, the government had nurtured and safeguarded Jewish Palestine. But that changed with the 1939 White Paper and its strangling provisions. The idea of an independent Jewish state, always present but always a distant dream for the Zionists, took on greater immediacy.

For England, 1940 was a grim year of standing almost alone against the Nazi march toward world conquest. Like a house of cards, Denmark, Norway, Belgium, Luxembourg, and the Netherlands collapsed before Hitler's armies. In June, most of France fell, and soon thereafter Italy entered the war on Germany's side. The British fought on heroically, their Royal Air Force (RAF) battling the German Luftwaffe in the skies and their population enduring destructive bombings on the ground. Yet even in that struggle for life and liberty, British authorities zealously pursued their White Paper regulations, especially when it came to admitting refugees. They resolved now not to permit a soul into Palestine beyond the quota figures and to turn back every illegal ship caught or send its passengers to special detention camps. Golda did not believe—nor did anybody in the Yishuv—the British claim that they had to protect themselves from dangerous spies the Germans might plant among fleeing refugees. For the Zionists, that was just one more excuse for placating the Arabs, and this at a time of the greatest Jewish need.

The struggle became heartrending and brutal. On November 11, the British intercepted two ramshackle ships, the *Milos* and the *Pacific*, carrying 1,750 refugees. They transferred the passengers to a third ship, the S.S. *Patria*, in Haifa port, to be deported to the remote colony of Mauritius in the Indian Ocean. Bent on stopping them, the Haganah had explosives smuggled aboard the *Patria*, intending to damage part of it and in the subsequent commotion spirit away its passengers. They miscalculated. The explosives blew a huge hole in the ship, and it quickly went down, drowning some 250 refugees. "We were looking through a window . . . and we saw the boat sinking," Berl Repetur recalled, "and we all ran to the port to begin saving what we could." With British help, they saved 1,500 immigrants. Winston Churchill, a Zionist sympathizer and now prime minister, intervened to have the survivors remain in the land and avoid a British "act of inhumanity."

After the *Patria* disaster, angry Mapai executives clamored to know who had given the Haganah permission to smuggle the explosives onto the ship. Golda staunchly defended the Haganah, in spite of the dreadful results. As sad as she felt about the loss of lives, she never wavered in her conviction that the immigration needed to continue under all circumstances, even when tragedy hits. Her "demeanor at that meeting," Repetur said, "it was one of her strongest moments ever in the way she bore herself."

Golda's unequivocal commitment to the immigration in defiance of the British put her in the same camp as Berl Katznelson, David Ben-Gurion, the Haganah chief, Eliyahu Golomb, and other "activists" in the Mapai Party. The "moderates," who opposed them, argued that a British victory in the war had to take precedence over everything and the Jews needed to desist from their illegal activities. Joseph Sprinzak, who would become the first speaker of the Israeli Knesset, adhered to that camp, as did David Remez, Golda's closest ally in so many other areas. She would keep her emotional ties to Remez, but as the debates mounted, she found herself leaning more often toward Ben-Gurion's militant approach.

That approach would guide her in a new assignment she assumed at the end of 1940. Dov Hoz, head of the Histadrut's political department, died in a horrendous automobile accident, and Golda inherited his position. Hoz had been related by marriage to Eliyahu Golomb, Shaul Avigur, and Golda's old friend Moshe Sharett, all of them leading Zionist figures and all known collectively as the brothers-in-law. A tough but amiable man, Hoz would puncture the airs of the falsely modest by saying, "Listen, my friend, you're not big enough to make yourself that small," a line that might have later inspired one of the best-known Golda quips, "Don't be so humble, you're not that great."

Around this time, Golda also became a member of the mandate's War Economic Advisory Council, which dealt with all matters relating to the country's economy. Her new positions brought her in closer contact than ever with the British, but that proximity did little to soften her attitude toward the authorities. "We must do all in our power to help the illegal immigrants," she impressed upon her colleagues. "Britain is trying to prevent the growth and expansion of the Jewish community in Palestine, but it should remember that Jews were here 2,000 years before the British came." As if to drive home her point, she took on yet another role, as one of the heads of a Histadrut committee devoted to Aliyah Bet activities.

Still, as Ben-Gurion said, while defying the White Paper, the Yishuv also had to help England win the war. The way to do that, Golda firmly believed, was to recruit Palestinian Jews for the British army. She regarded enlistment as a moral and political imperative, and for more than one reason. Of course, she and other Yishuv leaders wanted to aid the battle against the Nazis. They also recognized, however, that the training their soldiers received in fighting alongside the British would stand them in good stead later. ("Later" was always in the back of Zionist minds: later when they had a state; later when they had a legitimate Jewish army.)

Although neither the Histadrut nor the Jewish Agency had the legal right to draft anyone into the British army, they issued conscription orders for people between the ages of twenty and thirty, pressuring them to enlist. Golda supported every recruiting scheme. The party "can do what it wants" to get volunteers, she said coldly, including coercing men who hesitated to enlist by threatening to take away their Histadrut membership.

Overall, the Yishuv succeeded in its recruitment drives. Eventually, about thirty thousand men enlisted in all branches of the British armed forces. Jewish women were accepted in the forces beginning in 1942, their numbers reaching more than four thousand by war's end. Always fearful of giving Jews too much power or prominence, the British had hoped to balance their Palestine forces with one Arab for every Jew who joined. That hope fell through when few Arabs signed up. The "Palestine Buffs" consisted almost entirely of Jews.

The British well understood Zionist long-term hopes for statehood, and they suspected—rightly—that the Jews would expect concessions after the war because of their military cooperation. So, through the ups and downs of the war, they also seesawed in their attitude toward Jewish help. At the beginning, they doggedly seized weapons hidden in Jewish settlements, as they always had, and arrested officers of the underground Haganah. Their outlook began to change when France fell to Germany in 1940 and the French Vichy government—Germany's puppet—took control of Morocco, Tunisia, and Algeria to the west of Palestine and the mandates over Syria and Lebanon to the north. Now the British accepted, even cooperated with, the Haganah, closing their eyes to its "illegality."

By the spring of 1941, the Axis appeared unstoppable. Italy had rained bombs on Haifa and Tel Aviv and seemed on its way to controlling Egypt. Germany occupied Greece and Yugoslavia and forced Bulgaria, Hungary, and Romania into joining the Axis powers. Rumors circulated that England was poised to pull out of the Middle East, sending waves of fear through the Yishuv and the British forces stationed there. What would happen if the British retreated? Would the Germans annihilate Palestine's Jews? Would the Arabs launch a massacre with aid from the Axis powers? Should the Jews abandon the country to save their lives? In defense, the Haganah formed an elite new combat corps to protect the Yishuv against Arab attacks if the British left and fight a guerrilla war if the Nazis moved in. They called it Palmach, a strike force. Its members lived on kibbutzim and earned their keep working part-time on the farms while they trained for their military missions. Always a strong backer of the Haganah, Golda was among the new corps's most avid supporters in the Histadrut. And the British openly collaborated with it, relying on its members to infiltrate enemy lines and gather intelligence information for His Majesty's army.

The second half of 1942 brought another panic for the Jewish public and the British in Palestine, even greater than before. A year earlier, Hitler had invaded the Soviet Union, dissolving the nonaggression pact the two nations had, and as the German army smashed its way to one victory after another, the Russian bear seemed doomed. In North Africa, the wily and brilliant German "Desert Fox," Erwin Rommel, shattered British defense lines and reached El Alamein, Egypt, only two hundred miles from the Suez Canal. This time the invasion of Palestine loomed as almost inevitable. Sitting in the Histadrut secretariat, Golda wrote to her daughter, Sarah, that if the "evil" reached the land, "for us there is no alternative but to fight to the end." At the meeting, she pleaded to head a special committee to deal with the danger. "From the day I joined the secretariat, this is the first time I am asking for an assignment," she said. "I am asking for an assignment tied to this hour of emergency."

By fall, before the committee could materialize, everything changed. The Germans became bogged down in Stalingrad, and the British, under General Bernard Montgomery, halted Rommel's advance. Once the danger to Palestine dissipated, the British attitude, like Pharaoh's heart, hardened again. They reverted to their earlier practices in regard to Yishuv military action, shutting Palmach training bases and cracking down on weapons held by the Haganah. Eliyahu Sacharov would

The Mabovitch family in Milwaukee in 1906, shortly after coming to America from Pinsk. *(Left to right)* Golda; her father, Moshe; elder sister, Sheyna; mother, Bluma; and little sister, Clara (Tzipka). *(Family of Golda Meir)*

At age eleven, Golda *(top row, fourth from left)* created and became president of the American Young Sisters' Society, whose purpose was to raise money to provide textbooks for poor children. This photograph appeared in *The Milwaukee Journal* on September 2, 1909, accompanied by an article praising the "little children who give their play time and scant pennies to charity." *(Wisconsin Historical Society)*

Golda *(seated, farthest right)* attended the Fourth Street School in Milwaukee, from which she graduated in 1912 as class valedictorian. It was renamed the Golda Meir School in 1979. *(Historic Photo Collection/Milwaukee Public Library)*

A page from the 1916 *Tattler*, Milwaukee's North Division High School yearbook. The quotation alongside Golda's photograph ("Those about her / From her shall read the perfect ways of honor") is from Shakespeare's *Henry VIII* and refers to his newborn daughter, the future Queen Elizabeth I. *(Family of Golda Meir)*

Golda, age nineteen, and Morris Meyerson, age twenty-four, after their wedding in December 1917. Golda later said that what initially drew her to Morris was "his gentleness, his intelligence, and his soul." *(Family of Golda Meir)*

While attending sessions at the first American Jewish Congress in Philadelphia in 1918, Golda had her picture taken by a professional photographer. Sheyna once described her younger sister as having deep-set eyes; a head of thick, chestnut hair, a nose that suited her face, although it was "a little too large," and a firm mouth, where her "obstinacy resided." *(Family of Golda Meir)*

Golda as the Statue of Liberty in an "Americanization" pageant held in Milwaukee in 1919 to welcome new citizens. "Here I found freedom, kindness, and cleanliness," Golda later said of the city in which she grew up. *(Wisconsin Historical Society)*

At a picnic in 1919 with members of the Milwaukee branch of Poalei Zion, the international Labor Zionist organization. Golda is seated at the extreme right in the first row, alongside Yossel Kopilov and Regina Hamburger, who would remain lifelong friends. Morris is seated directly behind her and Meir Dubinsky, one of her many rejected suitors, is standing in the middle of the last row. *(Courtesy of Miriam Copilove Frumkin)*

Feeding chickens on the kibbutz Merhavia. Accepted only after their third application, Golda and Morris became full members of the socialist kibbutz in the fall of 1921, a few months after immigrating to Palestine. Placed in charge of the chicken house and its new incubator, she succeeded in producing more chickens than the collective had ever bred. *(Family of Golda Meir)*

Golda and Morris with their children, Menahem and Sarah, sometime in the 1930s. Menahem would become a professional cellist, and Sarah spent most of her life on kibbutz Revivim. Golda and Morris permanently separated around 1940, but they never officially divorced and she always kept his photo at her bedside. *(Family of Golda Meir)*

Israel's first ambassador to the USSR presents her credentials to the deputy chairman of the Supreme Soviet, Ivan Alekseevich Vlasov, at the Kremlin, September 1948. Copies of the photograph, which appeared in the Russian magazine *Ogonek*, found their way into Jewish homes throughout Russia. (*Archive Department/University of Wisconsin-Milwaukee Libraries*)

Tens of thousands of Soviet Jews defied their government's warning to keep their distance from the Israeli delegation and mobbed Golda as she left Moscow's Choral Synagogue following Rosh Hashanah services in 1948. Deeply moved, all she could say was "A dank eich vos ihr seit geblieben Yidden" (Thank you for having remained Jews), after someone protectively shoved her into a taxi.

With David Remez at the official opening of the first Knesset in Jerusalem, February 1949. Golda's earliest political mentor, Remez was also the great love of her life. "Do you know how dear you are to me? Do you have any clue about all the things in my heart?" she wrote to him in 1946. *(Photograph by Hans Pinn, Government Press Office, State of Israel)*

Prime Minister David Ben-Gurion's first cabinet, May 1949. Golda, minister of labor, was the only woman in it. Seated next to her is Zalman Shazar, minister of education and culture, with whom she also had a long-term romantic relationship. Ben-Gurion sits at the head of the table. To his right is Moshe Sharett, minister of foreign affairs. David Remez, minister of transportation, sits directly under the portrait of Theodor Herzl. *(Photograph by Hugo Mendelson, Government Press Office, State of Israel)*

Opening the Tel Aviv–Netanya Road in 1950. Known as Highway 2, this road began inside Tel Aviv and ran north along the Mediterranean coast to the town of Netanya. *(Photograph by Rudi Weissenstein, The Photo House. All rights reserved.)*

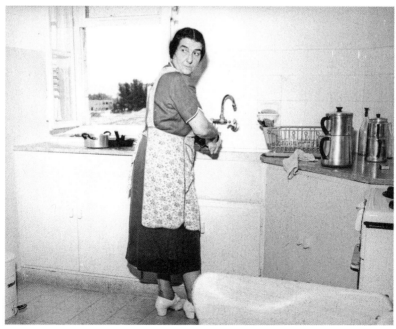

The kitchen of the apartment in Jerusalem's Talbieh neighborhood where Golda lived while she was labor minister was the first "Golda's kitchen." That was the name—sometimes complimentary, sometimes not—given by the public to the room where, it was said, she both cooked meals and "cooked up" deals with her political allies. *(Photograph by David Rubinger,* Yediot Aharonot *Archive)*

With David Ben-Gurion in 1959. It is unlikely that he actually referred to her as "the only man in my cabinet," but his deep admiration of her oratorical, organizational, and diplomatic skills propelled her career upward. *(Photograph by Hans Pinn, Government Press Office, State of Israel)*

With Israel's ambassador to the United Nations Abba Eban at a meeting of the General Assembly in July 1957, a year after Ben-Gurion named her foreign minister. One of her hardest tasks at the UN was to announce, on March 1, 1957, Israel's withdrawal from the territory it had captured during the 1956 war with Egypt. *(Government Press Office, State of Israel)*

With her sisters, sometime in the 1950s. Clara *(left)*, the only member of the Mabovitch family who did not immigrate to Israel, lived in Connecticut. Sheyna *(center)*, Golda's childhood idol, would admonish her as she rose to the highest levels in the Israeli government: "Don't forget that you are the daughter of a carpenter." *(Family of Golda Meir)*

receive a seven-year jail sentence from a British military court on suspicion that he had helped organize a network that smuggled weapons
to the Haganah from British warehouses in Egypt. The only concrete
evidence prosecutors could produce to convict him were thirteen bullets he owned—one more than he was legally allowed for his licensed
revolver. An Arab charged in a civilian court of possessing an illegal rifle
and eighty-six bullets would be given a six-month jail sentence.

That was the atmosphere in September 1943, when Golda appeared
in a Jerusalem military court at the trial of two men, Leib Sirkin and
Abraham Rachlin, accused of stealing three hundred rifles and 105,000
rounds of ammunition from the British to transfer to the Haganah. As a
Histadrut executive representative, she was one of three witnesses called
by Sirkin's defense lawyer, Dr. Bernard Joseph (later Dov Yosef, Israeli
attorney). Turned over to the prosecutor, Major R. L. Baxter, she faced
hostile questioning.

"You are a nice, peaceful, law-abiding lady, are you not?" he began.

"I think I am," she replied, ignoring his condescension.

He then read from a speech she had given on May 2, 1940, in which
she said, "For twenty years we were led to trust the British government,
but we have been betrayed." And again, "We have never taught our
youth the use of firearms for offense but for defensive purpose only . . .
And if they are criminals, then all the Jews in Palestine are criminals."

"What about that?" he asked.

"If a Jew who is armed in self-defense is a criminal, then all the Jews
in Palestine are criminals," she answered calmly.

Trying to trip her up, Baxter asked whether she had heard of the Palmach. She responded as though she knew of it only from afar—although
she had promoted its creation. "I first heard of the Palmach as groups of
young people, organized with the knowledge of the authorities, and who
were specially trained at the time the German army was drawing near to
Palestine," she said, and when pressed about whether it was a legal body,
she repeated that "these groups were organized to help the British army
and with the knowledge of the authorities." She would not let the British
forget that they had needed the help of Jewish forces. Nor should they
overlook the importance of Jewish self-defense during the Arab disturbances of the 1920s and 1930s.

Partway through the questioning, the president of the court, Major
Russell-Lawrence, joined in to criticize Golda about the Yishuv's pressure on young Jews to enlist in the British army, even though the British

government had not called for conscription in the land. Without missing a beat, she reminded the court that "both the Government and the army asked for Jews to go into the forces and asked the [Jewish] Agency to help."

Her self-confidence as she fended off every question must have irritated the court president. When, in response to something the defense attorney asked, she began to speak about earlier Arab riots, the president cut in. If they continued in the same vein, he said, "we'll soon be back to a period of 2,000 years ago." To which she countered, "If the Jewish question had been solved 2,000 years ago."

"Keep quiet!" the president shouted.

Golda: "I object to being addressed in that manner."

President: "You should know how to conduct yourself in court."

Golda: "I beg your pardon if I interrupted you, but you should not address me in that manner."

The next day *The Palestine Post* printed a large part of Mrs. Meyerson's testimony, omitting, however, the last part—probably on orders from the military censors. Nonetheless, Golda's appearance in that way in the paper bolstered her reputation as a symbol of strength and defiance. Much later, in 1975, after she had retired as prime minister, Golda Meir received a letter from Major Baxter congratulating her on an honor she had been given. He'd always had "the greatest admiration" for her "since we crossed swords at the Military Court in Jerusalem," he wrote. "We both knew each other when we were not worth knowing." He also teasingly suggested that if she ever needed a job, "I can get you one here in Ulster, where your talents would be invaluable!" (At the time, the British were trying to help subdue violent battles between Catholics and Protestants in Northern Ireland.)

In these years, her talents were being stretched in every direction as she involved herself in myriad assignments as part of her Histadrut work. One of those assignments called for balancing the needs of civilian laborers working in British army camps in Palestine with Britain's wartime needs. Existing camps grew larger and new ones sprouted with the war, requiring additional people to build roads, repair railways, clean, cook, and supply the daily necessities of army camp life for the soldiers. The hired laborers, called Raji workers, came from all over the land, Jews and Arabs, skilled and unskilled, Histadrut members and nonmembers such as Revisionists and religious Zionists. Golda became the voice of all of them in seeking better working conditions.

At their peak, about seventy-five army camps throughout the country employed almost fifteen thousand Jews and some twenty-eight thousand Arabs. Both groups lived under austere conditions, often with insufficient food, inadequate sleeping arrangements, and low pay. Through polite requests and impatient demands, Golda got the British commanders to improve those conditions, including installing a kosher kitchen for the religious Jews. After months of negotiations, she also won basic pay raises for both Jews and Arabs. To be sure, a fixed gap separated the wages of the two groups: the Jews went from eighteen *grush* (pennies) a day to twenty-five, the Arabs from fourteen to eighteen *grush* a day. Even at those low rates, the British complained that the increases, particularly for the Arabs, would lead to similar bids in the civilian workplace and crop up again at the end of the war.

Ignoring all complaints, Golda persisted. After winning the basic salary increases, she set out on the harder job of wresting cost-of-living raises comparable to those in civilian industries. The British commanders never directly rejected her requests; they simply continued to postpone making a commitment. Finally, when told she needed to have more patience, Golda burst out, "Patience. Negotiations. This matter has gone on for years. Almost every day . . . with the captain, with the colonel, with the brigadier, with the financial advisor in the head secretary's office, and afterwards . . . the matter even reached . . . the war cabinet in London. What more could we do?"

Through all the nerve-racking delays, she had refused to allow the workers to go on strike, impressing on them that they must not interfere with the British war effort. In May 1943, with the British still holding back, she gave in and asked the Histadrut executive for permission to stage a warning strike. Its purpose, she emphasized, was strictly for a cost-of-living increase, and as such it extended to Arab workers equally with Jewish ones. Here was Golda at her socialist best, disregarding politics to champion the rights of every worker: "We have a responsibility to the Arab workers . . . And if the Army will try to distinguish in a cost of living increase between Jewish and Arab workers, we will have to help the Arabs in staging their own strike . . . I have promised the Arabs that we will help them get an equal cost of living raise."

To persuade Arab laborers to join the strike, Golda met with their union heads and leaders, including some of the most nationalistic who had no love for Zionists. And at a joint gathering of Jewish and Arab representatives in the Histadrut office in Tel Aviv, she spoke openly about wage disparities between Arabs and Jews. Everybody interprets the concept of a single salary differently, she said. To Jewish leaders it meant raising Arab wages to the level of Jewish workers, but to the military authorities it meant lowering Jewish salaries to the current level of Arab workers. The purpose of the strike was to combat such thinking. With the approval of the Histadrut executive, a joint Arab and Jewish work stoppage took place as a one-day protest and warning on May 10, 1943. A cost-of-living increase at an equal rate for Jews and Arabs went into effect soon afterward.

In September 1971, Prime Minister Golda Meir received a letter from an Arab man living in a refugee camp in Ramallah. He knew her, he wrote, from the days when she was in the Histadrut and he was there alongside her. "I am the person who went with you to Jerusalem to secure workers' rights," he reminded her. He would like to meet with her now to wish her well on the Jewish New Year.

Golda's grit and stubbornness earned her the grudging respect of the British military officials. At a meeting she attended in a brigadier general's office with her delegation of Arab and Jewish workers, the officer remained seated while keeping the delegates standing. As a gentleman, however, he offered Golda a chair. She turned it down and refused to participate in the meeting until all the delegates received seats. The "nice, peaceful, law-abiding lady," in Major Baxter's words, made a lasting impression. And the "saga of the chair" spread through the army camps, becoming part of Golda lore.

Toward the end of the war, the workers held a party in Haifa. "With great feeling a woman comrade stood up and gave Golda Meyerson a gift from the camp workers." They'd had her name inscribed in the golden book of the Jewish National Fund, in gratitude.

THERE WAS ALWAYS TALK in the Histadrut of sending Golda overseas. The American Labor Zionists requested at the end of 1942 that she organize a fund-raising campaign there for the Yishuv as she had in the 1930s, and the Pioneer Women of Baltimore hoped that she would speak at their "Donor Supper." Yet through all the war years, whenever her colleagues reviewed calls for her to go abroad, they decided that it was too difficult or too dangerous and she had important work to do in Palestine. It was one of the ironies of her life that when her children were small, she traveled constantly and suffered constant guilt at the long separations from them, and now that they had reached ages when she could leave them without that guilt, she would remain at home while they began to fly from the nest.

Devoting himself to his cello studies, Menahem became the youngest member of the Palestine Symphony Orchestra in 1943 before leaving to join the Jewish Settlement Police. The police force had been established under the British in 1936 to protect Jewish agricultural settlements against Arab attacks. When Menahem joined, during the war, it aided the British by keeping watch over their arsenals, radar stations, and strategic plants. More exciting for Menahem, his job called for guarding German and Italian prisoners of war and learning to use a military rifle. Sarah, however, took the hardest road and one that led to her permanent departure from home.

At seventeen, she left high school a year before graduation and along with others in her Labor Zionist youth group began a grueling training program to prepare for living and working on a kibbutz. Many parents of the young people in the group objected to their children dropping out of school. Morris vehemently opposed Sarah's plans, and Sheyna warned Golda that Sarah would regret the decision for the rest of her life. Golda remained calm and for the most part accepting. Her own experience on the Merhavia kibbutz had been one of the high points in her life, she always said, so how could she stand in the way of her daughter's choice? She was also proud. Sarah would become part of the much-admired kibbutz movement, its members still regarded as the cream of the nation's Zionists. For years, Golda would pepper her speeches with sly references to "my daughter in the kibbutz." The only question she asked when the subject first came up, Sarah later said, was whether she and her friends were "going to the settlements because we want to fulfill a national mission or because we simply don't want to study." Convinced of her daughter's sincerity, Golda gave her approval.

A shy and studious teenager, with owl glasses, Sarah tried to keep out of the limelight and hide her mother's growing fame: when asked on questionnaires about her parents' occupations, she responded that her mother "worked in the Histadrut." Her own work would be part of a plan developed by the Jewish Agency to reclaim the scorched, desolate Negev area in the south. She settled in Revivim, a small, isolated Negev outpost at the time, far more primitive than Golda's Merhavia. Kibbutz members "lived in tents," Sarah remembered, "in constant heat and dust and loneliness." The first time Golda and Menahem visited her, after driving through bleak, sandy roads, Golda turned to her son in dismay at the barrenness all around. "How in the world will Sarah ever manage here?" she asked him, but she never entreated her daughter to return to Tel Aviv.

Instead, from the day Sarah began her training, Golda sent her bits of advice sprinkled like salt through her letters. "You probably know about the typhus epidemic," she wrote in one letter. "Your hands, especially, have always to be clean when you eat and in general after work. Don't eat raw fruit, and do whatever else the doctor tells you." In another, she mentioned having heard that Sarah and her comrades were not getting enough sleep. "That's not good," she wrote. "You're working hard, and you also need to get a nice rest." She often reminded Sarah to "write to Father," with whom Golda had broken and who was away working for Solel Boneh in the Middle East. Occasionally, warm compliments accompanied her motherly counsel: after Eliyahu Golomb visited Sarah, Golda wrote to her that "everybody says the same thing; you are lovely." On other occasions, she couldn't resist hinting at her own loneliness: "The house is very strange without you. So quiet and sometimes even a little sad." The tables had been turned. No longer the absent mother, Golda felt the absence of her children.

But she was also intensely preoccupied with news reaching the Yishuv about the decimation of Europe's Jews. As early as 1935, with Hitler's Third Reich firmly entrenched, Golda spoke of the need to rescue as many Jews as possible from the "ovens of Germany." She could not know then, nor could anybody, that the words she used rhetorically would become reality as the Nazi cauldron consumed millions of victims. For Jews in the Yishuv, as for Jews everywhere, Nazi anti-Semitism, vicious as it was, seemed at first but an extreme of the persecutions that had marked all of Jewish history. Jews expelled from countries they had lived in for centuries, Jews herded into ghettos, beaten, starved, murdered— lamentably such things had happened before. But no stretch of the imagination would picture real ovens, mass shootings, or the likes of death camps. "In a way, I suppose, it should be chalked up to the credit of normal decent men and women that we couldn't believe that such a monstrously evil thing would ever actually happen," Golda was to say of the Holocaust. "It wasn't that we were gullible. It was simply that we couldn't conceive of what was then still inconceivable."

Even when the truth of Nazi killings began drifting into the Yishuv, people had trouble accepting it, so fantastical did it seem. In mid-March 1942, a group of sixty-nine Yishuv members who had been trapped in Poland when the war broke out returned home, freed as part of an exchange arrangement in which Britain released German nationals it had held. Jewish Agency executives questioned group members extensively about their accounts of German shootings, deportations, and death factories. Eliyahu Dobkin, involved in gathering news, asked a woman with whom he'd had a long conversation whether she wasn't actually exaggerating what she had witnessed. She stood up, slapped him across the face, and left.

In the United States, Golda's friend Marie Syrkin received an account of the mass gassing of Jews in the Polish town of Chelmno and—unable to believe it—buried it in small type on the back page of the *Jewish Frontier*, the journal she edited.

Proof of how difficult it was to absorb reports of the Nazi atrocities was "the fact that we were able to continue our work, to eat and sleep and sometimes even to laugh," Golda said. She had been no more clairvoyant than other leaders and just as wrapped up as they in her everyday duties. She differed from many of them, however, in that once she grasped the "inconceivable" information flowing in, she was able to digest and act on it. "We can no longer speak of aliyah the same way we did ten years ago," she advised her comrades. "Now it is a matter of bringing in every Jew, not because he's a farmer [who could work the land] but because he's a Jew."

DEVOTION TO RESCUE OPERATIONS became her credo and her passion. And the source of a sharp and sensitive debate between the Histadrut and the Jewish Agency Executive, in particular David Ben-Gurion, its secretary; Eliezer Kaplan, its treasurer; and Yitzhak Gruenbaum, head of its rescue committee. How much of its limited resources should the Jewish Agency allot to rescuing the Jews of Europe? How much should be used for building Eretz Israel—the long-standing Zionist ideal—to serve the Jewish remnant after the war?

Golda had no doubt about the answers. "There is no other Zionism now except for the rescue of Jews," she declared. "This is Zionism." She meant that at this moment in history the primary goal for all Zionist leaders had to be the act of saving Jews. Her words seemed a direct rebuttal to Gruenbaum, who had argued that "this tendency to consider Zionist activities second must be resisted." Even in these catastrophic times, "Zionism comes first": building the land and creating settlements had to take precedence over all other activities. Both their statements would become well-known in the annals of Israeli history. Gruenbaum would modify his somewhat. Golda repeated hers often.

After knowledge of the systematic mass murder of Jews became indisputable, Golda and others in the Histadrut secretariat proposed that the Jewish Agency become headquarters for raising and distributing money for rescue. They offered fifty thousand Palestinian pounds from their own budget to get started and asked the Jewish Agency to match those funds. Agency officials argued that their funds would be just a drop in the bucket, and in any event the British did not allow them to send money out of the country for fear it would fall into enemy hands. Most important, the chances for rescue appeared so slim that "before any money was allocated, it had to be proved that rescue was somehow possible." It would be better, agency leaders still maintained, to use their budget to continue developing a homeland so that when the nightmare ended, a safe haven would exist for all Jews. They proffered not fifty thousand pounds but fifteen thousand toward a rescue fund.

The disagreement went on for months, a "tragic misunderstanding," Golda called it. She and other Histadrut chiefs traveled tirelessly back and forth from their offices in Tel Aviv to the Jewish Agency offices in Jerusalem to argue their case. At one point, Meir Ya'ari, a Hashomer Hatzair leader, simply refused to go to Jerusalem one more time to plead futilely with the agency. Golda went anyway, with a small team she organized dedicated to rescue. In her perseverance, she also devised a novel fund-raising scheme: gather a hundred rich Jews from Palestine into a room and do not allow them to leave until each signs a check for a thousand pounds. "I'm positive that within two or three hours it will be possible to exit this room with 100,000 pounds." The technique worked. Several "parlor meetings" took place, where members of the Jewish Agency spoke and the audience donated money for rescue operations.

Increasingly anguished by the news from Europe, Golda grabbed at any straw. When a special "Yishuv to the Rescue" campaign was held, none of the major leaders showed up at its opening meeting. She appeared and worked hard with campaign organizers on fund-raising activities. She "was the only person we could turn to for help," one of them said. As the Holocaust historian Dina Porat put it, the actions of some leaders didn't match their fervent expressions of sorrow. With Golda, words and deeds went hand in hand.

The occasional arrival of Zionist emissaries stationed in neutral Istanbul, Turkey, fueled her zeal. The Istanbul of World War II had the feel of Rick's Café in the classic film *Casablanca*. Criminals mingled with spies, partisans rubbed shoulders with Nazi agents, and the air hung heavy with rumors and international intrigue. With money, the emissaries felt they could establish contacts that might lead to at least a few lives saved, and even if much of their funds fell into the wrong hands, some would be available for forged documents and bribes to lift people out of the depths of hell. The emissaries asked again and again for someone to manage their activities, and Golda's name frequently came up. Although she could not take on that job herself, she encouraged others in the Yishuv to make periodic trips to Istanbul. She was especially pleased when the Jewish Agency's treasurer, Eliezer Kaplan, returned from one visit sufficiently convinced of the possibility of some rescue that he allocated an extra eighty thousand pounds toward it. After some time, even Gruenbaum agreed that "if we are able to do something without hurting essential Zionist interests, we must do it."

Yet behind Golda's unceasing efforts and the rescue attempts of other Yishuv leaders lay a harsh truth. The Jews of Palestine represented but a small, powerless people living under the rule of a government that had grown increasingly unfriendly toward them. Ultimately, while they might do some good on their own, they could do little to save the masses of Jews trapped in the Nazi extermination system. "Ironically, the new Jews, standing tall in Palestine . . . were as powerless" as "the persecuted Jews of the Exile," writes the journalist Tom Segev.

Their aspirations and weakness came to the fore during the uprising in Poland's Warsaw ghetto, which began on Monday, April 19, 1943, the eve of Passover. Knowing the fate that awaited them, the fifty-five thousand or so Jews still in Warsaw after others had been deported accepted their underground leaders' decision to resist the Nazis. A month beforehand, the leaders sent a coded letter to the Yishuv using Hebrew words with Polish endings to appeal for funds. A wedding was soon to take place, it read, and if "Mr. Hatsalska" (rescue) wanted to send a greeting card, he'd better hurry. Urged by Golda, the Histadrut immediately dispatched five thousand pounds to the rebels.

A few days after the uprising burst out, the top managers of Palestine's transportation unions received an urgent phone call summoning them away from their regular Friday morning meeting to the Histadrut offices. There they were ushered into a room, where Golda Meyerson delivered the first news they heard about the rebellion in the Warsaw ghetto. The partisans desperately needed money to buy arms, she told them. A person had been found to transport the funds, and "although there is no guarantee that the money will reach them, we have to try."

This meeting had to be kept secret, she cautioned, because the mandatory government forbade transferring money to enemy territory. Nor could she reveal whom else she planned to approach. From this group she hoped to collect the sum of fifteen thousand pounds. "Divide the figure among yourselves," she directed them, "and I will return in half an hour to accept your checks." Then a warning: "If you plan to argue with me about the amount, I will cancel this appeal to you. And the stain on your conscience will remain forever."

The checks were ready within fifteen minutes, recalled Zvi Or Hof, who attended the meeting.

Other efforts proved less successful. Soon after receiving word of the Warsaw uprising, Golda and Remez suggested organizing a petition for help to the Allies, to be signed by every Jew in Palestine. Golda thought it should also be sent to Jews and non-Jews in the United States, Great Britain, and South Africa, the English-speaking countries where it might amass millions of signatures. The Histadrut turned down the idea as too time consuming and difficult to execute. The Bermuda conference on refugees brought another disappointment. Convened by the United States and Britain to discuss aiding refugees, it opened on April 19, the very day of the Warsaw ghetto uprising. It met in Bermuda for nine days and ended with nothing achieved. Or less than nothing. Among other decisions, the conference concluded that no ships could be made available for taking refugees out of Europe, that—with the Allies' policy of "unconditional surrender" for the Axis powers—no negotiations with Hitler for the release of Jews could take place, and that the White Paper could not be changed.

Golda and Remez began desperately cabling Zionist Labor Party members in England and the United States to protest and put pressure on the Allies. "Greatly Astonished Lack Public Mass Actions American Jewry for Saving Jews Europe," a telegram to the Poalei Zion Party in New York read. It concluded, "American Jewry Must Change Ordinary Way of Life and Mobilise All and Everything to Save Brethren Nazi Occupied Territory." The protest meetings and demonstrations American Jews did hold and the streams of letters and appeals they sent to government officials were insufficient in Golda's view.

They "could have done so much and didn't," she rebuked Joseph Schwartz of the Joint Distribution Committee, an American-based organization that helped Jews all over the world. They in the Yishuv understood that the United States had laws, like those in Britain, against sending money into enemy-occupied territory. They also understood that American Jews "are afraid," because of the blatant anti-Semitism in the country at the time. But "for Jews of the world there are no laws and no boundaries now—there is only one law: millions of Jews are being destroyed . . . If we do not do something—there is nobody who will." (The question of how much American Jews and their leaders did to stop Hitler remains an open sore within the American Jewish community, painfully and continually examined and reexamined.)

In her own backyard, and after her initial headway, Golda faced disillusionment with Histadrut workers. She, Remez, and others in the executive committee organized a conference early in May to kick off a week dedicated to collecting donations for rescue. "Woe to us that we are so weak," she began an emotional talk, "and blessed are we that we have a corner of a homeland, that we can offer our help to the best of our ability." The purpose of their meeting was to unite with the "comrades who are rebelling in the Diaspora who do not want to die silently and submissively but to die bravely in order to save the honor of Israel for generations to come." Ultimately, the responsibility for aiding Europe's Jews rested with them, she said, and she called on working people to join the fight by aiding every Jew possible.

The next day *Davar* ran the speech in its entirety. But neither it nor the conference motivated the workers to contribute a day's pay to the rescue fund, as Golda requested. Many had lost interest or did not believe their donations would reach the proper hands. Their response irritated her. "It's clear that our working public didn't stand in line" to pay up, she reported bitterly to her colleagues. "They won't do anything until they get receipts from the ghettos."

Her optimism was fading and so was her strength. Working day and night and smoking incessantly, she began to suffer from acute gallbladder attacks sometimes so excruciating that the family doctor, Else Ascher, had to relieve them with a shot of morphine. "One can always push oneself a little bit beyond what only yesterday was thought to be the absolute limit of one's endurance," she wrote later. So she pushed on, with growing despondency at the unceasing flow of terrible news. After a heroic battle, Warsaw would fall on May 16. One by one, the Nazis were to liquidate other ghettos—Cracow, Vilna, L'vov, later Lodz—and in the end the thousand-year-old Jewish community of Poland would be blotted out. Golda could not know all the details or the destruction yet to come, but as the horror mounted and hope for rescue dimmed, she blamed herself and her comrades for not having done enough.

"I'm deeply ashamed," she said after the failure in Bermuda. "Day after day we received telegrams on the proceedings of the Bermuda conference and life continued here as if nothing had happened." When Jews themselves fall short, "What do we want from the gentiles?" she asked. The Yishuv "should have turned the world upside down" for rescue operations, but it did not. Its failure gave her "no rest."

Her disappointments about large-scale rescues aside, she felt that through its emissaries the Yishuv had at least pursued every "shadow of hope" to try to reach individual Jews in Nazi-occupied Europe and provide whatever firsthand help they could. A new opportunity, or more accurately a "shadow" of opportunity, opened up in the second half of 1944. For years during the war, Yishuv leaders had tried to persuade the British to help them send commando units into occupied lands to establish contact with the Jews there. They hoped to parachute about a thousand soldiers, who could fan out into Jewish communities and, where feasible, set up underground units to fight the Nazis. The British repeatedly turned down their requests, using many excuses, most likely because they did not want to strengthen the Yishuv's hand. Finally, they agreed to have RAF planes drop a meager thirty-two young Jewish parachutists into Italy, Austria, and some of the Balkan countries to aid captured Allied pilots and encourage Jewish partisans. The commandos carried out their mission between March and September 1944 after an intensive training period. Of the group, twelve were captured, seven of these executed.

Hannah Senesh, the most famous of the parachutists and one of three women on the mission, was captured in her native Hungary, imprisoned, tortured, and then shot. She was only twenty-three, a poet who has remained a symbol of courage for generations of Israelis. After the war, Golda met Hannah's mother and spoke of the guilt she felt at the loss of that young woman and others: "They obeyed our call, they went, and they did not return." Enzo Sereni, at age thirty-nine one of the oldest in the group, was caught when he parachuted into Nazi-held northern Italy and later murdered at Dachau. A sophisticated man—his father had been personal physician to the king of Italy—he had come to Palestine in the 1920s and helped found the kibbutz Givat Brenner. Having shared a warm friendship with him, Golda felt deeply bereaved at his death.

All the parachutists came to say good-bye to key leaders of the Yishuv before their departures. Several wrote memoirs afterward, and what remained uppermost in their memories about the leaders was that none gave them specific guidelines, only words of admiration and encouragement. Even so, Yeshayahu Dan, known as Shaike, felt inspired by Ben-Gurion's instructions to spread the word about the Land of Israel wherever they went. "If you get there safely, if you stay alive," the leader directed them, "try to help every Jew you meet to get to the Land of Israel. Whoever crosses your path, whatever his party, youth movement, faction, or worldview, young or old—help him!"

When Shaike went to see Golda, he was outraged to find several party leaders with her. Wasn't this supposed to be a secret mission? Why were he and the other parachutists being paraded in front of these officials? Golda sensed his anger and calmed him. These people deserve to see you, she whispered. "They have their hand on the pulse of what's going on in this country." David Remez spoke about his son, Aharon, a pilot in the Royal Air Force, and the dangers he faced. Then he wished the parachutists well and beseeched them to carry word of Zionism wherever they went. Golda, who had sat quietly through the meeting, began to weep openly—"the tears flowed from her eyes like water, but she didn't utter a sound," Shaike wrote. He noticed tears in the eyes of some of the other officials also. "I thought, before we've even embarked on our mission, they are already mourning us."

Other parachutists also recalled seeing Golda weep and say little at their leave-taking. The woman who could turn into ice when crossed even slightly also cried easily—often too easily, to get her way, her opponents would say. But her tears when sending young soldiers into danger were real. If they upset Shaike, they also drew him near to her. When asked to list his next of kin on official papers in case he suffered a disaster, he gave Golda Meyerson's name. Unmarried, with no immediate relatives in Palestine, he chose the person who seemed "most sensitive, understanding, and trustworthy."

Shaike managed to contact Romanian Jews and arrange to have hundreds of orphans sent to Palestine. Other parachutists fought alongside Yugoslav partisan groups. Some made connections with Zionist youth movements, and some carried out intelligence missions. Their presence behind enemy lines and their message about Palestine offered hope to Jews still struggling to stay alive. Their deeds became part of Zionist mythology and history. As for rescue operations, however, they could not change the course of events. Millions of Jews had been annihilated, and even as the war reached its final stages, hundreds of thousands of others would be exterminated.

In March 1944, the Germans invaded Hungary, and by early July they had deported more than 437,000 Jews to Auschwitz. By this time, the Third Reich knew, as did the rest of the world, that the Nazis faced defeat. Yet the transports from Hungary barreled on, and the furnaces in the death camps burned as fiercely as ever. Zionist leaders had hoped earlier at least to save a good number of Hungarian children. As part of that attempt, Golda approached the British chief secretary for help. "I came to him and said . . . that it was possible to bring in thousands of children from Hungary," she recalled. "What we needed was a ship." He responded as if she were asking for the moon. "Don't you know there's a war on? And that all our ships are needed for the war?" Yes, Golda replied wearily, "I have heard there is a war." But, she continued, "if they were British children, would you find a ship for them"? The secretary didn't answer.

On July 28, 1944, Golda and Hershel Frumkin, a prominent Histadrut leader, sent a telegram to Moshe Sharett in London about a letter they had received from a "hidden rabbi living in Lvov written one month ago." The rabbi's letter gave details about the deportations of Hungarian Jews, Golda's telegram noted: "Four trains consisting 45 coaches each containing total 1200 people arrived daily Oswienzien [Auschwitz] for annihilation." The cable indicated that the "rabbi demands bombing railway transporting Jews also Oswienzien gives particulars plan." Rabbi Michael Dov-Beer Weissmandel, who had been involved in various rescue operations, seems to have learned about the terrors of Auschwitz from two escapees and sent calls for help to Jews throughout the free world, including the Yishuv. With that information and more from various sources, Golda and other Jewish leaders appealed to the Allies to bomb the roads and tracks leading to Auschwitz and the death machinery in the camp itself. They hoped in that way to thwart the rolling of the trains and, in the commotion, give inmates a chance to escape. The Allies turned down all the requests, arguing that the bombings would divert planes from their regular missions and would also kill many Jews in the camp.

That refusal by Allied governments to bomb Auschwitz endures as one of the most controversial and haunting issues of the Holocaust years.

THROUGH ALL THE WARTIME TRIBULATIONS, the internal political tensions in Jewish Palestine never let up. Party disputes quieted down for a short while early in the war, but as threat of a German invasion of the land subsided, clashes flared again, as if nothing else in the world mattered. Faction B, the discontented minority in Mapai, remained unhappy with party chiefs. Led by Hakibbutz Hameuhad—the country's largest kibbutz movement—the group continued to accuse the chiefs of having moved too close to the mainstream and too far from the party's earlier socialist ideals. Many Faction B members, enamored of the Soviet Union in its fierce fight against German forces, now also embraced Soviet ideology, further separating them from the Mapai majority. For several years, Ben-Gurion tried to keep aloof of party squabbles while he devoted himself almost exclusively to plans for a Jewish state in Palestine after the war. Berl Katznelson, fearing that Faction B would draw young people from the party if it left, sought to prevent a schism. It fell to the next level of leaders, loyal followers of Berl and Ben-Gurion, to oppose Faction B openly. Calling itself Faction C, this group asked Golda to join it as its head.

True to form, once she accepted that role, she jumped into the battle with both feet, vigorously fighting against Faction B's attacks and divisiveness. When Faction B linked arms with small left-wing parties in the Histadrut to vote against the Mapai majority there, Golda became convinced that a rift was inevitable. "I don't want a split, but I don't want a fake unity either," she said. And when a party member suggested that they try still harder to maintain unity, she snapped, "The party is not divided between those who want a separation and those who want unity." Clearly everyone preferred unity, but they had reached a point of such infighting that "not only would I not join this party if I had not been in it for many years . . . but the moment is coming when I have almost decided to leave it." Her words carried the usual threat of resignation, but her concern for the party was sincerely felt. She saw what Ben-Gurion and others tried not to acknowledge: the party could no longer function effectively with Faction B in it.

When the final rupture came, in May 1944, it marked one of the saddest moments in the Labor Zionist movement. The Mapai Party had been formed to establish unity and inclusiveness in the movement, and it had marched steadily toward those goals, only to have them fall apart in the end. As if to rub salt in the party wounds, the breakaway Faction B called itself l'Ahdut Ha'avoda (toward the Unity of Labor) from the name of the party Ben-Gurion and Berl had founded almost twenty-five years earlier and then folded into Mapai. (The *l* would soon be dropped and the group known again as Ahdut Ha'avoda.) The new party members included young kibbutz activists and many of the elite of the Haganah and the Palmach.

For the present, however, Mapai had something to celebrate and so did Golda. The party won an overwhelming majority in elections to the Histadrut on August 6, leaving l'Ahdut Ha'avoda far behind. In September, Golda was chosen for the Elected Assembly (Asefat Hanivharim), a governing body of the entire Yishuv, where Mapai had also scored a victory. The election gave her a national position, her first outside the Histadrut. At the same time, she rose several notches within the party itself. Almost more than anyone, she had always embodied the Socialist Zionist ideals Faction B so clamored about. With those opponents gone, party members regarded Golda as the keeper of their values. She had more room to expand, and she moved up, closer to Ben-Gurion, nearer the top in the party hierarchy, and with a firmer grip than ever on its helm.

Yet she might have characterized 1944 as a year of sorrow, not success. The party infighting wore her out, and the destruction of Europe's Jews tore at her guts. Added to that was the grief of personal loss.

Berl Katznelson died suddenly of a stroke on August 12, a few months after the Mapai Party schism, his death almost emblematic of that wrenching separation. Berl had been the Palestine labor movement's inspiration, its visionary and ideologist. The division in Mapai sickened him, and the exodus of young people behind Faction B broke his heart. Two days before his death, Golda attended a meeting with him in Jerusalem. As they walked out together, he turned to her and said with despair, "They are taking the young away from me."

Berl had been protective of Golda from her earliest days in the land. Over time, he became her confidant and teacher, the two sometimes walking and talking for hours. When he organized a "study month"—a seminar on all aspects of Jewish life and culture—he handpicked a high caliber of lecturers, including Golda, who spoke about the Histadrut. His biographer Anita Shapira describes how in one session, while he spoke off the record about his life, Golda hid a young stenographer behind a curtain to write down his story, knowing he would not object.

Golda heard the news of Berl's death after returning from a play in Tel Aviv. She quickly left for Jerusalem, where he had died and where dozens of people now streamed into his small apartment. He was not only a much-loved leader, she was to say, but in their contentious Yishuv circles "the one man whom all of us, including Ben-Gurion, deeply revered."

Yossel Kopilov's death two months after Berl's brought new pain. The friend of her youth, the philosopher-barber, Yossel had followed her to the Land of Israel, lived near her, worked across the street from her, and probably never stopped loving her. He died of a brain tumor at age fifty-five. Toward the end, Golda arranged for his admission to Hadassah Hospital in Jerusalem and was with him when he was being escorted in. In the corridor, before she left, Yossel took her hand and held it a long time. Then he kissed it gently—his final farewell to her.

One other sadness in that fateful year might have touched Golda more deeply than any. Her father, Moshe Mabovitch, died on April 13, during the Passover week. He had become something of a leader in his town of Herzliya, the owner of orange groves, a helper to the Haganah, and an "upright, good-hearted Jew who loved people as they loved him," Golda said.

Moshe rarely expressed his sentiments to his daughter, but she sensed his great affection for her. When she was elected to the executive committee of the Histadrut, a neighbor congratulated him on that honor. He breathed deeply, the neighbor later told Golda, and responded slowly in Yiddish: "There is no one like Golda . . . I am saying this as someone standing on the sidelines" and not as a father. "From her childhood Golda was smart, with much personality . . . she will advance even further . . . you understand?" He became excited, walked toward the door, and turned back. "Mark my words. Golda will advance even further!"

12

Ein Breira—No Alternative

Hundreds of thousands of people thronged into New York's Times Square on May 8, 1945. Torn scraps of paper thrown gleefully from office windows fluttered through the air like so many dancing snowflakes, car horns honked loudly, strangers hugged one another, and smiles transformed war-weary faces. The day before, Germany had unconditionally surrendered to the Allied nations, and throughout the world people jubilantly marked VE day, the end of the war in Europe. Alone in a hotel room in London, Ben-Gurion wrote in his diary, "Victory day—sad, very sad."

Six million Jews had been murdered, and untold thousands of others, many only recently liberated from concentration camps, had no place to go. Golda, too, had little heart for celebration. "We could not go out into the streets with a sense of triumph," she said, "knowing that one third of our people was wiped out." She had a vision, though, which she spoke about at a meeting after VE day. She hoped the Jewish Brigade, a Zionist unit of the British army formed toward the war's end, would remain in Europe with the Allied forces.

"I want the German man and the German youth and the German Nazi to see Jews as Hebrew soldiers from the land of Israel, and particularly as part of the conquering army," she said. Generally, talk of revenge against the Germans had not interested her, except in the context of the war. But "if this is revenge—it is the kind of revenge I want."

In her everyday life, she threw herself into work more excessively than ever, perhaps to compensate for "the curse of helplessness," as she dubbed it, that she and the others had experienced during the war. One after another, she assumed new assignments without giving up old ones. One of those assignments, which she began toward the end of the war, involved working with the Histadrut's labor council in Tel Aviv, formerly the hotbed of Faction B and Mapai Party conflicts. Housed in Beit

Brenner, the council was responsible for about forty thousand working people, many of them in construction industries. Before the party split and even after it, Ben-Gurion wanted a strong hand to oversee this council and called on Golda for the task. She, in turn, invited Levi Eshkol (at that time Shkolnik) to serve as the council's secretary.

A gentle, pragmatic, somewhat colorless man just a few years older than Golda, Eshkol had lived in the kibbutz Degania, the country's first Zionist settlement, worked with agriculture and water problems, and had limited understanding of city workers or their hostility when unemployed. One of the first things he did on the job was to remove the door of his office to create a kibbutz-like atmosphere of openness and informality. He got more "informality" than he bargained for, Golda recalled years later. One unemployed worker and his family began camping out in his open office, including cooking meals there on a small Primus (kerosene) stove. When Eshkol arrived for work, the embittered laborer threw the Primus at him, stunning Eshkol with his rage.

Golda had been working unofficially with the Histadrut council. After the Primus stove incident, and to strengthen the organization, she made her position official and moved in to an office next to Eshkol's, which did not thrill him. A question lurked behind the move: Who would serve as number one, the council's actual head? One evening Eshkol poured out his heart to his friend Aharon Becker, also part of the labor council. "Golda mixes into everything," he complained. "It's impossible to know who is responsible for what." Together, they hatched a plan. A few days later, when the three were at a meeting, Becker announced that the time had come to name a permanent secretary. "What do you suggest?" Eshkol asked in seeming innocence. "I think we should give the job to Shkolnik," Becker answered. "What do you think, Golda?" Put on the spot, she had no choice but to agree.

Giving Eshkol the top title in the council didn't prevent Golda from involving herself in its hard, draining work or from continuing to mix into everything about it for the next two years. Then, in June 1945, when Eliyahu Golomb, the Haganah commander and Histadrut activist—and one of the Sharett brothers-in-law—died suddenly of a heart attack, she piled many of his responsibilities onto her already over-heavy workload. Not long afterward, she, Sharett, and Joseph Sprinzak became a committee of three to reorganize the supreme command of the Haganah and choose a replacement for Golomb.

Remez, who was in London for political meetings, wrote to Golda to commiserate about Golomb. They had all admired the man greatly and felt bereft at losing him. "We had hoped for a saving miracle," he wrote, "instead we got the phone ringing" with the bad news. After the death, Remez had a conversation with a physician who had treated Golomb and held that his passing could have been avoided. When Golomb was in London, the doctor had prescribed one basic medicine that would have kept him alive—"rest, a decent amount of rest."

The words should have been a warning. Rest was what Golda lacked. Even on Friday night and Saturday, the Sabbath, she busily bustled about her apartment, serving meals or sweets to an array of people who dropped in, often unannounced—visitors from America, friends from the kibbutzim in town for a weekend, party members come to discuss business or simply gossip. Her male counterparts had wives who shopped and cooked for them. Golda did the chores herself, with some help from Leah Biskin when she lived with the family. As exhausted as she might have been, however, she loved the hum of activity in her home, loved turning her kitchen into a communal gathering place. In later years, her kitchen would be a symbol of power, a center for high-level "political cooking." She was laying the foundation for that day now.

But her grueling daily schedule and nonstop weekend entertaining did their damage. Although she had become heavier, her face looked drawn and tight much of the time, her deep-set eyes ringed in shadows. Remez's letter about Golomb, dated July 5, crossed with two letters sent to him from people in the Histadrut office. Both spoke worriedly of the "hard pressure" on Golda. With Dov Hoz and Golomb gone and Remez and Shazar abroad, she had remained almost alone in Palestine among the Histadrut's senior people. Most recently, she had become involved in Iggud Hamikzoi (Workers' Union), the Histadrut department that bargained and negotiated with employers on behalf of the workers, and the general consensus was that she should head it. In addition, Sprinzak, feeling ill himself from overwork, took a vacation on the advice of his doctor, leaving many of his responsibilities to Golda.

A week later, the Histadrut comrades had dire news for Remez. That morning, July 11, Golda had lost consciousness, and when she came to, she said she "could not move at all." Doctors summoned took her immediately to Beilinson Hospital. There was "no surprise in the matter," the letter writer, Simcha, opined. Golda's work "crosses all boundaries . . . there is no day or night for her, and all our talk about the need to rest . . . naturally is not the kind of thing that influences Golda." Indeed, at age forty-seven, her routine response to warnings that she slow down was a flippant "A lot of us die at around fifty."

She had been in fine fettle just the night before, admonishing her colleagues at a Mapai meeting that if they wanted to convey their ideas to the general public, they had better learn to shorten their long, ponderous speeches. She joked that after one of her talks when she told her daughter, Sarah, that she'd spoken for less than an hour, Sarah asked in amazement, "What's wrong with you, didn't you have anything to say?" Sarah and her youth movement friends had become so accustomed to lengthy orations from party members that her mother's relatively short talk embarrassed her. Golda informed the meeting that in America, where she came from—which, after all, "is not a land of complete boors"— anyone who speaks more than fifty-five minutes is removed from the platform, a practice the party here may want to follow. Nothing in her cheerful, self-assured tone hinted at the next day's events.

Yet months earlier, Dr. Yosef Meyer, from the Kupat Holim health service, had cautioned the Histadrut leaders about the pace Golda was keeping. With her gallbladder attacks and migraines, she was not in good health to begin with. If anything happens to her, the doctor wrote to the executive committee, "who will be to blame, if not you"? The committee ignored the doctor's warning. It was easier to scold Golda about working too hard than to make a serious effort to try to stop her.

Two days after the incident in her office, its ramifications became clear. Only a miracle had rescued her from what could have been a "fatal" heart attack, Dr. Meyer said. A letter from the Histadrut staff informed Remez that the physicians who had carried her out of the office had been concerned about moving her at all and had used extreme caution in lifting her. Now they anticipated a hospital stay of some weeks and after that several months of recuperation in a rest home before she could return to work. Even then, the letter writer remonstrated, everybody, including Golda, will have to think seriously about whether there was any justification for her to continue working as she had been and in that way "shorten the days of her life."

Subsequent letters from the office to Remez filled in more details. Golda would be required to live a quiet and normal life after her complete recovery. She would absolutely have to give up her chain-smoking, cut down her coffee consumption to just two cups a day, and rest a great deal. "It's unclear how she will do this, but she will have to learn," wrote Chaim Berman. Thirty years later, Golda Meir might have looked back in amusement at how anybody could have imagined she would conform to those rules.

While she recuperated, Golda wrote to Remez from the hospital, and he in turn gave her news from abroad. He sent big news on July 26, the day results from the British general elections came in: The British Labour Party had roundly defeated Winston Churchill's Conservatives. Out of office, Labour had severely criticized the White Paper and had taken a strong stand in favor of opening the doors of Palestine to Jewish refugees, even to the extent of encouraging the Arab population to immigrate to other lands. Churchill, who spoke of himself as a Zionist, had done nothing to undo the White Paper regulations. With Clement Attlee as prime minister and Ernest Bevin as foreign secretary, the Zionists believed they had reason to be optimistic. This was a historic day, Remez wrote to Golda. From her hospital bed, she began making happy plans. As soon as the doctors permitted her, she would join Remez and other comrades in London and start meeting and working with Parliament members. She would ask Marie Syrkin to come to Palestine for a few months to help out while she was gone.

The plans came to naught. On July 28, 1945, she suffered a severe headache and weakness. She would have to remain in the hospital for several more weeks, with no visitors and total rest. Then she would go to a rest home in Cyprus for some months.

"Goldenyu," Zalman Shazar wrote to her from Cairo a day later. He had seen her in the hospital before he left home. "I have never left you with so heavy a heart as I did this time," he said. "If I had any hope that you would permit me to go with you to Cyprus and be with you during these months of rest, to watch over you and especially your rest, I would cancel my trip to London and travel with you . . . And I have no doubt that I would fulfill my role. But what good is it for me to complain . . . and I'm not even sure whether you believe me. And who knows if this is what you want?"

During her hospital stay, both he and Remez, the rival lovers, wrote to her. Both sent their letters to the Histadrut office, where others could read what they said, but Shazar labeled his "private," and in contrast to Remez's crisp, businesslike notes his conveyed warmth and love. "Please, Goldenyu," he wrote in one letter, "in the name of the best days we had, take a complete and thorough rest." When he returned from his travels, he hoped to visit her, if she permitted. It would be "my payment," he said. "For what? . . . Perhaps for my suffering."

Golda's recovery followed an uneven path. Discharged from the hospital on August 9, she was prepared to move to the rest home in Cyprus, when at the last moment it had no available room for her. She went to her sister Sheyna's house in Holon for a short while, suffered a mild attack there, and returned home to rest. On August 23, she moved to a rest home in Safed. She felt so well, she told a visitor, that she expected to attend a labor union conference in Paris the following month. Dr. Meyer absolutely forbade it, and she remained in Safed, planning to stay through the Jewish holidays, which ended on October 1.

In far-off Abadan, where Morris worked for Solel Boneh, he received two letters from their son, Menahem, informing him of Golda's illness, but because the mails were slow, a telegram saying she was much better arrived before them. He'd also heard from a colleague who had been home on vacation that she was recovering well. From "the depths of my heart," he told Menahem, he hoped that was the case. More than that, he had nothing to say about Golda, or to her, permanently separated as they now were. He sent regards only to Leah Biskin.

Remez and Shazar, on the other hand, continued to provide her with information. From Remez, she learned about the World Zionist conference in London that she had missed, and in one letter she found a small, personal hint of the emotions they had once shared in that city. "Today my taxi driver took me by chance to Torrington Square and that wave [of feeling] passed over me again." From Shazar, she learned about the Paris conference, in a letter packed with passion. He thought he heard her voice from a distance, from the stage at the conference. Although he knew that was not possible and that her doctors had prohibited her attending, he "drank in" those words, and they brought "comfort" and "glad tidings" to him. Many people care and worry about her, he wrote, "but if only you knew how my heart trembles when I think about you." And many people missed her at the Paris conference, but he wondered if she knew how much he personally missed her. Through all the days of the conference, "I felt from afar your spirit and your soul with us, with me, even if distances separated us." In a postscript he added, "Did you arrange to have the letter I sent to you in Cyprus returned? Please!" It was one thing for her to receive his loving words, another for them to be floating around the rest home in Cyprus to which she did not go. That letter has disappeared. This one she kept.

In his letter, Shazar guessed that Golda had left the rest home and returned to work before she should have. "I assumed from the beginning that the storms of these days would take you out of your loneliness and bring you . . . into the midst of the cauldron," he wrote. He understood that she, of all people, would not be able to resist the anticipation and anxiety accompanying the new British Labour government. "Blessed is your return, Goldenyu, and doubly blessed is your recovery," he continued, followed by what he really wanted to say: "And please do not be angry at me if I add my request, my fear: Please, Goldenyu, be careful and measured." For his sake and that of her children, "take care, take care."

Shazar had good reason to urge caution. On September 29, days before Golda was supposed to leave the rest home in Safed, her name appears in the minutes of a Mapai meeting as an active participant. She had cut her recuperation short and returned to the fray. By October 11, when Shazar wrote to her, she was in the thick of Yishuv doings as though nothing need change in her life's tempo. At the core of much of her frenzy now lay one overwhelming emotion: disappointment. It was fast becoming evident that the British Labour government, which she and her colleagues had so enthusiastically welcomed, had no intention of canceling the White Paper. She could not avoid jumping into the cauldron.

One major indication of the changed British Labour attitude was its response to a plea by the new American president, Harry S. Truman, to allow 100,000 Jewish refugees to enter Palestine immediately. Truman was not particularly a Zionist sympathizer: he had said at a press conference that if a Jewish state were to be established in Palestine, he had no intention of sending 500,000 American troops there to keep the peace. But he had a strong humanitarian impulse. Earlier, on July 14, during the Potsdam conference in which he met with Winston Churchill and Joseph Stalin to discuss the postwar world, he sent a memo to Churchill asking that the restrictions of the White Paper be lifted. Two days later, Churchill lost his job as prime minister. Attlee, his replacement, replied vaguely that the government needed time to review the situation in Palestine. Truman escalated his request after receiving a report on the desperate circumstances of Jewish Holocaust survivors, now called displaced persons, or DPs.

Earl G. Harrison, author of the report, had led a mission to the refugee camps in Germany and Austria during the summer of 1945. Dean of the University of Pennsylvania Law School and former U.S. commissioner of immigration, he was shocked by what he saw among the Jewish refugees. "As matters now stand," he wrote, "we appear to be treating the Jews as the Nazis treated them except we do not exterminate them."

Some of the DP camps Harrison visited were former concentration camps, including the notorious Dachau and Bergen-Belsen. In many, he saw refugees languishing behind barbed wire under American armed guards, some still dressed in the "hideous" striped camp pajamas of Nazi days, all with insufficient food and medical supplies. After speaking to the survivors, he concluded that most wanted to leave Germany and Austria and go to Palestine, where they would feel safe. He recommended that 100,000 Jewish refugees—a figure that originally came from the Jewish Agency—be admitted to Palestine as quickly as possible. Truman's plea to the Attlee government written at the end of August grew directly from Harrison's findings.

The aloof, urbane Attlee was to exchange correspondence with the president on the matter, but his brusque foreign secretary would become most identified with the government's Palestine policies. Ernie Bevin, as many called him, "was a large, powerfully built man with heavy shell-rimmed spectacles" and a bullish manner that had served him well in his earlier years as a dockworker and trade union organizer. Golda would speak of him as either "a little insane, or just anti-Semitic, or both" in his dealings with the Jewish refugee issue. He might not have been anti-Semitic, but he was like a brick wall when it came to understanding the depth of the refugees' suffering or the significance of the Land of Israel to the Jewish people.

Bevin considered the Jews a religious community, not a nation like the Arabs, and therefore in no need of their own land. Therefore, also, the refugees could be repatriated to the countries they had come from, despite the devastation they had experienced in many of those places. Moreover, Bevin made a point of linking Jewish victims to the larger refugee problem, downplaying the distinctive situation of Holocaust survivors. Besides that, England had emerged battered and bruised from the war, teetering on the edge of bankruptcy and financially dependent on its wealthy American ally. Its once great empire was falling apart— within the next few years it would withdraw from India, Egypt, Kenya, Cyprus, and other regions—while the Soviet Union aggressively pushed to make inroads into the Middle East. Eager to keep strong ties to the Arab regimes, suppliers of his nation's oil, Bevin had no intention of alienating Arab rulers or inciting Palestinian Arabs by placating the Jews.

As for Truman, Bevin regarded his insistence on admitting 100,000

Jewish refugees to Palestine a ploy to win Jewish votes in America. He was not altogether wrong in that. As Truman himself said, "I have to answer to the hundreds of thousands who are anxious for the success of Zionism; I do not have hundreds of thousands of Arabs in my constituents." Yet horrified by the Harrison report, Truman also sincerely wished "to do what's right."

During the next two months, while Truman and Attlee exchanged letters and arguments over the proposed 100,000 certificates, England didn't budge from a new quota it had set after the White Paper total of 75,000 had run out: 1,500 Jewish immigrants a month and no more would be admitted to Palestine. The future looked ominous to the Jews of the Yishuv. Better than anyone, Golda put into words the anger and disillusionment they all felt. She appeared on October 1, before a Histadrut conference, where her colleagues welcomed her back from her illness with extended applause. "For over twenty years British Labour supported the Jewish Labor movement in Palestine," she said, directing her remarks to the British government as well as her comrades. "Throughout these years British Labour constantly reiterated its faith in the justice of our cause . . . Who among us can now dare speak of labor solidarity, when after the great misfortune that has befallen our people, our friends and comrades in the British Labour government promise to treat us as they do?"

Her anger mounted as her words flowed. "Comrades of the Labour Party and of the Labour Government in England," she announced in a firm, steady voice, "you are facing a test. The 100,000 certificates for Jewish immigration into Palestine that are demanded of you are the test of your sincerity . . . You will not frighten us. We do not want to fight you. We want to build. We want to enable the small remnant of European Jewry to come to Palestine in peace . . . But should you persist in preventing us from doing this, we wish to make our position as clear as possible: We have no alternative."

Ein breira, "there is no alternative." Yishuv leaders used the phrase again and again, none more often or more effectively than Golda. It became part of her repertoire: there was no alternative to fighting the White Paper; no alternative to bringing in illegal immigrants; no alternative to creating a Jewish state. Over the years she would speak of "no alternative" as "Israel's secret weapon": it had no alternative but to survive.

"The hour has struck," she warned. "At this time we declare to our

comrades in the British Labour movement and to working people everywhere: it is the zero hour. You can save not only us but also yourselves
from a great misfortune." Even weakened, the British Empire towered
giantlike over the small Yishuv, but Golda felt no compunction about
threatening it. In our own way, we can make trouble for you, she was
implying.

Britain's response to the agitation about its policies came on Tuesday,
November 13, 1945, with a speech Bevin gave to the House of Commons. In a gesture of politeness, the government invited eleven Yishuv
leaders, including Golda, to Chief Secretary John Shaw's office in Jerusalem at five o'clock that afternoon, when Bevin's statement would be
read to them moments before he delivered it. To contemplate what they
might hear and how to react, the leaders convened with a broader group
at 4:05, fifty-five minutes ahead of the scheduled government meeting,
at the Jewish Agency headquarters. The room seemed to tremble with
tension and Talmudic-like speculation.

"We will not have to react to the talk, except in regard to one
subject—if they do not announce that they are repealing the White
Paper," one participant said. "If they say that the White Paper remains
but they will issue [additional] certificates, maybe we should react,"
another suggested. Golda Meyerson listened, then threw cold water on
whatever degree of optimism the others felt. She had no doubt that "we
will not receive good news today." Furthermore, she suspected that with
the bad news they would also receive a warning, and they "should not be
silent about that."

At 4:40 the pre-meeting ended. A little over an hour later, at 5:45, the
group gathered again at the Jewish Agency building, sober, distraught,
shaken by what they had heard from Bevin. Golda had been right. Britain had no intention of repealing the White Paper. Instead, it had invited
the United States to join it in forming the Anglo-American Committee
of Inquiry to seek a solution to the Jewish refugee problem, and the
American government had agreed. Nothing had changed. Another committee had been formed—another Évian, another Bermuda, another way
to dodge the desperate refugee situation and maintain the status quo.

A journalist who observed Bevin as he spoke that day described him as
"a squat, broad-shouldered, elderly figure, slightly incongruous in formal dress," who pounded on a table to make his points, especially when
he wanted to emphasize his own goodwill. His speech to Parliament
not only announced the Anglo-American committee; it also enunciated

some of his pet ideas about the refugee situation. "The plight of the victims of Nazi persecution, among whom were a large number of Jews, is unprecedented in the history of the world," he said, and "we cannot accept the view that the Jews should be driven out of Europe," and "Palestine, while it may be able to make a contribution, does not, by itself provide sufficient opportunity for grappling with the whole problem." He described the strong support the Zionist cause had "in the United States, in Great Britain and in the Dominions and elsewhere," but he emphasized that "the cause of the Palestinian Arabs has been espoused by the whole Arab world and . . . had become a matter of keen interest to their ninety million co-religionists in India," a hard number to match.

From a British perspective, what Bevin said might have sounded reasonable. Britain had been coping unsuccessfully with the conflict between Jews and Arabs for more than twenty years. By involving the United States, the government hoped to share the responsibility of finding a resolution that would satisfy both groups. Afterward, however, at a press conference, Bevin's anger at the Jews burst through. "I want suppression of racial warfare," he said, "and therefore if the Jews with all their sufferings want to get too much at the head of the queue you have the danger of another anti-Semitic reaction through it all." The crassness of the words and the distorted cartoon image of Jews pushing to "the head of the queue" set Jewish teeth on edge. The veiled threat about the danger of renewed anti-Semitism infuriated.

The Yishuv exploded with rage the next day as thousands mounted protests and the National Council called for a general strike. The chief rabbinate declared a day of fasting. During a Mapai Center meeting, Golda fired back with a statement of her own. She was the first speaker on the agenda in an atmosphere of gloom bordering on despair. She began slowly by reminding her comrades that simple common sense had told them to expect a hard blow from the British. The blow that hit them, however, was harder than they could have anticipated and made more bitter by coming from people who professed to be their friends—a message she would hammer home at every opportunity. Then she ripped apart the "socialist minister," as she called him with cutting sarcasm, pointing up his lack of a socialist conscience. Among other things, he lacked even the most elementary understanding of the refugee situation when he implied that Europe would be the best place for the displaced Jews. "This he says in the year 1945, after this war," when millions of Jews were slaughtered on European soil.

Her answer to Bevin's statement: "There will be no silence!" She would tell Britain and the United States that "we do not have ninety million Moslems in India standing behind us; we have six million graves in Europe." Nevertheless, they dare not write off the Jews in the Yishuv. The British "have a navy, army and air force, atomic bombs and secret weapons and open weapons. We know what our strength is. Our strength is the strength of a despairing nation that is fighting and struggling now for its life . . . Many of us face the question of whether to die with honor or to die as cowards . . . When England faced this question during the war, she chose to fight and to die if necessary with pride and honor and not to live lives of subservience and slavery. We are ready to accept this teaching from her."

She concluded with a call to arms: "We have received the declaration of war by the English government—we will not answer it by giving in."

If the rhetoric sounds melodramatic today, it reached its listeners at that melancholy meeting. High in the party hierarchy now, Golda rallied the troops into action.

Two weeks later, she spoke about action at a Mapai council meeting, a broader group than the more exclusive party center. Here her tone was more contemplative. They had never wanted to fight the government, she said. For years, despite Arab attacks and British restrictions, they had followed their path of *havlagah*, restraining themselves from initiating violence or retaliating against it. "We took the path we did not because we thought this way would make a great impression on the world. We took this path because this was our nature." The world, however, did not understand the Jewish ties to the land. "The good world, the enlightened, the just, the world of conscience," she said with the sarcasm that had become integral to her oratory, had not grasped the great need of the Jewish people for its own land, not even in their hour of desperation during the Holocaust. If that world once had a conscience, it "has gone underground."

The only way to arouse that conscience was to be active, to fight the British "not in the ghettos, not in gas chambers, but here in the Land of Israel," where the world will hear and know about it. She could not guarantee success, but after much soul-searching she had concluded that in the old way of restraint there "was no hope."

BY THE TIME GOLDA SPOKE those words, she well knew that the Haganah and its elite Palmach strike force had already embarked on an armed struggle against the British. She also knew that—in an astonishing turnaround—they had joined hands with two radical underground forces on the right whom until now the mainstream had vehemently opposed: the Irgun—the defense unit of the Revisionist movement—and an even more extremist breakaway group from the Irgun, Lohamei Herut Israel (Freedom Fighters of Israel), known by the acronym Lehi. The British called that group the Stern Gang, after their leader Abraham Stern, whom the police had shot and killed. In consultation with Haganah heads, and after lengthy debate, the party leadership had agreed to put aside powerful enmities with these organizations to form the unified Jewish Resistance Movement.

For Golda, as well as the others, that alliance with the radical Right required a conscious reorientation of thinking, or more: a negation of their long history of antipathy toward those groups, whom they called "dissidents." Through all the years of their existence, Golda had disagreed with them. These people "were wrong . . . from start to finish," she would say and repeat in various ways her opposition to the violence "both on moral grounds and tactically." She had never strayed from her belief that Revisionists were responsible for the murder of Chaim Arlosoroff in 1933 and had spoken out so forcefully against them that she landed high on their enemies list. She softened her hostility toward the dissident groups slightly during the war years, when the Irgun agreed to refrain from anti-British activity and cooperate in the struggle against Hitler. Late in 1940, after the disaster of the *Patria* ship, she opened her apartment to secret talks between the Irgun commander, David Raziel, and the Haganah chief, Eliyahu Golomb, who met to explore the possibility of unifying their two underground forces. The talks were short-lived; when Ben-Gurion got wind of them, he quickly quashed the idea.

After that, relations between the Yishuv and the dissidents had remained antagonistic. The Irgun truce with the British did not last out the war. (Lehi never made a truce.) Early in 1944, under its steely new commander, Menachem Begin (later to become Israel's sixth prime minister), it announced a revolt against the British government in Palestine. Posters plastered on buildings around the country displayed the group's emblem of a hand grasping a rifle against a map of mandatory Palestine, including Transjordan. Irgun members blew up British immigration and tax offices, raided intelligence headquarters, and attacked government broadcasting stations. Within the Yishuv, they intimidated merchants and extorted money from individuals and institutions to acquire funds for their operations.

During those months of terror, some young people had been attracted by the romantic boldness of these radical militants, but the bulk of the organized Jewish community had been repelled by their tactics. Golda, Ben-Gurion, and other Yishuv leaders had regarded them as irresponsible and destructive to Jewish interests. Just how destructive Golda had indicated at a chilling meeting of the Mapai political department in March 1944.

"In my opinion they pose a severe danger for us," she had said. "The British do not want to put an end to this," calculating that the dissidents' actions would turn world opinion against the Jewish cause. By doing nothing themselves to put an end to the militancy, Golda said, "to my mind this makes me something of a partner with them."

"Define what you mean by 'putting an end' to it," Ben-Gurion interrupted.

"Our job is to find a way, with whom to work to put an end to them, to put an end in every manner," she replied.

"Does putting an end to them mean destroying men?" Ben-Gurion interrupted again, as though testing Golda to see how far she was willing to go.

"All right then, even to destroy men," she answered, taking up his challenge. "I have no moral constraints in regard to this group." They are bringing disaster not only to the British but also to the Jewish community, she repeated.

One possibility for controlling the dissidents, she had suggested, was to cooperate with the British in capturing them, if Haganah heads agreed to that. "I know what it means to turn someone in," she said, softening her manner for a moment. "I'm not so lacking in feelings toward these things, what it means to give them up to the government." But, she emphasized, with the situation so dangerous to the entire Yishuv, something needed to be done.

Ben-Gurion broke in again: "But one thing no—Jews will not slaughter one another in the Land of Israel."

"They already have slaughtered Jews," she replied, remaining calm in the face of his goading. "I know that it is very bad to shoot people from the Irgun or the Stern group, but if they bring it to that point . . . we have to do everything to make them stop in this work."

It was a tough, implacable performance, probably shocking to some Mapai members. It might have been here that the myth of Ben-Gurion's famous "only man in the cabinet" remark about Golda first took root. In her blunt manner, she had put into words what many in the room, including Ben-Gurion (or especially Ben-Gurion), might have felt but didn't dare utter. To her mind, if the Jewish leaders truly believed that the dissidents undermined the Zionist cause and endangered Jewish lives, they needed to stop the radicals, using whatever means that called for.

Not long after that session, Golda's concept of cooperating with the British government in dealing with the dissidents had become Yishuv policy. The catalyst was the assassination of Walter Guinness, Lord Moyne, the highest-ranking British official in the Middle East, stationed in Cairo. The two assassins, Eliyahu Beit-Zuri and Eliyahu Hakim, members of Lehi, were quickly apprehended, convicted, and hanged. A millionaire owner of the Guinness beverage company, Lord Moyne had been a close friend of Winston Churchill's. The Zionists had long regarded him as unfriendly toward them and their nationalistic goals. But just two days before the murder, Churchill suggested to Chaim Weizmann that Moyne had changed his attitude and urged Weizmann to visit the minister in Egypt. Weizmann never got the chance. The murder shocked the world and infuriated Churchill. In a statement to the House of Commons, he warned that if his efforts on behalf of the Zionists were to "produce only a new set of gangsters worthy of Nazi Germany," he and others would have to reconsider their positions.

Horrified by the assassination, the Yishuv leaders had fiercely condemned it and launched what became known, awkwardly, as the *saison*, hunting season. Although Lehi was behind the murder, Yishuv leaders targeted the Irgun, the larger and more powerful movement. This time Ben-Gurion stated the goal: "To spew forth all the members of this harmful, destructive gang." Led by him, the Jewish Agency informed the British authorities that it would cooperate fully with them in rounding up members of the radical group. Through that autumn and winter, the Haganah and the Palmach kidnapped Irgun members, interrogated them, and handed numbers of them over to the British or gave the police lists of names. The "hunt" lasted until March 1945, but the anger and resentment it created lingered for decades.

Nevertheless, nine months after the *saison* ended, the Jewish Resistance Movement was born, with its remarkable sea change of cooperation among the longtime enemies. It would be an uneasy partnership. In many cases, the Haganah warned the British before blowing up an installation so that occupants could escape without losing their lives. Less scrupulous in their operations, the Irgun and Lehi rarely even expressed regret at having killed British police or army officers. Still, the three sides worked together for the next several months in their war against Britain. Part of that war involved a determined effort to bring boatloads of refugees to the land in direct defiance of British quotas. The other part called for the kind of sabotage and use of force the Yishuv leaders had previously condemned. "We kept hearing the argument, 'The Arabs can create so much trouble, therefore you have to give in.' So in the end we decided, very well, *we'll* create trouble," Golda said.

Golda's position on the Haganah committee with Moshe Sharett and Yosef Sprinzak placed her at the center of decision making for the underground forces. She also took part in professional meetings with the Haganah heads, Moshe Sneh and Israel Galili, to plan specific Haganah and Palmach operations. In one of the first and most celebrated of those operations, Palmach units infiltrated the British detention camp at Atlit and released the 208 illegal immigrants being held there. As deputy commander, Yitzhak Rabin led the daring assault that brought the immigrants to a kibbutz in Haifa, where they stymied the police by quickly dispersing among the local population. They were never recaptured. In a joint venture with the Irgun and Lehi a short while after that, the Palmach sabotaged railway tracks at 153 points around the country, paralyzing all rail travel. Later it sank British patrol ships and blew up two British coast guard stations and a radar installation in Haifa used to detect immigrant ships. Periodically the unified forces attacked British airfields and lighthouses. The Jews called their fight *ma'avak*, the struggle, and publicized their resistance through an underground radio station, Kol Israel, the Voice of Israel. To keep the Yishuv abreast and press the Jewish viewpoint on the British and Arabs, they broadcast in Hebrew, English, and Arabic.

The British struck back at the resistance movement with arrests and curfews that closed roads and prevented people from leaving their homes. (Those days were "among the most restful," Marie Syrkin recalled from her visits, when Golda would catch up with mending and ironing, although still "receiving or giving directives" by telephone.) British police forces regularly searched settlements for Haganah soldiers, hidden weapons, and illegal immigrants. To bolster their security forces, they summoned their crack Sixth Airborne Division, paratroopers and pilots who had been in the Normandy landing. In line with the men's red berets, the Jews nicknamed them *kalaniyot*, after the local red anemone flower with its black heart.

Around March 1946, the Jewish Resistance Movement paused in its assaults on the British. The Anglo-American committee had begun its work and was coming to town.

THE BRITISH AND THE AMERICANS each chose six men—and no women—to be on the Anglo-American committee. The American group included its chairman, a conservative Texas judge, Joseph Hutcheson; the editor of the *Boston Herald*, Frank W. Buxton; a former ambassador to Italy, William Phillips; the director of the Institute for Advanced Study in Princeton, New Jersey, Frank Aydelotte; and two people Golda would describe later as "fast friends"—James G. McDonald, the former League of Nations high commissioner for refugees, who was to become the first U.S. ambassador to the State of Israel; and Bartley Crum, a left-leaning San Francisco lawyer. Crum would become good friends with his British counterpart, Richard Crossman, a Labour member of Parliament. Bright, witty, unpredictable, both were the youngest in their respective groups, and both wrote books about their experience with the committee soon after it completed its work. By that time, they had become sympathetic to the Jewish cause. Ironically, Bevin had handpicked Crossman for the commission, expecting his total allegiance, and the younger man began the investigation with the same attitude as the other five British members of the committee—an acceptance of the White Paper and a bent away from Zionism or the centrality of Palestine for the Jews. His ideas changed radically as the committee took testimony from Jews and Arabs and traveled to the DP camps of Europe.

The committee members from the two countries met for the first time in Washington, D.C., and began their hearings at the Statler Hotel there on January 7, 1946. Truman requested that they complete their investigation and present their conclusions within 120 days. Bevin promised that if their recommendations were unanimous, he would do everything in his power to implement them. Among the people who testified in Washington, Albert Einstein stood out, his presence causing a loud stir of excitement in the audience. The Zionists thought he would bring great cachet to their side, so the impresario Meyer Weisgal spent hours persuading the reluctant scientist to appear. He might have saved his energies. Based on limited knowledge of the situation in Palestine, Einstein didn't do the Zionists any favors by saying that he disapproved of all forms of nationalism and didn't support the concept of a Jewish majority in Palestine. "I was not impressed by the testimony of Einstein," Golda remarked sardonically as she prepared for her own testimony.

Before that testimony in Jerusalem, the commission members crossed the Atlantic on the *Queen Elizabeth* to hold hearings with Jews and Arabs in London. To a person, Arab witnesses opposed further Jewish immigration into Palestine. Although some expressed sympathy for Jewish survivors of the death camps, they emphasized that the Europeans and not they had created the Jewish plight. One witness, Fares el-Khoury, chief of the Syrian delegation to the UN, exclaimed to Judge Hutcheson, "Why don't you give the Jews part of Texas?"

From London the committee fanned out to the displaced persons camps in Germany, Austria, and Poland, where they were deeply moved by the survivors they met. They found in these people, Crum wrote, a desire to go to Palestine so strong that "little less than death could destroy it." Some committee members questioned whether Zionist representatives visiting the camps had indoctrinated the refugees. In truth, the Jewish Agency had sent emissaries to the camps to teach the survivors about Zionism and offer them assistance if they were to settle in Palestine. But it is also true that the majority of survivors did not wish to stay in Europe; they wanted to go where they could feel wanted. Would they have preferred the United States if they had a choice? It was a moot question: the doors of that land were shut to them.

As the committee moved on to the Middle East, Golda and her Mapai comrades debated their approach. Ben-Gurion initially opposed any cooperation with the committee, regarding it as a cynical tool to maintain the status quo. In the United States, the activist rabbi Abba Hillel Silver had also refused to testify at what he considered just another delaying tactic. Some Mapai leaders had the same attitude. Why not simply boycott the committee? Golda answered with a shrewd sense of public relations and her old authority as an expert on all things American.

There is a big difference between England and America, she explained. For years, the empire had appointed one committee after another in every part of the world, and it mattered little to the local population what the committee decided. As a young country, the United States had little experience in such committees. "I have no doubt," she said, "that it would make a very bad impression on American public opinion" if their group boycotted the committee. It would be impossible to justify "to the newspapers, to members of Congress who supported us, and to other American friends why the Jews refused to appear before the committee to explain the rightness of their demands." In the end, Ben-Gurion decided to participate; he and Sharett gave their testimonies ahead of Golda.

The committee arrived in Palestine on March 8, staying at the

King David Hotel and conducting their hearings across the street in the imposing YMCA. British soldiers holding tommy guns guarded the building's entrance, while armed tanks patrolled the streets. Crum thought it was England's way of calling the committee's attention to the dangers of the Jewish Resistance Movement. In the elegant lecture hall inside, witnesses gave testimony while seated at a large round table facing committee members. The men who spoke dressed in dark suits and ties—uncomfortable garb for Ben-Gurion and the others, used to open collars and rolled-up shirtsleeves. Golda looked equally businesslike but also feminine in her proper dark skirt and jacket with a white blouse, her hair, as always, pulled back loosely in a bun and soft around her face. Representing the Histadrut, she was the only woman from the Yishuv to testify.

Her testimony, on March 25, lasted for an hour and a half, and during that time, *Davar* reported the next day, she spoke with "pride," "intelligence," and "warm emotion." Not "one ear in the packed auditorium stopped listening for even a moment," the story gushed. *The Palestine Post* praised her "direct approach" and "clear and unevasive replies," which "dispelled the uncomfortable court-room atmosphere, the irritation and the boredom" of the hearings. Avoiding the pomp that had weighed down other speakers, Golda began by giving the background of the pioneers who had come to the land from Eastern Europe, some of them forty or more years earlier. They had grown up "in an environment of persecution" but had decided "that there must be an end to senseless living and senseless dying among Jews." The only way to do that was "in creating an independent Jewish life in the Jewish homeland."

During the war years, she told the committee, they in Palestine felt helpless as they watched millions of Jews being slaughtered. Now they would do anything to save the remnant. "Gentlemen," she said, "I am authorized on behalf of the close to 160,000 members of our federation to say here in the clearest terms, there is nothing that Jewish labor is not prepared to do in this country in order to meet and accept large masses of Jewish immigration . . . That is the purpose for which we have come." In a moving moment, she tried to reach into the heads of her listeners and wrap their minds around the meaning of being Jewish:

I don't know, gentlemen, whether you who are fortunate to belong to the two great democratic nations, the British and the American, can realize what it means . . . to be a member of a people who is forever being questioned . . . on its very existence, its very right to be; what it means to be constantly questioned whether we have a right to be Jews as we are, not better, but not worse, than others . . . We only want that which is given naturally to all peoples of the world, to be masters of our own fate . . . to live as of right and not on sufferance.

She had read much of the formal statement from a prepared text. She answered the questions that followed extemporaneously. Many centered on relations with the Arabs. Should there be Arab immigration comparable to Jewish immigration? No, Golda answered. "I don't think that those Arabs outside of Palestine can put up a case for the necessity of immigrating into Palestine, whereas Jews are in quite a different position." What about the exclusion of Arab laborers from some Jewish plantations? Places of work "created by Jewish initiative and Jewish capital must be safeguarded for Jewish workers so long as the entire Arab economy is almost 100 percent closed to Jewish workers," Golda replied. Suppose you were "masters of your own fate" and there were a Jewish state, how would the Arab minority fare? "It would be more than foolish to expect that we could live here in comfort and in peace and not do everything for the Arab minority," Golda said. When the Labour minister, Sir Frederick Leggett, asked whether the use of Hebrew prevented unity, Golda—trying not to show her annoyance—answered, "Hebrew is our language, just as English is your language, just as French is the language of the French and Chinese, of China. None of these probably would be questioned as to why they spoke their language."

"Her walk, her talk, were like soldiers marching," Ruth Gruber, who attended the hearings, recalled. "Everything was in order. She knew exactly what she wanted to say and said it with great passion."

The committee completed its investigations on March 28, 1946, and flew to Lausanne, Switzerland, to work out its final report. Before leaving, Richard Crossman noted in his diary how comfortable he had felt with the testimonies of David Ben-Gurion, Golda Meyerson, and some of the other Jewish labor leaders. He regarded them as true socialists, idealistically wishing to build "the only free socialist society in the world." He had traveled far from his beginnings as "Bevin's man" on the committee.

Crossman and the rest of the committee had barely settled into their deliberations when a new crisis captured international attention. On

April 1, 1946, at the port of La Spezia on the Italian Riviera, the British intercepted a schooner packed with survivors and about to make a run for Palestine. In response, its eleven hundred passengers began a hunger strike. Palestine, they stated in a telegram to the Jewish Agency, is "the land of our last and only hope . . . we shall not leave this ship."

The boat, the *Fede*, was one of dozens attempting to carry clandestine immigrants to Palestine. After World War II, when the seas opened to maritime traffic again, shiploads of immigrants tried to reach Palestine, in much larger numbers than before. Tens of thousands of survivors fled from Poland (where, after World War II, they had encountered virulent anti-Semitism) to American-occupied Germany. From the DP camps there, illegal immigration leaders—many of them posing as British soldiers—commandeered trucks that smuggled the survivors to French and Austrian borders. The fleeing refugees were then escorted on foot across mountain passes, to the coast of Italy, where they jammed into old prewar boats to make the hazardous voyage to Palestine. The operation went under the name *bricha*, flight. Only a small percentage reached their destination; British tanks and destroyers blockading the waters around Palestine impounded the ships and forcibly brought their passengers to the detention camp at Atlit. The British acted differently with the *Fede*. They stopped the refugee ship before it sailed from La Spezia. In turn, its passengers not only undertook a hunger strike but also threatened mass suicide—ten persons a day—if they were prevented from sailing and entering Palestine. As the vessel sat in port surrounded by the British, its passengers fainting on deck from starvation, swarms of Italians came to gaze at it, and newspaper reporters from many lands sent home stories that stirred world sympathy for the refugees.

Although Golda was still recuperating from her heart attack some months earlier, she persuaded the National Council to allow her and other leaders to mount a hunger strike in sympathy with the refugees. Hoping to sway the British, she and a few others presented that decision to the chief secretary of Palestine. Golda remembered him saying, "Mrs. Meyerson, do you think for a moment that His Majesty's government will change its policy because *you* are not going to eat?" She answered, "No, I have no such illusions. If the death of six million didn't change government policy, I don't expect that my not eating will do so."

But Golda also knew the public relations value of the event, with the eyes of the world on it. She and fourteen other Yishuv leaders chosen by the National Council agreed among themselves to eat nothing and drink only unsweetened tea until the *Fede* was released. (Golda did make sure that cigarettes were permitted.) All the fasters had beds in the National Council office but at first spent most of their time together. The group included two women aside from Golda—Elisheva Vroma Snape, a survivor herself, and Yehudit Simhonit, whom Golda had worked with in the Women Workers' Council. The two men closest to Golda, Zalman Shazar and David Remez, sat alongside her in the strike.

While the Yishuv leaders fasted, people gathered outside the building, and delegations from kibbutzim and major organizations arrived regularly to show their support. As the days progressed and the fasters weakened, medical supervisors limited visitors to family members only and for just an hour or two in the afternoon. Three days into the hunger strike, Golda and the others rallied for the Passover holiday that would begin that evening. Although the chief rabbis urged them to eat in honor of the festival, they consented to nibble on only a symbolic piece of matzo, "the size of an olive," in keeping with Jewish law.

As the holiday began, thousands of people from every part of the country crowded into the courtyards around the national buildings in Jerusalem, chanting and praying for the fasting leaders and the refugees in La Spezia. Inside, Golda and her companions, joined by family members and Yishuv notables, conducted a traditional seder. The chief rabbis sat at the head of the table along with David Remez, who had become the chairman of the National Council. When the youngest in the group, Rabbi Isaac Werfel, asked the traditional four questions, beginning "Why is this night different from all other nights?," the others had to choke back their tears. The words in the answer, "In every generation each person is obliged to see himself as though he had personally left Egypt," had powerful meaning that night, Golda recalled.

At 6:00 p.m. the following day, Tuesday, April 16, the hunger strikes ended. The British had agreed to allow the *Fede* and all its refugees into Palestine. (The ship's name had been changed to the *Dov Hoz* and the passengers divided between it and a second ship, the *Fenice*, renamed *Eliyahu Golomb*, both names honoring the late Haganah heads.) After 101 hours of fasting, Golda and the other hunger strikers ate a meal of matzos and milk and returned home. Shazar entered Hadassah Hospital, suffering from heart problems as a result of the ordeal.

"There seems to be no end to the implications of this," a British official wrote angrily. Would every ship that wanted to get through now stage hunger strikes? Would the Jews do it again, to cancel the White

Paper? Would the Arabs use the same technique to have their leaders who had been banned for helping the Nazis during the war readmitted? He thought the Foreign Office should be warned of all possible consequences. But for the Jewish leaders, the admission of the refugees from La Spezia was a great victory—and for Golda a personal triumph. She had initiated the Yishuv fast and remained visible throughout, speaking constantly to the individuals and groups that visited. "There was nobody who didn't know who Golda was," an aide said.

THE ANGLO-AMERICAN COMMITTEE'S unanimous report came out on May 1 and satisfied no one completely. It called for issuing 100,000 immigration certificates immediately to allow the refugees into Palestine and recommended abolishing immigration and land regulations in the White Paper, both suggestions a victory for the Yishuv leaders. But it rejected any proposals for a Jewish or an Arab state, preferring a binational one under a UN trusteeship, a great disappointment to the Zionists. The Arabs turned down the report and its recommendations out of hand as "against the wish of . . . the Arab states and peoples." Truman welcomed its recommendations for accepting the 100,000 refugees and essentially abrogating the White Paper but advised that the rest of the report would have to be studied carefully before further comment. The British simply reneged on Bevin's promise to implement the report if it were unanimous.

Prime Minister Attlee declared that before a large contingent of new immigrants could be allowed into the country, Jewish military organizations would have to turn in their arms and disband, virtually an impossible condition to accept, given the settlements' need for protection against Arab hostility. That demand, Golda said, reflected the government's desire to "purge" the Jews and denude them of any ability to act on their own.

Bevin was enraged at the British members of the committee, particularly Richard Crossman, whom he had counted on to toe the anti-immigration line. He was also furious at Truman, who publicly urged England to admit the refugees into Palestine as quickly as possible but made no offer to accept any into the United States. At a speech to a Labour Party conference at Bournemouth, England, on June 12, Bevin made another statement that, like his "front of queue" comment, branded him in Jewish minds as an outright anti-Semite. The United States was clamoring for the admission of the 100,000 into Palestine, he said, because "they did not want too many of them in New York." The next day, a massive Jewish rally took place in New York's Madison Square Garden, with speaker after speaker denouncing Bevin. A few months later, the British foreign secretary took in a football game while visiting New York. When his name was announced over the loudspeaker, the stadium crowd hissed and booed.

In answer to the British, on June 17, the Jewish Resistance Movement carried out its last—and boldest—unified action. On that "Night of the Bridges," Palmach units stationed around the country blew up ten of the eleven bridges that linked Palestine to such neighboring lands as Transjordan, Syria, and Lebanon. The operation left the British isolated in Palestine and forced them to spend weeks rebuilding these structures. A day later, acting on their own, the Irgun kidnapped five British officers as hostages to prevent the British from hanging two of their men who had been condemned to death. Eventually, they released the officers, and the British commuted the Jewish men's sentences to life in prison, but for the present the kidnappings heightened the jittery atmosphere pervading the Yishuv. British authorities censored the press and regularly arrested people suspected of terrorism. Armed British soldiers appeared everywhere, and British tanks and military trucks rolled through the streets and roads, holding up traffic and arousing fear. Everyone waited nervously for the other shoe to drop.

It happened before dawn on Saturday, June 29, 1946. Backed by tanks and armored cars, some seventeen thousand British soldiers and policemen raided more than two dozen Jewish settlements throughout the country, searching for weapons and arresting hundreds of kibbutz members suspected of being in the Haganah. Golda and some colleagues had been tipped off beforehand by Haganah intelligence that the British were planning a large-scale military operation against the Yishuv, and that gave them a little time to hide arms and change some codes. But they didn't have a date for the attack, which the British would call Operation Agatha and the Jews label Black Saturday.

The British cleverly chose the Jewish Sabbath for their raid, because it would be easier to enforce a stringent curfew at that time, when people were at home. Also, with offices and factories closed, they expected less chance of organized resistance. Actually, they met fierce resistance, with people using their tractors and their bodies to block the entrances to their settlements, shouting and throwing whatever they could at the invaders. At the kibbutz Yagur, settlers fought desperately, but the British subdued them with teargas and water bombs. Soldiers ripped apart the floor, walls, and ceiling and after several days found a huge cache of Haganah weapons, which they confiscated.

In Jerusalem, armed soldiers broke in to the Jewish Agency headquarters and other official Jewish buildings and loaded boxes of papers and documents onto three large trucks headed for British headquarters. Time and again, when the British had questioned Golda, Ben-Gurion, or others about the Haganah, they claimed they knew little about it and that it had no connection to the Jewish Agency or other Jewish institutions. With the documents it now possessed, the government set out to destroy the Jewish Agency's legitimacy by proving that ties existed between it and the Haganah and between the Haganah and the Irgun and Lehi.

By the time Black Saturday ended, twenty-seven hundred people had been arrested and sent to internment camps. Among them were David Remez and Moshe Sharett. These leaders and other members of the Jewish Agency Executive—so-called VIJs (very important Jews)—were locked up behind barbed wire in Latrun, a detention center halfway between Jerusalem and Tel Aviv. But two of the most important men had eluded the British. Ben-Gurion was in Paris. He had been in London, meeting with British officials, but from the nature of their questions he became suspicious that they wanted to arrest him and took off for Paris. Moshe Sneh, head of the Haganah command, went underground at the last moment and later slipped out of the country. One of the few leaders of the organized Yishuv in Palestine who had not been arrested or attempted to escape was Mrs. Golda Meyerson. She would take the place of the others.

13

"Nevertheless: A Woman"

Golda, are you still at home? They didn't come to take you?" Paula Ben-Gurion called regularly to check on whether the British had arrested Golda along with other Yishuv chiefs during the Black Saturday raids in June 1946. Outspoken, sharp-tongued, and somewhat eccentric, Ben-Gurion's wife was not inquiring innocently. She understood, as did others, that—in a perverse way—being arrested was a good thing and being left behind bad. By rounding up the top leaders, the British aimed to rid the Yishuv of its key policy makers in the hope that an alternative group more willing to cooperate with them would take over. They did not, for example, touch the venerable Chaim Weizmann, who had long called for moderation in dealing with the government. With her oversolicitous phone calls, Paula implied that Golda fell into the category of alternative leadership or moderation, or, at the very least, that she simply wasn't important enough for the British to arrest.

On a humorous note, two months later the poet Nathan Alterman labeled a compliment from the British their most potent weapon. By complimenting a Jewish leader, British authorities cast suspicion on that person, neutralizing his or her opposition. Even activists like Golda Meyerson and others who were not picked up on Black Saturday, he wrote, felt they had been hit by a clap of thunder, their reputations damaged because of that British "compliment." Golda herself always reacted defensively to being left out. Abba Eban, foreign minister when she was prime minister, wrote—not without malice—that "Golda fiercely resented her exclusion from arrest. For the rest of her eventful life she considered this to be an unsuccessful plot to reduce her subsequent eligibility for prime ministerial office in a decolonized Land of Israel." Indeed, as late as 1959, she still felt compelled to explain to a group of high school students that the British probably did not arrest her because she was a woman and they didn't have a jail for women. Actually, the British did jail women in various locations, including Latrun, but the area of Latrun that held the important male leaders might not have had comparable women's facilities.

That could have been the British reason for not arresting Golda. Or, with her perfect English, they might have felt more comfortable dealing with her as a leader than with others in the Yishuv. But Eban erred on one score. Her exclusion from arrest made her *more* eligible, not less, for her ultimate office as prime minister. With Ben-Gurion, Sharett, Remez, and others either locked up or exiled in Europe, she quickly filled the leadership vacuum they had left, seizing every opportunity to be seen and heard and in the process garnering newspaper headlines. On June 30, a day after the British operation, she spoke at a memorial gathering marking the first anniversary of Eliyahu Golomb's death. Addressing the deceased Haganah leader, she promised that they who were left "would not buy life with the price of slavery." They would sacrifice their lives for freedom in their land, as "you taught us, Eliyahu." When she finished speaking, the mourners dispersed wet-eyed, "with silent sadness," *Davar* reported.

At a talk the next day, she called on American Jews to join the struggle in Palestine. "If we are defeated," she warned, "you, too, will lose your standing." Moshe Sharett's wife, Zipporah, wrote to her husband in Latrun that Golda was "excellent. Strong and straightforward." Sharett, who had replaced Arlosoroff as secretary of the Jewish Agency's political department, was a major catch for the British. His wife's endorsement was a major coup for Golda.

On July 2, she addressed an assembly of newspaper editors in Tel Aviv. "We will win if we utilize all our strength," *Davar*'s headline quoted her, with a prominent article covering her call for unity in fighting the enemy. The Mizrachi newspaper, *Hatzofeh*, cited her criticisms of the gentiles in that talk, the "goyim," who had failed the Jews twice in recent times, once during the Holocaust and now, with the British invasion of the Yishuv. In one of her bitterest statements along those lines, she declared, "The worst Jew is better than the good gentiles."

That declaration notwithstanding, she did not hesitate to ring up her English gentile friend Richard Crossman, who was scheduled to speak at a large gathering protesting the British Black Saturday actions. She and the Jewish Agency economist David Horowitz gave Crossman details to convey to his audience about the havoc the British had inflicted on the settlements during their raids. *Davar* devoted several columns to Crossman's talk and Golda's help.

Within a week after Black Saturday, Golda's name had appeared in the Hebrew newspapers every day, and she had been seen at almost every major political event. It followed that Moshe Sharett's letter of July 10 from Latrun to his assistant Zeev Sharef and the Jewish Agency official Eliyahu Dobkin, both in Jerusalem, would not have come as a surprise to them: "Ben-Porat suggested, and I latched on to the suggestion with enthusiasm, that we advise Zehava to move to Jerusalem or visit from time to time in order to support the political department." Zehava, meaning "Golda" in Hebrew, was one of the code names used for her. Ben-Porat was code for the lawyer Dov Yosef, Sharett's senior assistant, locked up with him in Latrun. Sharett wanted others to know that he had enthusiastically accepted the idea of Golda's going to Jerusalem and temporarily filling his job. Golda knew Zeev Sharef from years earlier and would have felt comfortable working with him. When her parents first moved to Herzliya, he had belonged to the nearby kibbutz Shefayim. Her father, an observant Jew, objected to the kibbutzniks working their fields on the Sabbath in full view of local synagogue worshippers. To prevent a fight, a young Golda negotiated a settlement: kibbutz members could work on Saturdays but only indoors, where their labor would not be visible to Sabbath observers.

With Sharett's support, she was to become acting head of the political department of the Jewish Agency for Palestine, a position comparable to foreign minister in an established government. Some months would pass before the position became official, but for all intents and purposes Golda now headed a national office for the first time in her career.

Not everybody expressed delight. Golda was well-known and admired by many in the labor movement, but could she replace Sharett on a national level? A broadly educated man fluent in eight languages and at home in Arab culture, Sharett was low-key, cerebral, and cautious. He descended from a distinguished family, which added to his luster in negotiating with the British. Golda had little formal education, spoke Hebrew poorly, and in her straightforward manner could also be impulsive and emotional. (In some ways, their different styles and intellects echoed differences between their grandfathers two generations earlier. The reader will recall that the two men, who owned taverns near each other in Pinsk, got along well, but Sharett's grandfather Leibe Shertok loved learning and literature; Menachem Naiditch, Golda's grandfather, could barely read or write.) Her total devotion to the party, so impressive to its leaders, also created enemies outside it. If it weren't for Mapai's backing, one nonparty man said, she would not have gotten the Jewish Agency position. She "was unfit for the post."

And she was a woman.

The religious *Hatzofeh* voiced strong opinions about that. She may be "wise, sharp, devoted, Lapidot's wife"—a reference to the biblical judge Deborah—an editorial read. "Nevertheless: a woman." No other country in the world had a woman in such a leadership role, although those countries also had wise and capable women in their midst. "It is impossible for a woman to head the most central mechanism of the Jewish community," the paper proclaimed. The Jewish way was to follow the teaching of the psalmist: "The honor of the king's daughter is within." Women's honor came from their homes, not the larger world.

Which only proves, *The Pioneer Woman* responded, "that even in the advanced, modern and liberal social structure of Jewish Palestine there still are elements, with old-fashioned ideas on womanhood . . . , who are trying to put back the clock of progress."

Brushing aside criticisms, Golda had her own concerns in moving from an advisory role to a broad decision-making one. "It's terrible to be responsible for other people's lives," she told her son. As always, she quickly immersed herself in work, gaining confidence as she proceeded. In one of the Yishuv's first orders of business, deciding how to respond to Black Saturday, she had no doubts. The Jews needed to adhere to a policy of civil disobedience toward the British, she argued, which might entail boycotting government functions, minimally using government services, handling disputes in rabbinic courts instead of British ones, and avoiding British goods. And when the Yishuv moderates argued, as they had for years, that Palestine's Jews could get more from Britain by cooperation and diplomacy than by resistance, she warned that if the Jewish Agency Executive did not behave decisively now, the extremist Irgun and Lehi surely would, with disastrous results. Even the Haganah, incensed at the British operation, might forgo its customary discipline and take matters into its own hands.

During their deliberations, she and other leaders—some thirty in all—met with Chaim Weizmann at his home in Rehovot. As president of the Zionist Organization and chairman of the Jewish Agency, he was the Jewish community's most prestigious figure. Golda wanted his help in her civil disobedience campaign, and he agreed to give it if his own conditions were met. With the authority of his presidency, he regarded himself as supreme head of the Yishuv's armed forces, and as such he demanded an end to the Jewish Resistance Movement and violence against Britain. He called on Golda to help implement his orders, threatening that if they were not followed, he would resign and let it be known why he did.

Despite her inclination toward active resistance, Golda felt obliged to follow Weizmann's directives. She enlisted the aid of Levi Eshkol, who had joined the civilian committee—called Committee X—that decided on Haganah and Palmach operations. Although he had voted to continue the resistance, she persuaded him to change his vote, weighting the committee against action. Moshe Sneh, who was still in hiding, resented Weizmann's dictating Haganah policy in that way and angrily resigned his position as head of the Haganah national command. Pressured by Golda and Eshkol, he changed the resignation to a leave of absence and escaped from Palestine to join Ben-Gurion in Paris and discuss the matter further.

Weizmann's imperiousness in commanding the Haganah irritated Ben-Gurion as well as Sneh, feeding into a long-standing conflict between the two men about the use of force against the British. A man of great charm and wit, with a proper British mustache and goatee, Weizmann had, over the years, gained the trust of the British and in turn trusted them. He remained steadfast in his belief that the only way to deal with Britain was through negotiation, avoiding any form of violence. Ben-Gurion was in a greater hurry and more willing to use physical force. With his large head, flying hair, and short, squat body, he lacked Weizmann's elegant appearance or grace. He rarely made small talk or went out of his way to butter up British diplomats. And his insights often flew ahead of the realities. When others cheered the victory of the British Labour Party, he sensed that they would betray their campaign promises to the Zionists, and began planning to oppose them. When others focused solely on battling the British, he prepared for an armed clash with the Arabs, which he believed inevitable. He respected Weizmann and probably also envied his influence with the British, but he was certain diplomacy alone would not open the gates of Palestine to Jewish refugees or pave the road to a state.

In her every bone, Golda identified with Ben-Gurion and his militant approach. Yet she stopped short of openly criticizing Weizmann or publicly supporting Ben-Gurion in his attacks on the older man (which grew more virulent with time). Her ties to Weizmann traced back to childhood, when her sister Sheyna met with other Zionist revolutionary groups in his family's house in Pinsk. During those years of turmoil in Palestine, Golda visited Weizmann and his wife, Vera, in Rehovot from time to time. Much later, she would recall that when he wanted to "pour out his heart," he would talk to her in Yiddish, the rejected language of the Yishuv but one they both loved. At the moment, however, her disappointment in him mounted as it became clear that even though she had conformed to his demands, he had no intention of speaking out on behalf of her civil disobedience program.

Very soon the issue moved to the back burner. The Yishuv's attention—and global attention—turned to the King David Hotel in Jerusalem. On July 22, 1946, the Irgun gave its response to Britain's Black Saturday by setting off a huge explosion that reduced the hotel's southwestern wing to a heap of rubble. Considered the gem of the Middle East, the hotel made an especially fitting target for a terrorist attack because of both its prominence and its use as British military and administrative headquarters. Irgun men, dressed as Arab porters, had smuggled explosives hidden in seven large milk containers into the hotel. At 12:37 p.m., the explosives went off, killing ninety-two people and injuring scores of others. It was the largest and most deadly attack against the British the Irgun ever undertook.

Through a notice in *Davar*, the Jewish Agency and National Council expressed "their horror at the dastardly crime perpetrated by the gang of desperadoes." From Paris, Ben-Gurion condemned the act as "anti-Jewish and non-human," but the British denounced him along with the extremist organizations. In fact, the Haganah does not emerge spotless, although the details of what happened and what went wrong have remained open to debate.

The operation was to be the joint Jewish Resistance Movement's answer to Black Saturday. Moshe Sneh had approved it for the Haganah but left it to Menachem Begin and his Irgun organization to implement. According to the Haganah, Sneh and others had insisted that the explosion take place after working hours, when offices had emptied. The Irgun chiefs argued that they had no way of smuggling in bombs late in the day; they needed people to be coming and going into the building. At some point later, in line with the decision of Committee X outlawing violence against the British, Sneh delivered orders to the Irgun to delay the action. And this is where the situation becomes murky. How clear were his orders? Why didn't Sneh simply forbid the project to take place instead of deferring it? In any case, the Irgun commanders decided to ignore the orders and proceed. They always maintained that they made phone calls ahead of time warning the British to evacuate the building and that those warnings went unheeded. Chief Secretary John Shaw denied that his office received such a call in time to save anyone.

Given Golda's position in the Yishuv, it might be assumed that she had a part in planning the bombing. However, Israel Galili, Haganah chief of staff, testified years later that he met her a few days after the explosion and was astonished that she knew nothing about the plans. "She was surprised to hear," Galili said, "that the Irgun received two directives in writing—the first regarding the execution of it and the second deferring it." Furious about the event, Golda discussed it with Sneh during a trip to Paris. "He said not to worry," she recalled. "The note [to Begin authorizing the operation] was not signed and was typed on a typewriter, not handwritten." That meant it could not be proven to have come from the Haganah. Golda had more on her mind than that. Bombing the hotel, she said, "was a terrible tragedy . . . a great shock to all of us." She wanted the Jewish Agency to investigate Sneh's role in the attack. It never did, and he and Ben-Gurion maintained warm ties for some time after the catastrophe.

Still shaken from the events of Black Saturday, the Yishuv reeled with shock and shame after the King David bombing. To make matters worse, a few days after the event two articles appeared in *Haaretz* blaming all the Yishuv leaders. Although unsigned, everyone knew they were written by the paper's senior writer Moshe Medzini, second husband of Golda's long-standing friend Regina.

"The establishment must resign!" one article cried. The Jewish Agency and its leaders needed to be held accountable for what had happened. Even if they did not personally implement the terror, they bore the responsibility and "should disappear, with all possible haste." Their job was to lead and not to follow others in the "terrible slide to the depths of the firmament." The second article argued that the mainstream must suppress the dissidents. "Is it above our capability to control those murderous people who live among us?" it asked. Seeking unity instead of "burning the evil from our midst," it continued, made everybody liable for the resulting disasters. The articles touched a raw nerve among readers. In this period of tension and fear, with their leaders locked up and the British arresting dozens of men and women after the terror, many accused Medzini of betraying his own people with his wide net of blame. If the British reprise their Operation Agatha, someone said, they're likely to shut down all the Hebrew newspapers except *Haaretz*, which supported them with its criticisms of Jewish leaders.

Regina was "very sad," Zipporah wrote to Sharett, because she heard what people said about her husband yet lacked sufficient knowledge to defend him. In later years, Regina would say that Golda and Medzini "didn't see eye to eye on politics," but the women remained friends.

Meanwhile, the British reacted swiftly to the King David disaster, instituting strict curfews and going from house to house searching for perpetrators. On July 24, they hit back more forcefully by rushing into print the evidence they had found linking the Jewish Agency to the Haganah and the Palmach, and those forces to the terrorist organizations. Golda understood that they were seeking to influence world opinion against the Jewish leaders in Palestine, especially the thinking of the U.S. president, Harry Truman. At a meeting the next day, she deliberately ignored the new paper but spoke forcefully about the need to prepare for "a bitter political struggle" against the government. When some members called for the resignation of Jewish Agency leaders, she retorted that any change in the Yishuv's national bodies at this point would only further Britain's interests. She would not give the British an inch.

A fresh blow struck the Yishuv a few days later. A joint British and American committee devised a new proposal in place of the rejected Anglo-American commission's recommendations. This one was named the Morrison-Grady Plan, after its heads—Herbert Morrison, a deputy prime minister of England; and Henry F. Grady, an American career diplomat. Their plan divided Palestine into four areas or cantons: separate Arab and Jewish provinces and British-controlled districts of Jerusalem and the Negev. The British jurisdiction would cover almost half the country, the Arab would be somewhat smaller, and the Jewish, smaller still, would consist of only fifteen hundred square miles, about 17 percent of the mandated area. The British would have authority over the central government, in charge of defense, foreign affairs, and finance, and the Jews and Arabs would have a degree of autonomy over local matters in their provinces, such as education and agriculture. Ultimately, all the cantons would be federated under a UN-British trusteeship. The one recommendation designed to please the Zionists and President Truman was the admittance of 100,000 Jewish refugees into Palestine after both the Jews and the Arabs accepted the plan.

Delighted with that recommendation, Truman was prepared to approve the proposal until he learned that American Jews hated it as much as the Palestinian Jews did. The plan would give the Jews less control than they already had and increase the British hold on Palestine. Even the Peel Commission report of 1937 calling for partition had allotted the Jews more land and given them more autonomy in a state of their own.

The Arabs expressed "unalterable opposition" to the plan. In spite of Jewish leaders' vehement opposition, they decided to discuss it along with other matters at a forthcoming conference of the Jewish Agency Executive, to be held in Paris.

"Pazit," another code name for Golda, needed to be at that Paris conference, Sharett wrote from Latrun. She had lived through Black Saturday and, better than anyone, could give a firsthand report of it. Accordingly, on Monday morning, July 29, 1946, Golda boarded a plane for Paris, taking her first voyage outside Palestine in seven years. Despite her new position in the agency's political department, she attended the conference as a delegate of the National Council. Moshe Sharett wanted it clear that he was still the political department head.

Golda painted a graphic picture of Black Saturday to the conference on the following Friday. She had never seen a pogrom in her life, she told the audience, but she had heard a great deal about them, and what had happened in Palestine on June 29 was what she imagined a pogrom to be. (In later years, she would not be quite as forthcoming about lacking experience with a pogrom; her public recollections always began with her childhood fear of pogroms close to home.) She saw villages wrecked, she said, and homes torn up, with quilts and pillows ripped apart, feathers flying about. In the kibbutz Yagur, where the British searched for hidden arms (and found them), she'd heard that the military had sprayed hot oil on members. She described finding photographs of children with their eyes pierced by pins in the wreckage after the troops left, an expression of the soldiers' rage. In Tel Aviv, the British military had blasted open the WIZO headquarters and smashed the Histadrut doors.

Decades after she settled in Palestine, Golda continued to use the pogroms of Eastern Europe as her frame of reference. True, the term still had immediate relevance. Only a few weeks earlier, forty Jews had been beaten to death in a vicious pogrom in the town of Kielce, Poland, particularly horrifying for having occurred so soon after the Holocaust. Even so, Golda's comparison of the British Operation Agatha to a pogrom was questionable. Palestine was not a Polish shtetl, and the British troops were not wild bands of civilians lawlessly killing and raping Jews. The military represented the colonial British government's attempt—although too often excessive—to keep order in the land it ruled. Much later Golda would recall telling the high commissioner that she realized no other army would have behaved better. "I hate to think what the French army would have done to us," she said. At the time, she was too angry for such a concession. Her analogy to a pogrom was even more problematic in identifying the Jews of Palestine with helpless Diaspora Jewish victims, the very condition she and other Palestinian Jews had been devoting their lives to undoing.

Nonetheless, Golda felt comfortable with the image and confident that it would resonate with her listeners. For them, too, the pogrom still aroused fearful memories, even as they shaped themselves into "new Jews." The Yishuv community would respond to the British "pogrom" in its own way, she told the conference, emphasizing the passive resistance program she advocated. To her great disappointment, that policy of noncooperation would never take off. The Yishuv depended too much on Britain for its economic, political, and security needs to turn its back on the government.

But bigger things were brewing. The idea of forming an independent Jewish state—not only a national home for the Jewish people—that had bubbled beneath the surface for some time was about to burst out as an immediate goal. The idea had been officially articulated four years earlier, when Hitler's murderous rampage had begun taking its toll and the British White Paper blocked the entry of Jewish refugees into Palestine. In May 1942, almost six hundred American Zionists and several from other lands had attended a conference at the Biltmore Hotel in New York City and declared the postwar goal of the Jewish community to be an independent Jewish "commonwealth" in Palestine. Weizmann and Ben-Gurion both had a hand in formulating this "Biltmore program," which left the concept of commonwealth vague enough to be open to future interpretation. Most mainstream Zionists accepted the Biltmore ideal yet saw it fade away as relations between the Jews and the British in Palestine deteriorated. Now the Morrison-Grady proposal had been put on the table, and the executive group meeting in Paris needed to come up with a statement about it.

Golda knew exactly how she felt. Morrison-Grady was a "trap," she said. "What the government intends to grant us now is something like the Municipal Council of Tel Aviv," nothing more than a city council, with little autonomy. In harsh tones she had not used before, she laced into Chaim Weizmann, who was planning to meet with Bevin and the colonial secretary, George Hall, to negotiate on Morrison-Grady. "Dr. Weizmann has nothing to say to Hall at present," she said. "There is no hope whatever that negotiations may result in substantial improvements of the plan . . . the only way is to reject the plan as a basis of discussion."

Most of the leaders present agreed with her, but how could they get from the untenable Morrison-Grady to some semblance of their ideal Biltmore plan? Nahum Goldmann, head of the agency's political office in Washington, argued for the course the Peel Commission had suggested almost a decade earlier: partitioning the land into Jewish and Arab states. Along with Berl Katznelson, Golda had rejected the plan then. This time, she supported Goldmann.

It was Monday morning, August 5, 1946. Goldmann had been in touch with David K. Niles, special assistant to President Truman for minority affairs and Jewish himself. Niles warned the conference that the president had threatened to "wash his hands" of the whole Palestine matter unless the Jewish Agency Executive came up with a reasonable plan of its own. The agency needed to send someone to Washington with a plan, Goldmann told the delegates. The plane would be leaving soon. If they wanted him to go, they had to decide on a resolution that day to deliver to Truman: "We must tell the President what immediate action is to be taken . . . The 100,000 must be admitted; Jews must have power over immigration, economic freedom, better boundaries."

Golda spoke next: "We must state clearly that the proposal of a province in Palestine [as recommended by Morrison-Grady] . . . cannot be a basis for negotiations, but that Jews are ready to negotiate if the proposal is a Jewish state in Palestine. In that case, we shall discuss everything: boundaries, immigration, economics, etc. . . . And if there is a state, we will negotiate also with the Arabs and come to an agreement."

If she'd once dreamed of a large state in all of Palestine, she put that aside. She would not negotiate on Morrison-Grady, but she would negotiate on any offer that began with a state, including a state in only part of Palestine. Later, as prime minister, she would appear inflexible when it came to that state, but the inflexibility was always about the state and its security, never about the old dreams of possessing all of the Land of Israel.

Along with others at the conference, she voted for the resolution Goldmann would carry with him to Washington. The second and most important paragraph in it stated, "The Executive is prepared to discuss a proposal for the establishment of a viable Jewish State in an adequate area of Palestine." It did not use the word "partition" or designate what would be "viable" or "adequate," but it made Morrison-Grady a non-starter and partition a possibility.

Although Golda backed Goldmann's mission to Washington, she and Ben-Gurion had their suspicions about him, a distrust she would carry through life. Personable, with a broad, intelligent-looking forehead and wide smile, Goldmann was a good talker and an extremely clever diplomat, but he had an independent mind that could edge on recklessness. Politically, his heart belonged to Weizmann, not Ben-Gurion, raising the fear that he would not stick to the Jewish Agency stand against dealing with Morrison-Grady. To some extent, that fear turned out to be warranted. In his meetings with Truman's aides (he never got to see the president), he specified borders for the proposed Jewish state, a subject he had not been authorized to raise at this early stage because it might lead to bargaining around the Morrison-Grady boundaries. Nevertheless, Goldmann did gain the president's endorsement for the concept of partition. In a dramatic moment, David Niles, with tears in his eyes, told him that Truman had accepted the plan without reservation.

Weizmann did not attend the Paris conference, but at Golda's suggestion she and several others flew to London in the middle of the conference to visit him at the home of a friend in Tring, where he was recuperating from an eye operation. Near blind and still grieving for a son killed in the war, he had little patience for their recommendations. He called the Paris conference "irresponsible" in its refusal to consider Morrison-Grady. Enraged at his obstinacy, Golda stormed out of the room. It would be years before he forgave her for that.

The group returned to Paris the same day. In reporting on the visit, Golda began with gentle praise. "I believe Dr. Weizmann is one of the greats of the Jewish people," she said, then changed her tone. "I saw him on Sunday. He seemed in a depression, not only physically but also mentally; he looks like a man who was beaten up and overpowered. He thinks we are responsible ourselves to a great extent for what has happened in the land. I asked myself then whether he has the strength to negotiate." She answered her own question. "There should be no doubt: Ben-Gurion is the man for negotiations." She had hitched her wagon more firmly than ever to the Ben-Gurion star.

In the volatile, tumultuous Paris conference, racked by the tensions of the times, tempers soon flared over another issue: The British had called for a roundtable conference in London, with Arabs and Jews, using Morrison-Grady as the foundation for a solution to the region's problems. How should the Jews respond? Moderates, including Goldmann and the Jewish Agency's treasurer, Eliezer Kaplan, urged that they attend. Ben-Gurion, Golda, and other activists opposed participating. A meeting on Saturday night, August 17, became a shouting match of viewpoints, lasting until one in the morning. Among other arguments, Goldmann maintained that a refusal to negotiate would lead to an outright battle with Britain, and Golda countered that not participating would allow the Jews a free hand to engage in that battle, which she saw as inevitable. She was certain the British had made commitments to the Arabs so that "through Bevin and Hall we are negotiating also with Jamal Husseini and the mufti."

The executive finally voted with Golda and Ben-Gurion against attending unless the British met three conditions Ben-Gurion had proposed earlier: negotiations would start from the concept of a Jewish state in Palestine; jailed Jewish leaders would be freed; and the Jews would choose their own delegates to the conference.

The Arabs also had conditions for participating. One was to invite as head of their delegation the mufti, Haj Amin al-Husseini, who had collaborated with the Nazis during the war. A second was that they would not attend any conference with the Jews present.

GOLDA LEFT PARIS ON Thursday, August 22, at the end of the agency conference, flying first to Beirut and then to Lod Airport near Tel Aviv. The flight gave her a good opportunity to sort out the tangle of pressures she would need to cope with the minute her plane touched ground. She had officially received her title as acting head of the Jewish Agency's political department at the Paris conference. She would have to continue treading a fine line between asserting her authority in that position and acceding to Sharett, whose job she held while he was away. She would also have to serve as emissary for Ben-Gurion, who did not dare set foot in London for fear of being arrested. The two had drawn close in Paris arguing for their activist position. Then there was David Remez, jailed with Sharett and looking to her for support and sympathy.

She had barely stepped off the plane when Zeev Sharef called on her for a detailed report about Paris to send on to their boss in Latrun. Sharett had been thirsting for that report, waiting impatiently for "Pazit's" return. Golda did her best, speaking with Sharef until two in the morning of her arrival. He transmitted her account in great detail and related also that Golda wished to know whether Sharett truly wanted her to enter the political department as its head. She herself had no desire for the job, she had insisted to him, but if ordered to take it, she would accept. It was the old party technique: deny your worth or interest until forced into the job you desired all along. This time the routine pushed Sharett into saying clearly in a return letter that he wanted Golda to fill his place. Then he listed twenty-six questions he still wanted answered. He might have been happy to have her hold down his position, but he meant to keep tight control over every inch of his domain.

About two weeks after she returned home, Golda appeared at a Mapai convention, where she gave a long talk about her thinking and Ben-Gurion's. She stressed again the need to reject the Morrison-Grady plan and demand a Jewish state. In an emotional moment, she speculated that perhaps hundreds of thousands of Jews among those slaughtered during the Holocaust had gone to their deaths comforted by the thought that one day the Jewish people would prevail in a home of their own. It was a far-fetched, sentimental imagining, but she stirred her audience with it. She spoke, with regret, about the need to continue resisting the British with a show of strength they would take seriously. At the same time, she cautioned members of the military, the Palmach, and the Haganah, who were chomping at the bit to follow the Revisionist pattern of fighting violently and ruthlessly, to restrain their impatience and recognize that if the moment was not right for military action, "then we don't act."

Always Golda conveyed ambivalence toward the use of force. She argued for it, opposed Weizmann and the moderates who would do away with it, and didn't hesitate to apply it when necessary. But she wanted it known that she would prefer not to have to use it. To her mind, armed strength had to be utilized selectively, to achieve political ends, and even then carefully and sparingly. In one of her first encounters with Shimon Peres, then a young man named Persky, he and another party member criticized her for not fighting forcefully enough to prevent the British from exiling illegal immigrants. She responded that if she had to choose between a physical struggle and successful negotiations, she would always choose the latter. As long as negotiations are alive, there is hope, she said.

That did not mean, of course, negotiating on Morrison-Grady, which had to be resisted. Ben-Gurion expressed some of the same thoughts in a passionate, poetic letter he sent to the convention. In it, he opposed both the moderate way of waiting until the British were ready to come to an agreement and the extremist way of constant armed combat with no limitations. He labeled the first path "Vichy," after the French surrender to the Nazis during World War II, and the second "Masada," after the battle at that ancient fortress that ended with the suicide of the Jewish fighters. "Neither Masada nor Vichy" became a credo for the activists.

The Mapai convention ended with an overwhelming show of confidence for the Ben-Gurion/Golda position—75 percent of the votes as opposed to those of the Weizmann faction. "The decision follows in your spirit," Golda cabled Ben-Gurion triumphantly. From Latrun, Sharett wrote to congratulate her on the victory.

Like a host whose dinner guests fail to show up, the British Palestine conference opened in London on September 9 with barely a handful of delegates. Knowing the Jewish Agency Executive would not appear, the government had invited representatives from other Jewish organizations. In a demonstration of solidarity, not one accepted the invitation. Nor did the Palestinian Arabs participate. A few Arab delegates from other countries—Egypt, Syria, and Iraq—came and flatly turned down the Morrison-Grady Plan or any suggestion of an autonomous area for Jews in Palestine.

Even with the conference's poor start, Weizmann and Goldmann continued to press the Jewish Agency executives to join it. Given Arab intransigence, they argued, a change had occurred in the British attitude toward the Jews. Acting on his own again, Goldmann assured the British that the agency was ready to reopen the question of participating in the conference and even gave them a list of prospective representatives, Golda Meyerson among them. Around the same time, Weizmann wrote to his friend J. M. Martin in the British Colonial Office urging that the men "shut up in Latrun for nearly three months" be released so that they could come to the conference, which most of them "are in favor" of attending.

Moshe Sharett had supported Ben-Gurion and Golda in their position against the London conference, but from the start he'd had mixed feelings. He took a more positive stand when rumors cropped up in the middle of September that Ben-Gurion had changed his mind and now leaned toward attending. When Zipporah asked Sharett whether he, too, had reversed himself, he explained that he had not actually changed positions. From the beginning, he had favored going to the conference and had opposed the tough line adopted in Paris, but after that line had been accepted and publicized, he did not see any point in defying the majority. Now that Ben-Gurion seemed to have changed, he felt free to say what he really thought: he approved entering negotiations with the British, if he and the others were released.

The rumors about Ben-Gurion's change of heart caused a crisis within the Jewish Agency Executive. For days, a frenzy of phone calls and cables shot through the wires, and letters traveled back and forth to Latrun, Paris, London, Jerusalem, and wherever else members were located: Should a new vote be taken on whether to enter the London conference? If Ben-Gurion had changed his mind, other activists reasoned, they, too, might agree to participate in the meetings. But had he? Nobody could say exactly where he stood, and he was in Stockholm, unavailable for questioning.

Golda wouldn't budge. In the midst of the commotion about change, and almost alone among the Jewish Agency Executive, she insisted that *all* the conditions laid down in Paris be met, especially the requirement to build the discussion around a Jewish state and not the Morrison-Grady proposal. As for Ben-Gurion, she had her doubts about whether he had, in fact, changed. She staked out her position at a stormy Mapai political committee meeting on September 18, questioning sharply what gave any of the moderates the right to speak for Ben-Gurion when they knew little about him. They had opposed his leadership, she charged coldly, and dismissed him and the Paris conference. She was closer to Ben-Gurion's thinking than they, yet she really did not know what he wanted to do. Then again, even if he had clearly said yes to attending the conference, it would not suffice for her.

"I have never taken it upon myself to say yes or no to everything Ben-Gurion . . . says," she stated. She wanted it in the minutes that she did not merely rubber-stamp Ben-Gurion's decisions, or anybody's; she made her own judgments. As for the conference, before agreeing that they attend it, she demanded to hear directly from one of the agency's emissaries in London that the British had indeed become more receptive toward the Jewish viewpoint. The political committee agreed to have Berl Locker come from London to speak at the next meeting.

IN HIS LATRUN PRISON CAMP, Sharett seethed with anger at Golda's independent stance. Where did she get the self-confidence to oppose his position and what appeared to be Ben-Gurion's? To Zipporah, he wrote with irritation that Golda "lacked all flexibility. Instead of easing this crisis, she made it infinitely worse. She did everything to build up the negative position of the party, and now she chokes it." His letter crossed with one from Zipporah to him, with a very different portrayal of Golda Meyerson.

Zipporah had received a phone call from Golda a day earlier asking if she might visit. The request delighted her; she had wanted to call on Golda for some time herself but had hesitated to intrude on the political leader's busy schedule. Golda visited for two hours, from seven until nine o'clock, through dinnertime, so that "the entire evening was taken up by Golda," Zipporah wrote, with some pride.

Golda, Zipporah continued, "is very lovely, filled with charm. She related that it was with a sense of honor that she entered the [Sharetts'] office, that the assistants there, Zeev and Aryeh, accepted her with love and warmth, and help her with everything." Golda particularly enjoys Aryeh—whom Sharett found somewhat boring—because he pays attention to her, Zipporah wrote wryly. But she was pleased that Golda praised the "devotion of these fellows to you, and it's not just devotion . . . but actual love."

Aware of her boss's anger at her, Golda was craftily wooing his wife and, through her, reassuring him that she was not trying to replace him in his staff's loyalty.

She also reassured Zipporah of her own dedication to achieving Sharett's freedom. He was stuck in Latrun. Ben-Gurion was alone and miserable in Paris. And Zipporah worried, she wrote, that people like Nahum Goldmann, eager to make common cause with the British, might agree to enter the London conference without insisting first on the leaders' freedom. But Golda felt sure (and would make sure, she implied) that the Jewish Agency would agree to no talks until the British met that condition.

Touched by his wife's account, Sharett modulated his tone. "It was very nice of Golda to visit you, and not in haste," he wrote to her in his next letter. "I have thanked her for that. My words toward her in my previous letter might have been too sharp. Don't let such outbursts disturb you." He still had complaints, however. Did Golda understand that Ben-Gurion's position in the first place was flawed? That the way the Paris resolutions were structured, with their insistence on partition as a starting point for discussion, left little room for negotiations? He suspected that she did not understand or want to admit that, and therein lay her "stubbornness." He wrote to Golda thanking her for visiting Zipporah but also expressing regret that she had taken such a definitive position against the London conference before hearing from him. She answered immediately that she might be wrong (a qualification she used often, especially when convinced she was right), but she had no choice except to stay with her beliefs.

Her directness seemed to mollify him. He understood that being on the scene, she had information that he didn't have, he wrote, and he supported her in making decisions according to her understanding. He did hope, however—he couldn't resist adding—that as much as possible she made her decisions after listening to other opinions. With that, he sent warm wishes for the Jewish New Year, arriving in two days.

Golda clung to her opinion during two more critical meetings. Following her request, the Mapai political committee invited Berl Locker, the London emissary, to speak to them. To Golda's mind, he said nothing that demonstrated a change in the British attitude toward the Jews. If Weizmann and Goldmann had their way, she said caustically, the agency would have joined the conference a week earlier while the Jewish leaders would still be sitting "quietly and comfortably" in Latrun. After much arguing, the Mapai committee agreed to leave the final decision about the conference to the Zionist Inner Actions Committee, the leading Zionist authority in the Yishuv, that would meet later that night.

The clock had already struck eleven in the evening, but before going on to that meeting, Golda and several party members joined a political gathering at a nearby rooftop. Zipporah, also at the gathering, chatted with her for a while and later reported the conversation in a letter to Sharett. Golda emphasized that from the beginning she had independently opposed joining the conference in London, Zipporah wrote. The fact that Ben-Gurion also opposed it strengthened her and led her to do everything she could to bend the party toward her view. When Ben-Gurion seemed to back away from his opposition, she didn't change, but party members became confused. She confided to Zipporah that she was worn out and no longer willing to explain the issues to the party. In fact, she thought the party was falling apart with its internal struggles. Zipporah implored Sharett not to repeat her words to anyone. Golda lived in terror that Ben-Gurion would appear one day and be furious if he knew what she said.

Leaving the gathering, Golda and her companions headed to the Zionist Inner Actions Committee meeting, which lasted into the early morning hours. Once again she argued against attending the London conference, and this time, with the backing of Levi Eshkol, she won a decisive victory. A majority on the committee voted to turn down the invitation.

From Paris, Ben-Gurion cabled Golda on September 29, five days after the Zionist Inner Actions Committee decision, instructing her to inform Sharett and others that the rumors that he would participate in the London conference had no foundation. It is anybody's guess why Ben-Gurion took almost two weeks to clarify his position. He might have tried to manipulate the British by appearing to be more flexible about the conference than he really was, or he might have genuinely vacillated, alone and despairing in Paris and unsure of what to do until the Zionist Inner Actions Committee made its decision. His full commitment to all the Paris resolutions—late as it came—vindicated Golda in her unwavering commitment all along.

BEHIND THE BARBED WIRE enclosing Latrun, David Remez looked forward to the letters he received from Golda, smuggled in with other Yishuv correspondence. At times she sent him two or three letters a day—she, who had been notorious among her friends for not answering her mail. In them, she revealed a side of herself that few others would ever see. The strong, opinionated woman who vehemently defended her views could also be frightened and vulnerable, filled with self-doubt; the hard-edged politician adept at manipulating people could also be pliant and passionate, even poetic in her emotions.

Over the years since Golda and Remez had become close, rumors had cropped up regularly about other lovers she had, within the Mapai Party and outside it, even with an aristocratic Palestinian Arab. Whatever the truth of those rumors, she had always kept deep, intense ties to Remez, the one person in whom she could unhesitatingly confide. Her letters to him, always in Hebrew, brimmed with tenderness and shared secrets. Once, she wrote about seeing her son, Menahem, off on a ship from Haifa on his way to the United States, where he would prepare to study at the Manhattan School of Music. Under pressure from the British and torn apart by the grim situation in the Yishuv, she felt herself "close to the edge," almost at the point of a mental and physical breakdown. She did a "strange thing" then. She stayed on alone in Haifa for two days, "simply to sleep." She told nobody else about the episode.

In almost every letter she sent Remez, she used code words and clues only the two understood. She signed many with the Hebrew word *ahat*, "one," or sometimes just the last letter of the word, *tuf*, certain that he knew what it meant. She wrote of reading the book *The River Jordan*, by the great archaeologist Nelson Glueck, a literary and scientific study of the river, which she promised to send to him. In her letters, she made constant allusions to antiquity—"blessings, blessings, and more in the way of the ancients," she ended one letter. They might have referred to the couple's mutual interest in the archaeology of ancient times, or they might have been a message about the ancient, idyllic days of their long, intimate relationship.

Separated from Remez, unable to see or speak to him, and in a position of greater responsibility than she'd ever had, she felt "terribly sad" and alone, having to fill a role that she "could not fill, yet could not recommend anyone else for either." The fact that she and Remez disagreed on basic issues made her sense of isolation worse. It is "very, very hard that we are not together on this," she wrote. He sided with the moderates and the Weizmann camp urging attendance at the London conference. Moreover, he was angry about the differences that separated them and angrier still at her loyalty to Ben-Gurion. His anger—and jealousy—showed through in a letter he wrote accusing her of being too dependent on Ben-Gurion. He fumed at her also because she had not answered his queries at length after she returned from the Paris conference. Later she would explain that she had been overwhelmed with work and "meetings without limits" so that she had no time to write the way she would have wanted to. Her immediate response to his accusations, though, was astonishment at his charges, rage at his assumptions, and profound hurt.

She referred to herself in the third person, as though taking distance from his invectives: "Is it really so that this woman did not answer, and if she did answer, her only response was Paris [code here for Ben-Gurion, hidden away in Paris]? And this from you? Is this woman so lacking in self-esteem that she blindly follows Paris?" Maybe she was wrong; she hoped she had misunderstood him. Nevertheless, "why was the woman's companion allowed to maintain his opinion, but not the woman?"

It was an everywoman's cri de coeur. Why, she wanted to know, was it assumed that a woman could not hold an opinion of her own? Why did Remez and his group suppose that Golda's ideas all derived from Ben-Gurion? "Lord of the universe, what have I done?" she shouted on the paper. She'd had strong feelings about the lenient position Weizmann, Goldmann, and other "London men" took in regard to the London conference, and she didn't agree with them. "It's possible I'm mistaken," she wrote, as she had to Sharett, "but if I think this way am I forbidden to speak out and fight for my thoughts as do others who think differently?"

She could not have been clearer in her message: She was nobody's puppet. She had her own opinions, and as a woman she had as much right to them as did any man to his.

Having asserted her rights and dignity, she could lower her voice. She described how much it had cost her emotionally to hold her ground against him and the others who disagreed with her. "Forgive me for my words," she wrote. "I would happily give my right hand to have you here with me now and we could talk about this. Do you still believe in me? Or is everything destroyed?" As for herself, nothing had changed in her feelings toward him, "except for a deep pain in the heart, but the heart still exists."

In subsequent letters, she revealed the feelings of that heart more openly. She must have understood that much of Remez's anger at her grew not only from their political disagreements but also from the differences he sensed in their balance of power. He had been her mentor and guide, she his adoring student. He had been in the top level of leadership, she only on her way. Now she stood near the top, Ben-Gurion's right hand, while he, Remez, remained locked up, asserting little influence. On both a personal and a political level, he resented her closeness to Ben-Gurion. She set out to convince him (and perhaps herself) that he had no reason to be concerned; she needed and cared for him as much as ever.

In a moment of quiet contemplation one night, she wrote of the differences between him and Ben-Gurion. She had become accustomed over many years, "for me, marvelous ones," to doing important things with Remez. "Generally we walked in one direction, but even when it was not that way, we walked together." She would never forget the Zionist Congress of 1937. They had different positions (he favored partition then; she opposed it), but their steps were always entwined. She gave him the credit for that. "You created this precious thing," she wrote. He had to know, then, how difficult it had been for her to be at the Paris conference without him. "I am not a conversational partner for the neighbor [Ben-Gurion]. Here the situation is completely opposite. Even when our thoughts do not differ, there is no connection, no simple and good talk." This time in Paris, however, she suddenly found herself assisting Ben-Gurion, someone he could lean on. But to have done this without Remez at her side was terrible for her, just as now every activity without him was like "a high mountain that I am overcoming with difficulty."

She ended with warm memories again, of "ancient days." Were he at home now, she would have phoned him, although they had agreed not to do that. She would have invited him in for "a conversation and a cup of tea" near the table on which she was writing.

One of her most emotional letters greeted him with the words "my hand in your hand." She wrote it on Rosh Hashanah eve, September 25, 1946, and she seemed enveloped in love and longing as the Jewish New Year approached. "Do you know how dear you are to me?" she wrote. "Do you have any clue about all the things in my heart? It seems to me that if we were to meet now, I would say everything to you, even though we forbade ourselves to use the known word." She had sent him a book of poems, which she hoped would express her feelings better than she could. For her, she wrote, "every word of yours, every letter is holy to me." She compared this holiday to another, Passover eve. "How good it was for me then. We were together. Day after day, hour after hour, night after night: I look forward to that." She ended with the same warm sentiments: "If only a shred of what is in my heart reaches you today, it will be a small part of the contents of my wishes for a good year."

Day after day, in letter after letter, Golda wrote to Remez about the latest political news, the anxieties about England, the party quarrels. "I do not want a day to pass without a sign," she noted. Interspersed were her longings to see him. Alone in her temporary quarters in Jerusalem, where she frequently slept over because of work, or at home by herself in Tel Aviv, and far past midnight, she sat and wrote to him. "My heart jumps at the thought of a live conversation," she wrote in one letter. "Only God knows how I am waiting for such a conversation." In another, she spoke of how filled her heart was with only good things. "How did you say it once, as if it were peeled, so sensitive and throbbing is it toward the good." She added a postscript to that letter, in their private code: "In general everything old gives me a warm feeling." When she heard that family members were permitted to visit relatives in Latrun, she wrote, "What a pity that there is not some family connection. Were I a sister I could have spoken with you today."

On October 7, she wrote to him from the hospital. The terrible strains of the past few months—the all-night meetings, the crisis over the London conference, the constant fights with British authorities about immigration, the absence of Remez, Sharett, and Ben-Gurion—all weighed heavily on her. She collapsed, from exhaustion and her old heart problems. "Once more I did a stupid thing that sent me to the hospital," she wrote to Remez, referring to her around-the-clock work schedule. She felt despairing about the work and the internal disputes over negotiating with the British. Even before she got sick, she had been thinking about how to untangle herself from the fray. "It seems to me that with this illness, it might be possible," she wrote. "I'm pleading with you, help me to get away from a situation I cannot bear. There may be no great honor in running away, but worse than that is continuing like an idiot." She had come close to the breaking point again, sick, depleted, needy.

She was still in the hospital a few days later, the first day of the festival of Sukkot. Rested and feeling better, she no longer spoke about running away. Her mind was abuzz again, caught up in the struggle with England. "What did my mother always say?" she wrote to Remez in describing the bitterness of that battle. "It's a calamity of the heart." She wrote the phrase in Yiddish, adding in Hebrew, "very, very much." But, the holiday had arrived, and "I tell you, there will still one day be a happy holiday for us. There will be."

THE DECISION OF THE Zionist Inner Actions Committee to decline the British invitation to the London conference distressed Chaim Weizmann. He spoke of resigning as chair of the Jewish Agency Executive, but after consulting with the colonial secretary, he agreed "to make one further effort to secure a change of attitude." He arranged to have key members of the Jewish Agency Executive flown to London to hold informal talks with British authorities. Two of the three people Weizmann invited, Eliezer Kaplan and Rabbi Yehuda Leib Fishman, accepted. Golda Meyerson did not. "I oppose any negotiations formal or informal without detainees and you," she wired Ben-Gurion. "Convinced their suggestion now merely a trap."

If the invitation was a trap to lure the Jews into the conference, it was also an indication of the trapped feeling the British had. The government needed the talks to show the world that the Jews and Arabs were participating in planning their own future, but the standoff in Palestine was taking its toll. The Irgun had stepped up its terrorist attacks, assassinating soldiers, blowing up buildings, and dynamiting railways. And if the British had hoped that by locking up Yishuv leaders, others, more sympathetic to them, would emerge as replacements, they found themselves sorely mistaken. Even in informal talks, the Jewish representatives insisted they could make no commitments until their leaders were freed. Adding to the mix, on October 4, a day before Yom Kippur, Harry Truman issued a statement calling for the immediate admission of 100,000 refugees into Palestine and for the first time publicly endorsing the concept of partition. Furious at the president's interference, Prime Minister Attlee accused him, as he had in the past, of using the Palestine issue to win over Jewish voters, especially during their High Holiday season, but he felt the weighty hand of American power on his back.

On November 5, 1946, four months after incarcerating the Yishuv leaders at Latrun, the British released them and lifted the ban on Ben-Gurion and Sneh. As a condition of release, they had demanded that the Jewish Agency strongly condemn all armed actions, including those of the Haganah and the Palmach. They accepted, instead, a general, watered-down antiterrorist resolution by the Inner Actions Committee. Even then, the Hebrew newspapers emphasized that the release was not a quid pro quo for any declarations by the committee or the Yishuv leaders. Moshe Sharett said that the release should be regarded as a measure "forced upon the British government" and not a gesture of its goodwill.

In many ways, the freed leaders found nothing changed outside their prison grounds. Hundreds of thousands of refugees still languished in DP camps; the British still forcefully intercepted ships trying to sneak some of them into the land; armed British soldiers could still be seen everywhere; and the issues of the Morrison-Grady Plan and the London conference would still appear on the agenda of the forthcoming Zionist Congress. Yet the Zionists could celebrate a victory of sorts. They had stood up to the British and forced them to free their leaders. Golda could take special satisfaction in that. More than anyone, she had held firm in her conviction that the Morrison-Grady Plan could never be the path to a state. In the face of Ben-Gurion's wavering and Sharett's disagreement, she held firm in opposing the London conference as the British proposed it. And she held firm in demanding the release of the prisoners before the Jewish Agency would even consider attending such a conference.

"To my regret," she wrote to Remez, "I was right."

14

1947: The Turning Point

Golda traveled to the Twenty-Second Zionist Congress in Basel, Switzerland, with a heavy heart. Seven years had passed since the last congress was held in Geneva during the summer of 1939. When she had said good-bye to delegates then, the scent of war permeated the atmosphere, but no one imagined that during that war a third of the Jewish people would be annihilated. Zionists she had worked with at that congress, from Germany, Poland, Czechoslovakia, and other parts of Eastern Europe, were gone now. With their absence and after the misery of the past years, gloom seemed to seep into every corner of the *Mustermesse*, where the congress met. In this city, Theodor Herzl had convened the First Zionist Congress in 1897. Now black bunting framed the stage in the hall with its portrait of Herzl gazing down on the events. "The shadow of tragic bereavement is upon us tonight," Chaim Weizmann intoned in his opening address on Monday, December 9, 1946. People sobbed aloud as he spoke. Among those who heard him were survivors who came to the congress from displaced persons camps.

Golda arrived several days early to attend pre-congress sessions of Ihud, the Labor World Alliance. Its three hundred or so delegates represented Poalei Zion organizations around the world, still only a remnant of what had once been a much larger, dynamic movement. The Poalei Zion made up Mapai's counterpart outside Palestine, and Golda had the task of mobilizing its members to support Ben-Gurion and his militant position toward the British. After Sharett's release from Latrun, she had resumed her old job in the Histadrut executive while he returned to heading the Jewish Agency's political department. She was now seen throughout the Yishuv as nearly on a par with him and other national leaders. Like the others, she delivered her talks in Yiddish, still the language of most of the world's Jews.

As she stood at the lectern for an Ihud meeting, she tried to make the delegates and hundreds of visitors from various lands understand that attempts to accommodate the British had brought the Yishuv no gains. Many leaders had concluded, therefore, that the only language the government understood was the language of force. Although they regarded armed resistance mainly as a tool for negotiating, unlike the indiscriminate violence of the Irgun and Lehi, they had to act now. Their restraint had only strengthened the hand of those radical groups. If asked, she told her listeners, an average Jew in Palestine would say that he disapproved of the extremists, yet "at least they're doing something." Therefore they, the more responsible activists, also had to do something.

She would repeat the theme of acting and fighting back many times during the congress itself. The World Zionist Congress functioned as the highest policy-making body in international Zionism, and here the final vote would be taken on the problems that had roiled the Yishuv for months: whether to attend the London roundtable, how to respond definitively to the Morrison-Grady proposal, and what position to take on various partition plans. Golda attended meetings, chaired party caucuses, and hovered in the corridors in a ceaseless round of day and night activities. Cigarette smoke veiling her eyes and nose, she listened intently to all sides, then fought for every word of the resolutions she wanted. In a speech on December 11, she hammered away at the necessity for a Jewish state in the immediate future—now.

She began by recounting British provocations: how, during wartime, the White Paper "stood as an iron wall" between the Jews of Palestine and Hitler's millions of victims; how after the war the British locked up "the elected representatives of the Jewish community"; how they had continued to drive away immigrants "with brutal force." At every turn, she told her audience, it "became obvious to us that a state was a necessity . . . not as a last resort but as an immediate instrument for the rescue of Jews and the building of Palestine."

With her knack for mixing hard facts with purple prose, she drew a touching picture of young sabras, boys and girls born in the Land of Israel, "plain and pure as the sun of Palestine," who risked their lives to help illegal immigrants leave their ships and steal into the country. "They go down to the sea . . . ford the waves to reach the boats and bear these Jews ashore on their shoulders," she said. Survivors of the Holocaust who had not been able to cry through all the years of their pain "shed tears," they told Golda, when they saw the "youth bearing grown men and women to the soil of the homeland." She followed through by calling on the delegates, particularly those from America—who now made up the largest proportion of the congress—to "hurry and send your sons and daughters . . . We need *halutzim*." She was to make that appeal to American Jews time and again in the years ahead and always be disappointed that large numbers of American Jewish youth did not heed her call.

Turning to the Revisionists, who sat together in the front rows of the hall, she described eleven settlements that had sprung up in the Negev all at once in an amazing night of construction. "You who always mocked at the efforts of settlement, at the idea of slow construction," had to recognize the wonder of those settlements, she said. Workers would go on building, "for these are the guarantee of our victory."

The next day's *Davar* newspaper overflowed with superlatives. "Waves of applause resounded without end from all parts of the hall, even in the rows of the Revisionists," it recorded. Golda had "mesmerized the hall" with her "great wisdom, clarity, and grace" and received the warmest response of any speaker at a plenum. *The Pioneer Woman* called her "The Woman of the Hour" and featured her dressed in an embroidered blouse, the fashion of the young pioneer women in Palestine.

Golda's brand of sentiment and drama added life to the congress, but the real drama unfolded away from the podium and the public. It featured an all-out battle between David Ben-Gurion and Chaim Weizmann, the two men most responsible for building the Zionist movement in Palestine and now at odds about how to proceed.

Unarticulated but ever present was the question of whether Weizmann should continue as president of the Zionist Organization. "Almost nobody could think of anything else," Golda later told a Mapai meeting. In his second speech to the convention, Weizmann had criticized the Jews for their militant actions but never said a word against the British behavior on Black Saturday, infuriating many of his listeners. Nevertheless, even those who opposed his presidency felt heartsick about pushing him out. Golda and Ben-Gurion had hoped he would accept a position as honorary president, but he turned that down. ("I have enough honor," he said irritably when asked.)

At the Hôtel Les Trois Rois, where some of the meetings took place, Golda chaired a Mapai Party caucus on the issue of Weizmann's presidency. Weizmann had requested one last chance to negotiate with Britain; if that failed, he would resign and blame it on the British government. In an effort to give him that chance but also assure the activist position, Golda presented a compromise proposition for decision: "We vote in favor of Dr. Weizmann if he will accept our program," meaning militant resistance to the British. Tempers soared as arguments on the motion raged through the night between moderates in the party who backed Weizmann and others who opposed him.

With the controversy seething, Ben-Gurion worked himself into a fit. He had clearly indicated that he wanted Weizmann out. Feeling betrayed by colleagues who promoted Weizmann's presidency, he rushed from the caucus to his hotel room. When a party member, Mordechai Sorkis, entered, a distraught Ben-Gurion wanted to know when the next train departed for Paris. He was leaving the congress. "I can no longer work with Weizmann," he shouted. Sorkis ran back to the meeting and found Golda, who enlisted Sharett and another Mapai leader, David Hacohen. The three hurried to Ben-Gurion, and for the next hour, with everyone yelling to the rooftops, they finally persuaded him to return to the congress. At three in the morning, Golda's motion in the party caucus passed by a strong majority.

After that, a new round of manipulations took place. Before the congress began, Ben-Gurion had been scrambling behind the scenes to form an alliance with the American leader Abba Hillel Silver that would give him enough votes against Weizmann at the congress. Golda considered that a dangerous liaison. Powerful, charismatic, and aggressive, Silver did not support partition; he had his eye on all of Palestine as a Jewish state. In that and in his extreme activist stand, he was closer to the Revisionists than to the Labor Party. Golda regarded him as the Labor Zionists' most formidable opponent because of the vast influence he wielded over American Jews. From Ben-Gurion's perspective, however, Silver and his Zionist Organization of America could be a great help at this congress.

Still hoping to preserve party unity and enable Weizmann to hold on to his presidency, Golda tried to have the congress elect a president and executive officers before voting on whether to participate in the London talks. She didn't succeed. By a tiny margin, the congress chose to vote on attending the London conference first. With that, Weizmann decided not to run for president as a candidate but to have his presidency hinge on whether the congress voted in favor of the conference. Paradoxically, Golda, who had originally opposed the London talks more vehemently than anyone, reversed herself and supported them now, largely out of sympathy for Weizmann. Many in the party agreed with her. With only a small minority of the Mapai delegation on his side, Ben-Gurion teamed up with Silver to amass votes against attending the conference. The religious Zionist Mizrachi Party joined their coalition, and the Shomer Hatzair delegation, which usually followed Weizmann, abstained this time. The motion to go to London was defeated by a vote of 171 to 154. Its defeat meant the defeat of Weizmann, a wrenching end to his leadership of the Zionist Organization. As he left the congress and made his way slowly into the street, the delegates stood up and applauded. In deference to him, the congress did not select a new president.

A small postscript to the Weizmann affair happened a few days after the congress ended. The Mapai's treasurer, Eliezer Kaplan, always a Weizmann follower, proposed at a Zionist Inner Actions Committee meeting that Weizmann be quietly reelected president of the Zionist Organization. Ben-Gurion flew into a rage at the suggestion, and the two men got into a yelling match that came close to a fistfight. Sitting a short way from them, Golda Meyerson leaped from her chair. "You should be ashamed of yourselves," she scolded loudly. "Look how you're speaking to each other, what kind of behavior is this?" Using all her strength, she physically separated them. Golda, the party whip, had also become its mother.

Ironically, about four weeks after the congress ended, Ben-Gurion and other leaders participated in the London roundtable after all, and despite the intense trauma that had surrounded the subject, the discussions amounted to nothing worthwhile. What had been so burning and divisive an issue to Zionist leaders for months would become with time little more than a footnote to the creation of the State of Israel. Even so, footnotes sometimes hold important nuggets of meaning. The Jewish refusal to attend the London conference at its start or to negotiate there on the Morrison-Grady Plan—both consuming causes led by Golda—might have helped speed up Britain's ultimate decision to withdraw from Palestine.

The congress changed lives. Ben-Gurion became the undisputed leader of the Zionist movement and received the defense portfolio in addition to heading the Jewish Agency Executive. Golda was appointed co-head of the Jewish Agency political department, with headquarters in Jerusalem. Moshe Sharett, still the head, would be based in the United States, now the center of Zionist activity. Abba Hillel Silver became chairman of the American branch of the Jewish Agency.

After the congress, Golda spoke to the press in tones of hope and enthusiasm, pushing aside the sadness and discord that had pulled at its seams. "Zionism and pessimism are not compatible," she declared, a slogan she would repeat often, especially in cheerless times.

WHEN GOLDA MOVED TO JERUSALEM to head the Jewish Agency political department there, the city teemed with British troops. Barbed wire ringed government buildings, piles of sandbags blocked roadways, and machine gun posts stood ready for split-second combat. People took to calling the British compound in the Russian quarter of town "Bev-ingrad," an armed fortress designed to protect the government against ever-mounting Jewish terror attacks. The Irgun and Lehi had ceased their operations for a month, until the end of the congress in December, swinging back into action in early January 1947. British nerves neared the snapping point as incidents of shootings, kidnappings, and explo-sions piled up.

From her new apartment on Keren Kayemet Street in the Rehavia section of town, Golda had only a short walk to the building where she worked. For the first time in her life, however, she had a car and driver at her disposal, useful for rounds of meetings with British officials on the one hand and Jewish leaders on the other to seek ways of stopping the extremists. To the British, she emphasized the Yishuv's anger at their restrictions on immigration, a fury that for young people in the militant Revisionist groups translated into terror attacks. Disgusted with the ter-ror herself, she still argued that most of those committing it were not murderers. They are "people who have gone out of their minds because of the sufferings of the Jews," she would say. To Jewish leaders, she took the opposite tack. "It's a lie" to hold that the dissidents are anguished by the sorrows of their people, she said at a meeting of the National Coun-cil. "I don't believe the people of Etzel or Lehi suffer more from the pain of Israel than I or you." Instead, they are coldly obeying orders, and as such the Jewish community needed to do all it could to stop them.

But hers was a thankless job, and she felt it. Both the British and the dissidents had decided to act in their own way, "with a strong hand, no matter what," Golda told a Mapai meeting. And the mainstream Jewish community was squeezed in the middle.

In early 1947, much of the contest between the two sides revolved around the case of Dov Gruner. An Irgun fighter, he had been wounded and captured by the British on April 23, 1946, while he and others raided the Ramat Gan police station. The men had shot at the police before removing arms for their group's use. After recovering from his wounds,

Gruner was brought to trial, convicted, and, on January 2, sentenced to death. Proclaiming that he did not recognize the authority of the British government, he refused all legal counsel or appeals. Two days before his scheduled execution, set for January 28, the Irgun kidnapped two Englishmen, a retired intelligence officer, Major H. A. Collins, and a judge, Ralph Windham, to hold as hostages until Gruner was released.

Soon after Golda assumed her new position and before the kidnappings, she and Remez had met with the new chief secretary, Henry Gurney, who sought the Jewish Agency's cooperation against the terrorists. Both emphasized their own opposition to terror and their belief that a change in the British immigration policy would go far to thwart it. They also warned that if the British carried out the death sentence against Gruner, they knew the dissidents would create great trouble. Gurney replied drily that the British government did not take kindly to terrorist threats. The British response hardened after the abduction of the two hostages. High Commissioner Sir Alan Cunningham called Golda, Kaplan, and Tel Aviv's mayor, Israel Rokach, to his office and gave them forty-eight hours to find the hostages. If not, the British would impose martial law on large swaths of the Yishuv, with extensive curtailing of citizens' rights. Frightened, Golda cautioned her colleagues that it would take years for the Yishuv to recover from such a blow. The Jewish Agency offered to have the Haganah search for the hostages. With that, and word that the British had postponed Gruner's hanging, the Irgun released its prisoners.

But the British wanted more. They wanted the Jewish Agency to give them the names of the kidnappers. And more. They wanted the agency's full cooperation in finding and reporting Irgun and Lehi members to them—a repeat of the *saison*, the hunting season on the dissidents, the Jewish leadership had participated in two years earlier. This time Golda refused. "You want us to tell the Jews to give information," she said to the chief secretary at one of their meetings. "We can say, 'let's fight the terror' and at that moment a ship of immigrants will come and be driven from the land." How could she encourage Jews to collaborate with the British while desperate Jewish refugees were being turned away from Palestine? The more restrictive the British became, the more heroic the dissidents seemed to ordinary people, especially the young.

Still the British pressed. In what they called Operation Polly, they began evacuating their civilians from Palestine, particularly women and children, implying that they were about to embark on an extensive operation to fight the terrorists that might also endanger the Yishuv. Golda countered by holding a press conference on February 2, 1947.

"There is a need now for wise statesmanship and wise administration," she said, in a swipe at the current statesmen and administrators. She explained that the government had asked the Jewish Agency to cooperate in the fight against terrorism by calling on the Yishuv to become "informers." This, they could not do. "We cannot make informers out of 600,000 Jews, each watching his neighbor and friend."

A day later, Gurney wrote to her arguing that the Jewish Agency had "openly refused its cooperation with the government" and giving it seven days to cooperate properly. Again Golda feared the worst: martial law, perhaps even a new White Paper dismantling the Jewish Agency. On February 9, she and Kaplan met with Cunningham, who calmed the waters for a while. The high commissioner assured the two that the government had no intention of imposing military rule at the moment and wished to help the Jewish Agency stop the terror.

GOLDA LIKED SIR ALAN CUNNINGHAM. The thin, mustached general was "a very, very fine individual," she once said. "He followed policy, he had no alternative, but personally he understood." He liked her also. "Goldie used to come up to see me to ask if I could not increase the quota of immigrants," he recalled later of his days as high commissioner, "but of course I couldn't . . . That was decided by the Foreign Office. I could pass on her comments, but that was all I could do. She used to weep a little and curse the ACD [aide-de-camp] when she went out, because she hadn't gotten her way . . . but I liked her generally."

The "liking" did not signify real friendship. An emotional distance always existed between Jewish leaders like Golda and the British, yet for all the conflict between them they lived in proximity through highly charged times and had to adjust to each other. For Cunningham and a few other officers, shared experiences allowed them to see the people they dealt with, both Jews and Arabs, as human beings and not only as adversaries. He sensed the same attitude in Golda and appreciated it. "I think she understood that I was trying to do what I could for both sides," he said of her.

Long after the mandate period, after Golda had become prime minister of Israel and Cunningham had retired, he wrote to urge her not to "budge from any of the territories" Israel had captured in the 1967 Six-Day War until the country was guaranteed secure and defensible borders. She was "touched" by his letter.

In her everyday life, Golda dealt with numbers of British officials from the Colonial Office. As one secretary left and another replaced him, she had to adapt to new personalities and try to win their sympathy for the Jewish cause. Generally, she got along well with those officials. That was not the case with Sir Henry Gurney, the last chief secretary before the British mandate ended. Gurney had replaced John Shaw, who seemed to quietly admire the Zionists but after discovering that he was high on the Irgun hit list left Palestine secretly.

Golda considered Gurney "one of the worst in the administration." At one of their meetings, she mentioned the aloneness of the Jews during the Holocaust, when no nation came to their aid. Gurney asked whether she had ever wondered why the nations of the world had that attitude toward the Jews. Golda snapped, "Are you hinting that they were justified?" To which Gurney quickly responded, "God forbid, that's not what I meant." She thought he did mean it and tabbed him an anti-Semite. She probably was not wrong. When, in a different context, she repeated the charge of Gurney's anti-Semitism to the colonial secretary, Arthur Creech Jones, he did not deny it.

"In the autumn of 1947," she recalled of Gurney, "he kept summoning me to see him during the evening, when the streets were deserted and when it was dangerous to travel from the Jewish Agency to the King David [British headquarters]. I think it was just spite; he could easily have called me in the morning."

Gurney left Palestine when the British pulled out in May 1948 and became high commissioner in Malaya. Three years later, members of the Malayan Communist underground assassinated him. In all his official positions, he had been known as cool and unflappable; no matter what happened, he could always relax with a round of golf. When asked about those qualities in him years after his assassination, Golda replied, "Yes, that was why we hated him. No one in that position had any right to be unruffled. He ought to have been pacing his room day and night, trying to find a solution to the Jewish problem." She remained unforgiving, with limited sympathy for his tragic end.

Aside from her official duties, Golda made a point of involving herself in the lives of everyday people in her charge, people like the English-woman Jane Lancaster, whose name crops up in one of her files. A devout Christian, Miss Lancaster grew medicinal herbs and plants in her garden in Talpiot, in southern Jerusalem. "I am a hundred percent pro Jewish, and always have been and always will be," she wrote to Golda. "I believe that one day Palestine will be all Jewish, because the Bible says so." She intended to live on a settlement and work the land after the British left, she said. When the British evacuated their citizens temporarily because of the deteriorating situation, she asked for Golda's help in having someone watch over her garden. She had received only forty-eight hours' notice to pack up and depart, and she worried that things might be stolen from it. Her medicinal plants were her "life-work," which she did "as a service to the country both for Jews and for Arabs." Golda arranged to have a *mukhtar*, a neighborhood guard, protect Miss Lancaster's garden until her return.

Acts like that enhanced Golda Meyerson's reputation. People noticed that despite the monumental events swirling about her, she still made time for small deeds of kindness.

AFTER THE FAILURE OF THE London talks, Ernest Bevin gave up any thought of solving the Palestine problem as it existed. On February 18, 1947, he announced in the House of Commons that he planned to turn the question over to the recently formed United Nations.

By then, the British had so barricaded themselves behind barbed wire and sandbags that the *New York Times* reporter Clifton Daniel could compare Jerusalem to a "medieval walled and moated city." So many Britons lived closed off within security zones that Jews joked about British ghettos and displaced persons. Back home, the British public had come to resent having 100,000 of its troops stationed in Palestine for months, even years, and always in danger of extremist attacks. The opposition leader, Winston Churchill, spoke for many when he labeled the nation's Labour Party policy in Palestine "a senseless dumb abyss—nothing."

Nevertheless, nobody knew what Bevin had in mind in throwing the Palestine problem into the lap of the United Nations. Certainly, he did not envision the actual creation of an independent Jewish state. Among other things, in the icy atmosphere that had grown up between Russia and the United States (soon to be called the Cold War), it seemed almost impossible that the Soviet Union would ever sanction such a Zionist state. Ben-Gurion, Golda, and the other Jewish authorities suspected that the British hoped to have the international community prop up their mandate in Palestine while freeing them from having to form a Jewish national home there.

As winter slipped into spring, their speculation about the British move intensified. On April 2, 1947, England formally asked to have the Palestine question placed on the UN General Assembly agenda; a special session on the issue took place on April 28; and on May 15, UNSCOP, the United Nations Special Committee on Palestine, came into being. Composed of eleven members representing Western and Eastern Europe, the British Commonwealth, Latin America, and Asia, it would be the twentieth committee to probe that land. Yet to Jewish leaders it had a different feel about it; the official legislative body of the world had set out to determine their nation's fate. So while Palestinian Arabs boycotted it, as they had other committees, the Jews determined to make the most of it.

An astonishing announcement by the Soviet Union on May 14 made the situation even more critical. Andrei Gromyko, Soviet ambassador to the United Nations, proclaimed to the General Assembly Russia's openness toward partitioning Palestine into Jewish and Arab states if a single state did not prove feasible. Until that moment, Stalin had opposed Zionism as a tool of the West and had appeared consistently hostile to Jewish aspirations for a state of their own. This sudden reversal, which astounded all sides, reflected the Soviets' internal conviction that with a weakened British Empire pulling back from Palestine, Russia could exert its influence on the Middle East. To Stalin's mind, backing the Jews helped undermine Britain even further. For the Zionist leadership, the Soviet surprise opened fresh possibilities.

Oddly, with the race of events moving swiftly forward, Golda seemed to be stuck in place. Despite her participation at meetings and her strong opinions, she somehow found herself on the periphery of the UNSCOP story. The "big guns," Ben-Gurion, Sharett, and Weizmann, served as the main spokesmen for the Jewish position, with a young Aubrey (later Abba) Eban among the liaisons to the committee. Golda functioned primarily as an administrator, receiving letters and reports from agency people around the world, sending off telegrams, organizing appointments—busy but not central to the unfolding drama. At a Jewish Agency Executive meeting in April, she spoke plaintively of the division of labor in the organization. Moshe Sharett, stationed in Washington, ran the show at the UN; Moshe Sneh, formerly of the Haganah, had been suggested as the person to handle Middle Eastern and European matters. It remained for her only to sit in her office and wait to be called for a discussion with the British high commissioner or the chief secretary. For that her position seemed hardly worthwhile.

About a month later, she announced that she would attend the Socialist International conference in Zurich. In that at least, she could play a meaningful part.

Representatives from nineteen countries participated in the conference which met during the first week of June. Golda and her delegation came eager to bring up the topic of Jewish immigration into Palestine. Just as eager to squelch that topic, Morgan Phillips, head of the British delegation, argued that the scheduling of the meetings did not allow him ample time to speak. Backed by most of the European delegates, the conference voted to extend its meetings for another day, and Golda received half an hour to give her presentation. "I spoke what was on my heart," she reported afterward to a party meeting. In her talk, she attacked the British authorities' treatment of the refugees and noted that the first Jews killed in Palestine in many years were victims of the Labour government's policies. People listened attentively to her words—something she noticed they did not do with other speakers—making her feel she had attained a diplomatic victory over the British delegates.

A troubling question hovered over the meetings, however, sapping some of that goodwill. Should this socialist conference admit the German Social Democratic Party? The party had been restored after the war, and under its head, Kurt Schumacher, it had strong working-class socialist ideals. With a two-thirds majority necessary for the admission of new member nations, the conference buzzed with speculation about how Golda and her delegation would vote. Schumacher spoke at length about the party's scrupulous investigations before accepting members, especially former Nazis applying for membership. He mentioned Hitler and the slaughter of the Jews briefly and when asked about them afterward passed over the question. Pressed further about why he had not addressed the subject more fully, he said he had forgotten to do so. That and the presence of former Nazis in his party would have been enough for Golda and her group to vote against admitting it, but their minds had been made up anyway. Their vote blocked the acceptance of the German Social Democratic Party at this conference, angering delegates from France, Britain, Belgium, and other countries who felt it imperative to support the Social Democrats in their opposition to the German Communist Party.

Ferociously anti-Nazi, Schumacher had suffered ten years in brutal Nazi concentration camps, much of them in Dachau. Golda might not have known that or that he was the first German politician to mention Holocaust victims in his speeches at home and to speak about compensation for German Jews. Given his history, he felt offended and enraged over her rejection. But the Holocaust was still too raw for her and the other Jewish delegates. They couldn't bring themselves to include a German political party in the socialist organization so important to them, let alone work with its members as colleagues.

THE UNSCOP GROUP ARRIVED IN Palestine on June 15, a few days after Golda's return from Zurich. They would spend five weeks touring Jewish and Arab areas, holding public hearings, and taking private testimonies. Golda accompanied members on some of their trips, as she had previous committees, making the Jewish case wherever possible. She did not testify officially, however, nor did she play a more pivotal role than she had earlier. Ben-Gurion and Sharett preferred to have her run the agency's political department while they handled the UNSCOP members. Her exclusion incensed her, and in the tiny Jewish Yishuv community everyone knew that. She had felt a "serious hurt" over it, the American Jewish Committee's Palestine correspondent wrote home. And when Moshe Sharett came from Washington to the political department's Jerusalem office—probably to supervise Jewish testimonies to UNSCOP—Mrs. Golda Meyerson staged "an indignant walk-out."

Hurt and frustrated at being sidelined, and feeling ill as she frequently did, Golda submitted her resignation from the Jewish Agency Executive to Ben-Gurion on June 29, claiming that her doctors had ordered her to take a complete rest for an indefinite period. ("It's not a matter of a week or weeks.") No stranger to such resignations himself, Ben-Gurion told her to take as much time off as she needed, wished her a full recovery, and refused to accept her resignation. A Lehi publication charged that Golda had "exploded" at a meeting, exclaiming that she had nothing to do at the agency and would not be reduced to a "technical secretary." According to the Lehi paper, she angrily left the political department for a time, returning only after Sharett and UNSCOP had both departed.

By the time she came back, world attention was focused on the saga of the refugee ship *Exodus 1947*. Of the more than sixty ships that tried to make their way into Palestine after World War II, it would become the most famous example of the suffering and heroism of the illegal immigrants. And Golda would be caught up in the politics surrounding it.

Originally named the *President Warfield*, the American ship had begun as an excursion steamer on the Baltimore–Norfolk line. The Haganah's Mossad l'Aliyah Bet, which purchased it in the United States, changed its name to *Exodus* and refitted it to hold—albeit under terrible conditions—the forty-five hundred refugees who crammed into it at the French harbor of Port-de-Bouc, near Marseilles. Soon after it set out on its voyage, British destroyers began to shadow it, and about twenty miles off the coast of Palestine, British sailors forcibly boarded it. The passengers and crew fought them fiercely, using cans of food, potatoes, bottles, buckets, or whatever else they could get their hands on. Three were killed by British bullets, twenty-eight badly wounded, and many others overcome with teargas before the ship's Palmach captain, Yitzhak "Ike" Aharonovich, surrendered. British destroyers towed the broken boat and its passengers to the Haifa port. That evening and the next day, British soldiers herded the exhausted refugees onto three prison ships and out to sea again.

"There were dead people on board when the ship reached our shores," Golda bitterly told a National Council meeting a little later, "and the British government observes one rule: a dead Jew has the right to enter the land legally and be buried in it . . . The government brings him in at its own expense, and in its great kindness does not deduct the corpse from our quota of immigration certificates . . . But only a Jew murdered by a British bullet may benefit from this privilege. Any Jew who reaches the shores of this land alive—his lot is to be deported."

Throughout their ordeal of capture and deportation, the refugees sent detailed broadcasts to the Kol Israel radio station in Palestine using equipment the Haganah had given them. Transmitted from there to the world press, their reports splashed across headlines everywhere. At the suggestion of Abba Eban, two members of the UNSCOP team visited the Haifa port. There they watched with horror as British soldiers using rifle butts, teargas, and their full weight pushed and pulled recalcitrant refugees into the prison ships.

Ernest Bevin, architect of the operation, might have recognized too late the blunder he had made. But he had earlier decided to make an example of this ship with the aim of stopping others. Or, in Golda's analysis, in his rage against the Jews, "he lost control altogether." As part of his plan, he did not send the three vessels with the captured refugees to Cyprus, where previous ones had gone and from where, eventually, deportees received certificates to enter Palestine. He sent them back to France, where the *Exodus* voyage had begun, hoping to end the journey there, with the Jews resettled in France or other parts of Europe. Instead, in support of the passengers, the French announced that nobody would be forced to land in that country, although those who voluntarily left the ships would be fully accepted there. In spite of their misery, and bolstered by Haganah representatives who surreptitiously made contact with them, only about 130 left the ships.

In Jerusalem, the British turned to Golda Meyerson for help in persuading the refugees to stay in France. She replied simply that the mission of the Jewish Agency was to bring Jews to Palestine, not to aid them in going to other lands. She would not intervene.

When Bevin realized that he could not pry the refugees from the boats, he chose a solution so insensitive that a collective gasp seemed to rise from the world community. He would send them to Hamburg, in the British zone of occupied Germany, the cursed land where so many had suffered. Ben-Gurion and Sharett, in Geneva, instantly grasped the profound public relations ramifications of Bevin's coldhearted decision. Sharett sent a cable to Golda saying that England itself felt "revulsion" at the decision to send *Exodus 1947* to Hamburg, and the British cabinet was meeting to reconsider it. He added, however, "Important nothing should happen Palestine spoil chances." It was an equivocal sentence. What "chances" was he referring to? Did he mean, as some historians have suggested, that he did not want the chances of the ship completing the voyage to Hamburg spoiled by the dissidents or anyone else? With the UNSCOP report hanging in the balance, the Hamburg decision had such a powerful, symbolic effect that in reality the Jewish leaders might not have wanted the British to reconsider it. For them, the larger goal of a Jewish state outweighed the immigrants' suffering—an outlook others, later, would condemn.

A protest rally about the fate of the *Exodus* took place in Tel Aviv, and a general fast was held throughout the Yishuv. Speaking to the National Council, Golda laced into the British, who did not seem to understand that "the whole problem of the hundreds of thousands of surviving Jews in Europe . . . was not created for the sole purpose of making trouble for the British government." She called on the world's nations to join the battle to bring displaced persons to Palestine, but she did not specifically bid them to pressure Britain to reverse its Hamburg decision. The refugees were forced off the ships in that city and placed in DP camps.

ON THE DAY THE *Exodus* arrived in France, July 29, 1947, the British executed three Irgun members they had captured and convicted. A day later, in retaliation, the Irgun hanged two British army sergeants they had kidnapped. The sergeants' booby-trapped bodies, which blew up when cut down, injured a British captain and mutilated one corpse beyond recognition.

The path to that gruesome scene began on May 4, after months of spi-

raling underground attacks and British reprisals. On that Sunday afternoon, Irgun fighters pulled off a spectacular raid on the British fortress
prison at Acre, freeing more than two dozen Jewish inmates (and, unin-
tentionally, almost two hundred Arabs). In attempting to stop them, the
British killed several Irgun and Lehi men and captured five of the attackers. A British court tried the captured men, sentencing three of them to
death and the other two to life in prison. Irgun gunmen responded by
kidnapping the two young British army sergeants, Clifford Martin and
Mervyn Paice, in Netanya, a beach town between Tel Aviv and Haifa.
They hid the men in a sealed cell beneath a diamond factory there, while
the British conducted a furious search for them.

In consultation with Golda, the Haganah undertook a search of its
own. At this point, the Yishuv simmered with anxiety. With the UNSCOP
team touring the country, a crisis brought on by Jewish extremists could
severely damage the Jewish cause and convince the committee that the
Zionists were not ready for self-government. Added to that, Chief Secretary Gurney had told Golda months earlier that as long as the terror
continued, there would be no possibility of increasing immigration quotas. The disappearance of the sergeants strengthened Gurney's hand.

News of the British hanging of the three Irgun men devastated the
Yishuv. Their families had pleaded with the UNSCOP group to intercede
for the men's lives, but mandate authorities had refused to budge. Young
people especially, many of whom had a romantic view of the underground
as valiant Davids fighting the British Goliath, raged against the execu-
tions. The Irgun's hanging of the young sergeants (the father of one had
pleaded with the Irgun's head, Menachem Begin, to release them) and the
mining of their bodies changed those feelings. Even among the young,
fury at the British turned into "horrified disgust" at the brutality of the
underground fighters. Many despaired at how quickly the Irgun had
undermined the worldwide sympathy the *Exodus* affair had generated.

Golda, Ben-Gurion, Sharett, and other agency heads fumed. The
Jewish Agency Executive and the National Council issued an open declaration against the Irgun condemning "the abominable deed of murdering two innocent people by a band of criminals." They called on the
entire nation to fight "the terrible malady which has infected us until it
is utterly eradicated." In a separate statement, the Haganah advised the
public to warn Yishuv authorities of any signs of provocative acts by the
terror organizations.

"We have never been so ashamed," Golda told High Commissioner

Alan Cunningham at a difficult meeting on July 31, after the bodies of the two sergeants were found. She promised him that the entire Yishuv leadership had agreed to embark on an all-out war against the extremists. Yet she stopped short, as she had earlier, of agreeing to the full and "open cooperation" with the British that he demanded. If they were to do that, she said, their energies would be siphoned into internal battles with many in the Yishuv who opposed such collaboration. "You are thinking only of the Jewish side," the high commissioner accused her. "I have to think also of the Arab side and the British side and especially the soldiers." A few minutes later, he added, "You come from America, and I think you can imagine what would happen if it were an American force stationed here. How long will I be able to restrain the army?"

Not long, as it turned out. On the night after their meeting, British soldiers and policemen went on a rampage in Tel Aviv as revenge for their dead comrades. They destroyed Jewish shops, beat up passersby, and shot at buses and cafés, killing five people and wounding many others, heightening passions in the country.

Golda left the meeting with Cunningham feeling drained but satisfied that she had calmed him down and bought time for the leadership and the Haganah to act against the dissidents. Less than a week later, the British government arrested forty Revisionists, along with the mayors of Tel Aviv, Ramat Gan, and Netanya, and sent them to the Latrun detention camp. None of the mayors belonged to the Revisionist Party or its militant groups but might have sought their support in the previous election. Golda and the Jewish Agency insisted they had nothing to do with the arrests; this was purely British doing. Few believed them. Some saw the move as the beginning of a "small *saison*," the agency's and the Haganah's means of rooting out the underground by managing to help the British without openly collaborating with them this time.

The dissident groups had no doubts about the source of the arrests. They branded it Operation Golda and launched into a vitriolic campaign against her. As head of the political department, she had regular contact with the British; as the only woman in the Yishuv with real power, she made an easy target. Posters plastered on walls and buildings denounced "this ambitious woman," and articles vilifying her spread across Irgun and Lehi newspapers. One, titled "How the General [Cunningham] Gave In to Golda," featured a crude cartoon drawing of Golda with an upraised arm guided by the British general and writing the words, "With our own hands we will subdue the crime," as though she were a puppet taking orders from him. A nearby heart shows the "love" relationship between Golda and the British. In crude sexual terms, another article portrayed her as shaking the hands of British officials "dirtied with the blood of the immigrants," seducing the "uncircumcised," and whispering to the general words that his "ears and his heart" want to hear: "We will take care of them," the dissidents.

Sometimes she needed Haganah bodyguards to walk her home in the evenings because of threats she received from the extremist groups. But she refused to back off in her unyielding opposition to them. She told her son that these people "degrade the moral stature of every Jew." To the public she said, "We need to gather our strength to burn this evil from our midst." Later, in 1948, when she went to America to raise money for the newly created State of Israel, a member of the Irgun was there for the same purpose. "The head of Macy's department store said he would contribute a million dollars and Golda and I could split it for our different organizations," the man recalled. "She refused. She said she would not share money with the Irgun or have anything to do with us. She lost half a million dollars that way. It was so foolish."

The Revisionists could not understand that her disagreement with them did not stem only from their belonging to a competing political party, although it certainly included that. Her disagreement with them came from deep within her, an intense and uncompromising disapproval of their philosophy and techniques that prevented her from even sharing much-needed money with them. She never discarded that attitude.

THE UNSCOP GROUP, meeting in Geneva, completed its report for the United Nations late on August 31, 1947. The majority of the committee had decided to recommend to the General Assembly that the British mandate be ended and Palestine be partitioned into Jewish and Arab states, with Jerusalem as an international city. That evening, Sharett, Eban, and others who had come to Geneva opened a bottle of champagne to toast the news. In Palestine, Golda celebrated also. The committee had done something "miraculous" in a very short time, she exulted at a press conference. Still, she felt it necessary to point out that "the Jewish people all over the world will receive the plan with pangs of sorrow . . . at the fact that little Palestine is again divided." She objected to losing Jerusalem as part of the Jewish state and to giving up the hill country in the western Galilee, important for climate and defense purposes. She hoped, therefore, that the UN General Assembly would accept the special committee's recommendations but would also "improve" on them.

The United States agreed to the partition plan after weeks of hesitating. The Soviet Union enthusiastically endorsed it. Great Britain stated glumly that it would take no responsibility for enforcing partition, nor would it cooperate with other nations in doing so, and that it would quit Palestine as soon as its mandate ended.

In the meantime, as if nothing had changed, His Majesty's government continued its battle against illegal immigration. After the *Exodus* affair, it returned to deporting refugees on captured ships to its colony of Cyprus. From 1946 until the birth of Israel, some fifty-two thousand Jewish deportees lived behind barbed wire in the Cyprus camps, guarded by British soldiers.

Rows of aluminum Quonset huts lined the section of the island set aside for the camps. In the summer their interiors baked under the burning sun, and in winter freezing winds whistled through their cracks. Some of the orphaned children in the camps were packed twenty-five to a bunk. Others lived in overcrowded tents, where they inhaled sand and dust with every breath. Each month, 750 inmates left the camps for Palestine, in the order in which they arrived—a "first in, first out" policy. Deportees waited for months, some for more than a year, for their turn to receive an immigration certificate to Palestine.

Into this "suburb of sorrow," as the journalist Ruth Gruber called it, Golda Meyerson stepped on November 10, 1947, with what seemed an outrageous request. Deeply concerned about the health of the youngest children in the camps, the Jewish Agency wished to push some fifteen hundred of them up to the front of the line for their certificates. In order to free children and their parents, however, groups of adult inmates, high on the waiting list, would have to waive their turn for that month. Only Golda had the temerity and confidence to volunteer for this thorny assignment that nobody else in the Jewish Agency wanted to touch.

The story of her arrival at the camps has become another part of Golda mythology: inmates pressed behind barbed-wire fences straining to see her; two little children welcoming her with a bouquet of paper flowers; the British camp commander told to be careful because Mrs. Meyerson was a "formidable person." Less known is the opposition and violence she faced from deportees of two ships, *Rafiah* and *La'Negev*, whose turn it was to leave. Some of these DPs belonged to the Irgun youth group Betar, far from admirers of Golda Meyerson. As she began presenting her proposal at a meeting of the ships' detainees, shouts and catcalls drowned out her words. When she tried to leave after managing to finish her talk, they physically blocked her path and would not budge unless she promised not to take their turn away from them. Holocaust survivors, desperate to escape the miseries of Cyprus, they had counted the hours and days for their exit moment; they would not forfeit that moment for anyone. Acting quickly, a special unit of refugees affiliated with the Palmach and organized to keep order in the camps forcefully held the rioters back, freeing Golda. "I'm proud of you," she whispered to them as she walked out, ignoring her attackers.

The rioting continued for several days. The agitators gained control of the camp, locked the gates so that nobody could leave, and took over the distribution of food and water. A Palmach unit finally subdued them, with aid from the outside. At the end of November, 912 parents, 609 babies, and 42 orphans left for Palestine on the British ship *Ocean Vigour*. Under terrible conditions and out of sheer determination, Golda had persuaded groups of inmates to give up their turn for the children.

SHE HAD ONE MORE major mission in the fall of 1947: to persuade King Abdullah of Jordan not to wage war against the Jews if the United Nations voted for partition. While Moshe Sharett, assisted by Abba Eban and other diplomats, worked feverishly in New York to line up votes in the General Assembly, Ben-Gurion looked beyond the voting to its immediate aftermath. Convinced that the Arabs of Palestine and neighboring lands would invade the new state the minute the British left the country, he had set the groundwork for buying arms and preparing the Haganah for the impending war. During the past two years, he had immersed himself in studying all aspects of warfare and assessing the capabilities and shortcomings of the defense forces. In October, he created a new body to determine how much manpower would be needed to deal with the coming crisis and placed Golda at its head. By mid-November, as part of his war preparations, he sent her to see King Abdullah.

Later critics would say she was a bad choice for that assignment. Surely Ben-Gurion was aware of the low status women held in Arab society. Why then would he choose a woman for such a sensitive and critical mission? He might have answered—as Abdullah was told—that with Sharett away, Golda occupied the highest position in the Jewish Agency's political department and was the most prestigious person for the job. But his decision probably involved more. Ben-Gurion would have wanted to demonstrate to Abdullah—and to history—that in the democratic, socialist state his Labor Party planned, women would have equal rights with men as they already did in the Yishuv. He would not compromise that principle to accommodate another country's prejudice. Beyond that, as the historian Boaz Lev Tov has shown, the Jews who came to Palestine truly believed that along with fulfilling their Zionist dreams, they brought modernity and progress to the Arab inhabitants. As a woman who had reached the top echelons of political authority, Golda symbolized to Ben-Gurion the kind of progress he wanted the Arab world to see, starting with the king of Jordan.

Golda might have had her own qualms about the meeting, not as a woman, but because she knew no Arabic and had no experience in dealing with Arab rulers. To make up for those lacks, two experts in Arab culture, Ezra Danin and Eliyahu Sasson, accompanied her and acted as interpreters. On November 17, she traveled secretly to the village of Naharayim on the Jordan River, where Pinhas Rutenberg had founded a hydroelectric power station in 1932. Rutenberg's son Avraham and the station manager, Avraham Daskal, had long-standing relationships with the king, and it was Daskal who arranged the meeting. After separate lunches, Golda and Abdullah sat down in the Rutenberg home to sip strong coffee and talk seriously.

The monarch Golda met was short, overweight, fairly unattractive, and exceedingly charming. Visitors knew him to be a great raconteur, a bad poet, and a gracious host. The woman Abdullah saw looked drab and unappealing at forty-nine, with nondescript clothes, a heavyset body, and thick ankles, puffed out of shape from various illnesses. He appeared startled at first by meeting with a woman but seemed placated when told of her rank in the Jewish Agency. He needed to be on good terms with the Zionists, even if he disapproved of their representative.

Abdullah reigned over a monarchy with shallow roots in the region. He had been born in Mecca, then part of the Ottoman Empire, into an aristocratic Bedouin family known as the Hashemites. As a way of gaining the support of Bedouin tribes, in 1921 Winston Churchill—Britain's colonial secretary at the time—carved out an area from the British mandate over Palestine for Abdullah to administer. Called the Emirate of Transjordan (later Jordan), it extended from the Jordan River eastward to the Arabian Desert. To Abdullah's younger brother, Faisal, the British gave the kingdom of Iraq. Common wisdom held that Abdullah envied his handsomer, courtlier brother. He longed to rule over a much broader area than the poor, barren Transjordan, short on resources and lacking an outlet to the sea. He hoped the Zionists would help him in his ambitions.

To many Jewish minds of the time, Churchill had given Abdullah what had legitimately been part of the Jewish homeland as set forth in the Balfour Declaration. Vladimir Jabotinsky and his Revisionist followers never stopped referring to the two banks of the Jordan, east and west, as Jewish territory. Ben-Gurion, Golda, and other Labor Party leaders made their peace with the existence of Transjordan, and over the years kept up contacts with Abdullah, whom the British crowned as king in 1946. The two countries had much in common: both fell under the British mandate; both fought on Britain's side during World War II; and both had a hated enemy—Haj Amin al-Husseini, the mufti of Jerusalem. The mufti, who had collaborated with Hitler, made it clear that he wanted the Zionists out of Palestine. For his part, Abdullah rightly feared that the mufti hoped to dominate all of Palestine and probably Jordan as well.

Golda knew Abdullah's fears and desires when she met with him. In earlier meetings, with other leaders, he had spoken of creating a Greater Syria that would unite Syria, Lebanon, Transjordan, and Palestine under one kingdom ruled by him. He alluded to that dream in this meeting but focused on more immediate thoughts. What did they think, he asked, of forming an autonomous Hebrew Republic within a larger Transjordanian kingdom, with him at its helm? Golda emphatically explained that the United Nations was now considering the Palestine question, and she and the others hoped it would resolve to form two states, one Jewish and one Arab. They wished to speak to him about an agreement based on that resolution. The king said he understood and suggested they meet again after the UN decision.

The most striking part of the conversation came next. How would the Jews feel if Abdullah seized the Arab part of Palestine? Golda replied that they would "look on that favorably," but she added qualifications: First, if he did not interfere with the creation of the Jewish state and avoided any confrontation between his forces and theirs. And second, if he declared that the action was solely to maintain law and order and preserve the peace until the United Nations could establish a government in that area. To that idea, the king responded heatedly, "But I want that area for myself, to annex it to my kingdom. I do not want to create a new Arab state that will upset my plans and use the opportunity to ride on me. I want to ride and not be ridden!" He then shrugged off a suggestion that he hold a referendum among the Arabs of Palestine, in which his influence would be decisive. He also dismissed the thought, raised a little later, that he invite Arab leaders who also opposed the mufti to join him. He was not sure those leaders could stand the test of defying the mufti.

The exchange at that meeting became famous, and controversial. Did Abdullah and the Zionists "collude," as some historians hold, to prevent the Palestinian Arabs from having a state of their own by agreeing to give the Palestinian area to Jordan? The evidence does not seem to support that. Danin wrote a long report of the meeting, Sasson a short one, and Golda later gave a verbal statement about it. Undoubtedly, all the accounts show that the Jewish side would have favored Abdullah's gaining control of the Arab area after partition. (If not he, Golda and the others knew, the mufti would rule it.) But the reports also show that the Jewish participants would not help him attain that goal; all emphasize the need to abide by the UN charter. Golda told Abdullah that "we could not promise to help his incursion into the country since we would be obliged to observe the UN resolution . . . We said that we could not therefore give active support to the violation of this resolution." Had she collaborated with him, he would not have had to insist as forcefully as he did that he did not want a new Arab state created in Palestine.

After that impassioned discussion, the conversation ranged over several topics, with Abdullah doing most of the talking. Most critical for the Jewish side was his avowal that he had told the Arab countries, including Iraq, that he would not permit their armies to pass through his land to invade the Jewish state. He also assured Golda and the others that he would personally see to it that no clashes occurred on the Jewish-Arab border in Palestine. As for the mufti, "this man needs to disappear off the face of the earth."

Golda left the meeting satisfied with the encounter. Before they parted, Abdullah had insisted that they meet again very soon after the UN reached its decision, a sign of his continued friendship. Ezra Danin warned her, however, that although Abdullah probably meant what he said at the moment, she should not be overly optimistic.

GOLDA RETURNED TO HER POST in Jerusalem to await the UN decision. In New York, Arabs and Jews lobbied frantically during the last week before the General Assembly vote—the Arabs to defeat the partition resolution, the Jews to uphold it. Through the months of anxiety leading to this week, Sharett had corresponded with Golda regularly about his meetings, his worries, his rare moments of optimism. He and the other Jewish delegates had enlisted whatever help they could to sway votes to their side, meeting again and again with delegates from borderline countries. Albert Einstein wrote to India's prime minister,

Jawaharlal Nehru, in an appeal for support. Chaim Weizmann visited Harry Truman and won his backing for partition and for including the Negev within the proposed Jewish state. By the time the voting came, on the Saturday after Thanksgiving, November 29, 1947, at 5:35 p.m. New York time, the suspense had become agonizing for everyone.

Like millions of people in the world, Golda stayed "glued" to her radio, paper and pencil in hand, recording the voting, "yes," "no," "abstention." When the roll call ended, thirty-three nations had voted yes, including the United States, the Soviet Union, and most of Latin America. Thirteen had voted no, among them India, Greece, and Cuba, as well as the Arab and Muslim states. Britain had been one of ten countries to abstain. The partition resolution dividing Palestine into sovereign Jewish and Arab states passed with the necessary two-thirds votes. On hearing that, Prince Faisal of Saudi Arabia and Abdul Rahman Azzam, secretary of the Arab League, swept out of the hall, most of the Arab delegates behind them. "Any line of partition drawn in Palestine will be a line of fire and blood," they told the press.

It was well past midnight in Jerusalem. People began pouring out of their homes, some still clad in pajamas, calling out to each other, banging on the doors of neighbors to wake them up. Lines of ecstatic men, women, and children snaked through the streets, shouting, singing, crying, kissing, forming circles within circles as they danced their way to the Jewish Agency courtyard. At 2:00 a.m., Golda arrived at her office there and stepped out on the balcony to speak to the ever-thickening crowds. Wild cheers greeted her.

Overcome at first with emotion, she could barely choke out the words "Mazaltov." "It's hard to express the feelings in the heart of a Jew at this moment," she managed to say. "We worked hard and we looked forward to this hour. We made many sacrifices. But we believed with full faith that this great time would come." She felt herself part of a miracle that generations before her had dreamed of and for which many had given up their lives. More soberly, she directed her words to the Arabs. "You have fought your battle against us in the United Nations," she said. "The partition plan is a compromise: not what you wanted, not what we wanted. But now let us live in friendship and peace together." She ended by sending warm greetings to the immigrants in Cyprus and the European DP camps. The crowds had stopped dancing. People stood still, linked arms, and sang "Hatikvah," the Jewish national anthem.

A few days later, a letter arrived at the Jewish Agency with Golda's picture in *The Palestine Post* as she appeared that Saturday night. In it she stands on the balcony among a crush of men. She is wearing black. Her face looks grim, her eyes watery. The caption above the photograph reads, "Rejoicing in Jerusalem." The letter writer complained, "Does this picture of victory really demonstrate joy?" It looks more "like a mother standing at her child's grave, being held up by two relatives. I think the time has come when people responsible for our public affairs start to pay more attention to their missions."

"I was looking very, very sad that day," Golda admitted afterward, "because the Arabs had rejected it [the UN resolution]. And we expected that there will be war."

15

"The Time Is Now"

They were still dancing in the streets, waving little blue and white flags, when Golda's fears came true. On November 30, 1947, the morning after the UN partition decision, a band of Arabs ambushed a bus near Lod Airport, killing five Jews and wounding many others. Less than half an hour later, Arabs assaulted a second bus, slaying two more people, and soon after that they murdered a Jew near the border between Tel Aviv and Jaffa. Thus, before the day of celebration ended, the Arabs in Palestine had killed eight Jews.

Two days later, Arab mobs pushed through to the commercial center of Jerusalem, set buildings ablaze, smashed store windows, and looted shops and galleries, while British troops stood aside, observing but doing little to stop the violence.

"Golda is not in Jerusalem," Ben-Gurion wrote in his diary, both relieved that she had avoided the mayhem and surprised by her absence.

She was, instead, in Holon, at her sister Sheyna's home, outside Tel Aviv. She had slipped away to host Sheyna's son Yona's wedding. Sheyna had gone to the States for stomach surgery, and with Shamai there as well, Golda had made all the wedding arrangements, including bringing her mother in from Herzliya. "It was a beautiful wedding," Yona recalled. "We knew there would be a war, and I wanted to marry before it began. Golda went out of her way to fill in for my parents."

That happy Tuesday afternoon provided the only respite Golda was to have from the anxieties of the next several months. The mob scene in Jerusalem marked the beginning of what some called a civil war and the historian Michael Bar-Zohar dubbed "the war before the war." In this war, bands of Palestinian Arabs set upon regions with large Jewish populations or with a mixture of Jews and Arabs—Jerusalem, Tel Aviv, Jaffa, Haifa—exploding bombs, murdering civilians, blocking roads, and disrupting all areas of normal life. Within a short time, volunteers from neighboring Arab countries crossed into Palestine to join the local Arabs. The most aggressive belonged to the Arab Liberation Army, led by Fawzi el Kaukji, who had spent the World War II years in Nazi Germany.

For months, the Haganah fought a defensive war, retaliating against Arab attacks but rarely initiating actions. In its force of about thirty-five thousand men, fewer than three thousand, most members of the Palmach, knew how to deal with real warfare. For arms, the fighters had about ten thousand rifles and several thousand other light weapons, but they had no tanks, airplanes, or other heavy armaments, and only a small number of rickety armored vehicles.

With violence flaring, the Jewish Agency voted to provide extra protection to its key leaders in Palestine: David Ben-Gurion, David Remez, and Golda Meyerson. Golda needed it. The only one of the three stationed full-time in Jerusalem, she had taken on a dozen responsibilities for the Yishuv that kept her visible and on the go. At one moment, she might huddle with other members of the newly formed Committee B, created to outline plans for the state-to-be; at the next, she might be hurriedly required to review an operation the Haganah had hatched for that evening. Every two days, she traveled the dangerous road to Tel Aviv and back for Jewish Agency or Mapai Party meetings, sitting in an armored car or a bus run by the Egged company, in a long convoy of vehicles protected by the Haganah. Even so, Arab snipers shot at the cars and trucks in the convoy or showered them with hand grenades. Occasionally, the British escorted the convoys with their own well-armored cars and offered their protection; often they did not. They were looking ahead to leaving the country as early as possible after their mandate ended. Jewish security was not a priority.

Golda pressed for that security by appearing routinely at the offices of British authorities, dodging Arab upheavals in the city to get to where she needed to be. At one meeting with Chief Secretary Gurney, she pulled out photographs of his police force sent to the Haganah by a reporter for the United Press International, Yehezkel Noam. He had been in Jerusalem when the Arab raids began and photographed Arab masses trashing and plundering stores with no British interference. "The police and soldiers are standing around with their arms folded," Golda showed Gurney, "while the Arabs are throwing stones and looting." He promised to look into the matter. He also promised to investigate the police practice of searching Haganah members and confiscating their weapons. With the mandate ending, his men had orders to stop those searches, he said.

On December 8, as Jews around the city kindled the second light of the Hanukkah festival, Golda sat in his office again, frustrated and impatient. During the first week of December, fifty-nine Jews had lost their lives to Arab terror. The British police had done little to rein in the attacks, and even assisted them at times. She didn't know what to make of Gurney these days. "He can be hard and mean and stubborn," she said afterward, "but I don't take him to be a liar." So why couldn't he protect the Jewish population as he promised?

Determined to get that protection, she carried her complaints to Alan Cunningham, the high commissioner. Moshe Sharett had cautioned her that the growing number of Jewish deaths at Arab hands was making Jews around the world "panic" that the state would never come into being. One of the conditions of the UN partition plan had been the ability of the Jews to maintain order in the land. No country wanted to send troops to keep peace there.

Ben-Gurion had phoned Golda from Tel Aviv to bolster her before confronting Cunningham. Although still head of the Jewish Agency, with its headquarters in Jerusalem, he had moved to Tel Aviv to lead the military battle from there. He urged her to insist that the British send the Arab Legion out of the country. Not to be confused with the Arab League, a union of Arab states in the area, the legion was a powerful Transjordanian army of fifteen thousand soldiers that served as part of the regular British forces and had at its head the British commander John Glubb. Its soldiers could not be trusted to desist from attacking Jews, let alone expected to protect them. Golda raised strong concerns about the legion at the meeting, but she pushed hardest on the British searches for weapons that had continued, in spite of Gurney's promises. The British claimed not to be taking sides, she argued, but what did they think they were doing when they confiscated Haganah weapons and not those of the Arabs?

Cunningham responded angrily to her accusations by pulling out the latest casualty figures. A hundred and six Arabs had been killed in the fighting compared with ninety-six Jews. "What does that tell you?" he demanded. The explanation was simple, Golda answered calmly. The Jews died defending themselves against Arab attacks. The Arabs died when the Jews fought back, and "our people were more capable." Why was it, Golda asked, that when the British suspected the Jews of harboring weapons in 1946, they sent their leaders to Latrun and tore apart the Jewish Agency building, but they won't even search the Arabs?

"Are you suggesting that we search both Jews and Arabs?" Cunningham asked.

"No," Golda answered.

"To search for weapons only among the Arabs, that's your proposal?" he asked irritably.

"Exactly. When Jews will attack Arabs you can search them."

Some of the conversation was less belligerent. He admitted that he was glad the Jews were getting a state, and she admitted that the British army in the Negev had done its work well. They agreed to cooperate more fully, and that evening she sent him a long list of security matters that required "urgent action." A written answer did not arrive until February, a month and a half later, and little of the action she called for was taken.

Throughout the dickering with the British, two immigrant ships preparing to set sail from Bulgaria preoccupied Golda. The *Pan York* and the *Pan Crescent*, together known as the *Pans*, were the largest ships in the history of the Mossad l'Aliyah Bet, the illegal immigrant enterprise. They had been banana boats, used by the United Fruit Company, before Haganah agents in the United States purchased them, planning to pack them with fifteen thousand Jews from Romania—the greatest number of illegal immigrants ever to be carried to Palestine.

Golda had warm ties to two of the men most intricately involved in the expedition. Shaike Dan, in direct charge, had been one of the parachutists who landed behind Nazi lines and contacted Romanian Jews in 1944. Shaul Avigur, head of the entire Aliyah Bet operation and Moshe Sharett's brother-in-law, was already one of the legendary figures of Zionism, known for the kind of closemouthed courage that heroes are made of. He and Golda had a strong relationship from the earliest days of the immigration, when she operated an illegal radio set. Shaike helped win the Romanian government's permission for the Jews to leave that country. Because the government would not allow them to sail from a Romanian port, he organized a complex system of trains to carry all of them to the port of Burgas in Bulgaria.

With everything set to go, Avigur suddenly received word from the Jewish Agency in Palestine not to sail. The British had put great pressure on the American government to prevent the ships from embarking, and the American secretary of state, George C. Marshall, had asked Moshe

Sharett to halt the operation immediately. America did not wish to be at war with England over the immigration issue, Marshall emphasized. Moreover, the nations of the world, having just voted to create a Jewish state, would be irritated at this provocation.

Shocked by the order to cancel the sailing after months of planning, Avigur and Dan appeared at a Mapai meeting in Tel Aviv to argue their case. They were disappointed that Golda, whom they had counted on for backing, didn't show up. Shaike explained to party members that the fifteen thousand Romanian Jews didn't come from displaced persons camps. They were Romanian citizens who had given up their homes and possessions to go to Palestine. With the Soviet takeover of Eastern Europe and the Iron Curtain rapidly descending over those lands, this might be their last chance to leave. How could they be deprived of that opportunity?

Ben-Gurion spoke after Shaike. With a nod to the difficulty of the Romanian situation, he fully backed Moshe Sharett in his struggles with the American State Department. If a Jewish state did not come into being because of this incident, there would be no immigration from any place in the world, not only Romania. He seemed assertive and resolute in his talk. But at five o'clock the next morning, the men received a phone call inviting them to his home. Instead of the self-confident leader of the night before, they found a soft-spoken man, "tragically torn" over the Romanian immigrant situation. He wanted them to fly to the United States and present their side to Moshe Sharett. He would accept whatever decision Sharett arrived at.

The men rushed to the American consulate in Jerusalem for visas and stopped off to discuss the situation with Golda, fully expecting her backing. To their dismay, she stood firmly against them. They needed to unite behind Sharett and not alienate the American government in any way, she told them. They argued heatedly, and the men left in anger. Golda did not even wish them well. "It seems to me that until the very last day of his life, Shaul did not forget the harsh things that were said at that meeting," Shaike Dan remembered. Shaul even thought of writing a book about the *Pans* episode, with a chapter called "Golda and the Boats."

Always the realist, Golda had placed Jewish hopes for a state above the hopes of the Romanian immigrants. It was one of the saddest ironies of the mandate period that the illegal boats, which the Jews long considered their most effective weapon in pushing Britain out of Palestine, had now become an obstacle to achieving their independence in it. Golda understood that and acted accordingly, unfeeling as that made her in the eyes of her friends.

As it happened, the men did not go to America, because Sharett planned to come to Palestine. Without a clear-cut directive to scratch the operation, the boats sailed off on their journey, but the Haganah arranged with the British to have them go directly to Cyprus and not try to land in Palestine. They steamed out of Bulgaria on December 27 and arrived in Cyprus on January 1, 1948. En route, they received Hebrew names: *Kibbutz Galuyot* (Ingathering of Exiles) and *Atzmaut* (Independence).

IN JERUSALEM, THE DANGERS WORSENED. Every time Golda entered a car or climbed into a bus to go to Tel Aviv, she put her life in peril. The road between the two cities, narrow and poorly paved in those days, twisted around forests and sharp inclines. Arab guerrillas regularly swept down from the hilltops and hid behind rocks until ready to storm a convoy of cars and buses with bombs and bullets, then disappeared as quickly as they had appeared. The burned-out frames of ambushed buses remain on the roadside to this day, ghostly reminders of those hazardous times.

Golda skirted catastrophe on one trip. On the chilly Friday afternoon of December 26, 1947, she sat in the Chrysler used by members of the National Council as it made its way from Tel Aviv to Jerusalem as part of a convoy of buses and trucks. Among the passengers in her car were Yitzhak Gruenbaum of the Jewish Agency and Hans Beyth, head of Youth Aliyah (an organization that cared for young immigrants). Near an Arab village on the way to Latrun, they met with heavy gunfire. The tires of Golda's car were hit and the car stuck in front of an Arab building. She and the others dashed out into one of the buses, where Beyth used his rifle to shoot back at the attackers. He was hit in the head and died on the spot—in her arms, Golda would later tell his son.

In another incident, Jewish Agency people were en route to their regular meeting in Tel Aviv when British soldiers halted their convoy to look for arms. They found a Sten gun hidden on one young woman and were about to arrest her. Golda demanded to see the search orders of the British major making the arrest. "I don't have written orders," he said, "but I have orders from the brigadier." Under those circumstances, Golda told him, he had no right to search any of the vehicles. When the officer saw her name on her identity papers, he walked away and left the matter to his lieutenant.

Having completed their search, the British signaled the convoy to move on. But first Golda wanted to know where they were taking the young woman. "To a police station in the Arab town of Majdal," the lieutenant said. "In that case," Golda announced, "I will go with her." Annoyed at her intrusion, the lieutenant arrested her, the young woman, and the driver of the car where the weapon had been found. After more than an hour of arguing among themselves, the officers decided to take their prisoners to a station in the Jewish town of Hadera. There the police chief instantly recognized Golda. He freed everyone, offered her a glass of wine to toast the New Year, and sent her to Tel Aviv with a special police escort.

During the long delay, Ben-Gurion had been nervously waiting for her in Tel Aviv, worried about her safety. When news of her arrest reached him, he also received word from her to inform Gurney of what had happened. She was not going to let the incident pass without calling the chief secretary on his vow to stop the searches and arrests. He would have heard of the matter in any case. The story of Golda Meyerson's arrest made the London newspapers, sharing headlines with the arrival of the *Pans* ships in Cyprus.

Slowly at first, then more drastically as the days and weeks passed, the 100,000 Jews of Jerusalem became victims of a deadly siege. Arab roadblocks choked off vital supplies from reaching Jewish sections, particularly in the Jewish Quarter of the Old City. Water became scarce, and food disappeared from marketplaces, while parents scrounged for a little milk or eggs to feed their children. Soon the city lacked fuel for heat in the middle of an unusually cold winter. "Jerusalem is on the front lines," Golda told Jewish Agency leaders. In the Old City, groups of ultra-Orthodox Jews held a large demonstration and planned to go out to the Arabs carrying a white flag of surrender in their hands. With great effort, Golda and Haganah members calmed them.

The spreading dangers in the city and on the roads led to prolonged discussions at Jewish Agency Executive meetings about whether to move the organization's headquarters to Tel Aviv. As it was, the meetings in Jerusalem were attended mostly by those who lived there; it had become too dangerous for others to make the trip. Golda steadfastly opposed such a move. "The center is in Jerusalem," she argued. With all the suffering, Jerusalem was still the pivot of Jewish life. As for the dangers, "in war," she said philosophically, "there is no way to avoid tragedies."

The Jewish Agency headquarters remained in Jerusalem, and Jerusalem remained Golda's territory. In addition to her other duties, when Ben-Gurion moved to Tel Aviv, he appointed her head of a security committee, responsible for security issues in Jerusalem and with final approval over all military actions there. Despite her authority, she couldn't always keep the Haganah under control. On the night of January 5, without consulting her, Haganah operatives bombed the Semiramis Hotel in the prosperous Arab neighborhood of Katamon, believing it to be an Arab headquarters and a center for many irregulars—those fighters who had slipped into Palestine from neighboring Arab countries. The bomb killed twenty-six people, among them a young Spanish deputy consul, causing outraged protests from Spain. When Golda learned of the operation, she lashed out at the Haganah personnel involved, not, she said, because she thought there were no irregulars at the hotel—there were—but because most of the people who died were innocent. Stoking her anger, cablegrams from the Jewish Agency office in America complained that the operation had badly hurt Jewish interests in the State Department and with the public. On her advice, Ben-Gurion removed the commander responsible for the bombing from his post.

But graver problems loomed. The Jews desperately needed money. Rumors circulated among American military strategists that the Jewish side had already lost the war, outnumbered, outfinanced, and outmaneuvered by the Arabs. If the Jews could not hold their own against the Palestinian Arabs, the thinking went, how could they fight the organized Arab states that would soon invade? To make matters worse, the United States slapped an embargo on the sale of arms to the entire Middle East. To be sure, the Jews had other sources for procuring arms: Czechoslovakia, with the blessings of the Soviet Union, was becoming a major supplier. And in the United States itself, a clandestine Haganah operation acquired the machinery and equipment needed to produce arms and managed to smuggle them into Palestine. What the Yishuv most lacked was cash, the large amounts necessary to pay for the materials and the black market operators who dealt in them.

Everyone knew the money had to come from Jews in the United States, now the wealthiest and strongest Jewish community in the world. Ben-Gurion had sent the Jewish Agency's treasurer, Eliezer Kaplan, there to raise at least seven million dollars. Golda attended the meeting in Tel Aviv after Kaplan's return when he reported that he could not raise that amount. American Jews, he said with resignation, felt they had given enough through the war years and afterward. Looking at Ben-

Gurion, Golda saw him "boil" at Kaplan's passivity. Slowly, he stood up and announced that he would go to the States with Kaplan to try again.

In the iconic narrative of the next moments, told by Golda and repeated many times, she proposed that she make the trip instead of Ben-Gurion. "What you can do here, I cannot do, but what you can do in the United States, I can do," she said. When Ben-Gurion adamantly resisted, she called for a vote of the executive, which backed her.

The story behind the story is slightly different. Ben-Gurion certainly understood how crucial his leadership was in Palestine during these tense days of fighting. That he would consider leaving to go to the States demonstrates how desperate he felt about the financial situation. Golda's volunteering to replace him suddenly opened up a viable alternative. He trusted her and relied on her to do jobs others could not or would not do. Were it not for that, the votes of the agency executives would not have swayed the stubborn, autocratic Ben-Gurion. For her, the situation fed into a gnawing desire to get away from fruitless meetings with British officials. It also placed her in a precarious position. Could she succeed where Kaplan had failed?

In his diary entry for January 13, 1948, Ben-Gurion simply recorded that "it was decided that Golda would go to America," omitting the tangled path to that decision.

In Golda's memory, she left for the States immediately after that fateful meeting. So urgent was her going that she did not have time to return to Jerusalem, change clothes, or pack her bags. In reality, she did not leave until January 22, nine days later. She was in Palestine long enough to learn of the slaughter of thirty-five young Haganah men, most of them Hebrew University students from prominent families in the Yishuv. Arab forces had cut off the road to the Etzion Bloc, a group of settlements south of Jerusalem, and the young men had set out on foot through the hills to bypass the road and try to reach the stranded people with supplies. An Arab shepherd spotted them, and soon hundreds of villagers and townspeople ambushed them. The fighting continued for seven hours. With the last man dead, the Arabs mutilated the bodies.

The slaughter of the young men took a terrible toll on the Yishuv. Nothing on that scale had ever happened before, and it fed into the despair and pessimism many had begun to feel about the prospects for partition. In Jerusalem, Golda met with the anguished parents, sharing their grief and their tears. She would carry their story with her to the States.

In a final meeting with Ben-Gurion in Tel Aviv, she received a wish list of arms and equipment he wanted. They included jeeps, rockets, cargo planes, speedboats, and an aircraft carrier to transport the material, all to arrive on the day the British left Palestine.

MENAHEM REMEMBERED MEETING HIS MOTHER at the airport. Golda remembered being greeted by her two sisters, Sheyna, still in America because of the surgery she had, and Clara, who had never left the States for Palestine. The most vivid memory, for everyone, was of a bitter-cold Friday, with winds howling and snow mounting. Golda spent the night at the Brooklyn home of Sheyna's married daughter, Judith Bauman, and the two sisters sat up all night talking.

Clara still lived in Bridgeport, Connecticut, where she had become head of the local Jewish Federation, a broad-based philanthropy. She suggested that to raise money, Golda speak at the annual conference of the parent organization, the Council of Jewish Federations and Welfare Funds, meeting at the Sheraton Hotel in Chicago. The person to arrange that was Henry Montor, executive vice-chairman of the United Jewish Appeal (UJA). Golda knew of Montor but had never met him. Three years earlier, in 1945, he had gathered a group of seventeen wealthy Jewish businessmen to meet with Ben-Gurion, then visiting New York, at the apartment of the millionaire Rudolf G. Sonneborn. At the meeting, the group formed a secret "club" to raise money and purchase armaments and equipment for the future state. During the next several years, the "Sonneborn Institute," its cover name, contributed hundreds of thousands of dollars toward buying and stockpiling military materials, to be shipped later to Palestine.

Montor was in Chicago when Golda arrived in the States. He knew little about her except that in the past she had been "an impecunious, unimportant representative, a 'schnorrer,'" who stayed in people's houses instead of hotels. Now she arrived "without a dime in her pocketbook even to take a taxi" and wanted to speak at the federation conference. Out of concern for Israel, he pressured the federation to fit her into a luncheon spot on Sunday, January 25, 1948, when the big donors would be present. But how was he going to sell her to that well-heeled crowd?

For two days, the snowstorm shut down airports and stalled trains, but during a brief break in the weather on Saturday, Golda found a plane to carry her to Chicago, probably the only one to leave that day. She had not been to the States in ten years. Although reports about her had appeared in American newspapers from time to time, she was hardly a household name. "I was terribly afraid of going to these people who didn't know me from Adam," she recalled. "I admit I was shaking. I had no idea what was going to happen."

It could not have been easy to meet Montor either. At forty-two, almost eight years younger than she, he had a reputation as a demon when it came to fund-raising. In 1946, he had set a goal of $100 million for the UJA, the largest campaign of any Jewish organization in history, anywhere in the world, and met it. After that he became for other fund-raisers "a Pied Piper. He played the tune and we all danced." Impatient, seemingly always in motion, his dark eyes snapping, Montor didn't suffer fools gladly. He was giving Golda this opportunity. She sensed that she had to live up to it or there would be no others.

She delivered her talk without notes, her favorite form of public speaking. "Friends," she said, looking out at the audience in the way she had of making every listener feel personally addressed. "The mufti and his people have declared war upon us. We have no alternative but . . . to fight for our lives, for our safety, for what we have accomplished in Palestine, for Jewish honor, for Jewish independence." She told them of the young people, seventeen- and eighteen-year-olds, Haganah members, who fearlessly escorted Jews over the dangerous road from Tel Aviv to Jerusalem, and of others, more than twenty thousand young men and women, who registered to join the military organization. She told them of the thirty-five who "fought to the very end" on the road to Kfar Etzion and of the last one killed. He had run out of ammunition but died with a stone in his hand, prepared to continue fighting.

The Jewish community in Palestine "is going to fight to the very end" also, she said. "If we have something to fight with, we will fight with that, and if not, we will fight with stones." The spirit of the young people fighting remained high, she related, but "this spirit alone cannot face rifles and machine guns. Rifles and machine guns without spirit are not worth very much, but spirit without arms can in time be broken with the body." They needed arms and they needed them immediately.

"Our problem is time," she emphasized. "Millions of dollars that we may get in three or four months will mean very little in deciding the present issue. The question is what can we get immediately. And, my friends, when I say immediately, this does not mean next month. It does not mean two months from now. It means now."

She considered herself "not as a guest, but as one of you," she told them, repeating the word "friends" several times. And without apology, she gave them the sum of between twenty-five and thirty million dollars in cash the Yishuv needed in the next few weeks.

"We are not a better breed; we are not the best Jews of the Jewish people," she said. "It so happened we are there and you are here. I am certain that if you were in Palestine and we were in the United States, you would be doing what we are doing there." Paraphrasing Winston Churchill, she promised that the Yishuv in Palestine "will fight in the Negev and will fight in Galilee and will fight on the outskirts of Jerusalem until the very end."

In closing, she gave the audience its charge: "You cannot decide whether we should fight or not. We will . . . That decision is taken. Nobody can change it. You can only decide one thing: whether we shall be victorious in this fight or whether the mufti will be victorious. That decision American Jews can make."

And, a final reminder: "I beg of you—don't be too late. Don't be bitterly sorry three months from now for what you failed to do today. The time is now."

The talk lasted thirty-five minutes. "The normal noises of a great crowd were paralyzed," a contemporary report of the event said. When she finished, the audience rose to its feet, some people weeping openly while they applauded. "Sometimes things occur, for reasons you don't know why," Montor recalled. "You don't know what combination of words has done it, but an electric atmosphere generates. People are ready to kill somebody or to embrace each other. And that is still vivid in my mind, that particular afternoon . . . She had swept the whole conference."

In her plain dark dress, without a speck of makeup, her hair austerely parted in the middle and pulled tightly back, she seemed to some like a woman out of the Bible. Others marveled at her "genius" for speaking without a prepared text. Her pauses, one man noted, were as meaningful as the words she used. The Dallas delegation—strongly non-Zionist—became so fired up that its members planned to "get so much money they won't know what to do with it."

By any measure, Chicago had been a triumph; her speech one of the best in her life.

BACK IN NEW YORK, reality set in. Golda participated in a small meeting Montor arranged with the administrative committee of the UJA, powerful leaders such as William Rosenwald and Edward Warburg. The

UJA had been formed in the late 1930s as an umbrella for two groups, the United Palestine Appeal (UPA), which focused on Palestine's Jews, and the Joint Distribution Committee, geared to Diaspora Jewry. Golda agreed to split the money she raised through the UJA on a fifty-fifty basis, half going to Palestine and half for world Jewry. She had announced from the start that she needed at least twenty-five million dollars and suggested that they set a goal of fifty million dollars so that she could get her full share. As they sat around the table eating kosher delicatessen sandwiches, objections to her request arose. The UJA was a philanthropic organization and should not be involved in funding arms, several of the men argued, especially in light of the American embargo against arms for the Middle East. As they spoke, tears rolled down Golda's cheeks, a true expression of her feelings—also meant for the others to see.

Henry Morgenthau Jr., board chairman of the UJA and former U.S. secretary of the Treasury, sat at the head of the table. "I feel just as deeply about America as you do," he told the others. "But the United Jewish Appeal is here for the purpose of saving the Jewish people and we can't save the Jewish people unless the Jews in Palestine . . . are able to defend themselves . . . If Golda Meyerson says that they have to have arms, and we are the only place where they can get the money to buy the arms, I'm afraid . . . you'll have to accept my decision. We are going to include Golda Meyerson and her request in this year's campaign."

The next day, Golda took off on a whirlwind fund-raising tour, traveling the country from coast to coast, visiting seventeen cities in a haze of meetings and meals: breakfast with a small group in a town, lunch with a larger one, dinner, usually, with the largest, and on to the next city. Morgenthau traveled with her to some cities, Montor to some, various organizational leaders to others. "These men had to change off. They couldn't take the schedule," she said, laughing. And some of them were much younger than she. Sam Rothberg, Julian Venezky, Lou Boyar—wealthy, philanthropic men with whom she would remain connected all her life—were in their early thirties at the time. Montor was a paid professional, but these men and most of the others she traveled with served as volunteers. Rothberg, who would become one of Golda's closest friends, had visited the Nazi death camps after the war. At fund-raising events, he would pluck at people's heartstrings as he described in detail what he saw.

Just as often he and the others would "terrorize" audiences. Golda marveled at how Montor seemed to know how much money every Jew in every community had. If he or the others felt people weren't giving enough, they would demand it. "We didn't beg, we didn't ask nicely . . . We insulted people and we got money," Lou Boyar said. Golda learned from the men's hard-line tactics. In Youngstown, Ohio, she, Rothberg, and Venezky walked out of a meeting because the numbers were too low. They came back an hour later and found people waiting for them, ready to open their purses wider than before.

Sometimes the task seemed overwhelming. At a dinner in a luxurious Miami Beach hotel, she felt tears rising as she looked at the sun-tanned people in their beautiful clothes and thought about presenting the grim situation at home. She was sure that when she got up to talk, everybody would walk out. "I didn't eat anything," she recalled. "I drank black coffee and smoked my cigarettes." Morgenthau, who was with her, took over. "We intend to do business tonight," he announced brusquely, ignoring hotel rules against solicitations. "Anybody that wants to walk out . . . you can just get up and walk out." Nobody did. Golda spoke, and they raised about $1.5 million that evening and close to $5 million for the entire day in Miami.

In New York and surrounding areas, the influential Reform rabbi Stephen S. Wise showed up frequently at Golda's fund-raising meetings. Occasionally, he spoke, in his sonorous voice, but more often he just sat in the room, and Golda sensed that his presence alone spurred people to contribute. In California, the famous radio and film star Eddie Cantor opened his home for a gathering and promised to devote himself to the spring campaign.

On February 11, Golda was able to cable Ben-Gurion that she had raised fifteen million dollars and hoped by the end of the month to have twenty million. Two days later, the sum raised had gone up to sixteen million dollars. On February 19, Sharett, cabling Kaplan in Jerusalem, wanted to know whether the "absurd" split with the UJA could be eliminated. It could not. But on February 24, Morgenthau cabled to say that he expected the campaign for fifty million dollars to come to a successful conclusion in the next few weeks and that "Mrs. Meyerson has done an outstanding job." Within four days, he was happy to report that the goal had been achieved. Golda's "iron campaign," as Sharett called it, had garnered the Jewish Agency twenty-five million dollars, three times what Kaplan had tried and failed to obtain.

While Golda campaigned, Ben-Gurion purchased guns, airplanes, cars, and other equipment, anticipating the funds that would come in and agonizing over events in Palestine. Some time before she left for America, he had phoned her to come to his home. "I tell you," he said as he paced up and down. "I feel as though I were going mad. What's going to happen to us? I'm sure the Arabs will attack us and we're not prepared for it. We have nothing." In early March, he wrote in his diary that "the only ray of light for the present is Golda's success."

She should have felt like a conquering hero when she returned to Palestine on March 19. His worries notwithstanding, Ben-Gurion lavished praise on her fund-raising feat. "Someday when history will be written, it will be said that there was a Jewish woman who got the money which made the state possible," he said to her. As recognition of her accomplishment spread to other institutions in the Yishuv, her only regret, she would say, was that she and those with her had not had the courage to ask for twice as much as they had. Next time she would not hesitate.

Yet for all her success, she came home to bitter disappointment. It had started while she was in America. In anticipation of the new state, executives of the Jewish Agency and the National Council decided to set up two bodies to govern the country until democratic elections could be held. One, a provisional state council, with thirty-seven members, would serve as a kind of parliament. The second, an administrative council, with thirteen members taken from the thirty-seven, would be the actual provisional government, the cabinet, of the state when it came into being. After prolonged negotiations among all the political parties in the Yishuv to determine the number of seats each would hold, a Mapai committee chose its representatives for both councils. Golda was included among the thirty-seven in the State Council but not in the—more important— thirteen-member Administrative Council. Mapai had received four seats in that council, and after lengthy party deliberations they were given to the four top chiefs, all male: David Ben-Gurion, Moshe Sharett, Eliezer Kaplan, and David Remez.

In early March, with Golda still away, Ben-Gurion upset the applecart. "It is essential to have a woman in the government," he declared at a Mapai meeting, "first of all because she is suited to it." Everyone understood that he was speaking about Golda. Moreover, he continued, "it is inconceivable that half the Yishuv, half the Jewish people, will not be represented in the first government we are attempting to build in the Land of Israel." Even more, "a woman in the first Jewish government will be . . . an important political banner for the entire Arab world." Just as Golda had personified the Yishuv's progressiveness in meeting with

Abdullah, she would signify the equality women held within the Jewish state.

The concept of a woman in the government—of Golda in the government—did not come as a surprise to anyone. It had been in the air for some time; Ben-Gurion had suggested it before; David Remez had suggested it. The others were astounded, however, that Ben-Gurion would raise the issue again at this late point, after tough bargaining with other parties and wrangling within Mapai had led to a final slate of names for the new provisional government. In his talk, Ben-Gurion offered to step aside and have Golda fill his place, but nobody took that offer seriously. They knew and he knew that he had to be in the government.

A long discussion followed his statement, and the only possibility for including Golda that emerged was to have her replace David Remez. As treasurer and financial expert, Kaplan had to be in the government. Sharett was indispensable in his dealings with the Americans and the United Nations. Although Remez headed the National Council, perhaps, some suggested, he could have a key role in the "Thirty-Seven" and Golda could replace him in the "Thirteen." In the end, with twenty-one votes for Remez and ten for Golda, the Mapai Party accepted the committee's recommendations. On March 6, Ben-Gurion wrote in his diary, "I sought to have Golda accepted—because she deserves it and because there is moral and political importance to her inclusion in the 'first government.' But I suspected that my demands would not be fulfilled."

Ben-Gurion was very fond of Golda and admired her many abilities. He would sincerely have wanted her in his government. Yet the commotion he caused about including her at a time when there was no longer much chance of that happening might also have been motivated by his desire to keep Remez out. Politically moderate, Remez often opposed Ben-Gurion's activism. Ben-Gurion might have wanted to manipulate Mapai into pushing Remez away from the center of power even at this late date. At the same time, his call to have Golda in the Administrative Council was also a message to history: from the start, the head of the new Jewish state wanted a woman in the highest ranks of government.

It was a good message, but it put Golda in an untenable position. Although she was in America when the Mapai deliberations took place, she had followed them carefully. She had longed to be in that first government, but how could she pit herself against Remez, the man who had been her adviser, mentor, and lover? Deeply hurt by being excluded and torn between her closeness to Remez and her loyalty to Ben-Gurion, once home she turned to Israel Galili, head of the Haganah, who had become a good friend, and wept on his shoulder.

A short time later, she offered to withdraw even from the "Thirty-Seven." A new political party had been formed in Tel Aviv in January. Calling itself Mapam, the United Workers' Party, it united two other parties, Hashomer Hatzair and l'Ahdut Ha'avoda, which had broken away from Mapai in 1944. It now dropped the *l* from its name and became simply Ahdut Ha'avoda, the name once used by an earlier organization. Radical socialists, Mapam's founders regarded themselves as heirs to the Russian Revolution and accused Mapai—Golda and Ben-Gurion's party—of being retrograde, too moderate and middle class. Mapai viewed Mapam as too far left and blind to the brutalities of the Soviets. Nevertheless, Ben-Gurion wanted the party represented in the new coalition government and sent Golda to talk to its leaders. In the kind of horse-trading that would become typical of forming later Israeli governments, Golda suggested that Mapai give one of its seats in the Administrative Council of thirty-seven to Mapam. The seat she proposed giving up was her own.

The party agreed it could offer to relinquish a seat, but it could no more be Golda's than Ben-Gurion's. She knew that, but like him she wanted to show herself the dedicated party leader. She might also have wanted to test the waters, because, in fact, her role at the Jewish Agency was becoming increasingly superfluous.

After all she had accomplished in raising money overseas, back home she had almost nothing official to do. With the British concentrating on withdrawing from Palestine—they had set May 15 as the date—and the Yishuv mapping out plans for a provisional government, the work of the political department in Jerusalem receded in importance. And with the siege of Jerusalem tightening every day, Tel Aviv became more than ever the action center of the Jewish Agency. Indeed, after she returned from America, it made more sense for her to remain in Tel Aviv for a while than go directly to Jerusalem. Years later, Shimon Peres found a note from Golda to Ben-Gurion buried in the drawer of an old desk he inherited. It read, "I have been home for several weeks and am not doing anything." It was signed, "The woman who saved the state."

MEANWHILE, EVENTS WERE UNFOLDING RAPIDLY in the Yishuv's struggle for statehood. On Golda's first day back from the States, shocking news came from that country: it was reneging on its commitment to partition. Speaking to the Security Council, the U.S. ambassador to the United Nations, Warren Austin, announced that the United States believed that a "temporary trusteeship" over Palestine should be established to stop the violence and maintain peace in that land. A trusteeship instead of the partition plan meant the undoing of an independent Jewish state and implied a continued British, or perhaps UN, presence in the land. President Harry Truman seemed as surprised as anyone by Austin's words, which he claimed to have known nothing about until he read them in the newspapers. "I am now in the position of a liar and a double-crosser," he wrote in his diary. The State Department later argued that he had approved the statement, and it is conceivable that he did, signing it along with other documents without realizing its implications. The blame hardly mattered; the blow shattered hopes and plans.

Ben-Gurion quickly arranged a press conference on March 20 in which he affirmed the Jewish decision to form a state and predicted that independence would be declared within the next six months. A week later, Golda reassured an overflow audience in Tel Aviv's Ohel Theater that "nothing has changed." The Jews had gained the legal right to declare a state from the UN's November 29 vote for partition, and as long as that international body did not alter its ruling, they were on safe ground. "We are fighting a war of national liberation," she said and, in one of her least prescient statements, added, "This is our last war for generations." In winning it, they would fulfill "the last hope of our people."

It was brave talk when in every way the Arabs were winning this "last war," beating down the Haganah and strangling the country's soul, Jerusalem. On the night of February 1, while Golda was in America, two British deserters blew up the *Palestine Post* building in West Jerusalem. Three weeks later, British army and police deserters rigged three trucks and an armored car, drove them into Ben-Yehuda Street, the city's main shopping center, and blew up two hotels and the entire street, leaving fifty-eight dead. Another bombing in Jerusalem followed that—this one at the Jewish Agency compound, a symbol of the Yishuv itself—and then another.

On the roads, the most ferocious battlegrounds, by the end of March Arab assaults had turned even the largest convoys into death traps. In one of the fiercest battles, on March 27, thousands of Arab troops fell on a convoy with dozens of trucks and armored cars trying to make its way back to Jerusalem from the Etzion Bloc, where it had dropped off supplies. The fighting continued for thirty hours, and after the British finally intervened to rescue the beaten Jews, they handed over Jewish weapons and armored vehicles to the Arabs.

And Jerusalem's Jews starved. With the city under complete siege,

Dov Yosef, who governed it, imposed a tight food ration. "A few noodles, two pieces of bread, and an occasional sardine kept us alive," recalled Marlin Levin, then a reporter for *The Palestine Post*. People scrounged in the fields for the edible weed *khubeizeh*, similar to a dandelion. For water, they depended on tank-laden trucks—one pail per person per day. Golda managed to visit the city on March 29 and cabled Ben-Gurion that the "situation has become worse than ever. The lack of necessities and fuel because of the siege is creating chaos." Speaking to the Zionist Executive back in Tel Aviv, she described "mothers sending their children to school, even when they have to think about which streets it is possible to cross without being struck down."

Ben-Gurion came to realize that the image to the world of the Jews as fighting only defensively no longer worked to their advantage, if ever it had. In a series of meetings with the heads of the Haganah, he ordered arms and men concentrated on breaking the Arab hold over Jerusalem. When the operations chief, Yigael Yadin, offered five hundred additional troops for that battle, Ben-Gurion demanded thousands. After arguing vehemently that they did not have thousands of men available, Yadin finally agreed to assign an unprecedented fifteen hundred fighters to the struggle for Jerusalem. With that, Operation Nachshon was launched. It bore the same name as the plan for a navy that Golda and Remez had once dreamed of. This time it meant taking the offensive, using arms and soldiers to break the enemy's grip on Jerusalem.

That ambitious plan became possible because arms purchased in Czechoslovakia with the money Golda had raised had begun to arrive. On April 1, a plane carrying two hundred rifles, forty machine guns, and 160,000 bullets landed secretly. The next day, forty-five hundred rifles, two hundred machine guns, and millions of bullets arrived in the ship *Nora* at Tel Aviv port, hidden under bushels of onions and potatoes. Unknowingly, the British let the ship and its precious cargo through.

Nachshon proved to be a major turning point in the war. It succeeded in opening main roads to Jerusalem long enough to send food and supplies there, before the Arabs cut it off again. It also succeeded in giving the Haganah control of villages and cities the partition plan had assigned to the Jewish state—Tiberias, Safed, Haifa, and others. To the amazement of the Jewish leaders, as Haganah forces approached these cities, tens of thousands of Arabs fled. Later, and for decades after the war, controversy would swirl around the question of whether the Arabs had abandoned their homes because their leaders ordered them to, Jewish forces expelled them, or fears of a Jewish conquest overwhelmed them. At various times, all these factors came into play. In this early stage, however, the Haganah seems to have forcibly evacuated very few villages; inhabitants of others fled on their own.

The most important conquest was the port city of Haifa, which fell to the Haganah between April 21 and April 22, although wealthy Arab merchants and landowners had bolted before that. Those who remained and wanted to surrender to the Jewish forces were warned by their leaders that they would be branded as traitors if they did. The loud noise of Haganah mortar shells and wild rumors about how the soldiers might treat them also terrified the population. On April 9, Irgun and Lehi forces had captured the Arab village of Deir Yassin, outside Jerusalem, and massacred more than a hundred villagers. Horrified, the Haganah and Jewish Agency strongly condemned the action, but accounts of the massacre sowed panic through the Arab world. The exodus from Haifa swelled even as the Haganah assured the Arabs that they could live there "as equal and free citizens" and the town's mayor pleaded with them to stay. In a city that had been home to seventy thousand Arabs along with seventy thousand Jews, only about six thousand Arabs remained.

Golda came to Haifa in the middle of the conquest and chaos. A few weeks earlier, she had suffered a mild heart attack, but she recovered quickly enough to accept Ben-Gurion's request that she investigate the situation in that city. When she went down to the city's port, she found "children, women, old people, waiting for a way to leave." She begged people not to go, but they were bent on escaping. On her way up, she entered houses, "where the coffee and *pitot* were left on the table" in the residents' haste to flee.

Yaakov Lubliani, the Haganah city commander, invited her for a tour of the old city, which had been badly damaged during the fighting. Rather than examining destruction, she wanted to visit an area that still held Arabs. He took her to the Arab neighborhood of Wadi Nisnas. As they walked through Muchlis Street, Golda stopped at a partially destroyed house and led Lubliani and others with them up an outer staircase. The flats on the first two levels were abandoned. On the third-floor landing, an old Arab woman came toward them, carrying bundles of what were probably all her possessions. When she saw Golda, she burst into tears. Taken aback for a moment, Golda looked at her and dissolved into tears also. The two women stood there facing each other and weeping, until Lubliani ushered Golda away.

He said nothing as they walked on, but he was angry. "We've been fighting and feeling happy that we were stronger and overcame the Arabs," he thought to himself, "and we can walk through the city without fear of being shot or attacked. And this one stands there and cries." From a soldier's viewpoint, Golda's tears were silly, a betrayal after the relief of victory. For Golda, they were a spontaneous expression of compassion for a woman who had lost everything.

"It is a dreadful thing to see the dead city," she told a Jewish Agency Executive meeting after she returned. She described some of what she had observed, and added, "I could not avoid thinking in my mind's eye that surely this must have been the picture in many Jewish towns." In the old Arab woman, she saw the image of the Jews of World War II fleeing Nazis. It took some courage to say that out loud at a time when most Jews felt little sympathy for an enemy that had initiated a war against them.

After her sympathetic description, she turned crisply to business, putting all sentiment aside. How were they to deal with the Arab exodus? "Should the Jews make an effort to bring the Arabs back to Haifa or not?" For the time being, she and Haifa authorities had decided "not to go to Acre or Nazareth to bring back the Arabs, but at the same time our behavior should be such that if because of it they do come back—let them come back." On principle, she continued, "we should not behave badly toward the Arabs [who remained] so that others won't return."

She sharpened the alternatives at a Mapai Center meeting a few days later. The country's leaders had to face what was happening around them. The Arabs were deserting their villages in droves. Many of them were friendly Arabs, running away because of the war. What should the Jews do about the empty villages they left behind? "Are we prepared to preserve these villages so that their inhabitants may return," she asked, "or do we want to erase any record that there had been a village in that place?" They would have to formulate far-reaching decisions, and Golda was putting the options to them bluntly.

Speaking about Haifa, she said, "I am not of those extremists—and there are such, and all power to them—who want to do everything that can be done to bring back the Arabs. I am not prepared to go to extraordinary lengths to bring the Arabs back." But the question remained of how to deal with those who had stayed behind or those returning of their own goodwill. Again, difficult choices existed and needed to be thought through. "If we treat them badly, others won't come and maybe those who had remained will pick up and go, and we would be rid of all of them," she reasoned harshly. On the other hand, the Jews could make an effort to treat the Arabs well, as they always said they would, and in that way encourage refugees to return, without considering the consequences to the country.

Sounding calculating, almost brutal, she meant to shake up her listeners, jar the party and its heads into grappling with a situation most would do anything to avoid. "It seems to me that we entered this war unprepared for many things," she said, "but also unprepared for victories." She called on the central committee to hold a full-scale open and serious discussion about the Arab refugees and, in so doing, steer the party's course on this troubling subject. This, too, required courage. She was confronting colleagues who spent hours debating every possible subject relating to the state that would be formed but who bypassed the most disturbing topic: how to relate to the Arabs in that state.

Golda Meyerson broke the silence in the party on the subject of the Arab refugees, says the historian Benny Morris, an authority on the birth of the refugee problem, but nobody picked up on her questions. It wasn't until June, after the Pan-Arab invasion of the Jewish state, that Ben-Gurion and Sharett made it known that while the war was on, Israel would not allow refugees to return to their homes, where they could serve as a fifth column. The policy, which gradually evolved, extended later to after the war as well.

THROUGH IT ALL, GOLDA STAYED in Tel Aviv, although everyone concerned wanted her back in Jerusalem heading the political department again. "Golda has to come here," Ben-Gurion wrote in his diary on April 21 during a visit to the city. Almost all members of the department would be sent to Tel Aviv, where they were most needed, and Golda would have a small staff to help her. She may not have enough to do, but after all "Jerusalem is Jerusalem from a Jewish and international viewpoint," he wrote, "and may become the capital of the state."

Five days later, he simply "did not know why she feels so deprived." He might, of course, have thought about the backseat Jerusalem had taken to Tel Aviv in all things that mattered and about Golda, with her energy and ambition, being isolated from major policy making. He probably did think about those things but preferred to ignore them. "It is right for her to go to Jerusalem if she receives that assignment—actually she has already received that assignment," he noted. So why wasn't she in Jerusalem?

Months earlier, she had fought for the centrality of Jerusalem in Jewish Agency operations. There was nothing left to fight for now; everything had moved to Tel Aviv. She would take her own sweet time about going to Jerusalem.

May 2: Records show that Golda Meyerson still had not moved to Jerusalem. At a meeting of the Jewish Agency Executive, Eliyahu Dobkin said, "We must *demand* that Mrs. Meyerson comes, and until she does, Mr. Kaplan will have to stay." The meeting resolved "to notify Mrs. Meyerson that she must come at once to Jerusalem."

May 6: Mrs. Meyerson had finally reached Jerusalem. At a meeting with Eliezer Kaplan and other Jewish Agency executives, she spoke of the need to be realistic in decision making. With most members of the agency executive now in Tel Aviv and the Administrative Council "Thirteen" also situated there, they needed to agree that all political decisions be made in Tel Aviv. She asked only that decisions made there be relayed as quickly as possible to Jerusalem so that they in that city do not say anything that contradicts Tel Aviv.

Proper as they seem, her words carried an undercurrent of martyrdom and rage. She had obeyed orders and moved back to Jerusalem. But by insisting that decisions be made only in Tel Aviv, she reminded the agency chiefs present that she was neither in the "Thirteen" nor part of the Tel Aviv power center, both places where she deserved to be. When others at the meeting disagreed about placing all decisions in the hands of Tel Aviv, she merely said, "I would like my comrades going to Tel Aviv to convey my message." She knew the leaders in Tel Aviv would get her message—the underlying one of feeling pushed aside.

MORE THAN INTERNAL POLITICS, however, worried Golda in these final days of the British mandate. With reports rolling in that the surrounding Arab states were prepared to invade Palestine as soon as the British left, she thought about King Abdullah of Jordan (whom the Jews had code-named "the friend"). He had as much as given his word to her in November that he would not attack the Jewish state, but rumors since then had Jordan planning to join the Arab League in their fighting. She had sent several messages to him, which he answered with positive reassurances: he was a Bedouin and therefore a man of honor; he was a king, making him doubly honorable; and he would never break a promise made to a woman.

Sharett had kept in touch with Abdullah when Golda was in America, but the contact had waned. She was eager to renew it, although neither she nor Ben-Gurion held much hope for it. Two things from her first meeting with the king still troubled her. Almost incidentally he had asked what the Jews thought of including their state, which he called the Hebrew Republic, within his kingdom, under his rule. He had also mentioned, in passing, that he hoped the Arabs would not be disappointed by the size of their state. Another disturbing question arose after the meeting. An emissary had inquired whether the Jews were prepared to cede to the king some of the area allotted to them by the partition agreement. In that way, he could show the Arab world that he had gained more territory for them than assigned by the United Nations, raising his prestige. Jewish leaders responded that they would not give up any part of their tiny state—"a border is a border," Golda affirmed. Furthermore, they would honor their assigned boundaries so long as peace reigned. If the Arabs made war, each side would take what was in its power to take.

With all that, Golda wanted one more chance to persuade the king to stay out of the war. A meeting could be worth the effort; Transjordan's Arab Legion was the strongest and best-trained army the Arabs had. Fearful of other Arab leaders, Abdullah agreed to the meeting reluctantly and on condition that Golda go to him in Amman this time. He had much to fear. Ben-Gurion had received a report from a French source that Saudi Arabia, Syria, and Egypt had decided that (1) Abdullah was to enter the war in Palestine, (2) they would murder him, and (3) they would set up a government headed by the mufti.

A plane Ben-Gurion had arranged to carry Golda directly to Haifa had broken down, and instead a tiny Piper Cub flew her out of besieged Jerusalem to Tel Aviv, while hurricane-like winds buffeted it from side to side. With the iron stomach that saved her from seasickness as a child, she kept her balance. After meeting with Ben-Gurion, she went on to Haifa, where Ezra Danin, the Arab expert she had traveled with before, joined her. From there, the two began a long, hazardous trip. Danin asked her why she was taking the risk, because the mission would probably fail. "If there is the slightest chance of saving one Jewish soldier, I'm going," she answered, and they pushed on. In Naharayim, Danin donned the traditional headgear of an Arab man. Golda disguised herself as an Arab woman in a long black dress and veil that her friend Regina had helped prepare. The pair would appear as "husband and wife" for the benefit of Arab legionnaires who lined the borders between the two countries. Muhammad Zubati, the king's close confidant, arrived after dark to drive them to Amman. On the way, they were stopped at least ten times while legionnaires checked their identity and Zubati called out his name to carry them through.

In Amman, Zubati took them to his home in a car whose windows had been covered with heavy black fabric. The king received them there in a friendly manner, but to Golda he seemed a different person—pale, depressed, tense. He had sent a proposal beforehand of what he wanted: Palestine would remain undivided, and the Jews given autonomy in the areas they inhabited. At the end of a year, the entire country would be merged with Transjordan under Abdullah's rule, with a single parliament in which Jews would have 50 percent of the seats.

Abdullah declared right off that the only way to avoid war was to agree to his offer, and Golda indicated immediately that it could not be accepted. Why, he wanted to know, were the Jews in such haste to declare an independent state? A people who had waited two thousand years could hardly be described as hasty, she answered. She reminded him of the agreement they had made and of their many years of friendship. "We are your only friends in the Middle East," she said, and advised him to stay with the original plan they had agreed on.

The king did not deny that he wished for that, but things had happened since then. He mentioned the massacre at Deir Yassin, which had infuriated the Arab world, and added, sadly, "Then I was alone, now I am one among five. I have no choice, and I cannot act differently." When Golda pointed out that if there had to be war, the Jews would fight with all their strength, Abdullah agreed that they would have to resist any attack. When he suggested holding a meeting of moderate Jews and Arabs to discuss his proposal, Golda rejected the idea out of hand. Not even "ten responsible Jews" would support his plan, she said. If, in fact, there was to be a war, the Jews would win it, and perhaps they could meet again after the Jewish state existed.

In spite of hard words, the tenor of the conversation remained friendly. As they prepared to leave, the Iraqi-born Danin, whom the king knew well, warned him that he was relying too much on his tanks, as the French had relied on the Maginot Line during World War II, but the Jews would smash those tanks and he would lose everything. On a personal note, Danin cautioned the king about allowing people to come close and kiss the hem of his robe. Someone might try to harm him. "I shall never depart from the custom of my father," he replied. "I was born a Bedouin, a free man, and . . . I shall not prevent my subjects from expressing their affection for me." (He would be assassinated three years later.)

Abdullah bade his guests farewell and left. Sick at heart, knowing war was inevitable, Golda wanted to leave immediately, but Danin advised that refusing the bountiful dinner arranged for them would insult the king. She dutifully heaped her plate full and barely ate, and the two left as soon as feasible. It was near midnight, Monday, May 10, 1948. From their car window, they saw Iraqi forces preparing to invade Palestine. Their Arab driver, frightened by all the checkpoints, dropped them off about two miles short of their destination in Naharayim. They groped their way in the dark through dangerous Arab territory until, about three in the morning, they met up with a Haganah scout who led them to Naharayim.

With little rest, Golda headed from there to Tel Aviv and a meeting of the Mapai central committee. As she entered the room, Ben-Gurion looked up expectantly. Rather than interrupt the meeting, she scribbled a note and handed it to him. "We met in friendship," she wrote. "He is very worried, and he looks terrible. He did not deny that there had been talks and an understanding between us regarding a desirable arrangement . . . but now he is only one of five." She could barely look at Ben-Gurion's face as he read.

Instantly, he left the meeting and rushed to Haganah headquarters. He summoned his chief commanders, Yigael Yadin, Yohanan Ratner, and Israel Galili, and ordered them to mobilize their forces and prepare to fight against an all-out Arab invasion. The last shred of hope that the king would refrain from war had vanished.

According to Moshe Dayan, after their second meeting, Abdullah forever bore a grudge against Golda. She had placed him in an impossible position, he said, by giving him the alternatives of either agreeing to an ultimatum that came from the lips of a woman or going to war. In such a situation, he had "of course" to take the second option.

On another occasion, Abdullah argued that Golda was responsible for the war, because she had been too proud to accept his offer. His physician told the Arabist Eliyahu Sasson that His Majesty found Golda very "rigid." Had he been able to speak with Sasson—who had been trapped in Jerusalem—"it might have been possible to arrive at an understanding." Sir Alec Kirkbride, the British minister in Amman, attributed Abdullah's behavior to the fact that the monarch "could not be wholly at his ease when talking business to a woman."

True, His Majesty would probably have felt more comfortable with a Sharett or a Sasson, men who knew Arabic and Arab culture. But Golda reflected the leadership's thinking: neither Ben-Gurion, Sharett, nor any

Yishuv leader would have agreed to the king's terms. In fact, Ben-Gurion dismissed a last-minute appeal from Abdullah to accept his proposal before declaring a state. Nothing Golda said, or who she was, led the king to join with the Arab League against the Jewish state. Intense pressure from other Arab leaders and the Arab public drew him into battle.

Golda accurately summed up Abdullah's situation at a meeting of the Administrative Council in Tel Aviv. "He is going into this matter [the war] not out of joy or confidence, but as a person who is caught in a trap and can't get out," she said.

Although not a member of the "Thirteen," she had been invited to this critical meeting on May 12, two days before the final British pullout, to report on Abdullah. Her report over, Ezra Danin, who had been with her, left, but Golda remained. Three of the thirteen members of this provisional government were absent, one in the United States and two stuck in Jerusalem. The ten present, and guests like Golda, sat around a large square table in the Jewish National Fund office building on a quiet street in Tel Aviv, thrashing out the most critical problems facing the Yishuv. She must have felt a sly satisfaction sitting with this group at such a decisive moment after the pain of having been excluded from it as an official member. When the discussion turned to a proposed cease-fire for Jerusalem, she became central to it.

High Commissioner Cunningham had proposed the cease-fire to her and Eliezer Kaplan a week earlier, and she had been adamant that certain conditions needed to be fulfilled first: an open road from Tel Aviv to Jerusalem so that food and supplies could be delivered and free access given to the Jewish Quarter of the Old City and its holy places. The Arabs had initially rejected those terms, yet they seemed more pliant when the tide began to turn against them. Both sides had stopped the fighting in Jerusalem for a few days, but the debate at hand concerned how useful a cease-fire would be for the Jewish side.

"I cannot go to Jerusalem tomorrow without a clear decision," Golda said. "Do we want a ceasefire? Is this good for the Jews or not?" She had placed decision making in the hands of this high-level governing body, and now she needed an answer from it. Instead, Kaplan and others suggested that she decide herself what she deemed best for the city, giving her total authority (and more personal satisfaction). She stayed on as the discussion turned to the most crucial subject at hand: whether to declare the state as soon as the British left.

Hesitation and anxiety gripped the group. Moods and statements swung from one extreme to another, often in the same person—joy at freedom from British rule, fear of the looming Arab invasion. For the first time, there would be no third party to act as a buffer between the Jewish and the Arab populations. The questions of when and how to proclaim the state had been agonized over for months, but now the moment of truth had arrived. The United States had proposed a truce that would delay the declaration of a state. This body had to decide.

"It is doubtful that a quorum of ten Jews was ever before summoned to determine the course of Jewish history in such manner," Zeev Sharef wrote.

Earlier, Sharett had delivered a message from the U.S. secretary of state, George C. Marshall, warning that Jewish leaders should not rely on their military people, for "flushed by victory, their counsel was liable to be misleading." Undersecretary of State Robert Lovett remarked that the Jews will be in a tight spot when the Arabs invaded, and they should not "blame us then."

Ben-Gurion called on the heads of the Haganah, Yigael Yadin and Israel Galili, both at the meeting, to assess Arab strength versus Jewish. "At this moment I would say that our chances are fifty-fifty," Yadin said. "To be more honest, I would say they have a big advantage." It was a daunting statement. Perhaps, some members argued, they could stop short of actually proclaiming the state, find a compromise, announce an interim position. Golda disagreed. "We cannot zigzag," she told her colleagues. Once they decided to create a state, they could not go partway. They had to follow through fully, with "every detail of the details" in place. "This is what the world is waiting for," she said.

When the issue was put to a vote, six of the ten members voted for declaring the state. Golda did not have a vote, but her outspoken support for statehood helped sway others and once again put her at odds with David Remez. He had voted to postpone the declaration.

THE BRITISH WERE SCHEDULED to leave at midnight on Friday, May 14, 1948, the fifth day of Iyar 5708 on the Hebrew calendar. The state would be proclaimed that afternoon so that no gap in governing existed. Ben-Gurion insisted that Golda return to Jerusalem on Thursday, to confer for a final time with Cunningham, and remain there. It broke her heart to have to miss the ceremony establishing the state that was to take place in Tel Aviv. The two-seater Piper Cub that would carry her to Jerusalem was scheduled to return immediately with Yitzhak Gruenbaum, slated to become minister of interior in the provisional government. Soon after takeoff, the plane developed severe engine problems, forcing the pilot to turn back. With the engine almost gone, he landed in Tel Aviv. And that is how it happened that Golda Meyerson signed Israel's Declaration of Independence while Yitzhak Gruenbaum remained in Jerusalem.

She washed her hair and put on her best dress. A car and driver took her to the Tel Aviv Museum at 16 Rothschild Boulevard, formerly the home of Tel Aviv's first mayor, Meir Dizengoff. There David Ben-Gurion, wearing a dark suit, white shirt, and tie with a tie clip, would read the declaration. Although the time and place of the ceremony had been kept secret for security reasons, word leaked out, and at least half the city thronged outside the museum that Friday. Inside, the hall had been scrubbed clean and new pictures hung on the walls with a large portrait of Theodor Herzl in the center. At exactly four o'clock, the ceremony began.

Ben-Gurion rapped his gavel, and the more than two hundred guests packed into the almost unbearably hot hall rose spontaneously and sang "Hatikvah." "I shall now read to you the Scroll of the Establishment of the State," he began softly. He read from the preamble, of the beginnings of the Jewish people in the Land of Israel, of their exile, and of their history from that time until the present. His voice rose slightly as he read the eleventh paragraph ending with the words "We hereby declare the establishment of a Jewish state in Eretz Israel, to be known as *Medinat Yisrael*, the State of Israel." Almost as one, the audience rose again, clapping, singing, and sobbing with joy and excitement.

After the entire proclamation was read and adopted, signers walked to the desk one by one in alphabetical order to write their names on a sheet of parchment Moshe Sharett and Ben-Gurion held between them. Golda's hands shook and tears flowed from her eyes as she signed "Golda Meyerson." She thought about the signers of the American Declaration of Independence she had learned about as a child, and about her journey from Russia to this moment. She thought about people who were missing, who should have been there, and she couldn't stop weeping. That evening, she and two colleagues went to Ben-Gurion's home with a bouquet of flowers to congratulate him for all he had done to make this day happen.

When asked in later years what her most important day in Israel was, Golda replied without hesitation, "Friday afternoon, when the State was declared. It was the greatest moment."

PART THREE

MADAM MINISTER

16

Moscow

At 6:11 p.m. Washington time, eleven minutes after the British mandate ended, President Harry S. Truman recognized the State of Israel, the first nation in the world to do so and at a speed that stunned his State Department. The Soviet Union accorded its recognition three days later. By that time, the armies of five Arab countries had invaded the new state.

The Pan-Arab assault began at dawn on May 15, 1948, less than twenty-four hours after the state came into being. During the following days, Egypt attacked from the south while its planes bombed and strafed Tel Aviv. Syria and Lebanon charged from the north and Iraq from the east. The Arab Legion, Abdullah's powerful Transjordanian army, penetrated Jerusalem, where the Haganah had occupied positions abandoned by the British. Reversing Haganah gains, the Arab Legion held the city's Jewish sections in a steel grip, pushing residents ever closer to starvation. There was "no coffee to make, no food to eat, no radio to tune in to—nothing but terror," Marlin Levin wrote. Earlier, while the state was being proclaimed, legion troops had destroyed all the settlements that made up the Etzion Bloc between Jerusalem and Hebron. Two weeks after the fighting began, the legion conquered the Jewish Quarter of the Old City and took its defenders captive.

With Jerusalem cut off and few official duties for her in Israel, Golda decided that the best help she could give her embattled country was to return to the States and raise money for more armaments. The army—which soon changed its name from Haganah to Israel Defense Forces (IDF)—urgently needed tanks, planes, and other heavy equipment and the money to buy them. She worried about leaving the country at this critical time, and about Sarah, in her small, poorly armed Negev settlement of Revivim in the path of Egyptian advances through the desert. Menahem was still in the States studying at the Manhattan School of

Music, but he would be returning soon to join the army, another source of anxiety.

She packed a light bag—this time she could not get to Jerusalem and her clothes—and got a laissez-passer, a pre-passport document, the first travel document issued by the new state. She flew from Haifa to Paris on Monday, May 17, in a small plane rented from a group of French journalists who had come to cover the war. Her Paris visa bore the word "Palestine" crossed out and "Israel" written in Hebrew script next to it. There had not been time to print new visas. On board with her were the Jewish Agency diplomat Gideon Rafael and Teddy Kollek—later mayor of Jerusalem—in charge of acquiring weapons in the United States. From Paris, the three flew together the next day on a commercial airliner to New York.

"I stand here this morning as a citizen of the State of Israel," Golda began her address to a United Jewish Appeal conference at New York City's Hotel Astor. She liked rolling the words "State of Israel" around her tongue. To people who knew her, she appeared more buoyant than she had on her last trip, more confident of herself. Nobody could call her a "schnorrer" anymore; she was the emissary of an independent Jewish government.

"Why are we, this generation, privileged to achieve that which so many generations of Jews before us—probably much better generations than ourselves—fought for, dreamt of, died for, and were not privileged to achieve?" she asked, making members of her audience feel special, singled out to witness the miraculous rebirth of Jewish sovereignty after two thousand years. She described the brave soldiers fighting against all odds, the bombs dropping over Tel Aviv, and the tens of thousands of immigrants who had begun streaming into the country. Israel needed money for arms and immigration. It also needed to take care of its Arab population. "We cannot have Arab villages in the Jewish State in the terrible condition that they have endured under British administration," she said, appealing to the liberal bent of most American Jews.

In one form or another, she carried the same message everywhere, as she crisscrossed the land, speaking until she was hoarse at breakfasts, lunches, and dinner gatherings. And people responded, even more generously than before. "My husband and I gave everything," recalled a woman who heard Golda at the Astor. "He said to me, 'The only thing we have left, honey, is some paid life insurance policies. Do you want them now or when I'm gone?' I said, 'Of course, I'll take them now.' We got up and announced the additional money."

She traveled with UJA leaders she had traveled with before: Sam Rothberg, Julian Venezky, Henry Morgenthau Jr., and especially Henry Montor. The two developed a close working relationship, a "give and take" that made them an extraordinary team, another fund-raiser remarked: "She inspired Montor, Montor inspired her, and this relationship grew." In every community, Montor pinpointed people for her to meet. Although he could "mesmerize" an audience himself, he was awkward in "eyeball-to-eyeball" confrontations. Golda, on the other hand, charmed people at parlor meetings and one-on-one encounters, which netted her millions.

In the midst of her whirlwind travel schedule, she still managed to reach beyond the Jewish community to cultivate public relations for the nascent state, and herself. "Henry Morgenthau brought a Mrs. Meyerson from Palestine to breakfast last Tuesday," Eleanor Roosevelt wrote to a friend. "A woman of great strength & calm & for me she symbolizes the best spirit of Palestine." In subsequent years, she and Mrs. Roosevelt became fast friends. Whenever Golda came to America, "I would run in to have a cup of tea with her between having come from somewhere by plane and before she took off to somewhere else by another plane," Golda recalled.

She also met with David Dubinsky, president of the ILGWU, to arrange an unprecedented loan of $1 million. American labor unions, with their large contingent of Jewish members, had been loyal supporters of labor in the Yishuv as early as the 1920s. During the Holocaust, they had contributed to the Histadrut and other organizations trying to save Jews and helped afterward in the illegal immigration struggle. Although Golda had corresponded with Dubinsky over the years, she had never before met him in person. A million-dollar loan to the fledgling state was a gamble for the union, but with Golda's assurance that it would be repaid on time, he encouraged his executive board to approve it. The loan was secured in June, and five months later, on December 1, Dr. Israel Goldstein, treasurer of the Jewish Agency, handed Dubinsky a check for $1 million. So pleased was the union with the quick repayment that it extended a new loan to Israel of $500,000, to be repaid in six months.

All the while Golda was collecting money, Teddy Kollek and his associates were spending large sums on arms and equipment they smuggled out of the United States. Despite Truman's instant recognition of Israel, he steadfastly refused to lift America's arms embargo to the Middle East. Ensconced at Hotel Fourteen on East Sixtieth Street in Manhattan—

above the famed Copacabana club, where Frank Sinatra performed—Kollek supervised a network of illegal arms procurement essential to Israel's defense. He worked closely with Al Schwimmer, who had been a U.S. Army flight engineer (and later founded Israel Aircraft), Alan Greenspun, a fearless Las Vegas businessman, and a cadre of colorful characters, including such underworld ones as Bugsy Siegel and Meyer Lansky. Whether Golda knew of Kollek's shady connections, she certainly knew and approved of the clandestine arms operations.

In the course of their work, Kollek and his team had the opportunity to buy large quantities of Flying Fortresses, B-17 bombers that the U.S. Army had stripped of their weapons and sold to junk dealers after World War II. The plan was to fly the planes under a subterfuge to Žatec airfield in Czechoslovakia, where they would be armed and flown to Israel. In the midst of planning, Israel's Foreign Ministry got cold feet; if the plan failed, it would jeopardize Israel's relationship with America. From Israel, Ben-Gurion gave Golda Meyerson, as the state's highest representative in America, final authority on the matter. Kollek, Eliyahu Sacharov—a member of his team—and Abba Eban met with her at the Hotel Sulgrave on East Sixty-Seventh Street off Park Avenue, where she was staying. After a long debate, with Eban presenting the Foreign Ministry viewpoint, she decided that whatever the risks they must go ahead with the operation. "On the scales are the fate, future, the very life of our people," she said, closing off the discussion. The plans for the Flying Fortresses proceeded. On their way from Czechoslovakia to Israel, the planes added a mission: they bombed Cairo.

While Golda traveled around the States, Remez kept her in touch with current events in Israel. In late May, to her great relief, he cabled her in Hebrew, using Latin letters: "Nothing happened in Revivim." The Egyptians had not attacked the kibbutz in their drive toward Tel Aviv, and Sarah was safe. Other news was disturbing, however. Jerusalem is fighting with "unimaginable strength," he wrote of the army's battles against the Arab Legion. The legion had occupied the fortress at Latrun, which controlled the route into the city, and all attempts to retake it had failed. The situation had become grim when Remez sent his cable, with just a few days of food and water left in Jewish Jerusalem. Then, in early June, the IDF discovered a rocky back road leading to the city, and with enormous effort cleared it to allow supply trucks through. The "Burma Road," as the soldiers dubbed it, saved Jerusalem from collapse. A few days later, on June 11, the UN called a monthlong cease-fire, which Israeli forces welcomed as a chance to regain their strength.

EVEN BEFORE GOLDA HAD LEFT for America, Moshe Sharett let it be known that he planned to make her the country's first minister to the Soviet Union, a plan that dismayed her. She had hoped to return from the States after a short time and take her place in the government, sharing in the excitement, and power, of creating new institutions. Nor did she wish to go back to the land she had left in poverty and fear as a child.

Plenty of others did want that position. Now head of the Foreign Ministry, Sharett was organizing consulates and embassies in the countries that recognized Israel, opening up diplomatic posts that many people regarded as plum jobs. The Moscow ministry was particularly desirable, given Russia's enthusiastic support for the new state and its satellites' role in providing weapons. (The actual position was minister plenipotentiary, slightly lower than ambassador.) Competition in the coalition government between Mapai and the left-wing Mapam Party flared over choosing the Moscow minister, but with Mapai dominant the decision fell to Sharett. Even so, most people would have expected Mapai's choice to be Mordechai Namir, who had done diplomatic work in Eastern Europe and asked Ben-Gurion for the position. Sharett, however, favored Golda for the post.

With Golda the front-runner, Azriel Carlebach, editor of the newspaper *Maariv*, raised objections that many shared. "It's hard to understand the matter," he wrote. Certainly, Golda Meyerson was very accomplished and beloved by the labor community in Israel. But "she has no connection at all to Russia. She has no personal experience with Russians . . . Golda was always to us 'the American,' even though she was born in Kiev." Furthermore, the article argued, Soviet support for Israel did not come out of love for that nation. It came because in backing Israel, Soviet leaders saw a way of keeping England and the United States out of the region. Given Golda Meyerson's strong American ties, choosing her might alienate the Russians.

Golda could have agreed with much of the column. She did not speak Russian, she had no interest in the fine points of diplomatic life, and she was among the most anti-Communist of all her colleagues. Time and again, during World War II, she reminded her comrades of the anti-Zionist positions the Soviet Union had taken and warned that young people, dazzled by the heroics of the Red Army, might lose faith in their own country's ideals. She even placed the Bund, the early socialist party that had opposed Zionism, above Jewish Communists. "They are Jews," she said, "in my eyes, the Communists are not Jews." The Bundists had rejected Zionism, but they had maintained their Jewishness; many of the Communists had tried to obliterate all traces of their Jewish identities.

Nevertheless, Sharett insisted on Golda as Israel's representative in Moscow. It may be that her strong pro-American and anti-Communist stances were the very features that made her an attractive choice for him and Ben-Gurion. Though these leaders frequently proclaimed Israel's neutrality in the Cold War between America and Russia, both leaned firmly toward the West. They could assume that Golda would not be seduced to the Soviet side, as others more enamored of Communism might. Aside from that, as one of the country's senior leaders, she brought to the position the kind of prestige the Russians expected.

In early June, she received the telegram from Sharett she had dreaded, asking her to take the position. She cabled Remez unhappily, and when he wired back, "Regarding your plea, it is not a mission but a challenge—nothing should impede you from accepting it," she saw that she had no choice. "Why did they pick me in particular?" she said facetiously to party members. "Because I am of the wrong age for the draft [and] they are not taking me into the army or the Palmach . . . Such a person has an obligation to accept any assignment given—and I accepted." Soon after she accepted, the newspapers announced an exchange of ministers with the Soviet Union, Golda Meyerson to Russia and Pavlov I. Yershov to Israel.

On a steamy July 1, she and Menahem (who was to return to Israel shortly) headed to Brooklyn to say good-bye to their friends Fanny and Jacob Goodman, whose apartment the family had stayed in when Golda visited the United States with the children in 1932. She leaned back and stretched out her legs in the taxicab, weary from travel. At the cross section of Flatbush and Eighth Avenues, a car suddenly collided with the cab and Golda was thrown forward, fracturing her right leg. She was taken to the New York Hospital for Joint Diseases, where, with a huge plaster cast on her leg, she spent her time in forced immobility and great impatience. She was not the only impatient person. The Russians conveyed their displeasure, as though she had intentionally staged the accident to postpone her mission. And Sharett hounded her with cables and phone calls about when she would be released from the hospital.

The leg began to heal, but she had developed phlebitis and blood clots, which could be dangerous if left unresolved. Confined to the hospital, she was at the mercy of journalists converging on her for interviews and well-meaning friends who dropped in when they pleased. "We experienced a perverse pleasure from getting to spend time with Golda as she recovered," an acquaintance from her Pioneer Women days wrote. "For how else would we have been able to find this common time for chatting—had it not been for her accident?"

She had downplayed the accident in a cable to Sheyna, now back in Israel, saying only that she had a sprained ankle. To Remez, she cabled that she'd had a "minor automobile accident" and would have to delay her departure probably by a week. The delay, which stretched almost into a month, meant giving up a rendezvous in Paris the two had secretly planned. After learning what had happened, he penned a sympathetic letter. "My life is empty when you are far away," he wrote. Whatever else went on in their professional and private lives, the two never lost the thread of intimacy that bound them to each other.

Remez wired Golda on July 22 to "beg" her to have patience with her leg, but her patience had run out. Disregarding doctor's orders, she left the United States on July 25, her leg not yet completely healed. She was to pay for her brashness with an operation a few years later and chronic leg problems. The night before she left, she had dinner in her hotel's elegant restaurant with old friends. While they ate, a waiter brought over a bottle of champagne, an unsigned gift from a group of strangers seated at a table in the corner of the room. They had recognized Golda and wanted to honor her, the representative of the new State of Israel.

"Golda has returned," Ben-Gurion noted in his diary on July 29. "More than $50 million has been collected."

The Israel she returned to was no longer the frightened country she had left. Refreshed from the June 11 cease-fire, which ended on July 8, and with hundreds of thousands of dollars of arms it had purchased now in place, the military was able to take the initiative in the fighting. By July 18 and a second cease-fire, it had become evident that the country would survive the Arab onslaught. The Egyptians had been stopped in their drive toward Tel Aviv. Israel controlled the lower Galilee, including the town of Nazareth, with the front line now in the center of the Galilee and in the Negev. In Jerusalem, the Jews had lost the Old City to Jordan, but the modern western part was no longer in danger and had clear passage to Tel Aviv.

Golda could turn her full attention to Moscow. While still in America, she had received a cable from Sharett asking permission to appoint Sarah and her fiancé, Zecharia Rehabi, to her Moscow staff as wireless radio operators, a field in which both had experience. She was delighted with the suggestion, Sharett's way of sweetening the Russian deal. Sarah and Zecharia had met at Revivim, where he was one of the kibbutz founders. Less than a week before leaving the country with Golda, they were married in Sheyna and Shamai's home in Holon. Regina pressed Sarah's dress for her and attended the celebration along with the family and close friends. Golda's mother, now suffering from dementia and living in a home for the aged, was brought to the event. Morris was there also and stood next to Golda for the ceremony under the chuppa. Zecharia, slightly built and dark-skinned, was of Yemenite descent, and his uneducated, devout parents sat shyly to the side, a bit intimidated by the august company. The marriage of a Western Jew with one from an Eastern background in Asian or African countries was not commonplace at the time. (A year later, in 1949, when Golda was in America again, a woman in Atlanta, Georgia, approached her. The son of the black singer Paul Robeson had just married a Jewish woman. "How do you feel about this?" the woman demanded. "You know my daughter is married to a young man, and he's dark, and we're very proud of him," Golda rejoined.) Unlike Golda's marriage, Sarah's lasted almost sixty years, until Zecharia's death.

At a going-away reception for Golda and the delegation accompanying her to Moscow, a reporter noted that many members of the group spoke Russian, except for the minister to Russia herself, Golda Meyerson.

"Is it on principle that you don't speak the language?" he asked Mrs. Meyerson.

"Yes," she replied drily. "It is a principle for me not to speak languages I don't know."

Having heard enough comments about her ignorance of Russian, Golda made sure to include Russian experts in her delegation. Mordechai Namir, who had requested a position in Moscow, served as the delegation adviser, Arieh Levavi and Arieh Lapid as first and second secretaries, Brigadier Yohanan Ratner as military attaché, and Moshe Bejerano as the trade attaché. For her personal assistant, Golda chose Eiga Shapiro, an elegant, Russian-speaking woman adept at handling the kinds of diplomatic details Golda cared nothing about. French-born Lou Kadar filled the role of French translator. Although everybody in the group spoke English, Israeli authorities decided to make French their diplomatic language. After their experience with the British, "they didn't want to hear the English language anymore," Kadar said.

Tall and thin, with thick lips, wide eyes, and a sharp wit, Kadar had come to Palestine in 1935 to visit her sister and remained to live on a kibbutz and then work at the Jewish Agency. During World War II, she served in the British army preparing educational materials for its soldiers. After the war, she was badly injured when Arabs blew up the Jewish Agency building in Jerusalem. She had recently recovered when Golda interviewed her for the Moscow assignment. Her first impression of Golda Meyerson was of an enormous woman, very tall and very stout. She later realized that Golda was not tall, but she was quite heavy at the time. She also seemed to be in a highly emotional state, having just met with the widow of a soldier killed in battle. The interview lasted less than fifteen minutes. Kadar was thirty-five, Golda fifty. For the next thirty years, she would serve as Golda's closest assistant, travel companion, and friend.

With Eiga, Lou, Sarah and Zecharia, the diplomatic staff and their families, and Golda, the Israeli legation consisted of twenty-six people. Before they left for Moscow, Golda attended a string of farewell parties in her honor. In the excitement of her departure, *Maariv*, which had criticized her lack of Russian expertise, waxed eloquent about her "blessed talent," her "levelheadedness," and the "strength of her convictions." It praised the fact that a woman had been chosen to represent the young state and enthused that Golda "symbolized all aspects of the arrival of the pioneer woman in the land of Israel." Her appointment would have special meaning in Russia, the "land of workers and of equal opportunities."

On August 29, 1948, Sharett, Remez, and other dignitaries saw her and her delegation off from the Tel Aviv airport as they began their journey on a Czechoslovakian Dakota airplane. They stopped in Rome for a night, and from there to Prague, where the Russians arranged a private plane (for which they charged $124 a person) to Moscow by way of L'vov. When the contingent arrived in Moscow on a gloomy Thursday, September 2, it seemed the entire city had turned out for the funeral of Andrei Zhdanov, a high Communist official. In a gesture of welcome, the funeral procession stopped for a moment to allow the small cavalcade of cars carrying the Israelis to pass through on their way to the Hotel Metropol, their home until an embassy house would become available to them. Golda's first official act was to write a letter of condolence to the Soviet foreign minister, Vyacheslav Molotov, on Zhdanov's death. It was an important move: the Soviet press published the names of diplomats who had sent condolences. The Russian newspapers *Izvestia* and *Pravda* also briefly noted Golda's arrival.

Before leaving Israel, Golda had decided to run their legation like a kibbutz as a way of presenting Israel as she wanted it seen—a small pioneering nation living simply according to its socialist ideals. Nobody on the staff took a salary; they would each receive housing, meals, cigarettes, and pocket money, kibbutz style, and have to manage with that. They quickly discovered that with no money for tipping, they had to wait interminably for their breakfasts to arrive and their rooms to be made up. Golda shrugged off such inconveniences. She became incensed, however, when the first hotel bill arrived and she discovered how expensive living there was. At a staff meeting, she decreed that members were to take just one meal a day—lunch—in the hotel dining room and prepare the others themselves. With Sarah at her side, she bought pots and pans, hot plates and other electrical goods at a store that sold stolen German war supplies cheaply, and distributed them to the staff. Twice a week, at seven in the morning, she and Kadar ventured out in the cold and dark to the local kolkhoz, a collective farm, to load their shopping bags with milk, cheese, bread, butter, sausages, and other necessities for the delegates. Friday nights the group ate together, and on Saturdays, Golda cooked for her family and the singles, Lou Kadar and Eiga Shapiro, on an electric plate in her bathroom.

The elegant Hotel Metropol draped in Art Deco architecture, with hanging crystal chandeliers and plush furniture, had never housed a legation like that of Golda Meyerson and her Israelis. What other guests and diplomats might have said about the group's unconventional style and the cooking odors that emanated from some of its rooms has been lost to history.

But a British chargé d'affaires, G. W. Harrison, had a strong opinion about Golda and her early weeks in Moscow that he conveyed to the British Foreign Office. He "fully endorsed" the description he had received of Mrs. Meyerson ahead of time from the British consul general in Jerusalem as a "tough American Trades Union and Labour boss . . . not over intelligent but honest." (Decades later, a friend sent Lou Kadar a copy of Harrison's letter from the British files. She read it to Golda, who lay close to death. "So at least he thought me honest, if not intelligent," the retired prime minister said, with a weak smile.) Harrison's letter also described Golda as "circularizing the whole of the Diplomatic Corps," which "caused some flutter" among diplomats whose countries had not recognized the State of Israel, "and they are the majority." Because England was among those countries, he agreed to exchange visits with her only on a personal and not an official basis. He had the feeling during their visit that Mrs. Meyerson's first impressions of Moscow "had been unexpectedly pleasant" and that she had been surprised to find Moscow's shops "so well stocked with food and goods," having believed that Communist austerity would keep them empty. She spoke of how difficult it was to build a state from the start, he reported. " 'But,' she said, 'it's worth it.' "

About five months after arriving in Moscow, Golda and her delegation took over the eleven-room former embassy of the Indian ambassador Mrs. Vijaya Lakshmi Pandit and her legation, which moved to larger quarters. A chef sent from Israel prepared meals for them, freeing Golda from cooking in her bathroom. She also let up a bit on her economic restrictions so that people had enough money to get their clothes cleaned and their hair cut, and even to give occasional tips. Lou Kadar introduced her to manicures at this time. She had never had her nails done before and she loved it. From then on, getting regular manicures became a necessity of her life. "Even in the hospital, I would bring a manicurist to her," Kadar said.

Diplomatic life in the U.S.S.R. began for Golda on Tuesday, September 7, with a visit to the Kremlin to meet the foreign minister, Molotov, who reviewed her credentials before she officially delivered them. With his rimless round spectacles and neat mustache, the small, stocky minister had the look of a fastidious schoolmaster devoted to details. He also had a reputation for cold cruelty when crossed. He was, however, "very cordial" to Golda during their talk, she wrote to Sharett. *Pravda*, the official Communist Party organ, reported the meeting on its front page.

Four days later, she formally submitted her letter of credentials to the deputy chairman of the Supreme Soviet, Ivan Alekseevich Vlasov, in a ceremony at the Kremlin. Before leaving Israel, she and Eiga Shapiro had held nervous consultations over what she should wear for that auspicious occasion, the kind of problem no male diplomat had to think about. They finally settled on a floor-length black dress made for her by a Tel Aviv dressmaker to be worn with a small black velvet turban. She later added a string of artificial pearls borrowed from Eiga. A photographer snapped a picture of her presenting her papers in that outfit, a black purse dangling from her wrist, and it appeared in the Russian magazine *Ogonek*. Copies of that photograph would find their way into Jewish homes throughout Russia, a token of pride in the Jewish state.

Everything about the ceremony seemed magical. Golda and her delegates were driven in official cars to the Kremlin complex, she in the first car, the others behind her. An elaborate entrance and many iron gates led inside to the meeting rooms. Soldiers opened the gates for them, and as they passed through, bells chimed, announcing their arrival.

Golda resolved to speak only in Hebrew at this formal event. Accordingly, aides sent Vlasov her speech translated into Russian beforehand. It presented her credentials, sent greetings from Israel, and expressed the hope that the friendship between the two nations would grow to their mutual benefit. She read the Hebrew out loud at the ceremony, her heart "pounding" with nervousness and excitement. When she finished, after ten minutes, Vlasov responded at somewhat greater length in Russian. His staff had suggested earlier that his words be translated into English for Golda and the delegates with her. She refused: she represented the State of Israel, whose language was Hebrew, not English. After a futile attempt by the Soviets to find a Russian translator who knew Hebrew, they agreed to have Arieh Levavi translate Vlasov's words into Hebrew. It was the first time the Russians allowed a translator in the Kremlin who was not one of their own. After the ceremony and a small reception, Golda and the other delegates returned to her room in the Metropol, exhausted, but ready for a festive supper and a glass of vodka to toast their formal acceptance into the diplomatic corps.

"The ceremony was very impressive, a complete success, and conducted in a friendly atmosphere," Golda wrote happily to Sharett, adding in the next day's cable, "Ceremony of presenting credentials reported in press on page one."

This, she was to say, was the "honeymoon" period of Israel's relationship with the Soviet Union. Ever since Gromyko's surprise UN speech in 1947 favoring partition, and especially with Russia's full recognition of Israel, Jewish leaders had basked in that country's friendship. Golda continued to feel that glow during these first days in Moscow. Even the usually stern Molotov seemed to go out of his way after their first meeting to show his approval of the young state. When they viewed a parade commemorating the anniversary of the Bolshevik Revolution, Golda looked with awe at the weapons on display. "If only we had just a few of the weapons," she said with a sigh. "You will have," Molotov answered sympathetically. "We too began with little."

Walter Bedell Smith, the American ambassador to Moscow, advised her not to fool herself about the Soviet attitude. "It will change," he warned. To be sure, Golda and her comrades were not oblivious to the shadowy Soviet world they now inhabited. They understood that they lived in a closed society, so distrustful of outsiders that citizens were forbidden to associate with foreigners. Every time they left the hotel, they handed their keys to a dour old woman who sat on the landing and, they assumed, reported their every move to the MGB (Ministry for State Security, later KGB). They knew their phones were tapped and walls bugged, so they wrote notes or walked outside when they wanted to have a private conversation. Sometimes they went into the bathroom and pulled the toilet chain while they whispered to each other. They sensed being followed whenever they left the premises. The chauffeur they brought with them from Israel, a man with years of experience, mysteriously failed the driver's test, no matter how often he took it, forcing them to hire a driver provided by the Foreign Ministry. Their maid, electrician, and other household help also came from the Foreign Ministry, as they did in other diplomatic missions.

BUT GOLDA AND HER MISSION differed from the others in the extent of Soviet friendship they enjoyed and the hidden dangers they faced in accepting that apparent friendship. A convoluted history lay behind Soviet-Jewish relations.

Jews in Russia had hailed the Bolshevik Revolution of 1917 and been part of it. To many it appeared to sweep away generations of Jewish persecution and degradation and place Jews on an equal footing with all Soviet citizens. Jewish cultural institutions flourished. Yiddish newspapers and publishing houses cropped up in major cities, and the newly founded Moscow State Yiddish Theater celebrated the changing world order in drama and song. But while Jews and Jewish culture began to find a place in Russian society, Zionism became anathema to revolutionary leaders, including Jewish ones. To them Zionist ideals represented the bourgeois past and an unredeemed nationalism; the Jewish future they beheld lay only in Communism and assimilation into the Soviet Union. Thousands of Zionists were jailed or exiled, some for years, cut off from Jews in the rest of the world. They were the first, but far from the last, to become known as "prisoners of Zion."

With Joseph Stalin's rise to power in the late 1920s and the 1930s, the dream of equality for Jews in Soviet Russia quickly evaporated. In securing his dictatorship, he purged Jews from public office, closed Jewish cultural institutions, and denounced the slightest sign of Jewish "nationalism" or "cosmopolitanism." Anti-Semitism might have become state policy had not World War II interceded. Desperately in need of Allied help and world Jewish support, Stalin toned down his animosity toward Jews. He established the Jewish Anti-Fascist Committee (JAFC), which was headed by the esteemed Yiddish actor Solomon Mikhoels, included the most prominent Jewish authors and intellectuals in the country, and became a vibrant Jewish cultural center. He also authorized a Yiddish daily newspaper, *Einikeit* (Unity), which carried great weight among Jewish readers. On the surface, that friendly attitude toward Jews continued after peace was declared, although, with the Cold War intensifying in 1947, fear and suspicion spread through the land, and Soviet Jewry became ever more isolated from the West. And then came Soviet recognition of Israel and Golda's arrival in Moscow. Soviet Jews had greeted the establishment of the state with tremendous enthusiasm. Within a few days, the JAFC sent a congratulatory telegram to Chaim Weizmann, and prominent Russian Jewish journalists wrote letters to the JAFC lauding Israel and expressing gratitude for the Soviet role in its creation. Hundreds of other Jews wrote to the JAFC to offer financial aid to the new state or ask about enlisting in the Israeli army or inquire about immigrating to Israel. Several wrote to the embassy, or directly to Golda, sending greetings and congratulations. At a special service in honor of Israel, twenty thousand people gathered at the Choral Synagogue of Moscow, spilling onto the streets outside. Flowers decorated the sanctuary, and blue and white banners hung for the occasion proclaimed, THE PEOPLE OF ISRAEL LIVES and LONG LIVE THE STATE OF ISRAEL.

Golda's mission began in that atmosphere of euphoria, "as if the Messiah had come," she was to say. On the second Sabbath after their arrival, she and several of the Israeli envoys walked to the great Choral Synagogue on Arkhipov Street for the ten o'clock services. She had been eager to meet Russian Jews, and she reasoned that the synagogue was the best place to begin. Namir arranged the visit ahead of time with the synagogue's rabbi, Shlomo Shleifer, and when the legation arrived, two members of the congregation welcomed them in front of the building. The Israeli men, each carrying his prayer shawl and prayer book, were seated downstairs on the dais and received the honor of being called up to bless the Torah.

Golda and the other women were ushered up the steps to two special boxes in the women's gallery. Looking around, Golda noticed how elderly and shabby looking most of the three hundred or so congregants were, with just a smattering of young people among them. When the cantor added a blessing for her along with the traditional blessing for the head of the Soviet government, she could feel people silently staring at her. At the end of the service, however, when she descended the stairs, loud applause and shouts of "bravo" and "shalom" broke out. Women hugged her, some sobbing, some kissing her hands and the hem of her dress. Filled with emotion, she, too, burst into tears as she bowed ceremoniously to the rabbi and chatted with him in Hebrew.

The excited crowd followed the delegation into the streets, and when it split up, a group stayed with Golda until she reached the Metropol. Near the hotel, an elderly man turned to her and whispered in Hebrew the *shehehiyanu* prayer that gives thanks for living to see that day, then quickly slipped away.

Two weeks later, Arieh Lapid, the delegation's second secretary, gave the rabbi a Torah scroll as a gift from Israel. He asked to have a date set for a festive ceremony when the legation could present the scroll officially. Lapid also gave the rabbi a package of fifteen hundred rubles along with Golda's personal card and an invitation for him and some of his congregants to visit with her.

During this springtime of Soviet friendship, Golda approached her diplomatic meetings with the Soviet hierarchy optimistically. Ivan Bakulin, the young head of the Middle and Near Eastern departments in the Soviet Foreign Ministry, most impressed her with his charm and intelligence. She spoke to him at length about Israel's pressing need for immigration to help fight in the present war but, more important, for hands and minds to build the budding state. Carefully avoiding the sensitive subject of an exodus of Jews from the Soviet Union itself, she hinted that many Jews would like to leave Soviet bloc countries, such as Romania and Bulgaria, and she hoped that anyone who wanted to go to Israel would be allowed to do so. Bakulin's pleasant and gracious manner notwithstanding, he offered her nothing more than the standard Soviet position: immigration had nothing to do with Russia's Jews, for only Jews from "non-democratic countries"—the capitalist West—had any reason to want to leave their homes and go to Israel.

Despite such rhetoric, Golda continued to hope that she might meet and talk to ordinary Russian Jews, learn about their lives, and tell them about the Jewish state. She knew the Yiddish theater, like the synagogue, served as a gathering place for Moscow's Jews, including secret Zionist activists. So in mid-September, she and her entourage went to the Moscow State Jewish Theater for the first time to see the play *Freylekhs*

(Joy), a celebration of Jewish perseverance. All the young women in her legation dressed in blouses trimmed with Yemenite embroidery, a way to be easily recognized. During intermission, as audience members circled the theater, they stopped near Golda, some touching her clothing, others softly murmuring greetings and blessings. After the play ended, so many people in the foyer thronged about her and her party that the Israelis could barely get to their coats. In the midst of the commotion, she heard someone say in perfect Hebrew, "Mother, this is she." Turning swiftly, she saw a man in his forties with an elderly woman on his arm. Within seconds they vanished. A few minutes later, another woman sidled up to her, whispered in Yiddish, "Take us with you," and disappeared into the crowd.

She longed to speak to such people, not in fleeting moments at public places, but in real conversations. Almost immediately after settling into the Metropol, she had begun holding open houses in her suite on Friday evenings, serving tea and cake as they did at home. The guests who appeared were pleasant enough: foreign journalists, Jewish tourists or businessmen, diplomats, but never any Russians and certainly not Russian Jews. Although Jewish community members might hover outside the hotel, they didn't dare step inside.

Golda might have thought at times that she had moved into an Alice in Wonderland world where nothing was as it appeared to be. Showered with attention on the one hand—many in the diplomatic corps regarded the Israelis as the Russians' favorites—on the other she and her staff felt themselves even more restricted from contact with local residents than other legations. In reality, there was much about the Soviet world in which she lived that Golda did not know.

She did not know that the MGB had investigated her past after she received the Moscow assignment. With bureaucratic incompetence, Ukrainian security uncovered four Goldas born in Kiev around the same time and could not determine which one she was. Of her duties as ambassador, the MGB report said that she had a "special assignment from the Mapai Party to make contact with Jews in the U.S.S.R. and find a way to get them actively involved in all Zionist activities." Behind official smiles, therefore, lay orders to monitor her every step.

She did not know that since 1946 the Soviet security apparatus had been gathering information about the Jewish Anti-Fascist Committee with increasing suspicion that it had "nationalist" and Zionist leanings. At the beginning of 1948, eight months before Golda arrived in Moscow,

Stalin had Solomon Mikhoels, the committee's famous head, murdered and his death covered up as an automobile accident. She did not know that the hundreds of letters sent to the JAFC in the excitement of Israel's establishment were sent on to (or confiscated by) the government, with the names, addresses, and phone numbers of the senders, who would suffer the consequences later.

She did not know that not long after Arieh Lapid invited Rabbi Shleifer to visit with her and to arrange a ceremony for accepting the Torah scroll the legation had brought, the rabbi received a series of "recommendations" from the Soviet Foreign Ministry. They included limiting his contacts with Israeli legation members, declining the invitation from Mrs. Meyerson, and accepting the Torah scroll in the presence of only a few people without calling attention to the occasion. Not knowing, Golda and the others had been puzzled by the rabbi's repeated postponements of the Torah celebration. They were disappointed when it finally did take place that only eighteen synagogue people had been invited, all from the executive committee. After a brief ceremony, the guests sat silently with the Israeli delegates in a small, dimly lit library, hesitating to speak as though unsure of whom they could trust. When someone began to sing a Zionist song, another stopped him. "Shah, shah," the man said, and silence descended again.

Most important, she did not know, or fully comprehend, the distinctions Stalin made between the Soviet Union's relationship with Israel and Soviet Jewry's relationship with it, between the government's policies toward the Jewish state and its policies toward the Jews in its domain. Whereas the government had its own reasons for backing Israel, it did not expect its actions to stir Soviet Jews to identify with the state. When, after Israel's creation, an audience member asked a lecturer how a Soviet citizen might arrange to move there, he was told that it would be highly unlikely for anyone to wish to leave the Soviet motherland. Russia's leaders believed, or wanted to believe, that Jews were thoroughly integrated into the Soviet Union.

Nevertheless, the government's firm political support of Israel misled many Jews into concluding that it approved of their enthusiastic Zionist response. The Soviet leaders' cordial reception of Golda and her legation misled her into concluding that they were more committed to her country's needs and aspirations than they truly were.

On September 21, both Golda and Soviet Jewry had their conclusions shattered by an article that appeared in *Pravda* by the prominent

Russian Jewish journalist Ilya Ehrenburg. In the form of a letter to one "Alexander R." from Munich, who had asked about the Jewish state, the article laid out the government's position on Soviet Jews and Israel. It wasn't pretty.

Although the Soviet government and its people had great sympathy for the State of Israel in its struggle against the British and the Arabs, Ehrenburg wrote, the creation of the state did not offer a real solution to the "Jewish question." That question could be solved "not by utopians or diplomats" but only by "the victory of socialism over capitalism." More to the point, the article continued, "obscurantists" invented "ridiculous stories" about the Jews as "some sort of chosen beings" and claimed that "there is some mystical link between all the Jews in the world." That claim was false. Jewish solidarity resulted only from anti-Semitism and persecution, which pushed Jews to regard themselves as connected. "If tomorrow some madman were to appear and announce that everyone with red hair or a snub nose should be persecuted and destroyed, we would see a natural solidarity among all the red-heads and all the snub-nosed," Ehrenburg stated. As for Israel, the article concluded, it had still not emerged out of the "dark forest" of capitalism. Therefore "the fate of Jewish workers in all countries is not linked with the fate of the State of Israel." Soviet Jews and those in the "People's Democracies," such as Poland and Bulgaria, should not "look to the Middle East," but "to the future," as embodied in the Soviet Union.

Everybody understood the article's clear-cut warning to Soviet Jews: keep your distance from Israel and its delegation. "It was so sudden that we were surprised and shocked," recalled Amos Manor. "Suddenly Ilya Ehrenburg writes to tell the Jews of the Soviet Union and Communists all over the world, 'Forget about Israel! This is not for you.' We understood Communist Party jargon. The support the Soviet Union had given us until that day was finished."

Stalin had ordered the article to attack the "active behavior" of the Jews since Golda Meyerson arrived in Moscow, Ehrenburg told a friend. Its message reverberated rapidly throughout the Eastern European countries. Overnight, it seemed, the warm relations Jewish emissaries had established with the Romanian government turned to ice. Jews would no longer be easily allowed out of that land or out of Poland and Hungary for some time. A small trickle would still flow from Czechoslovakia and on and off from Bulgaria. But for most Eastern European Jews, the Iron Curtain had been sealed.

"THIS IS THE ANSWER OF Moscow's Jews to Ehrenburg," a man whispered to Golda as she tried to make her way through a mass of thousands upon thousands of Jews who defied the journalist's warnings and turned out to see her at the Choral Synagogue on Rosh Hashanah, October 4, 1948, the Jewish New Year. She had not returned to the synagogue for two weeks after her first visit there, to allow the excitement of that appearance to simmer down, but she had to be there on Rosh Hashanah and Yom Kippur, the holiest days on the Jewish calendar. There might have been twenty thousand or as many as fifty thousand people in and around the synagogue when she and her legation arrived on that first holiday morning. They included droves of young people this time, and people from other synagogues, people from outside Moscow, organized groups of people, all come to see the Israelis. It was as if all the murdered Jews of the Nazi camps had returned to life and were shouting and trembling with the depths of their emotions, the Hebrew newspaper *Maariv* reflected.

The crowds applauded loudly, shouting "shalom" and "hurrah," while they opened a narrow path for the Israelis to enter the building. In the balcony, crushed on all sides by women calling her name, kissing her hands, touching her dress, Golda sat stiffly, shaken to the core by the scene around her. In the tumult, she noticed that the two banners celebrating Israel that had hung in the synagogue previously were gone. That was the only outward concession to Ehrenburg's warning. For the rest, people threw caution to the wind in their open embrace of Golda and her legation.

The service over, she struggled toward the door, almost smothered by the mass of congregants pushing to see and touch her. When she finally reached the outside, an amateur photographer snapped a picture of her, a black hat and white face bobbing up from a quicksand of heads. It would become an underground best seller along with the earlier photograph of her presenting her credentials. When she tried to walk, she heard a din of voices calling out to her, "A gut yahr" (Happy New Year), and again and again, "Golda" and "Goldele," and "nasha Golda" (Russian for "our Golda"). She was grateful when someone protectively shoved her into a taxi. Overwhelmed with emotion, all she could utter as she stuck her head out the window was "A dank eich vos ihr seit geblieben Yidden" (Thank you for having remained Jews).

The synagogue scene was repeated ten days later on Yom Kippur eve. Although the police escorted Golda and her staff this time, hordes of people mobbed them again. When the service ended and the rabbi urged, then pleaded with, congregants to go home, no one budged. They would not leave until Golda and her entourage did, and when that group walked out, hundreds joined them and escorted them to their hotel. On Yom Kippur itself, as is traditional, Golda stayed in the synagogue all day with other congregants. During the memorial service, Brigadier Ratner in full uniform stood before the congregants as they recited a somber prayer for Israel's fallen soldiers. At the end of the long day, when the shofar was blown and the people called out the traditional "Next year in Jerusalem," all eyes fixed on her. "It was as though an electric current had charged a thousand times through the synagogue and into the street," she said. "It was the most passionate expression of Zionism I have ever heard."

Her experience in Moscow's Choral Synagogue on those holy days in the fall of 1948 became a defining moment for Golda. Like most Israelis, she had believed that Russian Jews were lost to the Jewish people, completely assimilated and unconnected. She felt guilty, she would say after that holiday, that she had doubted them as she did. She never would again. Of all Israel's leaders, Golda Meir would become the most directly involved and most devoted to the cause of freeing Soviet Jewry.

Stalin and his cohorts were also taken by surprise by the numbers and ardor of the Jews who turned out for Golda and the Israeli legation. Moscow had not seen a spontaneous demonstration like that since 1927, when Trotskyites and others had protested Stalin's assumption of absolute power, and that one did not match this. The outpouring of feeling toward Israel infuriated Stalin, stirring his suspicions that Soviet Jews were disloyal to "Mother Russia" after all, a fifth column with an allegiance to another land. To keep tabs on the demonstrators, MGB agents liberally sprinkled among them made notes of their names and activities. The historian Yaacov Ro'i even raises the possibility that the secret police initiated the vast demonstrations "to provoke Jews into exposing themselves and their dreams of emigration" and to be able to blame Golda and the Israeli legation for causing trouble. It would be some weeks before Stalin acted on the information gathered, but in time and with various trumped-up charges people from those crowds would be arrested and imprisoned or exiled to remote areas.

A few days after Ehrenburg's article ran in *Pravda*, the Yiddish Communist paper *Einikeit*, jumping on the bandwagon, reprinted it. Then, in the wake of the holiday turnout at the synagogue, leading members of the Jewish Anti-Fascist Committee began to attack Soviet Jewish sympathy for Israel and the Israeli delegation, some out of conviction, some to counter the dangerous effects of the demonstrations. At a meeting of the JAFC presidium on October 21, Itzik Feffer, later discovered to have been an informer for the MGB, spoke of the need to "shatter the myths" about Ben-Gurion and other Israeli leaders. Leiba Kvitko asserted that "more suitable candidates than Golda Meyerson could have been found to head the Moscow mission." He wanted to inform the Jewish public openly that "this is a narrow-minded woman and that only the more ignorant elements regard her with reverence."

Ehrenburg himself behaved rudely to Golda when they met at a Czechoslovak embassy party in late October. She had wanted to meet to tell him in no uncertain terms what she thought of his article. As soon as the foreign correspondent Ralph Parker introduced them, Ehrenburg launched into a loud diatribe against the English language, especially when spoken by Russian-born Jews, a clear swipe at Golda. She proposed that they speak Yiddish, to which he responded that he didn't know Yiddish and anyway it derived from German, another inappropriate language for Jews. He showed no interest in visiting Israel, and after some further attacks on the English language he turned away. She and Namir thought he must have been drunk.

In the growing anti-Israel climate, Golda got support from an unexpected source. At a reception in Molotov's home commemorating the Bolshevik Revolution, she met Polina Zhemchuzhina (born Perl Karpovskaya), Molotov's wife, who held a powerful position in Soviet circles. During their conversation, she astounded Golda by switching from the Russian she had been speaking with a translator to Yiddish, saying several times, "Ich bin a yiddishe tochter" (I am a daughter of the Jewish people). She praised Golda for having gone to the synagogue and encouraged her to "go, go, the Jews want to see you." When she met Sarah, she asked a slew of questions about kibbutz living, which seemed to her implausible. Even Stalin—whom she greatly admired—opposed the idea of sharing everything, she said, and suggested that the young woman read Stalin's writings. Golda detected tears in Zhemchuzhina's eyes when she said good-bye to Sarah. If "it will be well with you, it will be well with all Jews in the world," the Russian woman said.

Golda couldn't have known that the secret police were looking into Zhemchuzhina's correspondence with her brother Sam Carp, an

American businessman, and her closeness to the slain actor Mikhoels. Zhemchuzhina herself had no inkling that she had fallen under serious suspicion. In the weeks after her meeting with Golda, the secret police accumulated new evidence against her, and in January they arrested her. During her interrogation, her enthusiastic welcome to Golda Meyerson was raised as an example of her improper behavior. She was expelled from the Communist Party and sentenced to five years of exile in Kazakhstan. Golda heard nothing about the arrest or sentence until years later. Like other Soviet punishments, this one was kept secret.

Even before Zhemchuzhina's arrest, the Ministry of State Security received orders to dismantle the Jewish Anti-Fascist Committee. Within a few days, the publication of *Einikeit* came to a halt, the Yiddish printing press was demolished, and Der Emes, a publisher of Yiddish literature, was shut down. Over the next few months, many of the leaders of the JAFC were arrested, including Leiba Kvitko and Itzik Feffer, whose criticisms of Ben-Gurion and Golda Meyerson at the October 21 JAFC presidium meeting were twisted around as though they had been words of praise. Tortured and sleep deprived, these men and the others confessed to their "crimes" of promoting Zionism and nationalism. They languished for years in the Lubianka jail until they were tried, convicted, and secretly executed in August 1952.

How responsible was the Israeli mission for Stalin's increasing paranoia about Soviet Jewish ties to Zionism and Israel? Certainly, his distrust began long before they arrived in Moscow—as evidenced by the murder of Mikhoels and the early investigations of the JAFC—and the results would have been the same had the Israelis not appeared. But the tumultuous events of September and October 1948, when thousands of Jews poured out to see Golda and the other envoys, most probably exacerbated his fears of an immediate Zionist plot and might have been the catalyst for his actions at that time against the JAFC and other Jewish institutions. As for Golda, critics have blamed her personally for attending services on the High Holidays, knowing that her appearance would cause a sensation. Others, like Amos Manor, argue that to the Jews of Soviet Russia, Golda "was the embodiment of Israel." In that capacity, "anyone who came would have received the same reception." Besides, "how could the Israeli ambassador *not* be in synagogue on the holiest days of the Jewish year?"

ON THE DAY THE ORDER went out to eradicate the Jewish Anti-Fascist Committee, Golda Meyerson boarded a plane to Paris, unaware of the fate of that organization or its members. From there she went on to Israel, where the campaign for elections to the country's first government was getting under way. Rumors flew in Russia that Israel had recalled her because Moscow was displeased with the way she had handled her synagogue visits. The rumors in Israel were just the opposite: that Golda wanted to resign from her position in Moscow, but Israeli leaders wouldn't let her. Neither was true, but that story came closer to her actual feelings. She told Regina that she had nothing much to do in Moscow aside from attending diplomatic receptions, which bored her to death, and would like to return home permanently.

In one of her first acts after arriving in Israel, she reported to the provisional government in great detail about her Moscow experiences. Although the press had already recounted some of them, Ben-Gurion decreed that everything discussed in the room must remain secret. When reporters bombarded Golda with questions about what she had said, she smiled enigmatically and answered in Yiddish, "My mother taught me that you can never get into trouble by not talking."

The election would take place in late January, after her return to Moscow. On her final evening in Israel, which fell on the last night of Hanukkah, Moshe Sharett held a farewell party for her and Abba Eban, who was heading back to his post at the United Nations in New York. Together with the party guests, she and Sharett, and the more buttoned-up Eban, sang old songs and danced the traditional hora. With their new government, they would be entering the global diplomatic arena, but they still clung to their earlier, simpler world, the world of pioneers and laborers, of informality and comradely closeness. Golda might have wished for the music to go on forever as she stamped her feet to the rhythms she had followed since her early kibbutz days. By the next morning, she was flying on the first leg of a difficult flight that would take her to Rome, Budapest, Prague, and finally, again, Moscow, "the vast, cold land of suspicion, hostility and silence." Everything there now seemed bleaker than it had before she left. No crowds showed up when she went to the synagogue, and the people who did come barely dared glance at her. When she and her staff attended the theater in January, Soviet security agents kept audience members away from them. Soon after that, Stalin had all the Yiddish theaters in Russia shut down.

Few people sent letters to the legation anymore, and fewer still tried to visit. Heart-wrenching stories became part of the envoys' everyday fare. One of the saddest concerned Pinhas Hefetz, who came to the embassy one day, emaciated, disheveled, and dressed in rags. He had left his home in Jerusalem in 1936 to fight in the Spanish Civil War. Wounded, he had been sent to Russia for treatment. He had a British mandate passport that he hoped would allow him into Israel to be reunited with his aged mother, who still lived in the Old City. Golda accepted the passport but said he would need the approval of the Soviets to leave the country. She received no response when she tried to get that approval from the Foreign Ministry. A month or so later, Hefetz reappeared, desperate for help. The police had severely punished him after his first visit, and he pleaded this time to stay at the embassy. Bypassing protocol, Golda phoned Molotov and insisted on seeing him immediately. When she returned, "she couldn't say a word," Lou Kadar recalled. "We saw her tight, pale face and we knew the answer." Looking back to that day some sixty years later, ninety-year-old Kadar broke down in tears. "We told him he had to leave," she said, sobbing. "We never saw him again. He committed suicide."

Daily, Golda suffered agonizing decisions. Was it safe to send greetings to a Russian woman whose family lived in Israel? How might she, as head of the legation, respond to a man who had slipped a note to her in the synagogue? When, if ever, should they try to make contact with Chaim Weizmann's sister Maria, who lived in Russia (and would be arrested in 1953)? Fear stalked the Jewish community during Golda's final months in Moscow, and she needed to exert extreme caution to avoid stoking it. As it was, the deputy foreign minister, Valerian Zorin, chastised her in February for distributing a bulletin about Israel to Russian Jews. His tone, Golda reported to Sharett, was "polite and cool," and she understood that the "narrow wedge has now been closed . . . it is completely forbidden to reply to a letter from any local Jew." It would take great discipline and personal anguish for Golda to refrain from responding to people who contacted her.

The Israeli elections were held on January 25, 1949. Mapai won more than 35 percent of the vote, giving it 46 of the 120 seats in the legislature, now called the Knesset. Mapam, with only 19 seats, refused to join a coalition government, which forced Mapai to form a coalition with smaller parties. Along with her old friends and rivals from the Women Workers' Council, Ada Maimon, Beba Idelson, and Yehudit Simhonit, Golda had campaigned hard to have women elected to the government. Even so, only seven out of Mapai's fourteen female candidates won election. Golda topped the list, and the other three came after her.

She flew to Israel in mid-February to participate in forming the government. Ben-Gurion had cabled her in Moscow, "I am not going to have a cabinet without you." After long negotiations, she received the cabinet position of minister of labor and social insurance. Pleased, she went back to Moscow for the last time at the end of March, packed up her belongings, made the rounds of diplomatic farewells, and announced officially that the mission had been one of the "greatest experiences" of her life. With a sense of relief, she returned to Israel and her new post on April 20, 1949. Sarah and Zecharia were to remain in Moscow for several more months, as would Lou Kadar. Namir replaced Golda as head of the legation.

IN THE SPRING OF 1975, the former prime minister Golda Meir filed a three-million-dollar lawsuit against the editor of *Commentary*, an intellectual Jewish magazine, and the American Jewish Committee, its publishers. Some months earlier, a Soviet Jewish émigré, Lev Navrozov, had written in an article that at Stalin's request Mrs. Meir gave the ruler the names of Soviet Jews who wished to serve in Israel's War of Independence. He then turned the lists over to his secret police, which arrested the would-be volunteers and sent them to concentration camps to be starved or murdered. The point of the article, "Notes on American Innocence," was that Western leaders did not understand the totalitarian mentality, putting them at a disadvantage in dealing with countries like the Soviet Union. "Even so tough-minded and unblinkered a figure as Golda Meir," Navrozov wrote, provided a "particularly painful" illustration of that lack of understanding. Furious, Golda denied in a letter to the editor that she had ever handed lists to Stalin and demanded an apology for "so serious and shocking" an allegation. When the editors stood by Navrozov, she instituted her lawsuit.

Navrozov was not the first person to cite lists of names that Golda might have given to Soviet authorities. Rumors circulated from prison to prison that during the anniversary celebration of the Bolshevik Revolution Golda provided Mrs. Molotov with the names of people who wanted to leave Russia. People arrested were sometimes called "Golda's Prisoners," because of the widespread belief that her activities had led to their incarceration. The Soviet rumor mill probably cranked out and circulated most of the rumors that implicated Golda or the legation; it served the authorities' purpose to denigrate the Israelis. Golda did discuss family reunification with Soviet authorities—having relatives of Israeli citizens join their families—and she did receive names of such people from Israel's Foreign Ministry. It's unlikely, however, that such lists ever reached Soviet authorities. When she tried to pin down Molotov or others to do something in this area, she was told, "We'll consider it," and never heard about the matter again.

The Soviets didn't need lists from Golda. They had many ways of collecting the names of Jews interested in Israel. There were the hundreds of people who wrote to the Jewish Anti-Fascist Committee and the thousands who turned out to see Golda on the holidays. According to a letter Golda received, there was even a chairman of the Moscow Jewish community who claimed the embassy had secretly instructed him to assemble lists of volunteers for Israel's War of Independence but who was actually working undercover for the MGB.

Ultimately, how the authorities obtained their names mattered little. By the time Golda left Moscow, darkness had descended on the Jewish community, blotting out its one brief Camelot moment, when Stalin supported the Jewish state and the Jews believed they could show their support for it also. The tragedy of the Soviet Jews was that they had erred. In reality, Camelot had never existed. It had been an illusion, a misguided fantasy, and their belief in it had made them more vulnerable than ever. The tragedy for Golda was her inability to influence the rulers of the Soviet Union and her inability to make things right for the Jews there. For a person who viewed herself as connected to all the Jews of the world, that tragedy cut deep.

She settled the lawsuit with *Commentary* in February 1976 after the editor ran an apology regretting "any distress the article may have caused her."

17

"Either Immigrants or Shoes"

Rumors followed Golda from Russia. The foreign press reported that she returned home after so few months because she had failed in her mission. It also stated that the Soviets had recalled Pavlov Yershov, because Israel had delayed in appointing Golda's successor. Israeli sources denied the truth of such reports. (In fact, Yershov had taken a short leave and returned to Tel Aviv in October.) Golda ignored everything said. She was too happy to be back in Israel at the heart of the action again, happy to be the first woman in the first cabinet of the country's first self-government in two thousand years. Aside from a historical statistic, for her that number signaled greater power and influence than she'd ever known. As labor minister, she would have a hand in shaping every aspect of the new state, its housing, its jobs, its social services. From her years of experience in the Histadrut, she felt more comfortable about handling those issues than she had in the rarefied atmosphere of international diplomacy. She was, in fact, in her element.

Every detail of the new government, from the trivial to the monumental, had to be thought through. How, people asked Mrs. Meyerson, should the only woman in the cabinet be addressed in Hebrew? As *sar*, "minister," or *sara*, a feminized version? "Let's compromise," she answered with a laugh. "Call me Golda." She was later addressed as *sara*. And how, in general, should members of the Knesset be designated during sessions? British and American lawmakers were referred to by the localities they represented, but the Israeli electoral system did not allow for that. Should Knesset members, then, be called by their first names, family names, or both? David Remez suggested the method used in traditional synagogues—the member's first name followed by his father's name, as in "David ben [son of] Yehiel." Golda made a counterproposal: "Why not use the mother's name instead of the father's?" The matter was tabled for future discussion.

Remez, who had been minister of transportation in the provisional government, continued in that role in the established one. Sitting at party or government meetings, he and Golda sometimes exchanged notes on scraps of paper, the way they had some twenty years earlier in the Histadrut executive committee. "I heard from Sharef," she wrote teasingly in one note, "the minister whom the prime minister most values is the transportation minister. His esteem for him is extraordinary." More moderate than Ben-Gurion, Remez had often disagreed with the prime minister, but under the overwhelming conditions of the first government he might have won the grudging admiration of the "old man," as Ben-Gurion, now at the peak of his career, was called.

Conditions *were* overwhelming. Israel's War of Independence had ended when it signed armistice agreements with Egypt in February 1949, Lebanon in March, Jordan in April, and Syria in July. In the course of the fighting, the young nation had expanded the territory allotted it by the UN partition resolution, gaining ground in the Galilee and taking control of the entire Negev to its southernmost tip, excluding the Gaza Strip. But even before the war drew to a close, thousands upon thousands of Jewish immigrants had begun pouring into the land. The free flow of immigrants, the Yishuv's most impassioned demand of the British, had come to pass, and it was about to drown the country.

In little over a year of statehood, from May 1948 to the end of 1949, more than 340,000 immigrants sought refuge in Israel, often at the rate of a thousand a day. By the end of 1951, that number had swelled to 700,000, doubling the country's population to more than 1 million, a full one-third of them immigrants. No other nation in history had absorbed that many newcomers in that short a time, their homeland suddenly swamped with strangers who spoke a dozen disparate languages and could not fathom one another's customs or cultures.

Each group had its own near-miraculous story. The survivors in the DP camps and the refugees in Cyprus arrived on planes and trains, many ill, many still ravaged in their bodies and minds from their Holocaust experiences. Yemenite community members were secretly airlifted to Israel over the course of two years, in what became known as Operation Magic Carpet. Almost 50,000 of them stepped off planes somewhat dazed by their flights, men with long, picturesque side locks, women in modest, hooded garments. Many could not read or write; large numbers were infected with trachoma, tuberculosis, and other diseases that forced them to be isolated. In contrast, thousands of Jewish families from Iraq, among them well-dressed upper- and middle-class men and women, sneaked across the border to Iran and headed to Israel from there. When the Iraqi parliament unexpectedly legalized Jewish immigration to Israel, a new wave began, and it continued to jump as the government piled on anti-Jewish restrictions. Other groups made their way to Israel from Turkey and Morocco, from Egypt, Tunis, and Algeria, all fleeing the anti-Semitism that intensified in these lands after the State of Israel was declared. In Eastern Europe, Jews rushed to escape Stalin's grip before all the gates closed. Scores of newcomers relocated from Czechoslovakia, and in the Balkan states of Bulgaria and Yugoslavia entire communities picked up and boarded ships to Haifa. In a move that surprised Golda and other Israeli leaders, the Communist governments of Poland and Romania agreed briefly to let their Jews go, adding 100,000 or more immigrants to the mix by the end of 1951.

When Golda returned from Moscow, she saw across the land acres of immigrant camps covered with shacks and tents crammed with newcomers. Many in the first groups to come to the state had settled into the neighborhoods and houses abandoned by Arabs during the war. Others found shelter in old British army camps. But as the numbers skyrocketed, the Jewish Agency—which still functioned alongside the new government—hastily set up the immigrant quarters. Misery ruled the camps. Occupants shared their sparse tents with strangers from other lands and traditions. They waited in long lines to get food or take a shower, and they constantly suffered thirst because of water shortages. They felt deprived, degraded, and—in many cases—hopeless.

Within weeks of assuming her role as labor minister, Golda stood before the Knesset describing with cool confidence her plan to get large numbers of immigrants out of the camps and into more livable homes. Her department would build thirty thousand single-family units during the next year. Following building techniques used in other countries that had erected prefabricated housing, she envisioned "ten, twenty, thirty" houses rising a day. And the immigrants themselves would help construct these homes, thus finding employment while investing in their future. They would also cultivate the plots around their houses, in that way working the land itself.

True, the buildings would not be large. Generally, each would consist of one room of about 320 square feet and no smaller than about 230 square feet. (Both substandard by American norms.) The room would include a lavatory and a tiny kitchen area, and if necessary it could be partitioned to provide a separate space for children. Over time, the inhabitants could add more rooms to the building as needed. Experts who had reviewed the plans, Golda emphasized, felt that such an arrangement, with its possibilities for growth, "is not at all bad . . . even quite good."

To criticisms that her proposed houses sounded more like one-room huts than "quite good," Golda responded decisively: "We have only one alternative: either to build fewer houses of better quality or more houses of slightly less quality." The immediate challenge was to find the capital to build these houses, inadequate as they might be. The Jewish Agency was almost bankrupt, and the government itself had close to nothing in hard currency reserves.

Indeed, even before contemplating new housing, but simply to make ends meet, the government had instituted a food-rationing program, the hated *tsena*, or austerity. Dov Yosef, who had been the military governor of besieged Jerusalem during the war, ran the program like a general, unsmilingly meticulous about quantities of food permitted. Everybody, from top government officials to the newest immigrants, received coupon books issued by the Ministry of Commerce and Industry. With those coupons, a shopper might come home from the grocers—after waiting endlessly in line—with little more than some potatoes, a few dehydrated eggs, maybe a little hard cheese. Only eggplant, *leben*, and frozen fish did not hit the ration list, and the fish was falling into short supply. Golda wholeheartedly approved of the program, and when people groused about shortages, she offered a moral spin: rationing was a small sacrifice to make compared with the supreme sacrifice of those who gave their lives so that others could have a country. Nobody could argue with that, but Golda's pious lecturing didn't prevent a black market in foodstuffs from thriving.

She took to dressing poorly to promote the spirit of austerity. At a tea party in honor of Hadassah's president, Rose Halprin, Golda's shabby clothes drew the attention of a group of French nuns invited from St. Joseph's Convent, which Hadassah had used as a hospital during the siege of Jerusalem. "Had I not known that she wasn't Catholic," said Sister Elisabeth admiringly, "I would have thought she had been educated in a convent." Interviewing Golda some time later, a reporter described her as "an austere looking woman" who wore "black utilitarian oxfords, a doubled breasted black suit, and a tailored white blouse," identical to clothes she had worn three years earlier in a magazine photograph.

To get her housing program under way, Golda flew to America in June, less than two months after she returned from Russia. To colleagues who criticized her for leaving in the middle of the country's housing crisis, she shot back that she would "not withhold from any Knesset member this great joy of going from city to city trying to raise money," if anyone so wished it.

She spent a month and a half in the States on those grueling tours. "Yours is the responsibility," she charged a Pioneer Women's convention in Philadelphia on June 12, using the technique that had always worked well for her: making American Jews feel like equal partners in forming the Jewish state while jabbing them with guilt for not being there themselves. Israel's citizens had no choice but to absorb the immigrants flocking to them, she told her audience, but as part of the world's largest Jewish community American Jews also had "the responsibility directly upon their shoulders."

At other meetings, she spoke of the thirty thousand houses she had promised the Knesset. "I did a strange thing," she would say slyly. "I presented a project for which I didn't have the money." Then the pitch: "It is an awful thing to do—to forge a signature to a check—but I have done it." It was up to American Jews to make the check good and "restore . . . dignity and self-respect" to the newcomers. Usually, she got the money she asked for. If she didn't, she "raised unholy hell," Harry Beale recalled. When her speech at the Shamrock Hotel in Houston, Texas, garnered only fifty-six thousand dollars, she fumed and became even more incensed when the chairman asked the four hundred guests present to put ten dollars each in a champagne bucket to round out the sum to sixty thousand dollars. She stormed out of the room, enraged at the idea of passing a hat for the State of Israel. In her suite, "she clawed the chaise, the cushion there, and she was speechless," while the others tried to calm her. When she returned home on July 19, she brought with her pledges for new millions.

In August, Golda reported to the Knesset that the thirty thousand units she had promised would be completed that year, with additional building programs carried out by the Jewish Agency and Amidar, a consortium of contractors formed to handle immigrant housing. She also spoke positively about unemployment figures, distinguishing between people who were seeking work and the hard-core unemployed. Although the numbers of the former would climb in the next several months, largely because of returning war veterans, many would find work in agricultural settlements and on irrigation projects in the Negev. The number of the steadily unemployed stood at around ten thousand, and her department was seeking ways to lower it.

Opposition members attacked her on all counts. Beryl Raptor, from Mapam, argued that his party's studies had turned up not ten thousand unemployed but between ten and twenty thousand. Yosef Serlin, from the center-to-right General Zionists Party, agreed that the blockhouses Golda promised might be a little better than the shacks the Jewish Agency had built, but "neither these nor these are suitable for living." Israel Rokach, mayor of Tel Aviv, objected strongly to the idea of housing an entire family in one room. To read the Knesset minutes of these arguments and others is to witness Golda in classic form, firing back at attack after attack without giving an inch. She didn't raise her voice or interrupt other speakers. Her most potent weapon was sarcasm, and she utilized it with dread precision.

"I am simply filled with envy for MK Serlin," she said, alluding to his ability to pass judgment on different forms of housing: "Huts—they should never have come into existence; blockhouses—no good, impossible to live in. Mr. Serlin approves only of good things; and he should be praised for his aesthetic sense. Only a large solid house finds favor in his eyes—and in my eyes also." But, if he is so aesthetically attuned, why didn't he advise the government months earlier on how to build tens of thousands of big, beautiful houses in the course of just a few months and with little money? There seemed to be competition, she continued, between Mr. Serlin and Mr. Rokach, whose "aesthetic sense is even more highly developed . . . MK Rokach says that one room is not enough for a family. I won't argue. It is also clear to me that two rooms are the minimal requirement for a family." However, given his position as mayor "of this great Hebrew city," she wondered why so many families in Tel Aviv itself had not yet risen even to the level of a blockhouse. As for Raptor, his larger numbers of unemployed were simply not true.

Sarcastic, tough, threatening, Golda pushed back the constant assaults. Yet an element of truth marked the criticisms of her housing plans. With waves of immigrants landing ceaselessly, she and her staff flailed about from one housing solution to another, trying hurriedly to find the right combination of materials, structures, and locations. Production of the thirty thousand one-room homes she promised fell far behind schedule. For a while, she touted steel houses, like ones she had seen in Detroit, but they were too expensive. Then there were designs for concrete houses similar to those being built in India. Under duress, as the immigrant population exploded, houses of fabric with wooden frames were built, and more tents were ordered.

An especially severe winter battered the country in 1950, making everything worse. Soaking rains fell for days, flooding the roads to and from the immigrant camps. Tents too flimsy to protect against the burning sun in summertime were buffeted by wind and water in the winter. The ground turned into swamps of mud that reached people's knees, adding to the wretchedness of having to queue up three times a day to get the small amounts of food allotted each immigrant. And aside from the physical toll of the camps, the immigrants' total dependency on the Jewish Agency and the government for food and services took a painful psychological toll. "The life of idleness is destroying the souls of even the best individuals," Manya Shochat wrote to Golda. Now in her seventies and ailing, Shochat—the early revolutionary Golda had known since her first days in the land—visited the immigrants regularly to offer her help. But little anyone did relieved the desperation within the immigrant centers.

Ma'abarot, transit camps, became the next solution, the first of them built in the spring of 1950. Made up of tents and tin huts not unlike those in the immigrant camps, the *ma'abarot* had the advantage of placing each family in its own unit. They also forced the immigrants to become as self-sufficient as possible. Instead of receiving handouts from the Jewish Agency, newcomers were expected to work to support themselves. For that reason, many of the transit camps were built on the outskirts of towns, where people might find jobs. Others grew up near agricultural settlements in the hope that the newcomers would learn to farm and cultivate the land.

In charge of the *ma'abarot* and their occupants, Golda labored feverishly to scout out tents for living that could be bought at a low enough price, to coax reluctant people to leave the immigration centers and learn to fend for themselves, and to find employment to help them do so. She was gratified that within two years the immigrant centers emptied and the numbers in the *ma'abarot* jumped to a quarter of a million. Yet these camps had severe problems of their own. Overcrowded and hastily built, they, too, lacked all semblance of comfort. With unemployment rife, many families still had to live hand to mouth or depend on the government for subsistence. Of those newcomers sent to work in kibbutzim and agricultural villages, many showed no interest in farming. Mostly small shopkeepers and artisans, they wanted to peddle their wares in the marketplace, not pick oranges in the fields.

The *ma'abarot* would come to symbolize the country's growing pains in these early years. They would also symbolize the gap between groups of immigrants. European newcomers, especially the educated and skilled, managed to find work and move on to permanent homes fairly quickly. Others, mostly from Islamic lands, who lacked skills and training and whose background differed from the dominant Germanic and Ashkenazi one of veteran Israelis, remained in the *ma'abarot* and in the poor neighborhoods long after overall housing improved.

THROUGHOUT THE TURMOIL OF IMMIGRATION, Golda held firm to one principle: every Jew who wanted to immigrate to Israel should be welcomed. On July 5, 1950, the Knesset passed its Law of Return, offering the rights of citizenship to any Jew who wished to settle in the Jewish state. But many a Zionist leader questioned whether Zionist emissaries should push forward mass immigration as they had been doing or whether the pace should be slowed, the numbers staggered. As finance minister, Eliezer Kaplan spoke of budgets and absorption capacities and of limited resources available for hordes of new immigrants. Israel Goldstein, the Jewish Agency treasurer, suggested that constraints be put on immigration from countries where Jews were not in danger. Levi Eshkol, head of the settlement department of the Jewish Agency, called for quotas on the number of immigrants permitted each year. Golda Meyerson remained adamant about free immigration. She fully backed Ben-Gurion's demand for "the return of the exiles." Every Jew who did not dwell in Israel was an exile, and every Jew, weak, old, or sick, should be allowed—nay, encouraged—to settle in the land, she insisted.

In the United States, when speaking to the Pioneer Women, she labeled restrictions on immigration "the Bevin way." It meant that they would have to tell Jews in North Africa or Yemen, "We can't take you in, although Bevin has nothing to say over our country anymore."

In Israel, she spelled out her feelings to the Knesset: "For me, this state with its Knesset, with its honored members from all the parties—they have meaning and worth and intelligence . . . only if there will be immigration of hundreds of thousands, not merely on paper or in speech, but in practice." When the debate turned to extending rationing to clothes, she gave her comrades a choice: "Either immigrants or shoes . . . either limitations on immigration or limitations on clothing." For her no contest existed; large-scale immigration took precedence over everything. Even as the situation deteriorated.

With every passing week and every new onslaught of immigrants, the suffering in the *ma'abarot* became more acute. Flimsy huts, filthy outhouses, and insufficient water intensified the diseases and epidemics many immigrants brought with them, and spread illnesses rapidly through the camps. Adding to the misery, especially in camps far from towns and settlements, a physician might visit once, or at most twice, a week, while pediatricians, eye doctors, or other specialists hardly ever showed up. The very sick, the old, the children, had almost no access to medical care. The camps also lacked ambulances and in numerous cases telephone connections for emergency help. Horror stories abounded in the press, and on the Knesset floor opposition party members hurled more damning accusations than ever at Golda. Yaakov Gil, of the General Zionists Party, compared life in the camps to the degradations in the slaughterhouses of Chicago that the American writer Upton Sinclair described in his book *The Jungle*.

Golda countered attacks with her usual daggers. "We have all read books in our lifetimes," she shot back at Gil. She wondered, however, whether this was the right opportunity "to prove our literary knowledge" by making inapt comparisons. But she also acknowledged the severity of the crisis and the heavy burden mass immigration placed on the young country. Her solution was not to limit immigration but to delegate greater responsibility to the rest of society, especially those who lived in comfort and security.

"What direction do we propose to take?" she challenged a workers' council. At present, she continued, the country was split into two nations, "the old timers" and "the new immigrants." Old-time workers and their families wanted refrigerators, washing machines, cars, and "all the other good things that every person in the country is entitled to." But a poor Yemenite family needed a roof over its head. It needed food and clothing. By forgoing their refrigerators and other luxuries and providing for the immigrants, the old-timers could turn the two nations into one. "I fully confess publicly," she said, "that I have no need for a Jewish state with a high standard of living but without a large, unlimited, Jewish immigration."

For the sake of the immigrants, she pressed the Knesset to call on doctors, nurses, and schoolteachers throughout the country to volunteer their services in the *ma'abarot* "part of every week or part of the year." They should see such service as their "top and most elementary obligation." By the same token, she lacerated doctors and engineers for striking for higher salaries, just as she had once refused the salary demands of nurses in the Histadrut. She sided with working people except when, to her mind, that side hurt the rest of society.

For the sake of the immigrants, she demanded that building laborers increase their productivity. "Shall I be told that four hundred bricks a day is the maximum that can be laid?" she scoffed. She frequently deplored the scarcity of skilled construction workers necessary to build permanent housing for the newcomers, threatening at one point to hire Italian workmen to do the job Israelis were not doing quickly enough.

The immigrants were her cause and socialism her abiding image of how the state should be run. "We cannot take pleasure in the great absorption of immigrants unless we participate in it ourselves," she said at a Mapai meeting. "We don't need a new ideology . . . we need to shed light on the old things that we have forgotten somewhat or pushed into a corner." The "old things" to her included a just society without social classes that cared for all its citizens.

Opponents would argue that her ideology was not as pure as she made it out to be, that it bore tinges of her party's politics and a paternalism born of power. She had complained bitterly, for example, that the owners of orange groves in Petach Tikvah exploited Yemenite immigrants from the Rosh Ha'ayin camp by avoiding the employment bureaus and hiring them at subminimum wages. At a Knesset meeting in November, Chaim Cohen-Meguri of the religious Herut Party blew up at her. "You yelled about exploitation," he charged. "Is the matter of *how* they are being exploited important?" By dint of its dominance in the government and the Histadrut, Mapai controlled the labor bureaus, the workers' wages, and the immigrants themselves, who could not get jobs unless they held membership cards in the party. Was that not exploitation? Golda paid no heed. Whatever its faults, she would always see Mapai as a democratic party devoted to the public interest, and therefore deserving of its dominant position.

To provide for the immigrants, she traveled back and forth to the United States, London, and South America, seeking contributions. She was in the United States on June 3, 1950, when her son, Menahem, married Chana Lutsky at a ceremony in Passaic, New Jersey. Golda had known Chana's mother, Sara Kessler Lutsky, since her Poalei Zion days in America, and Morris had been friendly with Chana's father. Menahem had returned to the States to continue his music studies, and Chana, a graduate of New York's Hunter College, had already made plans to settle in Israel, an arrangement that pleased Golda. To Menahem's disappointment, Morris, who'd had a heart attack some time earlier, did not attend the wedding. The young couple had a traditional Jewish ceremony, the bride pretty in white, the groom in a proper dark suit. At fifty-two, Golda appeared heavy and matronly in her ankle-length "mother of the groom" dress and open-toe shoes whose thick straps crisscrossing the instep drew attention to her swollen ankles.

Countering the joy of Menahem's marriage, Sarah came close to death in November, when Golda was back in Israel. During a dangerously complicated pregnancy, she was taken from her kibbutz, Revivim, to the Hadassah clinic in Beersheba. Her husband, Zecharia, phoned Golda, who dropped everything and rushed to Beersheba. Given little hope that Sarah would survive, Golda sat on a bench in the courtyard, weeping, while she waited for word from the doctors. Finally it came: the baby had been stillborn, but Sarah lived. "I want to express my deepest appreciation of Hadassah Hospital Beersheba," Golda cabled the Hadassah organization in New York, crediting the hospital staff with saving her daughter's life. Always the government official, she added, "I wonder whether even you realize what your hospital there means for the lives and welfare of all in the settlements of the Negev," her way of encouraging Hadassah to maintain that clinic far from the country's center.

Golda's own health was none too good. Her gallbladder attacks recurred, with severe pain, and the old migraine headaches plagued her. Her weight yo-yoed, sometimes low enough to make her appear almost svelte, at other times climbing high. She returned from one of her American trips with a detailed diet plan of just twelve hundred calories a day and strict instructions not to eat "nuts, olives, olive oil, chocolate and cocoa," foods rationed in Israel but not in the United States, where she spent so much time. "She loved chocolate ice cream," recalled Harry Beale, who traveled with her on many fund-raising trips in America. No matter how late at night, she would insist on finding an open coffee shop where she could eat ice cream, drink coffee, smoke her cigarettes, and talk to her traveling companions, frequently into the early morning hours. Hers was not a life conducive to disciplined dieting.

When she found a free moment in the States, she would squeeze in some shopping for personal and household necessities hard to find in Israel. One of her shopping lists included a "house dress" for Sarah, shirts for Zecharia, a shower curtain, Kleenex, furniture polish, white shoe polish, and "corset strings" and garters for herself. At least for official events, Golda, like most women of the period, wore a corset that cinched in her stomach and held up her stockings. Around this time, she began having orthopedic shoes made at a specialty shoe shop, M. Braverman & Sons on Third Avenue and East Seventy-Eighth Street in New York City. Similar-looking mid-heel shoes with laces worn by women in the Israeli army would become known as "Golda shoes."

ON HER CURRENT American trips, she had a new goal to energize her: selling Israel government bonds to American Jews, a more satisfying assignment than asking them for outright contributions. Many Jews in the United States had become irritated with the constant appeals for donations pitched at them from Israel. Added to that, America's involvement in a new war in Korea made businesspeople anxious and wary about doling out their money. The kernel of the bonds idea came from a deal she, Eliezer Kaplan, and others had worked out with David Dubinsky, head of the International Ladies' Garment Workers' Union, for a low-cost housing venture, the Amun-Israeli Housing Corporation. It would be financed by selling bonds backed by the Israeli government; to get it going, the union bought the first million dollars' worth of bonds.

The Israel Bonds concept as a national money raiser was simple: the state would sell government bonds, similar to U.S. saving bonds, and, when they came due, repay them with interest. Besides adding foreign currency to the government's coffers, the bonds offered a way for Israel to extricate itself from its total dependency on philanthropy. "We want to free ourselves of these kind and generous shackles," Golda announced. The UJA, through which Golda had raised millions for Israel, fought the plan tooth and nail, as did other charitable organizations. As far as they were concerned, the bonds program was just another form of competition for the hard-won American Jewish dollar. But Golda's close friend Henry Montor sided with her. He gave up his position as executive director of the UJA and became head of the bonds enterprise, persuading Henry Morgenthau Jr., UJA's president, to join him.

Golda was in constant touch with Montor. He organized her trips to the United States and wrote to her regularly when they were apart, single-spaced, multipage, obsessive letters about everyone and everything in the Zionist world. In his brash manner, he didn't hesitate to knock people whom he regarded as hurting Israel or his fund-raising activities. He referred mockingly to the towering American rabbi Abba Hillel Silver as "the Pope." He distrusted Israel's ambassador to Washington, Abba Eban, "with the shiny black hair, the little round face, and

With Eleanor Roosevelt in 1960. Roosevelt described Golda to a friend as "a woman of great strength & calm." They would get together for tea whenever Golda was in America. *(Franklin D. Roosevelt Presidential Library and Museum, Hyde Park, New York)*

With President John F. Kennedy in Palm Beach, December 1962. The United States had a "special relationship" with Israel in the Middle East, he told her, "really comparable only to its relationship with Britain." No previous president had spoken that way to an Israeli leader. *(White House Photographs, John F. Kennedy Presidential Library and Museum, Boston)*

With Moshe Dayan, sometime in the 1960s. The charismatic hero of the 1967 Six-Day War later served as minister of defense in Golda's government. They had a complex relationship, respecting—but not completely trusting—each other. *(Courtesy of Carolyn Hessel)*

Dancing with Momolu Dukuly, the foreign minister of Liberia, at a reception during her first trip to West Africa in November 1958. Providing agricultural and technical aid to the emerging nations of Africa became one of her primary goals as foreign minister. *(Government Press Office, State of Israel)*

Golda's trips to Africa as foreign minister in the 1960s often included doing a spirited hora with local African women. *(Government Press Office, State of Israel)*

When Golda visited the Western Wall in Jerusalem's Old City shortly after the Six-Day War, a paratrooper spontaneously embraced her, both of them overcome with emotion at Israel's victory. A note she squeezed into a crevice said, simply, *shalom*, peace. *(Government Press Office, State of Israel)*

When she was elected the Labor Party's candidate for prime minister on March 7, 1969, Golda sobbed quietly in her seat. "I always assumed a position with awe and trepidation, and endless doubts as to whether I was worthy of it," she said in her acceptance speech. *(Government Press Office, State of Israel)*

Prime Minister Meir, Zalman Shazar (who had become Israel's third president in 1963), Deputy Prime Minister Yigal Allon, and Interior Minister Moses Haim Shapira celebrate the swearing-in of the members of Israel's fourteenth government, March 17, 1969. *(Photograph by Fritz Cohen, Government Press Office, State of Israel)*

Saluting as she reviews an Israel Defense Forces color guard, Independence Day, 1969. The "boys," she said of the IDF, are the "glory of humankind." *(Government Press Office, State of Israel)*

Meeting with representatives from Israel's Muslim and Christian communities, April 1969. Her solution for the Arabs living on the West Bank was that most of the area be federated with Jordan, and that would comprise a Palestinian state. The Jordanians didn't accept the idea of Israel retaining any part of the West Bank, and Palestinian leaders did not accept the "Jordanian option." *(Photograph by Fritz Cohen, Government Press Office, State of Israel)*

With Pope Paul VI at the Vatican, January 1973. The first Israeli prime minister invited to have an audience with the pope, she responded to his criticisms of Israel by reminding him of the pogroms Jews suffered when they did not have a state. *(Government Press Office, State of Israel)*

With President Richard Nixon at the White House, September 1969. As soon as the press left the room, Nixon recalled, she "crossed her leg, lit a cigarette," and asked him what he was going to do about the planes Israel needed. From then on, they "had a very good relationship." *(Photograph by Moshe Milner, Government Press Office, State of Israel)*

With Yitzhak Rabin, then Israel's ambassador to the United States; Henry Kissinger, then Richard Nixon's national security adviser; and Leah Rabin, at the ambassador's residence in Washington, D.C., February 1973. Rabin and Kissinger would communicate directly, which violated protocol and infuriated Minister of Foreign Affairs Abba Eban. *(Photograph by Moshe Milner, Government Press Office, State of Israel)*

With Margaret Thatcher, then head of the United Kingdom's Conservative Party, during Thatcher's visit to Israel in March 1976. When a reporter asked Britain's "iron lady" whether she had learned anything from Golda about being a woman prime minister, she snapped back that they had more important issues to discuss. *(Photograph by Moshe Milner, Government Press Office, State of Israel)*

But can she type?

This poster, circa 1970, became an icon for women's groups throughout the United States. Ironically, Golda refused to call herself a feminist or identify with the women's rights movement in Israel. *(National Organization for Women, Seattle–King County Chapter/Prints and Photographs Division, Library of Congress)*

CBS makeup artist Sara Buchman helps Golda arrange her hair just prior to an appearance on *Face the Nation* in the 1970s. When Buchman asked if she wanted makeup, Golda replied, "No—I'm a realist." *(Courtesy of Judith Buchman-Ziv)*

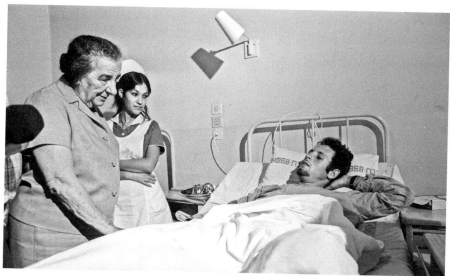

Visiting soldiers wounded in the 1973 Yom Kippur War. Even though she had received assurances from her generals that Egypt and Syria had no intention of attacking Israel, Golda blamed herself for not following her intuition and fully mobilizing the IDF, including the reserves. The war's casualties included more than 2,500 dead and more than 9,000 wounded. *(Photograph by Herman Chanania, Government Press Office, State of Israel)*

On October 29, 1973, just days after the cease-fire, Golda helicoptered to the western bank of the Suez Canal to hear about the war firsthand from IDF commanders and their troops. With her were her close adviser Israel Galili *(left, in white shirt)* and Minister of Defense Moshe Dayan *(right, with cap)*. Soldiers spoke of having to fight off overpowering enemy forces. *(Photograph by Yehuda Tzion, Government Press Office, State of Israel)*

With Egyptian president Anwar Sadat and Shimon Peres at the Knesset during Sadat's groundbreaking trip to Israel, November 1977. "I want to live to see that day that peace reigns between you and us," she said to him. *(Photograph by Yaakov Saar, Government Press Office, State of Israel)*

Receiving an honorary degree from Brandeis University, March 1973. Over the years, the woman who never finished college received many honorary degrees and awards. *(Photograph by Moshe Milner, Government Press Office, State of Israel)*

the chubby hands." Hadassah's president, Rose Halprin, was "rather a strange person." But he adored Golda. Whenever he felt discouraged, "the battles" she had "carried—and lost, without despairing"—inspired him to keep going.

Together, Golda and Montor pushed forcefully for the bonds program at a conference Ben-Gurion convened at the King David Hotel in Jerusalem on September 3, 1950. The prime minister invited fifty Jewish leaders, most from the United States and a few from Britain and South Africa, to discuss Israel's monetary needs. After three days of meetings, at which Montor, "usually ice cold and tightly reined in, exploded" at those who feared a bond drive, a participant wrote, and Golda Meyerson assured everyone that Israel would "achieve prosperity and repay any loans," the conference adopted a $1.5 billion fund-raising program. It included UJA gifts, private investments, and, at its center, the new borrowing mechanism, Israel Bonds.

The next month, Golda helped introduce the billion-dollar program to American Jews at the Statler Hotel in Washington. A record number of more than eleven hundred delegates attended this conference, which had "the longest dais of dignitaries ever seen by mortal man," the journalist Hal Lehrman wrote. Golda's "uplifting" talk, better than most, offered as security for repaying the loan the "thousands and thousands of children of Israel, the children of the old-timers and the little Yemenite children and Iraqi children and the Rumanian children," all growing up proud and free.

Ben-Gurion officially launched the bonds drive on May 10, 1951, at a gigantic rally in New York's Madison Square Garden, organized by Montor. Golda, who had arrived in the States a few weeks earlier, carried the message from community to community. The investment people made in Israel Bonds, she predicted, would finance a huge economic expansion in that country, creating a "20th century industrial revolution" there that would benefit everyone. In an effort to please her in her hard work, Israel Bonds leaders in Pittsburgh sought out people who could speak to her in Hebrew. Standing at the lectern afterward, she looked at the audience in mock seriousness. "Doesn't *anyone* here speak English?" she asked, to a roar of laughter.

On Friday, May 18, 1951, she appeared in New Jersey as the guest of the B. Manischewitz Company, makers of matzo, wine, and other kosher products. She gave no indication as she spoke of the anxiety that gripped her. She had received a telegram earlier in the day notifying her that David Remez had suffered a heart attack and was in Jerusalem's Hadassah Hospital. She had immediately cabled back asking to be kept informed about his health. The next day, at two in the morning Israel time, he suddenly took a turn for the worse and within moments passed away. Notified in New York of his death, Abba Eban broke the news to Golda and Ben-Gurion, who was still on his bonds tour.

With money in short supply and no official reason for her to return to Israel, Golda did not attend Remez's funeral, which brought out thousands of Israelis. But she had suffered a grievous loss. Remez had guided her career in its beginnings, and they had been friends and lovers for more than two decades. She never spoke publicly about their relationship. The most she allowed herself were the words that appear in her autobiography: that she and Remez saw a great deal of each other and had much in common and that he was one of the few colleagues with whom she discussed personal matters. And that she continued to miss him "to this day."

She was in Chicago when she received word that Morris Meyerson had died on Friday, May 25. In an eerie twist of fate, his death came on the final day of the seven-day shiva ritual for David Remez; she had lost the two men within a week of each other. Morris also died of a heart attack, and in another irony it happened in Golda's home. Menahem's mother-in-law, Sara Lutsky, had recently moved to Israel and was living in Golda's Tel Aviv apartment while Golda was away. Friendly with the Lutskys, Morris came to visit her on occasion. That day he felt ill, lay down to rest after lunch, and never awoke. He was fifty-seven years old.

Golda arranged to have the funeral delayed until she reached home. She, Menahem, and Menahem's wife, Chana, boarded an El Al plane in New York late Saturday night, when she promptly fainted and had to be given oxygen. Morris's death, so soon after that of Remez, crushed her. On top of that, she had fallen during a trip to St. Louis and dislocated her shoulder, which was causing her pain. Sarah, who, with Zecharia, drove up from the Negev through a thick fog to meet her mother at the airport, remembered her as "just miserable" that night.

"It was a great moment of sorrow to me," Golda was to say. "It was a feeling that somebody who was very close to me, and was the father of my children, and who was very sad the last years of his life" had died. She had not "for one moment lost a deep feeling of appreciation and friendship and respect" for him, she also said, and never veered from that line, even though she'd had no contact with Morris in those last, sad years of his life.

THOUGH GOLDA WAS KNOWN to cry easily and actually to love tear-jerker movies, she did not shed tears in public about her most personal hurts. After the deaths of Remez and Morris, she threw herself into her duties more tirelessly than ever. Since beginning her ministry, she had traveled from one end of Israel to the other, planting the first trees in Eilat, inspecting public works in Haifa, visiting Lod and Ramla, and distributing food in the *ma'abarot* everywhere. She picked up those travels again, and with a new election at hand in the summer of 1951 she also became a workhorse for her party.

The first coalition government had collapsed in February under the weight of a conflict between the secular and the religious parties about education in the *ma'abarot*. From the first, religious tensions had swirled around the new immigrants. In one instance, Golda was called in when army personnel at the Jassir *ma'abara* thoughtlessly cut off the side locks and beards of Yemenite immigrants and ordered women to strip for general disinfection. She ordered that soldiers be educated about Yemenite sensibilities and that female doctors deal with health issues among women. The government dispute about education concerned the religious parties' insistence on conducting their own religious classes in the camps, with exclusive responsibility for Yemenite education. Ben-Gurion, who advocated a unified state education system, refused their demands. When religious representatives in his cabinet voted against him, he resigned and dissolved the government. Elections were scheduled for July 30, 1951.

Campaigning became fierce, pitting the General Zionists against Mapai. "Let us live in this land," the General Zionist slogan beckoned, promising a better life than the austerity program Labor offered. In contrast, Golda and her colleagues made immigration the center of their platform. "Mapai does not promise you an easy life after July 30," she told voters. "On the contrary, it promises to bring many more Jews to this land, and the little that we have here we will divide equally among us." Mapai won, validating Golda's unbudging stand on immigration.

The immigrant flow slowed for a time in early 1952, partly because word of the hardships in Israel dampened people's zeal for that land, but also because the government had begun to put some restrictions on accepting the very sick and disabled. With the slowdown, Golda had a chance to catch her breath a little and concentrate on the myriad programs on her plate. Her one ministry encompassed responsibilities that would later be divided among several—housing, public works, labor legislation, and social insurance among them. Each division in her department had its own staff. Golda created a collegial atmosphere throughout the office so that staff members freely exchanged ideas with each other and her. She also encouraged people to go into the field, as she did, to meet immigrants in the camps or laborers at work and report on their findings. Sitting at her desk, a cigarette in the nicotine-stained fingers of her left hand, she listened intently to every idea, rarely taking a note. "Golda was not a reader or writer. Everything was through the ears," said David Harman, a family friend. In her office as in other meetings, only after listening and discussing would she make up her mind, almost never to be changed.

As a boss, she could be generous and motherly. When the father of one of her secretaries took ill, she chided the young woman for not notifying her. "How can we work together when you know so much about my life and you don't even tell me about your father?" she said, as though they had equal status. She appeared at the father's hospital bedside the next morning, winning the woman's lifelong adoration. She could also be cruel and unforgiving, especially when she decided an aide didn't care enough about an assignment. "Golda was impatient with stupidity and lack of preparation," said Zena Harman, who later became a Knesset member. "If she liked you, she liked you very much. If she didn't like you, God help you!"

THE HOUSING DIVISION, one of the most important in Golda's ministry, had the task of moving immigrants out of the *ma'abarot* into permanent housing. In keeping with a government decision to disperse the population, Golda tried to spread the new housing outward, into "development towns" and agricultural settlements around the country. Mapai's slogan, "from the town to the village," called on people to move away from large urban centers into small villages made up of several settlements. Not everyone agreed with that philosophy. Some newcomers refused to leave their *ma'abarot*, having found employment in nearby towns. Critics attacked Golda for pushing the immigrants into isolated areas with no infrastructure. "It's stupid, I told her," recalled the political commentator Zvi Kesse. "No good doctor, no good engineer, no good teacher, will come there. We are a state now, not a colony. We don't need to settle in distant places." But for her and other party leaders, building up settlements not only provided new areas for immigrant housing; it also fulfilled the Zionist ideal of continually developing the land.

She involved herself in the smallest details of the houses being erected, becoming the dread of contractors and engineers as she went about inspecting doors, windows, closets, room layouts, everything. If she thought a wall in a model house blocked the flow of space, she ordered it taken down. When she couldn't see through a kitchen window because it was placed too high, she decreed that it be lowered. ("A woman stands in the kitchen five hours cooking, and you are forcing her to see the wall and not the Kinneret?" she reprimanded the contractor.) In the new desert town of Dimona, she saw two apartment houses built close to each other, with no park or playground between them, and demanded to know how that had happened. When the architects told her it was the cheapest way to build, she immediately informed Levi Eshkol, who had become finance minister, that he would have to avoid such mistakes in the future. In the northern development town of Kiryat Shmona, she noticed that the lowest step in houses under construction was too high for a child or elderly person and ordered another step added. She took a firm stand against Jewish Agency engineers who argued that immigrants from Yemen and North Africa did not need indoor showers and toilets, because they never before had them. Once, inspecting the new home of a Yemenite family with some of those engineers, she saw a cooking pot placed in the toilet. "We told you so," the engineers gloated. Golda held her ground, and all houses built needed indoor bathrooms with flush toilets.

"These neighborhoods will not turn into slums," she vowed at a Knesset session. Schools, kindergartens, infirmaries, assembly halls, and the like would be built near new housing projects so that communities could grow and flourish. In the sad reality, poorly built with cheap materials, most of the buildings Golda hovered over so caringly did turn into slum dwellings, and the neighborhoods went down with them. Twenty years later, some of Prime Minister Meir's most ferocious opponents arose from those slum areas and from the development towns.

Building roads became another of Golda's passions, part of a vast program of public works. When economists argued that road building was too expensive, she sneered at them. "This has cost a lot of money. But I don't know what was more expensive: the months when tens of thousands of Jews sat in the camps and did nothing, and we provided them with food, clothing, and all their needs, or when by a tremendous upheaval and effort we took them out of the camps and put them to work." When the same experts maintained that rather than building roads, the country needed to invest in productive industries, she showed why they erred. "If we have to choose between making a road and vegetable growing—certainly vegetables!" she said. "If we have to choose between a road and clearing land for cultivation—clearing land, definitely! If we have to choose between a road and planting new orange groves—no question new orange groves! But the upshot is that we haven't one or the other." Much productive work was still in the planning stage, and with "even the finest paper plans, you can't feed people and support children."

Because of Golda, a visitor traveling through Israel in the early 1950s would see outdoor laborers at work everywhere, blasting through mountains, digging up the ground, clearing rocks, and laying asphalt as they broadened the road between Tel Aviv and the Galilee, created new roads to the south, repaired the highway to Jerusalem, opened arteries between one settlement and another. "If we decide to establish a new settlement in the Negev," Golda said, "we must first build the roads. First you pave a road, and only then can you settle immigrants on both sides of the road." And she made a special effort to extend the roads to communities of Arabs, who still lived under military rule and struggled to find a place for themselves in the new state.

Of her many activities during those years as labor minister—which she later labeled her "seven good years"—Golda gained the most satisfaction from wide-ranging social legislation she introduced and put into effect. In August 1950, she presented the nation's first labor laws to the Knesset. Unlike her usual talks without notes, in her more formal parliamentary addresses she generally read from a text prepared by her staff. When her legal adviser opened one of her speeches with a quotation from the great Jewish scholar Maimonides, she glared at him. "Have pity on me and get rid of that immediately," she commanded in Yiddish. "I never in my life studied Maimonides . . . Don't make me out to be what I am not." Yet in introducing the labor laws, she went back into history and spoke of their origins in the concerns of early Jewish teachings "for the worker—his rest, his wages, the conditions of his work." The new laws limited the workday to eight hours, mandated a day off every week, and guaranteed a paid vacation to working people. Many of the laws were based on long-standing Histadrut practices, and many reflected current modes in the West. But some, such as a paid vacation, Golda proudly emphasized, proved the young State of Israel more progressive than even the venerable Great Britain, which did not at that time have such a law.

The showpiece of Golda's proposed legislation was the national insurance plan, a social security system that she presented to the Knesset in stages, beginning in February 1952. Again, she mined Jewish history, citing the prophets who fought "for the cause of the poor and the widowed." In keeping with that, the first steps in the plan called for widows' and orphans' benefits, old-age pensions, industrial accident insurance, and maternity protection. Later she would introduce health and unemployment insurance, disability laws, and many other aspects of social insurance. Eshkol and other treasury people argued that the state was too burdened with other pressing problems to undertake the momentous expenses involved in the program. Golda fought them and won, giving Israel one of the world's most advanced social security systems of the time and one that remained the basis for all its later social laws.

The National Insurance Act became law in April 1954. A year later, on its first anniversary, Golda addressed the nation over the radio. She spoke of how the social security program had helped fulfill the socialist dreams of the pioneers for "a system based on justice and fraternity, for . . . a state where there would be no one neglected, no widows and orphans hungry for bread or people cast out in their old age."

Many of the new laws concerned women at work and in their family lives, some more enlightened than existing laws in the United States. A woman giving birth in Israel received six days of state-paid hospitalization, with 75 percent of the cost of the birth covered. A working mother enjoyed a paid maternity leave of twelve weeks, and when she returned to work, she was permitted an hour off a day for nursing her child, with no pay loss. To encourage Arab and Jewish women to have their babies in the hospital and not at home—a medically risky practice—the government offered monetary grants for hospital deliveries. With much fanfare and emotion, Golda gave the first grant to a Jewish child born in Hadassah Hospital on April 1, 1954, the day the National Insurance Act went into effect. As it happened, the child was the fourth girl born into a Sephardic family. As photographers snapped pictures and movie cameras rolled, the father struggled to muster enthusiasm for another daughter, when he lacked even one son. Golda had not been able to locate an Arab child born in a hospital that day, but shortly afterward she went to Nazareth to hand a check to the first Arab woman to give birth in the hospital after the law began operating. She felt more excited by the event than the woman herself, she commented.

Other laws protected working women by forbidding most forms of night work, from 11:00 p.m. until 6:00 a.m. The Labor Ministry walked a thin line, Golda explained. It wanted to protect women, yet it did not want to prevent them from finding work. "The greatest enemy of the good is the very good," she said, quoting Remez. Even so, some feminists later objected that the laws overprotected. "It was an old-fashioned attitude," said the activist Tamar Eshel. "It kept women down and they couldn't compete for jobs. The men didn't want them in the factory, because they couldn't take turns on the night shift." Those restrictive laws eventually disappeared.

Golda wanted Arab women as well as Jewish to benefit from the social security laws. She urged delegations of Arab women with whom she met to unite and stand up for their rights within their own communities, assuring them that the Labor Ministry would treat Arab women equally with Jewish ones. At the opening of a handicraft school in Jaffa, she admired the weaving, dyeing, and knitting young girls had learned to do, and promised full support of her ministry for the school. In an incident she liked to relate, a young Arab woman from a village on a hillside in the lower Galilee told her that a new road her crews had built for the village helped the men but not the women. She hoped the labor minister could ease the burden "of the heads of our women" who had to carry heavy jars of water on their heads up the road from a well below. Golda had a water pipeline installed that brought running water to the village.

It was in connection with a woman's issue that Golda wrangled with the ultra-Orthodox establishment in a way neither she nor anyone in the government had before. The issue was women's conscription in the army and the related subject of national service for Orthodox young women. During the early days of the government, Ben-Gurion made several concessions to the Orthodox rabbinate, including giving it control over marriage and divorce. He aimed to avoid fractious fighting with religious groups when so many other problems plagued the state. He also needed Orthodox support to form his first coalition government. After heated debate, the First Knesset voted to draft women into military service but agreed to exempt Orthodox women. The issue came up again in 1951 during the election campaign for the Second Knesset. There had been abuses of the system—girls pretending to be Orthodox to wiggle out of service—and indignation by the rest of the population about Orthodox privileges.

As they had from the start, ultra-Orthodox rabbis railed against the idea of religious women serving in any capacity and portrayed the army in such degrading terms that Golda went on the attack. Is an army camp so despicable that a modest, delicate girl didn't dare stand within four feet of it? And, if it is so morally corrupt, why do religious parents allow their sons to serve? She also warned that people deeply resented the extreme Orthodox. "In this land there are many young people and not so young who are not religious," she said. "If you think you are going to force your beliefs on them—you are expecting the impossible."

In the spring of 1953, after consulting with moderate Orthodox groups, she introduced a national service bill designed for women exempted from military duties. Instead of going to the army, these young women would devote their service to working in schools and nurseries, helping the immigrants, assisting in the health clinics, and the like. When debates on the bill opened in the Knesset, the ultra-Orthodox world went wild. The clamor that spread from the Mea Shearim quarter in Jerusalem to the streets of Brooklyn, New York, gave the impression that Orthodox girls were being yanked away from their homes to be raped and defiled. Crowds of shrieking men and women marched on the Knesset, and posters plastered on the walls warned parents to protect their daughters from the iniquities being visited upon them.

Golda was incensed. "You will not terrorize a legislative body with demonstrations of hysterical women or by mob violence," she berated the extreme Orthodox members of the Knesset. And she lashed out in disgust at the rabbis who led the verbal attacks on the army: "I know of no enemy of Israel . . . who would be capable of making the kind of statements concerning tens of thousands of sons and daughters of the State of Israel as have been made by residents of Israel, people who profess to be spiritual leaders of the people." The Knesset passed the national service act Golda had presented, but it was never implemented. With time, national service became a voluntary commitment for Orthodox young women who chose to fulfill it. Few remembered that technically the law required it.

THE BITTEREST CONTROVERSY OF ALL centered on the question of whether to seek reparations from Germany for its atrocities against the Jews during the Holocaust. Israel continued to need massive sums of money to absorb immigrants and build up the state, and no matter how many millions Golda raised in her forays to America, it was not nearly enough. As foreign minister, Moshe Sharett led in urging that Israel negotiate with the German Federal Republic (West Germany) for compensation for the wartime devastation of Jewish lives and property.

In this, he had the full support of Ben-Gurion and the help of Nahum Goldmann, head of the World Jewish Congress. For the rest of Israel, with its hundreds of thousands of Holocaust survivors, and for much of world Jewry, direct contacts with the country that murdered six million Jews seemed like nothing less than making a deal with the devil. Since the end of World War II, Israel had boycotted Germany and banished all things German from the land.

When the concept of negotiating directly with Germany first surfaced, Golda opposed it. She had no qualms about taking money the "cursed" land owed the Jewish people, but the thought of negotiating face-to-face with anyone in that land revolted her. "It is inconceivable that a State of Israel delegation sit in a German government ministry and speak with German government representatives," she declared. She suggested instead that Israel submit its claim to the four powers occupying Germany—the United States, Great Britain, France, and the Soviet Union—and have them handle the matter on its behalf. The cabinet agreed to that proposal, and the government sent a formal note to the four on March 12, 1951. Three of them turned down the request, citing their own financial issues with Germany. The Soviets never responded.

Step by step the nation began moving closer to direct negotiations. In April 1951, at a secret meeting in Paris with Jewish representatives, Chancellor Konrad Adenauer of West Germany agreed to acknowledge the crimes Germany had committed against the Jewish people and to accept Israel's claim of $1.5 billion as the basis for negotiations. In December, he signed a letter to that effect. Sharett and Ben-Gurion now had to present the idea of direct negotiations to the cabinet and the Knesset, and with that to the nation.

As word of the plan leaked out, emotions in the country flared. In the Knesset, the far-left Mapam Party joined with the far-right Herut, headed by Menachem Begin, in fiercely opposing the talks. With its leanings toward Communism, Mapam disapproved of the Western powers' growing rehabilitation of West Germany; Begin had a visceral hatred of Germany, which he labeled Amalek, the ancient and perpetual biblical enemy of the Jewish people.

Golda was torn between her antipathy to Germany and her appreciation—perhaps better than anybody's—of the state's need for funds. Gradually, she came to accept negotiations between Israel and Germany, but always with caveats and misgivings. "I realize that we must enter direct negotiations," she allowed during a government debate in the fall of 1951. Still, "we must be careful in our manner of speech with them." It should "not be that used when meeting with friendly countries." But what if the negotiators had been decent people all along? the moderate Levi Eshkol asked. "It is immaterial," she responded. "A German is a German."

At a Mapai meeting, where she felt more comfortable speaking freely, she elaborated on that thought. "I hold a racist view," she said without shame. "As far as I am concerned, all Germans are by definition Nazis; only later will I be prepared to find out whether this or that individual German is guiltless." To make her point, she recalled the Socialist International conference in Zurich in 1947, when she and the Mapai mission she headed had blocked the acceptance of Kurt Schumacher and his German Social Democratic Party into the organization. Even though he had fought against the Nazis and been in a concentration camp, she was not yet prepared, she said, "to divide the Germans into 'good' and 'bad.'" For the present, "they are all one and the same." She could accept the practical necessity of seeking reparations. In doing so, however, Israel needed to figuratively hold its nose while collecting "a detestable, repelling debt" from the "hands of murderers."

With the vote in the Knesset approaching, feelings reached a bursting point. Newspaper columnists lobbed invectives against Mapai, antireparations rallies filled the streets, and the threat of barely contained violence shadowed government proceedings. Before final debates began on January 7, 1952, Menachem Begin and his Herut followers staged a massive demonstration in Jerusalem's Zion Square, close to the Knesset, then housed on King George Street. Standing in a cold drizzle, thousands of protesters heard Begin denounce Ben-Gurion, "that maniac who is now Prime Minister," and vow, with screaming emotion, that "all of us are ready to give up our lives" to go to concentration camps or torture chambers to stop negotiations with Germany. As Begin made his way to the Knesset, the crowd surged after him, stoning the Knesset building and smashing windows while trying to get inside. For more than two hours, the police, armed with shields, batons, and teargas, struggled to contain the rioters. By the time the violence ended, ninety-two policemen and thirty-six civilians had been injured, cars were overturned, fires burned, and shattered glass lay everywhere.

Inside, speakers could hear the shrieking sirens of the Red Magen David mingling with the wails of police cars and the shouts of the mobs. Some Knesset members were wounded by the flying stones and shattered glass. Still, the speeches went on, including a long, raging one by Begin. Talks continued for two more days, while the rioting outside gradually subsided. When Golda stood up to speak, she first thanked the police for defending the Knesset. Then she repeated her condemnation of all Germans—every one of them, East or West, guilty, she said. Yet "reparations are our due," and Israel must receive them. A strong and independent nation, it would make its claims not by asking for favors but as "a victorious people with a defeated one." Israel's negotiators would deal with Germany not for the sake of friendship or forgetting but so "that we can strengthen ourselves, so that we may live."

On January 9, by a vote of 61 to 50, the Knesset accepted the government's proposal to negotiate with Germany on the matter of reparations. Golda voted with the majority.

SOME SIX MONTHS AFTER she became Israel's first minister of labor, Golda Meyerson received an award from the Women's National Institute naming her an "outstanding woman of the year." She shared the award with four other women from around the world, among them India's Madame Pandit, whom she had met in Moscow. Busy with the first wave of immigrants in Israel, Golda was not present at the rites held in New York on November 11, 1949. She received her gold medallion at a festive Tel Aviv ceremony attended by the sculptor Hana Orloff and other noted Israeli women and men. Dressed in her perennial black suit and white blouse, she spoke in her acceptance talk about gaining the greatest satisfaction from feeling she had done her best at whatever job she undertook. She meant it. Hard work had become her trademark and her passageway to ever more responsibility and control in the party and the country.

18

The Politician

R ussia again. Golda's workload as labor minister pulled her in many directions—one of them backward. As demanding as her current responsibilities were, she could not put her experiences as minister to Russia completely behind her.

She had left Moscow in 1949 knowing that fear enveloped the Jewish community. She had received reports about the disappearance of prominent Jewish writers and members of the Jewish Anti-Fascist Committee and like others assumed they had been arrested and deported. She would not know until 1955 that they had been tried and murdered in the cellar of the Lubianka Prison in the summer of 1952. Nevertheless, she knew that there was too much at stake to criticize the Soviet Union openly at this time. For one thing, she did not want to put the Jews in that land in greater danger. Then she had to be careful not to jeopardize Israel's standing with the Soviet satellite countries that sold it arms. Before departing from Russia, she had met with the minister of foreign affairs, Andrei Vyshinski, and assured him that although Israel had strong links to American Jews, it planned to maintain a neutral position between East and West.

Inside Israel, where the left-leaning Mapam Party bitterly attacked the centrist Mapai leaders, she found it especially hard not to speak out about her months in Moscow. Mapam, said its chief, Yaakov Hazan, was a "typical revolutionary" party as opposed to the bourgeois, "opportunistic" Mapai. The majority of elite soldiers who had served in the Palmach supported Mapam, as did most kibbutz members. Downplaying reports about the mistreatment of Jews, these people viewed the Soviet Union as the "world of tomorrow," when Communism would overtake the reactionary forces of capitalism, poverty would be eliminated, and workers would rule society. Whereas in the United States fear of Communism reached almost paranoid proportions with the rise of Senator

Joseph R. McCarthy, in Israel Communist ideology continued to dominate the thinking of large swaths of people, especially the young. In that environment, Mapam leaders blamed the Mapai government and not the Russians for growing tensions between the two countries.

Those tensions soared with two events that shocked Mapam and led Golda and her Mapai comrades to criticize the Soviets openly. The first happened in November 1952, when Rudolf Slansky, the Jewish former secretary-general of the Czechoslovak Communist Party, was brought to trial in Prague, along with thirteen other high-ranking officials, eleven of them Jewish. Accused of espionage, treason, and encouraging the "subversive activities of Zionism," eleven of the defendants were executed, including Slansky, and the other three given life sentences. An Israeli left-wing leader, Mordechai Oren, arrested earlier in Czechoslovakia, was made to testify against the accused, rattling his Mapam colleagues in Israel.

The second event, the "Doctors' Plot," had an even more sinister story line. Under Stalin's orders, nine prominent Soviet physicians, six of them Jewish, were arrested and accused of plotting to kill the country's top military commanders and key leaders through false diagnoses and bad treatment. They were also charged with having caused the death of Andrei Zhdanov, the high Communist official whose funeral Golda and her group drove past when they arrived in Moscow in 1948. Announced in *Pravda* on January 13, 1953, the accusations also tied the doctors in a diabolical manner to the Joint Distribution Committee and other "Jewish espionage" organizations. Stalin had declared all-out war on the Jews.

As a stunned Israeli and world media began searching for the source of this new vendetta, some thought to look back toward Golda Meyerson and the wild excitement with which Jews in Russia had greeted her in 1948. Ten days after the Doctors' Plot was "exposed," the weekend edition of *Davar* carried on its cover the iconic photograph of Golda in her black hat mobbed by thousands of people outside the Choral Synagogue on the High Holidays. Although the photograph had been sold underground in Russia for years, *Davar* proudly announced its first appearance in print in any newspaper. The paper had acquired it from the photographer himself, David Havkin, who had escaped from the Soviet Union and lived in Italy. Beneath the picture, boldfaced words cried, "Let My People Go," tying Golda at the synagogue to Soviet repression and the beginnings of a campaign to free Soviet Jews. More pointedly, a few days later, *Maariv* ran the headline "Meyerson Refuses to Reveal the Secret," with a story quoting Sefton Delmer, a well-known foreign correspondent for the London *Daily Express*. Delmer had tried to get Golda to reminisce for the *Express* about her experiences as minister to Moscow. She declined, he wrote, and he understood that she would never forgive herself if something she said hurt a single Jew behind the Iron Curtain. Nevertheless, he believed she held the key to the anti-Semitic campaign the Kremlin had unleashed. As Delmer saw it, Stalin drew two conclusions from Golda's ministry and the demonstrations for her: first, that despite Israel's avowals of neutrality, it essentially belonged to the West, and, second, that the vast numbers who appeared raised doubts about the loyalty of the Jews to the Soviet Union. He acted on those conclusions, which fed into his long-standing anti-Jewishness and growing desire to move closer to the Arab world.

After four years of stubborn silence about her visit to the synagogue on Arkhipov Street, Golda had to face its rediscovery in the press and the widespread assumption that it had led in some way to Stalin's current terror. For someone who cared as deeply as she did about Russia's Jews, the implication in the newspapers that she personally bore responsibility for the Kremlin's rampage against them was like a dagger to her heart. Hurt and angry, she asked Nechemia Levanon, at the Israeli embassy in Moscow, to investigate the fate of the people who had thronged around her outside the synagogue. He reported that no proof could be found that those people had been arrested and deported. In truth, such arrests and deportations *did* take place, but the Soviets masked their motives by officially charging the people they seized with economic offenses or the all-purpose crime of "cosmopolitanism." Levanon's assurance gave Golda some relief, but she never completely shook off a sense of guilt the accusations aroused.

Under the guise of an embassy staff member, Nechemia Levanon did secret work in Moscow, spreading educational materials about Israel and Judaism to Jews behind the Iron Curtain and ultimately trying to get them out. His assignment grew from a meeting about Jews in Communist lands that he and a small group of former Soviet Jews held with the Mossad's chief, Isser Harel, and Shaul Avigur, who had smuggled thousands of Jews into Palestine under the British mandate. Authorized by Ben-Gurion, this group established a bureau in Tel Aviv for Soviet Jewish affairs, with vague official duties and widespread covert ones. Although it was generally known as Lishkat Hakesher, the Liaison Bureau, or simply Lishka, the Bureau, those on the inside referred to it as the "office without a name," or, under their breaths with the code name Nativ, path. Housed in the same building as the Foreign Office, it supposedly reported to that minister, but it actually had direct accountability to the prime minister. Avigur headed the entire bureau; Levanon served at the Moscow embassy and later in Washington. Golda's name does not appear in the earliest accounts of this clandestine organization, yet people closely connected with the Soviet Jewish movement have verified her involvement from the start.

Nativ functioned as Israel's behind-the-scenes answer to Soviet anti-Semitism. Responding openly as a state to that government's latest anti-Jewish accusations was a more difficult task. Israeli leaders were not sure what motivated the Russians. "I don't even know whether what they did . . . came from hatred," Golda said at a Mapai meeting. "When Stalin made a pact with Hitler it wasn't because he loved Hitler so much, but because he had some plan. That's how it is now, probably some plan connected to the Arabs . . . And no matter what we do, we're not going to be able to influence them."

The quandary deepened on February 9, when a small bomb was hurled at the Soviet legation office in Tel Aviv, slightly injuring three employees. Israel quickly condemned the act, apologized profusely, and promised to catch the culprits. Disregarding that, the Soviets broke off diplomatic relations with the state, recalled their minister from Tel Aviv, and ousted the Israeli legation from Moscow. Sadly, *Maariv* noted, the flag the legation had first raised on September 2, 1948, the day Golda arrived in Moscow, had now been lowered by the Soviets.

Taken aback by the Soviet behavior over a relatively minor incident, Ben-Gurion, Golda, and Sharett began to speak more freely against the Communist treatment of Jews in Soviet lands. The time had come for Golda to tell her story. At a tense Knesset debate in which Mapam and other left-wing opposition groups faulted Israel for what had happened, she somberly rose from her seat, walked to the podium, and spoke slowly and emphatically of the "spiritual pogrom" in the Soviet Union against "Judaism in general, and Zionism in particular" that began long before the bomb exploded in the Soviet embassy. She used biting words to describe Ilya Ehrenburg, a Jew who had warned other Jews in his *Pravda* article to stay away from the Israel legation when she was in Russia: "A person who has lost all semblance not only of a Jew, but also of a self-respecting human being."

Ben-Gurion decided that the Soviet Union had to be denounced in the United Nations, and Golda was the person to do it. He and Moshe Sharett arranged for her to head Israel's UN delegation for that purpose, working with Abba Eban, who held the dual position of ambassador to the United States and the United Nations.

The assignment came at a good moment for her. Along with her sincere empathy for Soviet Jews, she had begun feeling herself pushed to the edge in her labor ministerial work. There would soon be thirty thousand to forty thousand people out of jobs, she informed a Mapai political committee. It was a staggering number that pained her deeply, yet despite all efforts she could find no solution for it. Moreover, she felt battered by her relentless squabbles with doctors, nurses, engineers, and municipal workers whose demands for higher wages she had to refuse in the current economic situation. "I have no strength for this," she told her colleagues, announcing that she wished to resign. Choose "someone who is stronger than I . . . someone who will look at these things rationally and will not feel them as deeply as I." Led by Ben-Gurion, they, of course, rejected any thought of her resigning, bolstering her with words she wanted to hear: nobody could do the job better than she. (She once advised an aspiring young politician that the threat of resignation was a "dangerous tool. One must use it with utmost care, never too often and always ready to take the risk." It never failed her.) She kept her position as labor minister but gladly turned her attention to the UN assignment.

Something else also motivated her in accepting that assignment. She thought often and spoke frequently of the helplessness that had gripped the Yishuv during the Holocaust. She had tried, to a greater extent than many others, to rescue Jews from the grinding death machines of those years, but so little could be done, so few saved. Now the Jews had a state of their own. When others in the free world asked why this small, weak state, with its wagonload of problems, was mixing into Soviet Jewish affairs, Golda replied that the state came into being not only for its citizens but to "protect Jewish lives and the honor of Jews wherever they are endangered." Israel might be small and weak, but "it has a voice among the family of nations," she would say, and that voice should be heard just as clearly as the louder ones of other nations.

By the time she left for the States to speak on behalf of Soviet Jews, the climate had changed. Stalin died on March 5, 1953, and a month later the Soviets made the dramatic announcement that the charges against the doctors had been false. The prisoners would be released and exonerated. The speech Golda had planned to give denouncing the Soviet

Union and its "doctors' plot" had to be hurriedly revised. Nevertheless she had things she wanted to say.

"I saw in the newspaper that next Tuesday you will be appearing before the United Nations," Sheyna wrote to her sister. "If I believed in God, I would pray to Him on your behalf. But I'm sure you will know what to say and how to say it, and that you will be a success."

Standing before the political committee of the UN General Assembly, not on the Tuesday Sheyna supposed, but about three weeks later, on April 13, Golda read from the new text she and her staff had carefully prepared. She began by expressing the "deep satisfaction and relief" of Israel's government that Moscow had dropped the case against the doctors. Even so, the Soviet Union's "revival of anti-Jewish incitement as an instrument of policy" should remind the United Nations of something very close to its memory, the "act of savagery" that was the Holocaust. "In the history of our people's unparalleled martyrdom," she went on, "we have observed . . . that the libel of the 'world Jewish conspiracy,' sponsored or tolerated by governments, has never remained confined to hostile words, but has invariably degenerated into daily acts which have brought untold sufferings upon the Jewish people."

Andrei Vyshinski blasted Golda's talk along with a follow-up Eban gave three days later. The Soviets had thought to gain worldwide approval by repudiating the doctors' trials. Golda sent a message that undoing one injustice did not eliminate other wrongs the Soviet Union was committing against the Jewish people. It was the first time anyone had called world attention to the extent of Soviet anti-Jewishness. Another three months would pass before the U.S.S.R. would resume diplomatic relations with Israel, announced by both countries on July 21, 1953. The antagonism between the two nations subsided for a short time after that.

Golda celebrated Passover in the United States and stayed on for two months after her UN talk. She spoke to Pioneer Women groups, raised money for Israel Bonds, outlined Israel's employment difficulties to groups of union leaders, breakfasted with Eleanor Roosevelt, and had an emergency operation on her gallbladder at Mount Sinai Hospital in New York. She had been suffering from gallstones before she arrived in the States in March, leaving Beilinson Hospital in Petach Tikvah prematurely to take up her UN duties. In America, she ignored her symptoms until the pain became too excruciating to bear. After surgery, she had to spend several weeks at Mount Sinai recuperating.

She did manage on this trip to attend her son Menahem's debut cello concert at Carnegie Hall in New York. She devoured the fine reviews, especially one in *The New York Times* that raved about the young musician's "firm, brilliant tone of considerable power," and cabled the good news to Sheyna, who immediately wrote back to say how "ecstatic" she was. The two women corresponded regularly, usually in Yiddish, whenever Golda left home for any length of time. Although Sheyna followed her younger sister's activities with pride, she treated domestic issues as equal to political ones, never allowing Golda to get carried away with her importance. "Golda," she wrote in one letter, "do not forget the refrigerator part!" In another, she included the address of her neighbor's brother, exhorting the very busy labor minister to "look him up and give him our regards." In her own life, Sheyna dealt with the loss of her husband, Shamai, a year earlier as stoically as she did with everything else, hoping, she wrote to Golda, that she had the strength to keep her "misfortune" from spoiling the family seder that year.

Upon returning to Jerusalem at the end of June, Golda moved in to an apartment she would speak of lovingly all her life. It was built for her in the rooftop of a romantic two-story stone villa in the Talbieh section of the city, and from its large bay window she had a sweeping view of Jerusalem. Ceramic tiles on the building's facade honored the name of Harun al-Rashid, a caliph of Baghdad and a hero of *The Thousand and One Nights*. A Christian Arab businessman, Hanna Ibrahim Bisharat, had built the villa in 1926 and during the 1930s and 1940s leased it to the British, who housed Royal Air Force officers in it. When they left, they turned the house over to the Haganah. Golda lived in a tiny room while her apartment was being readied, and when it was done, it became more than a home. Its kitchen has been said to be the original "Golda's kitchen," where meals were cooked and deals "cooked up" with Mapai colleagues, who visited frequently and held meetings in one of its high-ceilinged rooms.

She needed that home in Jerusalem, because the city had become the nation's capital and seat of the Knesset. At the end of Israel's War of Independence, with Jerusalem divided between Israel and Jordan, the United Nations voted to turn it into an international city. A furious Ben-Gurion, who had no intention of giving up the Jewish part of Jerusalem, quickly had Israel's capital moved there from Tel Aviv. He knew, he said later, that as angry as the nations of the world might be by his decision, they would do nothing to stop him, and particularly because Jordan would not give up the part of the city it was holding. Golda ignored warnings from friends that her new home stood dangerously close to the Jordanian border. She settled in, with full-time help to clean and cook because of her heavy work schedule.

Leah Biskin, who had lived with the family and cared for the children when they were little, moved in with her again and helped around the house until she became too ill with cancer to work. An assortment of guests appeared regularly. "Sunday night dinner . . . a total of ten people," Leah wrote to her friend Aliza London. "However, after lunch and in the evening there will be a hundred people present . . . On Tuesday, once again ten people for lunch." With the shortage of food, Golda never served meat, even at official dinners when she was allowed to. She specialized in preparing gefilte fish, "grinding, cleaning, and cutting," while Leah put the parts together. Golda also became friendly with her neighbors and especially fond of young Efi Arazi, who grew up to become a well-known electronics entrepreneur in Israel. When he moved away, she told his mother, Giselle, that she missed the sounds of the loud parties he'd held.

She was lonely. Sarah lived in far-off Revivim, and Menahem and Chana occupied her Tel Aviv apartment. When all the guests had gone from her home, she felt essentially alone, even with Leah Biskin asleep in another room. She liked having people around at all times. Jerry Goodman, who became founding executive director of the National Conference on Soviet Jewry, recalls walking along a road in Jerusalem as a young student, tired and covered with dust, when a large official-looking car pulled up. "Get in," he heard a voice say. As he did, he gazed with amazement at the passenger. "Are you . . . ?" he started asking. "Yes, I am," Golda answered. "Where can we take you?" The car itself was becoming famous. A big, shiny black 1950 DeSoto with seven seats, it had been a gift from Sam Rothberg and the other wealthy Americans who helped her raise money for Israel. It carried the license plate 600, her official ministry number. Sometimes it served as her office, where she reviewed papers and held meetings, sometimes she just stretched out and napped, a pillow propped behind her head, and as often as she could, she gave lifts to hitchhiking soldiers, farmers, construction workers, or students, chatting with them as her driver, Itzhak Philosoph, drove them all to or from Tel Aviv.

"WHAT WILL WE DO WITHOUT Ben-Gurion?" Golda asked Itzhak one day in the fall of 1953. The prime minister had informed his cabinet that he was resigning for at least two years to live and work on a new kibbutz, Sdeh Boker, in the heart of the Negev. He had already taken a three-month leave, from July 19 to October 18, when he and his wife, Paula, stayed on the kibbutz, and he traveled about the country examining army units and working out a system to strengthen the armed forces. But he needed more time; he was exhausted from his years of shaping the state, leading its war for existence, and overseeing the absorption of hundreds of thousands of immigrants. He wanted to work the land, read and write, and live the life of a "simple philosopher-shepherd," as Golda put it. He submitted his formal resignation on December 7 to his old friend Yitzhak Ben-Zvi, now Israel's second president, and a week later he and Paula set off for their new home in the desert.

From the first, Ben-Gurion's plans to resign sent Mapai leaders into a frenzy of fear and confusion. He had not prepared them for his leaving, nor had he asked any of them for advice in formulating his plans. Their immediate reaction was to plead with him to stay. His strength and obstinacy and his far-reaching vision had guided the people and the party for more than twenty years. How could any of them manage without him? They met with him as a group and as individuals, pressing the case for his remaining in office. Sounding like a mother comforting her children, Golda assured her colleagues that they had a right to their feelings. "Nobody should try to stifle the pain in his heart," she told them. For her, aside from the war they had endured, nothing would be "as great a blow to the state" as Ben-Gurion's departure.

Finally, when she and others realized that his plans would not change, the question changed. Who would—who could—replace Ben-Gurion for however long he would be gone? During the "old man's" extended leave, the foreign minister, Moshe Sharett, had been acting prime minister, and Pinhas Lavon, a younger Mapai member, had been acting defense minister, dividing between them the two positions he had held alone. Most people assumed that the same personalities would again replace him, but Ben-Gurion seemed equivocal about Sharett.

The two men had labored together through the long struggle that led to the state, with Ben-Gurion the activist fighter for Israel and Sharett, though equally nationalistic, moderate in his approach and far less charismatic than his older colleague. Ben-Gurion made decisions based on what he believed would support and advance Israel's sovereignty, with less concern for world opinion. He had not hesitated to defy the United Nations and declare Jerusalem the country's capital because he deemed that necessary for the future. Sharett, who as foreign minister paid keen attention to the world's reactions to the state, sought ways to use diplomacy and work through the United Nations wherever possible. He angrily resigned when Ben-Gurion moved the capital to Jerusalem, and stayed on only because the prime minister refused to accept the resignation or tell anyone about it. "I am quiet, reserved, careful," Sharett once said. "Ben-Gurion is impulsive, impetuous and intuitive."

Ben-Gurion did not want "reserved" and "careful" in his seat of power, and he made no effort to hide his feelings. Aware of the pulls between the two men, newspapers began speculating on possible successors to the prime minister, with Golda Meyerson and the finance minister, Levi Eshkol, leading the pack. When the "old man" proposed to the party—with unfeeling cruelty to Sharett—that Eshkol be named his successor, the rumor machines went into high gear. One story had it that the party was leaning toward Golda, in spite of Ben-Gurion's proposal. Another that Pinhas Lavon, whom Ben-Gurion named defense minister again, was promoting Golda's candidacy, arguing that neither Sharett nor Eshkol would relinquish his current position even if he became premier. Yet another recorded an announcement by the religious parties that they categorically opposed having a woman at the helm of the government.

Golda said nothing. Eshkol firmly turned down Ben-Gurion's invitation. Sharett spilled his hurt feelings into his diary. He jotted his suspicions of Golda, having heard rumors that Ben-Gurion planned to appoint her the next prime minister. He personally thought her well suited to become secretary-general of the party, but he would not dare suggest that so long as the possibility existed that she would inherit the premiership. "In my mind that possibility exists and remains," he wrote, in a kind of self-torture. "Her voice comes from the heart and goes to the heart," he admitted in one diary entry, but in her "simple English" her words were devoid of any intellectual content. In another, he allowed that she had a "formidable personality," yet she lacked "insight into herself." He asked Mordechai Namir, who had been in Russia with Golda, whether he had the impression that she felt prepared to be prime minister, and Namir affirmed that she did, causing Sharett more agony. Later Sharett heard from Yitzhak Navon, Ben-Gurion's secretary, that not only did Golda think herself worthy of inheriting the "old man's" mantle, but she believed that with two candidates, Eshkol and Sharett, vying against each other, she would emerge as the clearest solution. Ignoring her good friend Zeev Sharef's denial that she harbored such aspirations, Sharett convinced himself she did.

Golda and Sharett had worked side by side for years, he in the senior position and she a loyal second. In the race for prime minister, the power relationship between them showed signs of reversing, with her political ambitions and his insecurities beginning to reshape their alliance.

For the present, Sharett got the prize. A three-man committee selected to review the candidacies chose him as the most suitable person to be prime minister and persuaded Ben-Gurion to back him after all. On November 25, the Mapai central committee voted for Sharett as premier, allowing him to retain also his title of foreign minister. With the requisite sigh of helplessness, as if the position had been forced on him, Sharett told the newspapers that he "waited for the moment when he could return the assignment to Ben-Gurion." At the end of the new prime minister's first official meeting with his cabinet, Golda asked to say a few words. When Ben-Gurion decided to step down, "the Jewish people in Zion and the Jewish people in the Diaspora saw it as natural that Moshe Sharett would take his place," she said, ignoring the past weeks of crisis and competition. She promised Sharett the support of everyone in the government and concluded, "I want to express my personal joy that Moshe Sharett has attained what he deserved." If she believed it was really she who deserved that position, she pushed that belief away for the time being and resumed her work alongside him.

She felt less benign toward some of Ben-Gurion's other appointees. He named Moshe Dayan chief of staff of the Israel Defense Forces and Shimon Peres director general of the Defense Ministry. Dayan, the tough, handsome army hero with a black patch over an eye lost while fighting for the British during World War II, exuded confidence bordering on arrogance and the self-reliance of a young generation of sabras, born in the Land of Israel. Peres, with roots in Eastern Europe, looked to the broader world beyond Israel to form new alliances and strengthen the nation. Smooth and more low-key than the blunt-speaking Dayan, and more nakedly ambitious, he tended to work behind the scenes to gain his ends. These men, devoted to Ben-Gurion, dazzled him with their youth, energy, and willingness to take risks. For Golda and her party cohorts—Levi Eshkol, Pinhas Sapir, Zalman Aranne, and other "elders"—their appointments carried the whiff of a threat. Did Ben-Gurion mean to push aside his colleagues and choose a new generation as Israel's leaders?

The most problematic appointment was of Pinhas Lavon, a thin, attractive man with silver hair, intense eyes, and an air of disdain for all around him. A charismatic speaker and clever thinker, he felt himself above the need to consult with others in making key decisions. He also drank too much. Berl Katznelson, the Zionist icon, had described him as having "a brilliant mind in a murky soul." Golda regarded him as "one of the most capable if least stable members of Mapai, who nevertheless had "neither the necessary experience nor . . . the necessary powers of judgment" for the sensitive post of defense minister that Ben Gurion had given him. She and others argued with the "old man" about his choice, to no avail.

In short order, friction developed among the new appointees, much of it caused by Israel's deteriorating situation with neighboring Arabs, much radiating from Lavon.

Although Israel had signed armistice agreements in 1949 with each of the Arab states that had fought against it, hundreds of Arab infiltrators—many of them fedayeen, or suicide fighters—had begun sneaking across Israel's borders to ambush buses, blow up houses, and murder Jewish farmers and villagers. With Ben-Gurion's approval, the Defense Ministry adopted a policy of reprisals; the army struck back hard after every attack to send the message that infiltrators would not be tolerated. True to his nature, Sharett disapproved of that policy, preferring to use diplomatic channels to stop the border raids. Most times he was overruled. On October 14, 1953, while Ben-Gurion was on his predeparture leave, one of Israel's counterattacks went tragically awry. Reacting to an infiltrator's murder of a woman and her two children, the IDF's elite Unit 101 undertook a punishing retaliation. Commanded by a young major, Ariel Sharon, the unit converged on the Jordanian village of Kibiya and blew up dozens of its houses. The soldiers swore later that they believed the homes to be empty. But in the light of day, returning villagers found seventy bodies in the rubble, many of them women and children. The victims had been silently hiding in the darkened houses.

The operation evoked worldwide condemnation. Back from his leave, Ben-Gurion insisted at a cabinet meeting that the IDF had nothing to do with the episode. He had been told by Lavon, he said, that angry Israeli border settlers had acted on their own. Both men knew the truth but used Lavon's ploy to shield the military. Golda did not lie or try to cover up for the slaughter, as Ben-Gurion did, but neither did she side with those in the cabinet who spoke of Israel's shame at what had happened.

"If I were asked," she said coolly, "I would say, yes, retaliate, but if possible do so with only a small number of victims." Still, if a village with a thousand inhabitants is captured in a battle, "how can someone anticipate whether a bomb or a bullet will wound only a young man and not, God forbid, a woman or a child? Either you act or you don't act." She didn't doubt for a minute that acting on behalf of Jews trumped the damage from mistakes made.

Sharett was horrified by the massacre that had occurred and sickened by Ben-Gurion's attempt to conceal the army's culpability. "I would have resigned" before falsifying the facts, he told his wife. He was also enraged that Lavon, who had planned the operation with Dayan and others, had not bothered to keep him informed. That situation—his relationship to Lavon—declined further once Ben-Gurion's resignation went into effect and Sharett became prime minister. The defense minister ignored him on almost every major security matter. Moreover, Lavon, who had once been a "great dove," according to Golda, now "turned into the most ferocious sort of hawk." He responded to even the slightest border incident with extensive military action, openly mocking Sharett's moderate stance and undermining him at every turn.

Lavon did not treat Moshe Dayan or Shimon Peres much better. Activists like him, these men might have been his natural allies, but he kept them at a distance, fearful of their gaining too much power. They, in turn, came to despise and distrust him. Within two months after Ben-Gurion retired to Sdeh Boker, they drove there to complain bitterly to him about Lavon. The "old man" said little. A few months later, in late July 1954, Golda, feeling energetic after returning from a stay at Dr. Schlegel's clinic in Zurich (where she lost weight consuming nothing but juice and raw vegetables), went with Levi Eshkol and Zalman Aranne to fill Ben-Gurion in on the dreadful relationship between Lavon and Sharett. He refused their pleas for his return.

The atmosphere since Ben-Gurion's departure could not have been worse: a head of state battered and insulted by his defense minister, a defense minister suspicious of his deputy and jealous of his chief of staff, and both of them lacking faith in him but also in their indecisive prime minister. And all this mistrust and intrigue being played out against increasingly violent Arab border raids. The stage was set for a crisis of major proportions, and Lavon provided it.

The "mishap" or "shameful business," as its first phase came to be known, began in Egypt. Gamal Abdel Nasser, who had seized full power in that country in the spring of 1954, wanted all foreign troops out of his land. When England agreed to withdraw its forces from the Suez Canal and other bases, Israelis feared that without the British buffer Egypt would gear up for another war with them. In secret talks, Lavon and the chief of Israeli military intelligence, Colonel Benyamin Gibli, hatched a far-fetched plan to make the Egyptian government appear too weak to maintain order and in that way persuade the British not to pull out. The plan called for setting off explosions in British and American libraries, movie theaters, and other cultural centers and making it seem that radical Muslims had done this. A group of young Egyptian Jews, part of a spy network, handled the operation, which began on July 23, 1954, and quickly failed. Within a few days, the Egyptian police rounded up and jailed most of the people involved. Egyptian newspapers crowed about the capture of "Zionist spies," shocking the Israeli public and its leaders, who knew nothing about the plot.

When Sharett, Golda, and the other key ministers did learn about it, they publicly denied any wrongdoing on Israel's part and privately decided to keep the details of the failed operation secret. Peres told Golda that Lavon had spoken to him about setting off explosions in several Arab capitals in order to spark tensions and "make things lively" in the Middle East. He also told her that after he described Lavon's behavior to Ben-Gurion, the "old man" had grabbed his head in despair. Ben-Gurion had as little understanding of people as did her baby granddaughter, Golda remarked. She would take it upon herself to demand that he order Lavon to resign.

The show trial of the accused Jewish spies opened in Cairo on December 11, 1954, and six weeks later the Egyptian court handed down shockingly harsh sentences. Six of the prisoners received long jail terms, and two—Shmuel Azar and Dr. Moshe Marzouk—were condemned to death. Meir Max Binnet, a Mossad agent who might have led the foiled plot, killed himself. The hanging of Azar and Marzouk in their prison courtyard on January 31, 1955, startled and revolted Israelis, who had just begun to learn details of the disaster.

Lavon and Gibli refused to take responsibility for their botched adventure. Gibli insisted that Lavon had given him the order to put the scheme in motion, and Lavon categorically denied this. Stymied about what to do and pressured, especially by Golda, to investigate the mishap in a formal way, Sharett appointed a secret commission composed of Yitzhak Olshan, a Supreme Court justice, and Yaakov Dori, a former IDF chief of staff, to get at the truth. After speaking to everyone involved, the Olshan-Dori commission could not reach a definitive conclusion about who had given the order. It had accomplished nothing.

Throughout, Sharett held countless meetings with his most senior advisers—Golda, Aranne, and Eshkol—to thrash out the situation. After visiting Ben-Gurion again, the group agreed that even if Lavon had not directly given the order, the mishap had occurred in his office during his ministry, making him accountable for it. Lavon resisted every argument. He threatened blackmail, he threatened suicide, he blamed Peres, who he believed had betrayed him. He drank excessively in front of his Mapai colleagues. Finally, on February 17, 1955, with the entire press now calling for his dismissal, Lavon resigned.

The Mossad's head, Isser Harel, suggested that Golda replace him as defense minister. But she knew, as did the others, that the only way to bring order into their lives was for Ben-Gurion to take over the defense establishment. All day, after Lavon's resignation, party leaders headed to his kibbutz to persuade him to become defense minister. But it was not until early evening, when Golda and Mordechai Namir "unexpectedly" appeared, that, as Ben-Gurion noted in his diary, "I decided I must give in to their demand and return to the defense ministry. Defense and the army take priority over everything." That night Golda excitedly told Sharett, "Ben-Gurion accepts!" With those words, "a wave of joy engulfed me," he exulted. His wife, Zipporah, envisioning her husband's future now, said prophetically, "This is the end of peace and quiet."

WITHIN HER FAMILY, GOLDA CARRIED "a very heavy stone on her heart." Her son Menahem's marriage began falling apart about four years on. The biggest crisis flared when the couple lived in Zagreb, Yugoslavia, where Menahem was studying for three months with the famous cellist Antonio Janigro. As he remembered it, Chana suddenly informed him that she wanted a separation, taking him by surprise. "I didn't know she was that unhappy," he said. "He didn't love her enough," Ruth Weinberg, her daughter from her second marriage, observed. Pregnant at the time, Chana had begun to hemorrhage but rejected her physician's suggestion of an abortion. The couple returned to Israel, barely on speaking terms.

On January 3, 1956, Chana gave birth prematurely to a girl, whom the family named Meira, after Menahem's father, Morris Meyerson. Golda visited her daughter-in-law in the hospital briefly, the only time she would see that grandchild. The doctors told Menahem almost immediately that the child had Down syndrome, keeping the news from Chana for a few months. Once she found out, she was determined to raise the

child at home, an unusual course in an era when most families insti-
tutionalized mentally retarded children. Convinced that Meira needed
institutional care, Golda adamantly opposed Chana's decision.

Six months after Meira's birth, Menahem and Chana were divorced.
When Meira was about seven, Chana married Isaiah "Sheike" Weinberg,
who accepted the child as his own. He already had a daughter from a
previous marriage, and he and Chana subsequently had a son, Benjamin,
and their daughter Ruth. Younger than Meira, Ruthie drew close to her
half sister, loving and protecting her. In the spring of 1956, Menahem
married Aya Pinkerfeld, an early school friend and later a child psychiatrist. The couple would have three sons, who grew up knowing nothing
about the existence of their half sister, although Menahem paid half the
cost of rearing Meira, with financial help from Golda. For a while, he
visited her in Chana's home, but feeling unwelcome there, he stopped
going.

Golda "had no contact whatsoever with Meira," in Ruth Weinberg's
words. Menahem disagreed. "Mother always sent her gifts and postcards," he said, although she did not see her granddaughter. She also
kept Meira's existence hidden from the public; mental illness still bore
a mantle of shame. In interviews all her life, she spoke lovingly of her
five grandchildren, Menahem's three sons and Sarah's daughter and son,
without uttering a word about her sixth, a neglect that Chana bitterly
resented. At the age of eighteen, Meira moved from home to Kfar Tikvah, near Haifa, a community for young disabled people. Menahem's
wife, Aya, visited her there, and later Menahem went also. Occasionally,
they took her out to the movies or a café, and Menahem phoned her
regularly. Golda still kept her distance.

During Golda's lifetime, Chana revealed nothing publicly about the
relationship, but on the day of the prime minister's funeral, December 12, 1978, a mourning notice in the popular newspaper *Yediot Aharonot*
read, "On the death of my dear grandmother Golda Meir, her bereaved
granddaughter Meira Meyerson Weinberg." The notice dumbfounded
Israelis. One or two journalists had known about Meira but had kept
Golda's secret. People reacted with amazement, and some with condemnation, to the news that Golda Meir had another grandchild. "It was a
terrible shame," said Shulamit Aloni. "She ignored this girl in the most
brutal way."

Both Meira's families, Menahem's and Chana's, created a trust fund to
care for her. She and a young man she met at Kfar Tikvah continued to
live together in their sheltered community.

Her personal life darkened by Menahem's marital problems, her political life more frenetic than ever during Ben-Gurion's absence, Golda also became enmeshed in conflicts that swirled around Henry Montor and the Israel Bonds organization. She and Montor had drawn ever closer during her fund-raising tours of the United States. When she was in the hospital having gallbladder surgery, he visited her twice a day, barely able to pull himself away. And in his long letters to her, he delved into his innermost feelings, which he could "tell no one else."

Regina once asked Golda whether she would consider marrying Montor. The answer was "Never." She had no interest in marrying anyone; she valued her freedom too much. But Montor exuded the kind of electric energy that had attracted her to men like Remez and Shazar, and Regina suspected, as did others, that their relationship had moved beyond friendship.

Moshe Sharett was convinced of that, his son was to say. He confided his views to his diary during a fight between UJA leaders and Montor, then head of the Israel Bonds enterprise. Sharett had prepared a schedule for the two groups to launch their money-raising campaigns at different times of the year, thus avoiding competition between them. But in Montor's single-minded devotion to the bonds effort, he paid little attention to the schedule, organizing events that spilled over into UJA's time frame. Matters came to a head in early 1955 after he circulated a short article called "The Nonsense of Timing," arguing for the right to raise money anytime he wished. Infuriated, officials of UJA bombarded Sharett and the finance minister, Levi Eshkol, with protests against Montor. When they, in turn, insisted that Montor curtail his plans, he and his supporters accused the Israeli government of favoring the UJA.

Officially, Golda kept a low profile, leaving the mudslinging to others. She could not be seen as openly opposing her government in favor of her American friends or denigrating UJA. But no one doubted her position. Golda, Sharett wrote, was "emotionally incapable of reflecting on Montor's actions." She regarded his outbursts as "holy" and attempts to rein him in as "a direct personal blow to her." After threatening to resign several times, Montor submitted his resignation in March 1955, and to his surprise and great dismay Eshkol accepted it. When Sharett told Golda about Eshkol's decision, she was "annoyed to the depth of her soul," he wrote.

Montor's resignation was followed by the resignations of Golda's "boys"—Sam Rothberg, Julian Venezky, Lou Boyar, and a few others—men who devoted their time and wealth to Israel's cause, traveled with

Golda on her fund-raising expeditions, and, largely because of her and Montor, had become staunch supporters of Israel Bonds. Rothberg was so incensed about what had happened that he became "wildly, screamingly bitter," Montor wrote to Golda. On Israel Independence Day, a dinner held in New York's Waldorf Astoria hotel paid tribute to these men. Golda couldn't make it, but she sent a group letter to her "very dear Friends" that Montor read aloud. "I am sure you will understand and forgive if I do not say much of how I feel about what has been done to you," she wrote. "If I were a private citizen, I would say it loudly and clearly. But I'm sure you understand." She praised the men for what they had contributed to Israel and asked them not to be "bitter," although they had been "wronged and hurt" by what had taken place. "I love you all dearly," she concluded.

A few months later, Montor returned her sentiments: "Sam, Julian— all of us—are full of such deep feeling for you that you cannot possibly measure the extent of it. A communication from you is like a benediction from the high priest secluded in the sanctum sanctorum throughout the year." He personally missed terribly being with her in Israel, "peeling the endless mandarins in your house, and shooting my mouth off at 2 A.M." These were almost his farewell words to Golda and the intensity of their relationship. Feeling himself "pushed away" by Israel, he moved to Rome, Italy, where he opened an investment firm. In 1956, he divorced his wife of thirty years, and sometime after that married an Italian woman. Golda was "devastated" that the woman, Astrid, was not Jewish, recalled Esther Herlitz, a consul in New York then. Or simply by the marriage. Her correspondence with Montor dropped off, and there is no evidence that they had much—or any—contact after that, although he visited Israel frequently. Dr. Joseph Schwartz replaced Montor as head of Israel Bonds, and after several months Rothberg, Venezky, and most of the other "boys" returned to the bonds fold.

WITH THE MONTOR COMMOTION STILL in full throttle, Golda Meyerson ran for mayor of Tel Aviv. She let everyone know that she did this for the party. She had no interest in giving up her job as labor minister, she said, but Ben-Gurion wanted someone from Mapai to gain control of this key post, and he chose her. "I have a suspicion that you may enjoy it much more than your current job," Montor wrote to her, which probably came closer to the truth, regardless of her protests. But getting the job was not so easy, even for the popular Mrs. Meyerson.

Chaim Levanon, the current mayor, belonged to the General Zionists Party. To wrest control of the city from that party, Golda and her comrades turned to Mapam, Ahdut Ha'avoda (which had split from Mapam in 1954), and the small but influential religious parties. In exchange for the religious parties' support, Ben-Gurion had reached agreements with them on matters of religion in the state even before the state officially came into being. Under those agreements, the Jewish Sabbath became the legal day of rest in the land and kosher food the fare served at every state eating facility. The most controversial agreement concerned the Orthodox chief rabbinate's control over Jewish marriage and divorce.

Though Golda accepted the arrangement with the religious groups as a political necessity, she was frank about her own secular attitude toward religious rules. After she returned from Moscow, the Orthodox Knesset member Benjamin Mintz invited her to the Great Synagogue in Tel Aviv, knowing that she rarely, if ever, attended services except for official purposes. "Do you go to synagogue only in Moscow?" he asked jokingly. Without missing a beat, she replied, "In Moscow I wanted to be with Jews, so I agreed to sit even in the segregated women's section upstairs, but here in Tel Aviv, I am prepared to go tomorrow and every Sabbath if there will be equality and you arrange a seat for me downstairs in the sanctuary among the men!" That, she knew, would not happen in an Orthodox synagogue.

More seriously, she openly resented the authority the rabbis held over marital issues. Time and again, she informed her colleagues that she had never in her public life felt as ashamed of anything as she had when she voted to legalize the Orthodox rabbinate's monopoly over marriage and divorce. For a moment, she had even considered withdrawing from the Knesset to avoid raising her hand for the law. She didn't hold back about other religious rulings either. "I have never eaten pork in Israel," she once said, implying that she might have eaten it elsewhere. But should breeding pigs and selling pork be banned so that nobody could eat it? Such laws "begin with pork and reach into all sorts of other things. And what a person does in his private life is not anyone's business, not the business of one single rabbi."

Those antireligious statements notwithstanding, Golda joined her Mapai comrades in coalition talks with the religious parties. At the same time, she campaigned hard in Tel Aviv for the party and her candidacy. On the go nonstop from one neighborhood to the next, she gave speeches, made promises, and directed special appeals to women to vote for her party and clean up the city, whose dirty streets and poor hygiene endangered children. When the nationwide elections were held on July 26, 1955, Mapai remained the largest faction, but it lost seats in the 120-member Knesset, dropping from 45 to 40. In Tel Aviv, the party won 57,400 out of 188,822 votes cast, making it seem likely that Golda would become the city's next mayor.

"Dear Golda—or should I call you 'Madame Mayor'?" Montor wrote on July 30. The title was premature. Mayors were not elected directly in those years, and although Mapai won the most votes, it did not get a majority on the Tel Aviv city council. As negotiations for the religious parties' support on the council heated up, their leaders spread the word that they would not elect a woman as Tel Aviv's mayor, regardless of how much pressure they came under. On the evening of September 8, after almost two months of again running herself ragged electioneering (and landing in the hospital for several days, exhausted), Golda sat in the front row of the city council auditorium looking "sad and emotional." The vote had been taken: sixteen hands shot up for Chaim Levanon; fourteen were raised for Golda Meyerson. She had lost the election. Mapai had lost. The two decisive votes had been cast by Hapoel Hamizrachi, the religious labor party.

With almost sixty thousand popular votes, Golda had to relinquish her dreams of victory because of a minority religious vote. "You have undermined the elementary principles of democracy," she accused her opponents in her concession speech. She spoke without a text, in measured tones, but her anger burned through. As a labor party, Hapoel Hamizrachi should have voted with Mapai, its secular counterpart. Yet "you were not ashamed . . . to exploit the fact that a woman was put forward as a candidate." Women had participated in every aspect of building the Jewish state, she continued, but through their actions the religious parties had declared that women do not have equal rights in Israel. "If there is anyone who causes religious hatred among the young, the workers, and the little children," she spat out, "it is the religious parties."

She had suffered her first major political defeat. Undoubtedly, her earlier proclamations against religion had not helped the situation, but her gender lay at the core of the defeat. When she insisted years later that in her political climb men had never "put obstacles in my way," she willfully downplayed this painful episode in her life. Despite her disclaimers that she never wanted the mayoral post, losing it hurt badly. She resumed her position as labor minister and took her place in the cabinet again. After much haggling, Mapai formed a coalition government on the national level that once more included the religious parties.

ABOUT TWO MONTHS AFTER LOSING the Tel Aviv race, Golda sat at a special late night meeting of the Mapai political committee. Party members from the Women Workers' Council had come to discuss their forthcoming participation in a nationwide conference on women's position in the state. They despised rabbinic control over women's lives in Israel, particularly its jurisdiction over marital issues. Should they join with women from other political parties in demanding a change in the law? Joseph Sprinzak, speaker of the Knesset, suggested that this was a woman's matter, not one for the entire political committee to judge. Golda disagreed. "If the law is good for the women it is also good for Sprinzak; if it is bad for the women it is also bad for Sprinzak," she rebuked him. They had not two parties, one for women and one for men, but a single party whose concerns affected everybody. She made it eminently clear, as she had stated many times before, that she, too, resented the rabbinic grip on marriage and divorce.

But there was something the women needed to think about. If they wanted to call attention to the many negative aspects of the current marital laws, fine, she said. If, however, they wished to demand changes in the law, that would entail something more. Mapai members would have to go to the cabinet and call for the law to be altered. With that, Mapai's fragile coalition with the religious parties would fall apart, threatening the labor party's dominance in the government. After a long discussion in the committee, the women agreed to voice strong complaints against the rabbinate but not to insist on immediate changes in the law.

Ever political, Golda had put her rage at the religious bloc behind her for the benefit of the party. She also put the welfare of the party ahead of the issues she and the women cared about greatly. Long ago, when she left the Women Workers' Council, she chose to give the party and all that it represented top priority in her life, even if on occasion that required compromising on principle.

19

"Golda Meir"

The excitement of the mayoral campaign behind her with only the bitter aftertaste of defeat remaining, Golda resigned herself once again to her labor minister's role. She would admit to no one, not even herself, that after seven years she had become restless in that role. A year earlier, after she had made "a terrific impression" in England during an Israel Bonds trip, the perceptive Montor had asked, "Ever think of becoming Israel's foreign minister?" She might not have thought of it, not consciously, but she was already often living the part. Ben-Gurion's return as defense minister under Prime Minister Sharett had lasted less than a year. After Mapai's victory in the November 1955 elections, the "old man" resumed his earlier position as prime minister, making Sharett foreign minister again. As one of the most senior members of the party, Golda filled in for Sharett whenever he left the country.

He left frequently these days. In September, Egypt had stunned Israel by purchasing massive quantities of state-of-the-art Soviet weapons from Czechoslovakia, far exceeding anything the Israel Defense Forces had. Buoyed by the arms deal, Gamal Abdel Nasser increased the pressure on Israel by inciting more fedayeen attacks on civilians across the country's borders. He had already closed the Suez Canal to Israeli navigation and blockaded the Straits of Tiran, shutting off shipping from the port of Eilat. Hoping to balance Egypt's expanding power, Sharett went abroad in search of arms and Western support.

And Golda appeared in his place at weekly Sunday cabinet meetings to deliver foreign relations reports. At one session, she reviewed a conversation she'd had with the British ambassador John Nicholls, who wanted to learn Israel's reaction to Prime Minister Anthony Eden's speech at the Guildhall on November 9, 1955. Eden had called on Israel to establish a compromise border somewhere between the partition lines of 1947 set by the United Nations and the armistice lines of 1949 that reflected the country's gains in the war. His plan stemmed from an earlier British proposal—supported by the U.S. secretary of state, John Foster Dulles—that Israel give up territory in the Negev to allow Egypt and Jordan to build a land bridge between them. In the Cold War climate that now colored every action of the world's powers, Western leaders regarded the Czech arms deal with Egypt as a Soviet ploy to get a foothold in the Middle East. They reasoned that by having Israel cede land to the Arabs, they might halt the Soviet march into the region. Golda answered Nicholls quickly and decisively, as Ben-Gurion would soon answer Eden. With not the slightest hint of compromise on the Arab side, Israel would not give up "an inch" of its land. It would, however, agree, with no preconditions, to negotiate directly with Egypt to arrive at a peace treaty and final borders. Nicholls replied as Golda expected. Nasser would not negotiate with Israel, for fear of giving the impression that he recognized its legitimacy.

Golda's conversation with Nicholls ranged over many other topics of foreign policy: arms, Arab refugees, the fedayeen raids, and more. As she reported the discussion at the cabinet meeting, nobody seemed surprised that the labor minister sounded like a foreign minister. She appeared at home in the role.

Sharett seemed less comfortable. What earlier had been differences between him and Ben-Gurion stretched ever wider to form a chasm between them. Even as Arab infiltrators increased in number and violence, Sharett continued to oppose strong-handed reprisals against them and to rely on diplomacy to work with the Arab states. He became particularly irate after a bloody confrontation in December between Israeli and Syrian soldiers at the Sea of Galilee in northern Israel. In response to several Syrian attacks against Israeli fishermen along the lakeshore, Ariel Sharon, with Ben-Gurion's approval, conducted a large-scale raid that left thirty-seven Syrian soldiers and twelve civilians dead and brought condemnation from the United Nations. Sharett was in the United States at the time, trying to persuade the government to sell weapons to Israel. To his mind, the raid "murdered" any possibility of that happening. "I was horrified," he wrote in his diary. "More evidence of Israel as bloodthirsty."

That attitude grated on Ben-Gurion. The two men, who had worked together for decades and agreed on many policies, were coming now to despise each other. Paradoxically, after the elections, when Ben-Gurion had formed his new government, Sharett at first refused to be his foreign minister, fed up with always having to accede to the "old man's" will. Fearing that Sharett's departure would hurt the party, Ben-Gurion had threatened not to serve as premier unless he joined the cabinet as foreign minister. Sharett gave in. Now he tried to hold on for dear life to his ministry, while Ben-Gurion thrashed about for ways to get rid of him.

The situation worsened when Israel's troubles with Egypt accelerated in April 1956. After several months of quiet, Egyptian shelling and fedayeen raids triggered heated battles in Gaza and around the kibbutzim in the area. The night after the UN secretary-general, Dag Hammarskjöld, arrived to try to calm the region, terrorists attacked a bus on the road from Tel Aviv to Jerusalem and lobbed hand grenades into the synagogue of a nearby settlement, killing several children and wounding many others. Fevers ran high at cabinet meetings as the ministers debated how to respond to these assaults, with Sharett and his supporters stressing diplomacy and the Ben-Gurion camp calling for action.

More than anyone, Golda represented Ben-Gurion's viewpoint. "They need to know that they have to pay and to pay dearly," she argued. "I am not saying this because in Gaza Arab children were killed and here we are speaking of Jewish children, but because we did not start this." The following week, with the world's nations hounding Israel to resist retaliating against the raids, she went further. "It doesn't interest me if we cannot explain [our actions] to the world. It will not be because the world doesn't understand, but because it doesn't want to understand." Dulles and other world leaders would surely convey their sympathy if the state were destroyed, she said caustically, but that "doesn't interest us. If we remain alive we will explain all sorts of things." She would return to this theme many times during the years ahead: staying alive at the cost of world opinion meant much more than arousing world pity when dead.

Sharett, in contrast, cautioned that when Israel retaliated forcefully after an attack and killed large numbers of the enemy, it gave the impression that its soldiers wanted to expand the conflict, and that was not desirable. Ben-Gurion, who, pressed by Moshe Dayan, had been mulling the pros and cons of launching a preemptive strike against Egypt, seethed at Sharett's words. "My thoughts are not your thoughts," he barked at one meeting, brusquely interrupting the foreign minister. The cabinet finally concluded that the time was not right for another war and therefore Israel should resist extensive reprisals, but it did not rule out war in the future.

Almost accidentally, Ben-Gurion soon found an opportunity to push Sharett out of his way. The Mapai Party was looking to replace its secretary-general, Yona Kesse, with a senior person strong enough to reform and reorganize it, considering that it had lost Knesset seats in the last election. Golda's name had cropped up for the job a number of times. Unwilling to relinquish her powerful cabinet position or the Labor Ministry for the narrower party role, she had turned down the appointment. It was too hard for her, she claimed, although, of course, she would take it if the party insisted. On April 28, Ben-Gurion held a meeting at his residence in Jerusalem to discuss the matter. As Sharett later described events, in order to encourage Golda to accept the party's wishes and to "show her that she was not the only sacrificial lamb," he made a "chivalrous gesture" and lightheartedly volunteered himself to be party secretary.

"Marvelous," Ben-Gurion jumped in immediately. "A wonderful idea!"

Everyone was astounded, most of all Sharett. It had never occurred to him that his gesture would be taken seriously. "I was sure that no one in his right mind . . . would even consider my departure or dismissal from my post at the Foreign Ministry at this time," he wrote to Abba Eban. But the die was cast. Ben-Gurion had ruthlessly taken advantage of an offhand remark to drive Sharett out of the government. Later Sharett would refuse to become secretary-general of the party in any event.

In Golda's telling, a few days after the episode, she asked Ben-Gurion who would become foreign minister in Sharett's place. "You," he replied, to her surprise. In reality, the appointment was not unexpected. Ben-Gurion had broached the idea to her a number of times over the past year as his wrangling with Sharett became increasingly acrimonious.

For two months after the fateful meeting in April, while Sharett struggled with when and how to resign officially, Golda said nothing to her staff or in public about assuming his post. Nor did she say a single word to Sharett himself about what had happened, too embarrassed or uncomfortable to face him. Meanwhile, word of a major change in the government leaked to the nation's press. Day after day, news reports vacillated about whether Meyerson or Sharett would head the Foreign Ministry. By early June, before any official announcement, all the papers concluded that Sharett was out and Meyerson in, making Sharett even more heartsick.

He revealed his searing pain to his diary. He was a "condemned" man "awaiting execution," he wrote. "There was all the difference in the world between leaving of my own accord and being forced to leave, not by the public, but by one man to whom all bowed." As for Golda, her behavior was "incomprehensible." How could she have accepted the position when "she knew full well that the office was beyond her capabilities"? She had "an inferiority complex" that stemmed from "her half-baked education" and was unable "to put her thoughts down on paper" or to prepare a speech properly. How was she going to dictate a cable "with instructions on a complex matter"? And there was "the moral issue of her role" in his dismissal. He was convinced that claims she made to various people of being "miserable" because of his ouster were just so much blather, as was her explanation that she accepted the post because, as she often said, she would do anything Ben-Gurion requested, even jump out a fifth-story window.

Sharett's wife, Zipporah, suspected that "deep in her heart," Golda felt she was truly worthy of the mantle of foreign minister and that all her misery was nothing but a "facade, to camouflage the truth even from herself." Zipporah was not wrong. Golda might have felt guilty about taking the job from Sharett, but she also felt capable of filling it. She had already proven herself when she substituted for him. Filled with his sense of superiority, Moshe Sharett failed to see that behind her demeanor of self-doubt lay a confident and driven Golda Meyerson.

He never forgave her. He believed that had she refused to head the Foreign Ministry, or had she and others asserted that they would not serve under any foreign minister but him, Ben-Gurion would have "knuckled under." He was mistaken. If not Golda, Ben-Gurion would certainly have found someone else for the position; he could no longer abide Sharett in it.

On Sunday, June 17, 1956, Sharett announced his resignation to the Mapai central committee, giving no reason for it. The committee accepted it and approved the candidacy of Golda Meyerson as foreign minister and Mordechai Namir as minister of labor. In her brief talk, following the formula of modesty expected of new appointees, Golda lamented, "I hope this post will be temporary with me." The next evening, Ben-Gurion officially informed the Knesset of Sharett's resignation and Golda's appointment as foreign minister. Speaking slowly and sadly to the Knesset himself, Sharett related that he had reached the "absolute conclusion" that it was impossible for him to remain any longer in a government headed by David Ben-Gurion. Shortly before his

Knesset appearance, he met with his staff on the lawn of the Foreign Ministry compound in Jerusalem. Three hundred people crowded in to hear him take his leave of them, while he made "a supreme effort" to hold back his tears and appear composed. This was Sharett's loyal staff that Golda would inherit.

The news of Sharett's resignation and Golda's appointment traveled rapidly around the world. "Sharett Ousted; Israeli Job Given to Mrs. Myerson," *The New York Times* blared on page 1 the next day, adding in a subhead, "Premier Ben-Gurion Drops Foreign Minister as Too Cautious and Temporizing." *The Christian Science Monitor* headed its story "Adventurous New Foreign Minister" and contrasted Golda's preference to "tackle obstacles by head-on attacks" with Sharett's pattern of "patient persuasion." A Swiss newspaper spoke of the "calm before the storm," wondering whether the change meant that Israel was preparing for war. No one missed the signal that Golda's appointment ushered in a more muscular foreign policy.

The New York Times accompanied its news report with a profile of the new foreign minister headed "Motherly Diplomat." The story must have pleased Golda, portraying her in an image she had cultivated for years and that would endear her to people everywhere: the dedicated pioneer with a warm smile and crinkly eyes who had risen by dint of "time and talent" to become the only female foreign minister in the world.

She began her new job immediately, eerily exactly ten years after she had taken over as head of the Jewish Agency political department while Sharett was incarcerated in Latrun. A day after his resignation, she spent two hours with him and some of his staff, from 10:00 a.m. until noon, being briefed on the workings of the department. Although she listened attentively, "she did not take a single note," Sharett recorded with irritation. It was "a very strange phenomenon in the Foreign Ministry as we knew it." Not so strange for Golda, who habitually absorbed information by listening intently rather than reading or writing. The atmosphere between them that day was surprisingly "extremely pleasant," Sharett noted, as though he were merely turning over matters to her prior to a trip abroad. Hoping to maintain that pleasantness, Golda requested through their mutual friend Zeev Sharef that Sharett accompany her to the office and formally turn it over to her, the customary practice of an outgoing minister. Sharett refused. "To appear with her at the ministry before all the staff? That would be a display of conciliation and friendship that do not exist," he wrote in his diary.

Golda made her entry into the Foreign Ministry office alone on June 21, 1956, "feeling and probably looking miserable." It helped some that the staff welcomed her with red roses and a greeting card. A week later, she walked gingerly into the charged atmosphere of the Foreign Affairs and Defense Committee of the Knesset, her first appearance in the legislature as foreign minister. The chair read aloud a farewell from Sharett wishing the group success. Golda spoke briefly of how "extraordinary" he was and how hard it was to fill his shoes. "There is nobody in this country, without exception, who feels worse than I that I am sitting here instead of the former foreign minister, Moshe Sharett," she said. In the sadness of the moment, she might have believed that herself.

During the next days, she plunged into nonstop work. After appearing at the Knesset, she met individually with foreign ambassadors in Israel who called on her, and set out to establish her own relationship with world powers. ("The memories of my childhood and youth in your great country," she began her first official letter to John Foster Dulles, her mind on Israel's need for American arms.) She also held her first press conference in her new capacity.

A record number of local and foreign press corps members gathered in the Jerusalem Press Club on July 2 at a reception arranged for them to meet her. Peace would be a "blessing, not only for the State of Israel but also for the neighboring countries," she told them. Nevertheless, Israel had to protect its independence and the integrity of its territory. "It is our policy not to hurt anyone," she said, "but at the same time we shall not allow anyone to injure us . . . We cannot acquiesce in a state of affairs in which the lives of honest people, farmers working their land near the borders, shall be in constant danger." Israel did not and would not initiate border conflicts, she emphasized. "If there were actions on our part they always came after long and severe provocation. This policy is still in force."

Nothing she said was new, but the way she said it was. The press picked up on a clarity of conviction and a firmness when she spoke of the policy of reprisals that it had not gotten from Sharett. The audience—among them senior officials of Israel's Foreign Ministry—also heard a tone they had not heard from either Ben-Gurion or Sharett. "There was an air of warmth, almost intimacy," without a hint of "oppressive formality," *Maariv* enthused. On the whole, this first meeting took place with "smiles, goodwill, and mutual understanding," a promising sign for the future. She had passed an important test.

Not, however, in Moshe Sharett's view. "Simple, straightforward, and warm; extremely shallow Hebrew; a totally new style of presenting Israel's foreign policy in completely simplistic terms," he entered in his diary, disapproving of the very things the press admired. "Peace, reciprocity, sovereignty, and other such hackneyed terms."

Many of his devoted staff in the Foreign Ministry felt the same. "I'm not among my own," Golda wailed to her son. Most of the people she had worked with at the Labor Ministry had backgrounds similar to hers, with kibbutz or labor union histories behind them. Most of those in the foreign service had much more formal education than she or her cronies, some in elite British schools. Like Sharett, many spoke several languages, including the sophisticated language of diplomacy. As she settled into her everyday duties and the red roses that had greeted her faded and died, she could feel the staff's hostility. She could feel people's disdain for her direct manner of speaking and her inexperience in formal diplomacy. She could feel, and understand, their longing for the personal touch of Sharett, who knew everyone's name and family, interests and problems. "They were all children of Sharett," said Tamar Eshel, who worked in Israel's UN mission at the time. "I used to think of Daphne du Maurier's book *Rebecca*. Golda was like the second wife when everybody was calling for Rebecca, the first wife."

Abba Eban, Israel's ambassador to the United States and the United Nations, personified the kind of diplomat Foreign Ministry officers most admired. Cambridge educated, eloquent, and erudite, he had the bearing of a statesman and the British accent of the upper classes. Ben-Gurion himself admired Eban enough that after appointing Golda foreign minister, he asked the young diplomat to serve as his personal adviser on foreign affairs. Eban had enough sense to see the potential danger in such an arrangement. Over lunch, he and Golda decided that he should turn down the offer, deciding also that they "would be happy and creative in proportion to the geographic distance separating us from each other," Eban wrote.

BEN-GURION'S ATTEMPT TO RECRUIT EBAN as a "kind of watchdog" over Golda had to have hurt her and exacerbated her unease in the Foreign Ministry. As he often did, the prime minister sent out mixed signals. A few weeks after Golda began her new work, he wrote her an affectionate letter about the need to change her name. At his insistence, many people in the government had Hebraized their names (Sharett had originally been Shertok), but she had resisted. "For quite a long time your foreign family name has disturbed my peace of mind," he wrote, quite seriously. "Now, when you have been chosen to fill the position of foreign minister, which is the second most important job in the government, at a time when the entire public looks up to your standing in the state, it is appropriate to change your Diaspora name to an Israeli name—Meir." Having anointed her with that name (which means "illuminated"), he concluded with authority, "I am absolutely sure that your friends in the government will be able to call you Golda Meir." To his satisfaction, she accepted the revised name immediately, always holding on, however, to "Golda," a common Diaspora first name. Yet while recognizing Golda's new job as "second most important," Ben-Gurion had still tried to enlist Eban to supplement her work. And while acknowledging her "standing," he met regularly with Moshe Dayan, his chief of staff, and Shimon Peres, director general of the Defense Ministry, on matters that should have fallen in her domain as foreign minister.

There had been bad blood between Golda and Peres for a long time. He always traced their differences to the Zionist Congress of 1946. Moshe Sneh, then national head of the Haganah, had been one of the speakers at the congress. Listening to him laud the Soviet Union, Peres suspected that he was headed toward Communism and wrote that in a Mapai Party newspaper, *Ashmoret*. The article provoked a storm of controversy, and an angry Golda berated Peres for attacking a Haganah chief in that way. Peres remembered that tongue-lashing several years later, when Sneh proved him right by becoming a leader of the Communist Party in Israel. Golda probably didn't give as much weight to that incident as Peres did. She simply didn't trust him, viewing him as voraciously ambitious and self-serving. A Mapai colleague, Yitzhak Bareli, once tried to persuade her to change her mind about Peres. "He is a very gifted man," Bareli said. "So was Al Capone," Golda snapped.

More than a year before Golda became foreign minister, she invited a young journalist, Levi Yitzhak Hayerushalmi, to her home in Jerusalem on Rosh Hashanah, the Jewish New Year. To his amazement, she spent almost the entire day with him, pouring out her wrath against Shimon Peres. "He's dangerous," she told the journalist. "He's using public relations to make himself known so that he can take over the Mapai leadership. He can't be trusted." Relatively new at his profession, Hayerushalmi could not understand why this powerful woman had chosen him as the receptacle for her anxieties or why she would sacrifice her holiday to dwell on her fears about Peres. But with shrewd insight, Golda had rightly sensed that this journalist had his own public relations skills, and she needed to win him to her side.

Her side was that of the veterans, the "old guard" that felt increasingly pushed away by the Young Turks, Peres, and Dayan. Having gained Ben-Gurion's ear and confidence, the two young men bypassed official routes as they sought new means to deal with Nasser and the fedayeen terrorist raids. For all Sharett's efforts, the United States had turned down Israel's requests for weapons, hoping to woo Nasser to the West. But a new source of arms was opening up—France—and Peres was to become the face of Israel to the French.

ALTHOUGH AS FOREIGN MINISTER, Sharett had made an initial agreement with France to buy a dozen Mystère 4 fighter planes, it was Peres who pursued the relationship. Encouraged by Ben-Gurion, but without consulting Sharett or Golda when she took over the Foreign Ministry, Peres flew back and forth to France, cultivating friendships with high-level government officials. Smooth and sophisticated, he also wined, dined, and went "on the town" with his new friends, with the single-minded aim of acquiring weapons for Israel. He had great success, especially after the Socialist Party headed by Guy Mollet came into power in January 1956. The French cabinet found common cause with Israel's socialist government and especially with its struggle against Nasser. The French blamed the Egyptian leader for inciting and bankrolling a fierce rebellion by Arab forces in Algeria, which France ruled, and imagined that if he were overthrown, the rebellion would end. Selling arms to Israel constituted one step toward that goal.

On June 22, barely four days after Sharett resigned, Peres, Dayan, and the chief of military intelligence, Colonel Yehoshafat Harkabi, flew to Paris for a secret conference on a possible joint venture with the French against Egypt. Minister of Foreign Affairs Golda Meyerson (she had not yet changed her name) was not included in the secret. Held at an old castle in Vémars, outside Paris, the meeting centered on joint intelligence and other activities the newfound allies could do to thwart Nasser. In that context, Peres and Dayan could barely believe their ears when the French agreed to supply Israel with its dream list of weapons, among them two hundred light tanks, seventy-two Mystère 4 jet fighters, and a huge amount of ammunition. Even the steep cost to Israel—eighty million dollars—could not take the edge off the men's triumph.

After the group returned from France, Ben-Gurion filled Golda in about the trip and the agreement reached (known as the Vémars Agreement). He also confided in Levi Eshkol, the finance minister, who would have to raise money to pay for the deal. The arms from France began arriving on July 24, unloaded at a small port near Haifa, to keep their presence unknown. Golda visited the port to witness the unloading, relieved to have the weapons even if she had no great love for the men who had acquired them.

Within days after the first French arms reached Israel, a new event made arms more crucial than ever. On July 26, Nasser stood before a cheering crowd of thousands in Alexandria and declared that his government was nationalizing the Suez Canal. The canal had been privately owned by an Anglo-French company, and Nasser's announcement, putting it under government control, came as a sharp slap at the once great colonial powers. Like mortally wounded animals rearing their heads for a final kill, England and France roared in their old imperialist tones and secretly spoke of joining forces to topple Nasser. In Israel, with the specter of an Egyptian attack hanging over the country and the intriguing prospect of aligning with world powers, Ben-Gurion began to listen more attentively to Peres and Dayan, who had been pushing for a preemptive strike against Egypt.

During the next weeks, Peres met several times with French officials, who proposed that Israel join France and Britain in an operation against Egypt the two nations had dubbed Operation Musketeer. Knowing they would enrage the United States and the United Nations if they simply invaded Egypt, the collaborators needed a pretext to cover their plans. Israel, in their eyes, could provide one. Accordingly, the Israelis were invited to France on a secret mission to meet with that country's top leaders: Prime Minister Guy Mollet; Minister of Foreign Affairs Christian Pineau; and Minister of Defense Maurice Bourgès-Maunoury. Ben-Gurion hesitated. Faced with actually putting Israel at war again, he needed more information than the rosy evaluations he had been receiving from Peres and Dayan. This time, instead of bypassing Golda, he appointed her head of the Israeli delegation to France. Her mission was to convey his concerns to the French and ferret out answers from them.

Before leaving, Golda received a long memo from Ben-Gurion with a list of items he wanted discussed. He began by stating that Israel would not start the action on its own. Nor would it participate in any action unless England agreed to that participation and guaranteed that Iraq and

Jordan, with whom the British had a defense treaty, did not open a second front against Israel. In one part of the memo, he outlined Israel's war goals: control of the shoreline of the Straits of Tiran so that its ships had free passage to the Red Sea; demilitarization of the Sinai Peninsula, except for Israeli positions on the Red Sea shores; and peace negotiations between Israel and any regime that replaced Nasser if he were overthrown. He also demanded that the United States be told of the planned operation. Above all, he wanted Golda to explain that failure for England and France might affect their prestige in the world. Failure for Israel could mean its destruction.

The memo ended with some personal advice. The conversation should begin on a positive note, emphasizing Israel's wish to participate in the operation and expressing gratitude to France for the help it had provided the country ever since the War of Independence. But, the prime minister added, Golda should not be too humble or "flatter too much."

Memo in hand, Golda boarded a rickety and badly lit old French naval bomber at an out-of-the-way airfield in Israel late on Friday evening, September 28, 1956, after the long Sukkot holiday. With her were Moshe Dayan, Shimon Peres, Minister of Transportation Moshe Carmel, and Colonel Mordechai Bar-On, who headed Dayan's office as chief of bureau. "I can picture to myself Golda's suffering in this suffocating space," Ben-Gurion wrote in his diary. "In a few more days perhaps we'll know whether it was worthwhile."

Most of the plane's passengers sat on the floor or on shaky wooden chairs; only Golda had a proper seat, in the pilot's cabin. Sometime after midnight, the plane landed at the French naval base in Bizerta, Tunisia. The base commander, a French admiral, had received orders to host the group but had not been told who the guests were. He arranged a sumptuous meal for them and rooms at a charming guesthouse. When he and some of his officers saw Golda, they assumed that as the only woman in the delegation she must be its secretary. Accustomed to pretty young female secretaries accompanying official French missions, they exchanged crude jokes among themselves in French about her unstylish grandmotherly appearance. She didn't understand what they said, but she could sense they were talking about her and probably noticed that Peres, who knew French, did not stop them. Hurt and humiliated by the snickering and apprehensive about the meetings ahead, she barely touched her food.

She and the others retired around three in the morning and by six took to the air again, on a more comfortable flight to France. The French chief of staff, Colonel Louis Mangin, and the deputy chief, General Maurice Challe, met them at the Villacoublay military air base and whisked them to the Pavillon Henri IV, a palace that had been converted to a luxury hotel in St.-Germain-en-Laye on the outskirts of Paris. (The meetings became known as the St. Germain conference.) On Sunday morning, the French sent a car to fetch Golda and her companions to Colonel Mangin's private residence in Paris. Most of the French ministers who greeted them there had served in the French underground during World War II. Observing them, Mordechai Bar-On sensed that as they contemplated going to war against Egypt, they relived in their minds the heroism of those earlier days. To them, Nasser had become another Mussolini, to be stopped and destroyed in order to maintain French honor.

The foreign minister, Christian Pineau, chaired the first session. Sitting next to him at a long table, Golda listened carefully to his forty-five-minute talk. He spoke of France's wish to start the war by mid-October, before elections in the United States, reasoning that Dwight D. Eisenhower, running for reelection, would be too distracted to oppose the operation. As he went on, Golda had the uneasy feeling that the French did not yet know whether England would join in the plan and they intended to explore various options themselves with the Israelis.

When Pineau finished his opening remarks, soberly raising questions but giving few answers, Golda presented the Israeli position. "Golda handled the meeting very carefully," Bar-On recalled. She began positively, as Ben-Gurion had recommended, then went through his memo point by point. She spoke "warmly, yet productively." In Pineau's response, he emphasized that the French did not believe America should be notified ahead of time. He presented different scenarios, but the one that cropped up most often had Israel making the first moves against Egypt, with France or France and England joining later. By the end of the political part of the conference, Dayan, still keen on having Israel fight alongside the European powers, felt let down. "The one point that emerged clearly was that the situation was unclear," he said.

Dayan took center stage at the afternoon sessions, which focused on military and strategic planning, although Golda sat in on most of the discussions. The next morning she met privately with the French prime minister, Guy Mollet. She had been disappointed that he had not shown up at the earlier sessions, and Peres hastily arranged their meeting. With the ill will between Golda and him, he was certain she would use Mollet's absence as a mark against him in her report to Ben-Gurion. Golda valued the meeting greatly. As foreign minister of a small country so often dependent on large ones, she felt good that in this operation a world power needed little Israel. Nevertheless, as the conference ended, the French leaders had not made a final commitment to the project or to Britain's participation in it. Nor had they revealed details of their own military plans.

For the trip home on the evening of October 1, Golda and her delegation flew in a luxurious DC-4 plane that President Truman had earlier presented as a gift to General Charles de Gaulle. Along with the Israelis, the flight carried General Challe and a high-level French military delegation that would spend two days in Israel assessing the country's wartime capabilities. As soon as the plane landed the next morning, Golda and her group drove directly to Ben-Gurion's office in Jerusalem to deliver their reports on the conference.

Peres believed with certainty that Golda gave a negative report. She had been "skeptical and dour" as the talks proceeded, he wrote, and when she returned to Israel, she "reported to Ben-Gurion that my assertions that the French wanted a joint operation were groundless, or at least wildly exaggerated." In fact, nothing in Ben-Gurion's diary or other writings substantiates that accusation or suggests that she urged him to kill the deal with the French. Undoubtedly, she took a dimmer view than Peres or Dayan of Israel's venturing into a partnership with France at this time. She had told Mollet, she reported, that Israel's cabinet had not yet made a decision about the operation, and he had responded that neither had the French. He was to bring the matter to his government only at the close of the current UN Security Council meetings about the Suez crisis. That information did not awaken new doubts in Ben-Gurion; it confirmed already existing ones and his reason for sending Golda to the meetings.

For weeks after the St. Germain conference, Ben-Gurion circled around the French plans. At one point, he made a list of the pros and cons of Israel joining the enterprise and discussed it with Golda and Dayan. When he learned that the scheme had Israel launch a war with Egypt as a pretext for the French and English to intervene, he was ready to drop out of the game altogether. Urged by Dayan and Peres, he finally agreed to meet with the French prime minister. He did not invite Golda to this meeting, although he consulted with her and Levi Eshkol before leaving for Paris on October 21. He might have wanted her at home while he was away, but she had to swallow the bitter pill of learning that the French foreign minister, Christian Pineau, attended the sessions and the British foreign secretary, Selwyn Lloyd, showed up for a while. Of the three countries involved, she was the only foreign minister not included.

The conference convened in a beautiful villa in Sèvres, a wealthy suburb of Paris. After much discussion, Dayan came up with a proposal for a limited Israeli operation that swayed Ben-Gurion: IDF forces would drop paratroopers into the Mitla Pass, an area in the Sinai desert about twenty-five miles from the Suez Canal. That night, a second battalion would fight its way through Egyptian border defenses in the Sinai to link up with the paratroopers. Because the action would appear to be a large retaliatory raid rather than the opening salvos of a war, it might not lead to world censure against Israel. At the same time, it would give the French and British enough of a pretext to "protect" the canal by calling on Israel and Egypt to pull their forces back from it. When Nasser refused, as everyone expected he would, the French and British would bomb Egyptian airfields and occupy the canal while Israel moved ahead with its own strategies. It was an adventurous plan, "grotesquely eccentric," Abba Eban was to say, but each of the parties wanted its ends badly enough that all three signed on to the Sèvres Agreement.

At home, Golda kept mum about the activity afoot. Before Ben-Gurion left for Sèvres, she held a meeting in Jerusalem for Israel's ambassadors to major countries. Speaking about flare-ups along the Jordanian border and the movement of Iraqi troops into Jordan to bolster it, she gave the impression that Israel might take action against Jordan. The ruse, which Ben-Gurion also perpetrated, worked so well that President Eisenhower sent a message to Ben-Gurion disapproving of Israel's "mobilization" of forces near the Jordanian border. In a second message, he indicated that France and Britain would be asked to help stop Israel, revealing his ignorance of the tripartite alliance and a severe failure of American intelligence.

It took enormous effort for Golda to hide the conspiracy from her family. She spent the weekend before the start of the operation at Revivim. She knew that if something went wrong, this kibbutz in the Negev would be one of the first places Egyptian forces attacked on their way into Israel. She said nothing to her daughter or son-in-law and tried to appear relaxed. As she prepared to leave, a young man in charge of security approached her. He had heard something about army mobilization orders. "I know that you can't tell me anything," he said. "But should we start to dig trenches?" Golda answered softly, "I think perhaps I would if I were you."

On October 28, 1956, one day before the launch of the operation, the cabinet gathered for its regular Sunday meeting. While the ministers met, the armed forces were being mobilized for war, but the cabinet as a whole still needed to approve the campaign. Ben-Gurion opened the meeting by spelling out the reasons for Israel's actions, the casus belli: Egypt's closing of the Suez Canal to Israeli navigation, its blockade of the Straits of Tiran, its responsibility for organizing the fedayeen attacks. He emphasized Israel's unique opportunity to ally itself with Britain and France, and with them, he hoped, to overthrow Nasser.

Golda marveled at the last point when she spoke. "I am standing in amazement," she said excitedly. "I cannot fathom what happened there, that we, the weak, the small, the humble suddenly became a focal point." Whatever her earlier doubts, she now backed the prime minister all the way. After heated debate, so did the cabinet. Relieved but exhausted, Ben-Gurion spiked a high fever and took to his bed, where he remained during the first, crucial week of the war. Golda ran the next day's cabinet meeting, waiting nervously for the campaign to begin.

At 5:00 p.m. that day, Monday, October 29, 395 Israeli paratroopers dropped from sixteen Dakota transport planes into the Sinai, at the eastern entrance to the Mitla Pass. At the same time, three other IDF battalions crossed the border into Sinai, moving across the desert toward the parachutists. Before Egyptian commanders could grasp what was happening, Israeli airplanes, flying very low, cut the telephone wires in Sinai with their propellers, isolating the Egyptian forces from contact with headquarters. "Israel this evening took security measures to eliminate the Egyptian fedayeen bases in the Sinai Peninsula," a spokesman from the Foreign Ministry announced, presenting the operation as a retaliatory measure.

As agreed at Sèvres, a day later British and French envoys warned Egypt and Israel to pull back from the canal or the two powers would have to act to "restore peace." Israel accepted the ultimatum; Egypt, as expected, rejected it. In the next step according to plan, the British Royal Air Force was to start bombing Egyptian airfields at dawn on Wednesday, October 31. But the British delayed their attack for twelve hours, leaving Israel on its own and causing Israeli leaders great anxiety. In the meantime, however, Israeli ground forces gained control of large parts of Sinai, and by the time the combined Anglo-French armies landed in Alexandria and Port Said near the Suez Canal on November 5, the Israel Defense Forces had conquered the entire Sinai Peninsula, including the Gaza Strip, and lifted the blockade of the Straits of Tiran. They took thousands of Egyptians as prisoners, while the Egyptians seized only four Israelis. More than a thousand Egyptian soldiers died in the fighting; Israel lost 172 lives.

"The military says there has never been anything like it, and there is nothing like it," Golda exulted as she spoke at a Mapai meeting about the IDF's lightning victory. "That in such a short time, they would take such a large area against weapons like that and with so few losses." Of course, she continued, not to appear coldhearted, "every life lost is a world darkened for someone." Still, there was great "honor" and "glory" and "wonder" in what the armed forces achieved. A euphoric Ben-Gurion rejoiced in "the greatest and most glorious military operation in the annals of our people and one of the greatest in the history of the world."

Unfortunately, the diplomatic scene did not reflect the military triumph. Outraged at Israel's offensive, and the more so because it took place behind his back and just a week before the American election, President Eisenhower summoned an emergency session of the UN Security Council on October 30, soon after Israel began its assault. When England and France vetoed the council's resolution demanding a cease-fire and Israel's withdrawal from Egypt, the president transferred the issue to the General Assembly. He exploded with even greater fury when he realized that those two European nations, America's World War II allies, had colluded with Israel, "double-crossing" him with their secret operation. He became a prime mover in spurring the United Nations to take a stand against the three conspirators.

On November 4 and 5, as Israeli forces wound up their conquest of the Sinai Peninsula, Dag Hammarskjöld and Golda Meir exchanged messages. The UN secretary-general informed Israel's foreign minister of the General Assembly's resolution for an "immediate cease fire" and Israel's withdrawal "behind the Armistice Lines" established in 1949. In response, Mrs. Meir addressed five questions to the secretary-general, which could be boiled down to one: Would the status quo with Egypt change? That is, would Egypt recall its fedayeen gangs and lift the blockade of Israeli shipping? The questions went unanswered. But in a cable on November 5, Hammarskjöld informed Golda that the General Assembly had voted to establish the United Nations Emergency Force to supervise a cease-fire. That evening, with its military success assured, Israel accepted the cease-fire.

But now a new menacing factor colored the picture. The Soviet Union had been preoccupied during the first days of the Sinai fighting with an uprising in Hungary, which it brutally crushed on November 4. Free to turn their attention elsewhere—and wishing to turn world attention away from the Hungarian revolution—Soviet leaders jumped into the Middle East crisis, on Egypt's side. The Soviet prime minister, Nikolai Bulganin, sent harsh messages to France, Britain, and Israel. The severest went to Israel, accusing it of "sowing hatred for the State of Israel among the Middle East nations" and warning that it was "putting in jeopardy the very existence of Israel as a state." To drive home that point, the note added that the U.S.S.R. was "taking measures now to put an end to the war and curb the aggressors."

The Soviet posture terrified the Western world. A day after receiving Bulganin's telegram, Ben-Gurion secretly sent Golda and Peres to Paris to probe the French reaction. Their accounts, as usual, reflected their attitudes to each other. Peres portrayed Golda as asking Pineau foolish questions, and she simply ignored his having been there with her. Both relayed, however, that the French regarded the Soviets with great apprehension. "When I left Pineau at eight in the evening he was in despair," Golda told the cabinet. Aside from the Soviet threats, the French ambassador in Washington had received a chilling warning from the United States that if France did not obey the United Nations, America would not come to its aid if Russia attacked it. "They look terrible," Golda said of the French leaders. "They don't sleep at all."

Her report to the cabinet became part of a larger, anguished debate about what Israel should do. In the most recent General Assembly vote, ninety-five nations supported a resolution to have Israel leave Sinai and the Gaza Strip immediately, and only one nation—Israel—opposed it. (Britain and France abstained.) And with Russia in the picture, Eisenhower was squeezing the country harder than ever, threatening to cut off government aid or even sever all ties if it didn't give in. Aside from the president's angst about the possibilities of a nuclear confrontation in light of the Soviet threats, he and his advisers worried that the Russians would use the crisis to spread their influence across the Arab world. As a result, for the only time since 1947, when the two nations supported the partition of Palestine, the United States and the Soviet Union had a common cause: to oppose Israel, France, and Britain, America's friends.

The two European nations gave in almost instantly to the superpower pressures. Less than forty-eight hours after their troops landed near Suez, France and England announced their intention to pull out. They had gained nothing. Nasser had not been overthrown, the Suez Canal remained under Egyptian control, and the two countries appeared before the world as weak and inept. A day later, on November 8, Golda Meir cabled Dag Hammarskjöld, "The Government of Israel will willingly withdraw its forces from Egypt immediately upon the conclusion of satisfactory arrangements with the United Nations in connection with its international force." Israel, too, had buckled under international pressure. But it still had some fight left, and Golda would be on the front line.

That line moved to the United States. Golda's message to Hammarskjöld (and a similar one Ben-Gurion sent to Eisenhower) included a loophole: Israel's withdrawal depended on "satisfactory arrangements" for an international force in the areas it would leave. That meant that Israeli troops would not depart from Sinai without UN assurance that the Red Sea would remain open to Israeli shipping and that Egypt would not reoccupy the Gaza Strip, the source of the fedayeen raids. Abba Eban would negotiate these security needs feverishly with Dulles and others in the U.S. State Department. Much of Golda's work during the next four months involved making Israel's case at the United Nations in New York.

She left Israel on November 13 and walked into a hornet's nest of angry Israeli Foreign Ministry officials in the United States. These people had been among Sharett's strongest supporters. "She was detested and hated and unwelcome by all the Israeli diplomats," recalled Tamar Eshel. "They turned their backs and didn't help her at all." Her speaking skills, the unique ability she had to touch an audience, didn't serve her in this atmosphere either. She could not ad lib or display her emotions in her UN talks. Those speeches had to be precisely crafted, with staff members writing the various sections, which Golda reviewed and then read from a prepared text. "She couldn't stand it," Eshel said. "She liked to speak directly to people, not read from a paper."

Neither could she stand what seemed to her the overrefined routes of diplomacy. Abba Eban would say that his "worst moments" came when he had to meet Hammarskjöld together with Golda. "Her directness clashed excruciatingly with his subtlety." In one of her first meetings with the UN secretary-general, they had a confrontation that left them barely on speaking terms. Golda had joined Eban and other Israeli diplomats in a late night negotiating session with Hammarskjöld. When he remained adamant in his insistence that Israel withdraw unconditionally from the areas it had captured, she openly showed her disapproval of his stance and of him personally. Flushed and irritated by her criticisms, he lost his diplomatic aplomb and snapped, "Why are you so bitter, madam?" Taken aback for a moment, she quickly recovered. "Because I am anguished by the bitter fate awaiting our people if we are deprived of the capacity to defend ourselves," she replied.

Having heard about the clash, probably from Golda, Ben-Gurion noted to his cabinet that she was trying to repair the relationship. Making amends, she was to learn, was a large part of diplomacy, especially with the powerful and prickly. About Hammarskjöld, Ben-Gurion sympathized with her, convinced that the UN secretary-general "hated Israel in his heart."

Ben-Gurion planned to withdraw Israel's troops from the Sinai and Gaza in phases, over time, and to use that time to bargain with the UN and the Americans for conditions that would guarantee the country's security. Golda argued for those guarantees in speech after speech before the UN General Assembly. In one, on December 5, she spoke dramatically of the reasons Israel went to war. "For eight years now Israel has been subjected to the unremitting violence of physical assault and to an equally unremitting intent to destroy the country economically through blockade, through boycott, and through lawless interference with the development of its natural resources," she said. She raised her voice as she described the series of murders the fedayeen had committed, the massive stock of arms Egypt had amassed from Czechoslovakia, and the fact that "the soldiers of Nasser had an Arabic translation of *Mein Kampf* in their knapsacks." She asked, "What ought to be done now? Are we, in our relations to Egypt, to go back to an armistice regime which has brought anything but peace and which Egypt has derisively flouted? Shall the Sinai Desert again breed nests of fedayeen . . . ?"

Walking back to her seat with blank, disinterested faces all around her, she heard the applause of one person. She turned to nod gratefully to the delegate from Holland, one of the few nations that supported Israel. More acutely than ever, she felt the isolation of her country in that great forum of nations, "like an unloved orphan at somebody else's party," she said to Menahem.

In an effort to win diplomatic and public support for Israel, she set out to carry her message beyond the walls of the United Nations.

To the National Press Club in Washington, she reviewed the history of Nasser's rise to power, his alliance with the Soviet Union, and his constant threats to annihilate Israel. "At the Security Council, the Arab-Israel conflict had been discussed two hundred times in all these years," she said. "The United Nations seemed powerless to do more than consider each isolated incident after it had arisen." So Israel acted on its own, before "Nasser chose the day for the final blow." Now the United Nations needed to prevent Egypt from conducting hostilities against Israel. "That is the crux of the issue," she said, and her words were reported in newspapers throughout the country.

Flying to and from Washington and New York, she met constantly with key diplomats. Selwyn Lloyd, Britain's foreign secretary, found her "the easiest Israeli with whom to deal since Sharett's resignation." And as she did on every American trip, she spoke at UJA and Israel Bonds events, hopping from one city to another around the country. American Jews had been divided about Israel's Sinai campaign, many of them distressed by Eisenhower's ire and fearful of its effects on Israel, and on themselves. But large numbers united behind Israel's demand for security guarantees, and they showed their support by contributing greater sums to the philanthropies than they had in years. A series of rallies at New York's Madison Square Garden during the Hanukkah festival in December attracted twenty thousand people a night, the price of admission a minimum of a hundred-dollar Israel bond. When Golda or Eban rose to speak, the entire audience jumped to its feet, applauding. American Jews had not been as unified in their support of Israel since 1948, she told the crowds, and they cheered her wildly.

In a quieter mode, she won friends for Israel, and herself, at endless bonds dinners she attended. In Chicago, she shared the dais with George Meany, president of the AFL-CIO labor federation. An unflinching supporter of Israel, he compared Nasser to Hitler, to the applause of the audience. In California, she so impressed Harry M. Warner, a founder of Warner Bros., that he sent a letter to the White House asking the president to meet with her. "The dining room, which seats twelve hundred people, was filled to capacity and there were hundreds of people outside trying to get in to listen to her talk," he wrote. When she finished, "there wasn't a dry eye in the dining room, men and women alike." Mrs. Meir, he said, "was a very brilliant woman with a thorough understanding of a serious world problem." He could not think "of anything in the world that I would appreciate more" than an invitation to her from the president. At the risk of losing Warner's appreciation, Eisenhower turned him down. With the UN in session and foreign ministers from around the world in town, he received many such requests and had to refuse them, he explained. Besides, given the current Middle East crisis, if he saw Mrs. Meir, "the delicate and difficult negotiations . . . might be open to misunderstanding." We will never know whether a meeting with Golda Meir might have softened Eisenhower's attitude toward Israel, as it later would that of his successor, John F. Kennedy.

As it was, the president did not budge from his demand that Israel withdraw completely from all the territories it had occupied, and Golda did not budge from Israel's position that a UN force had to be in place before it withdrew from any of them. She appeared on television as often as possible, her face becoming familiar to millions of Americans. In whatever free moments she could find, she sandwiched in interviews with the press, sometimes sitting with a reporter on the white leather chairs outside the General Assembly Hall between sessions. Asked by one correspondent about comments that she represented a "tough" policy in contrast to Moshe Sharett, she replied, "I'd hate to call myself tough." Nevertheless, the correspondent wrote, "around the sometimes hostile UN, the general opinion is that she is."

Ben-Gurion glowed in the coverage she received. "I've heard many good things about Golda's performance," he told his cabinet. She is especially effective "when she appears before non-Jews, but even among Jews she makes a strong impression." Eban was a "genius," a man "of great intuition," he explained, but being away from Israel so long, he fell out of touch with the people; he lacked a sense of how they felt and what they wanted. Golda had that sense, which was why both were needed on the American scene.

Golda flew to Israel on January 10 to report to the cabinet on the situation at the UN. She'd had a "reconciliation meeting" with Hammarskjöld after their falling-out, but she saw no sign that his position had changed. He said little about the fedayeen attacks that had driven Israel to its actions in Gaza, and he ignored Nasser's stepped-up persecution of Egypt's Jews, forcing thousands out of the country and destroying the centuries-old Egyptian Jewish community. The next day she boarded a plane back to the States. The UN was taking up its resolution for Israel to withdraw from its captured territory, and the cabinet wanted Golda there.

Standing before the General Assembly on Thursday, January 17, 1957, she looked worn as she spoke, slowly and deliberately. Israeli troops had already withdrawn from most of the Sinai, she reminded the assembly. The issues that remained to be negotiated concerned the areas around the Straits of Tiran and the Gaza Strip. Israel would not leave those regions without ironclad assurances from the United Nations of its freedom to navigate through the straits and its freedom from "the nightmare of the previous eight years" of raids from Gaza. Hammarskjöld and Eisenhower responded to Golda's appeal by threatening sanctions if Israel's troops did not leave those last two areas, unconditionally.

A WEEK LATER, GOLDA MEIR was admitted to Mount Sinai Hospital in New York. She had fainted in her room at the Savoy Plaza Hotel during a late Wednesday night discussion with one of Israel's key ministers, Gideon Rafael. After administering two electrocardiograms, physicians at the hospital determined that she had not suffered a heart attack, as they originally suspected, but had collapsed from "exhaustion," a result of overwork. The diagnosis didn't surprise anyone on her staff. They had seen her return from Israel at two in the morning a week earlier, grab a few hours of sleep while she prepared for her UN talk, and spend every day after that huddled at meetings. And they well knew her habit of staying up most of the night, smoking, drinking dark coffee, and talking to whomever she could nab as company. "Whoever brought her the latest cables got stuck. She wouldn't let the person go home," recalled Esther Herlitz. "So we took turns for who would go to her at 10:00 or 11:00 when the latest cables came in."

Passing Golda's empty office while she was in the hospital, Tamar Eshel noticed letters, newspapers, and other papers that had come for her in the diplomatic pouch. "Nobody had bothered to take them to her," Eshel said. "Nobody wanted to help her." Eshel went to the hospital. She found Golda "terribly dejected" lying in bed. "Listen," Eshel said to her, "I'm one of the few women around here. I can help you a lot in this situation if you will let me." Golda declined the help, emphasizing that Eshel, divorced and with a young daughter, had her own responsibilities, probably Golda's way of avoiding having to feel beholden to a staff member. "I didn't offer again," Eshel remembered, her nose out of joint by being put off.

Golda left the hospital after three days, against doctors' orders, claiming that she felt fine. Back home in Israel, Sarah had given birth to a baby boy, and this was the day of his circumcision. Golda had airmailed a special outfit she bought in New York for the baby to wear at the ceremony. An hour before the event, she phoned Sarah to send her congratulations and assure her daughter that she felt well. A few days earlier, she had received a bittersweet letter from her close friend Henya Sharef describing the "charming" baby. "What a shame that you are not here to see Sarah so happy, actually beaming with joy," Henya wrote. "You have a lovely and happy family, and that is not a small thing," she added, as though to comfort Golda for her absence from yet another family milestone.

Making the absence even harder to bear, in early February Eisenhower turned the screws tighter than ever with a sharp warning that if Israel did not withdraw unconditionally from the Sinai and the Gaza Strip, the United States would stop the flow of money to that country, including private funds, such as those from Israel Bonds and the UJA. The president even went on television to take his case to the American people and put additional pressure on Israel.

But Israel also had friends in America. Newspaper articles that had been critical of its initial actions protested the thought of sanctions against the small country. Two powerful congressional leaders openly opposed the president. The Republican Senate minority leader, William F. Knowland of California, decried the idea that Israel would be slapped with sanctions while the Soviet Union got away with its cruel suppression of the Hungarian revolt. The Democratic Senate majority leader, Lyndon B. Johnson of Texas, wrote to Dulles with strong objections to the administration's threats. Eleanor Roosevelt, Harry S. Truman, and others spoke out on Israel's behalf. Unmoved, Eisenhower would not change his position.

At the suggestion of Christian Pineau, a compromise was reached at the end of February. Israel would announce its full withdrawal on the "assumption" of its free passage through the Straits of Tiran and the establishment of UN control in the Gaza Strip. If Egypt violated this arrangement, Israel would retain its right of self-defense. Eban and his staff met with Dulles and his staff to hammer out every word of this agreement, which the United States would endorse in the UN after Golda spoke. She did not take part in the initial writing of the text, but when it came close to completion, she joined Eban and Dulles to review the speech, make amendments, and add her own ideas. Word in Israel had it that Ben-Gurion had not accepted several of Eban's recommendations to withdraw, but after Golda informed him that withdrawal had become necessary—reluctant as she was—he gave in. She now had the unenviable task of announcing Israel's decision from the rostrum of the United Nations.

The night before she was to speak, Golda had her staff make copies of her text to be placed on every delegate's desk so that everyone knew the exact terms of the pullout. On the afternoon of March 1, in the ornate General Assembly auditorium, she read the agreed-upon words: "The Government of Israel is now in a position to announce its plans for full and prompt withdrawal from the Sharm El Sheikh area and the Gaza Strip in compliance with resolution (1) of Feb. 2, 1957." She went on to stipulate all the "assumptions" and "expectations" Israel had been promised, including its right of self-defense if its ships did not receive free passage through the Straits of Tiran or if conditions in Gaza reverted to where they had been previously.

When she finished her prepared statement, she put down her notes, paused, then added a personal appeal to the Arab states: "Can we . . . all of us, turn a new leaf, and instead of fighting among each other can we all, united, fight poverty, disease, illiteracy?"

She returned to her seat, followed to the podium by Henry Cabot Lodge, head of the U.S. delegation. To her horror, Lodge did not say the words that had been so carefully negotiated. He hedged. He called Israel's conditions for withdrawal "not unreasonable." Worse, he spoke of working out the future of the Gaza Strip "within the framework of the armistice agreement" of 1949 that gave Egypt the legal right to the area, in Israel's eyes an almost open invitation for the Egyptians to return and start their attacks again. Listening to Lodge, it struck Golda that all the months of secret planning, all the military triumph, all the negotiations, the hours and hours of discussions, the obsessive dwelling on every word to be said—all of them had been futile. Israel had lost its battle that day, and she would never forget it. Many of her actions in the future would resonate with the memory of that loss.

Late that evening, in a state of agitation, she summoned Eban and Gideon Rafael to her suite on the twenty-seventh floor of the Savoy Plaza Hotel. She had received a confidential report that Hammarskjöld was discussing arrangements for Egypt's return to the Gaza Strip, and she wanted to ask Ben-Gurion to cancel orders for Israel to evacuate it. Eban argued that Israel had made a solemn pledge to the United Nations and could not go back on it. The two got into a shouting match, and when she ordered him to cable Ben-Gurion on the spot to postpone the withdrawal, Eban stormed out of the room, slamming the door behind him. "Golda slumped down in an armchair and held her head between her hands," Rafael wrote. After a while, she calmed herself, offered him a cup of coffee, and reviewed the day's events with him quietly.

20

Conflict and Charisma

W hat was will not be again," Golda Meir told journalists at the airport upon her return to Israel on the evening of March 9, 1957. Egypt will not behave in Gaza as it had before the Suez campaign, and Israel's ships will no longer encounter the difficulties they had experienced going through the Straits of Tiran. With that declaration, which she repeated three times to the press and again at a cabinet meeting the next day, Mrs. Meir hoped to mitigate the disappointment the nation and its leaders felt in the outcome of the Sinai campaign.

She looked good stepping off the plane, healthy, with no sign of her recent illness or of fatigue after the long battle at the UN. Having rallied from her despair after delivering her withdrawal speech to the General Assembly, she now tried to put the best face possible on Israel's retreat. The small nation had gained international recognition by standing up for what it believed even under the threat of sanctions, she emphasized in all her talks. Israel had not withdrawn out of fear of sanctions. In fact, many Americans had disapproved of Eisenhower's bullying, and the American Jewish community had stood solidly behind the Jewish state. Indeed, when the president tried to enlist prominent Zionist and non-Zionist Jewish leaders to his side, they opposed him with "strength and pride," she relayed.

Israel evacuated Sinai and other areas, Golda explained, because it had found itself isolated in the United Nations. It could not win votes for its cause and could not stand up forever against the UN demands. Only France had backed it. (Whatever Golda's attitude at the beginning of the operation, she had come to see France as a "true friend.") So when the French minister Pineau came up with a compromise that gave Israel the right to self-defense if Egypt were to revert to its original practices, she and the others agreed to accept it.

Golda's explanation at the cabinet meeting did not convince everybody. Casting about for someone to blame, Israel Bar-Yehuda from the Ahdut Ha'avoda Party, wondered about Abba Eban. Had the time come to replace the ambassador in light of his failure to convince Dulles or Eisenhower of the justice of Israel's cause? Golda instantly leaped to his defense. "If any hint comes out of this meeting that Eban is going to be recalled, I will not remain in this government even one hour longer," she threatened several times. It was a surprisingly vehement response in light of her blowout with Eban a week earlier, when she screamed at him and he slammed the door on her. In the best tradition of a benevolent boss, she felt called upon in this setting to protect and defend a member of her team. In the process, she also established that *she* was the boss. "I am responsible," she averred. "I was there. I am responsible, and I will not allow anyone to blame Eban." Regardless of how visible Eban had become or how many meetings he held with Dulles or Hammarskjöld, she wanted it understood that *she* bore the ultimate authority. "There is not another nation that has an ambassador or official in Washington or the United Nations who, by any measure, can equal Eban," she stated. That is not to say that the two always agreed on political matters. No, "we argued day and night." Nevertheless, *she* made the decisions, and *she* took responsibility for them. Eban could not be faulted.

"If you will ask me: are you a hundred percent sure of your position," she said, adding a dab of modesty to her unequivocal assertion of authority, "I am not a hundred percent sure. I am sure only that under the circumstances we did what we could do. Perhaps others would have acted differently. I . . . could not run things differently than I did."

With that and her reassurance that the government had behaved honorably even under the peril of sanctions, she hoped to calm criticisms of the Sinai campaign and its aftermath.

She had one more series of vexing confrontations in regard to that campaign, however. Ten days after her statement at the United Nations, the Egyptians moved back into Gaza, contrary to the agreement to have UN peacekeeping forces in control there. Golda hastily flew to Washington and New York to hold a flurry of angry meetings with Dulles and Hammarskjöld but made no headway. The UN was not going to fight Egypt, and Ben-Gurion decided that Israel would not either. The best it could do was to stay on guard against fedayeen attacks.

Neither Golda nor Ben-Gurion could foresee that those attacks would not recur, and her prediction that "what was will not be again" would hold true for the next decade. The war in Sinai had sent a message to Nasser of Israel's strength. The personnel he sent to Gaza held administrative, not military, positions, so Israel's borders remained free from incursions. The Straits of Tiran stayed open to Israeli shipping and commerce, allowing the country a period of economic growth and expansion. During that time, Israel's friendship with France held steady. Israel's relations with the United States, at their lowest ebb during the war, became stronger because of it. Americans admired the plucky little country that had stuck to its principles even against the giant Uncle Sam, and the administration took note of the power of the Israeli army that had captured the entire Sinai Peninsula within a hundred hours.

WITH TRANQUILLITY IN THE LAND, Golda turned her full attention to her Foreign Ministry work. On July 25, 1957, she received the prestigious Stephen Wise Award of the American Jewish Congress at a ceremony held at the King David Hotel in Jerusalem. She spoke about the blessings of her life, punctuating descriptions of each phase of her existence in the Land of Israel with the words "how much more can a Jew ask?" or "what more can a Jewish woman desire?" She hoped "never to lose the feeling that it is I who am indebted for what has been given me."

She meant what she said. Yet going to her office every day, she might have hoped for a little more in her dealings with staff members, many of them still hostile toward her because she was not Moshe Sharett. For her part, she did not go out of her way to win over the office staff or the foreign officers. "I found Golda a hard woman," said Anne Marie Lambert, a deputy director in the ministry. "She had some people she liked and others she didn't like, and you couldn't convince her that she was wrong." It was a pattern Golda carried through all her professional positions: a "black and white" personality, everybody said about her. Those she liked basked in her approbation; the disliked felt a shudder of rejection. But even her favorites often tiptoed around her. "She was the kind of person with whom you did not readily disagree," recalled Michael Arnon, who worked with her in many capacities. "When there was a discussion, the way she would sort of look at you was frightening."

"She didn't like women, especially pretty women, and she intimidated many of the men," remembered Colette Avital, who was then a young assistant in the foreign office. "She could be cutting and punitive, but she was also pragmatic." The foreign office space was very "primitive, almost like a barracks." Once, when a meeting room became too cold, Golda asked to have the air conditioner turned off. "Ten men tried to turn off the mechanism, which was old, and couldn't." Finally, with an air of disdain, Golda walked over to the machine and pulled out the plug. "Nobody else had thought to do that," Avital said with a laugh.

Annoyed with a laxness she sensed in the department she inherited, Golda took to showing up when people clocked in and out of work, reprimanding those who arrived late or left early, guaranteeing resentment against her. Nor did she endear herself to the foreign service officers when she decreed that nobody in the ministry was to have a romantic liaison at any post outside Israel. "I am not the pope," she said. "What members of the ministry do at home is none of my business. But it must be understood that when stationed abroad they represent the people of Israel." When she heard that an Israeli diplomat in Brazil was having an affair with a local woman, she had him recalled. "I'm sending you to Russia with your wife," she scolded. "You need to have a child. If not, you will lose your job." The man obeyed orders.

The relationship between Golda and her staff became so poor that at one time staff members threatened to go on strike. They were particularly incensed that she had been filling vacancies in the diplomatic corps by bringing in people she knew and trusted from the Mossad and other divisions instead of following the protocol of promoting people from within. Eventually, the staff came to an agreement with the management of the ministry that limited the number of noncareer diplomats a minister could appoint. Esther Herlitz, who had become chair of the ministry's staff committee, also encouraged Golda to invite staff members to her official residence in Jerusalem. It was the kind of thing Sharett did regularly but Golda had avoided. An event was planned, and the evening went off well enough, although basic strains lingered.

Golda had moved in to the two-story stone house in Rehavia, the old part of modern Jerusalem, in 1957, a few months after Sharett moved out. He had loved the spacious quarters on the quiet corner of Balfour and Smolensky Streets. For her the building became a lonely palace, which she filled by inviting young university students—the children of her friends—and others to live there at various times. She invited her son and his family to use the residence as their vacation home. An indulgent grandmother, she allowed the children free run of the house.

In the formal ground-floor dining room, she held innumerable dinner parties for distinguished guests, its food cooked in a well-appointed kitchen by the housekeeper Yehudit. She entertained visiting dignitaries and gave less formal lunches in the broad reception room with its silk draperies and doors that opened into a lovely garden. Students might stay in one of the three small maids' rooms on that floor or upstairs in the attic. Golda occupied the second floor, which had several bedrooms; a library stacked with books and mementos from her trips abroad; and a large modern kitchen, where she prepared simple meals. Contrary to myth, "she wasn't much of a cook," recalled David Harman, who lived in her house for four years and frequently "noshed" with her. Late at night, maybe twelve, one o'clock, she would wash her hair, comb it out, then sit at the green-vinyl-covered table at one end of her kitchen reading papers and cables she brought home from the office or having tea and cake with one of her live-in guests. Sometimes she invited close friends upstairs to help her thrash out an issue or just talk. One of them was Zalman Shazar, with whom she maintained a deep and long friendship, and a romance, through much of her life. "When I saw Shazar's hat and cane in the entrance lobby, I knew not to go upstairs," recalled Ben Rabinovitch, another of Golda's student boarders. "It seemed different with him than with some of the others."

Moshe Sharett visited Golda once in the house he had been forced to vacate. He and Zipporah paid a courtesy call after Golda suffered an injury from a hand grenade thrown from the balcony of the Knesset on October 29, 1957, the first anniversary of the Sinai campaign. A mentally deranged young man, Moshe Duek, had hurled the grenade from the last row of the visitors' gallery to a table below occupied by Golda, Ben-Gurion, and other cabinet members. Caught and beaten by spectators, he could give the police no coherent reason for his actions. Golda and Ben-Gurion were rushed to Hadassah Hospital, she with grenade splinters in her leg and he with splinters in his arm and leg. Discharged soon afterward, she had to rest in bed for several weeks and permanently suffered additional swelling in her already swollen leg.

She was still bedridden when Moshe and Zipporah Sharett came to call on November 9, their first return to the foreign minister's residence since they had left it. They spoke casually, avoiding anything serious. But for Sharett, being in the house again was devastating, as though he had revisited a "beautiful view whose appearance had changed with time and become one of desolation." More than a year after Ben-Gurion ousted him as foreign minister and Golda Meir replaced him, he still smarted from the insult, on both accounts. Sometimes he dreamed about the two leaders, disturbing dreams that startled him awake. In one, Golda was at the center of a scandal in which a friend had been cast out of his Tel Aviv apartment, a reflection of Sharett's feeling of being forced away from his beloved foreign minister's home.

EVEN IF SHARETT HAD TRIED to put the painful episode of losing the Foreign Ministry behind him, Ben-Gurion did not let it rest. In an insensitive (some might say cruelly conceived) public address he gave at a large gathering at the kibbutz Givat Haim, he described the changeover from Moshe Sharett to Golda Meir in terms that insulted and infuriated both of them. It was January 18, 1957, after the Sinai campaign but before Golda and Eban had finalized Israel's withdrawal from the captured regions. Relieved that the armed forces had procured weapons from France that made victory possible, Ben-Gurion spoke of two phases in that process. In the first, the country obtained only a small amount of armor and munitions. The second began when "Golda entered the Foreign Ministry at the end of June," he explained, giving the impression that she had acquired the weapons. He went on from there to contrast Golda with Sharett, without mentioning the latter by name. He was sure, he said, that Golda would not mind his remarking that the minister who preceded her in the foreign office excelled her in diplomatic experience, in general and Jewish knowledge, and even in many abilities. But, aside from her own talents, Golda's advantage lay in "not having any experience in the Foreign Ministry." Because of that lack, Israel was able to conduct its diplomacy without standard "formalities" and "protocol." As a result, its "most unorthodox efforts bore fruit," and Israel acquired the arms it needed.

The words took Sharett's breath away with their inference that were it not for his prissy "protocol" and "formalities," Israel might have filled its military needs sooner. He brooded over Ben-Gurion's speech for months before writing to him. When Ben-Gurion answered that he had intended no criticism, Sharett cited chapter and verse of the offensive remarks. After a time, he stopped corresponding with the prime minister and did not speak to him for the rest of his life.

Golda had an immediate, visceral reaction to Ben-Gurion's talk. "He's a wild savage!" she burst out to a colleague. Aside from demeaning the diplomatic experience she had gained from years of meeting with foreign leaders, he was rewriting history. "How could I have changed anything and arranged for these weapons?" she told friends. "The matter was concluded only days before I took on the assignment as foreign minister." She well understood the real meaning behind the "most unorthodox efforts" he spoke of: because of her inexperience, he and his aides could go around her to achieve their ends, as they could not with Sharett.

Golda was caught in a trap. She adored Ben-Gurion. She regarded him as probably the greatest leader and most "astute and courageous statesman" the Jewish people would ever produce. Her colleagues knew her to be a "true Ben-Gurionist," passionately in favor of his activist positions and supporting him "a hundred percent" on security as well as international matters. Yet, increasingly, she felt shunted aside in the role he had given her. In part that came from the nature of Israel's government, with its blurry lines between the Ministries of Foreign Affairs and Defense in a country always beset by security problems. Added to that, in his dual posts as prime minister and defense minister, Ben-Gurion wielded enormous power and thought nothing of handling important foreign policy matters himself, often leaving Golda out in the cold. In a typical incident, he gave a ninety-five-minute report on foreign policy to the Mapai Center one evening. When Golda's turn to speak came, she refused to utter a word. The prime minister had covered everything she was to say, including details of talks she had held with officials in Paris, London, and Rome. She then marched out of the meeting before it ended.

But from her viewpoint, the greatest impediment to her work as foreign minister was Shimon Peres with his penchant for launching out on his own into foreign affairs while skirting around her to deal directly with Ben-Gurion.

"What are you doing?" Isser Harel, head of Israel's intelligence, once asked Peres. "Golda and Ben-Gurion have a camaraderie that goes back years . . . Are you trying to split them?" Peres shrugged. "That doesn't interest me," he said. "She has issues she can complain about to Ben-Gurion; I have his approval."

Peres did have the "old man's" approval and more. Having secured weapons from the French and cemented a strong relationship with them, he also became the architect of Israel's nuclear program. With much cleverness and many backroom meetings, he persuaded the French to assist Israel in building a nuclear reactor, which, under great secrecy, was constructed in the desert town of Dimona. Still in his thirties, he had become Ben-Gurion's fair-haired boy, admired for his self-confidence, creativity, and daring. Intoxicated with his successes, Peres moved with impunity into foreign policy areas Golda viewed as her domain and kept her in the dark about most of his dealings. When she flew to Paris in

July 1957, to meet the economist Jean Monnet and discuss integrating Israel into NATO, she discovered that Peres had beaten her to that conversation without telling her. Enraged, she wept bitter tears to Israel's Defense Ministry's envoy in Paris, Arthur Ben-Nathan, canceled her meeting with Monnet, and returned to Israel. When she went to Vienna for a Socialist International conference, she found Peres on the same airplane. Earlier, Ben-Gurion had instructed him to report to her about his plans. Put off by his neglect to do so until that moment, she told him sharply that she felt too ill to talk to him.

Nothing provoked her more than Peres's pattern of going behind her back to speak to Ben-Gurion about matters concerning her or her envoys. On one occasion, the prime minister wrote to tell her that Shimon Peres had been in Italy, and though excited by the Italian government's friendship toward Israel, he felt that Israel's ambassador to Rome, Elyahu Sasson, "did nothing" to sway the Italian community as a whole toward Israel. In the state's quest to be accepted into NATO, it was important to develop friendships with countries like Italy, Ben-Gurion advised.

Golda saw the letter as a rebuke to her in her choice of ambassador and instantly lobbed back a barbed response. "How can a man who came to Rome for one day . . . know that Sasson does nothing in regard to public relations?" she asked. She had also been in Rome, she continued, and in the course of two days she had meetings with the president, the prime minister, the foreign minister, and members of the foreign service—all organized by Sasson. Furthermore, she held a press conference in Sasson's home with journalists from newspapers of all stripes, and she could see the positive attitude they had toward him. And by the way, she threw in, the very day that Shimon gave his report to Ben-Gurion, he gave a detailed accounting of his trip to Golda and her office and did not even hint at any criticism. When she later asked Peres about the discrepancy between his two reports, he answered that she had not asked him a specific question about the embassy, as Ben-Gurion had. A lame excuse, she held, for going behind her back.

She saved her zinger for last. She was not writing to Ben-Gurion because everything in the foreign office pleased her. Nobody was more critical of her department than she. She was writing to point out the traits of talented people "who cannot be satisfied with their own success unless they denigrate the worth of their opponent." And, she concluded, "I am pained by the fact that you accepted his viewpoint about this uncritically."

Generally, she did not have to compose such letters. She went to see Ben-Gurion regularly with complaints about Peres and his intrusions, on more than one occasion threatening to quit if the situation did not improve. "I told Golda that I am worried and saddened by her suspicions, which are totally groundless," the "old man" jotted in his diary. In one instance, he asked her to sit down with Peres and try to work things out, which she did, but their meeting of minds didn't last long. Most times Ben-Gurion tried to placate her with flattery and promises. He, too, was trapped, caught between his admiration and need for Peres and his affection and respect for Golda. So while giving Peres a freer hand than he knew she could tolerate, he sent encomiums her way at every possible opportunity.

When she was ill in the States during the Sinai campaign, he urged Eban to do his best to have her limit her activities, including fundraising. "Golda is more important to Israel than several million dollars," he wrote, probably hoping Eban would show those words to her. For the Stephen Wise Award ceremony, which he could not attend, he prepared a flowery letter of praise in honor of the "dear woman" Golda Meir, to be read aloud by Dr. Israel Goldstein, president of the American Jewish Congress. As it had had with the biblical Deborah, Israel's leader at the time of the Judges, he wrote, Israel had the privilege now at the dawning of the "third Temple" (a term frequently used for the young state) to have a "noble spirited, accomplished, and wise" woman like Golda in its top echelons. "She is the most precious gift American Jewry has awarded us." On her sixtieth birthday, in 1958, he mailed greetings to a "devoted pioneer," a "proud Jewess," a "strong and courageous fighter," and a good comrade, "strict and forgiving at the same time." He addressed his good wishes to "precious and beloved Golda."

In spite of the exaggerated prose, the warmth Ben-Gurion expressed toward Golda reflected real feelings on his part. He genuinely appreciated her many skills and loved her in his own way. After the death of Joseph Sprinzak, he noted in his diary how the eulogies went on endlessly, until Golda took the stand as the last speaker. "The whole evening was worthwhile just to hear her words," he wrote. "How does she know from her very first sentence to touch the heart of her listeners, straight into the depths of the heart and soul, and not to move from there until her final word?" He admired and valued such qualities.

And there was something else, less tangible. Ben-Gurion had lost his mother shortly after his eleventh birthday, and according to his biographers throughout his life he carried within him an idealized image of women as mothers and protectors. When Golda's mother died in 1952, he sent her a touching note about how he still "felt orphaned" so many years after the death of his own mother. A mother's passing is the greatest loss anyone can suffer, he wrote, because nobody else can ever substitute for the love and intimacy she provided. Golda might have been an old warhorse, a hardened politician, a severe critic, but she never stopped being a woman to him and, like all women, idealized on some level, the way his mother had been. "He didn't treat her the way he treated men," Yariv Ben-Eliezer, Ben-Gurion's grandson, said. "He was tender to her, mainly because she was a woman."

The other side of that coin, of course, was a certain degree of condescension that Ben-Gurion also projected toward Golda. It was the kind of condescension that allowed him to describe her publicly as inexperienced in foreign affairs, although he had appointed her foreign minister, that led him to listen with only half an ear to her bitter complaints while permitting Shimon Peres to pursue matters that rightfully belonged in her realm, and that would soon enable him once again to try to have Abba Eban supplement her foreign policy activities. Golda never wanted to be treated differently because she was a woman, idealized or not. When asked time and again how it felt to be the only woman foreign minister in the world, she invariably answered, "I don't know. I was never a man." She refused to be defined by gender, to the dismay of later feminists. She built her self-image around the work she did, her loyalty to her party, and her devotion to Israel and the Jewish people. So while Ben-Gurion's flattery pleased her, it didn't prevent her from asserting herself to him about her disagreements with Peres or from fighting for her goals with the strength and political savvy few of her colleagues could muster.

THE FIGHTS WOULD NOW center on the Mapai Party and the next general election, coming up in the fall of 1959. The rancor between younger members of the party and older ones that had been contained with difficulty over the last several years swelled in the late 1950s into a full-scale generational war. On one side, Golda Meir, Pinhas Sapir, Zalman Aranne, Pinhas Lavon, Giora Josephthal, and other elders lined up with the Bloc, mayors and party secretaries in Tel Aviv and local party branches. On the other side, Shimon Peres, Moshe Dayan, Abba Eban, Teddy Kollek, and other young party members clamored for a change of the guard. The impetus for their agitation came from Ben-Gurion himself. Aware of passing time and the infirmities of age, the "old man" hoped to infuse the party leadership with young blood, to invigorate it and perpetuate its premier position in Israel. Besides, he liked associating with the dynamic young men who worshipped him, clinging to his every word like disciples at the foot of the master.

Did he mean to push away his long-standing comrades? Probably not; he aimed to make space for the young while holding on to the veterans. But Ben-Gurion was hard to read, even for those who had worked with him over decades. He was known to speak out of both sides of his mouth, thus urging on the youngsters, as they were called, but still expecting complete loyalty from the elders, shunting off their fears and hurt reactions.

Golda led the pack of the angry old guard, in close alignment with Sapir, then minister of trade, and Aranne, minister of education and culture. The troika, people called them. She had already felt the heat of Peres breathing down her neck in foreign affairs. Now Dayan set off on a "biological campaign" against the establishment leaders. Hero of the Sinai campaign, Dayan had resigned as army chief of staff and was looking toward a career in government. At a students' club in Tel Aviv, he spoke bluntly of replacing the older generation with his new one. The early party leaders, he said, "look back proudly on their achievements of 1902 . . . before we were born . . . but we are interested in 1962." Not once, in a long rambling talk, did he mention socialism, the labor movement, or the Mapai Party, all the things that meant most to Golda. As disturbing, at a Mapai convention a little earlier, he slammed into the party's sacred cow, the Histadrut labor organization, demanding that it be made over more efficiently.

With every new blow directed at them, the veterans became more convinced that Dayan, Peres, and the other youngsters were intent on a putsch, a military takeover of the government, backed by Ben-Gurion. "I could not believe my ears," the "old man" wrote, after Levi Eshkol told him how threatened the elders felt. "I explained the absurdity of the notion." Still, the veterans clung to their suspicions and their determination to fend off the Young Turks.

Golda had a special and personal battle to wage. In the middle of June, she entered Beilinson Hospital, this time with a severe case of gallstones. When Ben-Gurion visited, the doctors urged him to persuade her to fly immediately to a hospital in Boston noted for gallbladder surgery. Without that, her life might be in danger. She refused to leave Israel, and fortunately on June 19 she survived a successful operation at Beilinson. As she might have expected, news of her illness quickly spread to Israeli newspapers. She did not expect, however, that it would also reach the London-based *Jewish Observer and Middle East Review* or that the paper would suggest that because of her illness she was giving up her Foreign Ministry post. Nor did she expect the American television personality Ed Sullivan, who wrote for New York's *Daily News*, to report that Abba Eban would most likely replace her if she were to leave. Distraught at these reports, she accused Peres of having planted them. He had cultivated the press for years in every land he visited and was especially close to Jon Kimche, editor of the *Jewish Observer*. Peres categorically denied the accusations. "I was Golda's greatest victim," he was to say later. "Nobody suffered from her as I did."

In an effort to calm the waters between the warring groups of young and old, Ben-Gurion held two "reconciliation" meetings at the Kfar Hayarok (Green Village) Agricultural School. Golda attended the first on November 22, 1958. Worn out by her illness and emotionally drained by the rumors about her, she listened to the arguments on both sides but said nothing. By the second meeting, on December 6, she had gathered new energy and plotted a new course. She was not an "idiot" who didn't like the young, she assured her comrades. "I like the young. I also like old people, but not the old just because they are old and not the young because they are young." What she liked was an "honest, sympathetic person who does something for its own sake" and not for the sake of furthering himself. Her meaning was obvious: The young she rejected were not "honest, sympathetic" people. In fact, they were people "who think there is no need for ideology," an unacceptable stance in a party built around the ideology of labor.

Then she dropped a bombshell. After the elections, she would accept no position in the party, not in the cabinet, not in the Knesset, and not in any other institution. "I was incapable of thinking of anything," Ben-Gurion entered in his diary. "I was stunned." He had good reason to be. This was not the usual threat to resign that she—and he—regularly brandished to get their way. Her voice, her scathing language, the suddenness of her announcement, indicated that she meant what she said this time: You want to reject me for your youngsters? Good. I will reject you first, and let us see how well you manage without me.

Wherever Ben-Gurion turned after that, he saw evidence of Golda's burgeoning power and his need for her. In internal elections to the

Mapai labor council in Tel Aviv, the largest branch of the party, she won more votes than anyone, including every young candidate. Too old? Not satisfied with simply casting their ballots for her, many voters added written messages near her name on the order of "long live Golda" or "Golda—until 120 years," thumbing their noses at the idea that she was expendable because of her age or illness. Her popularity was such that party leaders in Tel Aviv offered her any slot she might want, if, indeed, she planned to give up the Foreign Ministry. Why not run for mayor again, or take over as secretary of the party or head of the Tel Aviv Mapai branch? The important thing was not to lose Golda Meir.

She rejected every offer, although as a loyal party member she worked hard for Mapai during the election campaign. On a stifling-hot Tuesday, November 3, 1959, the party won the largest victory in its history, gaining 47 of the Knesset's 120 seats, 7 more than it had before. Bypassing the triumphant win, Golda stuck to her resolve not to resume her Foreign Ministry position. Zalman Aranne joined her by turning down his post as minister of education and culture. There had been stories over the years identifying Aranne as one of Golda's lovers. A dedicated laborite, good looking, with large almond-shaped eyes and strong cheekbones, he spoke a rich, self-taught Hebrew that probably impressed Golda and was highly sensitive and emotional, which might have touched her soul. Lovers or not, they were good friends, and she appreciated his comparison of the youngsters' treatment of the veterans to the Eskimos, who, "when they grow old and their teeth drop out," are taken far away into the snow to die. "But we veterans still have teeth!" he would say.

Golda had teeth, and she used them to hold on tightly to her refusal to join the cabinet, while Ben-Gurion tried in every way to woo her. Not only did he want her in his government for her own sake, but he also realized that, like Aranne, other veterans would follow her out if she did not stay and he would be unable to form a coalition with other parties without the old guard predominant in his cabinet. Time and again, he made a special effort to show his respect for Golda; even before the elections, he appeared at the airport with a contingent of dignitaries to welcome her home after one of her trips abroad, something he rarely did for other ministers. At one private meeting, he asked her to be open with him. What did she have against him? Why was she so angry? She reminded him that she had not sought the job of foreign minister. He had given it to her, yet he had "no faith in her authority." In the fraught days before the Sinai campaign, he had dispatched Dayan and Peres to

France and not her. And although she had worked with all her strength at the United Nations, he spoke only about Abba Eban's role at that international body.

"Nothing I said helped," Ben-Gurion wrote, still unable to understand how she could feel so wounded by acts to which he had probably given little thought. To Golda, that was exactly the point. They were thoughtless acts.

For six weeks, Golda Meir refused to resume the role of foreign minister, while newspapers speculated on how Mapai would form a government. When she finally told Levi Eshkol that she would return to the government, but only as labor minister, Ben-Gurion sensed a crack in her armor and persuaded her to remain as foreign minister and not confuse the world by switching ministries. On November 29, she agreed to do so. She had made her point: Ben-Gurion and her party needed her unequivocally.

There was still, however, some unfinished business to be attended to. When Golda first announced that she would not continue as foreign minister, Ben-Gurion had signaled to Abba Eban that he would replace her, an arrangement that began circulating widely in the press. After twelve years of representing Israel abroad, Eban had resigned from his ambassadorial positions and returned home to preside over the Weizmann Institute in Rehovot. At the same time, he eagerly entered politics, one of Ben-Gurion's young men hoping to change the face of the Mapai Party. After the elections, when Ben-Gurion recognized that he needed Golda Meir as foreign minister, he offered Eban a cabinet position as minister without portfolio. He planned—without consulting Golda—to have Eban work closely with her, as a deputy minister. The young man would represent Israeli policies abroad, take on special diplomatic missions, and generally assist her in her work. His suave diplomacy would balance her earthiness.

On December 1, Eban called on Mrs. Meir to discuss his assignments in the foreign office. She didn't beat around the bush. Someday he would probably be a fine foreign minister, she said sweetly. For now, anything he did in the Foreign Ministry would only interfere with her responsibilities. She was sure he could occupy himself with other matters and in a different location. She saw no reason for him to situate his office in the Foreign Ministry building. Greatly disappointed, Eban spoke to Ben-Gurion, who advised him that he needed to learn more about the country and its people, after having been away for so long. "Maybe over time, Golda will change her mind—or maybe not."

When the prime minister presented his cabinet to the Knesset on December 16, three fresh young Mapai faces appeared in it. Moshe Dayan held the relatively minor portfolio of minister of agriculture, Abba Eban had been named minister without portfolio, and Shimon Peres was to become deputy defense minister, not fully in charge of the department. The elders in the party filled most of the other key positions. (Zalman Aranne returned as education and culture minister after Golda accepted the Foreign Ministry.) For now, in the battle of the generations, Golda and her comrades had come out ahead.

THROUGHOUT THE INTERNAL POLITICAL WRANGLES, Golda managed to perform her Foreign Ministry duties without interruption. She was particularly attentive to an unexpected wave of immigrants arriving from Poland. In 1956, the Soviets signed a repatriation agreement with Poland that allowed people who had fled from there to the U.S.S.R. during the Nazi invasion to return to their homeland. Under the reformist Polish president, Władysław Gomułka, Jews who arrived in Poland from Russia through repatriation received permission to continue on to Israel or to Western countries if they wished. Tens of thousands of Jews took advantage of that arrangement, many going directly from Poland to Vienna or Naples and from there to Israel. Although Israel encouraged and welcomed the immigration, the sudden large influx put a burden on the young state, which was also coping with streams of immigrants from Romania, Morocco, and other countries.

Golda wholeheartedly supported the immigration in spite of difficulties. "I cannot recall a situation in Israel in which all the immigrants had work, and everything was good and beautiful," she said to government leaders who complained about the difficulties of finding work for the many newcomers. And she was irritated that HIAS (the Hebrew Immigrant Aid Society) had obtained permits for numbers of Polish Jews to go to Canada and Australia, steering them to those countries instead of Israel. Worse, because those governments had strict health regulations for admitting immigrants, some of the youngest and strongest Polish Jews headed there, which left many of the weakest and sickest for Israel.

The health of the Polish immigrants troubled Israel's leaders. Many were aging Holocaust survivors, some elderly men and women whose families in Poland, reluctant to care for them, urged them to go to Israel after they returned from Russia. How does a state meant to be a refuge for Jews from all parts of the world cope with the large numbers of old and sick pouring in? In a highly charged meeting of the "coordination committee," a joint panel of representatives of the government and the Jewish Agency, Ben-Gurion spoke frankly. "We need the Jews no less than the Jews need us," he said. The question, however, was not the "size of the immigration, but its quality." Israel wanted children and young people who could work and protect the country. Instead of simply accepting sick people from Poland, shouldn't the country's representatives try to regulate immigration from various lands to admit mostly healthy people?

As a result of this and other discussions, in April 1958 Minister of Foreign Affairs Golda Meir was given the task of writing to Israel's ambassador in Poland, Katriel Katz. "A proposal was raised in the coordination committee to inform the Polish government that we want to institute selection in aliyah, because we cannot continue accepting sick and handicapped people," she wrote. She went on to ask the ambassador whether he thought this limitation could be explained to the Poles without its hurting the flow of immigration in general. More than fifty years later, that letter was rediscovered and Golda was severely and personally attacked for asking to halt the "aliyah of sick, disabled Polish Jews." For the record, then: the criticism was unwarranted. Golda's letter reflected a difficult committee decision led by Ben-Gurion, which she conveyed. She, more than any government official, consistently called for unlimited immigration into Israel. In the end, the matter seems to have been dropped, and the immigration continued without limitation.

Her travels as foreign minister aroused less controversy. In August 1958, she became the first Israeli foreign minister officially invited to London. Ten years after the creation of the state, the coldness between the two countries had finally begun to thaw. In a whirlwind four-day tour, Golda made the rounds of television, radio, and newspaper interviews and was feted by the Jewish community, which regarded her visit as "an outstanding success." The same month, she visited General Charles de Gaulle, who had become prime minister of France in June. Somewhat intimidated by his heroic reputation and the pomp of the Élysée Palace, where they met, Golda felt anxious about not being able to speak to him in French. But the general put her at ease, vowing through an interpreter his undying friendship for Israel; it was a friendship that would shrivel up before the end of the next decade. For the time being, as the French foreign minister, Maurice Couve de Murville, told Golda, de Gaulle had a soft spot in his heart for her. When they next met—at President Kennedy's funeral—he strode across the room to greet her, a sign of esteem from someone who expected others to kowtow to him, and spoke to her in English, an even rarer gesture.

She visited nine Latin American countries, a turning point in Israel's relations with those nations. In Japan, she met the emperor Hirohito and, at her request, attended a traditional geisha party, where she sat on cushions on the floor. In the Philippines, she received an honorary degree from the Catholic University of Manila, and in northern Burma (now Myanmar) she inspected farming villages built on the model of the Israeli *moshav* (cooperative farming village) by people who—at her invitation—had gone to Israel to learn about those border settlements. Wherever she traveled, she sent home picture postcards with short greetings to her grandchildren, and when she returned, she invariably had a bagful of inexpensive gifts for everyone in the family.

Hers was the work of any foreign minister: confer with world leaders, negotiate treaties, grant interminable interviews, and win friends for one's country. Yet for someone who never discarded—and frequently fell back on—the image of herself as a child coping with poverty and hunger, those world travels carried an extra dimension of awe: here am I, Goldie Mabovitch of Pinsk, meeting with the queen mother of Cambodia, the president of Italy, the emperor of Japan. When she received an honorary doctorate degree from a South American university, she cabled home that she was proud it had been given to the daughter of a carpenter. That attitude of awe (even if sometimes exaggerated for public consumption) reinforced her ability to connect with people by being herself, without the trappings of traditional diplomacy.

Most rewarding to her and fruitful for Israel were the ties she established with the emerging nations of Africa. "Representing the Jewish state can be a very lonely experience," she told a group of trainees entering the Foreign Ministry. Encircled by hostile Arab nations, "Israel is entirely by itself in the international community." It needed friends, and the new nations of Africa, in the process of gaining independence from colonial rule, offered attractive sources for that friendship. Israel, in turn, had much to give those nations from its experience as a small new country that had worked hard to build its economy, feed its people, and create a national culture. Beyond the rhetoric, this partnership became for Golda a personal and emotional commitment.

Ehud Avriel, Israel's first ambassador to an African country, went to Ghana in 1957. A year later, Golda visited Monrovia, the capital of Liberia, which had become independent years before any other African state.

Its president, William Tubman, had a historic connection with Israel. In November 1947, he had cast the decisive vote in the UN General Assembly that created the State of Israel. When Golda asked him why he had done that, given Arab pressure on him to vote against Israel, he told of coming to the United States as a young man to plead his country's cause in Washington, which had accused it of slave labor and cut off all relations. A congressional committee questioned him brutally and treated him with derision, except for one congressman, Emanuel Celler, a Jew who befriended him and helped him present his case. With that, he became a lifelong friend of the Jews. The story delighted Golda, and the two developed a warm and lasting relationship. As the high point of her visit, the Liberian tribe of Gola made her a paramount chief, bestowing on her the title of honorary queen mother. After a secret initiation rite in a tiny straw hut, she emerged proudly flaunting her bright, colorful tribal robes.

Her reception in Ghana had darker tones. It coincided with the All-African People's Conference in Accra, a gathering of delegates from national liberation movements across the continent, including the Algerian FLN, the rebel organization that had fought France in Algeria. At the invitation of George Padmore, chief theoretician behind the Pan-African movement, Golda met with sixty key conference leaders. The first question thrown at her mirrored the antagonism in the room: How could Israel justify accepting arms from France, the "Satan" that had sought to thwart African self-determination?

She chose her words carefully. "Our neighbors are out to destroy us. They get more weapons than they know how to use from the Soviet Union, free." France alone stood ready to sell Israel arms. "Even if de Gaulle *was* the devil," she said, "I would regard it as our duty to buy arms from him to keep my people from being annihilated once again." Her directness worked. Appreciative of the foreign minister's candor, the revolutionaries applauded her.

That meeting laid the foundation for Israel's International Cooperation Program (MASHAV in the Hebrew acronym), a plan of aid to developing countries. The aid took many forms. In Ghana, Israel helped create and run the country's Black Star shipping line and brought in Solel Boneh for joint housing and public works projects. In Mali, it developed a fish-processing program; in Tanzania, it began a pilot project for irrigating cotton; in Tanganyika, it established a youth leadership training center. Over the years, thousands of Israelis went to Africa to teach and advise workers in agriculture, industry, commerce, and medical practices. In many cases, Golda ignored protocol and bypassed professional diplomats to place Mossad agents in the African countries, infuriating her Foreign Ministry staff. With the large Muslim population there, she considered those operatives necessary for Israel's security even while they worked with the local people. She chose kibbutzniks to fill various roles, because of their expertise in agricultural techniques and their down-to-earth outlook. (For an African party that called for "formal dress or national costume," one kibbutz-born ambassador donned khaki pants and khaki shirt. "What's that?" the host asked. "National costume," the man replied.) In turn, hundreds of Africans went to Israel to be educated in specialized fields.

"Africamania," the former Shin Bet chief Amos Manor dubbed the phenomenon. Israel buzzed with the novelty of its newfound enterprise. African students attended Israeli universities, doctors and nurses trained in its hospitals, farmers lived on agricultural cooperatives, all of them now part of the country's landscape. "Relations with Africa are the central point in Israel's life, not merely her foreign policy," Golda said at a dinner party she threw in New York's Essex House for representatives from fifteen African nations attending UN General Assembly meetings. But, she emphasized whenever she had the opportunity, Israel had no desire to become a colonial power, seeking to exploit the Africans as the Europeans had. "We are not trying to establish ourselves in Africa . . . As soon as our work of assisting is completed, we will move out and on," she promised.

She did not mention publicly, nor did anyone, that a chunk of the money the country needed for its assistance to that continent came from the United States. Still in the throes of the Cold War, the Soviets attempted to influence the African countries by sending technicians there regularly. And Arab leaders, backed by the Soviets, were determined to break Israeli-African friendships and establish strongholds of their own. With that climate, the United States realized that helping Israel form alliances with Africa served its national interests as well. As President David Dacko of the Central African Republic told Ehud Avriel, "Israel was a small country without a colonialistic past and with an original social structure." While providing funds but remaining in the background, America could depend on Israel, with its strong Western orientation, to help stave off Communist ambitions in the African continent.

Golda loved going to Africa. In two extensive tours, she flew from one country to another: Cameroon to the Ivory Coast to Liberia to Sierra Leone to Guinea to Ghana one year, within little more than two weeks. Appearing the proper minister with a small white pillbox hat perched on her head, white shoes and gloves, she often alighted from small airplanes that might turn someone else's stomach and smilingly returned the greetings of officials come to welcome her. At a gala farewell party in Ghana, she led African leaders and Israeli delegates in a spirited hora, which turned into the highlife, the traditional, rhythmic African dance. From then on, photographs of her dancing the hora with African dignitaries and ordinary folk, in exotic locations or at her home office, became iconic testaments to the love affair she and Israel had with the African nations. If some of the heads of state she dealt with were corrupt, she didn't see that or, more likely, chose not to. "We don't mix in," she told reporters. Nor could she imagine that one by one her African friends would abandon Israel for their Arab "brothers" and be gone by 1973.

For the present, the Africans adored her country and her, a happy relief from her turf wars at home with Peres and the wrestling between veterans and youngsters. This was *Golda's* turf, and even though Peres made military deals with African leaders and Dayan received a hero's welcome when he toured the African countries as minister of agriculture, she earned the greatest accolades. "It's very hard to understand logically how accepted she was by the Africans," said Hanan Aynor, a key Israeli adviser on African affairs. "A woman in Africa at that time . . . was nothing more than a work mule, with no education." When Golda came along, one might have thought African leaders would not relate to her in any way. "Yet just the opposite happened . . . They treated her with such deep respect."

That respect and admiration flowed from ordinary people as well. She visited schools and hospitals, met with labor leaders and social workers, and people responded as though she belonged to their family. "Little Africans called Golda Meir are running around the bush," wrote the journalist Marlin Levin in his background notes to a story about her. Lou Kadar, who had worked with her in Moscow, served as her French translator and all-around secretary in Africa. Every time a new Golda or Golda Meir was born in Congo or Ghana, Togo or Sierra Leone, she sent a small gift from the foreign minister to the parents and new baby.

The women of Africa felt a special connection to Golda, and she took a genuine interest in them. Together with Mina Ben-Zvi, a social activist, and Inga Thorsson, later the Swedish ambassador to Israel, she organized a seminar in Haifa titled "The Role of Women in a Developing Society" that attracted delegates from twenty-two Asian and African countries, many of them from states in which less than 1 percent of the female population was literate. "The world will not know peace, and there will be no real happiness until we, the new peoples of the world, reach a standard of living and education that is comparable with that of the old and wealthy nations," she said. "And since the problems are so great, fifty percent of the people, that is only the male population by itself, cannot solve it."

Out of this seminar grew the International Training Centre in Haifa, which continues to train people from Asia, Africa, and Latin America in skills that will help women play vital roles in their country's development. Eventually, it carried Golda's name in its title.

Over the years, Golda logged more than 100,000 miles on her trips to Africa. After one tour, the Reverend Billy Graham asked for the secret of her success. Her quip, "Maybe it's because we go there to teach, not to preach," became part of the Golda Meir quotables.

SHE DIDN'T PREACH HER socialist principles in Africa, but she tried to demonstrate them. After attending Zambia's Independence Day celebration in 1964, a group of foreign dignitaries were taken by buses to visit the spectacular Victoria Falls, which meant crossing the border into Southern Rhodesia (today Zimbabwe). At the border, Rhodesian police refused entry to black leaders on Golda's bus. "In that case," she said indignantly, "I'm sorry, but I won't be able to enter Southern Rhodesia either." The other guests, from such countries as the United States, Britain, Germany, and France, followed her lead and traveled with her back to Zambia. As word of her action spread, she became a hero in the fight for African independence.

Along those lines, she stood firmly behind the fight against apartheid in South Africa, a country she refused to visit because of that policy. At the United Nations, she consistently sided with the black African nations against South Africa. When South Africa's foreign minister, Eric Louw, defended his government's policies in the General Assembly, at Golda's instructions Israel voted with the African nations in favor of censuring him, although all the Western states, with the exception of Holland, either abstained or absented themselves from the vote. The perception that a person should be "stamped as inferior" because of the color of his skin, she said at one UN session, defies the most basic human premise that "all men are created equal." In 1964, when Nelson Mandela and other leaders of the African National Congress—many of them Jewish—were arrested and tried for their anti-apartheid activities (known as the Rivonia trial), Golda instructed the Israeli Foreign Ministry to prepare a manifesto denouncing the trial. The ministry secured the philosopher Martin Buber and the author Haim Hazaz to create it. Of Hazaz, Golda avowed in the Knesset, "Without doubt his words expressed what all Israel feels." She described Mandela as making a "brilliant" appearance at the trial, "which bravely and powerfully expressed the pain of millions of Africans," and quoted parts of his speech.

Golda's strong stand against the South African apartheid government embarrassed South African Jews, who were staunch supporters of Israel but did not want to appear disloyal to their country. While they did not expect Israel to put their interests above its own, some said, they wondered why "it always had to be at the head of the queue in taking measures against South Africa." After the Yom Kippur War, when most African countries broke with Israel, its relations with South Africa improved, although it continued to oppose apartheid.

While they lasted, Golda's friendships with the African nations provided a bulwark against Arab attempts to condemn Israel and isolate it. When Arab delegates banged their tables after she spoke at the UN or shouted at her to go back to Milwaukee, the Africans applauded her. On a personal level, her all-out efforts brought her popularity and recognition around the globe. She had come into her own as Israel's foreign minister, "the highest ranking political official woman in the world today," in the words of a Liberian woman, "except that of Her Majesty Queen Juliana of the Netherlands and Her Majesty Queen Elizabeth of Great Britain."

21

"A Mutual Distancing"

Golda learned about the capture of the Nazi war criminal Adolf Eichmann before anyone in the government. The Mossad chief, Isser Harel, had planned his seizure for months after others had located him hiding in Buenos Aires under a false name. Ben-Gurion had approved the plans to snatch the notorious Nazi and Golda knew of them, but neither could know exactly how the drama would unfold: how, on the night of May 11, 1960, a team of men from the Shin Bet, the internal security service, would wait for "Ricardo Klement" to return from his work at a Mercedes-Benz assembly plant; how a car parked near the secluded street where he lived would shine its headlights into his eyes, blinding him for a moment, while four men jumped him and forced him, "squealing like a slaughtered animal," into another car; and how they would drive him frantically to a "safe house" some distance from the abduction, fearful of getting caught by the Argentinean police. Only after "Klement" admitted to being Eichmann did Harel have a coded message sent to a Mossad operative in Israel, Ya'akov Caroz, who had instructions to notify David Ben-Gurion, Golda Meir, and the IDF chief of staff, Haim Laskov, in person of the mission's success. Told by Ben-Gurion's secretary that the prime minister was at his kibbutz in Sdeh Boker, Caroz headed to Mrs. Meir's government office in Jerusalem. It was Friday, May 13. In the middle of a meeting, she stepped away from her desk and invited the Mossad messenger to join her on the balcony for privacy. When he gave her the news about Eichmann's capture, she caught her breath, overcome with emotion, and, pressing her hand to her chest, grasped for something to lean on.

"I beg of you," she said, putting her other hand on Caroz's shoulder, "if you hear anything more, come and tell me without fail."

Caroz next carried his message to the chief of staff, and that Sunday he drove to Sdeh Boker to deliver it to Ben-Gurion. In his diary entry of May 15, the "old man" wrote, with cautious understatement, "This morning I met a messenger from Isser who told me that Eichmann had been identified and captured and will be flown here next week (if they manage to get him onto the plane)." This would be an "important" and "successful" mission, he continued, if it did not turn out to be a case of mistaken identity.

After interrogating Eichmann, Harel and his captors had no doubt about his identity. They spirited him out of the country, drugged and dressed in an El Al uniform, aboard a special El Al noncommercial airliner Abba Eban had arrived in to represent the government at a celebration of 150 years of Argentina's independence from Spain. Eban, who had been briefed about the planned operation beforehand, would return later on a different plane.

At four o'clock in the afternoon on the sultry Monday of May 23, 1960, Ben-Gurion stood before the Knesset and tersely announced Eichmann's capture. One of "the greatest Nazi war criminals, who was responsible, together with the Nazi leaders, for what they called 'the final solution of the Jewish problem,'" was under arrest in Israel, the prime minister said, and "would stand trial soon, under the terms of the law for the trial of Nazis and Nazi collaborators."

The short statement so amazed the Knesset that for a few moments nobody uttered a word. Then the room went wild with excitement. As the news quickly spread, the entire country rejoiced. Eichmann had not single-handedly devised the "Final Solution" of exterminating Europe's Jews, but he had executed it, organizing the transports that carried millions to the death camps and overseeing the efficiency of the killing systems. People regarded him almost as villainous as Hitler himself. Word of Eichmann's capture also electrified the world, making headlines everywhere, but not necessarily approving ones. Typical of several other newspapers, *The Washington Post* chastised Israel for wanting to "wreak vengeance," rather than seek justice, and *The New York Times*, while recognizing the "heinousness of Eichmann's crimes," condemned the state for violating Argentina's sovereignty and international law. "No immoral or illegal act justifies another," an editorial sanctimoniously declared.

While most American Jews voiced pride in Israel's bold action, the influential American Jewish Committee, with its upper-crust, establishment members, echoed many of the newspapers' criticisms. Fearful that a trial in Israel would cast both the Jewish state and American Jews in a bad light, they sought to play down the Jewish nature of the Holocaust.

When Golda came to the States in June to speak at the UN, a group of AJC leaders met with her in their New York office. In their "consensus" opinion, they told her, "Eichmann committed unspeakable crimes against humanity, not only against Jews." Therefore, it would be best for Israel and Jews everywhere to have him tried before a German court or a special international tribunal. In that way, Nazism would be seen by the world as "the enemy of mankind." As might be expected, Golda vigorously rejected those arguments. In the fifteen years since the Holocaust, she reminded them, nobody except Israel had shown the slightest interest in finding Eichmann or other war criminals. Moreover, during the war, the world had been indifferent to Jewish suffering. Wasn't it only proper for the Jews to judge Eichmann's deeds? When, later that evening, an AJC member phoned Golda—who was by then in Miami—to inform her that a group of prominent judges and lawyers had independently recommended that once Israel completed its investigation of Eichmann, it turn over its evidence to an international tribunal, she dismissed the idea out of hand.

Neither Golda nor Ben-Gurion nor most Israelis had the slightest doubt that Eichmann should be tried in their country. Nor did Israel's leaders fear world opinion about something they believed in so strongly. Israel was almost thirteen years old, on the cusp of its bar mitzvah. This was not the weak nation that had quaked in helplessness when the Nazis steamrolled their way across Europe. Israel had proved itself in the war of 1956 and afterward as a strong and resolute country, certain that the fate of the world's Jews was tied to its fate and that it had to be the voice of those Jews, past and present. In the government, Ben-Gurion had consolidated his power and the power of Mapai as a result of the last election, and Golda had emerged stronger than ever. When she shrugged off the American Jewish Committee's pressures to hold Eichmann's trial elsewhere, she did so out of strength as well as conviction.

On June 1, a furious Argentinean government summoned Arieh Levavi, Israel's ambassador to that country, to explain Eichmann's kidnapping and have him returned immediately. Two days later, Israel sent an official letter of apology relating that a group of "volunteers," themselves survivors, uncovered Eichmann's whereabouts, transported him from Argentina, and persuaded him to agree to stand trial in Israel. In other words, neither Israeli security forces nor the government itself had any official involvement in the abduction. Nobody bought the story. And though Ben-Gurion wrote a personal, conciliatory letter to Argentina's president, Arturo Frondizi, delineating the importance of Eichmann to Israel, nationalists in that country—many with fascist connections—pressed for action against the Jewish state.

In New York, Golda met privately with Mario Amadeo, head of Argentina's delegation to the United Nations, hoping to head off a full-blown confrontation. A hard-liner who had supported the Italian dictator, Benito Mussolini, during the war, he had no interest in reconciliation. He lodged a formal complaint against Israel with the Security Council and launched a virulent assault on it. Among other things, he argued that Israel's actions posed a threat to world peace, and he appeared to equate Jewish refugees who sought asylum in Argentina during the war with Nazis who sought refuge there after the war.

Golda bristled with indignation as she stood before the Security Council to respond. In the course of her talk, she quoted from the memoirs of Rudolf Höss, the commander of Auschwitz, about how "obsessed" Eichmann had been with destroying the Jews, "without pity and in cold blood." How, then, could Amadeo speak in the same breath about Eichmann and the Jewish refugees, the Nazis' victims, as both benefiting from his country's acceptance of them? And how could the Argentinean foreign minister use the term "armed bands" about the people who had seized Eichmann? "Far from lynching Eichmann or hanging him on the nearest tree," they had handed him over to a court of law, she pointed out. Did Eichmann's captors pose a threat to peace, or, rather, did the threat to peace lie in "Eichmann at large . . . Eichmann free to spread the poison of his twisted soul to a new generation"?

The speech touched a nerve for many in the audience, *Maariv* reported. Nevertheless, Golda's was a "voice crying in the wilderness." Eight nations, including the United States, voted for a Security Council resolution declaring that Israel had violated Argentina's sovereignty and requesting that it make reparations. Argentina expelled Israel's ambassador, but by August it accepted a joint statement that included an apology by Israel, drafted by Argentinean officials and the legal adviser to Israel's Foreign Ministry. With that, the political dispute died down. For some time afterward, however, the Jewish community in Argentina suffered violent anti-Semitic attacks from right-wing nationalists and Nazi sympathizers.

Golda wanted something from Eichmann's trial aside from exposing the "monster's" deeds. She wanted Gideon Hausner, the attorney general and prosecutor, to link Eichmann to the grand mufti of Jerusalem,

Haj Amin al-Husseini, and in that way link Israel's Arab enemies to the Nazis. To her mind, the public relations advantage of such a linkage outweighed the risk that it would encourage accusations—already being made—that Israel was staging a show trial for political purposes. The mufti had, in fact, been received by Hitler in Berlin during the war and sought advice from the Nazis on how to use their techniques in dealing with the Jews in Palestine. But how close were his ties to Eichmann? Under pressure from Golda, Hausner had Avraham Zellinger, head of the police unit responsible for investigating Eichmann's activities, search for that data. Zellinger found a few ambiguous connections, such as an entry in the mufti's diary that speaks of the "best of the Arab friends," with the name "Eichmann" written beneath it. Following Golda's directive, Hausner submitted the documents he had obtained to the judges, but to her disappointment her case did not hold up. The court went no further than to recognize that Eichmann had met the mufti once, with no evidence of a close relationship between them.

A balding man with big ears, thick-rimmed glasses, and a thin line of a mouth that twitched at the corners, Eichmann stood in a bulletproof-glass booth with two guards behind him throughout what *Time* magazine later labeled one of the "top ten trials that shook the world." Hundreds of journalists from dozens of countries crammed into the Beit Ha'Am (People's House), Jerusalem's newly constructed cultural center, when the trial opened there on April 11, 1961. During the next eight months, 110 witnesses would testify before the three-man tribunal, 100 of them survivors of the death camps. Although the atrocities of the Holocaust had been known—Elie Wiesel's book *Night* had already been published in French and English—for the first time, the full extent of their horror penetrated world consciousness. For the first time, people everywhere understood how trapped the Jews had been and how most victims could not fight back, because they were unarmed, or because they did not know the fate that awaited them, or because the physical punishment meted out by the Nazis for even the slightest sign of resistance was inhuman. For the first time, young Israelis who had belittled the Jewish victims as symbols of Diaspora weakness and fear understood that they did not go to their deaths as sheep to the slaughter but had shown their own kind of courage by attempting to stay alive under unimaginable conditions.

One observer of the courtroom drama whose name would forever be linked to it was the German Jewish philosopher Hannah Arendt, herself a refugee from Nazi Germany. Arendt had become widely known for her book *The Origins of Totalitarianism*, a study of National Socialism and anti-Semitism. Now she came to cover part of Eichmann's trial for *The New Yorker*. Her five-part series would become a book, *Eichmann in Jerusalem*, published in 1963. She devoted much of it to accusing leaders of Europe's Jewish councils (*Judenräte*) of collaborating in the destruction of their communities by cooperating with the Nazis instead of defying them. The accusation triggered fierce controversy, minimizing as it did the impossible choices Jewish leaders had in trying to save their people and the trickery the Nazis constantly used to deceive them. As disturbing was Arendt's thesis about the "banality of evil," a term she coined, which later became almost a cliché. Colorless and ordinary looking in his dark suit and tie, Eichmann might have been any bank clerk or shoe salesman. Yet this "average" man had committed some of the most atrocious crimes in history. In Arendt's thinking, he could do that because in carrying out his duties as diligently as he did, he lost the ability to distinguish between right and wrong. The very ordinariness of the man and his empty outlook made his evil banal.

It was an interpretation that ignored Eichmann's ideological commitment to his work and genuine pleasure in it. He once described the deportation of 400,000 Hungarian Jews as one of his greatest feats. "It was actually an achievement that was never matched before or since," he boasted. Arendt's concept of the "banality of evil" might have been her way of showing contempt for the entire Nazi enterprise, but it deeply pained many Holocaust survivors, who took it seriously and still mourned friends and relatives murdered by Eichmann's "banality."

Golda Meir met Hannah Arendt once. The two women spent an evening together at the home of Leni Yahil, a historian and Holocaust researcher, and her husband, Haim Yahil, director general of Israel's foreign office. The couple had invited Arendt for dinner, and because she wanted to meet Golda, they asked the foreign minister to join them afterward. The Eichmann trial had begun a week earlier, but Arendt revealed nothing of her thinking. Instead, the women spoke more generally, late into the night, about their lives and beliefs.

The differences between them could not have been greater: Golda, the unschooled, down-to-earth politician, had devoted her life to the causes of Zionism and Israel. Arendt, the urbane Diaspora intellectual, detested nationalism in any form. Mrs. Meir was "pleasant and polite" that evening, the Yahils' son Amos recalled, but a little "on her guard" with the noted philosopher. Arendt was fatigued and impatient, having spent all day at the trial. "My problem was, simply, how to get a foreign minister to stop talking and go off to bed," she wrote to her husband, Heinrich Blücher. Golda, the night owl, would have loved to stay up talking many more hours.

Some two years later, after *Eichmann in Jerusalem* was published, Arendt described part of her conversation with Golda that evening in a letter to the great scholar of Jewish mysticism Gershom Scholem, with whom she had an ongoing correspondence. She recalled Golda making a "shocking statement" by saying that as a socialist she did not believe in God; she believed in the Jewish people. "The greatness of this people," Arendt wrote to Scholem, "was once that it believed in God, and believed in Him in such a way that its trust and love towards Him was greater than its fear. And now this people believes only in itself? What good can come of that?" Arendt had already touched on these ideas in a letter she wrote to Leni Yahil not long after the evening with Golda. Believing only in the Jewish people was a form of believing in nothing but oneself, she wrote then, "actual idol worship." As a concession to Yahil, she added, "However pleasant the idol worshipers may be, as your friend is and was."

While agreeing that people face the "danger of idol worship" in many areas, Leni Yahil quickly came to Golda's defense. "If there is a single person . . . who does not cross this boundary, it is this very woman to whom you ascribe a term I would not presume to use—my friend," she wrote, and referred to the "special and unvarying effect" Golda had on everyone she met, "irrespective of their skin color, culture or intellectuality." Among such people were "Negroes in new African states and sophisticated people like the Swedes, or a simple Yemenite woman, and Hannah Arendt." Yahil attributed Golda's impact on such a diverse range of people not to her "Americanism," as Arendt would have it, but largely to her "desire not to coin new rules arbitrarily," that is, *not* to regard herself as a god who capriciously imposes her will on others.

Leni Yahil felt betrayed after Arendt's *New Yorker* pieces appeared. She whipped off an angry letter to the philosopher, in which she spoke of publishing a response to the magazine series. She never did, but the correspondence ended shortly thereafter. We have no record of Golda Meir's impressions of Hannah Arendt or her writings. One can only imagine her fury after reading *Eichmann in Jerusalem*.

The court found Eichmann guilty on December 11, 1961, eight months after his trial began, and condemned him to death four days later. Like everything else surrounding the trial, the sentence provoked wide debate. Eichmann's German lawyer, Dr. Robert Servatius, hired for him by the state, appealed the verdict. When the court turned the appeal down, Eichmann submitted a handwritten plea for a pardon, arguing, as he had earlier, that he had simply obeyed orders. A group of prominent intellectuals, among them Martin Buber, Gershom Scholem, and Hugo Bergmann, supported his plea. A death sentence, they maintained, would only brutalize Israel. Attorney General Gideon Hausner sent the question to the cabinet, which held a secret session in the Knesset on May 29, 1962.

Only two of the thirteen ministers present, Levi Eshkol and Joseph Burg, called for commuting the punishment to life in prison. Golda Meir spoke vehemently in favor of the death sentence. She had always opposed capital punishment in the state, but trying the Nazis was a different matter. "There has been a trial, there has been a ruling in accordance with the law of the State of Israel—this has been done by all nations," she said. She then gave examples from other nations: the Poles put Rudolf Höss to death, the Czechs hanged Dieter Wisliceny, the Norwegians passed a death decree against Vidkun Quisling. "Nobody told them that they had to show some sort of supreme sensitivity," she said. "Only from us do they demand this, because the world has not yet become accustomed to viewing the nation of Israel like other nations." She continued, "I am not ready to go with the philosophers . . . I have only one other misgiving on this matter—that a young Jewish man will have to do it, but it will bring him honor."

Two months earlier, Golda and the others had agreed that Eichmann's wife should be allowed to visit her husband secretly. "I have no sentiment toward his wife," she had said during the debate, but she saw no point in denying the visit if doing so might hurt the state's reputation and allowing it would cause no harm. The visit, however, had to be carefully monitored so that Mrs. Eichmann could not slip her husband anything that might ease his death.

Now, in the final reckoning on Eichmann's fate, Eshkol and Burg reversed themselves after two rounds of votes, and the cabinet agreed unanimously to reject his plea for clemency. Two days later, on May 31, 1962, Adolf Eichmann was hanged, his body cremated and his ashes scattered in the Mediterranean Sea, beyond Israel's territorial boundaries.

WHILE THE EICHMANN SAGA played itself out, Israel's internal politics took a turn for the worse. What had begun earlier as the "mishap" exploded into the full-fledged "Lavon Affair," which ate away at the heart of the Mapai Party, and soon the country.

The reader will recall that in 1955 Pinhas Lavon had been forced to resign as defense minister after the failure of a misconceived sabotage plot in Egypt. Five years later, Lavon learned that witnesses at the Olshan-Dori committee investigating the Egyptian blunder had committed forgery and given false evidence against him. Although in the interim Lavon had become secretary-general of the Histadrut, Israel's powerful labor federation, he still felt himself under suspicion because of the scandal in Egypt. Nobody had ever solved the question of who gave the final order to carry out the sabotage operation, Lavon or Benyamin Gibli, chief of military intelligence. Convinced that the new findings cleared his name, Lavon went to Ben-Gurion on September 26, 1960, and demanded that the prime minister issue a statement freeing him from all blame in the Egyptian affair. Ben-Gurion refused.

"I told him that I had not accused him and if others had, I was not a judge who could clear him of wrongdoing," the "old man" wrote in his diary. In his view, only a court of law could do that. Lavon was furious.

To Ben-Gurion's astonishment, specifics of his talk with Lavon appeared in the popular Israeli newspaper *Maariv* and rapidly spread to others. Until then, almost all information about the original debacle had been censored, so that the public knew little of its specifics. Lavon went even further by taking his case to the Knesset's Foreign Affairs and Defense Committee. In copious detail, he described the fiasco in Egypt, attacked the armed forces and military intelligence service— Ben-Gurion's bailiwick—and shared his conviction that Dayan and Peres had framed him in the episode. Each time he testified, his words popped up immediately in the press, throwing the country into turmoil. Never before in Israel had the press been privy to such secret government activities. Clearly Lavon or a source close to him was leaking this information to it. Ben-Gurion suspected the journalist Levi Yitzhak Hayerushalmi, then Lavon's secretary. (This was the same Hayerushalmi to whom Golda had vented her rage against Peres on Rosh Hashanah some eight years earlier.)

Golda had been in America attending to her UN duties when this phase of the Egyptian scandal burst into public consciousness. Before returning home, she conferred with Levi Eshkol, also there on state business. Both had followed the story as it unfolded in the Israeli newspapers and concluded that with all his blabbing Lavon would have to be eased out of his Histadrut position. By the time she left the States on October 27, 1960, the Lavon storm was in full blast. Among other things, in his rage, he threatened to publicly release a "secret file" he possessed if he were not vindicated, and Eshkol worried that such a file might open a "Pandora's box," probably about internal party activities and finances.

Golda had no great love for Lavon. She had thought it a mistake for Ben-Gurion to appoint him defense minister back in 1953 and had worked to have him discharged from that position two years later. She did not seem frightened by his "secret file" threat, but she recoiled at his airing dirty laundry to the Knesset. Mostly, she wanted the disastrous affair with its sensational newspaper headlines to disappear and knew that would not happen with a judicial inquiry, which would take months to examine and cross-examine witnesses. Instead, she cast her vote at a cabinet meeting to have a committee of seven ministers, from within the cabinet and not the larger Knesset, investigate the Egyptian affair.

On a tense December 25—Christmas Day for much of the world—the Israeli cabinet heard the committee of seven's report delivered by its head, Minister of Justice Pinhas Rosen. After holding nineteen meetings between November 3 and December 21, the committee concluded that Lavon was innocent of wrongdoing. By implication, that meant that the military intelligence chief, Gibli, had given the order for the ill-fated operation in Egypt. Although the committee did not believe it had the power to call witnesses, it felt that its investigation had been thorough enough to regard the affair as "concluded and completed." As soon as Rosen ended his report, Ben-Gurion exploded in anger, lambasting the committee and ripping apart its conclusions. His reaction took the meeting by surprise. The prime minister had not actively opposed forming the committee of seven; he had simply not participated in the discussion or voted on the proposal. Now he complained that only a judicial inquiry could reach a legally viable conclusion.

Incensed at his response, Golda conspicuously rose from her seat and left the room while he was still talking. Her face pale with tension, she lit a cigarette in the hallway and stood there smoking for a while. Then she strode into the next room and scribbled her resignation on a piece of paper, which she had someone deliver to the cabinet secretary to be held for a later time. Meanwhile, Ben-Gurion informed the cabinet that he was taking a long vacation and that Levi Eshkol would replace him while he was gone. Neither he nor Golda appeared at the cabinet session that afternoon.

The battle of resignations was on again.

On New Year's Eve, a Saturday, Golda showed up at a Mapai secretariat meeting. Ben-Gurion did not, but the party secretary, Yosef Almogi, read aloud a letter of resignation the prime minister had drafted. During the course of the meeting, which lasted almost twenty-four hours, Golda criticized Lavon for his revelations to the Knesset Foreign Affairs and Defense Committee, behavior that "under no circumstances could be forgiven." Nevertheless, she emphasized, she and others had pleaded with Ben-Gurion to investigate the mishap when it first occurred in 1954, and he had refused to get involved. Had he done so, the party might have avoided the situation it was in, with the press all over the affair and the nation in an uproar. "Isn't it possible," she asked with bitter sarcasm, "to believe that a man—even the most honored among us—is capable of error, or is that heresy and forbidden to think of?" If such thinking were permitted, the Mapai colleagues knew that "Ben-Gurion is proposing something in which he errs."

She was angry that Ben-Gurion clung so stubbornly to his insistence on a judicial inquiry. Even if he could justify his stand in principle, he ignored the more important point of how greatly he damaged the party because of it. In recent weeks, newspapers, intellectuals, and many organizations had criticized the prime minister's "implacable" opposition to Lavon, some papers comparing Lavon to Alfred Dreyfus, the nineteenth-century French Jewish officer falsely convicted of treason. Such attacks weakened the party as a whole, not only its leader. She was angry at the way Ben-Gurion had removed himself from the discussion about choosing the committee of seven and announced his resignation only—she believed—when it presented conclusions he didn't like. She was also angry, still, at the "old man's" continued embrace of Dayan and Peres, who, she was convinced, had more than a little to do with planting the accusations against Lavon.

Ben-Gurion must not resign, she told the Mapai secretariat. "He has the right to form a government as he wishes." But she would not be part of that government; she was implementing her resignation. She knew full well, as she did the last time she resigned, that Ben-Gurion could not form a government without her and the other party veterans. As it was, Sapir would hand in his resignation in early January, and Aranne would back everything she did.

Hoping to heal the party, now in shreds, Yosef Almogi arranged a meeting at the Sharon Hotel in Herzliya with Ben-Gurion as chair. "Two comrades are destroying Mapai—Ziama Aranne and Golda Meir," the prime minister stated coldly soon after the gathering convened. Golda burst into tears and stormed out of the room. She calmed down after sipping some whiskey Almogi gave her and returned to the meeting. She was shaken but far from defeated.

That became clear at two more fateful meetings held in the first week of February 1961. Levi Eshkol, who had assumed the role of party peacemaker, surmised after speaking to Ben-Gurion that the "old man" would agree to head a new government if Lavon were removed from his position as secretary-general of the Histadrut. To accommodate the prime minister, he submitted a proposal to the Mapai secretariat that essentially dismissed Lavon from his post, and won its approval on February 3. A day later, Mapai's larger and more authoritative central committee met at the Ohel Theater in Tel Aviv to take up the proposal. Outside, mobs of students, intellectuals, and opposition party members demonstrated noisily in support of Lavon. Inside, after much debate, the committee voted to oust the Histadrut secretary.

Golda did not attend either meeting. On two of the most memorable days in the party's history, she visited the kibbutz Revivim to see her daughter and family in the Negev.

Her absence, wrote the journalists Eliyahu Hasin and Dan Horwitz, "was understood as a protest." Though most observers took it to be a protest in support of Lavon, she had never before demonstrated any feeling for him; she had helped push him out of one job and had spoken to Levi Eshkol early about removing him from this one. Her protest was directed not *for* Lavon but *against* Ben-Gurion, who had gotten his way and had Lavon ousted in spite of the findings of the committee of seven. By not appearing at the meetings, she avoided having to vote for Lavon and in that sense undermining Eshkol's attempts to bring peace to the party by having him dismissed. And she avoided having to vote against Lavon and for Ben-Gurion, with whom she was furious. So she stayed away, miles away, playing with her grandchildren, while the pundits rightly saw her absence as a protest, even if they did not fully comprehend the motives behind it.

BUT POLITICIANS REVERSE THEMSELVES when necessary, and Golda Meir was nothing if not a consummate politician. After Lavon's dismissal, Ben-Gurion agreed, yet again, to form a new government, and Golda and Sapir agreed to be part of it, putting their resignations aside. This time, however, the parties that had helped make up Mapai's coalition in the previous government did not agree to do so again. The prime minister's refusal to accept the verdict of the committee of seven had turned them against him, giving them hope at the same time that with the nation up in arms about the Lavon Affair, they might overthrow the weakened ruling party. Unable to form a government and wishing to avoid new elections, Ben-Gurion sent a letter to each of the Mapai ministers, suggesting that he withdraw and give that task to Levi Eshkol, who would then head the party. Golda became one of the most outspoken opponents of that proposal. Gone (for now) were the name-calling and sharp retorts between her and the "old man." They might fight among themselves, but rival parties were not going to dictate who should or should not lead Mapai.

"Ben-Gurion's suggestion is unacceptable, both rationally and emotionally," she told her colleagues at a party meeting at her home in Jerusalem. "Should Mapai allow others to put words in its mouth?" she demanded. No, the party needed to set its own agenda. "I'm for Ben-Gurion," she said, "and for a government with Ben-Gurion only. There is no other proposal."

With Ben-Gurion at an impasse to form a new government, the country went to the polls on August 8, 1961. Fueled by the fear of losing their top government position, the warring groups within Mapai pulled together to campaign intensely. The results were better than expected. Although the party lost five seats, it held on to forty-two, thus remaining dominant. When the other parties still would not allow Ben-Gurion to form a government, Levi Eshkol put together a coalition and established a government that not he but Ben-Gurion headed as prime minister. It was a strange and difficult arrangement. Golda kept her position as foreign minister.

She never stopped insisting that she hated that position. She much preferred being labor minister, she still told anyone who cared to listen, preferred building homes for immigrants in Israel to flying around the world meeting diplomats. As late as 1963, seven years into her term as foreign minister, she interviewed Simcha Dinitz to work with her. "Young man, why would you want the job?" she asked, taking off her glasses to stare at him. "Honestly speaking, I really don't," he answered. "Well, that makes two of us, because I don't like my job either," she said.

Despite the constant disclaimers, during the second half of her time as foreign minister she blossomed. To be sure, her troubles with Peres did not let up, and her disputes with Ben-Gurion shadowed all their dealings, but as her experience as foreign minister expanded, so did her confidence in her post. "She ruled with an iron fist," recalled Yoram Dinstein, who had worked in the foreign office. "But she was much admired. She was the kind of person who when she walked into a room everybody stood up, a kind of legend in her lifetime." Staff members who discounted her ability at first had either left or come to respect her authority. She ran meetings as she always had, by listening and consensus, but now no one doubted who was in charge. "Here is the problem, let's go around the table," she would begin. If she did not agree with the general conclusion, she might say—with her signature sarcasm—"Look, I'm a very simple woman, so explain to me how this brilliant idea matches our policy." By the end of the meeting, the decision would be what she wanted. "Her logic was incisive," Dinstein said. "But instead of throwing an idea at us and have everyone fight her, she would say, 'You tell me what to do.'"

Her later detractors had a different view of her methods. "If you told Golda she was 99 percent right, she would never forgive you until the end of her days," wrote the muckraking newspaper *Haolam Hazeh* (This world). Telling her she is 99 percent right "means you are implying she is 1 percent wrong. That's a complete lie," the paper parodied her, "and only an anti-Semite could have such a thought in his mind!"

Everyone, admirers and detractors, had a field day with her poor Hebrew. "She has a vocabulary of two thousand words, okay, but why doesn't she use them?" Abba Eban is reputed to have said, and some turned that into "five hundred" or "three hundred" words. (She returned the "compliment." When someone told her that Eban spoke five languages, she quipped, "So does the waiter at the King David Hotel.") Whatever their limitations, her words were quoted regularly. Her "Don't be so humble, you're not that great" became so famous that when she wanted to use it, she would begin, "As I like to say." And her standard answer in her mid-sixties and onward to friends and doctors who nagged her to stop smoking, "There's no point in my giving up cigarettes now; I won't die young," took its place in the growing library of Golda gems.

Her workday usually extended to sixteen or eighteen hours. If not scheduled for a formal meal, she ate her lunch at staff meetings, a simple salad that Lou Kadar prepared for her or her favorite sandwich—two pieces of bread smeared with margarine and orange marmalade—sent in from a local Tnuva restaurant. She tried not to keep her staff in the office after hours but carried piles of papers home in her briefcase—which she called by the Russian term *chimidunchik*—to work on in the evenings. After Simcha Dinitz became her political secretary, he would go home for an hour at the end of the day, then come back to her house to work with her until twelve, one o'clock in the morning, returning home again, exhausted. In one of his favorite Golda Meir anecdotes, he once suggested to her that she take a vacation. "Why?" she asked. "Do you think I'm tired?" "No," he replied, "but I am." "So you take a vacation," she ordered.

"She is a brilliant success in a post usually a man's," gushed *Life*, America's most popular magazine. She succeeded most conspicuously outside Israel, where she turned world leaders into friends with "the charm of a born diplomat." One of the people she charmed was Russia's pugnacious premier, Nikita Khrushchev, whom she met at a Soviet embassy reception. She told him that she had been born in Kiev, and had been very young when she left, but had heard from her mother and sister about its great beauty. She would love to see the city, she said ingratiatingly, and the premier, whose country was arming Israel's enemies, immediately invited her to visit. In tiny Luxembourg, which some foreign ministers might not have bothered about, Golda called on the duke and duchess and was warmly welcomed and "very much hugged."

But her closest ties were, as they had always been, with the United States. She received honorary degrees from Smith College and the University of Wisconsin, appeared on television and radio, and became for many far beyond the Jewish community a household name. "Are you the Golda we know you are?" asked an African American saleswoman at Macy's, where Golda loved to shop when in the States. She didn't need to answer; the saleswomen hovered over her. The media enjoyed contrasting the hard-hitting professional in the UN General Assembly with the sweet-smiling domestic woman. In its six-page spread of photographs, *Life* showed her as authoritative in a business meeting as she was "joyful" in her kitchen. (In truth, said Simcha Dinitz, "she had no culinary talent, but it fitted the Jewish mother image attributed to her . . . I was never served nor tasted her famous gefilte fish. The most I got was salami and a fried omelet.") She liked projecting a maternal image, as much a part of her as the other. Within the Jewish community, where she had long been adulated, she felt freer than ever to make demands for UJA and Israel Bonds and to speak her mind openly.

She refused to be reconciled to the idea that the vast majority of American Jews had no intention of immigrating to Israel even if they passionately supported the Jewish state. That fact was a tragedy so profound, she said, with unabashed exaggeration, that it ranked alongside two other tragedies of Jewish life: the Holocaust and the current repression of Soviet Jewry. "I simply cannot understand the instinctive lack of responsiveness when we speak about *aliyah*," she chided a group of American leaders. When one suggested that immigration to Israel usually resulted from some emergency and American Jews did not face an emergency, she replied heatedly that such an attitude was "inadmissible and untenable." What should Israel do to entice American Jewish youth? she asked. How can it become "an attractive force for the Jews who are not compelled to leave their homes"?

They were the kinds of questions that made Jacob Blaustein's blood boil. Blaustein had been president of the American Jewish Committee in the early years of the state and remained active in it. At a time when American Jews still did not feel totally secure in the United States, he and others on the committee worried that calls for immigration to Israel created anti-Semitism in America and led to accusations of Jewish dual loyalty. In the summer of 1950, Blaustein negotiated an agreement with Ben-Gurion: The prime minister declared that his country would not "interfere" with the internal affairs of other Jewish communities. Nor would it demand immigration from American Jews, much as it desired their technical skills.

A decade later, Blaustein complained to Ben-Gurion about his foreign minister, Golda Meir, whose statement to an Anglo-Jewish association that "Israel will continue to speak for Jewry" had violated the 1950 agreement. Reluctantly, the prime minister reaffirmed the agreement with Blaustein, as did Levi Eshkol when he became prime minister and Golda Meir when she took over the office. "I was privy to the talks which you conducted on the occasion of your visit to Israel in 1950, and to the understanding which flowed from those talks," she wrote to Blaustein in 1972. "This has been a continuing understanding. On my part, there has been no deviation from it, and it is my intention that there will not be."

It didn't much matter that she stretched the truth then and actually deviated from the agreement constantly as foreign minister. Even though American Jews adored her, they were not about to move to Israel en masse regardless of what she said. And her popularity with the American people at large was such that the committee's worries about anti-Semitism resulting from her aliyah statements became irrelevant, if they had ever had any significance.

DEALING WITH THE U.S. GOVERNMENT posed a different challenge. Israel had been seeking to buy arms from America since its founding and had always been rebuffed. Unlike France, which, during and after the Sinai campaign in 1956, was a major supplier of armaments to Israel, the United States refused to sell weapons to any Middle Eastern nation to prevent an arms race in the region. President Harry S. Truman kept that arms embargo even during Israel's worst days, in the 1948 war, and President Eisenhower continued the policy, even though the Soviets supplied arms to Egypt and Syria. When Golda met with Eisenhower's secretary of state, John Foster Dulles, on October 2, 1958, to request tanks, submarines, and anti-aircraft missiles, he turned her down flat. And though two years later she received somewhat more sympathy from Dulles's successor, Christian A. Herter, when she asked to buy Hawk anti-aircraft missiles, nothing came of that attempt either. Not until John F. Kennedy agreed to sell Israel the state-of-the-art Hawks did American policy change.

Ben-Gurion pressed Kennedy directly for the Hawks when they met at the Waldorf Astoria in New York at the end of May 1961, and Golda and her ambassador to the United States, Abraham Harman, kept up a campaign for the weapons. The Israelis anticipated that their supply of arms from France would dry up soon. Having made peace with Algeria, Charles de Gaulle no longer viewed Nasser as an enemy, and the French president would probably now strengthen his country's ties with the Arab states. Given her own closeness to the United States, Golda wanted to create American alliances and move away from total dependence on France. Kennedy finally relented when he became convinced that the Hawk would be a defensive weapon for Israel, necessary to rebut the advanced bombers the Soviets had sent the Arabs.

"President Kennedy had strong feelings for Israel," said Myer "Mike" Feldman, deputy special counsel to the president and his adviser on Israel. "He identified it with Ireland," a country he loved because of his own background. "The Irish have that problem, too," he would remark about one or another Israeli issue.

But Kennedy had larger motives in making his decision than a soft spot for Israel. He believed that solving the problem of the Arab refugees who had fled Israel during the war of 1948 was the key to resolving the entire Arab-Israeli conflict. And he had strong reservations about Israel's nuclear reactor in Dimona, which he wanted to monitor carefully. Although he did not make the sale of the Hawks contingent on either of these matters, he hoped that by supplying them to Israel, he could get that country's cooperation in the other areas.

Golda, Ben-Gurion, and Teddy Kollek received the good news of the sea change in America's arms policy at a meeting in Tel Aviv with Mike Feldman on Sunday afternoon, August 19, 1962. Kennedy had sent Feldman to this meeting, considered so secret that the envoy used a cover story even for America's Tel Aviv embassy, pretending that he and his wife had visited Rhodes and then come to Israel at the invitation of the Weizmann Institute. He could get away with it. A pleasant-looking chap with a receding hairline, round face, and horn-rimmed glasses, he was the White House's "anonymous man," a behind-the-scenes operator, unknown to the public but with full access to the president. Aside from delivering his announcement about the Hawks, he had come to negotiate with the Israeli leaders on the "Johnson plan" for handling the Arab refugees.

Dr. Joseph Johnson, head of the Carnegie Endowment for International Peace, was appointed by the UN Palestine Conciliation Commission, with strong American backing, to solve the issue of the Arab refugees, most of whom still lived in miserable refugee camps in Egypt, Jordan, Syria, and other Arab lands. Johnson's plan called for giving the refugees a choice between repatriation to Israel, resettlement in some other country, or compensation for loss of their property. Golda and Ben-Gurion took a dim view of the plan, convinced that Arab leaders would pressure the refugees toward repatriation, thus flooding Israel with Arabs, who might serve as a fifth column and undermine the country's security. Jordan, on the other hand, objected that too many refugees would choose to live there, causing turmoil.

Johnson made two trips to the Middle East, and Golda met with him then and again in the States. Among other things, their talks led to a "mutual antipathy." She viewed him as pro-Arab; he viewed her as inordinately stubborn.

Israel maintained that the refugee problem represented one part of the overall dispute between the Arab countries and Israel and that peace could be attained only through face-to-face negotiations among the parties involved. "I am prepared to meet with Nasser at any moment, to discuss peace," Golda said at every chance she could. She also regularly made the case that Israel had absorbed 500,000 Jewish refugees from Arab countries and integrated them into Israeli society in contrast to the Palestinian refugees who remained in cramped refugee camps.

Determined to make some headway on Johnson's plan, Kennedy sent Feldman to Israel on that August day, bearing the "carrot" of the promised Hawk sale. Feldman's meeting with Ben-Gurion, Golda, and Kollek lasted three and a half hours. His meeting with Golda alone two days later went on for six hours. "Golda Meir was a very difficult person to bargain with," he was to say. On the other hand, he developed "great admiration for her," although they "were on the opposite side of almost everything." In these meetings, "she was stronger than Ben-Gurion. He would give in while she remained firm." She "measured everything against the standard of Israel's safety," Feldman said, and he respected that. "She was a real patriot."

Golda had serious reservations about the Johnson plan, as did Ben-Gurion, who had prepared a six-page letter outlining its "impracticability," before leaving town. Still, with assurances from Feldman that not more than one refugee in ten would seek repatriation, Golda agreed to have the plan discussed with Nasser. Through a coded message, Feldman contacted John Badeau, U.S. ambassador to Cairo, who presented the proposal to the Egyptian president. Nasser's response was "moderate and slightly encouraging," although he insisted that ultimately the majority of refugees would have to be permitted to return to Israel, making it a binational state, even if it took "seventy years to accomplish."

Despite their lack of enthusiasm, neither side rejected the plan outright, and Kennedy decided it should be presented to the United Nations. Before doing so, Johnson showed his final version to the Arab and Israeli delegations. Golda turned "livid" when she read it. Feldman flew from Washington to New York, and over dinner they compared the detailed notes both had kept of their earlier conversations with what Johnson had given her. They didn't match. Johnson had given his plan to the American State Department—which traditionally leaned toward the Arab states—and officials there had put changes into the document that made it more favorable to the Arab side. Feldman later contended that instead of accepting Nasser's response, knowing that he could sway the other Arab states, the State Department had sent the document to all the Arab leaders and incorporated their changes. With more than sixty discrepancies from the original draft, this one no longer had safeguards against Israel's having to take in more refugees than it felt it could handle. "I was pretty mad," Feldman said. "It was disgraceful that a presidential mission would be undermined" in that way.

Golda refused to sign the document, but so did the Arab leaders. By the end of the year, Kennedy "buried" the plan. This could have been "a force that would permit peace in the Middle East," Feldman reflected years later. "I told the president that if it went through, he would deserve a Nobel Prize. Well, it never happened." Nor would it in the decades ahead.

President Kennedy raised the issue of the Arab refugees when Golda met with him on December 27, 1962, at his vacation home in Palm Beach, Florida. Looking almost svelte in her light summery outfit, her weight swing on the low side, she was quite taken with the handsome Kennedy, who looked so boyish "it was hard for me to remember that I was talking to the president of the United States," she recalled. They had a substantive meeting of seventy minutes, attended also by Mike Feldman, Abe Harman, and two State Department officials.

On the porch of his house as he sat on his rocking chair, dressed informally with shirtsleeves rolled up and no tie, President Kennedy made a historic statement to Golda Meir that came to define the fundamental bond between the United States and Israel. His country, he said, had a "special relationship" with Israel in the Middle East, "really comparable only to its relationship with Britain over a wide range of world affairs." He also told her that it was "quite clear that in case of an invasion the United States would come to the support of Israel," adding, "We have that capacity and it is growing." No previous American president had spoken that way to an Israeli leader. None before Kennedy had made a commitment to aid Israel if it suffered an Arab invasion. Golda's meeting with him marked a milestone in the ties between the countries that would, over time, be taken almost for granted.

Kennedy had some other things on his mind during that historic meeting. The briefing report he had received beforehand about the foreign minister described her as just as "tough and driving" as Ben-Gurion but "less intellectually flexible" and cautioned that it would take "determined persistence" to persuade her to "accept an opinion contrary to her own." So while he listened carefully to Israel's security problems, and while he sympathized with Golda's description of how the Jewish people had lost their sovereignty twice before in history and must not lose their third and perhaps final chance, he also spoke firmly of the burden the United States carried for the entire free world. Their relationship, he told her, was a "two-way street" in which Israel also needed to consider U.S. interests. It was important for America to keep its ties to the Arab countries as well as to Israel, he said, and those ties were also in Israel's interest. He hoped, therefore, that Israel would "proceed in such a way as to lessen collisions between us." In that context, he brought up the refugee question again. The Johnson plan, he admitted, "is gone," but they should keep trying. A settlement "might seem impossible to achieve, but it is equally impossible to let this dispute run on and blow up," he said, accurately predicting a future he would not see. Golda agreed to continue the quest for a solution, returning, as always, to the necessity of direct talks between Arab and Israeli leaders.

Almost in passing, the president raised the subject of America's "problems" with Israel's atomic reactor. "We are opposed to nuclear proliferation," he reminded her. She assured him that "there would not be any difficulty between us" on the nuclear reactor, then changed the subject.

She left pleased that "we are dealing with a friend and the representative of a great and friendly country." She felt more at ease with Kennedy than had Ben-Gurion, who told his aides disapprovingly, "To me, he looks like a politician." She also enjoyed playing the wise Jewish mother to the young president. In her memory, as she was leaving, Kennedy took her hand, looked her in the eyes, and said, "Don't worry. *Nothing* will happen to Israel."

Golda had not been completely honest with the American president when she shrugged off his nuclear concerns. They were her concerns also. Back in October 1956, at Sèvres, where Israel and France worked out strategies for the Suez campaign, Shimon Peres finalized arrangements to purchase a nuclear reactor from the French. "I want a nuclear option," Ben-Gurion had said, an option on one level to counter Israel's lack of oil and shortage of natural resources and on another to offset its existential threat from hostile neighbors. In the nuclear project Peres negotiated with the French during the next year, the reactor was to be built outside the Negev development town of Dimona, with French financing and scientists to guide it.

Only a few cabinet members were allowed in on the top secret project, and most of them opposed it. Levi Eshkol and Pinhas Sapir argued that it would eat up the entire state budget, Moshe Dayan had doubts that it could be executed, Yitzhak Rabin and other military heads held that it would overwhelm defense spending, and Yigal Allon and Israel Galili, young members of the Ahdut Ha'avoda Party, believed Israel should rely on conventional weapons. Of them all, Golda Meir did not oppose the plan, but she worried about the consequences of lying about it to the United States. She was to explain her position a few years after the project got under way.

"There is no need to stop the activities at Dimona," she said in a

Foreign Ministry policy meeting. "I was always of the opinion that we should tell them the truth and explain why, and it does not interest us whether the Americans think, as we do, that Nasser represents a danger for us . . . But if we deny that Dimona exists, we cannot use it as a bargaining point, because it is impossible to bargain about something that does not exist."

By early December 1960, the United States had become aware of Dimona and its reactor. Soon afterward, with leaks from American government sources, *Time* magazine, *The New York Times*, London's *Daily Express*, and other newspapers suddenly carried eye-opening stories about the American government's "mounting concern" that Israel, with French assistance, may be developing the capacity to produce atomic weapons. The revelations baffled Israelis, who had been given no information about the reactor, as much as they astounded the rest of the world. Ben-Gurion would have preferred to keep Dimona a secret indefinitely, but with those revelations he announced in the Knesset that Israel was building a "research reactor" in the Negev to be used "only for peaceful purposes." When Ogden Reid, the American ambassador in Tel Aviv, delivered five questions from the then president, Eisenhower, concerning the nuclear reactor, Ben-Gurion gave vague responses about the use of plutonium and about Israel's plans for allowing inspections of the Dimona site. He stated clearly, however, that what he had announced in the Knesset about the peaceful purpose of the reactor "still stands."

Never happy with Ben-Gurion's vagueness to the Americans about Dimona, Golda was dismayed when the "old man" agreed to the demands of President Kennedy, who succeeded Eisenhower on January 20, 1961, to have two American scientists visit the site. She believed that in the end misleading the Americans there, as Ben-Gurion planned to do, would hurt Israel. For the time being, however, after seeing only what the Israelis wanted them to see, the American scientists confirmed Israel's claims of peaceful plans for the reactor. Kennedy's moderate approach to the nuclear subject with Golda in Palm Beach reflected that report and others by American experts who turned up nothing suspicious (probably because of false panels and bricked-over hallways that concealed what needed concealing). But the president remained doubtful and soon began to exert intense and unrelenting pressure on Ben-Gurion to allow twice-yearly inspections of the facility, a plan the "old man" adamantly resisted.

He and Peres "were willing to bluff a great power," says the political scientist Shlomo Aronson. "Golda was not." She believed strongly that allies should not deceive one another. Whether she was right at the time is a moot question, says Aronson. It's possible that the United States needed the bluff. By openly acknowledging and accepting Israel's true nuclear capability, it would run the danger of pushing the Soviet Union into providing the Arab states with the same option. It might therefore have been more prudent to keep the situation murky. Almost a decade was to pass before Golda achieved the honest approach to nuclear capability that she sought with the American government. It happened when she served as prime minister of Israel and Richard Nixon as president of the United States.

KENNEDY'S DECISION TO SELL Hawks to Israel came at a crucial moment. Just about a month earlier, on Saturday, July 21, 1962, Nasser's Egypt launched four ballistic missiles that he boasted had the capacity to hit any target "south of Beirut," meaning within Israel's range. Anxious Israelis speculated wildly about the destruction these missiles might cause, not knowing whether they were designed to carry nuclear materials, germ cultures, or other terrifying nonconventional warheads. On top of that, Israel's intelligence chief, Isser Harel—criticized for being taken unawares by Nasser—discovered that the missiles had been secretly developed in Egypt by German scientists recruited for the job, some with Nazi-era backgrounds.

The German connection with Egypt could not have arisen at a worse time for Ben-Gurion. For almost four years, he and Shimon Peres had been cultivating West Germany as a major source of arms, knowing that they would have to replace the waning French market. At a momentous meeting in New York's Waldorf Astoria in March 1960, the Israeli prime minister shook hands with West Germany's chancellor, Konrad Adenauer. The gesture symbolized Israel's acceptance of what Ben-Gurion called a "different Germany," one that had broken with its Nazi past and sincerely wanted to reconcile with the Jewish nation. The two men agreed on a German loan to Israel of half a billion dollars and sealed an arms deal, negotiated earlier by Peres, for large deliveries to Israel of weapons and military equipment. Other secret negotiations continued after that meeting, possibly even concerning German help with Israel's nuclear endeavors. With those sensitive ties in progress, Ben-Gurion did not want to rock the boat in any way. He refused Harel's request that he ask Adenauer directly to recall the German scientists.

By no means did Golda share Ben-Gurion's enthusiasm for a new Germany. Although she had voted—reluctantly—to accept German reparations in 1952, she could muster no warmth for the country or its people. When, in 1956, Israel's ambassador to France, Yaakov Tsur, had raised the topic of Israel's establishing diplomatic relations with Germany, a "pale and tense" Golda told him that she could not discuss the subject in "any logical way" even if it made sense. The Holocaust was always her first frame of reference, the lens through which she judged all Germans, including those born long after it. It was an attitude that grated on Ben-Gurion.

The Shoah "lives within me no less than" within Golda, he told a group of students. "But I am more given to looking toward the future, and I'm not so taken with psychological complexities. I weigh matters, and sometimes I come to such a conclusion that I am forced to uproot all my feelings from my heart."

Eventually, Golda accepted the fact that Israel had to deal with post-war Germany, even to establish diplomatic relations with West Germany. For the present, however, she could not extend her hand to the Germans as Ben-Gurion had extended his to Adenauer. This difference in approach to Germany was the one major policy on which Golda and Ben-Gurion fiercely disagreed. Through all their years of building the state, they had shared the same basic outlook. She didn't simply agree with him; she believed in his vision and ideals. For all their political bickering about youngsters and veterans, for all the bitterness of the Lavon Affair and their serial resignations, they had been able to continue working together because of their mutual goals. The painful issue of Germany would finally split them apart.

With Ben-Gurion's permission and Golda's knowledge, Isser Harel tried to scare the German scientists out of Egypt. Some received booby-trapped packages or letter bombs that blew up in their faces. One disappeared, his car found abandoned. Several opened threatening letters. In March 1963, Harel's agents went too far. Two of them traveled to Basel, Switzerland, to meet with a woman named Heidi Goercke, daughter of a German electronics expert working in Egypt. They warned her that her father would face serious problems if he did not leave Egypt. But Goercke had notified the Swiss police before meeting the men, and with hidden microphones they recorded the entire conversation. A few hours later, the police arrested the two Mossad agents, and shortly after that the German police requested their extradition.

From then on, pandemonium reigned. On Golda's advice, Harel went to Tiberias, where Ben-Gurion was vacationing, and urged that he appeal to Adenauer to have the men freed. That was the only way to keep a lid on the brewing scandal. Again, not wanting to jeopardize Israel's relations with Germany, Ben-Gurion refused. Within days, the United Press news service broke the story of the arrested agents, sending it to newspapers everywhere. After consulting with Golda, a frantic Harel returned to Ben-Gurion, who ordered him not to respond to the official Swiss arrests but to explain those arrests in general terms to the media. In an attempt to present his case, Harel called a press conference in Israel and dramatically revealed everything about the German scientists and the danger they posed.

With that, panic gripped the country. Headlines about germ warfare and radioactive chemicals, about poison gas and nuclear bombs, blared from newspapers in Israel and across the world. Nothing had changed, people said. The Nazis were still bent on destroying the Jews. Where was Ben-Gurion's "different Germany" now?

To quell the storm, the Israeli cabinet decided to make a statement in the Knesset. As a show of unity to the Israeli public and the world, all the political parties in the Foreign Affairs and Defense Committee agreed to a joint draft resolution that would criticize the Germans and assure the country that the government was on top of the situation. With Ben-Gurion away, it fell to Golda Meir to submit the resolution, which he saw beforehand, to the Knesset.

On March 20, 1963, she stood before the Knesset and spoke of the "group of scientists and hundreds of German technicians" who were helping Egypt develop missiles and "even weapons forbidden by international law," whose sole purpose was "the extermination of the living." Those scientists came to Egypt to make money, she said, but also out of hatred for Israel. She made a point of distinguishing the current West German republic from the Nazi past and mentioning the majority of innocent German people who wanted "a different Germany." Still, "eighteen years after the fall of Hitler's regime that brought about the decimation of millions of Jews, members of this nation are again associated with deeds designed to destroy the State of Israel." She closed by calling on the Bonn government to end the activities of the German scientists in Egypt.

It was a harsh speech, which Golda always insisted she would not have given had Ben-Gurion not approved it, although later he changed his mind. Yet it was not harsh enough for his critics. Although all the factions had agreed to accept the statement, virulent attacks against Germany and Ben-Gurion followed it, none more virulent than those of Menachem Begin, head of the Herut Party. Begin had vociferously opposed Israel's acceptance of German reparations eleven years earlier. Now he argued that Ben-Gurion's reconciliation with Germany provided that country with an "alibi" for its past and present actions. West Germany, not individual scientists, was aiding Egypt, he charged. "You invite German education experts here and Germany sends Nasser experts in death," he shouted. "You send our Uzi [submachine guns] to the Germans, and the Germans put microbes in the hands of our enemies."

When Golda rose to end the debate, she rebuked Begin for a harangue that shook the room. Nevertheless, she made no attempt to respond directly to him or to any of Ben-Gurion's critics. She did not want to be dragged down to Begin's level, she implied. The larger truth was that she could not bring herself to defend Ben-Gurion's German policy, which in her heart of hearts she, too, opposed. Instead, she let the personal charges against him float in the air, like so many unpunctured balloons. By doing so, she left the "old man" isolated, with no one from his own Mapai Party defending him. Isolated, hurt, and angry, especially at his foreign minister.

A few days later, with the press and the people still overwrought about the German scientists, Ben-Gurion returned from his long vacation. Peres, who had been abroad, also returned and appeared in the prime minister's office with the chief of military intelligence, Meir Amit. On Peres's initiative, the military had conducted its own investigation of the crisis and found it to be highly exaggerated. The scientists were mediocre; the Egyptian missiles lacked the proper fuel and warheads. There was no evidence of biological weapons and no means to develop nuclear ones. The public hysteria had been far out of proportion, and the attacks on Germany unjustified.

That same day, Ben-Gurion summoned Isser Harel and presented him with Amit's findings. Harel disagreed strongly and defended the Mossad, his intelligence agency, against Amit's military one. A vehement argument ensued, and the next day Harel sent Ben-Gurion his letter of resignation. Harel's departure sent new shock waves through the country. The public found it hard to believe that the man who had captured Adolf Eichmann, the man who epitomized Israel's courageous intelligence service, had been allowed to quit so abruptly. Many blamed the misfortune on the prime minister and his insistent friendship with Germany.

Harel's resignation hit Golda hard. She had been his chief ally in the crisis of the German scientists, and the two of them had been allies in their opposition to Shimon Peres. Now Peres had won the latest battle, Harel was out, and Golda, tired and sick again (she would spend several weeks in the hospital in April and early May), began to talk once more about resigning.

She didn't have to make good on the talk. On Saturday night, June 15, 1963, she left her Jerusalem home for Ben-Gurion's official residence in Rehavia. The prime minister was there preparing for the weekly Bible study group he held, to convene in an hour. Visibly agitated, Golda told him that the German News Agency had reported that Israeli soldiers were being trained in West Germany on the use of new weapons Israel had acquired from that country. She urged Ben-Gurion to have the military censor prevent that news from being published in Israel. After the agony the public had suffered over the German scientists affair, she felt it should be spared from learning about another provocative connection to Germany. Ben-Gurion countered that he could not dictate rules to the military censor and refused to act.

Golda rushed to Levi Eshkol's home, requesting that he influence the "old man." Eshkol suggested she speak to Teddy Kollek, now director of the prime minister's office. Close to eleven o'clock, after the Bible study group had left, Teddy Kollek accompanied Golda to another face-off with Ben-Gurion. The three sat down at the kitchen table to a heated argument. Golda attacked Ben-Gurion's German policy, and he became impatient and dejected because he could not sway her to his point of view. Kollek would later write that their dispute about the German question turned as sharp as it did because "there was already a rift between them . . . Their conversation did not end with a bang—it seemed more like a mutual distancing."

The next day Ben-Gurion resigned. "I called Golda, Eshkol, Aranne and others," recalled Uri Lubrani, who was filling in for Yitzhak Navon, Ben-Gurion's bureau chief. "They could not convince him, and he gave in his resignation." A parade of colleagues and army generals also failed in their attempts to change his mind.

Ben-Gurion's confrontation with Golda had been "no more than the last straw," writes Michael Bar-Zohar. Many other factors went into his sudden resignation. He was tired and under attack by a large segment of the public because of his German policy. In this and the Lavon Affair, he felt unsupported by his closest colleagues: Golda, Sapir, Eshkol. At the same time, he suffered constant pressure from John F. Kennedy on the nuclear issue. And, all around, he was slowing down, his mind sometimes confused, his decisions impulsive or inappropriate.

He resigned at the right time. Golda wept copiously (and publicly) when the news became official. Like others, she had dutifully tried to persuade him not to leave. But she didn't try as hard as she might have. Their time together had ended.

22

Seat of Power

L evi Eshkol became Israel's third prime minister (Sharett had been second for a brief time), handpicked by David Ben-Gurion, then unanimously elected by the Mapai central committee. Anyone following Golda Meir's long career might wonder why Eshkol and not she. She might have asked herself the same question, and though declaring her unworthiness for that position—as protocol dictated—she would have accepted it if offered. After all, her success as foreign minister had made her a world-renowned figure, much better known internationally than the finance minister, Eshkol, and the power she wielded at home was unmatched, except, perhaps, by Ben-Gurion himself.

So, why Eshkol and not Golda? The answer lay in Ben-Gurion's continued influence and Eshkol's personality. For Ben-Gurion, Golda had become toxic. It was she who had spoken out most forcefully against his attacks on Lavon, she who had aligned herself most closely with the Mossad chief, Isser Harel, in the German scientists frenzy, and she who most openly opposed Shimon Peres, the prime minister's protégé. After years of taking her loyalty for granted, Ben-Gurion felt betrayed by her. "It had become a love-agony relationship," explained Yitzhak Navon. "He loved her, she admired him, and then it all fell apart." Undoubtedly Ben-Gurion retained some of the devotion he'd had toward her during their long history together—he wrote her solicitous letters when she fell ill even in the midst of their fights—but at this point he recoiled at the thought of having her replace him.

Eshkol offered something different. A plain-looking man with a thick fleshy face and sweet smile, he was self-effacing, even-tempered, and a seeker of compromise. His ironic sense of humor and old-country love for Yiddish made him likable and unthreatening. With a background as a kibbutznik and labor union leader, he played the realist to Ben-Gurion's visionary. The "old man" had faith in him. Besides, from his perspective,

Eshkol seemed more malleable than Golda, easier to manipulate, or even push aside, if the former premier decided to make a comeback.

Golda kept her position as foreign minister in Eshkol's government. Years later, Isser Harel, who, at her suggestion, became a special assistant to Eshkol for a while, alleged that she did not consider Eshkol "worthy" of being prime minister. At meetings, she and Harel would impatiently roll their eyes at each other whenever the new prime minister spoke. "She was ashamed of him," Harel said. If so, Golda kept such feelings hidden from others, and for all intents and purposes she and Eshkol developed a strong working relationship. She might not have included him in her inner circle of good friends, as she did Zalman Aranne or Pinhas Sapir, but she consistently supported him within the party. For his part, Eshkol respected Golda and relied on her. He frequently traveled to her home to get her advice, which he valued greatly, but also, according to his aide, Brigadier General Yisrael Lior, because he feared her wrath if he didn't include her in his deliberations. Eshkol called Golda in Yiddish *de malka*, the queen, Israel's royalty. (When he felt annoyed with her, he privately dubbed her *de klafte*, the shrew, or worse, *de machashefa*, the witch.)

Like Golda, Eshkol placed his hopes and trust in the United States, more than in France or other parts of Europe. Even so, almost before he had settled in as prime minister, President John F. Kennedy began pressing him as hard as he had his predecessor in regard to Israel's nuclear project. With Golda's backing, Eshkol managed to buy time, accepting the president's demands for additional inspections of Dimona without firmly committing himself to the semiannual visits the administration wanted. Within a few months, Kennedy became somewhat more conciliatory toward Eshkol than he had been toward Ben-Gurion, possibly because of Eshkol's low-key style or because the American administration did not want to unbalance Israel's new government by leaning too heavily on it. In an exchange of letters with Eshkol, Kennedy acknowledged the threat Israel faced from the Arab countries and assured the prime minister of America's commitment to Israel's security. Those assurances and his more moderate tone relieved some of the stress the Israelis felt.

Golda met with the American secretary of state, Dean Rusk, when she came to the States in September 1963 for the opening of the UN General Assembly. After she painted a grim picture of Nasser's military capabilities, a skeptical Rusk suggested that Israel and the United States compare notes on Egypt's preparedness for war. Golda leaped at the opportunity. With her American antennae always attuned, she quickly grasped that such an exchange of information would put the two countries on a more equal footing. At her initiative, Yitzhak Rabin, then IDF deputy chief of staff, and other key Israelis joined American officials at the State Department in November. As she had hoped, the meeting strengthened U.S.-Israel ties and set an important precedent for future consultations on regional security.

On November 22, 1963, a shattered and grieving American nation learned that an assassin's bullet had cut down their popular young leader. As foreign minister, Golda Meir represented Israel at Kennedy's funeral and attended a state dinner in the White House given by the new president, Lyndon B. Johnson. He bent his towering body down toward her as she approached him in the receiving line, enveloped her with one arm, and said, "I know you have lost a friend, but I hope you understand that I, too, am a friend." Assistant Secretary of State Phillips Talbot confided to her that any policy change toward Israel would only be for the better.

On her return home, she reported these promises and her impressions of the funeral to the government. Americans perceived the assassination as a "personal loss," she told them. American Jews heaved a sigh of relief that the assassin, Lee Harvey Oswald, wasn't Jewish and were distressed that his murderer, Jack Ruby, was. The whole issue had many "dark corners," she said, and went on to speculate—as millions of Americans did—on the "strangeness" of it: "I'm not a detective. I don't even like detective stories, but I have to ask myself whether Ruby was working for someone, either some political underground, or the Dallas police." Conspiracy theories along those lines and others have never abated in the United States.

Good to his word, Lyndon Johnson became the first American president to invite an Israeli prime minister on an official visit to the White House. He and Eshkol met there on June 1, 1964, with their various advisers, and again the next day. While the president asked Eshkol about Dimona and reiterated America's opposition to the proliferation of nuclear weapons, he did not threaten the prime minister, as Kennedy had, or even give the subject his highest priority—to the annoyance of some of his own people, who wanted him to take a tougher stand. He also agreed in principle to sell Israel tanks and Skyhawk bombers, although there would be many ups and downs before that deal actually went through. Eshkol left feeling "greatly exhilarated," he told the former Supreme Court justice Felix Frankfurter, a strong Israel supporter. He returned home "confident and cheered by the knowledge that the man in the White House is a friend of our cause."

He did not find the same friendly atmosphere awaiting him in Israel.

Within days of Ben-Gurion's resignation, the "old man" again began demanding a judicial inquiry into the Lavon Affair. Sometime earlier, he had commissioned a journalist, Haggai Eshed, to examine all the material relating to the scandal, going back to its beginnings in 1954. Eshed's book *Who Gave the Order,* published about the time Ben-Gurion left office, blamed that botched espionage attempt in Egypt on Pinhas Lavon after all and criticized the committee of seven ministers that had absolved him. With that, Ben-Gurion became obsessed—the only accurate word to use—with a driving wish to have a committee of judges reexamine the entire sorry business. At one point, Eshkol agreed to a judicial inquiry into the first stages of the episode, but Golda objected strongly. The country was fed up with the Lavon Affair, she argued. Nobody wanted to hear another word about it, regardless of how justified Ben-Gurion might have been in his demand for a judicial investigation. Privately, she feared that a new investigation might churn up all sorts of party dirt she could not even anticipate and cast a shadow over Eshkol and the veteran leaders. Swayed by Golda's disapproval, Eshkol withdrew his agreement to the inquiry.

Golda and Eshkol took another step away from Ben-Gurion when they arranged an alignment—*maarach* in Hebrew—between Mapai and Ahdut Ha'avoda. (The history of this small but highly influential party can boggle the mind, so here is a brief recap: In 1930, Ahdut Ha'avoda joined with Hapoel Hatzair to form the Mapai Party. In 1944, a group from Mapai—mostly from the kibbutz movement—split from it to create a new party, adopting the old name, Ahdut Ha'avoda. In 1948, this Ahdut Ha'avoda and yet another party, Hashomer Hatzair, together formed the left-leaning Marxist party called Mapam. In 1954, Ahdut Ha'avoda left Mapam and became independent again. Now, in 1965, that independent party agreed to vote with Mapai, although not to join it formally.) That alignment strengthened Mapai's influence in the Knesset. In return, and after much debate, Mapai agreed to rehabilitate Pinhas Lavon, whom Ahdut Ha'avoda members had supported all along, by allowing him back into the party. Mapai members also agreed to oppose several electoral reforms that Ben-Gurion wanted but that would weaken Ahdut Ha'avoda.

"I am committed . . . with all my heart," Golda wrote to the secretary-general of Mapai, asking that he count her in when the vote on alignment was taken, because she would be out of the country that day. She was committed to the unity among labor parties that the alignment represented. More to the point, although unspoken, she was committed to the new balance of power among young and old the partnership created. Yigal Allon, Israel Galili, and other young Ahdut Ha'avoda leaders offset the influence of Mapai's young princes, Shimon Peres and Moshe Dayan. On the one hand, with the Ahdut Ha'avoda men now on board, nobody could accuse the Mapai veterans of not wanting new blood in their mix. On the other, the newcomers posed no threat to the old-timers, as the Mapai young did. Some of these men had long been rivals of Peres and Dayan themselves while on good terms with Golda and the Mapai elders. In the years ahead, she was to become especially close to Galili, relying on him as her personal adviser.

Golda and Ben-Gurion still exchanged occasional letters and notes, but with little warmth. One such case centered on a biography Marie Syrkin had written of her, first published in 1955 and revised and expanded in 1963 with the title *Golda Meir: Woman with a Cause.* Reviewing the book in *Commentary,* the critic Alfred Sherman described Golda as having "joined forces with Levi Eshkol and Zalman Aranne to . . . cut the 'Young Turks' (like Shimon Peres and Moshe Dayan) down to size . . . and finally, last summer, eased Ben-Gurion out of office." The instant he saw the review, Ben-Gurion sent those lines to Golda, referring to the "falsehoods" in it and his sorrow that her name had become mixed up with such "dirty affairs." Ostensibly written to commiserate with Golda for the misuse of her name, his words read more like a rebuke, a hint that he blamed her for the reviewer's perception. She immediately dashed off a blistering letter to the editor of *Commentary,* objecting to the "vicious" passage about her that had "not one iota of truth" in it. She, Eshkol, and Aranne had been and still were "among the greatest admirers of Mr. Ben-Gurion," she wrote, even if they did not always agree with him.

Writing to the "old man," she expressed her regrets about the Sherman piece and hoped he did not hold her responsible. She then inquired archly about an article that had appeared in the popular Israeli newspaper *Yediot Aharonot.* A reporter for the paper, Isaiah Ben-Porat, wrote that Ben-Gurion had been forced to quit the government because of Golda Meir. Not only had nobody written to the newspaper to contradict that statement, she pointed out in her letter, but the person who spread such "despicable lies" had received the privilege of being given an interview with Ben-Gurion. She did not need to elaborate on her implication: Ben-Gurion had fed Ben-Porat the information that Golda Meir had pushed him out of office.

Thus the former friends picked at each other, with civil words on the surface (Golda ended her letter with "warm greetings" for the New Year to Ben-Gurion and his family) and a deep and expanding hostility beneath it.

Ben-Gurion's hostility to Levi Eshkol was more open, public, and unyielding. The man he had designated as his successor had become, in his eyes, incompetent and unfit for the office, in large part because of his refusal to open a new inquiry into the Lavon Affair. Pulling a trick out of his predecessor's hat, Eshkol resigned. In essence, he gave Mapai a choice: either support him or commission Ben-Gurion's judicial investigation. After a raucous meeting, the Mapai central committee voted in favor of Eshkol and against Ben-Gurion, to Eshkol and Golda's great relief.

The turmoil in the party came to a head at the tenth Mapai convention, held at the Mann Auditorium in Tel Aviv. Flags lined the square fronting the large cultural center and spotlights illumined the building as more than three thousand delegates and guests packed the auditorium on opening night, Tuesday, February 16, 1965. The festive air outside contrasted with the palpable tension inside. All the issues the party had been fighting about would be debated and brought to a vote during the next four days. Golda sat on the large dais, with other ministers. Zalman Shazar, now the country's president, had a place at the center of the table, with Eshkol and Ben-Gurion on either side of him.

The delegates watched with fascination bordering on horror as their most revered party leaders verbally ripped each other to pieces. The drama reached its height on Wednesday evening, when Ben-Gurion approached the rostrum, to tumultuous applause. Repeatedly sniping at Levi Eshkol and his refusal to open the Lavon Affair again, the former prime minister denied that the country wanted to put the matter behind it. "I don't know what the people want, but I know what it should want— that truth and justice shall reign in our land," he thundered. He, too, cared about party unity, a chief concern of the conference, he said. "But many forget that the party is not an end in itself. Truth comes before the party."

Moshe Sharett spoke next. Gaunt and fragile, his body riddled with cancer, he had been brought to the conference in a wheelchair and tended throughout by his wife and children. From that chair he mustered enough energy to assail Ben-Gurion and call on the party to "come to its senses" about the Lavon Affair. "We must free ourselves of this dybbuk," he cried. "The public is sick of it." And Ben-Gurion must either "forsake the issue and join the main stream" or "relinquish the crown of leadership." Nearly a decade had passed since Ben-Gurion had forced Sharett out of his position as foreign minister and given it to Golda. Sharett had never forgiven either of them for that recasting. Nevertheless, when he finished speaking, Golda Meir walked to his chair, leaned over him with her right hand gripping his, and kissed him on the head. "We called it the kiss of death," said Yitzhak Navon. "Sharett hated her and she didn't like him, but since he made a speech against Ben-Gurion, she kissed him." Sharett smiled in return.

Golda's speech, given close to midnight, enraged Ben-Gurion more than anybody's. She stepped up to the rostrum dressed all in black, her face pale and drawn from her recent illnesses. She spoke first about disagreements that had always existed in the party, yet its ability to overcome those and live by its ideals. "The first curse that hovered over the threshold of our home," she then said, "came when people began to talk about favorites and non-favorites." Although she didn't mention Peres or Dayan, everyone understood the reference to them. "Where there are favorites and non-favorites, there is no comradeship," she said. When she moved into the Lavon Affair and Ben-Gurion's demands, her tone became "sharp and slashing, like a knife," the newspaper *Yediot Aharonot* reported. (Later, Ben-Gurion's followers would label this evening "the night of the long knives," evoking Hitler's murderous purge of his opposition in 1934.) If Ben-Gurion so opposed the creation of the committee of seven ministers, and not only its conclusions, she asked, as she had before, why didn't he quit as soon as it was formed? And why, when Eshkol first told him about the committee, did he say it should proceed, with blessings? She was implying, none too subtly, that had the committee reached a decision Ben-Gurion wanted, he would not have resigned. She flung her questions directly at the "old man," his face flushing as her biting words pelted him. "You don't remember, Ben-Gurion," she exclaimed, turning to glare at the former prime minister. "But I remember."

This was Golda's final, tragic "reckoning" with Ben-Gurion. All her disappointments with her former idol, all her stored-up hurts, coalesced into one of the harshest speeches of the convention. The two would not reconcile for another six years, and by then "Ben-Gurion wasn't really Ben-Gurion anymore," she was to say.

Immediately after she finished her talk, Ben-Gurion stalked out of the convention hall, even though he had been scheduled to reply to the debate that evening. When he did speak, the next morning, he responded to Sharett but conspicuously avoided answering Golda. Her speech "was filled with poison," he would say. "And I doubt if speeches of that sort contribute to comradeship." A few months later, he told a journalist that he would not have believed Golda spoke as she did had he not heard it with his own ears. Her words carried "venom and hatred . . . why she hates me, I do not know." Afterward, he wrote, "I think she lives in a contaminated environment and drinks from muddy springs."

Eshkol's turn to provide drama came at the Thursday morning session. Facing the first prime minister, who had been steadily hammering away at him, he pleaded with passion, "Ben-Gurion, give me a chance," and the audience responded with loud and sustained clapping. When a vote was taken in the evening, a majority of the Mapai Party—63 percent—supported Eshkol's resolution to align with Ahdut Ha'avoda. There was less support for Eshkol and Golda's adamant opposition to reopening the Lavon investigation. A large minority, 41 percent, voted in favor of a judicial inquiry into the beginnings of the mishap in 1954. The "old man's" persistence had swayed more voters on that subject than his opponents had expected.

Ben-Gurion's young supporters regarded that strong vote as a victory of sorts and secretly hoped it would end their leader's obsession with the Lavon Affair. But Ben-Gurion would have none of that. He continued to attack Eshkol mercilessly as unfit to be premier, indicating to his followers that he would return to that post if asked. When the party rejected his overtures, he organized an independent slate of candidates within Mapai to run in the next election, scheduled for November 1965. And when the party moved to oust members who did not accept Eshkol's premiership, he formed a new party, the Israel Workers' List, with the Hebrew acronym, Rafi (Reshimat Poalei Yisrael). Out of a sense of loyalty to the "old man," Shimon Peres, who had not wanted to split Mapai or lose his cabinet position, reluctantly joined the new party. After waffling for three months, so did Moshe Dayan. Yosef Almogi, Teddy Kollek, Yitzhak Navon, and other young Ben-Gurion acolytes also shifted their allegiance from Mapai to Rafi, none of them happily. Abba Eban stayed with the Mapai majority.

Profoundly upset about the split in the party she had nurtured, Golda never completely forgave those who followed Ben-Gurion into Rafi. In the early 1970s, when she was prime minister, Yitzhak Navon, by then a Knesset member, planned to run for president of the state. Golda's assistant, Simcha Dinitz, assured him in her name that she would not stand in his way. Then she had second thoughts. Although by that time Rafi and Mapai had come together again as part of the larger Labor Party, Navon had been a devoted Ben-Gurionite and Rafi member. How could she trust him not to favor his old Rafi buddies, like Shimon Peres and Moshe Dayan? She phoned Ephraim Katzir, an eminent Israeli scientist teaching at Harvard, and asked him to return and run for president. Katzir did and won, and Navon had to wait five more years, until Golda had left office, to become Israel's fifth president. He would always resent her for that.

In 1965, Rafi competed with Mapai in the "longest, costliest, and dirtiest campaign in Israel's seventeen-year history," wrote the *Time* correspondent Marlin Levin. When the votes were counted on November 2, Rafi suffered an overwhelming defeat, collecting only ten Knesset seats to forty-five for Mapai and its alignment partner.

With the election, Eshkol became his own person, no longer simply Ben-Gurion's chosen successor. Like Ben-Gurion, he held the dual titles of prime minister and defense minister. But the strain of the long, bitter campaign took its toll. Soon after his victory, he suffered a heart attack and landed in the hospital for several weeks, delaying the process of forming a government. When he finally presented his government to the Knesset on January 12, 1966, one change stood out: Abba Eban replaced Golda Meir as minister of foreign affairs. She had decided to retire, and this time the party took her at her word.

Golda's friends and colleagues knew she was very ill. In the last few years, she had been in and out of hospitals. At various times, she'd been diagnosed with kidney stones, gallbladder attacks, migraine headaches, shingles, phlebitis, heart troubles, and simple exhaustion. She usually tried to make light of her medical problems. When asked about her health, she would quip, "Nothing serious. A touch of cancer here, a little tuberculosis there." And when, after one of her stays at Beilinson Hospital, her friend Rose Halprin wrote that she'd been happy to hear that Golda was planning a "period of convalescence" and hoped she was following her doctor's orders to stop smoking, Golda returned the letter with a handwritten note on the bottom: "You are mistaken on two points. I did not take a period of convalescence and I did not stop smoking. The doctor gave up, I won."

She no longer had much to joke about, however. She had been diagnosed with lymphoma, a cancer of the lymphatic system, and begun exhausting chemotherapy treatments. The actual nature of her illness would be kept hidden from all but her family and closest associates. In an age when newspapers still maintained a code of silence about the personal lives of national leaders, any investigative reporter who might have discovered the truth kept it under wraps. For the record, Golda spoke of needing a rest after more than thirty years of public service and thousands of miles of travel. She was bone weary and genuinely eager to stay home, read books, go to concerts, and bake cookies for her grandchildren. Besides, she would tell people, "As my mother used to say, 'It's always better to leave before they tell you to go.'"

She also had another, even more hidden motive for retiring: there was no place left for her to go. She'd been foreign minister for almost a decade, long enough, she felt. She and Eshkol were contemporaries: she sixty-eight, he seventy-one. Because she was not likely ever to succeed him, what other worthy roles remained for her? She kept her Knesset seat, promising Eshkol, "I won't go into a political nunnery," but she turned down his offer to make her deputy prime minister. "Better . . . to be a full-time grandmother than a part-time minister," she quipped.

Her retirement hit newspapers all over the world. The *New York Herald Tribune* lauded her as "Israel's First Lady," and *The Milwaukee Journal* editorialized that Golda Meir "is too valuable to be tied to a rocking chair." Hundreds upon hundreds of tribute letters piled up in her office. A UN official wrote that everywhere on earth, "in the game of 'association of ideas' the immediate reaction to the word 'Israel' has been the reply 'Golda Meir.'" And at her final session in the cabinet, Abba Eban praised her "glorious service" as foreign minister.

Eban had been waiting breathlessly in the wings for her job for years. Whatever her personal feelings about him, she knew he was well qualified to fill her shoes. He had been Israel's ambassador to the United Nations, where he gained an international reputation for his eloquence in defending the country's actions, and now served as Eshkol's deputy prime minister. His style differed vastly from hers: his Shakespearean English, impeccable Hebrew, and meticulous diplomatic rhetoric contrasted sharply with her homey, Jewish mother persona, and her willingness to go for the jugular when she deemed it necessary. Now that he no longer represented a threat to her career, she was happy to hand him the keys to her office. Unlike Sharett, who had left her fending for herself a decade earlier, she ceremoniously escorted Eban to his desk, introduced him to the senior staff, and shook hands with him for the cameras.

At the first session of the new Knesset, on January 26, 1966, Golda Meir entered the Knesset chamber smiling and nodding as usual as she walked to the chair she had occupied for ten years as foreign minister. Suddenly she stopped, remembering that she had resigned. "Oy vey," she moaned, and quickly moved to the back benches, where her Mapai colleagues greeted her with affectionate laughter. "It's hard to teach an old horse the way to a new stall," she said.

ABBA EBAN'S WIFE, SUZY, found the big, stone foreign minister's house "chilling" and in "uncared-for condition." It had been scheduled for renovations, but Golda had left that dirty work for its new occupants. She had her hands full enough transporting her belongings to the modest home she owned in Ramat Aviv, a Tel Aviv suburb. She and Menahem had purchased twin semi-attached houses there in 1959, when it was a low-cost neighborhood inhabited mostly by struggling writers and young professionals. "Very few people had cars then," Menahem's wife, Aya, recalled, "and with Golda ill so much of the time we thought it best for the family to live near each other." It would remain Golda's private home for the rest of her life.

To fit her belongings into its small spaces, she gave away most of the mementos and gifts she had accumulated through her years as foreign minister, many of them elaborate and expensive sculptures and jewelry. Some went to the government, others to museums. The drawings and small statues she kept filled the shelves of the combination living room and dining area on the first floor, and books—many of them presents from their authors—lined the shelves of her compact study on the second floor. In the living room, a comfortable sofa and a few upholstered chairs were grouped around a round copper coffee table, with Golda's favorite chair closest to the small kitchen, where she made strong coffee for a constant stream of visitors. On Saturday mornings, Menahem's three little sons came over for brunch in that kitchen; at other times, they wandered in and out of her apartment, to her delight.

When she could, she visited her sister Sheyna, who still lived in Holon, outside Tel Aviv. Like their mother, Sheyna was succumbing to Alzheimer's disease, "a most agonizing heartbreaking experience for me and the family," Golda wrote to Marie Syrkin. She dreaded falling prey herself. "I never wanted to live long," she once said. "To die—to live only as long as my mind is clear and not one minute after that." Sheyna had written her memoirs in Yiddish, and Golda would arrange to have the work published before her sister died. In much happier circumstances, Golda spent some weekends with Sarah and her family in the kibbutz Revivim.

It was a fantasy come true, the visits, the rest, the grandchildren—and it lasted less than a month. That's when, in early February 1966, she agreed to become secretary-general of the Mapai Party to replace the retiring secretary, Reuven Barkatt. Sapir, Aranne, and other regulars in her kitchen pressed her to head the party, which had a dire need for strong leadership. With her cancer fairly under control, she felt up to the new assignment. Or, as Simcha Dinitz was to say, Golda's ambition had been to leave public office and spend her life with her grandchildren. When she did, if the phone didn't ring and cables didn't arrive, she missed it all terribly.

Katzav Kaduri remembered the day Golda consented to become secretary-general. Kaduri was building manager of Mapai Party headquarters at 110 Hayarkon Street in the heart of Tel Aviv. It was pouring rain that day. Eshkol, Sapir, and others from the party were waiting in the building for Golda to officially accept the new position. "Suddenly, through the rain, I saw a woman coming from Frishman Street, from the number 62 bus," Kaduri recalled. "From the distance I recognized Golda's nose." He went up to her and asked why she had taken that bus, and in such terrible weather, and she told him she had been in Beilinson Hospital visiting Sheyna. "What?" she barked. "I should have taken a taxi?"

Frugal Golda would not dream of spending her own or the party's money on a taxi. (In the government, she was known for turning the lights out every time she left her office, to save on the electricity bill.) When she retired from the Foreign Ministry, she'd had to give up all the perquisites that went with government service. The police detachment posted outside her official residence bade her farewell with a bouquet of flowers, and the driver who had shepherded her around for years reluctantly transferred to a different post. Neighbors spotted her carrying bags of groceries and taking buses (although bus drivers frequently changed their routes to drop her off close to home). When she had to go to Jerusalem, she sometimes got a lift from Zevi Dinstein, who had become deputy defense minister in Eshkol's cabinet. The young man found it embarrassing to have a car and driver while the eminent former foreign minister did not. But Golda didn't mind. She liked being seen as one of the people, the intrepid pioneer.

With her new position came immense power. Despite internal cracks,

Mapai still dominated the country as the largest political party and still pulled most of the strings that kept the government, the labor unions, and much of society going. In moving from world-famous foreign minister to party head, Golda endowed the office with even greater prestige and influence than it had before. Her position became the second most important in the state, after that of the prime minister. Some would say more important, given her charismatic personality and strong convictions compared with Eshkol's temperate and hesitant manner.

In her acceptance speech as secretary-general, she described Mapai as the party of all the people, the "entire community of workers," historically so vital to the country that it could be identified simply as "the party," without having to give its name. She aimed to restore the party to its former glory, before its troubles began. In the hope of unifying it again, she urged Ahdut Ha'avoda to take the next step and not only align with Mapai in the Knesset but also fully merge with it. It was different with Rafi. Too much had happened, too much anger between the Mapai veterans and the young Rafi elite, too much acrimony between Golda and Ben-Gurion for her to open Mapai's arms to the breakaway party. She might be willing to negotiate with individual Rafi members for their return to the fold, but not yet with the group as a whole.

Golda's closeness to Ahdut Ha'avoda and distance from Rafi incensed that party's heads. Precisely because of the power she held, they aimed their fiercest attacks at her rather than at Eshkol. "Madame Disunity," a Rafi newspaper branded her. "It is doubtful," the editor wrote, "whether any single person contributed more to the split in Mapai than Golda Meir."

WHILE GOLDA FOUGHT HER BATTLES with Rafi, fear of another war with the Arab countries gripped the land. Over the past few years, Fatah guerrillas, part of the newly formed Palestine Liberation Organization, had been attacking targets in Israel, many of them civilian. Most of these militants had come from Syria but carried out their raids across Israel's Jordanian border. At the same time, the Syrians laid mines in Israel and repeatedly shelled the country's farms and villages along its northern frontier. Israel retaliated with attacks against Jordanian villages and, in one large-scale reprisal, on April 7, shot down six Syrian MiG-21 fighter planes. Already mired in gloom from a severe economic recession, Israelis worried that the rapidly escalating tensions on their borders might explode any day into full-fledged hostilities.

On May 15, 1967, while watching the Israel Independence Day

parade, the chief of staff, Yitzhak Rabin, received a whispered report that Egypt was moving thousands of armed troops along with a huge supply of tanks and other arms into the Sinai desert, an area that had been demilitarized after the 1956 Sinai campaign. Several days earlier, Russia had falsely warned Syria that Israel was prepared to launch an all-out strike against it. The Syrians passed the information on to their Egyptian allies, triggering Nasser's moves into Sinai as a show of strength against Israel. There have been a number of theories about why the Russians would have spread that misleading report. If, as many historians believe, Moscow had simply intended to frighten Israel away from Syria, the strategy backfired. Egypt's president, Nasser, vowed loudly to annihilate Israel and within two days ordered the UN Emergency Force out of the Sinai, the Gaza Strip, and Sharm El Sheikh. The forces had been stationed in those areas since 1957, as a buffer between Egypt and Israel. To everyone's surprise and shock—probably even Nasser's—the UN secretary-general, U Thant, immediately complied, without consulting the General Assembly or the major powers. By May 19, the last UN units had pulled out, leaving a shaky standoff between Israeli and Egyptian troops.

U Thant's decision hit Golda harder than anything that came earlier. She could still taste the bitter bile of having to stand up at the UN after the Sinai campaign and announce the pullout of Israeli troops from the territories taken. At the time, "she felt we had surrendered," the Israeli diplomat Gideon Rafael recalled. "We should never have withdrawn from Sinai and Gaza without a peace treaty with Egypt." Now, as the UN Emergency Force left those areas, she remembered her warnings ten years earlier, "in an almost intolerable rush of pain and anxiety."

Giddy with his success, Nasser upped the ante. On May 23, he announced that the Straits of Tiran would be closed to Israeli shipping and to ships bound to and from Israel, effectively cutting the country off from commerce with Africa and Asia. Israel considered that act a direct violation of the freedom of passage guaranteed it after the Sinai campaign. The threat of war permeated the air and with it the existential fears that always lay at the core of Israeli consciousness. Could the country defend itself against Arab armies once again, or would it be annihilated this time, as Cairo radio blared day and night? "It is now a question of our national survival, of to be or not to be," Yitzhak Rabin told his generals.

Levi Eshkol desperately hoped to avoid another war with Egypt by finding a diplomatic solution to the crisis, and for that he needed help from the major powers. Word had already come from President Lyndon Johnson that Israel should not fire the first shot or take any military action without consulting the United States. Now the Americans were asking for at least a forty-eight-hour delay before Israel made any move. With their nerves on edge, the ministerial defense committee, composed of cabinet members, met in Eshkol's office. Rabin pressed for an attack on Egypt as quickly as possible. Israel's army was strong enough to overcome the enemy, he argued, especially if allowed to strike first. The fighting would be hard and long, and tens of thousands of soldiers and civilians might lose their lives, he admitted, but they had no choice.

Because of the gravity of the situation, Eshkol invited opposition party leaders—Menachem Begin, head of the right-wing bloc, and Moshe Dayan, Shimon Peres, and others from Rafi—to a briefing at the end of the committee's meeting. Golda was invited also, and her voice became the most prominent in the group. She opposed Abba Eban's suggestion that American warships might escort Israeli ships through the straits to Eilat. Egypt might not shoot with the Americans present, she argued, but either Israel had freedom of navigation or it did not. On the other hand, she strongly supported the forty-eight-hour delay the Americans had requested, so as not to give them any grounds for blaming Israel.

After considerable debate, Rabin and other military leaders reluctantly accepted the delay and agreed with a government decision to dispatch Minister of Foreign Affairs Abba Eban overseas to assess Israel's support among the major powers. It was no secret that Eshkol and some of the ministers would have preferred to see Golda Meir in that role. Her experience as foreign minister and knowledge of America, they believed, made her a more suitable emissary than Eban (whose elitist language was to lead Lyndon Johnson to mimic him as "a miniature Winston Churchill"). And she was more skilled than anyone at mobilizing American Jews to pressure their government into aiding Israel. Eban, of course, resented any such substitution, hinting that he would resign if that happened, and Eshkol did not need another crisis on his hands.

These nerve-racking weeks became known as *ha'hamtana*, the waiting. The reserves were called up, and as the days slipped by, a doomsday mentality engulfed Israeli society. A country filled with Holocaust survivors took seriously Egypt's triumphant boasts of pushing them into the sea. Everywhere, people dug trenches around their homes and filled sandbags in preparation for the oncoming disaster. Basements were turned into air raid shelters and schoolchildren drilled in taking cover. Hotels were emptied of guests so that they could be used as emergency hospitals, massive blood drives were launched, and supplies of bandages, medicines, and stretchers were stockpiled. Grimmest of all, almost ten thousand graves were dug in fields and parks, anticipating the worst.

Levi Eshkol became the most convenient whipping boy for the fear and foreboding that filled every home. Although the people did not want war, the more intensely he sought a peaceful solution to the crisis, the less they seemed to respect him. He appeared weak and uncertain, lacking the courage of the nation's founder and father figure, David Ben-Gurion. The "old man" heightened the loss of faith in Eshkol by continuing to harp on the latter's faults. He accused Eshkol of causing the economic slump the country had experienced and of escalating the tensions with Egypt and Syria. He called the prime minister a liar and cheat and equated him with Chamberlain, who had misled the British before World War II. Although he stated that he had no interest in replacing Eshkol himself, he let it be known among close associates that he would, indeed, be willing to take command again. Shimon Peres led the bandwagon for his return, and the press and public followed suit. Even Menachem Begin, his fiercest opponent for two decades, called on the former prime minister to return and head a new government.

"I don't believe . . . that Golda will agree to it," Ben-Gurion noted in his diary, but he didn't withdraw from the pursuit; he even agreed to form a government with Eshkol as his deputy prime minister. When Begin suggested that change to Eshkol, he famously replied, "These two horses cannot be hitched to the same wagon."

Golda received a phone call from Paula Ben-Gurion one day. "Golda," she said in English, "come to Ben-Gurion. He loves you." She also received a letter from Shimon Peres, asking for a meeting to discuss an expanded national unity government that would include Rafi and the other opposition parties. Golda would have no part of either idea. An expanded cabinet, she argued, was "counter-productive" at a time of crisis when only "shared ideologies" and backgrounds make it possible for a government to work "in the most efficient and harmonious way." On a less grand scale, for Golda to have Rafi back in the fold, with its Peres and Dayan leadership, was to give the impression that the veteran Mapai chiefs needed that party's help in this crisis. And certainly, she did not want Ben-Gurion holding the reins of government again.

She became Eshkol's strongest supporter, and under her direction the

Mapai secretariat reaffirmed its faith in his leadership. She remained his supporter during the next crucial days as the waiting dragged on.

Eban returned from his exploratory trip on May 27 with essentially empty hands. He had stopped off in France and England before going to the United States. The French premier, Charles de Gaulle, greeted him coolly and instructed him imperiously that Israel must not make the first move, no matter how beleaguered it felt. It was evident that with the Algerian problem solved and France's need for Arab oil, the warm French friendship toward Israel in 1957 no longer existed in 1967. The British prime minister, Harold Wilson, although an admirer of Israel, had little to offer. In the United States, Eban held talks with Secretary of State Dean Rusk and Secretary of Defense Robert McNamara before finally seeing President Johnson. Based on their own intelligence reports, the American leaders disputed Israel's assertion that it faced an imminent attack by Egypt. They urged patience and informed Eban that the United States was trying to organize an international fleet of vessels, called Regatta, to break through the Egyptian blockade of the straits. They, too, warned against Israel's being the first to open hostilities. Johnson reiterated that warning when he and Eban met in the Oval Office on Friday evening, May 26. "Israel will not be alone unless it decides to go it alone," he said, a formula he repeated twice, with great emphasis. He also informed Eban that in the opinion of American intelligence sources, even if Egypt attacked Israel, "you will whip the hell out of them."

Johnson had always shown sympathy toward Israel, and been a true friend, as Golda said. He had appeared on television three nights before his meeting with Eban to deny Egypt's right to interfere with the shipping of any nation through the Gulf of Aqaba and the straits. "I am not a feeble mouse or a coward," he said to Eban. "I am going to do what is right." Yet Johnson was weakened by the morass of the Vietnam War. He needed time, he said, to get congressional approval for the armada he was putting together and to work through the United Nations to launch that plan.

The Israeli cabinet met to hear and discuss Eban's report late into the Saturday night of May 27 and again the next day. Between meetings, Eshkol received a message from Johnson, again warning Israel not to initiate a war and urging it to give the United States time to explore other options. With that, and Eban's conviction that America would pull away from Israel if it started the fighting, the cabinet agreed to wait a while longer to see what the Americans could do, and Eshkol decided to inform the nation. That Sunday, May 28, people throughout the country gathered nervously around their radios, tuned to the Voice of Israel station. To their dismay, they heard a stammering, stumbling prime minister tell them that the waiting period had to continue. They didn't know that the script he received from staff members had been so marked up with corrections that it was almost illegible, or that he'd recently had cataract surgery in one eye and had difficulty seeing, or that he'd had very little sleep for the past few days. They heard fumbling and weakness when they longed for clarity and strength. And they were alarmed and angry. While criticisms of Eshkol rained down from all sides, Golda stood by him and later defended him with words that would enter her lexicon of aphorisms: "A leader who does not hesitate before he sends his nation into battle is not fit to be a leader."

But Eshkol's clumsy speech reinforced the already existing agitation to have someone take his place. The movement to appoint Ben-Gurion in his stead had begun to lose steam when Begin and others discovered that the former prime minister opposed going to war even more strongly than did the present one. Isolated in his Negev kibbutz and away from the center of power, the "old man" misjudged Israel's preparedness for battle and underestimated the ability of its army. Then again, so did others who wanted Eshkol replaced. Steeped in derision for the prime minister, they did not realize that over the years he had built up, modernized, and substantially strengthened the armed forces. The country needed a hero, and, if not Ben-Gurion, who was better suited for that role in the popular mind than the black-patched Moshe Dayan, champion of the 1956 Suez campaign? Now the cry went up for Eshkol to relinquish his position as defense minister to Dayan, while he remained prime minister.

Golda was willing to offer Dayan a slot as deputy prime minister for defense matters, which he didn't even deign to consider. But she stood firm against splitting Eshkol's roles of prime minister and defense minister, and she stood firm against expanding the government to include Rafi and Begin's Gahal faction (composed of his Herut Party and the centrist Liberal Party), as the opposition parties were demanding.

"Everything was ready for victory," she told a reporter later. "I didn't have a moment of doubt that the IDF would win and that the defense forces were prepared as they should be. Therefore it would be a crime to take the defense portfolio away from Eshkol." At one meeting after another, many in her office, she smoked her chain of cigarettes, answered ever-ringing phones, and argued her case. She was the party head, not a member of the cabinet, a reporter observed, but her power appeared formidable.

Despite her efforts, the din for change grew louder and more urgent, especially after Jordan moved closer to an alliance with Egypt, thus menacing Israel from three directions: Egypt in the south, Syria in the north, and Jordan in the east. From politicians to the man in the street, the nation clamored for a national unity government with Dayan and only Dayan as defense minister. One day Golda heard a ruckus outside her home in Ramat Aviv. She looked through the window and saw her son and her driver fighting with one of the neighbors. The man was standing in front of her car and yelling, "I won't let her go! Don't take her. She should stay home." He didn't want her at her office, fighting against appointing Dayan.

On one of the worst days, more than a hundred women rallied outside her office on Hayarkon Street. Some carried placards that read, GOLDA, ENOUGH HATRED, others signs that called for Dayan and a national unity government. Concerned about the mobs, the police wanted to enter the building to protect her, but she refused. "I already stood up to demonstrations by men," she said to the officer in charge. "Women—big deal!" (When she related that insulting statement to the party, she apologized to her female colleagues.)

Protests against Golda began to appear regularly in the nation's newspapers. Under the heading "A Woman Who Is a Stumbling Block," Yitzhak Ziv-Av, a columnist for *Haaretz*, wrote, "I accuse Golda Meir of destructive political fanaticism . . . I accuse as a citizen, as a Jew, as a Zionist." *Yediot Aharonot* went further. In a column dripping sarcasm, the columnist Herzl Rosenblum questioned why Moshe Dayan could not become defense minister. Is it because he is the most experienced general in the state, or can command the greatest loyalty, or has a worldwide reputation? No, "it is Golda, and again Golda, and once more Golda," who bore the responsibility for keeping him out. Golda is a "femme fatale," Rosenblum wrote, mocking her with this sexist image, which everyone knew came not from her beauty but from her power to manipulate men. "She doesn't leave Eshkol alone . . . may God help him."

To Golda's mind, the protests and press attacks against her did not appear "from the heavens." They grew from a sophisticated campaign led by the opposition, particularly the Rafi leaders, Peres and Dayan, who had strong connections to the press. Pained by the accusations, she nevertheless steeled herself against reacting publicly. With her comrades, she compared the situation to what she had experienced in the 1940s, when the Revisionists had plastered satirical posters about her on public walls. She ignored the current attacks as she had ignored those. "It has been ten days of wild incitements against me by the newspapers . . . but I push away these incitements with vigor," she told colleagues.

Tensions reached new heights in the last week of May as one day tumbled chaotically into another with seemingly no beginning or end. To prevent Eshkol from having to give up his defense portfolio, Golda urged him to appoint Yigal Allon as his special assistant for defense matters. Currently labor minister, Allon had been the top field commander and hero of Israel's War of Independence. He was a well-liked leader of Ahdut Ha'avoda, Mapai's alignment partner, and Golda reasoned that giving him a spot next to Eshkol in the Defense Ministry would put a lid on the frenzy for Dayan. The prime minister, however, rejected the proposal, hoping that somehow the Dayan turmoil would taper off by itself. It didn't, and Golda blamed herself for not putting greater pressure on Eshkol to take Allon as his assistant and blamed Eshkol even more for not accepting her advice. She was angry enough at Eshkol that she did not appear at a meeting of Knesset alignment members, when his Mapai colleagues—supposedly his good friends—joined the chorus calling for Moshe Dayan to become defense minister. Hurt and alone, without Golda's support, Eshkol listened stone-faced to the speeches, not uttering a word.

Golda's absence from that meeting and the fact that Eshkol's other major supporter, Pinhas Sapir, was away, having gone to the States to raise money, might have precipitated the prime minister's next big mistake. Weary, isolated, and harassed, Eshkol decided to offer Allon the position of minister of defense. That meant that he would be willing, finally, to separate his functions as prime minister from those of defense minister. The meaning immediately became obvious to others. "I could understand your wanting to keep Eshkol as defense minister," said Moses Haim Shapira, head of the National Religious Party, at a Knesset meeting, "because you do not want to remove the defense portfolio from the prime minister. But now that you have decided to separate it, why not give the Defense Ministry to Dayan?" Having opened the door to relinquishing the Defense Ministry, he opened the way for Dayan's backers to push their candidate into that position. Eshkol had undermined himself.

Even so, Golda did not give up searching for ways to prevent Dayan from becoming defense minister. After one meeting, she and Eshkol thought to offer him the position of foreign minister and make Abba Eban a deputy prime minister. Eban refused to go along with that change. After another meeting, Eshkol offered Allon the Defense Ministry and Dayan command of combat forces in the south, a position he had requested earlier, causing awkwardness for the chief of staff, Yitzhak Rabin, who had faith in his current head of the southern command. A turning point came when Shapira threatened that his National Religious Party would quit the government coalition altogether if a national unity government were not formed, with Dayan as defense minister. Eshkol finally folded, and with that Golda could no longer hold out. After two stormy meetings on June 1, the Mapai secretariat agreed to appoint Moshe Dayan as defense minister, and it accepted a national unity government that would include Rafi and Gahal as well as the religious parties. With the expansion, Menachem Begin became a minister without portfolio, and Mapai was granted an additional seat in the cabinet.

"Where it says a man [for the new Mapai seat] it also means a woman," Eshkol said, suggesting in that way that Golda join the cabinet as a minister without portfolio. "Please tell them the woman's answer," Golda interjected. "Wherever it says a woman, it also means a man," Eshkol responded, indicating that Golda had rejected the offer.

THE DECISION TO GO to war ultimately belonged to Eshkol, and he made one last effort to find a diplomatic solution to the crisis. He sent the Mossad head, Meir Amit, on a secret mission to Washington to assess the situation. Was the United States truly going to help Israel, or would it, at the least, not stand in the way if Israel were to act alone? Meeting privately with the CIA director, Richard Helms, and other senior CIA staff, Amit received the impression that the armada idea had come to naught and that the United States would secretly welcome an Israeli initiative as long as it did not have to get involved itself. For the United States, knocking out Nasser would also be a way of keeping the Soviet Union out of the region. His impressions were strengthened at a more official meeting with Secretary of Defense Robert McNamara. "I hear you loud and clear," McNamara said after Amit described the situation. And when Amit said he was returning to Israel with a recommendation for war, McNamara didn't seem to react. "For me that was a green light," Amit recalled. Furthermore, Johnson called twice during that meeting and knew of its substance. When Amit returned to Israel on Saturday night, June 3, he went directly to Eshkol's home, where the prime minister, Dayan, and others waited with "unbearable" tension for him and the Israeli ambassador Abraham Harman. Amit believed, he told them, that the Americans will bless "any action that succeeds in sticking it to Nasser." His view that nothing would be gained from further waiting set the wheels of war in motion.

On Sunday morning, June 4, the Israeli cabinet voted in favor of launching a war against the Arab nations encircling the country, at a time and place the army considered appropriate. Like other Israelis, in the expectation of Egyptian air raids on Tel Aviv, Golda and her son, Menahem, had blacked out a room in their connected homes where they could turn on a light when the rest of the house was darkened. And she had packed an overnight bag of essentials to carry with her to a shelter in readiness for when sirens wailed their warnings. One evening, she ordered Menahem to tape up his windows immediately. He suspected, although she did not say so openly, that war was about to begin.

At 7:45 on Monday morning, June 5, Israeli fighter planes took off for Egypt's airfields. Egyptian pilots ate breakfast at that time, and almost all their planes were on the ground. A little over an hour later, half the Egyptian air force—204 planes—had been destroyed. By the end of the day, Jordan had lost its entire air force and Syria almost half of its: a total of 400 enemy planes had been demolished. Israeli forces had also made significant breakthroughs in the Sinai desert and the West Bank.

The White House counsel, Harry C. McPherson Jr., had arrived in Tel Aviv that morning, unaware, like everyone else, of the precise war plans. He followed the news as the morning progressed. Around noon, as he sat outside Levi Eshkol's office, sirens went on. Worried, he asked an intelligence chief with him whether he should go to a shelter. The man looked at his watch, looked up, and said, "It won't be necessary." By that time, on that first day of fighting, "the war was essentially won," McPherson wrote to Lyndon Johnson a few days later.

The war would last five more days. When it ended, on June 10, Israel had conquered a vast expanse of territory that was more than three times its original size. The Straits of Tiran were back under its control, as were the Gaza Strip, the Sinai desert, the West Bank, and—the last takeover—the Golan Heights.

The euphoria that swept the country now contrasted wildly with the panic that had consumed it before this Six-Day War (as Israel called it). For many Israelis, the most emotional and significant conquest was of East Jerusalem and the Old City, which the IDF took from Jordan after a hard battle and many casualties. Eshkol had promised Jordan's king, Hussein, that if he stayed out of the war, Israel would not attack his lands. But on the first day, Hussein's troops began shelling Jerusalem and the Jewish settlements on the border of Jordan and Israel. Israel struck back, and by Wednesday, June 7, all of Jerusalem had fallen into its hands.

Golda went to the Old City two days later. The paratroopers and other soldiers who swarmed there after the city was captured could not have predicted the depth of their feelings as their fingers touched the ancient stones of the Western Wall, which had been in Jordanian hands since 1948. Many of these young men were not religiously observant, yet the sight and feel of this monument, the last visible remnant of the Second Temple that had stood there almost two thousand years earlier, reached into the essence of their being. Like generations of people before her, Golda squeezed a *kvitl*, a piece of paper holding her wish, into a cranny of the wall. On it she had written the word *shalom*, peace. As she stood there, one of the soldiers put his arms around her, laid his head on her shoulder, and wept. She wept with him.

The next day, she flew to the United States for fund-raising and speaking obligations she had made months earlier. At a huge rally in Madison Square Garden organized by the UJA, she spoke with emotion. "Once again we have won a war, the third in a very brief history of independence," she began. "We don't want wars. We want peace more than all else." But the Arabs had to learn a lesson, she said, evoking an image that always haunted her: "Those that perished in Hitler's gas chambers were the last Jews to die without standing up to defend themselves." She described Israel's lightning victory and the young soldiers she had seen at the wall putting their guns aside to pray at the ancient site.

"Here we are," she said sardonically. "We're a wonderful people, they tell us . . . wonderful people—these Israelis. Look what they can achieve against such odds. Now that they have won this battle, let them go back where they came from so that the hills of Syria will again be open for Syrian guns; so that Jordanian Legionnaires, who shoot and shell at will, can again stand on the towers of the Old City of Jerusalem; so that the Gaza Strip will again become a place from which infiltrators are sent to kill and ambush." She looked at the thousands of faces in the audience. "Is there anybody who has the boldness to say to the Israelis: 'Go home! Begin preparing your nine and ten year olds for the next war, perhaps in ten years.'" Shouts of "No" resounded through the stadium. "You say,

'No,'" Golda continued. "I am sure that every fair person in the world in power and out of power, will say, 'No,' and forgive me for my impudence, more important than all—the Israelis say, 'NO!'"

A FEW DAYS BEFORE that speech, while she was still in Israel, Golda heard Levi Eshkol describe his visit to the Old City and Israel Galili talk of organizing the Jewish settlement there. "I assume we will not be able to stay in the Old City," she had responded, looking ahead. "And therefore Jews who settle in the Old City will need to be prepared to leave it in the future."

For Golda and other Israeli leaders, the elation after the country's astounding victory in its Six-Day War would give way to confusion and contradictions about what to do with the regions captured during that war, including Jerusalem.

PART FOUR

PREMIER

23

The Chosen

Golda sneaked away to a health spa on the outer edge of Zurich, Switzerland, during the summer of 1967. Situated on a hill near a wooded area, and not far from the elegant Dolder hotel, it provided her with rest, seclusion, and a strictly regulated diet. While there, she had a visit from her old friend Zeev Sharef, now minister of commerce and industry. Levi Eshkol, ill with cancer, had recently suffered another heart attack, both being kept secret from the public. "Look, Golda," Sharef said to her, "you will be the next prime minister." She demurred properly, but Sharef insisted that if there were to be a fight and split in the party about who would replace Eshkol, she would have to take the position. "Meanwhile, he's alive," she said, "let's leave this." She did not rule out the idea of becoming Eshkol's successor, however.

This was not the first time someone had spoken to her about filling the country's top position. The former Mossad chief Isser Harel, who disliked Eshkol, had broached the subject soon after she became Mapai's secretary-general. Eshkol needed to go, he told her, and she was the person to replace him. "I, an old, weak woman," she had replied. "What are you talking about?" But she did not rule out the idea.

For now, with Eshkol still in office, she immersed herself in strengthening and unifying the party. She had successfully kept the Rafi crowd at bay while creating the alignment between Mapai and Ahdut Ha'avoda. But with the extravagant success of the Six-Day War, Minister of Defense Moshe Dayan became Israel's larger-than-life hero, and his Rafi Party glowed in his reflected glory. Shimon Peres had been trying to have Rafi reunite with Mapai, and Golda could no longer ignore that effort. For Peres, Dayan, and the other Rafi princes, reunion with Mapai would provide a stronger base than they now had to siphon power away from the veterans and gain control of the labor government. For Golda, Sapir, Aranne, and the other elders, Rafi, with its newfound popularity, posed a danger to Mapai's hegemony over Israel's political life. If it split the labor vote, Menachem Begin and his right-wing Gahal Party might end up on top. Best to absorb it despite the risks.

Only Ben-Gurion, still head of Rafi, refused to rejoin Mapai. In an effort to persuade him, the Rafi spokesman Yosef Almogi prevailed on Golda to meet with the "old man" at the King David Hotel. After sitting through a two-hour harangue from him about Eshkol's inadequacies, she knew the attempt was fruitless. She entered hard negotiations instead with Peres, Almogi, and other Rafi members. Knesset member Shulamit Aloni, one of the youngest and most outspoken of that group, was particularly antagonistic toward Golda. More committed to individual rights than party solidarity, Aloni regarded Golda as quintessentially old guard. She used the current negotiations to suggest that Shazar, nearing seventy-nine, retire as Israel's president and Golda Meir replace him. No naïf of course, Golda understood the suggestion to be Aloni's way of shutting her out of active politics by confining her to the largely ceremonial role of president. "You're not stupid enough to think that I don't know the purpose of your suggestion," she snapped at Aloni. Maintaining her innocence, Aloni replied, "I meant what I said. Why is it always necessary to surround things with intentions that aren't there?" Few believed her.

At 3:00 p.m. on January 21, 1968, Elisheva House (named for Levi Eshkol's second wife, Elisheva Kaplan) in Jerusalem bustled with excitement. Delegates had arrived at that sprawling modernist center to sign the final papers merging Mapai, Ahdut Ha'avoda, and Rafi into a single new unit, the Israel Labor Party. Seated at the center of a table at the front of the hall and flanked by members of the three parties, Golda Meir chaired the large assembly of government ministers, political leaders, and guests. "These three parties have come together this evening to proclaim our unity," she announced to loud applause as she opened the formal part of the proceedings. The party that had first split two dozen years earlier was becoming whole and brimming with optimism for the future.

Barely three weeks later, the three factions within the new Labor Party were lashing out at each other again, and Golda announced irritably that she had changed her mind and would not serve as secretary-general of the united party, as she had agreed to do. She had accepted the position, she said, largely because of the urgings of her daughter, Sarah. But looking back at her two years as secretary-general of Mapai, she regarded them as the worst in her life. People had taken her for granted, and nobody came to her defense when she was "persecuted" by the news-papers and in the street (in her attempt to block Dayan from becoming defense minister). "What do I need it for?" she growled, dismissing the new position as an extension of the old. In a repeat of a well-worn rou-tine, her colleagues argued with her, flattered her, and pleaded with her to take the job. After a long talk with Levi Eshkol and a meeting with party members that lasted until three in the morning, she gave in. On February 7, she was voted secretary-general of the united Labor Party. Shimon Peres became deputy secretary-general.

With this role, her power and prestige reached an all-time high. A diagram in *Yediot Aharonot* placed her at the top of the Labor Party pyra-mid, with Pinhas Sapir just below her and Levi Eshkol off to his side. The title "strong man" of the organization doesn't do her justice, the accompanying article held. In her most recent exercise of power, she had Eshkol appoint Yigal Allon as his deputy prime minister, although Peres, Dayan, and other former Rafi members objected and the prime minister himself argued that he didn't need or want a deputy to help him. "Golda decided, and that's how it was," the article concluded.

Then, suddenly, on July 8, with her influence at its peak, Golda stunned the nation by announcing her resignation as secretary-general of the Labor Party. Scarcely six months had passed since the party had been established and she had consented to head it. Once again, Eshkol, Sapir, Aranne, Galili, and others trekked to her home or spent hours at her office begging her not to leave, but to no avail. "It would take a com-puter to determine how many times Golda has quit the numerous high posts she has held . . . and later retracted," a journalist wrote. "This time it does look like the real thing." She would resign as of August 1, and "nothing will change my mind," she said, leaving the press as bewildered as the public. "Why and especially why now?" asked *Maariv*, which first broke the story of her resignation. Nobody bought her explanation that she truly wanted the time to enjoy herself. "At seventy, one is entitled to some of the pleasures of life," she said, while everybody searched for deeper motives.

It could be her health, some said. It could be, as she frequently prom-ised, that "when the time comes" because of age, she "will demonstrate how a politician steps down." It could be that she was annoyed at party leaders who did not support her plan to include the leftist Mapam in the Labor Party umbrella. Or it could be her disappointment and anger at having lost a battle about electoral reforms to Peres and other former

Rafi members. The reforms instituted the direct election of mayors and secret ballots for internal voting, both of which she opposed because they limited party authority. It could be all those things, and it could also be that she had decided to bide her time. Having been caught up in the demanding work of running the party, she wanted distance, a quiet period in which to gather her resources and plan the future.

She had some hard thinking to do. Nobody could know how much more time the gravely ill Eshkol had, but party leadership loomed as the next big issue. Because of Labor's strength and dominance, whoever led the party also led the nation. Word of mouth pitted Moshe Dayan against Yigal Allon as the two most likely candidates for the top job. Charismatic Dayan, with his showy self-confidence, was the people's favorite, but Golda and the other elders didn't trust him. He could be moody and unpredictable, contradict himself without compunction, and think nothing of attacking the old guard while offering no alternatives of his own. She had opposed his being named defense minister, and now she opposed his inheriting the prime minister's mantle. By maneuvering to have Allon appointed deputy prime minister, she had positioned him as a strong challenger to Dayan. Yet she recognized that for all his courage during the War of Independence, Allon would not be able to withstand a Dayan political onslaught. He lacked "the killer instinct," as the British prime minister, Harold Wilson, who knew him well, once said. If not Dayan or Allon, who then? In her head, Golda could hear echoes of Sharef, Harel, and other friends telling her that she needed to assume the top job. She had pushed those voices away for the time being, but she had also told Eshkol that she did "not intend to retire to a political nunnery." She had kept her Knesset seat and would still be involved in party affairs. Just a few years earlier, she had been hurt when Ben-Gurion bypassed her to crown Eshkol prime minister. Now Ben-Gurion was gone from the political scene, Eshkol was dying, and she could afford to pull back, regain her strength, and wait to see how matters unfolded.

Pinhas Sapir was voted in as secretary-general of the united Labor Party on August 1, 1968, the day Golda retired. Buoyant and relieved to turn the work over to him, she commented wryly that she could see how indispensable she was in that the minute she walked out of her position, he walked in to fill it. Sapir had the appearance of the party boss he was. Bald, heavy-featured, and gruff-voiced, with a slight speech impediment, he seemed never to sit still, exuding tireless energy. In their years of working together, he and Golda had pulled most of the strings that made Mapai function. Although they differed politically—he held more dovish views than she—he had deep affection for her. He admired the fact that unlike the other founders, who had immigrated to Palestine directly from Eastern Europe, she had given up America with its many opportunities to go there. She had accepted every assignment the party gave her, no matter how demanding, and had filled most of the key positions in the land. In some ways, he held her in awe; at the same time, he had the power to shape her life.

In the autumn of 1968, Sapir visited Golda, who was again at the spa in Zurich where Sharef had called on her about a year earlier. Eshkol was fading, Sapir told her, and he proposed that she replace the prime minister when the moment came. This time she agreed, on condition that all the cabinet ministers remain in their appointed positions so that she would not have to renegotiate those appointments.

In turning to Golda, Sapir hoped to avoid an all-out war between Dayan and Allon that would split the newly united Labor Party. If either won, the other's faction—Dayan's Rafi or Allon's Ahdut Ha'avoda— would undoubtedly break away. He also reasoned that to keep the former Mapai faction dominant within the Labor Party, the next leader needed to come from its ranks and not from one of the smaller groups. Although pundits speculated constantly that he was angling for the top slot himself, in fact he did not aspire to be prime minister. He had neither the temperament for that job nor sufficient foreign policy experience. He preferred to be the kingmaker, manipulating from behind the scenes for the ends he wanted.

And he wanted Golda Meir as prime minister. Some weeks after meeting with her, he spoke with Allon privately as the two drove from Jerusalem to Tel Aviv. He recognized the younger man's abilities, he said, but only Golda could hold the party together. To soften his decision, he promised that Allon would become prime minister after Golda, a promise he had no intention of keeping. With Allon agreeing to back Golda, Sapir went to Abba Eban, another, less obvious contender for the premiership. (When Golda later heard from a friend that Eban had ambitions to be prime minister, she retorted, "Interesting. Of which country?") He assured Eban that after Eshkol died, Golda would serve only as interim prime minister, until the next elections, another distortion of his intentions. Eban consented, but later offered his support to Allon, who turned it down. Having given Sapir his word to back Golda,

Allon was too "intimidated," as Eban saw it, to retract it. Sapir also informed Israel Galili of his plans for Golda, thus forestalling a Galili campaign for Allon, his Ahdut Ha'avoda colleague.

Meanwhile, Eshkol still lived, and to quell rumors about his health, he declared that he would run again in the general elections coming up in the fall of 1969. He continued as prime minister for several months into the winter, chairing committees and attending meetings but growing weaker all the time. In his last days, aware of the machinations behind his back, he is said to have mumbled to himself in Yiddish about the *klafte*, shrew, Golda Meir, who was sitting at home waiting for him to die. After another heart attack, he passed away on the morning of February 26, 1969, at the age of seventy-three.

As soon as she received word of his death, Golda traveled to the prime minister's residence in Jerusalem, looking "numbed with grief." Many government ministers had already gathered there to pay their respects, including the rivals Allon and Dayan. After privately taking her final leave of Eshkol, Golda sat on a sofa in the guest room, cigarette in hand, and listened to an ongoing argument about where the prime minister should be buried. He was the first prime minister to die in office, and no precedent had yet been set concerning the burial of a government head. Some thought that as one of the founders of the kibbutz Degania, he should be interred in the kibbutz cemetery, where his first two wives were buried. Others argued for Mount Herzl in Jerusalem, which has a special section set aside for leaders. Arie Lova Eliav, a deputy cabinet minister, watched with amused wonder at how quickly Golda became the center of the discussion, with ministers moving to either side of her on the sofa to present their opinions. After listening to both sides, she decreed that Eshkol be buried in Jerusalem, and so it would be. It struck Eliav at that moment that Golda Meir would be the next prime minister.

The general public did not yet know that or have any idea about Sapir's behind-the-scenes scheming. Speculation about who would replace Eshkol became everybody's favorite pastime. In a move for continuity, the cabinet—with Golda present, although she was not a member—immediately named the deputy premier Yigal Allon as acting prime minister, seeming to put him in the lead. Popularity polls, however, showed Dayan ahead of him. When, two days after Eshkol's death, pollsters asked a cross section of Israelis whom they would select to head the country if they had a choice, 45 percent said Dayan, 32 percent chose Allon, 3 percent Abba Eban, 3 percent Menachem Begin, and 1 percent Pinhas

Sapir. Golda's name did not even appear among the responses. It never occurred to people that the elderly, retired secretary-general could, or should, be a real option. When another poll asked respondents whom the party itself might choose, only 1 percent named her. "She was very unpopular at the time," the journalist Yossi Sarid recalled. "Israelis saw her as a bitter politician who had stood in Dayan's way. Besides, nobody likes the person who runs a political party."

Ignoring the polls, Sapir pushed forward with his plans. In Israel, he said, "the prime minister is chosen by the Knesset and not by signatures in the street," a dig at the petitions that were being widely circulated on Dayan's behalf. To stave off the Dayan forces and promote Golda for premier, Sapir quickly organized several meetings of party leaders without waiting until the end of the traditional seven-day mourning period for Eshkol. At one of these, Eliav, having seen Golda in action, turned toward her. "Golda," he said out loud, "I propose that you be our candidate . . . because you are absolutely determined to be prime minister. You want it with all your heart and all your soul." The others gasped, dumbfounded at his directness. In the party ethos, nobody "wanted" a position; candidates simply obeyed the movement's decree. Golda turned red with embarrassment and rage. "I want something?" she practically screamed. "I don't want anything." Then everybody chimed in that she should be the party's candidate.

On March 2, as a result of the meetings, Labor's leadership bureau announced its decision to propose Golda as prime minister to the party's central committee, its main decision-making body. Without wasting a moment, Sapir stated publicly the next day that Golda Meir had the widest support in the party, not only as a stopgap premier, but also as its candidate for the forthcoming fall elections. When asked by journalists how she felt about the nomination, Golda said predictably, "I have always accepted decisions of party institutions. I will consider what I heard at this meeting and then decide." She did manage to slip in a subtle retort to those who might grumble about her age and health: "Being seventy is not a sin."

As she would later present the story, the request for her to be prime minister came unexpectedly and as something she "didn't want" but was pressed on her by the party. To help her decide, she spoke at length by phone with Menahem and Aya, who were then living in Connecticut, and with Sarah and Zecharia, who drove up from their kibbutz in Revivim. They argued that she had no choice and had to say yes. Sapir would laugh at that account. She already knew for half a year that she would be prime minister, he confided to a reporter.

Golda agreed to the nomination and, on the morning of March 7, appeared in Tel Aviv's Ohel Theater, her face wreathed in smiles as she accepted flowers from well-wishers. After some debate, Labor's central committee overwhelmingly elected her their candidate, automatically ensuring that she would be Israel's next prime minister. In the final count, 287 members voted for her, and 45 abstained, all of them from the Rafi faction. Not one person voted against her. Seated in the third row, between the deputy mayor of Tel Aviv and his young daughter, Golda put her head in her hands when the voting ended and made no effort to hold back the tears rolling down her cheeks. Almost half a century after coming to the Land of Israel, she had reached the pinnacle of her career, the highest position in the state. She would occupy the seat the great Ben-Gurion held for so many years, second to no one in the land she had chosen for her own. She walked to the podium to booming applause, stopping only to hug one colleague after another.

"I always assumed a position with awe and trepidation, and endless doubts as to whether I was worthy of it," she said in her acceptance speech. "But nothing in the past resembles this day." She earnestly assured her comrades that she had "never dreamed" that she would be faced with the moment when she "would have to accept this ruling of the party," and she ended by appealing to them to give her and her government team "all the help it needs" in "this difficult period." The first person to shake her hand when she finished speaking was Shimon Peres, her longtime adversary. As she left the hall, the crowds outside shouted, "Golda, Golda," and she waved to them briefly before driving off with Sapir in his blue ministerial limousine.

In an interview before Golda was voted in, Sapir described her as the "most outstanding . . . personality in the Jewish world," beloved by Jews everywhere. "I cannot overlook the sentimental thought that now at the head of this nation, where once stood Deborah the Prophetess, Golda Meir will stand," he said. He was not alone in making that comparison. The Orthodox labor party, Poalei Agudat Israel, which had once blocked her from becoming mayor of Tel Aviv because of her gender, now cited passages about Deborah in the biblical book of Judges and from the prophet Jeremiah to justify accepting a female prime minister. Only the most ultra-Orthodox parties still maintained that they could not support a woman as premier.

Other groups had their own doubts. During the debate before the final decision, some Labor Party members complained loudly about being "railroaded" into the vote, without being given a choice among several candidates. The press weighed in with concerns on everyone's mind about Golda's age and health. Israel "deserved a prime minister who above all will be a healthy person," *Haaretz* editorialized, warning that this prime minister's poor health could seriously endanger her and the country if a crisis hit. Several newspapers featured a drawing by the popular cartoonist "Dosh" in which the young, boyish figure he used to symbolize the Israeli sabra—known as Yisraelik or Skulik—gazes into a mirror held by a party leader and sees an old woman's face reflected back to him. No one could miss the meaning: Did that worn, wrinkled face really reflect this exuberant young nation, flying high after its victory in the Six-Day War?

Overall, however, enthusiasm for the choice overshadowed the reservations. A *Maariv* headline labeled Golda "One in Her Generation," an honor previously bestowed only on Ben-Gurion, for years singled out as unique even among the founders' generation. Women, especially, hailed her selection. She was, after all, one of only three women in the world to have become prime ministers. Sirimavo Bandaranaike of Ceylon rose to power after her husband's assassination, and Indira Gandhi became premier of India shortly after her father's death. But Golda Meir had climbed to the top of the ladder on her own, step by painstaking step. Rachel Shazar, who devoted herself to women's causes all her life (and made a point of ignoring her husband's romantic links with Golda), said it well when she wrote of the "deep mental satisfaction" she felt at the choice of Golda to head the state, "not only because of my relationship with her, but also because I accept this event as a justification of my own life's path." In the United States, after *Time* magazine portrayed Golda in a profile as "the 70-year-old grandmother," a reader wrote, "Did you ever refer to [President] Johnson by saying 'so said the grandfather . . . ?'" She went on, "Hooray for Golda! She is a great inspiration to womankind."

Golda accepted her nomination as premier from President Shazar, who formally invited her to organize a new government. While speculation continued about whether Dayan would run against her in the future, he told reporters that he would "consider it an honor to serve in Mrs. Meir's cabinet if she asks me." In a festive setting, on March 17, she presented her cabinet to the Knesset, which approved it by a vote of 84 to

12. Only one Knesset member abstained: David Ben-Gurion stood up and accused Golda of being "instrumental in concealing a serious moral defect," a reference to the Lavon Affair, which still haunted him. Asked afterward how she felt about the attack, she mumbled through clenched teeth, "No comment."

Wearing a simple white blouse, black skirt, and black sweater, Golda Meir was sworn in that day as Israel's fourth prime minister. After declaring her allegiance to the state, she sat for the first time in the prime minister's chair at the center of the cabinet table. Somewhat tense and tired from a week of political bargaining with coalition partners, she read her acceptance speech haltingly, her voice becoming husky with emotion at times. She spoke of Israel's strong desire for peace in spite of the wars that had been "forced upon" it, and she called for "face-to-face" negotiations with Arab leaders, as she had many times before. In the gallery, Sarah and her family watched the proceedings along with some of Golda's old friends who had traveled to Jerusalem for the occasion. Missing from that circle was the person who had started the young Goldie Meyerson on the path that led her to this day. Her sister Sheyna, the strongest influence of her youth, her inspiration (and perpetually nagging conscience), lay in a nursing home, her mind ravaged by Alzheimer's disease, oblivious of her sister's remarkable fate.

AHARON REMEZ, SON OF GOLDA'S longtime lover, David Remez, visited her at home a few weeks before she was nominated for prime minister. Although he had been told that she was extremely ill, he was taken aback by what he saw. Her face was drawn and dark, her hair disheveled, her energy depleted. She smoked constantly and spoke despairingly, and he felt he was looking at someone close to life's end. He saw her again, not long afterward, when she visited London as prime minister and he served as Israel's ambassador there. She hopped off the plane "like a young woman of twenty" and arranged a schedule that kept her busy from six in the morning until twelve at night. When he tried to limit her meetings, she scolded him: "I didn't come here to play games."

From the moment she took her oath of office, Golda was all energy and drive and firmly in control. In a television interview the following day, she appeared relaxed and self-confident, sure of her ability to run the country as though she had been prime minister all her life. In one of her first acts in office, she asked Lou Kadar, who had been her secretary on and off through the years, to return as a personal assistant. When

Kadar, now working in the Foreign Ministry, declined, not wanting that much responsibility, Golda pressed hard. It would be for six months only, she promised, until the fall elections. Lou reluctantly consented and would remain at Golda's side for the next four years. A few months later, Kadar sent a personal letter to Simcha Dinitz, who was working at the Israeli embassy in Washington. The "old lady" needs you, she wrote, but she doesn't want you to feel that this is a command performance. Dinitz immediately called Golda. "I want you back not because you're so good, but because I'm too old to change," she quipped, which he understood as a backhanded compliment. He returned to Israel to be her political secretary and then director general of the prime minister's office. (Years later, after working for Menachem Begin, Dinitz was to say that he received more compliments from Begin in four days than from Golda in four years.)

During her first few months in office, Golda lived in Jerusalem with her friends Zeev and Henya Sharef while Miriam Eshkol cleared out the late prime minister's belongings from the official residence at 46 Ben Maimon Street. On the job, the new prime minister quickly reverted to old habits, working on stacks of papers until two or three in the morning, puffing on her ever-present cigarettes, and consuming one cup of coffee after another. More often than not, one or more of the ministers she felt closest to—Israel Galili, Pinhas Sapir, Zeev Sharef—dropped in to talk and gossip with her well into the night. In the morning, Lou Kadar woke her around 7:00 or 7:30, late by Israeli standards, and the two shared a breakfast of toast with margarine or jam while Golda read the morning newspapers, her eyes flitting quickly to what was written about her. Sometimes Kadar had to stop her from phoning an editor or reporter early in the morning to chew the person out about a story she didn't like or considered unfair. After spending most of the week in Jerusalem, her days filled with meetings, she traveled to Tel Aviv on Thursday for conferences there. Friday night Shabbat dinners in her home at Ramat Aviv were for family and friends, and Saturday mornings she prepared brunch there for her grandchildren before returning in the afternoon to Jerusalem to get ready for Sunday morning's cabinet meeting.

She presided over those cabinet meetings with the same iron fist she had used as party secretary. In Eshkol's footsteps, she felt compelled to assemble a national unity government as he had, with ministers ranging from the right-wing Gahal to the left Mapam Party, all with vociferous opinions, many with fierce personal rivalries. But if Eshkol had the face of hesitation and easy compromise, Golda's demeanor was one of conviction and decisiveness. When she wanted order, she thumped on the table. When someone spoke out of turn or went on too long, she looked up and scowled, enough to cut him short. Nor did she hesitate to enforce her opinions. In her characteristic way, she patiently listened to all sides of a dispute, arrived at a decision, and stuck to it with "bulldog tenacity." She'd had a strained relationship with Moshe Dayan ever since she tried to stop him from taking over the Defense Ministry before the war. At a Labor Party meeting in her earliest days as prime minister, he threatened to bolt the party if he weren't more fully included in its decision making, and she warned him sternly that "conditional party membership is unacceptable." As a cabinet member, however, he became so aware of her strength that after one intensive policy dispute he sidled up to her and asked, "Do you still love me, Golda?" And at a Tel Aviv theater one evening, he conspicuously changed his seat for one next to hers, publicly signaling his acceptance of her leadership. The audience roared approval.

Although many differences between them remained, Golda accepted Dayan into her inner circle of advisers, her "kitchen cabinet." The term "kitchen cabinet" goes back much earlier than Golda; it was first used in the nineteenth century for the American president Andrew Jackson and his most intimate advisers. But it became widely associated with her, even before she was prime minister. When Golda resigned as secretary-general of Labor, Shulamit Aloni, not unhappy to see her go, remarked to a reporter that she was glad problems of the country and the Jewish people would no longer be decided in Golda's kitchen. The term caught on and became the source of dozens of cartoons and just as many angry attacks. "All government decisions are cooked in Golda's kitchen," the saying went. On Saturday evenings, Yigal Allon, Pinhas Sapir, Israel Galili, Dayan, and a select few others would meet in Golda's Jerusalem home to thrash out ideas and policies. They usually sat in the living room, drinking tea or strong coffee that Golda prepared herself in the kitchen, nibbling on cookies or cake she had baked or bought, and freely speaking their minds, without stenographers present to record their words or the press eavesdropping. Many of the issues discussed would then be presented at the larger and more formal cabinet meeting the next morning. Critics complained that the process was undemocratic, concentrating too much influence in the hands of a small, unrepresentative group. For Golda, it was a useful way to get advice and arrive at decisions with people whose ideas she trusted or needed. It was also, as the historian Anita Shapira noted, a process that transformed "the traditional term that indicated women's banishment to housekeeping jobs ('a woman's place is in the kitchen') into a center of 'political cooking,' a symbol of power."

THE MOST INTENSE DISCUSSION in the kitchen cabinet and in the full cabinet, in the Knesset and at corner cafés, centered on what to do with the territories captured during the Six-Day War. The discussion had begun as soon as the war ended, when Israel found itself in control of more than a million Arabs and an area more than three times its original size. From the perspective of later decades, when every debate about peace between Israel and its Arab neighbors seems to hinge on the status of the occupied territories and Israeli settlements in them, it is hard to grasp the degree of uncertainty that existed about them after the war. Overwhelmed by the army's staggering victory, Israeli leaders simply had no plan for how to handle its conquests. The government's first impulse had been to pull back to prewar lines from most of the conquered areas in exchange for peace treaties with the Arab states. After fierce debates, the cabinet voted on June 19, 1967, to return the Sinai Peninsula to Egypt and the Golan Heights to Syria if those countries agreed to full peace and security arrangements. It made no commitment about the Gaza Strip, which Egypt had administered but never annexed, or the West Bank of the Jordan River—the heart of ancient Judaism—which Israeli forces took from Jordan. Jerusalem, most Israelis agreed, should be reunited as one city and their capital. Even so, as Golda had observed when Levi Eshkol and Israel Galili spoke of settlements in the Old City, doubt existed about whether, with international pressure, Israel would be able to keep control of the city's contested areas.

Israel's willingness to withdraw to the prewar borders with Egypt and Syria dissolved during the next few months. "We're waiting for a phone call from King Hussein," Dayan said, triumphantly expecting concessions from the defeated Arab leaders. The call didn't come. Instead, Israel received three angry "noes" from eight Arab states attending a conference in Khartoum in September: no recognition, no negotiations, and no peace. There were small hints in the conference documents of possible interest in using diplomacy to regain Arab territory, but from what the Israelis could tell, the "noes" overshadowed them. Voices in Israel rose louder than ever, and ideas about what to do, especially concerning the West Bank and Gaza, competed with each other. "I am not shocked that we haven't set a date for making a final decision," Golda said, while still party secretary. "I'm shocked by all the talk in the country up until now . . . Everyone's got a magic formula."

The most prominent of those formulas, and diametrically opposed to each other, came from Yigal Allon and Moshe Dayan, the perpetual rivals. Allon proposed creating a Palestinian Arab enclave along the densely populated mountain ridge of the West Bank and annexing only the sparsely populated region along the Jordan valley and in the lowlands next to the Dead Sea. Israelis would then build settlements in these annexed lands for security purposes, which he named "defensible borders." Later his proposal, known as the Allon Plan, included annexing some parts of Sinai and the Golan Heights and small areas very close to the Green Line (the cease-fire border of 1949, which existed until the 1967 war), also to maintain secure boundaries. Dayan, on the other hand, called for building military bases and eventually a string of civilian settlements precisely in the Arab-populated mountain ridge of the West Bank, near major Arab cities such as Ramallah, Nablus, and Jenin. It was important to create "facts," he said, to establish Israel's permanent presence by planting roots in those areas. In his plan, Israel would rule—but not annex—the entire West Bank, integrating its economy with the Israeli one. It would be an "enlightened" rule, however, in which the Palestinians would retain their Jordanian citizenship, be free to travel across bridges throughout Israel and Jordan, and manage their own affairs.

Both plans had other vagaries and flaws, but most people viewed Dayan's, with its emphasis on Israeli centers in the heart of Palestinian regions, as more hawkish than Allon's. At one point, in November 1968, Pinhas Sapir, considered a dove in the Labor Party, vehemently criticized Dayan in the press. Sapir objected to Dayan's idea of expanding Israel's borders to integrate hundreds of thousands of Palestinians, which would change the state's demographic makeup and also flood it with Arab workers. In response to Dayan's insistence that he aimed only for economic and not political integration, Sapir argued that the first would inevitably lead to the second and eventually to the annexation of the entire West Bank, leaving nothing to negotiate with Arab leaders. As their war of words escalated, Golda stepped in to try to end the fighting. "This public debate between Dayan and Sapir is destructive," she stated. "It's bound to give ammunition to our enemies and raise questions and speculation among friends." As far as she was concerned, such outright conflict should be kept under wraps. It could only fracture the party, so recently unified, and dangerously clue the outside world to Israel's internal divisions. She sincerely hoped that "both sides in this dispute come to the conclusion that they *have* to stop it." They didn't. In one of the few times Sapir publicly disagreed with her, he argued that these fundamental differences in approach needed to be aired and not buried from view. The dispute continued for some weeks and was picked up again in 1972.

Golda is "a great believer in secret diplomacy," the *Time* correspondent Marlin Levin wrote to his New York bureau chief. She had told him that Israel needed strength not only to stand fast along its borders but also "to keep quiet" and develop the power of silence. "We have too many people who talk too much," she said. For her, part of keeping silent was deciding *not* to decide at this time what Israel should do with the captured lands. When Levi Eshkol was interviewed by *Newsweek* magazine a few weeks before he died and implied that he was prepared to relinquish Judaea and Samaria (the ancient Hebrew names for the West Bank) in exchange for peace, Menachem Begin and his nationalistic Gahal Party threatened to break away from the unity government. They would not yield one inch of that territory. Nor would the religious parties, advocates of the Greater Israel of biblical promise. Golda knew that, and although publicly she gave "unqualified" support to Eshkol, she would not make the same mistake. Why exacerbate internal party strife when negotiations with Arab leaders had yet to materialize? "We don't draw maps," she said. "Why should I create a Jewish war before there is any hope whatsoever of peace with the Arabs?"

She did have some basic principles she repeated at every opportunity. At their core lay her determination that Israel would not return to the 1967 borders as they existed until June 5, when the Six-Day War broke out. They had not provided security then, so why would they in the future? Israel would not replay what happened in 1957, after the Sinai campaign, she emphasized to the Press Club about a month after she took office. It would not pull back from the lands it had conquered as it had then with only UN promises for peace and no concrete agreements with the Arab states. The shame and resentment of that pullout never left her. "I have reason to envy Mr. Eban as Foreign Minister for many things," she recalled once. "But I envy him more for one thing, namely, he will never have to do what I had to do in 1957: to stand before the United Nations and say, we will withdraw." Israel was stronger now than it had been a decade earlier, and strong enough this time to stand up to the "Big Four"—the United States, Britain, France, and Russia—who were trying to work out a peace settlement for the region among themselves. "I do not . . . accept the right of any powers large or small to decide the fate of others," she would say. And it wouldn't matter whether "four or forty nations meet"; Israel's position would not change.

She insisted on direct negotiations with Arab leaders, which would imply their recognition of Israel, a plan they steadfastly refused. "Suppose we want to return territory we have taken," she said more than once. "To whom? We can't send it to Nasser by parcel post."

When asked what exactly Israel hoped to achieve from direct negotiations, Golda would say no more than an equivocal "agreed, secure borders," matching the equally equivocal UN Resolution 242, from which the phrase stemmed. The resolution, passed on November 22, 1967, after months of negotiations, called on the Arab states to acknowledge the right of countries in the region "to live in peace within secure and recognized boundaries," without naming Israel per se. It called on Israel to withdraw from "territories occupied in the recent conflict," without specifying "the" territories or "all the" territories, leaving Israel room to negotiate on its withdrawal. Given those ambiguities and the Arab opposition to direct meetings, Golda had no desire to spell out beforehand what she expected from negotiations. With no interest at all in a Greater Israel, or simply acquiring more land, she viewed the territories as bargaining chips she could use to arrive at stronger, more secure borders. The details of those borders would have to wait for the bargaining.

In the privacy of government and party meetings, she inclined more toward Allon's plan than Dayan's. The sheer numbers of Palestinian Arabs who would become Israel's responsibility if it were to integrate the West Bank and Gaza into it reinforced her aversion to that idea. "I want a Jewish state without any doubt," she said on various occasions, "a Jewish state without having to count the population, the Jews and the non-Jews, every morning for fear the figures had changed." For her, a Jewish state meant also maintaining the socialist ideal of "Hebrew labor" that had motivated Israel's founders. They had insisted on working the land and building the country with their own hands, not those of others. Now, with Dayan's "open bridges" policy between Israel and Jordan and Arab laborers pouring into the country to seek work, Israelis found it easy to ignore that ideal. "They will not be the professors or heads of hospitals," she warned of these Arabs. Unskilled as many of them were, they would do the "black labor," the lowest menial jobs. "To me this is the complete antithesis of Zionist thinking. Shall we remain the intelligentsia with clean hands while they dirty their hands?" To many Israelis, the argument, so burning in the country's pioneer days, now sounded outdated. Unemployed in their own lands, Arab laborers welcomed the work, and Israelis welcomed their labor in the expanding economy. But for Golda, the principle of Hebrew labor was still more honest and equitable.

Settling into her role as head of the nation, she preferred to say little else about the captured lands than to reiterate these principles. Her focus—and anxieties—remained fixed on the state's survival. Conditioned by the pogrom fears of her childhood and the Holocaust nightmare of adult life, she still viewed Israel's existence as precarious, in spite of its brilliant victory and powerful military. When Amos Oz and other young writers and intellectuals raised questions about the morality of occupying the conquered territories, she blasted them. "For me, the greatest morality consists of the Jewish people's right to exist," she retorted. "Without that, there is no morality in the world." While such certitude did not win her many friends among intellectuals, it reassured much of the public. The tough old bird was in charge, and she would be a bulwark against whatever the Arabs or anyone else threw at Israel.

24

A Different Kind of War

The new prime minister had hardly settled in to her official residence in the spring of 1969 when Gamal Abdel Nasser launched a brutal war against Israel. This was not a conventional war. It did not involve the massing of troops or deployment of the entire Egyptian air force. It was not heralded by marching bands blaring martial music. Yet it was cruel and bloody and lasted longer than any of Israel's previous wars. Nasser called it a "war of attrition," and its aim was to wear down the Jewish state's strength and morale until it withdrew from all the territories it had captured in 1967. Six months earlier, in September 1968, Egyptian soldiers stationed along the west side of the Suez Canal had shelled Israeli troops stationed on the other side, killing ten and injuring eighteen others. Taken by surprise, Israeli forces built fortifications all along the canal and returned Egyptian artillery fire whenever it erupted. In March, Nasser made the war official by announcing that he no longer recognized the cease-fire established after the Six-Day War. "What was taken by force will be returned by force," he vowed. Shootings and harassment of Israeli soldiers along the canal became incessant, one operation following another, like water steadily dripping on a rock, eating away at its surface.

In response to the intense Egyptian bombardments, Israel stepped up its military activities, initiating raids of its own, shooting at radar stations, blowing up fuel storage tanks, and bombing strategic areas. If Egypt and the neighboring Arab countries abide by the 1967 cease-fire arrangements, "they will find full reciprocity on our part," Golda asserted. If not, Israel would continue to reciprocate in kind.

Against the backdrop of the new war, she found herself and her country squeezed by superpower manipulations that often had less to do with Israel and more with their own jockeying for dominance in the Middle East. President Richard Nixon of the United States and his national security adviser, Henry Kissinger, viewed the Middle East as part of their "linkages" principle, in which they placed regional problems into the context of their broader relationship with the Soviet Union. From their perspective, Soviet involvement in Arab-Israeli issues was simply a way for that country to furrow deeper into the region, or as Nixon put it, "We want peace. *They* want the Middle East." Nevertheless, while still belligerent toward each other, the two nations had embarked on a path of détente. Through it they opened a back channel of discussion designed to relax tensions and prevent conflicts between their client states from exploding into full-fledged wars.

The superpower machinations placed Israel in a strange position. While Russian representatives met in New York with the French, British, and Americans for Big Four deliberations on solving the Arab-Israeli conflict, or held sessions with the United States alone in Washington, the Soviet Union armed Egypt with tanks, guns, mines, and missiles. How, Golda wanted to know, could her country possibly accept a solution arrived at under these circumstances? "I am especially impressed when we are told that a partner to this search for peace . . . is the Soviet Union," she said sarcastically at a press conference, "since its contribution to peace in the area has been so outstanding."

Against the backdrop of the war of attrition, Golda sought to tighten her grip on politics at home. Elections would be held in October 1969, and she was intent on keeping the Labor Party strengthened and unified, no easy task. It pleased her that after much give-and-take, the leftist Mapam Party had allied itself with Labor. That party, composed of the former Mapai, Ahdut Ha'avoda, and Rafi Parties, now had a partner. Together they formed the enlarged Maarach, the new Alignment. Such a broad-based alliance consolidated Golda's power and secured Labor's position as the premier force in Israeli politics. Yet constant grumblings within the partnership put the Alignment on shaky ground. Differences about security and the territories between the dovish Mapam and the hawkish former Rafi Party members had the two groups tearing at each other. Even more divisive, the Rafi faction, with Moshe Dayan at its head, again threatened to split from the united Labor Party if its members did not receive a greater role in decision making. Dayan griped that he felt like a "subtenant" in his own house, with the old guard totally in charge. He himself vacillated regularly between remaining in the government as defense minister and heeding the thousands of voices in Rafi clamoring for him to quit the Labor Party and run for prime minister.

At Dayan's invitation, Golda attended a large Rafi faction rally at the Cinerama hall in Tel Aviv. "We were born to live together," she told the audience, in an appeal for unity. "We are bound in a common fate—a great, tragic wonderful fate." While others spoke, she listened quietly, even when they attacked the former Mapai Party leadership. But when the Knesset member Mordechai Ben-Porat accusingly dredged up her past opposition to Dayan's appointment as defense minister, she stalked out of the meeting indignantly, Israel Galili trailing behind her. Dayan apologetically escorted her to the door. Returning to the podium, he told the crowd that he did not want Rafi to leave the Labor tent. He couldn't help feeling, however, that there had never been a real merger in the party, because Rafi leaders had always been treated as outsiders.

In that atmosphere of rancor, Golda prepared for the party's convention on August 3, 1969, the kickoff for the election campaign. Consciously putting insults behind her, she hammered home her message of unity. "Let us eliminate the very word 'split' from our vocabularies," she pleaded. "We are willing to accept discussions and arguments without limit . . . But 'split'? Never." At the convention, doves and hawks haggled over every word of the party's platform while she tried to appear above the fray, singing her song of togetherness. The main thing, she said several times, "was to seek that which unites, rather than points of division."

In the name of party unity, she made a great political concession in the weeks after the convention. To accommodate Dayan and the Rafi contingent, she agreed to install Shimon Peres as a minister in the next cabinet. "I accept this with love," she told doubtful former Mapai colleagues some months later. "It is much better than splitting the party." Then she added what they all knew: "It is not exactly to my taste, but even so I went along with it." Golda, who by all accounts held grudges indefinitely and saw the world only in black and white, adjusted her vision to include a man who had been a political foe for decades. In a choice between personal feelings and party unity, she went for the pragmatic.

She achieved what she wanted. The Rafi people finally dropped their threats and voted to remain in the Labor-Alignment group. Dayan assured them that a government with Golda as prime minister and him as defense minister would carry out its programs well. With the party united behind her, Golda could turn her attention to a forthcoming trip to the United States. She was eager to take the measure of Richard Nixon, who assumed office a short time before she did and to whom she planned to deliver a list of arms her country needed. Six months after she took office, the idea of Golda Meir as a stopgap premier seemed almost ludicrous. There is "nothing interim, nothing temporary, nothing equivocal" about her, wrote the journalist Erwin Frenkel. Like Ben-Gurion, she had become a fixture on the scene.

THE VISIT TO AMERICA WAS a fantasy come true. Wherever Golda set foot, she was received with a bursting exuberance no Israeli premier before her had experienced. In Philadelphia, where she arrived on September 24, 1969, a crowd of five thousand met her at the airport, many of them schoolchildren carrying posters that read, GOLDA A GO GO or WE DIG YOU, GOLDA. Afterward, more than twenty thousand people packed Independence Hall and applauded wildly at the end of her brief speech about Israel's desire for peace. "I am wise enough to understand that the applause was not directed to me . . . It was rather an ovation for the State of Israel," she said, with required modesty. She knew as well as anyone that the men, women, and children who swarmed to see her in Philadelphia and every other city she visited were as intrigued by the "71-year-old grandmother" (as the press frequently referred to her) who headed the State of Israel as they were loyal to that state. Her simple bearing—she appeared time and again in the same black-and-white herringbone tweed suit—and midwestern twang with its faint echo of Eastern Europe made her seem the American dream come true, the local girl made good. The "former Milwaukee schoolteacher" (another favorite press nomenclature) from an impoverished family had risen against all odds—including the odds of being a woman—to the highest office in her land. Americans, and especially American Jews, who had admired her earlier as Israel's foreign minister, were swept away by her presence as prime minister. No one doubted that she would hold her own with the president of the most powerful nation on earth. "What can you do? She's irresistible," one observer commented. Most people who saw and heard her agreed.

Menahem, who was studying in America, came to Philadelphia with his family to meet his mother, as did her sister Clara, who still lived in Connecticut. They had all been invited to the state dinner President Richard Nixon was giving for Mrs. Meir in Washington the next night. On Thursday morning, September 25, a marine helicopter carried her and her party to the South Lawn of the White House, where the president greeted her before three hundred guests and the first lady handed her a bouquet of roses. She had been apprehensive about this meeting with a new president, Lou Kadar recalled. "That changed the minute they met. She looked relieved and so did he." Often withdrawn and suspicious, Nixon was all smiles as the two leaders mounted a red-carpeted platform for a brief exchange of greetings. Later he wrote that she "conveyed simultaneously the qualities of extreme toughness and extreme warmth." He responded to both, treating her with dignity but also with friendly ease.

Her welcome had all the trappings of a grand occasion: a nineteen-gun salute on the White House lawn; the marine band playing "Hatikvah" and "The Star-Spangled Banner" (in that order); and a ceremonial review of the troops, with Golda in her thick orthopedic shoes and carrying her ever-present black handbag as she hurried to keep pace with the president and a bemedaled adjutant army general. At the gala dinner in her honor that evening, she wore a long coffee-colored lace and velvet gown and a strand of pearls, not nearly as chic as Mrs. Nixon in her pink velvet-trimmed dress designed by Geoffrey Beene, but more elegantly turned out than she had ever been. In his toast, the president spoke of the honor of receiving for the first time "the head of government of another state who also is a woman" and pulled out an "old Jewish proverb" that "man was made out of the soft earth and woman was made out of a hard rib," a corny nod to her proverbial strength. He went on to compare her to the biblical Deborah, under whose leadership peace graced the land for forty years. At the much-coveted dinner, 129 guests dined on sole Véronique and Chateaubriand, with a dessert of "Charlotte Revivim," named for Sarah's kibbutz. Afterward, everyone attended a concert by Isaac Stern and Leonard Bernstein in the East Room, Golda hugging both of them when it ended.

The real work of her American visit came in two meetings she had with the president. The Phantom jet fighters President Johnson had consented to sell Levi Eshkol had begun to arrive, but Israel needed more to counter the surface-to-air missiles and other arms the Soviets were sending Egypt. She asked Nixon for an additional twenty-five Phantoms, eighty Skyhawk attack bombers, and low-interest loans of $200 million a year for periods of up to five years. She received "no concrete, direct promise" about those requests, she told a news conference, but she found that President Nixon had "sensitivity" toward Israel's problems and the balance of power in the Middle East, and she was satisfied with his assurances.

She and Nixon discussed Israel's arms and economic needs in the Oval Office on September 25 and 26. Nixon would later recall his impressions of her at those talks. Indira Gandhi of India, he said, "acted like a man, with the ruthlessness of a man, but wanted always to be treated like a woman." In contrast, Golda Meir "acted like a man and wanted to be treated like a man," with no special concessions to her womanhood, and he appreciated that. When their meeting began, she smiled for the photographers and made the proper conversation, but as soon as the press left the room, she "crossed her leg, lit a cigarette, and said, 'Now, Mr. President, what are you going to do about those planes that we want and we need very much?'" From then on, they "had a very good relationship."

Indicative of that relationship, they arranged a more direct way of staying in touch. Yitzhak Rabin, who had become Israel's ambassador to Washington a short time earlier, would communicate with Henry Kissinger, Nixon's national security adviser, and vice versa, bypassing both countries' foreign policy departments. Minister of Foreign Affairs Abba Eban fumed at this arrangement, as had Golda when Ben-Gurion bypassed her to work with Shimon Peres. Happy with the president's wish for directness, however, she brushed aside Eban's unhappiness.

Nobody but Golda and Nixon knew what transpired at their most private meeting, when they spent part of their time conversing on the White House lawn, where they could not be heard or recorded. "As to the more substantive matters that I discussed with Mr. Nixon," she was to write in her memoir, "I can only say that I would not quote him at the time, and I will not quote him now." They each claimed to have kept notes on their conversation; the president told Undersecretary Elliot Richardson that he had dictated a memorandum about the meeting. Apparently, neither that memorandum nor any other notes were sent to a state archive. They remain hidden or deeply classified. Yet based on memos from Kissinger and others speculating about the meeting, historians have concluded that the top secret subject the two discussed that fall day was Israel's nuclear capability. And through that discussion, they arrived at a historic turning point in America's attitude toward Israel and the bomb.

In the early 1960s, after Israel had built its nuclear reactor in Dimona with the help of the French, Golda had pleaded with Ben-Gurion to "tell the Americans the truth and explain why" in regard to their nuclear program. Ben-Gurion dismissed such truth telling as naive and dangerous and then found himself hounded by President John F. Kennedy to allow American experts to inspect Dimona regularly. The pressure shifted to Levi Eshkol after Ben-Gurion resigned, and even though Lyndon Johnson had less interest in the matter when he took office, the American visits continued, with Israel doing its best to hide every trace of its nuclear capacity. Eshkol was also pressed to join the nuclear Non-proliferation Treaty. All that changed after Golda's meeting with Nixon. In February 1970, Rabin informed Kissinger that Israel would not sign the Non-proliferation Treaty, and not long after that talk of American visits to Dimona ceased. Exactly what the two leaders said to each other at that mysterious meeting stayed secret, but Golda presumably acknowledged that Israel had the capability to produce nuclear weapons. Nixon seems to have accepted this fact on condition that Israel keep the program under wraps, carrying out no public tests and making no public statements about it.

Whatever the precise terms of the Meir-Nixon agreement, from then on Israel maintained a policy of vagueness, *amimut*, or "nuclear opacity," in the words of Avner Cohen, a leading expert on the subject, neither admitting to having the capability nor denying it. That policy has continued to govern Israel's handling of the bomb and to shape America's acceptance of it as a reality in that country. Ironically, at a National Press Club appearance in Washington, a journalist asked Golda whether Israel would ever employ nuclear weapons if its survival were in jeopardy, to which she quipped, "We haven't done so badly with conventional weapons."

Their two days of meetings ended, Golda Meir and Richard Nixon spoke to the Washington press corps. They had no new decisions to announce, Nixon said, but they had made progress toward a better understanding of each other. Golda said she was going home with a lighter heart than she had coming. She had "found in the President of the United States a friend of Israel" with full understanding of the country's "problems and difficulties."

She did not go directly home. After two more days of meetings with various government officials, appearing on the prestigious television show *Meet the Press*, and visiting with Jewish community leaders, she headed to New York City and a whirlwind lovefest. A crowd of fifteen thousand turned out at City Hall Park, many arriving in chartered buses from New Jersey and Connecticut, to catch a glimpse of her. On Tuesday evening, September 30, Mayor John Lindsay hosted a black-tie dinner for her at the Brooklyn Museum (she wore the same gown as she had in Washington). With twelve hundred guests, several hundred more than had been invited for the shah of Iran, it was the largest and most expensive dinner the city had ever given. "Sure, it's very high," the commissioner of public events replied to criticism of its cost. "But you had the head of Israel here and the expense of kosher cooking." (In contrast to the nonkosher presidential dinner at the White House.)

During her three jam-packed days in New York, Golda attended a luncheon in her honor given by the UN's secretary-general, U Thant, hosted Governor Nelson Rockefeller at her Waldorf Astoria suite, conferred with Secretary of State William Rogers, appeared on the *Today* show, held private sessions with the editors of *Time* and *Life* and executives of *The New York Times*, had breakfast with *Newsweek* editors, and lunched with broadcasting executives. When she appeared at a rally of almost four thousand Jewish high school and college students at Madison Square Garden, she received a ten-minute standing ovation. An overflow audience of two thousand massed outside to cheer her as she came and left. "It's overwhelming," she said, beaming, of her New York reception. "It's beyond anything I ever dreamed of."

And off she flew, in an El Al airplane, to a star-studded dinner in Los Angeles, where Governor Ronald Reagan shared the dais with her and the actor Gregory Peck asked her to dance. (She declined, regretfully.) Addressing the glittering audience, she told of how she had been kept so busy in New York that she did not have time to go to Macy's basement to buy pots and pans, the way she used to. They loved it. When she turned serious, she spoke of her willingness to travel anywhere to make peace with Arab leaders. The problem was that what the Arabs wanted "could not be settled by compromise—they want us dead. We have decided to stay alive." It was a line she repeated often, with variations, especially to the press.

She made Milwaukee, her next stop, a sentimental journey to her roots. As its highlight, she visited the Fourth Street School she had attended as a child. The building looked much the same, but the students, in Golda's youth largely white and Jewish, were now all African American. Her eyes glistened when she pinned a paper carnation the children had made to her lapel, and when they assembled in the auditorium and sang "Hatikvah" and "Heveinu Shalom Aleichem" in Hebrew, she ignored her security guards and dove in to hug them and shake their hands. She left the school on a wave of nostalgia, which continued at the

City Center for the Performing Arts, where she addressed an audience of more than four thousand. "Here I found freedom, kindness, and cleanliness," she said of the town where she had grown up. "And later I learned from Zionist friends here that . . . we could build for the Jewish people a home of our own." From a place of honor on the stage, the old-time Labor Zionist Isadore Tuchman listened attentively. Over half a century earlier, he had inspired young Goldie Meyerson to join Poalei Zion and begin her Zionist odyssey. Now the circle was completed.

Outside the center, noisy demonstrators shouted anti-Israel slogans, but Golda looked past them as she entered her limousine and was whisked to the airport for her flight to New York.

She had been scheduled to leave the States on October 5 but stayed an extra day to address the AFL-CIO convention in Atlantic City, New Jersey. For the first time since she left Israel, she felt "on home territory." Trade unionism was in her blood, the Histadrut a part of her DNA from her earliest days in Israel. After invoking her father's union and receiving a tumultuous standing ovation, she conveyed the same message she had throughout her trip. Israel needed arms to combat the weapons Egypt received from the Soviets, although Israel's greatest ambition was to have peace in the area. By dint of his position, George Meany, president of the labor federation, had direct access to Richard Nixon. It didn't hurt that over the years Meany had become a close and "dear old friend" to Golda.

She returned to Israel on October 7, her American tour a triumph. Her views about Russia and Egypt, Israel and the United States, had made headlines from one end of the land to the next. Hordes of people had come out to see her wherever she appeared, and thousands more had seen or heard her on television or radio. For American Jews, long-standing delight in this down-to-earth woman had taken on a new dimension: awe. They were awed by her popularity in the non-Jewish world and awed by her fearlessness in speaking her mind, even to the president of the United States. More than Ben-Gurion or Levi Eshkol, Golda Meir had begun to establish herself as the leader of all the Jewish people, not only of Israel. "They saw her as one of them, but not really one of them," said the former Mossad chief Efraim Halevy. "She was the boss, and they learned to tiptoe in her presence. The equation had changed."

Her loving reception in the United States spilled over into Israel. In public opinion polls, her approval rating soared to more than 75 percent and would jump another ten points in the next few months. Ephraim

Kishon, the country's best-known humorist, later described the change of heart that gripped young people like him. When she became prime minister, he published a sarcastic letter to her in the newspaper written in mock-biblical style, describing the public's request for "an old and exceedingly weary woman to reign over us now." After half a year, he said, "we really felt pretty stupid: Golda at 71 displayed a tireless energy, a wholly new style, and oodles of charisma." In about a year, he found "Golda's simplicity magnificent, endearing," and within two years "I found her beautiful, too."

Her first order of business was the national election, coming up on Tuesday, October 28. Having put the party in order before leaving for America, she hoped that with its Mapam alignment it would win a clear majority of votes, eliminating the need to form a coalition government. As Election Day approached, she campaigned around the clock, drawing the biggest crowds and longest ovations of any Labor Party leader. "Even when there is peace," she told admiring audiences, "I will always hold one thing against Nasser. He made killers out of our boys." The party plastered thousands of billboards across the nation with colored posters of the prime minister. She looked matriarchal, a kindly but commanding presence urging voters to cast their ballots for the Alignment.

Tuesday evening, she rode from Jerusalem to Tel Aviv to await the results at Labor Party headquarters with Pinhas Sapir, Abba Eban, and other party members. Four hours after the polls closed, they raised glasses of Israeli champagne and munched on corned beef sandwiches to celebrate victory. It was not quite the victory she had hoped for. Labor won fifty-six seats, five fewer than it had before, and Gahal increased its seats, from twenty-two to twenty-six. Labor still dominated by a large margin, but Golda had to face hard bargaining sessions to form a national unity government that once again would include both the right-wing Gahal and the left-wing Mapam.

BACK IN WASHINGTON, Ambassador Yitzhak Rabin received a troubling top secret document from one of his key aides, Amos Eiran. Secretary of State Rogers, looking for Senate endorsement of a new Middle East policy he planned to introduce, gave a copy of his speech to Hugh Scott, Republican senator from Pennsylvania. The plan called for Israel's withdrawal from Egyptian lands to the pre-1967 boundaries between the two countries in return for an Egyptian agreement to a peace settlement. It also spoke of a unified Jerusalem, with roles for both Israel and Jordan, and of Israel solving the Arab refugee problem. Too busy to read the speech, Scott asked Eiran—a good friend—for his reaction. Eiran was stunned. Nobody had conferred with Rabin or Golda about going ahead with this plan or indicated that it would soon be made public. He sent it on to Rabin, who considered it unacceptable: it ignored Israel's demands for face-to-face negotiations with Arab leaders and undermined its negotiating position by making its withdrawal a precondition for peace with Egypt. Even so, in cabling the plan to Golda, Rabin suggested that they not reject it outright but insert revisions in it before responding to the Americans. Golda phoned him immediately on receiving the cable.

"Have you gone out of your mind?" she shouted. "Do you represent Israel or America?"

Furious that this proposal had been sprung on her, she felt betrayed by Nixon and Kissinger. There had been talk when she was in Washington of Israel delivering "software" in exchange for the "hardware" it wanted from the United States—concessions on the occupied lands as a trade-off for the planes and munitions she had requested—but Kissinger had downplayed that equation. Now, after she had argued for months against an imposed settlement by the four powers or two powers, Rogers was planning exactly that. How much of this plan, she wondered, had been brewed as a concession to the Soviet Union in America's quest for détente?

Despite Golda's strong objections, Rogers publicly unveiled his proposal on December 9 at the Galaxy Conference on Adult Education in Washington. The next day Israel's cabinet denounced the plan. Soon afterward, it authorized Rabin and Israeli consuls throughout the United States to organize Jewish community demonstrations against it. A few weeks later, Rabin brought Kissinger a message for President Nixon from Golda Meir. It didn't mince words. She had returned from her visit with the president three months earlier feeling that "indeed Israel has a friend in the White House." Although she continued to believe that, "recent developments had caused her grave concern," particularly her perception of a "serious deterioration" in America's policy toward Israel. The president responded with reassurances about America's "unmistakable moral commitment to Israel's survival" and a vague defense of the Rogers plan, which, in fact, he didn't have much faith in himself.

The only good to come for Israel from the Rogers brouhaha was the national unity government Golda managed to put together. The warring parties pushed aside their differences long enough to form a "wall to wall" coalition representing nearly 90 percent of the electorate. On December 15, the prime minister officially presented her unity government to the Knesset. One by one, the ministers shook her hand as she sat at the cabinet table dressed in her white blouse and dark suit, smoking nonstop. With twenty-four ministers, she had the largest cabinet in Israeli history, and also the largest number of ministers without portfolio. The latter included Israel Galili, among her closest advisers; Shimon Peres, among her least favorite officials; and Menachem Begin, Labor's strongest rival. Yigal Allon remained deputy prime minister but also assumed the education portfolio, Pinhas Sapir became finance minister again, and Moshe Dayan remained defense minister and Abba Eban foreign minister. The two men, worlds apart in outlook—Dayan a hawk and Eban a dove—barely spoke to each other. Her hardest problem in assembling the cabinet, Golda is reported to have said with a smile, was how to get Dayan to desist from picking up a newspaper and reading it every time Eban began to speak to the cabinet.

Happy smiles were rare for her these days. The Arabs and the Soviets had also rejected the Rogers plan, and the war of attrition continued without letup. Soon after she took office, Golda left orders for her military secretary, Yisrael Lior, to inform her about every action Israel took and every "boy" killed or wounded no matter the time of day or night. Sometimes she'd be awakened in the early morning hours with phone calls bringing the latest casualty figures. Unable to fall asleep again, she'd prepare tea for the bodyguards who stood watch outside her house, sipping from her cup with a sugar cube in her mouth as she always did, and chatting with the men until she felt calm enough to go back to bed. She had a recurring nightmare, she told the Mapam leader, Yaakov Hazan, a close friend, also rumored to have been among her lovers. "Suddenly all the telephones in my home start to ring. There are a lot of phones, located in every corner of the house, and they don't stop ringing. I know what that ringing means, and I'm afraid to pick up all the receivers. I wake up covered in a cold sweat." Fearfully, she stays awake.

As often as she could, she attended the funerals of fallen soldiers and visited their bereaved families, the hardest thing to do, she told Lou Kadar. When unable to visit, she wrote to parents and spouses, expressing her anguish, feeling as though she were personally responsible.

Early in January 1970, at the urging of Yitzhak Rabin and in the hope of ending the war, Golda ordered bombing raids deep inside Egypt, with Israeli planes destroying military installations and crushing cities along the Suez Canal. Now, she said, Nasser could no longer lie to his people about Egypt's victories and Israel's weakness. The war had come home to them. As Israeli bombs neared Cairo, Nasser made a secret trip to Moscow to ask for help. The Russians obliged by providing him with highly sophisticated fighter planes and up-to-the-minute SAM-3 surface-to-air missiles. They also sent thousands of advisers to Egypt to train its military in operating the new weapons. But in the United States, Richard Nixon still did not approve the sale of the planes and arms Mrs. Meir had asked for when they met. Convinced that Israel was strong enough to fend off its enemies, he did not want to further escalate the Middle East arms race, he said. He also hoped that by denying Israel additional weapons, he might improve America's diplomatic relationship with Egypt and Syria and thus its influence in the region.

By March, Golda felt desperate. "I know you have been advised about my new anxieties," she wrote to the evangelist Billy Graham, who had close ties to the president. "Israel must be assured and our adversaries convinced that the United States will continue to stand by us." With Nixon, she was more graphic: "It is true that our pilots are very good, but they can be good only when they have planes." If the president decided not to fill her requests, Israel "would feel really forsaken." Israel called off its deep penetration raids in early April; the Soviet missiles proved too effective to continue. Nixon promised Rabin that as president he would always maintain the balance of power between Israel and its neighbors by replacing Israeli equipment lost through attrition or fighting. As for selling it the additional planes and weapons the prime minister so persistently solicited—well, that would still have to wait.

Into the mix of tensions and worries with which Golda had to cope in the spring of 1970, a new element suddenly appeared. Nahum Goldmann, president of the World Jewish Congress, wanted to meet with Egypt's president, Nasser, to talk peace. Goldmann had been a strong supporter of the UN partition plan that established the state in 1947 and later played a key role in negotiating the reparations agreement with West Germany. Well spoken and charismatic, with an outsized ego, he never hesitated to offer advice to Israeli leaders, although he had not settled in the state or spent much time there. Over the years, he became an influential leader of Diaspora Jewry, with entrée to heads of nations around the globe. In March 1970, he seems to have wrested an invitation to Cairo. The precise story is murky, involving several intermediaries, including Yugoslavia's president, Marshal Tito. His most direct contact was Nasser's emissary Ahmed Hamrush, who arranged the invitation under certain conditions: Goldmann was to visit as an individual and not as a representative of the Israeli government, but he needed to inform the prime minister of the invitation. Also, after the meeting, Egypt had the right to choose a time to publicize the fact that it took place. Later the meaning of these conditions became murky also.

In Goldmann's view, Golda combined "human kindness" with "ruthless firmness," but he was also "allergic" to her "rigidity." He once told her that he envied the cheap fake alligator handbag she carried because in it she held all the truths and solutions to problems that troubled her. That gave her the strength to believe she was 100 percent correct in everything. He, on the other hand, was never convinced that he was 100 percent correct about anything, and that was the basis for their many disputes.

Goldmann sought out Golda, who was at a rest home in Motza outside Jerusalem. "I cannot simply decide this on my own," she told him after he presented his Nasser plan. "It is the kind of thing that must be decided by the government." Knowing that a positive response was unlikely from the cabinet as a whole—certainly Menachem Begin would vote against any contact with Nasser—he asked that she consult only her small kitchen cabinet. A few days later, with Abba Eban's encouragement, she ignored his request and presented the issue to the full cabinet. As expected, the ministers vetoed the meeting with Nasser.

An irate Goldmann claimed in widespread interviews and lectures that he had not asked for permission and had simply intended to make Golda aware of the invitation. By taking his plan to the entire cabinet, she had torpedoed it.

Golda replied that no matter how informal Goldmann considered his mission, he would have been seen in Cairo as representing Israel. "It wasn't that Dr. Goldmann wanted the government to know that he was going to Cairo," she told the press. "This was a condition from the other side." What, she asked, did Nasser have in mind when he insisted that the Israeli government know of Goldmann's visit? "Nasser, all of a sudden, is so worried about the Israel government that no Jew and no Israeli citizen should come to see him without the permission of the Israel government? Where's the reason in all this?" And what would Goldmann have done at such a meeting? Just listen to Nasser and not present his own views? What if Nasser had asked about refugees or Jerusalem? "I have never heard of two people meeting, two sides, and then there is a monologue. Nobody in their senses would accept such a mission."

On April 2, 1970, a day after Goldmann received word of the government's decision, *Haaretz* published the first of a series of six articles he had written earlier, calling for greater flexibility in the government's foreign policy, especially in its insistence on direct negotiations with Arab leaders. About the same time, a long article he wrote for *Foreign Affairs*, "The Future of Israel," suggested that Israel become a neutral state protected by broad international guarantees rather than its own military. Goldmann might have postponed publishing those positions had he been permitted to meet with Nasser. For Israeli leaders, the publications reaffirmed their decision to quash his mission to Cairo. "Not an iota of Zionism remains in him," Golda seethed.

The Goldmann affair electrified the Israeli public. Having kept the matter secret for weeks, Golda had to acknowledge it after it leaked to the French newspaper *Le Monde* and other sources. The Kol Israel radio station broadcast the story at 11:00 p.m. on Sunday, April 5. The next day, all hell broke loose, with newspapers and politicians vehemently taking sides for or against the government decision. Those who disagreed felt they had been deceived. Through the many months of war, Golda had vowed that she would move heaven and earth, if she could, to find an opening toward peace. Now Goldmann might have found that opening, or at least a sliver of it, and had been stifled. *Haaretz* branded the cabinet's action "a mistake that needs to be rectified." In a poll it took of sixty-four respondents, 63 percent favored Goldmann's meeting Nasser, and 37 percent opposed, representing the country's attitude, the paper held. "Did you ever see a poll in *Haaretz* that is different from the editorial policy of *Haaretz*?" Golda countered. In contrast, a government-sponsored survey of two thousand respondents found that 62 percent thought the government had been correct and 35 percent that it had not.

Small as it might have been, the opposition made itself heard. Fifty-six Jerusalem high school students, "about to be inducted into the army," signed a letter to Golda Meir warning that they did not see how they could fight in a "permanent, futureless war," while the government "misses chances for peace." It ended "Give Goldmann a chance," echoing the American anti-Vietnam war chant, "Give peace a chance." University professors in Tel Aviv and Jerusalem sent telegrams to the prime minister sharply objecting to the cabinet decision, and students and faculty members waved banners that proclaimed, GOLDMANN TO CAIRO, GOLDA TO THE KITCHEN, or GOLDA'S AFRAID OF PEACE. Demonstrators held sit-ins at three major intersections and stopped traffic for half an hour, until the police hauled them away. More than a hundred protesters tried to break in to Golda's home in Jerusalem, with some reaching the courtyard before the police intervened.

On April 17, at the Cameri Theatre in Tel Aviv, a satiric review by Hanoch Levin, *The Queen of the Bathtub*, scandalized audiences with its mockery of Golda Meir—who was simply "exhausted" by being "right all the time"—and its powerful antiwar message. In one sketch, the biblical Isaac pleads with his father, Abraham, to sacrifice him, a biting reference to fathers sacrificing their sons to a futile war. Israelis had never experienced such openly antigovernment vitriol before, and certainly not in wartime.

A public outcry against the obscene language and crude images in Levin's play forced it to close after only nineteen performances. The young students who wrote to Golda—in what came to be called "The Twelfth Graders' Letter"—soon served in combat units, as did their peers who had not protested. Nasser denied that he had invited Goldmann, and with time that fracas quieted down. As it had before, Golda's national unity government kept the support of the majority of Israelis. But a deep crack had appeared in that support, and a protest movement, which had been stirring below the surface, now became a permanent factor in Israeli society.

Years later, after she had retired and after Anwar Sadat—Nasser's successor—visited Jerusalem, Golda Meir told Dov Goldstein, a journalist whom she liked and trusted, that she regretted not having permitted Goldmann to meet with Nasser after all. He could not represent the government, but he could have said that she had allowed him to speak with the Egyptian president. She doubted anything would have come of that conversation, but she might have made a mistake in forbidding it.

THE ATTRITION WAR RAGED ON. The body count grew. On their radios every evening, Israelis heard the names of soldiers lost, and in their morning papers they saw black-bordered photographs of the fallen. Five killed, twenty wounded one day; seven more dead, a dozen hurt the next. Palestinian fedayeen crossing into Israel from Jordan murdered children and adults in terror attacks, and Syrian artillery fire hit Jewish settlements in border towns and along the Golan Heights. The phones never stopped ringing in Golda's home; the reality was fast approaching the nightmare.

In mid-April, the U.S. assistant secretary of state Joseph Sisco traveled to Cairo and Israel to sound out possible peace prospects. Still anxiously hoping for American arms, Golda, Dayan, Eban, Galili, and others spent several hours beforehand working out the best strategy to use for the secretary's visit. Golda suggested that the most effective tour would be to take him to the Jordan valley settlements, which were being shelled regularly from Jordan. Let him see how the children had to sleep in shelters every night and how the adults held up in spite of constant assaults. She intended not to play on Mr. Sisco's sympathy, she insisted, but to show him "the type of person" an Israeli is. That wasn't quite true. Golda had always found calling attention to Jewish suffering an effective means to her ends. Unfortunately, it didn't work this time.

Sisco visited the Jordan valley settlements, held talks with Golda, Dayan, and Eban, and returned to the States with little accomplished and no sign of weapons forthcoming. Around the same time, word came that Soviet pilots, supposedly only instructors, were actually flying Soviet-made combat planes in Egypt, posing a serious threat to Israeli aircraft. Golda sent an urgent message to Nixon, strongly advising him to state publicly that the United States "will not acquiesce in provocative Soviet actions" and expressing hope that Israel would receive the military equipment it had asked for. Nixon responded orally through Abba Eban with the usual soothing words and no commitment. A Dosh cartoon a little later showed Nasser sitting in the cusp of a large Soviet hand, comfortably smoking a cigar, while a small perspiring Yisraelik dangles by one foot from the fingers of an American hand. The caption reads, "Some people's friends are friendlier than others'."

On May 26, Golda Meir stood before the Knesset to read a carefully prepared report on the political situation in Israel. The visible strain in her face reflected the pressures piling up from all directions—the war with Egypt, the withholding Americans, the conniving Russians, the Palestinian terrorists, and, on an everyday basis, the hassle to hold her national unity government together. Although firm in her convictions, she constantly had to find a middle course between the doves on the left in her own Labor Party, such as Eban and Sapir, and the hard-liners on the extreme right in the Gahal faction led by Menachem Begin.

She spoke for an hour and forty minutes, the longest speech she had ever given in the Knesset. During most of it, she reviewed the history of Israel's relationship with Egypt, heaping scorn on Nasser and his Soviet props. In passing, she mentioned Israel's acceptance of Security Council Resolution 242, with its call for the nation's withdrawal from occupied territories and guarantees to it of secure and recognized boundaries. She also mentioned a formula for negotiations (the Rhodes formula) that had been used after the war of 1948 and included mediation along with direct talks between the belligerents. These mentions might have been a nod to the government doves, and maybe to world opinion. Two television journalists who recently interviewed both Nasser and Golda told her that Egypt appeared more flexible than Israel and more open to a political settlement. Such a reputation could only hurt Israel, so she slipped in these references in an altogether moderate speech.

A hue and cry rose from Begin and the Gahal ministers. The references to Resolution 242 and the negotiation formula raised the specter of withdrawal from the territories. If so, they would have to quit the coalition government. They quieted down only after they were allowed to abstain from a vote endorsing the speech, but the noise foreshadowed problems ahead.

The problems came soon enough. In June, Secretary of State Rogers introduced a new initiative, which proposed a ninety-day cease-fire during which Israel would negotiate with Egypt and Jordan within the framework of Resolution 242 and under the auspices of the UN envoy Dr. Gunnar Jarring. It aimed to get the parties to "stop shooting and start talking." When Walworth Barbour, U.S. ambassador to Israel, presented the new Rogers plan to Golda on June 19, she "almost jumped out of her chair" with agitation. She ardently opposed short-term cease-fires, convinced that they did nothing but give Nasser time to replenish his forces. She also objected to the idea of opening negotiations while firing continued and Soviet arms flowed to Egypt. When Barbour pleaded with her not to reject the new plan before an answer came from Egypt and Jordan, she replied coldly that her view was "entirely negative," although she would bring the matter to the cabinet. The next day, she received a personal letter from President Nixon also urging her not to respond until the other side reacted so that the onus of a rejection did not fall on either Israel or the United States.

Rogers went public with his plan on June 25, and the same day Golda told her cabinet that with the delay of arms supplies from the United States the cease-fire was a "death trap" for Israel. Distressed by what they all recognized as an American link between arms supplies and Israel's agreeing to Rogers's proposal—although Nixon denied that in his letter—the cabinet grappled at meeting after meeting with what to do. Golda's first inclination had been to send a harsh reply to the president. But in Washington, the Israeli ambassador, Rabin, was so horrified by the extreme negative tone of her letter that he took it upon himself not to deliver it, a daring decision. Instead, he flew to Israel, where he spent hours prevailing upon Golda to soften her response. She finally agreed to a more nuanced answer in which she did not reject Rogers's proposal outright, but nor did she accept it.

Meanwhile, the military situation was becoming dire. On June 30, a day before Golda wrote to Nixon, a new, advanced Russian-made SAM-2 missile shot down two Israeli Phantom jets over the Suez Canal, startling a nation that thought of its air force as invincible. As perilous, the Egyptians were steadily moving their Soviet-made missiles toward the canal, where they could be used to cover a canal crossing by Egyptian forces. Then, on Wednesday, July 22, Nasser astonished the world by accepting the Rogers proposal. He had returned from a two-week visit to Moscow, where the Soviets might have warned him that they wanted no further entanglement in the Middle East conflict. Or he and they might have concluded—as Golda suspected—that a cease-fire offered him an opportunity to improve Egypt's military position. In any case, the prime minister and her cabinet had to make a decision about the Rogers initiative.

Two days after Egypt's acceptance, Golda received another secret letter from Nixon, this one filled with promises. Among other things, the president promised that America would not press Israel to accept a solution to the Arab refugee problem that would fundamentally alter the Jewish nature of the state. He acknowledged that Israel's final borders needed to be arrived at through negotiations, which the Israelis took to mean that he did not expect their borders to be identical to those before the Six-Day War. He also agreed that no Israeli soldier should be withdrawn from the present lines until a binding peace agreement had been achieved. Added to all that, he pledged to continue supplying arms to Israel and provide large-scale economic aid.

That letter and a dramatic event a week later finally pushed Golda and her government to a decision. Toward the end of July, Soviet pilots began to tangle directly with Israeli aircraft flying combat missions over the Suez Canal. In a dogfight on July 30, the Israelis shot down five Russian-piloted MiGs, killing three pilots. The terrifying specter of a war with the Soviets now entered into cabinet deliberations and led the ministers toward accepting the cease-fire. "I must admit I am taking this step with an aching heart," Golda said. "It is not the greatest joy for me to accept it but God did not promise me that in this land I would have only joys." A day later, the Israeli cabinet voted to accept the latest Rogers peace initiative, slightly altered.

The decision was finalized on Friday, August 7, 1970, and with that Menachem Begin and his Gahal ministers resigned from the unity government. After hours of debate in their central committee, their party had voted to leave the coalition and return to the opposition rather than assent to the Rogers initiative with its expectation of Israeli withdrawal from occupied territories. Before leaving, Begin praised Golda's leadership and the mutual trust he had felt. "I at all events will always view these three years [in the government] as the best chapters of my life," he said. "We will go into opposition." In her response, Golda said she had hoped to preserve the partnership as Eshkol did and was very sorry "that it was my lot to head a government that lost a group of its members."

Later that day, she read in the Knesset her government's formal response to the American proposal. It was a bittersweet moment for her. With the cease-fire, the mounting deaths of Israeli soldiers would stop; her worst nightmares taper off. But to arrive at this point, she had to compromise firm beliefs. She had accepted a temporary cease-fire, although to her mind that aided the enemy. She had agreed to negotiations under the auspices of a mediator—Dr. Gunnar Jarring—although she had always insisted on face-to-face talks with Arab leaders. And she had forfeited her coalition government, although she had worked ceaselessly to keep it intact.

Denouement: The cease-fire officially began at midnight, August 8. As part of the agreement, both parties were to maintain the status quo within an area of thirty-two miles along either side of the Suez Canal, with no military equipment to be moved into that area. In the hours before the agreement became official and for several nights afterward, Israeli aerial surveillance reported seeing the Egyptians moving Russian SAM-2 and SAM-3 missiles into the cease-fire zone on their side, about thirteen to eighteen miles from the banks of the canal. The ink had barely dried on the cease-fire agreement, and it was already being violated. Under orders from Golda, Ambassador Rabin reported the violations to the American State Department. Weeks of quibbling ensued, with the United States arguing that its evidence did not conclusively show the Egyptian missile movements that Israel claimed. Frustrated and irritated, Golda told a group of correspondents that Israelis were being treated "like half-wits." "What does the U.S. want us to do," she exclaimed, "sit still while the missiles move?" She asked to meet with Nixon to review the situation but was told that the time was "inopportune" for such a meeting.

In early September, the State Department publicly acknowledged that the Egyptians and Soviets had indeed violated the cease-fire agreement. The Israeli cabinet pondered whether to pull out of the prospective Jarring peace talks, or at least postpone them, until the missiles were removed. Golda received a promise that the United States would supply Israel with sophisticated antimissile equipment and restore the military balance in the region. With that, the president turned his attention elsewhere, the cease-fire took hold, and the Egyptian missiles remained standing close to the canal, silent sentries ominously anticipating the next crisis.

25

"What Has Happened to Us?"

The war of attrition was still in full swing on November 10, 1969, when Golda Meir stood before television cameras and radio microphones to read a letter addressed to her from the heads of eighteen Jewish families in Georgia, a province of the Soviet Union. The letter, she told her audiences, was a "cry from the depths." Ignoring the consequences they would face at home, the Georgian families appealed to the Israeli government to help them leave the Soviet Union and immigrate to Israel. They had turned to the Jewish state after countless attempts to get the necessary exit permits from their government and enclosed a copy of their letter to be sent to the UN Commission on Human Rights.

"We will wait months and years and if necessary all our lives but we will never give up our beliefs and our hopes," Golda read to rapt listeners. She closed by reciting the name of each family as it appeared with its address at the letter's end.

Nine days later, she spoke about that letter to a packed opening session of the Seventh Knesset. "We are declaring from this podium," she announced, "we shall not lag behind the Jews of the Soviet Union. We will . . . see to it that every person of conscience—Jew and non-Jew, all to whom freedom is precious—will raise his voice in defense of the freedom of others as well." At the meeting's end, the Knesset resolved to call on parliaments throughout the world to use their influence to help Soviet Jews emigrate.

In reading the letter from the Georgians publicly and presenting it to the Knesset, Golda broke radically with Israel's long-standing policy of secrecy in its dealings with Soviet Jews, pushing the subject out of the shadows and into the spotlight.

Through all the years and all her activities, she had never lost sight of the plight of the Jews in that land. Although the violent anti-Semitism she witnessed in Stalin's day had been reined in, a strong anti-Jewish bias still ran through the country. Jews were forbidden Yiddish and Hebrew books, had no national theater (as other ethnic groups did) or seminaries for training rabbis, and faced strict quotas that kept most of them from universities and high-level positions. Those who tried to immigrate to Israel usually lost their jobs and homes and risked being exiled or thrown into jail for having rejected their country. As foreign minister and then party secretary, Golda had stayed in close touch with Nativ, Israel's clandestine organization that spread Jewish culture and Zionist ideas to Soviet Jews. Some of its key leaders—Shaike Dan, Shaul Avigur, and Nechemia Levanon—who had been her comrades in the pre-state illegal immigration movement, frequently turned to her for advice. She was one of the few in the government to devote herself so fully to the Soviet Jewish cause; others argued that Israel already had more on its plate than it could handle.

Within a few months of becoming prime minister, she had determined that it was time for Israel to support the Soviet Jewish cause openly. In the United States, a grassroots movement inspired to some extent by the American civil rights struggle had organized protests and demonstrations on behalf of Soviet Jewry, attracting wide publicity. About the same time, the Soviets severed diplomatic ties with Israel because of the 1967 war. Their doing so freed the state to be more confrontational than it had been. Among Soviet Jews themselves, Israel's lightning victory in that war sparked pride and excitement and a desire to leave for their "homeland," Israel.

"Golda's response to the Georgian Jews validated their activities and those of others," Yaakov Kedmi said. "No other prime minister would have done what she did that day. No other cared that much about all Jews, not only Israelis."

Kedmi spoke from experience. Born Yasha Kazakov, he was one of the first Soviet Jews to openly defy the regime. On June 13, 1967, as a twenty-year-old Moscow student, he renounced his Soviet citizenship and declared his intention to live in Israel. After being turned down for emigration, threatened by Soviet authorities, and drafted into the army (he tore up the draft notice), he was suddenly—in February 1969—given two weeks to get out of the country. About a year later, now an Israeli citizen, Kedmi erected a tent in front of the UN building in New York City and staged a hunger strike to have his parents freed from Russia. Officially, the Israeli government considered the action extreme and called for the strike to end, but Yoram Dinstein, who served in Nativ, received a personal cable from Golda ordering him to go to the tent, shake Kedmi's hand, and express sympathy in her name.

Once she had shattered the secrecy, Golda continued to use her bully pulpit as prime minister to speak out for the Soviet Jewish cause. "Soviet Jews are not alone and are not forgotten—we are with them shoulder to shoulder," she promised at a solidarity rally of some twenty thousand students. "Not pity but justice is what we demand," she proclaimed at a later mass gathering. In return, Kremlin leaders began to attack her personally. At a large Soviet press conference, organized as a showpiece for world consumption, the few Jews who had risen to high positions in the U.S.S.R. were put forward to deny having a "Jewish problem" in their country. "I did not ask Golda Meir to be my sister," one of them declared. "My brothers and sisters are Russians, Ukrainians and other Soviet nationalities."

In the spring of 1970, Golda became enmeshed in one of the more spectacular undertakings of the Soviet struggle. Nechemia Levanon, who had become head of Nativ, brought her a request from a group of Jews in Leningrad. For months, they had been plotting to hijack a small, twelve-seat Soviet airplane, fly it to Sweden, and from there make their way to Israel. It would be a dramatic means of drawing the West's attention to the Soviet Jewish predicament. Would the Israeli government approve of this plan? Instantly recognizing the scheme as destined to fail, Golda gave a negative response, which was relayed by a coded phone message to the Leningrad group: "The highest medical expert is unable to recommend the use of this medication."

To their amazement, Golda and Levanon received news on June 15 that the KGB had arrested a group of Jews as they walked onto the tarmac of the Smolny Airport near Leningrad, planning to commandeer a plane. The determined plotters had ignored Golda's directive, and the Soviets had discovered the plan almost at its start.

The captives' trial at the Leningrad City Court began six months after the arrests, and a week later, on Christmas Eve 1970, the verdict was announced. Two of the defendants were to be executed by shooting and the rest given long prison terms at hard labor camps. The sentences so out of proportion to the crime—the hijacking had never occurred—elicited worldwide reactions. From New York to Paris to Rome and Berlin, newspaper editorials and mass demonstrations denounced the Soviets and demanded freedom for Russia's Jews. In Israel, Golda appeared at gatherings everywhere, her voice raspy from shouting, reminding the crowds that Jews had sung of their hope "for two thousand years" and would not lose it now. At the Western Wall, where thousands gathered every night and groups held hunger strikes, she predicted that "the tears of sorrow will one day become tears of joy" after Soviet Jews will be allowed out. Behind the scenes, she contacted lawmakers in the United States and other Western countries and leaders of major Jewish organizations, appealing to them to show support for the prisoners. On New Year's Eve, a week after the verdict was pronounced, Moscow announced that the two death sentences had been commuted and most of the others reduced. Even the closed-off Soviet Union could not remain oblivious to world opinion.

The impact of the Leningrad trial encouraged Levanon to pursue another goal he had been aiming for: a worldwide conference of Jewish organizations in support of Soviet Jews. When he suggested the idea to Premier Levi Eshkol in early 1969, he received an unenthusiastic response. Golda Meir, on the other hand, warmly welcomed the plan and worked diligently to make it happen. Held in Brussels on February 23–25, 1971, the conference brought together more than six hundred delegates from thirty-eight countries, representing dozens of Jewish organizations, many of them fighting turf wars among themselves over who had control of the Soviet struggle. For the time being at least, they united under the biblical cry that had become the movement slogan: "Let my people go." At the closing ceremony, a stooped, barely coherent Ben-Gurion appeared briefly to wildly cheering delegates. Golda did not attend, feeling that her presence as Israel's prime minister might be seen as a direct confrontation with the Soviets. Throughout the conference, however, she served as the "driving force behind it."

In 1970, 1,000 Jews received exit visas from the Soviet Union, a vast increase from previous years. In 1971, the number reached 13,000, and by the mid-1970s a total of about 200,000 Jews had left that country, most headed for Israel. As often as she could, Golda went to the airport to greet the new arrivals, sometimes inviting individuals or groups to her home for tea. On one occasion, she stared silently at a group of young Russian immigrants before asking them in Yiddish, "Would you tell me what preserved your Jewish consciousness through all those years?" Since her days as Israel's envoy to Moscow, she had marveled at the persistence of that consciousness in spite of Soviet repression. Her wonder at and commitment to Soviet Jews remained an undercurrent in her life regardless of what else occupied her.

IN MANY WAYS, HER LIFE took a turn for the better after the cease-fire in the attrition war. Her ratings in Israeli opinion polls reached 90 percent in 1970, up five percentage points since she was voted prime minister. Americans named her the woman they most admired in the world in 1971 and again in 1973. In 1972, only Pat Nixon topped her. She headed the charts in England also, outranking Queen Elizabeth one year. Her recipe for chicken soup had become world famous; when a Los Angeles television personality referred to it on a show, eighteen thousand people called in for it, and another three thousand wrote to the prime minister's office in Jerusalem. At home or abroad, when she entered a theater, audiences invariably stood up to give her a long ovation.

Anecdotes about her abounded, her clever quips repeated like legendary folklore. "Let me tell you something about Moses," she would say, not with total originality, and be quoted in *The New York Times*. "He took us forty years through the desert in order to bring us to the one spot in the Middle East that has no oil." Or, to Oriana Fallaci, "Old age is like an airplane flying in a storm. Once you're in it, there's nothing you can do." The magician Uri Geller, noted for bending spoons through sheer concentration, credited her with jump-starting his career, because when asked at a press conference about Israel's future, she replied, "Don't ask me. Ask that young fellow—Uri Geller." Iphigenia Sulzberger, mother of the *New York Times* publisher, never forgot how Golda greeted her when she came for coffee by opening the door herself, smiling, and shaking hands so warmly that within moments the two women were embracing like old friends. An oft-repeated story went that after welcoming Senator Frank Church personally when he arrived to join other guests for breakfast one morning, Golda disappeared. Walking into the kitchen, Church found her arranging the food and dishes for everyone herself. Surprised, he offered to help, but she shooed him back into the living room. "If you really want to help," she told him, "you can help Israel get the Phantoms and surface to air missiles it needs."

Her private life never ceased to fascinate a public hungry for juicy gossip. So when the muckraking weekly *Haolam Hazeh* published a news item in 1971 that the prime minister was going to marry the retired multimillionaire Lou Boyar, the news spread rapidly, picked up by the *Los Angeles Times* and other American newspapers. The two had been seen dining alone frequently at a secluded Hungarian restaurant on the outskirts of Jerusalem. A Los Angeles builder, Boyar had been one of the founders of the Israel Bonds organization along with Henry Montor and Sam Rothberg and now spent several months a year in Israel. He named a high school in Jerusalem for his wife, Mae, who died in 1962 and had been confined to a wheelchair for years because of severe rheumatoid arthritis. Golda stayed with the Boyars whenever she went to Los Angeles, leading to rumors about a romance between her and Lou Boyar that circulated for years. The marriage story took hold when the magazine reported that at a birthday party Golda gave for Boyar—he was four months older than she—he proposed marriage and she replied with a kiss. He dismissed the report as "unfortunately not true." Golda's secretary, Lou Kadar, called it "absolutely ridiculous." Golda didn't comment.

A real source of satisfaction for her and the public was her reconciliation with David Ben-Gurion. After six years of almost no contact between them, she visited him at his desert home in Sdeh Boker on a hot July day in 1971. His eighty-fifth birthday was approaching; she had refused to attend his eightieth birthday party, when the Lavon Affair still soured her thoughts about him. That had quieted down finally. His strength had declined, his mind clouded; she was struggling with her lymphoma and the secret, painful treatments it entailed. They needed to make up. In a brightly printed summer dress, her features softened by emotion, she shook hands warmly with a smiling Ben-Gurion. The two went into his green hut and spoke alone for an hour and twenty minutes. On the way to lunch afterward at a nearby college, they paused at the grave of his wife, Paula, where Golda laid a wreath of red roses.

On the fiftieth anniversary of Golda's arrival in Israel, Revivim—Sarah's kibbutz—gave a big party for her. In spite of their reconciliation, Ben-Gurion had hesitated about going, agreeing only after some friends urged him to attend. As Golda entered the room, she spotted him sitting down. Within moments, they fell into each other's arms, kissing like the long-lost friends they were. They held hands as they walked into the dining room for the ceremonies.

Instead of a speech, Ben-Gurion read aloud three letters he had sent her in the past, among them his congratulations in 1958, on her sixtieth birthday, when he conveyed his deepest feelings of friendship and love to a "true pioneer" filled with "wisdom in everything she does." In her talk, Golda referred to a birthday cable she had once sent him when she was out of the country. Despite arguments they'd had in the past and would probably continue to have, she had written, she would always be grateful for the "enormous privilege" of working alongside the "one man who more than any other individual was responsible for the fact that we have a state of our own." She still felt the same way, she said, and thanked him for "the gift of his presence."

She launched the nation's celebration of Ben-Gurion's eighty-fifth birthday with a party at the end of September at Beit Berl, Mapai's education center. This time she spoke about two lessons she had learned from her former chief during the nation's years of struggle: the need to be afraid in times of danger, and the courage necessary to continue, though afraid. At the end, she called on Ben-Gurion to return to the Labor Party, a request he refused. A week later, she led the entire cabinet to Sdeh Boker to pay its birthday tribute to the "old man."

In these years of her greatest popularity, Golda Meir equaled and might have surpassed Ben-Gurion in the kind of absolute power he had enjoyed. At the Beit Berl celebration, she repeated a story she enjoyed telling about her old boss. It concerned a discussion that took place in her home about whether the party was run democratically. Ben-Gurion asked one of the party leaders, Peretz Naphtali, what he thought. Naphtali replied with a smile and said, "Ben-Gurion I want to tell you. The movement in the most democratic fashion always accepts what you propose." Ben-Gurion probably missed the humor in the statement. Golda didn't, but it would not have occurred to her that someone might tell a similar story about her. With her power and prominence, she was also becoming more autocratic than ever.

Her style differed greatly from Ben-Gurion's. She spoke about gefilte fish and grandchildren. She shared meals with the help who cleaned her house, and remembered her bodyguards' birthdays—things that were out of the "old man's" ken. No one, however, doubted her authority or control. "When I got a phone call from Golda Meir, I stood at attention," Yoram Dinstein said, only half jokingly. "She would say things like, 'In my poor judgment,' or 'I'm just an old lady,'" recalled Yoram Peri, who had been a spokesman for Israel's Labor Party, "but that was because she was so tough and filled with self-righteousness. People didn't dare confront her. She would gaze at them and they would begin to lisp." Uri Savir, architect of the Oslo Accords, whose father served many years in the foreign service, labeled her "ruthless." She had "incredible charisma," he said, "but she was very much feared."

When Julie Nixon, the president's daughter, interviewed Golda for a *Ladies' Home Journal* article, the prime minister asked warmly about her mother, Pat. But if the young interviewer posed a question she didn't want to answer, "she became absolutely rock-like . . . She did not respond. She seemed rooted to her chair. Immobile. Silent. Her eyes cold and dark."

In her imperial position, she could also be insensitive to the feelings of people closest to her. She thought nothing of calling her friend Regina at eleven o'clock at night. "What are you doing now? Come visit me," she would say, and then stretch the visit out for hours, because she hated to be alone. When she went to Revivim, she arrived by car or helicopter and instantly became the center of attention, greeting everyone as though it were her home rather than her daughter's. Shy by nature, Sarah would walk behind her with "tiny little steps," her head bowed, embarrassed by her mother's conspicuousness and feeling left out herself. Golda never noticed.

"She retained many of her virtues," her friend and biographer Marie Syrkin said of Golda, "but to say that power doesn't go to your head is nonsense. It . . . did not corrupt her, but it certainly altered her . . . You become so inured to praise that it doesn't mean anything anymore and you take for granted all these endless compliments and these multitudes chasing you."

INUNDATED WITH PRAISE AND COMPLIMENTS, Golda chafed when criticisms began cropping up more frequently alongside the accolades. The media, which in the earlier days of state building had been a tool of government leaders in mobilizing the nation, had become more independent as the country gained its confidence. As in any democracy, the press now felt free to attack politicians and leaders for their perceived failures and to publicize secret information leaked by inside sources. Golda regularly railed against leaks and didn't hesitate to chastise journalists when she felt she'd been wronged. But she was particularly troubled in these years by the social changes beginning to grip the country. The rebellions against authority sweeping across Europe and the United States in the 1960s and 1970s made a profound impression on young Israelis. The twelfth-grade students' letter objecting to military service and the anti-government demonstrations that followed the Nahum Goldmann affair tore into a society that had always been united in its wars for survival. As dissent spread to many areas and a new left wing gained followers—albeit still a small minority—Golda worried that the very essence of that society was being threatened.

"What has happened to us in the last year?" she cried out at a Knesset meeting. "What has happened to our understanding? To our good sense?" Among the last remaining founders of the state, she was determined to conserve the ideals that had molded it—socialism, Zionism, self-sacrifice—against the powerful forces buffeting them about.

She'd had a brush in the States during her trip in 1969 with the kind of resistance she would encounter in Israel. Elie Wiesel had invited her to his Manhattan apartment to meet with a group of professors and editors, the sorts of intellectuals who always made her uncomfortable. Sitting in an easy chair, the guests spread on the floor around her, she spoke warmly about Nixon as a friend of Israel and immediately came under fierce attack for supporting his Vietnam policy. She had backed that policy largely because of how desperately Israel needed the president on its side, but she had not been prepared for the degree of hostility she would arouse. To cut through the tension, the humorist Herbert Tarr called out, "Mrs. Meir, will you marry me?" Relieved by the group's laughter, she replied, "Would *you* be embarrassed if I said yes."

No humor lightened the situation at home when, in December 1971, she received a cable signed by thirty-four academics, many of them professors at Hebrew University, complaining that the government had not "exhausted all possibilities for opening negotiations with Egypt and avoiding the danger of another war." She was incensed. What did these ivory-tower professors know about running a country or dealing with diplomacy? The cable quickly reached *Haaretz*, which published its contents the next day. Just as quickly, another telegram arrived for Golda, this one from five Tel Aviv professors who supported the government's actions. Most of these men belonged to the Greater Israel movement with its ideal of retaining all the territories Israel had captured. Golda had never held that position and still didn't, but in anger—and spite— she let it be known that she would be happy to meet with the second group of professors, but not the first. Some in the rejected group shot back that they had not even asked to meet with her and that her response reflected her ill will toward most of the intellectual community.

The gap between her outlook and the new attitudes these protesting professors represented became even more obvious at a gathering she held in her Jerusalem home about a year later with young writers and poets, among them Israel's most prominent literary voices, Amos Oz, A. B. Yehoshua, Yoram Kaniuk, Yehuda Amichai, and others. She had called the meeting to discuss a controversy swirling around two largely Christian Arab villages in the Galilee, Ikrit and Berem. During the war of 1948, its inhabitants had consented to the IDF's request that they evacuate their homes "temporarily," with the promise that they would be allowed back after the war. That never happened, in spite of their appeals to subsequent Israeli governments. Over the years, the former villagers became Israeli citizens, and many served in the army and police force, yet many still wished to return to their towns. This time, when the issue came up again, the writers espoused the villagers' cause and students rallied to their side.

She served tea. She smoked almost three packs of her unfiltered Chesterfields while she talked with her guests for seven hours. "We went round and round in circles and got nowhere," one participant, Hanoch Bartov, recalled. The writers argued that Israel had a moral responsibility to the villagers. Golda gave the standard government rebuttal: Allowing these villagers to return would set a precedent for thousands of other Arab refugees that Israel could not possibly absorb. Moreover, although an "injustice" had been done—and she acknowledged that it had—the army still considered the return of Arabs to these villages near the Lebanese border a security risk. Then she added her own interpretation, which more than anything staked out the contrasts between her and her guests. She was concerned about a crisis of Zionist ideology, she said, concerned that the young people marching for Ikrit and Berem had learned to doubt the utter rightness of the Zionist cause, and that posed a greater danger than war itself. It was as though she were looking backward while the world around her moved forward.

"She wanted us to drop the subject and talk about general problems, about Zionism," A. B. Yehoshua observed, "but we constantly returned to Ikrit and Berem." These writers had little interest in theoretical discussions of ideology. Most of them sabras, born in the Land of Israel, they took their Zionism for granted and felt confident enough in themselves and their country to sympathize with the displaced Arabs among them. Golda, on the other hand, part of an immigrant generation propelled by the Zionist dream, feared an erosion of that dream as young people adopted new causes and appeared to turn their backs on the goals of their own country.

"We had no common language," Hanoch Bartov said.

They had no common language on many social issues these days, even where they might have been expected to agree. Like the writers and professors, like most Israelis, Golda regarded herself as a secular Jew. She loved the Chinese food Lou Kadar brought her when she felt ill, unkosher as it might be, never gave up smoking on the Sabbath or any holiday, and made no bones about her beliefs. Years earlier, she had objected when a small religious party asked to have Sabbath observance written into an agreement it was negotiating with Mapai. Certainly not, she had declared. Mapai members might honor an occasional request not to hold a meeting on the Sabbath, but she would never put such a ruling in writing. And more than once, she spoke of her shame at having signed the personal status law that placed marriage, divorce, and other family matters into the hands of the Orthodox rabbinate.

Now, however, she was prime minister, and like Ben-Gurion and the others before her she had to compromise with the religious parties or risk their leaving her coalition. That put her at odds with the writers and intellectuals and many Israelis who felt choked by the ever-tightening grip of the rabbinate on their lives. In the current restive atmosphere, she had to contend with attacks against religious compromises that her predecessors had not.

When, in 1969, a debate broke out about extending Israeli television programming—still in its infancy—from three nights a week to seven, including the Sabbath, Golda naturally inclined toward supporting the extension. Television was like radio, which operated seven days a week, she said. The religiously observant did not have to listen or watch on the Sabbath if they didn't want to. Under massive pressure from the religious parties, she changed her tune and asked the government to postpone Sabbath television transmission. An outraged television set owner appealed that decision, and a Supreme Court justice ordered the premier to show cause why the Israel Broadcasting Authority should not proceed with its Friday night programming, essentially overruling her. It was an embarrassing defeat for Golda, but one that she eventually shrugged off as Friday night television became part of the Israeli scene.

More serious was the dispute that raged about a case involving religion and Jewish identity in the state—what became known as the "Who is a Jew?" question. This case—there would be others—centered on an Israeli naval officer, Benjamin Shalit, his non-Jewish Scottish wife, and their two children, who had been born and raised in Israel. Although the parents rejected any form of religion, they sought to have the children listed as Jews by nationality on their identity cards. The rabbis opposed this, arguing that in halacha, or traditional Jewish law, only a child born to a Jewish mother or a female convert to Judaism may be considered Jewish, and Shalit's wife had not converted. Nevertheless, the high court ruled in Shalit's favor, holding, in effect, that a Jew is anyone who says he or she is a Jew, even if that person disavows Judaism as a religion. At first Golda gladly accepted the court's ruling, but virulent Orthodox protests and pressure, both in Israel and in the United States, pushed her to the other side. Within days, at her behest, the cabinet rushed a bill through the Knesset reversing the court's decision and defining Jewish identity by religion only. Shutting her ears to the thousands of demonstrators who marched outside the Knesset protesting "religious coercion" and calling for "a free country," Golda defended the bill. With intermarriage and assimilation decimating Jewish communities, she said, she was willing to compromise with the religious parties "for the sake of the survival and unity of the Jewish people." To many secular and non-Orthodox Israelis, her explanation sounded more like political appeasement of the rabbinate without touching the core issue of the case, defining Jewish identity in a Jewish state.

An amendment to the Law of Return enacted by the Knesset in March 1970 incorporated the religious definition of a Jew. It did not specify, however, that conversion had to be according to halacha or Orthodox standards, a benefit to the American Reform and Conservative denominations, which were working to establish a foothold in Israel. In public life, Golda respected and encouraged the liberal movements. As a show of her approval, she accepted an honorary degree from Hebrew Union College, the Reform seminary, despite the Israeli rabbinate's refusal to recognize the non-Orthodox movements. Yet on a personal level she felt as uncomfortable with religious change as she did with other forms of change. At a dinner she attended of the Conference of Presidents of Major American Jewish Organizations in the States, some leaders of the liberal Reconstructionist movement presented her with a copy of their new Passover Haggadah. She thanked them but immediately added that though she was not religious, when she had a Passover seder with her grandchildren, she wanted them to read the same words their grandparents and generations of Jews before them had read, not a new version.

"WHAT HAS HAPPENED TO US?" Her question in the Knesset could have been her theme song as she looked around at the political protests and antireligious demonstrations that had never before been seen in Israel. What had happened to discipline? she wanted to know, deeply troubled especially about young people, who, she feared, took America as their model.

After a visit to the States in 1970, she spoke with horror of a country whose youth had lost their moral compass. They are against the community, against the home, against the family, she told a gathering at Revivim. "If their parents take showers every day, then their rebellion demands that a shower is something forbidden, and to wash is forbidden and to cut one's hair is forbidden." She dreaded the impact those rebellious young people might have on the more sheltered Israeli young. When one of her grandsons showed up with an "Afro" hairdo, popular in the States, and another sported hippie beads around his neck, she almost exploded with agitation. Asked by an interviewer what negatives she saw in Israeli life, the first thing that came to her mind was "imitation," mainly of the United States. The revolts by the young there had led to "nihilism," a situation she certainly hoped did not reach Israel.

She had cause to be apprehensive about the turbulence of America's youth, the druggies and flower children who wandered aimlessly through San Francisco's Haight-Ashbury, the students who burned American flags in their anti-Vietnam rage. But with little understanding of popular culture, she also tended to confuse the radical extremes of behavior in the United States and other countries with the high spirits of a baby boom generation come of age. In 1965, an earnest Israeli ministerial committee banned the Beatles from entering the country because the group caused "disorder among young people." A few years later, with the Beatles a worldwide phenomenon, Golda was asked about the ban during a visit to London. She glanced quizzically at an assistant; she had no idea who the Beatles were. After watching them on television later in the day, she asked the assistant incredulously, "How could they imagine that the government of Israel would give permission to these people to come in and give us culture?" To her mind, the Liverpool lads hardly differed from the long-haired hippie types she so derided.

She also melded the marginal with the mainstream in her response to one of the most far-reaching social revolutions of her time: the women's movement. "Do you mean those crazy women who burn their bras and go around all disheveled and hate men?" she famously said to Oriana Fallaci in 1972, making no distinction between the radical fringes and a Betty Friedan, whose *Feminine Mystique*, published a decade earlier, had sold millions of copies. (In fact, she would refuse to meet with Betty Friedan during Friedan's first visit to Israel in 1974.) She had made a similar identification of the radical with the more moderate almost forty years earlier in the newspaper *Der Yiddisher Kaempfer* when she equated all feminists with women who regarded men as "the enemy." At that time, struggling to find her way in the male-dominated world, she exaggerated in order to distinguish herself from women like Ada Maimon and Hanna Chizick, who devoted their lives to women's causes. Now, as prime minister, she had reached the pinnacle of success but chose not to alter her attitude substantially. She still did not wish to be seen as a "woman" leader, but like any man, simply as a leader whose achievements resulted from hard work and devotion to ideals. "Men have never given me special treatment," she said, nor did she expect special privileges as a woman. Her words carried the underlying message that any woman willing to dedicate herself to her goals could do the same as she without the need for a separate, organized movement. Feminists would argue that she was the exception to the struggle women underwent to make their mark in a male-dominated world.

So determined was Golda to set herself apart from women as a group that she told Fallaci she had "never belonged to a women's organization," although she had actually headed two women's organizations, the Women Workers' Council in Israel and the Pioneer Women, its American counterpart, both her first stepping-stones into active political life. She also insisted that being a woman had never "been an obstacle" in her career, ignoring that she had to run away from home as a child because her parents did not approve of educating a girl, ignoring, too, that as an adult she lost the election to be mayor of Tel Aviv because the religious labor party had, in her words, exploited "the fact that a woman was put forward as a candidate."

She did acknowledge women's special problems and qualities. When as foreign minister she met with Margaret Meagher, Canada's first ambassador to Israel, and the media harped on their importance as female ministers, she whispered to Meagher, "The fact that they're making such a fuss proves that women still have a long way to go to get equal status with men." It bothered her that the Knesset did not have more women, and she helped three important women get there—Zena Harman, Esther Herlitz, and Tamar Eshel. She also admitted that "to be successful a woman has to be much more capable than a man," although, she added, that was not men's fault. She took pride in her pronouncement years earlier when, as a result of a spate of rapes in the land, male ministers suggested that women not be allowed on the streets after dark. Because men were attacking women, men, and not women, should be given a curfew, Golda had said, repeating the story often to interviewers. And she was pleased to receive a copy of a poster that had become iconic among American women's groups with her image and the legend "But Can She Type?" beneath it, and to learn that thousands of copies had been distributed.

None of that translated, however, into Golda's identifying with feminism as a political movement or trying to elevate the overall status of women in the state. For her, the face of feminism in Israel, and one that she disliked, was Shulamit Aloni. The brash, outspoken, and fearless Aloni became well-known through a popular radio call-in show she hosted. Highly educated and trained as a lawyer, she regarded Golda as "boorish" and "self-righteous," part of the old guard that had contributed to building the state but whose time had passed. Golda viewed Aloni as arrogant and provocative. In one of their many clashes, she rebuked the younger woman for referring to Israel in the Knesset as "conquerors" after the 1967 war. "How dare you call Jews conquerors?" she scolded. "We Jews are always underdogs." And even if Aloni thought that way, she had no business saying so publicly. "You think you can say anything, because you're a lawyer!" the prime minister shouted. Aloni had been a Mapai Knesset member, but in the election of 1969 Golda insisted on having her name placed sixty-fourth in the list of Labor Party candidates, guaranteeing that she would not be elected. In 1973, Aloni left Labor to form her own party, driven away, many felt, by Golda's venom.

As one of the founders of Israel's feminist movement, Aloni pushed through a variety of laws benefiting women. She also initiated civil rights legislation for consumers, minorities, secular Jews, and others. When she spoke about civil rights, she often said, Golda accused her of being "bourgeois," indulging in a luxury the country could not yet allow itself. Aside from their personal animosity, that difference in perspective kept these two strong women—similar in their confidence and conviction—far apart. In Golda's view, the individual rights Aloni promoted had to grow from the larger enterprise, the socialism, the nationalism, the collective goals that, when achieved, would provide for individuals within the community. Singling out any one group, such as women, took energy away from the strivings of the nation as a whole. While she might compromise with her coalition partners on specific issues, she refused to compromise on those founding principles of the state—even if others thought the time had long since come for her to do so.

IN A THREE-WAY INTERVIEW, Golda, her daughter, and her granddaughter were questioned about the place of socialism in their country. Golda answered at length that she remained as much a socialist as she had been in 1949: now as then that meant fighting poverty and providing equal opportunity for all. True, the dream had not been totally realized, and crime and poverty still existed in the land, yet she continued to believe in socialism as the best path for the state. Her daughter, Sarah, thought the socialist ideal was alive in Israel only in kibbutzim, such as hers in Revivim. Her granddaughter Naomi replied with a shrug that socialism did not concern her at the moment. "I am interested in other subjects," she said.

Most young Israelis, and plenty of older ones, would have agreed with Naomi that they did not have socialism on their minds. With the country's enormous expansion after the 1967 war, the economy flourished. A new middle class rose, builders and businesspeople, industrialists, technologists, and professionals, most of them city dwellers interested in making money and enjoying the luxuries it brought. Golda's socialist slogans appeared old-fashioned as some people accumulated fortunes and the gap between haves and have-nots stretched wider than it ever had. The old dogmas didn't work with large segments of the laboring classes either, the very core constituents of Golda's Labor Party. The relative calm on the battlefield after the cease-fire opened the way for labor disputes to explode in almost every corner of society. In June 1971, electrical utility repairmen went on work stoppages that plunged neighborhoods into darkness, and striking hospital maintenance workers closed down government medical services for days. In September, postmen demanding higher wages held a "go slow" strike, which tied up the postal system, and on-again, off-again strikes by customs officials and dockworkers led to pileups of imported goods. Most disruptive, a wildcat strike by eight hundred civil aviation workers paralyzed Lod Airport, the country's one international airport.

"Pure hooliganism," Golda snapped. As a long-standing labor advocate, she had always resisted legislation that limited workers' rights to seek higher wages. Now, however, she, Sapir, and others in her cabinet tried to push through tough labor laws that would restrain wildcat strikes. "I simply cannot stand by and watch everything deteriorate into a political and moral catastrophe," she said as the anarchy grew, adding, "The situation is deteriorating into a rebellion, not by the Arabs but by our own hands." She was especially irked that many of the strikers did not come from the lowest rungs of society, but were skilled workers and professionals who wanted to reap the benefits of middle-class life. In pre-state days, she had forced employed workers to pay the special *mifdeh* tax to help the unemployed. In the current situation, she would not put up with the demands for increased wages from people relatively high in the economic scale. "I will not spend my last days at the head of a government that only considers how to make some people millionaires," she huffed.

She showed her impatience in her speech to the Knesset on July 28, 1971, the last day before its summer recess. "We are a wise, sensible and patriotic people, who can reach the heights of self-sacrifice," she said, yet are "behaving as if there were no danger ahead of us, as if we had already . . . eliminated poverty and completed the development of the country." She had no tolerance for "people in Israel who live above the standard of living we can permit ourselves," and she warned against "a life-style imported from abroad" and influenced by wealthy foreigners. Her sympathy lay with workers "on the verge of poverty, earning the lowest salaries." Only they had the right to receive salary increases. Everyone else needed to remain within existing standards of living until pressures on the country let up.

She tried to maintain that utopian view while one union after another agitated for higher wages. More often than she liked, she found herself in opposition to the formidable, independent, and highly respected Yitzhak Ben-Aharon, secretary-general of the Histadrut, the large, unruly labor federation that still dominated the employment scene as it had in the pre-state era. He was no less a socialist than she, but he represented and fought for all the laboring classes, while her heart remained fixed on the lowest strata of the economy. Sadly, in one of the more painful ironies of her life, the most vocal members of those low-income groups turned their frustration and wrath against her, making her a pariah within their community.

They called themselves the Black Panthers (Pantherim Shechorim), a name adopted from radical blacks in the American civil rights movement and chosen for its shock value. Most were young people who had come to Israel as children with their parents from Morocco, Algeria, Iran, and other Arab countries in North Africa and the Middle East, cast out of their homes and lands after the establishment of the state or during the Sinai campaign in 1956. They watched as the new Soviet immigrants received clean, relatively spacious garden apartments while they lived in cramped, deteriorating flats in slum neighborhoods, the same neighborhoods where their families had been settled when they first arrived in a less prosperous Israel. They watched as the Ashkenazi Jews from Eastern European and Western countries rose ever higher on the economic scale and continued to dominate every aspect of the nation's political, financial, and cultural life while they and their people, called Sephardim, and later Mizrahim, held the most menial jobs. Few in their communities finished high school, and those who did might go on to vocational schools, rarely to a university. About 20 percent lived below the poverty level.

Their parents might have passively accepted their lot in life, but in the revolutionary spirit of the times these young people protested loudly, and sometimes violently, against their second-class status, directing much of their rage toward Golda Meir, the most prominent supporter of Soviet Jewish immigration. When the group first came to attention, in February and March 1971, the police, with Golda's approval, tried to prevent their demonstrations, out of fear of riots. They demonstrated anyway, beginning in Jerusalem's poverty-stricken Musrara section, which had been predominantly Arab before 1948 and was now home to most of the protesters. ENOUGH OF NOT HAVING WORK, their posters proclaimed. ENOUGH SLEEPING TEN TO A ROOM. ENOUGH OF BROKEN PROMISES FROM THE GOVERNMENT. ENOUGH DISCRIMINATION.

In the spring, they demanded a meeting with the prime minister, threatening to hold a hunger strike at the Western Wall until she agreed. On April 13, she met with five Panther leaders, joined by the education minister, Yigal Allon, and the welfare minister, Michael Hazony. Mostly dark-skinned, dressed in jeans, T-shirts, and sneakers, they assembled in her Jerusalem office to make their case, some of them having been coached by sympathetic university lecturers. Golda began in a friendly manner, offering them all cigarettes, which they quickly accepted, and speaking to them personally. She turned first to Reuven Abergil, one of the most outspoken of the group.

"Were you born here?" she asked.

"We are all from Morocco—I am from Rabat," he answered.

"What school did you attend?"

"I studied only until third grade . . ."

"What did you do after that?"

"I was on the street, in court, in jail . . ."

"You didn't work?"

"Yes, when I could. I did only construction work . . ."

"And what do you do now?"

"Street cleaning . . ."

On and on she pressed—how old was his son, what kind of work did his wife do before having a child, where did he work prior to his marriage? Finally, he burst out, "We didn't come here to speak about my individual work. It would be great if this were my problem. This is the problem of the entire Sephardic community . . . The situation of this group is terrible, and its people live on the edge of poverty." But Golda persisted in questioning individuals. "What kind of work do you do?" she asked each man and received similar answers. Most were drifters. One had a jail record that prevented him from getting work or going into the army; another shared a room with ten brothers growing up, with no opportunity for any form of education; "nobody ever taught us that it is necessary to work hard," said another. As her queries mounted, one or another tried to cut in by insisting, as Abergil had, that he spoke in the name of the people he came to represent and not in his own name, and again she ignored that assertion.

They talked at each other, not to each other. These young men saw themselves as leaders of a revolutionary new movement, with thousands of followers, as Saadia Marciano told Golda. True, he didn't have a paying job, but he had made the Panthers his life's work, to help others like him. She fully empathized with the poverty with which they had grown up. After all, hadn't she also been poor? Hadn't she suffered dire deprivation in her early years in Jerusalem with two young children? Yet no matter how wretched these men's existence, she could not comprehend why they didn't work or make an effort to find work. She had grown up with the Protestant ethic of working hard to improve one's life. Why weren't they doing that, as countless other immigrants and children of immigrants had? Going further, she refused to regard them as a new movement, with people like Marciano at its head. "This government and this state were not born yesterday," she told them with some annoyance. She and others in the government had been fighting poverty long before the Panthers arrived on the scene. Nor was this a matter of Sephardim and Ashkenazim, but of raising the living standard of all the underprivileged.

Besides everything else, she could not tolerate their use of the name Black Panthers. "Why did you choose this name?" she asked irritably several times. Didn't they know that the American Panthers were anti-Semitic? It was not about ideology, they argued. They chose the name to attract attention. Had they asked her, she offered stiffly, she would have advised them not to take such a name. Later, Kochavi Shemesh, an attorney and former Panther secretary, said they chose the name specifically to frighten Golda.

They left the meeting angry and convinced that she had not the slightest understanding of their complaints or community. She left angry and convinced that these young men should be off the streets, in school or working instead of organizing protests. Of course, she recognized the difficulties of their home lives, she told a cabinet meeting. "One thing is clear—their background is terrible and pathetic. The background is large families, impossible housing . . . and the eldest child takes to the streets and all the others follow." Even so, she could not accept their claim that the Sephardic Jews suffered discrimination. And she resented their refusal to recognize the government's efforts to eliminate poverty.

Maybe if she had agreed to investigate discrimination against this ethnic group, maybe if she had appeared to take these young people seriously as leaders of a political movement instead of questioning them individually and speaking to them—as she said—the way she might speak to a son or grandson, the follow-up would have been different. As it was, they made her the butt of their unmitigated hatred. "She was Mama Russia," said Shemesh. "She cared nothing about us but went out to greet all the Soviet immigrants. We became extreme because of her."

The demonstrations became more violent and more frequently targeted at her. She had to cancel an appearance at a Maimouna celebration, a post-Passover North African Jewish festival, after a group of Panthers burst into the festivities and brawled with the police, leading to several arrests. Two weeks later, scores of Black Panthers waving banners with the words GOLDA TEACH US YIDDISH marched down Dizengoff Street in Tel Aviv, then sat down on the pavement, disrupting traffic. As they saw it, she regarded only people who spoke Yiddish, like the Soviet immigrants, as real Jews. A demonstration known as the Night of the Panthers that began on Tuesday, May 18, with a small group of protesters in Jerusalem's Davidka Square, turned into a wild melee as demonstrators marched down Jaffa Road against police orders. By the time the crowd reached Zion Square, thousands had joined the procession. Helmeted policemen tried to disperse the mobs with nightsticks and powerful jets of water, while protesters pelted them with stones, bottles, and Molotov cocktails. Shopwindows were smashed, cars overturned, and dozens of people injured. The police hauled more than a hundred protesters off to jail before the rioting ended late at night. The next morning, relatives of some of those imprisoned demonstrated for their release in front of Golda Meir's home in Rehavia.

A day after the rioting, Golda spoke to the Moroccan Immigrants Association. She did not regret meeting with the Panthers a few weeks earlier, she said, although some people had criticized her for that. The meeting had given her insight into their nature. "They were once good boys and I hope there are some among them who will yet be good boys, but there are others I suspect will not change," she said, hinting also that the demonstrators might have been manipulated by extreme left-wing elements. When the association's president, Shaul Ben-Simhon, referred to the Panthers as "nice guys" whom he had visited in jail, she quickly jumped in. "People who throw Molotov cocktails at Jewish police are not nice."

In the collective memory of Mizrahim and then the public at large, her words at that meeting, "once good boys" and "not nice," became forever associated with each other. The phrase "they are not nice boys," or, more often, "they are not nice," would attach itself to Golda Meir for the rest of her life and long after her death. The context would be forgotten, as would any subtleties. Some insisted she dubbed the Panthers "not nice" immediately after meeting with the five leaders; others that she labeled them that way in a radio broadcast. It didn't matter that she wrote to Ben-Simhon to clarify the situation. "For months, a campaign of slander has been conducted against me because of my remark that the 'Panthers are not nice,'" she wrote, reminding him that she had said what she did only in response to his referring to them as "nice" and only in connection with those who threw Molotov cocktails. She wondered also why he had not spoken out in her defense. It didn't matter that he acknowledged the accuracy of her description, had seemed surprised that the words had taken on a life of their own, and expressed his regret that "there are people who spread slanders based on distortion of the facts." Nothing changed. For the young Black Panthers and many Middle Eastern Jews in Israel, being referred to as "boys" and "not nice" symbolized the condescension and lack of respect they attributed to Ashkenazim in general and the prime minister in particular.

The demonstrations escalated through the spring and summer of 1971. At a meeting of the Knesset's Foreign Affairs and Defense Committee in June, Golda described how the police prevented some Black Panthers from knocking down her fence and entering her house. They did not wish to hurt her, the men explained; they only wanted to break in and toss her furniture around. "That's legitimate," she said with her usual sarcasm, "but that the police didn't allow them to do it—that makes the police brutal." She had grown impatient with their tactics and their accusations of police brutality after each demonstration. "I don't know why poverty and Panthers are being treated as though they are one and the same thing," she went on. "They are not the same. The war on poverty is the war on poverty, and the Panthers did not invent it." She blamed the media for drawing attention to the Panthers instead of highlighting true pockets of poverty in the land. She could not bring herself to give these young people the one thing they craved: validation for their cause and their conviction that with their background they had a role to play in building the state—validation they believed she gave Russian immigrants.

They flaunted their disdain toward her. In July, more than three thousand members and supporters from all over the country converged on Jerusalem, this time in an orderly and quiet demonstration, licensed by the police. The signs they carried in Hebrew, English, and Yiddish called on Israelis to "throw Golda Meir out of the government" and get rid of her ruling party. For the first time, posters also displayed the American Black Panthers' clenched-fist salute, a special provocation for the prime minister.

A month later, all sense of order disappeared when several hundred Panthers swelled into a mob of more than two thousand as they headed to Davidka Square, stopping traffic and almost paralyzing downtown Jerusalem. GOLDA, GOLDA, GET LOST ALREADY, EVERYONE'S HAD ENOUGH OF YOU, banners blared. Some demonstrators carried a satiric caricature of a naked Golda Meir with angel's wings, which they burned in effigy. Soon afterward, they set fire to three black coffins painted with the words "Democracy" and "Justice," while posters proclaimed, A STATE IN WHICH HALF THE POPULATION ARE KINGS AND THE OTHER HALF ARE EXPLOITED SLAVES WE WILL SEND UP IN FLAMES. After four tumultuous hours, mounted and foot police moved in with batons and water trucks, eventually scattering the marchers and clearing the square.

Through the months of ruckus, a commission initiated by Golda and approved by the government in February 1971 met regularly to investigate poverty and recommend reforms. Named the Prime Minister's Committee for Children and Youth in Distress, and known as the Katz Committee after its chairman, Yisrael Katz, it included 129 experts from a broad range of fields, such as housing, education, health, and labor. "Golda was very active in the commission's work," recalled Baruch Levy, responsible for implementing changes recommended. "She didn't want this to be just another report to put on the shelf. She would sit for six or seven hours at plenary sessions, smoking, drinking coffee, and concentrating on the deliberations."

The committee worked for two years before presenting its report to the government in June 1973. It called for bigger allowances for each child in large families, more low-income housing, tax benefits for the poor, subsidized rentals, and many other welfare programs. A few months after it appeared, the Yom Kippur War pushed social problems to the back burner while security and defense took top priority. Golda remained involved in the commission's work for a while after the war, and over time several of its suggestions came to fruition. Community centers and playgrounds for disadvantaged youth ranked high among them.

The Panthers split after a year or two into competing factions. Although their attempts to form a political party failed, their protests pushed the problems of North African and Middle Eastern Jews into public consciousness for the first time. "The State of Israel after the Panthers' rebellion is an altogether different place than it had been," says Kochavi Shemesh, "and the Katz Committee deserves credit for many of the changes that have taken place."

And Golda, who formed the commission and cared so profoundly about poverty in Israel?

"We give her no credit. She never understood that Sephardic Jews wanted to share the cake, to be partners with the administration. She just thought we were not nice."

26

Terror, Territories, and the Palestinian Question

For all the domestic demands pressing on Golda, violence on the outside most frightened and tormented her. As prime minister, she would have to contend with terrorist skyjackings, explosions, kidnappings, assassination attempts, and other assaults to a degree that no world leader before her could have imagined.

They began with the takeover of an El Al airliner in 1968, while she was still secretary-general of Israel's Labor Party. A little after midnight on July 23, two men burst into the cockpit of flight 426 flying from Rome to Tel Aviv. Waving guns and attacking crew members, they forced the pilot to redirect the plane to Algiers. After weeks of negotiations, all the hostages were freed and the Boeing 707 returned to the Israelis. But the men, along with a third accomplice, had pulled off the first and only successful hijacking of an El Al airplane. With that, they drew the world's attention to the cause of the Palestinian Arabs.

The organization behind the El Al hijacking was the Popular Front for the Liberation of Palestine (PFLP), an extremist Marxist group founded a year earlier by George Habash. The Palestine Liberation Organization (PLO), a larger and more moderate group (although Golda would hardly make that distinction), already existed, having been formed in 1964 at an Arab League summit in Cairo, with Ahmad Shukeiri as its chairman. An ineffectual leader, he would be replaced five years later by the wily and aggressive Yasser Arafat. Back in 1959, Arafat had founded the underground Fatah group dedicated to guerrilla warfare inside Israel. When he became chairman of the PLO, he turned it into an umbrella that included the PFLP, Fatah, and several smaller terrorist groups. They frequently operated independently, especially the PFLP, which made airplane hijacking its weapon of choice. But the PLO and Arafat would be the names Golda invoked most often as the personifications of terror against Israel.

Arafat had clear-cut plans: rid the region of Israel, gain control of the West Bank of the Jordan River, which Israel had captured from Jordan in 1967, and establish a Palestinian state in all of western Palestine. "The end of Israel is the goal of our struggle," he told Oriana Fallaci, "and it allows for neither compromise nor mediation." To help achieve that goal, he received financial backing from the established Arab states Egypt, Lebanon, and Syria.

The attacks came with the swiftness of machine gun fire. Golda had just begun her premiership when two pounds of TNT exploded in a Hebrew University cafeteria, wounding twenty-nine. In the same week, an explosion rocked a Jerusalem supermarket, killing two, and a grenade hurled at the Ramallah branch of Israel's Bank Leumi hurt an Arab depositor. In the weeks and months that followed, guerrillas launched Soviet-made Katyusha rockets against kibbutzim in the Jordan valley, massacred nine children and three adults in a school bus shelling near the *moshav* Avivim, and slipped across the borders into Israel to attack civilians and soldiers.

But the most sensational and deadly feats happened outside Israel itself. Terrorists opened fire on an El Al plane in Zurich, threw hand grenades at the airline's offices in Brussels and Athens—killing a Greek child—and assaulted passengers at Munich's airport lounge. They killed the wife of an Israeli diplomat at the embassy in Paraguay and—in one of their more brazen actions—attempted to assassinate David Ben-Gurion in Copenhagen.

On February 21, 1970, a Swissair jet headed for Tel Aviv exploded in midair after having taken off from Zurich Airport, killing all forty-seven passengers and crew members. As Israel mourned twenty Israeli and Jewish victims of the crash, Golda spoke bitterly of the "grief and rage" burning in her heart. The terror organizations that committed the act had "put themselves outside the laws and morality of human society," she said at a cabinet meeting. In the Knesset, she reviewed the series of attacks and called on the nations of the world and civil aviation boards to stop the murders by not agreeing to the terrorists' terms.

Among the Arab nations, only Jordan issued a statement of regret for the Swissair disaster, a courageous move in light of Egypt's and Syria's support for the militant organizations but in keeping with ties King Hussein had established with the West. The terrorists held no great love for Jordan. Some twenty years earlier, Hussein's grandfather King Abdullah had annexed the West Bank of the Jordan River, the territory designated for a Palestinian state in the UN resolution of 1947, absorbing a million Palestinian Arabs into his realm. Although Hussein lost that territory to Israel during the Six-Day War, half the population of Jordan was still of Palestinian origin. In an attempt to integrate all his subjects into a united kingdom, Hussein became the only Arab leader to grant citizenship to the Palestinian refugees who fled there during the Arab-Israeli wars. The rise of the PLO and other radical organizations undermined his unity goal. The militant young leaders, eager to build a power base in Jordan as well as the West Bank, opposed Hussein's rule.

Twice Palestinian terrorists tried to assassinate the king, but both times his loyalist Bedouin troops protected him. Short of being able to get rid of Hussein, the PLO built a state within a state for its own use in Jordan, putting its stamp on the country's daily life and providing training camps for the fedayeen. The guerrillas themselves strutted around Amman with loaded guns as if they owned it. Hussein seemed to be a drowning man, flailing about while he lost political control of his country.

A bloody showdown would change that. It began on September 6, 1970, with a spectacular PFLP hijacking of three airliners from different countries. Two of the hijacked aircraft, TWA and Swissair flights, were flown to a remote, scorching-hot landing strip in the Jordanian desert called Dawson's Field, which the jubilant terrorists dubbed "Revolution Airport." The third plane, a Pan American jet, was taken to Cairo and the next day, with passengers and crew barely escaping through emergency chutes, blown up, a coded warning to Egypt's president, Nasser, for having accepted the American-brokered cease-fire in the attrition war and drawn closer to Hussein. Another hijacked aircraft joined the two at Dawson's Field on September 9. With more than five hundred hostages in captivity, the hijackers demanded the release of Palestinian prisoners in Israeli and European jails. By September 12, they had freed all the hostages, except for fifty-five Jewish ones and some crew members, whom they hid in various locations. Then they blew up the three empty airliners, one after another, in an extravaganza the entire world's media witnessed. The last hostages were soon exchanged for seven jailed PFLP militants.

For Hussein, the hijackings and landings on Jordanian soil were a final insult, a direct challenge to his authority. After months of trying to make peace with the militants in his land, he decided to rid himself of them. With tanks and heavy artillery, his Bedouin army moved against strategic guerrilla positions in Amman and other cities, slaughtering thousands. In response, Syria, ally of the terrorist organizations, began sending tanks and other armored units across Jordan's northern border and occupied the town of Irbid. With "extreme anxiety," knowing that his forces were no match for the powerful Syrian army, Hussein appealed to Great Britain and the United States to enlist the help of Israel, the only neighboring power that could respond quickly. The British held off, but the Americans passed the appeal on.

In the grand ballroom of the New York Hilton hotel, Golda Meir was speaking to a thousand people at a United Jewish Appeal gala on the last day of a state visit to the United States, September 20, 1970. About ten minutes before she was to finish, Secret Service agents received an urgent phone call for her from America's national security adviser, Henry Kissinger. Rabbi Herbert Friedman, UJA head, explained that she could not take the call at that moment. When Israel's ambassador to Washington, Yitzhak Rabin, called back, Kissinger told him that King Hussein asked to have Israel's air force attack the Syrian invaders.

"Are you recommending that we respond to the Jordanian request?" Rabin asked. Israel would not act on this extraordinary plea without assurances that the United States approved.

Kissinger hesitated. He would bring an answer from the president in half an hour, he said. Rabin, with Golda now, was ushered into a small private room with a telephone.

She sat there, "a tired woman slumped in a chair, worn out from a week of traveling . . . having finished a tense, hour-long TV speech," Rabbi Friedman recalled, "to be faced with an agonizing request." Golda and Rabin decided to consult with the deputy prime minister, Yigal Allon, and the defense minister, Moshe Dayan, in Israel. They received a split opinion. Allon, who'd had several contacts with Hussein, advocated rescuing the "little king." Dayan had reservations. "We won't mourn if Hussein is replaced by someone willing to make peace with us," he later told a television audience. Golda and Rabin favored saving the king.

After conferring with the president, Kissinger assured Rabin that the United States would "look favorably upon an Israeli air attack," make good any material losses Israel suffered, and do its best to prevent Soviet interference on behalf of Syria. An hour later, Rabin gave him Golda's answer: Israel would send a reconnaissance flight over Jordan at first light to assess the situation. Within moments, Rabbi Friedman noted, she had reverted to "head of the government, commander-in-chief of the army . . . with a crisp authority in her voice."

In the end, Hussein didn't need help. Israel had massed troops on its border with Syria and flew Phantom jets low over the Syrian tanks in Jordan, sending a signal to Damascus not to pursue a war with its neighbor. At the same time, America's Sixth Fleet moved eastward in the Mediterranean toward the Syrian and Lebanon coasts, while its Eighty-Second Airborne Division stood poised on high alert, warnings to the Soviet Union not to intervene. With that support, the king used his own air and ground forces to drive the Syrians back to their own country. During the next months, he cracked down harder than ever on the Palestinian guerrillas who remained in Jordan. By mid-July 1971, his Bedouin army had routed the PLO from his land; a defeated Arafat fled to Lebanon with the remnants of his followers.

The terrorists would remember the month when Hussein began his onslaught against them as Black September.

For the larger Arab world, the civil war inside Jordan was the "biggest tragedy since the defeat of 1967," wrote Mahmoud Riad, Egypt's foreign minister. For Israel, the Jordanian-Syrian crisis marked a high point in its relations with the American administration. When it ended, Kissinger telephoned Rabin to convey President Nixon's gratitude to the prime minister. The United States, he said, was "fortunate in having an ally like Israel in the Middle East."

GOLDA MEIR HAD WARM FEELINGS for the king whose realm she helped save. From the earliest days of the Yishuv, his ancestral family, the Hashemite dynasty, had maintained cordial relations with Zionist leaders. In January 1919, Emir Faisal, Hussein's great-uncle, whom the British would name king of Iraq, reached an agreement with Chaim Weizmann that spoke of the "ancient bonds" between Arabs and Jews and urged that all necessary measures be taken to "encourage and stimulate immigration of Jews into Palestine." A few months later, he wrote an even more enthusiastic letter to Felix Frankfurter, asserting that Arabs and Jews were "cousins" and the Arabs looked "with the deepest sympathy" on the Zionist movement.

That ardor for Zionism cooled under pressure from Arab leaders in Syria and Palestine, and about a dozen years later Faisal denied having written "anything of that kind." Still, neither he nor his brother Abdullah, king of Transjordan, ever adopted the antagonistic attitude toward the Jews typical of Haj Amin al-Husseini, the mufti of Jerusalem. During the 1920s and 1930s, al-Husseini incited Arab riots against the Jews in

Palestine and later befriended Hitler. Al-Husseini's aggressiveness also threatened Abdullah's kingdom so that when the king and Golda met just before and after the UN partition of Palestine, their nations shared a common enemy. To Golda and Ben-Gurion's great disappointment, Abdullah joined the invading Arab forces against Israel in 1948, but the two countries found a relatively harmonious footing again after that war.

For his engagement with the Zionists and the West, Abdullah was shot dead by a Palestinian Arab as he walked to prayers at the al-Aqsa Mosque in the Old City of Jerusalem, his blood splattering on his fifteen-year-old grandson, Hussein bin Talal. In Hussein's recollection, a bullet aimed at him ricocheted off a medal fastened to a brand-new uniform he had worn that day at his grandfather's suggestion, sparing his life.

Hussein's memory of his beloved grandfather was frozen in time, Golda was to say, and the tragedy molded his life. As king—he was crowned at the age of seventeen—he learned to be cautious in dealing with the forces around him, whether Israel, the Arab states, the Western powers, or the Palestinians in his midst, skillfully balancing the competing pulls from all sides. But he made a disastrous error by entering the 1967 Arab-Israeli War after Levi Eshkol promised that nothing would happen to Jordan if he stayed out. By fighting alongside Egypt and Syria, he lost half his kingdom to Israel—the West Bank and East Jerusalem, which Abdullah had seized in 1948. Even so, during the postwar years, Golda and others secretly negotiated with him in an attempt to link much of the West Bank with Jordan again, the most logical solution they saw to the vast numbers of Palestinian Arabs in the region.

In the context of that "Jordanian option," as it became known, Golda made one of the most provocative statements of her career. "There was no such thing as Palestinians," she bluntly told Frank Giles of the London *Sunday Times*. She went on: "When was there an independent Palestinian people with a Palestinian state? It was either southern Syria before the First World War, and then it was a Palestine including Jordan. It was not as though there was a Palestinian people in Palestine considering itself as a Palestinian people and we threw them out and took their country away from them. They did not exist."

She meant that historically there had never been a cohesive Palestinian nation in the region, and she tried to explain that some years later. She had been misquoted, she wrote in *The New York Times*. "My actual words were, 'There is no Palestinian people. There are Palestinian refugees.'" And she elaborated: "When in 1921 I came to Palestine . . . we, the Jewish pioneers, were the avowed Palestinians. So we were named in the world."

She was not alone in equating Palestinian Arabs with refugees. The Security Council Resolution 242 about the territories spoke only of a refugee problem, with no mention of a political role for the Palestinians, and in discussions of the Middle East the nations of the world almost always focused on established states like Egypt and Syria and rarely on Palestinians. But Golda was after more than that in her pronouncement about the Palestinians. In denying the existence of a separate Palestinian identity, she also denied the need for a separate Palestinian state between Israel and Jordan, a subject that had begun to surface. When the British created Transjordan in 1921, she explained time and again, they sliced it out of the larger region that had historically been Palestine. "Now did that really make such a terrible cleavage between the people on the East Bank and the people on the West Bank?" she would ask, and answer, "They were the same people . . . what is the difference between an Arab that lived in Amman and an Arab that lived in Nablus?" Because, as she saw it, there was no ethnic difference, Jordan was the state for Palestinians, with no need for another.

"There will be no third state in the area," she said emphatically. "In that area there must be two states, one Jewish and one Arab. What the Arabs call theirs is not our business." In fact, they could call it "Palestine if they like."

Moreover, she frequently pointed out, "nobody heard of a Palestinian entity before 1967." Where were the Palestinian Arabs? "What makes them now more Palestinian than they were until 1967?" Their nationalism, she implied, had been aroused only since Israel took over, proof that a Palestinian state on the West Bank, undoubtedly run by the PLO, would be a "time bomb" against Israel. "Arafat says he doesn't want to liberate the West Bank. He wants to liberate the entire Palestinian area," she told interviewers. He also said he would negotiate with Arab countries to take back Israeli Jews who came from them. "Iraqi Jews should go back to Iraq . . . Libyan Jews should go back to . . . Libya . . . And I should go back to Milwaukee."

To Golda, Arafat bore shades of the mufti in his wish to eliminate Israel. Jordan's king, Hussein, on the other hand, represented moderation, like his grandfather Abdullah. Golda chose the Jordanian option, not the Palestinian. So did most Israeli leaders—Shimon Peres, Yigal Allon, Yitzhak Rabin, and Abba Eban among them—and the American Henry Kissinger.

Only minuscule numbers, generally on the far left, thought differently about the Palestinians. One of those was Arie Lova Eliav, a Knesset member and respected establishment figure. After the 1967 war, still a junior government minister, he received Prime Minister Levi Eshkol's permission to "roam around" the captured territories for six months and learn about the people in them. On returning from his tour, he said to Eshkol, "Look, there is an emerging Palestinian people there. They have their own heroes, their own bitterest enemies, but it is a national movement." Ill and worn out, Eshkol paid no heed. Eliav then put his ideas into a series of articles for *Davar* that he gathered into a booklet called *New Targets for Israel*. It spoke of the Palestinians as the key to solving Israel's problem with the Arab world and of the need for Israel to talk with Palestinian leaders. Most radically, it suggested that Israel give the West Bank and Gaza to the Palestinian national movement to create a state, although with all sorts of security arrangements. He sent the booklet to Golda and got no response.

A year later, Golda became prime minister and Eliav was elected secretary-general of the Labor Party. A few weeks after that, she received a copy of *Time* magazine that made her gasp. In an article titled "The Lion's Roar," Eliav told the correspondent Marlin Levin some of the ideas he had advocated in his booklet. "The first thing we have to do is to recognize that the Palestinian Arabs exist as an infant nation," he said. He referred to "two states" that can "live equally together," as the only solution to the Palestinian problem.

Golda phoned Eliav and invited him over. At five that evening, she personally greeted him at the door and ushered him into her kitchen, where she offered him tea and cake. On the table, she had placed a copy of *Time* opened to the article about him, with the most offending sentences underlined in "blazing red." She lit a cigarette. "Lova, have you seen *Time* magazine?" she asked. "Of course," he said. "And I assume you will deny several sentences in it?" she pressed on. "Why should I deny them? I think Levin did an excellent job," he answered. He reminded her of the booklet he had sent her, with the same ideas. "Really . . . I don't remember ever getting it," she said. "Maybe the mail . . ."

She remained silent. "So these are your views?" she finally said. "Yes, these are my views." Another long silence. And then Golda's zinger, which, in later years, Eliav would quote frequently. After asking him to call a meeting of the party's central committee, she said, "We'll both come and I will say, 'You have elected a young and clever secretary-general, but you have elected me as an old and foolish prime minister. So you have to choose. Either you want the young and clever secretary-general or you want the old and foolish prime minister.'" With some effort, Eliav talked her out of the meeting, convincing her that they should agree to disagree.

Things would never again be the same between them. Golda had once considered him her possible successor. He had a sterling record as a Haganah member in pre-state Israel, a soldier in the Jewish Brigade during World War II, a leader of the illegal immigrant movement, and a Mossad operative. She'd been close to his family; he proudly showed this author a photograph of her with his son as a young child. And he cherished a collection of her selected speeches that she sent him, signed "with admiration." After the *Time* piece, she no longer included him in the most sensitive of her kitchen cabinet meetings or treated him as an insider. "I was a litmus paper case in terms of the black-and-white judgments she made," he recalled. "I was white as snow one day, and then I was black as night." He resigned as party secretary-general in April 1971.

THE PARTY CONSENSUS was with Golda, not Eliav, but even he accepted the idea of linking a Palestinian state with Jordan. In the hope of solving the Palestinian problem through Jordan, Israeli officials held scores of secret meetings with King Hussein, many of which have come to light but probably not all. Some of those meetings were arranged through friends of the king, some through Israel's Mossad, and some through the American CIA, with whom the king clandestinely worked from time to time. The meetings took place in odd venues: at a private apartment in Paris, at the Dorchester hotel in London, on a ship in the Gulf of Aqaba, in the clinic of Hussein's private Jewish physician Dr. Emmanuel Herbert, in the king's own palace in Amman. The king, who loved to fly, once piloted an Israeli helicopter to Tel Aviv for a meeting and became emotional while flying over the Jerusalem sites he had lost. The Israelis used the code name "Charles" for him and kept the meetings top secret with only vague reports occasionally leaking out. When a *New York Times* reporter once asked Golda whether she had met the king, she answered, "I met his grandfather." "But have you met Hussein?" the correspondent persisted. "Let me be an advocate for Israel," she said, not denying any meetings but firmly changing the subject.

She met Hussein for the first time in Paris in 1965, when she was foreign minister. Territories were not the issue then, but both leaders wanted to maintain a cordial relationship. Over the years, their countries had cooperated in fighting terrorism, controlling mosquitoes, and handling economic issues, and just a year earlier they had concluded a treaty for sharing the waters of the Jordan River. The young king—he was only twenty-nine—was unusually short, but he stood ramrod straight and carried himself with an air of dignity softened by a wide, friendly smile. Golda liked him. "I have wanted to meet you for a long time," he said as they shook hands, "and I am pleased about this meeting." He spoke of her meetings with his grandfather and how much it meant to him to follow in that tradition. In the course of their talk, he assured Golda that he would not permit foreign troops on his soil and that he would work to keep the border between their countries quiet. He hoped Israel would use its influence in Washington to get his country economic aid. "It was a good meeting," the king recalled. They had talked about their dreams for their children and grandchildren "to live in an era of peace in the region."

A year after the 1967 war, as a sign of friendship, Golda sent a note to Hussein through Theodore Sorensen, who had been a senior adviser to President Kennedy and was visiting in the area: "I hope Your Majesty knows that Israel is your best friend in the Middle East." When Sorensen returned to Jerusalem, he reported that the king had smiled and replied, "There are some people who believe I am Israel's best friend in the Middle East."

They were, in fact, each other's best friend in the region, which is why they kept up their contacts. It helped also that the two leaders enjoyed and respected each other. Sometimes, in an almost motherly way, Golda told Hussein anecdotes—which he loved hearing—about himself as a little boy when she met with his grandfather. At one meeting, in May 1970, held at an abandoned castle on Coral Island in the Bay of Aqaba, they had a festive dinner, and Golda served the meal to him, his officers, and her own ministers. They had a good time, the king told an aide, but accomplished little. Golda, of course, was turning on her charm for more than a good time. She hoped these meetings would lead to an agreement about the West Bank and Jordan and with that a permanent peace settlement. Yigal Allon had already presented much of his plan to Hussein and his adviser, Zaid al-Rifai, at an earlier meeting. Pulling out a map, he had pointed to the areas Israel was willing to give back, about 70 percent of the West Bank, while it held on to the rest for security purposes. The king grew angry, and Rifai had jumped in to say that Israel's keeping 30 percent of the territory was "totally unacceptable." They could reach a peace deal only if Israel returned everything taken in 1967. Even later, for all the goodwill between them after Israel helped Jordan in its crisis with Syria, they failed to arrive at an agreement.

That was the situation when Hussein took Golda by surprise on March 15, 1972, by announcing to great fanfare on Jordanian radio his own plan for a "United Arab Kingdom." Speaking from his palace in Amman, the king called for a federation consisting of "Palestine" on the West Bank and Jordan on the East Bank, but open also to "any other liberated Palestinian territory whose inhabitants wish to join us," a probable reference to Gaza. His plan would have East Jerusalem serve as the capital of Palestine, and Amman the capital of both Jordan and the kingdom as a whole, which Hussein would rule. At first blush, the plan might have seemed just what Golda desired: a West Bank linkage with Jordan under Jordanian authority. Much of the Arab world thought so and vilified Hussein for his "grave collusion" with the Zionist enemy. In reality, the king's scheme fell far short of Israel's dream plan. Hussein had ignored what the London *Daily Telegraph* facetiously called "the little matter" of Israel's control over the West Bank. That failure gave Mrs. Meir more than enough grounds to blast his plan "ruthlessly."

Standing before the Knesset, she described the king's presentation of his program as a "pretentious and one-sided" pronouncement. "This is a plan dealing with territories that are not under his control and that he strives to obtain by 'liberation,'" she said. "No unilateral declaration . . . will bring Jordan one inch nearer to peace . . . There is only one way that has any prospects: namely serious negotiations for a peaceful solution."

Less than a week after that speech, she and Hussein met in secret again, in an air-conditioned tent in the Araba Desert. She berated him for not consulting her about his federation plan before announcing it, considering the many contacts they'd had, and considering also that the two shared a computerized direct phone line that he could have used to call her. He explained apologetically that he had not intended to implement the plan until he had a peace agreement with Israel. That prompted Golda to ask him whether he was prepared to make a deal with Israel, separate from the other Arab states, and if it could be based on border changes that Israel considered urgent to its security. Yes, he could make an agreement with Israel under the proper circumstances, Hussein said, but, no, he would never consent to border changes. The entire West Bank, including East Jerusalem, needed to be in his federation, although he was willing to demilitarize the region. He was also willing to have

Jerusalem serve as the capital of both nations without formally dividing it again, a suggestion Golda considered unacceptable to Israel, which regarded the united city as its "eternal capital."

The two leaders thrashed over the same subjects again—and again—at two more secret meetings that year. Moshe Dayan, who attended both, urged the king to arrange a settlement with Golda, because, he explained, no leader in Israel was more authoritative than she and none more willing to make far-reaching concessions. "Her line would be more convenient to you than my line," he said. That was true. Her "line" would have Israel keep only the unpopulated areas of the West Bank, where some Jewish settlements had been built. Dayan, the hard-liner, wanted to hold on to the entire bank, and the IDF bases that had been set up there. "I believe I have a majority in the Knesset and in the government for such a program," Golda said of her proposal, even if Gahal and the religious parties opposed it. Again, the king rejected the offer. He could not face the Arab world—and probably not survive—if he were to accede to the Israelis. Although he and Golda would meet several more times, talk of a peace settlement had reached a stalemate.

What, then, to do about the West Bank and other territories? The debate in Israel, low-key at first, became contentious, its divergent positions hardened with time.

Yigal Allon had been one of the first to formulate a plan, and although he changed and refined it several times, at its heart still lay the concept of keeping an Israeli presence in the captured territories for security purposes but restricting that presence to sparsely populated Arab areas. Yet, paradoxically, Allon became a champion of a group of religious settlers who planted themselves in the densely populated Arab town of Hebron. For Jews, that town was soaked in tradition, revered for centuries as the burial place of the biblical patriarchs and matriarchs. Jews had lived in Hebron for centuries, until they fled during the Arab massacre in 1929. Allon believed its rich Jewish history gave settlers the right to return. During Passover, in 1968, with the army's permission, a group led by Rabbi Moshe Levinger held a seder in the Park Hotel. The next day, against orders, they refused to leave the city. Allon arranged to have arms sent to them for their protection and was one of the first government ministers to visit them. The government finally forced them to move to quarters in a military compound and eventually permitted them to build the large settlement of Kiryat Arba on the city's outskirts.

Despite his hawkishness, Moshe Dayan opposed a Jewish settlement in Hebron, because he thought it raised unnecessary tensions. This was the same Dayan, however, who wanted Israel to govern as much of the West Bank as possible—without formally annexing it—and to build settlements that would become permanent even if there were to be a peace treaty. Allon's plan, he said, smacked of the British White Paper that had restricted Jewish settlement during the pre-state era. Born in the Land of Israel and educated in biblical lore, Dayan felt a strong emotional pull to the West Bank. Here lay the center of ancient Judaism. Here Joshua had blasted the walls of Jericho with his trumpets, here in the city of Beersheva the tomb of the matriarch Rachel still beckoned to the faithful, and here Israelite kings had ruled the northern tribes from their capital in Shomron. Dayan argued that if the government wanted to forbid Jews to live in those regions, it might just as well forbid the study of the Bible in school.

Dayan's admirer and Rafi colleague Shimon Peres hailed his comrade's military rule of the territories over the years as "one of the greatest successes and attainments of the state." Pinhas Sapir, who had opposed Dayan's plans for the territories in print in 1968, continued to rail against the "creeping annexation" they represented and the "masters and servants" society that would result from incorporating vast numbers of Arabs without giving them citizenship.

And Golda Meir tried to straddle all sides. In an interview with Louis Heren, deputy editor of *The Times* of London, in March 1971, she spoke of her willingness to negotiate "everything" for a peace agreement, including the final borders of the West Bank. The Gahal Party and religious groups wanted to retain the entire Judaea and Samaria, she said, but she had no interest in placing all of those territories, with their 600,000 Arabs, under Israeli control. She also spoke of withdrawing completely from a demilitarized Sinai Peninsula but including Israeli troops in an international patrol of the area. Although she insisted on keeping Jerusalem and the Golan Heights, her emphasis on what she was willing to give up rather than what she wanted to keep caused a minor sensation. Abroad, the international community attacked her for not speaking of a total withdrawal from all the occupied territories. At home, Gahal and the religious parties attacked her for her willingness to withdraw from any of the territories. In their anger, they attempted, and failed, to force a no-confidence vote against her. Most surprising to her, the Israeli Left, usually her harshest critics, enthusiastically praised her for her "sensible and reasonable" proposal, to their minds putting her in the camp of the doves.

Golda claimed she did not say anything she had not said before, but from the outside her plans seemed more explicit and compromising, and especially significant for being said to a foreign, instead of an Israeli, newspaper. Heren later recalled that she had been distraught and tearful that day, having just returned from the military funeral of a young soldier whose grandfather had been murdered during the Arab riots of the 1930s and whose father fell during the War of Independence. "Why can't they let us live in peace . . . ?" she had cried. When Heren asked if she wanted to delete anything from the record, considering the emotional strain she was under, she assured him she would stand by every word she had said, as she did. But the fuss that interview aroused reinforced for her the wisdom of not spelling out detailed borders until face-to-face peace talks took place. "I have to confess," she said at a party secretariat meeting a year later, "and maybe this is a sin, but . . . I still do not think the time for that has come."

There were a few things she did wish to make clear, however. Unlike Dayan and even Allon to some extent, she did not yearn for the biblical "land of the fathers." True, "after two thousand years of longing and dreaming," Israel had a right to celebrate what it had achieved in the Six-Day War, but deliberations about the territories needed to center strictly on matters of "security and peace," not nostalgia. She felt that way even about Hebron, laden as it was with history. She accepted the idea, which neither Dayan nor Allon did, that if Israel signed a peace treaty with Jordan, it would have to return that city. For the present, she argued, how could an Israeli government pass legislation banning Jews from any part of the Holy Land? For the future, she firmly supported forcing Jews out of other illegal settlements on the West Bank before they entrenched themselves, as had the Hebron group.

TO MILITANT PALESTINIAN ARABS, the fine print of differences between Golda Meir's approach to the settlements and Moshe Dayan's or Yigal Allon's meant little. They wanted Israel out of the territories, and the region, altogether, and they continued to hone their skills at forcing the world to pay attention to them. On May 8, 1972, Black September, an extremist offshoot of the PLO, named for the guerrilla expulsions from Jordan, embarked on a "grandiose" plan. Wielding pistols and explosives, four members—two men and two women—seized command of a Sabena airline Boeing 707 flying from Brussels to Tel Aviv. When they landed in Tel Aviv, they threatened to blow up the plane and its passengers unless Israel released more than three hundred Palestinian prisoners, to be flown to Cairo. In a daring Israeli operation, while the government pretended to bargain with the terrorists, commandos disguised as mechanics arrived to "repair" the plane (which they had secretly disabled). Within seconds, they burst inside, killed the two male terrorists, captured the women, and freed the passengers. "Our boys acted marvelously, just marvelously," Golda clucked, like a proud mother hen.

Furious after this humiliation, the terrorists quickly planned another spectacle, and this time they succeeded. Three members of the Japanese Red Army, an international group working with the Popular Front for the Liberation of Palestine, arrived at Lod Airport on an Air France flight in the evening of May 30, 1972. Dressed as businessmen, they waited with other passengers for their luggage. When it came, they calmly opened their cases, pulled out submachine guns and grenades, and started shooting all around. They massacred twenty-four people and wounded more than seventy before two of them were killed and the third captured. Most of the dead were Puerto Rican Catholics on a pilgrimage to Israel.

Golda received dozens of letters and cables from horrified heads of state, including an apology from the Japanese prime minister and a moving telegram from King Hussein. Using the code name "March" and addressing her as "April," he condemned the "sick souls that plan, execute, or praise" such an "atrocious crime." Golda replied that she was "deeply touched" by his message and appreciative of his public utterances condemning the murders.

Lod became a prelude to Munich.

At 8:45 a.m. on September 5, 1972, Golda Meir received word from the Israeli embassy in Bonn, Germany, that terrorists had invaded the Olympic Games in Munich and were holding Israeli athletes hostage. The heart-stopping news hit her at a particularly vulnerable time. Her sister Sheyna lay close to death after years of having suffered from Alzheimer's disease. Golda had visited her every Friday and probably planned to be at her bedside at Loewenstein Hospital in Ra'anana during these final days. Instead, she spent anxious hours on the phone tracking the harrowing events in Munich. After initial confusion and the sickening sense that once again Jews were unsafe in Germany, she and her ministers sorted out some of the details: In the dark, early dawn hours that Tuesday, eight Black September terrorists dressed as athletes had scaled the fence surrounding the Olympic Village. Changing clothes and blackening their faces, they stole toward building No. 31 on Connollystrasse, which housed the Israeli sportsmen. After breaking in to two of the apartments, they shot and killed two Israelis who tried to stop them— Moshe Weinberg and Yossef Romano—and, wielding pistols, bound and tethered another nine with heavy rope. Twenty years later, the athletes' wives would learn from secret German files that the men had been brutally beaten. Romano had also been castrated, probably after he died.

The terrorists demanded the release of 232 prisoners from Israeli jails and 2 from German prisons or they would begin executing their captives. After consulting with her cabinet, Golda responded through the Foreign Ministry that Israel did not negotiate with terrorists and that it expected the West German government to do everything in its power to rescue the hostages peacefully. "If we should give in," she told a reporter, "then no Israeli anywhere in the world will feel that his life is safe . . . It's blackmail of the worst kind."

A little later, at a meeting of the Knesset Foreign Affairs and Defense Committee, she called on the Olympic Organizing Committee to suspend the games, which had been continuing throughout the attack. When the committee finally and reluctantly agreed to a suspension, a number of players grew angry at the delay and Israel's refusal to accede to the terrorists. "Golda Meir, holding the fucking world to ransom again!" an Irish athlete shouted.

At her home in Jerusalem, Golda and her key aides followed every step of the terror, receiving regular bulletins from the Foreign Ministry, which had a hotline to the German government. With dozens of reporters and TV cameramen in Munich for the Olympics, viewers across the globe watched in horror as the macabre drama unfolded on their television screens. In the afternoon, Golda dispatched the Mossad head, Zvi Zamir, to Munich to monitor the situation and work with officials there. A thin, soft-spoken man not easily given to smiles, Zamir would later report that the police commander in charge treated him with "extreme impatience" and that the whole operation "was carried out badly and ineptly." The German police, he would say, "did not make even a minimal effort to save lives."

The terrorists had demanded two helicopters to carry them and the hostages from the Olympic Village to the military airfield of Fürstenfeldbruck and an airplane to fly them from there to Egypt. Thousands of spectators looked on silently as the terrorists led the bound and blindfolded hostages single file to the waiting helicopters. Zamir was taken to the airport together with German officials and could only watch help-lessly when the police prematurely opened fire against the terrorists. In the confusion and gun fighting that followed, the terrorists murdered all the hostages in the helicopters and then set one of the copters afire with a hand grenade.

At one in the morning, Israeli time, as the entire nation waited for news from Munich, German sources reported that the hostages had been rescued after an airport battle. Golda ordered a bottle of cognac for her and her advisers, and throughout the country people raised their glasses in toasts. By morning, the grim truth became known. "I am sorry to tell you," Zamir reported by phone to Golda, "but the athletes were not rescued . . . Not one of them survived."

In the United States, on the morning of September 6, President Rich-ard Nixon and his adviser Henry Kissinger consulted on how to handle the tragic news from Munich. "Mrs. Meir, and she's the only one that can do it," Nixon said, "should call upon the International Olympic Com-mittee to go forward with those games." Kissinger agreed. She can say, Nixon continued, " 'Well, that's what my boys would have wanted.' It will make them look good . . . you see, the trouble with the Jews is that they've always played these things in terms of outrage." Again Kissinger agreed. He said he had been on the phone half the night with the Israelis, who had wanted the Americans to appeal to the committee to cancel the games. "They're crazy," Nixon said. "But they want to look good, don't they? . . . You see that's exactly the reason Mrs. Meir should do it." As for the United States, Secretary of State Rogers had suggested that the pres-ident declare a national day of mourning and lower flags to half-staff. Kissinger disagreed. "It's not our day of mourning, Mr. President . . . God, I am Jewish. I've had thirteen members of my family killed . . . but I think you have to think also of the anti-Semitic woes in this country. If we let our policy be run by the Jewish community . . ." They decided that the president would call on Americans to go to church for a moment of silence during the funeral in Israel for the slain athletes. He himself would slip into a nearby church for five minutes. "That's my moment of silence," he said, moving on to other business.

In Israel, Golda received word that President Nixon did not want to be asked to pull America's athletes out of the games. Although angered and pained, she abided by those wishes. In Munich's Olympic Stadium, where the circle of flags flew at half-mast, a crowd of eighty-four thou-sand attended a memorial service for the murdered Israelis. Avery Brundage, president of the International Olympic Committee, announced that the games would go on again the next day so as not to allow the terrorists to win by destroying the "goodwill" of the Olympic movement. It could be said, of course, that the terrorists *had* won by pushing Israel out of the games while the rest of the world played on.

On Thursday, September 7, Israel held its mourning ceremony at Lod Airport, where the remains of the fallen athletes had arrived in an El Al plane. Thousands joined the men's families at the rites, many sobbing openly before the line of coffins, each covered with the nation's colors. Golda, so devastated by the murders, could not be at the ceremony. Sheyna had died late on Wednesday night, aged eighty-three, and the prime minister and her family gathered at the municipal funeral parlor in Tel Aviv before driving to the family plot at the Nahalat Yitzhak Cemetery for the burial. Zalman Shazar, Israel's president, embraced her warmly before he led the long cortege of mourners, including many government leaders who had come directly from the Lod Airport memorial. Haggard and sorrowing, Golda faced her sister's grave. In a low voice choked with emotion, she delivered a eulogy for the woman who had been the idol of her youth. "You were my guide ever since I was a little girl," she said. "You demanded a lot of me, you never gave in." And she spoke of Sheyna's humility and all she had done for the family. Among the condolence letters she received was one from King Hussein.

SHE HAD LITTLE TIME TO mourn her sister; the Munich massacre dominated everything, the government, the media, the street. Soon after the scope of the tragedy reached her, Golda received a telegram from the German ambassador in Israel conveying the sympathy of West Germany's chancellor, Willy Brandt. In her return cable, she praised Germany for its "desperate attempt to save the lives of our sportsmen without yielding to brutal intimidation." Golda, who broke with Ben-Gurion in part because of his friendship with West Germany, now recognized that country's importance to Israel as an ally and go-between with Egypt and the Soviet Union. She sought to dampen criticism of it and maintain good relations, especially with Brandt, a socialist leader with whom she felt a common bond. Then came Zvi Zamir's damning report about the Germans' incompetence and indifference to human life in handling the crisis.

The report led to an angry confrontation between the Israeli government and the West German, the very kind of dispute Golda most wanted to avoid. Zamir's evaluation was translated into English and sent to the West German government. About the same time, the Germans instituted an internal investigation, which cleared their police of any wrongdoing. While accusations and counteraccusations flew between the two countries, Golda appointed a committee, headed by Pinhas Koppel, to investigate Israel's own role in the disaster. In addition to the Germans' failures, the committee faulted Israel's intelligence agencies and other officers for not providing sufficient security for the Olympic athletes. Some government officials rejected the Koppel report as going too far in blaming Israel, but as the country's highest-ranking minister Golda accepted ultimate responsibility for the debacle. If she were just a regular minister, she would resign, she said, but she could not, knowing that her resignation would lead to the fall of the government and a political crisis. "It is sad and bitter for me," she said. Eventually, three Israeli security officials were asked for their resignations, and Golda turned her attention to tracking down terrorists "wherever we can reach them."

An appalling new event speeded up that work. Six weeks after the Munich catastrophe, three terrorists hijacked a German Lufthansa plane en route from Beirut to Munich. As their price for not exploding the plane with its passengers, the hijackers demanded freedom for the three captured Munich terrorists (the other five had been killed in the gunfight at the airport). Israel urged the German government not to yield to the demand, unaware that it had capitulated almost immediately. The hijackers and the three freed terrorists flew off in the Lufthansa plane from the city of Zagreb to Libya, where they let the passengers go. Forty years after the event, the German magazine *Der Spiegel* claimed that before the massacre Germany and Bavaria had ignored warnings of a terrorist attack. Afterward, German authorities cooperated with terrorist leaders in the hope of dissuading them from further attacks in their country.

The release of the terrorists awakened old hatreds. "Nazism," the "Holocaust," the "old Germany"—the terms flew from Israelis' minds into public condemnation. Although Golda strongly denounced the German action in the Knesset, she carefully avoided such linkage. She saw no point in alienating Brandt, who had opposed the Nazis and was now in the midst of a reelection campaign. Nevertheless, with deteriorating relations between the two countries, Brandt sent her an angry message expressing his pain at the things being said in Israel. "With all due force I must contradict parallels being drawn to a criminal period of German policy," he wrote. He explained that the government decided to release the terrorists to save lives and in the future would "oppose vigorously" any terrorist attack. The German ambassador in Israel presented the message to the prime minister, and she accepted it graciously, emphasizing in her return message that her country knew very well the difference between freeing the terrorists and the dreadful period of the Shoah. Her meeting with the ambassador and her conciliatory words defused the tensions. Less than a year later, Brandt made a state visit to Israel, smoothing out relations between the two nations again.

Israel initially struck back at the terrorists even more fiercely than people expected it to. Its warplanes flew punishing bombing missions on guerrilla camps and PLO bases in Syria and Lebanon, and its tank forces and armored units smashed bridges and destroyed houses in Lebanon suspected of harboring PLO operatives. But to many Israelis, that response fell short of the scope and brutality of events in Munich. And the world's general indifference to the mounting terror attacks— Germany was not the only country that surrendered to terrorists in a bargain for peace—made it seem to them that Israel needed to take matters into its own hands.

Within days of the Munich massacre, Golda spoke somberly of methodical warfare against the terrorists "with everything required for this far-flung and dangerous front line." At a meeting in her office, she also promised family members that Israel would hunt down all those responsible for the murders. To aid in that mission, she appointed Major General Aharon Yariv, who had retired as director of military intelligence, as her personal adviser on counterterrorist activities. If there were tensions between Yariv and the Mossad chief, Zvi Zamir, because of overlapping responsibilities, she ignored them, and the two still managed to work well together. Together they came to her with a plan for eliminating Black September leaders and other terror chiefs. It would be the first use in the world of "targeted assassinations" on a large scale.

"It was not about vengeance," Zamir insists, even though that is how most books and films on the subject have portrayed the operation. "It was about preventing terrorism in the future and deterring terrorists from considering attacks against Israeli targets." He had raised the possibility of carrying Israel's war against terror abroad before, but Golda wanted no part of it, certain that European countries would act against terrorists themselves once the hijackings began. She discovered soon enough that they did nothing. Terrorists roamed freely around Europe, and some countries did not even allow El Al security guards to be armed.

Too often, when European authorities did arrest terrorists, they quickly set them free, as the Germans had.

Even after Munich, Golda resisted the plan Zamir and Yariv presented. "As a woman she was not very exhilarated by the idea," Yariv told a BBC reporter. Golda might have said that being a woman had nothing to do with her lack of enthusiasm. Being head of a state, she was more concerned about her "boys" becoming involved in illegal activities on foreign soil. And other things bothered her. People would be killed without court trials. "If we do this, what makes us different from the Arabs?" she asked. With Zamir and Yariv's insistence and the consent of the entire cabinet, she finally relented, justifying her decision by blaming the terrorists for creating a situation in which Israel did what it felt it had to do.

The people marked for death were Black September operatives involved in Munich and others who posed severe threats to the country. After a long internal investigation, Zamir would submit a name to Golda, and she, along with a few cabinet members, would make the final decision. This secret "tribunal" came to be known as Committee X. Sometimes she merely nodded her head to indicate her acceptance of a name. Sometimes she and the others postponed judgment for months, even years. But gradually, the message reached the terrorists. A man might be shot on his way home, another answer a phone that exploded, cars would be blown up, an apartment stormed, rockets fired at a house. There was no place to hide from Israel's wrath.

Then, in the Norwegian town of Lillehammer, on July 21, 1973, Israeli agents made a dreadful mistake. They killed a Moroccan waiter, Ahmed Bouchiki, whom they mistook for Ali Hassan Salameh, the "Red Prince," mastermind of the Munich massacre. (They killed Salameh later, in 1979.) The scandal, a nightmare for Golda, shook the foundations of the Mossad. Yet even with that disaster, and several Mossad agents jailed in Norway as a result, Zvi Zamir maintains that the pursuit of the terrorists achieved its purpose. "We succeeded in putting an end to the type of terror that was perpetrated," he says, referring to international terrorism.

BUT THE TERRORISTS HAD ALSO achieved their goal: promoting Palestinian claims across the globe. Golda tasted the bitter fruits of their success during an audience with Pope Paul VI on January 15, 1973. Israel's ambassador to Rome, Amiel Najar, had arranged the audience to take place after Golda left a Socialist International conference in Paris. According to some reports, a terrorist plan to assassinate her in Paris as well as a plot to shoot missiles at the plane carrying her from Paris to Rome had both been foiled, thanks to sharp-eyed Mossad agents. Golda arrived safely at Rome's Leonardo da Vinci Airport, ringed for her protection by more than a thousand police armed with submachine guns. Other officers guarded her during her drive to the Villa Madama, a luxurious Renaissance palace reserved by the government for important visitors.

She was excited about meeting the pope. The Vatican did not have diplomatic relations with Israel, and although Abba Eban had met the pontiff in the past, she would be the first Israeli prime minister—and the first female head of state—to do so. In one of her "I, Goldie Mabovitch of Pinsk" moments of awe beforehand, she marveled that the daughter of a lowly carpenter was appearing before the head of the all-powerful Roman Catholic Church. "Just a minute, Golda," one of her aides kibbitzed. "Carpentry is a very respectable profession around here." She dressed in black, as required of women for papal audiences, and had planned to cover her head with a black lace mantilla like the ones she had seen the Kennedy sisters wear when the pope visited the United Nations. Told that only Catholics wear such shawls, she had an old black hat flown to her from her home in Tel Aviv. She was not about to buy a new hat for which she had no further use.

Honor guards lined the way as she entered the Apostolic Palace, at 12:15 p.m., along with Ambassador Najar. The Vatican foreign minister and a translator joined the pope. Golda spoke in English, the pope in Italian; she addressed him as "Your Holiness," and he called her "Your Excellency." At times, she couldn't shake off the sense that this man of the cross represented the symbol under which Jews had been murdered for generations. But the thought that the head of the church was sitting "face to face with a Jewess from Israel" also tickled her.

The meeting began courteously, with the pope lauding it as "a historic moment." It quickly slipped downhill when he began criticizing Israel for its handling of the Arab refugee situation, its dealings with the Palestinians, and its harsh reprisals against terrorists. In an interview later with *Maariv*, Golda quoted him as saying that the Jewish people, who should be merciful, behaved fiercely in its own country. "I can't stand it when we are talked to like that," she told the reporter Dov Goldstein. She responded with her well-worn memory of having been a child in

Kiev watching her father board up the door in fear of a pogrom. "When we were merciful, and we didn't have a homeland, and we were weak— then they led us to the gas chamber," she said. They spoke quietly, never raising their voices when they disagreed but gazing steadily at each other. "His eyes bored deep into me, and I looked back with an open, strong, and honest gaze," she recalled. "I decided I would not lower my eyes under any circumstances. And I didn't." The meeting ended on a better note at 1:30, with the pope thanking Golda for Israel's care of Christian holy places and presenting her with an inscribed silver dove.

The Israel embassy and the Vatican worked out a satisfactory press release about the meeting. As it was being published, the Vatican press officer, Federico Alessandrini, issued a "verbal note" that he wrote, undoubtedly with the approval of papal higher-ups. It emphasized that Golda Meir had not been invited by the pope, but had requested the audience, and that the pope had granted it because of his desire for peace and his interest in the defense of the weak, "most of all the Palestinian refugees." A "diplomatic slap in the face," as one journalist labeled it, the statement was plainly designed to reassure the Arab states of the papacy's closeness to them. At a press conference that evening, Golda said pointedly, "I did not break into the Vatican." The meeting had been arranged through discussions between the two sides. Despite the Alessandrini statement, she told the press that the papal audience had great "historic value" and was much appreciated by her and her people. The next day the pope sent her additional gifts, a rare edition of the Bible and a Vatican Library catalog. After she returned to Israel, she sent him a facsimile of a fragment from the Dead Sea Scrolls and a gracious thank-you note, for which the Vatican thanked her cordially. The air between them had cleared, at least somewhat.

BACK HOME, SHE FOUND Labor Party members gearing up for elections, scheduled for October 1973. A "grand debate" about the territories, begun within the party in October 1972, had gone public, with ministers presenting their views to newspapers and audiences around the country. Most outspoken, Moshe Dayan appeared almost nonstop at meeting after meeting to promote his ideas, and in the process he constantly upped his demands. On the assumption that the Arab states would not make peace for at least four years, and probably much more, he insisted on including a four-year program for the territories in the party's forthcoming platform. As he envisioned it, the program would emphasize creating large-scale settlements throughout the populated West Bank and Gaza, offering government support for business investments in the occupied regions, constructing a deepwater port in northern Sinai to be called Yamit, and building major Israeli industrial centers in parts of the territories. His latest, and most controversial, demand had been to allow Israeli firms and individuals to buy land from Arab landowners in the West Bank, something the government had prohibited. Each new proposal seemed to bring Dayan closer to the Right than to the centrist Labor Party. With each, he hinted that if he didn't get his way, he would split with Labor, sending shudders through Golda and other party leaders. If he were to leave, he might influence his Rafi colleagues and others to follow and, with his enormous popularity, tilt the scales against Labor in the next election.

Even so, Golda held out against his expansionist proposals. She denounced the idea of private purchases on the West Bank as "irresponsible," a scheme that would lead to wild land speculation. Like Abba Eban, Pinhas Sapir, and other moderates in her government, she continued to view the territories as bargaining chips to be exchanged for peace with the Arab states, but with border changes necessary for security purposes.

The more widely Dayan campaigned for his ideas, the greater the impression he gave at home and abroad that his views represented official government policy. And Golda's refusal to spell out a concrete proposal with actual borders for Israel fed into that impression. Although she spoke of areas that Israel needed to hold on to—Jerusalem, the Golan Heights, Gaza, Sharm El Sheikh—she did not have a "Golda plan," comparable to the Allon or Dayan plans, she said. Yet it was no longer sufficient for her to maintain that she did not want to create a war among the Jews by delineating new frontiers before engaging in peace negotiations. "It may not be convenient for a government faced with difficult negotiations and decisions to take the public into its confidence," editorialized The Jerusalem Post, which ordinarily supported Golda. "But we have reached a point at which the unwillingness of the prime minister to commit herself to anything more than a most general desire for peace undermines confidence."

There is evidence today that Golda was trying secretly to develop a comprehensive policy for the territories. In the hope of breaking the deadlock with King Hussein and entering serious negotiations, she asked the intelligence expert Aharon Yariv to work out a specific, long-range proposal for what Israel needed and didn't need in the West Bank. He submitted a confidential document to her, code-named "Spark," with detailed suggestions, an appendix, and three maps. Unfortunately, its contents have not been made public, and we don't know how much of it she incorporated into her thinking. She also commissioned a study of Palestinian refugee camps in the territories, with suggestions on how to raise the refugees' standard of living and integrate them into the economy of the region. None of this did she discuss publicly, nor did she elaborate on her thinking during the months of debate within the party. She left it to Israel Galili, government minister without portfolio, to formulate conclusions and compromises that she and the party as a whole could accept.

With his short, pudgy build and disheveled white hair, Galili projected a down-to-earth image that belied the enormous power he exercised as Golda's closest adviser. She valued his talent for smoothing over differences among opponents and depended on his common sense and bent toward secrecy, often seeking his opinion in scribbled notes during meetings. She also admired his modest lifestyle; he lived in a one-and-a-half-room apartment in the kibbutz Na'an near the city of Rehovot. When the formal party debates ended with little agreement in April 1973, after six months and 180 hours of talks, she asked him to formulate a policy on the territories for the party platform. The Galili document was a compromise between Dayan's radical demands and the line the party had held all along, what it called the "oral law." It proposed to develop new settlements in the territories, but still only in areas with a small Arab population, in keeping with the parameters of the Allon Plan. It limited Dayan's plans for a port, but as a concession to him, it allowed for some private purchase of land in the territories, subject to regulations by a cabinet committee. It also approved various industrial projects in parts of Judaea and Samaria.

The document did not sit well with the more dovish members of the party, and numbers of them stayed away when Galili presented it for approval to the party secretariat on September 3, 1973. From Lova Eliav's vantage point, its acceptance of settlement building closed out all chances of creating an autonomous Palestinian state and denied Palestinian nationalism. With unrepressed emotion, he read a prepared statement from the podium. "This document is brought before us with the lashing of the whip of time and the scourge of hastiness and panic," he cried out. "It goes against all that I understand to be the values of the

Labor Movement . . . There are many in this hall and in this land . . . whose souls weep in silence because of this document." His melodramatic words infuriated Golda. "I have lived through fifty years of political activity . . . and we never before had a comrade who set himself up as a messiah," she said, steaming, and took him to task for implying that Jews could not speak their minds in Israel. "What kind of picture is drawn here? Whip, lash, fear, silence . . . Are we speaking of the Jewry of Russia or Syria?"

The document was approved by those present in a vote of 78 to 0. In spite of Eliav's rejection and accusations from many quarters that the party had caved in to Dayan, Golda regarded that vote as a bulwark against Dayan's more extreme plans. True, it added settlements, but they would be confined to sparsely populated areas, and Israel would not have to cope with the overwhelming demographic problems she dreaded. Moreover, the program still left much of the West Bank open to negotiations. Dayan, who had no expectations of peace agreements with Jordan or any Arab countries for many years, wanted to integrate all of Judaea and Samaria into Israel. Golda, who continued to meet secretly with King Hussein, still regarded negotiations toward a territorial agreement and peace with Jordan as a serious option.

27

Premier Meir and President Sadat

In Egypt, the world seemed to have turned upside down. On September 28, 1970, while mediating an uneasy truce between King Hussein and Yasser Arafat after Jordan's violent civil war, the Egyptian president, Gamal Abdel Nasser, suddenly collapsed and died. He was fifty-two years old. The news stunned the world and his country, where millions poured into the streets to express their grief. To Golda Meir, the towering, charismatic Nasser represented Israel's archenemy and stumbling block toward peace. He brought his people no achievement, only war, she said after he died, although she allowed public expressions of mourning among Israel's Arab population.

Anwar el-Sadat, who replaced Nasser, cut a slight figure, with his lanky build, dark skin, and simple speech, a reflection of his humble beginnings in a poor village of the Nile delta. He had been in the officers' group that overthrew Egypt's monarchy and led to Nasser's takeover as president, but as second-in-command he seemed colorless. His election as president surprised almost everyone, with many in Egypt and abroad mocking him as a lightweight, a man of "low intellectual capacity," as an Israeli report said. Yet within months he began to consolidate his power by ridding his army and government of a group of rival Soviet supporters, most of them Nasser's cronies. And almost immediately after assuming his post, he informed the United States that he had no intention of dismounting the missile sites Egypt had advanced on the west bank of the Suez Canal in breach of the cease-fire that ended the attrition war.

In reaction to those missiles, Golda and the cabinet had decided to pull Israel out of peace talks conducted by the UN envoy Gunnar Jarring. A letter to Golda from Richard Nixon urging her to resume the talks promptly and promising Israel military supplies changed their minds. Jarring flew to Jerusalem for opening discussions with Golda and Abba Eban and afterward conferred with the Egyptians. When neither side offered anything new, he called on each to respond to a series of statements: Israel would withdraw from all captured Egyptian territory to the 1967 lines in return for the establishment of demilitarized zones and guaranteed free passage through the Suez Canal and the Straits of Tiran. Egypt would agree to a peace pact with Israel, acknowledge that nation's territorial integrity, and respect its right to secure and recognized borders in return for sovereignty over Sinai.

On February 4, 1971, a few days before Jarring's statements, Sadat announced "a new initiative" to the Egyptian National Assembly. In it, he agreed to add a thirty-day extension to the cease-fire that had halted the war of attrition. He also offered to open the Suez Canal to world shipping if, during that period, Israel started withdrawing its troops from the canal's eastern bank, which it had captured during the 1967 war. That withdrawal was to be but "a first step in a timetable" for a complete withdrawal from all the occupied Arab territories and the "restoration of the legitimate rights of the Palestinian people." The first step was contingent on agreeing to the whole package.

With that perspective, Sadat answered Jarring's statements. In part of his answer, he used a word Israel had been waiting to hear since 1948: "peace." Egypt would be "ready to enter into a peace agreement with Israel" and to recognize Israel's sovereignty, his reply said; it was the first time any Arab leader had even mentioned the concept of peace with Israel. That was the "good news," as Yitzhak Rabin put it. The "bad news" was that the peace agreement depended on the same preconditions the Egyptian president had laid down in his February 4 speech, and then some: Israel was to withdraw completely to the June 4, 1967, borders, pull out of Sinai, give up the West Bank—including East Jerusalem—leave the Golan Heights, return Gaza to Egypt, and settle the Arab refugee problem.

Israel "did not underestimate" Sadat's pronouncement about peace, Golda wrote to President Nixon sometime later, but it could not accept the Egyptian president's preconditions. "And all this without real negotiations on agreed borders!"

Responding to Jarring, Israel acknowledged Sadat's willingness to speak about a peace agreement and indicated its own readiness to withdraw some distance in Sinai, to "secure and recognized boundaries" that would be agreed on in negotiations. It would not, however, go back to the June 4, 1967, lines, a position Golda had held from the start, and would not tie an agreement with Egypt to agreements with other Arab states. With the gap between the two sides unbridgeable, the Jarring mission fell apart.

In the years since those talks, Golda Meir and her cabinet have been repeatedly criticized for having missed an opportunity for peace in 1971 that might have prevented the tragic Yom Kippur War in 1973. In the end, after its peace treaty with Egypt in 1979, Israel *did* withdraw from all of Sinai. Had Golda and the others been more receptive to Sadat's unprecedented offer of peace in 1971, the argument goes, so much bloodshed on both sides would have been avoided.

But 1971 was not 1979. And the Israeli mind-set before the Yom Kippur War contrasted significantly with the thinking after it. Almost no Israelis, including the "super dove" Lova Eliav, would have dreamed in the early 1970s of having their country simply pull away from all its achievements in the Six-Day War without negotiating to improve its position and security. "We had no peace with the old boundaries," Golda would say. "How can we have peace by returning to them?" Moreover, Sadat was far from the statesman earlier that he became later. His insistence that Israel agree to forfeit not only Sinai but also all the occupied territories before negotiations could even begin seemed preposterous, especially coming from the defeated nation.

The concept of an interim, or partial, agreement between Israel and Egypt had appeared before Sadat's February initiative and would be raised again afterward. Moshe Dayan had suggested in the fall of 1970 that both parties move back from their sides of the Suez Canal, taking their armor and artillery with them. Dayan, who famously declared that he preferred Israel to stay in Sharm El Sheikh (a strategic outpost at the tip of the Sinai Peninsula) "without peace" than to give back "Sharm El Sheikh with peace and return to the former lines," proposed not returning to those former lines but drawing back far enough to allow the Egyptians to clean the Suez Canal—which had been blocked by sunken ships—reopen it to international shipping, and rebuild nearby Egyptian towns that had been destroyed during the attrition war. Golda had mentioned Dayan's idea to Kissinger in October but lost her enthusiasm after Chief of Staff Chaim Bar-Lev labeled it dangerous. Without her backing, Dayan did not push his proposal.

Sadat's suggestion of an interim agreement in his February 4 speech, which he expanded on in an interview with *Newsweek*, came close to Dayan's concept but with greater requirements of Israel. He now demanded that Israeli forces withdraw more than halfway across the Sinai to a line behind the market town of El Arish and that Egyptian military forces cross the canal to replace them. And again, any agreement about a partial Israeli withdrawal from Sinai was to be predicated on a commitment to total withdrawal from all the captured lands.

DURING THE NEXT SEVERAL MONTHS, a confusing parade of proposals about an interim agreement bounced back and forth between Egypt, Israel, and the United States. Speaking to the Knesset on February 9 in response to Sadat's talk, Golda agreed to support the reopening of the Suez Canal to free shipping for all states and to some withdrawal of Israeli forces from the occupied eastern bank, with that area becoming demilitarized. She continued to insist on direct peace talks, however, before explicit borders could be discussed. In March, Dayan again suggested an Israeli pullback from the canal, this time of about twenty-nine to thirty kilometers (some eighteen miles), but an official paper the government submitted to the U.S. ambassador Walworth Barbour in mid-April carefully avoided pinpointing how far that pullback might be.

For his part, Sadat spoke of not giving up "one inch" of any Arab lands to Israel and of not allowing Israel passage through the canal until the refugee problem was resolved. As for establishing diplomatic relations with Israel, such as opening an embassy there, the answer was "never, never, never." So while the Egyptian president held out the prospect of peace with Israel, he consistently emphasized his preconditions before any peace talks could begin.

Into this morass stepped the U.S. secretary of state, William Rogers, and not very gingerly. He told a press conference in March that his original plan of 1969, which called for Israel to return to the 1967 border with Egypt, was essentially still American policy. Ignoring both Israeli and Egyptian rejection of his plan, he barreled on. In exchange for Israeli withdrawal, he said, various zones in the Sinai would be demilitarized, and an international force, including American troops, would guarantee peace by patrolling Gaza and Sharm El Sheikh. With that system in place, Israel's insistence on secure "defensible borders" was unnecessary. "An American guarantee to Israel is as good as geography," he bragged. Golda retorted that Israel had suffered its fill of American guarantees that didn't work. Most recently, the United States had done nothing when Egypt violated the standstill provisions of the cease-fire in the war of attrition.

An angry Rogers next appeared before a closed-door session of the U.S. Senate, complaining of Israel's rigidity. Israeli leaders, he said—and meant mostly Golda—never believed the Arab states would agree to make peace with them. Taken by surprise by Sadat's initiative, they had nothing of their own to offer. Nevertheless, the ever-hopeful Rogers arranged to hold peace discussions with the Egyptian president and the Israeli premier in early May. After two days of talks in Cairo, he flew to Jerusalem and a meeting with Golda on May 6 that Yitzhak Rabin described as "tough and unsatisfactory."

Sadat had sent Rogers a memo outlining a plan for Israel to withdraw from Sinai and the Gaza Strip in two stages. If Israel accepted that proposal, he agreed to extend the current cease-fire by six months. If, in the end, it did not completely withdraw, Egypt reserved the right to "liberate" its territory by force. Despite that war threat, Rogers was immensely impressed with Sadat's true desire for peace, he told Golda. She was suspicious. As far as she could tell, she said, the Egyptian president's partial agreement plan was nothing more than a trap for getting all his land back in whatever way he could. She had no intention of mapping out how far Israel would withdraw from the canal or the rest of Sinai in either an interim or a final agreement. Those matters, as she had been saying all along, needed to be negotiated by the two parties. She rejected Sadat's demand to have Egyptian forces cross to the eastern bank of the canal after Israel vacated it, even for symbolic purposes. And most adamantly, a cease-fire agreement had to be indefinite, not something that required constant renewal.

That last posed a particular sticking point between the two sides. For Golda and her ministers, a limited cease-fire was a smoking volcano poised over their land; nobody could know when war might erupt again. From Sadat's viewpoint, with a cease-fire in place indefinitely and without the fear of war, Israel would never withdraw from all of Sinai.

On the second day of meetings, while Rogers and Golda conferred coldly, Moshe Dayan met privately and on friendlier terms with Assistant Secretary of State Joseph Sisco. Emphasizing that what he said was his personal opinion and not official policy, Dayan suggested, as he had earlier, that Israel pull back some thirty kilometers from the canal, farther than Golda or the government had been willing to go. Later, Dayan again dropped his proposal either because he knew Golda still did not support it or because he recognized that an interim agreement had no meaning if Sadat remained wedded to linking it to a final withdrawal. When Sisco reported to Sadat about his talks with Israel, he tried to soften his news by presenting Dayan's withdrawal idea as if it were the government's position. Sadat rejected it anyway.

Sisco and Rogers had more than Israel and Egypt in mind in pursuing an interim agreement. Sadat had signaled to Rogers that he wanted to free his country from its dependence on the Soviet Union. If America helped Egypt reach a partial agreement with Israel on his terms, within six months he would expel the thousands of Soviet advisers and forces in his land. Rogers and Nixon—whom the secretary of state instantly informed of Sadat's proposal—leaped at the chance to get the Soviet Union out of Egypt. Golda Meir had "diddled us along," the president wrote in a secret memo to Rogers. Although the United States had always backed Israel, he wondered whether to tilt that policy "on the side of 100 million Arabs rather than the side of two million Israelis." It was the strongest support Nixon ever gave the Rogers State Department in its Middle East initiatives, and almost the last.

Sadat began purging his pro-Soviet government opponents in the middle of May, arresting and jailing the most powerful among them. A week later, the Soviet president, Nikolai Podgorny, came calling, aghast at the Egyptian leader's actions. The upshot was a fifteen-year treaty of friendship that Sadat signed with the Soviet Union on May 27, 1971. He was to write later that the treaty came too late to win back his loyalties to the Soviets, although that was their intention. In the meantime, it befuddled the American State Department and the White House, which didn't know what to make of the quixotic Egyptian president. "We thought he was Rigoletto," Kissinger once said. A jester, untouched by reality.

Golda brooded about Sadat's Soviet treaty and the increase in weapons that would flow to Egypt. Her anxiety deepened when the Egyptian president launched into a renewed spurt of anti-Israel bellicosity. To recover Arab lands, Egypt was prepared to have a million of its troops killed, he vowed, and even then it would continue to wage a war to wipe the "Zionist intrusion" off the earth. At every opportunity, he declared 1971 the "year of decision," with dark overtones of a new military assault. Golda branded Egypt the latest Soviet satellite. When Assistant Secretary of State Sisco opened yet another round of peace talks in Jerusalem, she sought to hinge the discussion on much-needed armaments.

Sisco had met with Nixon, Rogers, Kissinger, and others before leaving the States. The president told him to be conciliatory about Israel's request for arms yet remain firm about the need for diplomatic progress. "Don't promise a damned thing," Nixon ordered. "This is not going to be a free ride this time. From now on it is *quid pro quo*."

Sisco kept his meetings with Golda respectful while trying to nudge her to greater concessions. She kept her eye on the armaments ball, especially distressed that the United States had not shipped Phantoms and other aircraft for the past six months. She didn't feel quite as hostile toward Sisco as she did toward Rogers, so she approached him a little more openly, with her instinctive ability to recast even the most complex situation into personal terms.

Early in their first meeting, to illustrate Israel's fear of having Russia rearm Egypt, she embarked on a long, seemingly rambling anecdote from her stint as emissary to Moscow back in 1949. It concerned an elderly couple who had left two daughters behind in the Soviet Union when they came to mandatory Palestine years earlier. They pleaded with Golda before she went off to get their daughters out and into Israel. After she returned from Moscow empty-handed, she tried to explain to the wife the impossibilities of such an assignment. "I don't want to understand any explanation. I am a mother. I want my daughters here," the woman cried. "I understood her perfectly," Golda told Sisco. "No explanation was good enough for her without her daughters here." In the same vein, Israel did not want to understand America's calculations that a balance of power existed between the Jewish state and Egypt even without new Phantoms. Israel understood a different truth—the "terrifying" threat to its "very existence" if American calculations proved wrong.

It was vintage Golda: the subtle association of herself with the mother pleading for her children; the less than subtle reference to Israel's ever-present existential fears. Subliminally, there was also the association of Russia with cruelty toward Soviet Jews then and toward Israel now by arming Egypt. And in case Sisco still didn't get her message, Israel was "extremely concerned, worried and hurt" by the administration's continuing delay in delivering the planes. She also hoped he noted the difference between the sides. Sadat was willing to sacrifice a million Egyptians to destroy Israel. "I don't want to sacrifice one boy, not one," she said.

Sisco didn't stand a chance against her barrage of words and unabashed tug at the heartstrings. They met three times, on July 30, August 2, and August 4, accompanied by their ministers and aides. After the last meeting, Sisco cabled Nixon and Rogers that the prime minister had expressed "warm esteem" for the president, but "she made clear that for the time being at least she prefers to play a waiting game." The meetings had accomplished so little that the undersecretary of state decided not to stop off in Cairo to report about them.

AT THE UN GENERAL ASSEMBLY annual meeting, on October 4, 1971, Secretary of State William Rogers presented to the world's delegates a six-point American initiative for the Middle East designed to get the Suez Canal reopened and lead to peace in that region. As he spoke about his program, it sounded to Golda and her government like a reprisal yet again of the original Rogers plan. It called for a partial agreement that would be "merely a step" toward an overall settlement based on UN Resolution 242, essentially adopting the Egyptian viewpoint. It allowed for some Egyptian "personnel" to cross the canal to the east bank after Israel evacuated it, and it did not rule out an eventual Egyptian military presence on that bank. It encouraged an extended cease-fire, but not the indefinite one Golda had argued for, and it was vague about how any agreement was to be supervised.

Two days after the Rogers address, Golda Meir responded in a seething public statement. Among other things, she implied that the American official could not serve as an honest broker. "Mr. Rogers made it difficult for himself to render the good services he had no doubt intended," she said. "He erred greatly in several of the views he expressed." At a Knesset meeting about three weeks later, she repeated those criticisms of Rogers with equal rage and passion and added Sisco to her line of fire. Sadat, who monitored Golda's talks as she did his, had a few choice words in his autobiography for her "famous" Knesset speech and public rebuke of Rogers. Having studied Golda Meir's character, he wrote, "we knew that she was fond of dealing with ministers, both in daily life and at cabinet meetings, as though she was handling students in the Milwaukee classrooms where she worked as a schoolteacher." She treated Rogers that way, and her speech "terrified" him and influenced American opinion, according to Sadat.

In reality, Golda approached that speech with the conviction that the U.S. president would not penalize her for her brazen criticism of his secretary of state. About a year earlier, during a visit to the United States after Rogers had publicized his original plan of 1969, she was about to leave on a speaking tour to the American Jewish community when she received word that Leonard Garment wanted to meet her alone on the tarmac of LaGuardia Airport in New York City. Garment, Nixon's liaison to the Jewish community, had a secret message from the president. She was "to slam the hell out of Rogers and his plan," wherever she spoke. Cognizant of both Israel's and Egypt's opposition to the plan,

Nixon had held little faith in it, but rather than fight his secretary of state, he stood behind the plan officially while priming the Jewish community to do the fighting for him. Golda was aware in the fall of 1971 that in the most recent go-around with Sisco and Rogers, Nixon had supported his State Department's Middle East efforts. But the similarity between Rogers's UN talk and his 1969 plan gave her reason to suspect that the support would not last long.

She also knew that Henry Kissinger was gaining the upper hand in his power struggle with William Rogers. From the beginning of their political relationship, the two men had engaged in a visceral rivalry. The brilliant, German-born, Jewish Kissinger, national security adviser to the president, resented the proper, thoroughly American, self-controlled Rogers, who had the plum position of secretary of state, and the hostile feelings were mutual. Kissinger made no effort to hide his disdain for Rogers's various plans, which neither Israel nor Egypt accepted. A master manipulator, who had written his PhD dissertation on the cruelly practical Austrian diplomat Klemens von Metternich, Kissinger was exerting ever more influence over the president. In fact, within two years he would replace Rogers as secretary of state. With her keen political sense and her memory of the covert message she had received from Leonard Garment, Golda felt bold enough to attack Rogers publicly as she did.

The result was another invitation to the White House, where she went in December 1971. By the time she got there, Rogers's six-point program had petered out, unwelcomed in Egypt as it had been in Israel. And as she expected, Nixon had reverted to his dislike of the various Rogers initiatives. When they met in the Oval Office on December 2, he made it clear that in his eyes the State Department's Middle East diplomacy had failed. Going forward, such matters would be handled only by the White House. "Don't worry if sometimes the United States speaks in two voices," he said. The voice that counted was his own or, by proxy, Henry Kissinger's. The national security adviser had moved from the edges to the heart of Middle Eastern affairs.

Golda had met with Kissinger a day earlier at the Shoreham Hotel, where she was staying, to review the subjects that would come up in the presidential meeting, bolstering her confidence as she entered the Oval Office that the meeting would go well. It could not have gone better. In an about-face from his harsh directives to Sisco, Nixon reassured her several times that she could count on him for arms. When she told him that the original Rogers plan "hangs like a sword over our heads" and that it needed to be "removed" from the table, he agreed not to press Israel to return to the June 1967 borders. Nor, in a summit meeting between him and the Soviet general secretary, Leonid Brezhnev, planned for May, would he "squeeze" the Jewish state by imposing a deal it found unacceptable.

After almost two hours of conversation, Golda summarized in a few short sentences what Israel would regard as a new understanding: there would be no American-Russian pressure on the state; the Rogers plan would not be a basis for discussion with the United States; Israel was to give the United States its views for both partial and overall agreements; and the delivery of arms and airplanes would continue without disruption. "Everyone knows that you will succeed to leave the States with a full shopping bag," the president said, teasingly, picking up on a popular image of her. He cautioned her to keep its contents secret, even from Secretary of State Rogers.

The Israeli historian and archivist Hagai Tsoref has pointed out that Golda's approach to diplomacy in regard to Egypt changed in the fall of 1971 as Rogers's influence on American Middle East policy waned. Especially after the White House meeting, the "classic Golda"—stubborn and unyielding as she has often been seen—gave way to a more flexible personality increasingly willing to make concessions to achieve peace. Sadat's saber rattling about war in the near future had made her apprehensive, and because she expected war, she refused to go back to the insecure borders of June 4, 1967. At the same time, with the removal of pressure from Rogers—whom she distrusted—to return to those lines, she felt freer to pursue peace in other ways.

She demonstrated her more open attitude at a follow-up session with Kissinger at New York's Waldorf Astoria on December 10. Golda came bearing concessions that she and Dayan had secretly worked out before she left Israel. Instead of insisting on an indefinite cease-fire, she agreed to one lasting from eighteen months to two years. Instead of limiting a withdrawal of Israeli troops to nine or ten kilometers from the Suez Canal, she agreed to pull back far enough for the canal to be opened and six months later to withdraw about thirty kilometers to the Mitla and Gidi Passes—close to what Dayan had suggested. Instead of forbidding any Egyptian presence in the territory Israel vacated, she agreed to allow Egyptian technicians and a "uniformed force," meaning police, to cross into it. She also consented to have Rabin explore "proximity talks" with Sisco, an idea Rogers had raised in his UN speech. It meant

Sisco's shuttling between Israel and Egypt to find common ground. Real negotiations, however, would take place secretly between Kissinger and Rabin, on the one hand, and Kissinger and the Soviet ambassador Anatoly Dobrynin, on the other.

The proximity talks had barely left the ground when Egypt rejected them. Sadat had reason to turn down not only the talks but also the direction Israel and the United States were taking. They had moved far from linking an interim agreement to a final plan, as he had demanded. From his perspective, they had "twisted" his February initiative around. Rather than a comprehensive settlement with all the Arab states, they had moved to a partial settlement with Egypt alone. And even that turned into "a partial settlement of a partial settlement," with his broad plan reduced merely to "the reopening of the Suez Canal." He'd had "enough of this hide and seek game." He would never agree to opening the canal as an end goal, whether Israel pulled back nine or thirty kilometers. With calm restored to the area, ships navigating as usual, and the threat of war diminished, Israel would have no incentive to return all of Sinai or any Arab territories. He was not going to let that happen.

Although 1971, his "year of decision," had ended, Sadat still envisioned a battle ahead for the return of Arab lands and the "rights" of the Palestinian people. In February 1972, he flew to Moscow to obtain Soviet weapons, with the prospect of making war.

FOR GOLDA MEIR, THE END of President Sadat's "year of decision" with none of his threats implemented brought a sense of relief and security. She felt especially good about the closeness she had established with the United States at her December meeting with President Nixon, a true shift in their nations' relationship that went beyond the ties they had developed after Israel helped Jordan during its 1970 civil war. There were reasons for this shift. When Nixon lost faith in Rogers and Sisco and turned to Kissinger, he removed a large barrier between the two countries. Kissinger preferred to maintain the status quo and wait until Egypt became so disillusioned with its Soviet patron that it turned to the United States for aid. Accordingly, he didn't pressure Israel to arrive at a final settlement with the kind of intensity the State Department did, a strategy that suited Israel's own interests. Meanwhile, with the Soviets bolstering Egypt, the United States wished to demonstrate its strength by backing Israel, its one reliable friend in the Middle East. This was particularly true in view of American losses in Vietnam and a recent victory by India over Pakistan, the country the United States had backed. On the domestic front, Nixon faced an election in 1972, with the majority of Americans admiring Israel and its popular premier. He hoped his Israel stance would earn him votes and funding in the traditionally Democratic Jewish community, and his campaign was gearing up to present him as a firm advocate of the Jewish state.

Then there were the personalities. Golda had supported Nixon's Vietnam policy, to the disapproval of groups of Americans, including her sister Clara. ("How on earth can you like that man?" Clara would say, and Golda would answer that he "never broke a single promise he made to Israel.") Speaking to the press or the president himself, she consistently referred to him as "a true friend of Israel," stroking his ego while giving him a reputation to uphold. Nixon also developed a strong rapport with Israel's ambassador to Washington, Yitzhak Rabin. In fact, during the 1972 election campaign, *The Washington Post* criticized Rabin, and Golda reprimanded him, for interfering in domestic American politics by conspicuously favoring the president over the Democratic candidate, George McGovern. He denied any wrongdoing, but he didn't hide his gratitude for Nixon's pro-Israel comments. The president, in turn, always spoke highly of Rabin. When the Israeli ambassador prepared to leave the States at the end of his term, Nixon praised him lavishly to Golda and asked what post he would be offered next. "That depends on how he behaves," she answered, bringing a flush of embarrassment to Rabin's cheeks. Nixon responded that if Israel didn't want its envoy's services, the United States would be happy to have him.

The compatibility between Rabin and Golda also strengthened Israel's hand in Washington. She might assert her authority over him, as she did crudely in that conversation on his retirement, or call him to task when she believed he overstepped the bounds of his office, but she had great respect for him and he for her. "She treated him as a son, a chosen son, and they got on extremely well," recalls the former Mossad head Efraim Halevy, who worked closely with both of them. To Golda, he was "the dream of a sabra," says Yoram Peri, "the epitome of the young '48 generation, honest, shy, sincere. She liked his integrity and modesty." Kissinger understood that Rabin, not Eban, was her emissary and had her approval, and that enhanced the partnership between the two men. Together, Golda and Rabin "created the vocabulary of Israeli-American relations," and together they transformed the Israeli embassy into a "powerful influence in Washington, on the Hill, with the media, and in terms of the White House," says Halevy. By the end of 1971, no other embassy had the clout of Israel's, and Golda's repeated visits made Washington, rather than Tel Aviv, the main channel between Israel and the United States. Nixon was aware of this and enjoyed the rapport.

As the year closed, the flurry of American diplomatic activity centering on Israel and Egypt simmered down. The United States was preoccupied with other pressing matters: Vietnam, China, an upcoming summit in Moscow. The months ahead would open a period in which Israel "never had it so good," Golda Meir later told Nixon.

WITH LESS PRESSURE from the United States, the Jewish state could go about its normal activities, still glorying in its six-day victory, still boasting of the "ship shape condition of its defense forces." Certainly, the terror attacks that escalated in 1972, and especially the Munich massacre, sapped away at the nation's energy, but the cruelty and violence behind them also bolstered Israelis' conviction of the rightness of their cause. Certainly, internal arguments raged about how much of the territories Israel should keep and how far to go in building settlements, but they did not detract from the country's overall satisfaction and belief in itself. And if the outside world criticized Israel's refusal to give up its captured lands or give in to Sadat's demands, those criticisms only led many Israelis to dig in harder, convinced that they could go it alone if necessary. "The whole world is against us," a popular song proclaimed, half seriously, half mockingly. "Let the whole world go to hell." Where, after all, had the whole world been when Nasser threatened Israel's existence? Where, now, when Sadat constantly trumpeted the war he planned to demolish the Jewish state?

Golda set the pace for the confidence and defiance of the people and its generals. "The Arabs have tried and lost three times before and I have no doubt they will lose a fourth time, should they try it again," she told a Labor council assembly, and repeated at every opportunity. "We have an amazing nation!" she marveled. "Amazing!" The "boys" in the armed forces, the "glory of humankind." And she would often say, "The non-Jewish world has been in two groups—those that killed us and those that pitied us . . . If we have to have a choice between being dead and pitied and being alive with a bad image, we'd rather be alive and have the bad image."

On a personal level, she kept her appearance as bright as possible, although her lymphoma, which had been in remission, recurred from time to time. Throughout her premiership, the cancer remained a carefully guarded secret from everyone except family and the closest friends. Members of the press who guessed that she suffered a serious illness said nothing except to note on occasion that the premier appeared tired or frail from hard work.

In the middle of the night, often hiding her identity under a large scarf, Golda Meir would go to Hadassah Hospital to get the cobalt treatments that kept the illness under control. "She told me to call her Golda and to treat her like any other patient," recalled the radiotherapy technician Elhanan Reich. A nurse who cared for her remembered that "as soon as the doctor's back was turned, Golda would whisper to me, 'Get me a cigarette and take one for yourself.'" To the hospital staff, Golda was "outgoing," "modest," "motherly," "involved" in their personal lives, the way she always had been with her cleaning woman or the guards in front of her home. They adored her and kept her secret, "even from my wife," said Reich, who was sometimes called in the middle of the night to meet the prime minister at the hospital for an emergency treatment when the pain became too intense for her to handle. Her secret did not become public until after she died, when Lou Kadar, who often accompanied her to the treatments, acknowledged that Golda had been ill with lymphoma for fifteen years. "The treatments were very painful, and the doctors didn't know if she could go through with them," Kadar recalled. "But she did. She had the treatment at night and would go back to the office in the morning as if nothing had happened." She handled the lymphoma as she did other illnesses.

"She had to live with her headaches and she had to live with her bad legs and she had to live with her cancer. That was that," said Kadar.

Ill as she was, Golda still might have said of herself that she, too, "never had it so good." At the height of her popularity now, she kept a firm grip on the government. ("Her Meirship," some called her.) It would be her choice whether to run for office again, and while she made noises, as always, about wanting to retire, she could become prickly with anyone who suggested that she do so. When the *Jerusalem Post* editor Ted Lurie hinted at the end of 1972 that she might be entering her last year as prime minister, she quipped, "What! So you're sacking me?!"

Along with toughness and determination, her Jewish grandmother image had become etched onto the popular imagination, a craggy-faced old woman with shrewd peasant eyes and wispy hair who spoke with down-to-earth wisdom. Even Henry Kissinger, for all his cleverness, felt that she acted toward him "as a benevolent aunt toward an especially favored nephew," making disagreeing with her especially unpleasant. For Nixon, Leonard Garment was to say, Golda Meir was the "mother of all mothers," his own mother "squared—smart, spiky, resolute." Thousands of people throughout the world wrote intimately as though they had known her for years. After her meeting with Nixon in December, one correspondent enclosed a newspaper photograph of the event, concerned about her appearance. "Listen honey, take a little time off," the writer advised. "You look like you should go to the mountains for about three weeks, no phone, no nothing. Take it easy dear Friend." And dozens of letters solicited her favorite recipes, with her office invariably sending the one for chicken soup. ("Boil the chicken with parsley, celery, cut-up carrots, peeled onion, salt, pepper, and a pinch of paprika, until it is tender.")

As she looked ahead to a relatively quiet period in Israel, Golda also began to look back, to take stock of the long life she had led. Having made peace with Ben-Gurion after six years of anger, she guided the country in celebrating his eighty-fifth birthday. At the end of 1971, she held a second reunion—she had held one ten years earlier—for the survivors of the ill-fated *Pocahontas* ship that had brought her and the others to Palestine fifty years earlier. There weren't many of them left now, but they sang and reminisced, still proud of their decision to come there. She reminisced when she received the Freedom of Jerusalem prize, recapturing the first time she went to Jerusalem and the Western Wall. Nonreligious, she'd had no feeling for the wall until she saw men and women putting their *kvitlech*, little notes, into the crannies of the stones, praying and weeping. Suddenly she understood the "magic" of that old ruin. She reminisced about socialism and Zionism with her old friend Meyer Weisgal, chancellor of the Weizmann Institute, when he conferred an honorary fellowship on her.

The quality Jews always needed, the quality that made her life possible, Golda would say, was optimism. As she looked backward at her life and forward to her remaining years, she bore within her the contradictory attitudes of deep suspicion toward much of the world along with a stripe of optimism and hope. Optimism was the source of Jewish achievement despite obstacles, she would say. "A Jew cannot afford the luxury of not being optimistic."

OPTIMISM LED HER TO ROMANIA in the spring of 1972, with the hope of reaching a peace deal with Anwar Sadat. Nicolae Ceaușescu, head of

Romania's Communist Party, had secretly sent her an invitation to visit his country so that he could personally deliver a message he had received from Sadat during a recent trip to Cairo. Golda grabbed the opportunity. Israel had good relations with Romania, one of the few Eastern European countries that had not broken with it after the Six-Day War yet also managed to maintain diplomatic ties to the Arab countries. Moreover, she knew that Sadat had faced setbacks in Egypt that might make him more amenable to negotiations. The Soviets had not welcomed his call for war, as he widely claimed they did. Nor had they given him the military hardware he asked for during a trip to Russia in February. Instead, they advised him to tone down his belligerent rhetoric. On the eve of Nixon's visit to China—a breakthrough for an American president—and preparing for their summit with the United States, they had no wish to spark a new fire between Egypt and Israel. At home, Sadat had been coping with violent student demonstrations protesting his policies. Under such pressures, he might have been seeking a solution through Romanian mediation.

Golda arrived in Romania on Thursday, May 4, 1972, the first Israeli prime minister to visit a Communist country. After preliminary talks with Prime Minister Ion Maurer, she met alone with Ceaușescu in two long sessions that stretched into fourteen hours. He relayed that Sadat expressed willingness to meet directly with an Israeli, possibly her, or, alternatively, to arrange a meeting on a lower diplomatic level. Thrilled, she answered that Israel was ready to meet the Egyptian president at any time and place and on any level of diplomacy, without preconditions. Israel had no wish to keep all, or even most, of the territories it had captured and was willing to make deep compromises for peace. She suggested they begin by discussing a partial settlement rather than a final one. Ceaușescu promised to deliver that message to Sadat.

Then he mentioned terms Sadat had already given him for a partial settlement, and her hopes flitted away like so many frightened birds. The Egyptian president would have Israel withdraw a hundred kilometers from the east bank of the Suez Canal, farther than Dayan or anyone had proposed. Some part of the area Israel vacated would be supervised by international forces, but Egyptian troops would be stationed in others. Golda replied that her government opposed having Egyptian troops on that side of the canal, considering it dangerous to Israel. Ceaușescu agreed to contact her after he spoke to Sadat. She would never hear from him again.

On Friday evening, she attended services in the Choral Synagogue in

Bucharest (wearing the black hat she would later don to meet the pope) and in some ways found herself transported back to Moscow almost a quarter of a century earlier. Ten thousand Jews from all parts of Romania waited silently in the street, freer than the Moscow Jews had been but just as eager to glimpse her. As her car passed, thousands of hands waved to her, and when she stepped out and greeted the crowds with "Shabbat shalom," a roar of voices repeated the words. During the service, she wiped away tears as a choir of fifty young people sang "Jerusalem of Gold" and other Israeli songs in Hebrew. She didn't know then that Romanian intelligence had foiled a plot by four terrorists sent from Egypt to assassinate her in the evening as she walked to her car.

THAT SUMMER SADAT ASTOUNDED the world by ousting fifteen thousand Soviet experts and advisers from his country. Although he didn't totally sever relations with the Soviets, he blamed them for the ouster because they did not supply him with the weapons they promised. It would become clear later that ridding Egypt of a restraining Soviet presence also freed the country for war against Israel. But Sadat's opposition to the Russians was also an attempt on his part to draw closer to the United States. He had already indicated to Secretary of State Rogers that he would willingly drop the Soviets if the United States pushed Israel toward the settlement he wanted. He had also opened a secret channel with Henry Kissinger by proposing that Egypt's national security adviser visit the United States. Kissinger responded cautiously to the proposal, scheduling the visit for early in 1973 and observing the ouster of the Soviet advisers without much overt reaction. He still had not taken the measure of the Egyptian president, who publicly attacked the United States for its friendship with Israel yet secretly tried to sidle up to it. And in the ping-pong game of détente with the Soviets, he preferred to keep the score fairly even in public while working behind the scenes to try to push them out of the Middle East.

Golda made a dramatic pitch to Sadat in a Knesset speech about a week after his announcement. "It would seem that this hour in the history of Egypt can, indeed should, be the appropriate hour for change—and if it truly is the hour for change, let it not be missed," she said. "I appeal to the president of Egypt as the leader of a great people, a people with an ancient heritage whose future is ahead of it," she continued. "Let us meet as equals and make a joint supreme effort to arrive at an agreed solution." The words flowed elegantly; Israel was calling on Egypt again for direct negotiations. Sadat immediately rejected the call as "the same old tune" and reiterated that Egypt would not go to negotiations while its land was occupied.

That's where matters stood for the prime minister when she visited Washington again at the end of February 1973 to seek another American commitment for planes and arms. This time she was given residence in Blair House, the official presidential guesthouse, instead of in her usual Shoreham Hotel, a sign of her friendly relationship with President Nixon. But all was not as rosy at first as she anticipated.

She arrived in the American capital a few days after Hafez Ismail, Sadat's special adviser. Historians would later pinpoint Ismail's secret meeting with Henry Kissinger during that visit and another in May as stepping-stones toward the war that was to break out a few months later. Bearing himself with dignity and a slight aloofness, Ismail delivered Egypt's latest peace proposals when the two men met in a handsome private home in the town of Armonk, New York. Ismail categorically rejected any interim agreement about the Suez Canal unless it was part of a comprehensive plan for Israel to withdraw to prewar borders. He was more flexible, however, in regard to the other captured territories, suggesting that an Egyptian-Israeli settlement could be worked out first, provided negotiations were under way for agreements with Syria and Jordan. But even then he could not offer full peace with Israel until the Palestinian refugee problem was resolved. Instead, he proposed a "state of peace" that would end the belligerency between the countries, allowing Israeli ships free passage through the Suez Canal and Straits of Tiran and committing Egypt to preventing terrorist operations from Egyptian soil when possible. It would not include diplomatic relations of any kind or trade agreements between the countries. Ismail showed a degree of flexibility in acknowledging Israel's security needs. Egypt would allow some areas of the Sinai to be demilitarized and an international force to be stationed in regions of concern to Israel, such as Sharm El Sheikh. He was adamant that a settlement had to take place during 1973 and certainly by September.

Kissinger later wrote that he found little new in Ismail's proposal, which, in the end, did not offer much more than the existing cease-fire. He had not been expecting a great deal in any case. A few days before his meeting with Ismail, he had told Rabin that when the Egyptian adviser visited London, the British found him so "intransigent" they saw "no hope for any progress." His own strategy at the upcoming meeting, he said, would be to listen but "present no proposal of any kind." Indeed, he told Golda afterward that he had applied his "usual delaying tactics," committing himself to nothing.

Historians differ as to why as late as 1973 Kissinger delayed and did not press Israel toward further compromises for peace. Some argue that given Golda's unbudging stance Kissinger gave up trying and simply agreed to put the peace process on hold until after the Israeli elections in October. Others maintain that for the sake of détente both the United States and Russia accepted the status quo and refrained from pushing their client states toward greater activity. Then there was the rivalry between Kissinger and Rogers that led to a confused Middle East policy. Kissinger himself contended that he aimed to hold off until Sadat became so disenchanted with the Soviets' ability to get him what he wanted that he would turn fully to the United States.

Whatever his true motives, Kissinger disappointed Sadat by his low-key response to Ismail. And when, shortly after the Egyptian adviser returned to Cairo, word leaked to the press that as a result of Golda Meir's visit the United States had agreed to sell Israel additional Phantoms and Skyhawks, it caused an "explosion in Cairo." As the Egyptians saw it, Nixon had simply become a "hostage to Israeli pressure," moving them closer to war.

Nevertheless, Ismail's visit ranked high on Kissinger's agenda when Golda met with him in Washington for breakfast on February 28. The national security adviser tried to drive home to her that in light of that visit "there must be movement" on an agreement with the Egyptians when she saw the president the next day. Nixon had come to feel, he said, that America's oil supplies from Arab lands were in danger because of Israel and had told Kissinger to "quit pandering to Israel's intransigent position." Somewhat startled, Golda went on the offensive.

"It is simply incredible," she snapped. "The Egyptians behave as if they had won the war . . . There is no realism. Do we really have to take all this?" Israel had been willing to negotiate anything, but without the Egyptian preconditions. Besides, she asked, what does "a state of peace" mean? It means, she answered herself, "that after all the conditions have been met there still will be no normal relations." No government would accept such conditions. "Why should only Israel be forced to negotiate 'a state of peace,' which is not really peace?"

She argued effectively for a while, but instead of staying focused on what she might say to sway the president, she allowed her deep distrust of the Arabs to take over. "We just will not go along with this!" she said when Kissinger mentioned a linkage between an interim and a final agreement. It was nothing more than a plot by the Egyptians, "first to get us back to the '67 borders, then to the '47 borders, and then bring the Palestinians back, which means no more Israel." Impatiently, Kissinger ended the discussion by urging her to let him know what she intended to say to the president.

Two draining sessions with other government officials followed the Kissinger encounter. A week earlier, on February 21, the Israel air force had mistakenly shot down a Libyan passenger plane that had drifted into Israeli airspace in the Sinai Peninsula. One hundred and six people were killed, arousing world condemnation. The incident came up at the beginning of Golda's luncheon conversation with Deputy Secretary of State Kenneth Rush. With emotions in the region running high because of the downed plane, Rush said, the United States thought it wise not to announce a decision on selling Israel planes at this time. At an afternoon meeting, Secretary of Defense Elliot Richardson followed through by questioning whether Israel really needed additional planes, because its air force could easily overpower any in the region.

Feeling hurt and rebuffed, her face pale with fatigue, Golda considered returning to Israel without seeing the president. She had been through such haggling sessions before, and so had Rabin, who accompanied her; they typified the routine a small state had to endure in its constant pleas for aid from its powerful patron. Now, however, she was aware of a hostile tone that had not been present in her last few visits, and certainly not with Nixon. Rabin had never seen her so dispirited. Sensing that both the State Department and the White House had grown weary of Israel's lack of new initiatives for peace with Egypt, he suggested that the two work out some ideas together to present to Kissinger for transmission to the president. Their planning paid off when they met with Richard Nixon at the White House the next morning, March 1.

In high spirits, the chief executive greeted her pleasantly, wished Rabin a happy birthday (he turned fifty-one), and reassured her on the Libyan plane tragedy that "things like this can happen." Giving an example of how Israel was ready to "negotiate anytime, anywhere," she described the Ceauşescu episode, when she had expected Sadat to meet with her. "The reason Sadat doesn't want to talk with you, Mrs. Meir, is he is afraid you would gobble him up," Nixon said, smiling.

As a result of her working session with Rabin, Golda showed more flexibility about Egypt than she ever had. She agreed to have Kissinger continue talking secretly with the Egyptians and Soviets, although not to negotiate on Israel's behalf, and she agreed to an interim settlement on Suez. More significantly, she appeared ready at this point to connect the interim to a final agreement. To allay Sadat's fears, she promised that Israel's pullback from the canal would be not its final position but its initial one and open for further negotiations. "It shows we are prepared to take a risk for peace," she said.

In taking that risk, she also consented to have Israel move its troops back to the Sinai passes and, in accordance with a private telephone conversation she'd had with Dayan in August 1972, to allow a number of Egyptian soldiers to cross into the area vacated. Even with the Suez Canal opened, she proposed not having Israeli ships use it, to "save face for Sadat." They were not major concessions, but little by little she had moved away from her earlier unstinting stands, and for the time being they satisfied Kissinger and Nixon. The meeting ended after some twenty minutes with the president promising Israel at least a hundred Super Mirage planes and considerable military and economic aid for the next two years.

When Golda entered a packed National Press Club luncheon after the White House meeting, she received a standing ovation and another as she left. That evening, dressed in a simple light blue short-sleeved gown, she attended a state dinner of poached red snapper and supreme of squab. (Pat Nixon wore a posh long-sleeved pale green taffeta gown; the president, black tie.) Nixon joked about the large number of people beyond the 120 guests who wanted to be invited but had not made the cut, and Golda took as her theme "We are not alone; we have a friend" in the United States. In New York City, where she went a few days later, she escaped another assassination attempt, this one by a Black September terrorist who planted two powerful car bombs along Fifth Avenue and one at John F. Kennedy International Airport. The bombs failed to detonate, and Golda—fearless about such things—continued her visit, speaking around the country to wildly enthusiastic Jewish audiences as she raised funds for Israel Bonds.

It had been a good trip after all, and she returned to Israel satisfied with the results. Indeed, "satisfied" might best describe the mood that gripped the country. With the Watergate scandal rising to engulf Nixon, his sense of urgency about a Middle East peace initiative receded, lessening the pressure on Israel. Despite many utterances about wanting to retire, Golda told CBS television before she left the States that her future plans would be guided by her party's wishes. The hint that she might stay on as premier tamped down Israelis' fear of party infighting and of losing the one person capable of holding the nation together.

For Anwar Sadat, Golda's more flexible positions appeared to be too little, too late. He wanted all his land back, and he escalated his war threats to get it. In an interview with *Newsweek's* Arnaud de Borchgrave, he declared that the "resumption of the battle" was "now inevitable." Yet the more he threatened, the less seriously many took him or worried about the consequences if he were brash enough to act. At a pivotal meeting in Golda's Jerusalem home on April 18, 1973, she and her closest advisers, Moshe Dayan and Israel Galili, analyzed the possibilities of war and the costs of peace. To help assess the situation, she invited some key military and intelligence officers: Chief of Staff David Elazar and his office head, Avner Shalev; the Mossad chief, Zvi Zamir; the IDF's director of military intelligence, Eli Zeira; and the director general of Golda's office, Mordechai Gazit. General Zeira assured the group, as he would continually, that there was little chance of Egypt's starting hostilities. Zvi Zamir and David Elazar were less sure, and Moshe Dayan agreed with them that while Sadat had no hope of succeeding, he might plunge into war to break through the current "no peace no war" impasse.

Israel Galili seemed to grasp the dilemma the leaders faced more clearly than any present. "There is the possibility of avoiding this whole calamity if we are ready to enter into a series of agreements based on a return to the former boundary," he said. He understood the weightiness of the decision they were making and wanted the group to be fully aware of it. Yet like the others, he preferred to accept the concept of war over moving back to the insecurity of the 1967 borders. As the historian Uri Bar-Joseph explains, they were *that* sure that if Sadat actually carried out his threats, Israel would easily defeat his forces. They also knew that even with the prospect of warfare the majority of Israelis had no sentiment for totally undoing what had been won in 1967. In fact, a recent public opinion survey had found that 96 percent of Israelis opposed giving up Sharm El Sheikh under any circumstances. So the group in Golda's kitchen decided to inform the government of the possibility of another war.

As the session ended, the prime minister turned toward the stenographer. "I am announcing for the record that I do not want war," she stated. She knew the record would show that she and her advisers had chosen the option of war over conceding completely to Sadat. She wanted it to show also that as head of the state she did not want to go to war. She sincerely meant that and would continue to seek peace however she could. But if war were to come, she also meant something she had said earlier in the meeting: "We are quite sure of ourselves."

In the weeks that followed, Dayan instituted a "blue-white" state of readiness, code name for beefing up the army's preparedness for hostilities. The IDF mobilized reserve units, moved tanks and other equipment closer to the Suez Canal, and reinforced several army divisions, all at considerable cost. On May Day, Sadat seemed poised for action, stating that political solutions were now out of the question. Israel remained on high alert. As weeks passed and nothing happened, the defense minister gradually reduced the alert, and the atmosphere reverted to normal. Sadat seemed less to be believed than ever.

GOLDA CELEBRATED her seventy-fifth birthday on May 3 with a quiet party at the home of Meyer Weisgal, attended by her children and grandchildren, Lou Kadar, Simcha Dinitz and his wife, and a few other intimates. For the occasion, Jordan's king, Hussein, gave her a strand of perfectly matched pearls that she kept tucked away in a box in her drawer. The public celebration was modest. A group of high school seniors presented her with seventy-six long-stemmed pink roses, and several Hebrew newspapers recapped highlights of her life in Israel. *The Jerusalem Post* ran excerpts from her speeches, including some of her most popular quotations. Two of the best known, "Peace will come when the Arabs will love their children more than they hate us" and "When peace comes we will perhaps in time be able to forgive the Arabs for killing our sons, but it will be harder to forgive them for having forced us to kill their sons," fell into disfavor with later critics, who denounced them as expressing superiority toward Arabs. To Israelis, surrounded by implacable Arab states out to destroy them, they seemed for many years apt expressions.

Four days later, hundreds of thousands of Israelis and foreign tourists packed into Jerusalem to mark the nation's twenty-fifth anniversary. Soldiers paraded in their smart uniforms while jets streaked overhead, tanks rolled through the streets, and fireworks blazed in the skies. Nobody could doubt Israel's military might. The outlook of the country matched the exuberance of the parade. The economy was booming, the gross national product rising at the rate of about 9 percent a year and the country's exports forty-eight times greater than they had been in 1949. Despite domestic tensions and outside dangers, nothing could dampen the nation's pride and amazement at what it had achieved in the short span of twenty-five years.

On May 20, Henry Kissinger held his second meeting with Hafez Ismail in an old farmhouse south of Paris. After five hours of talks, nothing had changed. Kissinger urged a "step by step" approach to a peace agreement that might not be completed until 1974 or 1975. Ismail feared that once Egypt committed itself to the first steps, the United States would lose interest in pressing Israel any further. According to Egyptian sources, Kissinger insulted Sadat by advising him to be "realistic" and, as the defeated nation, not ask for "victor's spoils." Kissinger was to say that by the time the meeting took place, Ismail knew that Sadat had completed his plans for war against Israel. Unless Kissinger could have guaranteed that Israel would return to the 1967 borders, war would inevitably have broken out.

For Golda, June brought a new dimension to her peace quest. The German chancellor, Willy Brandt, visited Israel, the first official visit by a German chancellor in office, although Brandt had been to the country when he was mayor of West Berlin. Golda Meir and Willy Brandt had a cordial relationship, proper, but not particularly friendly. They had exchanged letters in 1971 after she congratulated him on winning the Nobel Peace Prize, and this year he sent her birthday congratulations. Emotions in Israel ran high on June 7, 1973, when Brandt's Luftwaffe 707 with its gleaming iron cross touched down at Lod International Airport and the IDF orchestra played the German national anthem. Searing memories of the Holocaust were entwined with more recent memories of the massacre of Israeli athletes in Munich less than a year earlier. For Golda, too, it was a hard moment. Just ten years before, she had split with Ben-Gurion over issues surrounding friendship with West Germany.

Ahead of the visit, she had assured a wary German ambassador that there would be no violent demonstrations against the chancellor. "In Israel we know who Brandt is," she told him about the leader who had fought underground against the Nazis. She hoped to involve Brandt in a Middle East peace process, although she knew that he had been skittish about serving as a mediator between Israel and Egypt. At two secret meetings in Jerusalem, she reviewed the situation as it stood and asked Brandt to submit a proposal from her to Sadat for private talks between Egypt and Israel. The chancellor could tell the Egyptian leader, she said, "that he is convinced that we truly want peace. That we don't want all of Sinai, or half of Sinai, or most of Sinai." She repeated, as she had to Kissinger and Nixon, that although Israel would not return to all the 1967 borders, it was more than willing to negotiate what the borders would be.

On the way to the airport for Brandt's flight back to Germany, he and Golda agreed to establish a secret channel between them, bypassing the Foreign Ministry, similar to the channel that existed in Washington between the prime minister's office and the Israeli embassy. Relations between the countries had grown warmer during the visit, and Brandt wrote to Golda through that secret channel that he had passed along to Richard Nixon, the Soviet leader, Leonid Brezhnev, and other world leaders his impression that Israel truly wanted peace. As it happened, the person on whom it fell to transmit her message to Sadat, Lothar Lahn, was a middle-ranking German diplomat and a critic of Israel. We don't know what he said or his tone of voice when he presented Golda's proposal for secret negotiations to Hafez Ismail. But Ismail turned him down with finality. Egypt was aware that Israel wanted such a meeting, he said, but it had no purpose. As long as the Jewish state did not agree ahead of time to return to the 1967 borders, it would simply be "talks about talks." Ultimately, Willy Brandt was too concerned about Germany's relations with the Arab countries to become involved in the Middle East conflict.

On June 17, Golda made it official: she would "bow to the will" of her party and run again for office. She has three basic reasons for running, a party member said. One, she believes the coming year will be crucial in Israel-U.S. relations and she is the only person to talk to Nixon. Two, she wants to prevent a bitter leadership battle among other potential candidates, and three, what else would she do? Retirement would kill her. Added another wag, only God and Nixon could keep Golda from running. God for obvious reasons and Nixon by suddenly forcing Israel to withdraw completely from the occupied territories. Golda wrote a letter with her decision "after considerable soul-searching" to the Labor Party secretary, Aharon Yadlin. When he read it to the party's central committee, listeners burst into applause. Given Golda's enormous popularity, her decision to head the Labor list of candidates virtually assured the party victory in the general election, scheduled for October 29, 1973.

For this election, a group of women in the party started a drive to have 20 percent of the local and national list consist of women's names. "We knew we couldn't get this through the party machine without Golda," recalled Esther Herlitz, "and she had no interest in it. It was quite a job, but we finally convinced her to speak up." Under pressure from Herlitz, Tamar Eshel, and other strong women in the party, Golda demanded a 20 percent quota for women on the party's lists. "I would rather speak up now than be ashamed later on for having no women on our lists," she said after being sold on the idea. The resolution passed, and urged by her, party members scrambled to come up with the requisite number of women's names.

Throughout the summer, Golda hit the campaign trail, speaking four or five times a week, flying in rickety helicopters to remote kibbutzim and neglected areas. "I must get out and have that contact with people. Otherwise I'd suffocate," she told a reporter. In September, she redoubled her efforts after the Labor Party alignment dropped by 4 percent against the right-wing opposition list in elections to the Histadrut. But neither she nor her party was really worried. In the few weeks left before elections, Labor placed ads in all the newspapers, with a picture of the party's leaders, Golda in the center, and reassuring words that spoke to the nation's satisfaction and the party's confidence: "Quiet reigns on the banks of the Suez. The lines are secure; the bridges are open; Jerusalem is united. New settlements spring up and our political position is strong. You know only the Labor alignment can achieve this and with your help, we shall continue."

28

"I Will Never Again Be the Person I Was"

On the afternoon of September 13, 1973, Golda Meir received word of an air battle in progress between Israeli and Syrian planes. Sixteen Syrian MiG-21s had attacked four Israeli Phantoms returning from a reconnaissance flight over Syria. Within moments, a covering force of Israeli Mirages shot down nine of the Syrian planes. Delighted with that news, the prime minister turned ashen when told that one Israeli Mirage had been hit and the fate of the pilot, who had parachuted into the Mediterranean, was as yet unknown. She immediately ordered a helicopter to rescue him. When Syrian planes tried to interfere with the rescue, the Israelis trounced four of them, making a total of thirteen Syrian planes downed. A smiling Golda celebrated the air victory with the rest of Israel, one more proof of the military's invincibility.

She also turned the incident to good use in her political campaign, boasting that because she had accepted the cease-fire in 1970, ending the war of attrition, Israel had received the American arms that made this victory possible. Menachem Begin and his Gahal group, she would point out, had left the government because of their opposition to the cease-fire. But even while basking in Israel's triumph in the skies, she worried that Syria might launch a revenge attack. She had been planning to go to Strasbourg, France, at the end of September to address the consultative assembly of the Council of Europe, and she asked Dayan whether, in view of the tensions on the Syrian front, she should cancel the trip. Having received reports from Major General Yitzhak Hofi, commander of Israel's northern forces, about a buildup of Syrian tanks and artillery in the Golan, Dayan had concerns himself. He suggested she discuss the situation with Jordan's king, Hussein, due to arrive for another clandestine meeting.

This was not a routine meeting. Hussein had urgently requested it after returning from a summit in Cairo with Anwar Sadat and the Syrian leader, Hafez al-Assad. He arrived by helicopter at a secure Mossad guesthouse north of Tel Aviv on September 25, accompanied by Zaid al-Rifai, who had become his prime minister. At a long table in the conference room, he and Rifai sat opposite Golda Meir and Mordechai Gazit, conducting their conversation in English. Closed-circuit television secretly filmed the meeting, with several Israeli intelligence officers in another room watching and listening.

Early in the meeting, the king described Sadat's and Assad's impatience with the stalemate in regard to Israel. But his urgency came from information he had learned from a "very, very sensitive source in Syria" that Syrian forces being built up on the Golan Heights were in a "position of pre-attack" and not there simply for training purposes. "Whether it means anything or not, nobody knows," he said of the report he'd received. "But I have my own doubts. However, one cannot be sure. One must take those as facts."

"Is it conceivable that the Syrians would start something without the full cooperation of the Egyptians?" Golda asked.

"I don't think so," Hussein replied. "I think they are cooperating."

Like so much else surrounding the Yom Kippur War, this conversation has become a source of controversy. Did Hussein's words constitute an actual warning that was ignored about the war that would erupt in ten days? The king later denied that he had issued a warning, as did Mordechai Gazit. Both might have had reasons for their denials—the king so as not to appear a traitor to his people and Gazit to protect Golda and himself. More pertinent is what Hussein actually said. He relayed no explicit war plans and gave no information about the time or place of a possible attack. Nor did he mention any preparedness of Egyptian troops along the Suez Canal. Having made it clear to the two Arab leaders that he would not participate in another war against Israel, after losing so much in 1967, he was not included in their specific plans.

Still, his intimation of war greatly troubled Golda. She phoned Moshe Dayan immediately after the meeting, close to midnight. After checking with his sources, the defense minister called back to assure her that the IDF already knew of the situation in the north and planned to reinforce Israeli troops there. Hussein had said nothing new. Golda left for her Jerusalem home with Lou Kadar, who had served hot drinks at the meeting. Kadar thought the king looked tense and frightened. She felt strongly that he was predicting war and was amazed that Golda did not seem to take his warning seriously. But Golda felt reassured by Dayan.

At Dayan's request, General Hofi reviewed the king's message with several of his generals. They all agreed that the Syrians would not launch an all-out war without Egypt and, in keeping with the "conception" the intelligence community held, Egypt would not start a war without Scud ballistic missiles and other weapons capable of striking Israel that it had not yet received from the Soviet Union. Nevertheless, Chief of Staff David "Dado" Elazar decided to send two tank companies from the Seventh Armored Brigade stationed in the south northward to the Golan. "We'll have a hundred tanks against eight hundred Syrian ones. That should be enough." he said, with the swashbuckling confidence of the Israeli military.

Accompanied by Elazar and others, Dayan flew to the Golan and at a news conference issued a warning: "Any blow from their side would hurt them more than it will us." Israel radio repeated those words again and again to make sure they reached Syrian ears.

Her fears stilled, Golda took some time for herself. A year had passed since her sister's death, and she and her family visited Sheyna's grave, then paid their respects at Morris's. It was the eve of Rosh Hashanah, the Jewish New Year, and the prime minister left the city to spend a quiet holiday at the kibbutz Revivim. On the following Sunday, September 30, caught up once again in the plight of Soviet Jewry, she would travel to Strasbourg as planned.

Those Jews never left her mind. About a year earlier, she had tried to fight an education tax the Soviets had imposed on Jews who wanted to immigrate to Israel. Aimed especially at preventing intellectuals from fleeing the Soviet Union, it required them to repay the government for the cost of their education—with figures that ranged from five thousand to twenty-five thousand dollars or more, far beyond the means of most Soviet citizens. Golda had tried to get Richard Nixon to intervene, but devoted as he was to détente with the Soviets, he had ignored her appeals. On the other hand, he voiced a strong opinion later when the Democratic senator Henry "Scoop" Jackson introduced an amendment to a new trade bill designed to deny most favored nation status and trade benefits to the Soviets if they did not change their emigration policies for Jews. The president was furious with Jackson and furious with the American Jewish community for supporting him. During Golda's visit to the White House in March 1973, he and Kissinger had tried to pressure her into squelching public backing for the Jackson amendment. "Congressmen say the linking has the support of Israel," Nixon accused, and Kissinger added, "The important thing is for you not to influence the congressmen." She was noncommittal. "I cannot tell the Jews of the United States not to concern themselves with their brethren in the Soviet Union," she had said. Although Israel could not openly back the Jackson amendment, no one doubted where its prime minister's heart lay.

Now a new issue concerning Soviet Jews had arisen. Two days before Golda's trip to Strasbourg, two Palestinian terrorists hijacked a train carrying Russian Jewish emigrants as it crossed the border from Czechoslovakia to Austria. Calling themselves Eagles of the Palestinian Revolution, they nabbed four people as hostages and threatened to kill them unless Austria shut down the Jewish Agency transit camp at Schönau Castle near Vienna, a stopping point for Russian Jews on their way to Israel. To world amazement, Austria quickly acceded to the terrorists' demand. The hostages were freed and the terrorists flown to Libya.

In Strasbourg, Golda discarded the formal speech she had prepared and spoke instead of the pitfalls of surrendering to terrorism. "To give in when one life is in danger only endangers more," she said. "There can be no deals with terrorists." She arranged to meet Austria's chancellor, Bruno Kreisky, on her way back from Strasbourg, expecting that when she asked him in person to reverse his decision, he would do so.

Instead, iciness and tension shaped their meeting. "He didn't even offer me a glass of water," she was to say whenever recounting the meeting. She had been acquainted with Kreisky over the years, with little friendship between them. Although he did not deny his Jewish background, he regarded himself primarily as an Austrian, with no interest in Zionism or Israel. He particularly irked her by asserting that they belonged to "two different worlds," hers one of war and his of peace. He refused to change his mind about Schönau, suggesting that the transit camp be placed under UN auspices. As for capitulating to the terrorists, "I would not be able to bear the loss of human life on my conscience," he argued.

Sitting on the edge of her chair, unsmiling, hands tightly folded, Golda knew she had lost the battle. After almost two hours of wrangling, she rose, said an abrupt good-bye, and headed to Schwechat Airport and home, refusing to meet the press with Kreisky. On her return to Israel, she had the "glassy-eyed, pasty-faced look of a beaten woman," a *Time* magazine correspondent reported. As it turned out, although the transit camp at Schönau was closed, individual Russian immigrants were permitted to go through Austria to Israel.

A few days after Golda Meir's visit, Ismail Fahmi, an Egyptian envoy, called on Kreisky to convey Anwar Sadat's gratitude for his decision to shut the Schönau transit camp. During their conversation, Fahmi told the Austrian chancellor that before 1973 ended, the Egyptians would go to war against Israel because they could no longer tolerate the existing situation. Kreisky didn't tell anyone of Fahmi's words; they seemed like so much talk.

THE KREISKY AFFAIR FILLED the newspapers at home and abroad. Occasionally, references to Syrian or Egyptian troop movements appeared, but they were generally dismissed as routine army exercises. And even if an increase in enemy troops might indicate some "hostile intent," *The Jerusalem Post* explained in a typical dispatch, Israel's strong borders could assure the nation a sense of "equanimity" as it approached the solemn Yom Kippur day.

Golda was not as sanguine. She had been receiving a stream of information the public did not have. Even as she set off for Strasbourg that Sunday, September 30, she was given an updated intelligence report at the airport about the continued strengthening of Syrian forces in the Golan. On Monday, at the bidding of a worried Dayan, Israel Galili had called her in Strasbourg to arrange for an urgent discussion about the Egyptian and Syrian fronts as soon as she returned. Tuesday night, past midnight and moments after her plane touched down in Tel Aviv, Dayan met with her in a corner of the airport to brief her on the situation. Neither of them knew that a day earlier a source in Cairo had warned the Mossad that under cover of a military exercise Egypt would launch a war against Israel in a week. Unconvinced, perhaps, of the reliability of the date—there had been other warnings and mistaken predictions—the Mossad did not pass on the information to the prime minister in a form that would call her attention to it.

On Wednesday morning, October 3, Golda convened a meeting in her Jerusalem home of her kitchen cabinet stalwarts, Moshe Dayan and Israel Galili, joined by Yigal Allon; David Elazar; the Israel air force commander, Benny Peled; and Brigadier General Arye Shalev, second-in-command to the military intelligence head, Eli Zeira, who was at home sick. They were puzzled about events on both the Syrian and the Egyptian fronts: the transfer of Syrian forces from the Jordanian border to the Golan, the large-scale military exercises of the Egyptian army, with a call-up of thousands. Yet an eerie tranquillity hung over the gathering. Arye Shalev assured the group, as Eli Zeira had consistently, that the likelihood of war remained low. Clinging to the "conception," he maintained that the Egyptians did not believe they were ready for war and Syria would not go to war without them. General Elazar agreed with his analysis.

After listening attentively to the generals, the prime minister raised some questions. Might Egypt undertake a diversionary activity as a cover for a Syrian attack? That didn't seem likely, Shalev replied. Both countries know their limitations. Did the United States have military equipment that Israel lacked and should acquire? No, Peled said. That was not necessary. But shouldn't Israel's defenses on the Golan be reinforced more than they had been? That would mean weakening defenses on the southern, Egyptian, front by moving forces away from there or, alternatively, mobilizing the reserves, Elazar explained, and he didn't wish to do either yet.

Golda still felt uneasy, but the confidence of her generals and security experts bolstered her. "Thank you for calming me," she said as she shook Shalev's hand. She was calm enough to hold a government meeting later that morning about her confrontation with Kreisky, without ever mentioning war tensions with Egypt and Syria. At Yigal Allon's suggestion, however, she placed the situation on the agenda of the next government session, to be held on the following Sunday, October 7, the day after Yom Kippur. "And maybe we can even send Assad to synagogue on Yom Kippur as an example for Kreisky," she joked.

In the afternoon, the Mossad head, Zvi Zamir, who had not been invited to the morning meeting, came to tell the prime minister that he disagreed with the opinion of the military intelligence leaders Zeira and Shalev. Based on information he had, he feared the Egyptians and Syrians were, indeed, preparing for war. Golda liked Zamir and trusted his judgment, although Zeira had the ultimate responsibility for evaluating intelligence data. When unsure of herself about security issues Zamir brought her, she would have him consult with Moshe Dayan or other army officers before she decided. On this day, she sent him to Dayan to present his viewpoint. Dayan continued to stand by Zeira. After all, the military intelligence chief exuded total confidence and had been right on earlier occasions when others thought Egypt might start hostilities. With no definitive proof of impending war, low-key, unassuming Zvi Zamir did not press his stand. Zeira's "low probability" remained the ruling position.

And nobody knew that Zeira was hiding something that might have made a difference in everybody's thinking. Israel had a top secret warning system, mysteriously called "the special means of collection." It consisted of highly sensitive electronic listening devices planted on the Egyptian side of the Suez Canal and fashioned to pick up "chatter" from telephone and cable lines, and even within rooms. The spy system was activated sparingly, so as not to use up its battery pack or be discovered by the Egyptians. Zeira had the sole authority to decide when to turn it on, and he decided it was not necessary to do so at this time. His subordinates, Colonel Menachem Digli and General Yoel Ben-Porat, pleaded with him that the electronic bugs were designed precisely for the kind of uncertain situation confronting them. Zeira wouldn't budge, absolutely convinced the Egyptians were not ready for war. Yet all along, during those tense days of late September and early October, he did not prevent Golda, Dayan, Elazar, and the others from believing that he had placed the listening devices in operation. To their minds, the special means provided insurance of at least a forty-eight-hour warning before an Egyptian attack, time enough to call up the reserves. When Dayan asked Zeira whether he had picked up anything unusual in the Egyptian chatter and the intelligence chief replied, "Totally quiet," the defense minister felt free to advise Mrs. Meir that the specter of war did not hover overhead.

Golda was giving a campaign speech in a basketball stadium in Givatayim, outside Tel Aviv, on the evening of October 4 when military intelligence intercepted a KGB radio transmission indicating that the families of Russian advisers in Egypt and Syria were being hurriedly evacuated. As the night wore on, the Israelis discovered that the Soviets had dispatched eleven cargo planes to the two countries for an emergency evacuation, among them six giant Antonov An-22s, each capable of carrying four hundred passengers. For the first time, a shadow of doubt crossed Eli Zeira's mind. Why would the Russian families be whisked out that way? The evacuations were "serious and problematic," he acknowledged, although that didn't necessarily mean the Soviets expected war.

Other bad news took the generals by surprise that Thursday evening. A reconnaissance plane sent out during the day returned late in the afternoon with photographs showing a buildup of Egyptian tanks, artillery, and forces along the west side of the Suez Canal. In the past nine days, artillery had jumped from about eight hundred pieces to more than a thousand, and tanks and armored trucks had been moved to the front lines. "From the numbers alone you can get a stroke," Dayan said.

ON EDGE ALL EVENING, Golda fell into a fitful sleep late in the night. Zvi Zamir did not wish to awaken her to say he was journeying to London in the morning, so he left word with his bureau chief, Alfred "Freddy" Eini, to inform her military secretary, Yisrael Lior. Eini had phoned Zamir at 2:30 a.m. with an urgent message received at Mossad headquarters that his most valuable—and most unlikely—spy in Egypt wanted to meet with him in person. The message included the word "chemicals," the code for war, and the spy was Ashraf Marwan, son-in-law of Gamal Abdel Nasser and a close associate of Anwar Sadat's. For reasons only he knew, probably financial, Marwan had approached the Mossad three years earlier to offer his services. After investigating him extensively, the agency recruited him and over the years found him to be an invaluable trove of information. Mossad personnel assigned him various code names: "Angel," "Babylon," "the In-Law," but usually referred to him simply as "the source." The scenario of this high-level Egyptian spying for the enemy seemed so bizarre that several in the intelligence community then and later questioned whether he was a double agent, working for Egypt while pretending to spy for Israel. Golda, who received copies of all his reports, had doubts also. "What's your opinion of this source?" she would ask Zamir from time to time. "Is he serious or not?" Or, "Do you believe him? Are you sure?" Because of Zamir's faith and the quality of the reports, she eventually came to regard her doubts as a "wrongdoing."

The Mossad chief kept that faith despite several false alarms sent out by Marwan, including one back in April when he had warned that Sadat was going to war in mid-May and Israel spent millions gearing up for hostilities that didn't happen. Zamir trusted Marwan enough to agree to meet him in London that day. In the early morning hours, before he left, he phoned Zeira, who asked him to call from overseas as soon as he had news.

Golda met with Zeira, Dayan, Elazar, and several others in her Tel Aviv office at 9:45 on Friday morning, October 5. She had learned about Zamir's departure just a little earlier from Yisrael Lior and was miffed that the Mossad chief had not notified her of his departure immediately, as he did Zeira. Her anger soon took a backseat to the disturbing tidings she heard about the reconnaissance photographs showing extensive deployment along the Egyptian and Syrian fronts and about the hasty flight of Russian families from those countries. The Russian exodus especially filled her with foreboding. Why the rush? What did the Soviets know that the Israelis didn't? Although still puzzled by the evacuation, Zeira found several nonthreatening explanations for it. The Soviets might have had a falling-out with the Egyptians again, or, more likely, they feared that Israel would attack the Arab countries and wanted their people out first. None of his rationalizations completely satisfied Golda. She remembered that just before the 1967 war, something similar had happened. What did it portend now?

Chief of Staff Elazar explained that he had put the army on C alert, the highest alert short of war. He had directed the armed forces to cancel all leaves, placed the air force on full readiness, and sent reinforcements to the Golan Heights. Yet neither he nor Dayan nor any of the generals present suggested calling up the reserves to supplement the regular army. Under the impression that the "special means" had been opened, they probably assumed they would have enough warning time to do that if necessary. And General Zeira, still wedded to his "conception," assumed there would be no attack. Zamir, who might have presented a different viewpoint, was in London, and Golda did not consider herself qualified to second-guess her top generals and intelligence experts.

After the meeting broke up, Zeira met Lou Kadar in the corridor. Placing his arm around her shoulder, he smiled and said, "Don't worry. There won't be a war."

At 11:30 a.m., Golda held an emergency meeting of her cabinet members who were in Tel Aviv to have them briefed by the generals. Only nine made it; most of the others had left for the holiday to their homes in Jerusalem, Haifa, or various kibbutzim. Later those omitted would complain that she should have sought them out anyway. Consumed with worry, she appeared drained, her face taut from tension. After listening to the reports again, she reviewed for the group what she had read in translations of the Arab press. Just as they had before the Six-Day War, Arab newspapers were spreading false reports that Israel had concentrated troops on the Syrian and Egyptian borders and warning that their forces were prepared to repulse any attack. At Galili's suggestion, the ministers gave Golda and Dayan permission to call up the reserves on Yom Kippur if necessary without convening the entire cabinet.

It was decided also to send a message to the United States to be passed on to the Soviets and through them to Egypt and Syria that Israel had no intention of attacking the Arab states. Golda wrote the first part, a personal note to Henry Kissinger, who had been appointed secretary of state two weeks earlier, assuring him that if Syria and Egypt had amassed troops on the borders out of fear of an Israeli assault, such fears were "totally baseless." If, on the other hand, those Arab countries intended to attack Israel, they needed to know that "Israel will react militarily, with firmness and great strength." The second part of the message, prepared by military intelligence, undermined the urgency in Golda's note by reiterating Zeira's slogan of the "low probability" of an Arab attack. Lulled by that report's confident tone and by similar reassuring reports from the CIA, Kissinger did not deliver Israel's message to the Soviets until the next day, Saturday, October 6. It arrived about an hour and a half before war exploded.

At the end of the cabinet meeting on October 5, the ministers left phone numbers where they could be reached if needed. Golda extended to each the traditional Yom Kippur greeting—"May you be inscribed well [in the Book of Life]." She planned to stay on in Tel Aviv instead of going to Revivim, to be easily reachable. With everybody gone, she sat in her office alone, staring into space, gripped by a sense of dread. By the time she left, quiet had begun to descend on the land, as Jews prepared for their holiest of days. On the way home, she paid a condolence visit to Simcha Dinitz, now ambassador to the United States, who was in Israel because his father had died a few days earlier, and instructed him to return to Washington immediately after Yom Kippur. In her house in Ramat Aviv, she joined her son and daughter-in-law and some of their friends in the last meal before the fast began. Too jumpy and nervous to eat, she went to bed early and lay there tossing and turning for hours. For all the convictions of her top generals, she couldn't push away her fear of a war.

THE PHONE CALL FROM Yisrael Lior at around 3:50 on Saturday morning woke her from a troubled sleep. "Today war will break out," she heard him say. He had just received the stunning news from Freddy Eini, Zvi Zamir's bureau chief. Zamir had met with Ashraf Marwan in a London hotel, where the Egyptian spy informed him that the Egyptian and Syrian armies would attack toward evening, the Egyptians bombarding Israeli targets in Sinai and crossing the Suez Canal while the Syrians stormed the Golan Heights. Zamir raced to a Mossad station to phone his coded message. "You won't get through. In Israel there is a holiday," the operator said cheerily. When he finally did get through, he had Eini deliver his message to Eli Zeira and the military aides of Golda, Moshe Dayan and Dado Elazar.

"I knew it would happen," Golda said after a moment's silence. "Yisrael, what do we do now?" She was Hamlet, crying, "O my prophetic soul." In her heart of hearts, she had distrusted Zeira's soothing "low probability of war" mantra. She had been profoundly disturbed by Russia's evacuation of its civilian families from Egypt. Why had she not acted on the glaring realities? And the reserves. At the government meeting the previous day, she had felt in her gut that the reserve forces should be mobilized, yet she allowed herself to be persuaded by the military men that they would have time if that became necessary. Why had she, who had always relied on her intuition, not done so in this most crucial time? Why had she not trusted her own judgment? She would never forgive herself for those blunders. "I will never again be the person I was before the Yom Kippur War," she was to say.

"I'm getting dressed and ready to go to my office immediately," she told Lior. She instructed him to arrange a meeting for her with the senior defense officials as quickly as possible. Dayan and Elazar had already met to begin war plans and already fallen into serious disagreement by the time they appeared in Golda's office at 8:05 a.m. Elazar firmly believed that the reserves needed to be fully mobilized to supplement the standing army, which had been put on alert. Dayan, still not completely convinced that war would break out, wanted a limited call-up, arguing that extensive mobilization would make Israel appear to be preparing for aggression. By the same token, he opposed Elazar's proposal for a preemptive strike against Syria. After the many assurances Israel had given the United States that the Arabs would not dare attack it, if it struck first, it would surely be blamed for initiating a war.

The two high-level generals stated their cases before the elderly, civilian prime minister, who had routinely deferred to them in military matters. "If you agree to a large mobilization, I won't resign," Dayan said—hedging his bets as usual—but 50,000 or 60,000 men should be sufficient. With greater determination, Elazar argued for a mobilization of at least 200,000 men. Because it took twenty-four hours to fully mobilize, they could be ready to fight by the next day, whereas if they were not called up and war broke out, an entire day would be lost. Because Israel did not keep a large standing army and the reserves made up 75 percent of its defense forces, the consequences could be severe. Golda had no problem accepting Elazar's argument. "We need to be in the best possible position," she said. "As far as the outside is concerned, if there is a war, it's all right for them to be angry at us, as long as our position is the best it can possibly be." They would begin by mobilizing 100,000 to 125,000 troops and increase that number as needed.

A preemptive blow raised different problems. Although Marwan had not given Zamir a specific hour for the beginning of hostilities, indicating only that it would be early evening, the Israelis calculated that the war would start at 6:00 p.m. On that assumption, Elazar told Golda she had time to think about preemption and possibly discuss it with the Americans. The Israeli Air Force could be ready to strike Syrian air bases by twelve noon. The action could save many lives. "My heart is drawn to it," the prime minister said. Yet she could not authorize a preemptive strike. This was not 1967, she explained. This time the world was watching and would hold Israel accountable for starting the war. If it needed help in the future, it would get nothing from the United States or anybody else. Against Dayan's recommendation, she also ordered that all children be evacuated immediately from settlements on the Golan Heights.

Having begun the meeting shocked by the news from Zamir and confused by the debate between her key generals, she emerged distinctly in charge, guided by her instincts and practical good sense. At 10:15 a.m., she met with Kenneth Keating, the U.S. ambassador to Israel. "We may be in trouble," she told the astounded diplomat. As she had in her letter to Kissinger, she asked that the United States inform the Soviets that Israel had no intention of attacking the two Arab countries. When he questioned her closely about a preemptive strike, she asserted again that Israel would not hit first, "although it would make things much easier for us." Keating rushed to cable the State Department, while Golda conferred with Menachem Begin.

Henry Kissinger would claim that he did not warn Golda against striking preemptively, though he believed she had made the right decision. Actually, she remembered that in the past he had told both Simcha Dinitz and Yitzhak Rabin that "whatever happens, don't be the one that strikes first." And on October 6, after being awakened at 6:15 a.m. in his Waldorf Astoria suite in New York City—his headquarters for the UN General Assembly meeting—and reading Keating's cable, he phoned the Soviet ambassador Anatoly Dobrynin to say that he had cautioned Israel against "a precipitous move" and he hoped Dobrynin would restrain his Arab "friends." Next, he sent word through Mordechai Shalev, Israel's chargé d'affaires in Washington, that Israel must avoid any preemptive action or the consequences would be "very serious." He then sent a cable to the president recounting those admonitions.

Certain she would need American help in the days ahead, Golda reasoned that she could not permit Israel to strike first. She explained her reasoning at a tense government meeting hastily convened at noon. This time cabinet members had been summoned from all parts of the country. Most had some idea of what was going on; everywhere, they could see young men leaving synagogues, some with prayer shawls still draped around their shoulders, rushing to cars or buses to respond to their call-up. Still, many of the ministers were shocked and irate that until now they had been told next to nothing about the looming crisis. Dayan and Elazar reviewed the situation for them as it existed, and Golda raised the possibility that the war might start even earlier than the expected 6:00 p.m., maybe as early as 4:00 in the afternoon. As she spoke, the wail of sirens sliced through the air. For a moment she went on, then sirens again.

"What is this?" she asked, startled. "It seems the war has begun," a stenographer near her answered. "Nor dos felt mir" (That's all I need), the prime minister muttered, slipping into her native Yiddish at this moment of truth. Lior rushed in seconds later to say that the Syrian army had opened fire and Syrian aircraft had been spotted taking off. "So they did surprise us after all," Golda said, and repeated it several times that day. "I'm angry that they surprised us." A little later she added, "We have to hit them back hard."

Anwar Sadat had planned his surprise well. He had decided to go to war as early as October 1972, although he sent his emissary Hafez Ismail to meet with Henry Kissinger twice in 1973 to seek a diplomatic way out of the deadlock with Israel. Convinced in his heart that it would not materialize, he enlisted Syria's Hafez Assad for a joint campaign against Israel. Both kept their decision tightly secret, even from their own military commanders, many of whom didn't know until shortly before going into battle that their military exercises were preparations for a real war. Sadat did not reveal his war plans to the Soviets until the end of September or give them the actual date until October 3. For Israel's consumption, he planted false stories in the Egyptian newspaper *Al-Ahram* about demobilizing troops and organizing soldiers for a pilgrimage to Mecca. And by constantly threatening an attack and not acting on his threats, he lulled Golda and her advisers into writing off his war talk as so much bluff.

Yet for all that, the Egyptians were amazed that Israel did not pick up their signals—the extent of the army's "training exercises" or the evacuation of the Russian dependents and the movement of their fleet away from the Egyptian coast. These actions did arouse Golda's suspicions, but she acceded to the intelligence experts' conviction that Egypt would not go to war without the planes it required, and she accepted her military advisers' self-satisfied sense of Israel's superior power in case the Egyptians foolishly attacked. Those beliefs prevented her and other Israeli and American leaders from perceiving Sadat's real intentions. In light of past experience, the Egyptian president had little expectation of winning back all his territory on the battlefield and certainly not of conquering Israel. He initiated the war to recapture the self-respect and pride his nation had lost in its humiliating 1967 defeat and to open the way to negotiating from strength and with U.S. involvement. In the words of his wife, Jehan, "Sadat needed one more war in order to win and enter into negotiations from a position of equality . . . he was not ready to meet with Israel feeling inferior."

GOLDA COULD NOT know any of that when the sirens screamed and confusion overtook her Tel Aviv office on the afternoon of October 6. Because Zamir had warned that war would begin that evening, nobody was prepared for it four hours early. When the Syrians and Egyptians struck with massive force in the north and south, Israeli tanks had not yet taken up their positions, reserve forces had not arrived, and soldiers found themselves struggling with hopelessly outdated equipment. Nevertheless, on that first evening, Golda received reports that Israeli forces had held their own on both fronts. At six o'clock, she spoke by radio, and later television, to a stupefied nation that, until that day, had been kept in the dark about the prospect of war.

"At two o'clock this afternoon, the armies of Egypt and Syria attacked Israel," listeners heard her say in a voice both somber and flat as she read from a prepared text. "They launched a series of offensives from the air, by armored forces, and by artillery, in Sinai and on the Golan Heights. The Israel Defense Forces are fighting and are repulsing the attack, and grave losses have been inflicted on the enemy." She spoke of Egyptian and Syrian hostilities as "an act of madness" that Israel had tried its best to prevent. With the nation again facing the "ordeal of a war imposed on us," she expressed confidence "in the spirit and strength of the IDF."

She spent most of that night poring over a large map spread out before her and trying to internalize the battlefields. "I, the great military expert," she recalled sardonically, following reports of which bridge had been crossed, which line breached. "It didn't make much sense, my sitting alongside the map, but where was home, what was home, who could go home?"

As night turned into day, calamitous reports from the front began to pile up. In the south, Egyptian forces established bridgeheads across the Suez Canal and streamed toward the Israeli-held eastern bank. They crashed through the Bar-Lev Line, a string of fortified strongholds along the canal named for the former army chief of staff Chaim Bar-Lev, giving them a foothold in Sinai. Israel suffered hundreds of casualties and hundreds more wounded or taken prisoner and lost dozens of tanks and 10 percent of its aircraft, blown apart by a barrage of Russian-made surface-to-air missiles. Many of the missile batteries had been standing in readiness since the end of the attrition war in 1970, when Egypt moved them close to the canal on its side in violation of the cease-fire. Complicating matters, IDF commanders transferred part of the air force to the Golan Heights, leaving many southern ground forces unassisted by aircraft.

All that day, October 7, Golda rushed from one meeting to the next, her emotions a roller coaster of hope and despair. At 7:35 a.m., after very little sleep, she visited the "Pit," the IDF's underground command center, where Elazar described the bleak conditions in the north that had forced him to transfer aircraft there. Even so, he tried to put a positive spin on the situation by recounting some small Israeli successes. At a 9:10 consultation of the "war cabinet"—composed of Golda, Moshe Dayan, Yigal Allon, and Israel Galili, with several other military and civilian leaders present—the discussion centered on persuading Henry Kissinger to postpone a UN Security Council vote on a cease-fire so Israel could have time to regain what it had lost, a pressing concern for Golda. To the question of what to tell Kissinger about Israel's condition, she urged honesty, disagreeing with a suggestion to emphasize only losses as a way to get American help. "We can't play hide and seek with him," she said. The secretary of state needed to know the difficulty of Israel's position but also that it would improve. "I don't get the impression that the situation is lost," she said, searching for optimism, although "tonight was a bad night."

Her true anxiety came through during her closing remarks, when she allowed that she regretted not having permitted the IDF to strike preemptively: "If, God forbid, we face such a situation again, we need to ignore the world and let the army get on with it." In an urgent message to Kissinger that afternoon requesting arms, she wrote, "You know the reasons why we took no preemptive action. Our failure to take such action is the reason for our situation now." She would never again express misgivings about that decision. In fact, she would testify after the war that she always knew she had done the right thing. She couldn't prove it, but she could say with confidence that had Israel preempted, it would not have received the crucial aid it needed from the United States. In this second dark day of fighting, however, she had to wonder whether she had made a terrible mistake.

Her feelings hit rock bottom at a war cabinet consultation that afternoon. Moshe Dayan, hero of the 1956 and 1967 wars, demigod to many, iconic symbol of the nation's power, a man who had exuded pride and confidence with every breath, spoke with unalloyed pessimism about both the southern and the northern fronts, which he had just toured.

"The canal line is lost," he said without a glimmer of hope, and proposed a deep withdrawal of Israeli troops to a second defensive line on the Israeli bank, about nineteen miles from the canal. In a chilling portrayal of what that involved, he explained that as the IDF abandoned its posts, it would have to leave behind wounded soldiers whom it could not evacuate. "Whoever gets through—gets through. If they decide to surrender—they will surrender. We have to tell them: 'We can't reach you. Try to break out or to surrender.'"

Golda listened in horror. "I underestimated the enemy's strength . . . and overestimated our forces and their ability to stand fast," Dayan admitted. Presently, he estimated that the Egyptians had two thousand tanks to Israel's eight hundred; the Syrians fifteen hundred to Israel's five hundred. In the air, Egypt had 600 planes to Israel's 250, about the same number as Syria had. And both enemies had missiles that were decimating Israel's air force. Moreover, the setbacks were not only about Egyptian and Syrian territories; they cast their shadow over Israel proper if other Arab states were to join in. "The Third Commonwealth is in danger," he had declared to the air force commander, Benny Peled, referring to the modern State of Israel, rebuilt after the destruction of the Second Commonwealth two thousand years earlier. "They have come to fight us for the Land of Israel itself," he continued. Golda agreed with him about the Arabs' motives. She had no doubt that they would view a victory in this war as a step toward the goal that had eluded them in previous wars, ridding the region of Israel. "There is no reason why they won't continue, and not only now," she said. "They have tasted blood . . . this is the second round since 1948."

In the depths of her soul, she probably realized that America would not permit Israel to be destroyed; it would order a standstill in the fighting if Israel were losing badly. But the impact of such an IDF defeat on Israelis would be disastrous and the view of Israel as less powerful than anyone had thought extremely dangerous in the international scene. The Jewish state would be seen as insignificant, not even worthy of receiving arms. "Jews in general are not loved; weak Jews even less so," she said. "They'll throw us to the dogs." She needed to know something from her generals, however, irritation in her voice. "I thought we would begin to hit them the moment they crossed the canal. What happened?" After the many assurances she had been given about Israel's strength and Sadat's weaknesses, how could they find themselves in the present state? Dayan had no answer. He had erroneously prepared for this war on the basis of the last one, he admitted, but the Arabs proved themselves much better fighters now, and they had many new Soviet-supplied weapons. Wrong judgment, overwhelming odds . . . The defense minister tripped over his explanations. The little ironic smile that often hovered around his lips had disappeared. He seemed to many in the room a broken man.

At some point, Golda walked out of the meeting into the corridor to speak with Lou Kadar. The color had left her face, which now appeared "green" with fatigue and fear. She told Kadar that Dayan wanted her and the others to consider conditions for "surrender." He had not actually used that word, but to Golda retreating from the Bar-Lev Line without attempting to retake the canal constituted a form of surrender. Reflecting on that dreadful afternoon a few years after the war, Golda told Avner Shalev, Elazar's bureau chief, that "on the second day of the war, I decided to commit suicide." She said something similar to Yaakov Hazan, her good friend (and possibly onetime lover), and from time to time mention of the prime minister's suicidal thoughts have surfaced. Despondent over Dayan's report, she might, indeed, have had such momentary thoughts, but it is inconceivable that this woman who had consistently shouldered the hardest tasks and put the nation above friends, family, and personal health would seriously have contemplated escaping responsibility when the situation turned desperate or abandoning her people when they needed her most. Lou Kadar later denied that Golda thought in earnest about suicide. It was she who rummaged her mind for a physician friend who might give her "a pill or something," she said, and for her, too, the fantasy passed quickly.

After spending a short time with Kadar, Golda went back to the meeting. Her color had returned, and her voice had become strong again.

Those first hours of shock and fear aside, she would become a "rock" throughout the war, a judgment even her severest critics held. She would be called on to make military decisions she never, in her wildest imaginings, thought she could, and she would make them with clear-eyed common sense and strategic insight. Her outward strength, in spite of inner turmoil, would keep the nation on a steady keel during some of the worst days of the conflict, and her steely determination would serve her well in navigating the shoals of big-power pressures and everyday crises.

Toward the end of the war cabinet meeting on that Sunday, October 7, she had Elazar called in, and while he presented the same grim facts as Dayan, instead of giving up the canal line, he recommended trying to oust the Egyptians from it. The council decided to send him to the southern front to plan a counterattack, and Dayan consented, although he did not generally respect Elazar's judgment and did not agree with the plan. Golda breathed a little easier.

In the afternoon, Dayan came to her office and offered to resign. She turned him down unequivocally; she wouldn't give up her defense minister in the middle of a war. Besides, she still believed in him, although when Chaim Bar-Lev came to see her, she placed her right hand on her elbow and, moving it side to side, said, "The great Moshe Dayan! One day like this. One day like that!" In truth, she had already begun to rely more on Elazar for help with decisions.

Encouraging news reached the prime minister on Monday morning, October 8, day three of the war. Elazar expected that the Egyptians would soon be pushed back across the Suez Canal, and he asked permission for an air attack on four targets along the coast. "Make them worry," he said. "We need to press them. After all, they are only human." The optimism stretched into the afternoon, with reports that in the south the IDF might actually be able to cross the canal to the Egyptian side, and in the north to reach the old cease-fire lines.

By evening, victory had turned into defeat and euphoria to despair. The reports had been mistaken; the counterattack in the south had failed miserably. Hundreds of tanks had been destroyed or abandoned, with heavy losses among their crews and not the slightest possibility of crossing the canal to the Egyptian side. In the north, although the IDF had made inroads in the Golan, the Syrians had received reinforcements that could lead to a new offensive. Golda struggled to make sense of the quick change in fortune. "Only this morning, we had to hold back Arik," she remarked, referring to Ariel Sharon, who led a reserve division in the south and had been chomping at the bit to cross the canal. And now, nothing?

The extent of the disaster became clearer on day four, Tuesday, October 9. In the south, there had been poor communication between soldiers on the ground and the command centers in the rear that had reported success. The generals had clashed among themselves, and—topping it off—Shmuel Gonen, commander of the southern front, had given contradictory and confused orders. He would soon be replaced by Chaim Bar-Lev. The situation in the north looked a little brighter, with Israeli forces repelling the enemy in some areas. During a 7:30 a.m. consultation, Dayan and Elazar asked permission to concentrate all their efforts on the northern front so as to win that battle and then be free to turn to the south. The order for the battle would include bombing military targets inside Damascus, Syria's capital. Golda had strong doubts, aware of the toll bombing the city might take on civilians and the criticisms of Israel that would follow. She finally gave in after her close adviser Israel Galili agreed with the operation.

Writing about that awful day, Dayan described Golda as living on cigarettes and coffee and almost no sleep, yet "I could not imagine anyone with a more attentive ear, open mind, and courageous heart than Golda at this meeting."

In their reports, both Dayan and Elazar presented a bleak picture of Israel's position in the south. It would be a longer war than anybody had anticipated, so extensive, Dayan warned, that they might have to mobilize older men and teenagers and even try to recruit Jews from the Diaspora. And the need for ammunition and armaments from the United States had become critical. Although Ambassador Dinitz had been pressing for military supplies, the Americans had been dragging their feet. Increasingly agitated by what she heard, Golda suddenly tossed out a "crazy idea." Suppose she flew incognito to Washington for twenty-four hours and appealed directly to Nixon for the tanks, Phantoms, and other weapons Israel so urgently required. "Maybe he'll say he can offer nothing but sympathy," she said, but she didn't think so. Given her friendship with the president, this was the "best card" they could play to get results.

During the consultation, Golda frantically phoned Ambassador Dinitz, although it was 1:45 a.m. Washington time, insisting that he call Kissinger immediately to impress on him the urgency of Israel's arms requests. She phoned again at 3:00 a.m. "I don't care what time it is," she shouted. "Call Kissinger now." Dinitz followed orders, much to Kissinger's annoyance, and the two men arranged to meet, with their aides, at 8:20 that morning in the White House Map Room. Kissinger was stunned when Dinitz spelled out the staggering number of Israeli losses over the past four days: five hundred tanks—four hundred of them on the Egyptian front alone—and some forty-nine planes, fourteen of them Phantoms. Obviously, the Americans would have to shift gears rapidly from expectations they had held of a swift Israeli victory.

At the end of the meeting, Dinitz asked to speak to Kissinger alone for five minutes. That request has led to speculation—and a popular play based on it—that at Golda's bidding, Dinitz threatened Kissinger with Israel's nuclear capability unless it received the weapons it needed. Kissinger has categorically denied any such threat. "Nonsense. Absolute nonsense," he says. "Had they raised that issue, they would have totally ruined themselves. We would have been forced by law to act on what we had not formally acknowledged and what they had not formally acknowledged. Any threat to use nuclear weapons would have changed the entire equation here to the disadvantage of Israel . . . it was never said; it was never hinted at. It didn't happen." The speculation has never been substantiated through interviews or documents of any kind.

What Dinitz spoke to him about privately, Kissinger says, was Golda's wish to make a lightning visit to the president, an idea he rejected out of hand, without even consulting Nixon. "For her to leave the country leaderless for forty-eight hours in the middle of a war," he says, "was a sign of panic. If it got out, the entire Arab world would become so confident that nothing could work. And there was nothing she could accomplish here."

ISRAEL'S NUCLEAR OPTION DID COME into play briefly during those nightmarish days. In his despondency, Dayan suggested to Golda that Israel use "unconventional weapons." Disturbed, she relayed the suggestion to Chaim Bar-Lev, who noted in his diary that Golda seemed more alarmed by Dayan's nervousness than by the war situation itself. The prime minister and her cabinet firmly turned down the request, but Dayan might have taken some minor actions that did not require her approval. On October 8 or 9, he seems to have increased the readiness of Israel's Jericho missiles, its main nuclear delivery system. "As far as I know," said James Schlesinger, American secretary of defense at that time, "Dayan did something. But he would have been remiss if he hadn't; it was a perfectly natural military precaution. When you're attacked, you put your forces on alert." Schlesinger maintained that whatever action Israel took was intended as a threat not to the United States but to the Arab world. "There was some evidence that the Russians were beginning to move nuclear weapons into Egypt. Israel sent an implicit warning: we have a major nuclear weapon here compared to you Egyptians, even though you've got some Soviet help," he said. "That's very different from saying to the United States, 'If you don't help us, we'll initiate.' That would have been a big mistake."

Golda nicknamed the nuclear facility at Dimona *varenye*, an engineer who worked there recalled. In Eastern Europe, *varenye* was a jar of fruit preserves Jews kept in reserve so they would have something to eat in times of trouble. Whatever the exact nature of Dayan's nuclear preparedness during those October days, Golda Meir had no intention of using the weapons. They remained her *varenye*. "Like John F. Kennedy a decade earlier," Avner Cohen writes, "Golda Meir had stared into the nuclear abyss and found a path back to sanity." Her behavior "demonstrated to the world that Israel was a responsible and trusted nuclear custodian."

In Israel on that Tuesday evening, October 9, Moshe Dayan went before the editors of Israel's daily newspapers and shook them to their core. He had told Golda at the morning meeting that they needed to be "straight" with the Israeli public and not mislead it into anticipating an easy win. On that note, he told the editors bluntly that although Israel was making some progress against the Syrians in the Golan, the IDF lacked the strength to throw the Egyptians back across the Suez Canal. He described the up-to-date Soviet weapons pouring into Egypt to the extent that "the war is now against Soviet weaponry more than against the Egyptians." By the time he finished his grim assessment, *Davar*'s editor, Hannah Zemer, was in tears, and *Haaretz*'s editor, Gershom Schocken, labeled his words an "earthquake" that would rock the nation. Dayan had been scheduled to appear on state television that night, but some of the editors appealed to Golda to stop him before he created panic in the land. At her request, he stepped aside and allowed General Aharon Yariv to replace him. Yariv did not hide the difficult facts, but he presented them in a way listeners could digest. Golda explained later that in the midst of a war she didn't feel it necessary to tell the nation the entire truth, for "situations can turn around and truths change."

The next day, the situation in the north did begin to turn around as the IDF pushed Syrian troops back, almost to the line Israel had held before the war. Israel's need for arms and planes was becoming acute, however. There had been little problem with the United States filling small requests for ammunition, Sidewinder air-to-air missiles, spare parts, and other equipment. El Al Airlines would pick these up in the States in total secrecy, landing at night with their insignia painted out. After Golda's appeals to Kissinger, via Dinitz, President Nixon had agreed also to replace Israel's war losses, including aircraft and tanks. In a personal letter, she thanked him, promising that when Israel came out victorious, "we will have you in mind."

But then nothing happened. Golda grew desperate as Israel's stock of planes and arms dwindled to a dangerous low, with no new arrivals from the United States. Two narratives have emerged on the subject. In one, which Golda, Dinitz, Eban, and other Israelis accepted, Kissinger did everything possible to get supplies to Israel but constantly hit road-blocks from Secretary of Defense James Schlesinger, who feared that a major rearming of Israel would provoke an Arab oil embargo. In the other, a Machiavellian Kissinger, playing all angles, delayed the ship-ments, while Schlesinger basically followed his directions. The reality is unclear either way. Kissinger surely did not want Israel to lose the war, but nor did he want another overwhelming victory that would again humiliate the Arabs and their Russian patrons. The best result would be "if Israel came out a little ahead but got bloodied in the process," he had told Nixon. Slowing down American aid to Israel was one way to gain his ends. And Schlesinger might have been less invested in Israel's success than in neutralizing the Arab oil weapon. But both men were also influ-enced by Israel's constant assurances that it would win the war rapidly. Golda would never allow Israel to appear weak, so that even at the worst time, when pleading for supplies, Dinitz told Kissinger that the future "looks promising." That double message of "we're strong, but help us" might have contributed to the delay.

To Golda, it made little difference who held up the arms or why: Israel needed supplies and needed them quickly. Having given his approval for the weapons, Nixon had become overwhelmed by Watergate issues, leaving the deliberations on how to resupply Israel to Kissinger. Only when it became clear to both of them that the Soviets had launched a monumental airlift of arms to the Egyptians and Syrians did he involve himself again. "We can't allow a Soviet-supported operation to succeed against an American-supported operation," he told Kissinger. "If it does, our credibility everywhere is severely shaken."

The series of decisions the president now made led to one of the most critical airlifts in history, code-named Operation Nickel Grass. Kissinger, who still hoped to keep America's hand hidden, had thought to have Israel charter commercial airliners to carry the supplies, but no airline would risk its pilots or aircraft in the dangerous Middle East war zone. Nixon decreed that the United States use its own aircraft—the Military Airlift Command—to fly ammunition, tanks, radar systems, even helicopters directly to Israel. "Whichever way we have to do it, get them in the air *now*," he ordered. When Schlesinger suggested sending only three C-5A military transports to avoid difficulties with the Arabs and Soviets, Nixon argued that the United States would take as much heat for three planes as for three hundred. And when a dispute broke out about the type of plane to use, he thundered, "Goddamn it, use every one we have. Tell them to send everything that can fly." After Nixon and Golda had both resigned, he wrote to her that he would "always be proud of" his decision to insist on a "massive airlift rather than the rather modest assistance which my military advisors had recommended."

The airlift began on Saturday, October 13. The plan had been for the planes to land at night, immediately unload, and fly out of Israel before daybreak to keep the secrecy. Crosswinds at Lajes Field in the Portuguese Azores islands, where the planes stopped to refuel, delayed the flights, and most arrived early Sunday morning in broad daylight. Half of Tel Aviv came out to cheer the great Galaxies and Starlifters that landed at Lod Airport. Golda cried—allowed herself to cry for the first time since the war began—then greeted the pilots with kisses. All told, the planes flew to Tel Aviv more than three hundred times, landing every fifteen minutes and delivering some twenty-two thousand tons of matériel.

WHILE THE AMERICANS WERE DITHERING about how and when to send out the airlift, Golda Meir was making far-reaching decisions of another kind. After recapturing much of the Golan, Israel's military leaders wrestled with what to do next on the Syrian front. Should they dig in and consolidate the positions they had won along the 1967 cease-fire line, known as the Purple Line? If they did that, they would be able to send one of their divisions to the south to help the troops there hold out against the Egyptians. Or should they use all their divisions to make a bold counterattack against the Syrians, push them back from the Purple Line, and head toward Damascus? They had to act quickly, because Iraqi troops were on their way to reinforce the Syrian army, and King Hussein might jump into the fray with his Jordanian forces. After hours of discussion without reaching a conclusion, the military men carried their dilemma to their civilian prime minister for her verdict. Golda chose to cross the old cease-fire line and push on to Damascus. In her elemental way, she reasoned that it would take four days to move forces from the north to the southern Egyptian front, and if during that time the UN ordered a cease-fire, Israel would have nothing to show for its grueling days of war. It would have lost territory in the south and gained nothing new in the north. Accordingly, on Thursday, October 11, Israeli forces began a counterattack in the north that after some days of fierce fighting brought them within twenty miles of the Syrian capital and left Syrian forces and armor decimated.

With the northern border relatively under control, Golda put that mission on hold while she and her commanders focused their attention on the Egyptian front. The airlift had not yet arrived, but the knowledge that supplies would be replaced boosted morale and gave the military the confidence to press on and use up the stockpiles it had. But in what way? What should be the next step in Sinai? It's not often that national or military leaders hit a moment in their activities that they intuitively recognize as a turning point. In the afternoon of October 12, Golda and her war committee reached such a moment at a meeting in her Jerusalem office.

The atmosphere had become gloomy again. Dayan, Elazar, Bar-Lev, and the others deliberating the army's next move wavered on the brink of discouragement. Exhausted from the intensive fighting in the south, the IDF needed a cease-fire to rebuild its strength, Elazar reported. But, Bar-Lev explained, the Egyptians, still securely ensconced on their bank of the Suez and with a foothold on the eastern, Israeli side, were not likely to sanction a cease-fire unless they faced a serious new danger. Among themselves, the generals had weighed the idea of creating that danger by sending Israeli troops across the canal to the Egyptian side. Such a crossing, however, would be fraught with risks for Israel. Two crack armored Egyptian divisions still stood on that side, still protected by the missile umbrella that had repulsed Israeli planes and tanks when the IDF attempted its first offensive.

While the committee debated the various options, an aide entered the room and signaled excitedly to the Mossad chief, Zvi Zamir, whom Golda had invited to the meeting, to step outside. At the other end of a secure phone, Zamir's bureau chief, Freddy Eini, gave him newly received intelligence information. The Egyptians planned to attack the Gidi and Mitla Passes deep in Sinai either the next day or the one after it. As part of the operation, the two formidable armored divisions would leave the Egyptian side of the canal and cross over to the Israeli side to join the offensive. A year earlier, the Egyptian spy Ashraf Marwan had described the same plan to the Mossad, and although it didn't happen then, Egypt's strategy now followed Marwan's plan exactly, validating the intelligence report. When Zamir returned with his news, a wave of excitement shot through the room. Everyone knew that the turning point in the war had arrived. The gloom dissipated and the air crackled with energy.

"Good," Golda said with satisfaction. "I understand that Zvika [Zamir's nickname] has ended the debate for us." She would take an aggressive stance toward moving ahead now.

Sadat had blundered. He had undertaken to move his forces away from their missile protection partly in response to pressure from Assad, who had been urging him to divert Israel from its attack on Syria, and partly out of hubris, so euphoric was he at his troops' early successes. On Sunday, October 14, the Egyptian armored divisions crossed into the Israeli eastern bank, to face bitter fighting from Israel. The ensuing struggle, involving 2,000 tanks, was "one of the largest tank battles ever to take place in history," wrote Chaim Herzog. The Egyptian army lost 250 tanks; the IDF 20. Bar-Lev phoned Golda, lifting her spirits. "Golda, it will be all right," he drawled. "We are back to being ourselves and they are back to being themselves."

That night, the IDF began its first secret steps toward laying bridges to cross the canal. During the next several days, the two sides would fight some of the cruelest and bloodiest battles of the war, with hundreds of soldiers killed or wounded, but led by General Ariel Sharon, Israel would succeed in its efforts to cross the canal and establish a stronghold in "Africa," as the IDF called the western, Egyptian bank of the Suez Canal. On October 17, the Soviet premier, Aleksei Kosygin, came to Cairo to persuade Sadat to seek a cease-fire or face total defeat. Just five days earlier, with her generals distressed and troops exhausted, Golda Meir had indicated to Henry Kissinger that Israel was leaning toward an immediate cease-fire, and Sadat had demanded a return to the June 1967 lines as his condition for it. Now, with Israeli forces across the Suez and their victory in sight, the roles reversed. The Soviets, and soon the Egyptians, pressed for a cease-fire; Israel could afford to take its time.

Meanwhile, Henry Kissinger had received an invitation to Moscow from the Soviet party secretary, Leonid Brezhnev, to work out cease-fire terms. The night he arrived in the Russian capital, October 20, the Watergate scandal in the American capital rose to a feverish pitch. In what the press dubbed the Saturday Night Massacre, President Nixon fired the special Watergate prosecutor, Archibald Cox, which led Attorney General Elliot Richardson and Deputy Attorney General William Ruckelshaus to resign immediately. The president tried to show he still had his hand on the tiller by staying in close touch with Kissinger during the secretary of state's negotiations with the Russians. As soon as they reached agreement, Nixon wrote to Golda Meir (in a letter prepared by Kissinger) urging her to accept their conditions. The terms Kissinger and Brezhnev agreed on, which that Sunday evening would become Security Council Resolution 338, included a cease-fire in place, a start to implementing UN Resolution 242, and an order for negotiations between the parties involved under the auspices of a third party. It was to be the UN's first call for the direct negotiations Golda had been demanding from the start.

At her insistence, Kissinger flew to Israel from Moscow to review the UN resolution. She was wary; she had always feared having the big powers impose their will on Israel, and with the reference to Resolution 242 she suspected a secret U.S.-Soviet deal to foist the June 1967 borders on the Jewish state. Kissinger assured her that the resolution's wording was vague enough to mean "nothing" until the various clauses were negotiated. She also had little faith in a standstill cease-fire. When Israel had agreed to that after the attrition war, Egypt had nevertheless moved its missiles up to the canal, causing much of the trauma early in this war. To this objection, Kissinger archly gave Israel a green light to continue its military action even after the cease-fire went into effect, ostensibly to compensate for an earlier communications delay. "You won't get violent protests from Washington if something happens during the night, while I'm flying," he said. When Golda said, "If they don't stop, we won't," he added, "Even if they do."

SEVERAL ISRAELI OFFICIALS joined Golda and Kissinger at lunch, when word came that Egypt had accepted the cease-fire. Golda knew Israel had no choice but to accept it also. To the Knesset, she emphasized that Israel had agreed "from a position of strength and military initiative" and out of "appreciation and esteem" for the United States and its "positive policy." The right-wing opposition objected, especially to the 242 clause, but the Knesset endorsed the cease-fire. It was to begin on October 22 at 6:52 p.m. Israel time.

It unraveled almost instantly. The Egyptians blamed the Israelis and the Israelis blamed the Egyptians for starting the fire again. Earlier, Israeli forces had almost completely ringed Egypt's elite Third Army—twenty thousand men and two hundred tanks—on the east bank of the canal. Within a day after the cease-fire, as the Third Army tried to break through its stranglehold, the IDF completed the work of encircling it and severing all its supply lines of food, water, and ammunition. In a paroxysm of rage, the Soviet Union demanded that Israel withdraw from any advances it had made and return to the October 22 cease-fire lines. When Kissinger suggested that Israel and Egypt negotiate a withdrawal line, Golda refused. Israel was not going to accept "Russian and Egyptian ultimatums . . . assented to by the United States," she had Dinitz tell Kissinger. Making no concessions, she finally agreed that if Egypt stopped shooting and accepted the cease-fire, Israel would do the same. Late on Tuesday, October 23, with Israeli forces some thirty miles from Damascus, Syria also agreed to end the fighting. A new cease-fire was scheduled to go into effect at 7:00 a.m. the next day.

But the Third Army was still entrapped. Desperate, Sadat appealed to both the Soviets and the Americans to send troops to the region to ensure that Israel adhered to the cease-fire, a move Kissinger strongly opposed for fear of a confrontation between the two powers. The Soviet leader, Brezhnev, who had been exchanging hotline phone calls and polite letters with Nixon about implementing the cease-fire, suddenly upped the ante. In a message of October 24, he attacked Israel for "drastically" violating the cease-fire and proposed that the two major powers jointly take action to curb the Israelis. If the United States did not agree to that, Moscow would consider "taking appropriate steps unilaterally." When the Soviet ambassador Dobrynin read the letter to Kissinger over the phone, the secretary of state interpreted it as a dangerous threat of Soviet military intervention in the Middle East. Nixon had gone to bed early, totally consumed by the Watergate affair. Rather than wake him, Kissinger and senior officials, among them Chief of Staff Alexander Haig, Secretary of Defense James Schlesinger, and others at the National Security Council, raised the state of alert of U.S. conventional and nuclear forces throughout the world to Defcon 3, the highest peacetime level of military readiness.

Kissinger informed Dinitz of the military alert, and a shocked Golda Meir called an emergency meeting of the cabinet, which lasted all night while the ministers debated Israel's next steps. The crisis gradually dissipated after Nixon and Brezhnev began to exchange conciliatory letters and agreed to have a UN force supervise the truce. But Golda and Israel were not off the hook about the Third Army. Kissinger emphasized that the United States would not allow Israel to capture that army and force a humiliating surrender by Sadat. He insisted that Golda permit food, water, and medical supplies to be brought to the beaten men. She resisted. A revitalized army might attempt a new offensive against Israeli forces. Kissinger pressed harder. If Israel didn't allow basic supplies to get through, the Soviets might embark on an airlift to the hemmed-in soldiers, or the United States itself might resupply them. "You will lose everything," he warned Dinitz, speaking, he said, "as a friend."

At one point, Golda suggested that representatives of Egypt and Israel meet face-to-face to negotiate about the Third Army, which Kissinger regarded as another stall. Irritated, he gave Dinitz a deadline: President Nixon required an answer from Israel by 8:00 a.m. Saturday, October 27, about how it proposed to deal with the Third Army. Golda responded with a scalding letter to him. "I have no illusions but that everything will be imposed on us by the two big powers," she wrote. The United States was rewarding Egypt for "her aggression," while "Israel is being punished, not for its deeds, but because of its size and because it is on its own." She was playing a clever strategic game. By complaining yet not giving an inch, she was forcing Egypt to negotiate on her terms. Her strategy paid off. At 4:07 a.m. that Saturday, the Egyptians amazed Kissinger by formally accepting Golda's proposal for face-to-face talks, to be held under UN supervision. They made two conditions: a complete cease-fire and the passage of one convoy of nonmilitary supplies to the Third Army.

Golda accepted both, and at 1:30 a.m. on Sunday, October 28, the Israeli major general Aharon Yariv and the Egyptian major general Mohamed El-Gamasy met at Kilometer 101 on the Cairo–Suez Road. They saluted each other, shook hands, and began in English the first direct talks ever held between representatives of the two countries.

On the morning of the historic meeting of the representatives of Egypt and Israel, Golda Meir appeared on the CBS television show *Face the Nation*. When asked about Israel's agreement to supply Egypt's Third Army with food and medical goods, she spoke of the pressures that had been exerted. Sadat should have been given time "to enjoy his defeat," she said. "He started a war, our people are killed, his in the many thousands are killed, and he has been defeated. And then by political arrangements he is handed a victory and has become or thinks he has become a hero in the eyes of the Egyptian people."

She knew he had not been handed a victory, but the image of Sadat as a hero haunted her. Earlier, when Kissinger had visited Israel, he asked her whether she thought Sadat would survive the setbacks his forces had suffered. "I do," she had said. "Because he is the hero. He dared." He had dared to take on Israel and puncture its myth of invincibility. Almost presciently, she understood that despite his defeat he would be celebrated. And despite her victory, she would never be the same. Neither she nor her nation would ever be the same.

29

An "Irrevocable" Decision

She alighted from the helicopter slowly, clothed in her standard warm-weather outfit: the simple short-sleeved beige dress, the white-laced orthopedic shoes, the big white handbag dangling from her arm. Never mind that she had come this Monday morning to the western bank of the Suez Canal, after a war that had scarcely ended and might burst out again at any moment. The prime minister maintained her proper appearance, even on the battlefield among exhausted men in grimy, rumpled uniforms. She had come to the front to hear firsthand reports of the war from commanders and their troops. Moshe Dayan had accompanied her, joined by Generals David Elazar, Shmuel Gonen, Chaim Bar-Lev, and others, and a slew of reporters and photographers pressed after her as she made her way painstakingly down the steps of a bunker that served as divisional headquarters. "How many times have I told you that I have not come for the newspapers? That's Tel Aviv or Jerusalem, but not here," she growled impatiently. With the press shooed away, she listened intently to descriptions of the fighting, especially alert to reports of enemy assaults after the cease-fire. She would take the reports with her to the United States in a few days, to drive home to Henry Kissinger that it was not Israel violating the truce.

One of the commanders related that of the ten trucks he inspected carrying supplies to the encircled Egyptian Third Army, three were filled with cartons of cigarettes for the officers and no water or food. "I can understand that," Golda said, to general laughter, as she lit up one of her chain of cigarettes. "They were all cigarettes with filters, so I didn't take a carton for you as a gift," the speaker continued in the same vein. "I know you wouldn't smoke filtered cigarettes." Golda chuckled. "It's good that you thought of me," she said. She liked being with the men, and especially liked meeting directly with the troops after speaking with their commanders. Sitting on a chair, the soldiers surrounding her on the ground, she found herself close to tears at times as they described having to fight off overpowering enemy forces. They spoke freely, and she answered their questions frankly. Even when they wanted to know why Israel had agreed to feed the trapped enemy army or accepted a cease-fire before the return of its prisoners of war, she felt comfortable with her "boys," in whom she took such great pride.

The questions that arose during this visit and another she was to make to the Syrian front a few weeks later reflected questions and comments she encountered wherever she went. Israel had won a clear-cut victory in the war that just ended. The army had overcome surprise attacks on two fronts, fully restored its position on the Golan Heights in the north, and aimed its artillery within twenty-five miles of Damascus. In the south, it had entrapped Egypt's Third Army on the east side of the Suez Canal and crossed to the west side, deep into Egyptian territory. Yet the mood in the country was glum. With so many reservists mobilized and no guarantee when they would return from the front, the economy struggled with severe manpower shortages and soaring inflation. More achingly, the war had taken a staggering toll in human lives. Some twenty-six hundred men had been killed and over seven thousand wounded, and the enemy still held several hundred soldiers prisoners. Jordanian television images of the barefoot, unshaven captives, their hands tied behind their backs, had ripped Israeli hearts, and the more so because those images seemed to symbolize the new image the nation had of itself: vulnerable, under mortal attack, and no longer infallible. To be sure, the Arabs suffered much greater losses—almost sixteen thousand troops dead and almost nine thousand taken prisoner—but in Israel, where everybody knew someone who had fallen or been hurt, the focus remained on the nation's grief.

In the political arena, questions cut closer to the bone. In the name of national unity, the opposition leader, Menachem Begin, had refrained throughout the war from attacking Golda's decisions or the military's actions. In a prelude of things to come, however, he alluded to the "frivolous" unpreparedness of the army, for which someone would have to answer. Within Golda's cabinet, Minister of Justice Ya'akov Shimshon Shapira blasted Moshe Dayan for his "failings in protecting the country." Dayan offered Golda his resignation (again), and she turned it down (again), stating publicly that he enjoyed her "full confidence." Members of the Alignment rallied to her side, with Mapam's leader, Yaakov Hazan, accusing Shapira of launching a "blood libel" that could destroy the party. The commotion died down when Shapira himself resigned, a loss for Golda, who had often turned to him for advice. Not yet prepared to deal directly with the discontent, Golda promised to take up war matters "when the time is right." For the present, she was headed for the United States.

She had initiated the visit; it's unlikely that either Nixon or Kissinger longed to see her. She had accepted the cease-fire and agreed under duress to begin resupplying the Egyptian Third Army, and they knew she would not spare them her ire about that. A State Department briefing paper described Mrs. Meir as "an outstanding organizer, a decisive leader and a skillful propagandist" who could be "friendly, tactful, and charming or stubborn and blunt." Kissinger expected more stubborn and blunt on this visit than tactful and charming.

As she viewed it, she needed the trip to affirm America's special relationship to Israel and be reassured that in its desire to win Egypt away from Russian dominance, the United States was not tilting too far toward the Arab side. She had no illusions about Israel's almost total dependence on the superpower. No European nation had come to her country's aid during the war, and even most of the African states she had worked so hard to cultivate had broken off diplomatic relations with Israel to stay on good terms with the oil-rich Arab lands. The United States was Israel's only "real friend," she had told cabinet members in agreeing to send the first convoys to Egypt's Third Army, and "there was nothing to be ashamed of" when sometimes a small country like it simply has to give in to that nation's demands. Still, Israel had its own demands that she was taking with her, high among them the release of its prisoners of war, direct negotiations with Egypt, and the lifting of an Egyptian blockade of the Bab el-Mandeb Strait at the southern end of the Red Sea, which cut off vital Iranian oil supplies for Israel.

The press wanted to know whether Mrs. Meir had come to the States to fend off American pressure for further concessions. Not at all, the premier answered firmly each time the query arose. But if there was no American pressure, why *did* she come to Washington now? "To find out there was no pressure," she finally snapped.

In reality, the pressure was becoming suffocating. Ismail Fahmi, soon to be Egypt's foreign minister, arrived in Washington on October 29, two days before she did. Meeting with Nixon and then Kissinger, he insisted that there could be no exchange of prisoners or lifting of the blockade until Israel agreed to return to the first cease-fire lines of October 22, before it had completely encircled Egypt's Third Army. "Nobody in the Arab world believes that you cannot tell Israel what it must do," he said drily, when Kissinger claimed he needed time to work on the matter. But being told what to do by the big powers was precisely what Golda most resented and would fight against during her three-day stay in America's capital.

She met with Kissinger once before she spoke with President Nixon and twice afterward, late night meetings at Blair House, where she was staying. With Nixon, she had established a pattern since their first conference in 1969. She would flatter him. "I told the troops of your help," she said when they met, warmly thanking him again for the airlift. He would speak in generalities: "You have to have some confidence in me and in Henry that we will do our best." He did warn that if the cease-fire broke down and "Europe and Japan freeze this winter" because the Arabs cut off their oil supplies, "Israel will be in a hell of a spot." And he bantered that if Israel did not begin negotiating with Egypt under American auspices, "I could leave you to the UN," which led Golda to crack, "That court of high injustice!" But for the most part the president left the detailed haggling for his secretary of state.

She trusted Kissinger, but up to a point. She was wary of the compromises she knew he would press on her so that he could win over Egypt. Kissinger sympathized with Golda, but up to a point. He noted that she looked "devastated" and "drained" by the war, yet he felt thwarted at every turn by her refusal to give in to what he regarded as crucial to the U.S. policy of luring the Arab world away from the Soviets. Like dueling fencers, they attacked and parried, lunged and retreated, circling each other to find the weak spots.

Israel did not want to be told, "You have to do this. Take your choice," Golda railed at the secretary of state right off. And she objected to the credence he gave Sadat. "Why believe the Egyptians? Why is it that everything we say isn't believed?" As for the original cease-fire line of October 22, she argued that nobody even knew exactly where the fighting had stopped at that time. She proposed instead that the two sides exchange positions—Egypt leave the eastern, Israeli-controlled bank of the Suez Canal and Israel leave the western, Egyptian bank, each side pulling back ten kilometers from the canal.

Sadat would never accept such a proposal, Kissinger countered. He'd be overthrown if he got nothing on the east bank and gave up territory on the west bank. On the other hand, Golda was being "too honest." If she used a little deviousness—one of Kissinger's own diplomatic techniques—she could accept the *principle* of the October 22 line, offer to negotiate with Egypt about its exact location, and in that way stall for time while tackling other matters important to each side. For Sadat, most crucial of those matters was to have Israel continue its convoys of food and medical supplies to the entrapped Third Army. For Golda, the return of Israeli prisoners overshadowed everything. At home, relatives of captured soldiers had been demonstrating for three days for a stronger government stand on getting its prisoners back. "We can't allow convoys through without our prisoners," she insisted. "We're one family. They don't care about their prisoners." Nor was she willing to have UN inspectors replace Israelis in monitoring the convoys, for fear they would allow the Egyptians to slip in military supplies.

Two nights in a row, America's secretary of state and Israel's prime minister dueled with each other into the early hours of the morning. A frustrated Kissinger barked at one point, "This is the lousiest assignment I've had since I've been here." Time and again he threatened, as he had before, that if Israel didn't allow the convoys to pass through its lines and reach the beleaguered Egyptian army, Russia would airlift supplies in, and the United States just might join it. "Madame Prime Minister," he said impatiently at their last meeting, on November 3, "you didn't start the war, but you face a need for wise decisions to protect the survival of Israel." And she, with shaky voice, replied morosely, "You're saying we have no choice." Yet by the time that night's meeting ended, Kissinger had a general framework of Israel's conditions for a formal cease-fire that he would take to Cairo, where he was going on November 6 to meet with President Sadat.

The secretary of state no longer thought of the Egyptian president as a clown; indeed, he would soon refer to him as a "remarkable man." Sadat surprised him by accepting a draft of a six-point agreement Kissinger had constructed, although it left the Third Army still encircled and had only vague wording about Israel's returning to the October 22 line. He could do so, Kissinger wrote, because the proposal had something in it for everyone. Sadat's Third Army would continue to receive nonmilitary supplies, and the UN would replace Israeli checkpoints on the Cairo–Suez Road, although at the Suez end Israeli officers could participate in checking the cargo. Golda got the longed-for release of Israeli prisoners in Egypt and relief from anxiety about withdrawing to the October 22 line. While not spelled out, the Egyptians also agreed to ease their blockade of the Bab el-Mandeb Strait. Joseph Sisco brought the plan to Golda, who was back in Israel. She examined it "with the thoroughness of a bloodhound" but, once satisfied, congratulated Kissinger on "a fantastic achievement."

At 3:00 p.m. on Sunday, November 11, 1973, General Aharon Yariv and his counterpart, Lieutenant General Mohamed El-Gamasy, sitting at a U-shaped table in their tent on Kilometer 101, with their aides present, signed the six-point cease-fire agreement that later became the basis for a separation of troops and paved the way for final peace talks.

GOLDA ANNOUNCED THE CEASE-FIRE AGREEMENT to the nation from Lod Airport before boarding a plane to London for a Socialist International meeting. Everything had changed since she attended the organization's last meeting in Paris about a year earlier. At that time, the French president, Georges Pompidou, angrily objected that the gathering had been designed to enhance the standing of France's Socialist Party, his political opponents, in a forthcoming election. He particularly objected to the presence of Golda Meir, who had become deputy chairman of the organization, given her popularity among the French despite the government's cold relations with Israel. This time it was she who came in anger at her socialist colleagues, whose countries had refused to sell Israel weapons or help in any way during the Yom Kippur War.

She had set the event in motion with a phone call to West Germany's chancellor, Willy Brandt, who organized it. Socialist leaders from twenty countries, including eight other heads of state, gathered at the Churchill Hotel, where they listened in stunned silence to her fifty-five-minute opening speech. After describing Egypt's surprise assault and Israel's losses—equating the numbers of Israelis killed proportionately to two and a half times America's losses in ten years of the Vietnam War—she lambasted the European nations for not permitting American planes to refuel on their territory during the airlift. Only Portugal had allowed the planes to land, at the Azores. "We are all old comrades, long-standing friends," she said, her bitterness almost tangible. "On what grounds did you make your decisions . . . ?" The European countries had a "Munich attitude," she continued, willing to sell out Israel for Arab oil, the way they had betrayed Czechoslovakia at Munich to appease Hitler in 1938. She had long ago determined to safeguard Israel from becoming like Czechoslovakia, a small country at the mercy of large ones.

"What did you think?" she concluded, according to a socialist leader who witnessed the closed session. "That confronted with death, Israel would go down alone?" Regarded by many as an allusion to Israel's nuclear capabilities, her words "sent shivers through the audience." Nobody applauded after she finished, and when the conference chairman, Bruno Pittermann, asked if anyone would like to speak, he got no response. After a long silence, someone—probably Harold Wilson—called out, "Of course they can't talk. Their throats are choked with oil."

That showdown out of the way, Golda visited the British prime minister, Edward Heath, at 10 Downing Street before returning to Israel, their first meeting in three years. Anticipating her criticism of Britain's embargo on arms to either side, a background paper advised Heath that while there was no "guaranteed method of handling Mrs. Meir successfully when she is in a contentious mood," she was "susceptible to compliments if she finds them plausible." Accordingly, Heath began by congratulating Golda on the cease-fire agreement with Egypt. She still got in some licks about British policy. "Had not the British government seen any difference between the situation of an aggressor and a country which was attacked?" she asked. But rather than dwell on that, she used part of their time together to enlist Heath's aid in arranging a prisoner exchange with Syria, which had not participated in the truce with Egypt. The plight of Israel's prisoners in Syria had become alarming; some had been found blindfolded and shot through the head, their hands bound behind their backs, and the Red Cross had made no headway with that government. Heath promised to do what he could.

On November 15, a few days after she returned from London, Golda elatedly witnessed the first prisoner exchange with Egypt. Special red-and-white planes chartered by the International Red Cross flew from Cairo to Tel Aviv with the most injured men first, then returned with the freed Egyptians. Over the next week, 238 Israelis were exchanged for about 8,400 Egyptians. While cameras clicked, thousands of Israelis greeted the arrivals, some weeping, some pressing bouquets of flowers into the men's arms. In contrast, the freed Egyptians were taken to a military section of the Cairo International Airport closed to public view, with newsmen and photographers barred from watching them disembark. After portraying himself as the victor in the war, Sadat did not want attention called to the disproportionate number of Egyptian prisoners compared with Israeli.

Perhaps more than anything, the arrival of the prisoners brought home to a still traumatized Israel the reality of what it had experienced.

From every direction now, Golda faced blame for the blunders and body counts the war had wrought.

In the Knesset, Menachem Begin removed his kid gloves and lunged for the jugular. On November 13, he "advised" the prime minister to submit her resignation because of "criminal negligence." Wagging his finger at her and her ministers, he introduced a slogan he was to repeat at every opportunity: "Why did you not call up the reserves?" "Why did you not advance the tanks?" Soon the refrain would be taken up throughout the country.

There had already been calls from the press and other quarters for an official investigation of why Israel had been so unprepared. Golda resisted at first, rebuking newspaper editors for wanting to "chop off" somebody's head so soon. "If we were a normal nation," she told a Mapai colleague, Moshe Baram, "we would not be required to have an investigative committee. England didn't have an investigative committee after Dunkirk," when British forces suffered a disastrous defeat by the Nazis. She gave in, Baram said, because she no longer had the emotional stamina to fight the demands. At her direction, the cabinet appointed a commission of inquiry, which was given judicial powers like that of a criminal court. Chief Justice Simon Agranat of the Supreme Court became the commission's chair, and he, in turn, named five members to it, among them two former generals, Yigael Yadin and Haim Laskov. Later, IDF officers and ordinary civilians would accuse the two of having been biased in Moshe Dayan's favor. Like everyone linked to the Yom Kippur War, Golda would be required to testify at length before the commission.

Within the Labor Party itself, she felt jabs of disapproval. After toning down their differences during the war, the doves and hawks clawed at each other again. The doves, most of them younger members of the party, rejected the Galili document she had approved in August as the platform for the next election. Because of the war, the election had been moved from October to December 31, and such party members as Lova Eliav, Pinhas Sapir, and Yigal Allon wanted to use the time to overhaul the platform and start again. They also argued for reopening the party election lists that had been prepared before the war to include more moderate candidates, which would entail postponing the elections. Golda opposed changing the slate of candidates or the election times. But she understood that if she wanted to hold the party together and block Begin and a newly formed Likud Party (composed of Gahal and some small right-wing parties), she needed to modify the Galili plan for a platform better suited to postwar conditions.

At the same time, the attacks on the Galili document, which included attacks on Galili, Golda's most trusted adviser, spilled over to attacks on her. A Labor Party magazine, *Ot*, carried an article by Zvi Kesse, then a young dove, calling outright for the resignations of Golda Meir and Moshe Dayan. Others in the party more subtly blamed Dayan but barely hid their unhappiness with Golda's reliance on her small kitchen cabinet for major wartime decisions. Worn out though she was, she was not going to be sidelined without a fight. She demanded a debate on the simmering issues, to determine "what kind of a party we have and what it stands for."

What began as rebellion ended in compromise. After hours of back-room discussions, the party's central committee arrived at a fourteen-point program for the platform designed to satisfy all sides. It spoke of "defensible borders" but also of "territorial compromise," of consolidating settlements, but with priority given to "security considerations." Although it rejected the idea of a separate Palestinian state, it acknowledged Palestinian "self-identity," which it said should be realized within the state of Jordan. Pleasing to Golda, it described a forthcoming Arab and Israeli peace conference in Geneva sponsored by the United States and the Soviet Union as a "major event in the history of the Middle East." Here was a chance to show Israel and the world the party's peaceful goals.

Despite the document's attempt at evenhandedness, when the party's central committee met on December 5 to vote on it, tensions ran high. Did the new paper actually replace the Galili plan? What should Israel demand of the peace conference? And, above all, should the leadership be changed? Golda sat in her front-row seat, puffing on her ever-present cigarette, listening to forty speakers, beginning at 9:00 a.m. with Yigal Allon calling for all the ministers except Mrs. Meir to resign and continuing with one after another criticizing the government or each other. For fifteen hours, she listened, occasionally commenting. At about 1:00 a.m., she rose to the podium.

Ignoring the hour, she launched into a long, meandering speech defending herself yet assuming responsibility for the war's mistakes. She highlighted peace feelers she had sent to Sadat before the war, with no response, and she mentioned Dayan's suggestion early to pull back from the Suez Canal so that the Egyptians could open it to shipping.

"I confess," she said, "that I did not understand what he was talking about. Retire from the canal? Just like that?" How, at the time, could she have withdrawn without an agreement from Sadat? And how to make an agreement when he demanded up front that Israel return everything captured in 1967?

Nevertheless, "if anyone should take parliamentary responsibility, I put myself first," she said. She had been told, she continued, that she looked sad on television, and that was bad for the nation's morale. "At my age should I start wearing makeup?" she joshed, veering off the subject. "I would, if I thought it would help. But I'm a realist in such matters, and I can't wear a mask." Then back: "I'm sad like everyone else, plus one thing—the fact that I am the prime minister." She went on, "There was a fatal mistake of evaluation. The information was in our hands, including mine, and I have tortured myself not a little since then."

When she finished her talk, she demanded a vote of confidence, a secret ballot so that nobody would feel intimidated. And, of course, she would be more than happy if other candidates for party leadership stepped forward. As expected, no alternative candidates appeared. Bleary-eyed party members (Golda still alert and energetic) cast their ballots at 3:00 a.m. to give their premier overwhelming approval. The final count was 291 for, 33 against, and 15 abstentions. Once again she had proven that, as the *New York Times* correspondent Terence Smith put it, "Mrs. Meir bestrides the Labor Party like a colossus."

IN THE MIDST OF THE postwar turmoil, David Ben-Gurion died on December 1, 1973, at the age of eighty-seven, after suffering a stroke some two weeks earlier. To many Israelis, he seemed a figure from the distant past, unconnected to their lives, but for Golda he would remain her idol, an intrinsic part of herself, and she a devoted "Ben-Gurionist." Even after their bitter quarrels, she regarded him as superior to any world leader, the giant of her age, the true colossus. "With all his faults, and he *had* faults," she was to say, "in critical hours, he was always right." At a cabinet memorial, hung with a black-bordered portrait of the "old man," she eulogized him as the nation's "chosen one" who knew "that our strength was in deeds."

Ben-Gurion's death symbolically marked the end of the heroic age of the state's creation. Only Golda remained from the founding generation of leaders, alone, ill, facing issues the others had not: a war almost lost, a nation doubting itself, leaders publicly maligned, isolation on the world stage. Yet she also had what Ben-Gurion never did: the tantalizing possibility of reconciliation with Israel's most formidable neighbor, Egypt.

Henry Kissinger viewed the road to that reconciliation in step-by-step terms. The cease-fire had been a first step, the planned Geneva peace conference the next. The war had ended much the way he wanted it to. Israel had won, but not with a smashing triumph. Egypt had regained its self-respect and leveled the field, placing the prospect of an agreement in the realm of reality. Golda had been moved by the negotiations between the Israeli and the Egyptian generals on Kilometer 101, "the first time Israeli soldiers and Egyptian soldiers sat in tents and talked," she said. Actually, with her support they had progressed from the cease-fire agreement to negotiations about the disengagement of their two armies. When they hit a stalemate, Sadat broke off the talks, probably instigated by Kissinger. The secretary of state had grown irritated with the military men for not keeping him informed of their progress. More to the point, he had planned disengagement to be the main agenda of the Geneva conference and would not allow that to be taken away from him. The conference was his show, and he wanted total control.

Kissinger traveled to the Middle East again, winning agreements from Egypt and Jordan to send representatives to the conference. As he told it, when he met with Assad, the Syrian president agreed to every condition he set down. Astonished, Kissinger congratulated him on his flexibility. To which Assad replied that it made little difference to him what went on at the conference, because he had no intention of having Syria attend. When the conference convened, Syria was represented by an empty chair and a nameplate at the table.

THE ISRAELI CABINET HAD ALREADY voted in principle to attend the peace conference; the hard bargaining was left to Golda and her negotiating team in meetings held with Kissinger in Jerusalem on December 16 and 17. Their first concern was the conference invitation. Always suspicious of the United Nations (which in two years would pass its "Zionism is racism" resolution), Golda objected to having the conference take place under the "auspices" of that international organization. After much debate it was agreed that the letter of invitation would have the United Nations convening the conference but not running it. The letter would also omit any reference to the Palestine Liberation Organization, which Israel regarded as a terrorist group. But overriding those specifics lay the most profound issue of the conference for Golda. To reconcile with

Egypt, Israel would have to withdraw from territory it had captured. Exactly when it would withdraw and from how much territory would be part of negotiations. One way or another, however, it would have to trade the concrete positions it now held on Egyptian soil for a more nebulous agreement of peace. To Golda, those positions represented security, a bulwark against any mischief Egypt might undertake. If at some point the peace fell apart, Egypt would have lost nothing, but Israel would have given up something real, something—Golda agonized—for which Israeli soldiers had sacrificed their lives.

"It is a unilateral step," she said to Kissinger. Israel desperately needed peace, but because she believed the Jewish state was at a disadvantage while seeking it, she determined to hold on as long as she could to every gain and fight tooth and nail to attain something in return before making any concession.

After ten hours of exhausting deliberations, Golda Meir accepted the letter of invitation and agreed to have Israel attend the Geneva conference. Her announcement of that decision in the Knesset incited an angry outburst from Menachem Begin. He didn't denounce the peace conference as such—that would have looked bad for his Likud coalition in the upcoming elections—but ignoring her marathon negotiations, he vehemently criticized the prime minister for having yielded too easily to Kissinger without demanding more before the conference. Golda chalked up his attacks to preelection rhetoric.

The conference opened on Friday morning, December 21, at the ornate Council Chamber of the Palais des Nations in Geneva. It was the week of Hanukkah, the festival of miracles, but anyone expecting miracles was in for a disappointment. The Egyptian delegate stipulated ahead of time that he would not shake hands or be photographed with Abba Eban, Israel's representative. He also demanded an empty table and chair to separate them; that issue was resolved by having individual tables for each country, with the UN secretary-general at a table in the middle. Public speeches consumed the entire first day, and the conference was formally adjourned the next day to await the Israeli elections. Despite that short duration, the very fact of the conference had symbolic significance. Israelis and Arabs had gathered in the same room to talk not about war but about settling their differences. They would hammer out solutions to some of those differences in the next weeks and months, but a beginning had been made. For Golda and the Labor Party, the conference offered an opportunity to associate themselves with hopes for peace and cast their Likud opponents as the party of war and fear.

Both parties had been running rather muted election campaigns, given the somber mood gripping the nation. A prestigious poll from the Institute of Applied Social Research found that ten days before the election a full 40 percent of voters had still not made up their minds. For the first time, both major parties used television, introduced into the country in 1968. The Labor Party put a different speaker on every night during the last two weeks of the campaign, Golda alternating with the others. Their theme on TV and in the ads that saturated newspapers cleverly combined self-criticism with criticism of the other side. "We Say: Nevertheless," proclaimed one ad directed at people who might want to express their anger by not voting. Such a path, the ad warned, could lead to the fall of Labor and increase the chances of war with the rise of Likud. Another ad cautioned that "punishing" Labor by voting against it would only strengthen the "'not one inch' policy" of the Right in its opposition to territorial compromise. "We Request Your Confidence," declared an advertisement featuring a motherly photograph of Golda with a heartfelt plea for a "mandate of peace and security."

The campaign paid off. In spite of their anger, over 80 percent of the more than two million eligible voters took to the voting booths on December 31 and returned Golda and the Labor Alignment to power. It was too hard in the aftermath of war and the insecurity of the present to drop Labor, the only ruling party the nation had ever known. Nonetheless, it was not a total victory. The Alignment lost 6 of its 57 Knesset seats, reducing it to 51 out of 120 seats, while Likud increased its seats from 31 to 39. With those numbers, Golda would have to woo disparate parties for her government.

But first she had to achieve a disengagement plan with Egypt. Almost immediately after the elections, she dispatched Moshe Dayan to Washington to present Kissinger with a plan he had devised and the cabinet had approved for separating the two armies. Dayan also invited Kissinger to the Middle East to help develop rules for several negotiation committees that had been formed during the Geneva conference. Although Kissinger consented, Sadat made it clear that he wanted an agreement quickly and he preferred to deal directly with the secretary of state, his "friend," than with negotiating teams. Geneva fell by the wayside, and Kissinger embarked on a frenetic "shuttle diplomacy" between Israel and Egypt.

Back and forth the secretary of state flew, from Jerusalem to Aswan, an Egyptian resort where Anwar Sadat had a villa, and back to Jerusalem. Sometimes he shuttled to both countries in one day, ultimately conducting three rounds of visits to each. Golda had come down with a nasty case of shingles, a painful viral infection of the nerves, which kept her from attending negotiating sessions with her team or the long working lunches and dinners Kissinger held with Abba Eban and Moshe Dayan. Even so, the secretary of state visited her at her Jerusalem home when he began his rounds and never left Israel for Egypt without consulting her about every idea on the table. In the course of two weeks, he managed to narrow the gap between the two countries' proposals. As wrenching as it was, Golda dropped talk of a final peace treaty at this time or even of Egypt's renouncing its state of war with Israel and concentrated strictly on the separation of military forces. For the first time, she agreed also to give up territory Israel had occupied since 1967. On his end, Sadat abandoned the conditions he had been adamant about two years earlier, such as a timetable for Israel's withdrawal from all Arab lands, and accepted the more limited pullbacks he had refused to consider at that time.

On the last day of Kissinger's shuttle, January 17, as he arrived in Israel to nail down the disengagement agreement, he delivered a personal message to Golda dictated to him by Anwar Sadat: "You must take my word seriously. When I made my initiative in 1971, I meant it. When I threatened war I meant it. When I now talk of permanent peace between us, I mean it. We have never had contact between us. We now have Henry Kissinger whom we both trust. Let us use him and talk to each other through him and then we will never lose contact with each other."

The next day Israel's premier gave Kissinger a return message for the Egyptian president: "I am deeply conscious of the significance of a message received by the Prime Minister of Israel from the President of Egypt. It is indeed a source of great satisfaction to me and I sincerely hope that these contacts between us through Dr. Kissinger will continue and prove to be an important turning point in our relations. I, on my part, will do my best to establish trust and understanding between us." Using Sadat's words, she reiterated, "When I talk of permanent peace between us I mean it."

On that Friday, January 18, 1974, in the army tent at Kilometer 101, with clear skies and a biting wind outside, Generals David Elazar and Mohamed El-Gamasy signed an agreement for the disengagement of their forces (known as the Sinai I Agreement). It called for Israel to withdraw completely from the western bank of the Suez Canal and from the eastern bank about twenty kilometers into the Sinai. The strategic Gidi and Mitla Passes would stay in its hands. Egypt remained in the eastern bank areas it had recaptured, separated from the Israelis by a UN buffer zone. Both nations had permission to keep seven thousand troops and thirty to forty tanks in their zones. It was understood also that Egypt would reopen the canal and rebuild the cities along its banks. "True," a relieved Golda told party members, "this is still not peace. But six years ago [after the 1967 war], they would not even listen to us, let alone sit with us." To a beaming Kissinger, she said, "I sincerely and honestly believe you have made history this week."

Pushed aside for the moment was the tortuous bargaining between the two leaders and the jokes each is said to have made about the other at times. Kissinger reputedly mimicked Golda and called her "Miss Israel" to Sadat. She reputedly responded to Nixon's observation that they both had Jewish foreign ministers, "Yes, but mine speaks English." Then, too, when Kissinger huffed at her that he was an American first, then secretary of state, and then a Jew, she shot back, "That's okay, Henry. In Hebrew we read from right to left." And when he complained that in Cairo Sadat hugged and kissed him but in Israel everyone always attacked him, she cracked, "If I were an Egyptian, I would kiss you also." In the long run, for all their differences, they were both pragmatists, bent on getting things done.

AS GOLDA MIGHT HAVE EXPECTED, she came under fierce fire from right-wing politicians as a result of the Sinai deal. Menachem Begin accused the government of "pursuing a path of capitulation in foreign policy" by making concessions without a peace treaty. Ariel Sharon, then a general turned politician, charged that by agreeing to leave the canal's western side, the government had cast away its "trump card."

Less expected was the far-reaching influence of a new phenomenon in the country. An amorphous group of young nationalist and religious Zionists had become newly unified and highly vocal in their opposition to giving up any territory Israel occupied in the Six-Day War. Calling themselves Gush Emunim (Bloc of the Faithful), they advocated building settlements throughout the territories and especially in the West Bank, the biblical Judaea and Samaria. Politically, many in this group were part of the young guard of the National Religious Party, which had traditionally been Labor's moderate coalition partner in the government. Influenced by the religious rulings of various Orthodox rabbis, these young people pressured their party's veterans to move away from Labor and affiliate more closely with right-wing political parties. They also called for changes in legislation about conversions to Judaism that would give the Orthodox greater control.

For Golda, the changed religious landscape made the task of fashioning a new coalition government more difficult than ever. Instead of being able to take for granted her party's alliance with the National Religious Party as she had in the past, she had to struggle to gain its participation in her government. For almost five weeks, she held wearying negotiations with its leaders, marked by frustrating on-again, off-again agreements. By February 20, just when she seemed to have a solid commitment from them, they pulled back, ordered by the chief rabbinate council not to accept any compromises on the conversion issue. Golda reluctantly began piecing together a minority government with two other small groups and altogether only fifty-eight seats in the Knesset.

Meanwhile, even more serious events began to disrupt the political scene. On a cold rainy morning, a young man with thick-rimmed glasses and windblown dark hair appeared in the parking lot opposite Golda's Jerusalem office holding a placard that read, DAYAN—RESIGN! The thirty-three-year-old reserve captain Motti Ashkenazi had commanded an outpost at the northern end of the Suez Canal, code-named Budapest, the only fortification on the Bar-Lev Line that did not fall to the Egyptians. In the thick of battle, after losing thirty-two men in his unit, he had vowed to protest the war's mistakes when he returned. Discharged from service on February 1, he took up his lone vigil two days later at what he called "From Budapest—in Protest." Two days after that, another reservist released from the army joined him. Then another and another in the days that followed as demobilized soldiers came home. Within a month, four thousand demonstrators, including many civilians, picketed Golda's office.

Golda understood the power of those protests and the moral sway of a Motti Ashkenazi. "If I live to be 150," she told Labor Party leaders, "I will not be able to compare myself to Motti Ashkenazi, who fought in the war and I did not." But why didn't the protesters understand how she and the others at the helm felt? "I cannot accept the idea that his pain and worry about the state are greater than my pain about all that happened," she continued. She understood the protesters' motivation but did not truly fathom the depth of their rage.

For the time being, Dayan had become the prime target for the intense emotions the war left in its wake. Parents of fallen soldiers spat at him and shouted "murderer." In a full-page *Haaretz* ad, a long list of professionals—doctors, teachers, psychologists—accused him of being "directly responsible" for the blunders early in the conflict. Within the party, activists held a rally demanding that Golda deny him the Defense Ministry in her new cabinet. Even in the army, accusing fingers pointed at Dayan, once their hero, now their fallen god.

While Golda scrambled to form a government, a hurt and angered Dayan notified her that he would not serve in her next cabinet as defense minister. In addition to the pain of the protests, he felt strongly that Golda should form a national unity government that included Likud, something the National Religious Party's young guard also demanded. She flatly refused. Such a coalition would be a "government of paralysis," she argued, at a time when compromises would have to be made with Egypt and Syria. But she needed Dayan and his Rafi faction to bolster the Labor Party. "I have asked him, I am asking him, and I will be asking him to be included," she told reporters. When Shimon Peres, out of loyalty to Dayan, also refused to serve in her cabinet, she reprimanded them, "You have no right to go—not at so difficult a time."

Disappointed, yet determined to keep her government afloat, Golda offered the post of defense minister to Yitzhak Rabin. By now, she was exhausted by the endless bargaining sessions and fed up with fractious party politics. Not fully recovered from her bout with shingles, she had suffered an inflammation of her eyelids, which confined her to her home for several days. On March 3, she presented her cabinet to a closed-door session of Labor Party leaders. After listening stoically for four hours while they tore apart her choices, she decided she'd had enough. "Had I resigned last August or September I would have been taking a wise step," she said, announcing moments later that she would not head the next government. With that, she marched out of the room, leaving her colleagues stunned and the party secretary, Aharon Yadlin, shouting, "Golda, come back, you must hear what we have to say."

"Like a silent Buddha," for an entire day she received the supplications of senior party leaders, as she had at other times. Finally, on Tuesday, March 5, she consented to return. On Wednesday, Moshe Dayan and Shimon Peres informed her that they would join her cabinet after all, claiming that a threatening Syrian buildup along the Golan Heights necessitated an immediate new government. Some people questioned whether the threat existed or whether the pair needed an excuse to return graciously. It made no difference. Having them back would make it possible for Golda to form a substantial government, and she welcomed them with tears of joy. "If I were an Arab, I would kiss you both," she joked. Indeed, their return prompted the National Religious Party to reverse itself and join her coalition. With sixty-eight seats, she presented her majority government to the Knesset on March 10, 1974. Dayan was again defense minister, Peres minister of information, and Rabin labor minister.

THEY STILL FACED serious war issues. Not long after Golda Meir and Anwar Sadat agreed on the separation of their forces in the Sinai, the Egyptian president sent another oral message to her and to Moshe Dayan urging them also to work out a disengagement deal with Syria's president, Assad. Ambassador Simcha Dinitz, who had delivered the message, suspected, he wrote to Golda, that Kissinger had induced Sadat to send it, in the hope that with the war ended, the Arab states would lift an oil embargo they had imposed on America a few months earlier. But Sadat was just as eager for a Syrian agreement so that he would not be isolated as the only Arab ruler to reconcile with Israel. The message conveyed his wish for Israel to proceed on the Syrian front and "not make any difficulties" for him in the Arab world. In her return message, Golda expressed Israel's desire to begin disengagement talks "at any moment," but not before Assad produced a list of Israeli prisoners of war in Syria and permitted the Red Cross to visit them.

Israel held over three hundred Syrian POWs, whose names it had given to the International Red Cross, but Assad refused to reciprocate unless Israel withdrew not only from the large areas it had conquered during the Yom Kippur War but also from territory on the Golan Heights it had taken during the 1967 war. That demand, an infuriated Golda told Kissinger, was "chutzpah of the nth degree." After starting a war and losing, how could he have the nerve to insist on more territory? In the meantime, families of Israeli POWs in Syria clamored for news of their loved ones. At one point, dozens stormed the Knesset and smashed some of its windows, demanding stronger government action to free the prisoners. And every day that Syrian and Israeli troops did not disengage, artillery and air fights continued on the Golan Heights.

In late February, Kissinger made a brief shuttle trip between Israel and Syria and returned from Damascus with good news. He had with him a list of sixty-two prisoners of war and three civilians who had been employed as watchmen on the Golan Heights. Eighteen other men were unaccounted for and now presumed dead. He also had Assad's consent for Red Cross visits to the captives. In a moment of high drama and tugging emotion, he called on Golda Meir in her Jerusalem office. For the prime minister, he was to write, "the list of surviving Israeli prisoners was not a negotiating counter or a political coup: it was a record of the life or death of members of her family." After examining the list, which was in Arabic, Golda said excitedly that she would have it translated into Hebrew and in the hands of the parents within two hours. When she gave the names to Chief of Staff David Elazar, he turned away from Kissinger while reading them so that the secretary of state would not see that he was crying. Turning back, he whispered in a hoarse voice, "Dr. Kissinger, we are very grateful."

Kissinger had extracted the names by agreeing to have Israel submit a disengagement plan to Assad that—despite Golda's objections—included pulling back from some areas of the Golan Heights captured in the Six-Day War. About a week earlier, at the peak of Golda's crisis in forming her government and with attacks zinging in from the Right, she had told a delegation of settlers from the Golan that she regarded the heights as an inseparable part of Israel and would not give up any territory within them. With the two sides so far apart, negotiations to go forward would be much tougher than they had been with Egypt.

But before bargaining could get under way seriously, Golda's life turned upside down.

She had testified for a full day on February 6 before the Agranat Commission of Inquiry investigating events leading to the Yom Kippur War. She had tried hard not to blame any key people for the war's mishaps. Yes, she wished the Mossad's chief, Zvi Zamir, had called her before going to London to meet with his chief Egyptian spy, but she understood how suddenly he had to leave. True, the head of military intelligence should have informed all cabinet ministers about the Russians evacuating Egypt and Syria just before the war, but there had been so many information leaks he took extra precautions. Mostly she blamed herself for not having proposed earlier that the reserve forces be mobilized. She could tell herself that as a civilian she was not expected to do what the generals had not deemed necessary, but that didn't stop her from agonizing about her decision. When the commission member Yigael Yadin asked her provocatively whether, in fact, she had not called up the troops because such a draft would look bad for her party in the upcoming elections, she replied indignantly, "I don't speak enough Hebrew to find the diplomatic words to appropriately reject that . . . It never crossed anyone's mind."

She was one of fifty-eight witnesses to testify before the commission. A nation on edge, eager to fix responsibility for the failures in the first days of the war, waited anxiously for the panel's first report. When it appeared on April 2, 1974, as an "interim report," it set off a blast that convulsed the country.

The commissioners had decided from the start that they would deal only with military matters and not political or parliamentary ones that involved civilian ministers. On that basis, they found Chief of Staff Lieutenant General David Elazar directly responsible for the errors committed on the eve of the war and recommended that he resign from the military. They also had severe criticisms for Major General Eli Zeira, head of military intelligence, and his deputy, Brigadier General Arye Shalev, both of whom had downplayed the threat of war with their "low probability" predictions, and recommended that they be removed from office. But the commission completely exonerated Moshe Dayan and Golda Meir of any negligence in carrying out their duties. It found that Golda had acted "fittingly" during the critical days before the war's outbreak and that she used her authority "properly and wisely when she ordered the mobilization of the reserves on Yom Kippur morning despite the weighty political factors involved." As for Dayan, the commission ruled that he "was not required to issue orders adding to or different from those proposed by the chief of staff and chief of intelligence," meaning that he had no responsibility for Elazar or Zeira's decisions.

Elazar immediately resigned, even while averring that an "injustice" had been done to him. He showed that as defense minister, Dayan, his superior, had full authority to make plans and decisions in all military matters before the war, and only in the actual fighting did he, Dado, become the decision maker. How, then, could he be blamed and Dayan not? Much of the nation agreed, and a cry went up throughout the land, louder than ever, for the defense minister to step down. The public viewed the popular Dado, who had brought the war to a successful end, as a scapegoat and Dayan as unduly favored, especially by the two generals on the commission.

Shocked and upset by the commission's harsh verdict against Elazar, Golda told him that he had been "a great and glorious commander." She later told Avner Shalev, his bureau chief, that "Dado saved the people of Israel." When Shalev asked why, then, she didn't defend him to the Agranat panel, she replied, "What would you have wanted—a new affair?" The Lavon Affair, which had split the nation, left behind years of hard feelings. Taking sides now, she implied, might cause a repeat of that trauma, and the more so if she pitted herself against Dayan and his followers. It was an insufficient answer that left Dado feeling painfully betrayed. Racked with sadness, he left the military and became head of Zim, Israel's national shipping line. Two years later, he died of a heart attack; some called it a broken heart. He was fifty years old.

When the report first came out, Dayan asked Golda for a third time if he should resign, and this time she didn't pressure him to stay. She answered, noncommittally, that the entire cabinet needed to make that decision. He decided not to resign and held on to that decision even as protests burst out everywhere and the Labor Party itself became chaotic. Yitzhak Rabin found the Agranat Report so flawed in evading the "real issue" of civilian responsibility that he wanted to send it back to the commission for reconsideration. Abba Eban would use the terms "eccentric" and "unacceptable favoritism" in describing it. Deputy Premier Yigal Allon, long Dayan's rival, spearheaded a campaign to oust the defense minister and elicited ready support from the leftist Mapam Party and Labor's Ahdut Ha'avoda faction. As always, Dayan's Rafi wing threatened to withdraw from the party and vote against the government if Dayan were driven out. "You realize that it won't end with Dayan," Haifa's mayor, Yosef Almogi, said to Golda. "They're really aiming at you." To which she replied, "You're telling me?"

With her party in crisis and the Likud opposition poised to send a no-confidence motion to the Knesset, which Labor could well lose, Golda Meir took matters into her own hands. On Wednesday evening, April 10, she stood before a meeting of Labor Party leaders and calmly announced her resignation. "Five years are enough. I have come to the end of the road. It is beyond my strength to continue carrying this burden," she said. She spoke for fifteen minutes to a packed and hushed room. Her decision to leave had nothing to do with Moshe Dayan, she insisted. Even if "yesterday, this morning, or right now" he decided to quit, she would resign anyway. She did not feel blameworthy for anything, she said, except for having given in two or three times in the past year— "against my better judgment"—to continue as party head and prime minister. She had done so because of the pleading of her colleagues and because, as she had since her youth, she accepted the will of the movement. Now, however, her decision was "irrevocable," and she wanted no delegations sent to try to change her mind.

None came. Golda's decision to quit "was the only one left to her,"

Lou Kadar wrote to Marie Syrkin. "As a matter of cold fact, she didn't take it, it was pushed down her throat, and not too gently either." Allies who might have been saddened by the decision accepted its finality. "Perhaps there was no other way out," said the party secretary-general, Aharon Yadlin. He and others began to plan for a new government in keeping with Israeli law that when a prime minister quits, the entire government falls.

This was not how Golda Meir envisioned leaving the post she had worked so many years to attain. A malaise had settled over her country since the Yom Kippur War. Along with taking the lives of thousands of soldiers, the war had cost more than seven billion dollars. To compensate, the government cut back on subsidies for bread, butter, milk, and rice. Families found their food costs rising more than 70 percent, while a bus ride cost twice as much as before. Golda's popularity dropped from 65 percent before the war to 21 percent in February. There had been times before the war when she considered resigning and times now when she wished she had. Yet her sense of duty to the party and her own desire to maintain her position (although she would deny that) had kept her at the job. She could not have escaped the abyss of this war.

A day after submitting her resignation to her party, Golda handed an official letter to Israel's president, Ephraim Katzir, and then spoke before the entire Knesset. That morning, three members of the Popular Front for the Liberation of Palestine had massacred eighteen persons in an apartment block in the northern Galilee town of Kiryat Shmona. As prime minister, Golda Meir had been the first world leader to encounter terrorism on the scale Israel suffered, and now, as her term of office drew to a close, she had to confront the worst attack that had taken place on Israeli soil. Profoundly shaken, she opened her Knesset talk by speaking about the slaughter, which she labeled "murder for murder's sake." She angrily blamed the government of Lebanon for harboring and aiding terrorists.

After a pause in the proceedings, she read the statement of her resignation, which she tied to "a ferment" among the public that could not be ignored and the need for a "new and stable" government. She listed Agranat Commission recommendations for improving that government and concluded by advising the nation to "live and act not as a defeated community but as a nation and state with a secure future ahead."

And for the next six hours, she sat and listened to a Knesset debate about her statement, her resignation, her handling of the war, and her government. Likud's head, Menachem Begin, always a gentleman, promised that when Mrs. Meir actually left the stage, he would proclaim from the Knesset rostrum his high esteem for her long service to the nation. "I can do without that," she called out bitterly from her seat. "I cannot," Begin answered. But meanwhile, he would point out her mistakes, which he did without restraint. Because she had described herself to her Labor colleagues as having reached the end of the road, he wondered how capable she was of heading even a caretaker government. He demanded, instead, early elections to replace her and her cabinet. He criticized her handling of the period before the war, and particularly the day before, when, he said, she neglected to inform the entire cabinet of the dangers the nation faced. "That's not true," Golda shouted, but Begin would not let up. He attacked her "kitchen cabinet" and the decisions she made with it and held her as responsible as Moshe Dayan for the war's early setbacks. Others in the opposition picked up his charges, ripping through her record as prime minister. Most members of her party had walked out during the debates, leaving her at the mercy of the opposition. One of the few who remained was Shimon Peres, who defended her briskly, citing the Agranat conclusion that at a crucial moment she made wise decisions. Years later, he still spoke proudly about having stood up for Mrs. Meir when others did not.

After six hours of discussion, the Knesset resolved to accept the prime minister's resignation and prepare for new elections. Golda Meir's political career of almost fifty years had ended. She left the Knesset with an overwhelming sense of relief and an enduring sadness.

30

"My Only Fear Is to Live Too Long"

Thrown off balance by Golda's resignation, the Labor Party fell into confusion. Party leaders overruled her wish for new elections, which would keep her caretaker government in place until the voting, opting instead to choose a new premier. Finance minister Pinhas Sapir, who had supported her position, changed and went along with the party's desire to appoint a prime minister and avoid elections, which it could lose. The powerful Sapir had seemed the most logical candidate to replace Golda Meir, but he adamantly refused. Given a choice between being prime minister and committing suicide, he would choose the latter, he told acquaintances. He still preferred his influential spot behind the scenes. The two people who did declare themselves candidates had been ferocious rivals for years: Shimon Peres and Yitzhak Rabin.

Golda had felt close to Rabin when he served as her ambassador in Washington, even though his streak of independence put her off at times. That streak, and her likely reservations about anybody who succeeded her, led her to refrain from openly endorsing either candidate, much to Rabin's disappointment. Knowing how greatly Golda disliked Peres, however, Sapir designated Rabin as his choice for prime minister. The former ambassador had several appealing qualities for the position. A native-born sabra, he had been in the Palmach, the elite pre-state strike force, and commanded Israel's army during the Six-Day War. With his clear blue eyes, square jaw, and straight talk, he seemed to embody the new generation of Israelis, the "sons" of the founders. Above all, he was untainted by either politics or the Yom Kippur War. He had been in Washington before the war and on his return headed an emergency fund-raising organization. Backed by Sapir, he won the party's election, with 298 votes against 254 for Peres. Because of Peres's strong showing, Rabin felt obliged to name him defense minister. In forming his cabinet, he shocked the party and the nation by appointing Yigal Allon foreign minister instead of Abba Eban, who had held the position for years, thus earning Eban's everlasting hatred.

Like Golda, Rabin felt hamstrung by the strong right-wing leanings of young members of the National Religious Party, Labor's past partner. To bypass that obstacle, Sapir recommended including Shulamit Aloni's Citizens Rights Movement (CRM, later called Ratz) in the government. Golda wouldn't hear of it. Although the women's mutual dislike was well-known, she insisted—to highly skeptical ears—that she had no personal objections to Aloni. No, not at all. Rather, adding the liberal CRM to the coalition would substantially increase the number of doves in the government, and that might lead to new policy battles. During a fraught all-night meeting at Tel Aviv party headquarters, Golda demanded that a vote be taken on her proposal to exclude Aloni's party from any Labor coalition. The party's secretary-general, Aharon Yadlin, refused her demand. With that, she stalked out in a rage, slamming the door behind her. She was not used to being overruled. An awkward silence followed. Then raucous fighting. And then, ignoring Golda's outburst, the Labor leaders voted to include the CRM in their coalition. With Aloni's party and other small ones, Rabin mustered a bare majority of 61 seats out of the 120 in the Knesset. He was to present his cabinet to the parliament on June 3, 1974.

While she was still prime minister, however, Golda Meir had one more major mission to accomplish, and she did not want to delegate it to anyone else. Racing against time, she needed to complete the work she and Henry Kissinger had begun of devising a separation of Syrian and Israeli troops and getting Israel's prisoners of war home from Syria. In Kissinger's words, now "the lioness rallied herself for one more heroic effort to bring about an agreement with the hated Syrians . . . which she recognized was essential for the security of her country."

The secretary of state had returned at the end of March from a "very brutal talk" in Moscow with the Soviet premier, Brezhnev, who was furious at America's attempt to squeeze the Soviets out of the Middle East. Kissinger knew that unless Israel and the United States produced an acceptable deal, Syria would fall right back into Russia's open arms. Among other concessions, Israel needed to offer Syria "some slice of the Golan Heights," he told Moshe Dayan, including the town of Kuneitra, which had been captured during the Six-Day War.

To gain his ends, in early May he embarked on another marathon shuttle, spending the next thirty-four days flying between Damascus and

Jerusalem, with occasional stops at other Arab capitals. Some nights in Israel, he and his team and Golda and hers argued until two or three in the morning, then picked up again early the next day. Once when he asked to speak to her for a few moments alone after a meeting, she said with a smile, "Sure. The young people want to go to sleep." The "young people" being Peres, Dayan, Dinitz, and Kissinger's negotiators.

Mobs of furious protesters greeted Kissinger on each of his trips to Israel. Angry protests against him had started during the Egyptian negotiations, but now what had been a few hundred demonstrators swelled to thousands as word spread of his pressures for concessions in the Golan. Unlike the Sinai desert, which separates Israel from Egypt by many miles, little distance exists between Syria and Israel proper and even less with the settlements that sprang up on the Golan after the war. Mostly young, mostly religious, many from the settlements, demonstrators gathered outside the Knesset or opposite Golda's office or in the street near her house, shouting, singing, stamping, as they denounced any kind of withdrawal from the captured area. They carried posters proclaiming, ERETZ YISRAEL IS OURS and NO SURRENDER, and they greeted Likud's leader, Menachem Begin, who egged them on, with excited cries of "Be-gin," "Be-gin." Hundreds denounced Kissinger as a traitor, at times screaming, "Jewboy, Jewboy, go home." The slur was a reference to anti-Semitic outbursts by Richard Nixon that had been heard on tapes of his conversations. Kissinger was shocked to encounter such taunts in the Jewish state, and Golda was outraged.

Some of Israel's intelligentsia also fought against any withdrawing from the Golan, with more than a dozen staging a hunger strike opposite Golda's residence. "Don't give a prize to the aggressors!" scholars demanded in a letter. "Don't breach the wall of the settlements!"

Golda moved ahead with the negotiations anyway. Greater Israel had never been her vision, but miles of the captured territories spelled security for her, and she would bargain even harder about Syrian disengagement than she had about Egyptian. She pulled out all the stops, ranging in her arguments with Kissinger from detailed haggling about every kilometer of land to emotional digressions about Israel's vulnerability. She was driven mad, she said at one meeting, when good, devoted friends of the Jewish state declared in their speeches, "And Israel is here to stay!" as if anyone could doubt that proposition. Does anybody question whether Canada is here to stay? Or Vietnam? Or Pakistan? Israel "is the only country in the world about which the best thing our friends can say is that it's here to stay," she complained. It should be understood that "Israel has as much right to live as anybody else."

When Kissinger spoke of the Arab leaders' frustration at not getting back land they felt was theirs, she responded that they were frustrated "because they could not destroy Israel." And when he needled her, "Is it a crime for a Syrian president to want a Syrian village back?" she retorted, "Yes. After a war, a Syrian president or an Israeli president or an American president that has attacked people twice in seven years, can't have what he wants."

As a negotiator, Kissinger used every technique he could muster. In one conversation, he poked at Golda's most sensitive nerve when he reflected vaguely that had they both "understood what could happen" and been "a little bit more active" in dealing with the Egyptians in 1973, just before the Yom Kippur War, perhaps that war "wouldn't have happened." His none-too-subtle warning: better to make concessions now than face another disastrous conflict.

For more than two weeks, Kissinger held contentious meetings in Damascus and Jerusalem, with little progress. Assad demanded that Kuneitra and some of the hills around it revert to Syria; Golda and her team were willing to give back part of the city and none of the hills. Assad wanted civilians to return to Kuneitra; Golda argued that those civilians might carry ammunition and lay mines to trap Israelis. The progress was so snail-like that an irate Kissinger expressed doubts about continuing. "I am wandering around here like a rug merchant . . . Like a peddler in the market!" he yelled at Golda. And he complained that "the people with the signs"—the protesters—were dominating Israeli positions. On the seventeenth day of the shuttle, he spoke to her about his plans to break off the talks.

THE NEXT DAY, Wednesday, May 15, 1974, a sickening terror attack pushed everything else to the background. In the early morning hours, three members of the Popular Front for the Liberation of Palestine crossed into Israel from Lebanon dressed like Israeli soldiers and carrying knapsacks loaded with explosives. In the town of Ma'alot in the Galilee, they randomly entered an apartment building and murdered a family, moving on from there to a school building, Netiv Meir, where more than a hundred teenage students and some teachers and nurses were sleeping. The group, most from a religious high school in Safed, had been on a three-day field trip. Some students and teachers managed to leap out the windows and escape, but the terrorists still held eighty-five students hostage. The men demanded the release of twenty terrorists in Israeli prisons by 6:00 p.m. or they would blow up the school with the children inside. Despite Israel's policy of not negotiating with terrorists, the cabinet agreed to do so, because, as Golda said, "one doesn't conduct wars on the backs of children." The French and Romanian ambassadors were sent as intermediaries, but the Palestinians refused to act until they received a code word from their organization in Bucharest. The code word never came, and with the 6:00 p.m. deadline approaching, Israeli soldiers stormed the schoolhouse. The terrorists were all killed, but they had managed to slaughter sixteen of the teenage hostages—most of them girls—and wound seventy, five of whom died later.

That evening, a grieving Golda spoke on national television about the "bitter" and "terrible" day. The cabinet had met all day, from 9:00 a.m. until 7:00 p.m., she said. When it became clear to the ministers that time was running out and the building would be blown up, they sent the army into action, with the grim results now known. She ended by promising that the government "will do everything in its power to cut off the hands that want to harm a child, an adult, a settlement, a town or a village." A week later, in a hushed, sad voice she spoke before the Knesset of the "wolves in human form" who had committed the Ma'alot atrocity and announced the appointment of a commission to investigate it. In the debate that followed, Moshe Dayan denounced the initial decision to give in to the terrorists, a rare public attack against the government by a minister in it.

Throughout the day of terror, Henry Kissinger and his wife, Nancy, remained in Jerusalem, following the events. That evening they visited Golda at her home to convey their condolences. Still shaken by the incident, she told the secretary of state that nevertheless they all had to get back to making peace. She would call a negotiating meeting for the next morning. That gesture meant more to him than anything that had come before, Kissinger was to say.

The tug-of-war picked up again, with neither side yielding. This time, Golda asked Kissinger to submit an American plan of possibilities. His proposal gave Syria slightly more control of the area around Kuneitra and Israel control of the surrounding hills, although with limited armaments. That plan now became the focus of several new shuttle go-arounds. Assad haggled for more territory; Israel demanded, in light of the Ma'alot tragedy, a promise that Syria would prevent Palestinian terrorists from crossing the line of separation between them. By Sunday night, May 26, when Assad again refused to budge on several details or to include a Palestinian terrorist statement, Kissinger told him he could do nothing more. The shuttle had failed, and he was going home. If this was a ploy on Kissinger's part, it worked. The next morning, as he and Assad shook hands to say good-bye, the Syrian president suddenly asked for one more effort—the way a good Arab merchant might begin to negotiate at the last moment. Back Kissinger went to Jerusalem and then to Damascus again.

On Wednesday, May 29, after another all-night session, Golda and her team accepted the final terms for disengagement with Syrian troops on the Golan. Based on the U.S. plan, the agreement included Syrian jurisdiction over Kuneitra and the return of civilian life there, Israeli control of the hills nearby, a thinning out of troops on both sides, and a special UN force in a buffer zone between the two armies. A paragraph at the beginning stipulated that both parties would scrupulously observe the cease-fire on land, sea, and air. A private memorandum of agreement from the United States to Israel stated that raids across the separation line would be considered a violation of the cease-fire, and Israel had the right to prevent them, with U.S. support for its actions.

Although they could not know it then, Golda Meir, Henry Kissinger, and Hafez al-Assad had constructed an agreement that would remain in effect for decades, lasting through much other turmoil in Arab-Israeli life. The Israeli prime minister and the American secretary of state congratulated each other at a party in her Jerusalem office attended by cabinet members and Knesset leaders. Golda told Kissinger it had been a "joy and a pleasure" to work with him—unlikely sentiments a few weeks earlier—and spoke of her hope that Syrian and Israeli mothers and wives and children would be able to sleep at night without fear. Kissinger praised Golda as the dominant figure in the negotiations, "towering over everybody." He closed his talk by kissing her on the cheek, and she uttered, in words that would join other Golda sayings, "Oh, Dr. Kissinger, I didn't think you kissed women." It was a dig at his many embraces of male Arab leaders.

Golda presented the terms of the disengagement agreement to the Knesset on Thursday, May 30. "I am happy that I can leave knowing that the government has succeeded in its very great efforts," she said, in this, her last appearance before the parliament as premier. Despite continued demonstrations and Menachem Begin's condemnation, Israeli and Syrian army officers signed the accord in Geneva the next day and began working out a detailed timetable for implementing it. The first step involved an exchange of prisoners of war, beginning with the wounded. As the bulk of Israeli POWs debarked in Tel Aviv on June 6 from the special DC-6 airplanes chartered by the International Red Cross, mobs of excited relatives and friends welcomed them with shouts of joy and tears of gladness. Golda Meir was on hand to greet them, as was Yitzhak Rabin, the new prime minister of Israel.

He had assumed that office on Monday evening, June 3, 1974. In presenting his government to the Knesset, he outlined a program that for the most part continued his predecessor's domestic and foreign policies. After a seven-hour debate, the Knesset endorsed his coalition, making him, at fifty-two, the country's youngest head of state and its first native-born one.

RABIN STEPPED FORWARD at 7:15 p.m. to sign his oath of office. At the same moment, Golda Meir rose from the premier's chair and turned toward the rear benches, where Labor Party delegates sat. Three other outgoing ministers also rose from their seats, Moshe Dayan, Abba Eban, and Pinhas Sapir, but all eyes were on her. "It was one of the most dramatic moments in my life," recalled the journalist Eitan Haber, who was in the Knesset that day. "She stood up, placed her handbag on her arm, and walked slowly, slowly toward the rear. I could see her back, slightly hunched, her swollen legs, and that bag hanging from her arm. Nobody shook her hand or said anything. Everybody knew it was the end of an era." Somebody made a place for her in the first row of the Labor Party's desks, and she sat down quietly, nodding to members on either side of her. The other three ministers found places in the last row of the Labor section.

Henry Kissinger phoned Golda Meir that evening. "How do you feel?" he asked. "Wonderful," she answered. "I feel so light-hearted and light headed. It's a good feeling."

On Tuesday morning, with the staff present, she raised a toast to Yitzhak Rabin as she officially turned the prime minister's office over to him. On Wednesday, she formally resigned from the Knesset. "I'm not going to enter a nunnery," she said on Israeli television, similar to words she had used when she retired years earlier as secretary-general of the party. "I'll take an interest in everything that happens." As a parting gift, the cabinet presented her with "a good, simple set of plates and dishes, no silver, just nice Israeli china," she wrote to a Hadassah friend.

As soon as she announced her retirement, Golda began receiving messages from admirers at home and abroad. Among them was a telegram from the British prime minister, Harold Wilson, that the British Foreign Office kept hidden from public knowledge for more than thirty years. Wilson called Golda's retirement a "terribly sad and moving moment." He spoke of their "closest personal and professional friendship" and the "priceless inheritance" she was leaving and ended with wishes for a "tireless" retirement. British officials classified the cable lest Arab leaders resent Wilson's affection for Israel's prime minister. The incident came to light when the British National Archives declassified that file in 2005.

Interviewing Golda Meir some years before her retirement, the Italian journalist Oriana Fallaci asked her if she feared death. The answer she received was "My only fear is to live too long." Golda had expressed that thought more than once. She had seen both her mother and her sister Sheyna ravaged by Alzheimer's disease, heartrending experiences for her. She had witnessed Ben-Gurion's mental deterioration, especially after he retired. She had gently suggested to her onetime lover Zalman Shazar that he retire from the presidency of the state after he'd had embarrassing moments of forgetfulness. She made people close to her promise that if they saw in her signs of mental decline, they would tell her, so she could withdraw from public view. "I want to die with my mind clear," she said to Fallaci.

She needn't have worried. At seventy-six, she not only had full control of her mind but, as Wilson had wished, was as "tireless" as ever. As a former premier, she was given a car and driver, a bodyguard, and secretarial staff. At first she wondered why she needed all those trappings of an office she had left, but she soon found out. Her phone never stopped ringing, and "hundreds and hundreds" of letters arrived regularly, with invitations for speaking engagements or requests to meet her now that she was "free." Although she spoke wistfully of wanting to wake up to an empty day, she rarely turned down an event. One day she might receive the keys to a city; another appear before a UJA or Pioneer Women mission visiting the country. Television and newspaper correspondents couldn't get enough of her, and everyone wanted to give her an award—from International Mother of the Decade to Israel's Man of the Year. The most prestigious Israeli award she received was the Israel Prize, the nation's highest honor, presented for her life's work.

And, of course, every dignitary who came to town called on her. Richard Nixon arrived about two weeks after she left office, the first sitting president to visit Israel. Golda had been in Hadassah Hospital for two days for a series of blood tests. She looked fit that Sunday afternoon, June 16, when she greeted Nixon and his wife, Pat, at the prime minister's residence in Jerusalem. She had planned to vacate that home as soon as she concluded the Syrian negotiations, when word came of Nixon's visit. She needed a grander space to greet him than the modest house in Ramat Aviv that she shared with Menahem and his family.

Drowning in the Watergate scandal, the president had hoped for a public relations boost with a trip to the Middle East, and he was rewarded with wildly exuberant crowds cheering him in the streets of Egypt, Saudi Arabia, and Syria. The Israeli greeting was a bit more low-key; his policy of seeking a more balanced American approach to the Arab states didn't sit well with many Israelis. Even so he received a warm enough welcome and an especially enthusiastic one from Golda. Toasting her at a state dinner that evening, Nixon said that of all the world leaders he had met, "none had greater courage, intelligence, stamina, determination or dedication" than she. In return, she praised him for "doing many things that nobody would have thought of doing," triggering peals of laughter in the press room in view of the accusations against him in the Watergate drama. She meant her words as a compliment and thanked him "as a great American president."

On the morning of August 9, 1974, Richard Nixon, having resigned the presidency, climbed into Marine One, the presidential helicopter, and left Washington in disgrace. Within a few days, he received a letter from Golda Meir. "I am writing to tell you that in your hour of difficulty I thought of you and, naturally, of what you have done for Israel," she wrote. "I personally wish to thank you most heartily for your kindness and graciousness and for your friendship." About a year later, Nixon wrote to thank her for "some very generous comments you made about me in your recently published book."

For years, Golda had rejected publishers' requests to write a book about her life. "What have I got to write about?" she said to her colleagues. "The interesting things I won't tell, and what I can tell is not interesting." After the trauma of the Yom Kippur War, she had a change of heart. A book about her life would transmit the history of her time and nation as she wanted it told. "When we began," recalled Rinna Samuel, a journalist from the Weizmann Institute whom she hired as a ghostwriter, "she seemed to me like a broken little old lady. The writing and the success of the book helped to heal her."

The British publishing house Weidenfeld and Nicolson paid an advance of $250,000 for the book, a great deal of money at the time (although it offered Moshe Dayan $450,000 for his memoirs). Golda reminisced into Samuel's tape recorder, and Samuel scrounged through boxes of papers and government sources for other material. She also contacted Golda's old friend Marie Syrkin for assistance. Syrkin, who had written two earlier biographies of Golda, felt somewhat hurt at not having been asked to write this book, but she agreed to review each chapter. Golda "will never tell the truth about lots of things: married life, love affairs (if any), party intrigue," Lou Kadar wrote to Syrkin. She was, indeed, a "stubborn censor," Samuel said. But in one of the boxes of papers Samuel received, she found a packet of Yiddish letters to Golda from Zalman Shazar, put there by mistake. Assuming they were love letters, and without reading them, she claimed, she placed them in an envelope, marked it "Not to Be Opened for 50 Years," and sent it to the Israel State Archives. Shazar died on October 5, 1974, while Golda's book was still in progress. Although his mental acumen had dulled, his death evoked great sadness in her.

Her autobiography, *My Life*, was published in Israel, England, France, Germany, and the United States in 1975, to great acclaim, and translated into more than twenty languages. "I could write another book with the many things left out of this one," Golda told her son.

THE IMAGE OF YASSER ARAFAT standing before the UN General Assembly wearing his military uniform and black-and-white-checked keffiyeh, with a holster around his waist, confirmed for Golda Meir and much of the Jewish world the one-sidedness of that international body, and she told that to President Gerald Ford when she met with him on December 18, 1974. She had made her first visit to Washington since resigning office, but the change in her status was hardly visible. The new president, accompanied by Henry Kissinger and Brent Scowcroft (Simcha Dinitz and Mordechai Shalev were with Golda), treated her with the respect and cordiality she had known throughout her premiership. It would be that way the next year and the one after that. Golda Meir's presence in the States meant an invitation to a private meeting at the White House. She had moved from prime minister to prime emissary of her country.

At this meeting, Arafat was much on her mind. She thanked Ford for having voted against inviting him to the UN and against giving the PLO "observer status" there. "It speaks much for Israel, the little line in the press that the U.S. didn't stand up for that butcher Arafat," she told the president. She also spoke sympathetically about King Hussein of Jordan, who had been pushed aside in October when a summit meeting of Arab leaders in Rabat, Morocco, designated the PLO the "sole legitimate representative of the Palestinian people." She and the Jordanian king had "a close and almost touching relationship," she said. She'd had maybe thirty "very friendly" meetings with him that she didn't report to her government "for fear of leaks" and maintained "close exchanges" throughout the Yom Kippur War.

The meeting ended with friendly handshakes all around. That evening Golda greeted more than a hundred guests—Supreme Court justices, members of Congress, Hollywood moguls, politicians, journalists, Jewish leaders, and others—at an elegant State Department dinner hosted by Henry Kissinger for someone "we all admire and we all love."

The events in Washington capped off a highly successful fund-raising trip through the States. She had shared ideas about Israel with her good friend the AFL-CIO head, George Meany, appeared on CBS-TV's *Face the Nation*, spoke at a Labor Zionist Alliance luncheon in her honor, and, most enjoyably, spent two days at Princeton University answering students' questions. She facetiously told members of the university's Whig-Cliosophic Society that rumors that Israel's prime minister and other officials didn't dare make a decision without first consulting her were "exaggerated." She didn't say untrue. In the same vein, she explained to an audience at the Woodrow Wilson School of Public and International Affairs that she could not speak for the Israeli government. "I can only speak for the Israel people," she said, to laughter. "In the 'Israel people,' I think I should include the Israel government," she added after a pause. She was playing it for laughs but conveying a clear message: retirement for her did not mean fading into the woodwork. On a more serious note, when the students asked about compromising with Arafat, she emphasized his aim of destroying Israel, repeating a favorite line: "To be or not to be is not a question of compromise. Either you be or you don't be." But what if Arafat were to recognize Israel? That recognition was so out of the range of possibility, Mrs. Meir suggested, that it reminded her of a Yiddish expression: "If my grandmother had wheels, she would have been a carriage." The students adored her.

Before returning to Israel, she was feted as guest of honor at a swanky Israel Bonds black-tie tribute dinner held in New York's Waldorf Astoria. She came home tired but in high spirits, a mood not matched by the country's new premier.

Yitzhak Rabin, heading a weak government with a narrow coalition, was having a difficult time. A cartoon in *Maariv* soon after he became prime minister showed the four "shadows" who had left the government, Golda Meir, Moshe Dayan, Pinhas Sapir, and Abba Eban, hovering disapprovingly over the new leadership. It had some truth. Not long after Rabin took office, Golda and Sapir prevented him from joining with Likud to form a national unity government, which they believed would weaken the Labor Party. But she also supported him personally and scrupulously avoided criticizing him publicly. He consulted her regularly, frequently turning up at her home on a Saturday morning to prepare for his Sunday cabinet meeting and spending hours talking to her before meetings with President Ford.

Unfortunately, Rabin lacked Golda's comfortable way with American politicians. He'd developed excellent relationships with Nixon and Kissinger when he served as her ambassador to Washington and knew Ford from those years but didn't quite click with him. The earnest and affable American president was put off by the Israeli prime minister's seeming aloofness on the one hand and sabra bluntness on the other. And whereas Golda Meir never fought openly with an American commander in chief, but directed her most biting barbs to his subordinates, from their earliest meeting in September 1974, Rabin confronted Ford head-on, to disastrous results.

The dispute between the two men, as it evolved over the next several months, centered on forging a new interim Israeli-Egyptian agreement beyond the separation of forces. Sadat demanded a further pullback of Israeli troops from the Gidi and Mitla Passes in the Sinai and the return of the Abu Rudeis oil fields on the southwestern coast of the peninsula. In exchange, Rabin insisted on greater security for Israel by way of a nonbelligerency agreement. With Ford's approval, Kissinger undertook another intense round of shuttle diplomacy, but this time he made little headway. On March 22, 1975, with negotiations deadlocked, he gave up. Within days, Ford wrote Rabin a blistering letter threatening to "reassess" America's relationship to Israel. He and Kissinger let it be known that they blamed Israel for the collapse of the talks.

Golda visited Rabin at his Jerusalem home and announced publicly that she was "100 percent" behind him. Privately, she fumed at Kissinger. She had lost respect for him, she told a friend. On the day he left, after the shuttle had broken down, he called on her to say good-bye and promised that he would never lead the American people to believe Israel was at fault for the failure of the talks. He then proceeded to do just that.

After excruciating negotiations and manipulations, including a strongly worded letter to Ford supporting Israel signed by seventy-six U.S. senators, the two sides reached a breakthrough. On September 1, 1975, Sadat and Rabin initialed a new agreement: Israel would return the oil field and withdraw from the length of the passes in return for an Egyptian commitment not to use force to settle disputes. Augmenting the deal for Israel, the United States agreed to give the Jewish state substantial financial aid and to send 150 civilian technicians to man warning stations in the passes. Golda had strengthened Rabin's resolve during the roughest haggling, yet she knew when to back down, as she had with the earlier disengagement agreement. When the Labor Party held its caucus to vote on the new accord (known as Sinai II), she made a point of attending. It was her first such meeting since retiring, and she spoke forcefully in favor of the agreement. With her support, the party overwhelmingly accepted it and guided it through the Knesset, overriding Menachem Begin's vehement opposition.

With the crisis behind Israel, Golda made another friendly visit to the White House in December 1975. President Ford referred to the "sharp words" of the previous months as having been spoken as "friends and not as opponents." Like Nixon, he felt relaxed with Golda's easy style and plain English, and for her the meeting served to smooth over any remaining rough spots the president had with Yitzhak Rabin. It didn't hurt either that at an earlier ceremony Raphael Soyer unveiled a portrait he had painted of her to be hung later in the National Gallery of Art. At the time, she was one of only three foreigners honored in that way.

She had come to the United States to attend her old friend Sam Rothberg's sixty-fifth birthday party and, as always, raise money for Israel Bonds and the UJA. But this time she added a new note of urgency. A year after the UN appearance of Yasser Arafat (who, she held, could never "wash from his hands the blood he has shed"), that international body passed Resolution 3379 equating Zionism with racism. Before leaving for the States, she had spoken at a rally in Tel Aviv to thousands of students protesting the resolution. Now as she traveled from city to city—New York, San Francisco, Los Angeles, Cleveland, Miami—she homed in on the decline of the United Nations into an organization without purpose, much like the League of Nations before it, and she urged Jews everywhere to mobilize to overturn the resolution: "I have a feeling that, instinctively, every Jew, individually, felt that this resolution at the United Nations meant him . . . It can mean something, and can drive us on to great acts, only if each one says, it means me, my son, my daughter, my grandchild." The UN did not rescind the resolution until 1991.

Golda immersed herself in another cause during these retirement years, one that she had never really left: the predicament of Soviet Jews. As prime minister, she'd spoken out openly against the restrictive emigration laws of the Soviet Union and been quietly instrumental in bringing individuals and families from that land to Israel. She had held back, however, from anything that smacked of Israel's direct interference in American or Soviet legislation. She had refrained, for example, from taking a public stand in the fight between the White House and the U.S. Congress about the Jackson-Vanik amendment that would tie U.S. trade benefits for the Soviet Union to that nation's immigration policies for Jews. Nixon and Kissinger had vehemently opposed the amendment as detrimental to détente with the Soviets. After it passed the House and the Senate, despite their opposition, citizen Golda Meir could cable her "appreciation and congratulations" to Senator Jackson and accept his recognition of "how much this cause means to you personally and how devotedly you have pursued it."

As prime minister, Mrs. Meir did not attend the first worldwide conference on Soviet Jewry held in Brussels in February 1971, because she did not want to appear to be confronting the Soviets. As a private citizen, she not only headed the Israeli delegation to the second Brussels conference in February 1976 but also served as the conference's honorary president. At a news conference, she urged the nations of the world to put pressure on the Soviets to ease their "irrational" laws against Jewish emigration. During her closing address, she called the gathering "one of the greatest emotional experiences of my life."

The numbers of Jews the Soviets permitted to emigrate fluctuated over the next several years, depending on internal Russian politics and relations between East and West. The dam broke in 1989, when the Cold War ended and tens of thousands of Jews began leaving the Soviet Union. By the 1990s, more than a million Soviet Jews had immigrated to Israel, bringing with them scientific and technological knowledge and a distinct culture that changed Israeli society. Golda was no longer alive then, but her years of dedication to the Soviet Jewish cause had paid off. Said Meir Rosenne, one of the prime figures in the Soviet Jewry movement, "I am willing to testify in a court of law: without Golda Meir you would not have in Israel today more than a million Jews from the former Soviet Union."

Before her stint in Brussels, Golda had been in London, where her autobiography was a runaway best seller and she a star, attracting a huge audience for a lecture to the Jewish community at Albert Hall and celebrated by members of Parliament with a reception at the Savoy Hotel. It's unclear whether she met Margaret Thatcher on this trip, but the two had a friendly tête-à-tête when Britain's "iron lady," then head of the Conservative Party, visited Israel in March 1976. When a newsman asked Thatcher whether she had learned anything about being a woman prime minister from speaking with Golda, she snapped back that they were too concerned with issues to dwell on such matters. Golda added scornfully, "They think that's all women think about." Both leaders wanted to be identified by their activities, not by gender, and neither ever spoke out in support of the organized women's movement in her country.

Golda was in the United States again in May 1976, picking up an honorary degree at Wellesley College and accepting the prestigious AFL-CIO Philip Murray–William Green Award, the first foreigner ever to receive that highest tribute of the American labor movement. As she walked slowly to the dais at the dinner in her honor, a thousand guests rose from their seats and sang the refrain of "You'll Never Walk Alone." To U.S. labor, she was Israel personified.

She met, as before, with President Ford, bringing several messages from Yitzhak Rabin. She also met with Jimmy Carter, who was running against Ford for president. Carter had asked for the meeting, hoping to impress Jewish voters by being seen with her, but she refused to be photographed with him and would not endorse his candidacy—not wanting to give the appearance of mixing into American politics. Anyway, she'd had a bizarre encounter with the born-again Christian Carter when he visited Israel in the spring of 1973. Golda had assigned him a driver and station wagon to tour the country. When he met with her afterward, his main observation was that he had "long taught lessons from the Hebrew Scriptures that a common historical pattern was that Israel was punished whenever the leaders turned away from devout worship of God." He asked her if she was concerned about the secular nature of her Labor government. Surprised by the question, she lit a cigarette, shrugged, and said with a laugh that "Orthodox" Jews still existed and could handle the nation's responsibility in that regard. Carter's preaching was not to her taste.

While Golda Meir traveled about from place to place meeting with politicians and Jewish leaders like an ambassador of goodwill for Israel, the atmosphere surrounding Prime Minister Rabin became grimmer and grimmer. The man who twenty years later would be viewed by many as a powerful leader and a martyr murdered because of his ideals at this time appeared increasingly ineffectual. Within the Labor Party, his fierce competition with Shimon Peres turned meetings into miserable face-offs between the two men and closed out any chance of party unity. Within the country as a whole, the badly hurt wartime economy still suffered from high unemployment and low living standards. In the religious sphere, the national religious group Gush Emunim, just finding its sea legs during Golda's premiership, aggressively defied government prohibitions against creating new settlements in crowded parts of the West Bank. With each attempt to settle in a densely populated area, each struggle with the IDF, the Gush gained more sympathizers. The settlement it finally founded in Sebastia, in the heart of the region, represented its victory over a weakened government. Protests and unrest among the Palestinians in the territories added to Rabin's woes, as did a string of corruption scandals among high-level government officials.

Invariably the former prime minister's confidence and charisma were compared with the current one's insecurities. In a telephone poll, 48 percent of respondents thought Golda should return to active political life, and some party leaders whispered among themselves about replacing Rabin with her. Almost two years after officially retiring, she agreed to the party's call to head a "steering forum" to guide and strengthen Rabin. Even Anwar Sadat weighed in on the prime minister's faltering position. Early on, he had asked Kissinger whether Rabin "had Golda's guts." Later he said publicly that Golda Meir had been a "true leader," able to make decisions and "stand up to her people," whereas Rabin was "extremely weak."

Rabin had a brief surge in popularity in July 1976, when, in a precisely planned operation, the IDF freed the hostages and crew held by terrorists in a hijacked airplane in Entebbe, Uganda. The success of the operation lifted the nation's spirits and momentarily made the prime minister a national hero. Golda sent him fifty red roses with a card that said, "Nothing succeeds like success. With appreciation, admiration, and respect, Golda." Five months later, after a dispute with the National Religious Party and hoping to capitalize on his newfound acclaim, Rabin resigned and dissolved his government. He called for new elections, assuming he would win with a larger majority than he had before. They would be held on May 17, 1977.

As might be expected, the best-laid plans and so on. Trouble for Rabin started immediately, when his rival, Shimon Peres, announced that he would run for party leadership, even though Rabin was still the prime minister. Golda pleaded with Peres not to divide the party by entering the race, and when he disregarded her request, she actively worked to have Rabin reelected as party head, standing beside him at public events. Rabin won the internal battle by only forty-one votes. Then, as he began his national campaign, he faced a powerful challenge to Labor's hegemony in the form of a new centrist party, composed mostly of an educated middle class, the kind of people who had traditionally backed Labor. Calling itself Dash (Democratic Movement for Change), it included a small group, Shinui, which had been ceaselessly demanding change since the end of the Yom Kippur War. Yigael Yadin, a well-known archaeologist and former army chief of staff, headed it.

As if these setbacks were not enough, Rabin himself got caught in a scandal. His wife, Leah, had failed to close a bank account in dollars the couple had kept in New York when he was ambassador, a violation of Israel's law, which forbade its citizens to hold foreign currency accounts abroad. Standing by his wife, Rabin resigned, yielding his place to Peres after all. "A *pisheke* [a pants wetter—a nothing]!" Golda ranted about Leah Rabin privately, enraged at her negligence, enraged at what the scandal did to a party already riddled with problems.

SHE JOINED OTHER party members at Labor headquarters in Tel Aviv on the night of May 17 to follow election returns. By 10:00 p.m., the results had become clear: "Ladies and Gentlemen, a 'Mahapach,'" a reversal, an earthquake, the national news anchor Chaim Yavin announced to an astounded populace. Menachem Begin and his Likud Party had swept the election, winning forty-four seats to Labor's thirty-two. Begin had rallied to his side the "second Israel," the Mizrahim from North Africa and the Middle East, who, for decades, had felt unrecognized in the Ashkenazi-dominated culture. He had also won over the Greater Israel crowd with his rhetoric against yielding even an inch of Judaea and Samaria.

The results crushed Golda. After ruling the nation's political life from before the state existed, the Labor Zionist movement, the center of her world, had been toppled. Moreover, the man she had once regarded as a terrorist, the man who had mercilessly criticized her for every compromise she made with Egypt or Syria, was to be the next prime minister of Israel. She might not have blamed herself for the shocking loss—after all, she was out of office—but she could not help but take it personally, as a repudiation of her deepest convictions. She carried the trauma of that lost election with her for the rest of her life.

On a private level, her world shrank relentlessly. A year after she lost Zalman Shazar, she mourned the death of Pinhas Sapir, the "kingmaker," who had first put her in office. As finance minister, he had remained one of the most trusted members of her inner circle, his death a "terrible blow," Lou Kadar said. Meyer Weisgal, former chancellor of the Weizmann Institute and one of her closest friends, died in September 1977. (He was said to be one of the very few people whose cursing Golda would tolerate.) She lost Moshe Dayan through defection, not death. On Election Day, aware of Labor's difficulties, she and the diplomat Gideon Rafael had speculated despondently on who among their Knesset comrades might cross to the other side. The one person who would never leave the Labor Party was Moshe Dayan, she asserted with confidence, especially because he had been a candidate on Labor's list. A few days later, Dayan accepted Begin's invitation to be his foreign minister. Among other things, he did not want to remain in the wilderness, always identified with the Yom Kippur War. Golda could not forgive him. Asked by an interviewer whether Dayan had contacted her after leaving the party, she shrugged and said, "It's not important, I haven't seen him." She had, in fact, ignored two requests from him to meet.

Humbled by its defeat, the Labor Party campaigned hard to keep control of the Histadrut, the national labor federation. Walking alongside Yitzhak Rabin, Yigal Allon, Shimon Peres, and other party stalwarts, Golda led a procession of some twenty-five thousand workers through the streets of Tel Aviv, her eyes staring sternly ahead, her lips fixed in a tense half smile. To boost morale, she called out in her address, "Do we look like a camp in despair?" and cheering voices shouted back, "No!" She went on to equate Menachem Begin with the hard line of Zeev Jabotinsky in pre-state days. It was how she thought of the new prime minister and how she consistently portrayed him, as a throwback to the early uncompromising policies of the Far Right. Labor won this election, offering Golda and the others at least a modicum of relief.

Another source of relief and joy seemed to be in the offing when she allowed the playwright William Gibson to stage her life in a new play called *Golda*. She had turned down other requests, including one from the British composer Lionel Bart, songwriter for *Oliver!*, to build a musical around her. But with Gibson—author of *The Miracle Worker*, which she admired—as writer, Arthur Penn as director, and Anne Bancroft in the starring role, Golda was excited about this production. The excitement mounted when Israel Bonds turned opening night at New York's Morosco Theatre into a glamorous fund-raising event. Golda invited seventeen guests to fly with her for the November 14 opening, only to sit stone-faced through a confused distortion of her history and the nation's. The play closed after three months, a flop.

FAR MORE DRAMA WAS HAPPENING outside than inside any theater that November 1977. Early in the month, Anwar Sadat announced to his parliament that he was willing to fly "to the ends of the earth" for peace. Secretly, he and Begin had opened a channel of communication through Romania's president, Nicolae Ceauşescu, whom Golda had approached in 1971 with no results. Begin invited Sadat to Jerusalem, and to widespread amazement the Egyptian president accepted. Golda, in America then, decided not to hurry back to Israel unless invited by the government to the big event. As it was, Sadat had instructed an advance guard preparing his trip to arrange a meeting specifically with her. Once invited, she left for Israel immediately. She had met earlier with President Carter, who asked if she thought Sadat really wanted peace. "I don't know whether he *wants* peace," she answered. "What is certain is that he *needs* it very much." Less starry-eyed than most about Sadat's visit, Golda understood that, overpopulated and impoverished, Egypt desperately needed the American aid that would come only with peace.

When Anwar Sadat stepped off his Egyptian airplane at Ben-Gurion Airport on November 19, 1977, and onto the red carpet laid out for him, millions of Israelis watching on television might have felt themselves transported to a magical land, a place where the wars that had taken so many of their sons had never happened and the deadly enmity that had blanketed the two countries for decades didn't exist. An honor guard carried Israeli and Egyptian flags, a band played the national anthems of both countries, and a twenty-one-gun salute heralded Israel's honored guest. Lined up to greet the elegant, dignified Egyptian were key government officials, none of whom had ever wished him well. Now everyone was smiling and shaking hands. Before he left Egypt, Sadat's wife had instructed him to "make a special effort with Mrs. Meir." She had felt both "dislike and respect" for Israel's former prime minister. He reported back that when they met, he told Mrs. Meir she had a reputation in Egypt as "the strongest man in Israel" and she smiled. But Yitzhak Rabin, standing next to Golda, overheard Sadat say, "For many, many years I have wanted to meet you," and Golda respond, "Why didn't you come?" His answer was revealing: "The time was not yet ripe." He had not been ready before the war to extend himself for peace in this way. The Egyptian *Al-Ahram* newspaper carried a picture of the two of them on its front page.

Dressed nattily in a dark blue suit and polka-dot tie, Sadat addressed the Knesset in Arabic on November 20, and though his presence beamed conciliation, his hard words hit all the most divisive issues between the former enemies. To achieve "permanent peace based on justice," he declared, Israel needed to "give up . . . the dream of conquest," withdraw from all the territories to the pre-1967 borders, and ensure the "legitimate rights of the Palestinian people," including their "right to statehood." In return, the Arabs would end the "state of belligerence in the region." Wearing his usual dark suit and somber tie, Begin responded in Hebrew, forcefully spelling out Jewish historical ties to the entire Land of Israel and emphasizing Israel's unreciprocated willingness from its beginnings to negotiate with the Arab nations. No one listening could doubt that the journey to peace was still long and rocky.

The next morning, Golda spoke in English to the Egyptian president at a small Knesset gathering of the Labor Party leadership. After congratulating him on having "the privilege of being the first" great Arab leader to come to Israel, she emphasized Israel's satisfaction in holding a face-to-face meeting with him, something she had always advocated. She responded to the issues he had raised, more to the point than Begin had: Israel's consent to territorial compromise, but its need also for secure borders; its agreement to a Palestinian state, but one connected to Jordan. It was the Labor Party platform, and if she personally "was deeply hurt" because Begin was running the show, she hid that well. She spoke simply and eloquently.

"We must all realize that the path leading to peace may be a difficult one, but not as difficult as that path which leads to war," she said, and with warmth and humor she cut through formalities. She hoped that "even an old lady like myself will live to see the day," she began, interrupted herself with a smile, and added, "Yes, you always call me an old lady," which sent Sadat into peals of laughter, and she continued, "I want to live to see that day that peace reigns between you and us."

She concluded by presenting him with a gold bracelet for his new granddaughter, "as a grandmother to a grandfather," and thanked him for the gift he had sent her, a silver cigarette box. This was Golda at her best: finding common ground with a once formidable enemy on the most fundamental human level, as loving grandparents. "She won't admit that she was impressed by him," Kadar wrote to Syrkin, "but I can assure you that she was."

That didn't prevent her from steadily criticizing both Begin and Sadat as they later inched toward an agreement. Sadat had implied in his Knesset speech that Israel had failed to respond to his peace initiative in February 1971, and though she had said nothing at the time, his words riled her. When he repeated that claim in a *Jerusalem Post* interview, she joined Labor Party leaders in pointing out that his proposal in 1971 had depended on Israel's committing to withdraw from all the territories before negotiations could begin. She continued to criticize Sadat's insistence on preconditions rather than agreeing to negotiate everything. As for Begin, if he accepted Sadat's conditions, he would be giving in "too early and too quickly." And he would be making the "fatal mistake" of believing that by returning Sinai to Egypt, Israel would be allowed to keep all of Judaea and Samaria, the territory that meant most to him.

At a Labor Party tribute on her eightieth birthday, Golda again criticized Begin for appearing to go along with Sadat's demands. Israel needed to keep some of Sinai for its own security—the town of Yamit, for example—and not trust that a peace treaty will always protect it, she argued. On the other hand, she could not condone the Likud's policy of building settlements throughout the West Bank, including populated Arab areas. "We don't want a million Arabs who don't want us," she declared, a position that had not changed since 1967.

Ironically, as the bargaining between Israel and Egypt hit a standstill, Sadat declared on American television that he had a better chance of attaining a peace agreement with Golda Meir than with Menachem Begin. He was posturing to pressure Begin, but it was also true that for all the hard lines Golda held, she had, in the end, reached accords with him on a cease-fire, troop withdrawals, and other interim arrangements, and he had great respect for her.

Some months after Sadat's visit, Golda wrote a letter to his wife, Jehan, regretting that she had not joined her husband in Israel. His words "no more wars," she wrote, "continue to reverberate in . . . the ears of all Israel." And she prayed that they would come true for "the sake of your country and mine."

AT EIGHTY, GOLDA TRIED TO remain as engaged as ever in the big events swirling around her, and she took pride in the fact that the news media still cited her speeches and opinions. A year earlier, she had been the subject of an Israeli *This Is Your Life* television show with appearances by Harold Wilson, Henry Kissinger, and other key people in her life. It was torture to sit through a seven-hour taping for the show without a cigarette, she said afterward, but she didn't want young people to see her smoking on television. On her eightieth birthday in May 1978, she received dozens of bouquets of flowers and requests for interviews from journalists around the world. A concert in her honor at the kibbutz Revivim attracted an audience of more than eight hundred, and a gala family party with dozens of friends stretched into hours of reminiscing.

But in the weeks and months that followed, she was in and out of the hospital. By September, when President Jimmy Carter invited Begin and Sadat to a summit at the presidential retreat in Camp David, her health had deteriorated badly. Even so, she followed the proceedings carefully. In a framework agreement announced on September 17, Israel consented to withdraw from Sinai, uprooting Jewish settlements there, in exchange for normal relations with Egypt. A day later, in her last public talk, Golda marveled, sarcastically, that Begin, who had balked at even the mention of UN Resolution 242 with its return of territories to the Arabs, had now agreed to give so much away. When told a little later that he and Sadat would receive Nobel Peace Prizes, she quipped, "I don't know about the Nobel Prize, but they certainly deserve an Oscar." She had never lost her suspicion of them both.

The Camp David Accords marked a bittersweet moment in Golda Meir's life. Although she would not live to see the final treaty between Israel and Egypt, she knew the peace she had sought with that country for so long was close at hand. But she could not claim the credit for it.

"I've Always Been a Realist"

A lmost three thousand delegates crushed into the Grand Ballroom and adjoining rooms of the Sheraton Hotel in Dallas, Texas, for what most suspected was Golda Meir's last appearance in the United States. It was Saturday afternoon, November 12, 1977. She had traveled to the States for the opening of *Golda* and had not planned on coming to the annual convention of the GA (General Assembly of the Jewish Federations of North America). A reminder from the convention chairman of her address to that organization thirty years earlier, in 1948, changed her mind. At that time, she had arrived in the middle of a blizzard to raise money for the fledgling Jewish state and returned home with pledges of fifty million dollars. She reminisced at this appearance about how her "knees were caving in" with terror back then as she addressed a roomful of people she didn't know and about the overwhelming response she had received. This time a Texas businessman had sent his private plane to carry her from New York to Dallas and back again. This time she was greeted with song and dance and excited, sustained applause. She spoke of how much American Jews and Israelis had accomplished together and of the importance of Israel in all of Jewish life.

"Look, people," she said as she concluded, "I was going to say 30 years from now, I'll come and we'll talk about this meeting. But I've always been a realist. I don't think I'll be able quite to make it." She spoke as she always had, without notes, and those who heard her that day never forgot the moment. "She was saying good-bye to American Jews," a communal leader recalled. "There was such a sense of intimacy, like sitting in her kitchen and talking to her."

Golda Meir's American connection set her apart from every Israeli prime minister before or after her. Like the other early leaders, she could trace her origins and many of her attitudes to Eastern Europe. The mostly insulated Jewish surroundings of her young childhood left her never quite trustful of gentiles, and the widespread anti-Jewishness there imprinted on her mind a lasting memory of violence and fear. But that background was filtered through her American experience. Enthusiasm, optimism, and self-belief also became part of her outlook, and the Yankee sense that through hard work and determination anyone can achieve success. As an Israeli leader, she used her fluency in English and insights into American culture to touch the hearts, and pocketbooks, of American Jews as no one else could. They took pride in her as one of their own, and she taught them to attach their destiny to the destiny of Israel. With her American know-how, she forged a more powerful bond between Israel and the United States than had ever existed. When asked by a reporter after the Yom Kippur War how she felt about Israel's dependency on the great superpower, she corrected him. "Instead of calling it dependency, I'd like to call it friendship," she said. It remained a tight strategic friendship from her day on.

Unlike the other early leaders and most of Israel's immigrants, she did not come to Palestine because of persecution. She chose to come and leave the abundance of America behind her. She loved America with its democracy, she said, but she needed to work for her own people. That sense of who she was and what she wanted for herself never left her, and it fueled her drive to get ahead. Throughout her career, she denied being motivated by ambition; "I have a lot of faults," she would say, "but the craziness of ambition, this sickness I do not have."

But while she might not have plotted each step on her way up, with political shrewdness she moved ever forward toward greater authority and power. In every period, she took on the most difficult missions, from collecting a special tax for the unemployed from workers with limited incomes themselves to creating housing for hundreds of thousands of homeless immigrants to developing a social security system to benefit her entire nation. Because she was astute and willing to devote herself completely to the job at hand, she usually succeeded, and her success enhanced her reputation. Comfortable as a leader, she didn't question whether she belonged in office. Even when she complained, as she did about becoming foreign minister, she always knew she would fit into whatever position she held.

She lived in a society dominated by men. "She is a great woman," Ben-Gurion once said, "but she is a woman!" He meant that she was different, hard to understand. She handled her differentness by being herself, exhibiting traditionally feminine traits in spite of—or perhaps because of—her male milieu. Although indifferent to the latest fashions, she cared about her appearance and carefully selected the simple clothes she wore, adding beads, pearls, or other basic jewelry. She always had manicured nails, made a point of serving guests herself with tea and homemade cookies, and relaxed by washing dishes or puttering about the kitchen, the locus also of her most important political decisions. "One can't even yell at her," wrote the humorist Ephraim Kishon. "She may burst into tears—part ham, part genuine." Her capacious handbag became her trademark, carried wherever she went, whether ceremonially inspecting an American honor guard on the White House lawn or meeting with grimy Israeli troops on the battlefield.

On the other hand, in her desire to secure her place within the male establishment, she eschewed any identification with organized feminism. Those "crazy women who burn their bras and . . . hate men," she labeled the feminist movement of the 1970s, at a time when her endorsement would have meant a great deal to its struggle for women's equality. She agreed that "to be successful, a woman has to be much more capable than a man" and that "so many injustices" toward women still existed. Yet she did not make a point of advancing women's causes and refused to acknowledge that she herself had experienced discrimination because of her gender, although from her youth onward she had. She argued that child rearing presented the greatest challenge for women who also wanted to work outside their homes or have careers, but would not recognize that easing those difficulties was a large part of the agenda of the women's movement.

Paradoxically, her refusal to be identified by gender reinforced some of feminism's ultimate goals. She bridled at being referred to as a woman minister, for example. The president of Israel didn't send for her to form a cabinet after the 1969 elections because she was a woman, she said, but because he thought she had the support of the majority of the Knesset. But paradox within paradox, the very fact that as a woman she had to overcome formidable barriers to achieve what she did inspired other women. In her own time and to this day, women have looked up to her as a model to be emulated. And as more and more women have entered occupations and professions once closed to them, she has served as a symbol of possibilities, "the mother of us all," an Israeli politician said.

In safeguarding the security of the state, Golda was ferocious. "I have a Masada complex. I have a pogrom complex. I have a Hitler complex," she would say when accused of maintaining a fortresslike mentality, and she would launch into a long discourse on Jewish suffering throughout history. She became known for her obduracy in negotiations, so often accused of being intransigent that she considered "Intransigent" her middle name, she joked. What has often been forgotten is how frequently, after tough bargaining, she compromised, standing up to fierce criticism from her political opponents—after the war of attrition, for example, or the disengagement of forces at the end of the Yom Kippur War.

To people with whom she worked, she could be less compromising and more autocratic and demanding. It was axiomatic that if she liked someone, the sun shone on that person, and if she didn't, her icy stare could cause frostbite. She never forgot a slight and could hold a grudge for years. "You have to forgive her," Ben-Gurion would say to her critics condescendingly. "She had a very difficult childhood." It *was* difficult, and its grinding poverty and constant squabbles between her feisty mother and her domineering older sister left their mark on her. But that mother also became a source of old-world wisdom for her, the sister initiated her into a lifelong passion for Socialist Zionism, and her early environment, impoverished as it was, steeped her in *Yiddishkeit*, a dedication to Jews and Jewishness. So along with the sternness, the stubbornness, and the cutting sarcasm toward people who crossed her went the Jewish mother softness, the self-deprecating humor, the true concern for all Jews.

Frequently referred to as the mother of the Jewish people, to a great extent Golda Meir saw herself that way. She regarded Israel as the center of Jewish life, and therefore responsible for Jews wherever they lived. She told a meeting of young soldiers after the Yom Kippur War that if they had fought only for the Jews in Israel, the struggle and sacrifice were not worth it. But if they recognized that fighting for Israel meant fighting for Jews everywhere, then "no sacrifice is too great." That broad connection between Jews in Israel and those in the Diaspora made the plight of Jews in the Soviet Union especially compelling to her.

With her eye on world Jewry, however, Golda sometimes missed important domestic changes. She continued to preach socialist values long after the country had moved toward capitalism and those principles appeared irrelevant to many Israelis, especially the young. Ironically, the one ethnic group that might have accepted her ideas rejected them and her as a symbol of the establishment. The Mizrahim, or Sephardim, who had come to Israel from Muslim lands, directed their anger toward her for their lack of mobility. She cared about their welfare, looked out for their health and housing, and, as prime minister, appointed a commission to investigate their social and economic needs. But she lacked the imagination to penetrate their culture and lives, so different from hers, and to see them as equals. She wanted them to pull themselves up by the bootstraps, out of poverty, through education and hard work, and considered them ungrateful for the government's willingness to help them. They considered her patronizing and blind to their aspirations and hopes. Their disappointment in her and her party helped Menachem Begin and his Likud Party gain power.

By the same token, she lacked the foresight to see the rising tide of nationalism among Palestine's Arabs. In this, she was not alone. In all its wars and negotiations, Israel had dealt with the established Arab nations: Egypt, Syria, Jordan, Lebanon. Most Israelis and much of the world viewed Palestinian Arabs mainly as refugees, victims of the wars. With the rise of Yasser Arafat and his Palestine Liberation Organization, they became identified also with terrorists bent on destroying Israel. Only a tiny segment of Israeli leaders recognized the desire of Palestinian Arabs for a national identity, and for the most part they were far out of the mainstream. It was Golda, however, who made the ill-conceived remark that "there was no such thing as Palestinians" and never lived it down despite her numerous attempts to explain that she did not deny the existence of Palestinians as a people. She had meant only that they had never in the past organized themselves into a nation.

Golda opposed the concept of a sovereign Palestinian state between Israel and Jordan, but she envisioned a union of Palestinian Arabs with the kingdom of Jordan, however they worked that out among themselves. To that end, she met secretly with King Hussein at least thirty times to try to arrive at an agreement about the West Bank. She would not have Israel go back to the 1967 borders, which she regarded as insecure, nor did she have any desire to occupy all of Judaea and Samaria, the dream of Begin and his Likud Party.

During much of her premiership, Golda's popularity ratings hit record highs. Basking in their smashing victory of 1967, Israelis applauded her fortitude and self-assurance, a reflection of their own sense of themselves. Even after the Yom Kippur War, they voted for her and her party, although the sounds of protest had begun to be heard in the land. She had pulled them through that war, made perceptive military and strategic decisions, and remained a pillar of strength even as her once heroic defense minister fell apart.

For the most part, regard for her life and work began to change after she died in 1978. Gradually, criticisms of her mounted, with the most virulent attacks centered on the Yom Kippur War and her failure to prevent it. Yet, as American and Israeli archives have steadily released once top secret documents, it has become increasingly clear that the Egyptian president, Anwar Sadat, would not have made peace without a guarantee ahead of time that Israel would relinquish all the territories it had captured in 1967. In hindsight, that might have been a fair price to pay for peace, or even for the lack of belligerence, short of full peace, that Sadat offered. At the time, it appeared to Golda and her cabinet, and the overwhelming majority of Israelis, foolish, even reckless, for Israel to consider returning to the borders that had led to the Six-Day War in the first place.

As documents have been released, they have revealed also Golda's clandestine attempts to open a dialogue with Arab leaders. She had sent secret messages to Anwar Sadat through the Romanian president, the German chancellor, and the American secretary of state, among others. In the end, Israelis and Egyptians negotiated a cease-fire face-to-face, and Sadat came to Israel to meet with its leaders, validating Golda's call all along for direct negotiations. But by then the war had happened. With his pride restored because of it and his hand strengthened in the Arab world, the Egyptian president felt freer than he had been to make a separate treaty with Israel. Had he responded to her feelers earlier, she would have been prepared to make serious concessions. That he didn't led to the greatest tragedy of her life.

GOLDA REMAINED DEEPLY SADDENED by the war and the downfall of the party to which she had devoted herself. Yet she did not live out her final years in bitterness and despair. She continued to be a voice of authority for her party and to maintain her busy involvement in national affairs until almost the end. As late as January 1978, she was writing letters to key American labor leaders asking for funding to help the Israeli Labor Party regain political vitality. Her steep physical decline began as she approached her eightieth birthday in May 1978, after the lymphoma that had plagued her for almost fifteen years worsened, sending her repeatedly to the hospital. She'd already had shingles, two eye operations, a frozen shoulder, and what appeared to be a mild heart attack but was later diagnosed as angina pectoris. In April, she had shared a stay at Hadassah Hospital in Jerusalem with her daughter, Sarah, who underwent open-heart surgery, causing Golda great anxiety. By Passover, the two were back in Golda's house in Ramat Aviv, celebrating the holiday surrounded by family. Sarah took a leave from her kibbutz to recuperate there, and Golda's sister Clara came from the States to help care for both of them. Clara had visited Golda frequently through the years, getting on her older sister's nerves with unsolicited advice. But as Golda's illnesses worsened and she was periodically confined to her bedroom on the second floor, Clara lugged trays of food up to her without complaint.

In a letter of July 30, Lou Kadar described to Marie Syrkin that with both legs swollen from the hips down, Golda walked with a cane and much difficulty and gulped down painkilling pills that did little good. At about this time, Golda began meeting weekly with Dov Goldstein, a journalist with the Hebrew newspaper *Maariv*. He had conducted six previous interviews with her, and she trusted him. "She needed a good ear to say what was in her heart," Goldstein says. There were things she would say that he could publish, she told him, but others never. She spoke again and again about the Yom Kippur War and her haunting regret that she had not followed her intuition, ignored the complacent reassurance of her generals, and mobilized the troops sooner. With tears in her eyes, she would repeat that she would never again be the Golda she had been before the war. "I smile. I laugh. I listen to music . . . But in my heart . . . it is not the same Golda." When she felt well, they sat in her living room, and she made him tea; other times, they spoke by phone. "She was so filled with humor, even when she was ill," he says. "She had more humor than any other prime minister, and I knew them all."

As Golda's disease spread, it affected her bones and made her "so thoroughly miserable" that she wanted to be in the hospital more than at home, Lou wrote to Marie. In late October, she canceled a meeting with Dov Goldstein, saying she was going to Hadassah Hospital. "I'll call you next week," he said. "I won't be here," she replied. She would enter the hospital for the last time on October 30. During her final weeks of life, she still managed to follow the news on television and accept visits from a few friends and party leaders. Her children and grandchildren visited regularly, and her niece, Sheyna's daughter, Judy Bauman, a nurse, helped care for her. On his last visit, Shimon Peres was kept waiting outside her room for ten or fifteen minutes. When he asked a bodyguard why, he was told that Golda had been putting on makeup so Peres would not see how sick she looked.

She died on Friday, December 8, 1978, at 4:30 in the afternoon, of liver failure, a complication of the lymphoma. At that moment, Menachem Begin was en route to Norway for his Nobel Peace Prize ceremony on Sunday.

Golda left a letter of instructions to be opened a day after her death, but she had revealed its contents to her Labor Party colleagues when she resigned. It specified that no eulogies be recited at her funeral: "After a death, people often say the opposite of what they really mean." And she wanted no monuments or institutions named for her, an order that continues to be ignored. Over a thousand people were invited to her funeral, four hundred of them dignitaries from abroad. President Carter sent his mother, Lillian, to represent him and invited Marie Syrkin to join the U.S. delegation.

Tens of thousands of people circled the coffin as it lay in state on the Knesset Plaza Monday and Monday night. On Tuesday morning, December 12, after a service in the Knesset's Chagall Hall, a long procession led by military jeeps wound its way up to Mount Herzl for the burial. Huddled under black umbrellas in an icy rain, five hundred mourners watched the simple wood coffin being lowered into the ground. For a brief moment, the sun burst through the clouds, then vanished, as though, some said, the heavens had opened to make way for Golda Meir. The least mystical of people, she would have dismissed that thought with a wave of her hand, and been secretly pleased by it.

IN HER FAREWELL TALK TO the American Jewish community, Golda told of being asked by a young man why she had left the America she loved to go to the Land of Israel. "I was selfish," she answered him. "I heard something was going on over there, something was being built, and I said: What? And I won't have a share in it? No. I'm going." She went. She shared in building a state out of a vision and for nearly sixty years helped shape every aspect of that state. In spite of faults or failures, she left a legacy for Israel, the Jewish people, and the world at large of courage, determination, and devotion to a cause in which one believes, however difficult the course. "Nothing in life just happens," she once said. "You have to have the stamina to meet obstacles and overcome them. To struggle."

She was buried near other national leaders in a section of Jerusalem's Mount Herzl Cemetery called the Burial Plot of the Nation's Greats.

Acknowledgments

Brief thank-yous on the page seem insufficient to express the profound gratitude I feel toward the researchers, experts, historians, archivists, librarians, and friends who have guided, aided, and reassured me during my many years of researching and writing this biography of Golda Meir. Nevertheless, the public recognition is meant to say, simply, "Without you, I could not have undertaken or completed this project."

Thank you to Boaz Lev Tov, my Israeli research assistant, who functioned more as a partner than an assistant. An accomplished historian, he contributed insights into Israel's past that were crucial to me in understanding the complexities of this country. In his research in the Israel State Archives, the Central Zionist Archives, the Israel Labor Party Archive, the Lavon Archive, and many others, he both filled and anticipated my needs as I moved from chapter to chapter. And the hours upon hours that we spent on the phone analyzing every aspect of Golda's life and character added clarity and depth to my own outlook. I am responsible for the viewpoints and any errors in this book, but his scholarship informed my thinking throughout.

Amos Eiran spent a great deal of time with me in Israel, directing me to key issues to be examined and introducing me to government leaders and scholars, and he has my deep appreciation. Robert Caro gave me the best advice as I launched my interviews, and continued to support, encourage, and advise me as the work progressed. I'm tremendously grateful to him for his help and friendship. I'm grateful also to Anita Shapira, who generously shared with me her research findings that related to Golda as she prepared her own acclaimed books on Israeli history and David Ben-Gurion. I thank her also for her thoughtfulness in waiting for me to complete this project. Abraham Ascher, historian of Russian history, guided me in pursuing Golda's abiding interest in Russian Jewry and led me to other helpful sources and historians, and I thank him warmly.

There are not enough words for me to convey my appreciation to Marlin Levin, former chief of the Time-Life News Bureau in Jerusalem, who, with enormous generosity, gave me his personal archival holdings on Golda Meir, a treasure trove of information and unpublished reports he had written during her lifetime. My appreciation also to two members of Golda's extended family, David Klein and Shmuel Katz, who provided letters from Morris Meyerson's family that had never before been published. They appear in the notes as "Family letters of David Klein."

I am indebted to Uri Savir, who arranged major interviews in Israel for me, including one with Shimon Peres. I thank Ellen Isler for putting me in touch with the late Amos Manor, former head of the Shin Bet, who was himself a fountain of knowledge and a conduit to significant figures in Golda's life and Israel's history. Special thanks to Hagai Tsoref of the Israel State Archives for his consistent help and insights, and especially for his thoughtfulness in allowing me to read his penetrating papers on Golda before they were published. My deepest gratitude goes also to Judith Reifen Ronen of the Golda Meir Memorial Association, who has been forthcoming and generous with materials and data from the very start. I am indebted to Yaakov Sharett, who went out of his way to provide me with texts of his father's unpublished writing.

In the United States, I enjoyed a rewarding visit to Golda's Milwaukee, where Cindy P. Benjamin welcomed me graciously, Tybie and Max Taglin kindly took me on an extensive tour of Golda's old neighborhood, and Herman Tuchman, his wife, Chai, and his sister, Dorothy Weingrod, shared family memories about Golda's early years. On a similar trip to Denver, Norman Provizer, director of the Golda Meir Center for Political Leadership at Metropolitan State University, most considerately devoted a day to showing me Golda's connections to that city.

Miriam Wallerstein did substantial research in New York in the files of Na'amat Woman, Hadassah, YIVO, and the Joint Distribution Committee. I thank her for that, for tracking down journal articles, and for her help in myriad other ways. Thank you to Jane Avner for her research in Milwaukee, Ben Fishman for his at the Library of Congress and presidential libraries, Grace Palladino at the George Meany Memorial Archives, Karen Pastorello at the Kheel Center, Cornell University Library, and Vicki Lipski at the American Jewish Archives. And thank you to Kathleen Bernstein and Jay Hyland at the Jewish Museum Milwaukee Archives, Mazx Yela at the UW-Milwaukee Libraries, and the staffs at the Dorot Jewish Division of the New York Public Library, the

Jewish Theological Seminary, and other libraries and archives used, particularly the Public Records Office of the British National Archives. A word of thanks also to the National Security Archive, which publishes indispensable electronic briefing books and declassified government documents online.

Robert H. Wolf translated large portions of Sheyna Korngold's Yiddish memoirs, *Zikhroynes*, into English for me, and my dear friend the late Maier Deshell translated numbers of Yiddish letters, all of great use. Other Yiddish translators, whom I thank, were Rivka Schiller, Lazer Mishulovin, and Yeshaya Metal. I was insecure in the beginning about my Hebrew skills and engaged several people to summarize sections of Hebrew books in English. They included Naomi Danis, Allon Pratt, Gahl Pratt, Orna Goldman, Rachel Shargal, and Tamar Fisher. After a short while, I became my own translator, and I thank them for getting me over the hump.

Throughout this project, Carolyn Hessel has been involved, enthusiastic, and supportive as only she—guardian angel of Jewish writers—can be. She read my manuscript more than once, made on-target suggestions, and went out of her way to make the book known to others. I am so grateful to her for so much. I'm indebted also to my editor, Altie Karper, who, in all the time I was writing this biography, never pressured or questioned me but always expressed calm confidence in the outcome and made herself available for any queries I might have had. Her judgment, insights, and knowledge have guided me throughout, and I feel blessed to have my work in her hands. I also want to thank Josefine Kals and Danielle Plafsky of Penguin Random House for the enthusiasm with which they immediately greeted this book and for their creativity, energy, and intelligence in promoting and marketing it. My agent, Charlotte Sheedy, has been at my side from the start—so many decades together, such a long friendship. Thank you.

Families seem to come last in book acknowledgments, and that is true here, too. But in reality, my husband comes first in my gratitude for his patience, love, and goodness, which sustained me through the years of this writing, as they have in every way.

Notes

OHD, ICJ Oral History Division, Institute of Contemporary Jewry, Hebrew University
    PRO Public Record Office
    PW *Pioneer Woman*
    RG Record Group
    UJA United Jewish Appeal
USNAM U.S. National Archives Microfilm
    WSAG Washington Special Actions Group
    WWC Women Workers' Council
    YTA Yad Tabenkin Archives

Introduction: "Call Me Golda"

xv "Your grandson": National press conference, Washington, D.C., *JP*, Oct. 3, 1969.
xviii She warned her assistants: Ovad Natan, interview with author, Feb. 10, 2006.

1. The Carpenter's Daughter

3 Eighth Constitutional Convention: "Proceedings of the Eighth Constitutional Convention of the AFL-CIO, Atlantic City, New Jersey, Oct. 2–7, 1969," vol. 1, Daily Proceedings.

4 "My dear friend": Ibid., 202.

4 "The applause continued": Eiran, interview with author, Aug. 2, 2006.

4 "Don't forget": GM speech at Israel Bonds National Tribute Dinner, Dec. 22, 1974, IBA.

4 Moshe Yitzhak Mabovitch: A record of his work as a carpenter appears in a file of I. Mabovitch in the State Archives of the City of Kiev, RG: Kiev Administration for Simple Crafts (1873–1904). The *I* derives from his middle name, probably Izok in Russian.

4 After the illness and death: Korngold, *Zikhroynes* (Yiddish, sections translated into English for author by Robert Wolf), 22–23.

4 For Russia's Jews: For early history of Kiev, see Henry Abramson, "Ukraine," in Hundert, *YIVO Encyclopedia*, 2:1930–37; Natan M. Meir, *Kiev*.

4 Khazaria: See Brook, *Jews of Khazaria*. See also Moshe Gil, "No Jewish Khazars" (Hebrew), *Haaretz*, April 28, 2009.

5 Pale of Jewish Settlement: Richard Pipes, "Catherine II and the Jews: The Origins of the Pale of Settlement," *Soviet Jewish Affairs* 5 (1975): 3–20; Michael Stanislawski, "Russian Empire," in Hundert, *YIVO Encyclopedia*, 2:1607–14.

5 "the increase of *zhidy*": Hamm, *Kiev*, 119–20.

5 chief of police: Natan M. Meir, *Kiev*, 29.

5 more than fourteen thousand members: Ibid., 26.

6 "one of the personalities": GM, *My Life*, 17.

6 kidnapping: For a discussion of mistaken notions about Russian conscription, see Litvak, *Conscription and the Search for Modern Russian Jewry*, 1–12.

6 convert them: Stanislawski, *Tsar Nicholas I and the Jews*, 10.

6 *khappers:* Ibid., 29–33.

7 "two men": Korngold, *Zikhroynes*, 14.

7 "an innocent": GM, *My Life*, 15.

8 "Jewish craftsmen": Hamm, *Kiev*, 122.

8 "cold and hunger": Korngold, *Zikhroynes*, 25–27.

8 "tall woman": GM, *My Father's House* (Hebrew), 14.

8 "There will be no artisans": Korngold, *Zikhroynes*, 15.

9 "it's not a tragedy": GM, *My Life*, 18.

9 Brodsky family: Hamm, *Kiev*, 129–31.

10 "enough milk": Korngold, *Zikhroynes*, 28.

10 "crisp white gown": Ibid., 34.

10 "a man's mind": Ibid., 13.

10 "What does it": Fallaci, *Interview with History*, 112.

11 "Whoever remembers": Korngold, *Zikhroynes*, 6.

11 "Promise to obey me": Ibid., 61–62.

11 "There's a *dybbuk*": Syrkin, *Golda Meir*, 17.

11 "like a little crown": Korngold, *Zikhroynes*, 49.

11 "It was streaked": Gruber, interview with author, Aug. 1, 2004.

11 "Somehow the washing": Harman, interview with author, Oct. 19, 2004.

12 "golden child": GM, *My Life*, 21.

12 "a little too cold": Ibid., 14.

13 "I can hear": GM, interview with Kenneth Harris, *London Observer*, Jan. 17, 1971. Variations appear in GM, *My Life*, 13; *My Father's House*, 16; and other places.

13 fried fish: Korngold, *Zikhroynes*, 55.

14 "In the early 1900's": Fallaci, *Interview with History*, 110.

14 City records: In *Ves Kiev* (All Kiev), a directory of Kiev residents, published between 1899 and 1915. The plaque appears on a column on the side of the building. It reads in Russian, "Here until 1903 lived the famous statesman of Israel, Golda Meir."

14 lifting his hat: Jewish Agency representative in Kiev, telephone interview with author, Dec. 13, 2006.

14 more than twenty thousand: Pinsk history and economy are discussed in depth in Rabinowitsch, *Pinsk*, a compilation of articles on the city. The English is abridged from a Hebrew text with the same title; both were used in this chapter.

14 "no one dared": Azriel Shohat, "The Character of Pinsk from the 1880s to the First World War," in ibid., 1:50.

15 "butchers, coachmen and porters": Ibid.

15 "was not a pleasant town": Weizmann, *Trial and Error*, 22.

15 *Pinsker blotte*: "Golda Meir on Her Childhood in Pinsk," GM speech in Hebrew at Haifa conference in memory of Pinsk, Dec. 15, 1965, in Rabinowitsch, *Pinsk*, vol. 1, pt. 2, p. 473.

16 market days: Shalom Tannenbaum, "The Market and the Taverns" (Hebrew), in Rabinowitsch, *Pinsk* (Tel Aviv: Pinsk-Karlin Association, 1966), 2:29–30.

16 large brick building: Korngold, *Zikhroynes*, 7–12.

16 Golda later remembered: "Golda Meir on Her Childhood in Pinsk," 473.

17 One of the taverns: Tannenbaum, "Market and the Taverns," 2:30.

17 "There was another Naiditch": "Golda Meir on Her Childhood in Pinsk," 476.

17 modern *heder*: Benjamin Lifton, unpublished memoir in possession of author, 1991, 10.

18 attend a primary school: Adler, *In Her Hands*.

18 "was a good woman": GM, interview with Harris.

18 only books: GM, *My Life*, 23.

18 "even beyond Pinsk": Jeffrey Veidlinger, "Even Beyond Pinsk," in Greenspoon, Simkins, and Horowitz, *Jews of Eastern Europe*, 175–89.

18 make an audience cry: Michael Arnon, interview with author, Oct. 20, 2004.

18 David Ben-Gurion: Teveth, *Ben-Gurion*, 5.

18 Berl Katznelson: Shapira, *Berl*, 4.

18 two nicknames: "Golda Meir on Her Childhood in Pinsk," 476.

19 "My mother": Ibid.

19 "wild-haired": GM, *My Life*, 21.

19 a murderous pogrom: See Monty Noam Penkower, "The Kishinev Pogrom of 1903," *Modern Judaism* 24, no. 3 (2004): 187–225.

20 "You fast": Clara Stern, "What Motivated Golda: Early Years in Russia," recording in *Golda Meir: Israel's Woman of Valor* (New York: Educational News Service, 1979).

21 Zionist groups: For an overview, see Scott Ury, "Zionism and Zionist Parties," in Hundert, *YIVO Encyclopedia*, 2125–32.

21 "bourgeois utopianism": Sachar, *History of Israel from the Rise of Zionism to Our Time*, 68.

21 "House of Jacob": Isaiah 2:5.

21 lovers of Zion: See Laqueur, *History of Zionism*, 75–83.

23 "Mother understood": Korngold, *Zikhroynes*, 61.

23 "I'll tell everything": Ibid.

23 "a shining example": GM, *My Life*, 21.

24 "Bloody Sunday": For events in 1905 and their aftermath, see Ascher, *Revolution of 1905*, vol. 1, *Russia in Disarray*.

24 "a troop of Cossacks": GM, interview with Harris. That they were not the same as Cossacks, see John Klier, "Cossacks and Pogroms: What Was Different About 'Military Pogroms'?," in Budnitsky et al., *World Crisis of 1914–1920* (Russian), 47–70.

25 "equality for the Jews": Frankel, *Prophecy and Politics*, 149.

25 "Mir hubin": "Golda Meir on Her Childhood in Pinsk," 474.

25 "For no group": Frankel, *Prophecy and Politics*, 149.

25 690 anti-Jewish pogroms: Ibid., 135.

25 "Take us away": "Golda Meir on Her Childhood in Pinsk," 475.

25 "So what did I take": GM, "My Beginnings" (from a 1969 radio interview in Hebrew), in *Land of Our Own*, 22.

26 "poverty, pogroms": GM, interview with Harris.

2. An American Girl

27 In leaving Russia: The pattern described is based on Gur Alroey, " 'And I Remained Alone in a Vast Land': Women in the Jewish Migration from Eastern Europe," *Jewish Social Studies: History, Culture, Society* 12, no. 3 (Spring/Summer 2006): 39–72; and Gur Alroey, "Bureaucracy, Agents, and Swindlers: The Hardships of Jewish Emigration from the Pale of Settlement in the Early 20th Century," in *Jews and the State: Dangerous Alliances and the Perils of Privilege*, ed. Ezra Mendelsohn (New York: Oxford University Press, 2003), 216–31.

28 It was nighttime: Description of their travels in Korngold, *Zikhroynes*, 77–84.

28 Moshe had sailed: U.S. of America Petition for Naturalization: "emigrated from Liverpool, England, the 17th day of November, 1903."

28 "Only last night": Korngold, *Zikhroynes*, 80.

29 S.S. *Montreal*: "List or Manifest of Alien Passengers . . . ," S.S. *Montreal*, sailing from Antwerp, May 16, 1906. Arriving at Port of Quebec, May 27, 1906, Ancestry .com.

29 sea voyage: See Steiner, *On the Trail of the Immigrant*, 30–47.

30 "Everybody who was anybody": Quoted in Howe and Libo, *How We Lived*, 18.

30 Moshe's move: Records of the Industrial Removal Office, American Jewish Historical Society, Newton Centre, Mass., and New York, Records, 1899–1922.

30 "their own salvation": Ibid., 3.

30 "ignorant, superstitious": Naomi W. Cohen, *Jacob H. Schiff*, 107.

30 seventy-nine thousand immigrants: Records of the IRO, 4.
31 One name and age: Records of the IRO, Removal Records (1899–1922), series 2, box 8, p. 12, ledger entry 9353.
31 300,000: Swichkow and Gartner, *History of the Jews of Milwaukee*.
31 "first time I saw": Meriel McCooey, "The Making of Golda Meir," *Sunday Times Magazine* (London), April 18, 1971.
32 Rachel Yanait: Ruth Kark, "'Not a Suffragist'? Rachel Yanait Ben-Zvi on Women and Gender," *Nashim*, no. 7 (Spring 2004): 139.
32 "This is how": Korngold, *Zikhroynes*, 87.
33 "It's the Cossacks": GM, *My Life*, 35.
33 Milwaukee's socialism: Mari Jo Buhle, Paul Buhle, and Dan Georgakas, eds., *Encyclopedia of the American Left* (Urbana: University of Illinois Press, 1992), s.v. "Milwaukee," 471–73.
34 "Jews ran small businesses": Hess interview, tape 1, Feb. 2, 1964, Jacob R. Marcus Center, AJA, HUC-JIR.
34 615–623 Walnut: *Milwaukee City Directory, 1907–1908*, Milwaukee Public Library.
34 "the Settlement": Swichkow and Gartner, *History of the Jews of Milwaukee*, 119.
35 ninety groceries: Ibid., 162.
35 "Suddenly become": Korngold, *Zikhroynes*, 90.
35 peeling frame houses: Swichkow and Gartner, *History of the Jews of Milwaukee*, 166–68.
35 "light dazzled": Korngold, *Zikhroynes*, 89.
35 "When it hurts": Ibid., 95.
36 "Brewers' Hill": History of Fourth Street School, author visit and interview with Tom Hanley (school principal), July 28, 2005.
36 "they will be glad": Griffin and Provines, *Civics for Young Americans*, 22.
36 "the bell": James Baldwin, *Four Great Americans: Washington, Franklin, Webster, Lincoln* (New York: Werner School Book Co., 1896, 1897), 59.
36 "When I studied": Israel Shenker, "Peace and Arab Acceptance Were Goals of Her Five Years as Premier," *NYT*, Dec. 9, 1978.
36 "She was always first": Regina Medzini, interview with Drora Beit-Or, Sept. 29, 1986, audio division, GMMA Archive.
37 "very serious minded": Ibid.
37 *Uncle Tom's Cabin:* GM, *My Life*, 38.
37 "school fame": Sara Feder, "I Remember Golda," *PW*, May–June 1973, 3.
37 *di Yiddishe:* Jacob Katzman, "Golda and America," *Jewish Frontier*, Jan. 1979, 8.
38 "If a daughter": Korngold, *Zikhroynes*, 118.
38 "I can tell you": Syrkin, *Golda Meir*, 24.
38 newspapers carried editorials: For example, in 1908 articles appeared in the *Evening Wisconsin*, April 14, *Milwaukee Sentinel*, May 20, and *Social Democratic Herald*, May 30.
39 "Russian Jewish section": *Milwaukee Journal*, Sept. 11, 1908.
39 "said a speech": Syrkin, *Golda Meir*, 26.
39 "We had the greatest success": Ibid.
39 "Packen Hall": There was no place called Packen Hall. Most likely this was Paschen Hall, located then at 525 Chestnut Street.
39 "Children Help": *Milwaukee Journal*, Sept. 2, 1909.
40 "We cannot": Friend to Jewish Consumptives' Relief Society, April 3, 1909, Beck Archives, Special Collections, Penrose Library, University of Denver.
40 "moist": GM, *My Life*, 40.
41 Colleagues rolled their eyes: Michael Arnon, interview with author.
41 "worse than death": GM, "My Beginnings," 26.

41 Men didn't like: GM, *My Life*, 41.

41 September 3, 1912: Record of Milwaukee Public Schools, confirmed in letter of Sharon P. Grant, program administrator, Nov. 29, 2006.

41 "I surely thought": Sheyna to Golda, Aug. 27, 1912. All the letters cited are in P-1886/29, ISA, except where otherwise noted.

41 "very happy": Sheyna to Golda, Oct. 8, 1912.

42 "Is there anybody": Sheyna to Golda, Oct. 8, 1912.

42 "My advice": Shamai to Golda, Nov. 15, 1912.

42 "almost a disease": Yossel to Golda, n.d. (Yiddish), P-1886/27, ISA.

42 "Don't know": Sheyna to Golda, Nov. 29, 1912.

42 "Well Goldie": Shamai to Golda, n.d. (signed "Sam").

43 "You have no idia [*sic*]": Sheyna to Golda, Dec. 13, 1912.

43 "I knew that Clara": Sheyna to Golda, Jan. 6, 1913.

43 "I am going to live": GM, *My Life*, 44.

43 "I had done something": Ibid., 45.

3. "Dearest Gogo"

All the letters cited are from P-1886/29, ISA, unless otherwise noted.

44 "a little too large": Korngold, *Zikhroynes*, 99–100.

44 1606 Julian: Preserved as Golda Meir House and Museum, Golda Meir Center for Political Leadership, Metropolitan State University, Denver, Norman Provizer, director.

44 "bury your dead chickens": Sign found in other half of duplex, 1608 Julian, and displayed at Golda Meir House.

44 German-speaking Jews: For history of Jews in Colorado, see Uchill, *Pioneers, Peddlers, and Tsadikim.*

45 National Jewish Hospital: Jeanne Abrams, interview with author, Aug. 15, 2006. For history of the sanatoria, see Jeanne Abrams, *Blazing the Tuberculosis Trail: The Religio-ethnic Role of Four Sanatoria in Early Denver* (Denver: Colorado Historical Society, 1990).

45 accumulating A's: "Record of Golda Mabowehz, North High School," box 6, folder 11, GMLA.

45 "a little flirtatiously": Joseph T. De Rose, interview with author, Aug. 16, 2006.

46 "I respect": Minnie to Golda, Sept. 15, 1914.

46 "a nice fellow": Minnie to Golda, Sept. 25, 1915.

46 "Say Goldie": Regina to Golda, Aug. 11, 1913.

46 "You just ought": Regina to Golda, Feb. 2, 1914.

46 "Clara and your mother": Regina to Golda, June 18, 1914.

47 Aid Association: Ball ticket for the association found in boards of the preserved Julian Street house, Golda Meir House. Shamai became secretary of the association. Sheyna to Golda, Aug. 27, 1912.

47 square oak kitchen table: Reconstructed in Golda Meir House and Museum.

47 Hegel: GM, *My Life*, 46.

48 Golda placated her: Ibid.

49 "four fell in love": Regina Medzini, *Panorama* TV, Aug. 9, 1971.

49 Yossel Kopilov: Miriam Copilove, telephone interview with author, June 28, 2008.

49 "By what fate": Yossel to Golda, Nov. 16, 1914, P-1886/27, ISA.

49 "flirting": Yossel to Golda, Feb. 27, 1919, P-1886/27, ISA.

49 "You are my sister": Yossel to Golda, n.d., P-1886/27, ISA.

49 Ida: Yossel to Golda, Dec. 15, 1914, P-1886/27, ISA.

49 "for his gentleness": GM, *My Life*, 50.

49 "From him": Fallaci, *Interview with History*, 115.
49 half sister Sarah: David Klein, interview with author, Aug. 25, 2006; Shmuel Katz, interview with author, Jan. 11, 2007.
50 His mother, Shifra: David Klein, interview with author, Aug. 25, 2006.
50 "it was an exertion": Sarah to Rae and Broudo, n.d., FLDK.
50 "I confess": Sarah to Rae, n.d., FLDK.
50 complete works: Sarah to Rae, May 21, 1915, FLDK.
50 "our family": Sarah to Rae, n.d., FLDK.
50 "Have you ever stopped": Morris to Golda, 1915, in Syrkin, *Golda Meir,* 36.
51 "cursed coldness": Sarah to Rae, Feb. 20, 1917, FLDK.
51 "He was one of the purest": Zuckerman, *Essays and Profiles* (Yiddish), 425.
51 "Ours was a great love": Fallaci, *Interview with History*, 116.
51 "beautiful soul": Syrkin, *Golda Meir,* 35.
51 "the matrimonial course": Regina to Golda, Aug. 4, 1914.
51 "hard person": Regina, interview with Beit-Or, Sept. 29, 1986, GMMA Archive.
51 "A real hard, tight pest": Zuckerman, interview with author, Feb. 20, 2006.
51 "like a hawk": GM, *My Life*, 50.
52 "Very well, I'll leave": Syrkin, *Golda Meir,* 34.
52 "Stubbornness": Korngold, *Zikhroynes,* 130.
52 "Now Goldie": Sheyna to Golda, Jan. 10, 1917.
52 "Dearest Goldie": Regina to Golda, June 18, 1914.
52 "as lonely": GM, *My Life*, 51. See also Polly Wilson Kemp, "Golda in Denver," *Denver Post*, Dec. 10, 1978.
53 "Well! The cat came back": Regina to Morris, Dec. 26, 1914.
53 no record: Sharon R. Grant to author, Nov. 29, 2006. "We have no information in our records that she ever left North Division."
53 living room couch: GM, "My Beginnings," 28.
53 "Her parents would give": Quoted in Linda Maiman, "Golda Meir's Milwaukee Years," *Insight, Milwaukee Journal*, Oct. 31, 1976, 1.
54 "The hall was fairly full": Quoted in McCooey, "Making of Golda Meir."
54 "Just learned about passing": Telegram, Herman and Chai Tuchman Collection, JMMA.
54 As a Zionist organization: For analysis of Poalei Zion in the United States, see Rojanski, *Conflicting Identities* (Hebrew).
55 "it is audacious": Louis Perchonok, "Memoirs," unpublished, 39, box 3, Louis J. Swichkow Collection, JMMA.
55 "Lincoln Park": Quoted in Maiman, "Golda Meir's Milwaukee Years," 10.
55 "arrangements committee": *Milwauker Wochenblat*, Sept. 1, 1916.
55 "the only girl there": Maiman, "Golda Meir's Milwaukee Years," 10.
55 *folkschule:* Folk schools are discussed at length in Raider, *Emergence of American Zionism*, 34–35.
55 120 students: 13th and 14th Annual Reports, Federated Jewish Charities, box 1, Federated Jewish Charities Collection, JMMA.
55 A photograph of the *folkschule:* Box 7, folder 8, GMLA.
56 "Darling Golda": Dubinsky to Golda, n.d., P-1886/28, ISA.
56 "lovely summer night": Dubinsky to Golda, July 3 no year, P-1886/27, ISA.
56 Buzie: Dubinsky to Golda, Aug. 10, 1916, P-1886/27, ISA.
56 "I'll remain": Dubinsky to Golda, Oct. 4 no year, P-1886/28, ISA.
56 "After a short stroll": Dubinsky to Golda, n.d., P-1886/28, ISA.
57 "Goga": Sheyna to Golda, Aug. 27, 1912.
57 "other people seem": Morris to Golda, Jan. 22, 1915.
57 "Getting up to ask": Ibid.

57 "You know well": Morris to Golda, June 1, 1915.

57 "very close": Yona Kama, interview with author, Jan. 11, 2007.

57 "Don't mind": Morris to Golda, Feb. 11, 1915.

57 "little girl": Morris to Golda, June 29, 1915.

57 "head over heels": Morris to Golda, July 17, 1915.

57 "fondle" and "kiss": Morris to Golda, June 21, 1915.

57 "sailing through": Morris to Golda, Jan. 22, 1915.

57 "dwell in the bughouse": Morris to Golda, Oct. 5, 1915.

58 Hechalutz: See Shapira, *Ben-Gurion*, 43.

58 "two Bens": Ibid.

58 "At the end": Yitzhak Ben-Zvi, *Selections from His Writings* (Hebrew), ed. Yemima Rosenthal (ISA, 1958), 69.

59 "get up": Rachel Yanait Ben-Zvi, *Coming Home* (New York: Herzl Press, 1964), 215.

59 "I do not know": Quoted in Syrkin, *Way of Valor*, 39–40.

59 "In principle": Menahem Meir, *My Mother*, 12.

59 "Yes, Gogele": Morris to Golda, Oct. 5, 1915.

60 "But of course": Ibid.

60 "the soul of one": Yossel to Golda, Jan. 19, 1915, P-1886/28, ISA.

60 "so very": Morris to Golda, Aug. 5, 1915.

60 "I would not": Morris to Golda, Oct. 5, 1915.

60 "all the necessary expenses": Morris to Golda, Oct. 12, 1915.

60 "be a burden" Morris to Golda, Oct. 19, 1915.

60 "Such an attitude": Ibid.

61 "I'm the luckiest": Golda to Regina, in Meron Medzini, *Golda* (Hebrew), 42. Medzini dates this Nov. 15, 1916, but it has to be 1915.

61 "Oh Goldie": Regina to Golda, Nov. 16, 1915.

61 "Goldie's intended": Perchonok, "Memoirs," 84, box 3.

61 "Those about": *The Tattler*, North Division High School, vol. 8 (Sept. 1915–June 1916).

61 "Goldie Mabovitz": *Milwauker Wochenblat*, Jan. 27, 1916, 4.

4. The Path to Palestine

62 newfound respectability: For the growth of Zionist groups, see Raider, *Emergence of American Zionism*, 41.

62 Even David Ben-Gurion: Teveth, *Ben-Gurion*, 100–103.

63 "personified the struggle": Perchonok, "Memoirs," 103, box 3.

63 "promised dangerous results": *NYT*, March 11, 1916.

64 "make a spectacle": GM, *My Life*, 61.

64 "She would move people": Rose Kader in McCooey, "Making of Golda Meir."

64 "free of stage fright": Perchonok, "Memoirs," 112, box 3.

64 "My dear fellow Jews": Ibid., 113.

65 Almost every account: "Representatives to the American Jewish Congress," in *Report of Proceedings of the American Jewish Congress, Philadelphia, Pa., December, 1918* (New York: American Jewish Congress, 1918, 73–78). Milwaukee delegates are "Chas. Friend, Nathan Sand, and E. Lisitsky."

65 "It was the beginning": Tuchman, interview with Bill Marten, Feb. 21, 1962, Tuchman Collection.

65 "In Milwaukee": Zerubavel, *In the Days of War* (Hebrew), 213.

66 "save": Ibid.

66 "Golda from Milwaukee": Ibid.

66 "I strongly wish": Zerubavel to Golda, Feb. 7, 1917, P-1886/28, ISA.

66 "colleague": Zerubavel to Golda from Minneapolis, n.d., P-1886/28, ISA.
66 "to talk things over": Zerubavel to Golda, March 14, 1917, P-1886/28, ISA.
66 "on behalf": Zerubavel to Golda, May 10, 1917, P-1886/27, ISA.
67 "with a sad and serious face": Zerubavel, *In the Days of War*, 213.
67 "in the flesh": Zerubavel to Golda, June 23, 1917, P-1886/27, ISA.
67 "bloodied, tragic place": Zerubavel to Golda, Dec. 29, 1917, P-1886/27, ISA.
67 "parlor Zionist": GM, *My Life*, 58.
67 "What if he hadn't": GM, interview with Harris.
67 "spreading yourself": Yossel to Golda, 1918, P-1886/27, ISA.
68 "excelled as an active worker": Perchonok, "Memoirs," 14, box 1.
68 "amorous adventures": Sarah to Rae, Aug. 17, 1917, SKC.
69 "Then she would take medication": Quoted in Martin, *Golda*, 77.
69 "noodge": Raizel to Golda, Nov. 11, 1917, P-1886/27, ISA.
69 "searching": Dubinsky to Golda, Sept. 16, 1917, P-1886/28, ISA.
69 "The boy is head over heels": Sarah to Rae, Oct. 31, 1917, SKC.
69 Much of the credit: Reinharz, *Chaim Weizmann: The Making of a Statesman*, 67–72.
70 "Can we be sure": Zuckerman, *Essays and Profiles*, 425.
70 gifts: Golda Meir, *My Life*, 54.
71 "I must join the fight": Dubinsky to Golda, May 6, 1918, P-1886/28, ISA.
71 "But if it is my fate": Dubinsky to Golda, July 3, 1918, P-1886/27, ISA.
71 marriage certificate: Milwaukee County Vital Records, Register of Deeds, 278:8.
71 "plainest of plain": Maiman, "Golda Meir's Milwaukee Years," 12.
71 "But I did powder my nose": Ibid.
71 *Encyclopaedia Britannica*: Menahem Meir and Sarah Rehabi, interview with author, Jan. 7, 2007.
72 "I was sure": Raizel to Golda, Jan. 14, 1918.
72 "Who leaves a new husband": GM, *My Life*, 66.
72 "couldn't say no": Ibid.
72 "to ensure the equal rights": Perchonok, "Memoirs," 123, box 3. On Yiddish, see also *Labor Zionist Handbook* (New York: Poalei Zion Zeire Zion of America, 1939), 36–37.
73 "wrote much faster": Regina to Golda, Feb. 17, 1919, P-1886/28, ISA.
73 "My dear, you are right": Golda to Morris, Dec. 8, 1919, 1886/28, ISA.
74 Abortions were illegal: Jeffrey S. Adler, "Halting the Slaughter of Innocents," *Social Science History* 25, no. 1 (Spring 2001): 1244–64.
74 "rushed off": Skoss to Golda, n.d., P-1886/28, ISA.
74 "I was thunderstruck": Sheyna to Golda, April 7, 1918, P-1886/29, ISA.
75 Five thousand people: For an analysis of the congress, see Frankel, *Prophecy and Politics*, 541–47. See also *AJY* (Philadelphia: Jewish Publication Society, 1919), 21:186–88.
75 For the Zionists: Frankel, *Prophecy and Politics*, 545.
75 "I tell you": Syrkin, *Way of Valor*, 45.
76 "when she appeared": Tuchman, interview with Marten.
76 "This is the life": Medzini, *Golda*, 46.
76 "like a religious Greek": Yossel to Golda, Dec. 26, 1918, P-1886/27, ISA.
76 Louis Marshall: "Jewish Rights in Eastern Europe, an Address Delivered Before the American Jewish Congress," Dec. 15, 1918.
76 National Committee: Reported in *Milwaukee Sentinel*, May 22, 1919.
76 parade: *Milwaukee Sentinel*, May 29, 1919.
78 "Hurry up": Regina to Golda, Feb. 4, 1919, P-1886/29, ISA.
78 "My deepest wish": Yossel to "the Myersons," n.d., P-1886/28, ISA.
78 "body and soul": Sarah to Morris, July 8, 1919, P-1886/29, ISA.

78 "bargains": Regina to Golda, Oct. 31, 1918, P-1886/29, ISA.

79 "there were another Goldie": Ibid.

80 "small and withdrawn": GM, *My Life*, 70.

80 "Milwaukeeans who have received": *Jewish Daily Press*, April 3, 1921.

80 "How would you explain": Szalita, interview with author, Nov. 18, 2004.

5. "New Jews"

83 "was too good a Catholic": Prendergast-Gallivan correspondence, July 9–July 12, 1921, American Consulate Index Bureau 365113/710-711, RG 59, NA.

83 The International Seamen's Union: Giles T. Brown, "The West Coast Phase of the Maritime Strike of 1921," *Pacific Historical Review* 19, no. 4 (Nov. 1950): 385–96.

83 And trouble they made: Sheyna Korngold, "The Journey of the *Pocahontas*," in Yehuda Erez, *Third Aliyah Book* (Hebrew), 1:208–12.

84 "I don't know": GM, interview on *Panorama*, Aug. 9, 1971.

84 "God damn": American Consul to Secretary of State, July 14, 1921, American Consulate Index Bureau 196, 32/340, RG 59, NA.

84 Forty years later: GM, *My Life*, 346–47.

84 About a decade after that: Elisha Kally, *Here and in Distant Lands: Autobiographical Stories* (Hebrew) (Tel Aviv: Leor), 93.

85 "new Jews . . . Real Hercules": Yossel to Shamai, in Syrkin, *Way of Valor*, 21.

85 "new Jew": See Segev, *One Palestine, Complete*, 257–69.

86 "none dared oppose her": Korngold, *Zikhroynes*, 139.

86 "Well, Golda": GM, "My Beginnings," 32.

87 Barash: Korngold, *Zikhroynes*, 144–45.

87 The Tel Aviv they saw: For history and descriptions of Tel Aviv, see Mann, *Place in History*; and Helman, *Young Tel Aviv*.

87 "has become the first Hebrew city": Morris to family and friends, Aug. 8, 1921, in Yehuda Erez, *Third Aliyah Book*, 1:237–38.

88 Eden cinema: Nirit Anderman, "Eden Now," *Haaretz*, July 24, 2008.

88 "with crowds of Jewish workers": Morris to family and friends, Aug. 8, 1921.

89 "True, one feels": Golda to Shamai, Aug. 24, 1921, in Syrkin, *Golda Meir*, 67.

89 "because they anticipated": Laqueur, *History of Zionism*, 227–28.

90 "feel the existence": Quoted in the Arab newspaper *Carmel* and reported in *Haaretz*, July 12, 1921.

90 "if we will not go": Golda to Shamai, Aug. 24, 1921, in Syrkin, *Golda Meir*, 67.

90 Golda chose Merhavia: GM, "From Milwaukee to Merhavia," in Yehuda Erez, *Third Aliyah Book*, 2:734–36, reprinted in English in *Wisconsin Jewish Chronicle*, July 11, 1969.

90 Dubinsky had helped: See Stephen Lawson, *One Square Mile in Israel* (London: Anglo-Israel Association, 1989).

91 "There was a need": Tsur, Zvulun, and Porat, *Here on Earth* (Hebrew), 187.

92 "even had warm water": Morris's depiction of Merhavia in letter to his mother, Dec. 13, 1921, in Yehuda Erez, *Third Aliyah Book*, 1:239–41.

92 *barhash*: GM, "First Days in Kibbutz Merhavia: A Memoir," *Midstream*, March 1970.

92 "spiritual satisfaction": Morris to his mother, Dec. 13, 1931, in Yehuda Erez, *Third Aliyah Book*, 1:239.

93 "no longer be constantly": GM, *My Life*, 68.

93 "who had arrived": Lishamski to Yanait, n.d., P-2283/16, ISA.

93 "How could one have": Korngold, *Zikhroynes*, 158–59.

93 "accept the dowry": GM, "How I Made It in My Kibbutz," in *Land of Our Own*, 39.

94 "It was not easy": Golda Myerson, "The World of Hanna Chizik," *PW,* Dec. 1952, 14.

95 "witch": GM, "From Milwaukee to Merhavia."

95 "there is only": Protocols of meetings from Dec. 1921 to Sept. 1923, 14–15 (Hebrew), Merhavia Archives.

95 constant turnover in membership: Ibid., 17.

95 Blumenfield: GM, "First Days," 28.

95 "impossible": Friedman in Merhavia protocols, 7, 17.

96 "with dead ducks": GM, "First Days," 27.

96 David Yizraeli: Ibid., 28.

96 Manya Shochat: Rachel Yanait Ben-Zvi, *Before Golda.*

96 Ada Maimon-Fishman: Ada Fishman and her brother Rabbi Juda Leib Fishman added the name Maimon to show their descent from Maimonides. She is referred to in this book as "Maimon," although she also appears as "Fishman" in the scholarly literature. Rachel Yanait added her married name, Ben-Zvi, to hers, but she is also referred to as Yanait.

97 Second Aliyah: In reality, immigration to Palestine was more fluid than the different aliyot would imply. There were farmers and shopkeepers as well as laborers among the Second Aliyah immigrants, and there were religious and ultrareligious individuals and families who came throughout the years to dwell in the land of their ancestors, but the divisions became useful in characterizing groups of immigrants.

97 "bequeathed": GM speech at Third Aliyah conference in Habimah Auditorium, 1960, in Yehuda Erez, *Third Aliyah Book,* 2:910–13.

97 women's movement: Dafna N. Izraeli, "The Zionist Women's Movement in Palestine, 1911–1927: A Sociological Analysis," *Signs* 7, no. 1 (Autumn 1981): 87–114.

98 "What happens": Minutes of the WWC conference, Sept. 1922, IV-230-5-1, LA.

98 permission from Merhavia: Mentioned in letter from Ada Maimon to Aliza Shidlansky, Oct. 16, 1922, IV-104-83-8, LA.

98 "as an American girl": Maimon to Bussel, Dec. 14, 1922, IV-104-83-6, LA.

99 Ada Maimon won that representation: Izraeli, "Zionist Women's Movement," 103.

99 "Ah, Palestine": Morris to family, 1923, in Syrkin, *Way of Valor,* 63.

99 "He couldn't stand": Fallaci, *Interview with History,* 116.

100 Histadrut convention: *The Second Convention of the Histadrut, Tel Aviv, 1923* (Hebrew), compiled by Mordechai Saver from handwritten minutes and other sources (1968).

100 The stage: A description of the convention is in Yehuda Sharett, "Letter to Moshe Sharett on the Second Histadrut Convention, Feb. 7–20, 1923," in Moshe Sharett, *London Days Letters* (Hebrew), 250–307.

100 "The future of this land": *Second Convention,* 11.

101 "The very existence": Ibid., 22.

101 "For us, the newcomers": Ibid., 49; other words appear on pp. 111–12.

101 "She was filled with grace": Yehuda Sharett's descriptions of Golda in *London Days Letters,* 261 and 288–89.

102 "conceited": Sharett to Katznelson, March 29, 1923, in ibid., 210–11.

103 "to further the cause": GM, *My Life,* 57.

103 "never had a special interest": Kark, " 'Not a Suffragist'?," 141.

103 In May, another conference: *Ha'Kvutza: A Collection of Kvutza Subjects* (Hebrew) (Tel Aviv: Histadrut Cultural Committee, 1925), 15–49.

103 "It's enough": GM, "With a Full Heart," in Yehuda Erez, *Third Aliyah Book,* 2:910.

103 "change attitudes": *Ha'Kvutza,* 30.

103 "Why is it so much better": GM, *My Life,* 88.

104 "Preparing food": Maimon, *Women Build a Land,* 72–73.

104 "men should also": *Ha'Kvutza*, 32.

104 "common sense": GM, "With a Full Heart," 2:910.

104 love affair: Medzini, *Golda*, 64.

105 "tragedy": Fallaci, *Interview with History*, 115.

105 enterprise collapsed: Merhavia was reconstituted in 1929 by a totally different group.

6. The Dark Years

106 Casino: Shchori, *Dream That Became a City* (Hebrew), 368.

106 "unbearably small": GM, *My Life*, 97.

106 "I found great satisfaction": Korngold, *Zikhroynes*, 154–55.

107 Shamai earned a decent living: Ibid., 161–62.

107 "was bound by his bondage": Syrkin, *Golda Meir*, 83.

107 met him again: Eliahu Biltsky, "Interview with Prime Minister Golda Meir" (Hebrew), 4, n.d., IV-104-38-2, LA.

107 coined Hebrew names: Herman, *Conquerors of the Seaways* (Hebrew), 65.

108 "intelligent, clever": Teveth, *Ben-Gurion*, 335.

108 Gusta Strumpf: See Sheva, *Road in the Wilderness* (Hebrew), 60–63.

108 Rabin's mother: When Golda, as prime minister, mentioned to Rabin that she had been a cashier at the buildings department, he said, "So was my mother." "No," she corrected him, "I was the cashier; your mother was the bookkeeper." Yitzhak Rabin, *Memoirs*, 6.

108 "whether a person": Minutes of committee preparing a book of Solel Boneh writings (Hebrew), July 29, 1971, 3, Eliahu Biltsky, IV-104-38-28, LA.

108 second story: GM, interview with Biltsky, 2, IV-104-38-2, LA.

108 "tail": Beit-Or and Rehabi, *In Close Company with Golda* (Hebrew), interviews by Drora Beit-Or and Sarah Rehabi, 10.

109 "If somebody": Minutes of committee for Solel Boneh book, 33, IV-104-38-28, LA.

109 "Why didn't you": Sheva, *Road in the Wilderness*, 90.

109 "a Jew on the corner": GM, interview with Biltsky, 5, IV-104-38-2, LA.

109 Solel Boneh: Yitzhak Greenberg, "Golda in the Histadrut," in Avizohar, *Golda* (Hebrew), 43.

110 tiny two-room apartment: Syrkin, *Golda Meir*, 84.

110 "beautiful lampshade": Quoted in Martin, *Golda*, 140.

110 alcohol in the tin bathtub: GM, "How I Made It in My Kibbutz," 41.

110 international workers' conference: BGD, May 5, 1924.

111 Officially, the Hashomer: Yehuda Erez, ed., *Letters of Ben-Gurion*, vol. 2, *1920–1928* (Hebrew) (Tel Aviv: Am Oved, 1972), Oct. 7, 1926, 343–46, describes earlier investigations, in which Golda participated.

111 "extremely close friends": GM, *My Life*, 120.

111 "no reason to believe": Histadrut Secretariat, May 14, 1925.

111 another Histadrut executive meeting: Beit-Or and Rehabi, *In Close Company with Golda*, 9.

112 "Her Hebrew was weak": Ibid.

112 "Golda is here": HaCohen to Remez, Aug. 9, 1925, David Remez, 1922–1944 (Hebrew), IV-104-113-34, LA.

112 "I would succeed": GM, *My Life*, 99.

112 alternated times: Hillel Dan, *On an Unpaved Road* (Hebrew) (Jerusalem: Schocken, 1963), 13.

112 unpaid bills: GM, *My Life*, 100–103.

112 "we lived in more poverty": GM, interview with Harris.

113 seven thousand left: Lossin, *Pillar of Fire*, 135.

113 "The reason we could fulfill": Solel Boneh secretariat minutes, Aug. 16, 1926, IV-124-2-8-B, LA.

113 "pioneer": GM, interview with Biltsky, 15, IV-104-38-2, LA.

113 "he no longer wanted": Gideon Lev-Ari, "Interview with Prime Minister Golda Meir on the Occasion of Fifty Years of Her Aliyah," 1971 (Hebrew), GMMA Archive.

113 Miss Kallen's: Syrkin, *Golda Meir*, 84.

113 "I received a letter": Shapira, *Berl Katznelson* (Hebrew), 2:705–6.

114 Katznelson's wife: Bili Muskana-Lehrman, "Golda Flesh and Blood: The Love, the Hatred, and the Men in the Middle" (Hebrew), *Maariv Supplement*, Feb. 26, 1988.

115 "listening intently": Michaeli, *Herzliya Beginnings and Development* (Hebrew), 76–77.

115 "good-hearted man": "Golda Meir on Her Childhood in Pinsk," 476.

115 She spoke to them: Menahem Meir and Sarah Rehabi, interview with author, Jan. 8, 2007.

116 also "not free": Bat-Sheva Margalit Stern, "'They Have Wings but No Strength to Fly': The Women Workers' Movement Between 'Feminine' Control and 'Masculine' Dominance," in Kark, Shilo, and Hasan-Rokem, *Jewish Women in Pre-state Israel*, 203–4.

116 One of the major battle arenas: For background, see Greenberg, "Golda in the Histadrut," 51–52.

116 In her account: GM, *My Life*, 111.

116 "swooping from above": Stern, "'They Have Wings,'" 205.

117 "Golda should never have married": Medzini, interview with Beit-Or, 14.

117 "the marriage was a failure": GM, *My Life*, 112.

7. A Star Is Born

118 "put me on the path": GM, interview with Harris.

118 "who cannot remain at home": Some of the essays in the book first appeared in Hebrew in 1928, with the title "The Woman Worker Speaks." An expanded Yiddish edition, in which Golda's essay appeared, signed G.M., was published in 1931 and edited by Rachel Katznelson-Shazar. The English translation by Maurice Samuel was called *The Plough Woman*, 205–7.

119 nanny: See Teveth, *David's Zeal* (Hebrew), 2:254.

119 "Don't have the cigarette": Thelma Ruby Frye, "Report from Pretoria," *Foto News*, n.d., YIVO archive, Bund file.

119 Her tasks as secretary: Greenberg, "Golda in the Histadrut," 46–57.

120 throbbing migraines: Lou Kadar, interview with author, Aug. 19, 2004.

120 Golda did not work: Golda to Rachel Yanait Ben-Zvi, 1928, P-2083/12, ISA.

120 frightened Golda: Sarah Rehabi, interview with I. Avi-Benjamin, *PW*, Sept.–Oct. 1969, 6.

120 "She would travel": Muskana-Lehrman, "Golda Flesh and Blood."

120 "resented it": Sarah Rehabi and Menahem Meir, interview with author, Feb. 4, 2006.

120 "really have in their hearts": GM, interview on *Panorama*.

120 Manya Shochat's daughter: *Haaretz* Supplement, Oct. 17, 1986.

121 "Meyerson was more": Muskana-Lehrman, "Golda Flesh and Blood."

121 "She is a public person": Syrkin, *Way of Valor*, 71.

121 "I ask only one thing": Ibid., 72.

121 "how it happened": HEC minutes, June 18, 1928, LA.

122 "It was very good": Shazar and Shazar, *On Two Shores* (Hebrew), 185.

122 "She had some unpleasant hours": Ibid., 187.

122 Golda had first noticed: GM, *My Life*, 119.

123 "Give me your hand": Shazar and Shazar, *On Two Shores*, 222.

123 "Goldenu": Shazar to Golda, P-1886/12, ISA.

124 "held hands": Itzhak Philosoph, interview with author, Jan. 18, 2007.

124 "the small nations": BGD, Aug. 5, 1928.

125 "Rhodela was sick": Shazar and Shazar, *On Two Shores*, 189.

125 "Sometimes I feel": Ibid., 190.

125 "Golda should . . . be involved": BGD, Sept. 22, 1928.

125 "Golda adamantly opposed": Shazar and Shazar, *On Two Shores*, 192.

125 "I do not understand": Dispute about going to America in HEC minutes, Sept. 20 and Nov. 5, 1928, LA.

127 "Always": GM, "Borrowed Mothers," in *Plough Woman*, 207.

127 "but she cannot depart": BGD, Oct. 8, 1928.

127 S.S. *Aquitania:* NY Passenger List 1928, T715 4392:21, USNAM.

128 convention: *Palestine Souvenir on the Occasion of the Fifth Anniversary of the Geverkshaften Palestine Campaign and the Fourth National Labor Convention for Palestine Held in New York, December 29/30, 1928.* Golda is listed in the program along with Arlosoroff, Marminski, and Bloch.

128 "greetings from a *chavera*": Ibid.

128 digging a tunnel: *New York Morgn Zhurnal,* Jan. 1, 1929.

128 "brought the convention": Ibid.

128 Pioneer Women: For a history of the organization, see Mark A. Raider, "The Romance and *Realpolitik* of Zionist Pioneering: The Case of the Pioneer Women's Organization," in Reinharz and Raider, *American Jewish Women and the Zionist Enterprise*, 114–32.

128 "were the first and last": GM, *My Life*, 113.

129 "I do not believe": GM to Yanait, 1928, P-2083/12, ISA.

129 in 1949: Esther Zackler, "She Was a Part of Our lives," *PW,* Jan.–Feb. 1979, 5–6.

130 three thousand members: *AJY: 1928–1929*, 30.

130 "The entire movement": Raider, "Romance and *Realpolitik*," 116.

130 "like a flash": Dvorah Rothbard, "When Peace Comes—Remember Me," *PW,* Jan.–Feb. 1979, 8.

130 "she didn't wash": Fannie Shoock, unpublished letter to *Na'amat Woman* magazine, Dec. 26, 1989, GM file, NUSA archive.

130 "do housework": Adele Patick Epstein, unpublished letter to *Na'amat Woman*, 1990, GM file, NUSA archive.

130 "greatly succeeded": Greenberg, "Golda in the Histadrut," 63.

131 $36,500: Ibid., 62.

131 Morris resigned: Meyerson to Kaplansky, March 20, 1929, IV-104-754-3, LA.

131 Golda had requested: Histadrut Finance Committee memo, April 14, 1929, IV-104-754-3, LA.

131 "She neglects herself": Syrkin, *Way of Valor,* 74.

131 "Perhaps you understand": Ibid., 71.

131 "If there was ever": Shapira, *Berl*, 166.

132 "suffered mostly dagger wounds": Levin, *It Takes a Dream*, 127.

132 Haganah members had used: "Golda Meir on Her Childhood in Pinsk," 476.

133 WIZO involvement: HEC minutes, Oct. 11, 1929, LA.

133 "as a formal matter": HEC minutes, Nov. 18, 1929, LA.

134 breaking point: The contentious meeting, with battles between Ben-Gurion, GM, and Maimon, in HEC minutes, Dec. 16, 1929, LA.

134 one of fifteen people: Mapai convention, Jan. 6, 1930, 2-21-1930-5, LA.

135 "I have had the feeling": WWC secretariat minutes, Jan. 9, 1930, IV-230-5-17, LA.

135 busy with her children: BGD, March 25 [, 1930]. She suggested hiring Gusta Strumpf in her place.

135 A year later: Stern, " 'They Have Wings,' " 383n23.

135 "Golda is conducting": Ben-Gurion to Paula, June 23, 1930, in Yehuda Erez, *Letters of Ben-Gurion*, 3:96.

135 "knew nothing": MC minutes, Aug. 3, 1930, P-811/4, ISA.

135 "one visit to Israel": GM, *My Life*, 134.

135 Ben-Gurion prevailed: Ben-Gurion to Eliyahu Golomb, July 17, 1930, in Yehuda Erez, *Letters of Ben-Gurion*, 3:116.

136 "without particular sharpness": MC minutes, Aug. 3, 1930, P-811/4, ISA.

136 Friedrich Adler: Ibid.

136 "tragic": Ben-Gurion, *kaf* A248-12061, Genazim archives. Ben-Gurion's reaction to GM's talk appears also in BGD, July 26, [1930,] and in the newspaper of *Hapoel Hatzair*, Aug. 15, 1930.

136 Gone too, Golda's shame: GM, *My Life*, 58.

8. Pioneer Woman

137 the matter of Zalman Shazar: Greenberg, "Golda in the Histadrut," 64.

137 "We always avoid": Remez to GM, June 14, 1930, in Martin, *Golda*, 171–72.

138 "I don't believe": Yossel to Morris, n.d., P-1888/28, ISA.

138 "You're impressed": Remez to GM, June 14, 1930, in Martin, *Golda*, 171–72.

138 "I'll suffer": Ibid., 173.

138 Shazar journeyed there: Shazar to Rachel, in Shazar and Shazar, *On Two Shores*, 222n1.

138 S.S. *Europa:* NY Passenger List 1931, T715 5057:1, USNAM.

138 Great Depression: For general statistics, see *Historical Statistics of the United States;* for New York, see Edward Robb Ellis, *The Epic of New York City* (New York: Basic Books, 2004), 532–33; Sachar, *History of the Jews in America*, 428–30.

139 They don't accept Jews: HEC minutes, July 21, 1938.

139 Membership in Zionist institutions: Halperin, *Political World of American Zionism*, 327.

139 tour schedule: "Goldie Myerson's Tour," unpublished typescript, GM file, NUSA archive.

140 reception for her at the Hotel Pennsylvania: Pioneer Women's Organization to Mary Robbins, April 12, 1932, GM file, NUSA archive.

140 she appeared in Philadelphia: *Davar*, May 30, 1932.

140 membership in the ILGWU: Sachar, *History of the Jews in America*, 460–61.

140 grueling pace of travels: "Goldie Myerson Visits a Number of Cities," *Yiddisher Kaempfer*, May 27, 1932.

140 "You undoubtedly already know": Greenberg, "Golda in the Histadrut," 65.

140 "Sarah ill": Menahem Meir, *My Mother*, 29.

140 Family lore: GM, *My Life*, 135–37.

141 "The knowledge": Greenberg, "Golda in the Histadrut," 67.

141 "hard situation": WWC secretariat minutes, July 12, 1932, in Nahalal, IV-104-83-15, LA.

141 bookstore on Jaffa Road: Menahem Meir and Sarah Rehabi, interview with author, Feb. 14, 2006.

141 "Everyone thought": Zuckerman, interview with author, Feb. 22, 2006.

142 They disembarked in New York: NY Passenger List, T715 5212:2, USNAM.

142 "in perfect health": GM, *My Life*, 137.

142 "It was not a good time": Sarah Rehabi and Menahem Meir, interview with author, Oct. 13, 2004.

142 Golda helped the children: Menahem Meir, *My Mother*, 31.

142 "went wild": Menahem Meir and Sarah Rehabi, interview with author, Feb. 14, 2006.

143 "big brother": Ibid., Oct. 13, 2004.

143 Her younger sister, Clara: Ibid., Jan. 8, 2007.

143 in twenty-five years: Clara Stern passport application and letter to Mrs. R. B. Shipley, Passport Division, U.S. Department of State, June 12, 1950.

143 Morris's family: David Klein, interview with author; Shmuel Katz, interview with author.

143 "We were always lonesome": Sarah Rehabi, interview with Avi-Benjamin, 6.

144 "the smell of railway stations": GM, *My Life*, 138.

144 1225 Broadway: Rothbard description of Golda's office, *PW*, Jan.–Feb. 1979, 9.

144 "It may be redundant": Rachel to Shazar, Dec. 5, 1932, in Shazar and Shazar, *On Two Shores*, 239.

144 "stay only in hotels": Shazar to Rachel, Dec. 30, 1932, in ibid., 242.

145 "Golda slept": Unpublished essay by Norma Salz, 1931, GM file, NUSA archive.

145 Newark, New Jersey, chapter: GM, *My Life*, 138.

145 "It's too bad": Beba to GM, March 5, 1933, IV-208-I-1830, LA.

146 "Golda Meyerson clubs": Rothbard, *PW*, Jan.–Feb. 1979, 9.

146 women's fair at the New York Armory: Jacob Katzman, "Golda and America," *Jewish Frontier*, Jan. 1979, 10.

147 "aggressive, impatient woman": Raider, "Romance and *Realpolitik*," 114.

147 "husbands closeted themselves": Zackler, *PW*, Jan.–Feb. 1979, 5.

147 "We were her family": Ibid.

147 "from her heart": Salz, GM file, NUSA archive.

147 "spell": Marie Syrkin, *The State of the Jews* (Washington, D.C.: New Republic Books, 1980), 163–64.

147 "She's everything I'm not": Kessner, *Marie Syrkin*, 402.

147 "impassioned and persuasive": Syrkin, *State of the Jews*, 163–64.

148 "who is a remarkable speaker": Kessner, *Marie Syrkin*, 229–30.

148 "I always come away": Menahem Meir, *My Mother*, 168.

148 "from the fact that": Syrkin to GM, July 27, 1954, addressed "Dearest Golda," P-812/26, ISA.

148 "privately influence": Syrkin to Sarah Rehabi and Menahem Meir, Nov. 5, 1988, box 5, folder 9, GMLA.

149 "harassed and tired": Sara Feder, "Remembering Golda . . . (on the Occasion of Her 75th Birthday)," *PW*, May–June 1973, 4.

149 "practically like an aunt": Menahem Meir, *My Mother*, 168.

149 Golda wrote an article: "Travel Impressions," *Yiddisher Kaempfer*, May 2, 1932, reprinted in Hebrew as "What My Eyes See (Impressions from My Travels in America)," *Davar*, May 25, 1932.

151 "very very feminist matter": Simhonit, interview with DroraBeit-Or and Sarah Rehabi, April 5, 1987, GMMA Archive.

151 "not a single *chavera*": *Davar*, June 2, 1931.

152 "I'm still doing": GM to Berl, Jan. 19, 1934, IV-104-754-1, LA.

152 despite pleas: See GM's letter to the Women Workers' Council, July 23, 1934, IV-208-1-1830, LA.

152 "liveliest and best-organized": *Davar*, July 31, 1934.

9. Black Clouds Rising

153 Chaim Arlosoroff: Mark A. Raider, "Emissaries in the Promised Land: Manya Shohat, Chaim Arlosoroff, and Enzo Sereni in the USA," *Judaism* (Winter 2000).

153 Jabotinsky: Katz, *Lone Wolf;* for Jabotinsky and Ben-Gurion, see Tsahor, *Shaping of the Israeli Ethos* (Hebrew). See also Halkin, *Jabotinsky.*

153 "dunam by dunam": Weizmann quoted in Laqueur, *History of Zionism,* 495.

154 praise for Hitler: Golda wrote about this in Yiddish in *PW,* Feb. 1934, in Greenberg, "Golda in the Histadrut," 70.

154 Behind the ideological clashes: For the quarrel between Labor and the Revisionists, see Sarid, *You Chose Us for Ruling* (Hebrew).

155 "general": *PW* (Yiddish), Feb. 1934.

155 disrupted a speech: "From the Campaign Meeting in America," *Davar,* Jan. 12, 1933.

155 "We had the suspicion": GM to WWC, June 24, 1933, in Greenberg, "Golda in the Histadrut," 69.

155 More than seventy thousand people: "Arlosoroff Funeral Attended by Throng," *NYT,* June 19, 1933.

155 "Tel Aviv Insists": *Davar,* April 18, 1933.

156 Fearful for the future: Anita Shapira, "The Debate in Mapai on the Use of Violence, 1932–1935," *Zionism* 2, nos. 3–4 (1981): 99–124.

156 "There are times": MC minutes, Oct. 21, 1934, P-811/1, ISA.

157 "Vladimir Hitler": Teveth, *Ben-Gurion,* 414.

157 Telegrams for and against: BGD, Oct. 30, 1934.

157 "most unfortunately": GM, *My Life,* 145.

157 Tel Aviv, that chameleonic city: Pinhas Yurman, "Tel Aviv 1934: Picture of a Place," in Naor, *Tel Aviv.*

158 "gown of concrete": Nathan Alterman, "Morning Song."

158 "hidden yearning": Rehabi, interview with Avi-Benjamin, 6.

158 Me'onot Ovdim: See Yurman, "Tel Aviv 1934"; see also Mann, *Place in History.*

158 254 Hayarkon Street: Menaham Meir and Sarah Rehabi, interview with author, Aug. 22, 2004.

159 barbershop: Kally, *Home and Hearth* (Hebrew).

159 James Joyce's *Ulysses:* Menahem Meir and Sarah Rehabi, interview with author, Aug. 22, 2004.

160 myriad activities: See, for example, *Davar,* Dec. 6, 21, and 27, 1934; April 30, 1935; Oct. 28, 1936; and Nov. 4, 1936.

160 Haboneh: IV-230-1-358, LA.

160 "good" editors: Rachel to Shazar, Feb. 2, 1935, in Shazar and Shazar, *On Two Shores,* 260.

160 Palestine Symphony: "Histadrut Representatives with Toscanini and Huberman," *Davar,* Dec. 25, 1936.

160 After hours of waiting: Menahem Meir, *My Mother,* 28.

161 "Everybody knew": Manor, interview with author, Oct. 12, 2004.

161 "one of the very few": GM, *My Life,* 124.

161 "she saw in him": Aharon Remez in Muskana-Lehrman, *Maariv,* Feb. 26, 1988.

161 "very attractive": Sacharov, e-mail interview with author, March 20, 2008.

162 "easy to get": Martin, *Golda,* 162; a nickname circulated about her was "the mattress."

162 "rapidly": Eilam, interview with Drora Beit-Or, Sept. 1985–Feb. 1986, GMMA Archive.

162 "She devoted herself": Sacharov, interview with author, March 20, 2008.

162 "important force": Aharon Remez in Muskana-Lehrman, *Maariv*, Feb. 26, 1988.

162 "I knew about it": Medzini, interview with Beit-Or.

163 "After I left": The notes between GM and Remez are in IV-104-113-37, LA.

163 "the warm, personal": Aharon Remez in Muskana-Lehrman, *Maariv*, Feb. 26, 1988.

164 "If only Golda": See, for example, BGD, May 1, 1935.

164 In September 1935: Her schedule is compiled from letters, speeches, minutes of meetings, newspaper articles, and ship manifests.

164 "reflected my mood": Menahem Meir, interview with author, Jan. 14, 2009.

164 "You told me": London to GM, March 28, 1976, GMMA Archive.

165 "When Golda was home": Zuckerman, interview with author, Feb. 22, 2006.

165 "What do you want": GM, radio interview with Yaakov Agmon, "Personal Questions," Sept. 14, 1977 A-RE1, GMMA Archive.

165 about 175,000 Jews: Population statistics from Dotan, *Struggle for Eretz Yisrael* (Hebrew), 135–36.

166 "I kissed the children": GM, *My Life*, 148.

166 their Revolt: Segev, *One Palestine, Complete*, 366. For an Arab viewpoint, see 360–74.

167 *havlagah:* See Shapira, *Land and Power*, 234–57.

167 top hats: Photograph in Lossin, *Pillars of Fire*, 234.

168 "Half a loaf": Peel Commission, Report Conclusions, July 7, 1937, in Rabinovich and Reinharz, *Israel in the Middle East*, 44.

168 "here and now": Teveth, *Ben-Gurion*, 609.

168 "A Jewish State": Weizmann, *Trial and Error*, 385.

168 "is not the end": Bar-Zohar, *Ben-Gurion*, 91.

169 "I want a Jewish state": GM's entire talk at the council is published with the others in *On Paths Toward Statehood* (Hebrew), July 29–Aug. 7, 1937 (Tel Aviv: Ihud Publication, 1938).

170 "I don't like it": Levin, *It Takes a Dream*, 161.

170 "We knew that many Arabs": *The Twentieth Zionist Congress, August 3–21, 1937* (Hebrew) (Jerusalem: Histadrut and Jewish Agency, 1937), 140.

170 "Ben-Gurion, in his greater wisdom": GM, *My Life*, 157.

170 "Had the partition scheme": GM, interview with Yaron London, Israel Television, Dec. 8, 1978.

171 "One must not": GM to Isaac Hamlin (Yiddish), Marcus Center, AJA, HUC-JIR.

171 "a sea psychology": "Mrs. Goldie Myerson Outlines Plans for Fleet of Jewish Ships," *Wisconsin Jewish Chronicle*, Dec. 10, 1937.

171 "Berl Katznelson created": Remez to GM, April 7, 1937, P-1886/1, ISA.

171 "tens of thousands": *Wisconsin Jewish Chronicle*, Dec. 10, 1937.

171 "ate, drank, slept": GM, *My Life*, 156.

171 A letter from London: IV-104-113-37-15, LA.

172 "bluff": Gusta to GM, May 10, 1938, GMMA Archive.

172 "to be as cautious": Boukstein to GM, May 13, 1938.

172 Zimori: Minutes of Nachshon administration center, Aug. 11, 1938.

172 "I very much want": Gusta to Remez, Dec. 13, 1939, IV-104-113-37-16, LA.

172 "The rich Jews": HEC minutes, March 2, 1939.

173 "Capitain": Shapira, *Berl Katznelson* (Hebrew), 2:706.

173 Évian-les-Bains: For background information, see S. Adler-Rudel, "The Evian Conference on the Refugee Question," in *Leo Baeck Institute: Year Book XIII* (London: East and West Library, 1968), 235–73.

173 "a man of good intentions": HEC minutes, July 21, 1938.

173 "would be expected": *FRUS 1938* (Washington, D.C., 1955), 1:740–41.

173 "no order to the day": HEC minutes, July 21, 1938.

174 "overseas territories": Adler-Rudel, "Evian Conference," 245.

174 "As we have no real": Avriel, *Open the Gates!*, 25. See same source for other countries' excuses.

174 "Everybody expresses sympathy": *Haaretz*, July 18, 1938.

174 "There is only one thing": GM, *My Life*, 159.

175 "I realized then": Julie Nixon Eisenhower, "Golda Meir," *Ladies' Home Journal*, March 1977, 159.

175 One group: Ervin Birnbaum, "Evian: The Most Fateful Conference of All Times in Jewish History," part 2, *Nativ*, November, 2008, 2.

10. "And the Heart Breaking"

All the letters from Morris to Golda are in the Golda Meir personal file in ISA P-1886/8. All are in English.

176 "bury the hatchet": Morris to GM, April 1, 1937.

176 "this day of days": Morris to GM, n.d.

176 "the days of silence": Morris to GM, April 1, 1937.

176 "What will you send": Morris to GM, April 4, 1937.

176 "Lovely, wonderfully lovely": Morris to GM, April 7, 1937.

177 "Let's lose our egos": Morris to GM, April 1, 1937.

177 "such trivialities": Ibid.

177 "The whole complex": Morris to GM, April 4, 1937.

178 "be happy in the knowledge": Morris to GM, April 5, 1937.

178 "cherished letter": Morris to GM, April 7, 1937.

178 "I no longer know": Morris to GM, April 15, 1937.

178 Rumor had it: Martin, *Golda*, 216.

179 "and the heart breaking": GM to Morris, ca. Nov. 15, 1938, P-1886/4, ISA.

179 failure of the Évian conference: Friling, *Arrows in the Dark*, 1:21.

179 Golda happened to be there: Burg, *Autobiographical Chapters* (Hebrew), 82.

179 "Tens of Hitler youth": Remez to his wife, Nov. 20, 1938, IV-104-113-8, LA.

179 "impossible to imagine": GM to Menaham, Nov. 16, 1938, P-1886/4, ISA.

179 "barbarous world": GM to Morris, ca. Nov. 15, 1938, P-1886/4, ISA.

179 "run down": GM to Morris, ca. Nov. 26, 1938, P-1886/4, ISA.

180 Yossel's son: Elisha Kally, interview with author, April 15, 2008.

180 "I would like you to consult": GM to children, Nov. 26, 1938, P-1886/4, ISA.

181 "Picture my reunion": Morris to children, Aug. 15, 1939, P-1886/4, ISA.

181 "hunched over": Martin, *Golda*, 225.

181 "impregnable wall": Morris to GM, April 15, 1937, P-1886/8, ISA.

181 "spite": Martin, *Golda*, 197.

181 "idea never entered": Fallaci, *Interview with History*, 116.

181 He pulled away: Menahem Meir, *My Mother*, 17.

182 "troubled existence": Morris to Menahem, in ibid., 19.

182 "become unbearable": Morris to Menahem, Jan. 26, 1946, P-1886/4, ISA.

182 "One can go crazy": GM to children, Nov. 16, 1938, P-1886/4, ISA.

183 "I was in London": "Golda Meir on Her Childhood in Pinsk," 484.

184 internal disagreements: See Michael J. Cohen, *Palestine to Israel: From Mandate to Independence* (London: Frank Cass, 1988), chap. 3.

184 "If we must offend": Chamberlain to Palestine cabinet committee, April 20, 1939, PRO CAB 24/285 CP89 (39), BNA.

184 "Even if Britain": Ben-Gurion to Paula, Feb. 9, 1939, in Ben-Gurion, *Letters to Paula* (Hebrew), 288.

184 The British hoped to buy them off: Laqueur and Rubin, *Israel-Arab Reader*, 44–50.

185 "What will our potential enemies": Gilbert, *Churchill and the Jews*, 159.
185 "Jewish children scattered": *Dvar Hapoelet*, May 3, 1939, 52–54. An abridged English translation appears in Christman, *This Is Our Strength*, 1–7.
185 *Kindertransports:* Harris and Oppenheimer, *Into the Arms of Strangers*.
187 illegal ship *Dora:* Avigur interview, Jan. 1967, 170.38, Haganah Archive.
187 "In the early morning hours": Ibid.
187 "Within an hour": Avriel, *Open the Gates!*, 272.
188 "The notion of attacking Arabs": GM, *My Life*, 149.
188 "Do Not Murder": Rabbi Benjamin and Yaakov Patrazil, eds., *Against the Terror* (Hebrew) (Jerusalem, 1939).
189 "Café Panic": Neumann, *In the Arena*, 144.
189 "are so very quiet": GM to Sarah, Aug. 14, 1939, P-1886/4, ISA.
189 "Thousands of Jews": *The Twenty-First Zionist Congress* (Hebrew) (Jerusalem, 1939), 14.
190 "A Rabbi from America": GM to children, Aug. 21, 1939, in Menahem Meir, *My Mother*, 56.
190 electrified the audience: For the dispute, see Marie Syrkin's report in *Jewish Frontier*, Sept. 1939, 10–13. For Berl's speech, see *Twenty-First Zionist Congress*, 147–49.
190 "The entire Congress": GM to children, Aug. 21, 1939, in Menahem Meir, *My Mother*, 56.
191 "prepare both": Minutes of HEC meeting, Aug. 25, 1939.
191 "all meet again": Weizmann's talk in *Twenty-First Zionist Congress*, 222–23.

11. Life and Death

192 Unemployment soared: Laqueur, *History of Zionism*, 534.
192 "should give up having kitchens": GM, "Mutual Aid Within the Workers' Community," in Christman, *This Is Our Strength*, 12.
192 battle with the nurses: Greenberg, "Golda in the Histadrut," 123–25.
193 "Generally, I'm not a coward": HEC minutes, Oct. 1, 1939, LA.
193 "We shall not go": Syrkin, *Way of Valor*, 94.
194 "Fifty or sixty men": MC minutes, Sept. 21, 1939, 2-23-1939-27, LPA.
194 "Do we have one party": MC minutes, Oct. 25, 1939, 2-23-1939-27, LPA.
195 "could not continue": MC minutes, Nov. 1, 1939, 2-23-1939-27, LPA.
195 "Ben-Gurion resigned": Friling, interview with author, May 19, 2005.
195 "There may be people": MC minutes, Nov. 22, 1939, 2-23-1939-28, LPA.
195 "to request": MC minutes, Dec. 6, 1939, 2-23-1939-28, LPA.
196 100,000 Palestinian pounds: HEC minutes, Dec. 24, 1939, LA; "Envisaged by Histadrut," *Palestine Post*, Dec. 26, 1939.
196 "not a single member": HEC minutes, Dec. 24, 1939, LA.
196 "sadistic streak": Syrkin, *Golda Meir*, 106.
196 "blot on the community": GM, "Mutual Aid Within the Workers' Community," 14.
196 "the loathed *mifdeh* drives": GM, *My Life*, 144.
196 "that this labor federation": HEC minutes, June 13, 1940, LA.
197 "to speak, to listen": GM entire testimony, July 1, 1940, in IV-104-113-118, LA.
198 "We must assist": There are several versions of Ben-Gurion's statement. This one is in Shapira, *Ben-Gurion*, 115–16.
198 "didn't laugh": Teveth, *Ben-Gurion*, 742.
198 "a small Pale of Settlement": Ibid., 736.
198 "He was a young": GM described the meeting in HEC minutes, March 10, 1940, 6/210, LA.
199 "We were looking": Repetur, interview with Drora Beit-Or, April 10, 1985, 2–4.

200 "act of inhumanity": Gilbert, *Churchill and the Jews*, 179.
200 "demeanor at that meeting": Repetur, interview with Beit-Or, 3.
200 "activists": Meir Chazan, "The *Patria* Affair: Moderates vs. Activists in Mapai in the 1940s," *Journal of Israeli History*, no. 2 (Autumn 2003): 61–95.
200 "Listen, my friend": Sacharov, *Out of the Limelight*, 48.
200 "We must do": GM speech, May 2, 1940, quoted in Sirkin-Rachlin trial, in *Land of Our Own*, 48.
201 "can do what it wants": HEC minutes, April 29, 1941, 9/41, LA.
202 "evil": GM to Sarah, n.d., P-1886/4, ISA.
202 "From the day": HEC secretariat minutes, July 2, 1942, LA.
203 "You are a nice": GM's testimony in *Land of Our Own*, 46–51.
204 "the greatest admiration": Baxter to GM, 1975, P-812/26, ISA.
205 At their peak: Greenberg, "Golda in the Histadrut," 112.
205 "Patience. Negotiations": HEC secretariat minutes, May 5–7, 1943, LA.
205 "We have a responsibility": Ibid.
206 a single salary: Greenberg, "Golda in the Histadrut," 115.
206 "I am the person": Letter from Ramallah, Sept. 1971, G-6467/7, ISA.
206 "saga of the chair": Greenberg, "Golda in the Histadrut," 115.
206 "With great feeling": *Davar*, Feb. 20, 1945.
206 fund-raising campaign: HEC secretariat minutes, Dec. 17, 1942, LA.
206 "Donor Supper": Yetta Surosky to "Chavera Dvora," Feb. 13, 1943, Pioneer Women's Organization, NUSA archive.
207 "my daughter in the kibbutz": Menahem Meir, *My Mother*, 71.
207 "going to the settlements": I. Avi-Benjamin, "My Mother, Golda Meir," *PW*, Sept.–Oct. 1969, 7.
207 "worked in the Histadrut": Ibid.
208 "How in the world": Menahem Meir, *My Mother*, 71.
208 "You probably know": None of the letters are dated and all are in file P-1886/4, ISA.
208 "ovens of Germany": GM speech at Nineteenth Zionist Congress in Lucerne, Sept. 1935.
208 "In a way": GM, *My Life*, 146.
209 Eliyahu Dobkin: Porat, *Blue and Yellow*, 37.
209 mass gassing of Jews: Kessel, *Marie Syrkin*, 341.
209 "the fact that we were able": HEC secretariat minutes, Aug. 12, 1943, 26/51, LA.
209 "We can no longer speak": HEC secretariat minutes, Aug. 5, 1943, 25/50, LA.
209 debate between the Histadrut and the Jewish Agency: For an in-depth analysis of Zionist attitudes to the Holocaust, see Porat, *Blue and Yellow*.
209 "There is no other Zionism": HEC secretariat minutes, Jan. 21, 1943, 3/28, LA; HEC secretariat minutes, Aug. 5, 1943, 25/50, LA.
209 "this tendency to consider": Porat, *Blue and Yellow*, 76.
210 "before any money": Ibid., 77.
210 "tragic misunderstanding": HEC secretariat minutes, Aug. 5, 1943, 25/50, LA.
210 Meir Ya'ari: HEC secretariat minutes, Feb. 11, 1943, 5/30, LA.
210 "I'm positive": HEC secretariat minutes, Jan. 21, 1943, 3/28, LA.
210 "was the only person": Porat, *Trapped Leadership* (Hebrew), 164. The "Yishuv to the Rescue" campaign occurred in April 1944.
210 words and deeds: Ibid., 171.
211 Golda's name: Ibid., 225.
211 extra eighty thousand pounds: Porat, *Blue and Yellow*, 81.
211 "if we are able": Ibid., 80.
211 "Ironically, the new Jews": Segev, *Seventh Million*, 110.

211 "although there is no guarantee": Zvi Or Hof, eulogy for GM in *Haaretz*, Dec. 13, 1978.

212 Golda and Remez: Brown, *Israeli-American Connection*, 191.

212 Bermuda conference: See Friling, *Arrows in the Dark*, 1:90–97.

212 "Greatly Astonished": Marcus Center, AJA, HUC-JIR.

212 "could have done": HEC secretariat minutes, Aug. 12, 1943, LA.

213 "Woe to us": HEC minutes, May 5–7, 1943, LA.

213 *Davar:* May 7, 1943.

213 "It's clear": HEC minutes, May 26, 1943, LA.

213 family doctor: Menahem Meir, *My Mother*, 74.

213 "One can always push": GM, *My Life*, 166.

213 "I'm deeply ashamed": HEC secretariat minutes, April 29, 1943, LA.

214 "should have turned the world": HEC secretariat minutes, Aug. 12, 1943, LA.

214 "shadow of hope": Ibid.

214 "They obeyed our call": Menahem Meir, *My Mother*, 67.

215 "If you get there safely": Ettinger, *Blind Jump*, 54.

215 "They have their hand": Ibid., 55.

215 "the tears flowed": Amos Ettinger, *Blind Jump* (Hebrew) (Tel Aviv: Zmora Bitan, 1986), 64.

215 "most sensitive": Ettinger, *Blind Jump*, 78.

215 Other parachutists also recalled: Palgi, *Great Wind Comes* (Hebrew), 17.

216 "I came to him": Lossin, *Pillar of Fire*, 293.

216 "hidden rabbi": Copy of cable sent to Golda on Dec. 29, 1972, by B. Vago, University of Haifa, in G-6479/15, ISA.

216 Michael Dov-Beer Weissmandel: See Porat, *Blue and Yellow*, 216–18.

217 "I don't want a split": MS minutes, May 3, 1942, 28, P-811/5, ISA.

218 Elected Assembly: For a detailed discussion of the party fights, see Meir Avizohar, "From Political Activity to National Leadership," in Avizohar, *Golda*, 151–57.

218 "study month": Shapira, *Berl*, 304–5.

218 "the one man": GM, *My Life*, 125.

219 Then he kissed it gently: "Yossel's Last Days," a memoir by his wife, Dina, in possession of his son Elisha Kally and shown to author.

219 "upright, good-hearted Jew": "Golda Meir on Her Childhood in Pinsk," 476.

219 "There is no one like Golda": Michaeli, *Herzliyah*, 77.

12. *Ein Breira*—No Alternative

220 "Victory day": BGD, May 8, 1945.

220 "We could not go out": Address before the Sixth Histadrut Conference, Oct. 1, 1945, translated in *PW,* Nov. 1945, 11.

220 "I want the German man": MS minutes, May 15, 1945.

220 "the curse of helplessness: "Testimony of Goldie Myerson at the Anglo-American Inquiry Hearings, March 25, 1946," *PW,* April 1946, 5.

221 Primus stove: L. Kuperstein, ed., *Beit Brenner* (Hebrew) (Tel Aviv: T.A. Workers' Council, 1973), 400.

221 "Golda mixes": Becker, *With the Times and the People* (Hebrew), 76–77.

222 "We had hoped": Remez to GM, July 5, 1945, P-1886/12, ISA.

222 "rest": Ibid.

222 "political cooking": Anita Shapira, "Golda: Femininity and Feminism," in Reinharz and Raider, *American Jewish Women and the Zionist Enterprise*, 307.

222 "hard pressure": Simcha to Remez, July 4, 1945; Chaim Berman to Remez, July 5, 1945, IV-104-113-117, LA.

222 "could not move": Histadrut staff to Remez, July 13, 1945, IV-104-113-117, LA.

222 "no surprise in the matter": Simcha to Remez, July 11, 1945, IV-104-113-117, LA.

223 "A lot of us": Syrkin, *Way of Valor*, 136.

223 "What's wrong": MC minutes, July 10, 1945.

223 "who will be to blame": Meyer to HEC, March 13, 1945, 1/4/NN, Kupat Holim Center.

223 "shorten the days": Histadrut staff to Remez, July 13, 1945, IV-104-113-117, LA.

223 "It's unclear": Berman to Remez, July 18, 1945, IV-104-113-117, LA.

224 big news: Remez to GM, July 26, 1945, P-1886/12, ISA.

224 As soon as the doctors: Berman to Remez, July 29, 1945, IV-104-113-117, LA.

224 severe headache: Ibid.

224 "Goldenyu": Shazar to GM, July 29, 1945, P-1886/12, ISA.

225 Golda's recovery: Chaim Berman and others to Remez, Aug. 9, Aug. 29, Sept. 8, 1945, IV-104-113-117, LA.

225 "the depths of my heart": Morris to Menahem, Oct. 13, 1945, P-1886/8, ISA.

225 "Today my taxi driver": Remez to GM, Sept. 28, 1945, P-1886/12, ISA.

225 "drank in": Shazar to GM, Oct. 11, 1945, P-1886/12.391, ISA.

225 "I assumed from the beginning": Ibid.

226 her name appears: MC minutes, Sept. 29, 1945, LA.

226 500,000 American troops: Radosh and Radosh, *Safe Haven*, 88.

227 "As matters now stand": Ibid., 93.

227 "hideous": Ibid.

227 "was a large, powerfully built": Crum, *Behind the Silken Curtain*, 61.

227 "a little insane": GM, *My Life*, 201.

227 Bevin considered the Jews: Crossman, *Nation Reborn*, 79.

228 "I have to answer": Alonzo L. Hamby, *Man of the People: A Life of Harry S. Truman* (New York: Oxford University Press, 1995), 405.

228 "to do what's right": Spiegel, *Other Arab-Israeli Conflict*, 20.

228 "For over twenty years": GM to Sixth Histadrut Conference, Oct. 1, 1945, *PW*, Nov. 1945, 11.

229 "We will not have to react": Meeting of Jewish Agency management, Nov. 13, 1945.

229 "a squat, broad-shouldered": T. R. Fyvel, review of *Ernest Bevin*, by Francis Williams, *Commentary*, Nov. 1953, 495–97.

230 "The plight of the victims": Bevin's statement to Parliament can be found online at hansard.millbanksystems.com/commons/1945/nov/13/palestine-anglo-american -committee-of.

230 "I want suppression": British Foreign Office to G. R. Strauss, Feb. 15, 1946, PRO FO 800/485, BNA.

230 "socialist minister": MC minutes, Nov. 14, 1945, 2-23-1945-46, LPA.

231 "We took the path": Mapai council minutes, Nov. 30, 1945, 2-22-1945-61, LPA.

232 "were wrong": GM, *My Life*, 196.

233 "In my opinion": Mapai political committee minutes, March 27, 1944, 2-26-1944-2, LPA.

234 "produce only a new set": Makovsky, *Churchill's Promised Land*, 217.

234 "To spew forth": Bar-Zohar, *Ben-Gurion*, 123.

235 "We kept hearing": Bethell, *Palestine Triangle*, 208.

235 British detention camp at Atlit: Yitzhak Rabin, *Memoirs*, 15–16.

235 "among the most restful": Syrkin, *Way of Valor*, 130.

235 *kalaniyot*: Dare Wilson, *With the 6th Airborne Division in Palestine, 1945–1948* (London: Pen and Sword, 2008).

236 The American group included: American statement about committee members, Washington to Foreign Office, cable, Dec. 7, 1945, PRO FO 371/45388, BNA.

236 "fast friends": GM, *My Life*, 192.

236 Richard Crossman: Crum, *Behind the Silken Curtain*, 8–9.

236 Bevin had handpicked Crossman: Weisgal, *So Far*, 223.

236 within 120 days: Washington to Foreign Office, telegram, Dec. 7, 1945, PRO FO 371/45388, BNA.

236 Einstein didn't do the Zionists: Weisgal, *So Far*, 222.

236 "I was not impressed": Mapai Council minutes, Feb. 4, 1946, 2-022-1946-62, LPA.

237 Arab witnesses opposed: Crum, *Behind the Silken Curtain*, 69–71.

237 "Why don't you give": Crossman, *Palestine Mission*, 70.

237 "little less than death": Crum, *Behind the Silken Curtain*, 127.

237 Ben-Gurion initially opposed: Teveth, *David's Zeal*, 4:673–77.

237 Silver had also refused to testify: Neumann, *In the Arena*, 216.

237 "I have no doubt": Mapai Council minutes, Feb. 4, 1946, 2-022-1946-62, LPA.

238 Crum thought it was England's way: Crum, *Behind the Silken Curtain*, 163.

238 "pride," "intelligence": *Davar*, March 26, 1946, 1.

238 "direct approach": *Palestine Post*, March 26, 1946, 1.

238 "Gentlemen": Golda's entire testimony, including questions, appears in "The Case of the Histadrut," *PW*, April 1946, 1.

239 "Her walk, her talk": Gruber, interview with author.

239 "the only free socialist society": Radosh and Radosh, *Safe Haven*, 138.

240 La Spezia: The saga of the *Fede* appears in Avriel, *Open the Gates!*, chap. 20, 275–86.

240 "the land of our last": Central refugee committee to Jewish Agency, London, cable, April 7, 1946, PRO CO 537/1805, BNA.

240 "Mrs. Meyerson": GM, *My Life*, 194.

241 As the days progressed: *Davar*, April 18, 1946.

241 Three days into the hunger strike: Palcor News Agency/Palestine Telegraphic Service Bulletin 58, vol. 9, Friday, April 19, 1946, PRO CO 537/1805, BNA.

241 "In every generation": Golda's memories, H-4310/2-3, ISA.

241 "There seems to be": I. N. Clayton to Sir Walter Smart, April 17, 1946, PRO CO 537/1805, BNA.

242 "There was nobody": Michael Arnon, interview with author.

242 "against the wish": King Abdullah's response in A. Cunningham to Secretary of State, June 19, 1946, PRO CO 537/1753, BNA.

242 "purge": *Davar*, June 17, 1946, 2.

243 "they did not want": *NYT*, June 13, 1946, 1.

243 hissed and booed: J. P. E. C. Henniker to P. F. R. Beards, Dec. 2, 1946, PRO FO 800/486, BNA.

243 Jewish Sabbath: Notes prepared for PM's Statement to House of Commons, July 1, 1946, PRO CO 537/ 1713, BNA.

244 Jewish Agency's legitimacy: From High Commissioner for Palestine to Secretary of State, July 9, 1946, outlining documents found, PRO CO 537/1715, BNA.

13. "Nevertheless: A Woman"

245 "Golda, are you still": GM, *My Life*, 195.

245 "compliment": Natan Alterman, "The Seventh Column," *Davar*, Sept. 6, 1946.

245 "Golda fiercely resented": Abba Eban, *Personal Witness*, 72.

245 as late as 1959: Simcha Raz, "Authors and Books" (Hebrew), *Face to Face*, Dec. 27, 1963, 13.

246 "would not buy life": *Davar*, July 1, 1946.

246 "If we are defeated": *Davar*, July 2, 1946.

246 "excellent": Zipporah to Moshe, July 2, 1946, in Sharett and Sharett, *Imprisoned with Paper and Pencil* (Hebrew), 31.

246 "We will win": *Davar,* July 3, 1946.

246 "The worst Jew": *Hatzofeh,* July 4, 1946.

247 "Ben-Porat suggested": Sharett to Dobkin and Sharef, July 10, 1946, in "Months in the Ayalon Valley," ed. Pini Opher, the unpublished letters of Moshe Sharett in 1946 (Hebrew), generously given to the author by Yaakov Sharett.

247 Golda knew Zeev: Menahem Meir, interview with author, June 9, 2010.

247 A broadly educated man: Sheffer, *Moshe Sharett.*

248 "was unfit for the post": Dr. Felix Rosenblueth at Aliya Hadasha meeting, British secret report, Sept. 7, 1946, PRO CO 537/1714, BNA.

248 "wise, sharp, devoted": *Hatzofeh,* Aug. 28, 1946.

248 "that even in the advanced": Malkah Raymist, "A Woman in Her Own Right," *PW,* March 1947, 10.

248 "It's terrible": Menahem Meir, *My Mother,* 87.

248 civil disobedience: Bethell, *Palestine Triangle,* 253.

248 met with Chaim Weizmann: Ben-Gurion, *Toward the End of the Mandate* (Hebrew), 8n23.

249 Committee X: Goldstein, *Eshkol* (Hebrew), 262–63.

250 "pour out his heart": "Golda Meir on Her Childhood in Pinsk," 473.

250 setting off a huge explosion: For a detailed account, see Bethell, *Palestine Triangle,* 253–69. For Begin's viewpoint, see Gordis, *Menachem Begin,* 48–54.

250 "their horror": *Davar,* July 23, 1946.

250 "anti-Jewish": Ben-Gurion, *Toward the End of the Mandate,* 86.

251 "She was surprised": Teveth, *David's Zeal,* 4:751–60.

251 "The establishment": *Haaretz,* July 24, 1946.

251 If the British reprise: Zipporah to Moshe, July 29, 1946, in Sharett and Sharett, *Imprisoned with Paper and Pencil,* 113.

252 "very sad": Ibid.

252 "didn't see eye to eye": Medzini, interview with Beit-Or, 16.

252 rushing into print: "Publication of the White Paper," *Davar,* July 25, 1946.

252 "a bitter political struggle": *Summary of Reports, Jewish Agency Affairs and the Attitude of the Moderate Parties,* PRO CO 537/1713, BNA.

252 Morrison-Grady Plan: See Siegel, *Other Arab-Israeli Conflict,* 22–23.

253 "unalterable opposition": Radosh and Radosh, *Safe Haven,* 180.

253 "Pazit": Sharett to Sharef, July 22, 1946, in *Months in Ayalon Valley.* The Hebrew word *paz* means "pure gold."

253 a pogrom: Jewish Agency Executive Paris Conference minutes, Aug. 2, 1946, CZA.

254 "I hate to think": GM interview with Bethell, May 24, 1977, P-1784/2, ISA

254 "Biltmore program": See Rabinovich and Reinharz, *Israel in the Middle East,* 54–55.

254 "trap": Jewish Agency Executive Paris Conference minutes, Aug. 4, 1946, CZA.

255 "wash his hands": Goldmann, *Autobiography of Nahum Goldmann,* 232.

255 "We must tell": Ibid.

255 "We must state": Ibid.

255 "The Executive is prepared": Ibid.

256 he specified borders: Evyatar Friesal, "Toward the Partition of Palestine," in Raider, *Nahum Goldmann,* 169–203.

256 "irresponsible": GM, *My Life,* 199.

256 "I believe Dr. Weizmann": Jewish Agency Executive Paris Conference minutes, Aug. 13, 1946, CZA.

257 "through Bevin and Hall": Ibid., Aug. 17, 1946.

257 three conditions: Ibid., Aug. 6, 1946.

257 The Arabs also had conditions: Bethell, *Palestine Triangle,* 278; *NYT,* Aug. 26, 1946.

258 Golda wished to know: Sharef to Sharett, Aug. 23, 1946, S25/10.016, CZA.

258 twenty-six questions: Sharett to Sharef, Aug. 24, 1946, in *Months in Ayalon Valley*.

258 "then we don't act": MS minutes, Sept. 6, 1946, 2-21-1946-27, LPA.

258 encounters with Shimon Peres: Ilana Kaufman, "Political Activity in the National Institutes," in Avizohar, *Golda*, 204.

259 "Neither Masada nor Vichy": Ben-Gurion, *Toward the End of the Mandate*, 159.

259 "The decision follows": MS minutes, Sept. 6, 1946, 2-21-1946-27, LPA.

259 A few Arab delegates: Bethell, *Palestine Triangle*, 278.

259 list of prospective representatives: Submitted on Sept. 20, 1946, London Conference, PRO CO 537/1779, BNA; N. Goldmann to G. H. Hall, Sept. 20, 1946, Z4/20279II, CZA.

259 "shut up in Latrun": Weizmann to Martin, Sept. 16, 1946, PRO CO 537/2517, BNA.

259 rumors cropped up: *Davar*, Sept. 17 and 19, 1946.

259 When Zipporah asked: Zipporah to Sharett, Sept. 16, 1946, in Sharett and Sharett, *Imprisoned with Paper and Pencil*, 269.

259 not actually changed: Sharett to Zipporah, Sept. 18, 1946, in ibid., 278.

260 Now that Ben-Gurion: Sharett to GM, Sept. 18, 1946, in "Months in the *Ayalon Valley*."

260 a crisis: Ben-Gurion sent several equivocal cables in which he seemed to hint that he might agree to attending the conference if the British released all the detainees. See Ben-Gurion to Z. Sharef, Sept. 22, 1946; Ben-Gurion to GM, Sept. 24, 1946, in Freundlich, *Political Documents of the Jewish Agency*, vol. 1, *May 1945–December 1946*, 614, 624.

260 "I have never": Mapai political committee minutes, Sept. 18, 1946, 2-26-1946-4, LPA.

260 "lacked all flexibility": Sharett to Zipporah, Sept. 19, 1946, in Sharett and Sharett, *Imprisoned with Paper and Pencil*, 284.

261 "the entire evening": Zipporah to Sharett, Sept. 20, 1946, in ibid., letter 131, addendum, 282–83.

261 "It was very nice": Sharett to Zipporah, Sept. 21, 1946, in ibid., 290–91.

261 He wrote to Golda: Sharett to GM, Sept. 21, 1946, in *Months in Ayalon Valley*.

262 She answered immediately: Sept. 23, 1946, in Freundlich, *Political Documents of the Jewish Agency*, 1:617–18.

262 He understood: Sharett to Golda, Sept. 23, 1946, in *Months in Ayalon Valley*.

262 "quietly and comfortably": Mapai political committee minutes, Sept. 24, 1946, 2-26-1946-4, LPA.

262 Zionist Inner Actions Committee: Minutes, Sept. 25, 1946, S 25/1780, CZA.

262 later reported the conversation: Zipporah to Sharett, Sept. 24, 1946, in Sharett and Sharett, *Imprisoned with Paper and Pencil*, 298.

263 Ben-Gurion cabled Golda: Sept. 29, 1946, in Freundlich, *Political Documents of the Jewish Agency*, 1:635.

263 "close to the edge": GM to Remez, Sept. 15, 1946, IV-104-113-37, LA.

263 *The River Jordan*: GM to Remez, Oct. 10, 1946, IV-104-113-37, LA.

264 "blessings": GM to Remez, Sept. 20, 1946, IV-104-113-37, LA.

264 "terribly sad": Ibid.

264 "very, very hard": GM to Remez, Sept. 15, 1946, IV-104-113-37, LA.

264 "meetings without limits": GM to Remez, Sept. 26, 1946, IV-104-113-37, LA.

264 "Is it really": GM to Remez, Sept. 22, 1946, IV-104-113-37, LA.

265 "Forgive me": Ibid.

265 "for me, marvelous ones": GM to Remez, Sept. 26, 1946, IV-104-113-37, LA.

266 "my hand": GM to Remez, Sept. 25, 1946, IV-104-113-37, LA.

266 "I do not want": GM to Remez, Sept. 30, 1946, IV-104-113-37, LA.

266 "My heart jumps": GM to Remez, Sept. 29, 1946, IV-104-113-37, LA.

266 "How did you": GM to Remez, Sept. 30, 1946, IV-104-113-37, LA.

266 "What a pity": GM to Remez, Oct. 3, 1946, IV-104-113-37, LA.

266 "Once more": GM to Remez, Oct. 7, 1946, IV-104-113-37, LA.

267 "What did my mother": GM to Remez, Oct. 10, 1946, IV-104-113-37, LA.

267 "to make one further effort": London Conference, PRO CO 537/1779, BNA.

267 "I oppose any negotiations": GM to Ben-Gurion, Sept. 28, 1946, in Freundlich, *Political Documents of the Jewish Agency*, 1:630.

267 Truman issued a statement: Radosh and Radosh, *Safe Haven*, 188–91.

268 watered-down antiterrorist resolution: Foreign Office to Washington, Nov. 4, 1946, PRO CO 537/1780, BNA.

268 "forced upon the British government": J. Gutch to Trafford Smith, Nov. 23, 1946, PRO CO 537/1780, BNA.

268 "To my regret": GM to Remez, Sept. 26, 1946, IV-104-113-37, LA.

14. 1947: The Turning Point

269 "The shadow of tragic": Abba Eban, *Personal Witness*, 81.

270 "at least they're doing": GM at Ihud conference, Dec. 7, 1946, 3-021-1946-8, LPA.

270 "stood as an iron wall": GM, "Why We Need a Jewish State," in *Land of Our Own*, 58–65; for the fuller version given here, see "Address by Mrs. Goldie Meyerson, 12/12/46," PRO CO 537/1733, BNA.

271 "Waves of applause": "The Zionist Congress," *Davar*, Dec. 22, 1946.

271 "Woman of the Hour": *PW*, Feb. 1947, 13.

271 "Almost nobody could think": MC minutes, Jan. 9, 1947.

271 "I have enough": Bar-Zohar, *Ben-Gurion*, 138.

272 "We vote in favor": Teveth, *David's Zeal*, 4:864.

272 "I can no longer": Ibid., 865.

272 Golda regarded him: MC minutes, Jan. 9, 1947.

273 "You should be ashamed": Teveth, *David's Zeal*, 4:865.

274 "Zionism and pessimism": Syrkin, *Golda Meir*, 159.

274 Keren Kayemet Street: Medzini, *Golda*, 153.

274 "people who have gone": Meeting of GM and Remez with chief secretary, Jan. 7, 1947, P-812/21, ISA.

274 "It's a lie": National Council minutes, April 1, 1947, P-812/4, ISA.

274 "with a strong hand": MS minutes, April 21, 1947, 2-24-1947-18, LPA.

275 "You want us to tell": GM meeting with chief secretary, Jan. 29, 1947, P-812/21, ISA.

275 Operation Polly: Bethell, *Palestine Triangle*, 301.

276 "There is a need": *Palestine Post*, Feb. 3, 1947.

276 "openly refused": Gurney to GM, Feb. 3, 1947, S25/5647, CZA.

276 she and Kaplan met with Cunningham: Jewish Agency Executive minutes, Feb. 9, 1947, P-812/21, ISA.

276 "very, very fine": GM address to International Inaugural Conference, Miami Beach, Fla., Feb. 20, 1966, IBA.

276 "Goldie used to come": Cunningham, interview with Bethell, Nov. 24, 1975, P-812/4, ISA.

276 "budge from any": GM, *My Life*, 205.

277 John Shaw: Bethell, *Palestine Triangle*, 279.

277 "one of the worst": Jewish Agency Executive minutes, March 7, 1947, P-812/21, ISA.

277 "Are you hinting": GM meeting with chief secretary, Jan. 29, 1947, P-812/21, ISA.

277 Arthur Creech Jones: MC minutes, June 11, 1947, 2-24-1947-19A, LPA.

277 "In the autumn of 1947": GM, interview with Bethell, May 24, 1977, P-1784/ 2, ISA.

277 cool and unflappable: Golani, *End of the British Mandate for Palestine*.

277 "Yes, that was why": GM, discussion with John Fletcher Cooke, April 18, 1973, in Hadara Lazarus, *In and Out of Palestine* (Hebrew) (Jerusalem, 2003), 206.

277 "I am a hundred percent": Lancaster to GM, n.d., S25/8178, CZA.

278 "life-work": Lancaster to GM, Feb. 3, 1947. For a different interpretation of the Lancaster story, see Segev, *One Palestine, Complete*, 11, 293, 445.

278 "medieval walled": Clifton Daniel, *NYT*, March 1, 1947, 4.

278 "a senseless dumb abyss": Makovsky, *Churchill's Promised Land*, 239.

279 she spoke plaintively: Jewish Agency Executive minutes, April 13, 1947, P-812/ 22, ISA.

279 Socialist International Conference: MS minutes, May 29, 1947, 2-24-1947- 18, LPA.

280 "I spoke what was": MS minutes, June 11, 1947, 2-24-1947-19'A, LPA.

280 first Jews killed: *Palestine Post*, June 10, 1947, 1.

280 Kurt Schumacher: Shafir, *Outstretched Hand* (Hebrew), 38–39.

281 "serious hurt": Palestine Report, Aug. 14, 1947, 2, in Palestine/Israel Reports 1947–1973, Digital Archive, AJCA.

281 "an indignant walk-out": H. Lowenberg to Milton Himmelfarb, Aug. 3, 1947, in ibid.

281 "It's not a matter": Ben-Gurion, *Chimes of Statehood* (Hebrew), 235.

281 "exploded": "Why Did We Pick on Golda Meyerson?," *HaMaas*, Aug. 17, 1947, in *Fighters for the Freedom of Israel, Collected Works* (Hebrew), 1:689–90.

281 *Exodus 1947:* For the *Exodus* story, see Halamish, Exodus *Affair*. See also Bethell, *Palestine Triangle*, 324–36.

282 "There were dead people": National Council minutes, Aug. 26, 1947, P-812/7, ISA.

282 "he lost control": GM, *My Life*, 201.

283 mission of the Jewish Agency: Syrkin, *Way of Valor*, 170.

283 "revulsion": M. Shertok and E. Sasson to GM, Aug. 23, 1947, in Freundlich, *Political Documents of the Jewish Agency*, 2:602.

283 "Important nothing": Halamish, Exodus *Affair*, 201.

283 "the whole problem": National Council minutes, Aug. 26, 1947, P-812/7, ISA.

284 "horrified disgust": Palestine Report, July 1947, 6, Digital Archive, AJCA.

284 "the abominable deed": Freundlich, *Political Documents of the Jewish Agency*, 2:229n1.

284 In a separate statement: S25/5645, CZA, made before bodies were found.

284 "We have never": GM meeting with high commissioner, July 31, 1947, S25/ 22, CZA.

285 along with the mayors: Palestine Report, Aug. 14, 1947, 1, Digital Archive, AJCA.

285 "small *saison*": Slutsky, *History of Hagana* (Hebrew) 3:954.

285 Operation Golda: Palestine Report, Aug. 14, 1947, 1.

285 "this ambitious woman": *HaMaas*, Aug. 17, 1947, in *Fighters*, 1:689–90.

285 "How the General": *HaMaas*, July 21, 1947, in ibid., 685–88.

286 "dirtied with the blood": *HaMaas*, Aug. 17, 1947, in ibid., 689–90.

286 "degrade the moral stature": Menahem Meir, *My Mother*, 90.

286 "We need to gather": National Council minutes, Aug. 7, 1947, P-812/7, ISA, and other places.

286 "The head of Macy's": Maks Birnbach, conversation with author, Oct. 27, 2005.

286 champagne: Abba Eban, *Personal Witness*, 105.

286 "miraculous": *Palestine Post*, Sept. 2, 1947, 1.

286 "improve": *NYT*, Sept. 2, 1947, 1.

287 fifty-two thousand Jewish deportees: Gruber, *Witness*, 120.

287 "suburb of sorrow": Ibid., 146.

287 The story of her arrival: GM, *My Life*, 202–4.

287 *Rafiah* and *La'Negev*: David Shaari, *Deportation to Cyprus* (Hebrew) (Jerusalem: World Zionist Organization, 1981), 152.

288 "I'm proud of you": Gilad and Meged, *Palmach Book* (Hebrew), 1:818.

288 *Ocean Vigour*: Ibid.

288 new body: It was called the Mobilization Center for National Service. See Medzini, *Golda*, 159.

288 Later critics would say: Moshe Dayan, *Story of My Life*, 168–69.

289 modernity and progress: Boaz Lev Tov, "Neighbors in Fact: Cultural Ties Between Jews and Arabs Toward the End of the Ottoman Period," *Zemanim*, no. 110 (2010): 42–54.

289 short, overweight: Dallas, *King Hussein*, 25.

289 Emirate of Transjordan: For Jordan's beginnings, see Mary C. Wilson, *King Abdullah, Britain, and the Making of Jordan* (New York: Cambridge University Press, 1987).

290 Greater Syria: See Morris, *1948*, 66–67.

290 "look on that favorably": Description of the meeting from Ezra Danin, "Meeting with Abdullah," Nov. 17, 1947, S25/4004, CZA.

291 "collude": See Shlaim, *Collusion*; see also Schueftan, *Jordanian Option* (Hebrew).

291 "we could not promise": Report to People's Administration, May 12, 1948, People's Administration Minutes, April 18–May 13, 1948, ISA.

291 not be overly optimistic: Danin in "Revivim: Fiftieth Anniversary of Golda's Coming to Israel," 1971, RE-72, GMMA Archive.

291 Albert Einstein wrote to: Morris, *1948*, 55.

292 Chaim Weizmann visited Harry Truman: Radosh and Radosh, *Safe Haven*, 264.

292 "Any line of partition": Abba Eban, *Personal Witness*, 123.

292 "It's hard to express": *Davar*, Dec. 1, 1947, 1.

292 "You have fought": GM, *My Life*, 211.

293 "Rejoicing in Jerusalem": Photograph, *Palestine Post*, Nov. 30, 1947; letter, Dec. 2, 1947, S25/825, CZA.

293 "I was looking": GM, interview on *Panorama*.

15. "The Time Is Now"

294 "Golda is not": Ben-Gurion, *War of Independence* (Hebrew), Dec. 2, 1947.

294 "It was a beautiful wedding": Yona Kama, interview with author.

294 "the war before the war": Bar-Zohar, *Ben-Gurion*, 143.

295 Committee B: Medzini, *Golda*, 171.

295 Yehezkel Noam: *Hatzofeh*, Nov. 25, 2007.

295 "The police and soldiers": Jewish Agency Executive minutes, Dec. 7, 1947, S53/1430, CZA.

296 fifty-nine Jews: Gedalia Yogev, ed., *Political and Diplomatic Documents, December 1947–May 1948*, vol. 1, no. 28, p. 42n1, ISA.

296 "He can be hard": National Council Executive minutes, Dec. 9, 1947, IV-104-754, LA.

296 "panic": Sharett to GM, Dec. 9, 1947, in Yogev, *Political and Diplomatic Documents*, 1:42.

296 "What does that tell you?": Report on Golda Meyerson's discussion with the high commissioner, Dec. 17, 1947, P-812/18, ISA.

297 *Pans*: For the story of the ships, see Ettinger, *Blind Jump*, 207–31; and Ben-Gurion, *War of Independence*, Dec. 9, 1947, 29–34.

298 "It seems to me": Ettinger, *Blind Jump*, 220.

299 Golda skirted catastrophe: There are varying accounts of where Golda and Beyth were sitting and who was with them. This one is from Avigdori-Avidav, *Road We Took* (Hebrew), entry of Dec. 26, 1947. See also Levin, *It Takes a Dream*, 211.

299 in her arms: Martin, *Golda*, 297.

299 "I don't have": This entire incident is described in *Davar*, Jan. 1, 1947, 2.

300 "Jerusalem is on the front lines": Jewish Agency Executive minutes, Jan. 4, 1948, S53/1430, CZA.

300 "The center is in Jerusalem": Jewish Agency Executive minutes, Dec. 27, 1947, S53/1430, CZA.

301 Semiramis Hotel: Jewish Agency Executive minutes, Jan. 11, 1948, S53/1430, CZA.

301 cablegrams from the Jewish Agency: E. Epstein to GM, Jan. 7, 1948, in Yogev, *Political and Diplomatic Documents*, 1:138.

301 already lost the war: Abba Eban, *Personal Witness*, 132.

301 the United States slapped an embargo: Radosh and Radosh, *Safe Haven*, 277–78.

301 clandestine Haganah operation: Sacharov, *Out of the Limelight*, 70–85.

301 seven million dollars: Ben-Gurion, *War of Independence*, Jan. 3, 1948, 107.

302 "boil": GM, UJA interview with Jeff Hodes, Shulamit Nardi, and Menahem Kaufman, June 8, 1975, 2, OHD, ICJ.

302 "What you can do here": Syrkin, *Golda Meir*, 184–85.

302 "it was decided": Ben-Gurion, *War of Independence*, Jan. 13, 1948, 143.

302 In Golda's memory: GM, *My Life*, 212; Syrkin, *Way of Valor*, 196.

302 until January 22: *Davar*, Jan. 23, 1948, 1.

302 Golda met with the anguished parents: *Davar*, Jan. 20, 1948, 1.

303 final meeting: Ben-Gurion, *War of Independence*, Jan. 21, 1948, 168.

303 Menahem remembered: Menahem Meir, *My Mother*, 114.

303 Golda remembered: GM, interview with Hodes et al., 2.

303 "an impecunious, unimportant": Montor, UJA interview with Jeff Hodes, Rome, Oct. 14, 1975, 54, OHD, ICJ.

304 "I was terribly afraid": GM, interview with Hodes et al., 3.

304 "a Pied Piper": Lou Boyar, UJA interview with Menahem Kaufman, March 14, 1976, 2, OHD, ICJ.

304 "Friends": For full talk, see Syrkin, *Way of Valor*, 200–208.

305 "The normal noises": "A Great Woman and a Great City," Excerpts from a report of members of the national campaign, UJA, Feb. 2, 1948, S53/1430, CZA.

305 "Sometimes things occur": Montor, interview with Hodes, 54.

305 "genius": Harry Beale, UJA interview with Jeff Hodes, June 27, 1975, 33, OHD, ICJ.

305 "get so much": Montor, interview with Hodes, 56.

306 "I feel just as deeply": Ibid., 59.

306 "These men had to change": GM, interview with Hodes et al.

306 "terrorize": Ibid., 10.

307 "We didn't beg": Boyar, interview with Kaufman, 5.

307 "I didn't eat anything": GM, interview with Hodes et al.

307 Stephen S. Wise: GM, interview with Melvin Urofsky, Oct. 6, 1975, 4, OHD, ICJ.

307 Eddie Cantor: *Davar*, March 21, 1948, 4.

307 fifteen million dollars: Ben-Gurion, *War of Independence*, Feb. 11, 1948, 232.

307 sixteen million dollars: Ibid., Feb. 13, 1948, 238.

307 "absurd": Sharett to Kaplan, Feb. 19, 1948, S53/1430, CZA.

307 "Mrs. Meyerson": Morgenthau to Kaplan, telegrams, S53/1430, CZA.

307 "iron campaign": Ben-Gurion, *War of Independence*, March 2, 1948, 274.

308 "I tell you": MS minutes, Sept. 30, 1971, 890/73, 89, IDFA.

308 "the only ray of light": Ben-Gurion, *War of Independence*, March 3, 1948, 276.

308 "Someday when history": GM, *My Life*, 214.

308 her only regret: Zionist Executive committee minutes, April 4, 1948, S5/2673, CZA.

308 Administrative Council: *Minhelet Ha'Am*, also called People's Administration.

308 "It is essential": MS minutes, March 3, 1948; Ben-Gurion, *War of Independence*, March 6, 1948, 282n3; MC minutes, March 6, 1948.

309 "I sought to have Golda": Ben-Gurion, *War of Independence*, March 6, 1948, 282.

310 wept on his shoulder: Anita Shapira, interview with author, Jan. 20, 2005.

310 "I have been home": Peres, *Battling for Peace*, 115.

311 "I am now in the position": Radosh and Radosh, *Safe Haven*, 303.

311 Ben-Gurion quickly arranged a press conference: Ben-Gurion, *War of Independence*, March 20, 1948, 313.

311 "nothing has changed": *Davar*, March 28, 1948, 2.

312 "A few noodles": Marlin Levin, "Ahuzat Bayit" memoir, MLA.

312 *khubeizeh*: Levin, *It Takes a Dream*, 220.

312 "situation has become worse": Slutzky, *Haganah Book*, 3:1403–4.

312 "mothers sending": Zionist Executive minutes, April 7, 1948, S5/2673, CZA.

312 arms purchased in Czechoslovakia: Figures in Morris, *1948*, 117.

313 branded as traitors: Morris, *Birth of the Palestinian Refugee Problem*, 87.

313 "as equal and free citizens": Morris, *1948*, 143–46.

313 In a city that had been home: Weiss, *Wadi Salib* (Hebrew), 8.

313 mild heart attack: Martin, *Golda*, 332.

313 "children, women, old people": Jewish Agency Executive minutes, May 6, 1948, CZA.

313 Yaakov Lubliani: Almogi, *Total Commitment*, 90–92.

314 "We've been fighting": Eshel, *Haganah Battles in Haifa* (Hebrew), 377.

314 "It is a dreadful thing": Jewish Agency Executive minutes, May 6, 1948, CZA.

314 "Are we prepared": MC minutes, May 11, 1948, CZA.

315 broke the silence: Benny Morris, *The Birth of the Palestinian Refugee Problem, 1947–1949* (Hebrew ed.) (Tel Aviv: Am Oved, 1991), 433.

315 "Golda has to come": Ben-Gurion, *War of Independence*, April 21, 1948, 363.

315 "did not know": Ibid., April 26, 1948, 371.

316 "We must *demand*": Jewish Agency Executive minutes, May 2, 1948, CZA.

316 finally reached Jerusalem: Ibid., May 6, 1948.

316 "I would like my comrades": Ibid.

316 he was a Bedouin: Syrkin, *Golda Meir*, 196.

317 "a border is a border": "Protocols of Administrative Council, April 18–May 13, 1948" (Hebrew) (Jerusalem: Israel State Archives, 1978), 41.

317 Ben-Gurion had received a report: Ben-Gurion, *War of Independence*, May 8, 1948, 401.

317 "If there is the slightest chance": Danin's memories in "Fifty Years After Golda Meir's Aliyah," Revivim, 1971, RE-72, GMMA Archive.

318 The king received them: In addition to Danin's memories, see GM's report in "Protocols of the Administrative Council, April 18–May 13, 1948," 40–44. See also Sharef, *Three Days*, 72–76; and Shlaim, *Politics of Partition*, 160–66.

319 "We met in friendship": Ben-Gurion, *War of Independence*, May 11, 1948, 409.

319 "of course": Dayan, *Story of My Life*, 169.

319 too proud: GM, *My Life*, 221.

319 "rigid": Schueftan, *Jordanian Option*, 5.

319 "could not be wholly": Kirkbride, *From the Wings*, 5.

320 "He is going into this matter": Administrative Council minutes, May 12, 1948, 43.

320 adamant that certain conditions: GM, E. Kaplan—Sir Alan Cunningham, May 6, 1948, in Yogev, *Political and Diplomatic Documents*, 1:744.

320 "I cannot go to Jerusalem": Administrative Council minutes, May 12, 1948, 60.

321 "It is doubtful": Sharef, *Three Days*, 121.

321 "flushed by victory": M. Shertok, E. Epstein, G. Marshall, R. Lovett, D. Rusk, May 8, in Yogev, *Political and Diplomatic Documents*, 1:757–69.

321 "blame us then": Ibid.

321 "At this moment": Administrative Council meeting, May 12, 1948, 63–64.

321 "We cannot zigzag": Ibid., 110.

322 "I shall now read to you": Sharef, *Three Days*, 282–85.

322 "Friday afternoon": GM, interview with Gideon Lev Ari, "Fifty Years After Her Aliyah," 1971, 6.

16. Moscow

325 "no coffee to make": Levin, "Ahuzat Bayit" memoir, MLA.

326 Her Paris visa: GM personal documents, P-812/25, ISA.

326 From Paris: Air Passenger Manifest, Transcontinental & Western Air Inc. New York Passenger List, T715 7598:42, USNAM.

326 "I stand here": Emergency Conference, UJA, May 23, 1948, Hotel Astor, Joint Distribution Committee archives, 45/54, 1954.

326 "My husband and I gave": Mathilde Brailove, interview with Jeff Hodes, April 25, 1973, 24, OHD, ICJ.

327 "give and take": Beale, interview with Hodes, 21.

327 "mesmerize": Ibid., 22.

327 "Henry Morgenthau brought": Roosevelt to David A. Gurewitsch, May 26, 1948, in Lash, *Eleanor*, 134.

327 "I would run in": GM at International Inaugural Conference, Miami Beach, Fla., Feb. 20, 1966, IBA.

327 an unprecedented loan: Third Quarterly Meeting, GEB, June 7–11, 1948, 5780/016, box 5, ILGWU Papers, Kheel Center, Cornell University.

327 new loan to Israel: Fourth Quarterly Meeting, GEB, Dec. 21–24, 1948, 5780/016, box 5, ILGWU Papers, ibid.

328 Flying Fortresses: Described in Sacharov, *Out of the Limelight*, 169–71.

328 "On the scales are the fate": Ibid., 170.

328 "Nothing happened": Remez to GM, May 25, 1948, P-1886/12, ISA.

329 "It's hard to understand": *Maariv*, June 16, 1948, 2.

329 "They are Jews": MC minutes, July 10, 1944, LPA.

330 "Regarding your plea": Remez to GM, n.d., P-1886/12, ISA.

330 "Why did they pick me": *Maariv*, Aug. 16, 1948, 4.

330 exchange of ministers: *Davar*, June 27, 1948, 1.

330 Flatbush and Eighth Avenues: *NYT*, July 2, 1948.

330 "We experienced a perverse": H. Yafe, "Our Woman Minister" (Yiddish), *PW*, April 1949, 5–6.

331 She had downplayed: GM to "Ovdim Korengold," handwritten for cable, P-1886/12, ISA.

331 "minor automobile accident": GM to Remez, handwritten note, P-1886/12, ISA.

331 "My life is empty": Remez to GM, July 3, 1948, P-1886/12, ISA.

331 Remez wired Golda: Remez to GM, July 22, 1948, P-1886/12, ISA.

331 The night before she left: Yafe, "Our Woman Minister," 5–6.

331 "Golda has returned": Ben-Gurion, *War of Independence*, July 29, 1948.

332 Regina pressed Sarah's dress: Medzini, interview with Beit-Or, 15.

332 "How do you feel": Beale, interview with Hodes, 25.

332 "Is it on principle": *Maariv*, Aug. 19, 1948, 4.

332 "they didn't want to hear": Lou Kadar, interview with author.

333 Her first impression: Kadar, interview with Drora Beit-Or (Hebrew), June 26, 1986, 31, GMMA Archive.

333 "blessed talent": *Maariv*, Aug. 27, 1948, 5.

334 "fully endorsed": Harrison to British Foreign Office, Sept. 17, 1948, box 4, file 5, GMLA.

334 "So at least he thought": Kadar to Marie Syrkin, Oct. 1978, box 5, file 6, GMLA.

335 chef sent from Israel: Erika Oyserman, "Personal Assistant to the Prime Minister," *PW*, Jan. 1974, 6–8.

335 "Even in the hospital": Kadar, interview with author.

335 "very cordial": GM to M. Shertok, Sept. 7, 1948, in *DISR* (London: Frank Cass, 2000), 1:336.

335 A photographer snapped: *Maariv*, Nov. 23, 1948, 2.

336 "pounding": Provisional Government minutes, Dec. 8, 1948, 8.

336 It was the first time: Namir, *Israeli Mission to Moscow* (Hebrew), 44–45. Namir is the basic source for events in Moscow.

336 "The ceremony was very impressive": GM to M. Shertok, Sept. 11, 1948, in *DISR*, 1:339.

336 "Ceremony of presenting": GM to M. Shertok, Sept. 12, 1948, in ibid.

336 "If only we had": GM to W. Eytan, Nov. 9, 1948, in ibid., 401.
   "It will change": Namir, *Israeli Mission to Moscow*, 77.

337 Their maid, electrician: GM, interview with Yaacov Ro'i, April 22, 1968, 4, OHD, ICJ.

338 prominent Russian Jewish journalists: Binyamin Pinkus, "Change and Continuity in Soviet Policy Towards Soviet Jewry and Israel," *Israel Studies* 10, no. 1 (Spring 2005): 96–123.

338 a special service: Ro'i, *Soviet Decision Making in Practice*, 190.

338 "as if the Messiah": *NYT*, Dec. 30, 1970, 25.

338 second Sabbath: She attended services on Sept. 11, 1948.

338 Namir arranged: The visit is described in Namir, *Israeli Mission to Moscow*, 48–50.

339 burst into tears: I. V. Polianskii to V. Molotov, Oct. 6, 1948, in *DISR*, 1:377.

339 *shehehiyanu* prayer: Syrkin, *Golda Meir*, 225.

339 Two weeks later: Polianskii to Molotov, Oct. 6, 1948, in *DISR*, 1:377.

339 Ivan Bakulin: Provisional Government minutes, Dec. 8, 1948, 9.

339 *Freylekhs*: Ala Zuskin-Perelman (daughter of the Russian Jewish actor Benjamin Zuskin) to the author, March 10, 2009. The play the legation saw that night is incorrectly identified as *The Travels of Benjamin the Third* in *Chagall and the Artists of the Russian Jewish Theater*, ed. Susan Tumarkin Goodman (New York: Jewish Museum; New Haven, Conn.: Yale University Press, 2008), 158.

340 All the young women: GM, interview with Ro'i, April 22, 1968, 8.

340 "Mother, this is she": Provisional Government minutes, Dec. 8, 1948, 13.

340 open houses: GM, *My Life*, 246.

340 MGB had investigated: Kostyrchenko, *State Anti-Semitism 1938–1953* (Russian), 388–89.

340 since 1946: Kostyrchenko, *Out of the Red Shadows*, 60–132,

341 "recommendations": Polianskii to Molotov, Oct. 6, 1948, in *DISR*, 1:377.

341 Not knowing, Golda and the others: Provisional Government minutes, Dec. 8, 1948, 14.

341 "Shah, shah": GM, interview with Ro'i, April 22, 1968, 8.

341 audience member asked: Ro'i, *Soviet Decision Making in Practice*, 188.

341 On September 21: Ilya Ehrenburg, "Concerning a Certain Letter," in *DISR*, 1:352–60.

342 "It was so sudden": Manor, interview with author, Oct. 12, 2004.

342 Stalin had ordered: G. M. Malenkov to Stalin, Sept. 18, 1948, in *DISR*, 1:352.

342 "active behavior": Kostyrchenko, *Out of the Red Shadows*, 110n235.

343 "This is the answer": Namir, *Israeli Mission to Moscow*, 66.

343 all the murdered Jews: *Maariv*, Nov. 23, 1948, 2.

343 "A gut yahr": *Davar*, Jan. 3, 1949, 4.

343 "A dank": GM, *My Life*, 251.

344 "It was as though an electric current": Ro'i interview with GM, July 10, 1968, 5.

344 "It was the most passionate": Provisional Government minutes, Dec. 8, 1948, 14.

344 Moscow had not seen: Gennadi Kostyrchenko, "Golda at the Metropol Hotel," *Russian Studies in History* 43, no. 2 (Fall 2004): 77–84.

344 "to provoke Jews": Ro'i, *Struggle for Soviet Jewish Emigration*, 34.

345 At a meeting of the JAFC presidium: Redlich, *War, Holocaust, and Stalinism*, 404–8.

345 Ehrenburg himself: Namir, *Israeli Mission to Moscow*, 68–69.

345 "go, go": Ibid., 84. Golda's meeting with Zhemchuzhina appears on 83–84.

346 She was expelled: Zhemchuzhina's arrest and interrogation are in Kostyrchenko, *Out of the Red Shadows*, 122–23.

346 leaders of the JAFC were arrested: For an account of arrests and interrogations, see Rubenstein and Naumov, *Stalin's Secret Pogrom*, esp. 41–43, 172, and 322–23.

346 critics have blamed her: Shulamit Aloni (one of her severest critics), interview with author, Oct. 17, 2004.

346 "was the embodiment": Manor, interview with author, Oct. 12, 2004.

347 Rumors flew: Namir, *Israeli Mission to Moscow*, 97–98.

347 Golda wanted to resign: *Davar*, Dec. 14, 1948, 1.

347 She told Regina: Medzini, *Golda*, 226.

347 one of her first acts: Provisional Government minutes, Dec. 8, 1948.

347 "My mother taught me": *Maariv*, Dec. 13, 1948, 6.

347 Together with the party guests: *Maariv*, Jan. 4, 1949.

347 "the vast, cold land": GM, *My Life*, 255.

347 One of the saddest: Kadar, interview with author. There are several variations of this story. See Namir, *Israeli Mission to Moscow*, 125–26.

348 chastised her in February: Meeting: V. A. Zorin—G. Meyerson, Feb. 7, 1949, in *DISR*, 1:436–38.

348 "polite and cool": GM to M. Sharett, Feb. 9, 1949, in ibid., 438–39.

349 "I am not going to have": Ben-Gurion to GM, Jan. 27, 1949, in Dan Giladi, "Immigration Absorption, Labor, and Social Legislation," in Avizohar, *Golda*, 297.

349 "greatest experiences": GM, Statement, April 18, 1949, in *DISR*, 1:465.

349 "Notes on American Innocence": *Commentary*, Aug. 1974, 34–40. I'm grateful to Neal Kozodoy, former editor of *Commentary*, for the magazine sources.

349 "Even so tough-minded": Ibid., 39.

349 "so serious and shocking": *Commentary*, April 1975, 26.

349 "Golda's Prisoners": Gilboa, *Black Years of Soviet Jewry*, 312.

349 Golda did discuss: See, for example, Sh. Friedman to GM, Sept. 28, 1948, in *DISR*, 1:371–73.

350 "We'll consider it": GM report, April 16, 1950, IV 104-53-94, LA.

350 According to a letter: Avraham Kalinsky to GM, Aug. 29, 1976, P-977/19, ISA.

350 "any distress the article": *Commentary*, Feb. 1976, 4.

17. "Either Immigrants or Shoes"

351 "Call me Golda": *Maariv*, March 6, 1949, 1.

351 "Why not use": *Palestine Post*, Sept. 15, 1949, 4.

352 "I heard from Sharef": GM to Remez, IV-194-113-37, LA.
352 more than 340,000: Hacohen, *Immigrants in Turmoil*, 118. Best source on immigration.
352 Jewish families from Iraq: See Hillel, *Operation Babylon*.
353 thirty thousand single-family units: *KR*, May 31, 1949.
353 "ten, twenty": Ibid.
353 Both substandard: Charles Abrams, "Israel Grapples with Its Housing Crisis," *Commentary*, April 1951, 348.
354 "is not at all bad": *KR*, May 31, 1949.
354 "We have only": *KR*, June 1, 1949.
354 rationing was a small sacrifice: *Davar*, May 12, 1949, 2.
354 black market in foodstuffs: J. L. Teller, "The Israeli Voter Ponders the 'Moral Crisis,'" *Commentary*, Feb. 1951, 145–52.
354 "Had I not known": *Maariv*, May 9, 1949, 2.
354 "an austere looking woman": Lucille Elfenbein, "Engine Trouble Launched Her Career," *Providence (R.I.) Bulletin*, May 16, 1951, Scrapbook, P-829/3, ISA.
355 "not withhold from any Knesset member": *KR*, June 1, 1949.
355 "Yours is the responsibility": *PW*, Sept. 1949, 7–13.
355 "I did a strange thing": GM, *My Life*, 264–65.
355 "raised unholy hell": Beale, interview with Hodes, 27.
355 "she clawed the chaise": Ibid., 25–26.
355 Golda reported to the Knesset: *KR*, Aug. 3, 1949.
356 "I am simply filled with envy": *KR*, Aug. 8, 1949.
356 steel houses: *Maariv*, Sept. 15, 1949, 3.
356 concrete houses: *Maariv*, Oct. 16, 1949, 2.
357 "The life of idleness": Rachel Yanait Ben-Zvi, *Before Golda*, 139.
358 "the Bevin way": *PW*, Sept. 1949, 8.
358 "For me, this state": *KR*, Aug. 7, 1950.
358 "Either immigrants or shoes": Ibid.
359 "We have all read books": *KR*, Jan. 1, 1951.
359 "What direction do we propose": Speech to National Council of Industrial Workers delegation, July 14, 1950, GMMA Archive.
359 "I fully confess": *Davar*, July 16, 1950, 1.
359 "part of every week": *KR*, Dec. 11, 1950.
359 lacerated doctors: Giladi, "Immigrant Absorption, Labor, and Social Legislation," 353–54.
360 "Shall I be told": *Palestine Post*, May 20, 1949.
360 Italian workmen: *Maariv*, Aug. 25, 1950, 2.
360 "We cannot take pleasure": *Davar*, Aug. 18, 1950, 1.
360 She had complained bitterly: *KR*, May 23, 1950.
360 "You yelled about exploitation": *KR*, Nov. 20, 1950.
361 "mother of the groom": Wedding photograph of Menahem, Chana, Golda, and Chana's mother, GM personal papers, P-1886/16, ISA.
361 weeping: Gruber, *Witness*, 246.
361 "I want to express": GM to Hadassah, cable, Dec. 28, 1950, in *Hadassah Newsletter* 31, no. 5, G-6465/23, ISA.
361 "nuts, olives": GM personal papers, P-1886/24, ISA.
361 "She loved chocolate": Beale, interview with Hodes, 28.
361 One of her shopping lists: GM personal papers, P-1886/24, ISA.
362 Amun-Israeli Housing: ILGWU minutes, Fifth Quarterly Meeting of GEB, June 3626–10, 1949, Kheel Center.
362 "We want to free ourselves": Syrkin, *Way of Valor*, 287.

362 "the Pope": Montor to GM, March 11, 1950, P-833/3, ISA.

362 "with the shiny black hair": Montor to GM, Dec. 12, 1951, P-833/3, ISA.

363 "rather a strange person": Montor to GM, Nov. 2, 1949, P-833/3, ISA.

363 "the battles": Montor to GM, Sept. 27, 1951, P-833/3, ISA.

363 "usually ice cold": Herbert A. Friedman, *Roots of the Future* (Jerusalem: Gefen, 1999), 165.

363 "achieve prosperity": Ibid., 169.

363 "the longest dais": Hal Lehrman, "A Billion Dollars for Israel," *Commentary*, Dec. 1950, 521.

363 "thousands and thousands": Syrkin, *Way of Valor*, 284–85.

363 "20th century": From a talk in Minneapolis, April 27, 1951, Scrapbook, P-829/3, ISA.

363 "Doesn't *anyone* here": Anne Copeland, in "Reflections on Golda on the 100th Anniversary of Her Birth," Israel Bonds, 1998, IBA.

363 B. Manischewitz: *Jewish Standard*, May 18, 1951, Scrapbook, P-829/3, ISA.

364 "to this day": GM, *My Life*, 124.

364 in Golda's home: Menahem Meir, interview with author, June 9, 2010.

364 promptly fainted: Ibid.

364 dislocated her shoulder: *Davar*, May 29, 1951, 4.

364 "just miserable": Sarah Rehabi, interview with author, Feb. 14, 2006.

364 "It was a great moment": GM, interview on *Panorama*.

365 side locks and beards: Zameret, *Melting Pot in Israel*, 110.

365 "Mapai does not promise": *Davar*, July 5, 1951, 2.

366 collegial atmosphere: See Chen, *Seven Happy Years* (Hebrew), and Beit-Or and Rehabi, *In Close Company with Golda*.

366 "Golda was not a reader": David Harman, interview with author.

366 "How can we work together": Chava Bar-Yosef, interview with author, Aug. 24, 2004.

366 "Golda was impatient": Zena Harman, interview with author, Oct. 19, 2004.

366 "It's stupid": Kesse, interview with author, Feb. 9, 2006.

367 "A woman stands": Slater, *Golda*, 101.

367 new desert town of Dimona: Chava Bar-Yosef, interview with author.

367 northern development town of Kiryat Shmona: Menahem Meir, *My Mother*, 140.

367 "We told you so": Beit-Or and Rehabi, *In Close Company with Golda*, Dec. 6, 1985, 42.

367 "These neighborhoods": *KR*, June 1, 1949.

367 "This has cost": Mapai executive council minutes, March 12, 1953, 42.

368 "If we have to choose": Ibid., 47.

368 "If we decide": *KR*, Jan. 14, 1952.

368 "Have pity on me": Zvi Bar-Niv, "Small Anecdotes," in Tamir, *Golda* (Hebrew), 72.

368 "for the worker": *KR*, Aug. 10, 1950.

369 "a system based on justice": "The First Anniversary of Israeli National Insurance," Radio address to the nation, March 30, 1955, in Christman, *This Is Our Strength*, 72–73.

369 She felt more excited: GM, *My Life*, 276.

370 "The greatest enemy": GM, address to WWC secretariat, July 27, 1952, in *Dvar Hapaoelet*.

370 "It was an old-fashioned attitude": Eshel, interview with author, Aug. 24, 2004.

370 Arab women equally: *Davar*, Aug. 2, 1949, 4.

370 "of the heads of our women": GM, *My Life*, 281.

371 "In this land": *KR*, March 6, 1951.

371 "You will not terrorize": Syrkin, *Golda Meir*, 263.

371 "I know of no enemy": GM, excerpts from address to Knesset, *PW,* March 1954, 22.
372 "It is inconceivable": Cabinet meeting minutes, Dec. 27, 1950. Complete deliberations appear in Sharett, *Reparations Controversy,* 38.
372 "I realize that we must": Cabinet meeting minutes, Oct. 28, 1951, in ibid., 97.
373 "I hold a racist view": MC minutes, Dec. 13, 1951, in ibid., 130.
373 "a detestable, repelling debt": Ibid., 132.
373 "that maniac": *JP,* Jan. 8, 1952.
374 "reparations are our due": *KR,* Jan. 8, 1952.
374 61 to 50: *KR,* Jan. 9, 1952.
374 "outstanding woman": *PW,* March 1950, 2.

18. The Politician

375 minister of foreign affairs, Andrei Vyshinski: April 14, 1949, *DISR,* 461–65.
375 "typical revolutionary": Tsahor, *Hazan,* 196.
376 "subversive activities of Zionism": Kostyrchenko, *Out of the Red Shadows,* 279.
376 Ten days after: *Dvar Hashavua,* Jan. 23, 1953.
376 "Meyerson Refuses": *Maariv,* Jan. 29, 1953, 1.
377 asked Nechemia Levanon: Levanon, *"Nativ" Was the Code Name* (Hebrew), 64.
377 Soviets masked their motives: Ro'i, *Soviet Decision Making in Practice,* 196, 200.
378 Nativ, path: Boaz, *Unseen yet Always Present* (Hebrew), 262–63.
378 involvement from the start: Meir Rosenne, interview with author, Jan. 10, 2007.
378 "I don't even know": Mapai political committee minutes, Jan. 16, 1953.
378 *Maariv* noted: *Maariv,* Feb. 13, 1953, 1.
378 "spiritual pogrom": Ibid.
379 "I have no strength": Mapai political committee minutes, Feb. 19, 1953.
379 "dangerous tool": Rafael, *Destination Peace,* 57.
379 "protect Jewish lives": *Davar,* May 7, 1953, 2.
380 "I saw in the newspaper": Sheyna to Golda (Yiddish), March 23, 1953, GMMA Archive.
380 "deep satisfaction": The talk is in Scrapbook, P-829/3, ISA.
380 emergency operation: *Davar,* May 3, 1953.
381 "firm, brilliant tone": *NYT,* March 24, 1953.
381 "ecstatic": Sheyna to GM (Yiddish), April 1, 1953, GMMA Archive.
381 "do not forget": Ibid.
381 "look him up": Sheyna to GM (Yiddish), March 23, 1953, GMMA Archive.
381 Harun al-Rashid: Background on the house, in *Haaretz,* Jan. 4, 2004, and May 3, 2006.
381 they would do nothing: Bar-Zohar, *Ben-Gurion,* 190–91.
382 "Sunday night dinner": Biskin to Aliza and Joseph London (Yiddish), Jan. 1, 1954, Na'amat files.
382 Efi Arazi: Giselle Arazi, interview with author, Jan. 19, 2007.
382 "Get in": Jerry Goodman, interview with author, Oct. 26, 2006.
382 "What will we do": Philosoph, interview with author.
383 "simple philosopher-shepherd": GM, *My Life,* 284.
383 "Nobody should try": MC minutes, Nov. 11, 1953.
384 "I am quiet": Yaakov Sharett, "A Dove Among Hawks: Moshe Sharett—the Political Tragedy of an Israeli Leader," *Midstream,* May/June 2004, 24.
384 "old man" proposed: Mapai political committee minutes, Nov. 2, 1953.
384 leaning toward Golda: *Maariv,* Nov. 15, 1953, 1.
384 Another that Pinhas Lavon: *Maariv,* Nov. 20, 1953, 1.
384 categorically opposed having a woman: *Maariv,* Nov. 23, 1953, 2.

384 Eshkol firmly turned down: Goldstein, *Eshkol*, 354. He did not want the position at this time.

384 having heard rumors: Sharett, *Political Diary* (Hebrew), Oct. 26, 1953.

384 "In my mind": Ibid., Nov. 9, 1953.

384 "Her voice comes from the heart": Ibid., Oct. 29, 1953.

384 "formidable personality": Ibid., Nov. 2, 1953.

384 asked Mordechai Namir: Ibid., Nov. 17, 1953.

384 heard from Yitzhak Navon: Ibid., Dec. 13, 1953.

384 Zeef Sharef's denial: Ibid., Dec. 14, 1953.

385 "waited for the moment": *Maariv*, Nov. 26, 1953, 2.

385 "the Jewish people": Sharett, *Political Diary*, Jan. 25, 1954.

386 "a brilliant mind": Teveth, *Ben-Gurion's Spy*, 66.

386 "one of the most capable": GM, *My Life*, 288–89.

386 IDF had nothing to do with: Cabinet meeting minutes, Oct. 18, 1953.

386 "If I were asked": Ibid.

387 "I would have resigned": Bar-Zohar, *Ben-Gurion*, 206.

387 "great dove": GM, *My Life*, 288.

387 Within two months: Bar-Zohar, *Shimon Peres*, 92.

387 Dr. Schlegel's clinic: L. Schlegel medical report on Mrs. Golda Myerson, July 19, 1954, Scrapbook, P-829/3, ISA.

388 "make things lively": Sharett, *Political Diary*, July 29, 1954.

388 grabbed his head: Ibid.

388 baby granddaughter: Ibid.

389 He drank excessively: Ibid., Feb. 12, 1955.

389 Isser Harel, suggested: Ibid., Jan. 14, 1955.

389 "unexpectedly": BGD, Feb. 17, 1955.

389 "Ben-Gurion accepts": Sharett, *Political Diary*, Feb. 17, 1955.

389 "This is the end": Sheffer, *Moshe Sharett*, 781.

389 "a very heavy stone": Lou Kadar, interview with author. The story of Meira appears in detail in Slater, *Golda*, 107–17, and in *Haolam Hazeh*, Dec. 20, 1978.

389 "I didn't know": Menahem Meir, interview with author, Oct. 13, 2004.

389 "He didn't love her enough": Weinberg, interview with author, May 19, 2005.

390 "had no contact whatsoever": Ibid.

390 "Mother always sent": Menahem Meir, interview with author, Jan. 14, 2009.

390 "On the death": *Yediot Aharonot*, Dec. 12, 1978.

390 "It was a terrible shame": Aloni, interview with author.

391 twice a day: Medzini, interview with Beit-Or.

391 "tell no one else": Montor to GM, April 19, 1954, P-833/3, ISA.

391 "Never": Medzini, interview with Beit-Or.

391 Sharett was convinced: Yaakov Sharett, correspondence with author, Aug. 7, 2010.

391 Matters came to a head: For details of the dispute, see "Statement Made by Julian Venezky," Thursday, March 3, 1955, A6, GMMA Archive.

391 "emotionally incapable": Sharett, *Political Diary*, Feb. 24, 1955.

391 "a direct personal blow": Ibid., Feb. 12, 1955.

391 "annoyed to the depth": Ibid., March 12, 1955.

392 "very dear Friends": The author is grateful to Gail Wertheimer, Julian Venezky's daughter, for a copy of that unpublished letter.

392 "Sam, Julian": Montor to GM, Aug. 19, 1955, P-833/3, ISA.

392 "pushed away": Montor to GM, June 16, 1955, P-833/3, ISA.

392 "devastated": Herlitz, interview with author, May 10, 2005.

392 "I have a suspicion": Montor to GM, Aug. 19, 1955, P-833/3, ISA.

393 To wrest control: Mapai political committee minutes, June 21, 1955.

393 "Do you go": *Maariv*, May 4, 1949, 1.
393 felt as ashamed: MC minutes, April 18, 1955; Mapai political committee, Aug. 21, 1954, and Nov. 15, 1955, and other occasions.
393 "I have never eaten pork": Mapai political committee minutes, Sept. 8, 1955.
393 special appeals to women: *Maariv*, July 22, 1955, 13.
394 the party won: *Maariv*, July 27, 1955, 5.
394 "Dear Golda": Montor to GM, July 30, 1955, P-833/3, ISA.
394 not elect a woman: *Maariv*, Aug. 19, 1955, 1.
394 "sad and emotional": *Maariv*, Sept. 9, 1955, 2.
394 "You have undermined": Ibid.
394 "put obstacles in my way": Fallaci, *Interview with History*, 113.
395 "If the law is good": Mapai political committee minutes, Nov. 15, 1955, 2-26-1955, LA.

19. "Golda Meir"

396 "a terrific impression": Montor to GM, Feb. 22, 1954, P-833/3, ISA.
396 she reviewed a conversation: Cabinet meeting minutes, Nov. 20, 1955.
397 "I was horrified": Sharett, *Political Diary*, Dec. 11, 1955.
398 The night after: Bar-On, *Gates of Gaza*, 118–21.
398 "They need to know": Cabinet meeting minutes, April 8, 1956.
398 "It doesn't interest me": Cabinet meeting minutes, April 13, 1956.
398 Sharett, in contrast, cautioned: Cabinet meeting minutes, April 8, 1956.
398 "My thoughts": Ibid.
399 too hard for her: *Maariv*, June 6, 1956.
399 "show her that she was not": Sharett, *Political Diary*, letter to Abba Eban, June 14, 1956.
399 "Marvelous": GM, *My Life*, 287.
399 "I was sure": Sharett, *Political Diary*, June 14, 1956.
399 refuse to become secretary-general: *Maariv*, June 6, 1956.
399 Ben-Gurion had broached the idea: Menahem Meir, *My Mother*, 156.
399 "condemned": Sharett, *Political Diary*, June 17, 1956.
400 "incomprehensible": Ibid., June 16, 1956.
400 "deep in her heart": Ibid.
400 "knuckled under": Ibid., June 24, 1956; GM, *My Life*, 288.
400 "I hope this post": *JP*, June 18, 1956.
400 "absolute conclusion": *JP*, June 19, 1956.
401 "a supreme effort": Sharett, *Political Diary*, June 18, 1956.
401 "Sharett Ousted": *NYT*, June 18, 1956.
401 "Adventurous": *Christian Science Monitor*, June 23, 1956.
401 "calm before the storm": Reported in *Maariv*, July 3, 1956.
401 "Motherly Diplomat": *NYT*, June 18, 1956.
401 "she did not take": Sharett, *Political Diary*, June 19, 1956.
401 "extremely pleasant": Ibid.
401 "To appear with her": Ibid., June 20, 1956.
402 "feeling and probably looking": GM, *My Life*, 292.
402 red roses: *Maariv*, June 21, 1956.
402 farewell from Sharett: *Maariv*, June 27, 1956.
402 "There is nobody": Ibid.
402 "The memories": GM to Dulles, July 4, 1956, in *Documents on the Foreign Policy of Israel, January–October 1956*, vol. 2, ed. Yehoshua Freundlich (Jerusalem, 2008).
402 "blessing": *JP*, July 3, 1956, 1.

402 "There was an air": *Maariv*, July 3, 1956, 2.
403 "Simple, straightforward": Sharett, *Political Diary*, July 2, 1956.
403 "I'm not among my own": Menaham Meir, *My Mother*, 157.
403 "They were all children": Eshel, interview with author.
403 "would be happy": Abba Eban, *Personal Witness*, 251.
403 "kind of watchdog": Ibid.
404 "For quite a long time": Ben-Gurion to GM, July 20, 1956, Letters, BGA.
404 traced their differences: Peres, *Battling for Peace*, 58.
404 "He is a very gifted man": Bareli, *From Ideology to Apparatus* (Hebrew), 168–69.
404 young journalist: Hayerushalmi, interview with author, Nov. 15, 2009.
405 Sharett had made an initial agreement: Sheffer, *Moshe Sharett*, 832.
405 "on the town": Bar-Zohar, *Shimon Peres*, 120.
405 dream list of weapons: Ibid., 129.
406 Vémars Agreement: On the Sinai campaign, including steps leading to it, see Bar-On, *Gates of Gaza*; Golani, *Israel in Search of a War*; and Tal, *1956 War*.
406 memo from Ben-Gurion: Ben-Gurion to GM, Sept. 27, 1956, Letters, BGA.
407 "I can picture to myself": BGD, Sept. 29, 1956.
407 Golda had a proper seat: Mordechai Bar-On, "With Golda Meir and Moshe Dayan at the St. Germain Conference," *Maariv*, June 8, 1973.
407 crude jokes: Bar-Zohar, *Like a Sandbird* (Hebrew), 201.
408 Observing them: Bar-On, interview with author, Feb. 15, 2006.
408 "Golda handled the meeting": Ibid.
408 "The one point": Moshe Dayan, *Story of My Life*, 254.
408 Peres hastily arranged their meeting: Peres, *Battling for Peace*, 123.
409 Golda valued the meeting: Mordechai Bar-On, interview with author.
409 "skeptical and dour": Peres, *Battling for Peace*, 123.
409 "reported to Ben-Gurion": Ibid., 113. Based on Peres's account, historians have pictured Golda as giving a completely negative account of the meetings. See, for example, Bar-Zohar, *Shimon Peres*, 141–42; Medzini, *Golda*, 294; Golani, *Israel in Search of a War*, 88.
409 She had told Mollet: BGD, Oct. 2, 1956.
409 pros and cons: BGD, Oct. 3, 1956.
409 consulted with her and Levi Eshkol: BGD, Oct. 19, 1956.
410 "grotesquely eccentric": Abba Eban, *Personal Witness*, 257.
410 meeting in Jerusalem: Ambassadors' meeting minutes, Oct. 18, 1956, Protocols, BGA.
410 message to Ben-Gurion: *FRUS*, Oct. 27, 1956, 16:795.
411 "I know that you can't": GM, *My Life*, 299.
411 cabinet gathered: Cabinet meeting minutes, Oct. 28, 1956.
411 "I am standing": Ibid.
411 Golda ran: Cabinet meeting minutes, Oct. 29, 1956.
411 cut the telephone wires: Herzog, *Living History*, 135.
411 "Israel this evening": *JP*, Oct. 30, 1956, 1.
412 "The military says": MS minutes, Nov. 4, 1956.
412 "the greatest and most glorious": *KR*, Nov. 7, 1956.
412 "double-crossing": Eisenhower, *Waging Peace*, 73. For Eisenhower's reactions, see also Nichols, *Eisenhower 1956*.
412 "immediate cease fire": Hammarskjöld to GM, Nov. 4, 1956, Letters, BGA.
412 five questions: GM to Hammarskjöld, Nov. 4, 1956, Letters, BGA.
413 "sowing hatred": Govrin, *Israeli-Soviet Relations*, 45.
413 Peres portrayed Golda: Bar-Zohar, *Shimon Peres*, 160.
413 she simply ignored: Cabinet meeting minutes, Nov. 8, 1956.

413 "When I left Pineau": Ibid.

414 "The Government of Israel": Nov. 8, 1956, 565/1300385, BGA.

414 "She was detested": Eshel, interview with author.

414 "worst moments": Abba Eban, *Personal Witness*, 267.

415 "Why are you so bitter": Rafael, *Destination Peace*, 63–64.

415 "hated Israel": Cabinet meeting minutes, Dec. 31, 1956.

415 "For eight years": GM, "The Israeli Action in Sinai," in *Land of Our Own*, 89–100.

415 "like an unloved orphan": Menahem Meir, *My Mother*, 165.

416 "At the Security Council": "Report to America," Address Before the National Press Club, Washington, Dec. 10, 1956, in Christman, *This Is Our Strength*, 77–86.

416 "the easiest Israeli": Lloyd, *Suez 1956*, 218.

416 series of rallies: *Maariv*, Dec. 23, 1956.

416 Nasser to Hitler: *Davar*, Dec. 14, 1956, 8.

416 "The dining room": Warner to Eisenhower, Nov. 30, 1956, GMMA Archive.

417 "the delicate and difficult": Eisenhower to Warner, Dec. 7, 1956, GMMA Archive.

417 "tough" policy: Thomas P. Whitney, "Mrs. Meir Hates to Call Herself 'Tough,'" *Wisconsin State Journal*, Nov. 25, 1956, 5.

417 "I've heard many good things": Cabinet meeting minutes, Dec. 31, 1956.

417 "genius": Cabinet meeting minutes, Jan. 13, 1957.

417 "reconciliation meeting": *Maariv*, Jan. 1, 1957.

418 "the nightmare": "Why Our Forces Stayed in Gaza-Aqaba: Excerpts from a Statement Before the UN General Assembly, January 17, 1957," *PW*, Feb. 1957, 5–6, 14, 22.

418 "exhaustion": *NYT*, Jan. 25, 1957.

418 "Whoever brought her": Herlitz, interview with author, May 10, 2005.

418 "Nobody had bothered": Eshel, interview with author.

418 Golda left the hospital: *Maariv*, Jan. 27, 1957.

418 An hour before the event: *Maariv*, Jan. 28, 1957. *My Life* mistakenly gives her grandson's age as six months at the time of the Sinai campaign. He was born on Jan. 19, 1957. I am grateful to Yona Kamma for the family tree genealogy.

419 "charming" baby: Henya Sharef to GM, Jan. 23, 1957, GMMA Archive.

419 friends in America: Isaac Alteras, "Eisenhower and the Sinai Campaign of 1956: The First Major Crisis in US-Israel Relations," in Tal, *1956 War*, 36–37.

419 Word in Israel: *Maariv*, March 10, 1957.

419 copies of her text: Esther Herlitz, interview with author, May 10, 2005.

420 "The Government of Israel": *NYT*, March 2, 1957.

420 put down her notes: *NYT*, May 5, 1973.

420 "Can we . . . all of us": GM, *My Life*, 308.

420 "not unreasonable": *NYT*, March 2, 1957.

420 state of agitation: Rafael, *Destination Peace*, 66–67.

20. Conflict and Charisma

421 "What was will not be": *Maariv*, March 10, 1957.

421 "strength and pride": Cabinet meeting minutes, March 10, 1957.

422 "If any hint": Ibid.

423 "how much more": "My Life's Course," July 25, 1957, in Christman, *This Is Our Strength*, 101–6.

423 "I found Golda": Lambert, interview with Geraldine Stern, March 4, 1981, tape 17, collection 21, GMLA.

423 "She was the kind": Arnon, interview with author.

423 "She didn't like women": Avital, interview with author, Feb. 7, 2006.

424 "I am not the pope": *JP* magazine, Jan. 18, 1977.
424 "I'm sending you": Avital, interview with author.
424 go on strike: Esther Herlitz, interview with author, Oct. 23, 2004.
425 "she wasn't much of a cook": Harman, interview with author.
425 "When I saw Shazar's hat": Rabinovitch, interview with author, May 15, 2005.
425 "beautiful view": Sharett, *Political Diary*, Nov. 9, 1957.
425 Sometimes he dreamed: Ibid., May 7, 1957.
426 "Golda entered": His speech is recapped in ibid., Jan. 18, 1957.
426 When Ben-Gurion answered: Ibid., April 7, 1959.
426 chapter and verse: Ibid., May 22, 1959.
426 did not speak: Teveth, *Ben-Gurion's Spy*, 186.
426 "He's a wild savage": Sharett, *Political Diary*, April 4, 1957.
427 "astute and courageous": GM, *My Life*, 151.
427 "true Ben-Gurionist": Isser Harel, interview with Drora Beit-Or, Feb. 14, 1986, GMMA Archive.
427 ninety-five-minute report: *Maariv*, Sept. 19, 1958.
427 "What are you doing?": Harel, interview with Beit-Or, Feb. 14, 1986.
428 Peres had beaten her: BGD, June 7, 1957.
428 she wept: Bar-Zohar, *Shimon Peres*, 203–4.
428 canceled her meeting: Matti Golan, *Road to Peace*, 85.
428 "did nothing": Ben-Gurion to GM, Dec. 3, 1957, P-833/7, ISA.
428 "How can a man": GM to Ben-Gurion, Dec. 4, 1957, P-833/7, ISA.
429 "I told Golda": BGD, July 23, 1957.
429 sit down with Peres: Matti Golan, *Road to Peace*, 85.
429 "Golda is more important": Ben-Gurion to Eban, Dec. 23, 1956, Letters, BGA.
429 "dear woman": Ben-Gurion to Israel Goldstein, July 25, 1957, Letters, BGA.
429 "devoted pioneer": Ben-Gurion to GM, May 3, 1958, Letters, BGA.
429 "The whole evening": BGD, Feb. 10, 1959.
430 "felt orphaned": Ben-Gurion to GM, Aug. 28, 1952, GMMA Archive.
430 "He didn't treat her": Ben-Eliezer, interview with author, Oct. 20, 2004.
431 "biological campaign": Teveth, *Moshe Dayan*, 370.
431 "look back proudly": Ibid.
431 "I could not believe": BGD, Nov. 26, 1958.
431 When Ben-Gurion visited: BGD, June 13, 1958.
432 successful operation: *Maariv*, June 19, 1958, 1.
432 giving up her Foreign Ministry post: *Maariv*, June 17, 1958.
432 Ed Sullivan: *Maariv*, June 16, 1958.
432 "I was Golda's greatest victim": Peres, interview with author, Aug. 18, 2004.
432 "idiot": MS minutes, Dec. 6, 1958.
432 "I was incapable": BGD, Dec. 6, 1958.
433 "long live Golda": *Maariv*, Jan. 6, 1959.
433 highly sensitive: GM, interview with Anita Shapira, July 15, 1975, a transcript kindly given to the author.
433 "when they grow old": Teveth, *Ben-Gurion's Spy*, 190.
433 appeared at the airport: *Maariv*, Aug. 2, 1959.
433 "no faith in her authority": BGD, Nov. 17, 1959.
434 "Nothing I said": Ibid.
434 she agreed to do so: BGD, Nov. 29, 1959.
434 Ben-Gurion had signaled: Abba Eban, *Personal Witness*, 292.
434 Eban called on Mrs. Meir: BGD, Dec. 2, 1959.
434 "Maybe over time": Ibid.
435 "I cannot recall": Coordination committee of the Jewish Agency and the government, Jan. 20, 1958, 100-513, CZA.

435 obtained permits for numbers: Coordination committee, Feb. 18, 1958, 100-513, CZA.

436 "We need the Jews": Ibid.

436 "A proposal was raised": *Haaretz*, Dec. 8, 2009. A Polish Jewish historian, Szymon Rudnicki, working on a book about Israeli-Polish relations, had uncovered Golda's letter to Katz. *Haaretz* ran an article about the letter, headlined "Golda Meir Asked to Halt Aliyah of Sick, Disabled Polish Jews," and quoted Rudnicki's description of her as a "brutal politician" who wrote a "very cynical document" calling for a limit to the immigration of needy Polish Jews.

436 "an outstanding success": *Jewish Vanguard*, Aug. 22, 1958, 5.

436 Charles de Gaulle: GM, *My Life*, 314–15.

437 "Representing the Jewish state": Yehuda Avner, "The First Word: The Case for 'Dwelling Alone,'" *JP*, Oct. 12, 2006.

437 Israel's first ambassador: Ehud Avriel, "Some Minute Circumstances," *Jerusalem Quarterly*, no. 14 (Winter 1980): 28–40.

438 "Our neighbors are out": Ibid., 38.

439 "formal dress or national costume": Esther Herlitz, interview with author, May 10, 2005.

439 "Africamania": Manor, interview with author, Jan. 11, 2007.

439 "Relations with Africa": *NYT*, Oct. 9, 1960.

439 "We are not trying": GM, interview with Marlin Levin, 1960, in Israel-Africa relations, MLA.

439 She did not mention: Yaakov Nitzan, interview with author, Feb. 20, 2006. See also BGD, Aug. 25, 1960.

439 "Israel was a small country": President's Deputy Special Counsel to President Kennedy, memorandum, Nov. 21, 1961, FRUS, *1961–1963*, vol. 15.

440 one country to another: Schedule of countries, G-6270/25, ISA.

440 "We don't mix in": GM, interview in *HaMahaneh*, Jan. 25, 1966.

440 "It's very hard to understand": Aynor, interview with Tova Shapira and Judith Reifan-Ronen, June 14, 1988, LA.

440 "Little Africans": GM backgrounder, Meir, MLA.

441 "The Role of Women": Mina Ben-Zvi, "Pilot Plant for African Women," *PW*, March 1962, 4–5. The seminar was held at Beit Ruttenberg, Haifa, April 17–May 31, 1961.

441 "The world will not know peace": *Shalom Magazine*, no. 3 (1997).

441 "In that case": GM, *My Life*, 336.

441 Eric Louw: See Shimoni, *Jews and Zionism*, 307–91.

441 "stamped as inferior": GM at the UN, Oct. 2, 1963, quoted in *KR*, June 17, 1964.

442 Golda instructed: "Israel and Nelson Mandela, 1962–1965: A Call for Freedom," ISA.

442 "Without doubt": *KR*, June 17, 1964. In June 1990, Mandela told a group of American Jewish Congress leaders that he was grateful to Golda Meir for her early denunciation of apartheid. See Lifton, *Entrepreneur's Journey*, 343.

442 "it always had to be": Michael Comay, interview with Gideon Shimoni, May 9, 1977, OHD, ICJ.

442 "highest ranking": Mrs. Sarah Simpson George, introductory remarks, Liberian women's reception, Feb. 27, 1958, P-812/31, ISA.

21. "A Mutual Distancing"

443 capture of the Nazi war criminal: See Bascomb, *Hunting Eichmann;* and Harel, *House on Garibaldi Street*. See also *Documents on the Foreign Policy of Israel*, vol. 14, *1960* (ISA: 1997).

443 "squealing like a slaughtered animal": *Haaretz*, May 7, 2010.

443 "I beg of you": Harel, *House on Garibaldi Street*, 189.

444 "This morning I met": BGD, May 15, 1960.

444 special El Al noncommercial airliner: Abba Eban, *Personal Witness*, 312.

444 "the greatest Nazi war criminals": *KR*, May 23, 1960.

444 "wreak vengeance": *Washington Post*, May 27, 1960.

444 "heinousness": *NYT*, June 18, 1960.

445 "Eichmann committed": Simon Segal to Dr. John Slawson, memo, June 16, 1960, Israel/Government/Meir file, FAD 1960, 1962, AJC Archives.

446 How, then, could Amadeo speak: *Maariv*, June 23, 1960.

446 "Far from lynching": GM, Statement to the Security Council, June 22, 1960, in *Land of Our Own*, 126–34.

446 "voice crying in the wilderness": *Maariv*, June 23, 1960.

446 Eichmann's trial: See Lipstadt, *Eichmann Trial*; and Yablonka, *State of Israel vs. Adolf Eichmann*.

447 "best of the Arab friends": Zellinger to police commissioner, memo, Nov. 25, 1960, A-3062, ISA.

447 "top ten trials": *Time*, April 8, 2011.

447 One observer: Arendt, *Eichmann in Jerusalem*.

448 "It was actually": Stangneth, *Eichmann Before Jerusalem*.

448 "pleasant and polite": Amos Yahil, interview with author, June 24, 2008.

449 "My problem was": Arendt to Blücher, April 26, 1961, in Young-Bruehl, *Hannah Arendt*, 332.

449 "shocking statement": Ibid., 333. Golda once told the *New Republic* editor, Martin Peretz, that she didn't believe in God, but believed "in a people which believes in God." *New Republic*, Dec. 23, 1978.

449 "actual idol worship": Arendt to Yahil (Hebrew), May 8, 1961, *Yad Vashem Studies* 37, no. 2 (2009): 34.

449 "If there is a single person": Yahil to Arendt, ibid., 36.

450 "There has been a trial": Cabinet meeting minutes, May 29, 1962. See also Yechiam Weitz, "We Have to Carry Out the Sentence," *Haaretz*, July 27, 2007.

450 "I have no sentiment": Foreign Affairs and Defense Committee minutes, *KR*, March 18, 1962.

451 "I told him": BGD, Sept. 26, 1960.

451 Levi Yitzhak Hayerushalmi: BGD, Oct. 4, 1960.

451 Before returning home: MC minutes, Nov. 11, 1964.

452 "secret file": Almogi, *Total Commitment*, 180.

452 "Pandora's box": Ibid., 182.

452 committee of seven ministers: Cabinet meeting minutes, Oct. 30 and Oct. 31, 1960.

452 "concluded and completed": Cabinet meeting minutes, Dec. 25, 1960.

452 she lit a cigarette: Hasin and Horwitz, *Lavon Affair* (Hebrew), 161.

453 "under no circumstances": MS minutes, Dec. 31, 1960.

453 "implacable": *JP*, Sept. 15, 1961.

453 "He has the right": MS minutes, Dec. 31, 1960.

453 "Two comrades are destroying": Almogi, *Total Commitment*, 187.

454 mobs of students: *Davar*, Feb. 7, 1961.

454 "was understood": Hasin and Horwitz, *Lavon Affair*, 204.

455 "Ben-Gurion's suggestion": *Davar*, March 1, 1961.

455 "I'm for Ben-Gurion": *Maariv*, Feb. 26, 1961.

455 "Young man": Dinitz interview with Geraldine Stern, March 2, 1981, tapes 8 and 9, collection 21, GMLA.

456 "She ruled with an iron fist": Dinstein, interview with author, Jan. 11, 2007.

456 "If you told Golda": *Haolam Hazeh*, Dec. 14, 1978.

456 "She has a vocabulary": Dinstein, interview with author, Jan. 11, 2007. Of Eban's two thousand words, Golda told her grandson, "Next time I see him, I won't say hello. I don't want to waste my few precious words." Gideon Meir, interview with author, Jan. 14, 2007.

456 "So does the waiter": Dinitz, interview with Tova Feldshuh, GMLA.

456 simple salad : Dinstein, interview with author, Jan. 11, 2007.

456 favorite sandwich: Marlin Levin, interview with author, Dec. 15, 2005.

457 "Why?": *NYT*, March 18, 1969.

457 "She is a brilliant success": *Life*, April 1963, 52–53.

457 Nikita Khrushchev: *Davar*, Oct. 30, 1960.

457 "very much hugged": Dan Patir, interview with author, April 22, 2009.

457 "Are you the Golda": Dinitz, MLA.

457 "joyful": *Life*, April 1963, 53.

457 "no culinary talent": Dinitz, MLA.

458 "I simply cannot understand": Third Dialogue in Israel, *Congress Bi-weekly*, Nov. 9, 1964, 7–11.

458 Blaustein negotiated an agreement: Charles S. Liebman, "Diaspora Influence on Israel: The Ben-Gurion-Blaustein 'Exchange' and Its Aftermath," *Jewish Social Studies* 36, nos. 3–4 (July–Oct. 1974).

458 "Israel will continue": Ibid., 279.

458 "I was privy": Ibid., 280.

459 When Golda met with: On her dealings with Dulles and Herter, see Abraham Ben-Zvi, *Decades of Transition: Eisenhower, Kennedy, and the Origins of the American-Israeli Alliance.*

459 "President Kennedy had strong feelings": Feldman, interview with author, June 7, 2006.

460 "anonymous man": *NYT*, March 3, 2007.

460 "Johnson plan": Feldman to Kennedy, memo, Aug. 10, 1962, FRUS, *1961–1963*, vol. 18.

460 "mutual antipathy": Spiegel, *Other Arab-Israeli Conflict*, 111.

460 "I am prepared to meet": *Maariv*, Sept. 28, 1960.

460 500,000 Jewish refugees: GM, "Toward a Solution of the Arab Refugee Problem," statement in the Special Political Committee of the General Assembly, Dec. 15, 1961, in *Land of Our Own*, 135–54.

461 "Golda Meir was a very difficult person": Feldman, interview with John F. Stewart, Aug. 20, 1966, KOHP.

461 "great admiration for her": Feldman, interview with author.

461 "impracticability": Feldman to JFK and Grant, Aug. 21, 1962, in FRUS, *1961–1963*, vol. 18.

461 one refugee in ten: Feldman to JFK, Rusk, and Grant, Aug. 19, 1962, in ibid.

461 "moderate": Cairo embassy to Department of State, Aug. 24, 1962, in ibid.

461 "livid": Feldman interview, Aug. 20, 1966, KOHP.

461 instead of accepting Nasser's response: Feldman, interview with author. See also *JP*, Nov. 29, 1961, on changes.

461 "I was pretty mad": Feldman interview, Aug. 20, 1966, KOHP.

461 "a force that would permit peace": Feldman, interview with author.

462 "it was hard for me": GM, *My Life*, 311.

462 "special relationship": The entire conversation with Kennedy is reported in Memcon: JFK meeting with Meir in Palm Beach, Dec. 27, 1962, NSF, box 118, Israel, General, John F. Kennedy Library.

462 milestone in the ties: See Bass, *Support Any Friend*, esp. 3 and 183.

462 "tough and driving": Ibid., 207.

463 "we are dealing": *PW*, Feb. 1963, 12.

463 "To me, he looks like": Bar-Zohar, *Ben-Gurion*, 274.

463 "Don't worry": GM, *My Life*, 313. This does not appear in the official memo of the meeting.

463 "I want a nuclear option": Karpin, *Bomb in the Basement*, 76.

463 the nuclear project: For a thorough discussion of the project, see Avner Cohen, *Israel and the Bomb*.

463 most of them opposed it: Bar-Zohar, *Shimon Peres*, 219–20.

463 consequences of lying: Avner Cohen, *Israel and the Bomb*, 142.

463 "There is no need to stop": GM at a Foreign Ministry discussion, June 13, 1963, in Karpin, *Bomb in the Basement*, 228–29.

464 become aware of Dimona: On Israel and America, see Shalom, *Israel's Nuclear Option*.

464 "mounting concern": *NYT*, Dec. 18, 1960.

464 "research reactor": Dec. 21, 1960, in Karpin, *Bomb in the Basement*, 161–62.

464 "still stands": Ibid., 179.

464 two American scientists: BGD, March 29, 1961.

464 "were willing to bluff": Aronson, interview with author, Feb. 19, 2006.

465 allies should not deceive: Avner Cohen, *Israel and the Bomb*, 282.

465 At a momentous meeting: March 14, 1960. Bar-Zohar, *Ben-Gurion*, 266–67.

466 "pale and tense": Yaakov Tsur, *Paris Diary* (Hebrew), 272.

466 "lives within me": Shabtai Teveth, *The Elusive Years and the Dark Hole* (Hebrew) (Tel Aviv: D'vir, 1999), 169.

466 scare the German scientists: See Harel, *German Scientists Crisis* (Hebrew), and Harel, interview with Beit-Or, Feb. 14, 1986.

467 Harel went to Tiberias: The sequence of events is in Bar-Zohar, *Ben-Gurion*, 300–301; and Bar-Zohar, *Ben-Gurion, a Political Biography* (Hebrew), 3:1534–38.

467 which he saw beforehand: Bar-Zohar, *Ben-Gurion*, 301.

467 "group of scientists": The speech and discussion in *KR*, March 20, 1963.

467 had Ben-Gurion not approved it: GM, interview at Revivim, July 7, 1978, Interviews, BGA.

468 lacked the proper fuel: Amit, interview with author, Feb. 16, 2006. See also Bar-Zohar, *Shimon Peres*, 260.

469 "there was already a rift": Teddy Kollek, *For Jerusalem* (London: Weidenfeld and Nicolson, 1978), 155.

469 "I called Golda": Lubrani, interview with Boaz Lev Tov, June 2, 2003, Rabin Center Archives.

469 "no more than the last straw": Bar-Zohar, *Ben-Gurion*, 306.

470 Golda wept copiously: *Yediot Aharonot*, May 29, 1964.

22. Seat of Power

471 "It had become": Navon, interview with author, May 19, 2005.

471 solicitous letters: See, for example, Ben-Gurion to GM, Feb. 10 and Oct. 10, 1965, Letters, BGA.

472 "worthy": Harel, interview with Beit-Or, Feb. 14, 1986.

472 he feared her wrath: Haber, *Today War Will Break Out* (Hebrew), 123.

472 *de malka*: Medzini, *Golda*, 405.

472 Kennedy began pressing him: See Shalom, *Israel's Nuclear Option*, 59, 62–63.

472 Golda met with the American secretary of state: Sept. 30, 1963, FRUS, *1961–1963*, 18:143–44.

473   an important precedent: Bass, *Support Any Friend*, 235–37.
473   "I know you have lost": Cabinet meeting minutes, Dec. 1, 1963.
473   "personal loss": Ibid.
473   tanks and Skyhawk bombers: Yitzhak Rabin, *Memoirs*, 64.
473   ups and downs: In February 1965, two high-level U.S. delegations came to Israel to negotiate about selling arms to Israel but also to Jordan. A deal was concluded on March 10, 1965, to sell Israel tanks and Skyhawk planes and Jordan tanks. Golda was deeply involved in all negotiations. "Israel's Documented Story: No Longer a Common Law Wife," ISA.
473   "greatly exhilarated": Frankfurter to LBJ, June 24, 1964, White House Famous Names, Frankfurter, Felix, box 2, Lyndon Baines Johnson Library.
474   At one point: Almogi, *Total Commitment*, 216–17.
474   "I am committed": GM to Reuven Barkatt, Oct. 21, 1964, Letters, BGA.
475   "joined forces": *Commentary*, July 1964.
475   "falsehoods": Ben-Gurion to GM, Sept. 2, 1964, Letters, BGA.
475   "vicious" passage: GM to *Commentary*, Sept. 1964.
475   She then inquired archly: GM to Ben-Gurion, Sept. 10, 1964, Letters, BGA.
476   in favor of Eshkol: MC minutes, Dec. 13, 1964.
476   opening night: *JP*, Feb. 17, 1965.
476   "I don't know what": *JP*, Feb. 18, 1965.
476   "come to its senses": Ibid.
477   kissed him on the head: *Maariv*, Feb. 18, 1965 (photograph).
477   "We called it the kiss of death": Navon, interview with author.
477   dressed all in black: *Yediot Aharonot*, Feb. 18, 1965.
477   "The first curse": GM's speech at tenth Mapai convention, Feb. 17, 1965, Conventions, BGA.
477   "sharp and slashing": *Yediot Aharonot*, Feb. 18, 1965.
477   "the night of the long knives": Bar-Zohar, *Ben-Gurion*, 309.
477   "You don't remember": Feb. 17, 1965, Conventions, BGA.
477   "reckoning": *Yediot Aharonot*, Feb. 18, 1965.
478   "was filled with poison": *JP*, Feb. 19, 1965.
478   "venom and hatred": *Yediot Aharonot*, April 16, 1965.
478   "I think she lives": Bar-Zohar, *Ben-Gurion*, 309.
478   "Ben-Gurion, give me a chance": *JP*, Feb. 19, 1965.
478   sense of loyalty: Matti Golan, *Road to Peace*, 104.
478   After waffling for three months: Teveth, *Moshe Dayan*, 404.
478   Golda never completely forgave: Navon, interview with author.
479   "longest, costliest": Levin to *Time* world bureau, Nov. 4, 1965, MLA.
479   presented his government: *JP*, Jan. 13, 1966.
479   "Nothing serious": *Reader's Digest*, July 1971.
479   "period of convalescence": Halprin to GM, May 10, 1963, box 4, file 5, GMLA.
480   "As my mother used to say": Yehuda Ben Meir, interview with author, Nov. 24, 2004.
480   "I won't go": GM, *My Life*, 348.
480   "Better . . . to be a full-time grandmother": Ibid.
480   "Israel's First Lady": *New York Herald Tribune*, Jan. 16, 1966.
480   "is too valuable": *Milwaukee Journal*, Jan. 4, 1966.
480   "in the game": B. Ross to GM, Jan. 16, 1966, A-12, GMMA Archive.
480   "glorious service": *JP*, Jan. 27, 1966.
480   shook hands with him: Photograph of GM and Eban, *JP*, Jan. 14, 1966.
481   "Oy vey": *New York Times Magazine*, April 17, 1966.
481   "chilling": Suzy Eban, *Sense of Purpose*, 261–62.

481 "Very few people": Aya Meir, interview with author, Feb. 14, 2006.

481 "a most agonizing": GM to Syrkin, July 21, 1965, P-812/26, ISA.

481 "I never wanted": GM, interview on *Panorama*.

482 to become secretary-general: *JP*, Feb. 2, 1966.

482 Simcha Dinitz was to say: Simcha Dinitz, MLA.

482 Katzav Kaduri: *Tel Aviv*, March 23, 1999.

482 turning the lights out: *NYT*, Oct. 26, 1969.

482 bouquet of flowers: *JP*, Feb. 8, 1966.

482 lift from Zevi Dinstein: Yoram Dinstein, interview with author, Jan. 11, 2007.

483 second most important: For Golda's work as party secretary, see Meir Chazan, "Golda Meir: A Female Leader, Chairwoman of the Party" (Hebrew), *Iyunim Bitkumat Israel* 20 (2010): 249–78.

483 "entire community of workers": MC minutes, Feb. 3, 1966.

483 individual Rafi members: See Aharon Harel, *Between Building and Destruction* (Hebrew), 494–96.

483 "Madame Disunity": Chazan, "Golda Meir," 256.

484 thousands of armed troops: For figures, see Herzog, *Arab-Israeli Wars*, 149.

484 number of theories: See, for example, Ginor and Remez, *Foxbats over Dimona*, which argues that the Soviets wanted to lure Israel into a preemptive attack that would give the Russians and Arabs an opportunity to bomb Israel's nuclear reactor at Dimona.

484 many historians believe: See Benny Morris, "Provocations," *New Republic*, July 23, 2007, 47–52.

484 "she felt we had": Rafael, *Destination Peace*, 66–67.

484 "in an almost intolerable rush": GM, *My Life*, 355.

484 "It is now a question": Haber, *Today War Will Break Out*, 164–65.

485 Golda was invited: MS minutes, Sept. 29, 1967.

485 most prominent: Haber, *Today War Will Break Out*, 170–71.

485 Eshkol and some of the ministers would have preferred: Zaki Shalom, *Policy in the Shadow of Controversy*, 282.

485 "a miniature Winston Churchill": Oren, *Six Days of War*, 115.

485 he would resign: Shalom, *Policy*, 282.

486 ten thousand graves: Oren, *Six Days of War*, 136.

486 liar and cheat: MS minutes, Sept. 28, 1967.

486 "I don't believe": BGD, May 24, 1967.

486 "These two horses": *Maariv*, Oct. 4, 1967.

486 "come to Ben-Gurion": Segev, *1967*, 251; Haber, *Today War Will Break Out*, 178.

486 letter from Shimon Peres: MS minutes, May 25, 1967.

486 "counter-productive": GM, *My Life*, 362.

487 reaffirmed its faith: *JP*, May 26, 1967.

487 "Israel will not be alone": See Zaki Shalom, "Lyndon Johnson's Meeting with Abba Eban: Introduction and Protocol," *Israel Studies* 4, no. 2 (Fall 1999): 221–36. See also Abba Eban, *Personal Witness*, 386–91.

487 "you will whip": Abba Eban, *Personal Witness*, 389.

487 "I am not a feeble mouse": Ibid., 388.

488 "A leader who does not hesitate": Dinitz quoting Golda in *NYT*, March 18, 1969. A variation on this is in GM, *My Life*, 362.

488 deputy prime minister for defense: Moshe Dayan, *Story of My Life*, 399.

488 "Everything was ready": Gilboa, *Six Years, Six Days* (Hebrew), 174.

488 the party head: Nakdimon, *Toward the Zero Hour* (Hebrew), 110.

489 "I won't let her go": MS minutes, Sept. 28, 1967.

489 GOLDA, ENOUGH HATRED: BGD, June 1, 1967; *JP*, June 2, 1967.

489 "I already stood up": MS minutes, Sept. 28, 1967.
489 "A Woman Who": *Haaretz*, May 30, 1967.
489 "it is Golda": *Yediot Aharonot*, May 30, 1967.
489 "from the heavens": MS minutes, Sept. 29, 1967.
490 "It has been ten days": Ibid.
490 Golda blamed herself: Nakdimon, *Toward the Zero Hour*, 112.
490 did not appear at a meeting: *Yediot Aharonot*, May 30, 1967.
490 Sapir, was away: Greenberg, *Pinhas Sapir* (Hebrew), 290.
490 "I could understand": Nakdimon, *Toward the Zero Hour*, 199.
491 two stormy meetings: MS minutes, June 1, 1967.
491 "Where it says a man": Ibid.
491 Amit received the impression: Oren, *Six Days of War*, 146–47.
491 "I hear you loud and clear": Amit, interview with author.
492 "any action that succeeds": Oren, *Six Days of War*, 156.
492 blacked out a room: GM, *My Life*, 359.
492 tape up his windows: Menahem Meir, *My Mother*, 181.
492 400 enemy planes: *U.S. News & World Report*, June 19, 1967. See also Yitzhak Rabin, *Memoirs*, 105–6.
492 "It won't be necessary": McPherson to Johnson, June 11, 1967, Harry McPherson office files, box 42, Johnson Library.
492 more than three times its original size: Oren, *Six Days of War*, 307.
493 a *kvitl*: GM, *My Life*, 105.
493 "Once again we have won": GM's speech, "In the Hour of Deliverance: 1967," in *Land of Our Own*, 155–62.
494 "I assume we will not be able": Haber, *Today War Will Break Out*, 235.

23. The Chosen

497 "Look, Golda": Tamir, *Golda*, 45.
497 "I, an old, weak woman": Isser Harel, interview with Beit-Or, Jan. 31, 1986, GMMA Archive.
498 In an effort to persuade him: Almogi, *Total Commitment*, 244.
498 "You're not stupid": *Maariv*, Dec. 20, 1967.
498 "These three parties": *Yediot Aharonot*, Jan. 22, 1968.
499 "persecuted": *Yediot Aharonot*, Feb. 4, 1968.
499 A diagram: *Yediot Aharonot*, June 20, 1968.
499 "It would take a computer": Levin to *Time* world bureau, July 9, 1968, Meir, MLA.
499 "nothing will change": *Maariv*, July 12, 1968.
499 "Why and especially": *Maariv*, July 9, 1968.
499 "At seventy": *JP*, July 14, 1968.
499 "when the time comes": *JP*, July 9, 1968.
499 electoral reforms: *Maariv*, July 5, 1968; see also Greenberg, *Pinhas Sapir*, 339.
500 "the killer instinct": Abba Eban, *Personal Witness*, 477.
500 "not intend to retire": *JP*, July 14, 1968.
500 Buoyant and relieved: Minutes of former Mapai members in the LPS, Aug. 1, 1968.
500 he seemed never to sit still: *JP*, Sept. 22, 1968.
501 He admired the fact: Greenberg, *Pinhas Sapir*, 354.
501 Sapir visited Golda: Beilin, *Price of Unity* (Hebrew), 52.
501 he promised that Allon: Greenberg, *Pinhas Sapir*, 356.
501 "Interesting": Medzini, *Golda*, 437.
501 He assured Eban: Abba Eban, *Personal Witness*, 476.
502 "intimidated": Ibid., 477.

502 he would run again: *JP*, Jan. 26, 1969.

502 *klafte:* Medzini, *Golda*, 437.

502 "numbed with grief": *JP*, Feb. 27, 1969.

502 where the prime minister should be buried: Amnon Barzilai, "Prime Time by Default," *Haaretz*, Oct. 10, 2003.

502 Yigal Allon as acting prime minister: *JP*, Feb. 27, 1969.

502 Popularity polls: *Haaretz*, Feb. 28, 1969.

503 "She was very unpopular": Sarid, interview with author, May 15, 2005.

503 "the prime minister is chosen": *Davar*, Feb. 23, 1969.

503 "I propose that you": Barzilai, "Prime Time by Default."

503 Sapir stated publicly: *JP*, March 3, 1969.

503 "I have always accepted": *JP*, March 4, 1969.

503 "didn't want": GM, *My Life*, 378.

504 She already knew: Avneri, *Sapir* (Hebrew), 267.

504 overwhelmingly elected her: Levin to *Time* world bureau, March 7, 1969, Meir, MLA.

504 tears rolling down: GM, *My Life*, 378.

504 "I always assumed": *JP*, March 9, 1969.

504 "Golda, Golda": Levin to *Time* world bureau, March 7, 1969.

504 "I cannot overlook": Levin to *Time* world bureau, March 6, 1969, Sapir, MLA.

504 cited passages about Deborah: Judges 4:5, 8; Jeremiah 31:22.

505 "railroaded": *JP*, March 7, 1969.

505 "deserved a prime minister": *Haaretz*, Feb. 28, 1969.

505 drawing by the popular cartoonist: *JP*, March 6, 1969.

505 "One in Her Generation": *Maariv*, March 7, 1969.

505 "deep mental satisfaction": Rachel Katznelson Shazar, "Pages from a notebook," A248-41182, Genazim archives.

505 "the 70-year-old grandmother": *Time*, March 14, 1969.

505 "Did you ever refer": Letters, *Time*, April 4, 1969.

505 "consider it an honor": Levin to *Time* world bureau, March 6, 1969, Meir, MLA.

506 "instrumental in concealing": Syrkin, *Golda Meir*, 352.

506 "No comment": *Orah* magazine, Hadassah-WIZO of Canada, April 1969.

506 tense and tired: *NYT*, March 17, 1969.

506 "forced upon" it: *JP*, March 18, 1969.

506 "like a young woman of twenty": Muskana-Lehrman, "Golda Flesh and Blood."

507 six months only: Kadar, interview with author.

507 "I want you back": Dinitz interview with Geraldine Stern, March 2, 1981, tapes 8 and 9, collection 21, GMLA.

507 During her first few months in office: *JP*, March 17, 1969.

507 On the job: Lou Kadar, interview with Yosef Shavit, *Yediot Aharonot*, Nov. 14, 1980.

507 she prepared brunch: Daniel Meir, interview with author, Jan. 14, 2007.

508 she thumped on the table: *Time*, Sept. 19, 1969.

508 "bulldog tenacity": Levin to *Time* world bureau, March 6, 1969, Meir, MLA.

508 "conditional party membership": *JP*, March 30, 1969.

508 "Do you still love me": *Time*, Sept. 19, 1969.

508 changed his seat: *NYT*, June 5, 1969.

508 decided in Golda's kitchen: Aloni, interview with author.

508 "All government decisions": *Time*, March 14, 1969.

509 "the traditional term": Shapira, "Golda: Femininity and Feminism," 306–7.

509 "We're waiting for a phone call": Dayan, interview with BBC, June 12, 1967.

510 "I am not shocked": Quoted in Shlomo Gazit, *Carrot and Stick*, 135.

510 "facts": *NYT*, March 9, 1969.

510 vehemently criticized Dayan: For the Sapir-Dayan conflict, see Greenberg, *Pinhas Sapir*, 299–301.

510 "This public debate": Greenberg, *Pinhas Sapir*, 299. See also *Davar*, Nov. 12, 1968.

511 "a great believer": Levin to *Time* world bureau, March 6, 1969, Meir, MLA.

511 Levi Eshkol was interviewed: *Newsweek*, Feb. 17, 1969; the interview was conducted on Feb. 3.

511 threatened to break away: *JP*, Feb. 11, 1969.

511 "unqualified": *JP*, Feb. 12, 1969.

511 "We don't draw maps": *Time*, May 23, 1969.

511 not replay what happened in 1957: *JP*, April 20, 1969.

511 "I have reason to envy": *Time*, May 23, 1969.

512 "I do not . . . accept": GM, interview with Clifton Daniel for National Education Television, April 27, 1969.

512 "four or forty nations": *Maariv*, April 20, 1969.

512 "Suppose we want to return": *Maariv*, Jan. 10, 1969.

512 "agreed, secure borders": *Time*, May 23, 1969.

512 "to live in peace": UN Security Council, Resolution 242, Nov. 22, 1967, in Rabinovich and Reinharz, *Israel in the Middle East*, 242.

512 "I want a Jewish state": GM meeting with students from Bar-Ian University, May 29, 1969, GMMA Archive.

512 "They will not be the professors": Meeting of Labor Party Knesset members, June 3, 1969, 2-011-1969-155, LPA.

513 "For me, the greatest morality": Shlomo Gazit, *Carrot and Stick*, 135.

24. A Different Kind of War

514 "What was taken": Aronson, *Conflict and Bargaining in the Middle East*, 89.

514 "they will find full reciprocity": *JP*, Sept. 10, 1969.

515 "We want peace": Nixon, *Memoirs*, 477.

515 "I am especially impressed": Levin to *Time* world bureau, March 20, 1969, Meir, MLA.

515 "subtenant": *NYT*, July 13, 1969.

516 "We were born": *JP*, July 8, 1969.

516 "Let us eliminate": *JP*, July 20, 1969.

516 "was to seek that which unites": *JP*, Aug. 6, 1969.

516 "I accept this with love": Greenberg, *Pinhas Sapir*, 361.

517 "nothing interim": *JP*, Independence Day Supplement, April 22, 1969.

517 In Philadelphia, where she arrived: *NYT*, Sept. 25, 1969.

517 "I am wise enough": *PW*, Jan. 1970, 10.

517 "What can you do?": *JP*, Oct. 3, 1969.

518 "That changed": Kadar, interview with Steve North for Kol Israel, Jan. 29, 1979.

518 "conveyed simultaneously": Nixon, *Memoirs*, 478.

518 nineteen-gun salute: For a description of the ceremony, see *JP* Weekend Magazine, Sept. 28, 1969.

518 At the gala dinner: Description of clothes and food in *Los Angeles Times*, Sept. 29, 1969.

518 "the head of government": Toasts of the President and Prime Minister Golda Meir of Israel, Sept. 25, 1969, in Public Papers of Richard Nixon.

518 twenty-five Phantoms: Nixon, *Memoirs*, 478.

518 "no concrete": *NYT*, Oct. 3, 1969.

519 "acted like a man": Nixon/Gannon interviews, May 27, 1983, Walter J. Brown Media Archives, University of Georgia Special Collections Libraries.

519   most private meeting: Avner Cohen and William Burr, "Israel Crosses the Threshold," *Bulletin of the Atomic Scientists*, May/June 2006, 22–30.

519   "As to the more substantive matters": GM, *My Life*, 390.

519   dictated a memorandum: Saunders to HAK, Dec. 8, 1969, box 605, Israel, vol. 3, NPMP, NSCF, cited in "Israel Crosses the Threshold," doc. 26, NSA.

519   nuclear capability: The main sources used here are Avner Cohen, *Israel and the Bomb;* Avner Cohen, *Worst-Kept Secret;* Karpin, *Bomb in the Basement;* and Shalom, *Israel's Nuclear Option.*

519   "tell the Americans": Avner Cohen, *Israel and the Bomb*, 336.

520   Rabin informed Kissinger: Memcon, HAK and Rabin, Feb. 23, 1970, HAK Office Files, box 134, Rabin/HAK 1969–1970, vol. 1, NPMP, cited in "Israel Crosses the Threshold," doc. 28, NSA.

520   Nixon seems to have accepted: Some historians hold that Nixon probably coordinated his acceptance of Israel's capability with Kissinger before meeting with Golda. See Avner Cohen, *Worst-Kept Secret*, 276n62.

520   *amimut:* See ibid., 1–33.

520   "We haven't done so badly": *JP*, Oct. 3, 1969.

520   "found in the President": Remarks on the Departure of Prime Minister Golda Meir of Israel, Sept. 26, 1969, Public Papers of Richard Nixon.

521   "Sure, it's very high": *NYT*, Dec. 31, 1969.

521   "It's overwhelming": *NYT*, Oct. 1, 1969.

521   Macy's basement: *PW*, Jan. 1970, 11.

521   "could not be settled": *JP*, Oct. 3, 1969.

522   "Here I found freedom": *NYT*, Oct. 4, 1969.

522   Isadore Tuchman: *JP*, Oct. 5, 1969.

522   "on home territory": GM, *My Life*, 394.

522   "They saw her": Halevy, interview with author, Feb. 8, 2006.

522   public opinion polls: *NYT*, April 19, 1970.

523   "an old and exceedingly weary": Kishon's memories in *JP*, Nov. 22, 1978.

523   biggest crowds: Levin to *Time* world bureau, Oct. 30, 1969, Meir, MLA.

523   "Even when there is peace": *Time*, Nov. 7, 1969, 31.

524   "Have you gone": The story of the Rogers document and GM's reaction come from Eiran, interview with author, May 9, 2005.

524   "software": Yitzhak Rabin, *Memoirs*, 155–56.

524   "recent developments": Memcon, Rabin, HAK, Saunders, Dec. 26, 1969, box 756, Meir, NPMP, NSCF.

524   "unmistakable moral commitment": HAK to Nixon, "Talking Points," Jan. 17, 1970, box 756, Meir, NPMP, NSCF.

525   ministers shook her hand: Margalit, *Dispatch from the White House* (Hebrew), 15.

525   Her hardest problem: Levin to *Time* world bureau, Dec. 1, 1969, Meir, MLA.

525   "Suddenly all the telephones": Amnon Barzilai, "Golda Meir's Nightmare," *Haaretz*, Oct. 3, 2003.

525   hardest thing to do: Kadar, interview with author.

526   further escalate: Nixon, *Memoirs*, 480.

526   "I know you have been": GM to Graham, March 11, 1970, Presidential Correspondence, box 756, Folder: Israel, Golda Meir 1970, NPMP, NSCF.

526   "It is true that our pilots": Nixon, *Memoirs*, 480.

526   Nixon promised Rabin: Yitzhak Rabin, *Memoirs*, 171.

526   Nahum Goldmann: For an analysis, see Meir Chazan, "Goldmann's Initiative to Meet with Nasser in 1970," in Raider, *Nahum Goldmann*, 297–324.

527   "human kindness": Goldmann, *Autobiography*, 303.

527   "allergic": Ben-Porat, *Dialogues* (Hebrew), 34.

527 fake alligator handbag: Ibid., 19–20.

527 "I cannot simply decide this": *JP*, April 10, 1970.

527 Eban's encouragement: Eban to GM, March 27, 1970, A-7054/19, ISA.

527 she had torpedoed it: See *JP*, April 7, 1970; *Maariv*, April 7, 1970.

527 "It wasn't that Dr. Goldmann": *JP*, April 20, 1970.

527 "I have never heard": *JP*, April 10, 1970.

528 series of six articles: *Haaretz*, April 2–9, 1970.

528 a long article he wrote: Nahum Goldmann, "The Future of Israel," *Foreign Affairs*, April 1970, 443–59.

528 "Not an iota": *Davar*, April 22, 1970.

528 "a mistake that needs": *Haaretz*, April 6, 1970.

528 "Did you ever see a poll": *JP*, April 20, 1970.

528 government-sponsored survey: "Survey Conducted on April 6, 1970 . . . ," presented to Yigal Allon, April 9, 1970, A-7054/19, ISA.

528 "about to be inducted": Twelfth-grade letter to GM, April 8, 1970, G-7442/4, ISA.

528 University professors: *Davar*, April 8, 1970.

528 GOLDMANN TO CAIRO: *NYT*, April 12, 1970.

528 GOLDA'S AFRAID: *Maariv*, April 13, 1970.

528 Demonstrators held sit-ins: *Davar*, April 9, 1970.

528 More than a hundred protesters: *Davar*, April 12, 1970.

529 Nasser denied: Margalit, *Dispatch from the White House*, 89.

529 she regretted: Goldstein, interview with author, Feb. 11, 2006.

530 "the type of person": Defense council minutes, April 9, 1970 A-7041/25, ISA.

530 Sisco visited: *JP*, April 16, 1970.

530 "will not acquiesce": GM to Nixon, April 27, 1970, Presidential Correspondence, box 756, Folder: Israel, Golda Meir, 1970, NPMP, NSCF.

530 Nixon responded orally: HAK, Memorandum for the President, "Reply to Prime Minister Meir," May 15, 1970, Presidential Correspondence, box 756, Folder: Israel, Golda Meir, 1970, NPMP, NSCF.

530 "Some people's friends": *JP*, June 28, 1970.

530 Golda Meir stood before the Knesset: *KR*, May 26, 1970.

531 Two television journalists: Margalit, *Dispatch from the White House*, 118.

531 "almost jumped out of her chair": Ibid., 123.

531 "entirely negative": Yitzhak Rabin, *Memoirs*, 177.

531 personal letter: Nixon to GM, June 20, 1970, Presidential Correspondence, box 756, Folder: Israel, Golda Meir, 1970 NPMP, NSCF.

531 "death trap": Cabinet meeting minutes, June 25, 1970.

531 the Israeli ambassador, Rabin, was so horrified: Yitzhak Rabin, *Memoirs*, 177.

532 another secret letter: Nixon to GM, July 24, 1970, Presidential Correspondence, box 756, Folder: Israel, Golda Meir, 1970, NPMP, NSCF.

532 "I must admit": Cabinet meeting minutes, July 30, 1970.

533 "I at all events": Cabinet meeting minutes, Aug. 4, 1970.

533 "that it was my lot": Ibid.

533 "like half-wits": John Shaw to *Time* world bureau, Sept. 2, 1970, Meir, MLA.

533 "inopportune": HAK, *White House Years*, 87.

25. "What Has Happened to Us?"

535 "cry from the depths": *Davar*, Nov. 11, 1969. The letter was written on Aug. 6, 1969.

535 "We will wait months": *Maariv*, Nov. 11, 1969.

535 "We are declaring": *KR*, Nov. 19, 1969.

536 She was one of the few: Meir Rosenne, interview with author.

536 "Golda's response": Kedmi, interview with author, Feb. 22, 2006.

537 shake Kedmi's hand: Dinstein, interview with author, Jan. 11, 2007.

537 "Soviet Jews are not alone": *Davar*, Dec. 3, 1969.

537 "Not pity but justice": *Maariv*, Dec. 27, 1970.

537 "I did not ask Golda Meir": *JP*, March 5, 1970.

537 "The highest medical expert": Levanon, *"Nativ" Was the Code Name*, 347.

538 "for two thousand years": JFA VT DA 56, Steven Spielberg Jewish Film Archive.

538 he received an unenthusiastic response: Levanon, *"Nativ" Was the Code Name*, 374.

538 barely coherent Ben-Gurion: Wiesel, *And the Sea Is Never Full*, 27.

538 "driving force": Ben Rabinovitch, interview with author.

538 13,000: *Forward*, June 17, 2010.

538 "Would you tell me": Marlev to *Time* world bureau, Jan. 13, 1971, Soviet Union, MLA.

539 90 percent: *NYT*, April 19, 1970.

539 woman they most admired: *Los Angeles Times*, Dec. 28, 1973.

539 outranking Queen Elizabeth: *Parade*, Jan. 20, 1974.

539 Her recipe for chicken soup: *Maariv*, Jan. 18, 1971.

539 "Let me tell you something": *NYT*, June 11, 1973.

539 "Old age is like an airplane": Fallaci, *Interview with History*, 121.

539 "Don't ask me": Geller interview, Dec. 2006, IDF radio station.

539 Iphigenia Sulzberger: Medzini, *Golda*, 482.

539 Senator Frank Church: Marlev to *Time* world bureau, n.d., Golda, MLA.

539 marry the retired multimillionaire Lou Boyar: *Los Angeles Times*, June 17, 1971.

540 "unfortunately not true": *Los Angeles Times*, Sept. 6, 1972.

540 "absolutely ridiculous": Parker to Jerusalem, June 18, 1971, Golda, MLA.

540 she shook hands warmly: *Davar*, July 18, 1971.

540 Ben-Gurion had hesitated: *Haaretz*, April 4, 2012.

540 fell into each other's arms: Moshe Olnick, interview with author at Revivim, May 19, 2005. He was present at the celebration.

540 "true pioneer": Transcript of party at Revivim, Sept. 10, 1971, RE-72, GMMA Archive.

540 "enormous privilege": Ibid.

541 the need to be afraid: MS minutes, Sept. 30, 1971.

541 she led the entire cabinet: *Davar*, Oct. 7, 1971.

541 "Ben-Gurion I want to tell you": *Jewish Frontier*, Nov. 1971, 5.

541 "When I got a phone call": Dinstein, interview with author, Jan. 11, 2007.

541 "She would say things like": Peri, interview with author, Feb. 22, 2006.

541 "ruthless": Savir, interview with author, Oct. 28, 2004.

542 "she became absolutely rock-like": Julie Nixon Eisenhower, "Golda Meir," 154.

542 "What are you doing": Medzini, *Golda*, 479.

542 "tiny little steps": Barry Solomon, interview with author, Revivim, May 19, 2005.

542 "She retained many of her virtues": Quoted in Kessner, *Marie Syrkin*, 402.

542 "What has happened": *KR*, July 28, 1971.

543 "Mrs. Meir, will you marry me?": Wiesel, *All Rivers Run to the Sea*, 310.

543 "exhausted all possibilities": The letter was sent Dec. 26, 1971; see *Al Hamishmar*, Jan. 18, 1972, G-7444/24, ISA.

543 ivory-tower professors: Yoram Dinstein, interview with author, Jan. 11, 2007.

543 The cable quickly reached: *Haaretz*, Dec. 27, 1971.

543 meet with the second group: *Al Hamishmar*, Jan. 13, 1972, G-7444/25, ISA.

544 "We went round and round": Bartov, interview with author, Dec. 20, 2006.

544 crisis of Zionist ideology: See Amos Elon, "Two Arab Towns That Plumb Israel's Conscience," *NYT*, Oct. 22, 1972.

544 "She wanted us to drop": *Haolam Hazeh*, Dec. 20, 1978.

544 "We had no common language": Bartov, interview with author.

544 Chinese food: Kadar, interview with author.

545 Certainly not: Sarid, *You Chose Us for Ruling* (Hebrew), 52–53.

545 Israeli television programming: *KR*, May 19, 1969.

545 postpone Sabbath television: *NYT*, Nov. 8, 1969.

546 cabinet rushed a bill: *JP*, Jan. 30, 1970.

546 "religious coercion": *Maariv*, Feb. 10, 1970.

546 "for the sake of the survival": *JP*, Jan. 29, 1970.

546 honorary degree: *NYT*, Oct. 14, 1970.

546 Passover Haggadah: Rabbi Shlomo Riskin, conversation with author, May 4, 2008.

546 never before been seen: Among some groups of protesters, there appeared supporters of Meyer Lansky, the American Jewish bootlegger and crime boss. Lansky had helped Israel by smuggling arms to it during its War of Independence. In 1970, about to be prosecuted in America for tax evasion, he fled to Israel. When Golda heard he had been connected to the Mafia, she denied his application for citizenship, and he was forced to return to the United States. See Lacey, *Little Man*, 334–35.

547 "If their parents": GM's talk at Revivim, Sept. 30, 1970, RE-71, GMMA Archive.

547 "Afro" hairdo: Lou Kadar, interview with Shavit, Nov. 14, 1980.

547 Asked by an interviewer: "Three Generations, Interview with Golda Meir," translated by Avi Amalia, *PW*, Dec. 1970; Hebrew original by Levi Yitzhak Hayerushalmi, *Maariv*, Sept. 30, 1970.

547 "disorder among young people": Alon Gan, "Crushing the Beatles," *Haaretz*, Sept. 19, 2008.

547 "How could they imagine": *Time*, Sept. 19, 1969.

547 "Do you mean": Fallaci, *Interview with History*, 112.

547 refuse to meet with Betty Friedan: Betty Friedan, "Women in the Frontline," *NYT*, Oct. 28, 1984.

548 "Men have never given me": Fallaci, *Interview with History*, 113.

548 "the fact that a woman": *Maariv*, Sept. 9, 1955.

548 "The fact that they're making": Nov. 1958, Meagher, MLA.

548 It bothered her: Fallaci, *Interview with History*, 113.

548 three important women: Zena Harman, interview with author; Herlitz, interview with author, May 10, 2005; and Eshel, interview with author.

548 "to be successful": Fallaci, *Interview with History*, 113.

549 "But Can She Type?": The Israeli consul in New York sent a poster to Golda. "I think she'll be pleased," he said. *Yediot Aharonot*, Sept. 19, 1973.

549 "boorish": Aloni, interview with author.

549 "conquerors": Aloni, *I Can Do No Other* (Hebrew), 50.

549 sixty-fourth: Greenberg, *Pinhas Sapir*, 366.

549 "bourgeois": Aloni, interview with author.

549 three-way interview: "Three Generations," *PW*, Dec. 1970.

550 fighting poverty: Socialism's meaning to her discussed in Levin to *Time* world bureau, March 6, 1969, Meir, MLA.

550 "Pure hooliganism": *JP*, Sept. 8, 1971.

551 "We are a wise": *KR*, July 28, 1971.

551 Black Panthers: For an inside view of the group, see Chetrit, *Intra-Jewish Conflict in Israel*. See also Amos Elon, "The Black Panthers of Israel," *NYT*, Sept. 12, 1971.

552 below the poverty level: *Time*, Feb. 14, 1972.

552 to prevent their demonstrations: Aaron Chelouche to Pinhas Koppel, March 10, 1971, IP-412/9, ISA.

552 ENOUGH OF NOT HAVING WORK: *JP*, Aug. 19, 2012.

552 demanded a meeting: Reuven Abergil to GM, April 7, 1971, IP-412/9, ISA.
552 sympathetic university lecturers: Leo Kopple to Yosef Ben-Porat, April 21, 1971, A-4479/2, ISA.
552 "Were you born here?": The complete minutes are given in Tali Lev, "'We Will Erase the Past of Those Who Have a Past': The Full Protocol of the Black Panthers' Meeting with the Prime Minister of Israel, April 1971" (Hebrew), *Theory and Criticism* 32 (Spring 2008): 197–226. Also in G-6465/2, ISA. GM's report to the cabinet in A-56/5, ISA.
553 to frighten Golda: Shemesh, interview with author, Feb. 20, 2006.
554 "One thing is clear": Cabinet meeting minutes, April 18, 1971, A-56/5, ISA.
554 "She was Mama Russia": Shemesh, interview with author.
554 Maimouna celebration: *JP*, April 19, 1971.
554 GOLDA TEACH US YIDDISH: *JP*, May 4, 1971.
554 Night of the Panthers: *JP*, May 19, 1971.
554 Golda Meir's home: *JP*, May 20, 1971.
555 "They were once good boys": *Maariv*, May 20, 1971.
555 "they are not nice": Shlomo Hillel, interview with author, Oct. 18, 2004.
555 "For months, a campaign": GM to Ben-Simhon, Nov. 1, 1971, A-7086/6, ISA.
555 "there are people": Ben-Simhon to GM, Nov. 5, 1971, G-6521/2, ISA.
555 "That's legitimate": Knesset Foreign Affairs and Defense Committee minutes, June 8, 1971, A-7118/4, ISA.
556 "throw Golda Meir out": *Maariv*, July 6, 1971.
556 clenched-fist salute: *JP*, July 6, 1971.
556 GOLDA, GOLDA: IP-412/10, ISA. See also *Maariv*, Aug. 24, 1971.
556 A STATE IN WHICH HALF: Chetrit, *Mizrahi Struggle Against Israel* (Hebrew), 154.
556 "Golda was very active": Levy, interview with author, Nov. 18, 2004.
557 worked for two years: See Prime Minister's Committee for Children and Youth in Distress, *Report to the Prime Minister* (Jerusalem, 1973).
557 "The State of Israel after": Shemesh, interview with author.

26. Terror, Territories, and the Palestinian Question

559 "The end of Israel": Fallaci, "Yasir Arafat," in *Interview with History*, 130–31.
559 "grief and rage": *NYT*, March 4, 1970.
559 "put themselves": *NYT*, Feb. 23, 1970.
559 In the Knesset: *KR*, Feb. 23, 1970.
560 to integrate all his subjects: Shlaim, *Lion of Jordan*, 206–7.
560 state within a state: Ibid., 316. See also Dallas, *King Hussein*, 131.
560 spectacular PFLP hijacking: A good description of these events is in Ashton, *King Hussein of Jordan*, 144–45.
561 "extreme anxiety": PRO, CAB 128/47, Sept. 21, 1970, BNA.
561 United Jewish Appeal gala: Friedman, *Roots of the Future*, 285–88; and author interview, Sept. 7, 2005.
561 "Are you recommending": Yitzhak Rabin, *Memoirs*, 187.
561 "a tired woman": Friedman, *Roots of the Future*, 287.
561 "We won't mourn": Zak, *Hussein Makes Peace* (Hebrew), 124.
561 "look favorably": HAK, *White House Years*, 623.
561 "head of the government": Friedman, *Roots of the Future*, 287.
562 "biggest tragedy": Riad, *Struggle for Peace in the Middle East*, 163.
562 "fortunate in having an ally": Yitzhak Rabin, *Memoirs*, 189. See also WSAG meeting, Sept. 24, 1970, with oral points for Rabin that the United States will take this event into account as it gives "prompt and sympathetic" consideration to Israel's requests for military assistance. WSAG and SRG Mtg. Jordan, box H-076, NSCF.

562 "ancient bonds": Jehuda Reinharz, *Chaim Weizmann: The Making of a Statesman*, 273.

562 "cousins": Ibid., 274.

562 "anything of that kind": Laqueur and Rubin, *Israel-Arab Reader*, 17.

563 In Hussein's recollection: Shlaim, *Lion of Jordan*, 47.

563 frozen in time: Edward J. Carlough, "Comments from the General President," *Sheet Metal Workers' Journal* (March/April 1991): 2–3.

563 "There was no such thing": *Sunday Times* (London), June 15, 1969, FCO 17/947, BNA.

563 "My actual words": *NYT*, Jan. 14, 1976.

564 focused on established states: HAK, *Years of Upheaval*, 624–25.

564 "Now did that really make": *JP*, April 22, 1969.

564 "There will be no third state": *NYT*, Aug. 27, 1972.

564 "nobody heard": *NYT*, Feb. 8, 1970.

564 "time bomb": *NYT*, Jan. 14, 1976.

564 "Arafat says": GM, interview with James Reston and James Feron, *NYT*, Feb. 8, 1970.

565 "roam around": Eliav, interview with author, Oct. 12, 2004.

565 "The first thing": "The Lion's Roar," *Time*, Jan. 26, 1970.

565 "blazing red": Eliav wrote up the incident in *Rings of Faith* (Hebrew), 293–97. See also Gorenberg, *Accidental Empire*, 203–5.

566 "I was a litmus paper case": Eliav, interview with author.

566 secret meetings: See Zak, *Hussein Makes Peace*; and Shlaim, *Lion of Jordan*. Shlaim lists dates and locations of Hussein's meetings with Golda and other Israeli officials on 671–72.

566 CIA: See Ashton, *King Hussein of Jordan*, 62–63 and throughout.

566 "I met his grandfather": *NYT*, Aug. 27, 1972.

567 "I have wanted to meet you": Zak, *Hussein Makes Peace*, 79–80.

567 "It was a good meeting": Shlaim, *Lion of Jordan*, 223.

567 "I hope Your Majesty": Zak, *Hussein Makes Peace*, 44.

567 Golda told Hussein anecdotes: Melman and Raviv, *Behind the Uprising*, 114.

567 Golda served the meal: O'Connell, *King's Counsel*, 90.

567 "totally unacceptable": Melman and Raviv, *Behind the Uprising*, 93–96.

568 "United Arab Kingdom": For the federation plan, see Lapidoth and Hirsch, *Jerusalem Question and Its Resolution*, 291–93.

568 "grave collusion": *JP*, March 16, 1972.

568 "the little matter": *Daily Telegraph* (London), March 16, 1972.

568 "ruthlessly": Levin to *Time* world bureau, March 23, 1972, Hussein, MLA.

568 "pretentious and one-sided": *JP*, March 17, 1972.

568 Less than a week: The meeting was on March 21, 1972. See Shlaim, *Lion of Jordan*, 353; Zak, *Hussein Makes Peace*, 161.

569 Her "line": Zak, *Hussein Makes Peace*, 162.

569 What, then, to do about the West Bank: See Gorenberg, *Accidental Empire*, for a survey of the growth of settlements on the West Bank.

569 Levinger held a seder: See Shlomo Gazit, *Trapped Fools*, 252–53.

570 forbid the study of the Bible: "Deliberations on the Territories in the Labor Party Secretariat" (Hebrew), May 1972–April 1973, 68, Galili 74-10, YTA.

570 "one of the greatest": Ibid., 29.

570 "creeping annexation": Ibid., 20.

570 interview with Louis Heren: *Times* (London), March 13, 1971, held in Golda's Jerusalem office.

570 "sensible and reasonable": *NYT*, April 18, 1971.

571 Heren later recalled: Related in Rafael, *Destination Peace*, 265.

571 "I have to confess": MS deliberations, May 1972–April 1973, 19, Galili, 74-10, YTA.

571 "after two thousand years": Ibid., 83.

571 about Hebron: GM, *My Life*, 405–6.

571 "grandiose": Foreign Affairs and Defense Committee minutes, May 9, 1972, A-7116/6, ISA.

572 "Our boys acted": Ibid.

572 "sick souls that plan": Hussein to GM, June 1, 1972, A-7043/4, ISA.

572 "deeply touched": GM to Hussein, June 4, 1972, A-704/4, ISA.

572 visited her every Friday: Ovad Natan (GM's driver), interview with author.

573 Twenty years later: *NYT*, Dec. 2, 2015.

573 not negotiate with terrorists: MFA-5334/4, ISA.

573 "If we should give in": Klein, *Striking Back*, 58.

573 to suspend the games: Foreign Affairs and Defense Committee minutes, Sept. 5, 1973, A-7056/9, ISA.

573 "Golda Meir, holding": Reeve, *One Day in September*, 66.

573 "extreme impatience": A-7056/9, ISA.

574 bottle of cognac: *JP*, Sept. 7, 1972.

574 "I am sorry": Sept. 6, 1972, A-7056/10, ISA.

574 "Mrs. Meir": The Nixon-HAK exchange in FRUS, *1969–1976*, vol. E-1, Sept. 6, 1972. See also *Haaretz*, Feb. 24, 2006.

575 "goodwill": *JP*, Sept. 7, 1972.

575 "You were my guide": *PW*, Nov. 1972, 13.

575 sympathy of West Germany's chancellor: Sept. 6, 1972, A-116/7, ISA.

575 "desperate attempt": GM to Brandt, Sept. 6, 1972, MFA-5331/1.

576 "It is sad": Consultation of the prime minister with a team of ministers about the conclusions of the inquiry team on the Munich disaster, Oct. 5, 1972, A-4079/10, ISA.

576 "wherever we can reach them": GM Knesset speech, *KR*, Oct. 16, 1972.

576 Forty years after: *Der Spiegel*, July 16 and Aug. 20, 2012. See also *Haaretz*, July 22 and Aug. 26, 2012. *Der Spiegel* based the claims on newly opened files in German archives.

576 "With all due force": Brandt to GM, Nov. 8, 1972, A-7056/10, ISA.

577 knew very well the difference: GM to Brandt, Nov. 8, 1972, MFA-5331/16, ISA.

577 "with everything required": *NYT*, Sept. 13, 1972.

577 tensions between Yariv and the Mossad chief: See Bar-Zohar and Haber, *Massacre in Munich*, 136.

577 "It was not about vengeance": Zamir, interview with author, Feb. 16, 2006.

578 "As a woman": Yariv, interview with Peter Taylor, 1993, cited in Reeve, *One Day in September*, 154.

578 "If we do this": Zamir, interview with author, Oct. 12, 2004.

578 Committee X: Hunting for the killers is based on Bar-Zohar and Haber, *Massacre in Munich*; and Klein, *Striking Back*. Also Zamir, interviews with author.

578 "We succeeded": *Haaretz* magazine, Feb. 17, 2006.

579 terrorist plan: *Maariv*, Jan. 18, 1973.

579 shoot missiles: Ostrovsky, *By Way of Deception*, 185–96.

579 more than a thousand police: *JP*, Jan. 15, 1973.

579 "Just a minute": *Maariv*, Jan. 19, 1973.

579 "face to face": The events and Golda's feelings are based on her interview with Dov Goldstein in *Maariv*, Jan. 19, 1973. See also Ambassador Najar's summary, with some differences in the order and content of the conversation. A-7053/5, ISA.

580 "verbal note": The writer Muriel Spark, who lived in Rome, described the Alessan-

drini affair best in "When Israel Went to the Vatican," *The Tablet*, March 24, 1973, 277–79.

580 "diplomatic slap": Press conference, Jan. 15, 1973, A-7028/5, ISA.

580 "I did not break into": Ibid.

580 facsimile of a fragment: On this and the exchange of letters, see A-7028/5, ISA.

580 "grand debate": See Kieval, *Party Politics in Israel and the Occupied Territories*, 70–87.

580 four-year program: Shlomo Gazit, *Trapped Fools*, 255–56.

581 "irresponsible": *NYT,* April 4, 1973.

581 "Golda plan": *Maariv,* Sept. 8, 1972.

581 "It may not be": *JP,* Sept. 3, 1972.

581 Aharon Yariv to work out: Amos Gilboa, *Mr. Intelligence—Ahrale Yariv* (Hebrew) (Tel Aviv: Yediot Aharonot, 2013), 565.

582 Palestinian refugee camps: G-6690/20, ISA.

582 scribbled notes: Galili 85-7, YTA.

582 Galili document: For terms, see Shlomo Gazit, *Trapped Fools*, 258; and Safran, *Israel, the Embattled Ally*, 179. For discussion about it, see A-7041/24, Aug.–Sept. 1973, ISA.

582 "This document is brought": *JP,* Sept. 4, 1973.

583 "I have lived": Ibid.

583 no expectations of peace: Dayan repeatedly took this position. One example is his speech to a conference of overseas Jewish student leaders, reported in *JP,* Sept. 15, 1973.

27. Premier Meir and President Sadat

584 no achievement: GM speech at Revivim, Oct. 1, 1970, GMMA Archive.

584 "low intellectual capacity": Israel Foreign Ministry Supplement on Anwar Sadat, Oct. 8, 1970, A-7062/5, ISA.

585 series of statements: Dr. Gunnar Jarring's Memorandum of Feb. 8, 1971, Aide-Mémoire, A-7042/9, ISA.

585 "a new initiative": Anwar Sadat, "Announcement of Peace Initiative," Feb. 4, 1971, Anwar Sadat Archives, Presidential Speeches, http://sadat.umd.edu/archives /speeches.

585 "good news": Yitzhak Rabin, *Memoirs*, 192–93; see also Raviv, *Israel at Fifty*, 141.

585 "did not underestimate": GM to Nixon, Aug. 17, 1971, G-7445/12, ISA.

585 Responding to Jarring: On Feb. 26, 1971. See Abba Eban, *Personal Witness*, 501.

586 repeatedly criticized: For criticisms and responses to them, see Mordechai Gazit, "Egypt and Israel—Was There a Peace Opportunity Missed in 1971?," *Journal of Contemporary History* 32, no. 1 (1997): 97–115.

586 "We had no peace": *Yediot Aharonot*, Feb. 7, 1971.

586 "without peace": Dayan quoted in *Davar,* June 27, 1969.

586 Golda had mentioned Dayan's idea: HAK, *White House Years*, 1280.

586 Without her backing: Dayan, interview with Rami Tal, Nov. 22, 1976, in *Yediot Aharonot*, April 27, 1997. According to Menahem Meir, Golda's son, Dayan came to their home every Saturday morning, before the Saturday evening kitchen cabinet meeting, and tried out his ideas with her. If she didn't agree with something, he would never fight for it. Menahem Meir, interview with author, Jan. 14, 2009.

586 he expanded on: *Newsweek*, Feb. 22, 1971.

587 Golda agreed: *NYT,* Feb. 10, 1971.

587 twenty-nine to thirty kilometers: Dayan, *Milestones* (Hebrew), 526.

587 an official paper: *JP,* April 23, 1971.

587 "one inch": *NYT,* Feb. 10, 1971.

587 "never, never": *NYT*, Dec. 28, 1970.

587 still American policy: *NYT*, March 17, 1971.

587 "An American guarantee": Levin to *Time* world bureau, March 23, 1971, MLA.

587 An angry Rogers: MFA-4549/7, ISA.

588 "tough and unsatisfactory": Memorandum for Record, May 12, 1971, box 997, Haig Memcons, NPMP, NSCF, NA.

588 Sadat had sent Rogers a memo: Vanetik and Shalom, *Nixon Administration and the Middle East Peace Process*, chap. 10, which analyzes the May meetings.

588 She was suspicious: Meir-Rogers meeting, May 6, 1971, MFA-7031/1, ISA.

588 second day of meetings: Meir-Rogers meeting, May 7, 1971, MFA-7031/1, ISA.

588 Dayan suggested: Rafael, *Destination Peace*, 267.

588 Sisco reported to Sadat: Yitzhak Rabin, *Memoirs*, 201.

589 "diddled us along": Nixon to Rogers, May 26, 1971, in Craig A. Daigle, "The Russians Are Going: Sadat, Nixon, and the Soviet Presence in Egypt, 1970–1971," *Middle East Review of International Affairs* 8, no. 1 (2004): 1–15.

589 the treaty came too late: Anwar el-Sadat, *In Search of Identity*, 284.

589 "We thought he was Rigoletto": HAK, interview with author, April 6, 2005.

589 "Zionist intrusion": *JP*, June 11, 1971.

589 "Don't promise a damned thing": NSC Minutes Originals, 1971 through June 20, 1974, box 10, NPMP, NSCF, NA.

590 "I don't want to understand": Meir-Sisco meeting, July 30, 1971, A-7029/7, ISA.

590 "extremely concerned": Ibid.

590 "warm esteem": Sisco to president and secretary, Aug. 4, 1971, Subject Numeric Files 1970–1973, Political and Defense box 2390, folder 4/20/71-12/31/71, RG 59, NA.

591 "Mr. Rogers made it difficult": *NYT*, Oct. 9, 1971.

591 At a Knesset meeting: *KR*, Oct. 26, 1971.

591 "famous": Anwar el-Sadat, *In Search of Identity*, 227.

591 "we knew that she was fond": Ibid., 286.

591 "to slam the hell": Garment, *Crazy Rhythm*, 192–93.

592 "Don't worry": Report of meeting of GM with Richard Nixon in the Oval Office, Dec. 2, 1971, A-4239/1, ISA.

592 Shoreham Hotel: Conversation between Prime Minister and Cardinal, Dec. 1, 1971, A-4239/3, ISA. Israeli secret documents sometimes refer to HAK by the code name "Cardinal." Other code names for him were "Shaul" and "Naftali." Nixon was "Robert."

592 "hangs like a sword": Meir-Nixon meeting, Dec. 2, 1971, A-4239/1, ISA.

593 "classic Golda": Hagai Tsoref, lecture at Haifa University, "Forty Years from the Yom Kippur War," June 6, 2013. With thanks to Dr. Tsoref for giving me his unpublished paper.

593 Waldorf Astoria: Conversation between Prime Minister and Cardinal, Dec. 10, 1971, A-4239/3, ISA. See also Yitzhak Rabin, *Memoirs*, 209.

594 "twisted": Sadat, "Address to the Nation," Jan. 13, 1972.

594 to maintain the status quo: HAK, *White House Years*, 326, 1290.

595 "How on earth": Menahem Meir, *My Mother*, 197.

595 Golda reprimanded him: GM to Rabin, June 1972, A-7061/3, ISA.

595 "That depends": Yitzhak Rabin, *Memoirs*, 217.

595 "She treated him": Halevy, interviews with author, Feb. 8, 2006, Jan. 21, 2007.

595 "the dream of a sabra": Peri, interview with author.

595 "created the vocabulary": Halevy, interviews with author, Feb. 8, 2006, Jan. 21, 2007.

596 "never had it so good": HAK, *Years of Upheaval*, 220.

596 "ship shape condition": Levin to *Time* world bureau, March 4, 1972, Rabin, MLA.

596 "The whole world": Music by Kobi Oshrat, lyrics by Yoram Taharlev.

596 "The Arabs have tried": *Time*, Jan. 18, 1971.

596 "We have an amazing": GM, interview with Dov Goldstein, *Maariv*, Sept. 8, 1972.

596 "The non-Jewish world": *NYT*, Oct. 7, 1969.

597 "She told me to call her": Reich, interview with author, Feb. 21, 2006.

597 "as soon as the doctor's back": Yetti Stein, telephone interview with author, Jan. 17, 2005.

597 "The treatments": Kadar, interview with Steve North, AP report, Jan. 12, 1979.

597 "What!": *JP*, Dec. 7, 1972.

598 "as a benevolent aunt": HAK, *White House Years*, 370.

598 "mother of all mothers": Garment, *Crazy Rhythm*, 191.

598 "Listen honey": M.V.T. to prime minister, Dec. 1971, from "Dear Golda," collection of letters to GM given to author by Lou Kadar.

598 "Boil the chicken": G-6479/28, ISA.

598 *kvitlech:* GM address at the Western Wall on receiving the Freedom of Jerusalem prize, 1971, in *Land of Our Own*, 232–35.

598 socialism and Zionism: *JP*, July 8, 1971.

598 "A Jew cannot afford": GM, interview with Gideon Lev-Ari, 1971, GMMA Archive.

598 Ceauşescu: For a description of the visit, see GM, *My Life*, 400–401; for the meetings, see Dinitz to Ephraim Evron, A-7061/3, ISA.

599 services in the Choral Synagogue: Chaim Leaf file, kof-541-40223, Genazim archives.

600 plot by four terrorists: Pacepa, *Red Horizons*, 94–97.

600 draw closer to the United States: Daigle, "Russians Are Going."

600 "It would seem that this hour": GM, "Let Us Meet as Equals," statement in the Knesset, July 26, 1972, GM Papers, YIVO archives.

601 "the same old tune": *JP*, July 28, 1972.

601 Historians would later pinpoint: See especially Kipnis, *1973*, chaps. 2 and 4.

601 Egypt's latest peace proposals: Summary of conversation between HAK and Ismail, A-7064/8, ISA.

601 little new: HAK, *Years of Upheaval*, 216.

601 "intransigent": HAK-Rabin conversation, Feb. 22, 1973, HAK Office Files, box 135, Rabin/Dinitz sensitive memcons, 1973, NPMP, NA.

602 "present no proposal": Meir-HAK meeting, Feb. 28, 1973, A-7064/8, ISA.

602 Historians differ: For varying explanations, see Kipnis, *1973*; Daigle, *Limits of Détente*; Vanetik and Shalom, *Nixon Administration and the Middle East Peace Process*; and Bar-Joseph, *Watchman Fell Asleep*. See also Meir-HAK meeting, Feb. 28, 1973, A-7064/8, ISA.

602 "explosion in Cairo": HAK, *Years of Upheaval*, 222.

602 "hostage to Israeli pressure": Mahmoud Riad, *Struggle for Peace in the Middle East*, 238.

602 "there must be movement": Meir-HAK meeting, Feb. 28, 1973, A-7064/8, ISA.

602 "quit pandering": HAK, *Years of Upheaval*, 212.

602 "It is simply incredible": Meir-HAK meeting, Feb. 28, 1973, A-7064/8, ISA.

603 Two draining sessions: Luncheon meeting with Deputy Secretary of State Kenneth Rush; meeting with Secretary of Defense Elliot Richardson, A-7064/8, ISA.

603 so dispirited: Yitzhak Rabin, *Memoirs*, 215.

603 "things like this": GM meeting with Richard Nixon at the White House, March 1, 1973, box 1026, NPMP, NSCF. Memoranda of Conversation-Presidential/HAK Jan.–March 1973, NA.

604 private telephone conversation: Aug. 15, 1972; they also took up the subject on Feb. 18, 1973, 105-953/85, IDFA. Cited by Hagai Tsoref in Haifa University lecture, "Forty Years from the Yom Kippur War," June 6, 2013.

604 National Press Club: *JP*, March 1, 1971.

604 poached red snapper: *NYT*, March 22, 1973.

604 "We are not alone": "Exchange of Toasts Between the President and Golda Meir," State Dining Room, March 1, 1973, IBA.

604 another assassination attempt: See *Haaretz*, Feb. 20, 2009.

605 "resumption of the battle": *Newsweek*, April 23, 1973.

605 At a pivotal meeting: Minutes in Bartov, *Dado* (Hebrew), 257–62.

605 "no peace no war": A term Sadat repeated often. See *Yediot Aharonot*, Sept. 27, 1973.

605 they were *that* sure: Uri Bar-Joseph, *The Watchman Fell Asleep*, preface to revised Hebrew ed., 15.

606 perfectly matched pearls: Rinna Samuel, interview with author, Jan. 8, 2006.

606 excerpts from her speeches: *JP*, May 3, 1973.

606 The economy was booming: *Time*, April 30, 1973.

607 "step by step": HAK, *Years of Upheaval*, 226–27.

607 According to Egyptian sources: El-Gamasy, *October War*, 176.

607 "In Israel we know": Michael Peled to Yohanan Marcoz, May 6, 1973, describes the conversation between GM and the German ambassador, von Puttkamer. It also mentions that the ambassador conveyed Brandt's birthday wishes to Golda. CHZ-66808/4, ISA.

608 "that he is convinced": "Points from the Prime Minister–Brandt Conversation, June 9, 1973," A-370/5, ISA.

608 On the way to the airport: "Brandt's Visit—Various Points," A-370/5, ISA.

608 Brandt wrote to Golda: Brandt to GM, June 28, 1973, A-7036/2, ISA.

608 "talks about talks": Elishev Ben-Horin to Mordechai Gazit, July 3, 1973, A-4239/15, ISA.

608 Germany's relations: For further details of Brandt's visit to Israel, see "Publication Commemorating the Fortieth Anniversary of the Historic Visit to Israel of Chancellor Willy Brandt of West Germany, June 9, 2013," ISA.

608 three basic reasons: *Time*, Feb. 12, 1973, 16.

608 only God and Nixon: Ibid.

608 "We knew we couldn't": Herlitz, interview with author, May 10, 2005; Eshel, interview with author.

609 "I would rather": Herlitz, interview with author; Eshel, interview with author.

609 "I must get out": *NYT*, July 4, 1973.

609 "Quiet reigns": Terence Smith, "The First Israeli Revolution," *NYT*, Dec. 30, 1973.

28. "I Will Never Again Be the Person I Was"

610 turned ashen: Eitan Haber, *Today War Will Break Out*, 16.

610 He suggested she discuss: Bar-Joseph, *Watchman Fell Asleep*, 89.

610 not a routine meeting: The meeting place is described in Rabinovich, *Yom Kippur War*, 47–50.

611 "very, very sensitive": Bregman and El-Tahri, *Fifty Years' War*, 118–19.

611 "Is it conceivable": Ibid.

611 "I think they are cooperating": In a later book, Bregman, who claims to have received a transcript of the conversation, has the king's answer as "I think they would cooperate." Bregman, *History of Israel*, 149.

611 constitute an actual warning: Lieutenant Colonel Zusia Kaniazher, head of the Jordanian desk of Israel's military intelligence and one of the people monitoring Hussein's words in the next room, believed they meant war. He conveyed that message to commanders in the field and was reprimanded. See Bar-Joseph, *Watchman Fell Asleep*, 90–92.

611   The king later denied: Shlaim, *Lion of Jordan*, 368.

611   no explicit war plans: Mordechai Gazit analyzed in detail the king's visit, which he attended, in an unpublished paper he kindly made available to the author: "The Yom Kippur War: A Critical Look at Commonly Accepted Assumptions."

611   Kadar thought the king looked tense: Gail Gavra, in *Yediot Aharonot*, Oct. 8, 2000, describes Kadar's astonishment at Golda's calm response to Hussein's news.

612   "We'll have a hundred tanks": Rabinovich, *Yom Kippur War*, 52–53.

612   "Any blow from their side": *Maariv*, Sept. 30, 1973.

612   Sheyna's grave: Medzini, *Golda*, 539.

612   Golda had tried to get Richard Nixon: GM to Nixon, Aug. 31, 1972, "Presidential Correspondence," box 756, Israel, Golda Meir, 1972, NSCF.

612   "Congressmen say the linking": Memcon-Presidential/HAK Jan.–March 1973, box 1026, NPMP, NSCF, NA. See also Yitzhak Rabin, *Memoirs*, 231.

613   "To give in": *NYT*, Oct. 2, 1973.

613   "He didn't even offer": Haber, *Today War Will Break Out*, 20.

613   "two different worlds": *NYT*, Oct. 6, 1973.

613   "I would not be able": Tom Segev, "Between Two Worlds," *Haaretz*, Sept. 22, 2006.

613   "glassy-eyed, pasty-faced": Levin to *Time* world bureau, Oct. 3, 1973, Schönau, Kreisky, MLA.

614   Ismail Fahmi: Segev, "Between Two Worlds."

614   "hostile intent": *JP*, Oct. 3, 1973.

614   Galili had called her: Braun, *Moshe Dayan and the Yom Kippur War* (Hebrew), 51.

614   Neither of them knew: Yisrael Lior morning testimony, Agranat Commission, Dec. 6, 1973, 78.

614   Wednesday morning: For details of the meeting of Oct. 3, see Bar-Joseph, *Watchman Fell Asleep*, 119–31.

615   "Thank you for calming me": Braun, *Moshe Dayan and the Yom Kippur War*, 54.

615   a government meeting: Nakdimon, *Low Probability* (Hebrew), 75.

615   "And maybe we can": Ibid., 72.

615   disagreed with the opinion: Bar-Joseph, *Watchman Fell Asleep*, 130.

615   When unsure of herself: Zamir morning testimony, Agranat Commission, Dec. 11, 1973, 92.

616   nobody knew: Uri Bar-Joseph, "The 'Special Means of Collection': The Missing Link in the Surprise of the Yom Kippur War," *Middle East Journal* 64, no. 4 (Autumn 2013): 531–46.

616   basketball stadium: Nakdimon, *Low Probability*, 77.

616   "serious and problematic": Bar-Joseph, *Watchman Fell Asleep*, 146.

616   about eight hundred pieces: Rabinovich, *Yom Kippur War*, 73.

616   "From the numbers": Braun, *Moshe Dayan and the Yom Kippur War*, 57.

617   "What's your opinion": Lior morning testimony, Agranat Commission, Dec. 6, 1973, 82.

617   "wrongdoing": GM morning testimony, Agranat Commission, Feb. 6, 1974, 40.

617   he phoned Zeira: Zamir morning testimony, Agranat Commission, Dec. 11, 1973, 86.

617   She had learned: GM morning testimony, Agranat Commission, Feb. 6, 1974, 35.

618   "Don't worry": GM, *My Life*, 423.

618   an emergency meeting: Bar-Joseph, *Watchman Fell Asleep*, 157–63.

618   her face taut: Haber, *Today War Will Break Out*, 22.

619   "totally baseless": Scowcroft to HAK, Oct. 5, 1973, HAK Office Files, box 136, June 4, 1973–Oct. 31, 1973, NPMP, NA.

619   Kissinger did not deliver: HAK, *Years of Upheaval*, 465.

619   condolence visit: Medzini, *Golda*, 544.

619 "Today war will break out": Haber, *Today War Will Break Out*, 13.

619 "You won't get through": Zamir morning testimony, Agranat Commission, Nov. 29, 1973, 82.

620 "I knew it would happen": Haber, *Today War Will Break Out*, 13.

620 "O my prophetic": William Shakespeare, *Hamlet*, act 1, scene 5.

620 persuaded by the military: Meir morning testimony, Agranat Commission, Feb. 6, 1974, 61.

620 relied on her intuition: Amir Lam, "In Golda's Shoes," *Yediot Aharonot*, Dec. 5, 2008.

620 "I will never again": GM, television interview with Zvi Gil, April 24, 1974, Film Archive, Channel 1, 13010/94. And many other times.

620 "I'm getting dressed": Haber, *Today War Will Break Out*, 13.

620 "If you agree": Minutes of consultation convened at 8:05 a.m., Oct. 6, 1973, in "Yom Kippur War, Special Publication [in Hebrew], Consultations in the Prime Minister's Bureau, 6–9 October 1973," ISA. Summaries of the consultations are given in English.

621 "We may be in trouble": Box 1173, 1973 War (Middle East), Oct. 6, 1973, File No. 1, NPMP, NSCF, NA.

621 "although it would make things": Keating to HAK and embassy in Washington, telegram, VL 762/A, ISA.

621 "whatever happens": Memcon, Dinitz and HAK, Oct. 7, 1973, Department of State Records, Records of HAK, 1973–1977, box 25, Cat C 1974 Arab-Israeli War, RG 59, NA.

621 "a precipitous move": HAK, *Crisis*, 16.

621 "very serious": Ibid., 18.

622 prayer shawls still draped: Haber, *Today War Will Break Out*, 30.

622 shocked and irate: Shlomo Hillel, interview with author.

622 "What is this?": Nakdimon, *Low Probability*, 130.

622 "So they did surprise us": Cabinet meeting, 12:00 p.m., Oct. 6, 1973, "Outbreak of Yom Kippur War," ISA.

622 false stories in the Egyptian newspaper: Heikal, *Road to Ramadan*, 32–33.

623 "Sadat needed": Jehan Sadat, interview in *Yediot Aharonot*, June 11, 1987.

623 "At two o'clock": Address to nation, Oct. 6, 1973, A-7045/10, ISA.

623 "I, the great military expert": GM, interview with Dov Goldstein, *Maariv*, Sept. 16, 1974.

624 "We can't play hide and seek": War cabinet consultation, 9:10 a.m., Oct. 7, 1973, "Yom Kippur War, Consultations," ISA.

624 "You know the reasons": HAK Memcon, Oct. 7, 1973, Department of State Subject-Numeric Files, 1970-73, box 2062, Po. 27, Arab-Isr., RG 59, NA. Also quoted in HAK, *Years of Upheaval*, 477.

625 testify after the war: GM morning testimony, Agranat Commission, Feb. 6, 1974, 95.

625 "The canal line is lost": War cabinet consultation, 2:50 p.m., Oct. 7, 1973, "Yom Kippur War, Consultations," ISA.

625 "The Third Commonwealth": Bar-On, *Moshe Dayan*, 171.

625 "There is no reason": War cabinet consultation, 2:50 p.m., Oct. 7, 1973, "Yom Kippur War, Consultations," ISA.

626 "Jews in general": Quoted in Hagai Tsoref, "Golda Meir in the Yom Kippur War," lecture on launching the ISA memorial volume on GM, Dec. 22, 2016.

626 "green": Kadar, interview with Joseph Shavit, *Yediot Aharonot*, Nov. 19, 1980.

626 "on the second day": Shalev, interview with author, Jan. 16, 2007.

626 to Yaakov Hazan: Nakdimon, *Low Probability*, 143.

626 "a pill or something": Kadar, interview with author.

627 severest critics: See, for example, Meir Pail, in Barzilai, "Golda Meir's Nightmare."

627 offered to resign: GM, *My Life*, 429.

627 "The great Moshe Dayan": Herzog, *War of Atonement*, 118.

627 "Make them worry": Consultation with COGS Elazar, 9:50 a.m., Oct. 8, 1973, "Yom Kippur War, Consultations," ISA.

627 "Only this morning": War cabinet consultation, 7:50 p.m., Oct. 8, 1973, "Yom Kippur War, Consultations," ISA.

628 "I could not imagine": Dayan, *Story of My Life*, 606.

628 "crazy idea": War cabinet consultation, 7:30 a.m., Oct. 9, 1973, "Yom Kippur War, Consultations," ISA.

628 "I don't care": GM, *My Life*, 430.

629 speculation: See Hersh, *Samson Option*, 225–30; William Gibson, *Golda's Balcony* (New York: Applause Theatre & Cinema Books, 2003). The play is based on Hersh's book.

629 "Nonsense": HAK, interview with author.

629 "unconventional weapons": *Yediot Aharonot*, July 12, 2013.

629 firmly turned down: See Amir Oren in *Haaretz*, Oct. 3, 2013.

629 minor actions: Elbridge Colby et al., *The Israeli "Nuclear Alert" of 1973: Deterrence and Signaling in Crisis* (Center for Naval Analysis, 2013), 34.

629 "As far as I know": Schlesinger, interview with author, May 23, 2006.

630 *varenye:* Shavit, *My Promised Land*, 193.

630 "Like John F. Kennedy": Avner Cohen, "The Last Nuclear Moment," *NYT*, Oct. 6, 2003.

630 "straight": War cabinet consultation, 7:30 a.m., Oct. 9, 1973, "Yom Kippur War, Consultations," ISA.

630 "the war is now": *Haaretz*, Feb. 15, 1974.

630 "earthquake": Nakdimon, *Low Probability*, 156.

630 "situations can turn": GM, interview with Goldstein, Sept. 16, 1974.

631 "we will have": GM to Nixon, Oct. 22, 1973, A-7249/8, ISA.

631 Machiavellian Kissinger: Edward Luttwak and Walter Laqueur, "Kissinger and the Yom Kippur War," *Commentary*, Sept. 1974, 33–49. See also Matti Golan, *Secret Conversations of Henry Kissinger*.

631 "if Israel came out": Gil Troy, "Happy Birthday, Mr. Kissinger," *Tablet*, May 23, 2013.

631 "looks promising": Memcon, Dinitz and HAK, Oct. 9, 1973, 8:20 a.m., Department of State Records of HAK, 1973–1977, box 25, Cat C 1974 Arab-Israel War, RG 59, NA.

631 double message: David Tal, "A Tested Alliance: The American Airlift to Israel in the 1973 Yom Kippur War," *Israel Studies* 19, no. 3 (Fall 2014): 29–54.

631 "We can't allow": WSAG Principals, box 92, WSAG Meeting ME, 10/17/73 (FOLDER 6), H files, NPMP, NSCF, NA.

632 "Whichever way": Nixon, *Memoirs*, 927.

632 "Goddamn it": Ibid.

632 "always be proud": Nixon to GM, Sept. 28, 1976, GMMA Archive.

632 more than three hundred times: Oren, *Power, Faith, and Fantasy*, 334.

633 Golda chose: The debate is described in Rabinovich, *Yom Kippur War*, 303–4.

634 turning point in the war had arrived: Bergman and Meltzer, *Yom Kippur War* (Hebrew), 173–74.

634 "Good": Golan, *Yom Kippur War* (Hebrew), 792.

634 "one of the largest tank battles": Herzog, *War of Atonement*, 205.

634 "Golda, it will be all right": GM, *My Life*, 432.

634 immediate cease-fire: She later denied that she had sought a cease-fire at that time. See Amir Oren, "New Lessons from 1973 . . . ," *Haaretz*, Sept. 13, 2013.

635 "nothing": HAK Memcon, Oct. 22, 1973, Department of State, SN 70-73, box 17, POL 7 US/HAK, RG 59, NA.

635 ostensibly to compensate: HAK, *Years of Upheaval*, 569.

635 "You won't get violent protests": HAK Memcon, Oct. 22, 1973, Department of State, SN 70-73, box 17, POL 7 US/HAK, RG 59, NA.

635 "from a position of strength": *KR*, Oct. 23, 1973.

636 "Russian and Egyptian ultimatums": HAK, *Years of Upheaval*, 573.

636 "drastically": Brezhnev's letter is in box 69, Dobrynin/HAK vol. 20 (Oct. 12–Nov. 27, 1973), NPMP, HAK Office Files, NA.

637 "You will lose everything": HAK, *Crisis*, 387.

637 "I have no illusions": Ibid., 398.

637 4:07 a.m.: Ibid., 400.

637 They saluted each other: El-Gamasy, *October War*, 321.

638 "to enjoy his defeat": GM, interview with *Face the Nation*, Oct. 28, 1973, G-6467/9, ISA.

29. An "Irrevocable" Decision

639 "How many times": Bergman and Meltzer, *Yom Kippur War*, 361.

639 "I can understand that": Ibid., 367.

640 "frivolous": Levin to *Time* world bureau, Oct. 25, 1973, MLA.

640 "failings in protecting": The Shapira episode is in *JP*, Oct. 26, 1973.

641 "an outstanding organizer": Briefing paper, Feb. 1973, Department of State Records, Records of HAK, 1973–1977, box 2, NODIS Action Memos, 1973–1976, RG 59, NA.

641 "real friend": GM, *My Life*, 441.

641 "To find out": *NYT*, Nov. 2, 1973.

642 "Nobody in the Arab world": HAK Memcon, Nov. 2, 1973, Department of State Records, Records of HAK, 1973–1977, box 1, Misc. Docs, Tabs, 1973–77, RG 59, NA.

642 "I told the troops": GM meeting with Nixon, Nov. 1, 1973, Department of State Records, Records of HAK, 1973–1977, box 2, NODIS Action Memos, 1973–1976, RG 59, NA.

642 "devastated": HAK, *Years of Upheaval*, 619.

642 "drained": Ibid., 620.

642 "You have to do this": GM meeting with HAK, Nov. 1, 1973, 8:10–10:25 a.m., Department of State Records, Records of HAK, 1973–1977, box 2, NODIS Action Memos 1973–1976, RG 59, NA.

643 "We can't allow convoys": GM meeting with HAK, Nov. 2, 1973, 10:00 p.m.–12:45 a.m., Department of State Subject-Numeric Files, 1970–1973, PL ISR-US, RG 59, NA.

643 "This is the lousiest": GM meeting with HAK, Nov. 1, 1973, 8:10–10:25 a.m.

643 "Madame Prime Minister": GM meeting with HAK, Nov. 3, 1973, Department of State Records, Records of HAK, 1973–1977, box 3, NODIS Action Memos, 1973–1976, RG 59, NA.

643 "remarkable man": HAK, *Years of Upheaval*, 638.

643 something in it for everyone: Ibid., 642.

644 "with the thoroughness": Ibid.

644 Georges Pompidou: *NYT*, Dec. 28, 1972.

644 stunned silence: *JP*, Nov. 12, 1973.

644 "We are all old comrades": GM, *My Life*, 446.

644 "What did you think": Wiesel, *And the Sea Is Never Full*, 55.

645 Harold Wilson: Yoram Peri, interview with author.

645 "guaranteed method": PREM 15/1715, BNA.

645 "Had not the British government": GM meeting with Heath, Nov. 12, 1973, PREM 15/1715, BNA.

645 freed Egyptians: *NYT*, Nov. 16, 1973.

646 "criminal negligence": *NYT*, Nov. 14, 1973.

646 "chop off": Tom Segev, *Haaretz*, Jan. 7, 2011.

646 "If we were": Nakdimon, *Low Probability*, 257.

647 Labor Party magazine: *NYT*, Nov. 26, 1973.

647 "what kind of a party": Ibid.

647 fourteen-point program: See Don Peretz, "The War Election and Israel's Eighth Knesset," *Middle East Journal* 28, no. 2 (Spring 1974): 111–25.

648 "I confess": Central committee minutes, Dec. 5, 1973, B-223-1973-108, LPA.

648 "Mrs. Meir bestrides": Smith, "First Israeli Revolution."

648 "With all his faults": GM, interview at the kibbutz Revivim (Hebrew), Aug. 7, 1977, Interviews, BGA.

648 "chosen one": *NYT*, Dec. 2, 1973.

649 "the first time Israeli soldiers": *JP*, Dec. 2, 1973.

649 met with Assad: HAK dinner meeting with GM and other Israelis, Dec. 16, 1973, Department of State Records, Records of HAK, 1973–1977, box 2, NODIS Action Memos 1973–1976, RG 59, NA.

650 "It is a unilateral step": Meeting of GM and HAK with delegations, Dec. 17, 1973, A-7025-20, ISA.

650 outburst from Menachem Begin: *JP*, Dec. 21, 1973.

650 not shake hands: Abba Eban, *Personal Witness*, 549.

651 40 percent of voters: *Time*, Jan. 7, 1974.

651 ads that saturated newspapers: They appear in *JP*, Dec. 23 and 27, 1973.

651 over 80 percent: *JP*, Jan. 1, 1974.

652 narrow the gap: For a good description of HAK's rounds, see Kalb and Kalb, *Kissinger*, 529–42.

652 "You must take my word": Sadat to GM, Jan. 16, 1974, A-7063/7, ISA.

652 "I am deeply conscious": GM to Sadat, Jan. 18, 1974, A-7063/7, ISA.

653 "this is still not peace": Labor Party bureau minutes, Feb. 21, 1974.

653 "I sincerely and honestly": HAK, *Years of Upheaval*, 841.

653 "Miss Israel": Isaacson, *Kissinger*, 553.

653 "That's okay, Henry": A version of this anecdote appears in HAK, *Years of Renewal*, 375.

653 "pursuing a path": *JP*, Jan. 21, 1974.

653 "trump card": Ibid.

654 DAYAN—RESIGN!: Bar-On, *Moshe Dayan*, 185.

654 Motti Ashkenazi: See *Time*, March 4, 1974. The texts of the signs Ashkenazi held are given in Motti Ashkenazi, Nurit Ashkenazi, and Baruch Nevo, *War Will Break Out This Evening at Six* (Hebrew) (Tel Aviv: Hakibbutz Hameuhad, 2003), 151.

654 "If I live to be 150": Labor Party bureau minutes, Feb. 21. 1974.

655 "directly responsible": *Haaretz*, Nov. 28, 1973.

655 activists held a rally: *JP*, Jan. 13, 1974.

655 Even in the army: Dayan, *Story of My Life*, 737.

655 "government of paralysis": *NYT*, Feb. 20, 1974.

655 "I have asked him": *JP*, Feb. 21, 1974.

655 "You have no right": Matti Golan, *Road to Peace*, 114.

655   "Had I resigned": *JP*, March 4, 1974.

655   "Golda, come back": *Time*, March 18, 1974.

655   "Like a silent Buddha": Levin to *Time* world bureau, March 7, 1974, Meir, MLA.

656   "If I were an Arab": *Time*, March 18, 1974.

656   "not make any difficulties": Sadat to GM, Jan. 1974, A-7069/7, ISA.

656   "at any moment": GM to Sadat, Jan. 1974, A-7069/7, ISA.

656   "chutzpah of the nth degree": HAK, *Years of Upheaval*, 1054.

657   "the list of surviving": Golda and Dado's reactions in ibid., 961–62.

657   inseparable part of Israel: *JP*, Feb. 10, 1974.

657   she wished the Mossad's chief: GM morning testimony, Agranat Commission, Feb. 6, 1974, 36, IDFA.

657   head of military intelligence: Ibid., 107.

657   blamed herself: GM afternoon testimony, Agranat Commission, Feb. 6, 1974, 57, IDFA.

657   "I don't speak enough Hebrew": Ibid.; see also *Israel Hayom*, Oct. 8, 2013.

658   "interim report": *Report of the Commission of Inquiry, Yom Kippur War* (Hebrew) (Tel Aviv: Am Oved, 1975). See also Lahav, *Judgment in Jerusalem*, 227–43.

658   "injustice": *JP*, April 3, 1974.

658   "a great and glorious commander": *NYT*, April 3, 1974.

658   "Dado saved the people": Barzilai, "Golda Meir's Nightmare"; and Shalev, interview with author.

659   "real issue": *JP*, April 4, 1974.

659   "eccentric": Abba Eban, *Personal Witness*, 564.

659   "You realize that it won't end": *Time*, April 22, 1974.

659   "Five years are enough": GM's resignation speech to party leaders, Labor Party bureau minutes, April 10, 1974, 2-2S-1974-58, LPA.

659   "was the only one left": Kadar to Syrkin, May 7, 1974, Marcus Center, AJA, HUC-JIR.

660   "Perhaps there was no other": *JP*, April 11, 1974.

660   "murder for murder's sake": GM's resignation speech and debate afterward in *KR*, April 11, 1974.

661   Years later, he still spoke proudly: Peres, interview with author.

30. "My Only Fear Is to Live Too Long"

662   Given a choice: Greenberg, *Pinchas Sapir*, 353.

662   Rabin felt obliged: Yitzhak Rabin, *Memoirs*, 240–41.

663   Golda demanded that a vote: *JP*, May 12, 1974.

663   "the lioness rallied": HAK, *Years of Upheaval*, 1044.

663   "very brutal talk": Memcon, Moshe Dayan, Simcha Dinitz, HAK, et al., March 29, 1974, HAK Memcons, doc. 15, NSA.

663   "some slice of the Golan Heights": Ibid.

664   "Sure. The young people": Memcon, GM, HAK, et al., May 29, 1974, FRUS, *Arab-Israeli Dispute, 1974–1976*, doc. 78, 26:360.

664   "Be-gin": *JP*, May 8, 1974.

664   "Jewboy": *JP*, May 14, 1974.

664   Kissinger was shocked: GM, interview with Goldstein, Sept. 16, 1974.

664   "Don't give a prize": Intellectuals to GM, May 6, 1974, ISA.

664   "And Israel is here to stay": Memcon, HAK, GM, et al., May 5, 1974, A-7038/5, 672 ISA.

665   "because they could not": Ibid.

665   "Is it a crime": Memcon, HAK, GM, et al., May 12, 1974, A-7038/5, ISA.

665 "understood what could happen": Memcon, HAK, GM, et al., May 5, 1974, A-7038/5, ISA.

665 "I am wandering around": Isaacson, *Kissinger*, 570.

665 "the people with the signs": Memcon, HAK, Meir, et al., May 13, 1974, A-7038/5, ISA.

665 On the seventeenth day: HAK, *Years of Upheaval*, 1076.

666 "one doesn't conduct wars": *NYT*, May 16, 1974.

666 "bitter": Ibid.

666 "wolves in human form": *JP*, May 21, 1974.

666 his wife, Nancy: HAK married Nancy Maginnes on March 30, 1974, and she accompanied him on part of his Syrian shuttle diplomacy. HAK, *Years of Upheaval*, 1032.

666 That gesture meant more to him: Ibid., 1076.

667 one more effort: Ibid., 1084.

667 Based on the U.S. plan: May 31, 1974, FRUS, *Arab-Israeli Dispute, 1974–1976*, doc. 88, 26:369–70.

667 private memorandum: May 30, 1974. Records of Joseph Sisco, box 32, Briefing Book: Syria-Israeli Disengagement Documents, Undersecretary Sisco, RG 59, NA.

667 "joy and a pleasure": *JP*, May 30, 1974.

667 "towering over everybody": HAK, *Years of Upheaval*, 1081.

667 "Oh, Dr. Kissinger": *JP*, May 30, 1974.

667 "I am happy": *KR*, May 30, 1974.

668 "It was one": Haber, interview with author, Jan. 9, 2007.

668 Somebody made a place: *Davar*, Sept. 13, 1974.

668 "How do you feel?": HAK to GM, June 3, 1974, in Lester, *Henry A. Kissinger Telephone Conversations on World Affairs*.

668 "I'm not going to enter": *JP*, June 2, 1974.

668 "a good, simple set": GM to Rebecca Shulman, Aug. 7, 1974, box 4, folder 6, GMLA.

669 "terribly sad": Wilson to GM, June 2, 1974, PREM 16/174, BNA. Ordinarily, the press would have made the telegram public when it was sent.

669 "My only fear": Fallaci, *Interview with History*, 122.

669 "hundreds and hundreds": GM, interview with Goldstein, Sept. 16, 1974.

669 Man of the Year: *Maariv*, Jan. 23, 1975.

669 Israel Prize: Received in 1975.

670 "none had greater courage": Nixon, *Memoirs*, 1016.

670 "I am writing to tell you": GM to Nixon, Aug. 13, 1974, box 4, folder 6, GMLA.

670 "some very generous comments": Nixon to GM, Sept. 10, 1975, GMMA Archive.

670 "What have I got to write about?": MS minutes, Feb. 1, 1961.

670 "When we began": Samuel, interview with author.

670 The British publishing house: *JP*, Feb. 20, 1974.

671 contacted Golda's old friend: Kessner, *Marie Syrkin*, 438.

671 "will never tell the truth": Kadar to Syrkin, Sept. 20, 1975, Marcus Center, AJA, HUC-JIR.

671 "stubborn censor": Samuel, interview with author.

671 "I could write another book": Menahem Meir, interview with author, Aug. 23, 2004.

671 "It speaks much": Memcon, GM, Ford, HAK, et al., Dec. 18, 1974, Gerald R. Ford Digital Library.

672 "a close and almost touching": Memcon, GM, Ford, HAK, et al., Dec. 18, 1974.

672 "we all admire": *JP*, Dec. 20, 1974.

672 "exaggerated": The two days at Princeton, in *NYT*, Dec. 12, 1974.

672 Israel Bonds black-tie tribute dinner: Held on Dec. 22, 1974.

673 four "shadows": *Maariv*, Aug. 5, 1974.

673 Golda and Sapir prevented: *Maariv*, Aug. 26, 1974.

673 consulted her regularly: Yitzhak Rabin interview with Geraldine Stern, tape 19, collection 21, GMLA.

673 Golda Meir never fought openly: HAK, *Years of Renewal*, 380.

673 "100 percent": *Davar*, March 24, 1975.

673 Privately, she fumed: Levin to *Time* world bureau, July 21, 1975, Meir, MLA.

674 excruciating negotiations: The ins and outs of those negotiations and the final agreement can be followed in detail on the ISA blog "Turning Point to Peace: The First Rabin Government and the Sinai II Agreement," pts. 1 and 2.

674 her first such meeting: *Davar*, Sept. 3, 1975.

674 "sharp words": Memcon, GM, Ford, HAK, et al., Dec. 19, 1975, Ford Digital Library.

674 Raphael Soyer: *Davar*, Dec. 21, 1975.

674 Sam Rothberg's sixty-fifth birthday: Kadar to Syrkin, Sept. 7, 1975, Marcus Center, AJA, HUC-JIR.

674 "wash from his hands": GM address to UJA study conference, Oct. 14, 1974.

674 "I have a feeling": GM, "Without Israel, There Is No Hope for the Jewish People," *PW*, Feb. 1976, 3, 9.

675 "appreciation and congratulations": GM to Jackson, n.d., A-171-5709 GMMA Archive.

675 "how much this cause": Jackson to GM, Oct. 30, 1974, A-171 5709 GMMA Archive.

675 "irrational": *NYT*, Feb. 19, 1976.

675 "one of the greatest": *JP*, Feb. 20, 1976.

675 "I am willing to testify": Rosenne, interview with author.

676 "They think that's all women": *JP*, March 23, 1976.

676 Philip Murray–William Green Award: *AFL-CIO Free Trade Union News*, June 1976, 1–3.

676 She also met with Jimmy Carter: *Davar*, May 28, 1976.

676 "long taught lessons": Carter describes the incident in Carter, *Palestine*, 32.

677 telephone poll: *Davar*, March 11, 1976.

677 "steering forum": *NYT*, March 10, 1976.

677 "had Golda's guts": HAK, *Years of Upheaval*, 1108.

677 "true leader": *Maariv*, Aug. 6, 1976.

677 "Nothing succeeds like success": *NYT*, July 16, 1976.

678 Golda pleaded with Peres: *Davar*, Jan. 9, 1977.

678 "A *pisheke*": Meron Medzini, interview with author, Aug. 22, 2004.

678 "Ladies and Gentlemen": Shapira, *Israel*, 357.

679 "terrible blow": Kadar to Syrkin, Sept. 7, 1975, Marcus Center, AJA, HUC-JIR.

679 cursing Golda would tolerate: Zevi Dinstein, interview with author, Jan. 18, 2007.

679 On Election Day: Rafael, *Destination Peace*, 317.

679 "It's not important": *Davar*, Sept. 23, 1977.

679 "Do we look like a camp": *JP*, June 16, 1977.

679 Lionel Bart: *Davar*, Oct. 19, 1975.

680 The play closed: On Feb. 16, 1978. In 2003, Gibson staged the successful *Golda's Balcony*.

680 "to the ends of the earth": Shilon, *Menachem Begin*, 284.

680 Secretly, he and Begin: Anwar el-Sadat, *In Search of Identity*, 306.

680 arrange a meeting specifically with her: *YNet News*, Nov. 16, 2007.

680 "I don't know": *Davar*, Nov. 22, 1977.

680 "make a special effort": Jehan Sadat, *Woman of Egypt*, 377.

680 "the strongest man": Ibid., 378.
680 "For many, many years": Rabin, interview with Geraldine Stern, tape 19, collection 21, GMLA.
681 *Al-Ahram:* In *Davar,* Nov. 21, 1977.
681 "permanent peace based on justice": Sadat's speech appears in Anwar el-Sadat, *In Search of Identity,* 330–43.
681 Begin responded: See Shilon, *Menachem Begin,* 289.
681 "the privilege of being the first": Knesset speech, Nov. 21, 1977, GMMA Archive.
681 "was deeply hurt": Kadar to Syrkin, Dec. 14, 1977, Marcus Center, AJA, HUC-JIR.
682 "She won't admit": Ibid.
682 repeated that claim: *JP,* Jan. 13, 1978.
682 joined Labor Party leaders: *Davar,* Jan. 15, 1978.
682 continued to criticize: *Davar,* June 1, 1978.
682 "too early and too quickly": Ibid.
682 "We don't want a million": Labor Party center minutes, May 21, 1978, A3 GMMA Archive.
682 Sadat declared on American television: *Davar,* March 14, 1978.
682 great respect: HAK, interview with author.
682 Golda wrote a letter to his wife: Jan. 13, 1978, in Tsoref, *Golda Meir Commemorative Book* (Hebrew), 632.
683 torture to sit: *JP,* Jan. 18, 1977.
683 eightieth birthday: *Davar,* June 13, 1978. See also Menahem Meir, *My Mother,* 238.
683 last public talk: LPS minutes, Sept. 18, 1978.
683 "I don't know about": Slater, *Golda,* 270, and other places.

Endings: "I've Always Been a Realist"

684 "knees were caving in": "Peace in Israel," Herbert R. Abeles Memorial Address, Nov. 12, 1977, Forty-Sixth GA, Dallas.
684 "She was saying good-bye": Stephen Solender, interview with author, Oct. 30, 2006.
685 "Instead of calling it dependency": *Face the Nation,* Oct. 28, 1973, National Jewish Archive of Broadcasting.
685 "I have a lot of faults": TV Channel 1 archive, 3049/78. She also said more than once, "I can say honestly that never throughout my life have I planned what position I would like to have." In Merhavia files, excerpts from speeches.
685 "She is a great woman": Herzog, *Living History,* 163.
685 feminine traits: See Shapira, "Golda: Femininity and Feminism," 303–12.
686 "One can't even yell": *JP,* Dec. 22, 1978.
686 "crazy women": Fallaci, *Interview with History,* 112.
686 "to be successful": Ibid., 113.
686 president of Israel: *Observer* (London), Jan. 17, 1971.
686 "the mother of us all": Ruth Calderon, conversation with author.
686 "I have a Masada complex": Stewart Alsop first mentioned accusations that Golda had a "Masada complex" in *Newsweek,* July 12, 1971. This was her personal response to him, quoted in *Newsweek,* March 19, 1973, and repeated at other times.
687 "Intransigent": GM, *My Life,* 373.
687 "You have to forgive her": quoted in *Time,* Dec. 18, 1978.
687 "no sacrifice is too great": *PW,* Feb. 1976, 3.
688 the existence of Palestinians: See, for example, *Davar,* Jan. 15, 1976.
689 criticisms of her mounted: One of the most vocal and influential critics of the 1980s was Yossi Beilin. See his book *Price of Unity* (Hebrew) and exchange of letters with Sarah Rehabi, Dec. 8, 1987–Jan. 10, 1988, GMMA Archive.

689 key American labor leaders: GM to Murray H. Finley, Jan. 20, 1978, GMMA Archive.

689 open-heart surgery: Kadar to Syrkin, April 12, 1978, Marcus Center, AJA, HUC-JIR.

690 Clara lugged trays: Kadar to Syrkin, March 30, 1978, Marcus Center, AJA, HUC-JIR.

690 both legs swollen: Kadar to Syrkin, July 30, 1978, Marcus Center, AJA, HUC-JIR.

690 "She needed a good ear": Goldstein, interview with author.

690 "I smile": GM, interview with Goldstein, *Maariv*, Dec. 10, 1978.

690 "so thoroughly miserable": Kadar to Syrkin, Oct. 2, 1978, Marcus Center, AJA, HUC-JIR.

690 "I'll call you next week": Goldstein, interview with author.

690 Peres was kept waiting: Peres, interview with author.

691 "After a death": Levin to *Time* world bureau, April 11, 1974, MLA.

691 "I was selfish": GM address to GA, Dallas, Nov. 12, 1977.

691 "Nothing in life": Julie Nixon Eisenhower, "Golda Meir," 176, and variations in other places.

Bibliography

Author's Interviews

Jeanne Abrams . Yitzhak Agassi . Shulamit Aloni . Meir Amit . Shimshon Arad . Giselle Arazi . Michael Arnon . Shlomo Aronson . Abraham Avihai . Colette Avital . Yehuda Avner . Aharon Barnea . Mordechai Bar-On . Hanoch Bartov . Michael Bar-Zohar . Yariv Ben-Eliezer . Yehuda Ben-Meir . Ted Comet . Miriam Copilove . Yael Dayan . Joe De Rose . Yoram Dinstein . Zevi Dinstein . Suzy Eban . Amos Eiran . Arie Lova Eliav . Tamar Eshel . Myer Feldman . Jonathan Frankel . Sara Frankel . Herbert Friedman . Tuvia Friling . Mordechai Gazit . Shlomo Gazit . Ralph Goldman . Dov Goldstein . Alice Golembo . Jerry Goodman . Ruth Gruber . Eitan Haber . Efraim Halevy . David Harman . Zena Harman . Levi Yitzhak Hayerushalmi . Esther Herlitz . Arthur Hertzberg . Shlomo Hillel . Lou Kadar . Elisha Kally . Yona Kama . Shmuel Katz . Yaakov Kedmi . Zvi Kesse . Henry A. Kissinger . Aaron Klein . David Klein . Mathilde Krim . Naftali Lavi . Marlin Levin . Baruch Levy . Nechama Lifshitz . Lior Lotan . Haggai Mann . Amos Manor . Meron Medzini . Amnon Meir . Aya Meir . Daniel Meir . Gideon Meir . Menahem Meir . Ernest Michel . Shlomo Nakdimon . Ora Namir . Ovad Natan . Yitzhak Navon . Yaakov Nitzan . Moshe Olnick . Dan Patir . Shimon Peres . Yoram Peri . Itzhak Philosoph . Norman Provizer . Ben Rabinovitch . Moshe Raviv . Sarah Rehabi . Shaul Rahabi . Elhanan Reich . Judith Ronen . Meir Rosenne . Raphael Rothstein . Rinna Samuel . Yossi Sarid . Uri Savir . James R. Schlesinger . Don Schuefton . Zohar Segev . Avner Shalev . Anita Shapira . Yaakov Sharett . Kohavi Shemesh . Steven Solender . Barry Solomon . Michael Stanislawski . Yetti Stein . Alberta Szalita . Herman Tuchman . Julian Venezy . Ruth Weinberg . Dorothy Weingrod . Elie Wiesel . Gad Yaakobi . Amos Yahil . Zvi Zameret . Zvi Zamir . Nomi Zuckerman

Archives and Libraries

American Jewish Archives
American Jewish Committee Archives
Ben-Gurion Archives
Elmer Holmes Bobst Library, New York University
British National Archives
Central Zionist Archives
Hadassah Archive
Israel Bonds Archive
Israel Defense Forces Archives
Israel State Archives
Jerusalem Post Archives
Jewish Museum Milwaukee Archives

Jewish Theological Seminary Library
Kheel Center Archives, Cornell University Library
Labor Party Archives
Lavon Archive
*Marlin Levin Archive
Library of Congress
George Meany Memorial Archives
Golda Meir Library Archives
Golda Meir Memorial Association Archive
Milwaukee Public Library
Na'amat USA Archive
National Security Archive
New York Public Library
Yad Tabenkin Archives
YIVO Archives
*The Marlin Levin Archive is housed with the Meitar Collection, Tel Aviv.

Film and Broadcast Archives

IBA Film Archives, Channel 1, Jerusalem
National Jewish Archive of Broadcasting, Jewish Museum, New York
Steven Spielberg Jewish Film Archive, Jerusalem

Special Collections

Lucy Dawidowicz Papers, American Jewish Historical Society
Muriel Spark Papers, McFarlin Library, University of Tulsa

Newspapers and Periodicals in English

Commentary
Foreign Policy
Jerusalem Post
Life
Look
New Republic
Newsweek
New York Times
Palestine Post
Pioneer Woman
Saturday Evening Post
Time
U.S. News and World Report
Washington Post
Wisconsin Jewish Chronicle

Newspapers and Periodicals in Hebrew

Al Hamishmar
Davar
Haaretz

Haolam Hazeh
Hatzofeh
Maariv
Yediot Aharonot

Oral Histories

Golda Meir Library Archives, University of Wisconsin at Milwaukee: Shulamit Aloni . Yehuda Avner . Simcha Dinitz . Tamar Eshel . Regina Hamburger-Medzini . Abraham Harman . Zena Harman . Robert A. Hess . Lou Kadar . Anne Marie Lambert . Meron Medzini . Eli Mizrachi . Yitzhak Rabin . Sarah Rehabi . Zeev Sharef . Isadore Tuchman

Oral History Division, Institute for Contemporary Jewry, Hebrew University of Jerusalem: Harry Beale . Lou Boyar . Mathilda Brailov . Michael Comay . Moshe Davis. Golda Meir . Henry Montor . Sam Rothberg . Benjamin Swig

Lyndon Baines Johnson Library Oral History Collection: Abe Feinberg . Arthur B. Krim

Official Reports and Documents

Agranat Inquiry Commission on the Yom Kippur War. Reports and testimonies.
American Jewish Yearbook, 1948–1978, Volumes 49-78.
Documents on Israeli-Soviet Relations, 1941–1953. 2 vols. London: Frank Cass, 2000.
U.S. Department of State. *Foreign Relations of the United States (FRUS)* Volumes on the Middle East, 1961–1976.
U.S. Department of State. *Soviet-American Relations: The Détente Years, 1969–1972.* Forewords by Henry Kissinger and Anatoly Dobrynin.

Selected Books in English

Adler, Eliyana R. *In Her Hands: The Education of Jewish Girls in Tsarist Russia.* Detroit: Wayne State University Press, 2011.
Ajami, Fouad. *The Arab Predicament: Arab Political Thought and Practice Since 1967.* Cambridge, U.K.: Cambridge University Press, 1981.
Allen, Peter. *The Yom Kippur War: The Epic Encounter That Transformed the Middle East.* New York: Scribner's, 1982.
Almogi, Yosef. *Total Commitment.* Translated by Ted Gorelick. New York: Cornwall, 1962.
Antonius, George. *The Arab Awakening: The Story of the Arab National Movement.* Safety Harbor, Fla.: Simon Publications, 2001.
Arendt, Hannah. *Eichmann in Jerusalem: A Report on the Banality of Evil.* New York: Viking Press, 1965.
Aronson, Shlomo. *Conflict and Bargaining in the Middle East: An Israeli Perspective.* Baltimore: Johns Hopkins University Press, 1978.
———. *David Ben-Gurion and the Jewish Renaissance.* Translated by Naftali Greenwood. Cambridge, U.K.: Cambridge University Press, 2011.
———. *The Politics and Strategy of Nuclear Weapons in the Middle East: Opacity, Theory, and Reality, 1960–1991: An Israeli Perspective.* With Oded Brosh. Albany: State University of New York Press, 1992.
Ascher, Abraham. *The Revolution of 1905.* 2 vols. Redwood, Calif.: Stanford University Press, 1988.
Ashton, Nigel. *King Hussein of Jordan.* New Haven, Conn.: Yale University Press, 2008.

Associated Press. *Lightning out of Israel: The Six Day War in the Middle East*. New York: Associated Press, 1967.

Avishai, Bernard. *The Tragedy of Zionism: How Its Revolutionary Past Haunts Israeli Democracy*. New York: Helios Press, 2002.

Avner, Yehuda. *The Prime Ministers: An Intimate Narrative of Israeli Leadership*. Introduction by Martin Gilbert. New Milford, Conn.: Toby Press, 2010.

Avriel, Ehud. *Open the Gates!* London: Weidenfeld and Nicolson, 1975.

Bar-Joseph, Uri. *The Watchman Fell Asleep: The Surprise of Yom Kippur and Its Sources*. Albany: State University of New York Press, 2005.

Bar-On, Mordechai. *The Gates of Gaza: Israel's Road to Suez and Back, 1955–1957*. New York: St. Martin's Griffin, 1994.

———. *Moshe Dayan: Israel's Controversial Hero*. New Haven, Conn.: Yale University Press, 2012.

Bar-Zohar, Michael. *Ben-Gurion: The New Millennium Edition*. Translated by Peretz Kidron. Tel Aviv: Magal Books, 2003.

———. *Facing a Cruel Mirror: Israel's Moment of Truth*. New York: Scribner, 1990.

———. *Shimon Peres: The Biography*. New York: Random House, 2007.

———. *Spies in the Promised Land: Iser Harel and the Israeli Secret Service*. Translated by Monroe Stearns. Boston: Houghton Mifflin, 1972.

Bar-Zohar, Michael, and Eitan Haber. *Massacre in Munich*. Guilford, Conn.: Lyons Press, 2005.

Bascomb, Neal. *Hunting Eichmann: How a Band of Survivors and a Young Spy Agency Chased Down the World's Most Notorious Nazi*. Boston: Houghton Mifflin Harcourt, 2009.

Bass, Warren. *Support Any Friend*. New York: Oxford University Press, 2003.

Bauer, Yehuda. *Flight and Rescue: Brichah*. New York: Random House, 1970.

Beckerman, Gal. *When They Come for Us We'll Be Gone: The Epic Struggle to Save Soviet Jewry*. Boston: Houghton Mifflin Harcourt, 2002.

Begin, Menachem. *The Revolt: Story of the Irgun*. Translated by Shmuel Katz. Tel Aviv: Steimatzky Agency, 1977.

Beilin, Yossi. *Israel: A Concise Political History*. New York: St. Martin's Press, 1992.

Ben-Gurion, David. *Israel: A Personal History*. New York: Funk & Wagnalls, 1971.

———. *Memoirs*. Compiled by Thomas R. Bransten. New York: World, 1970.

Ben-Zvi, Abraham. *Decades of Transition: Eisenhower, Kennedy, and the Origins of the American-Israeli Alliance*. New York: Columbia University Press, 1998.

Ben-Zvi, Rachel Yanait. *Before Golda: Manya Shochat*. Translated by Sandra Shurin. Introduction by Marie Syrkin. New York: Biblio Press, 1989.

Bernstein, Deborah. *The Struggle for Equality: Urban Women Workers in Pre-state Israeli Society*. New York: Praeger, 1987.

———, ed. *Pioneers and Homemakers: Jewish Women in Pre-state Israel*. Albany: State University of New York Press, 1992.

Bethell, Nicholas. *The Palestine Triangle: The Struggle Between the British, the Jews, and the Arabs, 1935–48*. London: Deutsch, 1979.

Black, Ian, and Benny Morris. *Israel's Secret Wars: A History of Israel's Intelligence Services*. New York: Grove Press, 1991.

Blum, Howard. *The Eve of Destruction: The Untold Story of the Yom Kippur War*. New York: HarperCollins, 2003.

Boyne, Walter J. *The Yom Kippur War and the Airlift That Saved Israel*. New York: Thomas Dunne, 2002.

Bregman, Ahron. *A History of Israel*. Hampshire, U.K.: Palgrave Macmillan, 2003.

Bregman, Ahron, and Jihan El-Tahri. *The Fifty Years' War: Israel and the Arabs*. London: Penguin, 1998.

Brinkley, Douglas, and Luke A. Nichter, eds. *The Nixon Tapes, 1973*. New York: Houghton Mifflin Harcourt, 2015.

Brook, Kevin Alan. *The Jews of Khazaria*. Lanham, Md.: Rowman & Littlefield, 2009.

Brown, Michael. *The Israeli-American Connection: Its Roots in the* Yishuv, *1914–1945*. Detroit: Wayne State University Press, 1996.

Burkett, Elinor. *Golda*. New York: HarperCollins, 2008.

Carter, Jimmy. *Palestine: Peace Not Apartheid*. New York: Simon & Schuster, 2006.

Chetrit, Sami Shalom. *Intra-Jewish Conflict in Israel: White Jews, Black Jews*. London: Routledge, 2009.

Christman, Henry, ed. *The State Papers of Levi Eshkol*. New York: Funk & Wagnalls, 1969.

———. *This Is Our Strength: Selected Papers of Golda Meir*. New York: Macmillan, 1962.

Cohen, Avner. *Israel and the Bomb*. New York: Columbia University Press, 1998.

———. *The Worst Kept Secret: Israel's Bargain with the Bomb*. New York: Columbia University Press, 2010.

Cohen, Naomi W. *Jacob H. Schiff: A Study in American Jewish Leadership*. Waltham, Mass.: Brandeis University Press, 1999.

Crossman, Richard H. S. *A Nation Reborn*. New York: Atheneum, 1960.

———. *Palestine Mission*. London: Hamish Hamilton, 1947.

Crum, Bartley C. *Behind the Silken Curtain*. New York: Simon & Schuster, 1947.

Daigle, Craig. *The Limits of Détente: The United States, the Soviet Union, and the Arab-Israeli Conflict, 1969–1973*. New Haven, Conn.: Yale University Press, 2012.

Dallas, Roland. *King Hussein: A Life on the Edge*. New York: Fromm International, 1999.

Dallek, Robert. *Nixon and Kissinger: Partners in Power*. New York: HarperCollins, 2007.

Dawidowicz, Lucy S. *The War Against the Jews, 1933–1945*. New York: Bantam Books, 1986.

Dayan, Moshe. *Breakthrough: A Personal Account of the Egypt-Israel Peace Negotiations*. New York: Alfred A. Knopf, 1981.

———. *Diary of the Sinai Campaign*. New York: Schocken Books, 1967.

———. *Story of My Life*. New York: Warner Books, 1976.

Dayan, Yael. *My Father, His Daughter*. New York: Farrar, Straus & Giroux, 1985.

Eban, Abba. *Abba Eban: An Autobiography*. New York: Random House, 1977.

———. *Personal Witness: Israel Through My Eyes*. New York: Putnam, 1992.

Eban, Suzy. *A Sense of Purpose*. London: Halban, 2008.

Eisenhower, Dwight D. *The White House Years: Waging Peace, 1956–1961*. Garden City, N.Y.: Doubleday, 1965.

El-Gamasy, Mohamed Abdel Ghani. *The October War: Memoirs of Field Marshal El-Gamasy of Egypt*. Translated by Gillian Potter, Nadra Morcos, and Rosette Frances. Cairo: American University in Cairo Press, 1993.

Eliav, Arie Lova. *Land of the Hart: Israelis, Arabs, the Territories, and a Vision for the Future*. Translated by Judith Yalon. Philadelphia: Jewish Publication Society, 1974.

Elon, Amos. *The Israelis: Founders and Sons*. New York: Holt, Rinehart and Winston, 1971.

———. *Jerusalem: City of Mirrors*. Boston: Little, Brown, 1989.

Eshed, Haggai. *Reuven Shiloah: The Man Behind the Mossad*. Translated by David and Leah Zinder. Forewords by Shimon Peres and Chaim Herzog. Portland, Ore.: Frank Cass, 1997.

Ettinger, Amos. *Blind Jump: The Story of Shaike Dan*. New York: Cornwall Books, 1992.

Fallaci, Oriana. *Interview with History*. Translated by John Shepley. Boston: Houghton Mifflin, 1977.

Ferrell, Robert H., ed. *The Eisenhower Diaries*. New York: W. W. Norton, 1981.

Frankel, Jonathan. *Prophecy and Politics: Socialism, Nationalism, and the Russian Jews, 1862–1917*. Cambridge, U.K.: Cambridge University Press, 1984.

Freundlich, Yehoshua, ed. *Political Documents of the Jewish Agency*. Jerusalem: World Zionist Organization, 1996–1998.

Friling, Tuvia. *Arrows in the Dark: David Ben-Gurion, the Yishuv Leadership, and Rescue*

Attempts During the Holocaust. 2 vols. Translated by Ora Cummings. Madison: University of Wisconsin Press, 2004.

Ganin, Zvi. *An Uneasy Relationship: American Jewish Leadership and Israel, 1948–1957.* Syracuse, N.Y.: Syracuse University Press, 2005.

Garment, Leonard. *Crazy Rhythm: From Brooklyn and Jazz to Nixon's White House, Watergate, and Beyond.* Cambridge, Mass.: Da Capo Press, 2001.

Gazit, Mordechai. *The Peace Process, 1969–1973: Efforts and Contacts.* Jerusalem: Magnes Press, 1983.

———. *President Kennedy's Policy Toward the Arab States and Israel: Analysis and Documents.* Tel Aviv: Shiloah Center, Tel Aviv University, 1983.

Gazit, Shlomo. *The Carrot and the Stick.* Washington, D.C.: B'nai B'rith Books, 1995.

———. *Trapped Fools: Thirty Years of Israeli Policy in the Territories.* Introduction by Shimon Peres. Portland, Ore.: Frank Cass, 2003.

Gilbert, Martin. *Churchill and the Jews.* New York: Holt, 2007.

———. *Exile and Return: The Struggle for a Jewish Homeland.* Philadelphia: Lippincott, 1978.

Gilboa, Yehoshua. *The Black Years of Soviet Jewry, 1939–1953.* Boston: Little, Brown, 1971.

Ginor, Isabella, and Gideon Remez. *Foxbats over Dimona: The Soviets' Nuclear Gamble in the Six-Day War.* New Haven, Conn.: Yale University Press, 2007.

Glenn, Susan A. *Daughters of the Shtetl: Life and Labor in the Immigrant Generation.* Ithaca, N.Y.: Cornell University Press, 1990.

Golan, Galia. *Soviet Politics in the Middle East: From World War II to Gorbachev.* Cambridge, U.K.: Cambridge University Press, 1990.

Golan, Matti. *The Road to Peace: A Biography of Shimon Peres.* Translated by Akiva Ron. New York: Warner Books, 1989.

———. *The Secret Conversations of Henry Kissinger: Step-by-Step Diplomacy in the Middle East.* Translated by Ruth Geyra Stern and Sol Stern. New York: Quadrangle Books, 1976.

Golani, Motti. *The End of the British Mandate for Palestine, 1948: The Diary of Sir Henry Gurney.* Hampshire, U.K.: Palgrave Macmillan, 2009.

———. *Israel in Search of a War: The Sinai Campaign, 1955–1956.* Portland, Ore.: Sussex Academic Press, 1998.

Golden, Peter. *Quiet Diplomat: A Biography of Max M. Fisher.* New York: Herzl Press, 1992.

Goldmann, Nahum. *The Autobiography of Nahum Goldmann.* Translated by Helen Sebba. New York: Holt, Rinehart and Winston, 1969.

Gordis, Daniel. *Menachem Begin: The Battle for Israel's Soul.* New York: Schocken Books, 2014.

Gorenberg, Gershom. *The Accidental Empire: Israel and the Birth of the Settlements, 1967–1977.* New York: Times Books, 2006.

Govrin, Yosef. *Israeli-Soviet Relations, 1953–1967: From Confrontation to Disruption.* London: Frank Cass, 1998.

Greenspoon, Leonard J., Ronald A. Simkins, and Brian J. Horowitz, eds. *The Jews of Eastern Europe.* Omaha: Creighton University Press, 2005.

Griffin, W. W., and Harris G. Provines. *Civics for Young Americans.* New York: Parker P. Simmons, 1905.

Gruber, Ruth. *Ahead of Time: My Early Years as a Foreign Correspondent.* New York: Carroll & Graf, 1991.

———. *Destination Palestine: The Story of the Haganah Ship* Exodus 1947. New York: Current Books, 1948.

———. *Witness.* New York: Schocken Books, 2007.

Hacohen, Devorah. *Immigrants in Turmoil: Mass Immigration to Israel and Its Repercussions in the 1950s and After*. Translated by Gila Brand. Syracuse, N.Y.: Syracuse University Press, 2003.

Halamish, Aviva. *The* Exodus *Affair*. Syracuse, N.Y.: Syracuse University Press, 1998.

Halevy, Efraim. *Man in the Shadows: Inside the Middle East Crisis with a Man Who Led the Mossad*. New York: St. Martin's Press, 2006.

Halkin, Hillel. *Jabotinsky: A Life*. New Haven, Conn.: Yale University Press, 2014.

Halperin, Samuel. *The Political World of American Zionism*. Silver Spring, Md.: Information Dynamics, 1985.

Hamm, Michael F. *Kiev: A Portrait, 1800–1917*. Princeton, N.J.: Princeton University Press, 1993.

Harel, Isser. *The House on Garibaldi Street*. New York: Bantam Books, 1976.

Harris, Mark Jonathan, and Deborah Oppenheimer, eds. *Into the Arms of Strangers*. New York: Bloomsbury, 2001.

Hazleton, Lesley. *Israeli Women: The Reality Behind the Myth*. New York: Simon & Schuster, 1977.

Hazony, Yoram. *The Jewish State: The Struggle for Israel's Soul*. New York: Basic Books, 2000.

Heikal, Mohamed. *The Road to Ramadan*. New York: Quadrangle Press, 1975.

Helman, Anat. *Young Tel Aviv: A Tale of Two Cities*. Waltham, Mass.: Brandeis University Press, 2012.

Hersh, Seymour M. *The Samson Option: Israel's Nuclear Arsenal and American Foreign Policy*. New York: Random House, 1991.

Hertzberg, Arthur. *The Zionist Idea: A Historical Analysis and Reader*. Philadelphia: Jewish Publication Society, 1997.

Herzog, Chaim. *The Arab-Israeli Wars: War and Peace in the Middle East*. New York: Random House, 1982.

———. *Living History: A Memoir*. New York: Pantheon, 1996.

———. *The War of Atonement: The Inside Story of the Yom Kippur War*. Boston: Little, Brown, 1975.

Hillel, Shlomo. *Operation Babylon: The Story of the Rescue of the Jews of Iraq*. Translated by Ina Friedman. Garden City, N.Y.: Doubleday, 1987.

Horne, Alistair. *Kissinger: 1973, the Crucial Year*. New York: Simon & Schuster, 2009.

Horowitz, Dan, and Moshe Lissak. *Origins of the Israeli Polity: Palestine Under the Mandate*. Translated by Charles Hoffman. Chicago: University of Chicago Press, 1978.

Horowitz, David. *State in the Making*. Translated by Julian Meltzer. New York: Alfred A. Knopf, 1953.

Howe, Irving, and Kenneth Libo. *How We Lived: A Documentary History of Immigrant Jews in America, 1880–1930*. New York: Richard Marek, 1979.

Hundert, Gershon David, ed. *YIVO Encyclopedia of Jews in Eastern Europe*. New Haven, Conn.: Yale University Press, 2008.

Hurwitz, Zvi Harry. *Begin: His Life, Words, and Deeds*. Jerusalem: Gefen, 2004.

Hussein, King of Jordan. *Uneasy Lies the Head: The Autobiography of His Majesty King Hussein of the Hashemite Kingdom of Jordan*. London: Heinemann, 1962.

Insight Team, Sunday Times. *The Yom Kippur War*. Rev. ed. New York: Ibooks, 2002.

Isaacson, Walter. *Kissinger: A Biography*. New York: Touchstone, 1996.

Israeli, Raphael. *Man of Defiance: A Political Biography of Anwar Sadat*. London: Weidenfeld & Nicolson, 1985.

Israelyan, Victor. *Inside the Kremlin During the Yom Kippur War*. Foreword by Alvin Z. Rubinstein. University Park: Pennsylvania State University Press, 1995.

Kalb, Marvin, and Bernard Kalb. *Kissinger*. Boston: Little, Brown, 1974.

Kark, Ruth, Margalit Shilo, and Galit Hasan-Rokem, eds. *Jewish Women in Pre-state*

Israel: Life History, Politics, and Culture. Waltham, Mass.: Brandeis University Press, 2008.

Karpin, Michael. *The Bomb in the Basement: How Israel Went Nuclear and What That Means for the World*. New York: Simon & Schuster, 2006.

Katz, Shmuel. *Lone Wolf: A Biography of Vladimir Jabotinsky*. 2 vols. New York: Barricade Books, 1996.

Katzman, Jacob. *Commitment: The Labor Zionist Life-Style in America: A Personal Memoir*. New York: Labor Zionist Letters, 1975.

Katznelson-Rubashow, Rachel, ed. *The Plough Woman: Records of the Pioneer Women of Palestine*. Rendered into English by Maurice Samuel. New York: Nicholas L. Brown, 1932.

Kessner, Carole S. *Marie Syrkin: Values Beyond the Self*. Waltham, Mass.: Brandeis University Press, 2008.

Khalidi, Rashid. *Palestinian Identity: The Construction of Modern National Consciousness*. New York: Columbia University Press, 2000.

Kieval, Gershon. *Party Politics in Israel and the Occupied Territories*. Westport, Conn.: Greenwood Press, 1983.

Kimche, David, and Dan Bawley. *The Sandstorm: The Arab-Israeli War of June 1967: Prelude and Aftermath*. New York: Stein and Day, 1968.

Kipnis, Yigal. *1973: The Road to War*. Translated by Barbara Doron. Foreword by William B. Quandt. Charlottesville, Va.: Just World Books, 2013.

Kirkbride, Sir Alec. *From the Wings: Amman Memoirs, 1947–1951*. London: Frank Cass, 1976.

Kissinger, Henry. *Crisis: The Anatomy of Two Major Foreign Policy Crises*. New York: Simon & Schuster, 2003.

———. *The White House Years*. Boston: Little, Brown, 1979.

———. *Years of Renewal*. New York: Touchstone, 1999.

———. *Years of Upheaval*. Boston: Little, Brown, 1982.

Klein, Aaron J. *Striking Back: The 1972 Munich Olympics Massacre and Israel's Deadly Response*. New York: Random House, 2005.

Kochavi, Noam. *Nixon and Israel: Forging a Conservative Partnership*. Albany: State University of New York Press, 2009.

Koestler, Arthur. *Promise and Fulfillment: Palestine, 1917–1949*. London: Macmillan, 1949.

Korn, David A. *Stalemate: The War of Attrition and Great Power Diplomacy in the Middle East*. Boulder, Colo.: Westview Press, 1992.

Kostyrchenko, Gennadi. *Out of the Red Shadows*. New York: Prometheus Books, 1995.

Kumaraswamy, P. R., ed. *Revisiting the Yom Kippur War*. Portland, Ore.: Frank Cass, 2001.

Kurzman, Dan. *Ben-Gurion, Prophet of Fire*. New York: Simon & Schuster, 1983.

Lacey, Robert. *Little Man: Meyer Lansky and the Gangster Life*. Boston: Little, Brown, 1991.

Lahav, Pnina. *Judgment in Jerusalem: Chief Justice Simon Agranat and the Zionist Century*. Berkeley: University of California Press, 1997.

Landau, David. *Arik: The Life of Ariel Sharon*. New York: Alfred A. Knopf, 2013.

Lapidoth, Ruth, and Moshe Hirsch, eds. *The Jerusalem Question and Its Resolution: Selected Documents*. Norwell, Mass.: Kluwer, 1994.

Laqueur, Walter. *Dying for Jerusalem: The Past, Present, and Future of the Holiest City*. New York: Sourcebooks, 2005.

———. *A History of Zionism*. New York: Schocken Books, 1972.

Laqueur, Walter, and Barry Rubin, eds. *The Israeli-Arab Reader: A Documentary History of the Middle East Conflict*. New York: Penguin Books, 2001.

Lash, Joseph P. *Dag Hammarskjold, Custodian of the Brushfire Peace*. Garden City, N.Y.: Doubleday, 1961.

———. *Eleanor: The Years Alone*. New York: Norton, 1972.

Lester, Robert E. *The Henry A. Kissinger Telephone Conversations on World Affairs, 1969–1974*. Bethesda, Md.: Lexis Nexis, 2006.

Levin, Marlin. *It Takes a Dream: The Story of Hadassah*. Abridged by Esther Kustanowitz. Foreword by Elie Wiesel. Jerusalem: Gefen, 2002.

Lifton, Robert K. *An Entrepreneur's Journey: Stories from a Life in Business and Personal Diplomacy*. Bloomington, Ind.: Author House, 2012.

Lipstadt, Deborah E. *The Eichmann Trial*. New York: Nextbook/Schocken, 2011.

Litvak, Olga. *Conscription and the Search for Modern Russian Jewry*. Bloomington: Indiana University Press, 2006.

Lloyd, Selwyn. *Suez 1956: A Personal Account*. New York: Mayflower Books, 1978.

Lossin, Yigal. *Pillar of Fire: The Rebirth of Israel—a Visual History*. Translated by Zvi Ofer. Jerusalem: Shikmona, 1983.

Lukacs, Yehuda. *Documents on the Israeli-Palestinian Conflict, 1967–1983*. Cambridge, U.K.: Cambridge University Press, 1984.

Maimon, Ada. *Women Build a Land*. Translated by Shulamith Schwarz-Nardi. New York: Herzl Press, 1967.

Makovsky, Michael. *Churchill's Promised Land: Zionism and Statecraft*. New Haven, Conn.: Yale University Press, 2007.

Mann, Barbara E. *A Place in History: Modernism, Tel Aviv, and the Creation of Jewish Urban Space*. Stanford, Calif.: Stanford University Press, 2006.

Martin, Ralph G. *Golda: Golda Meir, the Romantic Years*. New York: Scribner, 1988.

McCullough, David. *Truman*. New York: Simon & Schuster, 1992.

Meacham, Jon. *Franklin and Winston: An Intimate Portrait of an Epic Friendship*. New York: Random House, 2003.

Medding, Peter. *Mapai in Israel: Political Organisation and Government in a New Society*. Cambridge, U.K.: Cambridge University Press, 1972.

Medzini, Meron, ed. *Israel's Foreign Relations: Selected Documents, 1947–1974*. Jerusalem: Ministry of Foreign Affairs, 1977.

Meir, Golda. *A Land of Our Own: An Oral Autobiography*. Edited by Marie Syrkin. New York: Putnam, 1973.

———. *My Life*. New York: Putnam, 1975.

Meir, Menahem. *My Mother Golda Meir: A Son's Evocation of Life with Golda Meir*. New York: Arbor House, 1983.

Meir, Natan M. *Kiev, Jewish Metropolis: A History, 1859–1914*. Bloomington: Indiana University Press, 2010.

Melman, Yossi, and Dan Raviv. *Behind the Uprising: Israelis, Jordanians, and Palestinians*. New York: Greenwood Press, 1989.

Morris, Benny. *The Birth of the Palestinian Refugee Problem, 1947–1949*. Cambridge, U.K.: Cambridge University Press, 1987.

———. *The Birth of the Palestinian Refugee Problem Revisited*. Cambridge, U.K.: Cambridge University Press, 2004.

———. *Israel's Border Wars, 1949–1956: Arab Infiltration, Israeli Retaliation, and the Countdown to the Suez War*. Oxford: Clarendon Press, 1997.

———. *1948: A History of the First Arab-Israeli War*. New Haven, Conn.: Yale University Press, 2008.

———. *Righteous Victims: A History of the Zionist-Arab Conflict, 1881–2001*. New York: Alfred A. Knopf, 1999.

Naveh, Hannah, ed. *Gender and Israeli Society: Women's Time*. London: Vallentine Mitchell, 2003.

Neumann, Emanuel. *In the Arena: An Autobiographical Memoir*. New York: Herzl Press, 1976.

Nichols, David A. *Eisenhower 1956: The President's Year of Crisis: Suez and the Brink of War*. New York: Simon & Schuster, 2012.

Nixon, Richard. *The Memoirs of Richard Nixon*. New York: Grosset & Dunlap, 1978.

O'Connell, Jack. *King's Counsel: A Memoir of War, Espionage, and Diplomacy in the Middle East*. With Vernon Loeb. New York: Norton, 2011.

Oren, Michael. *Power, Faith, and Fantasy: America in the Middle East, 1776 to the Present*. New York: W.W. Norton, 2007.

———. *Six Days of War: June 1967 and the Making of the Modern Middle East*. New York: Ballantine, 2002.

Ostrovsky, Victor. *By Way of Deception: The Making of a Mossad Officer*. With Claire Hoy. Scottsdale, Ariz.: Wilshire Press, 1990.

Oz, Amos. *A Tale of Love and Darkness*. Translated by Nicholas de Lange. Orlando, Fla.: Harcourt, 2004.

Pacepa, Ion Mihai. *Red Horizons: The True Story of Nicolae and Elena Ceausescus' Crimes, Lifestyle, and Corruption*. Washington, D.C.: Regnery, 1987.

Parker, Richard B., ed. *The October War: A Retrospective*. Gainesville: University Press of Florida, 2001.

Peres, Shimon. *Battling for Peace: Memoirs*. Edited by David Landau. London: Weidenfeld & Nicolson, 1995.

———. *David's Sling*. London: Weidenfeld & Nicolson, 1970.

Pogrebin, Letty Cottin. *Deborah, Golda, and Me: Being Female and Jewish in America*. New York: Crown, 1991.

Porat, Dina. *The Blue and the Yellow Stars of David*. Cambridge, Mass.: Harvard University Press, 1990.

Prittie, Terence. *Eshkol: The Man and the Nation*. New York: Pitman, 1969.

Quandt, William B., Fuad Jabber, and Anne Mosely Lesch. *The Politics of Palestinian Nationalism*. Berkeley: University of California Press, 1973.

Rabin, Leah. *Rabin: Our Life, His Legacy*. New York: Putnam, 1997.

Rabin, Yitzhak. *The Rabin Memoirs*. Rev. ed. Translated by Dov Goldstein. Berkeley: University of California Press, 1996.

Rabinovich, Abraham. *The Yom Kippur War: The Epic Encounter That Transformed the Middle East*. New York: Schocken Books, 2004.

Rabinovich, Itamar, and Jehuda Reinharz, eds. *Israel in the Middle East: Documents and Readings on Society, Politics, and Foreign Relations, Pre-1948 to the Present*. Waltham, Mass.: Brandeis University Press, 2008.

Radosh, Allis, and Ronald Radosh. *A Safe Haven: Harry S. Truman and the Founding of Israel*. New York: HarperCollins, 2009.

Rafael, Gideon. *Destination Peace: Three Decades of Israeli Foreign Policy*. New York: Stein & Day, 1981.

Raider, Mark A. *The Emergence of American Zionism*. New York: New York University Press, 1998.

———. *Nahum Goldmann: Statesman Without a State*. Albany: State University of New York Press, 2009.

Raider, Mark A., and Miriam B. Raider-Roth, eds. *The Plough Woman: Records of the Palestinian Women of Palestine: A Critical Edition*. Waltham, Mass.: Brandeis University Press, 2002.

Raviv, Moshe. *Israel at Fifty*. London: Weidenfeld & Nicolson, 1998.

Redlich, Shimon. *War, the Holocaust, and Stalinism*. Australia: Harwood Academic, 1995.

Reeve, Simon. *One Day in September: The Full Story of the 1972 Munich Olympics Massacre and the Israeli Revenge Operation "Wrath of God."* New York: Arcade, 2000.

Reinharz, Jehuda. *Chaim Weizmann: The Making of a Statesman*. New York: Oxford University Press, 1993.

———. *Chaim Weizmann: The Making of a Zionist Leader*. New York: Oxford University Press, 1985.

Reinharz, Shulamit, and Mark A. Raider, eds. *American Jewish Women and the Zionist Enterprise*. Waltham, Mass.: Brandeis University Press, 2005.

Riad, Mahmoud. *The Struggle for Peace in the Middle East*. New York: Quartet Books, 1981.

Ro'i, Yaacov. *Soviet Decision Making in Practice*. New Brunswick, N.J.: Transaction Books, 1980.

———. *The Struggle for Soviet Jewish Emigration, 1948–1967*. Cambridge, U.K. : Cambridge University Press, 1991.

Ross, Dennis, and David Makovsky. *Myths, Illusions, and Peace: Finding a New Direction for America in the Middle East*. New York: Viking Press, 2009.

Rubenstein, Joshua, and Vladimir P. Naumov, eds. *Stalin's Secret Pogrom: The Postwar Inquisition of the Jewish Anti-Fascist Committee*. New Haven, Conn.: Yale University Press, 2001.

Sachar, Howard M. *A History of Israel from the Rise of Zionism to Our Time*. New York: Alfred A. Knopf, 2003.

———. *A History of the Jews in America*. New York: Alfred A. Knopf, 1992.

Sacharov, Eliyahu. *Out of the Limelight: Events, Operations, Missions, and Personalities in Israeli History*. Translated by Rachel Bar Yosef. Jerusalem: Gefen, 2004.

Sadat, Anwar el-. *In Search of Identity: An Autobiography*. New York: Harper & Row, 1977.

Sadat, Jehan. *A Woman of Egypt*. New York: Simon & Schuster, 1987.

Safran, Nadav. *Israel, the Embattled Ally*. With a new preface and postscript by the author. Cambridge, Mass.: Belknap Press, 1981.

Samuel, Maurice. *The Plough Woman*. New York: Nicholas L. Brown, 1932.

Schiff, Zeev. *October Earthquake: Yom Kippur 1973*. Translated by Louis Williams. Tel Aviv: University Publishing Projects, 1974.

Schlor, Joachim. *Tel Aviv: From Dream to City*. London: Reaktion Books, 1995.

Segev, Tom. *1949: The First Israelis*. Edited by Arlen Neal Weinstein. New York: Free Press, 1986.

———. *1967: Israel, the War, and the Year That Transformed the Middle East*. Translated by Jessica Cohen. New York: Henry Holt, 2007.

———. *One Palestine, Complete: Jews and Arabs Under the British Mandate*. Translated by Haim Watzman. New York: Metropolitan Books, 2001.

———. *The Seventh Million: The Israelis and the Holocaust*. Translated by Haim Watzman. New York: Hill and Wang, 1993.

Seltzer, Robert M., and Norman J. Cohen, eds. *The Americanization of the Jews*. New York: New York University Press, 1999.

Shalom, Zaki. *Israel's Nuclear Option: Behind the Scenes Diplomacy Between Dimona and Washington*. Portland, Ore.: Sussex Academic Press, 2005.

Shapira, Anita. *Ben-Gurion: Father of Modern Israel*. Translated by Anthony Berris. New Haven, Conn.: Yale University Press, 2014.

———. *Berl: The Biography of a Socialist Zionist*. Translated by Haya Galai. Cambridge, U.K.: Cambridge University Press, 1984.

———. *Israel: A History*. Translated by Anthony Berris. Waltham, Mass.: Brandeis University Press, 2012.

———. *Land and Power: The Zionist Resort to Force, 1881–1948*. Translated by William Templer. Stanford, Calif.: Stanford University Press, 1999.

———. *Yigal Allon, Native Son: A Biography*. Translated by Evelyn Abel. Philadelphia: University of Pennsylvania Press, 2008.

Sharef, Zeev. *Three Days*. Translated by Julian Louis Meltzer. Garden City, N.Y.: Doubleday, 1962.

Sharett, Yaakov, ed. *The Reparations Controversy: The Jewish State and German Money in the Shadow of the Holocaust, 1951–1952*. Berlin: Walter de Gruyter, 2011.

Shavit, Ari. *My Promised Land: The Triumph and Tragedy of Israel*. New York: Spiegel and Grau, 2013.

Sheffer, Gabriel. *Moshe Sharett: Biography of a Political Moderate*. Oxford: Clarendon Press, 1996.

Shilon, Avi. *Menachem Begin: A Life*. Translated by Danielle Zilberberg and Yoram Sharett. New Haven, Conn.: Yale University Press, 2012.

Shimoni, Gideon. *Jews and Zionism: The South African Experience (1910–1967)*. New York: Oxford University Press, 1980.

Shipler, David K. *Arab and Jew: Wounded Spirits in a Promised Land*. New York: Penguin Books, 2002.

Shlaim, Avi. *Collusion Across the Jordan: King Abdullah, the Zionist Movement, and the Partition of Palestine*. New York: Columbia University Press, 1988.

———. *The Iron Wall: Israel and the Arab World*. New York: W. W. Norton, 2000.

———. *Lion of Jordan: The Life of King Hussein in War and Peace*. New York: Alfred A. Knopf, 2007.

———. *The Politics of Partition: King Abdullah, the Zionists, and Palestine, 1921–1951*. New York: Oxford University Press, 1998.

Siniver, Asaf. *Abba Eban: A Biography*. New York: Overlook Duckworth, 2015.

Slater, Robert. *Golda: The Uncrowned Queen of Israel: A Pictorial History*. Middle Village, N.Y.: Jonathan David, 1981.

Spiegel, Steven L. *The Other Arab-Israeli Conflict: Making America's Middle East Policy, from Truman to Reagan*. Chicago: University of Chicago Press, 1985.

Stangneth, Bettina. *Eichmann Before Jerusalem: The Unexamined Life of a Mass Murderer*. Translated by Ruth Martin. New York: Alfred A. Knopf, 2014.

Stanislawski, Michael. *Tsar Nicholas I and the Jews*. Philadelphia: Jewish Publication Society, 1983.

Steiner, Edward. *On the Trail of the Immigrant*. New York: Revell, 1906.

Sternhell, Zeev. *The Founding Myths of Israel: Nationalism, Socialism, and the Making of the Jewish State*. Translated by David Maisel. Princeton, N.J.: Princeton University Press, 1998.

St. John, Robert. *Eban*. Garden City, N.Y.: Doubleday, 1972.

Swichkow, Louis J., and Lloyd P. Gartner. *The History of the Jews of Milwaukee*. Philadelphia: Jewish Publication Society, 1963.

Syrkin, Marie. *Blessed Is the Match: The Story of Jewish Resistance*. Philadelphia: Jewish Publication Society, 1947.

———. *Golda Meir: Israel's Leader*. New York: Putnam, 1969.

———. *Way of Valor: A Biography of Golda Myerson*. New York: Sharon Books, 1955.

Tal, David, ed. *The 1956 War: Collusion and Rivalry in the Middle East*. Portland, Ore.: Frank Cass, 2001.

Teveth, Shabtai. *Ben-Gurion: The Burning Ground, 1886–1948*. Boston: Houghton Mifflin, 1987.

———. *Ben-Gurion's Spy: The Story of the Political Scandal That Shaped Modern Israel*. New York: Columbia University Press, 1996.

———. *Moshe Dayan: The Soldier, the Man, the Legend*. Translated by Leah Zinder and David Zinder. New York: Dell, 1974.

Thomas, Gordon. *Gideon's Spies: The Secret History of the Mossad*. New York: St. Martin's Press, 1999.

Truman, Harry S. *Memoirs*. Garden City, N.Y.: Doubleday, 1978.

Tyler, Patrick. *Fortress Israel: The Inside Story of the Military Elite Who Run the Country—and Why They Can't Make Peace*. New York: Farrar, Straus and Giroux, 2012.

Uchill, Ida Libert. *Pioneers, Peddlers, and Tsadikim: The Story of Jews in Colorado*. Boulder: University Press of Colorado, 1979.

Urofsky, Melvin I. *Louis D. Brandeis: A Life*. New York: Pantheon Books, 2009.

Valeriani, Richard. *Travels with Henry*. Boston: Houghton Mifflin, 1979.

Vanetik, Boaz, and Zaki Shalom. *The Nixon Administration and the Middle East Peace Process, 1969–1973: From the Rogers Plan to the Outbreak of the Yom Kippur War*. Translated by Guy Solomon. Eastbourne, U.K.: Sussex Academic Press, 2014.

Weisgal, Meyer. *So Far: An Autobiography*. New York: Random House, 1971.

Weizman, Ezer. *The Battle for Peace*. New York: Bantam, 1981.

Weizmann, Chaim. *Trial and Error*. New York: Schocken Books, 1949.

Wiesel, Elie. *All Rivers Run to the Sea: Memoirs*. New York: Alfred A. Knopf, 1995.

———. *And the Sea Is Never Full: Memoirs, 1969*. Translated by Marion Wiesel. New York: Alfred A. Knopf, 1999.

Wyman, David S. *The Abandonment of the Jews*. New York: Pantheon, 1984.

Yaari, Ehud. *Strike Terror: The Story of Fatah*. New York: Sabra Books, 1970.

Yablonka, Hanna. *The State of Israel vs. Adolf Eichmann*. Translated by Ora Cummings with David Herman. New York: Schocken Books, 2004.

Young-Bruehl, Elisabeth. *Hannah Arendt: For Love of the World*. New Haven, Conn.: Yale University Press, 1982.

Zameret, Zvi. *The Melting Pot in Israel: The Commission of Inquiry Concerning the Education of Immigrant Children During the Early Years of the State*. Albany: State University of New York Press, 2002.

Zipperstein, Steven J. *Elusive Prophet: Ahad Ha'am and the Origins of Zionism*. Berkeley: University of California Press, 1993.

Selected Books in Hebrew

Book titles are given in English using the publishers' translations or the author's translation when not provided by the publisher.

Aloni, Shulamit. *I Can Do No Other*. Tel Aviv: Maariv Book Guild, 1997.

Avigdori-Avidav, Hadassah. *The Road We Took: Diary of a Convoy Escort*. Tel Aviv: Defense Ministry Publishing House, 1947.

Avizohar, Meir, ed. *Golda, Growth of a Leader*. Tel Aviv: Am Oved, 1994.

Avizohar, Meir, and Avi Bareli, eds. *Now or Never: Proceedings of Mapai in the Closing Years of the British Mandate, Introductions and Documents*. Kfar Saba: Beit Berl, 1989.

Avneri, Arye. *Sapir*. Givataim: Peleg, 1976.

Bareli, Meir. *From Ideology to Apparatus*. Tel Aviv: Elilav, 1994.

Bar-Joseph, Uri. *The Watchman Fell Asleep*. Or Yehuda: Zmora Bitan, 2013.

Bartov, Hanoch. *Dado: 48 Years and 20 More Days*. Or Yehuda: Dvir, 2002.

Bar-Zohar, Michael. *Ben-Gurion, a Political Biography*. Tel Aviv: Am Oved, 1977.

———. *Like a Sandbird: Shimon Peres—a Biography*. Tel Aviv: Yediot Aharonot, 2005.

Becker, Aharon. *With the Times and the People*. Tel Aviv: Am Oved, 1982.

Beilin, Yossi. *The Price of Unity: The Labor Party Until the Yom Kippur War*. Revivim: Leor, 1985.

Beit-Or, Drora, and Sarah Rehabi, eds. *In Close Company with Golda: Conversations with Yitzhak Eilam About Golda Meir*. Tel Aviv: Golda Meir Memorial Association, 1987.

Ben-Gurion, David. *Chimes of Statehood*. Edited by Meir Avizohar. Tel Aviv: Am Oved, 1993.

———. *Letters to Paula*. Tel Aviv: Am Oved, 1968.

———. *Toward the End of the Mandate*. Edited by Meir Avizohar. Tel Aviv: Am Oved, 1993.

———. *The War of Independence: Ben-Gurion Diary*. Edited by Gershon Rivlin and Elhanan Oren. Tel Aviv: Defense Ministry Publishing House, 1982.

Ben-Porat, Yeshayahu. *Dialogues*. Jerusalem: Edanim, 1981.

Ben-Zvi, Yitzhak. *Poalei Zion in the Second Aliya*. Tel Aviv: Mapai, 1950.

Bergman, Ronen, and Gil Meltzer. *The Yom Kippur War: Moment of Truth*. Tel Aviv: Yediot Aharonot and Chemed, 2003.

Boaz, Arieh. *Unseen yet Always Present: The Life Story of Shaul Avigur*. Tel Aviv: Defense Ministry Publishing House, 2001.

Braun, Arie. *Moshe Dayan and the Yom Kippur War*. Tel Aviv: Edanim, 1992.

Burg, Joseph. *Autobiographical Chapters*. Edited by Meir Hovav. Jerusalem: Yad Shapira, 2000.

Chen, Zalman. *The Seven Happy Years*. Tel Aviv: Lavon Institute, n.d.

Chetrit, Sami. *The Mizrahi Struggle Against Israel, 1948–2003*. Tel Aviv: Am Oved, 2004.

Cnaani, David, ed. *The Merhavia Book*. Merhavia: Sifriat Hapoalim, 1961.

Dayan, Moshe. *Milestones: An Autobiography*. Tel Aviv: Yediot Aharonot, 1976.

Dotan, Shmuel. *The Struggle for Eretz Yisrael*. Tel Aviv: Defense Ministry Publishing House, 1986.

Eliav, Arie Lova. *Rings of Faith*. Tel Aviv: Am Oved, 1983.

Erez, Sarah. *One Period in the Life of David Remez, 1934–1945*. Tel Aviv: David Remez Fund, 1977.

Erez, Yehuda, ed. *The Third Aliyah Book*. Tel Aviv: Am Oved, 1964.

Eshel, Tzadok. *Haganah Battles in Haifa*. Tel Aviv: Defense Ministry Publishing House, 1978.

Gilad, Zerubavel, and Megged Matti, eds. *The Palmach Book*. Vols. 1–2. Tel Aviv: Hakibbutz Hameuhad, 1953.

Gilboa, Moshe. *Six Years, Six Days: Sources of the Six-Day War*. Tel Aviv: Am Oved, 1969.

Golan, Shimon. *The Yom Kippur War: Decision Making of Israeli High Command*. Ben Shemen: Modan, 2013.

Goldstein, Yossi. *Eshkol: Biography*. Jerusalem: Keter, 2003.

———. *Golda—Biography*. Beersheba: Ben-Gurion University, 2012.

Greenberg, Yitzhak. *Pinhas Sapir: Economic and Political Biography*. Tel Aviv: Resling, 2011.

Haber, Eitan. *Today War Will Break Out: Memoirs of Brigadier General Yisrael Lior*. Tel Aviv: Yediot Aharonot, 1987.

Harel, Aharon. *Between Building and Destruction: The Histadrut and the Labor Movement, 1956–1965*. Tel Aviv: Am Oved, 2004.

Harel, Isser. *The German Scientists Crisis, 1962–1963*. Tel Aviv: Maariv, 1982.

Hasin, Eliyahu, and Dan Horwitz. *The Lavon Affair*. Tel Aviv: Am Hasefer, 1961.

Herman, Zvi. *Conquerors of the Seaways*. Tel Aviv: Hakibbutz Hameuhad, 1978.

Kally, Elisha. *Home and Hearth: Reminiscences of an Israeli Engineer*. Rehovot: Turgeman, 2001.

Lazar, Hadar. *In and Out of Palestine, 1940–1948*. Jerusalem: Keter, 2003.

Levanon, Nechemia. *"Nativ" Was the Code Name*. Tel Aviv: Am Oved, 1995.

Margalit, Dan. *Dispatch from the White House*. Tel Aviv: Otpaz, 1971.

———. *I Have Seen Them All*. Tel Aviv: Zmora-Bitan, 1997.

Medzini, Meron. *Golda: A Political Biography*. Tel Aviv: Yediot Aharonot Books and Chemed Books, 2008.

Meir, Golda. *My Father's House*. Tel Aviv: Hakibbutz Hameuhad, 1972.

Michaeli, Ben Zion. *Herzliya Beginnings and Development*. Herzliya: Milo, 1989.

Nakdimon, Shlomo. *Low Probability: The Background and Consequences of the Yom Kippur War*. Jerusalem: Revivim, 1982.

———. *Toward the Zero Hour*. Tel Aviv: Ramdor Press, 1968.

Namir, Mordechai. *The Israeli Mission to Moscow*. Tel Aviv: Am Oved, 1971.

Naor, Mordechai, ed. *Tel Aviv at Its Beginnings, 1909–1934*. Jerusalem: Yad Ben-Zvi, 1984.

Palgi, Yoel. *A Great Wind Comes*. Tel Aviv: Am Oved, 1978.

Porat, Dina. *Trapped Leadership*. Tel Aviv: Am Oved, 1986.

Rabinowitsch, Wolf Zeev, ed. *Pinsk: Historical Volume—History of the Jews of Pinsk, 1506–1941*. 2 vols. Tel Aviv and Haifa: Association of the Jews of Pinsk in Israel, 1966–1977.

Rojanski, Rachel. *Conflicting Identities: Poalei Zion in America, 1905–1931*. Tel Aviv: Ben Gurion University Press, 2004.

Rosenthal, Yemima, ed. *Documents of the Foreign Policy of Israel*. Vol. 8. Jerusalem: Government Printing Office, 1995.

Sarid, Menahem. *You Chose Us for Ruling: Ben-Gurion and Jabotinsky, 1930–1935*. Herzliya: Oren, 2004.

Schueftan, Dan. *Jordanian Option: The Yishuv and the State of Israel Vis-à-Vis the Hashemite Regime and the Palestinian National Movement*. Tel Aviv: Hakibbutz Hameuhad, 1986.

Shafir, Shlomo. *An Outstretched Hand*. Tel Aviv: Zmora, 1986.

Shalom, Zaki. *Policy in the Shadow of Controversy: Israel's Ongoing Security Policy, 1949–1956*. Tel Aviv: Ma'arachot, 1995.

Shapira, Anita. *Berl Katznelson: A Biography*. 4 vols. Tel Aviv: Am Oved, 1980.

———. *Brenner: A Life*. Tel Aviv: Am Oved, 2008.

———. *New Jews, Old Jews*. Tel Aviv: Am Oved, 1997.

Sharett, Moshe. *The London Days Letters, 1923–1925*. Tel Aviv: Hedkel, 2008.

———. *Political Diary*. 5 vols. Tel Aviv: Am Oved, 1968–1979.

Sharett, Rena, and Yaakov Sharett, eds. *Imprisoned with Paper and Pencil: The Letters of Moshe and Zipporah Sharett During the Period of His Detention by the British at Latrun, June–November 1946*. Tel Aviv: Moshe Sharett Memorial Foundation, 2000.

Shazar, Rachel, and Zalman Shazar. *On Two Shores: Letters, 1909–1963*. Edited by Michael Hagitti. Jerusalem: Mossad Bialik, 1999.

Shchori, Ilan. *The Dream That Became a City: Tel Aviv Birth and Growth: The City That Gave Birth to a State*. Tel Aviv: Avivim, 1991.

Sheva, Shlomo. *A Road in the Wilderness*. Tel Aviv: Am Oved, 1976.

Slutsky, Yehuda. *History of the Hagana*. Vol. 3. *From Resistance to War*. Tel Aviv: Am Oved, 1972.

Tamir, Nahman, ed. *Golda: A Collection in Her Memory*. Tel Aviv: Am Oved, 1981.

Teveth, Shabtai. *David's Zeal*. 4 vols. Jerusalem and Tel Aviv: Schocken, 1976.

Tsahor, Zeev. *Hazan*. Jerusalem: Yad Ben-Zvi, 1997.

———. *The Shaping of the Israeli Ethos*. Tel Aviv: Am Oved, 2009.

Tsoref, Hagai, ed. *Golda Meir Commemorative Book*. Jerusalem: Israel State Archives, 2016.

Tsur, Muki, Tair Zvulun, and Hanina Porat, eds. *Here on Earth*. Jerusalem: Hakibbutz Hameuhad, 1981.

Tsur, Yaakov. *Paris Diary*. Tel Aviv: Am Oved, 1968.

Weiss, Yfaat. *Wadi Salib: A Confiscated Memory*. Jerusalem: Hakibbutz Hameuhad, 2007.

Yaacobi, Gad. *Grace of Time: An Autobiography*. Tel Aviv: Yediot Aharonot and Chemed, 2002.

———. *On the Razor's Edge*. Tel Aviv: Edanim, 1989.

Zak, Moshe. *Hussein Makes Peace*. Ramat Gan: Bar-Ilan University Press, 1996.

———. *Israel and the Soviet Union: A Forty-Year Dialogue*. Tel Aviv: Maariv Book Guild, 1988.

Zameret, Zvi, and Hannah Yablonka, eds. *The First Decade, 1948–1958*. Jerusalem: Yad Ben-Zvi, 1997.

———. *The Second Decade, 1958–1968*. Jerusalem: Yad Ben-Zvi, 2000.

Zerubavel, Yaakov. *In the Days of War and Revolution*. Tel Aviv: I. L. Peretz, 1966.

Zuckerman, Baruch. *Essays and Profiles*. Tel Aviv: I. L. Peretz, 1967.

Works in Other Languages

Budnitsky, Oleg, et al. *World Crisis of 1914–1920 or the Fate of Eastern European Jewry.* Moscow, 2005. (Russian)

Korngold, Sheyna. *Zikhroynes.* Tel Aviv: Farlag Idpres, 1968. (Yiddish)

Kostyrchenko, Ginnadi. *State Anti-Semitism, 1938–1953.* Moscow: MSD, Materik, 2005. (Russian)

Index

A NOTE ON THE TYPE

This book was set in Janson, a typeface long thought to have been made by the Dutchman Anton Janson. However, it has been conclusively demonstrated that these types are actually the work of Nicholas Kis (1650–1702), a Hungarian, who most probably learned his trade from master Dutch typefounder Dirk Voskens.

Composed by North Market Street Graphics,
Lancaster, Pennsylvania

Printed and bound by Berryville Graphics,
Berryville, Virginia

Designed by M. Kristen Bearse